W9-AHS-205

VOLUME II

This book should be used in conjunction with Volume I of Motor's Emission Control Manual which contains complete information on 1968-73 models.

CONTENTS

VOLUME II

The contents of Volume II of Motor's Emission Control Manual is the result of suggestions, letters, interviews and contact with over 6500 independent repair shops, service stations, dealerships, governmental agencies and automobile dealerships. Funneling information through our extensive sales force and through our editorial staff, it was actually the mechanic in the field and the environmental government official who told us what should be in this book. In every case, we've attempted to incorporate the thousands of suggestions and reams of information into this volume. To all those who contributed ideas, we thank you, and we hope Volume II will be at least as informative as Volume I.—*Joe Oldham*

PUBLISHED BY

MOTOR
1790 Broadway
New York, NY 10019

ISBN 0-910992-42-8

VEHICLE IDENTIFICATION AND SPECIFICATIONS

1974-75

CONTENTS

Each section contains vehicle identification information, general engine specifications, tuneup specifications and distributor specifications. For models earlier than 1974, refer to your Emission Control Manual, Volume I.

AMERICAN MOTORS

SERIAL NUMBER LOCATION

1969-75: Plate is attached to top of instrument panel, on driver's side.

ENGINE IDENTIFICATION

6-232 & 6-258 (1971-74): The engine code is located on a pad between number two and three cylinders. The letter A denotes the 258 engine. The letter E denotes the 232 engine.

V8-304, 360, 390, & 401 (1970-74): The engine code is located on a tag attached to the right bank rocker cover. The letter H denotes the 304 engine. The letter N denotes the 360 engine with 2-barrel carburetor while the letter P denotes the 360 engine with 4-barrel carburetor. The letter X denotes the 390 engine. The letter Z denotes the 401 engine.

GENERAL ENGINE SPECIFICATIONS

Engine	Carburetor	Bore and Stroke	Piston Displacement, Cubic Inches	Compression Ratio	Maximum Brake HP @ rpm	Maximum Torque Lbs. Ft. @ rpm	Normal Oil Pressure Pounds
1974							
100 Horsepower②..........6-232	1 Barrel	3.75 x 3.50	232	8.0	100 @ 3600	185 @ 1800	75
110 Horsepower②..........6-258	1 Barrel	3.75 x 3.90	258	8.0	110 @ 3500	195 @ 2000	75
150 Horsepower②.........V8-304	2 Barrel	3.75 x 3.44	304	8.4	150 @ 4200	245 @ 2500	75
175 Horsepower②.........V8-360	2 Barrel	4.08 x 3.44	360	8.5	175 @ 4000	285 @ 2400	75
195 Horsepower②.........V8-360	4 Barrel	4.08 x 3.44	360	8.5	195 @ 4400	295 @ 2900	75
220 Horsepower②③........V8-360	4 Barrel	4.08 x 3.44	360	8.5	220 @ 4400	315 @ 3100	75
255 Horsepower②.........V8-401	4 Barrel	4.165 x 3.68	401	8.5	235 @ 4600	335 @ 3200	75
1975							
100 Horsepower...........6-232	1 Barrel	3.75 x 3.50	232	8.0	100 @ 3600	185 @ 1800	37–75
110 Horsepower...........6-258	1 Barrel	3.75 x 3.90	258	8.0	110 @ 3500	195 @ 2000	37–75
150 Horsepower..........V8-304	2 Barrel	3.75 x 3.44	304	8.4	150 @ 4200	245 @ 2500	37–75
175 Horsepower..........V8-360	2 Barrel	4.08 x 3.44	360	8.25	175 @ 4000	285 @ 2400	37–75
195 Horsepower..........V8-360	4 Barrel	4.08 x 3.44	360	8.25	195 @ 4400	295 @ 2900	37–75
220 Horsepower..........V8-360	4 Barrel	4.08 x 3.44	360	8.25	220 @ 4400	315 @ 3100	37–75

②—Ratings are net (as installed in the vehicle). ③—With dual exhausts.

(continued)

TUNEUP SPECIFICATIONS

★When using a timing light, disconnect vacuum hose or tube at distributor and plug opening in hose or tube so idle speed will not be affected.

● When checking compression, lowest cylinder must be within 80% of highest.

▲Before removing wires from distributor cap, determine location of the No. 1 wire in cap, as distributor position may have been altered from that shown at the end of this chart.

Engine	Spark Plug		Distributor		Ignition Timing★			Carb. Adjustments					
								Hot Idle Speed		Air Fuel Ratio		Idle CO%	
	Type	Gap Inch	Point Gap Inch	Dwell Angle Deg.	Firing Order Fig. ▲	Timing Degrees BTDC	Mark Fig.	Std. Trans.	Auto. Trans.	Std. Trans.	Auto. Trans.	Std. Trans.	Auto. Trans.
1974													
6-232 L/EGR	N12Y	.035	.016	31–34	A	5	D	700	600D	—	—	④	④
6-232 W/EGR	N12Y	.035	.016	31–34	A	5	D	600	550D	—	—	④	④
6-232 Calif.	N12Y	.035	.016	31–34	A	5	D	600	700D	—	—	④	④
6-258 L/EGR	N12Y	.035	.016	31–34	A	3	D	550	700D	—	—	④	④
6-258 W/EGR	N12Y	.035	.016	31–34	A	3	D	550	600D	—	—	④	④
6-258 Calif.	N12Y	.035	.016	31–34	A	3	D	600	700D	—	—	④	④
V8-304	N12Y	.035	.016	29–31	B	①	C	750	700D	—	—	0.5–1.0	0.5–1.0
V8-360	N12Y	.035	.016	29–31	B	5	C	750	700D	—	—	0.5–1.0	0.5–1.0
V8-401	N12Y	.035	.016	29–31	B	5	C	750	700D	—	—	0.5–1.0	0.5–1.0
1975													
6-232, 258	N12Y	.035	—	—	A	5	E	600	550D	—	—	—	—
6-232, 258 Calif.	N12Y	.035	—	—	A	3	E	600	700D	—	—	—	—
V8-304	N12Y	.035	—	—	B	5	C	750	700D	—	—	—	—
V8-360	N12Y	.035	—	—	B	5	C	—	700D	—	—	—	—

①—Exc. Calif. auto. trans., 5° BTDC; Calif. auto. trans., 2½° BTDC.

④—W/Air Guard 0.5–1.0%. W/O Air Guard 1.0–1.5%.

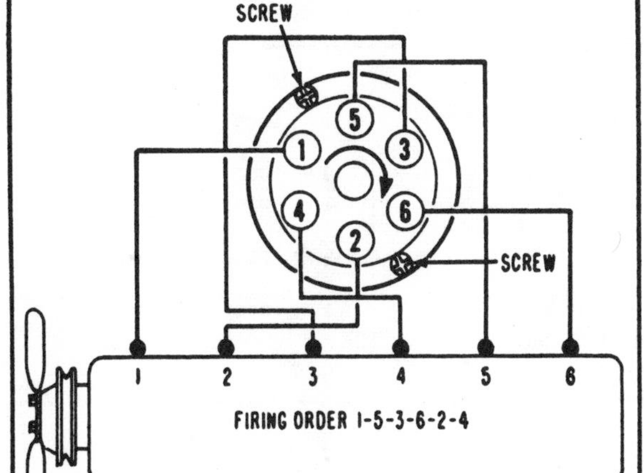

Fig. A

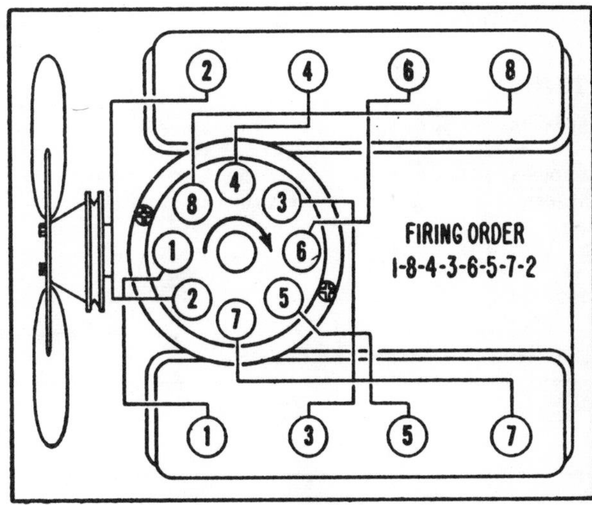

Fig. B

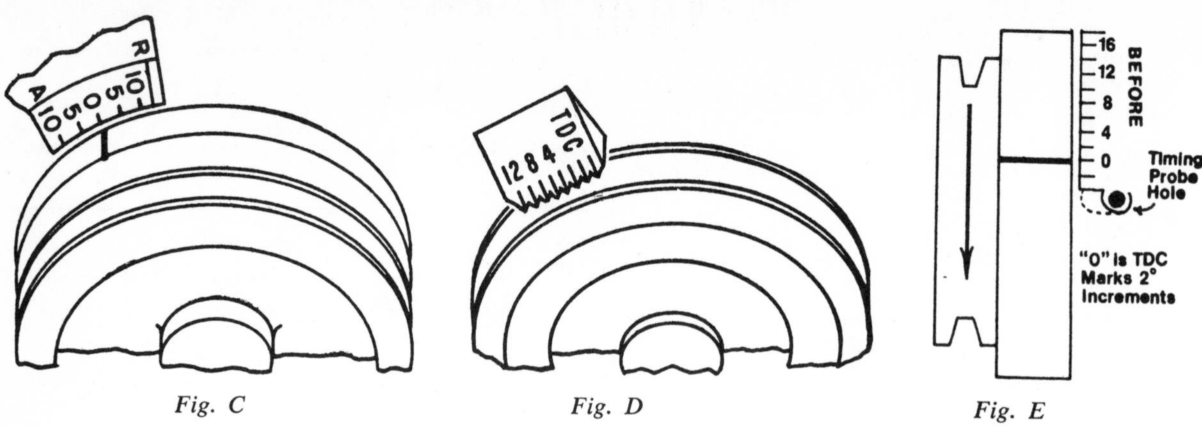

Fig. C *Fig. D* *Fig. E*

DISTRIBUTOR SPECIFICATIONS

★If unit is checked on vehicle, double the rpm and degrees to get crankshaft figures.

Breaker arm spring tension 17–21 oz.

Distributor Part No.①	Centrifugal Advance Degrees @ rpm of Distributor					Vacuum Advance		Distributor Retard	
	Advance Starts	Intermediate Advance			Full Advance	Inches of Vacuum to Start Plunger	Max. Adv. Dist. Deg. @ Vacuum	In. of Mercury Start Retard	Max. Retard Dist. Deg. @ Vacuum
1974									
1110528	0–2 @ 600	3–5.5 @ 800	6–8.5 @ 1000	6.5–9 @ 1500	15 @ 2200	5–7	9 @ 13	—	—
1110529	0–2 @ 500	4.5–7 @ 800	7–9 @ 1000	7–9.5 @ 1500	14 @ 2300	5–7	9 @ 13	—	—
1112112	0–2 @ 500	4.5–6.5 @ 800	7.5–9.5 @ 1000	9¾–11¾ @ 1500	14 @ 2200	5–7	8¼ @ 12¾	—	—
1112179	0–2 @ 500	4.5–6.5 @ 750	8–10 @ 1000	12.5–13.5 @ 1600	17 @ 2200	5–7	8¼ @ 12¾	—	—
1112214	0–2.5 @ 500	6.5–8.5 @ 700	—	11–13 @ 1500	17 @ 2200	4–6	8¼ @ 13	—	—
1112215	0–1.5 @ 400	4–6¾ @ 600	6.5–8.5 @ 1000	10–12 @ 1600	16 @ 2200	4–6	8¼ @ 13	—	—
1975									
3224746	0–1½ @ 400	5–7 @ 750	6½–8½ @ 1000	—	9¼–14 @ 1500	—	16¾ @ 1000	—	—
3224965	0–1 @ 400	4½–6 @ 750	8–10 @ 1000	—	11–13 @ 1500	—	18 @ 1000	—	—
3224966	0–2½ @ 450	6¼–8¾ @ 750	8¼–10¼ @ 1000	—	11–13 @ 1500	—	18¼ @ 1000	—	—
3224968	0–1 @ 500	2–4½ @ 750	6½–8½ @ 1500	—	6–9 @ 1500	—	17½ @ 1000	—	—
3223969	0–2 @ 500	3½–6 @ 750	7–9 @ 1000	—	7–9½ @ 1500	—	18 @ 1000	—	—

①—Stamped on distributor housing plate.

BUICK

All Intermediate & Full Size Models

ENGINE IDENTIFICATION

Buick engines are stamped with two different sets of numbers. One is the engine production code which identifies the engine and its approximate production date. The other is the engine serial number, which is the same number that is found on the vehicle identification plate attached to the left body hinge pillar. To identify an engine, look for the production code prefix letters, then refer to the following table for its identification.

On 1968-75 V8-350, 400, 430, 455 engines on left-bank cylinder head.

On V8-400 engines the code is stamped upside down on front of cylinder block when viewed from front of engine.

On V6-231, V8-300 and 340 engines the code is stamped on right side of crankcase between middle branches of right exhaust manifold.

Year	Engine	Code
1974	6-250 auto. trans.	CCW, CCX
	6-250 manual trans.	CCR
	V8-350 2-bbl.	ZC, ZP
	V8-350 4-bbl.	ZB, ZM
	V8-455 2-bbl.	ZI
	V8-455 4-bbl.	ZF, ZK
	V8-455 (Stage 1)	ZA, ZS
1975	V6-231	C
	6-250	D
	V8-260	F
	V8-350 2-bbl.	H
	V8-350 4-bbl.	J
	V8-400	S
	V8-455	T

GENERAL ENGINE SPECIFICATIONS

Engine ★	Carburetor	Bore and Stroke	Piston Displacement, Cubic Inches	Compression Ratio	Maximum Brake HP @ rpm	Maximum Torque Lbs. Ft. @ rpm	Normal Oil Pressure Pounds
1974							
100 Horsepower..........6-250①	1 Barrel	3.875 x 3.53	250	8.25	100 @ 3600	175 @ 1600	40
150 Horsepower..........V8-350	2 Barrel	3.800 x 3.85	350	8.5	150 @ 3600	270 @ 2000	37
165 Horsepower........V8-350②	2 Barrel	3.800 x 3.85	350	8.5	165 @ 3800	285 @ 2000	37
175 Horsepower..........V8-350	4 Barrel	3.800 x 3.85	350	8.5	175 @ 3800	260 @ 2000	37
195 Horsepower........V8-350②	4 Barrel	3.800 x 3.85	350	8.5	195 @ 4000	280 @ 2000	37
175 Horsepower..........V8-455	2 Barrel	4.3125 x 3.90	455	8.5	175 @ 3400	355 @ 2000	40
190 Horsepower........V8-455②	2 Barrel	4.3125 x 3.90	455	8.5	190 @ 3600	370 @ 2000	40
210 Horsepower..........V8-455	4 Barrel	4.3125 x 3.90	455	8.5	210 @ 3600	335 @ 2200	40
230 Horsepower........V8-455②	4 Barrel	4.3125 x 3.90	455	8.5	230 @ 3800	355 @ 2200	40
245 Horsepower........V8-455③	4 Barrel	4.3125 x 3.90	455	8.5	245 @ 4000	360 @ 2400	40
255 Horsepower........V8-455③	4 Barrel	4.3125 x 3.90	455	8.5	255 @ 4400	370 @ 2800	40
1975							
105 Horsepower..........6-250①	1 Barrel	3.875 x 3.53	250	8.0	105 @ 3800	185 @ 1200	36–41
110 Horsepower..........V6-231	2 Barrel	3.80 x 3.40	231	8.0	110 @ 4000	175 @ 2000	37
110 Horsepower........V8-260④	2 Barrel	3.80 x 3.385	260	8.5	110 @ 3400	205 @ 1600	—
145 Horsepower..........V8-350	2 Barrel	3.80 x 3.85	350	8.0	145 @ 3200	270 @ 2000	37
165 Horsepower..........V8-350	4 Barrel	3.80 x 3.85	350	8.0	165 @ 3800	260 @ 2200	37
170 Horsepower........V8-400⑤	2 Barrel	4.12 x 3.75	400	7.6	170 @ 4000	320 @ 2000	55–60
185 Horsepower........V8-400⑤	4 Barrel	4.12 x 3.75	400	7.6	185 @ 3600	320 @ 2400	55–60
205 Horsepower..........V8-455	4 Barrel	4.3125 x 3.90	455	7.9	205 @ 3800	345 @ 2000	40

★Net Rating—As installed in vehicle.
①—See Chevrolet chapter for service procedures on this engine.
②—Dual exhaust.
③—Stage 1.
④—See Oldsmobile chapter for service procedures on this engine.
⑤—See Pontiac chapter for service procedure on this engine.

TUNEUP SPECIFICATIONS

★When using a timing light, disconnect vacuum hose or tube at distributor and plug opening in tube or hose so idle speed will not be affected.

● When checking compression, lowest cylinder must be within 80% of highest.

▲Before removing wires from distributor cap, determine location of the No. 1 wire in cap, as distributor position may have been altered from that shown at the end of this chart.

TUNEUP SPECIFICATIONS

Year	Spark Plug		Distributor		Ignition Timing★			Carb. Adjustments					
								Hot Idle Speed		Air Fuel Ratio		Idle CO%	
	Type	Gap Inch	Point Gap Inch	Dwell Angle Deg.	Firing Order Fig. ▲	Timing Deg. BTDC ①	Mark Fig.	Std. Trans.	Auto. Trans.②	Std. Trans.	Auto. Trans.	Std. Trans.	Auto. Trans.
1974													
6-250②	R46T	.035	.019	31–34	A	③	C	950	600D	—	—	—	—
V8-350	R45TS	.040	.016	29–31	B⑨	4	J	—	650D	—	—	—	—
V8-455	R45TS	.040	.016	29–31	B⑨	④	J	—	650D	—	—	—	—
1975													
6-250⑥	R46TX	.060	—	—	D	10	C	800	600D	—	—	—	—
V6-231	R44SX	.060	—	—	E	12	F	800	700D	—	—	—	—
V8-260⑦	R46SX	.080	—	—	G	16	H	—	600D	—	—	—	—
V8-350	R45TSX	.060	—	—	I	12	J	—	600D	—	—	—	—
V8-400 2 bbl.⑧	R46TSX	.060	—	—	K	16	L	—	650D	—	—	—	—
V8-400 4 bbl.⑧	R45TSX	.060	—	—	K	16	L	—	650D	—	—	—	—
V8-455	R45TSX	.060	—	—	I	12	J	—	600D	—	—	—	—

TUNEUP NOTES

①—BTDC: Before top dead center.
②—D: Drive. N: Neutral.
③—Manual trans., 8° BTDC; auto. trans., 6° BTDC.
④—Exc. intermediate model Stage 1 eng., 4° BTDC; intermediate model Stage 1 eng., 10° BTDC.
⑥—See Chevrolet chapter for service procedures on this engine.
⑦—See Oldsmobile chapter for service procedures on this engine.
⑧—See Pontiac chapter for service procedures on this engine.
⑨—Except HEI, Fig. I

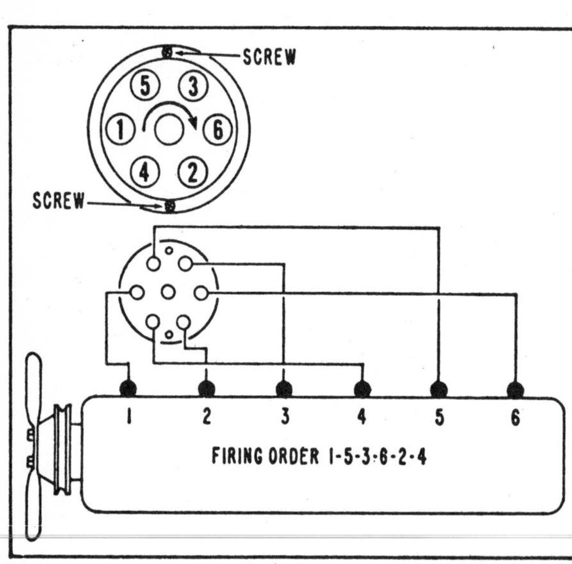

Fig. A

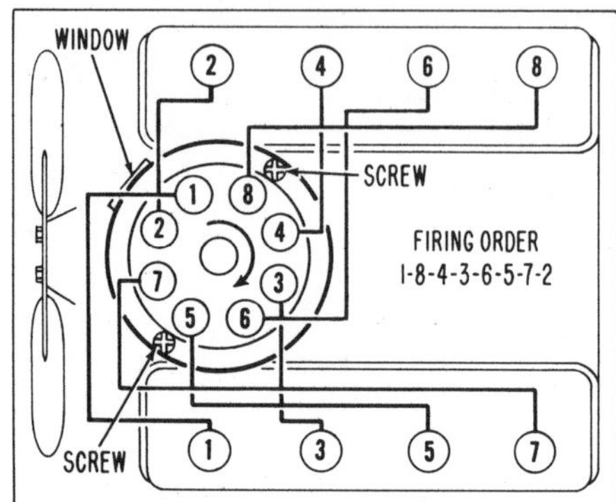

Fig. B

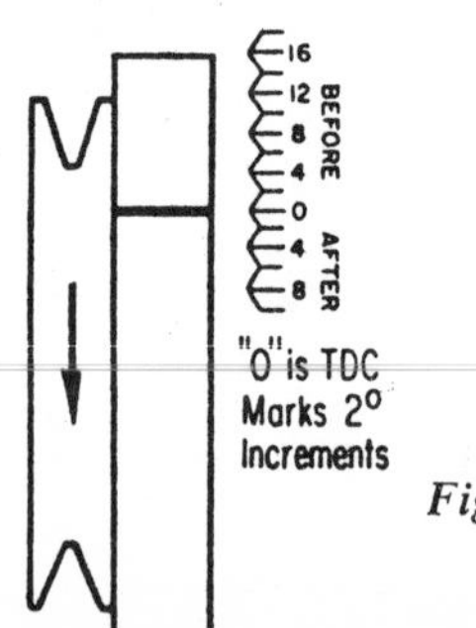

Fig. C

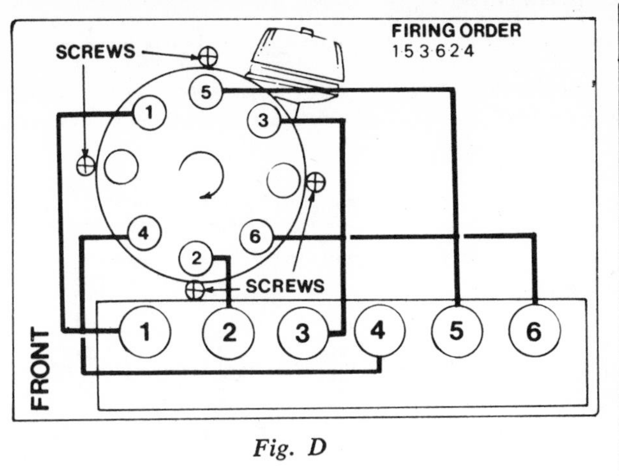

Fig. D

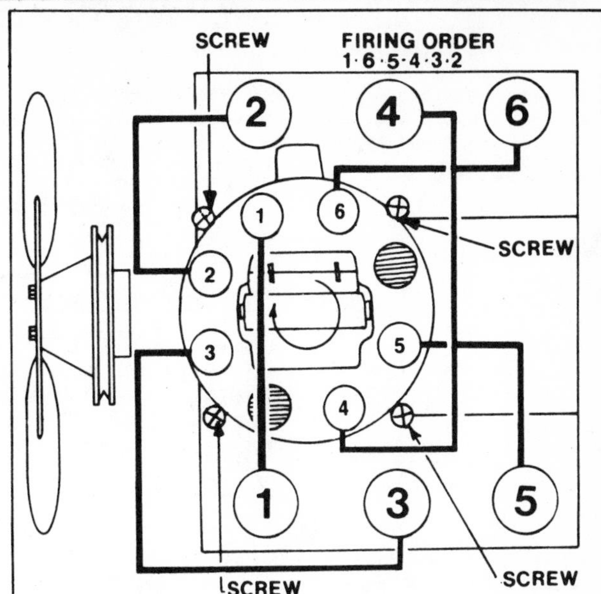

Fig. E

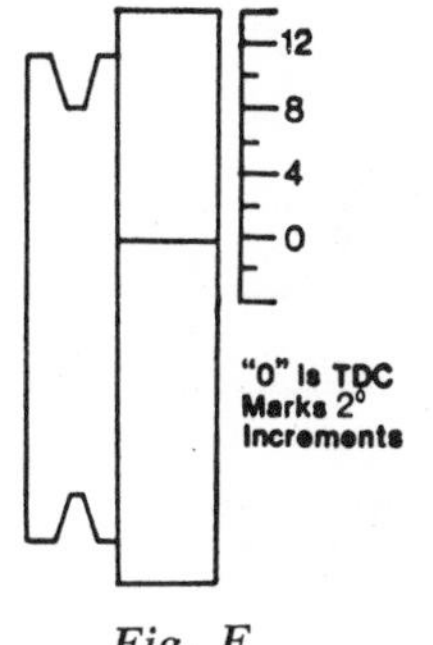

Fig. F

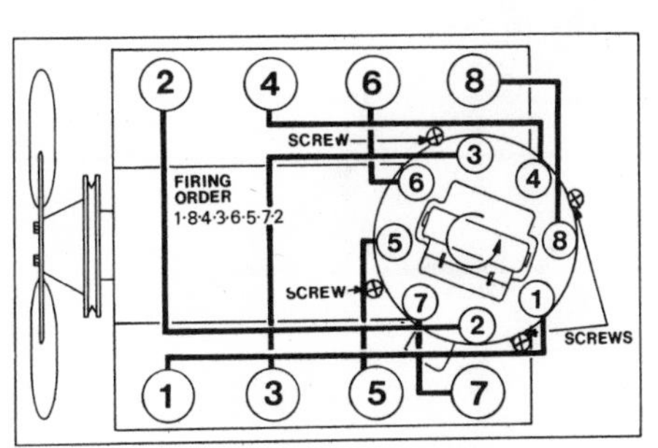

Fig. G

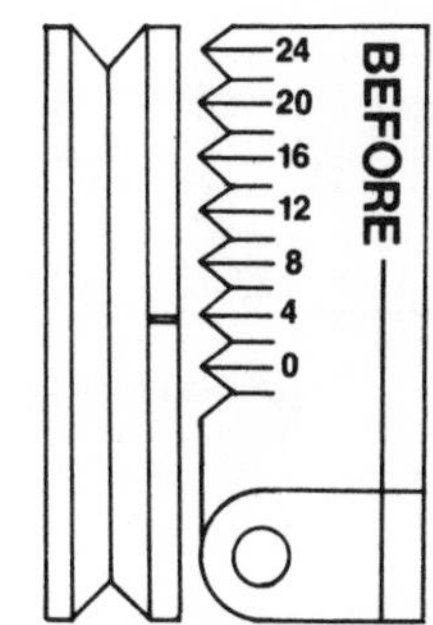

Fig. H

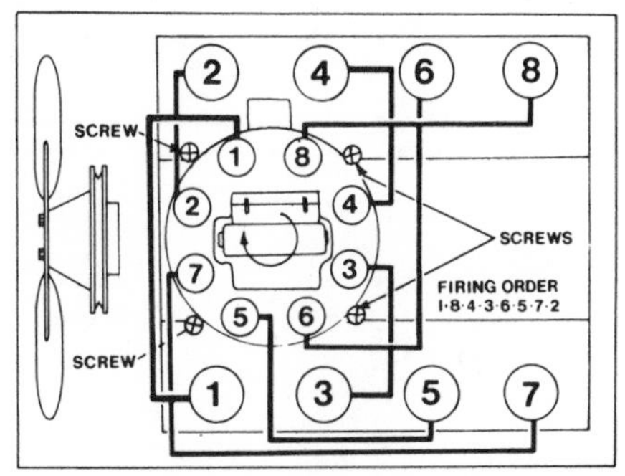

Fig. I

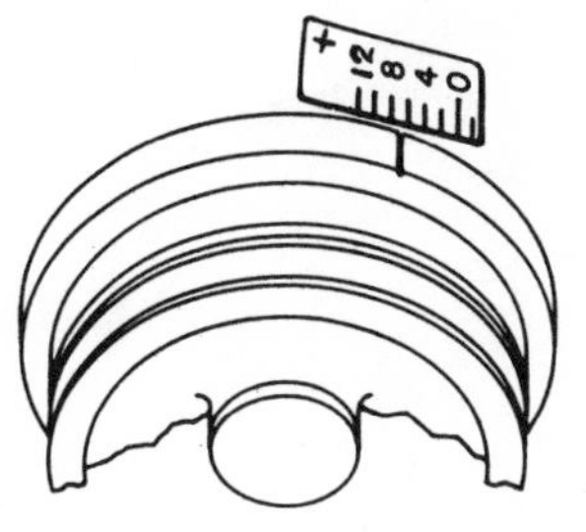

Fig. J

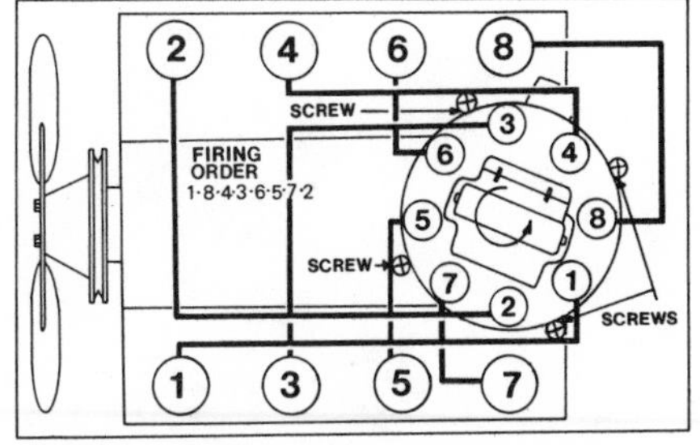

Fig. K

Fig. L

DISTRIBUTOR SPECIFICATIONS

Distributor Part No.①	Centrifugal Advance Degrees @ rpm of Distributor					Vacuum Advance	
	Advance Starts	Intermediate Advance			Full Advance	Inches of Vacuum to Start Plunger	Max. Adv. Dist. Deg. @ Vacuum
1974							
1110499	0–1 @ 550	7 @ 1150	—	—	10½ @ 2050	6	11 @ 14
1112520②	0–1 @ 450	7–9 @ 1200	—	—	10 @ 1500	6.5–8.5	9.5 @ 13
1112521②	0–1 @ 400	4½–6½ @ 900	—	—	12 @ 2300	6–8	9 @ 16
1112541	0–1 @ 450	5½–7½ @ 900	—	—	12 @ 1800	6–8	9 @ 16
1112542	0–1 @ 450	7–9 @ 1050	—	—	14 @ 2050	6.5–8.5	9.5 @ 13
1112802②	0–1 @ 450	5½–7½ @ 900	—	—	12 @ 1800	6–8	9 @ 16
1112803②	0–1 @ 450	7–9 @ 1050	—	—	14 @ 2050	6.5–8.5	9.5 @ 13
1975							
V6-231②	0 @ 500	5 @ 1000	—	—	8 @ 2050	6	9 @ 10
6-250②	0 @ 550	3½ @ 1150	—	—	8 @ 2100	4	13 @ 15½
V8-260②	0 @ 325	9½ @ 1200	—	—	14 @ 2200	4	12 @ 15
V8-350②	—	2–4 @ 1050	—	—	7 @ 2250	7½	8 @ 11½
V8-400②	0 @ 600	2 @ 700	—	—	8 @ 2200	7	13½ @ 13½
V8-455②	—	4½–6 @ 1500	—	—	9 @ 2200	5	7.1 @ 11

①—Stamped on distributor housing plate. ②—High Energy Ignition.

CADILLAC

VEHICLE IDENTIFICATION NUMBER LOCATION

On 1969-75 models it is located on rear upper portion of cylinder block, behind intake manifold and on left side of transmission.

ENGINE UNIT NUMBER LOCATION

On 1969-75 at rear of cylinder block.

GENERAL ENGINE SPECIFICATIONS

Engine	Carburetor	Bore and Stroke	Piston Displacement, Cubic Inches	Compression Ratio	Maximum Brake HP @ rpm	Maximum Torque Lbs. Ft. @ rpm	Normal Oil Pressure Pounds
1974							
205 Horsepower..........V8-472	4 Barrel	4.300 x 4.060	472	8.25	205 @ 3600	365 @ 2000	35–40
210 Horsepower..........V8-500	4 Barrel	4.300 x 4.304	500	8.25	210 @ 3600	380 @ 2000	35–40
1975							
190 Horsepower..........V8-500	4 Barrel	4.300 x 4.30	500	8.5	190 @ 3600	360 @ 2000	35–40

TUNEUP SPECIFICATIONS

★When using a timing light, disconnect vacuum hose or tube at distributor and plug opening in hose or tube so idle speed will not be affected.

●When checking compression, lowest cylinder must be within 80% of highest.

▲Before removing wires from distributor cap, determine location of No. 1 wire in cap, as distributor position may have been altered from that shown at the end of this chart.

Spark Plug		Distributor		Ignition Timing ★			Carb. Adjustments					
							Hot Idle Speed		Air Fuel Ratio		Idle CO%	
Type	Gap Inch	Point Gap Inch	Dwell Angle Deg.	Firing Order Fig. ▲	Timing Degrees BTDC ①	Mark Fig.	Std. Trans.	Auto. Trans.②	Std. Trans.	Auto. Trans.	Std. Trans.	Auto. Trans.
1974												
R45NS	.035	③	30	A⑤	10	B	—	600D④	—	—	—	.4
1975												
R45NSX	.060	—	—	C	6	D	—	600D	—	—	—	—

①—BTDC: Before top dead center.
②—D: Drive. N: Neutral.
③—Turn adjusting screw in (clockwise) until engine begins to misfire; then back screw out ½ turn.
④—When making adjustments, air conditioner must be turned off (if equipped). Also, hose must be disconnected at vacuum release cylinder. The hot idle compensator must be closed; this can be done by pressing finger or eraser end of pencil on compensator.
⑤—HEI, Fig. E.

(continued)

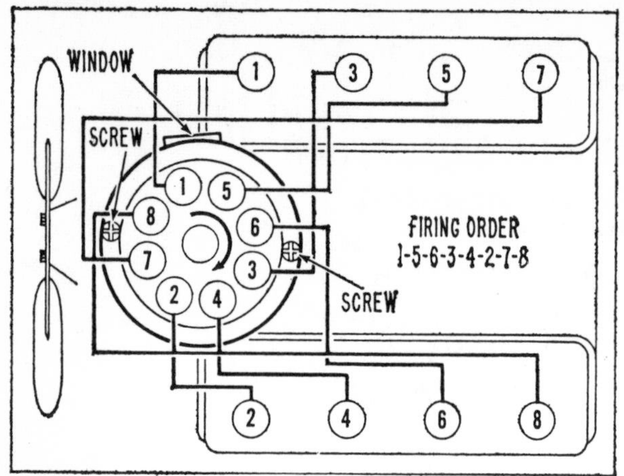

Fig. A

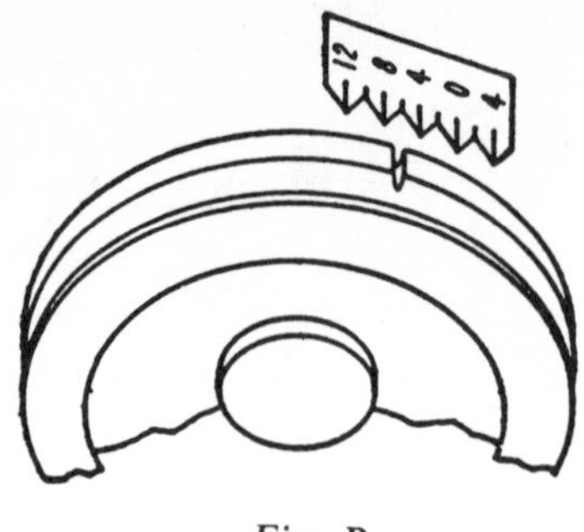

Fig. B

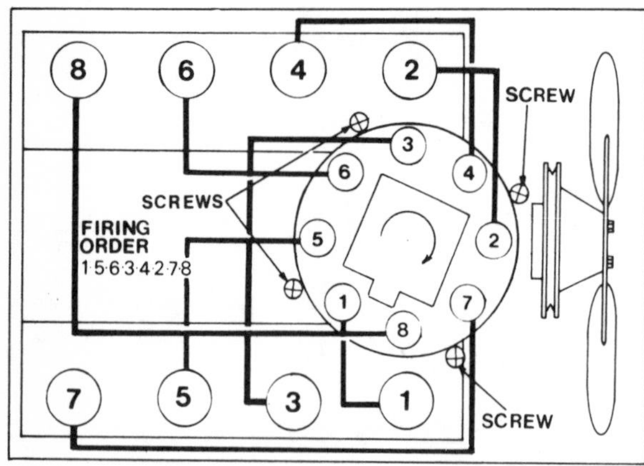

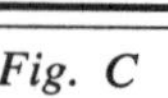

Fig. C

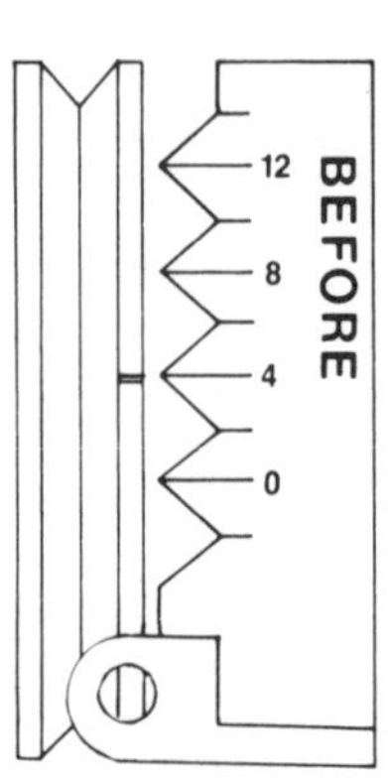

Fig. D

DISTRIBUTOR SPECIFICATIONS

★Note: If unit is checked on the vehicle, double the rpm and degrees to get crankshaft figures.

Breaker arm spring tension—19–23 oz.

Distributor Part No.①	Advance Starts	Centrifugal Advance Degrees @ rpm of Distributor — Intermediate Advance			Full Advance	Vacuum Advance — Inches of Vacuum to Start Plunger	Vacuum Advance — Max. Adv. Dist. Deg. @ Vacuum
1111262	0–2¼ @ 400	3¼–7¼ @ 800	4¾–8½ @ 1000	6¼–10 @ 1200	16 @ 2000	10–12	13¼–15¼ @ 11¼
1111939	0–2¼ @ 400	5.15–7.15 @ 800	7.40–9.40 @ 1000	8.40–10.30 @ 1200	14 @ 2000	8–10	11.30–12.60 @ 13
1112065	0–1 @ 400	3–5 @ 800	4¾–6¾ @ 1000	6–8 @ 1200	13 @ 2000	8–10	11.30–12.60 @ 13
1112108	0–1 @ 400	3–5 @ 800	4¾–6¾ @ 1000	6–8 @ 1200	13 @ 2000	8–10	11.30–12.60 @ 13
1112219	0 @ 400	—	4½–6½ @ 950	—	13 @ 2000	5–7	12 @ 13
1112835	0 @ 400	5 @ 600	—	—	10 @ 2500	5	16 @ 11.5
1112836	0 @ 400	5 @ 600	—	—	10 @ 2500	7	16 @ 13.5
1112837	0 @ 400	4 @ 600	—	—	9 @ 2500	5	16 @ 11.5
1112838	0 @ 400	4 @ 600	—	—	9 @ 2500	7	16 @ 13.5
1112839	0 @ 400	5 @ 600	—	—	10 @ 2500	5	16 @ 11.5
1112840	0 @ 400	5 @ 600	—	—	10 @ 2500	7	16 @ 13.5
1112841	0 @ 400	4 @ 600	—	—	9 @ 2500	5	16 @ 11.5
1112842	0 @ 400	4 @ 600	—	—	9 @ 2500	7	16 @ 13.5
1112845	1 @ 500	—	—	—	12 @ 2000	5	16 @ 11.5
1112855	1 @ 500	—	—	—	12 @ 2000	5	16 @ 11.5
1112892②	–½–0 @ 330	–1–2¼ @ 450	3–5 @ 600	5–7 @ 1400	10 @ 3000	6.5	9.5–10.5 @ 14
1112954②	–½–0 @ 330	–1–2¼ @ 450	3–5 @ 600	5–7 @ 1400	10 @ 3000	5.5	13.5–14.5 @ 16

①—Stamped on distributor housing plate. ②—High energy ignition.

CAMARO • CHEVELLE • CHEVROLET CORVETTE • MONTE CARLO • NOVA

SERIAL NUMBER LOCATION

Plate on left front door pillar on top of left side instrument panel

ENGINE NUMBER LOCATION

4 & 6 CYL.: Pad at front righthand side of cylinder block at rear of distributor

V8 ENGINES: Pad at front righthand side of cylinder block

ENGINE IDENTIFICATION CODE

Engines are identified in the following table by the code letter or letters immediately following the engine serial number.

CAMARO

CODE		
CCR	6-250 with M/T	1974
CCW	6-250 with T/H, E.E.C.	1974
CCX	6-250 with T/H	1974
CMA	8-350 with T/H	1974
CMC	8-350 with M/T	1974
CKB	8-350 with M/T, 185 H.P.	1974
CKH	8-350 with 4 BC, M/T	1974
CKH	8-350 with M/T, E.E.C., 185 H.P.	1974
CLJ	8-350 with M/T, 245 H.P.	1974
CKU	8-350 with T/H, 185 H.P.	1974
CKD	8-350 with 4BC, T/H	1974
CKD	8-350 with T/H, E.E.C., 185 H.P.	1974
CLK	8-350 with 4BC, T/H	1974
CMU	8-350	1975
CRC	8-350	1975
CMF	8-350	1975
CMH	8-350	1975
CRX	8-350	1975
CHW	8-350	1975
CHS	8-350	1975
CHT	8-350	1975
CJY	6-250	1975
CJZ	6-250	1975
CJL	6-250	1975
CJM	6-250	1975
CJR	6-250	1975
CJT	6-250	1975
CJU	6-250	1975
CJF	6-250	1975

CHEVROLET

CODE		
CMK	8-350 with 4BC, E.E.C., taxi & police	1974
CMA	8-350 with E.E.C., taxi & police	1974
CMD	8-350 with taxi & police	1974
CMH	8-350 with 4BC, E.E.C., police	1974
CMJ	8-350 with 4BC, police	1974
CMJ	8-350	1975
CKD	8-350 with 4BC, E.E.C.	1974
CRU	8-350	1975
CRW	8-350	1975
CRY	8-350	1975
CSA	8-400	1975
CTC	8-400 with 4BC, E.E.C., 180 H.P.	1974
CTD	8-400 with 4BC, 180 H.P.	1974
CTK	8-400 with 4BC, E.E.C., 180 H.P., police	1974
CTJ	8-400 with 4BC, 180 H.P., police	1974
CTA	8-400 with 150 H.P.	1974
CTB	8-400 with 150 H.P., police	1974
CTL	8-400	1975
CTM	8-400	1975
CTU	8-400	1975
CTW	8-400	1975
CTY	8-400	1975
CTZ	8-400	1975
CWU	8-454 with police	1974
CWW	8-454 with E.E.C., police	1974
CWY	8-544 with E.E.C.	1974
CXA	8-454	1974
CXX	8-454	1975
CXY	8-454	1975

CHEVELLE & MONTE CARLO

CODE		
CCR	6-250 with M/T	1974
CCW	6-250 with T/H, E.E.C.	1974
CCX	6-250 with T/H	1974
CCK	6-250	1974
CJL	6-250	1975
CLM	6-250	1975
CJR	6-250	1975
CJT	6-250	1975
CJU	6-250	1975
CJF	6-250	1975
CJZ	6-250	1975
CMC	8-350 with M/T	1974
CMA	8-350 with T/H	1974
CKH	8-350 with 4BC, M/T	1974
CKD	8-350 with 4BC, T/H	1974
CMF	8-350	1975
CMH	8-350	1975
CMJ	8-350	1975
CMU	8-350	1975
CTC	8-400 with T/H, E.E.C., 180 H.P.	1974
CTA	8-400 with T/H, 150 H.P.	1974
CWA	8-454 with M/T	1974
CWX	8-454 with T/H	1974
CWD	8-454 with T/H, E.E.C.	1974
CRT	8-350	1975
CRU	8-350	1975
CRX	8-350	1975
CSM	8-400	1975
CTL	8-400	1975
CTU	8-400	1975
CTX	8-400	1975
CXW	8-454	1975

(continued)

ENGINE IDENTIFICATION CODE—Continued

CHEVY NOVA

CODE		
CCR	6-250 with M/T	1974
CCW	6-250 with T/H, E.E.C.	1974
CCX	6-250 with T/H	1974
CCK	6-250	1974
CCS	6-250	1975
CCT	6-250	1975
CCU	6-250	1975
CCW	6-250	1975
CGC	8-262	1975
CGD	8-262	1975
CGF	8-262	1975
CGH	8-262	1975
CHW	8-350	1975
CJF	6-250	1975
CJL	6-250	1975
CJM	6-250	1975
CJR	6-250	1975
CJS	6-250	1975
CJT	6-250	1975
CJU	6-250	1975
CJW	6-250	1975
CJX	6-250	1975
CJZ	6-250	1975
CMC	8-350 with M/T	1974
CMA	8-350 with T/H	1974
CKB	8-350 with M/T, 185 H.P.	1974
CKH	8-350 with 4BC, M/T	1974
CKH	8-350 with M/T, E.E.C., 185 H.P.	1974
CKU	8-350 with T/H, 185 H.P.	1974
CKD	8-350 with 4 BC, T/H, E.E.C.	1974
CMF	8-350	1975
CMH	8-350	1975
CMU	8-350	1975
CRC	8-350	1975
CRX	8-350	1975
CZF	8-262	1975
CZH	8-262	1975
CZJ	8-262	1975
CZK	8-262	1975
CZL	8-262	1975
CZM	8-262	1975
CZY	8-262	1975
CZZ	8-262	1975

CORVETTE

CODE		
CHA	8-350	1975
CHB	8-350	1975
CHC	8-350	1975
CHR	8-350	1975
CHU	8-350	1975
CHZ	8-350	1975
CKZ	8-350 with M/T	1974
CLB	8-350 with M/T, E.E.C.	1974
CLR	8-350 with M/T, 245 H.P.	1974
CLA	8-350 with T/H	1974
CLC	8-350 with T/H, E.E.C	1974
CLD	8-350 with T/H, 245 H P.	1974
CWM	8-454 with M/T	1974
CWR	8-454 with T/H	1974
CWS	8-454 with T/H, E.E.C	1974

NOTES

A/C: Air Conditioned
A/H: Aluminum Heads
A/S: Air suspension
AIR: Air injection reactor
A/T: Automatic transmission
4BC: Four barrel carburetor
E.E.C.: Exhaust emission control
F/I: Fu el injection
H/D: Heavy Duty
HDC: Heavy duty clutch
HPE: High performance engine
H-L: Hydraulic lifters
M/T: Manual transmission
O/D: Overdrive
P/G: Powerglide
P/S: Power steering
P/V: Positive crankcase ventilation
SHPE: Special high perf. engine
S.S.: Super Sport
T/D: Torque Drive
T/H: Turbo Hydramatic
T/I: Transistor ignition

GENERAL ENGINE SPECIFICATIONS

Engine①	Carburetor	Bore and Stroke	Piston Displacement, Cubic Inches	Compression Ratio	Maximum Brake HP @ rpm	Maximum Torque Lbs. Ft. @ rpm	Normal Oil Pressure Pounds
1974							
100 Horsepower............6-250	1 Barrel	3.875 x 3.53	250	8.25	100 @ 3600	175 @ 1800	40
145 Horsepower..........V8-350	2 Barrel	4.00 x 3.48	350	8.50	145 @ 3600	250 @ 2200	40
160 Horsepower..........V8-350	4 Barrel	4.00 x 3.48	350	8.50	160 @ 3800	250 @ 2400	40
185 Horsepower..........V8-350	4 Barrel	4.00 x 3.48	350	8.50	185 @ 4000	270 @ 2600	40
195 Horsepower..........V8-350	4 Barrel	4.00 x 3.48	350	8.50	195 @ 4400	275 @ 2800	40
245 Horsepower..........V8-350	4 Barrel	4.00 x 3.48	350	9.0	245 @ 5200	280 @ 4000	40
250 Horsepower..........V8-350	4 Barrel	4.00 x 3.48	350	9.0	250 @ 5200	285 @ 4000	40
150 Horsepower..........V8-400	2 Barrel	4.125 x 3.75	400	8.50	150 @ 3200	295 @ 2000	40
180 Horsepower..........V8-400	4 Barrel	4.125 x 3.75	400	8.50	180 @ 3800	290 @ 2400	40
235 Horsepower..........V8-454	4 Barrel	4.250 x 4.00	454	8.50	235 @ 4000	360 @ 2800	45
270 Horsepower..........V8-454	4 Barrel	4.250 x 4.00	454	8.50	270 @ 4400	380 @ 2800	45

(continued)

GENERAL ENGINE SPECIFICATIONS—Continued

Engine	Carburetor	Bore and Stroke	Piston Displacement, Cubic Inches	Compression Ratio	Maximum Brake HP @ rpm	Maximum Torque Lbs. Ft. @ rpm	Normal Oil Pressure Pounds
1975							
105 Horsepower............6-250	1 Barrel	3.875 x 3.53	250	8.25	105 @ 3800	185 @ 1200	36-41
110 Horsepower..........V8-262	2 Barrel	3.671 x 3.10	262	8.5	110 @ 3600	200 @ 2000	32-40
145 Horsepower..........V8-350	2 Barrel	4.00 x 3.48	350	8.5	145 @ 3800	250 @ 2200	32-40
155 Horsepower..........V8-350	4 Barrel	4.00 x 3.48	350	8.5	155 @ 3800	250 @ 2400	32-40
165 Horsepower..........V8-350	4 Barrel	4.00 x 3.48	350	8.5	165 @ 3800	255 @ 2400	32-40
205 Horsepower..........V8-350	4 Barrel	4.00 x 3.48	350	9.0	205 @ 4800	255 @ 3600	32-40
175 Horsepower..........V8-400	4 Barrel	4.125 x 3.75	400	8.5	175 @ 3600	305 @ 2000	42-46
215 Horsepower..........V8-454	4 Barrel	4.251 x 4.00	454	8.15	215 @ 4000	350 @ 2400	42-46

(1)—Ratings are net—As installed in the vehicle.

TUNEUP SPECIFICATIONS

★When using a timing light, disconnect vacuum hose or tube at distributor and plug opening in hose or tube so idle speed will no be affected.

●When checking compression, lowest cylinder must be within 80% of highest.

▲Before removing wires from distributor cap, determine location of the No. 1 wire in cap, as distributor position may have been altered from that shown at the end of this chart.

Engine	Spark Plug		Distributor		Ignition Timing★			Carb. Adjustments					
								Hot Idle Speed(3)		Air Fuel Ratio		Idle CO%	
	Type	Gap Inch	Point Gap Inch	Dwell Angle Deg.	Firing Order Fig. ▲	Timing BTDC Deg. (1)	Mark Fig.	Std. Trans.	Auto. Trans.(2)	Std. Trans.	Auto. Trans.	Std. Trans.	Auto. Trans.
CAMARO													
1974													
6-250(18)	R46T	.035	(4)	31-34	C	8	A	850	—	—	—	.3	.3
6-250(19)	R46T	.035	(4)	31-34	C	6	A	—	600D	—	—	.3	.3
8-350, 145 HP(18)	R44T	.035	(4)	29-31	D	TDC	A	900	—	—	—	.5	.5
8-350, 145 HP(19)	R44T	.035	(4)	29-31	D	8	A	—	600D	—	—	.5	.5
8-350, 160 HP(18)	R44T	.035	(4)	29-31	D	4	A	900	—	—	—	.5	.5
8-350, 160 HP(19)	R44T	.035	(4)	29-31	D	8	A	—	600D	—	—	.5	.5
8-350, 185 HP(18)	R44T	.035	(4)	29-31	D	8(6)	A	900	—	—	—	.5	.5
8-350, 185 HP(19)	R44T	.035	(4)	29-31	D	8	A	—	600D	—	—	.5	.5
8-350, 245 HP	R44T	.035	(4)	29-31	D(23)	8	A	900	700D	—	—	.5	.5
1975													
6-250	R46TX	.060	—	—	E	8	A	850	600D	—	—	—	—
6-250(7)	R46TX	.060	—	—	E	10	A	850	550D(9)	—	—	—	—
8-350 2-bbl.	R44TX	.060	—	—	F	6	A	800	600D	—	—	—	—
8-350(18)	R44TX	.060	—	—	F	6(6)	A	800	—	—	—	—	—
8-350(19)	R44TX	.060	—	—	F	8(8)	A	—	600D	—	—	—	—

(continued)

TUNEUP SPECIFICATIONS—Continued

★When using a timing light, disconnect vacuum tube or hose at distributor and plug opening in hose or tube so idle speed will not be affected.

●When checking compression, lowest cylinder must be within 80% of highest.

▲Before removing wires from distributor cap, determine location of the No. 1 wire in cap, as distributor position may have been altered from that shown at the end of this chart.

Engine	Spark Plug		Distributor		Ignition Timing★			Carburetor Adjustments					
								Hot Idle Speed③		Air Fuel Ratio		Idle CO%	
	Type	Gap Inch	Point Gap Inch	Dwell Angle Deg.	Firing Order Fig. ▲	Timing BTDC Deg. ①	Mark Fig.	Std. Trans.	Auto. Trans.②	Std. Trans.	Auto. Trans.	Std. Trans.	Auto. Trans.
CHEVELLE & MONTE CARLO													
1974													
6-250⑱	R46T	.035	④	31–34	C	8	A	850	—	—	—	.3	.3
6-250⑲	R46T	.035	④	31–34	C	6	A	—	600D	—	—	.3	.3
8-350, 145 HP⑱	R44T	.035	④	29–31	D	TDC	A	900	—	—	—	.5	.5
8-350, 145 HP⑲	R44T	.035	④	29–31	D	8	A	—	600D	—	—	.5	.5
8-350, 160 HP⑱	R44T	.035	④	29–31	D	4	A	900	—	—	—	.5	.5
8-350, 160 HP⑲	R44T	.035	④	29–31	D	8	A	—	600D	—	—	.5	.5
8-350, 185 HP⑱	R44T	.035	④	29–31	D	8⑥	A	900	—	—	—	.5	.5
8-350, 185 HP⑲	R44T	.035	④	29–31	D	8	A	—	600D	—	—	.5	.5
8-400	R44T	.035	④	29–31	D	8	A	—	600D	—	—	.5	.5
8-454	R44T	.035	④	29–31	D	10	A	800	600D	—	—	.5	.5
1975													
6-250	R46TX	.060	—	—	E	8	A	850	600D	—	—	—	—
6-250⑦	R46TX	.060	—	—	E	10	A	850	550D⑨	—	—	—	—
8-350 2-bbl.	R44TX	.060	—	—	F	6	A	800	600D	—	—	—	—
8-350 4-bbl.⑱	R44TX	.060	—	—	F	6⑥	A	800	—	—	—	—	—
8-350 4-bbl.⑲	R44TX	.060	—	—	F	8⑧	A	—	600D	—	—	—	—
8-400	R44TX	.060	—	—	F	8	A	—	600D	—	—	—	—
8-454	R44TX	.060	—	—	F	16	A	—	600D	—	—	—	—
NOVA													
1974													
6-250⑱	R46T	.035	④	31–34	C	8	A	850	—	—	—	.3	.3
6-250⑲	R46T	.035	④	31–34	C	6	A	—	600D	—	—	.3	.3
8-350, 145 HP⑱	R44T	.035	④	29–31	D	TDC	A	900	—	—	—	.5	.5
8-350, 145 HP⑲	R44T	.035	④	29–31	D	8	A	—	600D	—	—	.5	.5
8-350, 160 HP⑱	R44T	.035	④	29–31	D	4	A	900	—	—	—	.5	.5
8-350, 160 HP⑲	R44T	.035	④	29–31	D	8	A	—	600D	—	—	.5	.5
8-350, 185 HP⑱	R44T	.035	④	29–31	D	8⑥	A	900	—	—	—	.5	.5
8-350, 185 HP⑲	R44T	.035	④	29–31	D	8	A	—	600D	—	—	.5	.5
1975													
6-250	R46TX	.060	—	—	E	8	A	850	600D	—	—	—	—
6-250⑦	R46TX	.060	—	—	E	10	A	850	550D⑨	—	—	—	—
8-262	R44TX	.060	—	—	F	8	G	800	600D	—	—	—	—
8-350 2-bbl.	R44TX	.060	—	—	F	6	A	800	600D	—	—	—	—
8-350 4-bbl.⑱	R44TX	.060	—	—	F	6⑥	A	800	—	—	—	—	—
8-350 4-bbl.⑲	R44TX	.060	—	—	F	8⑧	A	—	600D	—	—	—	—
CHEVROLET													
1974													
8-350, 145 HP	R44T	.035	④	29–31	D	8	A	—	600D	—	—	.5	.5
8-350, 160 HP	R44T	.035	④	29–31	D	8	A	—	600D	—	—	.5	.5
8-400	R44T	.035	④	29–31	D	8	A	—	600D	—	—	.5	.5
8-454	R44T	.035	④	29–31	D㉓	10	A	—	600D	—	—	.5	.5
1975													
8-350 2-bbl.	R44TX	.060	—	—	F	6	A	—	600D	—	—	—	—
8-350 4-bbl.	R44TX	.060	—	—	F	8⑧	A	—	600D	—	—	—	—
8-400	R44TX	.060	—	—	F	8	A	—	600D	—	—	—	—
8-454	R44TX	.060	—	—	F	16	A	—	600D	—	—	—	—

(continued)

TUNEUP SPECIFICATIONS—Continued

★When using a timing light, disconnect vacuum hose or tube at distributor and plug opening in hose or tube so idle speed will not be affected.

●When checking compression, lowest cylinder must be within 80% of highest.

▲When removing wires from distributor cap, determine location of the No. 1 wire in cap, as distributor position may have been altered from that shown at the end of this chart.

Engine	Spark Plug		Distributor		Ignition Timing★			Carb. Adjustments					
								Hot Idle Speed③		Air Fuel Ratio		Idle CO%	
	Type	Gap Inch	Point Gap Inch	Dwell Angle Deg.	Firing Order Fig. ▲	Timing BTDC Deg. ①	Mark Fig.	Std. Trans.	Auto. Trans.②	Std. Trans.	Auto. Trans.	Std. Trans.	Auto. Trans.
CORVETTE													
1974													
8-350, 195 HP⑱	R44T	.035	④	29–31	B	8⑥	A	900	—	—	—	.5	.5
8-350, 195 HP⑲	R44T	.035	④	29–31	B	8	A	—	600D	—	—	.5	.5
8-350, 250 HP	R44T	.035	④	29–31	B	8	A	900	700D	—	—	.5	.5
8-454	R44T	.035	④	29–31	D	10	A	800	600D	—	—	.5	.5
1975													
8-350⑱	R44TX	.060	—	—	F	6⑥	A	800	—	—	—	—	—
8-350⑲	R44TX	.060	—	—	F	6	A	—	600D	—	—	—	—

①—BTDC: Before top dead center.
②—D: Drive. N: Neutral.
③—Where two speeds are listed, lower speed indicates idle solenoid disconnected.
④—New points, .019″, used .016″. On V8s, turn adjusting screw in (clockwise) until engine misfires; then back off ½ turn.
⑥—For California set at 4° BTDC.
⑦—With integral intake manifold and all California models.
⑧—For California set at 6° BTDC.
⑨—For California 600 rpm.
⑱—With standard transmission.
⑲—With automatic transmission.
⑳—With distributor 1111496 set at 14°. All others set at 4°.
㉓—HEI, fig. H

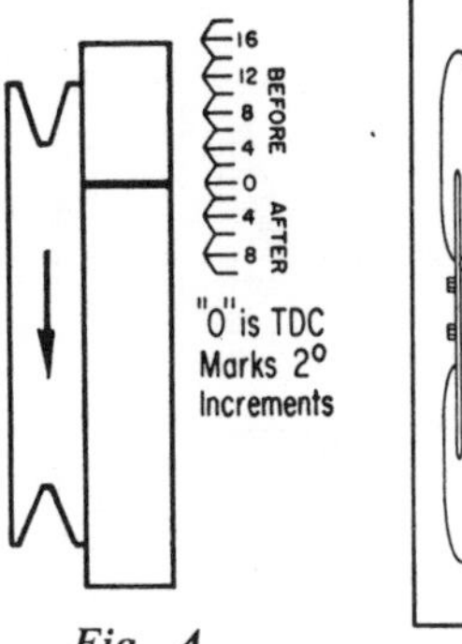

Fig. A

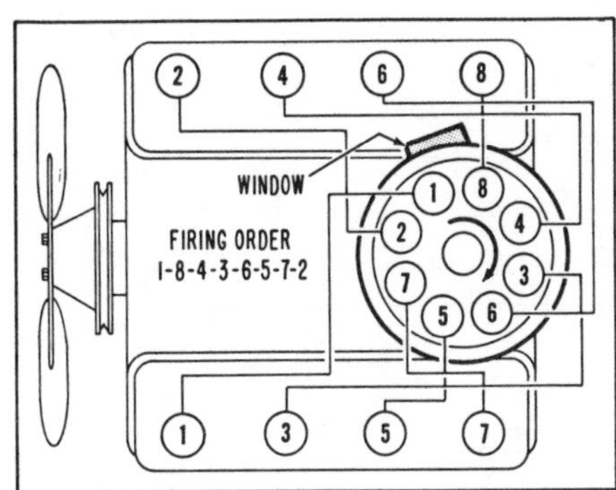

Fig. B

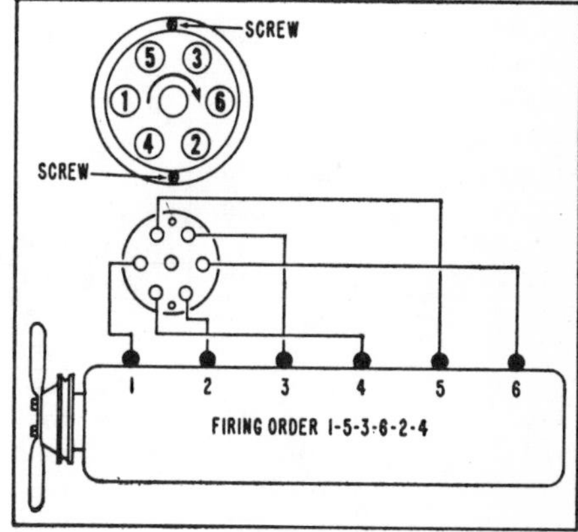

Fig. C

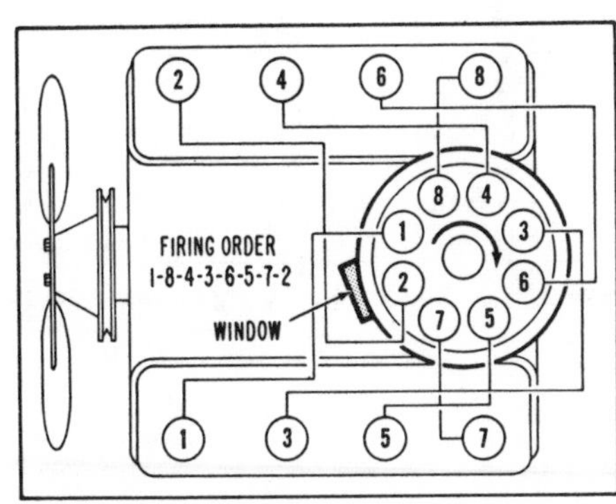

Fig. D

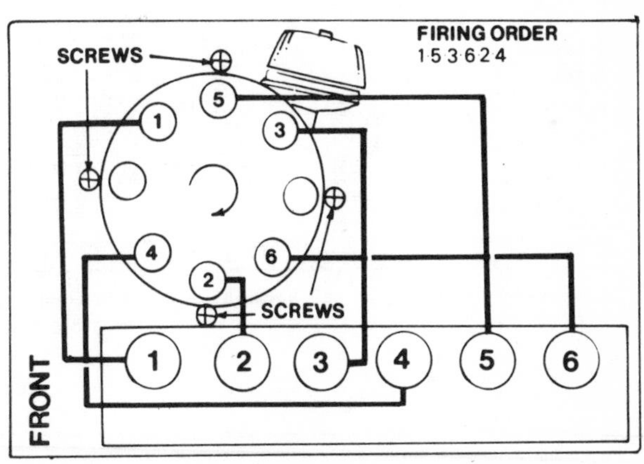

Fig. E

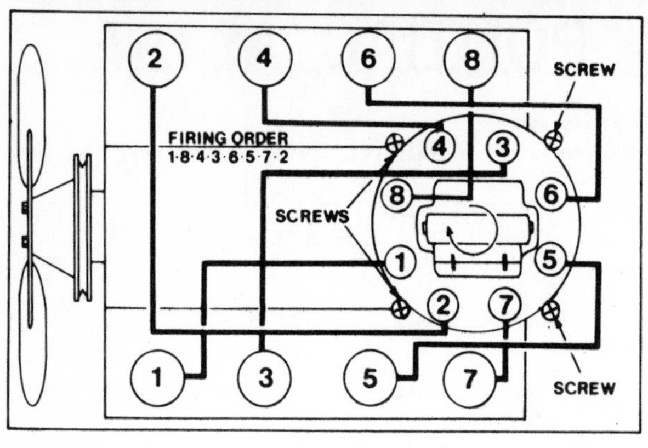

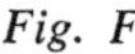
Fig. F

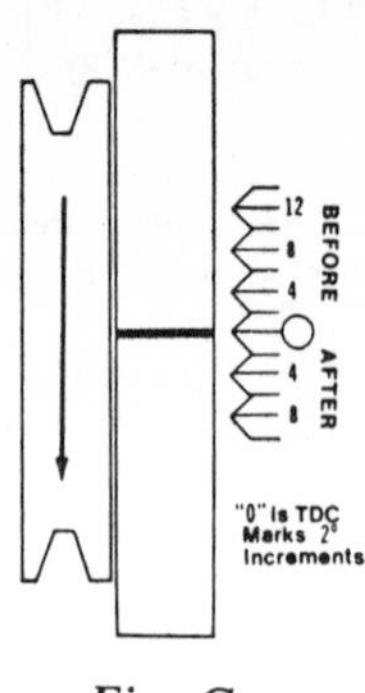

Fig. G

DISTRIBUTOR SPECIFICATIONS

★**Note: If unit is checked on vehicle, double the rpm and degrees to get crankshaft figures.**

Distributor Part No.①	Advance Starts	Centrifugal Advance Degrees @ rpm of Distributor — Intermediate Advance			Centrifugal Advance — Full Advance	Vacuum Advance — Inches of Vacuum to Start Plunger	Vacuum Advance — Max. Adv. Dist. Deg. @ Vacuum
1974							
1110499②	0 @ 550	7 @ 1150	—	—	12 @ 2050	7	12 @ 15.5
1112093③	0 @ 550	5½ @ 1200	—	—	9 @ 2100	6	7½ @ 14
1112113③	0 @ 550	5½ @ 1200	—	—	9 @ 2100	6	10 @ 15.7
1112114③	0 @ 550	5½ @ 1200	—	—	9 @ 2100	6	10 @ 15.7
1112844	0 @ 500	—	—	—	10 @ 1100	4	7 @ 8.5
1112247②	0 @ 550	5½ @ 1200	—	—	9 @ 2100	6	7½ @ 14
1112250②	0 @ 550	5½ @ 1200	—	—	9 @ 2100	10	5 @ 15.5
1112504③	0 @ 550	5½ @ 1200	—	—	9 @ 2100	8	8 @ 16
1112846	0 @ 500	—	—	—	10 @ 2100	4	15 @ 10.5
1112847	0 @ 550	5½ @ 1200	—	—	9 @ 2100	6	14 @ 8.5
1112849	0 @ 500	5 @ 900	7½ @ 1200	—	11 @ 2100	3	14 @ 8.5
1112850	0 @ 500	5 @ 900	7½ @ 1200	—	11 @ 2100	3	14 @ 8.5
1112851	0 @ 550	5½ @ 1200	—	—	9 @ 2100	3	14 @ 8.5
1112852	0 @ 600	1 @ 730	6 @ 1100	—	10 @ 2500	3	14 @ 8.5
1112853	0 @ 500	6 @ 1100	—	—	10 @ 2500	3	14 @ 8.5
1112854	0 @ 500	—	—	—	10 @ 2100	4	15 @ 10.5
1975							
1110650	0 @ 550	3½ @ 1150	—	—	8 @ 2100	4	9 @ 12
1112863	0 @ 800	3 @ 1100	—	—	7 @ 1900	4	9 @ 12
1112880	0 @ 600	6 @ 1000	—	—	11 @ 2100	4	9 @ 12
1112882	0 @ 500	4 @ 800	—	—	7½ @ 1400	8	7½ @ 15½
1112883	0 @ 550	6 @ 800	8 @ 1200	—	11 @ 2300	4	7½ @ 10
1112886	0 @ 900	—	—	—	6 @ 2100	4	9 @ 14
1112888	0 @ 550	6 @ 800	—	—	8 @ 2100	4	9 @ 12
1112933	0 @ 600	4½ @ 1000	—	—	11 @ 2000	3	8 @ 8

①—Stamped on distributor housing cover. ②—Breaker arm spring tension—19–23. ③—Breaker arm spring tension—28–32.

CHEVROLET VEGA • PONTIAC ASTRE

SERIAL NUMBER LOCATION

On top of instrument panel, left front.

ENGINE NUMBER LOCATION

On pad at right side of cylinder block, above starter.

ENGINE IDENTIFICATION CODE

Engines are identified in the following table by the code letter or letters immediately following the engine serial number.

Code		Code		Code	
CAB with TH 350, W/EEC	1974	CAD with M/T, W/EEC	1974	CAS 4-140	1975
CAA with M/T, W/EEC	1974	CAK with TH 350, W/EEC	1974	CAT 4-140	1975
CAH with TH 350, W/EEC	1974	CAL with M/T, W/EEC	1974	CBB 4-140	1975
CAJ with M/T, W/EEC	1974	CAM 4-140	1975	CBC 4-140	1975
CAC with TH 350, W/EEC	1974	CAR 4-140	1975		

M/T: Manual transmission
P/G: Powerglide
T/D: Torque drive
T/H: Turbo Hydramatic
L/ECC: Less Exhaust Emission Control
W/ECC: With Exhaust Emission Control

GENERAL ENGINE SPECIFICATIONS

Engine①	Carburetor	Bore and Stroke	Piston Displacement, Cubic Inches	Compression Ratio	Maximum Brake HP @ rpm	Maximum Torque Lbs. Ft. @ rpm	Normal Oil Pressure Pounds
1974							
75 Horsepower.............4-140	1 Barrel	3.500 x 3.625	140	8.00	75 @ 4400	115 @ 2400	40
85 Horsepower.............4-140	2 Barrel	3.500 x 3.625	140	8.00	85 @ 4400	122 @ 2400	40
1975							
78 Horsepower.............4-140	1 Barrel	3.500 x 3.625	140	8.00	78 @ 4200	120 @ 2000	40
87 Horsepower.............4-140	2 Barrel	3.500 x 3.625	140	8.00	87 @ 4400	122 @ 2800	40

①—Ratings Net—as installed in the vehicle.

TUNEUP SPECIFICATIONS

★When using a timing light, disconnect vacuum hose or tube at distributor and plug opening in hose or tube so idle speed will not be affected.

●When checking compression, lowest cylinder must be within 80% of highest.

▲Before removing wires from distributor cap, determine location of the No. 1 wire in cap, as distributor position may have been altered from that shown at the end of this chart.

Engine	Spark Plug		Distributor		Ignition Timing★			Carb. Adjustments					
								Hot Idle Speed		Air Fuel Ratio		Idle CO%	
	Type	Gap Inch	Point Gap Inch	Dwell Angle Deg.	Firing Order Fig. ▲	Timing Deg. BTDC ①	Mark Fig.	Std. Trans.	Auto. Trans.②	Std. Trans.	Auto. Trans.	Std. Trans.	Auto. Trans.
1974													
All	R42TS	.035	③	31–34	A	④	B	700	750D	—	—	0.5	0.5
1975													
78 Horsepower	R43TS	.060	—	—	C	⑤	D	700	550D	—	—	—	—
87 Horsepower	R43TS	.060	—	—	C	④	D	700	600D	—	—	—	—

①—BTDC—Before top dead center.
②—D—Drive.
③—New points .019″, used .016″.
④—Synchromesh trans. 10° BTDC; automatic trans. 12° BTDC.
⑤—Synchromesh trans. 8° BTDC, automatic trans. 10° BTDC.

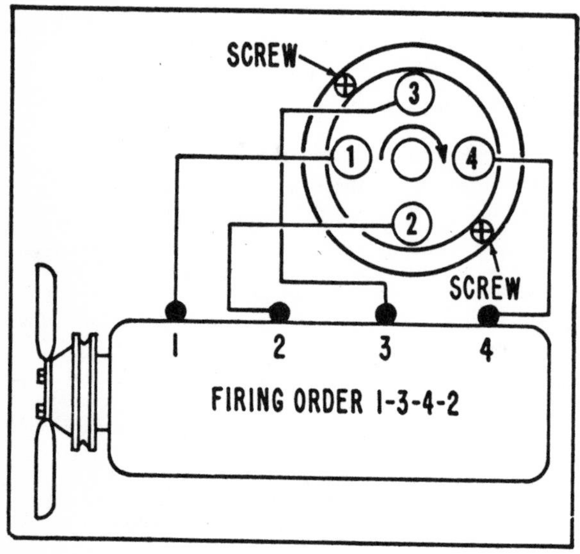

Fig. A

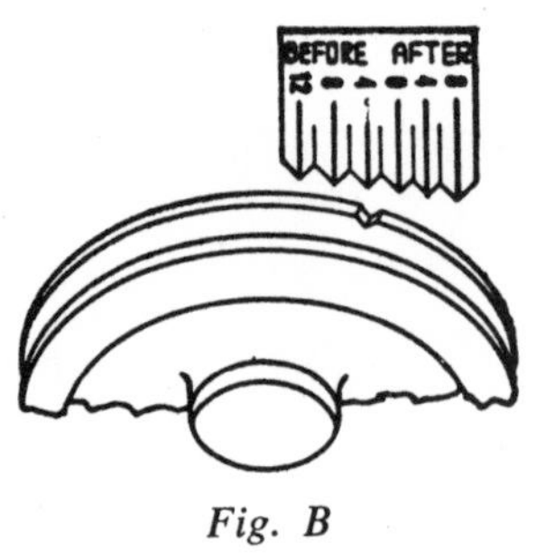

Fig. B

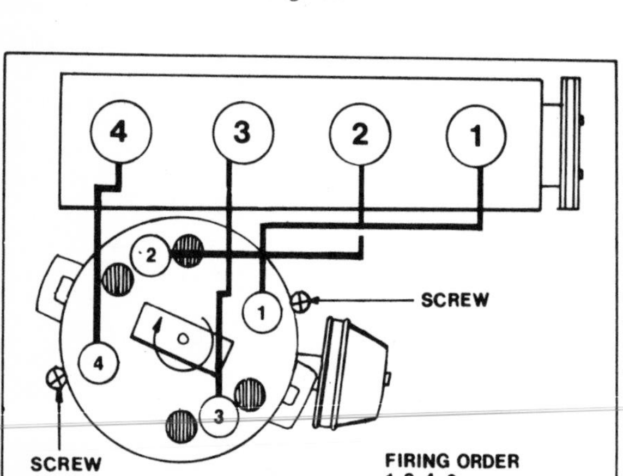

Fig. C

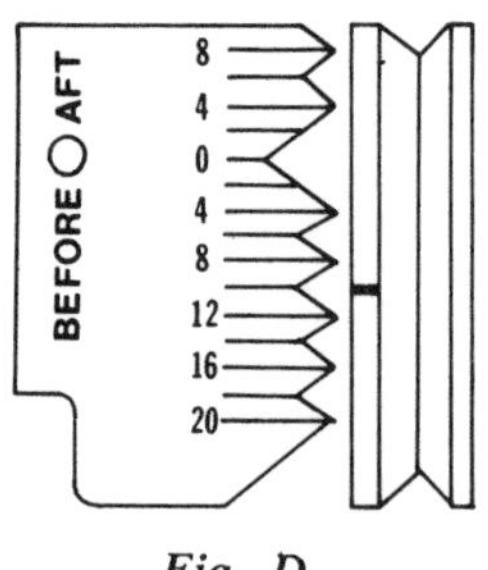

Fig. D

DISTRIBUTOR SPECIFICATIONS

★If unit is checked on vehicle double the rpm and degrees to get crankshaft figures.

	Centrifugal Advance Degrees @ rpm of Distributor					Vacuum Advance		Distributor Retard
Distributor Part No.①	Advance Starts	Intermediate Advance			Full Advance	Inches of Vacuum To Start Plunger	Max. Adv. Dist. Deg. @ Vacuum	Max. Ret. Dist. Deg. @ Vacuum
1973-74								
1110496	0 @ 800	1 @ 875	6 @ 1600	—	11 @ 2400	7½	12 @ 15	—
1975								
1112862②	0 @ 810	2½ @ 1000	—	—	11 @ 2400	5	12 @ 12	—

①—Located on distributor housing plate. ②—High Energy Ignition.

CHEVROLET MONZA 2+2
BUICK SKYHAWK • OLDS STARFIRE

SERIAL NUMBER LOCATION

On top of instrument panel, left front.

ENGINE NUMBER LOCATION

4 Cyl.: On pad at right side of cylinder block, above starter.

V-6:

V-8: Pad at front right hand side of cylinder block.

ENGINE IDENTIFICATION CODE

Engines are identified in the following table by the code letter or letters immediately following the engine serial number.

Year	Engine	Code	Engine	Code
1975	4-140③	CAM, CAR, CAS	V8-262 Std. Tr.③	CZA, CZB, CZC
	4-140	CAT, CBB, CBC	V8-262 Std. Tr ③	CZD, CZT, CZU
	V6-231 Std. Tr.①④	FP	V8-262 Auto. Tr.③	CZE, CZG
	V6-231 Auto Tr.①④	FR	V8-262 Auto. Tr.③	CGA, CGJ, CGK
	V6-231 Auto. Tr.②④	FS		

①—Except California.
②—California.
③—Monza.
④—Starfire.

GENERAL ENGINE SPECIFICATIONS

Engine	Carburetor	Bore and Stroke	Piston Displacement, Cubic Inches	Compression Ratio	Maximum Brake HP @ rpm	Maximum Torque Lbs. Ft. @ rpm	Normal Oil Pressure Pounds
1975							
87 Horsepower............4-140	2 Barrel	3.5 x 3.625	140	8.0	87 @ 4400	122 @ 2800	40
110 Horsepower...........V6-231	2 Barrel	3.3 x 3.4	231	8.0	110 @ 4000	175 @ 2000	37
110 Horsepower...........V8-262	2 Barrel	3.67 x 3.10	262	8.5	110 @ 3600	200 @ 2000	32–40

TUNEUP SPECIFICATIONS

★When using a timing light, disconnect vacuum hose or tube at distributor and plug opening in hose or tube so idle speed will not be affected.

●When checking compression, lowest cylinder must be within 80% of highest.

▲Before removing wires from distributor cap, determine location of No. 1 wire in cap, as distributor position may have been altered from that shown at the end of this chart.

Engine	Spark Plug		Distributor		Ignition Timing★			Carb. Adjustments					
								Hot Idle Speed		Air Fuel Ratio		Idle CO%	
	Type	Gap Inch	Point Gap Inch	Dwell Angle Deg.	Firing Order Fig. ▲	Timing BTDC Deg. ①	Mark Fig.	Std. Trans.	Auto. Trans.②	Std. Trans.	Auto. Trans.	Std. Trans.	Auto. Trans.
1975													
4-140	R43TSX	.060	—	—	A	③	B	700	750D	—	—	.5	.5
V6-231	R44SX	.060	—	—	C	12	D	800	700D	—	—	—	—
V8-262	R44TX	.060	—	—	E	8	F	800	600D	—	—	—	—

①—BTDC—Before Top Dead Center.
②—D—Drive.
③—Standard trans. 10°, Automatic trans. 12°.

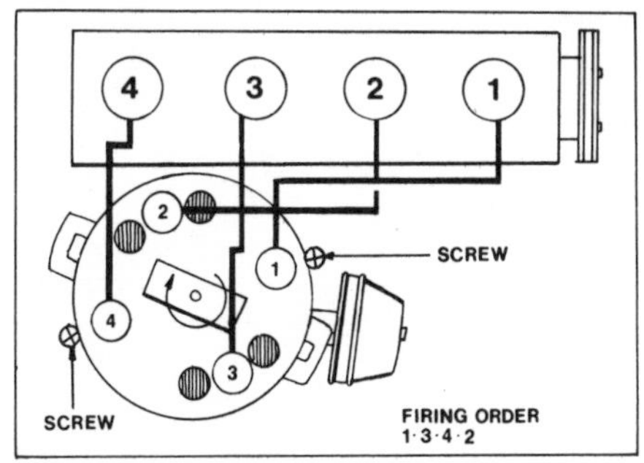

Fig. A

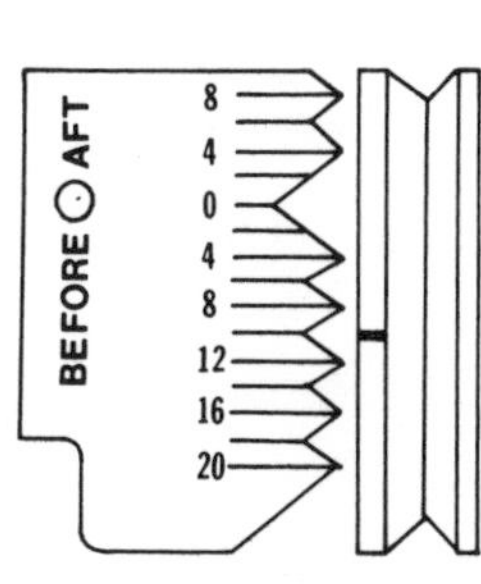

Fig. B

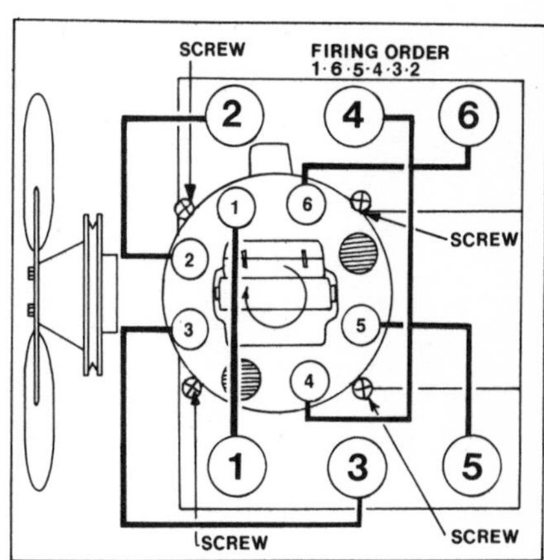

Fig. C

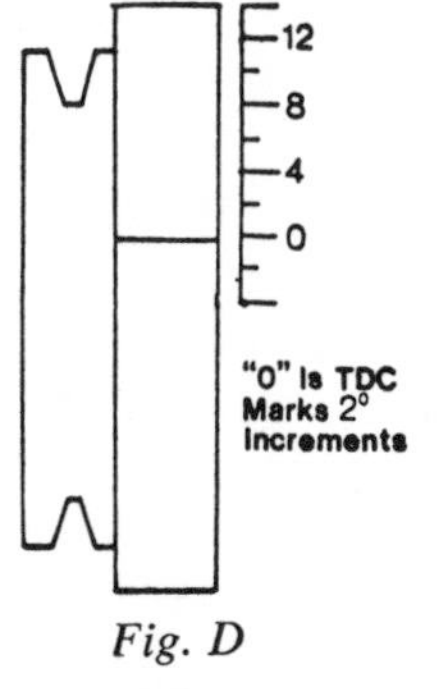

Fig. D

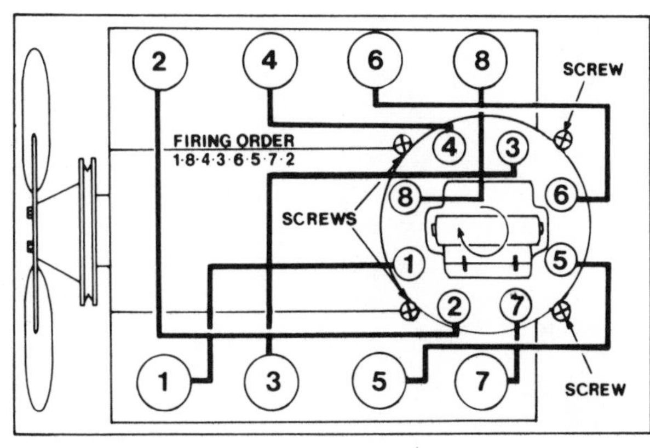

Fig. E

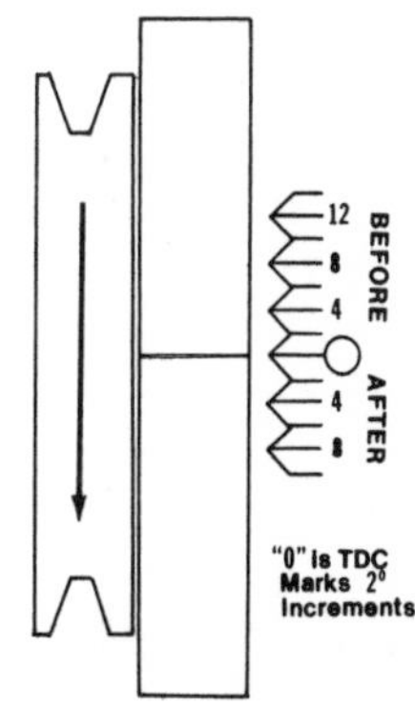

Fig. F

DISTRIBUTOR SPECIFICATIONS

★If unit is checked on vehicle double the rpm and degrees to get crankshaft figures.

Distributor Part No.①	Centrifugal Advance Degrees @ rpm of Distributor					Vacuum Advance		Distributor Retard
	Advance Starts	Intermediate Advance			Full Advance	Inches of Vacuum To Start Plunger	Max. Adv. Dist. Deg. @ Vacuum	Max. Ret. Dist. Deg. @ Vacuum
1975								
1112862	0 @ 810	2½ @ 1000	—	—	11 @ 2200	4	9 @ 12	—
1112933	0 @ 600	4½ @ 1000	—	—	11 @ 2000	3	8 @ 8	—
V6-231	0 @ 500	5 @ 1000	—	—	8 @ 2050	6	9 @ 10	—

①—Located on distributor housing plate.

CHRYSLER • DODGE IMPERIAL • PLYMOUTH

VEHICLE NUMBER LOCATION

1969-75: ON PLATE ATTACHED TO DASH PAD AND VISIBLE THROUGH WINDSHIELD.

ENGINE NUMBER LOCATION

1968-75 Six: Right front of block below cylinder head.
1969-75 V8-273, 318, 340, 360: Left front of block below cylinder head.
1969-71 V8-383 426, 440: Left side rear of block near oil pan flange.
1971-72 V8-400: Right front of block below cylinder head.
1972 V8-440: Upper left front of cylinder block.
1973-75 V8-400, 440: Upper right front of cylinder block.

ENGINE IDENTIFICATION CODE

1969-75 engines are identified by the cubic inch displacement found within the engine number stamped on the pad.

GENERAL ENGINE SPECIFICATIONS

CHRYSLER & IMPERIAL
1974

Engine	Carburetor	Bore and Stroke	Piston Displacement, Cubic Inches	Compression Ratio	Maximum Brake HP @ rpm	Maximum Torque Lbs. Ft. @ rpm	Normal Oil Pressure Pounds
185 Horsepower[1].........V8-400	2 Barrel	4.34 x 3.38	400	8.2	185 @ 4000	315 @ 2400	45–65
200 Horsepower[1]........V8-400[4]	4 Barrel	4.34 x 3.38	400	8.2	200 @ 4400	310 @ 2400	45–65
205 Horsepower[1]........V8-400[3]	4 Barrel	4.34 x 3.38	400	8.2	205 @ 4400	310 @ 2400	45–65
220 Horsepower[1]........V8-440[4]	4 Barrel	4.32 x 3.75	440	8.2	220 @ 4000	345 @ 3200	45–65
230 Horsepower[1]........V8-440[3]	4 Barrel	4.32 x 3.75	440	8.2	230 @ 4000	350 @ 3200	45–65
1975							
150 Horsepower...........V8-318	2 Barrel	3.91 x 3.31	318	8.6	150 @ 4000	255 @ 1600	30–80
180 Horsepower...........V8-360	2 Barrel	4.0 x 3.58	360	8.4	180 @ 4000	290 @ 2400	30–80
165 Horsepower...........V8-400	2 Barrel	4.342 x 3.375	400	8.2	165 @ 4000	295 @ 3200	30–80
190 Horsepower...........V8-400	4 Barrel	4.342 x 3.375	400	8.2	190 @ 4000	290 @ 3200	30–80
235 Horsepower...........V8-400	4 Barrel	4.342 x 3.375	400	8.2	235 @ 4200	320 @ 3200	30–80
215 Horsepower...........V8-440	4 Barrel	4.32 x 3.75	440	8.2	215 @ 4000	330 @ 3200	30–80

DODGE
1974

Engine	Carburetor	Bore and Stroke	Piston Displacement, Cubic Inches	Compression Ratio	Maximum Brake HP @ rpm	Maximum Torque Lbs. Ft. @ rpm	Normal Oil Pressure Pounds
95 Horsepower[1]...........6-198	1 Barrel	3.40 x 3.64	198	8.4	95 @ 4000	145 @ 2000	45–65
105 Horsepower[1]...........6-225	1 Barrel	3.40 x 4.12	225	8.4	105 @ 3600	180 @ 1600	45–65
150 Horsepower[1].........V8-318	2 Barrel	3.91 x 3.31	318	8.6	150 @ 4000	255 @ 2200	45–65
180 Horsepower[1]........V8-360[3]	2 Barrel	4.00 x 3.58	360	8.4	180 @ 4000	290 @ 2400	45–65
200 Horsepower[1]........V8-360[4]	4 Barrel	4.00 x 3.58	360	8.4	200 @ 4000	290 @ 3200	45–65
245 Horsepower[1][2]......V8-360[3]	4 Barrel	4.00 x 3.58	360	8.4	245 @ 4800	320 @ 3600	45–65
185 Horsepower[1]........V8-400[3]	2 Barrel	4.34 x 3.38	400	8.2	185 @ 4000	315 @ 2400	45–65
200 Horsepower[1]........V8-400[4]	4 Barrel	4.34 x 3.38	400	8.2	200 @ 4400	310 @ 2400	45–65
205 Horsepower[1]........V8-400[3]	4 Barrel	4.34 x 3.38	400	8.2	205 @ 4400	310 @ 2400	45–65
250 Horsepower[1][2]......V8-400[3]	4 Barrel	4.34 x 3.38	400	8.2	250 @ 4800	330 @ 3400	45–65
230 Horsepower[1]........V8-440[3]	4 Barrel	4.32 x 3.75	440	8.2	230 @ 4000	350 @ 3200	45–65
220 Horsepower[1]........V8-440[4]	4 Barrel	4.32 x 3.75	440	8.2	220 @ 4000	345 @ 3200	45–65
275 Horsepower[1][2]........V8-440	4 Barrel	4.32 x 3.75	440	8.2	275 @ 4400	375 @ 3200	45–65
1975							
95 Horsepower............6-225	1 Barrel	3.4 x 4.125	225	8.4	95 @ 3600	170 @ 1600	30–70
145 Horsepower...........V8-318	2 Barrel	3.91 x 3.31	318	8.6	145 @ 4000	255 @ 1600	30–80
180 Horsepower...........V8-360	2 Barrel	4.0 x 3.58	360	8.4	180 @ 4000	290 @ 2400	30–80
190 Horsepower...........V8-360	4 Barrel	4.0 x 3.58	360	8.4	190 @ 4000	270 @ 3200	30–80
230 Horsepower...........V8-360	4 Barrel	4.0 x 3.58	360	8.4	230 @ 4400	300 @ 3600	30–80

(continued)

GENERAL ENGINE SPECIFICATIONS—Continued

Engine	Carburetor	Bore and Stroke	Piston Displacement, Cubic Inches	Compression Ratio	Maximum Brake HP @ rpm	Maximum Torque Lbs. Ft. @ rpm	Normal Oil Pressure Pounds
DODGE—Continued							
175 Horsepower..........V8-400	2 Barrel	4.342 x 3.375	400	8.2	175 @ 4000	300 @ 2400	30–80
190 Horsepower..........V8-400	4 Barrel	4.342 x 3.375	400	8.2	190 @ 4000	290 @ 3200	30–80
235 Horsepower..........V8-400	4 Barrel	4.342 x 3.375	400	8.2	235 @ 4200	320 @ 3200	30–80
215 Horsepower..........V8-440	4 Barrel	4.32 x 3.75	440	8.2	215 @ 4000	330 @ 3200	30–80
PLYMOUTH 1974							
95 Horsepower(1)..........6-198	1 Barrel	3.40 x 3.64	198	8.4	95 @ 4000	145 @ 2000	45–65
105 Horsepower(1)..........6-225	1 Barrel	3.40 x 4.12	225	8.4	105 @ 3600	180 @ 1600	45–65
150 Horsepower(1).........V8-318	2 Barrel	3.91 x 3.31	318	8.6	150 @ 4000	255 @ 2200	45–65
170 Horsepower(1)(2).......V8-318	2 Barrel	3.91 x 3.31	318	8.6	170 @ 4000	265 @ 2600	45–65
180 Horsepower(1).........V8-360	2 Barrel	4.00 x 3.58	360	8.4	180 @ 4000	290 @ 2400	45–65
200 Horsepower(1)........V8-360(4)	4 Barrel	4.00 x 3.58	360	8.4	200 @ 4000	290 @ 3200	45–65
245 Horsepower(1)(2)......V8-360(3)	4 Barrel	4.00 x 3.58	360	8.4	245 @ 4800	320 @ 3600	45–65
185 Horsepower(1).........V8-400	2 Barrel	4.34 x 3.38	400	8.2	185 @ 4000	315 @ 2400	45–65
205 Horsepower(1).........V8-400	4 Barrel	4.34 x 3.38	400	8.2	205 @ 4400	310 @ 2400	45–65
250 Horsepower(1)(2).......V8-400	4 Barrel	4.34 x 3.38	400	8.2	250 @ 4800	330 @ 3400	45–65
230 Horsepower(1)........V8-440(3)	4 Barrel	4.32 x 3.75	440	8.2	230 @ 4000	350 @ 3200	45–65
220 Horsepower(1)........V8-440(4)	4 Barrel	4.32 x 3.75	440	8.2	220 @ 4000	345 @ 3200	45–65
275 Horsepower(1)(2).......V8-440	4 Barrel	4.32 x 3.75	440	8.2	275 @ 4400	375 @ 3200	45–65
1975							
95 Horsepower............6-225	1 Barrel	3.4 x 4.125	225	8.4	95 @ 3600	170 @ 1600	30–70
145 Horsepower..........V8-318	2 Barrel	3.91 x 3.31	318	8.6	145 @ 4000	255 @ 1600	30–80
180 Horsepower..........V8-360	2 Barrel	4.0 x 3.58	360	8.4	180 @ 4000	290 @ 2400	30–80
190 Horsepower..........V8-360	4 Barrel	4.0 x 3.58	360	8.4	190 @ 4000	270 @ 3200	30–80
230 Horsepower..........V8-360	4 Barrel	4.0 x 3.58	360	8.4	230 @ 4400	300 @ 3600	30–80
175 Horsepower..........V8-400	2 Barrel	4.342 x 3.375	400	8.2	175 @ 4000	300 @ 2400	30–80
190 Horsepower..........V8-400	4 Barrel	4.342 x 3.375	400	8.2	190 @ 4000	290 @ 3200	30–80
235 Horsepower..........V8-400	4 Barrel	4.342 x 3.375	400	8.2	235 @ 4200	320 @ 3200	30–80
215 Horsepower..........V8-440	4 Barrel	4.32 x 3.75	440	8.2	215 @ 4000	330 @ 3200	30–80

(1)—Ratings are NET—as installed in the vehicle.
(2)—With dual exhausts.
(3)—Exc. California.
(4)—California

TUNEUP SPECIFICATIONS

★When using a timing light, disconnect vacuum hose or tube at distributor and plug opening in hose or tube so idle speed will not be affected.

●When checking compression, lowest cylinder must be within 80 % of highest.

▲Before removing wires from distributor cap, determine location of the No. 1 wire in cap, as distributor position may have been altered from that shown at the end of this chart.

Engine	Spark Plug		Distributor		Ignition Timing★			Carb. Adjustments					
								Hot Idle Speed		Air Fuel Ratio		Idle CO%	
	Type (5)	Gap Inch	Point Gap Inch	Dwell Angle Deg.	Firing Order Fig. ▲	Timing Deg. BTDC (1)	Mark Fig.	Std. Trans.	Auto. Trans.(2)	Std. Trans.	Auto. Trans.	Std. Trans.	Auto. Trans.
CHRYSLER & IMPERIAL 1974													
V8-400(14)	J13Y	.035	—	—	H	7½(7)	E	—	750	—	14.3	—	—
V8-400(3)(16)	J13Y	.035	—	—	H	5	E	—	750	—	14.3	—	—
V8-400(3)(17)	J13Y	.035	—	—	H	5	E	—	750	—	14.1	—	—
V8-440(16)	J11Y	.035	—	—	H	10	E	—	750	—	14.3	—	—
V8-440(17)	J11Y	.035	—	—	H	10	E	—	750	—	14.1	—	—

TUNEUP SPECIFICATIONS—Continued

★When using a timing light, disconnect vacuum hose or tube at distributor and plug opening in hose or tube so idle speed will not be affected.

●When checking compression, lowest cylinder must be within 80% of highest.

▲When removing wires from distributor cap, determine location of the No. 1 wire in cap, as distributor position may have been altered from that shown at the end of this chart.

Engine	Spark Plug		Distributor		Ignition Timing★			Carb. Adjustments					
	Type (5)	Gap Inch	Point Gap Inch	Dwell Angle Deg.	Firing Order Fig. ▲	Timing BTDC Deg. (1)	Mark Fig.	Hot Idle Speed		Air Fuel Ratio		Idle CO%	
								Std. Trans.	Auto. Trans.(2)	Std. Trans.	Auto. Trans.	Std. Trans.	Auto. Trans.
CHRYSLER & IMPERIAL—Continued													
1975													
V8-318(4)(16)	N13Y	.035	—	—	G	2	B	800	750N	14.3 to 1	14.3 to 1	.3(12)	.3(12)
V8-318(6)(16)	N13Y	.035	—	—	G	2(10)	B	750	750N	—	14.3 to 1	—	.5(13)
V8-318(17)	N13Y	.035	—	—	G	TDC	B	—	750N	—	—	—	.5(13)
V8-360 2-bbl	N12Y	.035	—	—	G	6	B	—	750N	—	14.3 to 1	—	.3(12)
V8-360 4-bbl(16)	N12Y	.035	—	—	G	2	B	—	750N	—	14.3 to 1	—	.5(13)
V8-360 4-bbl(17)	N12Y	.035	—	—	G	6	B	—	750N	—	—	—	.5(13)
V8-400 2-bbl	J13Y	.035	—	—	H	10	E	—	750N	—	—	—	.3(12)
V8-400 4-bbl	J13Y	.035	—	—	H	8	D	—	750N	—	(32)	—	(19)
V8-440	RJ87P	.040	—	—	H	8	D	—	750N	—	(32)	—	(20)
V8-440(15)(16)	J11Y	.035	—	—	H	10	D	—	750N	—	14.3 to 1	—	.3(12)
V8-440(15)(17)	RJ87P	.035	—	—	H	8	D	—	750N	—	—	—	.5(13)
DODGE													
1974													
6-198	N14Y	.035	—	—	F	2½	C	800	750	14.3 to 1	14.3 to 1	—	—
6-225	N14Y	.035	—	—	F	TDC	C	800	750	14.3 to 1	14.3 to 1	—	—
V8-318	N13Y	.035	—	—	G	TDC	B	750	750	14.3 to 1	14.3 to 1	—	—
V8-360	N12Y	.035	—	—	G	5(8)	B	850	850	14.3 to 1	14.3 to 1	—	—
V8-400 Auto(14)	J13Y	.035	—	—	H	7½(7)	D	—	750	—	14.3 to 1	—	—
V8-400 Auto(3)	J13Y	.035	—	—	H	5	D	—	750	—	14.3 to 1	—	—
V8-400 Std(15)	J11Y	.035	—	—	H	5	D	900	—	14.3 to 1	—	—	—
V8-400 Auto(11)	J11Y	.035	—	—	H	5(9)	D	—	850	—	14.3 to 1	—	—
V8-440	J11Y	.035	—	—	H	10	D	—	850	—	14.3 to 1	—	—
1975													
6-225	BL13Y	.035	—	—	F	TDC	A	800	750N	(18)	(18)	.3(12)	(20)
V8-318(4)(16)	N13Y	.035	—	—	G	2	B	750	750N	14.3 to 1	14.3 to 1	.3(12)	.3(12)
V8-318(7)(16)	N13Y	.035	—	—	G	2(10)	B	—	900N	—	14.3 to 1	—	.5(13)
V8-318(17)	N13Y	.035	—	—	G	TDC	B	—	750N	—	—	—	.5(13)
V8-360 2-bbl	N12Y	.035	—	—	G	6	B	—	750N	—	14.3 to 1	—	.3(12)
V8-360 4-bbl(16)	N12Y	.035	—	—	G	2	B	—	850N	—	14.3 to 1	—	.5(13)
V8-360 4-bbl(17)	N12Y	.035	—	—	G	6	B	—	750N	—	—	—	.3(12)
V8-400 2-bbl	J13Y	.035	—	—	H	10	E	—	750N	—	14.3 to 1	—	.3(12)
V8-400 4-bbl	J13Y	.035	—	—	H	8	D	—	750N	—	(18)	—	(19)
V8-440	RJ87P	.040	—	—	H	8	D	—	750N	—	(18)	—	(20)
V8-440(15)(16)	J11Y	.035	—	—	H	10	D	—	750N	—	14.3 to 1	—	.3(12)
V8-440(15)(17)	RJ87P	.035	—	—	H	8	D	—	750N	—	—	—	.5(13)
PLYMOUTH													
1974													
6-198	N14Y	.035	—	—	F	2½	A	800	750	14.3 to 1	14.3 to 1	—	—
6-225	N14Y	.035	—	—	F	TDC	A	800	750	14.3 to 1	14.3 to 1	—	—
V8-318	N13Y	.035	—	—	G	TDC	B	750	750	14.3 to 1	14.3 to 1	—	—
V8-360	N12Y	.035	—	—	G	5(8)	B	850	850	14.3 to 1	14.3 to 1	—	—
V8-400 Auto.(14)	J13Y	.035	—	—	H	7½(7)	E	—	750	—	14.3 to 1	—	—
V8-400 Auto.(3)	J13Y	.035	—	—	H	5	D	—	750	—	14.3 to 1	—	—
V8-400 Std. (15)	J11Y	.035	—	—	H	5	D	900	—	14.3 to 1	—	—	—
V8-400 Auto.(11)	J11Y	.035	—	—	H	5(9)	D	—	850	—	14.3 to 1	—	—
V8-440	J11Y	.035	—	—	H	10	D	—	850	—	14.3 to 1	—	—

(continued)

TUNEUP SPECIFICATIONS—Continued

★When using a timing light, disconnect vacuum hose or tube at distributor and plug opening in hose or tube so idle speed will not be affected.

●When checking compression, lowest cylinder must be within 80% of highest.

▲When removing wires from distributor cap, determine location of the No. 1 wire in cap, as distributor position may have been altered from that shown at the end of this chart.

Engine	Spark Plug		Distributor		Ignition Timing★			Carb. Adjustments					
	Type (5)	Gap Inch	Point Gap Inch	Dwell Angle Deg.	Firing Order Fig. ▲	Timing BTDC Deg. (1)	Mark Fig.	Hot Idle Speed		Air Fuel Ratio		Idle CO%	
								Std. Trans.	Auto. Trans.(2)	Std. Trans.	Auto. Trans.	Std. Trans.	Auto. Trans.
1975													
6-225	BL13Y	.035	—	—	F	TDC	A	800	750N	(18)	(18)	.3(12)	(20)
V8-318(4)(16)	N13Y	.035	—	—	G	2	B	750	750N	14.3 to 1	14.3 to 1	.3(12)	.3(12)
V8-318(6)(16)	N13Y	.035	—	—	G	2(10)	B	—	900N	—	14.3 to 1	—	.5(13)
V8-318(17)	N13Y	.035	—	—	G	TDC	B	—	750N	—	—	—	.5(13)
V8-360 2-bbl	N12Y	.035	—	—	G	6	B	—	750N	—	14.3 to 1	—	.3(12)
V8-360 4-bbl(16)	N12Y	.035	—	—	G	2	B	—	850N	—	14.3 to 1	—	.5(13)
V8-360 4-bbl(17)	N12Y	.035	—	—	G	6	B	—	750N	—	—	—	.5(13)
V8-400 2-bbl	J13Y	.035	—	—	H	10	E	—	750N	—	14.3 to 1	—	.3(12)
V8-400 4-bbl	J13Y	.035	—	—	H	8	D	—	750N	—	(18)	—	(19)
V8-440	RJ87P	.040	—	—	H	8	D	—	750N	—	(18)	—	(20)
V8-440(15)(16)	J11Y	.035	—	—	H	10	D	—	750N	—	14.3 to 1	—	.3(12)
V8-440(15)(17)	RJ87P	.035	—	—	H	8	D	—	750N	—	—	—	.5(13)

TUNEUP NOTES

(1)—BTDC: Before top dead center.
(2)—D: Drive. N: Neutral.
(3)—4-barrel carburetor.
(4)—With catalytic converter.
(5)—Champion.
(6)—With air pump.
(7)—All except Station Wagons, Station Wagons 5° BTDC.
(8)—Calif. V8-360 Hi Perf. Manual Trans. 2½° BTDC.
(9)—Exc. Calif. auto. trans. & Police; Calif. auto. trans. & Police, 2½°.
(10)—ATDC: after top dead center.
(11)—High performance & Police.
(12)—Measured ahead of catalytic converter.
(13)—Measured in tailpipe.
(14)—2-barrel carburetor.
(15)—High performance engine.
(16)—Exc. California.
(17)—California only.
(18)—All except Calif. 14.3 to 1.
(19)—Except Calif. .3 (see note 19), Calif. .5 (see note 19).
(20)—Except Calif. .3 (see note 19), Calif. 1.5 (see note 20).

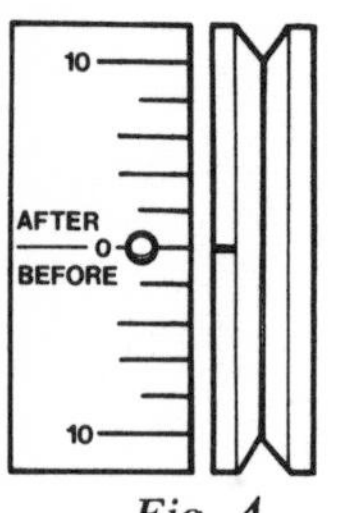

Fig. A

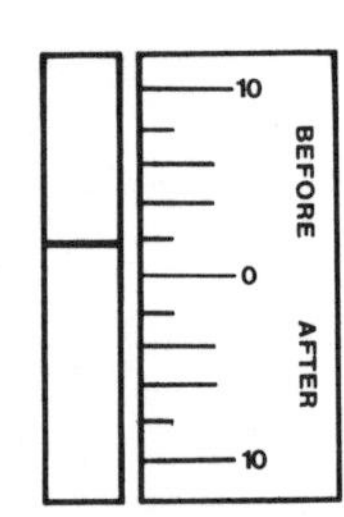

Fig. B

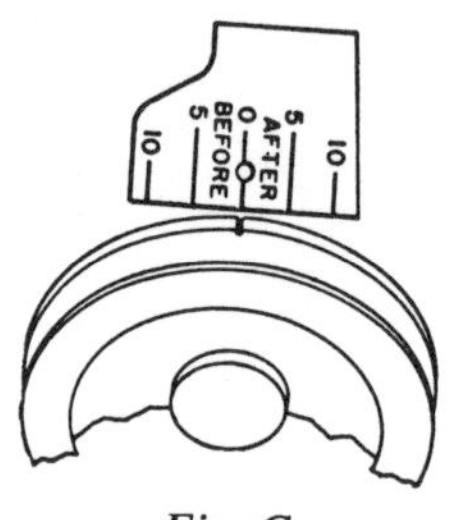

Fig. C

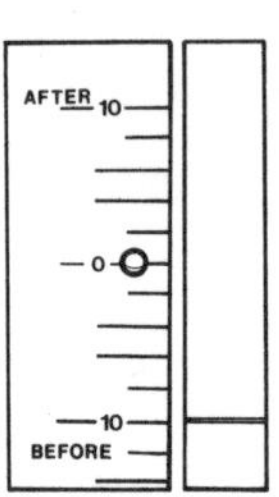

Fig. D

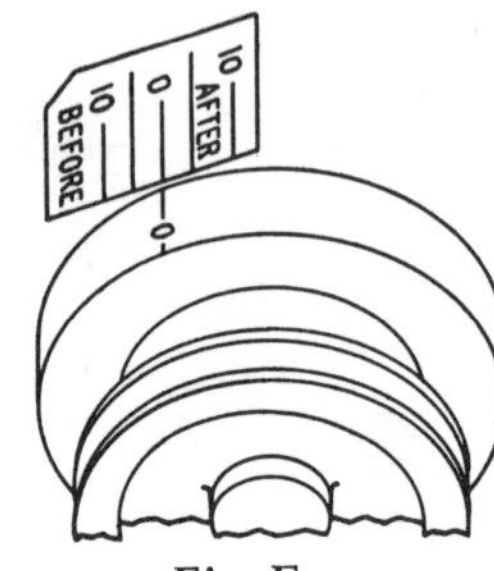

Fig. E

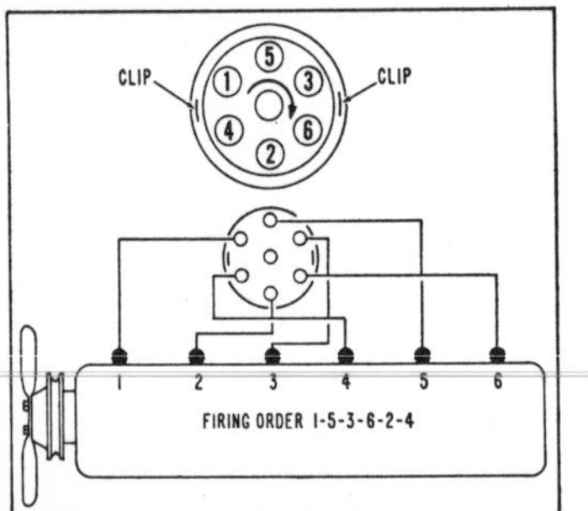

Fig. F

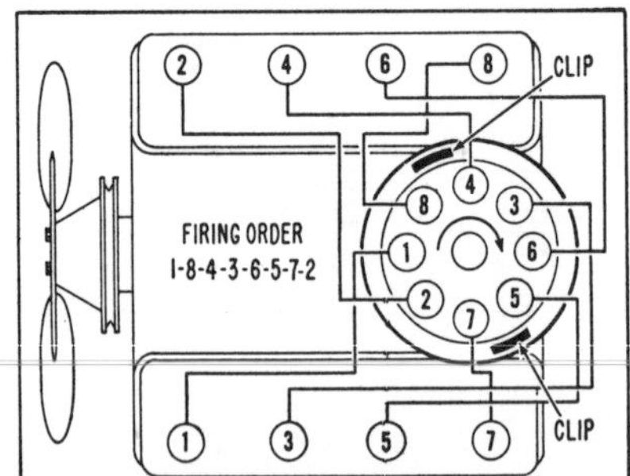

Fig. G

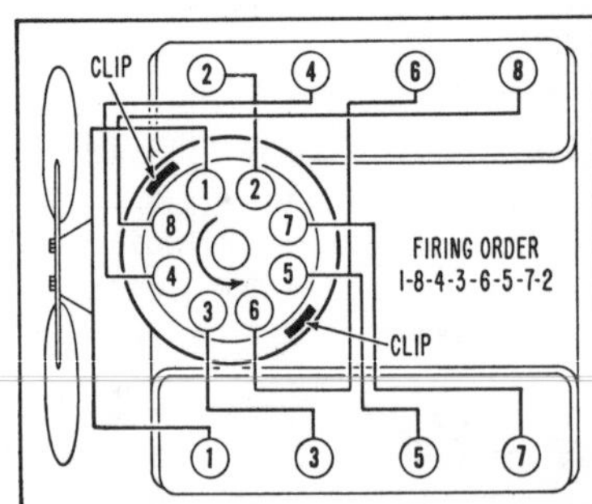

Fig. H

DISTRIBUTOR SPECIFICATIONS

★Note: If unit is checked on vehicle, double the rpm and degrees to get crankshaft figures.

Breaker arm spring tension—17–20oz.

Distributor Part No.①	Centrifugal Advance Degrees @ rpm of Distributor					Vacuum Advance		Distributor Retard
	Advance Starts	Intermediate Advance			Full Advance	Inches of Vacuum to Start Plunger	Max. Adv. Dist. Deg. @ Vacuum	Max. Retard Dist. Deg. @ Vacuum
CHRYSLER & IMPERIAL								
1974								
3755518	0.5–3.5 @ 650	5.5–8 @ 900	—	—	12 @ 2000	8	10 @ 14	—
3755522	0.5–3 @ 650	4–6.5 @ 900	—	—	10 @ 2000	8	10 @ 14	—
3755681	1–4.5 @ 650	8.5–11 @ 950	—	—	16 @ 2150	8	10 @ 14	—
1975								
3874090	1.5–5.5 @ 550	5.5–8 @ 700	—	—	14 @ 2200	7	12 @ 12.5	—
3874101	.5–3 @ 600	6–8.5 @ 950	—	—	12 @ 2000	8	11 @ 14	—
3874110	1–3.5 @ 600	6–8.5 @ 900	—	—	12 @ 2000	8	11 @ 14	—
3874115	1–3.5 @ 600	6–8.5 @ 900	—	—	12 @ 2000	7	12 @ 12.5	—
3874173	1–3.5 @ 600	3.5–6 @ 750	—	—	10 @ 2000	8	11 @ 14	—
3874298	.5–3.5 @ 700	7–10 @ 1100	—	—	16 @ 2100	9	12.5 @ 15.5	—

①—Stamped on distributor housing.

Distributor Part No.①	Advance Starts	Intermediate Advance			Full Advance	Inches of Vacuum to Start Plunger	Max. Adv. Dist. Deg. @ Vacuum	Max. Retard Dist. Deg. @ Vacuum
DODGE & PLYMOUTH								
1974								
3755037	1–4 @ 550	9–11.5 @ 900	—	—	14 @ 2000	9	8.5 @ 15.5	—
3755042	1–4 @ 550	9–11.5 @ 900	—	—	14 @ 2000	7	8.5 @ 11.5	—
3755467	0.5–3.5 @ 550	7–9.5 @ 950	—	—	14 @ 2000	9	8.5 @ 15.5	—
3755470	0.5–3.5 @ 550	7–9.5 @ 950	—	—	14 @ 2000	7	8.5 @ 11.5	—
3755475	0.5–4 @ 550	8–11.5 @ 800	—	—	14 @ 2000	7	11 @ 12.5	—
3755486	1–5 @ 600	8–10 @ 850	—	—	14 @ 2000	8	11 @ 13.5	—
3755503	0.5–4 @ 550	8–10.5 @ 850	—	—	16 @ 2200	8	10 @ 14	—
3755508	1–4.5 @ 650	8–10.5 @ 950	—	—	14 @ 2000	8	10¼ @ 16	—
3755512	0.5–3.5 @ 650	5.5–8 @ 900	—	—	12 @ 2000	8	10 @ 14	—
3755518	0.5–3.5 @ 650	5.5–8 @ 900	—	—	12 @ 2000	8	10 @ 14	—
3755522	0.5–3 @ 650	4–6.5 @ 900	—	—	10 @ 2000	8	10 @ 14	—
3755681	1–4.5 @ 650	8.5–11 @ 950	—	—	16 @ 2150	8	10 @ 14	—
3755686	0.5–4 @ 550	8–10.5 @ 850	—	—	16 @ 2200	8	10¼ @ 16	—
3656763	1.5–5.5 @ 550	6–8.5 @ 700	—	—	16 @ 2100	9	11 @ 15.5	—
3656859	0.5–4 @ 550	8–10.5 @ 800	—	—	14 @ 2000	7	8.5 @ 11.5	—
1975								
3874082	1–4.5 @ 600	8–10.5 @ 900	—	—	14 @ 2200	7	10 @ 11.5	—
3874090	1.5–5.5 @ 550	5.5–8 @ 700	—	—	14 @ 2200	7	12 @ 12.5	—
3874097	1–4.5 @ 650	8.5–11 @ 950	—	—	16 @ 2150	7	12 @ 12.5	—
3874101	.5–3 @ 600	6–8.5 @ 950	—	—	12 @ 2000	8	11 @ 14	—
3874110	1–3.5 @ 600	6–8.5 @ 900	—	—	12 @ 2000	8	11 @ 14	—
3874115	1–3.5 @ 600	6–8.5 @ 900	—	—	12 @ 2000	7	12 @ 12.5	—
3874173	1–3.5 @ 600	3.5–6 @ 750	—	—	10 @ 2000	8	11 @ 14	—
3874298	.5–3.5 @ 700	7–10 @ 1100	—	—	16 @ 2100	9	12.5 @ 15.5	—

①—Stamped on distributor housing.

FORD & MERCURY
Full Size Models

ENGINE & SERIAL NUMBER LOCATION
Plate On Left Front Door Pillar

ENGINE IDENTIFICATION
★Serial number on Vehicle Warranty Plate
Engine code for 1969-75 is the last letter in the serial number.

Year	Engine	Engine Code★
1974–75	V8-351	H
	V8-400	S
	V8-460	A

GENERAL ENGINE SPECIFICATIONS

FORD

Engine	Carburetor	Bore and Stroke	Piston Displacement, Cubic Inches	Compression Ratio	Maximum Brake HP @ rpm	Maximum Torque Lbs. Ft. @ rpm	Normal Oil Pressure Pounds
1974							
162 Horsepower..........V8-351	2 Barrel	4.00 x 3.50	351	8.0	162 @ 4000	275 @ 2200	45–75
163 Horsepower..........V8-351	2 Barrel	4.00 x 3.50	351	8.0	163 @ 4200	278 @ 2000	45–65
170 Horsepower..........V8-400	2 Barrel	4.00 x 4.00	400	8.0	170 @ 3400	330 @ 2000	45–75
195 Horsepower..........V8-460	4 Barrel	4.36 x 3.85	460	8.0	195 @ 3800	335 @ 2600	35–65
275 Horsepower..........V8-460	4 Barrel	4.36 x 3.85	460	8.8	275 @ 4400	395 @ 2800	35–65
1975							
148 Horsepower..........V8-351	2 Barrel	4.00 x 3.50	351	8.0	148 @ 3800	243 @ 2400	45–75
150 Horsepower..........V8-351	2 Barrel	4.00 x 3.50	351	8.0	150 @ 3800	244 @ 2800	45–75
158 Horsepower..........V8-400	2 Barrel	4.00 x 4.00	400	8.0	158 @ 3800	276 @ 2000	45–75
144 Horsepower..........V8-400	2 Barrel	4.00 x 4.00	400	8.0	144 @ 3600	255 @ 2200	45–75
218 Horsepower..........V8-460	4 Barrel	4.36 x 3.85	460	8.0	218 @ 4000	369 @ 2600	35–65

MERCURY

Engine①	Carburetor	Bore and Stroke	Piston Displacement, Cubic Inches	Compression Ratio	Maximum Brake HP @ rpm	Maximum Torque Lbs. Ft. @ rpm	Normal Oil Pressure Pounds
1974							
170 Horsepower..........V8-400	2 Barrel	4.00 x 4.00	400	8.0	170 @ 3400	330 @ 2000	45–75
195 Horsepower..........V8-460	4 Barrel	4.36 x 3.85	460	8.0	195 @ 3800	335 @ 2600	35–65
275 Horsepower..........V8-460	4 Barrel	4.36 x 3.85	460	8.8	275 @ 4400	395 @ 2800	35–65
1975							
148 Horsepower..........V8-351	2 Barrel	4.00 x 3.50	351	8.0	148 @ 3800	243 @ 2400	45–75
150 Horsepower..........V8-351	2 Barrel	4.00 x 3.50	351	8.0	150 @ 3800	244 @ 2800	45–75
144 Horsepower..........V8-400	2 Barrel	4.00 x 4.00	400	8.0	144 @ 3600	255 @ 2200	45–75
158 Horsepower..........V8-400	2 Barrel	4.00 x 4.00	400	8.0	158 @ 3800	276 @ 2000	45–75
218 Horsepower..........V8-460	4 Barrel	4.36 x 3.85	460	8.0	218 @ 4000	369 @ 2600	35–65

①—Ratings are NET—as installed in the vehicle.

TUNEUP SPECIFICATIONS

★When using a timing light, disconnect vacuum hose or tube at distributor and plug opening in hose or tube so idle speed will not be affected.

●When checking compression, lowest cylinder must be within 80% of highest.

▲Before removing wires from distributor cap, determine location of the No. 1 wire in cap, as distributor position may have been altered from that shown at the end of this chart.

Engine	Spark Plug		Distributor		Ignition Timing★			Carburetor Adjustments					
	Type ③	Gap Inch	Point Gap Inch	Dwell Angle Deg.	Firing Order Fig. ▲	Timing degrees BTDC ①	Mark Fig.	Hot Idle Speed Std. Trans.	Hot Idle Speed Auto. Trans.②	Air Fuel Ratio Std. Trans.	Air Fuel Ratio Auto. Trans.	Idle CO% Std. Trans.	Idle CO% Auto. Trans.
1974													
V8-351④	BRF-42	.044	.017	26–30	A	6	C	—	600	—	—	—	—
V8-351④⑦	BRF-42	.044	—	—	A	6	C	—	600	—	—	—	—
V8-351⑤	ARF-42	.044	.017	26–30	A	14	C	—	650	—	—	—	—
V8-351⑤⑦	ARF-42	.044	—	—	A	14	C	—	650	—	—	—	—
V8-400⑦	ARF-42	.044	—	—	A	12	C	—	625	—	—	—	—
V8-460⑦	ARF-52	.054	—	—	B	⑥	C	—	⑥	—	—	—	.25
1975													
V8-351	ARF-42	.044	—	—	A	14	C	—	700D	—	—	—	—
V8-400	ARF-42	.044	—	—	A	12	C	—	625D	—	—	—	—
V8-460	ARF-52	.044	—	—	B	14	C	—	650D	—	—	—	—

TUNEUP NOTES

①—BTDC: Before top dead center.
②—D: Drive. N: Neutral.
③—Autolite.
④—Windsor engine.
⑤—Cleveland engine.
⑥—Exc. Police Interceptor 14° at 650, Police Interceptor 10° at 700.
⑦—Breakerless distributor.

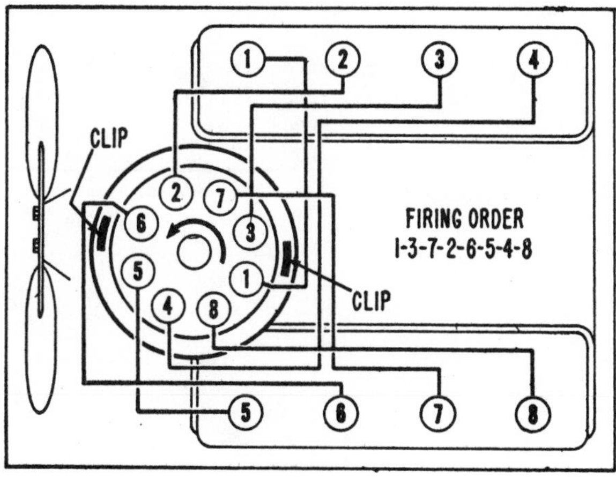

Fig. A

ATC 10 TC 10 20 30 BTC
ROTATION

Fig. C

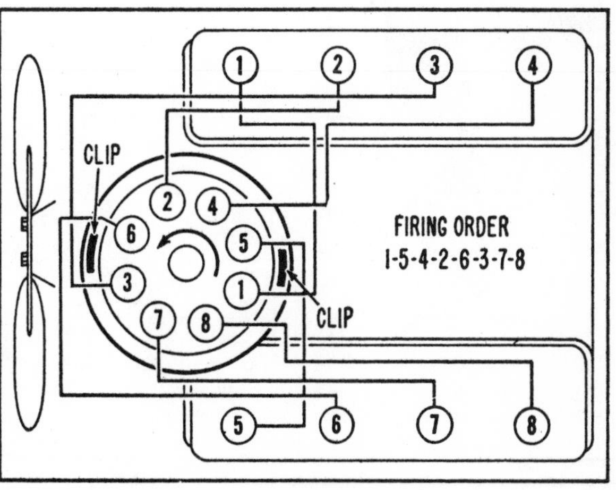

Fig. B

DISTRIBUTOR SPECIFICATIONS

★Note: If unit is checked on vehicle, double the rpm and degrees to get crankshaft figures.

Breaker arm spring tension—17–21 oz.

Distributor Part No.①	Centrifugal Advance Degrees @ rpm of Distributor					Vacuum Advance		Distributor Retard
	Advance Starts	Intermediate Advance			Full Advance	Inches of Vacuum to Start Plunger	Max. Adv. Dist. Deg. @ Vacuum	Max. Retard Dist. Deg. @ Vacuum
1974								
D3AF-AA	0–1½ @ 500	4–6 @ 750	6–8¼ @ 1000	10–12½ @ 1500	15¼ @ 2000	5	13¼ @ 20	—
D3ZF-GA	0–1 @ 500	0–2½ @ 750	2¼–4¼ @ 1000	5½–7½ @ 1500	9½ @ 2000	5	12½ @ 20	—
D4OE-CA	0–½ @ 500	0–1½ @ 750	2–4 @ 1000	5½–7½ @ 1500	9¼ @ 2000	5	13½ @ 20	—
D4VE-CA	0–½ @ 500	0–½ @ 750	3–5 @ 1000	7–9 @ 1500	9½ @ 2000	5	11¼ @ 20	—
1975								
D4AE-AA	0–2 @ 520	4½–7½ @ 800	10–12½ @ 1500	—	15¼ @ 2000	4	12¾ @ 17	—
D4OE-EA	0–2 @ 520	4½–7½ @ 800	10–12½ @ 1500	—	15¼ @ 2000	4	12¾ @ 17	—
D4VE-CA	−1½–+½ @ 800	3–5 @ 1000	—	—	19 @ 2000	4	19¾ @ 14	—

①—Basic part No. 12127.

FORD MUSTANG II & PINTO

ENGINE & SERIAL NUMBER LOCATION

Vehicle warranty plate on rear face of left front door.

ENGINE IDENTIFICATION

Engine code is last letter in serial number on vehicle warranty plate.

Year	Engine	Engine Code
1971–74	4-122①	X
1974–75	4-140②	Y
1974–75	V6-171③	Z
1975	V8-302	F

①—2000cc engine.
②—2300cc engine.
③—2800cc engine.

GENERAL ENGINE SPECIFICATIONS

Engine①	Carburetor	Bore and Stroke	Piston Displacement, Cubic Inches	Compression Ratio	Maximum Brake HP @ rpm	Maximum Torque Lbs. Ft. @ rpm	Normal Oil Pressure Pounds
1974							
4-122②	2 Barrel	3.575 x 3.029	122	8.2	80 @ 5400	98 @ 3000	45–65
4-140③	2 Barrel	3.781 x 3.126	140	8.4	82 @ 4600	113 @ 2600	40–60
4-140③	2 Barrel	3.781 x 3.126	140	8.4	88 @ 5000	116 @ 2600	40–60
V6-171④	2 Barrel	3.66 x 2.70	171	8.2	105 @ 4600	140 @ 3200	40–55
1975							
4-140③	2 Barrel	3.781 x 3.126	140	8.4	85.5 @ 4800	113 @ 2600	50
V6-171④	2 Barrel	3.66 x 2.70	171	8.2	110 @ 5000	135 @ 3200	40–55
V8-302⑤	2 Barrel	4.00 x 3.00	302	8.0	140 @ 3800	228 @ 2600	40–60

①—Net Rating—as installed in vehicle.
②—2000cc engine.
③—2300cc engine.
④—2800cc engine.
⑤—Refer to the Ford & Mercury—Compact & Intermediate Chapter for service procedures on this engine.

TUNEUP SPECIFICATIONS

★When using a timing light, disconnect vacuum hose or tube at distributor and plug opening in hose or tube so idle speed will not be affected.

●When checking compression, lowest cylinder must be within 75% of highest.

▲Before removing wires from distributor cap, determine location of the No. 1 wire in cap, as distributor position may have been altered from that shown at the end of this chart.

Engine	Spark Plug		Distributor		Ignition Timing★			Carb. Adjustments					
								Hot Idle Speed③		Air Fuel Ratio		Idle CO%	
	Type	Gap Inch	Point Gap Inch	Dwell Angle Deg.	Firing Order Fig. ▲	Timing degrees BTDC ①	Mark Fig.	Std. Trans.	Auto. Trans.②	Std. Trans.	Auto. Trans.	Std. Trans.	Auto. Trans.
1974													
4-122, 2000cc	BRF-42	.034	.025	35–41	A	6	B	750	650	④	④	—	—
4-140, 2300cc	AGRF-52	.034	.027	35–41	E	6	C	850	750	11 to 1	11 to 1	.15	.15
V6-171, 2800cc	AGR-42	.034	.027	35–41	F	12	D	750	650	12.7 to 1	12.7 to 1	.7	.4

(continued)

TUNEUP SPECIFICATIONS—Continued

Engine	Spark Plug Type	Spark Plug Gap Inch	Distributor Point Gap Inch	Distributor Dwell Angle Deg.	Ignition Timing★ Firing Order Fig. ▲	Ignition Timing★ Timing Deg. BTDC ①	Ignition Timing★ Mark Fig.	Hot Idle Speed③ Std. Trans.	Hot Idle Speed③ Auto. Trans.②	Air Fuel Ratio Std. Trans.	Air Fuel Ratio Auto. Trans.	Idle CO % Std. Trans.	Idle CO % Auto. Trans.
1975													
4-140, 2300cc	AGRF-52	.034	—	—	E	⑤	C	850	750D	—	—	—	—
V6-171, 2800cc	AGR-42	.034	—	—	F	⑥	D	850	700D	—	—	—	—
V8-302⑦	ARF-42	.044	—	—	G	6	H	—	700D	—	—	—	—

①—BTDC: Before top dead center.
②—D: Drive.
③—Headlamps on Hi Beam—Air Conditioner OFF. Where two speeds are listed, lower speed indicates solenoid disconnected.
④—11.7:1 Except Calif.; 10:1 Calif.
⑤—Exc. Calif. Auto. Trans., 6° BTDC; Calif. Auto. Trans., 10° BTDC.
⑥—Manual Trans., 6° BTDC; Exc. Calif. Auto. Trans., 10° BTDC; Calif. Auto. Trans., 8° BTDC.
⑦—Refer to the Ford & Mercury—Compact & Intermediate Chapter for service procedures on this engine.

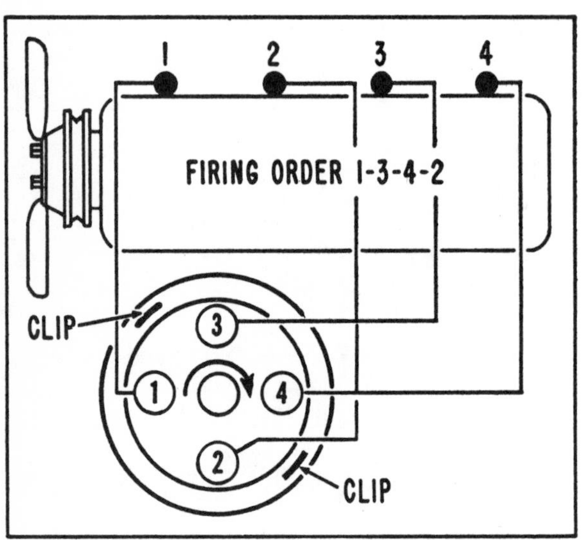

Fig. A

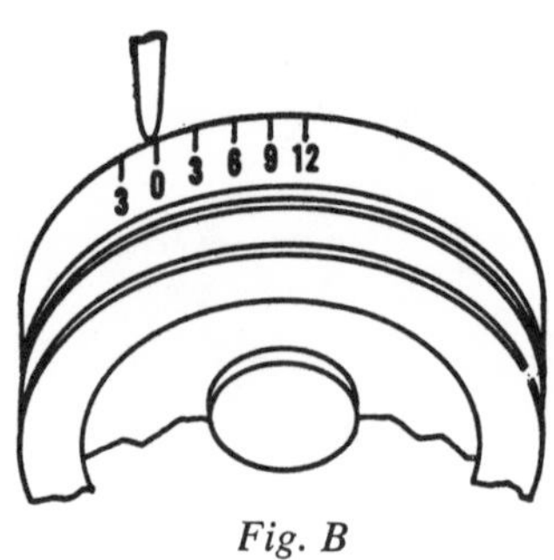

Fig. B

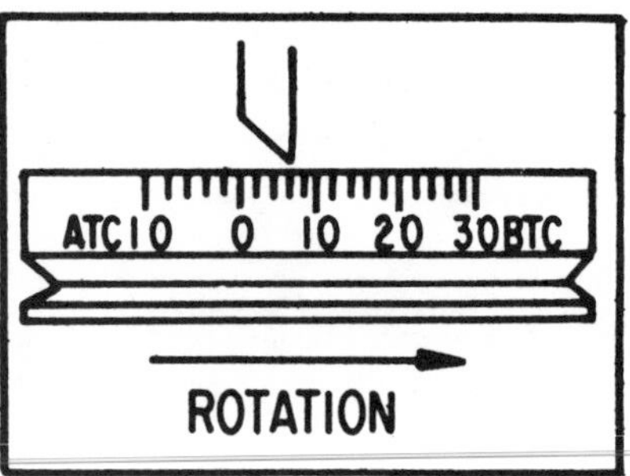

Fig. C

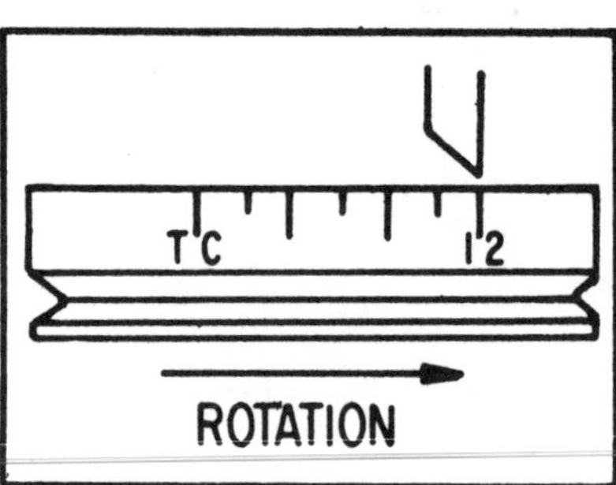

Fig. D

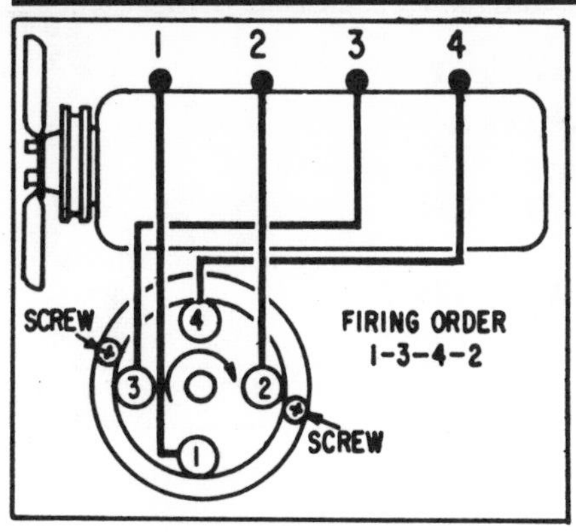

Fig. E

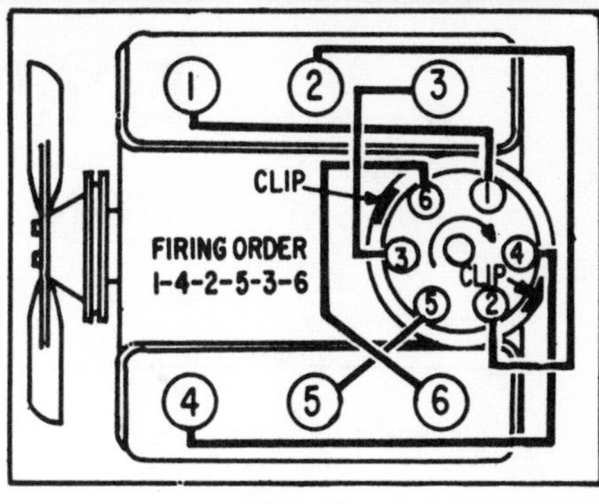

Fig. F

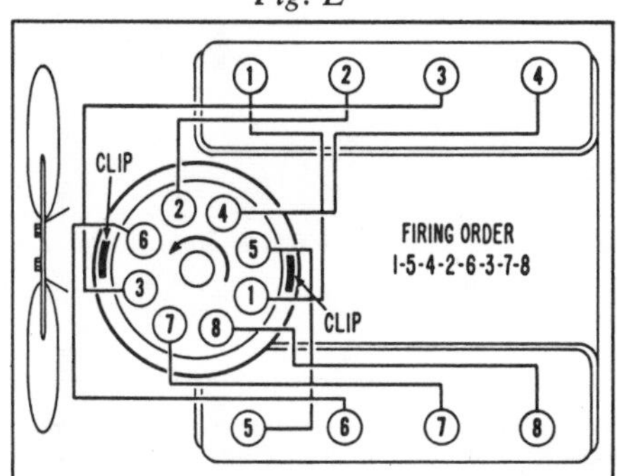

Fig. G

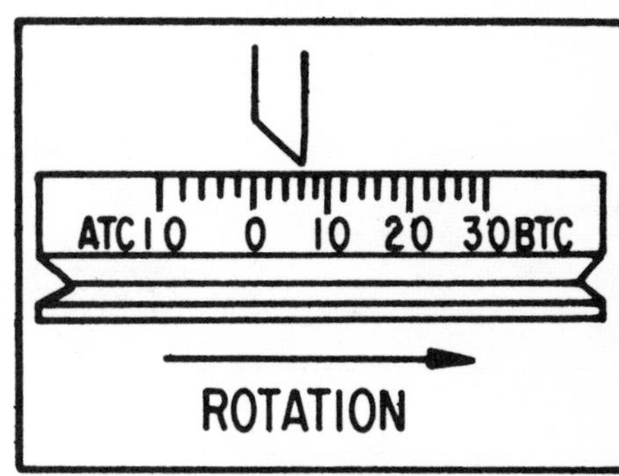

Fig. H

DISTRIBUTOR SPECIFICATIONS

Distributor Part No.①	Centrifugal Advance Degrees @ rpm of Distributor					Vacuum Advance		Distributor Retard
	Advance Starts	Intermediate Advance			Full Advance	Inches of Vacuum to Start Plunger	Max. Adv. Dist. Deg. @ Vacuum	Max. Retard Dist. Deg. @ Vacuum
1974								
74HF-EA	1–3 @ 500	5–7 @ 750	6½–8½ @ 1000	9½–11½ @ 1500	12–14 @ 2000	5	6 @ 20	—
74HF-LA	0–1 @ 500	1–3 @ 750	4–6 @ 1000	7–9 @ 1500	9½–11½ @ 2000	5	6 @ 20	—
D4ZE-AA	0–1 @ 500	4–6 @ 750	4–6 @ 1000	9½–11½ @ 1500	11½–14 @ 2000	5	7½ @ 20	—
D4ZE-BA	0–1 @ 500	4–6 @ 750	7–9 @ 1000	9¼–11½ @ 1500	11½–14 @ 2000	5	7½ @ 20	—
D4ZF-DA	0–1 @ 500	1½–3½ @ 750	6–8 @ 1000	9½–11½ @ 1500	11½–14 @ 2000	5	4½ @ 20	—
74TF-LA	0–½ @ 500	1–3 @ 750	3½–5½ @ 1000	7½–9½ @ 1500	8–10 @ 2000	5	4 @ 20	7 @ 20
74TF-MA	0–½ @ 500	1–3 @ 750	3½–5½ @ 1000	7½–9½ @ 1500	8–10 @ 2000	5	4 @ 20	4 @ 20
D4ZE-KA	0–1 @ 500	4–6½ @ 750	7–9 @ 1000	9¼–11½ @ 1500	12¾ @ 2000	5	6 @ 20	—
74TF-SA	0–½ @ 500	1–3 @ 750	3½–5½ @ 1000	7½–9½ @ 1500	9 @ 2000	5	3 @ 20	—
1975								
D5DE-KA	0–2 @ 775	2¾–4¾ @ 950	4¾–7 @ 1500	6¾–9¼ @ 2000	9½ @ 2350	4	10 @ 14½	3 @ 7
D5DE-NA	0–2 @ 550	2½–4½ @ 675	3¾–6 @ 1100	7–9½ @ 2000	10⅛ @ 2500	4	10 @ 14½	—
D5ZE-AA	0–2 @ 600	1–3 @ 650	2¾–5 @ 1000	5¼–7½ @ 1500	11⅝ @ 2500	4.8	4 @ 7½	—
D52E-EA	0–2 @ 675	5¼–7¼ @ 1025	7½–9¾ @ 1500	10–12½ @ 2000	12¾ @ 2250	4	4 @ 7	—
D52E-FA	0–2 @ 725	5½–7½ @ 1125	7¾–10 @ 1500	10¾–13¼ @ 2000	12¾ @ 2150	4	4 @ 7½	3 @ 7½
75TF-EA②	0–2 @ 650	2–4 @ 800	5–7 @ 1200	8–10 @ 1600	9 @ 2000	4¼	2½ @ 6¾	6 @ 10

①—Basic part No. 12127.

FORD THUNDERBIRD

ENGINE & SERIAL NUMBER LOCATION

Vehicle Warranty Plate On Left Front Door Pillar.

ENGINE IDENTIFICATION

Serial number on vehicle Warranty Plate.

Year	Engine	Engine Code
1973–75	V8-460	A

GENERAL ENGINE SPECIFICATIONS

Engine①	Carburetor	Bore and Stroke	Piston Displacement, Cubic Inches	Compression Ratio	Maximum Brake HP @ rpm	Maximum Torque Lbs. Ft. @ rpm	Normal Oil Pressure Pounds
1974							
220 Horsepower...........V8-460	4 Barrel	4.36 x 3.85	460	8.0	220 @ 4000	355 @ 2600	35–65
1975							
253 Horsepower...........V8-460	4 Barrel	4.36 x 3.85	460	8.0	253 @ 4400	386 @ 2600	35–65

①—Ratings are NET—as installed in the vehicle.

TUNEUP SPECIFICATIONS

★When using a timing light, disconnect vacuum hose or tube at distributor and plug opening in hose or tube so idle speed will not be affected.

● When checking compression, lowest cylinder must be within 75% of highest.

▲Before removing wires from distributor cap, determine location of the No. 1 wire in cap, as distributor position may have been altered from that shown at the end of this chart.

Engine	Spark Plug		Distributor		Ignition Timing★			Carb. Adjustments					
								Hot Idle Speed		Air Fuel Ratio		Idle CO%	
	Type	Gap Inch	Point Gap Inch	Dwell Angle Deg.	Firing Order Fig. ▲	Timing Degrees BTDC ①	Mark Fig.	Std. Trans.	Auto. Trans.②	Std. Trans.	Auto. Trans.	Std. Trans.	Auto. Trans.
1974													
8-460	ARF-52	③	⑤	—	A	14	B	—	650D④	—	—	—	—
1975													
8-460	ARF-52	③	⑤	—	A	14	B	—	650D	—	—	—	—

①—BTDC: Before top dead center.
②—D: Drive. N: Neutral.
③—Exc. Calif., .054 inch; Calif. .044 inch.
④—With lights and A/C off.
⑤—Breakerless distributor.

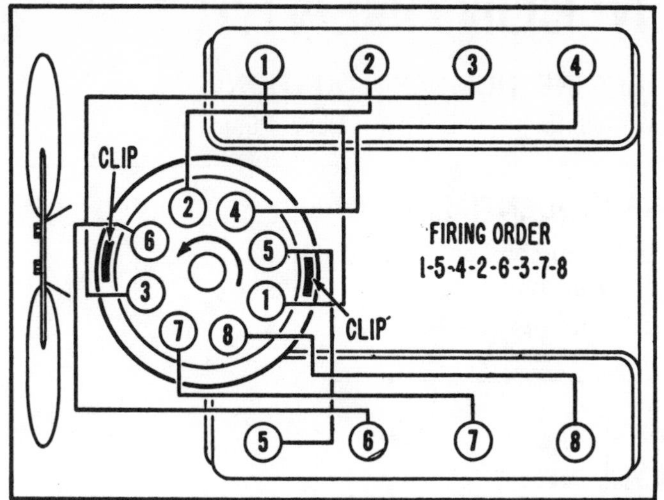

Fig. A

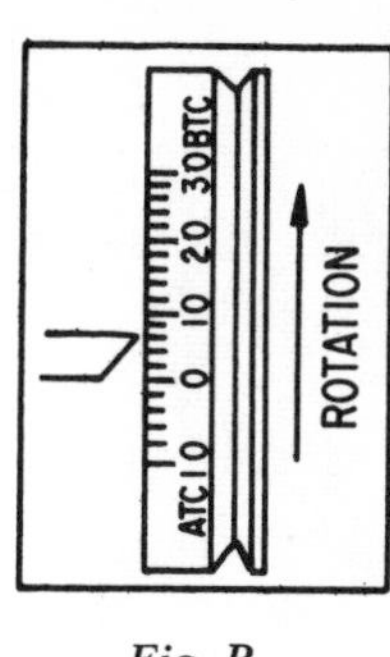

Fig. B

DISTRIBUTOR SPECIFICATIONS

★Note: If unit is checked on vehicle, double the rpm and degrees to get crankshaft figures.

Breaker arm spring tension—17–20 oz.

Distributor Part No.①	Centrifugal Advance Degrees @ rpm of Distributor					Vacuum Advance		Distributor Retard
	Advance Starts	Intermediate Advance			Full Advance	Inches of Vacuum to Start Plunger	Max. Adv. Dist. Deg. @ Vacuum	Max. Retard Dist. Deg. @ Vacuum
1974-75								
D4VE-CA	0–½ @ 500	0–½ @ 750	3–5 @ 1000	7–9 @ 1500	10½ @ 2000	5	11¼ @ 20	—

①—Basic part No. 12127.

LINCOLN CONTINENTAL

SERIAL & ENGINE NUMBER LOCATION

Vehicle Warranty Plate on Left Front Door Pillar

ENGINE IDENTIFICATION

*Serial number on vehicle Warranty Plate.

Engine code for 1969–75 is the last letter in the serial number.

Year	Engine	Engine Code*
1969–75	V8-460	A

GENERAL ENGINE SPECIFICATIONS

Engine①	Carburetor	Bore and Stroke	Piston Displacement, Cubic Inches	Compression Ratio	Maximum Brake HP @ rpm	Maximum Torque Lbs. Ft. @ rpm	Normal Oil Pressure Pounds
1974							
215 Horsepower..........V8-460	4 Barrel	4.362 x 3.850	460	8.0	215 @ 4000	350 @ 2600	35–65
220 Horsepower..........V8-460	4 Barrel	4.362 x 3.85	460	8.0	220 @ 4000	355 @ 2600	35–65
1975							
194 Horsepower..........V8-460	4 Barrel	4.362 x 3.85	460	8.0	194 @ 3800	347 @ 2600	35–62
206 Horsepower..........V8-460	4 Barrel	4.362 x 3.85	460	8.0	206 @ 3800	357 @ 2600	35–62

①—Ratings are NET—as installed in the vehicle.

TUNEUP SPECIFICATIONS

★When using a timing light, disconnect vacuum hose or tube at distributor and plug opening in hose or tube so idle speed will not be affected.

● When checking compression, lowest cylinder must be within 75% of highest.

▲Before removing wires from distributor cap, determine location of the No. 1 wire in cap, as distributor position may have been altered from that shown at the end of this chart.

Engine	Spark Plug		Distributor		Ignition Timing★			Carb. Adjustments					
								Hot Idle Speed		Air Fuel Ratio		Idle CO %	
	Type	Gap Inch	Point Gap Inch	Dwell Angle Deg.	Firing Order Fig. ▲	Timing Degrees BTDC ①	Mark Fig.	Std. Trans.	Auto. Trans.②	Std. Trans.	Auto. Trans.	Std. Trans.	Auto. Trans.
1974													
V8-460	ARF-52	.054	③	—	A	14	B	—	650D	—	—	—	—
1975													
V8-460	ARF-52	.044	③	—	A	14	B	—	650D	—	—	—	—

①—BTDC-Before top dead center.
②—D-Drive. N-Neutral.
③—Breakerless distributor.

(continued)

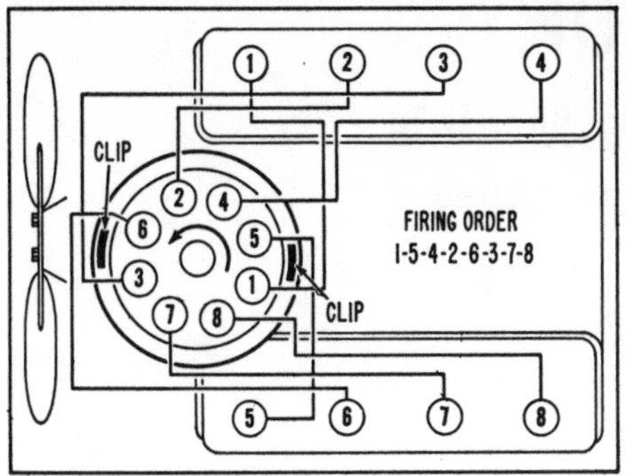

Fig. A

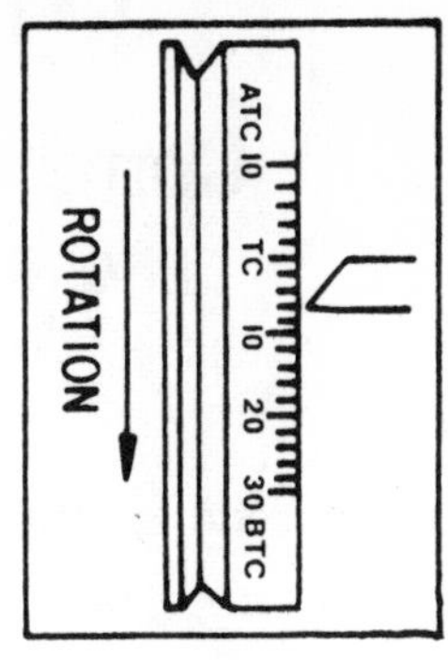

Fig. B

DISTRIBUTOR SPECIFICATIONS

★**Note: If unit is checked on vehicle, double the rpm and degrees to get crankshaft figures.**

Breaker arm spring tension—17–21.

Distributor Part No.①	Centrifugal Advance Degrees @ rpm of Distributor					Vacuum Advance		Distributor Retard
	Advance Starts	Intermediate Advance			Full Advance	Inches of Vacuum to Start Plunger	Max. Adv. Dist. Deg. @ Vacuum	Max. Retard Dist. Deg. @ Vacuum
1974-75								
D4VE-CA	0–½ @ 500	0–½ @ 750	3–5 @ 1000	7–9 @ 1500	9½ @ 2000	5	11¼ @ 20	—

①—Basic part No. 12127.

FORD & MERCURY

Compact & Intermediate Models

ENGINE & SERIAL NUMBER LOCATION

Vehicle warranty plate on rear face of left front door.

ENGINE IDENTIFICATION

Engine code is last letter in serial number on vehicle warranty plate.

Year	Engine	Code
1973–74	6-200	T
	6-250	L
	8-302	F
	8-351①	H
	8-351②	Q
	8-351③	R
	8-400	S
	8-429	N
	8-460	A
	8-460④	C

Year	Engine	Code
1975	6-200	T
	6-250	L
	8-302	F
	8-351	H
	8-400	S
	8-460	A
	8-460④	C

①—2-barrel carburetor.
②—4-barrel carburetor.
③—High Performance.
④—Police Interceptor.

GENERAL ENGINE SPECIFICATIONS

Engine①	Carburetor	Bore and Stroke	Piston Displacement, Cubic Inches	Compression Ratio	Maximum Brake HP @ rpm	Maximum Torque Lbs. Ft. @ rpm	Normal Oil Pressure Pounds
1974							
84 Horsepower............6-200	1 Barrel	3.68 x 3.13	200	8.0	84 @ 3800	150 @ 1800	30–50
91 Horsepower............6-250	1 Barrel	3.68 x 3.91	250	8.0	91 @ 3200	190 @ 1600	40–60
140 Horsepower..........V8-302	2 Barrel	4.00 x 3.00	302	8.0	140 @ 3800	230 @ 2600	40–60
162 Horsepower..........V8-351	2 Barrel	4.00 x 3.50	351	8.0	162 @ 4000	275 @ 2200	40–65
163 Horsepower..........V8-351	2 Barrel	4.00 x 3.50	351	8.0	163 @ 4200	278 @ 2000	45–75
255 Horsepower..........V8-351	4 Barrel	4.00 x 3.50	351	8.0	255 @ 5600	290 @ 3400	45–75
170 Horsepower..........V8-400	2 Barrel	4.00 x 4.00	400	8.0	170 @ 3400	330 @ 2000	45–75
195 Horsepower..........V8-460	4 Barrel	4.36 x 3.85	460	8.0	195 @ 3800	335 @ 2600	35–65
220 Horsepower②.........V8-460	4 Barrel	4.36 x 3.85	460	8.0	220 @ 4000	355 @ 2600	35–65
260 Horsepower..........V8-460	4 Barrel	4.36 x 3.85	460	8.0	260 @ 4400	355 @ 2700	35–65
1975							
74 Horsepower............6-200	1 Barrel	3.683 x 3.126	200	8.3	74 @ 3400④	132 @ 2400⑨	40–60
70 Horsepower④...........6-250	1 Barrel	3.682 x 3.910	250	8.0	70 @ 2800	175 @ 1400	40–60
72 Horsepower③...........6-250	1 Barrel	3.682 x 3.910	250	8.0	72 @ 2900	180 @ 1400	40–60
122 Horsepower⑤.........V8-302	2 Barrel	4.00 x 3.00	302	8.0	122 @ 3800⑤	208 @ 1800⑨	45–65
129 Horsepower⑥.........V8-302	2 Barrel	4.00 x 3.00	302	8.0	129 @ 3800⑥	220 @ 1800⑩	45–65
148 Horsepower③........V8-351M	2 Barrel	4.00 x 3.50	351	8.0	148 @ 3800	243 @ 2400	45–75
150 Horsepower④........V8-351M	2 Barrel	4.00 x 3.50	351	8.0	150 @ 3800	244 @ 2800	45–75
143 Horsepower⑦........V8-351W	2 Barrel	4.00 x 3.50	351	8.1	143 @ 3600⑦	255 @ 2200⑪	45–65
154 Horsepower⑧........V8-351W	2 Barrel	4.00 x 3.50	351	8.1	154 @ 3800⑧	268 @ 2200	45–65
144 Horsepower④.........V8-400	2 Barrel	4.00 x 4.00	400	8.0	144 @ 3600	255 @ 2200	35–65
158 Horsepower③.........V8-400	2 Barrel	4.00 x 4.00	400	8.0	158 @ 4000	276 @ 2000	35–65
216 Horsepower③.........V8-460	4 Barrel	4.36 x 3.85	460	8.0	216 @ 4000	366 @ 2600	35–65
217 Horsepower④.........V8-460	4 Barrel	4.36 x 3.85	460	8.0	217 @ 4000	365 @ 2600	35–65

①—Ratings are NET—as installed in the vehicle.
②—Cougar XR-7 requires A/C in California.
③—Except California.
④—California.
⑤—Comet & Maverick, California vehicles rated at 115 hp @ 3600 rpm.
⑥—Granada & Monarch, California vehicles rated at 115 hp @ 3600 rpm.
⑦—Granada, Monarch, Torino & Elite, California vehicles rated at 153 hp @ 3400 rpm.
⑧—Cougar & Montego, not available in California.
⑨—With man. trans., 75 hp @ 3200 rpm, 145 lbs. ft. @ 2000 rpm.
⑩—California vehicles rated at 203 @ 1800 rpm.
⑪—California vehicles rated at 270 @ 2400 rpm.

TUNEUP SPECIFICATIONS

★When using a timing light, disconnect vacuum hose or tube at distributor and plug opening in hose or tube so idle speed will not be affected.

●When checking compression, lowest cylinder must be within 75% of the highest.

▲Before removing wires from distributor cap, determine location of the No. 1 wire in cap, as distributor position may have been altered from that shown at the end of this chart.

Engine	Spark Plug		Distributor		Ignition Timing★			Carburetor Adjustments					
								Hot Idle Speed③		Air Fuel Ratio		Idle CO%	
	Type	Gap Inch	Point Gap Inch	Dwell Angle Deg.	Firing Order Fig. ▲	Timing degrees BTDC ①	Mark Fig.	Std. Trans.	Auto. Trans.②	Std. Trans.	Auto. Trans.	Std. Trans.	Auto. Trans.
1974													
6-200	BRF-82	.034	.025	33	D	6	A	750	550D	—	—	—	—
6-200⑧	BRF-82	.034	—	—	D	6	A	750	550D	—	—	—	—
6-250	BRF-82	.034	.025	33	D	6	A	600	600D	—	—	—	—
6-250⑧	BRF-82	.034	—	—	D	6	A	600	600D	—	—	—	—
8-302	BRF-42	.034	.017	26–30	B	6	E	850	575D	—	—	—	.5
8-302⑧	BRF-42	.034	—	—	B	6	E	850	575D	—	—	—	.5
8-351⑤⑬	BRF-42	.034	.017	26–30	C	6	E	—	600D	—	—	—	.4
8-351⑤⑬⑧	BRF-42	.034	—	—	C	6	E	—	600D	—	—	—	.4
8-351⑤⑫	ARF-42	.044	.017	26–30	C	10	E	—	650D	—	—	—	.5
8-351⑤⑫⑧	ARF-42	.044	—	—	C	10	E	—	650D	—	—	—	.5
8-351⑥	ARF-42	.034	.017⑪	26–31	C	⑩	E	900	800D	—	—	—	—
8-351⑥⑧	ARF-42	.034	—	—	C	⑩	E	900	800D	—	—	—	—
8-400⑧	ARF-42	.044	—	—	C	⑦	E	—	625D	—	—	—	—
8-460⑧	ARF-52	.054	—	—	B	⑨	E	—	650D	—	—	—	.25
1975													
6-200⑧	BRF-82	.044	—	—	D	6	A	750	600D	—	—	—	—
6-250⑧	BRF-82	.044	—	—	F	6	A	750	600D	—	—	—	—
V8-302⑧	ARF-42	.044	—	—	B	6	E	900	650D	—	—	—	—
V8-351⑧④	ARF-42	.044	—	—	C	14	E	—	650D	—	—	—	—
V8-351⑧⑬	ARF-42	.044	—	—	C	—	E	—	650D	—	—	—	—
V8-400⑧	ARF-42	.044	—	—	C	12	E	—	650D	—	—	—	—
V8-460⑧	ARF-52	.044	—	—	B	14	E	—	650D	—	—	—	—

①—BTDC: Before top dead center.
②—D: Drive.
③—For A/C add 50 rpm. Set with headlamps on high beam and A/C off.
④—Modified Engine.
⑤—With 2-barrel carburetor.
⑥—With 4-barrel carburetor.
⑦—Cougar 12°, all others 6°.
⑧—Breakerless distributor.
⑨—Cougar 14°, all others 10°.
⑩—Manual trans. 16° BTDC Auto trans 18° BTDC.
⑪—Manual trans .020 Auto trans .017.
⑫—Cleveland engine.
⑬—Windsor engine.

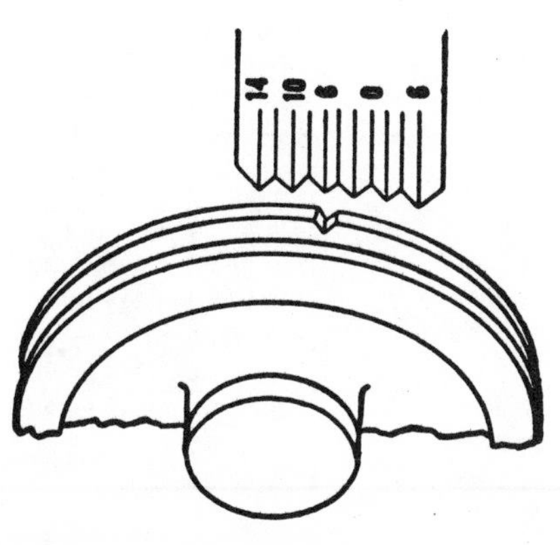

Fig. A

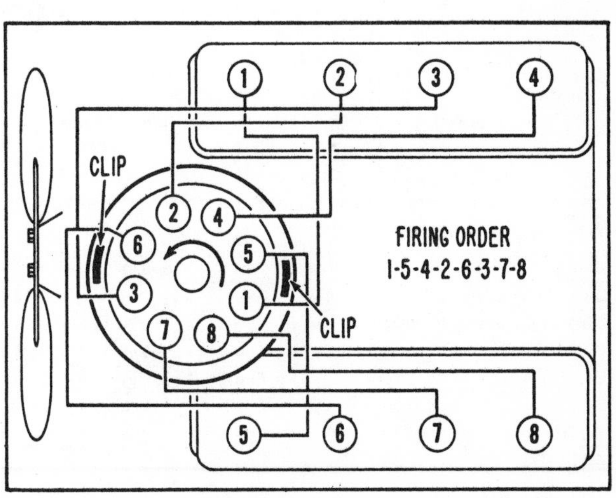

Fig. B

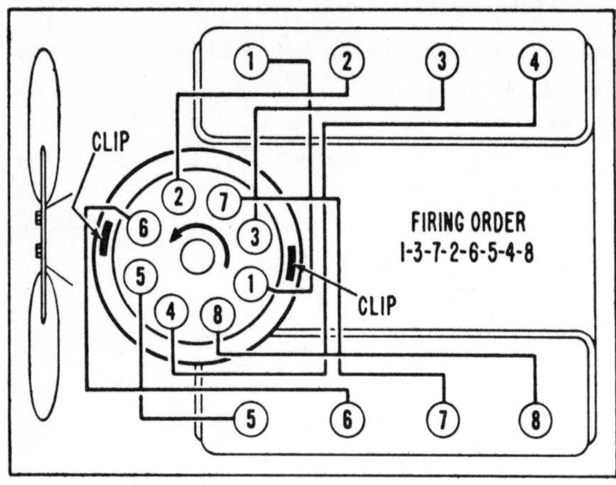

Fig. C

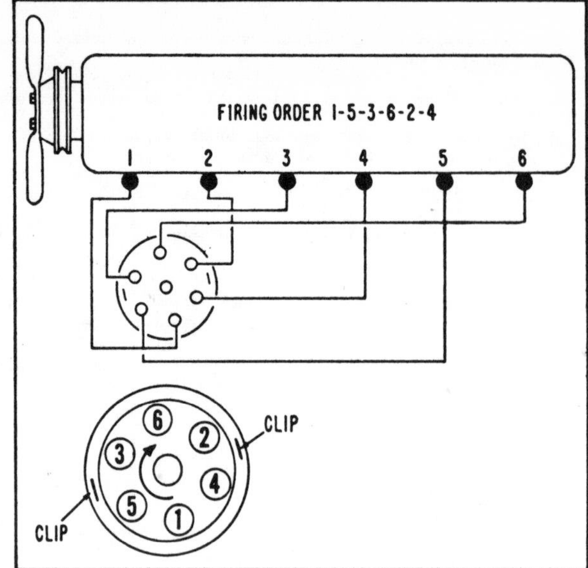

Fig. D

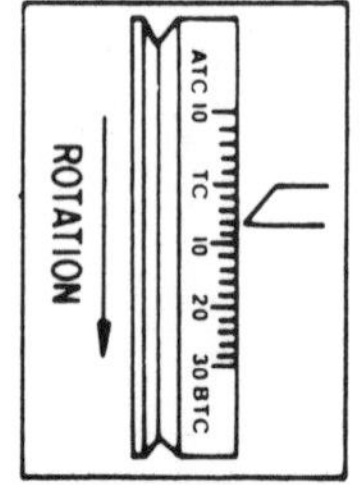

Fig. E

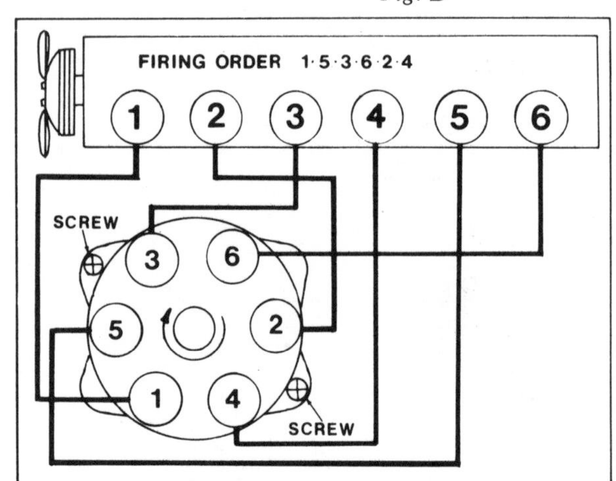

Fig. F

DISTRIBUTOR SPECIFICATIONS

Distributor Part No.①	Centrifugal Advance Degrees @ rpm of Distributor: Advance Starts	Intermediate Advance			Full Advance	Vacuum Advance: Inches of Vacuum to Start Plunger	Max. Adv. Dist. Deg. @ Vacuum	Distributor Retard: Max. Retard Dist. Deg. @ Vacuum
1974								
D3AF-AA	0–1½ @ 500	4–6 @ 750	6–8¼ @ 1000	10–12½ @ 1500	16½ @ 2000	5	13¼ @ 20	—
D3BF-DA	0–1¼ @ 500	2½–4½ @ 750	5½–7½ @ 1000	8½–10½ @ 1500	12 @ 2000	5	11¼ @ 20	5–7 @ 20
D3DF-FA	0–1½ @ 500	1½–3½ @ 750	4½–6½ @ 1000	6½–9 @ 1500	9¼ @ 2000	5	9¼ @ 20	2–4 @ 20
D3DF-HA	0–1½ @ 500	3½–5½ @ 750	7½–9½ @ 1000	9½–11½ @ 1500	11¼ @ 2000	5	7¼ @ 20	—
D3DF-KA	0–1½ @ 500	4½–6½ @ 750	7½–9½ @ 1000	8½–11 @ 1500	11¼ @ 2000	5	7¼ @ 20	2–4 @ 20
D3OF-FA	0–1 @ 500	0–1½ @ 750	1–3 @ 1000	5½–8½ @ 1500	13 @ 2000	5	5¼ @ 20	5–7 @ 20
D3OF-GA	0–1 @ 500	0–1½ @ 750	1–3½ @ 1000	6½–8½ @ 1500	13½ @ 2000	5	5¼ @ 20	—
D3OF-HB	0–1½ @ 500	½–3 @ 750	2½–5 @ 1000	6½–9 @ 1500	13½ @ 2000	5	11¼ @ 20	—

(continued)

DISTRIBUTOR SPECIFICATIONS—Continued

Distributor Part No.①	Centrifugal Advance Degrees @ rpm of Distributor					Vacuum Advance		Distributor Retard
	Advance Starts	Intermediate Advance			Full Advance	Inches of Vacuum to Start Plunger	Max. Adv. Dist. Deg. @ Vacuum	Max. Retard Dist. Deg. @ Vacuum
D3OF-RA	0-1½ @ 500	3½-5½ @ 750	5½-7½ @ 1000	6½-8½ @ 1500	10 @ 2000	5	9¼ @ 20	2-4 @ 20
D3UF-EA	0-1¼ @ 500	2½-4½ @ 750	5½-7½ @ 1000	9-11 @ 1500	14½ @ 2000	5	9¼ @ 20	5-7 @ 20
D3ZF-GA	0-1 @ 500	0-2½ @ 750	2¼- 4¼ @ 1000	5½-7½ @ 1500	11 @ 2000	5	12½ @ 20	—
D4AE-AA	0-½ @ 500	0-2 @ 750	2½-4½ @ 1000	5½-7½ @ 1500	11 @ 2000	5	12½ @ 20	—
D4AE-HA	0-1½ @ 500	5-7 @ 750	6-8 @ 1000	8-10½ @ 1500	12½ @ 2000	5	9½ @ 20	5-7 @ 20
D4DE-FA	0-1½ @ 500	4½-6½ @ 750	7½-9½ @ 1000	9-11 @ 1500	12½ @ 2000	5	7¼ @ 20	2-4 @ 20
D4DE-LA	0-1½ @ 500	4-6 @ 750	4½-6½ @ 1000	6-8 @ 1500	9½ @ 2000	5	•9 @ 20	2-4 @ 20
D4DE-MA	0-½ @ 500	½-2½ @ 750	3½-5½ @ 1000	7½-9½ @ 1500	13½ @ 2000	5	11½ @ 20	—
D4DE-NA	0-1½ @ 500	3½-5½ @ 750	5½-7½ @ 1000	6½-8½ @ 1500	10 @ 2000	5	9¼ @ 20	2-4 @ 20
D4DE-RA	0-1½ @ 500	3½-5½ @ 750	5½-7½ @ 1000	6½-8½ @ 1500	10½ @ 2000	5	9¼ @ 20	2-4 @ 20
D4OE-CA	0-½ @ 500	0-1½ @ 750	2-4 @ 1000	5½-7½ @ 1500	10½ @ 2000	5	13½ @ 20	—
D4VE-CA	0-½ @ 500	0-½ @ 750	3-5 @ 1000	7-9 @ 1500	10½ @ 2000	5	11¼ @ 20	—
1975								
D3ZF-GA	0-2 @ 775	2-4 @ 975	5.4-7.7 @ 1500	—	10¾ @ 2500	6	13¼ @ 24	—
D4OE-EA	0-2 @ 520	4½-7½ @ 800	10-12½ @ 1500	—	17¾ @ 2000	4	13 @ 17	—
D4VE-CA	0-2 @ 825	4-6 @ 1025	7-9¼ @ 1500	8⅓-11¼ @ 2000	12½ @ 2500	4	11¾ @ 14.6	—
D5AE-BA	0-2½ @ 975	—	3¾-6¼ @ 1500	—	11¼ @ 2150	4	13¼ @ 13	—
D5AE-DA	0-2½ @ 975	—	3¾-6¼ @ 1500	—	11¼ @ 2150	4.3	15¼ @ 13	—
D5AE-EA	0-2½ @ 975	—	3¾-6¼ @ 1500	—	11¼ @ 2150	3	13¼ @ 11	—
D5DE-HA	0-2 @ 550	3½-5½ @ 1000	7-9¼ @ 1500	10½-13 @ 2000	16½ @ 2500	4½	13¼ @ 19	—

①—Basic part No. 12127.

OLDSMOBILE
except Starfire

VEHICLE IDENTIFICATION PLATE

1969-1975 on left upper dash.

ENGINE NUMBER LOCATION

1969-71 & 1973-75 6-250: Right side of engine block directly to rear of distributor.

1969-74 V8s: Stamped on oil fill tube.
1975 Omega V8-350; on left bank cylinder head. V8-260, V8-455 & V8-350 Exc. Omega, stamped on oil filter tube.

ENGINE IDENTIFICATION CODE

YEAR	ENGINE	ENGINE PREFIX
1974	6-250 Std. Tr.	CCC, CCD
	6-250 Auto. Tr.	CCA, CCB
	V8-350 2-bbl.	QS, QT
	V8-350 4-bbl.	QB, QC, QL
	V8-350 4-bbl.	QO, QU, QW
	V8-350 4-bbl.	TB, TC, TL, TO
	V8-455 2-bbl.	UU, UW
	V8-455 4-bbl.	UA, UB, UC
	V8-455 4-bbl.	UD, UL, UO
	V8-455 4-bbl.	UP, UN, UR
	V8-455 4-bbl.	UV, UX, VP
	V8-455 4-bbl.	VA, VB, VC
	V8-455 4-bbl.	VD, VL, VO
1975	6-250 Std. Tr.①	CJU
	6-250 Auto. Tr.①	CJT
	6-250 Auto. Tr.②	CJL
	V8-260 Std. Tr.①	QA, QK
	V8-260 Std. Tr. a/c①	QD, QN
	V8-260 Std. Tr.②	TA, TK
	V8-260 Std. Tr. a/c②	TD, TN
	V8-260 Auto. Tr.①	QE, QP
	V8-260 Auto. Tr. a/c①	QJ, QQ
	V8-260 Auto. Tr.②	TE, TP
	V8-260 Auto. Tr. a/c②	TJ, TQ
	V8-350 Auto. Tr.①	RW, QL
	V8-350 Auto. Tr. a/c①	RX, QO, QX
	V8-350 Auto. Tr.②	RN, TL
	V8-350 Auto. Tr. a/c②	RO, TO, TX
	V8-400 Auto. Tr.①	YM, YT
	V8-455 Auto. Tr.①	UB, UE, UP
	V8-455 Auto. Tr. a/c①	UC, UD, UP
	V8-455 Auto. Tr.②	VB, VE, VP
	V8-455 Auto. Tr. a/c②	VC, VD, VP

①—Except California.
②—California.

GENERAL ENGINE SPECIFICATIONS

Engine①	Carburetor	Bore and Stroke	Piston Displacement, Cubic Inches	Compression Ratio	Maximum Brake HP @ rpm	Maximum Torque Lbs. Ft. @ rpm	Normal Oil Pressure Pounds
1974							
100 Horsepower ②6-250	1 Barrel	3.87 x 3.53	250	8.5	100 @ 3600	175 @ 1800	40
180 Horsepower V8-350	4 Barrel	4.057 x 3.385	350	8.5	180 @ 3800	275 @ 2800	30–45
200 Horsepower V8-350	4 Barrel	4.057 x 3.385	350	8.5	200 @ 4200	300 @ 3200	30–45
210 Horsepower V8-455	4 Barrel	4.126 x 4.250	455	8.5	210 @ 3600	350 @ 2400	30–45
230 Horsepower V8-455	4 Barrel	4.126 x 4.250	455	8.5	230 @ 3800	370 @ 2800	30–45
275 Horsepower V8-455	4 Barrel	4.126 x 4.250	455	8.5	275 @ 4200	395 @ 3200	30–45
1975							
105 Horsepower 6-250②	1 Barrel	3.87 x 3.53	250	8.25	105 @ 3800	185 @ 1200	36–41
110 Horsepower V8-260	2 Barrel	3.50 x 3.385	260	8.5	110 @ 3400	205 @ 1600	30–45
165 Horsepower V8-350③	4 Barrel	3.80 x 3.85	350	8.0	165 @ 3800	260 @ 2200	37
170 Horsepower V8-350	4 Barrel	4.057 x 3.385	350	8.5	170 @ 3800	275 @ 2400	30–45
190 Horsepower V8-400④	4 Barrel	4.1212 x 3.75	400	7.6	190 @ 3400	350 @ 2000	55–60
190 Horsepower V8-455⑤	4 Barrel	4.126 x 4.25	455	8.5	190 @ 3600	350 @ 2400	30–45
215 Horsepower V8-455⑥	4 Barrel	4.126 x 4.25	455	8.5	215 @ 3600	370 @ 2400	30–45

①—All horsepower and torque ratings are net.
②—See Chevrolet Chapter for service procedure on this engine.
③—Omega only. See Buick Chapter for service procedures on this engine.
④—See Pontiac Chapter for service procedures on this engine.
⑤—Exc. Toronado.
⑥—Toronado.

TUNEUP SPECIFICATIONS

★When using a timing light, disconnect vacuum hose or tube at distributor and plug opening in hose or tube so idle speed will not be affected. Timing should be set at 750 rpm on V8s.

● When checking compression, lowest cylinder must be within 70% of highest.

▲Before removing wires from distributor cap, determine location of the No. 1 wire in cap, as distributor position may have been altered from that shown at the end of this chart.

Engine	Spark Plug		Distributor		Ignition Timing★			Carb. Adjustments					
								Hot Idle Speed		Air Fuel Ratio		Idle CO%	
	Type	Gap Inch	Point Gap Inch	Dwell Angle Deg.	Firing Order Fig. ▲	Timing, Degrees BTDC ①	Mark Fig.	Std. Trans.	Auto. Trans.②	Std. Trans.	Auto. Trans.	Std. Trans.	Auto. Trans.
1974													
6-250⑦	R46TS	.035	.019	31–34	B	8③	D	850N	600D	—	—	0.3	0.3
8-350 4-bbl.	R46S	.040	.019	30	C	12⑧	A	—	650D	—	—	0.2	0.2
8-455, 275 hp	R45S	.040	.019	30	C	14⑧	A	—	650D	—	—	0.2	0.2
8-455 4-bbl.	R46S	.040	.019	30	C	8⑧	A	—	650D	—	—	0.2	0.2
8-455 4-bbl.④	R46SX	.080	—	—	F	8⑧	A	—	650D	—	—	0.2	0.2
8-455 4-bbl.⑥	R46S	.040	.019	30	C	10⑧	A	—	650D	—	—	0.2	0.2
8-455 4-bbl.④⑥	R46SX	.080	—	—	F	10⑧	A	—	650D	—	—	0.2	0.2
1975													
6-250⑦	R46TX	.060	—	—	E	10	D	850	⑪	—	—	—	—
V8-260	R46SX	.080	—	—	F	⑨	A	750	650D	—	—	—	—
V8-350⑤	R45TSX	.060	—	—	G	12	H	—	600D	—	—	—	—
V8-350	R46SX	.080	—	—	F	20⑧	A	—	650D	—	—	—	—
V8-400⑩	R45TSX	.060	—	—	I	16⑧	J	—	650D	—	—	—	—
V8-455	R46SX	.080	—	—	F	16⑧	A	—	650D	—	—	—	—
V8-455⑥	R46SX	.080	—	—	F	12⑧	A	—	650D	—	—	—	—

①—BTDC: Before top dead center.
②—D: Drive. N: Neutral. Add 50 rpm to slow idle speed for air conditioned cars with A/C off.
③—At 600 rpm with auto. trans. and 850 rpm with manual trans.
④—With High Energy Ignition system.
⑤—Omega only. See Buick Chapter for service procedures on this engine.
⑥—Toronado.
⑦—See Chevrolet Chapter for service procedures on this engine.
⑧—At 1100 rpm.
⑨—Exc. Calif., 16° BTDC; Calif., 18° BTDC. At 1100 rpm.
⑩—See Pontiac Chapter for service procedures on this engine.
⑪—Exc. Calif., 550D; Calif., 600D.

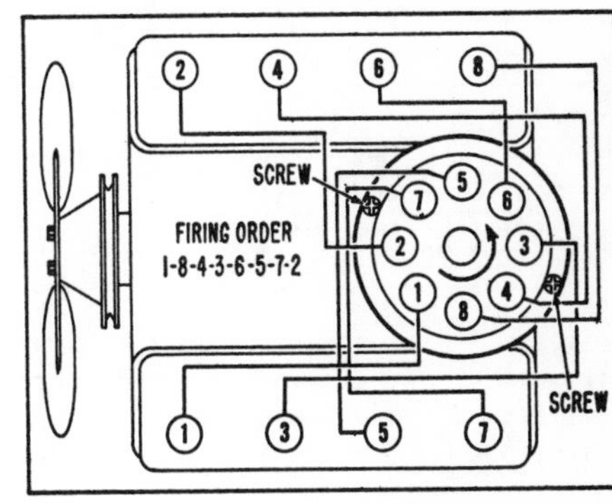

Fig. C

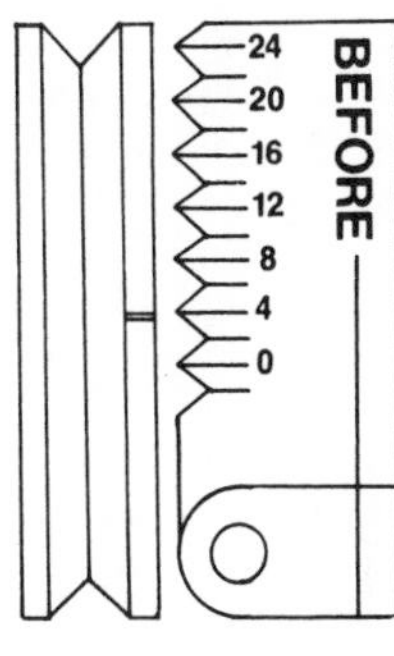

Fig. A

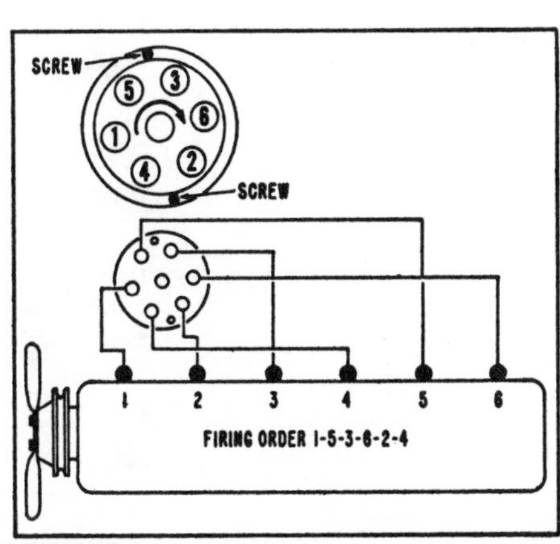

Fig. B

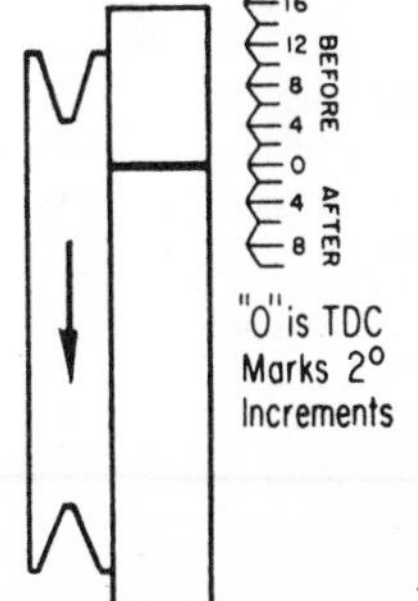

Fig. D

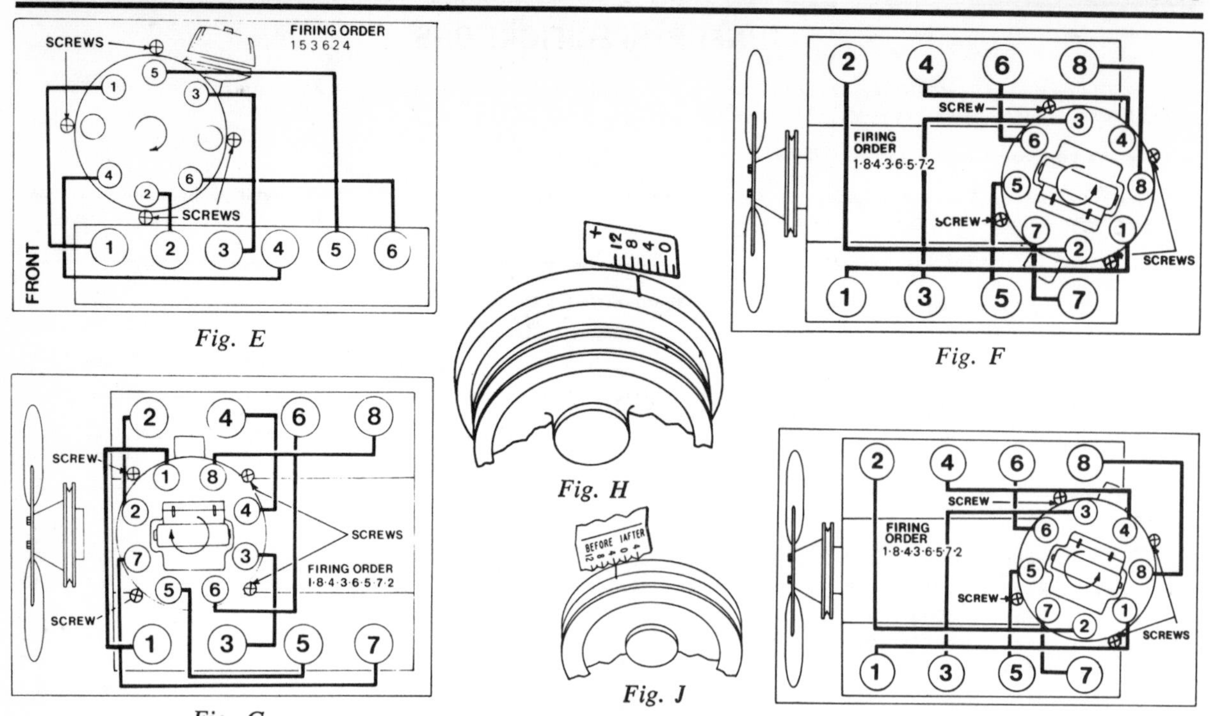

Fig. E

Fig. F

Fig. G

Fig. H

Fig. J

Fig. I

DISTRIBUTOR SPECIFICATIONS

★**Note: If unit is checked on vehicle, double the rpm and degrees to get crankshaft figures.**
Breaker arm spring tension—19–23 oz.

Distributor Part No.①	Centrifugal Advance Degrees @ rpm of Distributor					Vacuum Advance		Distributor Retard
	Advance Starts	Intermediate Advance			Full Advance	Inches of Vacuum to Start Plunger	Max. Adv. Dist. Deg. @ Vacuum	Max. Retard Dist. Deg. @ Vacuum
1973-74								
1110499	0 @ 465	1 @ 635	7 @ 1150	—	12 @ 2050	6–8	6 @ 15½	—
1112195	0-2 @ 400	8-10 @ 1050	—	—	16 @ 2000	5–7	8 @ 12	—
1112197	0-2 @ 540	5-7 @ 1000	—	—	11 @ 1800	7–9	9 @ 16.6	—
1112225	0-2 @ 380	5-7 @ 550	11-13 @ 1050	—	19 @ 2000	5–7	8 @ 12	—
1112226	0-2 @ 400	8-10 @ 1050	—	—	16 @ 2000	3½–4½	10 @ 13	—
1974								
1112506	0-2 @ 540	5-7 @ 1000	—	—	11 @ 1800	7–9	9 @ 16.6	—
1112531	0-2 @ 540	5-7 @ 1000	—	—	11 @ 1800	6	9 @ 10	—
1112532	0-2 @ 540	5-7 @ 1000	—	—	11 @ 1800	4	10 @ 13	—
1112550	0 @ 375	7 @ 600	—	—	13 @ 1500	12	8 @ 18	—
1112825	0-2 @ 575	3.5-5.5 @ 1000	—	—	9 @ 1700	6	9 @ 10	—
1112827	0-2 @ 575	3.5-5.5 @ 1000	—	—	9 @ 1700	7	12 @ 17	—
1112828	0-2 @ 400	8-10 @ 1050	—	—	16 @ 2000	3½–4½	10 @ 13	—
1112829	0-2 @ 575	3.5-5.5 @ 1000	—	—	9 @ 1700	4	10 @ 13	—
1112830	0-2 @ 575	3.5-5.5 @ 1000	—	—	9 @ 1700	7	12 @ 17	—
1975								
1110650	0 @ 550	3½ @ 1150	—	—	8 @ 2100	4	7½ @ 12	—
1112863	0 @ 550	3½ @ 1150	—	—	8 @ 2100	4	12 @ 14¼	—
1112896	0 @ 550	3 @ 1150	—	—	6 @ 2250	7	7 @ 11	—
1112928	0 @ 600	2 @ 700	—	—	8 @ 2200	7	12½ @ 12	—
1112936	0 @ 500	—	—	—	9½ @ 2000	6½	12 @ 16	—
1112937	0 @ 500	—	—	—	6½ @ 1800	8	9 @ 13	—
1112951	0 @ 325	9½ @ 1200	—	—	14 @ 2200	4	12 @ 15	—
1112952	0 @ 500	3½ @ 1050	—	—	7 @ 1800	8	9 @ 13	—
1112953	0 @ 500	—	—	—	9½ @ 2000	8	9 @ 16	—

①—Stamped on distributor housing plate.

PONTIAC
Except Astre

SERIAL NUMBER LOCATION

1969-75: On plate fastened to upper left instrument panel area, visible through windshield.

ENGINE IDENTIFICATION

The V8 engine code is located beneath the production engine number on a machined pad on the right-hand bank of the engine block.

The 6-cylinder engine code for 1969 vehicles is stamped on the cylinder head-to-block contact surface behind oil filler tube and on pad at front right-hand side of cylinder block at rear of distributor for 1970-75 vehicles.

CODE	TRANS.	ENGINE
1974		
CCR	③	6-250⑥
CCX	④	6-250⑥
CCW	④	6-250⑥
AA	④	V8-350①⑩
WB	③	V8-350①
WA	③	V8-350①
YB	④	V8-350①
YA	④	V8-350①
YC	④	V8-350①
YS	④	V8-350②⑦
AD	④	V8-400①⑦
ZB	④	V8-350①
ZA	④	V8-350①
WP	③	V8-350②
WN	③	V8-350②
YP	④	V8-350②
YN	④	V8-350②
ZP	④	V8-350②
AH	④	V8-400①⑦
AT	④	V8-400②⑦
A3	④	V8-400②⑦
YH	④	V8-400①
YJ	④	V8-400①
ZH	④	V8-400①
WR	③	V8-400②⑦
WT	③	V8-400②
YF	④	V8-400①⑦
YK	④	V8-400①⑦
YL	④	V8-400②⑦
YM	④	V8-400②⑦
YZ	④	V8-400②⑦
Y3	③	V8-400②⑦
YT	④	V8-400②
ZD	④	V8-400①⑦
ZJ	④	V8-400①⑦
ZK	④	V8-400①⑦
ZS	④	V8-400②⑦
ZT	④	V8-400②
AW	④	V8-455②⑦
A4	④	V8-455②⑦
YR	④	V8-455②⑦
YW	④	V8-455②⑦
YX	④	V8-455②⑦
YY	④	V8-455②⑦
Y4	④	V8-455②⑦
Y6	④	V8-455②⑦
Y9	④	V8-455②⑦
YU	④	V8-455②
ZU	④	V8-455②
ZW	④	V8-455②⑦
ZX	④	V8-455②⑦
Z4	④	V8-455②⑦
Z6	④	V8-455②⑦
W8	③	V8-455⑤
Y8	④	V8-455⑤

①—Two-barrel carburetor.
②—Four-barrel carburetor.
③—Manual trans.
④—Automatic trans.
⑤—Super Duty engine.
⑥—One-barrel carburetor.
⑦—High Energy Ignition System (H.E.I.).

GENERAL ENGINE SPECIFICATIONS

Engine③	Carburetor	Bore and Stroke	Piston Dis-place-ment, Cubic Inches	Com-pres-sion Ratio	Maximum Brake HP @ rpm	Maximum Torque Lbs. Ft. @ rpm	Normal Oil Pressure Pounds
1974							
100 Horsepower ①6-250	1 Barrel	3.88 x 3.53	250	8.2	100 @ 3600	175 @ 1600	30–45
155 Horsepower 8-350	2 Barrel	3.88 x 3.75	350	7.6	155 @ 3600	275 @ 2400	55–60
170 Horsepower ④8-350	2 Barrel	3.88 x 3.75	350	7.6	170 @ 4000	290 @ 2400	55–60
170 Horsepower 8-350	4 Barrel	3.88 x 3.75	350	7.6	170 @ 4000	280 @ 2000	55–60
200 Horsepower ④8-350	4 Barrel	3.88 x 3.75	350	7.6	200 @ 4400	295 @ 2800	55–60
175 Horsepower 8-400	2 Barrel	4.12 x 3.75	400	8.0	175 @ 3600	315 @ 2000	55–60
190 Horsepower ④8-400	2 Barrel	4.12 x 3.75	400	8.0	190 @ 4000	330 @ 2400	55–60
200 Horsepower 8-400	4 Barrel	4.12 x 3.75	400	8.0	200 @ 4000	320 @ 2400	55–60
225 Horsepower ④8-400	4 Barrel	4.12 x 3.75	400	8.0	225 @ 4000	330 @ 2800	55–60
215 Horsepower 8-455	4 Barrel	4.15 x 4.21	455	8.0	215 @ 3600	355 @ 2400	55–60
250 Horsepower ④8-455	4 Barrel	4.15 x 4.21	455	8.0	250 @ 4000	380 @ 2800	55–60
290 Horsepower ④8-455	4 Barrel	4.15 x 4.21	455	8.4	290 @ 4000	385 @ 3200	75–80

(continued)

GENERAL ENGINE SPECIFICATIONS—Continued

Engine③	Carburetor	Bore and Stroke	Piston Displacement, Cubic Inches	Compression Ratio	Maximum Brake HP @ rpm	Maximum Torque Lbs. Ft. @ rpm	Normal Oil Pressure Pounds
1975							
105 Horsepower............6-250①	1 Barrel	3.87 x 3.53	250	8.25	105 @ 3800	185 @ 1200	36–41
110 Horsepower..........V8-260⑤	2 Barrel	3.50 x 3.385	260	8.5	110 @ 3400	205 @ 1600	30–45
155 Horsepower............V8-350	2 Barrel	3.8762 x 3.75	350	7.6	155 @ 4000	—	55–60
175 Horsepower............V8-350	4 Barrel	3.8762 x 3.75	350	7.6	175 @ 4000	—	55–60
145 Horsepower............V8-350	2 Barrel	3.80 x 3.85	350	8.0	145 @ 3200	—	37
165 Horsepower..........V8-350⑥	4 Barrel	3.80 x 3.85	350	8.0	165 @ 3800	260 @ 2200	37
170 Horsepower............V8-400	2 Barrel	4.1212 x 3.75	400	7.6	170 @ 4000	—	55–60
185 Horsepower............V8-400	4 Barrel	4.1212 x 3.75	400	7.6	185 @ 3600	—	55–60
200 Horsepower............V8-455	4 Barrel	4.1522 x 4.21	455	7.6	200 @ 3500	—	55–60

①—For service on this engine, see Six Cylinder in Chevrolet Chapter.

③—Ratings are NET—as installed in the vehicle.

④—With dual exhausts.

⑤—See Oldsmobile Chapter for service procedures.

⑥—Ventura only. See Buick Chapter for service procedures.

TUNEUP SPECIFICATIONS

★When using a timing light, disconnect vacuum hose or tube at distributor and plug opening in hose or tube so idle speed will not be affected.

● When checking compression, lowest cylinder must be within 80% of highest.

▲Before removing wires from distributor cap, determine location of the No. 1 wire in cap, as distributor position may have been altered from that shown at the end of this chart.

Engine	Spark Plug		Distributor		Ignition Timing★			Carb. Adjustments					
								Hot Idle Speed③		Air Fuel Ratio		Idle CO%	
	Type	Gap Inch	Point Gap Inch	Dwell Angle Deg.	Firing Order Fig. ▲	Timing, Degrees BTDC ①	Mark Fig.	Std. Trans.	Auto. Trans.②	Std. Trans.	Auto. Trans.	Std. Trans.	Auto. Trans.
1974													
6-250	R46T	.035	⑪	32½	A	6	H	850	600D	—	—	0.2	0.2
V8-350 2-bbl.	R46TS	.040	⑪	30	D	⑫	I	900	650D	—	—	0.2	0.2
V8-350 2-bbl.④	R46TS	.040	⑪	30	D	10	I	—	625D	—	—	—	0.2
V8-350 4-bbl.	R46TS	.040	⑪	30	D	⑫	I	1000	650D	—	—	0.2	0.2
V8-350 4-bbl.④	R46TS	.040	⑪	30	D	10	I	—	625D	—	—	—	0.2
V8-400 2-bbl.	R46TS	.040	⑪	30	D	⑫	I	—	650D	—	—	—	0.2
V8-400 2-bbl.④	R46TS	.040	⑪	30	D	10	I	—	625D	—	—	—	0.2
V8-400 4-bbl.	R45TS	.040	⑪	30	D	⑫	I	1000	650D	—	—	0.2	0.2
V8-400 4-bbl.④	R45TS	.040	⑪	30	D	10	I	—	625D	—	—	—	0.2
V8-455	R45TS	.040	⑪	30	D	⑫	I	—	650D	—	—	—	0.2
V8-455④	R45TS	.040	⑪	30	D	10	I	—	625D	—	—	—	0.2
V8-455 SD	R44TS	.040	⑪	30	D	12	I	1000	750D	—	—	0.2	0.2
1975													
6-250⑨	R46TX	.060	—	—	B	10	H	800	650D	—	—	—	—
V8-260	R46SX	.080	—	—	C	16	G	750	650D	—	—	—	—
V8-260④	R46SX	.080	—	—	C	18	G	750	650D	—	—	—	—
V8-350	R46TSX	.060	—	—	E	⑦	I	800	⑮	—	—	—	—
V8-350⑥	R45TSX	.060	—	—	F	12	J	800	600D	—	—	—	—
V8-400 2-bbl.	R46TSX	.060	—	—	E	16	I	800	650D	—	—	—	—
V8-400 4-bbl.⑩	R45TSX	.060	—	—	E	16	I	800	650D	—	—	—	—
V8-400 4-bbl.⑬	R45TSX	.060	—	—	E	⑭	I	800	650D	—	—	—	—
V8-400 4-bbl.④	R45TSX	.060	—	—	E	12	I	800	650D	—	—	—	—
V8-455	R45TSX	.060	—	—	E	16	I	800	650D	—	—	—	—
V8-455④	R45TSX	.060	—	—	E	10	I	800	625D	—	—	—	—

(continued)

TUNEUP NOTES

①—BTDC: Before top dead center.
②—D: Drive. N: Neutral.
③—Where two figures are given, the higher is with solenoid active.
④—California.
⑤—Exc. H.E.I., Fig. D; H.E.I., Fig. E.
⑥—Ventura only.
⑦—Std. Trans. and all Calif. 12°, Auto. Trans. exc. Calif. 16°.
⑨—For service on this engine, see Six Cylinder in Chevrolet Chapter.
⑩—All except Firebird, Gran Prix and California.
⑪—New points .019″, used points .016″.
⑫—Std. trans. 10° BTDC. Auto trans. 12° BTDC.
⑬—Firebird and Grand Prix except California.
⑭—2-bbl. R46TSX; 4-bbl. R45TSX.
⑮—2 bbl. Carb. 600 rpm, 4 bbl. Carb. 650 rpm.
⑯—Man. trans. and all Calif.
⑰—Auto. trans. exc. Calif.
⑱—2 bbl. carb., 650 rpm; 4 bbl. carb.—Exc. Calif. Grand Safari sta. wag., 650 rpm; Grand Safari sta. wag. exc. Calif., 625 rpm; All Calif. models, 600 rpm.

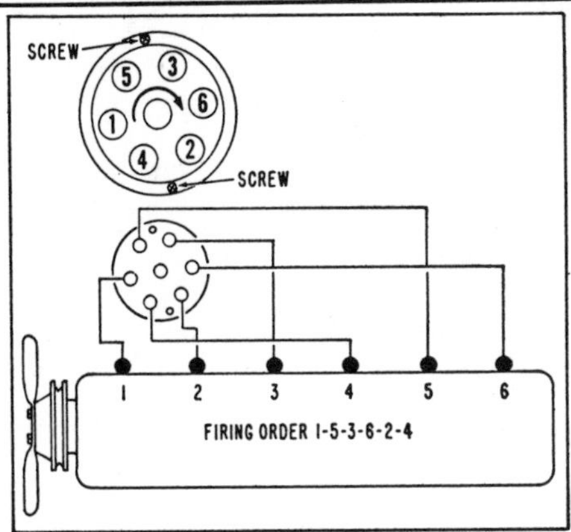

Fig. A

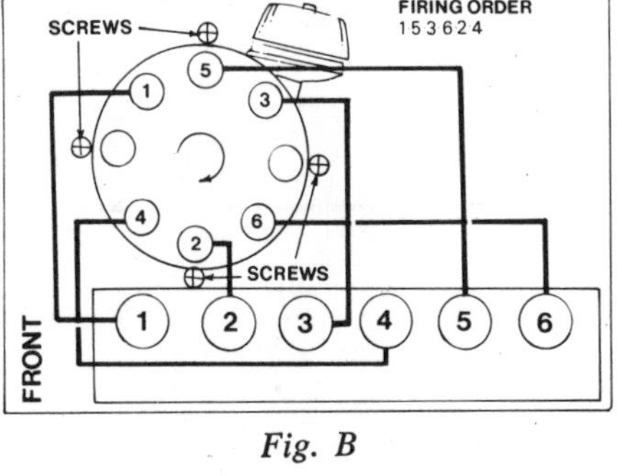

Fig. B

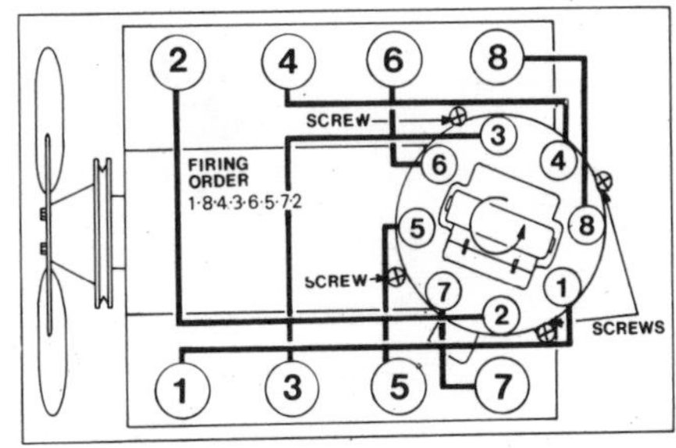

Fig. C

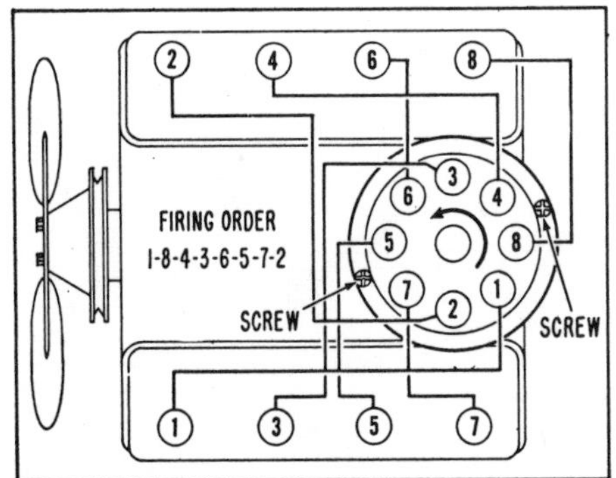

Fig. D

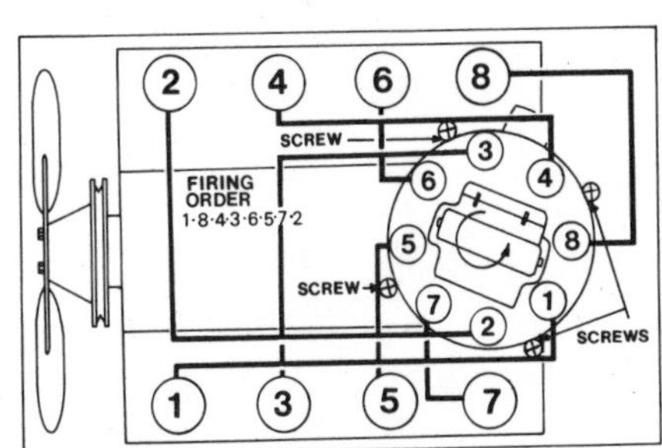

Fig. E

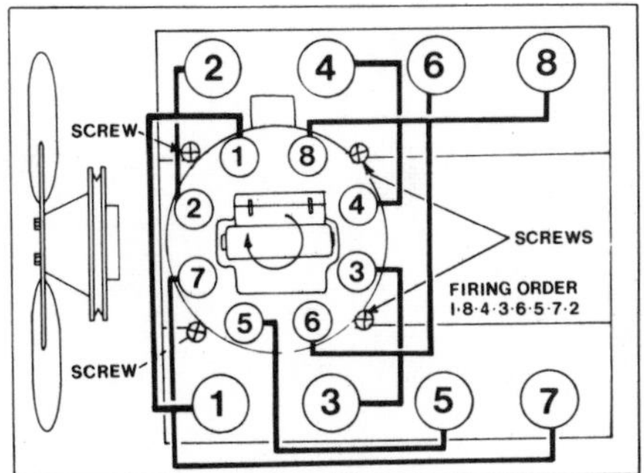

Fig. F

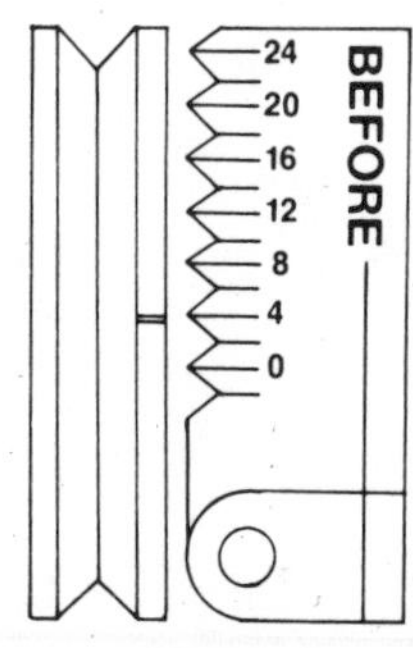

Fig. G

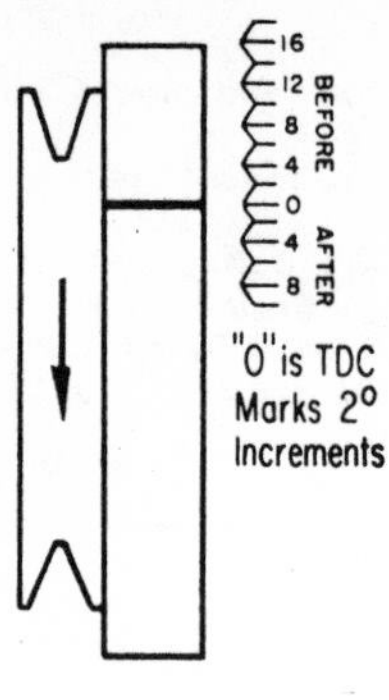

Fig. H

Fig. I

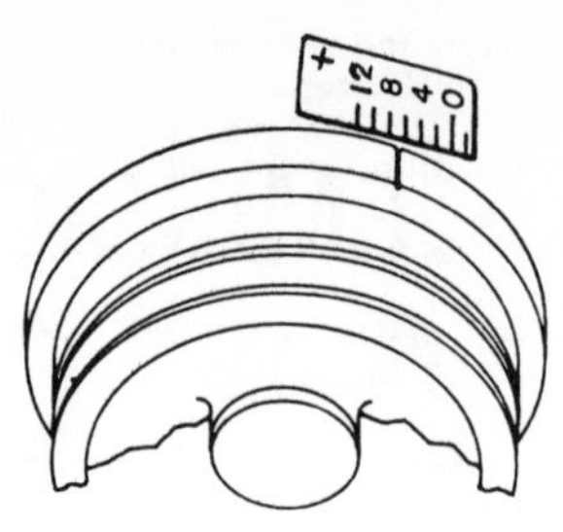

Fig. J

EMISSION CONTROL SYSTEMS

CONTENTS

Systems Application Charts

Universal Application Systems

Specific Application Systems

AMERICAN MOTORS

CHRYSLER CORPORATION

FORD MOTOR COMPANY

GENERAL MOTORS

EMISSION CONTROL SYSTEMS AND DEVICES

APPLICATION CHARTS

AMERICAN MOTORS

Year Model	Air Guard	Engine Model	EGR	Electric Choke	Evaporative Emission Control	Fuel Return	Thermostatically Controlled Air Cleaner	Transmission Controlled Spark	Back Pressure Sensor	EGR Coolant Temperature Override	Spark Coolant Temperature Override	Catalytic Converter	PCV
1974	①	All	②	360-401	All	—	All	③	④	All	All	—	All
1975	⑤	—	All	—	All	⑥	All	⑦	⑦	All	All	⑧	All

①—Matador 6-232, Matador 6-258 except Calif. with manual transmission or station wagon. All V8's except 304 Gremlin, Hornet and Javelin
②—All 6-232 for Calif. All station wagons with manual transmission except Calif.
③—All V8-401 except California with auto trans.
④—All Calif. except V8-401.
⑤—All except Hornet with 6-cylinder & auto trans and Gremlin with 6-cylinder.
⑥—Matador 6-258 with manual transmission except Calif. and all 6-232 exc. Calif.
⑦—California only.
⑧—All except Gremlin 6-cylinder except Calif. and Hornet 6-cylinder with auto trans.

CHRYSLER CORP.

Year Model	Air Injection System	Exhaust Gas Recirculation	Evaporative Control System	Orifice Spark Advance Control	Heated Air System	Electric Assist Choke	Electronic Ignition	Thermal Ignition Control	Venturi Vacuum Control	Ported Vacuum Control	Coolant Controlled EGR	Idle Enrichment	EGR Time Delay	Catalytic Converter	PCV
1974	①	All	All	All	All	All	All	②	③	③	All	—	—	—	All
1975	All	All	All	All	All	All	All	②	⑤	⑥	All	All	All	⑦	All

①—V8-440 California and emission control option in all other states.
②—Used with Maximum Cooling System and/or air conditioning.
③—V8-318 California only.
④—All V8 engines except California.
⑤—All except Calif. V8-318 with manual trans.
⑥—V8-318 with auto trans except California.
⑦—Except V8-318 2-bbl carb intermediate models, or V8-360 4-bbl carb.

FORD MOTOR CO.

Engine	Thermostatically Controlled Air Cleaner	EGR	Venturi Vacuum Amplifier	Spark Delay Valve	Distributor Vacuum Control	Thermactor	Electric Assist Choke	PCV	Fuel Decel Valve	Spark Deceleration Valve	Exhaust Heat Control	Catalytic Converter	Cold Weather Modulator	Evaporative Control System
1974														
2000 cc	All	All	All	(1)	(2)	(3)	All	All	(4)	—	—	—	—	All
2300 cc	All	All	All	(5)	All	(6)	All	All	—	—	—	—	—	All
2800 cc	All	All	All	All	All	All	All	All	(3)	—	—	—	—	All
6-200	All	All	(7)	(8)	All	(7)	All	All	—	—	—	—	—	All
6-250	All	All	(9)	(11)	(10)	(9)	All	All	—	—	—	—	—	All
V8-302	All	All	—	—	All	(7)	All	All	—	—	—	—	—	All
V8-351W	All	All	—	All	(12)	—	All	All	—	—	—	—	—	All
V8-351C(15)	All	All	—	(13)	(15)	All	All	All	—	—	—	—	—	All
V8-351C(16)	All	All	—	—	—	—	All	All	—	(17)	—	—	—	All
V8-400	All	All	—	(18)	(19)	(3)	All	All	—	—	—	—	—	All
V8-460	All	All	—	All	All	(3)	All	All	—	—	—	—	—	All
1975														
2300 cc	All	All	All	—	All	All	All	All	—	—	—	—	All	All
2800 cc	All	All	All	—	All	All	All	All	All	—	All	—	All	All
6-200	All	All	All	All	All	—	All	All	—	—	All	All	—	All
6-250	All	All	All	All	All	All	All	All	—	—	All	All	All	All
V8-302	All	All	All	All	All	All	All	All	—	—	All	All	All	All
V8-351W	All	All	—	—	All	All	All	All	—	—	All	All	All	All
V8-351M	All	All	—	—	—	All	All	All	—	—	All	All	All	All
V8-400	All	All	—	—	—	All	All	All	—	—	All	All	All	All
V8-460	All	All	—	—	—	All	All	All	—	—	—	All	—	All

(1)—Capri with auto trans for Calif. and Pinto for Calif.
(2)—Capri models.
(3)—California models.
(4)—All with manual trans.
(5)—All except Mustang & Pinto with man trans, & Pinto sta. wag. using carburetor #D42E-9510-KA.
(6)—Used on all models except those with carburetor numbers D42E-9510-CD, DB, GA & LA.
(7)—Maverick & Comet with auto trans for Calif.
(8)—Maverick & Comet with auto trans for Calif. & All except California with auto trans using carburetor numbers D4DE-9510-AFA, AGA, KB & KJ.
(9)—Maverick & Comet for California & Maverick except Calif. with auto trans using carburetor number D4DE-9510-ADA.
(10)—All except Montego & Torino.
(11)—All except Maverick using carburetor number D4DE-9510-ADA.
(12)—Except with carburetor number D4AE-9510-EA, KA.
(13)—Used on some applications.
(14)—Except Ford & Mercury full size models.
(15)—2 bar. carb.
(16)—4 bar. carb.
(17)—Torino with manual transmission except Calif.
(18)—Ford & Mercury sta. wag. and all Torino, Montego, Cougar, Ford & Mercury for California.
(19)—Except Ford & Mercury sta. wag.

GENERAL MOTORS

Year Model	Thermac Air Cleaner	Air Injection Reactor	Exhaust Gas Recirculation	Controlled Combustion System	Transmission Controlled Spark	PCV	Evaporative Emission Control	Back Pressure Transducer	Early Fuel Evaporation	Catalytic Converter
1974										
Buick	All	All	All	All	①	All	All	—	—	—
Cadillac	All	All	All	—	—	All	All	All	—	—
Chevrolet	All	All	All	All	②	All	All	—	—	—
Oldsmobile	All	⑮	All	All	③	All	All	⑤	—	—
Pontiac	All	⑯	All	All	⑦	All	All	—	—	—
1975										
Buick	All	All	All	All	—	All	All	⑨	⑧	All
Cadillac	All	⑩	All	—	—	All	All	⑪	All	All
Chevrolet	All	All	All	All	—	All	All	—	All	All
Oldsmobile	All	④	All	All	—	All	All	⑫	⑬	All
Pontiac	All	⑥	All	—	—	All	All	⑮	All	All

①—6-250 and V8-455 Stage 1.
②—With manual transmission.
③—Omega with 6-250 & manual transmission.
④—Omega 6-250.
⑤—California V8.
⑥—All 6-250 and 2-bbl V8 with manual transmission except California. All Calif. 6-250 and 2-bbl V8 with automatic transmission.
⑦—All 6-250 & V8 with manual transmission.
⑧—V8-350 except California.
⑨—V8-260.
⑩—California only; or all states when used with 145-amp alternator.
⑪—Used with AIR system.
⑫—V8-260 Cutlass and Omega; V8-350 Cutlass and 88 with auto trans for California; V8-455 Cutlass, 88 and 98 for California; Toronado except California.
⑬—All except the following: V8-350 Omega, Cutlass, and 88 California; V8-350 & 455 Cutlass, 88, 98 and Toronado non-California.
⑭—V6-231, 6-250 Cutlass and Omega; and V8-350 4-bbl Omega Calif.
⑮—All except V8-350.
⑯—Used where required.

Universal Application Systems

ELECTRIC ASSIST CHOKE

Cadillac

An electrically actuated ceramic resistor in an electric choke assembly, Fig. 1, heats the thermostatic coil which gradually relaxes coil tension to allow the choke valve to continue opening with both inlet air pressure pushing on the off-set choke valve and the weight of the choke linkage pulling the valve open allowing for precise timing of the choke valve opening for good engine warmup performance.

The electric choke operates as follows:

The electric choke receives an electric current operating through the engine oil pressure switch whenever the engine is running. The electric current flows to a ceramic resistor that is divided into separate sections—a small center section for gradual heating of the thermostatic coil, and a large outer section for additional rapid heating of the thermostatic coil.

The ceramic resistor functions as follows.

Air Temperature Below 50° F

Electric current, applied to the small section of the ceramic resistor, causes the section to heat up and warm the thermostatic coil which allows gradual opening of the choke valve for good cold engine warmup performance. As the small section of the ceramic resistor continues to produce heat, a temperature-sensitive bi-metal disk causes a spring loaded contact to close, applying electric current to the large section of the ceramic resistor thus causing it to heat up. Heat from the larger section of the ceramic resistor increases the rate of heat flow to the thermostatic coil for more rapid opening of the choke valve.

Air Temperature 70° F and Above

Electric current is applied directly to the small section, and through the spring contact, also to the large section of the ceramic resistor to provide a rapid heating of the thermostatic coil for greater choke valve opening when leaner air/fuel mixtures are desired at warmer ambient temperatures.

Air Temperature Between 50° F and 70° F

Electric current, applied to the small section or both the small and large sections of the ceramic resistor, depending upon the temperature, will produce the required heat to warm the thermostatic coil to control the choke valve position for good engine performance in these temperature ranges.

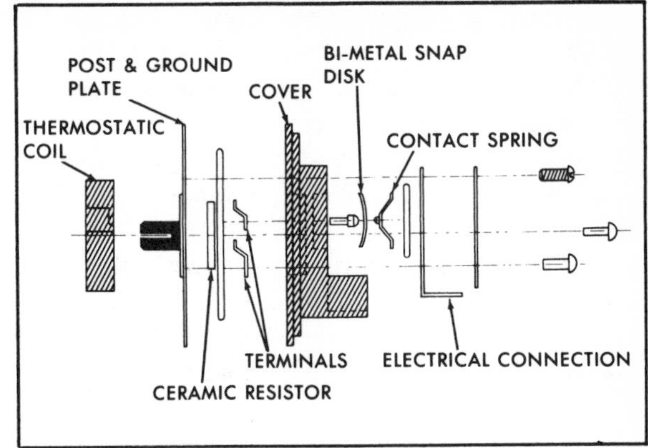

Fig. 1 Electric choke assembly

NOTE: Ground contact for the electric choke is provided by a metal plate located at the rear of the choke assembly. DO NOT INSTALL A CHOKE COVER GASKET BETWEEN THE ELECTRIC CHOKE ASSEMBLY AND THE CHOKE HOUSING.

The electric choke assembly is indexed properly by aligning the scribe mark on the front cover with the specified index mark on the choke housing.

Electric Choke Diagnosis

In order to have good engine performance during warmup and to be able to pass Federal or California exhaust emission standards, the electric choke must function properly.

Possible reasons for the choke not operating properly are listed below.

1. No engine oil pressure.
2. Malfunctioning oil pressure switch.
3. No current to oil pressure switch due to:
   Burned out 25 amp backup-Trans fuse.
   Broken wire to switch (18 orange, 18 orange/black or 18 dark green).
4. No current between the choke coil and the oil pressure switch due to:
   Broken 18 tan lead wire.
   Wire terminal not locked on coil terminal.
   Ground circuit incomplete between grounding plate of choke assembly and housing.
5. Failed choke coil assembly.

A voltmeter or continuity light may be used to check the circuits for continuity to the oil pressure switch and the choke coil.

If it is suspected that the choke coil assembly has

failed, the following check may be made.

1. Remove the coil from the carburetor and cool it to room temperature (above 60° F).
2. Attach a jumper wire between the positive battery terminal and the terminal of the coil assembly. Attach a second jumper wire between the negative battery terminal and the grounding plate of the choke coil assembly.
3. The tang of the coil should rotate 45° in 54 to 90 seconds.
4. If the coil fails to rotate or exceeds the above timing specification, replace the coil assembly.
5. If the coil is within the above timing specification then the coil is good and the problem is elsewhere.
6. Reinstall the coil and set it to the proper index. Refer to Carburetor Specifications.

If the coil is cooled off sufficiently the choke valve will close when the throttle is opened slightly. Attach a jumper wire between the positive battery terminal and the choke coil terminal. The choke coil should warm up and the choke blade can be observed opening, indicating a good and properly grounded choke coil assembly. At room temperature the choke blade should be wide open in approximately 90 seconds.

If the choke does not operate properly after the coil has been proven satisfactory, check out the other possibilities that prevent the current from getting to the choke coil.

Chrysler

The 1974-75 switch serves three purposes.

1. Below 58° F the control switch will partially energize the choke heater.
2. Above 58° F the control switch will fully energize the choke heater.
3. The control switch will de-energize the choke heater at approximately 110° F. During winter operations, engines will experience three stages of choke heat; partial heat during engine warmup, full heat after engine warmup and no heat well after engine warmup. Engine starts during summer temperatures will not experience the partial heat stage.

NOTE: The heating element should not be exposed to or immersed in any fluid for any purpose. An electric short in the wiring to the heater or within the heater will be a short of the ignition system.

Testing

1974-75 American Motors

1. Disconnect the electrical lead from the choke housing, then connect a test lamp between the choke housing terminal and the electrical lead.
2. Disconnect the choke heat tube from the choke housing and start the engine.
3. Using a small thermometer, position the thermometer bulb end inside the heat tube passage in the choke housing. Then read the thermometer and observe the test lamp.
4. Lamp should be out between 60-80° F and should be on at temperatures below or above these.

NOTE: If the test lamp did not light, check 7 volt source from alternator. If the test lamp did light within 60-80° F, replace the choke cover.

Chrysler

Testing for Chrysler is the same as for 1973 except that the electrical resistance for 1974-75 is 4-12 ohms.

1974-75 Ford

1. Remove the air cleaner and make certain that it was not interfering with the choke plate. Then check the linkages and fast idle cam for freedom of operation.
   NOTE: If delay valve is used, make certain it is operating properly.
2. On all except Mustang II and Pinto, disconnect the hot air supply tube from the choke housing. Then using the Choke Tester LRE-34618 or equivalent, check for correct operation of the choke.
3. Disconnect the stator lead and connect a 0-3 amp ammeter between the choke lead connector and stator lead, then start the engine and observe the reading.
4. On all except Mustang II and Pinto, cool the choke until the temperature is less than 55° F. If current flow is noted, the cap is defective.
5. At about 5 minutes of engine operation, a current reading of .3-1 amps should be noted for all except Mustang II and Pinto and .3-.75 amps for Mustang II and Pinto.
   NOTE: On Mustang II and Pinto, make certain that coolant is flowing through the choke housing. If the choke housing is not hot, check hoses for obstructions.
6. If no current draw is noted, check for proper operation of the alternator before replacing the choke housing.

AUTOMATIC CHOKE CHECK PROCEDURE

2150 2V Carburetor

2.8, 302, 351, 360, 390 and 400 CID Engines

Electric Choke Function Tests

1. Disconnect the stator lead at choke cap termi-

nal and connect a test light in series with ground.
2. The light should glow at all times while the engine is running.
3. If the light does not glow, either the alternator or the choke wire is defective and should be repaired as necessary.
4. Place the test light in series with the choke terminal and stator lead. If the light does not glow, replace the choke cap assembly. If the light glows, turn off the engine.
5. Manually open the throttle and set on fast idle cam. Remove the hot air supply tube at the choke housing and install a choke tester—Rotunda LRE-34618 or the equivalent. Cool the choke housing per choke tester manufacturer's instruction until bi-metal closes choke plate lightly in air horn.

NOTE: Do not use choke tester manufacturer's time specifications.

YF And YFA 1V Carburetors 250 And 300 CID Engines

Choke Functional Tests

1. Disconnect the stator lead at the choke cap terminal and connect a test light in series with the stator lead and ground.
2. The test light should glow with the engine running.
3. If light does not glow, either the alternator or the choke wire is defective. Correct as required.
4. Restart the engine and warm to normal operating temperature. Place the test light in series with choke terminal and alternator stator lead. If the light does not glow, replace the choke cap assembly. Engine and choke cap must be warmed to normal operating temperature whenever choke cap is replaced. If the light glows, turn off the engine. Reconnect the choke terminal and alternator stator lead.
5. Remove the hot air supply tube at the carburetor choke housing. Attach the Rotunda choke tester LRE-34518 or the equivalent. Manually set fast idle cam on high step. Cool the choke housing until the choke plate just closes.
   CAUTION: Use extreme care in removing, reinstalling and checking for leaks in the choke hot air supply tube. The retaining nut and/or choke housing can easily be cross threaded.
6. Check for choke resistance by securing an ohmmeter across the choke cap terminal and choke ground strap.
7. This value should be within specification. If range is exceeded, replace the choke cap and repeat the procedure beginning with Step 4.
8. Recool the choke housing until the choke plate just closes. If the choke plate is closed, this step should not be performed.
9. Remove the Rotunda choke tester LRE-34518 or the equivalent.
10. With the heat tube removed, the choke plate closed, and fast idle screw positioned on high step of cam, start the engine without touching the throttle and see that the choke opens to a vertical position with electrical assist only. Record the choke come-off time. If the choke does not open with electrical assist only, replace the choke cap and repeat the procedure beginning with Step 4.

CAUTION: Use extreme care in removing, reinstalling and checking for leaks in the choke hot air supply tube. The retaining nut and/or choke housing can easily be cross-threaded.

5200 2S/2V Carburetor 2.3L Engine

Electric Choke Functional Check

1. Disconnect the stator lead at the choke cap terminal or at the lead connector and connect it to one lead of a test light.
2. Connect the second test light lead to ground.
3. The light should glow at all times with the engine running.
4. If the light does not glow, either the alternator is not functioning or the automatic choke wire from the stator is an open circuit and should be repaired as necessary.
5. If the light glows, disconnect the test lead from ground and connect it to the choke lead connector.
6. If necessary, warm up the engine to normal operating temperature:
   (*a*) Verify that engine coolant is flowing through the choke housing. The housing should get hot. If not, check the hoses for restriction.
   (*b*) The choke unit should operate and the test light should glow. If not, the choke unit is defective and should be replaced.
7. If the light glows, an additional electrical check must be performed as outlined below. Remove the test light.
   (*a*) Stop the engine, release the cooling system pressure and disconnect the water hoses to the automatic choke housing.
   (*b*) Adapt the Rotunda choke tester LRE-34618, or equivalent, to one of the hose connections of the automatic choke housing.

(c) Cool the choke housing per the choke tester manufacturer's instructions until the bi-metal closes the choke plate lightly in the air horn. Maintain ¼ throttle opening while using the choke tester. If the choke plate is not lightly closed after five minutes, tap the plate lightly and continue. If the choke plate does not close in 10 minutes, recheck for binding and correct as required.

(d) Check electrical continuity between the choke cap terminal or the lead connector and ground at the choke bi-metal housing with an ohmmeter. Be sure above conditions are met and that adequate connections are made with the ohmmeter leads.

(e) The resistance should be within specs. If not, the electric choke unit should be replaced. Repeat the electric continuity check with the new choke cap and correct as required.

8. Reinstall the related system components to specs. Check the coolant level if required.

4350 4V Carburetor 460 CID Engines

Choke Functional Checks

1. Disconnect the stator lead at the choke cap terminal and connect a test light in series with ground.
2. The light should glow at all times while the engine is running.
3. If the light does not glow, either the alternator or the choke wire is defective and should be replaced as necessary.
4. Place the test light in series with choke terminal and stator lead. If the light does not glow, replace the choke cap assembly. If the light glows, turn off the engine.
5. Remove the hot air supply tube at the choke housing and install a choke tester Rotunda LRE-34518 or equivalent. Cool choke housing per choke tester manufacturer's instruction until the bi-metal closes the choke plate lightly in air horn.

   CAUTION: Use extreme care in removing, reinstalling and checking for leaks in the choke hot air supply tube. The retaining nut could be easily damaged.
6. Check for choke resistance by adequately securing an ohmmeter across the choke cap terminal and choke ground strap.
7. This value should be within specifications. If it is out of specifications, replace the choke cap assembly. Remove the ohmmeter.
8. Apply external vacuum 16 in ± 2 in. Hg to pulldown control diaphragm. Measure the choke plate opening at the lower edge. The pulldown setting should be within specifications for minimum choke plate opening. If the choke plate minimum opening is met, continue with the diagnosis. Reset the pulldown if it is found to be out of specification.
9. Reinstall the hot air supply tube.

   CAUTION: Exercise extreme care in removing, reinstalling and checking for leaks in the choke hot air supply tube as its retaining nut could be easily cross-threaded.
10. Start the engine without touching the throttle and observe the following.

    (a) If the diaphragm retracts.

    (b) On applicable models, the fast idle cam should rotate and the throttle should move to kickdown step of the cam in specified time.

    (c) The choke plate should open within specified time.

    If any of these conditions are not met, repair and/or replace accordingly.
11. Install shop air of specified psi or less to cold air inlet side of choke heat system. Use snoop or equivalent to check air leakage at the heat tube nut to the choke housing. No leakage acceptable. Repair or replace as necessary.
12. Stop the engine. Remove the instruments and reinstall the related system components.

CATALYTIC CONVERTERS

The major domestic automobile manufacturers have turned to the catalytic converter in 1975 in order to comply with HC and CO federal emissions standards. The 1975 acceptable standards of hydrocarbons (HC) and carbon monoxide (CO) emissions have been cut by 50% from their respective 1974 levels. California has been subjected to a 65% cut in these increasingly stringent standards.

HC and CO results from unburned or partially burned molecules of gasoline and motor oil. There were two possible methods available to automakers by which the federal standards for 1975 could be met. One solution could have been modifications upstream in the combustion chambers and the other was by downstream devices designed to function after the combustion process was completed. Catalytic converters were designed to suit the latter situation.

For 1975, General Motors has incorporated catalytic converters throughout their model line. Chrysler and FoMoCo have elected to meet federal

Fig. 2 Catalytic converter cutaway. GM

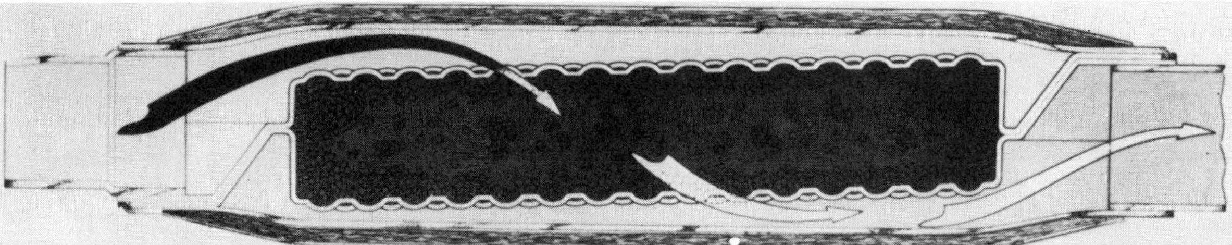

Fig. 3 Hydrocarbons and carbon monoxide are converted to water vapor and carbon dioxide

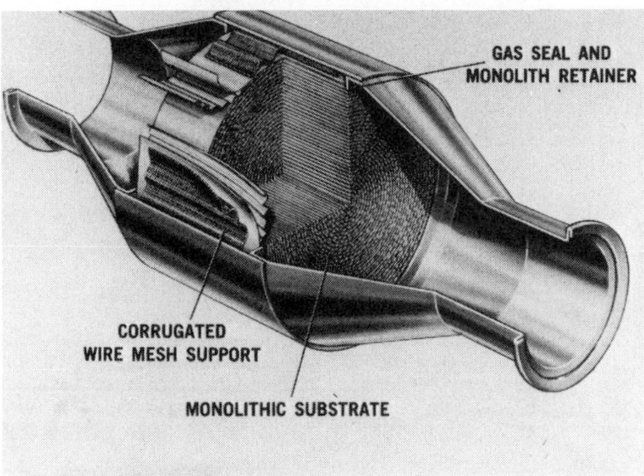

Fig. 4 Catalytic converter. Ford

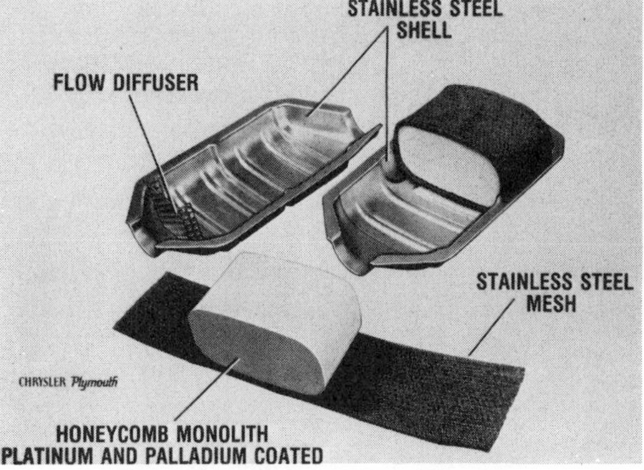

Fig. 5 Catalytic converter components. Chrysler-Plymouth

standards by way of a combined application of converters on 75% of their domestic products along with a more balanced utilization of pre-1975 emissions controls.

Description

The purpose of the catalyst is twofold. First, it is able to make a chemical reaction proceed at a quicker rate, and second, although it enters into the chemical reaction, it emerges unchanged. It is able to repeat the same process over and over. Emission control catalysts are being produced either in the form of pellets or as a unitized monolithic structure. Contained in a muffler-like chamber added to the exhaust system, a suitable catalyst will change HC and CO pollutants into harmless water vapor and carbon dioxide.

The catalyst itself consists of a relatively porous substrate of an inert material—alumina—in pellet or monolith form on which small amounts of catalytically active material are deposited. Few chemical elements have the type of chemical activity required of a proper catalytic agent. Two of the popular elements in use are noble metals—platinum and palladium. Resulting production catalysts have a relatively large surface area exposed to the exhaust stream.

Noble metal catalysts require the use of lead-free gasoline. Leaded fuel will coat the catalytic surface, rendering it ineffective.

To prevent inadvertent use of leaded fuels, 1975 model cars have a smaller diameter fuel tank filler neck opening. Federal regulations require most gasoline stations to provide unleaded fuels through pump nozzles of coordinated design. All major gasoline stations offer lead-free gas for 1975 models. The use of leaded gas in an emergency situation will not have any lasting effects on the converter. But there will be a temporary rise in emission levels. Catalyst durability is warranteed by the manufacturer for 50,000 miles.

The catalyst must be hot to do its job. Normal operating range is 900° to 1500° F, with peak temperatures in the 1800° range. Because of the close proximity of these high temperatures to the passenger compartment, insulation of the pellets or the monolith is critical. Substantial heat shielding is necessary to prevent abnormal heating of the car's interior. Grass shields are incorporated in order to shield the converter from undergrowth. Systems are also incorporated which protect the converter from backfire and from sub-freezing temperatures.

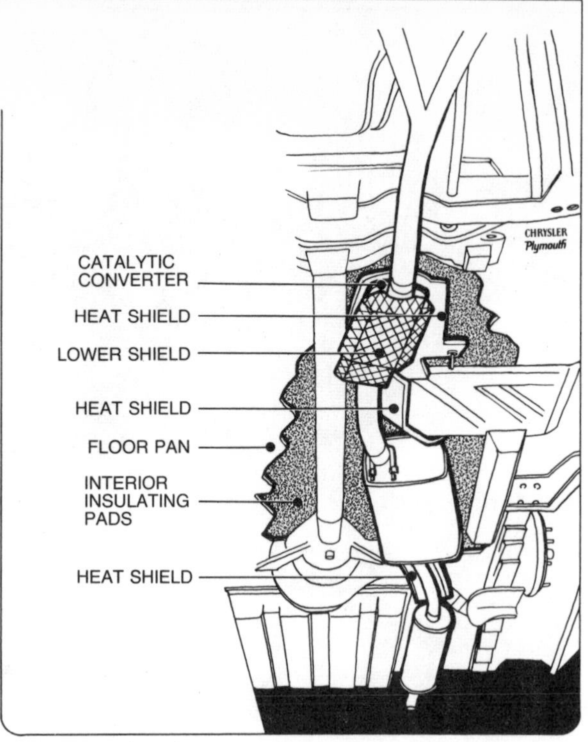

Fig. 6 Catalytic converter heat shield protection. Chrysler-Plymouth

Servicing

The catalytic converters that are used in Chrysler and Ford vehicles are not serviceable. After determining that the catalyst has lost its effectiveness, the complete catalytic converter assembly must be replaced. This operation is similar to replacing a muffler.

The converters used on General Motors and American Motors vehicles are serviceable. A special tool is used to remove a large drain plug after a vacuum is created within the converter. A special vibrator will help to drain the unit of pellets. Once emptied, the container can be refilled with recommended replacement catalyst pellets in a similar vacuum-assisted manner.

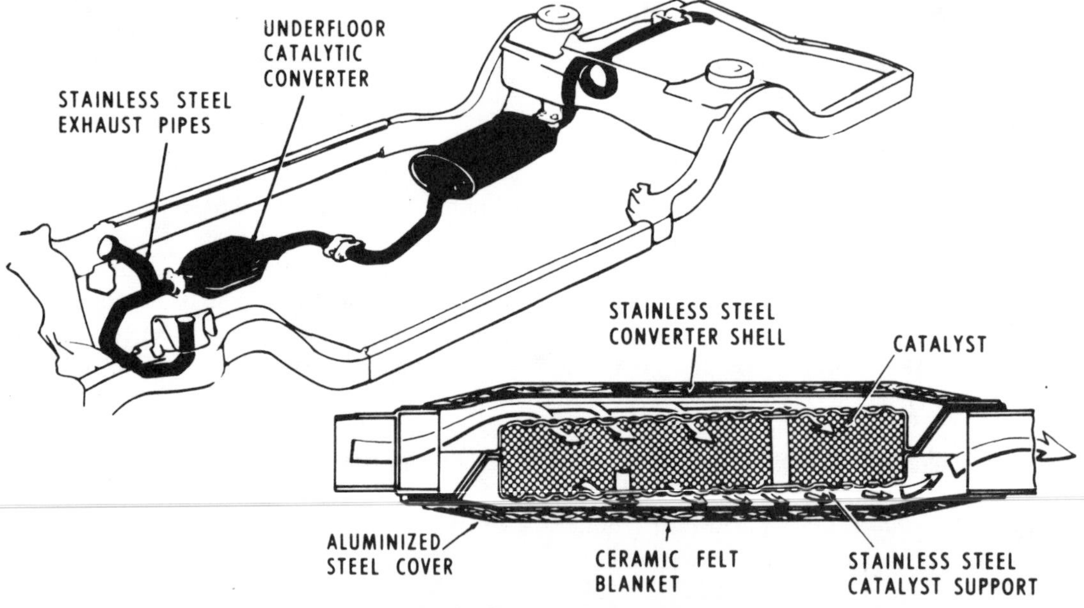

Fig. 7 Underfloor catalytic converter

Specific Application Systems

AMERICAN MOTORS EXHAUST GAS RECIRCULATION (EGR)

NOTE: EGR valves used with exhaust back pressure sensors have shorter and more tapered stems than those used without the sensor. The shorter stems are needed to match the EGR metering to back pressure sensor operation.

Exhaust Back Pressure Sensor

All 6-cylinder and some V8-304, 360 engines used on 1974 California vehicles and all 1975 vehicles are required to have an exhaust back pressure sensor, Fig. 8. This device consists of a diaphragm valve, a spacer and a metal tube. The EGR valve is mounted to the sensor spacer and is modulated by the sensor.

The EGR system, when equipped with a back pressure sensor, obtains a vacuum signal at the carburetor spark port and not the EGR port. The vacuum signal passes through the EGR/CTO (Coolant Temperature Override) switch when coolant temperature exceeds 115° F to the valve portion of the sensor where it is modulated by exhaust back pressure.

NOTE: The inlet nipple of the exhaust back pressure sensor has a .030-inch restriction, Fig. 8.

When exhaust back pressure is relatively high, as during acceleration and some cruising conditions, exhaust back pressure traveling through the metal tube overcomes spring tension on the diaphragm within the back pressure sensor valve, and closes the valve atmospheric vent.

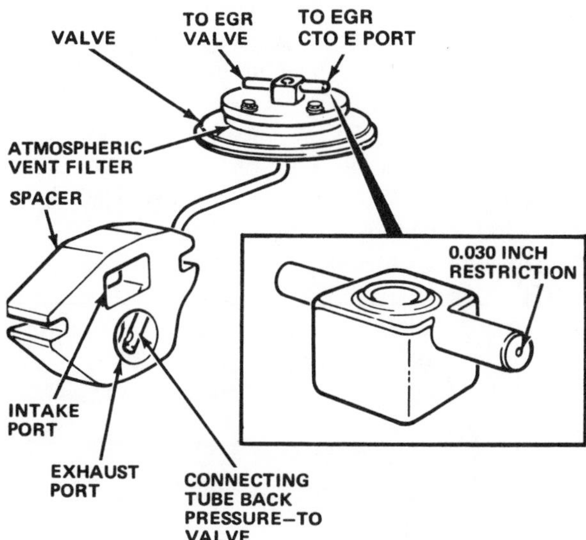

Fig. 8 Exhaust back pressure transducer sensor. (typical)

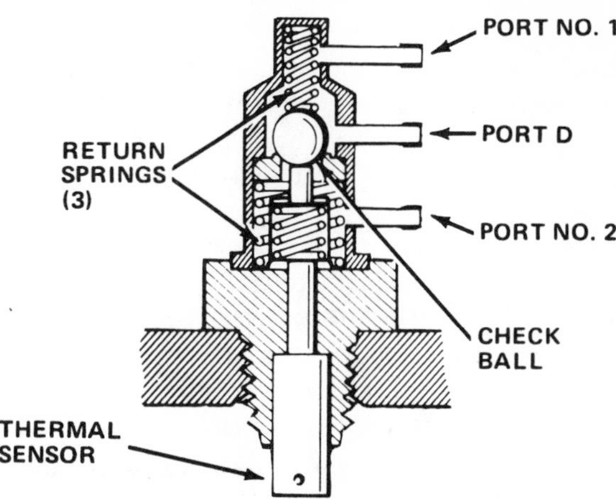

Fig. 9 Coolant temperature override switch. American Motors

With the back pressure sensor valve no longer vented to the atmosphere, the vacuum signal now passes through the back pressure sensor valve, and the EGR valve. When vacuum signals the EGR valve, exhaust gas recirculation commences.

When exhaust back pressure is too low to overcome diaphragm spring tension, the vacuum signal is vented to the atmosphere and does not pass through to the EGR valve. With no vacuum signal applied to the EGR valve, exhaust gas does not recirculate.

All 6-cylinder and some V8-304, 360 engines incorporate a steel restrictor plate under the exhaust back pressure sensor. The restrictor plate limits the rate of EGR flow, thereby improving driveability. Note that gaskets are used on both sides of the plate.

The back pressure sensor is not serviceable and must be replaced if defective.

TRANSMISSION CONTROLLED SPARK SYSTEM (TCS)

American Motors

The solenoid control switch closes and completes the ground circuit to the solenoid vacuum valve on automatic transmission equipped vehicles at speeds under 34 mph on 1974 models, 36 mph on 1975 models.

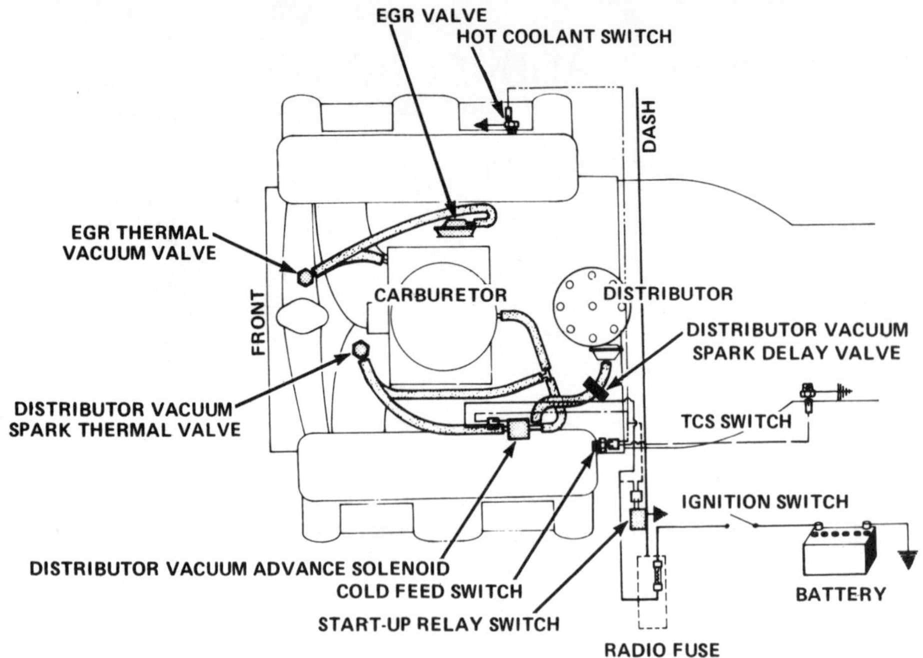

Fig. 10 1973 *Pontiac mid-year TCS system*

On automatic transmission equipped vehicles, the switch is operated by the transmission governor oil pressure on 1974-75 models.

The coolant temperature override switch, Fig. 9, is threaded into the thermostat housing on V8 engines or into the left rear side of the cylinder block on 6-cylinder engines. This switch provides full distributor vacuum advance until the engine coolant has reached 160° F on V8 engines or 115° F on 1974 California 6-cylinder engines.

General Motors

Fig. 10

A TCS system change on mid-year 1973 and all 1974 Pontiac models (vehicles manufactured after March 15, 1973) will incorporate the following revisions. A startup relay switch supplies full advance (ported advance on manual transmission vehicles) in any gear for 20 seconds after engine start.

A distributor vacuum spark thermal valve on 1973 models or distributor spark-EGR thermal vacuum switch on 1974 models, sensing air/fuel mixture temperature, provides full advance in any gear when the mixture temperature is below 62° F. When air/fuel mixture temperature rises above 62° F, the thermal valve closes, shutting off vacuum. To provide vacuum advance, the distributor must be energized, depending on condition, by the TCS switch, cold feed switch or the hot coolant switch.

The TCS switch grounds the distributor solenoid in high gear on all applications and in reverse gear on 1974 vehicles equipped with automatic transmissions only when the cold feed switch is closed. The cold feed switch, depending on application, closes when cylinder head temperature reaches 125°, 140° or 155° F. Regardless of TCS switch position, the hot coolant switch grounds the distributor solenoid when coolant temperature is over 240° F.

On some models, a distributor vacuum spark delay valve is installed between the distributor solenoid and distributor. This valve restricts the rate of initial vacuum supplied to the distributor, full vacuum will be supplied gradually.

The time relay is an electrical on-off type switch. When the coil is energized, it starts heating the bi-metal strip and opening the normally closed relay points within 20 seconds after the ignition switch is turned on. If for some reason the ignition key is left in the ON position and the vehicle is not started within 20 seconds and the relay completes its countdown, vacuum advance will be blocked off until the relay has cooled off.

NOTE: Once the relay has run one cycle (about 20 seconds), after the key has been turned on, the relay must cool off before it will reactivate, even if the key is switched OFF and then turned ON again.

Testing & Adjustments
1974-75 American Motors

Fig. 11

1. Disconnect wire from the solenoid control switch and connect a 12-volt test lamp in series

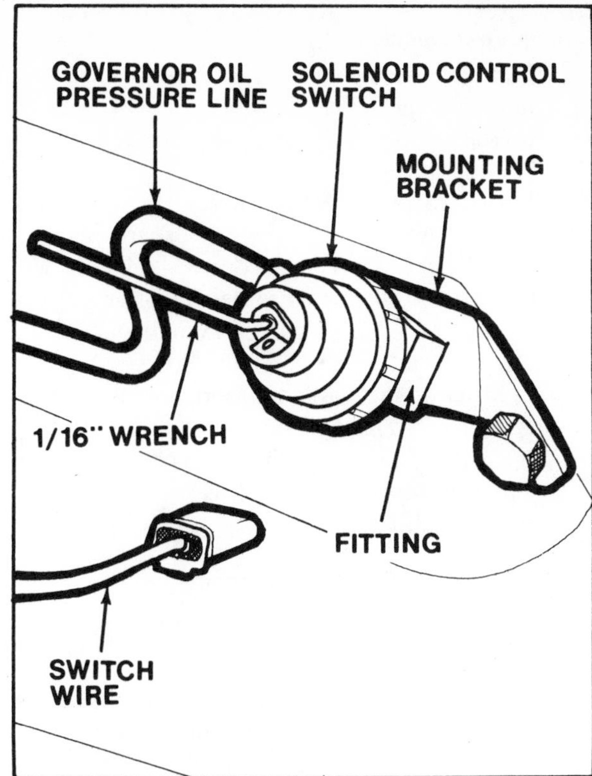

Fig. 11 *TCS solenoid adjustment* 1974-75

between switch wire and terminal.

2. Raise and support the vehicle so that the rear wheels are free to rotate.
3. Observe the speedometer and the test lamp. At speeds between 33-37 mph, the lamp should go off. If the test lamp remains on above this range, the solenoid control switch can be adjusted by turning the 1/16-inch allen head screw clockwise to increase opening speed and counterclockwise to decrease opening speed, Fig. 4. Adjust switch opening speed to 35 mph.

1973 Mid-Year & 1974 Pontiac System Diagnosis

Prior to performing any test, the engine must be at operating temperature and coolant temperature must not exceed 240° F. Insure that vacuum hose and electrical connections are correct. On models with distributor spark delay valve, connect a vacuum gauge to the DIST fitting on the delay valve. On models without delay valve, connect the vacuum gauge to the vertical fitting at the rear of the distributor vacuum advance solenoid.

NOTE: On models using a spark delay valve, vacuum will slowly rise to full in 10 to 15 seconds. Also, when performing the following tests on vehicles with a manual transmission, open the throttle slightly to uncover carburetor vacuum port.

Startup Vacuum Test

Start engine and observe vacuum gauge. Vacuum should be present for 20 seconds.

High Gear Vacuum Test

On manual transmission vehicles, shift into high gear and on automatic transmission vehicles, shift into reverse. Vacuum should be present in these gears.

If vacuum was observed at all times during the above tests, proceed with the following checks.

1. If no vacuum delay was present on vehicles equipped with spark delay valve, replace the delay valve.
2. Check for a stuck open distributor vacuum spark thermal valve by removing the vacuum hose running from the front fitting of the distributor solenoid and checking for vacuum at the hose. If vacuum is present, replace the thermal valve.
3. If no vacuum is noted at the front fitting of the distributor solenoid, the distributor solenoid plunger may be stuck in the energized position. To check, remove the electrical connector from the solenoid and if vacuum is still present, replace the distributor solenoid.
4. If vacuum is lost after disconnecting the solenoid electrical connector, the startup relay may be energizing the solenoid. To check, remove the electrical connector from the relay and if vacuum is lost again, replace the startup relay.
5. If vacuum is still present after disconnecting the startup relay electrical connector, the hot coolant switch may be energized or stuck in the closed position. To check, remove the electrical connector from the coolant switch and if vacuum is lost, replace the hot coolant switch if it has been determined that coolant temperature is over 240° F.
6. If vacuum is present after disconnecting the hot coolant switch electrical connector, the TCS switch may be stuck in the closed position. To check, remove the electrical connector from the TCS switch and if vacuum is lost again, replace the TCS switch.
7. If vacuum is still present after disconnecting the TCS switch electrical connector, check the system for grounded leads.

If no vacuum was observed during startup vacuum test proceed with the following checks.

1. Check for an open circuit in startup relay using a jumper wire connected between blue wire at startup relay and ground, energizing the relay. If the relay does energize, a vacuum

reading will be observed, indicating a defective startup relay which must be replaced. If startup relay does not energize, no vacuum reading will be observed, indicating that the failure of the relay is not due to lack of ground.

2. Connect a test lamp between the yellow wire of startup relay and ground to check if voltage is available to startup relay. If the lamp does not light, check the radio fuse and the wiring from the startup relay to battery as relay is not receiving voltage.
3. If the lamp lights in the above check, connect the test lamp between the yellow wire at the distributor solenoid and ground, to check if voltage is available to the solenoid. If lamp does not light, check the radio fuse and the wiring from the distributor solenoid to the battery.
4. If the lamp lights in the above check, connect a jumper wire between the blue wire at the distributor solenoid and ground with the engine running to energize the solenoid. If no vacuum reading was observed, the solenoid was not energized and may be internally plugged or has an open circuit. In turn, the solenoid must be replaced.
5. If a vacuum reading was observed and the solenoid was energized producing an audible click, the system is operating normally.

If no vacuum reading was observed during High Gear vacuum test, proceed with the following checks.

1. Remove TCS switch connector and ground the black wire with the engine running as the cold feed switch may be closed. If a vacuum reading is observed, the distributor solenoid is energized, indicating that the TCS switch is defective and must be replaced.
2. If no vacuum reading was observed in the above check, inspect black wire between the cold feed switch and the TCS switch for an open circuit.

DISTRIBUTOR VACUUM ADVANCE SYSTEM

1975 Pontiac

In conjunction with the catalytic converter, the distributor vacuum advance is no longer a function of speed or transmission gear. Under normal operation, some engines have a full advance system and other engines have a ported advance system.

Operation

Pontiac uses variations of full and ported vacuum advance, since the advance is no longer transmission gear position controlled.

1. Full advance means the distributor will receive manifold vacuum at all times. Advance will be present during idle, part throttle and closed throttle operation.
2. Ported vacuum advance means the distributor will receive vacuum when the spark port inside the carburetor is uncovered. Advance will be mainly at part throttle conditions. Very little or no advance will be available at idle or closed throttle.

Most of the basic full and ported vacuum advance systems have auxiliary devices to supplement or modulate the advance application. The following tabulation lists the systems and their variations.

System Components

Full Vacuum Advance System Variations

1. Retard delay cold.

   These engines contain a parallel system of hose plumbing in which one branch contains a spark retard delay valve and the other branch a thermal vacuum valve sensing engine coolant temperature.

   At cold engine coolant temperatures the TVV is closed, and the only vacuum path to the distributor is through the spark retard delay valve. At this condition, loss of vacuum advance when the throttle is opened will be gradual during a 4-second time period rather than immediate. This feature is to improve cold driveability.

   At warm engine coolant temperatures the TVV opens, and both vacuum paths to the distributor are available. Under these circumstances, the loss of vacuum advance with throttle opening will be instantaneous rather than delayed because vacuum will follow the path of least resistance.
2. Modulated full advance with retard delay cold.

   These engines are equipped with a vacuum advance modulator valve and a parallel system of hose routing between the modulator valve and full vacuum source in which one branch contains a spark retard delay valve and the other branch a thermal vacuum valve sensing coolant temperature.

   The distributor vacuum advance modulator valve provides a full vacuum signal to the distributor when the full vacuum source is in the zero to 10-inch range. When the full vacuum signal is greater than 10 inches, the valve modulates a constant vacuum signal of 10 inches as long as the ported vacuum signal is less than 10 inches. However, when both the full and ported signals are in excess of 10 inches, the ported vacuum source assumes control of distributor advance. The ported signal has a peak of about 15 inches.

The preceding description and chart has been rephrased below in terms of the modulating valve action during the driveaway of a car from a stop.

At idle and part throttle opening when there is less than a 10-inch spark port signal, the distributor receives a modulated constant 10-inch signal.

When the throttle is opened to the point that the spark port signal exceeds 10 inches, the valve switches so that the spark port signal controls the distributor vacuum advance.

As the throttle is opened to the point that the vacuum drops below 10 inches, the valve switches back to full vacuum source control of distributor advance.

At cold engine coolant temperatures, the TVV is closed and the only vacuum path from the full vacuum source is through the spark retard delay valve. Under these circumstances, loss of vacuum advance during a quick acceleration will be gradual during a 4-second time period rather than immediate. This feature is to improve cold driveability.

At warm engine coolant temperatures the TVV opens, and a vacuum path to the full vacuum source without a delay valve becomes available. No delay will be encountered with spark retard and a warm engine.

Ported Vacuum Advance System Variations

1. Normally ported with hot coolant override protection.

   These engines are equipped with a thermal vacuum valve located in the cylinder head and, under normal operating engine temperatures, the TVV allows ported vacuum to reach the distributor.

   To protect against overheating, the TVV will sense high coolant temperatures and open to provide full vacuum for the distributor with resultant improvement in cooling ability due to the engine speed increase.

2. Ported vacuum advance with hot coolant override protection plus full advance with retard delay cold.

   These engines are equipped with a thermal vacuum valve located in the cylinder head plus a rather complex parallel system of hose routing to the distributor in which one branch contains the spark retard delay valve from full vacuum and the other branch contains two thermal vacuum valves in series from a ported vacuum source.

   At cold engine coolant temperatures the only path to the distributor is through the spark retard delay valve since the TVV in the intake manifold denies other access. Full vacuum advance will be available and there will be a 4-second delay in retard.

   At warm engine coolant temperatures, the TVV in the intake manifold opens and now both a full and a ported vacuum signal are available to the distributor. But at idle the ported vacuum source acts as a bleed and the distributor will not advance. Therefore, this condition actually provides ported vacuum advance.

   As a protection against overheating, the TVV in the cylinder head opens when the coolant reaches high temperatures and supplies a full vacuum source to the distributor to provide for better cooling.

The vacuum source is generally at the rear of the carburetor. However, on some 4-barrel carburetors the vacuum source is at the front of the carburetor.

Functional Test for Vacuum Advance Systems

Full Vacuum Advance Systems

1. Warm up engine to normal operating temperature.
2. Hook up a timing light and observe for vacuum advance.

   Timing should be advanced beyond the initial setting.
3. Remove vacuum hose from distributor and observe for loss of vacuum advance.

   Engine should return to specified initial timing setting.
4. On engines equipped with a spark retard delay valve, verify the correct installation. Side marked DIST should be connected toward the distributor. Correct if needed.

   Locate the hose connected to port marked 1 on TVV in manifold water crossover. Remove the hose from the vacuum source. Plug the hose and cap the vacuum source.

   Tee a vacuum gauge into the hose between the distributor and the spark retard delay valve. Place the gauge so it can be observed from the driver's seat.

   Turn off the ignition and observe the vacuum gauge.

   Vacuum reading should not drop immediately, but should drop slowly (taking about 2 to 5 seconds to go from 15 to 5 inches).

   If the vacuum drops too fast, the TVV is

leaking or the spark retard delay valve is defective. Then remove the hose from TVV port marked 2 and plug hose. Turn off the ignition and observe the vacuum gauge.

If vacuum drops slowly, replace the TVV.

If vacuum still drops too fast, replace the spark retard delay valve.

Ported Vacuum Advance Systems

Ported vacuum advance engines can be identified by a TVV located in the right cylinder head between number 6 and 8 cylinders.

1. Hook up a timing light.
2. With a warm engine and the throttle closed, the timing should be at the specified initial setting.
3. Open the throttle and observe for vacuum advance.

   Timing should advance as the throttle is opened.
4. On engines equipped with a spark retard delay valve, verify the correct installation. Side marked DIST should be connected toward the distributor. Correct as needed.

   Locate the hose connected to port marked 1 on TVV in manifold water crossover. Remove the hose from lower port at right front of carburetor. Cap the port and plug the hose removed.

   Then Tee a vacuum gauge into the hose between the distributor and the spark retard delay valve. Place the gauge so it can be observed from the driver's seat.

   Turn off the ignition and observe the vacuum gauge.

   The vacuum reading should not drop immediately, but should drop slowly (taking about 2 to 5 seconds to go from 15 to 5 inches).

   If the vacuum drops too fast, the TVV is leaking or the spark retard delay valve is defective. Then remove the hose from TVV port marked 2 and plug the hose. Turn off the ignition and observe the vacuum gauge.

   If the vacuum drops slowly, replace the TVV in intake manifold water crossover.

   If the vacuum still drops too fast, remove the hose from D fitting of TVV located in right cylinder head and plug hose. Turn off the ignition and observe the vacuum gauge.

   If the vacuum drops slowly, replace the TVV in the right cylinder head.

   If the vacuum still drops too fast, replace the spark retard delay valve.

Functional Test of Individual Component Parts

Distributor Vacuum Advance Unit

1. Hook up a timing light.
2. With the engine running and at normal operating temperature, apply vacuum source in excess of 15 inches to the distributor and then seal off the vacuum source.
3. Vacuum advance unit should hold advance for 20 seconds.
4. Vacuum advance unit is unsatisfactory and must be replaced if the engine returns to initial timing setting in less than 20 seconds.

Distributor Vacuum Advance Modulator Valve (valve left on engine)

1. Remove the air cleaner and plug the manifold vacuum fitting. Do not disconnect the secondary vacuum break TVV hoses, but instead remove the TVV from the air cleaner body and leave the hoses intact.
2. Warm up the engine.
3. Remove the hose and attach a vacuum gauge to the DIST fitting which goes to the distributor. Tee a second vacuum gauge into the hose between the CARB fitting and the front of the carburetor.
4. At idle, the gauge connected to the DIST fitting should read 10 inches. Replace the valve if the gauge reading is less than 9 inches or above 11 inches.
5. In the Park position, gradually open the throttle and note that the DIST port gauge will be reading 10 inches as the CARB port gauge gradually increases to 10 inches. From then on, both gauges will read the same as the throttle is opened. Gauges will peak at about 15 inches before dropping off. Replace the valve if it does not conform.

Spark Retard Delay Valve

The checking procedure for this valve is covered in the function test procedure.

NOTE: Should the valve be checked under actual cold conditions in a car, the valve contains an orifice and consequently the vacuum rise will be rather slow. This is in addition to the slow loss in the vacuum when the car is accelerated.

EFE-DS TVV in Intake Manifold Water Crossover, 4 Port Type

1. The two lower ports marked 1 and 2 are a part of the distributor vacuum advance system. Ports are closed below 120° F and open above

FUNCTIONAL TEST FAILURE DIAGNOSIS GUIDE

Full Vacuum Advance System

No Advance at Idle

CAUSE	CORRECTION
1. Distributor advance unit not operating.	1. Replace part.
2. Plugged vacuum source.	2. Correct or replace part.
3. Vacuum hose off, pinched or plugged, or a T or F connector cracked and/or broken.	3. Check hoses, connectors and routing and correct.

Do Not Lose Advance When Removing Hose At Idle

CAUSE	CORRECTION
Damaged distributor advance unit.	Replace part.

No Retard Delay

CAUSE	CORRECTION
1. Defective spark retard delay valve.	1. Replace part.
2. Defective TVV in manifold.	2. Replace part.

Ported Vacuum Advance System

Has Advance at Idle

CAUSE	CORRECTION
1. Incorrect plumbing or pinched hoses.	1. Check hose routing.
2. Stuck TVV in cylinder head or intake manifold.	2. Replace part or parts.

No Advance When Throttle is Opened

CAUSE	CORRECTION
1. Distributor advance unit not operating.	1. Replace part.
2. Plugged vacuum source.	2. Correct or replace.
3. Vacuum hose off, pinched or plugged.	3. Check hoses and routing and correct.

No Retard Delay

CAUSE	CORRECTION
1. Defective spark retard delay valve.	1. Replace part.
2. Defective TVV in cylinder head or intake manifold.	2. Replace part or parts.

120° F.

2. Warm check, above 120° F with the valve left on the engine.

   Apply a vacuum source to the hose connected to the port marked 1.

   A vacuum gauge attached to the hose connected to the lowest port marked 2 should show a reading within 1 inch of the source vacuum. Replace valve if it does not conform.

3. Cold check, below 120° F. Remove from the engine or cool car overnight.

   Cool valve to below 120° F.

   Apply a vacuum source to a hose connected to or directly to the port marked 1. The valve in this mode has port 1 vented to the atmosphere and therefore the valve will not hold vacuum when the source is removed.

   A vacuum gauge attached to a hose connected to or directly to the lowest port marked 2 should not show a reading. Replace valve if a reading is obtained.

Distributor Vacuum Advance TVV in R.H. Cylinder Head, 3 Port Type

1. Valve provides ported advance below 227° F and full advance above 227° F.
2. Normal check, below 227° F with valve left on the engine.

   Apply a vacuum source to the center or C fitting.

   A vacuum gauge attached to the D fitting should show a reading within 1 inch of the source vacuum, and a gauge attached to the MT fitting should not show a reading. Replace valve if it does not conform.

3. Hot check, above 227° F. Remove the valve from engine.

   Use an external method to warm valve to above 227° F. It is recommended that the base of the valve be immersed in 100% glycol or oil, and the contents then heated. Never use a torch or an open flame directly to the base of the TVV.

   Apply a vacuum source to the MT fitting.

   A vacuum gauge attached to the D fitting should show a reading within 1 inch of the source vacuum, and a gauge attached to the C fitting should show no reading. Replace the valve if it does not conform.

GENERAL MOTORS CEC

Combined Emission Control System

The coolant temperature switch overrides the transmission switch to energize the solenoid and provide vacuum advance below 93° for 1973-74 vehicles. The time-delay relay is incorporated into the circuit to energize the solenoid for approximately 20 seconds on 1973-74 vehicles, after the ignition key is turned on.

GENERAL MOTORS EGR

Exhaust Gas Recirculation

1974-75 Dual Diaphragm EGR Valve

The dual diaphragm EGR valve, Fig. 12 is designed to provide increased exhaust gas recirculation rates when engine loads increase.

NOTE: Manifold vacuum is used as the signal to indicate the engine load.

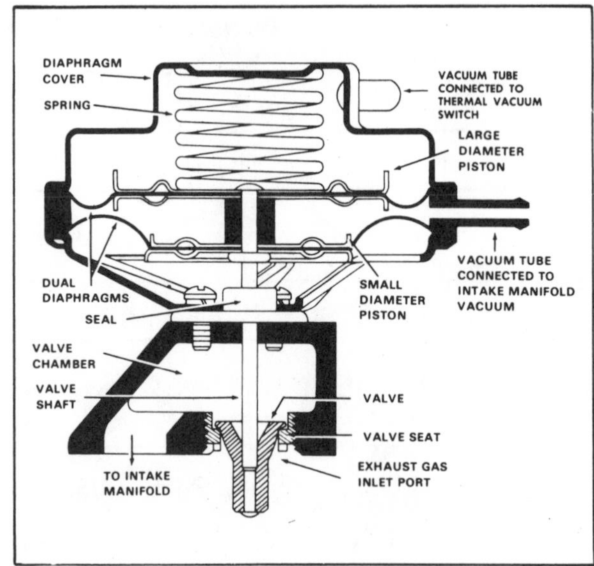

Fig. 12 Dual diaphragm EGR valve cross section

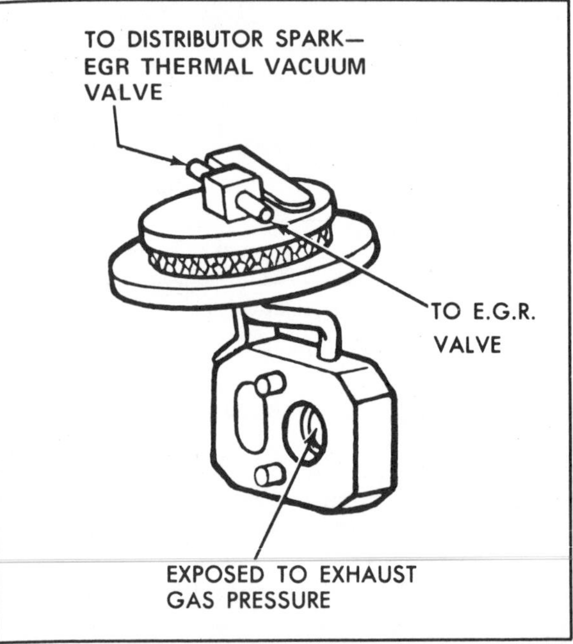

Fig. 13 Exhaust back pressure transducer. Pontiac

The valve is similar to the single diaphragm valve except that a second diaphragm has been added to the valve and is connected to the upper diaphragm with a spacer. Thus both diaphragms move together. A manifold vacuum signal is applied to the volume between the two diaphragms. The upper diaphragm has a larger diameter piston than the lower diaphragm, therefore the load caused by the manifold vacuum between the two diaphragms aids the spring load. Thus, as the engine load increases and manifold vacuum decreases the combined load of the spring and the vacuum chamber are reduced allowing the valve to open further for a given EGR vacuum signal.

Therefore, for high intake manifold vacuums such as during cruising, the opening is less than for low manifold vacuums obtained during accelerations. The valve now is capable of providing more recirculation on accelerations where loads are higher and the tendency to produce NOx is greater.

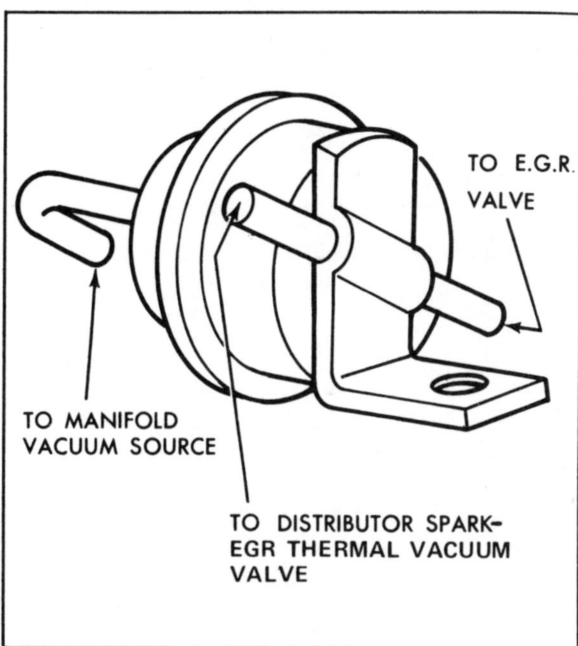

Fig. 14 Vacuum bias valve

Exhaust Back Pressure Transducer Valve

This valve, Figs. 13 and 17, used on some 1974-75 vehicles, modulates EGR flow according to engine load. The device consists of a diaphragm valve, a spacer and a metal tube.

The EGR system, when equipped with a back pressure transducer valve, obtains a vacuum signal at the carburetor spark port and not at the EGR port. This vacuum is modulated by the transducer and in turn activates the EGR valve.

When exhaust back pressure is relatively high, as during acceleration and some cruising conditions, exhaust back pressure traveling through the metal tube overcomes spring tension on the diaphragm within the back pressure transducer valve, and closes the valve atmospheric vent.

With the back pressure transducer valve no longer vented to atmosphere, the vacuum signal now passes through the back pressure transducer valve, and the EGR valve. When vacuum signals the EGR valve, exhaust gas recirculation commences.

When exhaust back pressure is too low to overcome diaphragm spring tension, the vacuum signal is vented to the atmosphere and does not pass through to the EGR valve. With no vacuum signal applied to the EGR valve, exhaust gas does not recirculate.

Vacuum Bias Valve

This valve, Fig. 14, used on some 1974-75 Pontiac vehicles, California models, is located between the EGR valve and the distributor spark-EGR thermal vacuum valve. At high manifold vacuum conditions such as cruising, the VBV decreases

EARLY PRODUCTION

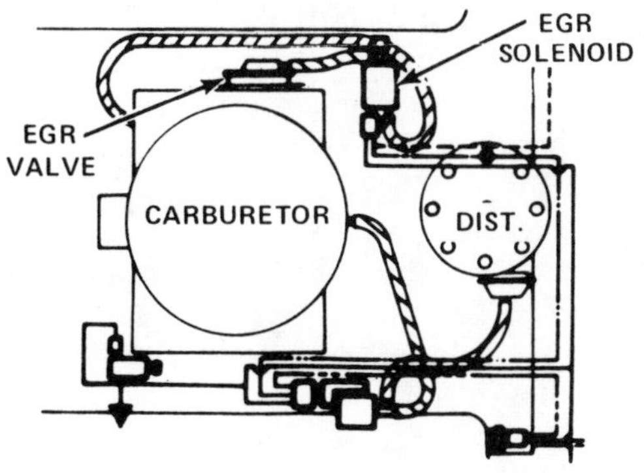

Fig. 15 Early 1973 Pontiac EGR system

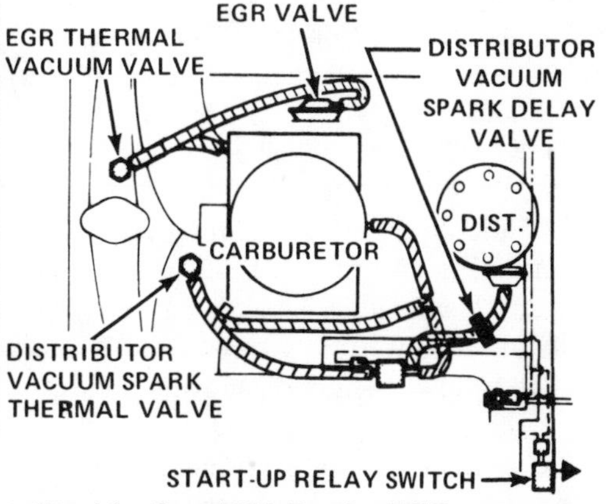

Fig. 16 Late 1973 Pontiac EGR system

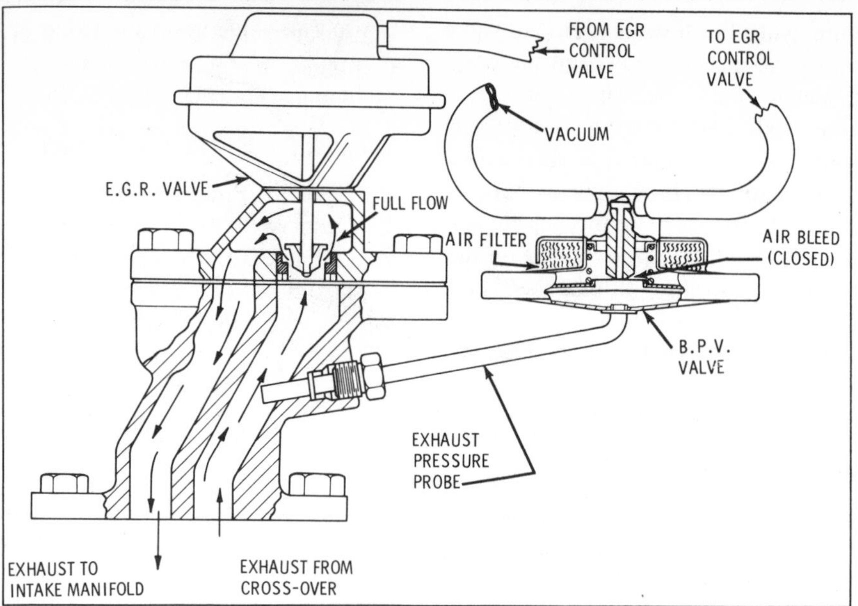

Fig. 17 Exhaust back pressure transducer. Oldsmobile

EGR flow and in turn, acts to reduce surge. When NOx formation is high and manifold vacuum is low as during acceleration, the VBV does not reduce EGR flow.

Fig. 15—An EGR system change on all mid-year 1973 V8 and 1974-75 6-cylinder Pontiac models (vehicles manufactured after March 15, 1973) will incorporate a new EGR thermal vacuum valve which senses engine coolant temperature. This thermal valve, located between the carburetor and the EGR valve, controls vacuum to the EGR valve. When coolant temperature is below 95° F on 1973 models or 100° F on 1974-75 models, the thermal valve isolates the EGR valve from the vacuum source, therefore eliminating exhaust gas recirculation. When coolant temperature is above 95° F on 1973 models or 100° F on 1974-75 models, the thermal valve opens and allows vacuum to actuate the EGR valve, allowing ported recirculation.

Fig. 16—On 1974-75 Pontiac vehicles equipped with V8 engines, the EGR thermal vacuum valve and the distributor spark thermal vacuum valve is incorporated into one assembly. This distributor spark-EGR thermal vacuum valve senses air fuel mixture temperature. This thermal valve is located between the EGR valve and its vacuum source. The valve prevents actuation of the EGR valve when air/fuel mixture temperature is below 62° F. When air/fuel mixture temperature exceeds 62° F, the valve opens and allows vacuum to activate the EGR valve.

The EGR valve cannot be disassembled and no actual service is required on it. However, it can be checked for proper operation as follows.

TESTING

Back Pressure Transducer Valve Except 1975 Pontiac

1. Remove air cleaner and plug manifold vacuum fitting, then with A/C off, and engine idling at operating temperature, place cam follower on fast idle step of cam.
2. Check the vacuum on back pressure transducer valve and record reading. Then using a tee fitting, connect a vacuum gauge to the EGR control valve side of the back pressure valve. If vacuum reading is not within 1.7-2.7 inches of mercury, disconnect and plug hose from the EGR valve. Vacuum reading should be the same or within 2 inches of mercury of that recorded previously. If not, replace back pressure transducer valve.

1975 Pontiac

Valve is to be left on the engine.

1. Preparation

   Remove the air cleaner and plug intake manifold air cleaner vacuum fitting.

   It is suggested that the choke secondary vacuum break TVV be unclipped and removed from the air cleaner body rather than removing hoses.

   Warm up the engine to operating temperature. Connect a vacuum gauge to carburetor side of BPT.
2. Place carburetor cam follower on high step of the fast idle cam with transmission in park.
3. Read and record the vacuum.

4. Tee a vacuum gauge into hose between BPT and EGR valve. Vacuum should read between 1.8 and 3.2 inches.

   Replace the BPT valve if not within specifications. Continue to the next step with vacuum gauge in the same location.
5. Remove the hose from the EGR valve and plug the hose. Read the vacuum gauge. This reading should be the same as or higher than the source reading in step 3.

   Replace BPT valve if reading is not within 3 inches of source reading from step 3.

All Except 1973 Mid-Year & 1974-75 Pontiac EGR System

1. Check the exhaust gas valve shaft for movement by opening the throttle to 1200-1500 rpm. The shaft should move upward and return to its original position when the engine speed is allowed to drop to idle.
2. An outside vacuum source can be connected to the vacuum supply port in the top of the EGR valve. The valve shaft should reach the top of its travel at 7 to 10 inches hg. of vacuum and the vacuum should not leak down.
3. If the EGR valve does not operate correctly, it must be replaced.

1973 Mid-Year & 1974 Pontiac EGR System

1. With engine at operating temperature, remove the air cleaner. Open throttle part way, release the throttle and observe EGR valve diaphragm movement through cut away portion on inboard side. The EGR valve should open with throttle opening.
2. If no diaphragm movement is observed, ensure that vacuum hoses are properly connected. If so, using a vacuum gauge, check for vacuum at hose connected to the EGR valve. If vacuum is present, the EGR valve is faulty and must be replaced.
3. If no vacuum was present at the EGR hose, check for vacuum at thermal valve side of hose running from the carburetor. If vacuum is present, the interconnecting hose or the EGR valve may be plugged if there is no obstruction.
4. If no vacuum is present at the thermal valve side of the hose running from the carburetor, the hose between the carburetor and thermal valve may be obstructed or the carburetor is faulty.

1975 Pontiac Except Ventura EGR System

1. Initial preparation.

   Remove air cleaner so EGR valve diaphragm movement can be observed or felt. Plug intake manifold air cleaner vacuum fitting and connect a tachometer.

   Warm up the engine to operating temperature.
2. Open the throttle part way and then release.
3. Observe the EGR diaphragm for movement.

   The valve should open slightly when the throttle is opened and close when it is released.
4. Remove the EGR hose from the EGR valve and plug the hose.
5. Place cam follower on second step of fast idle cam and note speed.
6. Attach a vacuum hose between air cleaner vacuum fitting and the EGR valve (or use an external source in excess of 11 inches) and note speed change. Speed should drop at least 200 rpm with auto or at least 150 rpm with manual.
7. A successful function test must meet the following criteria.

   EGR diaphragm must move and speed must drop when the diaphragm moves.

   If the system has a BPT, a separate check must be made on the BPT.

NOTE: When the air cleaner is removed, it is recommended that the choke secondary vacuum break TVV be unclipped and removed from the air cleaner body rather than removing hoses.

Functional Test of Individual EGR System Component Parts

The EGR valve can be left on or removed from the engine.

1. Depress the valve diaphragm.
2. With the diaphragm still depressed, plug the vacuum tube and release the diaphragm.
3. Observe diaphragm and/or pintle movement:

   The valve is satisfactory if it takes over 20 seconds for the pintle to seat or for the diaphragm to achieve full travel.

   The valve is unsatisfactory and must be replaced if it takes less than 20 seconds for the pintle to seat or for the diaphragm to achieve full travel.

Pontiac Ventura V8-260

1. Remove the air cleaner assembly and plug manifold vacuum fitting.
2. Remove the vacuum hose from the distributor and plug.
3. Install the tachometer.
4. Remove the EGR hose from the EGR valve and plug hose.

5. With A/C OFF, drive wheels blocked, transmission in park, start the engine and bring to operating temperature. Put cam follower on second step of fast idle cam and note engine speed.
6. Attach a vacuum hose between the air cleaner vacuum port on the intake manifold and the EGR valve or use external vacuum source of at least 9 inches. The diaphragm should rise and engine speed should drop at least 250 rpm with automatic transmission or at least 100 rpm with manual transmission.
7. If engine speed does not drop as specified in Step 6, clean the intake manifold EGR ports and EGR valve assembly. After cleaning, recheck function per Steps 5 & 6. If engine speed does not drop as specified, replace the EGR valve assembly.

V8-350

1. With the engine running, the car in PARK, set the fast idle cam on second step to hold throttle open. (Approx. 1400-1500 rpm.) Engine coolant temperature must be above 120° F.
2. Place your finger beneath the EGR valve in a manner to feel movement of the diaphragm.
3. Disconnect the vacuum hose and watch for movement of the diaphragm downward (valve closed). This should be accompanied by an increase in engine speed.
4. Reconnect the hose. The diaphragm should move upward (valve open). Engine rpm should decrease.

Failure Diagnosis

Diaphragm doesn't move.

1. Verify the engine speed. It should be approximately 1400-1600 rpm.
2. Verify the temperature. It should be above 120° F. Engine coolant temperature.
3. Check for vacuum at hose. If vacuum is present, change the valve. If no vacuum is present, find the cause for this condition. (Plugged or leaking hose or carburetor port, defective EFE/EGR switch.)

Diaphragm moves with no change in engine rpm.

1. Check manifold EGR passages for blockage.

EGR SYSTEM DIAGNOSIS

Buick

CONDITION	POSSIBLE CAUSE	CORRECTION
Part throttle engine detonation.	1. Insufficient exhaust gas recirculation flow during part throttle accelerations.	1. Check EGR valve hose routing. Check EGR valve operation. Repair or replace as required. Check EGR thermal vacuum switch. Replace switch as required. Check EGR passages and valve for excessive deposits. Clean as required.
NOTE: Detonation can be caused by several other engine variables. Perform ignition and carburetor related diagnosis.		
Engine starts but immediately stalls when cold.	1. EGR valve hoses misrouted.	1. Check EGR valve hose routings.
	2. EGR system malfunctioning when engine is cold.	1. Perform check to determine if EFE/EGR thermal vacuum switch is operational. Replace as required.
NOTE: Stalls after start can also be caused by carburetor problems. Refer to carburetor diagnosis section.		

EGR SYSTEM DIAGNOSIS

Buick

CONDITION	POSSIBLE CAUSE	CORRECTION
Engine idles abnormally rough and/or stalls.	1. EGR valve vacuum hoses misrouted.	1. Check EGR valve vacuum hose routing. Correct as required.
	2. Leaking EGR valve.	1. Check EGR valve for correct operation.
	3. Idle speed misadjusted.	1. Set idle rpm per engine label specification. Remove EGR vacuum hose from valve and observe effect on engine. Replace valve if speed is affected, reset rpm to specification and reconnect hose.
	4. Improper carburetor signal to EGR valve at idle.	1. Check vacuum signal from carburetor EGR port with engine at stabilized operating temperature and at curb idle speed. If signal is more than 2.0 in hg. vacuum, proceed to carburetor idle diagnosis.
	5. Failed EFE/EGR thermal vacuum switch.	1. Check vacuum signal into switch from carburetor EGR port with engine at normal operating temperature and at curb idle speed. Then check vacuum signal out of switch to EGR valve. If the two vacuum signals are not equal within ±½ in. hg., then proceed to EFE/EGR thermal vacuum switch diagnosis. Replace switch as required.
	6. EGR valve gasket failed or loose EGR attaching bolts.	1. Check EGR attaching bolts for tightness. Tighten as required. If not loose, remove EGR valve and inspect gasket. Replace as required.
Engine runs rough on light throttle acceleration, poor part load performance and poor fuel economy.	1. EGR valve vacuum hose misrouted.	1. Check EGR valve vacuum hose routing. Correct as required.
	2. Failed EFE/EGR thermal vacuum switch.	1. Same as Step 5 above under Engine Idles Abnormally Rough and/or stalls.
	3. EGR flow unbalanced due to deposit accumulation in EGR passages or under carburetor.	1. Clean EGR passages of all deposits.
	4. Sticky or binding EGR valve.	1. Remove EGR valve and inspect for proper operation. Clean or repair as required.
Engine stalls on decelerations.	1. Restriction in EGR vacuum line.	1. Check EGR vacuum lines for kinks, bends, etc. Remove or replace hoses as required. Check EGR thermal vacuum switch for excessive restriction. Replace as required. Check EGR valve for excessive deposits causing sticky or binding operation. Clean or repair as required.

EARLY FUEL EVAPORATION SYSTEM

This system is used to provide a source of rapid heat during cold driveaway. Rapid heat is more desirable because it provides for quicker fuel evaporation and more uniform mixture.

The EFE valve is a vacuum actuated heat valve which directs exhaust gases through the intake manifold and to the base of the carburetor during cold weather operation. The EFE valve is located at the flange of the exhaust manifold and is activated by a thermal vacuum switch which activates the EFE valve at below a predetermined engine temperature. Refer to chart below for temperatures.

	Temperature (Below)
Buick (Exc. Calif.)	120°
Cadillac	
Chevrolet	
V8 Exc. 454	180°
V8-454	180°
Six Cylinder	180°
Oldsmobile	120°
Pontiac	120°

Early Fuel Evaporation Distributor Thermal Vacuum Switch (EFE-DTVS) (400 C.I.D.)

Oldsmobile
Operation (Fig. 20)

Below 120° F coolant temperature, vacuum is supplied to the EFE valve which holds it closed, forcing all the exhaust gas from the left bank cylinders to pass under the carburetor. Above 120° F coolant temperature the EFE/DTVS closes, and the spring loaded EFE valve is open.

Distributor vacuum advance operation of the EFE-DTVS: Full vacuum advance is available at all times. The distributor vacuum advance diaphragm will be exposed to full intake manifold vacuum at all times.

A four second delay in loss of vacuum advance is controlled by the EFE/TVS which senses engine coolant temperature. Below coolant temperatures of 120° F, whenever the throttle is opened quickly, the vacuum advance is not lost immediately, but is gradually lost during four seconds, through the spark delay valve. Above coolant temperatures of 120° F, the thermal vacuum switch opens and provides a vacuum source which bypasses the spark delay valve, and the engine has full vacuum ad-

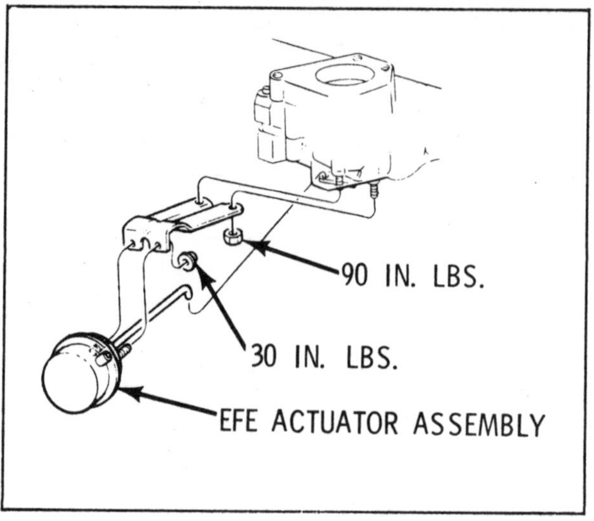

Fig. 19 EFE actuator (L-6)

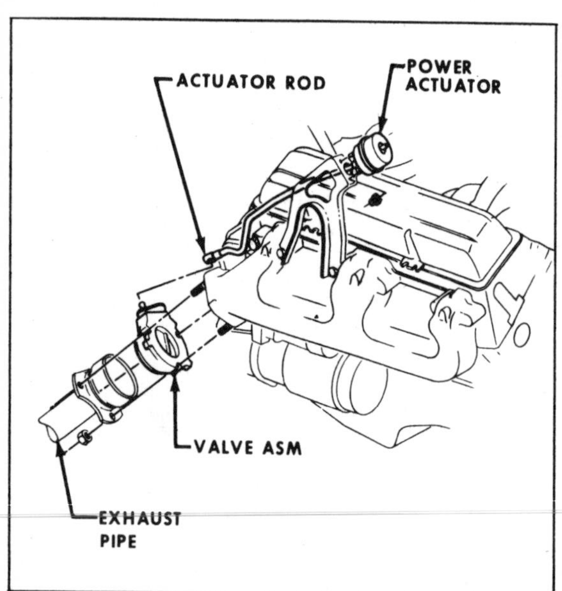

Fig. 18 Typical EFE valve

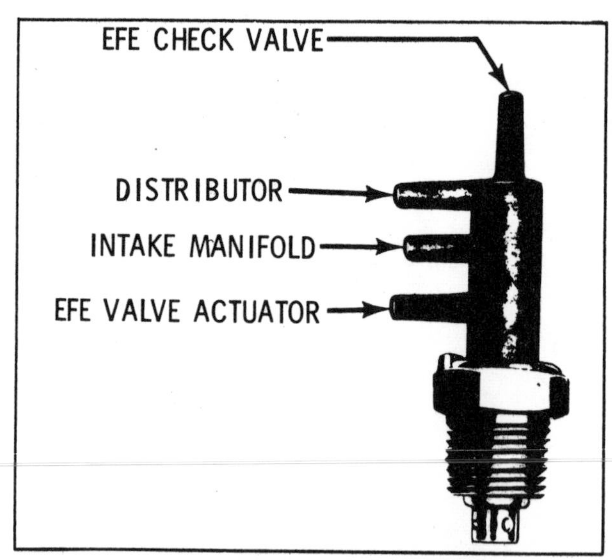

Fig. 20 EFE-DTVS (400 CID)

vance. On accelerations, the vacuum advance will now be lost immediately so the engine will not have spark knock at high temperatures.

Functional Checks

1. Cold engine (below 120° F) manifold vacuum is open to the EFE port.
2. Engine at normal operating temperature (above 120° F) manifold vacuum is open to the distributor port.

EFE Functional Test

Oldsmobile

Check valve for proper operation. A binding condition must be corrected. Check switch for proper operation. Check hoses for cracking, abrasion or deterioration. Replace parts as necessary.

1. Visually inspect the manifold heat valve for damaged valve or linkage, disconnected linkage, and cracked or deteriorated vacuum line.
2. Apply at least 10 inches of vacuum from an external vacuum source to EFE vacuum diaphragm.
3. Valve should move freely. Vacuum diaphragm must hold the plunger in retracted position for one minute without applying additional vacuum.
4. If the valve binds during test, free it with manifold heat valve lubricant, No. 1050422 or its equivalent. Use lubricant as directed on label. If the valve cannot be freed, replace the valve assembly.
5. If the diaphragm plunger leaks down within one minute, replace the vacuum diaphragm.

EFE/EGR Thermal Vacuum Switch (EFE/EGR TVS)

Buick, Oldsmobile V6 & Omega V8-350 (Fig. 21)

The EFE/EGR thermal vacuum switch (EFE/EGR TVS) located in the intake manifold coolant crossover passage has five nipples, four of which are marked as follows.

1. The nipple marked EGR has a hose connected which goes to the EGR valve.
2. The nipple marked EFE has a hose connected which goes to the EFE valve.
3. The nipple marked CARB has a hose connected to it which goes to a ported vacuum source in the carburetor.
4. The nipple marked CONN has a hose connected to it which goes to a connector in the engine vacuum harness for a manifold vacuum source.

The fifth nipple which is directly on top of the switch is connected to the air cleaner sensor on non-AIR cars and to the diverter valve on cars equipped with AIR.

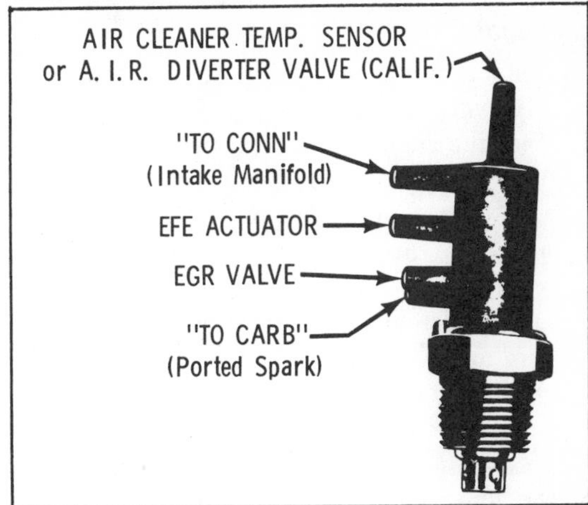

Fig. 21 *EGR/EFE-TVS* (231 *CID V*-6 *and Omega* 350)

The nipple on top of the switch has manifold vacuum present at all time regardless of coolant temperature.

When coolant temperatures are below 120° F ±3° the EFE/EGR TVS is switched internally to allow manifold vacuum to the EFE valve and top nipple only, closing off the ported vacuum supply to the EGR valve.

When coolant temperatures are above 120° F ±3° the EFE/EGR TVS is switched internally to allow manifold vacuum to the top nipple only, shutting off manifold vacuum to the EFE valve. The EGR port is uncovered and ported vacuum is now available to the EGR valve.

Early Fuel Evaporation Check Valve (EFE-CV)

Oldsmobile

Operation

A check valve is used in the vacuum line from the intake manifold to the EFE/TVS switch or the EFE/DTVS.

The valve holds the highest vacuum reached to keep the EFE heat valve closed until the TVS switches modes. The EFE heat valve could rattle without this valve under certain low vacuum conditions as during heavy acceleration.

Early Fuel Evaporation Solenoid (EFES)

All L-6

Operation (Fig. 19)

The L-6 engine has an EFE solenoid that is

electrically energized with the engine running when the oil temperature reaches 150° F. At this point the solenoid is energized which closes the vacuum supply to the EFE valve allowing the valve to open.

Functional Check

1. Connect a vacuum gauge to the hose at the EFE valve actuator.
2. With the engine running at operating temperature, energize the EFE vacuum solenoid with a 12-volt source. The vacuum gauge should read idle vacuum. If no vacuum is indicated, replace the solenoid.
3. Disconnect the lead from the engine oil temperature switch. With the engine running, ground the lead to the engine. The vacuum gauge should indicate idle vacuum. If no vacuum is indicated, check the continuity of the temperature switch to the solenoid lead. Repair or replace as necessary.
4. With the engine running and the engine oil at normal operating temperature, reconnect the lead to the engine oil temperature switch. The vacuum gauge should read zero. If vacuum is indicated, replace the engine oil temperature switch.

Pontiac

Before starting the test, the car should be cooled down so that the engine coolant temperature is below 120° F. Before starting engine to make system check, an extra person is required to start the engine while the tester observes the EFE valve for opening.

1. Locate the EFE valve and note the position of the actuator arm.
2. One man observes EFE valve when the engine is started.

   NOTE: Valve should close when engine is started cold. The actuator link will be pulled into the diaphragm housing.

3. If the valve does not close, remove the hose from EFE valve and apply an external vacuum source in excess of 8 inches. Valve should close.

   If valve still does not close, replace the EFE valve.

   If valve closes, the problem is not the EFE valve. See function test failure diagnosis for possible causes and repair the condition. Then proceed with function test.

4. Warm up the engine until coolant exceeds 120° F.
5. Observe the EFE valve to see if it has opened. The valve should open.
6. If valve does not open, remove the hose from EFE valve.

SYSTEM DIAGNOSIS

Pontiac

EFE valve does not close

POSSIBLE CAUSE	CORRECTION
1. Coolant not below 120° F.	1. Cool car overnight or remove TTV from engine for more rapid cooling.
2. Defective TVV.	2. Replace part.
3. Loose, kinked, pinched or plugged hoses, or cracked T.	3. Check hoses and connections and correct.
4. Defective EFE valve diaphragm or external damage to link or arm, etc.	4. Replace part.
5. Check valve installed incorrectly.	5. Install with tapered end toward vacuum source.

EFE valve does not open

POSSIBLE CAUSE	CORRECTION
1. Plugged vent in TVV.	1. Replace part.
2. Defective or stuck plunger in TVV.	2. Replace part.
3. Damaged EFE valve linkage parts.	3. Replace part.

SYSTEM DIAGNOSIS

Buick

EFE/EGR Thermo Vacuum Switch

CONDITION	POSSIBLE CAUSES	CORRECTION
Rough idle or stall during warm up.	1. No vacuum to EFE vacuum actuator with engine coolant temperature below 120° F ±3° F.	1. Check vacuum source for vacuum of 8 inches Hg or above.
		2. Correct improper vacuum hose routing, leak in connecting system, or EFE vacuum actuator diaphragm. Replace.
		3. Failed EFE/EGR thermo vacuum switch. Replace.
	2. Vacuum to EGR valve below 120° ±3° F.	1. Correct improper vacuum hose routing if necessary.
		2. Failed EFE/EGR thermo vacuum switch. Replace.
Rough idle, lack of performance, surge after warmup period.	1. Vacuum to EFE vacuum actuator with engine coolant temperature above 120° F ±3° F.	1. Correct improper vacuum hose routing.
		2. Failed EFE/EGR thermo vacuum switch. Replace.
Improper EGR operation.	1. Vacuum to EGR valve with engine coolant temperature below 120° F ±3° F.	1. Correct improper vacuum hose routing if necessary.
		2. Failed EFE/EGR thermo vacuum switch. Replace.

EFE System

CONDITION	POSSIBLE CAUSE	CORRECTION
Poor Operation during warmup such as—rough idle, stumble, etc.	1. No vacuum to vacuum actuator during warmup period for cold start.	1. Check vacuum source for vacuum of 8 inches Hg. or above. Repair improper vacuum hose routing, leak in connecting system, diaphragm, or EFE/EGR TVS. Failed EFE/EGR TVS. Replace.
	2. EFE valve linkage bent or binding.	1. Repair EFE valve linkage.
	3. EFE valve linkage disconnected.	1. Reconnect linkage.
	4. EFE valve shaft frozen in bearing.	1. Replace EFE valve.
	5. EFE valve loose on shaft.	1. Replace EFE valve.

Closed EFE Valve Diagnosis

CONDITION	POSSIBLE CAUSE	CORRECTION
Poor Operation after warmup —rough idle —lack of high speed performance —surge, misses at all speeds	1. Failed EFE/EGR TVS —vacuum present at vacuum actuator.	1. Replace EFE/EGR TVS.
	2. EFE valve asm. shaft frozen in bearing.	1. Replace EFE valve.
	3. EFE valve to housing interference.	1. Repair EFE valve.
	4. Vacuum actuator linkage bent or binding.	1. Repair EFE valve linkage.
	5. EFE valve separated from shaft.	1. Repair EFE valve linkage.
Noisy EFE valve asm.	1. Linkage stop failed.	1. Repair linkage stop tab.
	2. No vacuum actuator linkage over travel.	1. Replace vacuum actuator.
	3. Valve loose on shaft.	1. Replace EFE valve.
	4. Shaft loose in bushing, or bushing loose in housing.	1. Replace EFE valve.

SUB SYSTEMS

EGR Thermal Control Valve (EGR-TCV)

1975 Oldsmobile

All V8 engines use a temperature sensitive control valve in the vacuum line to the EGR valve.

The valve is closed below 61° (62°-400 CID) engine temperature blocking vacuum to the EGR valve giving better driveaway when the engine is cold.

The EGR control valve is open above 76° F engine temperature allowing EGR ported vacuum to be directed to the EGR valve.

Vacuum Delay Valve

1975 Oldsmobile & Pontiac Ventura V8-260

A vacuum delay valve is in the vacuum advance circuit on some V8 engines located in the vacuum hose between the carburetor port and the TVS C port.

NOTE: See Tuneup Specifications Chart for usage.

Distributor ported vacuum is metered through a .005-inch orifice in the valve, requiring up to 40 seconds for full vacuum advance.

When the valve is in the restricting position and ported vacuum drops, there is a pressure differential within the valve. The valve momentarily opens equalizing the vacuum between the vacuum advance and the distributor, retarding the distributor vacuum advance. When vacuum increases at the carburetor port the valve goes to the restricting position so vacuum to the advance will have to be metered to increase the distributor vacuum advance.

The valve is bypassed above 220° F coolant temperature when the TVS valve switches.

Functional Check

1. Connect a vacuum gauge to the TVS port of the valve and the hand operated vacuum device to the CARB port.
2. Draw a vacuum. There should be a slight hesitation on the gauge reading at the TVS port. The hand operated vacuum gauge should drop slightly and balance with the gauge reading at the TVS port. This should take 3 to 4 seconds to balance the readings.
3. If there is not a slight hesitation in readings the valve should be replaced.
4. Remove the gauge hose from the TVS port. Cover the port with a finger, draw a vacuum, 15 inches. The hand operated vacuum gauge reading should hold steady. If the vacuum reading should show a leak, replace the valve.
5. Remove the finger and the gauge reading should drop slowly, if the reading drops quickly to zero, replace the valve.

Spark Delay Valve (SDV)

1975 Oldsmobile

Operation

The 400 CID engine uses a spark delay valve allowing full manifold vacuum to be available to the distributor vacuum advance at all times.

The SDV causes a four second delay in loss of vacuum advance and is controlled by the EFE-distributor thermal vacuum switch which senses coolant temperature.

When the coolant temperature is below 120° F, and the throttle is opened quickly the vacuum is not lost immediately but is gradually lost in four seconds through the spark delay valve.

When the coolant temperature is above 120° F, the thermal vacuum switch opens and provides a vacuum source which bypasses the spark delay valve and the engine has full vacuum advance. On accelerations, the vacuum advance will now be lost immediately so the engine will not have spark knock at high temperatures.

Choke Thermal Vacuum Switch (CTVS)

Operation (Fig. 22)

The L-6 1-bbl. carburetor and all 4-bbl. carburetors (except the Omega 350) use a choke thermal vacuum switch to give a richer choke operation with engine coolant temperatures less than 57° (80° L-6). 400 CID has the CTVS in the air cleaner and has a switching temperature of 62°. The 1-bbl. and 4-bbl. carburetors are equipped with two vacuum breaks (primary and secondary). The choke thermal vacuum switch controls the vacuum to the carburetor secondary vacuum break. When the engine starts and the coolant temperature is greater than 57° F (80°-L-6), (400 CID air cleaner temperature is greater than 62°), both vacuum breaks pull the choke to its leanest position. If the coolant temperature is less than 57° F (80°-L-6), (400 CID air cleaner temperature less than 62°), the choke TVS closes and prevents the secondary vacuum break from pulling, giving a richer start and improved cold driveability.

Functional Check

Cold check. The valve should be closed. If it is a hot day, the valve can be chilled below the switching point.

Distributor Thermal Vacuum Switch (DTVS)

1975 Buick & Oldsmobile

Operator (Engines With Ported Spark) Fig. 23

A distributor thermal vacuum switch is used to advance the ignition timing at idle when the coolant temperature is high. At 220° a valve within the TVS moves, and if not equipped with a vacuum reducer valve, carburetor full manifold vacuum is directed to the distributor vacuum advance. On engines with a vacuum reducer valve, vacuum supplied will be 1½-inch less than manifold vacuum. The timing is then advanced allowing the engine to run cooler. This is the only time vacuum is directed to the distributor at idle. The 231 CID V-6 and the Omega 350 DTVS receives ported vacuum, switches at 231° F and does not use a vacuum reducer valve (VRV).

NOTE: To determine whether the engine has full manifold vacuum or ported spark, disconnect the hose at port C of the DTVS and connect a vacuum gauge. If vacuum is present at idle with the engine at normal operating temperature, the engine has manifold vacuum. If no vacuum, it has ported spark.

Functional Check

To test switch function, disconnect the distributor vacuum hose at port D of the TVS switch (Fig. 23).

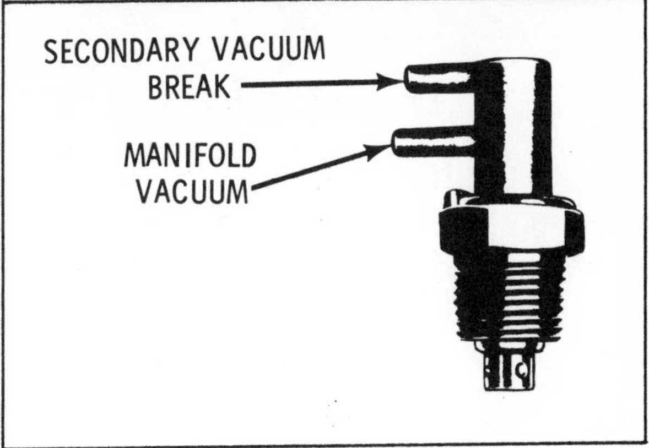

Fig. 22 CTVS (L-6 and 4 bbl except Omega 350)

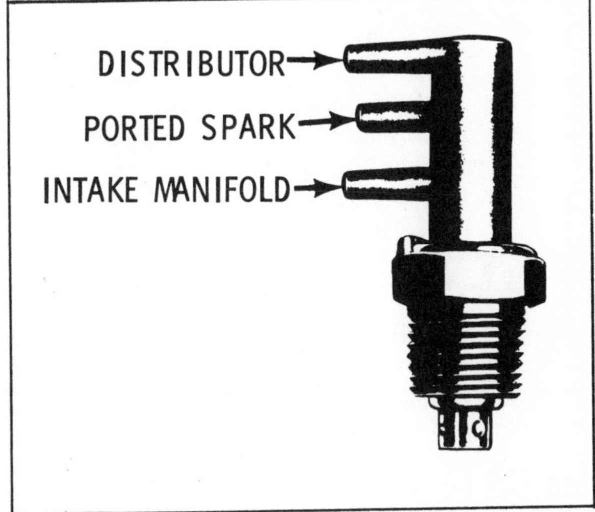

Fig 23 DTVS (ported spark) 1975 Oldsmobile

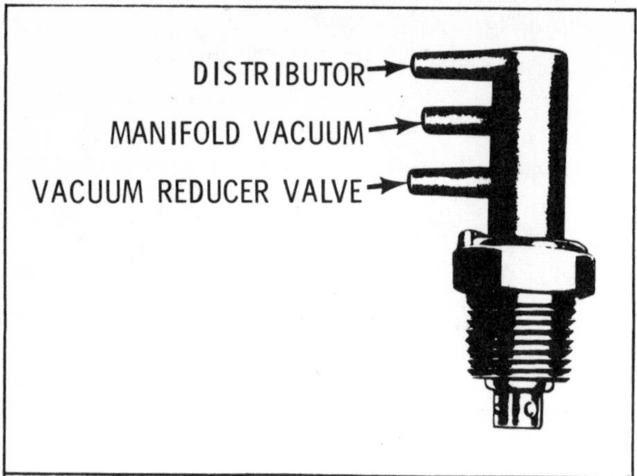

Fig. 24 DTVS (intake manifold vacuum) 1975 Oldsmobile

Connect a vacuum gauge and check for vacuum with the engine idling at normal operating temperature. If more than 5 inches of vacuum is present and the hoses are connected to the proper ports, check with Tool BT-7002 Tester. Replace the switch if not to specifications.

The TVS switch must be installed with a soft sealant on the threads.

Operation (Engines With Full Manifold Vacuum Spark) (Fig. 24)

Some V8 engines use a distributor thermal vacuum switch to allow increased ignition timing at normal operating temperatures. At higher coolant temperatures, 220° F and above, the DTVS switches the vacuum supplied to the distributor vacuum advance unit from manifold vacuum to vacuum which has been reduced 1.5-inch by the vacuum reducer valve (VRV). The reduced vacuum prevents detonation at the higher operating temperatures.

Functional Check

Test switch function as follows with engine idling at normal operating temperature.

1. Disconnect the distributor vacuum hose at port D and connect the vacuum gauge. Full manifold vacuum should be present. Reconnect the distributor vacuum hose.
2. Disconnect the vacuum reducer vacuum hose from the TVS switch and plug.
3. Connect a vacuum gauge to the vacuum reducer valve port of the TVS switch and check for vacuum with the engine idling at normal operating temperature.
4. If more than 5 inches of vacuum is present and the hoses are connected to the proper ports, replace the switch.

Install the TVS switch with a soft setting sealant on the threads.

CHRYSLER ORIFICE SPARK ADVANCE CONTROL (OSAC)

A tiny orifice is incorporated in the OSAC valve which delays the change in ported vacuum to the distributor by about 27 seconds on some 1974-75 applications when going from idle to part throttle.

CHRYSLER EXHAUST GAS RECIRCULATION (EGR)

Coolant Control Exhaust Gas Recirculation (CCEGR)

1974 engines using EGR are equipped with a CCEGR valve mounted in the radiator top tank. When coolant temperature in the top tank reaches 65° F, the valve opens so that vacuum is applied to open the EGR valve. On some engines, a similar CCEGR valve set for 90° F is mounted in the thermostat housing.

EGR Delay System

Some 1974 vehicles are equipped with an EGR Delay System, which has an electrical timer mounted on the dash panel in the engine compartment controlling an engine mounted solenoid. This solenoid which is connected with vacuum hoses to the carburetor venturi and vacuum amplifier, prevents EGR operation for about 35 seconds after engine start up.

EGR Maintenance Reminder System

The EGR Maintenance Reminder System consists of a switch counting device mounted in line with the speedometer cable about halfway between the transmission and the speedometer head (Fig. 25). The function of the system is to count the miles accumulated on the vehicle and at increments of 15,000 miles activate an indicator lamp in the instrument panel as a service reminder for the EGR system. The indicator lamp will remain illuminated (in the RUN position of the ignition switch) until the reset operation is performed.

The light reminds the driver that the EGR system should be checked as soon as possible. It is not intended to indicate that a state of urgency exists that must be corrected to insure safe vehicle operation.

To assure proper function of this system each of its components must be checked for proper operation as described. The following checks will assure that the system is operating properly.

1. Vacuum hose leakage check.
2. EGR valve functional check.
3. CCEGR valve check.
4. Timer and solenoid check.
5. Flow passage check.

In the event the switch counting device is replaced or reset for any reason the exhaust gas recirculation system maintenance service must be performed regardless of mileage.

Testing

Coolant Control Exhaust Gas Recirculation (CCEGR) Valve

The CCEGR valve can be tested for proper operation by placing it in ice and cooling it to below 40° F. Using vacuum pump and gauge tool C-4207 or equivalent, apply a vacuum of at least 10 inches of mercury to the valve nipple corresponding to the blue striped hose. If vacuum reading drops off more than 1 inch in one minute, the valve should be replaced.

FORD HIGH SPEED EGR MODULATOR SUBSYSTEM

The high speed EGR modulator subsystem used in some V8 engines, Fig. 26, is basically the same in operation as the ESC system described previously. This system cuts off exhaust gas recirculation flow by stopping vacuum flow from the EGR port to the EGR valve at speeds above 64 mph, in turn improving driveability.

The vacuum solenoid valve installed in the vacuum line is normally open (not energized), allowing vacuum flow from the EGR port to the EGR valve. The EGR system remains functional when the valve is not energized.

The speed sensor driven by the speedometer cable, produces an electric signal directly proportional to vehicle road speed, signalling the amplifier to energize the vacuum solenoid valve at which time the electronic module receives the signal from the speed sensor and amplifies it to provide a usable signal to the vacuum solenoid valve.

When the vehicle speed exceeds approximately 64 mph (trigger speed of the amplifier) the circuit to the ignition switch is completed and the normally open vacuum solenoid valve is energized. The plunger moves upwards and shuts off the EGR port vacuum and the vent at the bottom of the vacuum valve is opened, bleeding vacuum from the EGR valve and hose. Spring force closes the EGR valve which remains non functional until the vacuum solenoid valve is de-energized, at speeds below approximately 64 mph.

NOTE: There is a continuous internal vacuum bleed provided by the vent at the top of EGR valve. Whether the valve is in a closed or open position, this vent purges the vacuum supply hose from carburetor of any gasoline vapor.

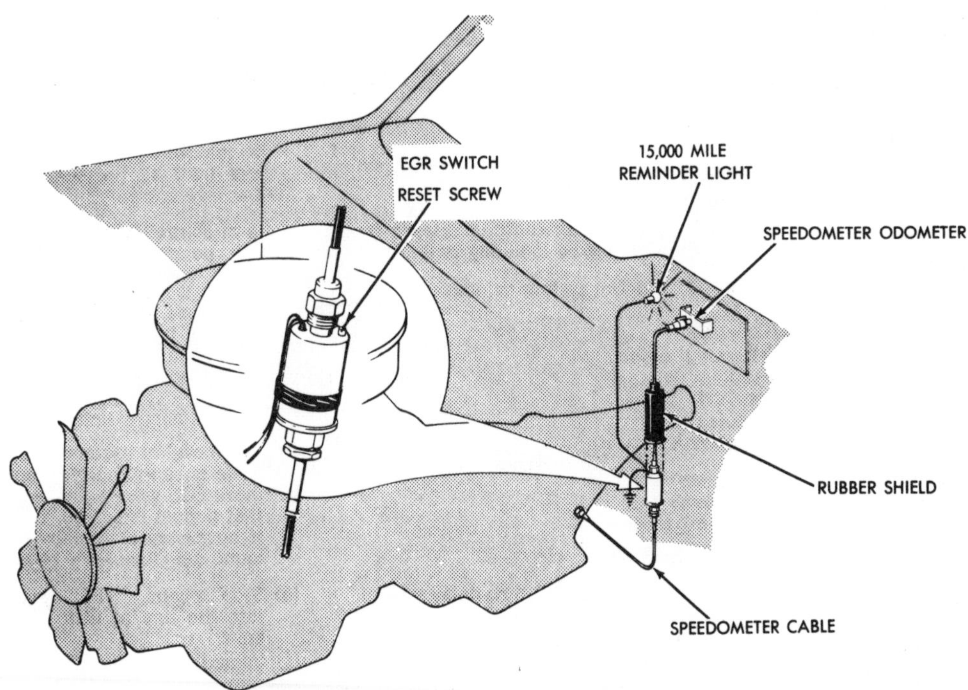

Fig. 25 EGR maintenance reminder system—1975 Chrysler

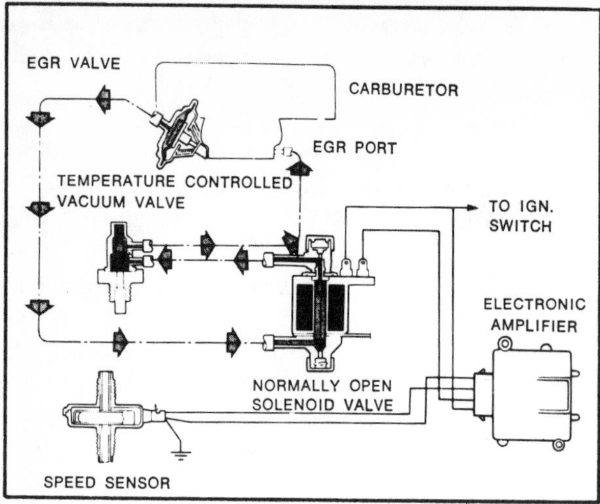

Fig. 26 Ford high speed EGR modulator sub-system components

Testing

1. Disconnect the vacuum hose from EGR valve and install a tee fitting and connect a vacuum gauge with a long hose into the vacuum line.
2. Raise the front and rear wheels off ground, with vacuum gauge visible from the driver's seat.
3. Start the engine and allow it to run at fast idle for about 3 to 4 minutes. At curb idle speed the vacuum gauge should read zero.
4. Place transmission in third gear for a manual transmission and in drive for an automatic transmission. Observe the speedometer and vacuum gauge. Increase the engine speed. The vacuum reading should increase. At about 67 mph the vacuum reading should drop to zero, indicating that the EGR high speed modulator subsystem is functioning properly.
5. If system is not functioning properly check the vacuum solenoid valve. Disconnect the electrical leads from the valve to isolate it from the electronic amplifier.
   CAUTION: Never connect any test jumper or test light to the valve unless it is isolated from the amplifier, as severe damage to the amplifier will result.
6. Connect jumper wires from the valve terminals to the battery and to a ground. Operate engine in neutral at about 1500 rpm. The valve should close when power is applied. If there is a vacuum reading replace the valve.
7. If there is no vacuum reading with the valve energized, check for power at the amplifier connector using a self powered test light. If there is no power, check and repair the ignition switch circuit. If there is power, check the ground connection. If grounded properly, check speed sensor for continuity with an ohmmeter placed across sensor. The resistance should be 40 to 60 ohms. If the speed sensor is functioning properly, replace the amplifier.

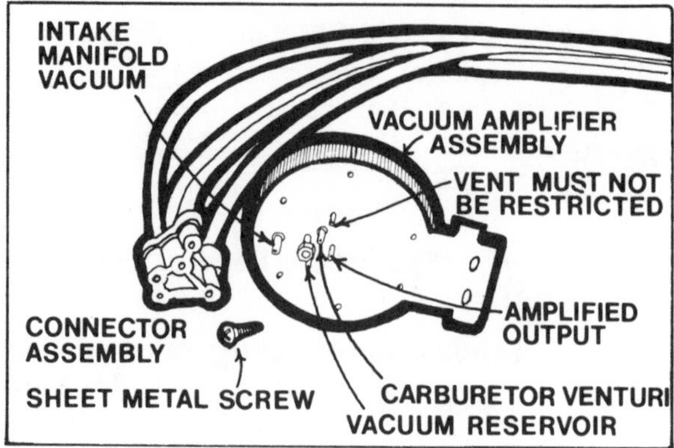

Fig. 27 Venturi vacuum amplifier

FORD EGR SYSTEM

Exhaust Gas Recirculation

Floor Entry EGR System

Some 1974 eight-cylinder engines use the Floor Entry EGR system, which has the EGR valve mounted on the rear of the intake manifold. The EGR valve controls the exhaust gases that enter specially cast passages in the manifold from the exhaust crossover passage. When the valve opens, the exhaust crossover is then opened to the two drilled passages in the floor of the intake manifold riser under the carburetor, Fig. 28.

Venturi Vacuum Amplifier

A Venturi Vacuum Amplifier, Fig. 27, used in 1974-75, uses a weak venturi vacuum signal to produce a strong intake manifold vacuum to operate the EGR valve, thereby achieving an accurate, repeatable and almost exact proportion between venturi airflow and EGR flow. This assists in controlling oxides of nitrogen with minimal sacrifice in driveability.

Tapered Stem EGR Valve

There is an additional EGR valve other than the poppet or the modulating type, which is the tapered stem type.

NOTE: If the tapered stem valve is plugged or causes rough idle due to leakage, it should be replaced.

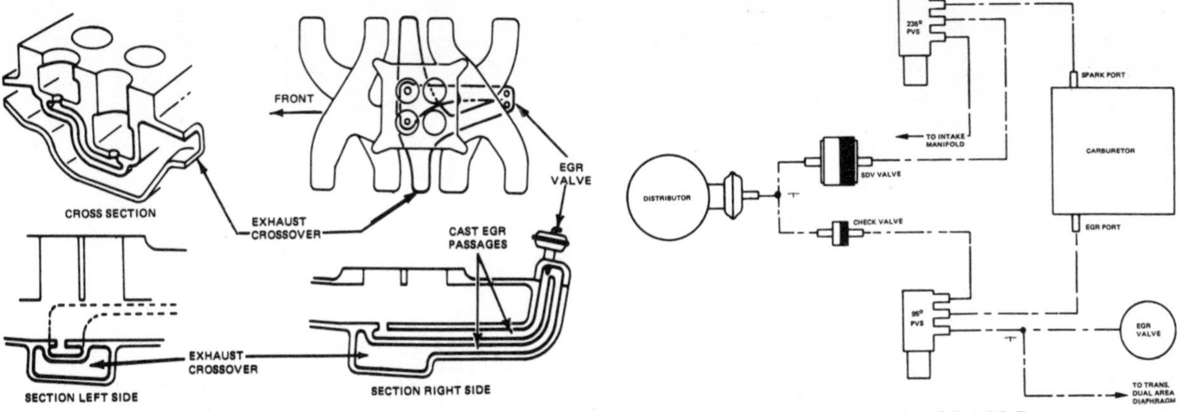

Fig. 28 Ford floor entry EGR system

Fig. 29 Ford EGR/CSC system

Cold Start Cycle (EGR/CSC)

The EGR/CSC System regulates both distributor advance and EGR valve operation according to coolant temperature by sequentially switching vacuum signals. The major system components are a 95° F EGR/PVS (ported vacuum switch) valve, a SDV (spark delay valve) and a vacuum check valve, Fig. 29.

When engine coolant temperature is below 82° F, the EGR/PVS valve admits carburetor EGR port vacuum (at about 2500 rpm) directly to the distributor advance diaphragm, through the one way check valve. At the same time, the EGR/PVS valve shuts off carburetor EGR vacuum to the EGR valve and transmission diaphragm.

When engine coolant temperature is 95° F and above, the EGR/PVS valve is actuated and directs carburetor EGR vacuum to the EGR valve and transmission diaphragm instead of the distributor. At temperatures between 82° and 95° F, the EGR/PVS valve may be open, closed or in mid-position.

The spark delay valve (SDV) delays carburetor vacuum to the distributor advance by restricting the vacuum signal through the SDV for a predetermined time. During normal acceleration, little or no vacuum is admitted to the distributor advance diaphragm until acceleration is completed and engine coolant temperature is 95° F or higher.

The check valve blocks off vacuum signal from the SDV to the EGR/PVS valve so that carburetor spark vacuum will not be dissipated when the EGR/PVS valve is actuated above 95° F.

The 235° F PVS valve which is not part of the EGR/PVS system is connected to the distributor vacuum advance to prevent engine overheating as on previous models.

DUAL-AREA DIAPHRAGM

On 1973-75 vehicles, new dual-area diaphragms are used, Fig. 31. These diaphragms offset effects of engines using the EGR system and equipped with automatic transmissions. The new diaphragms permit vehicles to function with satisfactory shift spacing and shift feel.

To test, remove the vacuum diaphragm and test unit using an outside vacuum source. Set regulator on tester to 18 inches Hg with end of vacuum hose blocked off. Then connect vacuum hose to vacuum diaphragm unit. If unit does not hold an 18-inch Hg reading, the diaphragm is leaking and must be replaced.

FORD DECEL VALVE

This valve, Fig. 30, used on the 1600cc, 2000cc, 2300cc and 2800cc engines, is mounted on the intake manifold adjacent to the carburetor and meters an additional amount of fuel and air during engine deceleration periods. This additional fuel and air, together with engine modifications, permits more complete combustion with the result being lower levels of exhaust emissions. During engine deceleration, manifold vacuum forces the diaphragm assembly against the spring in the decel valve, which in turn raises the decel valve (open position). With the valve open, existing manifold vacuum pulls a metered amount of fuel and air from the carburetor, which travels through the decel valve body assembly into the intake manifold. The decel valve remains open and continues to feed additional air and fuel for a specified time.

Adjustments

1600cc, 2000cc, 2300cc & 2800cc Engines

1. Connect tachometer to the engine and bring the engine up to operating temperature.

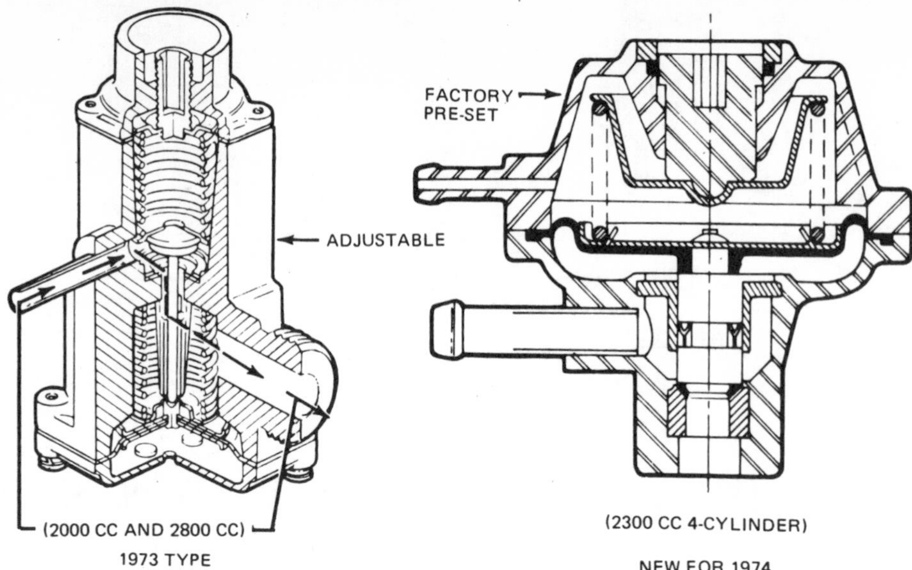

Fig. 30 *Ford decel valve*

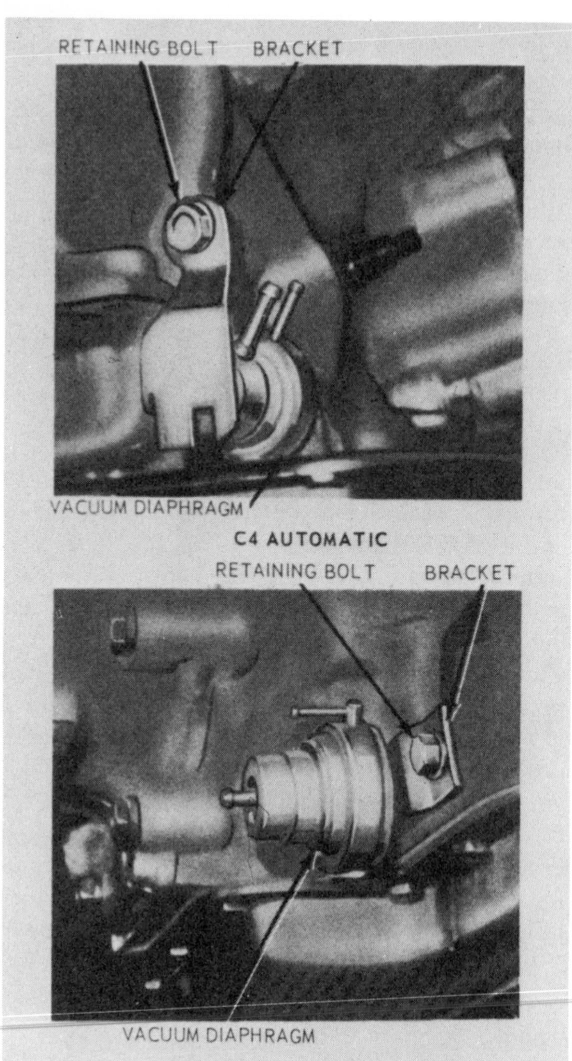

Fig. 31 *Dual diaphragm vacuum modulator. (typical)*

2. Disconnect the rubber hose between decel valve and carburetor at decel valve and cap nipple on valve.

   NOTE: Make certain that timing, CO or idle mixture and idle speed are set to specifications.
3. Raise engine speed to 3000 rpm and hold for about 5 seconds, then release the throttle. If the engine does not return to idle, check for binding linkage and correct as necessary.
4. Remove the cap from the decel valve and connect a vacuum gauge using a tee fitting so that valve remains operational.
5. Raise engine speed to 3000 rpm and hold for about 5 seconds, then release throttle and observe time required for vacuum to reach zero which should be 2-5 seconds.
6. On 2300cc engines, if valve is not within specifications, it must be replaced and retested. On 1600cc, 2000cc and 2800cc engines the decel valve may be adjusted by turning the adjusting screw inward to reduce the time the valve is opened and outward to increase it. If decel valve cannot be adjusted within the limits of the adjusting screw, it should be replaced.

FORD CTAV SYSTEM

Cold Temperature Activated Vacuum

This system operates basically the same as the TAV system previously discussed except that a latching relay, Fig. 32, has been added. The latching relay, activated by temperature switch closing remains energized regardless of temperature switch position which prevents system cycling due to minor ambient temperature changes.

The temperature switch energizes the three-way

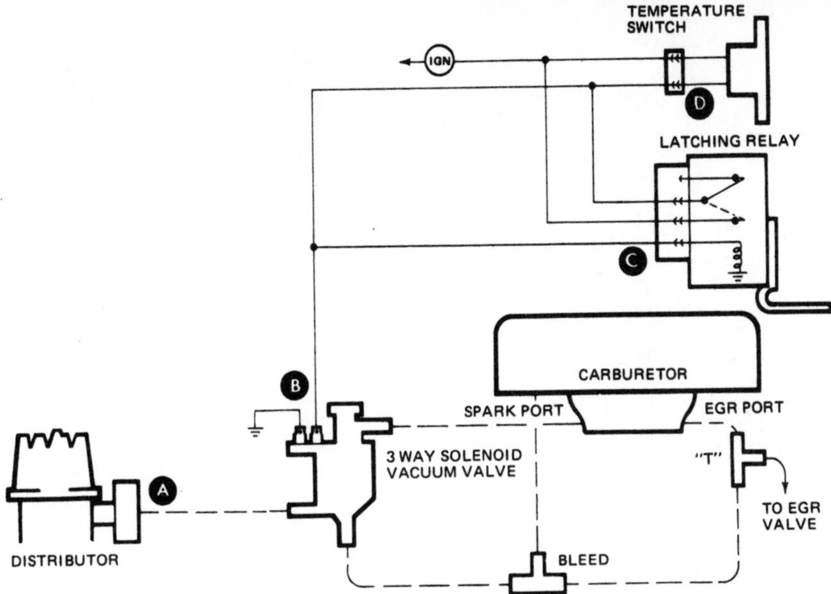

Fig. 32 Schematic of CTAV system above 65° F.

vacuum valve and latching relay when ambient temperature is above 65° F. When ambient temperature is below 49° F, the system is inoperative and the distributor diaphragm and EGR valve receives vacuum directly from its respective carburetor ports.

Testing

NOTE: Prior to performing any test on this system, ensure that temperature switch is about 65° F.

Vacuum System Test

1. With a tachometer connected, disconnect three-way solenoid vacuum valve ground lead. Connect a vacuum gauge to distributor end of hose running from solenoid vacuum valve and if no vacuum reading is observed at 1500 rpm, check vacuum source back to carburetor spark port.
2. If a vacuum reading of approximately 15 inches Hg was observed in above check, reconnect solenoid vacuum valve ground lead. If a vacuum reading is still noted, check solenoid vacuum valve ground and electrical leads back to ignition switch.
3. If after reconnecting solenoid vacuum valve ground lead, vacuum is low or non-existent run engine at 3000 rpm and if no vacuum is observed, check vacuum source back to carburetor EGR port.
4. If a vacuum reading of approximately 9 inches Hg was observed at 3000 rpm, system is functioning normally.

Electrical System Test

1. Disconnect temperature switch connector and connect a test lamp between the solenoid vacuum valve ground terminal and the ground. Turn ignition ON. If lamp lights, the latching relay is defective, requiring replacement.
2. If lamp does not light in above check, reconnect the temperature switch connector. If lamp still does not light, check temperature switch and wiring back to ignition switch.
3. If lamp lights in above check, again disconnect temperature switch connector. If the lamp goes out, replace latching relay. If lamp remains lit, connect the test lamp to temperature switch connector and cool temperature switch to below 49° F. If lamp lights, the temperature switch is faulty, requiring replacement.
4. If the lamp does not light when temperature switch is cooled to below 49° F, the system is operating normally.

Vacuum Operated Heat Control Valve (HCV)

For 1975, most 8-cylinder passenger car engines will have a vacuum operated heat control valve mounted between the exhaust pipe and the exhaust manifold (Fig. 33). Its function is the same as the bi-metal spring type heat control valve—preheat the fuel air mixture by directing a portion of the exhaust gas upward through passages in the intake manifold during engine warmup.

On cold starts, manifold vacuum is directed to the heat control valve (HCV) through the top two ports in the HCV PVS (ported vacuum switch),

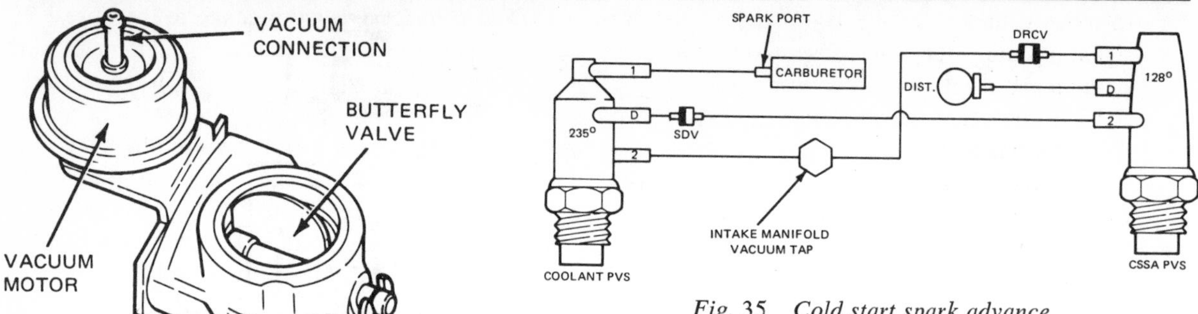

Fig. 33 Vacuum operated exhaust heat control valve

Fig. 35 Cold start spark advance (CSSA) system

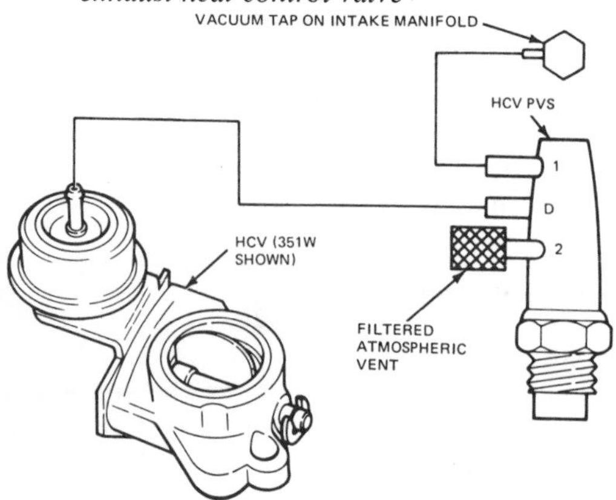

Fig. 34 HCV system schematic

PVS IDENTIFICATION CHART	
PVS Body Color	**Opening Temp. (°F.)**
Black	92–98
Blue	125–131
Purple	157–163

Fig. 36

Color Code	Temperature (°F.)
Green Top	Above 68°
Black Top	Above 100°
Plain Dichromate or Blue Top	Above 133°

Fig. 37

closing the HCV valve against the spring in the vacuum motor. When the engine coolant reaches a certain temperature, the PVS seals off the vacuum supply, venting the HCV vacuum motor to the atmosphere and allowing the spring to open the HCV butterfly valve (Fig. 34).

A separate Ported Vacuum Switch is used for each of three systems.

This system provides intake manifold vacuum to the distributor spark advance diaphragm when the engine coolant temperature is below 125° F. The vacuum path is from the intake manifold tap, through the Distributor Retard Control Valve (DRCV), through the CSSA PVS and to the distributor.

At 125° F, and above, the CSSA PVS is operated. Vacuum then reaches the distributor as follows—from the carburetor spark port, through the cooling PVS, through the SDV, through the CSSA PVS and to the distributor.

Above 235° F, the cooling PVS operates, directing intake manifold vacuum to the distributor through the SDV and CSSA PVS. In an over-temperature situation at idle, this will increase engine rpm by providing increased vacuum. When the engine temperature decreases, spark will once more be controlled from the spark port of the carburetor.

Cold Start Spark Advance System (CSSA)

On some 1975 460 CID V8 engines, a cold start spark advance system (CSSA) is added to the distributor spark control system (Fig. 35).

EGR System Diagnosis—EGR Valve, High Speed Modulator and Venturi Vacuum Amplifier

Check of EGR Valve When On The Engine

1. Start the engine and warm it up until engine coolant temperature is above the calibrated temperature of the EGR/PVS valve as shown in Fig. 36 and 37 according to the color code of the PVS valve.
2. Check all vacuum hoses in the system to be sure they are open and not broken, split or cracked and fit snugly onto connectors. Remove the EGR vacuum supply hose from the EGR valve and hook a vacuum hose from the EGR valve to an external, gauged, variable vacuum source with increments of 1-in. Hg, 0.10-in. Hg graduations and minimum 10-in. mercury capacity.
3. Gradually apply vacuum to the EGR valve and simultaneously observe the movement of the EGR valve stem.

   The stem should visually be observed to start

to move within ± 1.0-in. Hg of the diaphragm signal vacuum. To ease observation of valve stem, mark stem prior to observation.

If the EGR valve does not meet start to open specification, replace the valve.

With engine off, apply 8 inch Hg vacuum to EGR valve and trap. Vacuum should remain within 1-in. Hg for a minimum of 30 seconds. Replace the EGR valve if it is out of specification.

With engine at idle, apply vacuum to EGR valve of at least 8-inches Hg. The valve should move to the full extent of its travel and engine should roughen, rpm should decrease and/or stop completely. If idle quality doesn't change there is no EGR flow and if specifications have been met something is plugging the EGR system. Perform cleaning procedure to determine problem.

4. With hose routings properly connected, restart engine and stabilize temperature. If the engine idle quality is not acceptable, the EGR valve may not be sealing properly. If this condition is encountered, install a new EGR valve and new gasket. Recheck the idle condition of the engine. If there is no improvement in idle quality, the problem is elsewhere. The original EGR valve should be reinstalled and further engine diagnosis should be performed to determine the offending component. If there is improvement in idle quality, change EGR valve.

EGR PVS Functional Check

Verify that the EGR valve, external vacuum passages, and/or solenoid valve (if so equipped) are functional.

PVS With Two Connectors

1. Disconnect both vacuum hoses at the PVS valve. Connect vacuum gauge to either connector on the PVS. Connect manifold vacuum or auxiliary vacuum source of at least 10 inches Hg. to other connector.
2. Start engine and warm it up until engine coolant temperature is above the calibration temperature of the EGR/PVS as previously indicated. If no reading is noted on vacuum gauge —PVS has failed and should be replaced. If vacuum is noted—PVS is OK.

PVS With Three Connectors

1. Disconnect EGR vacuum hose at carburetor and connect manifold vacuum or auxiliary vacuum source to hose.
2. Disconnect EGR vacuum hose at EGR valve and connect a vacuum gauge to the hose.
   NOTE: If available, chassis dynamometer diagnostic equipment is beneficial when checking EGR valve function.
3. Start engine and warm it up until engine coolant temperature is above the calibration temperature of the EGR/PVS as previously indicated. If no reading is noted on vacuum gage—PVS has failed and should be replaced. If vacuum is noted—PVS is OK.

PVS With Four Connectors

1. Disconnect vacuum hoses at the PVS valve. Connect a vacuum gauge to either of the two ports marked D and M. Connect a vacuum supply to the other.
2. Start engine and warm it up until engine coolant temperature is above the calibration temperature of the EGR/PVS as previously indicated. If there is no vacuum reading—that portion of the PVS is OK. If vacuum is noted —the PVS is defective and should be replaced.
3. Connect the gauge to either one of the bottom two ports marked E and S and the vacuum supply to the other. If vacuum is noted—the PVS is OK. If there is no vacuum reading— the PVS is defective and should be replaced.

Spark Delay Valve

To determine if a delay valve is operating correctly, use the following procedure.

Equipment Required

1. Vacuum Gauge—USG Model 12121-1, 2 inches dia., 0-30 inches Hg vacuum gauge with 3/16-inch OD vacuum hose nipple adaptor and 24 inches of 3/16-inch ID distributor vacuum hose or equivalent.
2. Stop watch or wrist watch with a sweep second hand.
3. External vacuum source capable of maintaining a minimum constant 10 inches Hg vacuum.

NOTE: The vacuum gauge must have a small internal volume and be free from external leakage.

Procedure—Spark Delay Valve

1. Set external vacuum source to 10 inches Hg.
2. Connect black side of delay valve to vacuum source.
3. Connect the 24-inch section of vacuum hose to gauge and to colored side of delay valve.
4. Apply vacuum and observe time in seconds for gauge to read from 0-8 inches Hg with a constant 10 inches Hg vacuum source.
5. The minimum and maximum time for the

valve to reach 8 inches Hg should be as shown in Fig. 38.
When checking the delay valve, care must be exercised to prevent oil or dirt from getting into the valve as this will impair the functioning.

Trouble Shooting Guide

Replace delay valve if any of the above tests show the valve is defective.

Color	I.D. No.	Time in Seconds Minimum	Maximum
Black and Gray	1	1	4
Black and Brown	2	2	5
Black and White	5	4	12
Black and Yellow	10	5.8	14
Black and Blue	15	7	16
Black and Green	20	9	20
Black and Orange	30	13	24
Black and Red	40	15	28

Fig. 38

Color	I.D. No.	Time in Seconds Minimum	Maximum
Black and White	5	4	12
Black and Yellow	10	5.8	14
Black and Blue	15	7	16
Black and Green	20	9	20
White and Brown	2	2	2
White and Green	20	9	20

Fig. 39

Dual Delay Valve

1. Set external vacuum source to 10 inches Hg. Connect the 24-inch section of vacuum hose to gauge and to DIST nipple of delay valve. Connect black side of delay valve and CARB nipple of delay valve to vacuum source. Prevent vacuum from being applied to CARB nipple while applying 10 inches Hg vacuum to black side of valve. Apply vacuum to the CARB nipple and observe time in seconds for gauge to read from 0-8 inches Hg with a constant 10 inches Hg vacuum source.
2. The minimum and maximum time for the valve to reach 8 inches Hg should be as shown in Fig. 39. When checking the delay valve, care must be exercised to prevent oil or dirt from getting into the delay valve as this will impair the functioning.

Trouble Shooting Guide

Replace delay valve if any of the above tests show the valve is defective.

Retard Delay Valve

1. Set external vacuum source to 10 inches Hg. Connect colored side of delay valve to vacuum source. Connect the 24 inches section of vacuum hose to gauge and to white side of delay valve. Apply vacuum and observe time in seconds for gauge to read from 0-8 inches with a constant 10 inches Hg vacuum source.
2. The minimum and maximum time for the valve to reach 8 inches Hg should be as shown in Fig. 40. When checking the delay valve, care must be exercised to prevent oil or dirt from getting into the valve as this will impair the functioning.

Color	I.D. No.	Time in Seconds Minimum	Maximum
White and Brown	2	2	5
White and Green	20	9	20
Black and White	5	4	12
Black and Yellow	10	5.8	14
Black and Blue	15	7	16
Black and Green	20	9	20

Fig. 40

	I.D. No.	Time in Seconds Minimum	Maximum
White and Red	40	15	28

Fig. 41

Trouble Shooting Guide

Replace delay valve if any of the above tests show the valve is defective.

Procedure—Air Cleaner Delay Valve

1. Set external vacuum source to 10-inch Hg. Connect colored side of delay valve to vacuum source.
   NOTE: 20-inch OD to .27-inch OD adaptor may be required to connect colored side of valve to vacuum source.
   Connect the 24-inch section of vacuum hose to gauge and to white side of delay valve. Apply vacuum and observe time in seconds for gauge to read from 0-inch to 8-inch Hg with a constant 10-inch Hg vacuum source.
2. The minimum and maximum time for the valve to reach 8-inch Hg should be as shown in Fig. 41. When checking the delay valve care must be exercised to prevent oil or dirt from getting into the valve as this will impair its function.

Trouble Shooting Guide

Replace delay valve if any of the above tests show the valve is defective.

Spark Control Systems and Spark Delay Valve

Non-Thermal Control System

1. Remove air cleaner. Remove SDV if so equipped and repeat the Spark Delay Valve pro-

cedure. Install a connector in place of the SDV in order to carry out system checks.

2. Install T fittings and vacuum gauge at distributor.
3. With engine at normal operating temperature and with transmission in neutral, momentarily open throttle half way.
4. Observe the vacuum gauge for a quick rise and fall as the throttle is opened and closed. If a vacuum is evident, the system is OK. If no vacuum is evident, check the vacuum lines. T (if applicable) and port in carburetor for plugging and correct.
5. For vehicles with a cooling PVS, check vacuum reading at distributor at normal idle and engine operating temperature. If vacuum reading is 2-in. Hg or less, the PVS is OK. If vacuum reading is greater than 2 in. Hg, remove the top vacuum line that goes to the carburetor at PVS. If vacuum reading is still greater than 2 in. Hg, PVS is leaking and should be replaced.
6. Remove the vacuum gauge, T fitting, connector (where used), reinstall SDV (where used), and re-connect all vacuum lines.
7. Reinstall air cleaner and torque wing nut to specifications.

Cold Lock-Out Spark System

1. Remove air cleaner. Remove SDV if so equipped and repeat the Spark Delay Valve procedure. Install connector in place of SDV for system checks.
2. Install T fitting and vacuum gauge in primary side of distributor.
3. With engine at normal operating temperature and transmission in neutral, momentarily open the throttle half way.
4. Observe the vacuum gauge for a quick rise and fall as the throttle is opened and closed. If a vacuum is evident, the system is OK. If no vacuum is evident, check vacuum lines, cold lock-out PVS ports and carburetor port for plugging and leaks and correct.
5. Remove vacuum gage, T fitting, connector (if used) and install SDV (if used) and re-connect all vacuum lines.
6. Reinstall air cleaner and torque wing nut to specifications.

Dual Delay System

1. Remove air cleaner. Remove dual delay SDV (3-port) and repeat the Spark Delay Valve (Dual Delay Valve) procedure. Install a connector between the spark port line and the distributor line. Connect a vacuum gauge to the line removed from the manifold port (black side) of the dual delay valve.
2. Start engine and note if vacuum reading is obtained. If vacuum is evident, vacuum lines and connections to intake manifold are OK. If no vacuum is evident, check lines, Ts and manifold fitting for plugging and leaks and correct.
3. Remove gauge from line and plug line. Install T fitting at primary side of distributor and connect vacuum gauge.
4. With engine running and transmission in neutral, momentarily open throttle half way.
5. Observe the vacuum gauge for a quick rise and fall as the throttle is opened and closed. If a vacuum is evident, the system is OK. If no vacuum is evident, check the vacuum lines, and the spark port for plugging or leaking and correct.
6. Remove gauge and T fitting from primary side of distributor and install on secondary side. With engine running vacuum should be noted. If no vacuum, check vacuum line and connection to T for plugging and correct.
7. Remove T fitting, vacuum gauge, plug, and connector. Install dual delay valve and reconnect all vacuum lines.
8. Reinstall air cleaner and torque wing nut to specification.

Cold Start Spark Advance System

NOTE: Perform steps one through five only if engine complaint is spark knock or pinging.

CAUTION: Do not leave transmission in drive during steps two and four for longer than 15 seconds.

1. Connect a tachometer to the engine and start the engine.
2. With brake pedal depressed and transmission in drive (see Caution above), accelerate engine and record rpm at which spark knock or pinging occurs.
3. To allow transmission to cool, put engine in neutral and accelerate to 1500 rpm three times for 15-30 seconds each time.
4. Remove vacuum advance line from distributor and plug. Restart engine and repeat step two (see Caution above) to recorded rpm.
5. If spark knock or pinging re-occurred with vacuum advance line disconnected, stop engine and proceed to next step. If spark knock or pinging did not re-occur, the system has a faulty CSSA PVS and/or retard delay valve or check valve (if so equipped). Repair and/or replace as required.
6. Remove air cleaner. Remove SDV if so equipped and repeat the Spark Delay Valve

procedure. Install connector in place of SDV. Remove vacuum check valve or retard delay valve (if so equipped) and check per vacuum check valve or retard delay valve procedure. Install connector in place of check valve or retard delay valve.

7. Install T fitting and vacuum gauge at distributor primary.
8. Remove vacuum line from bottom port of Cold Start PVS and cap.
9. With engine at normal operating temperature and at idle the vacuum reading should be zero. If vacuum is not zero, the Cold Start PVS is defective and should be replaced.
10. Remove cap and reconnect the removed line to the bottom port of the Cold Start PVS.
11. Remove vacuum line from top port of the Cold Start PVS and plug.
12. For vehicles with a Cooling PVS, check vacuum reading at distributor at normal idle. If vacuum reading is 2 in. Hg or less the Cooling PVS is OK. If vacuum reading is greater than 2 in. Hg remove the top vacuum line (the line that goes to the carburetor) at Cooling PVS and plug. If vacuum reading is still greater than 2 in. Hg Cooling PVS is leaking and should be replaced.
13. With engine running and transmission in neutral momentarily open the controls (1/2 open).
14. Observe vacuum gauge for a quick rise and fall as the throttle is opened and closed. If vacuum is evident the spark advance system is OK. If no vacuum is evident, check the vacuum lines, ports in the Cold Start and Cooling PVSs, and the carburetor vacuum port for plugging and correct.
15. Remove T fitting, vacuum gauge, plug and connectors. Install SDV and check valve or retard delay valve (if used) and reconnect all vacuum lines.
16. Reinstall air cleaner and torque wing nut to specifications.

Delay Valve By-Pass System (PVS Operated)

1. Remove air cleaner.
2. Remove SDV and repeat the Spark Delay Valve Procedure. Install a connector in place of SDV. Remove vacuum line at distributor and install a T-fitting and vacuum gauge.
3. With engine idling at normal operating temperature and with transmission in neutral, momentarily open throttle (1/3 open).
4. Observe the vacuum gauge for a quick rise and fall as the throttle is opened and closed. If a vacuum is evident, the system is OK. If no vacuum is evident, check the vacuum lines, Ts and port in carburetor for plugging. Correct as required.
5. Shut engine off.
6. Remove vacuum gauge, T fitting, and connector. Reinstall SDV and reconnect vacuum hoses.
7. Remove vacuum check valve and check per Vacuum Check Valve Check Procedure.
8. Reinstall check valve in hose to distributor.
9. Install connector and vacuum gauge in vacuum hose from PVS to check valve.
10. With engine running at normal operating temperature and transmission in neutral, momentarily open throttle (1/2 open).
11. Observe the vacuum gauge for evidence of vacuum. If vacuum reading is two inches Hg or less, PVS is OK. If vacuum reading is greater than two inches Hg the PVS is defective and should be replaced.
12. Remove vacuum gauge, connector and plugs (where used), reinstall check valve and reconnect all vacuum hoses.
13. Reinstall air cleaner and torque to specifications. For flowing function:

    Set vacuum source at 5 in. Hg.

    Connect gauge to check which is the same side the vacuum source was connected to in Step 1 of this procedure.

    Apply vacuum to the opposite side used in Step 1. Reading on gauge should be same as source. If it is not, replace the valve.

Vacuum Check Valve Check Procedure

To determine if a check valve is operating correctly the following service procedure should be used.

Equipment Required:

1. Vacuum Gauge with 3/16-inch OD vacuum hose nipple adaptor.
2. Vacuum Source.

Procedure:

1. For checking function:

    Set vacuum source at 5 in. Hg.

    Apply vacuum to the check side of the check valve and trap. After 30 seconds the vacuum should not be less than 4 in. Hg. If it is, replace the valve.

Fuel Deceleration Valve Check Less Transmission Interlocked

Procedure—Marvel-Schebler Valve (Two hose connections)

For vehicles equipped with a PVS interlocked

fuel decel system, ensure that manifold idle vacuum is available at the fuel decel valve with the engine at normal operating temperature. If manifold vacuum is evident, the PVS and vacuum lines are OK. If no or low vacuum is evident, check vacuum lines, PVS ports and intake manifold fitting for plugging and leaks and correct.

1. Engine must be at normal operating temperature.
2. Connect tachometer and timing light.
3. Ignition timing and engine idle rpm must be as specified.
4. Remove air cleaner.
5. Visually inspect the hoses, connections and valve for any abnormal conditions. Repair or replace as necessary.
6. Check for vacuum leak at normal engine idle by placing finger over the small hole in the bottom of the valve. If a leak exists, replace valve.
7. Disconnect the rubber hose that connects the carburetor to the fuel decel valve at the carburetor and plug the hose.
8. With transmission in neutral and parking brake applied, increase engine speed to 3000 rpm and hold for five seconds. Release the throttle and note if engine immediately returns to normal idle speed. If engine speed does not return, check for linkage hang-up and correct before proceeding to the next step.
9. Remove plug from hose and install a T and a vacuum gauge into the hose between the valve and the carburetor.
10. Increase engine speed to 3000 rpm and hold for five seconds. Measure the time required for the vacuum to drop to zero when the throttle is released. This should be from 2 to 3.5 seconds. If less than 2 seconds, insure that vacuum is available from 3/16-inch hose. If out of specification, idle CO must be verified to specification before the fuel decel valve is adjusted. If the valve is still out of specification, adjust the valve until a time of 2 to 3.5 seconds is obtained. Replace the valve if it cannot be adjusted to specification. If the valve is the non-adjustable type, it must be replaced if it is not to specification.

NOTE: Fuel deceleration valve check must be done after idle fuel mixture adjustment.

Transmission Interlocked Fuel Decel System

For vehicles so equipped the following procedure should be used to check out the transmission interlock before checking the fuel decel valve.

Procedure—System Operational Test

To prepare for the system test, install a T fitting and a vacuum gauge with a long hose into the 3/16-inch vacuum line at the FDV diaphragm. Position the vacuum gauge so you can see it from the driver's seat.

Manual Transmission

1. With a manual shift, start the engine in neutral and check the vacuum gauge. There should not be any vacuum reading.
   If vacuum is noted, check fuse and electrical system. Repair or replace as required.
2. Holding the clutch disengaged and the engine idling, shift into a high gear—third or fourth. Two things should happen: the transmission switch should open the electrical circuit and at the same time, the vacuum gauge needle should move upscale. The vacuum valve opens when its electrical coil is de-energized. When these conditions check out during the operation test, the system is functioning properly. If no vacuum is evident, electro-mechanical switch located on front left side of transmission case has failed. Replace switch.

Automatic Transmission

1. To make the system operational test with an automatic transmission, start the engine in park or neutral. Observe that the vacuum gauge reads zero. If vacuum is noted, check fuse and electrical system. Repair or replace as required.
2. With an automatic transmission, the switch also opens in reverse. Therefore, with the engine operating at idle, apply the foot brake firmly and shift to reverse to actuate the transmission switch. If the system is operational, the transmission switch will open the circuit to de-energize the vacuum valve to allow vacuum to be applied to the FDV diaphragm. At this point, gauge should indicate a vacuum. If these conditions exist, system is OK.

   If no vacuum is evident in reverse gear, electrical pressure switch located at the back of transmission body housing has failed. Replace switch.

   After transmission interlock system check is completed, remove vacuum gauge and T fitting and disconnect one wire from the solenoid vacuum valve. This opens the switch and allows vacuum to reach the FDV diaphragm during the FDV procedure. Perform the FDV check per the procedure. After checking FDV

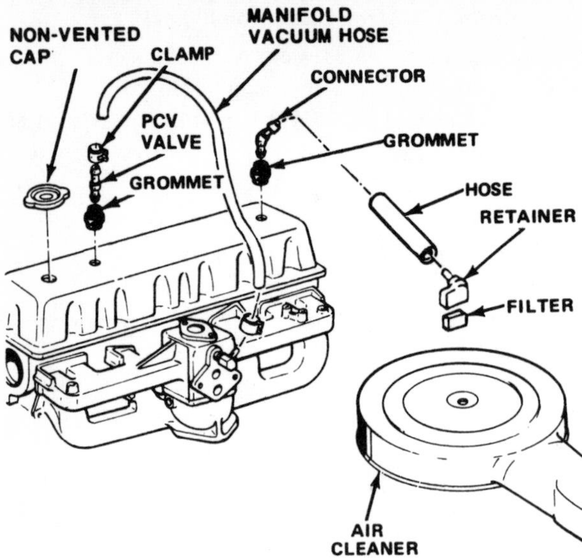

Fig. 42 PCV system—6 cylinder

according to the procedure, reconnect the wire to the solenoid.

FUEL EVAPORATIVE EMISSION CONTROLS

American Motors

Fuel vapors are drawn into the intake manifold through the carburetor air cleaner on all 1974 six cylinder engines, Fig. 42.

General Motors

NOTE: The purge valve (used on some applications), can be repaired without replacing complete vapor canister, using repair kit, part No. 7041344. The service is NOT a routine maintenance item and should be performed if damaged or parts are missing.

Ford Motor Co.

1971-75

The operation of the system is similar to the system used in 1970, but it has been simplified by the following modifications.

Fill Control Vent System

The fill control vent system which provides positive control of fuel height during fill operations is made possible by the design of the filler pipe and by vent lines within the filler neck or fuel tank. This system is designed so that about 10% of tank capacity will remain empty when the tank is filled. This space allows for thermal fuel expansion and temporary storage of fuel vapors.

Pressure and Vacuum Relief Valve

The pressure and vacuum system operates through the use of a sealed fill cap with a built-in pressure and vacuum relief valve. Under normal operating conditions, the valve opens to relieve pressure when it exceeds ¾ to 1¼ psi. When fuel-tank vacuum reaches ½-inch mercury maximum, the valve opens allowing air to enter the system.

Vapor Vent and Storage System

This system, on vertically mounted fuel tank, consists of a vapor separator mounted on the uppermost surface of the tank. The empty space at the top of the tank provides adequate breathing space for the vapor separator. Horizontally mounted fuel tanks use a raised mounting section for the vapor separator. This raised section provides additional breathing space for the vapor separator since the space allowed for thermal expansion of fuel is not as deep as it is on vertically mounted tanks.

The vapor separator which acts as a baffle to prevent fuel from entering the charcoal canister, Fig. 43, consists of a small hole in the outlet connected to the vapor tube plus open cell foam to separate liquid fuel and fuel vapors. The fuel vapors in the tank go through the opening in the vapor separator and into the vapor tube.

Fuel Vapor Return System

A fuel vapor return system is used on some engines to reduce the amount of fuel vapor entering the carburetor. It consists of a fuel vapor separator installed in the fuel supply line between the pump and carburetor and a one piece vapor return line from the separator to the fuel tank. Fuel vapors are collected in the separator and routed to the fuel tank where they recondense or are contained by the evaporative emission control system.

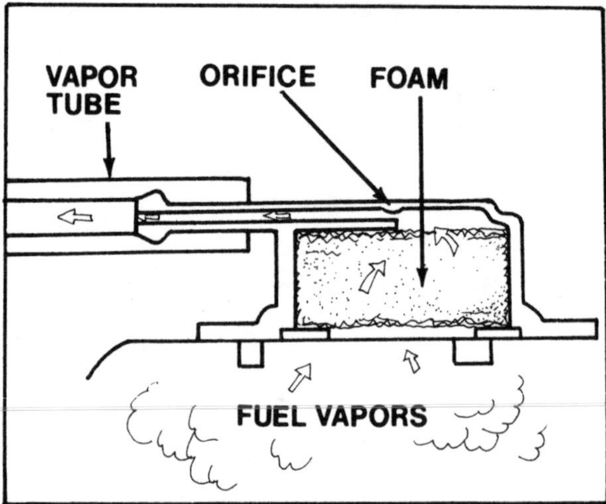

Fig. 43 Cross-section of vapor separator

VACUUM CIRCUITS AND COMPONENT LOCATIONS

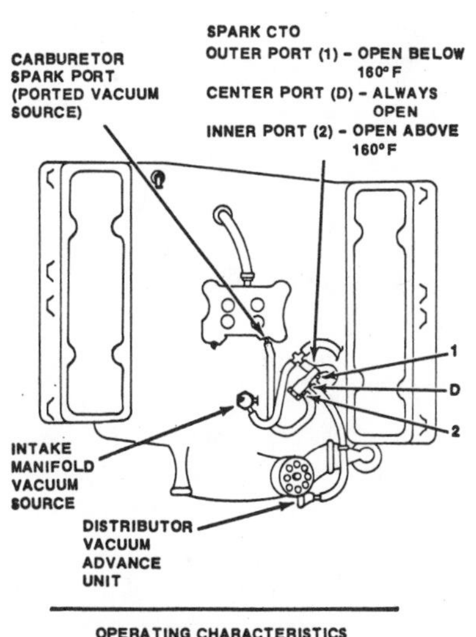

Fig. 1 Spark CTO system vacuum hose routing. 1974 American Motors V8-401

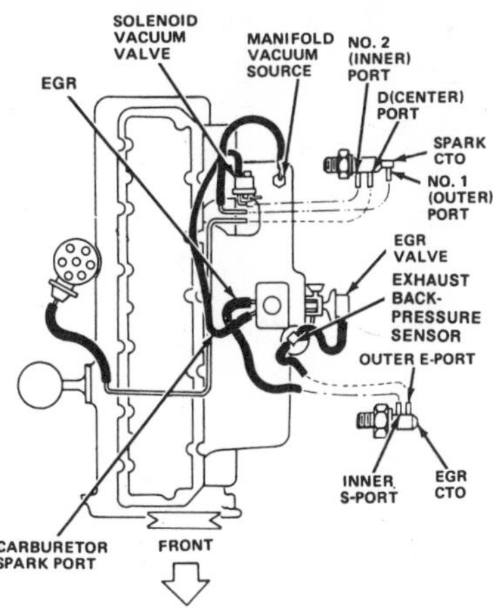

Fig. 2 1974 EGR vacuum line routing. 6 cyl. less Air Guard

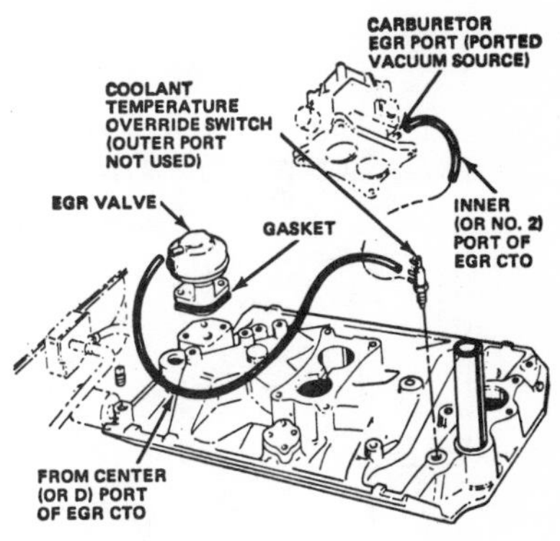

Fig. 3 EGR system vacuum hose mouting. 1974 American Motors V8

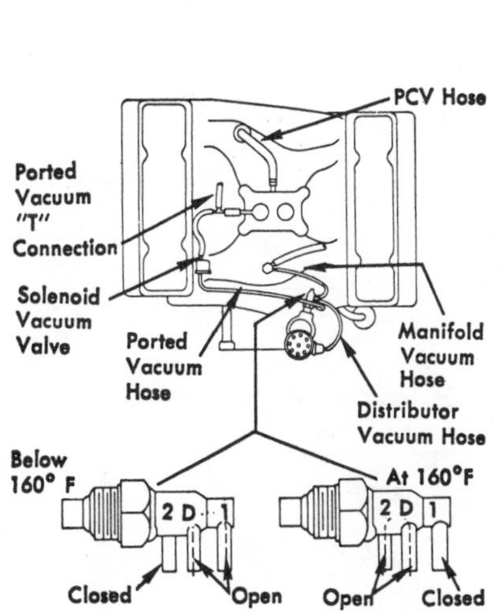

Fig. 4 CTO system vacuum hose routing. 1972 American Motors

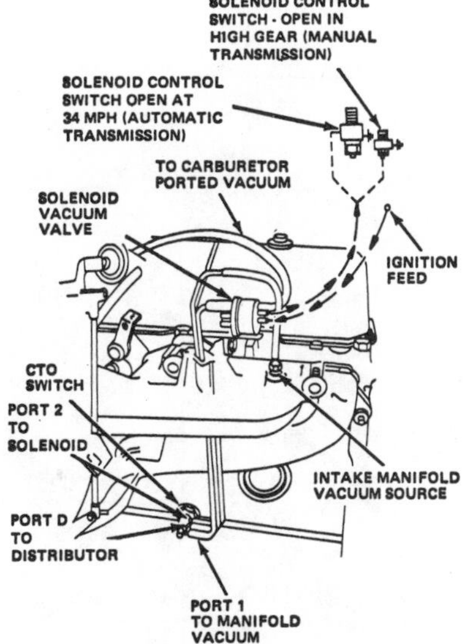

Fig. 5 TCS system vacuum and wiring. 1972-74 American Motors 6-232

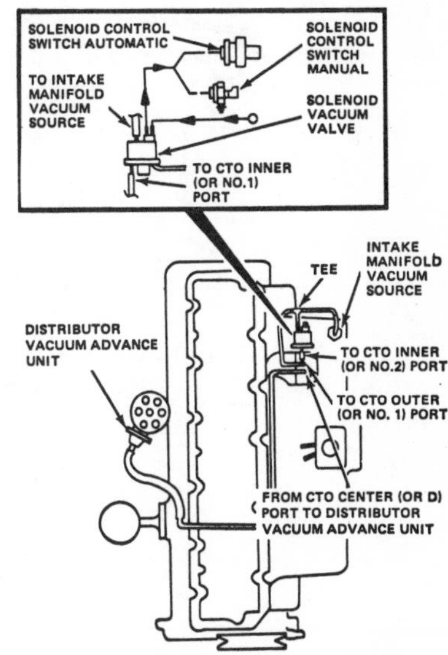

Fig. 6 TCS system vacuum and wiring. 1972-74 American Motors Matador with 6-258

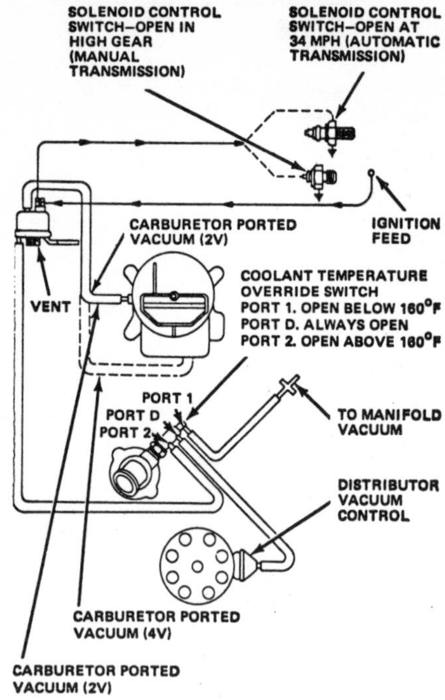

Fig. 7 TCS system vacuum and wiring. American Motors V8-390 & 401

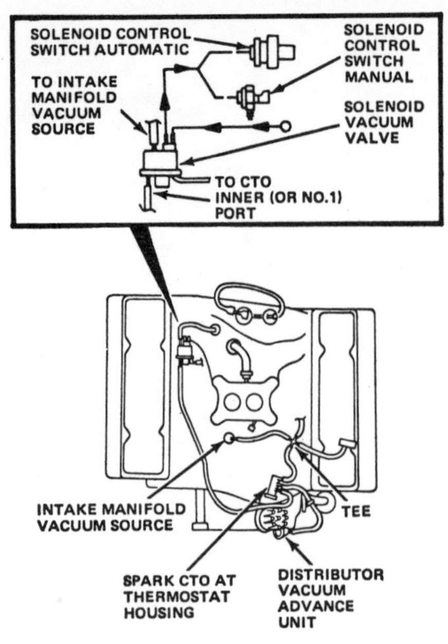

Fig. 8 TCS system vacuum and wiring. American Motors V8-304 & 360

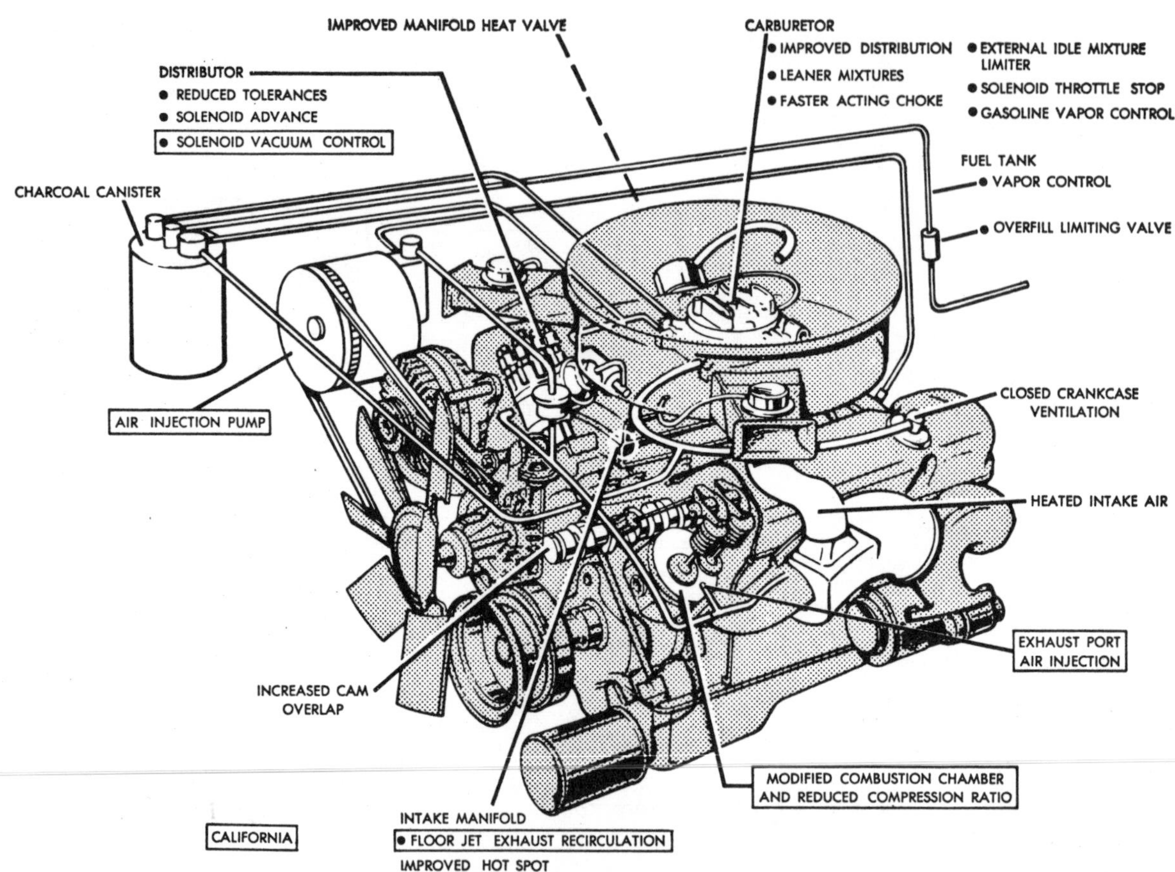

Fig. 9 Chrysler Emission Control System. 1972

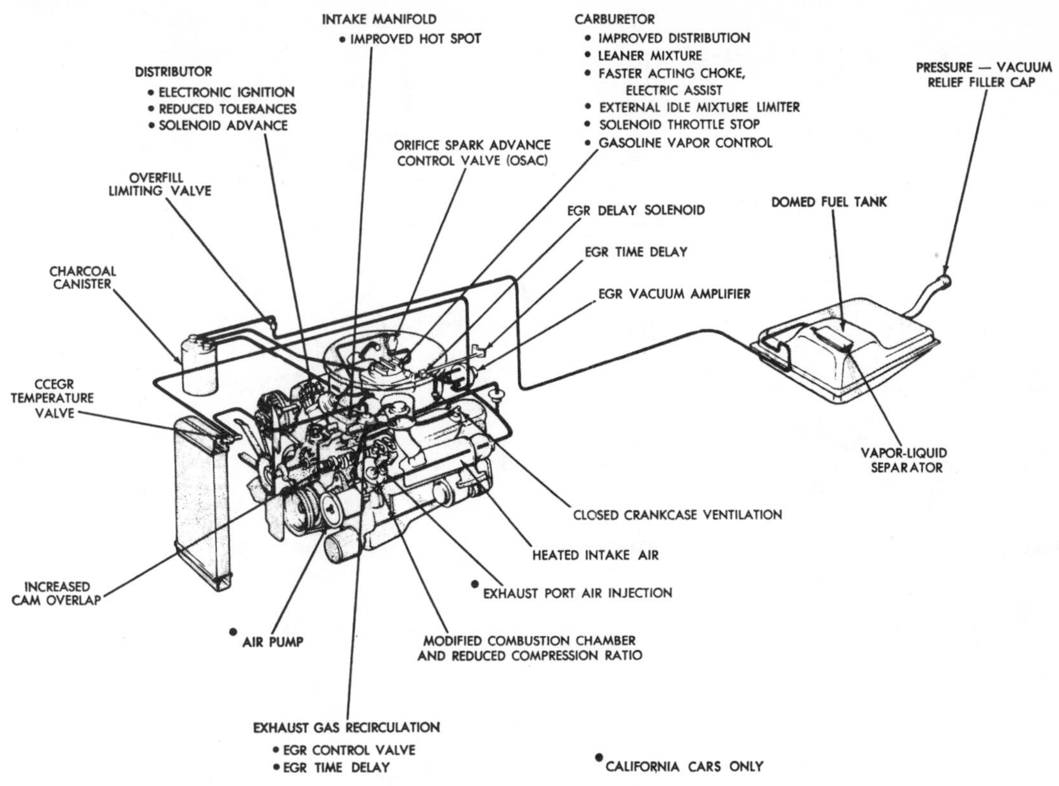

Fig. 10 *Chrysler Emission Control System.* 1973-74

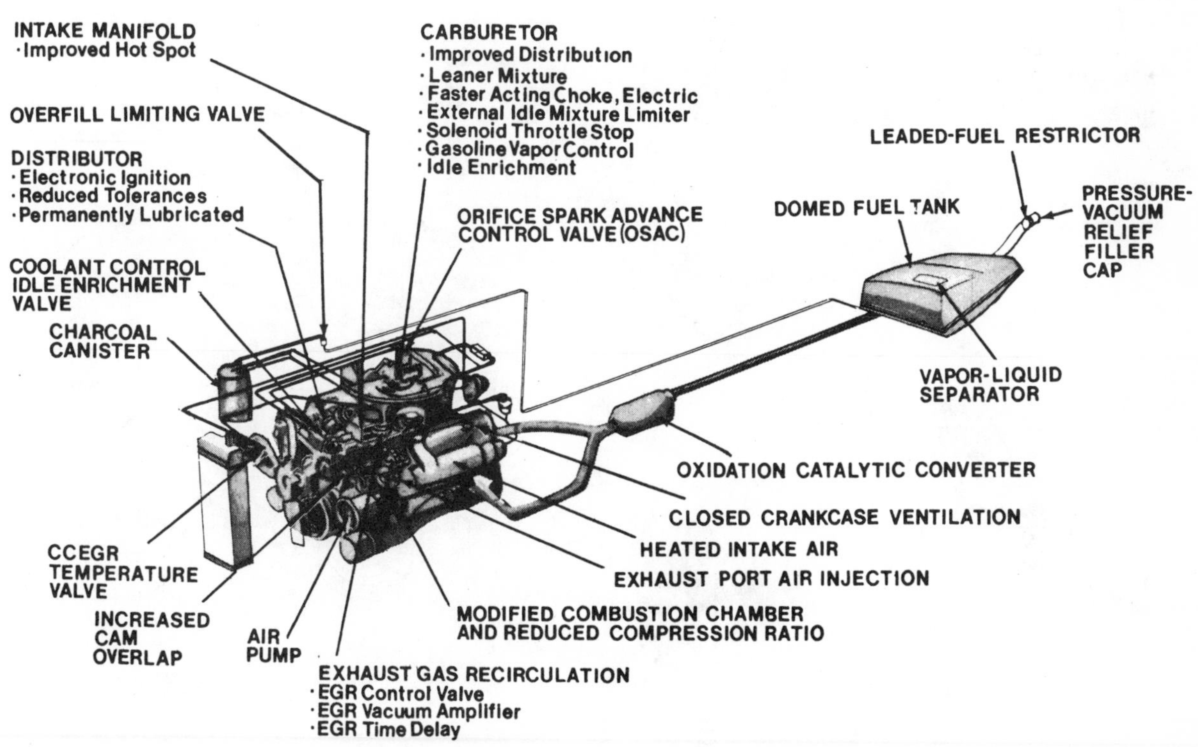

Fig. 11 *Chrysler Emission Control System.* 1975

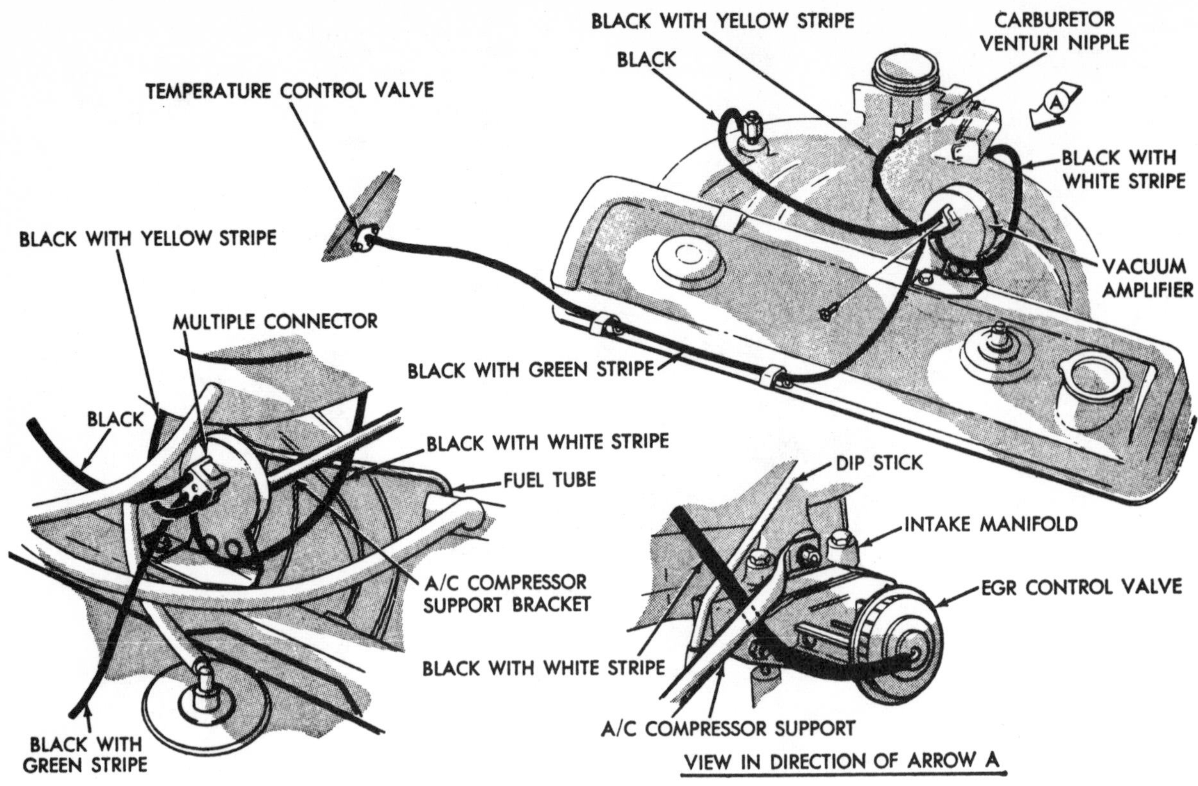

Fig. 12 *EGR system vacuum hose routing.* 1973 *Chrysler* 6-198, 225

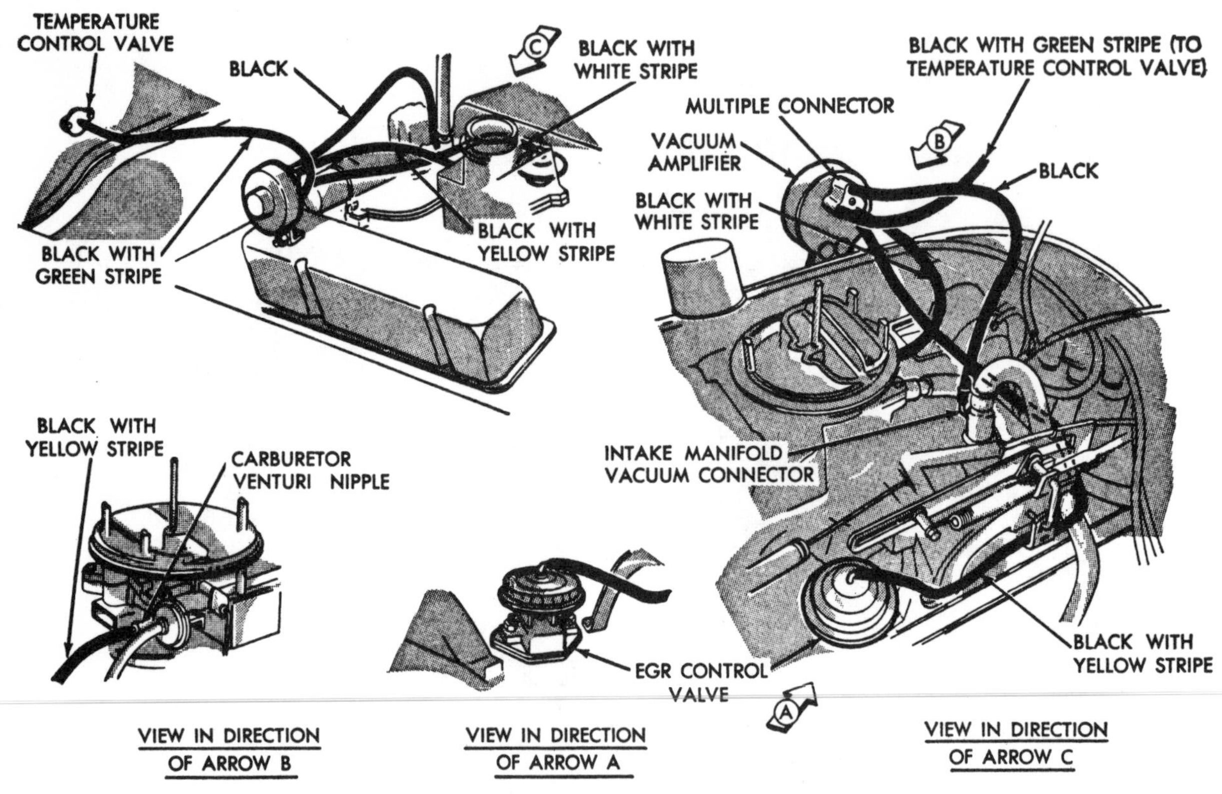

Fig. 13 *EGR system vacuum hose routing.* 1973 *Chrysler* V8-360

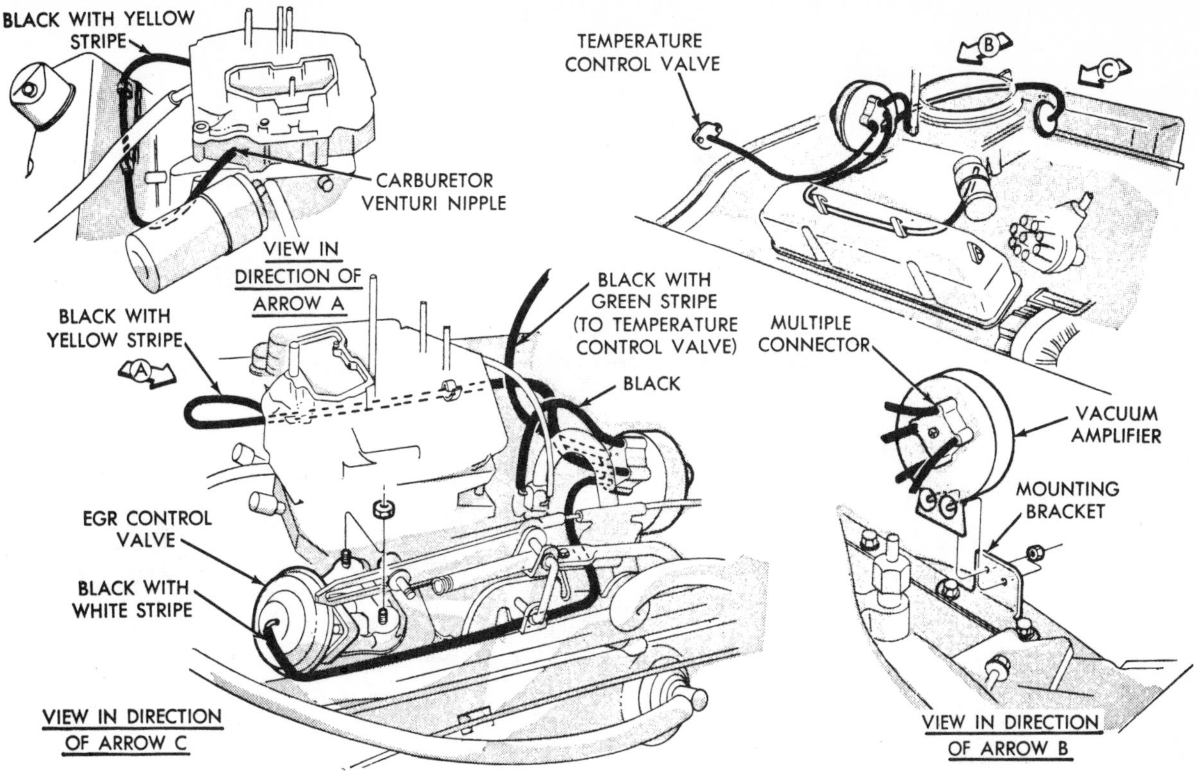

Fig. 14 *EGR system vacuum hose routing.* 1973 *Chrysler* V8-440

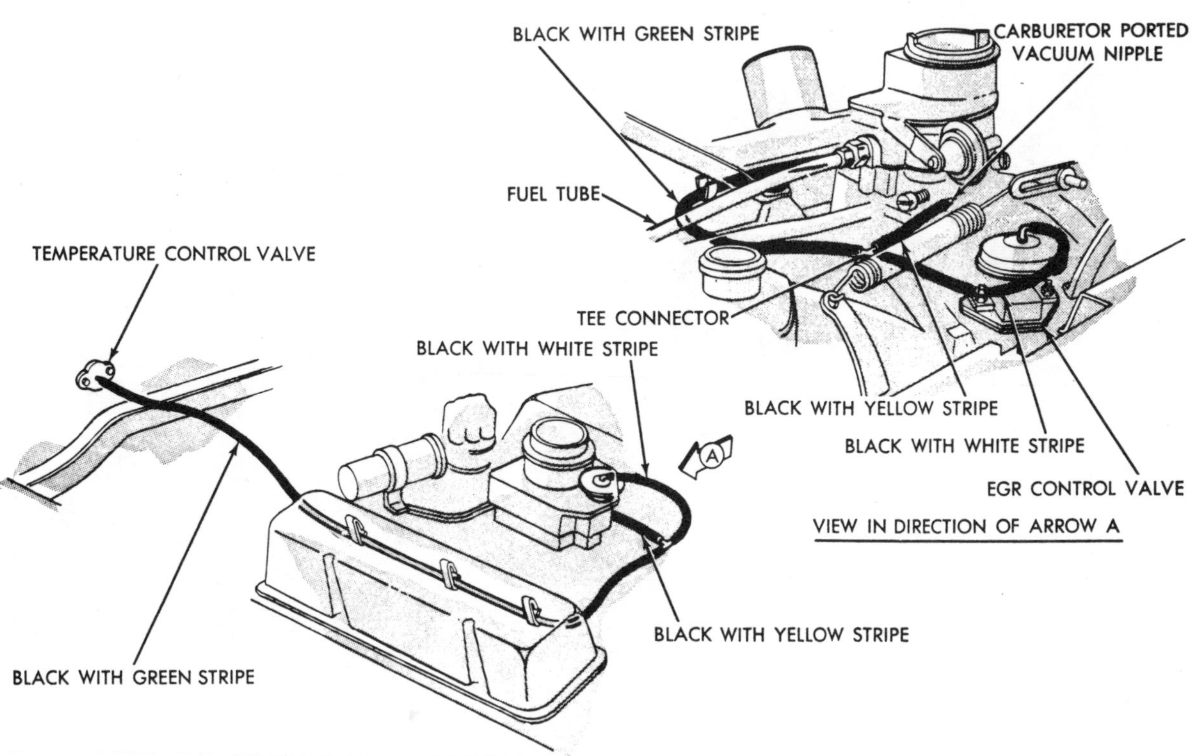

Fig. 15 *EGR system vacuum hose routing.* 1973 *Chrysler* V8-318

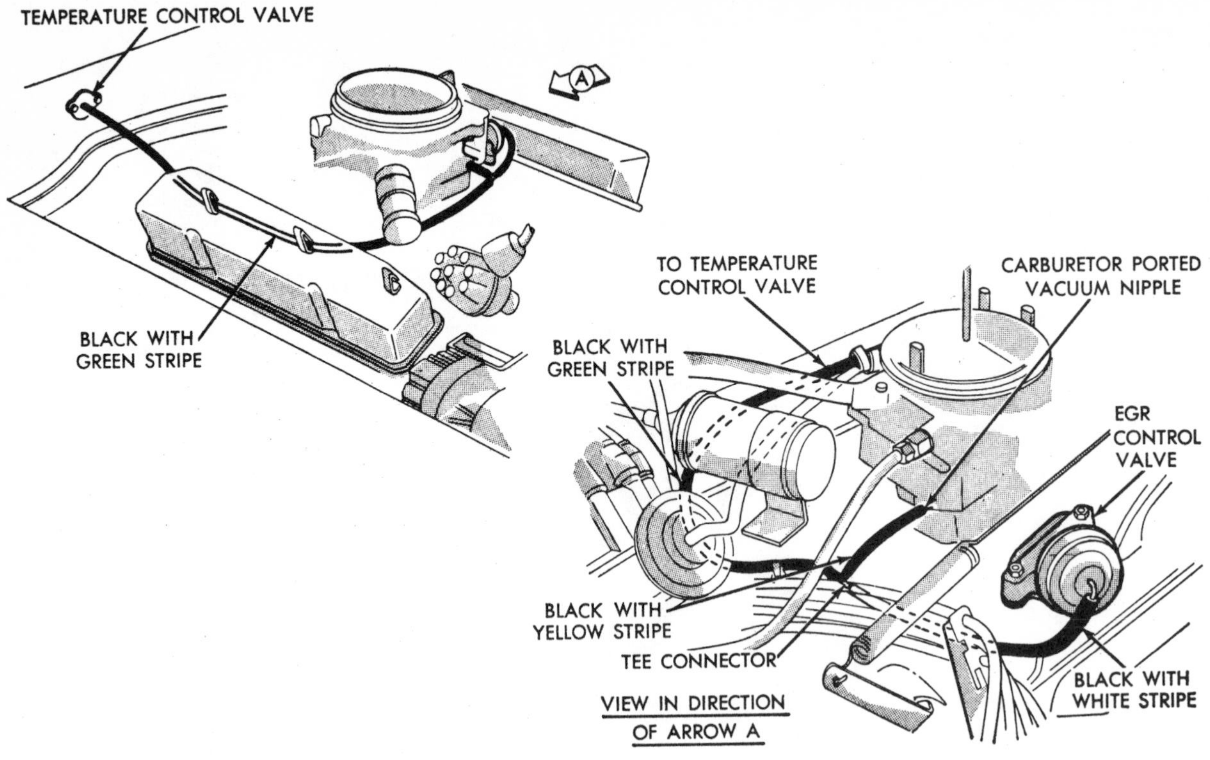

Fig. 16 *EGR system vacuum hose routing.* 1973 *Chrysler* V8-400

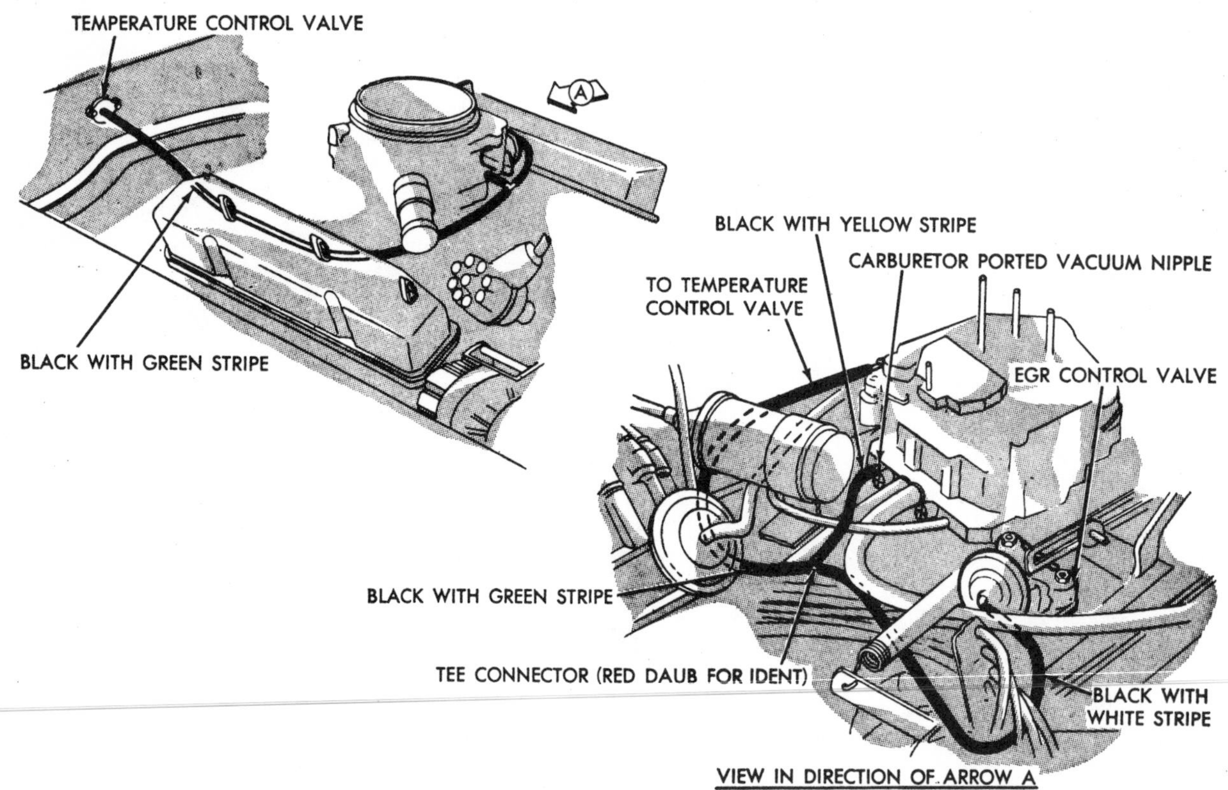

Fig. 17 *EGR system vacuum hose routing.* 1973 V8-440 *High Performance*

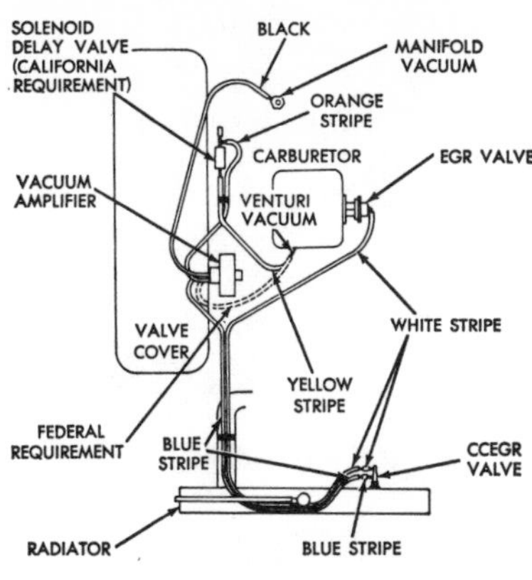

Fig. 18 *EGR system vacuum hose routing.* 1974 *Chrysler* 6-198, 225

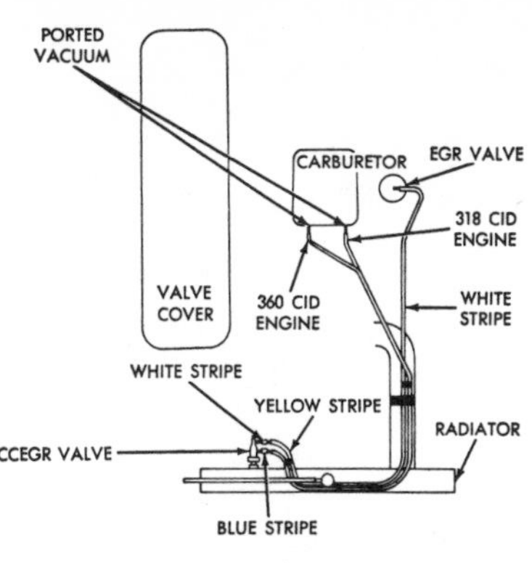

Fig. 19 *EGR system vacuum hose routing.* 1974 *Chrysler* V8-318, 360 (*ported vacuum*) *exc. California*

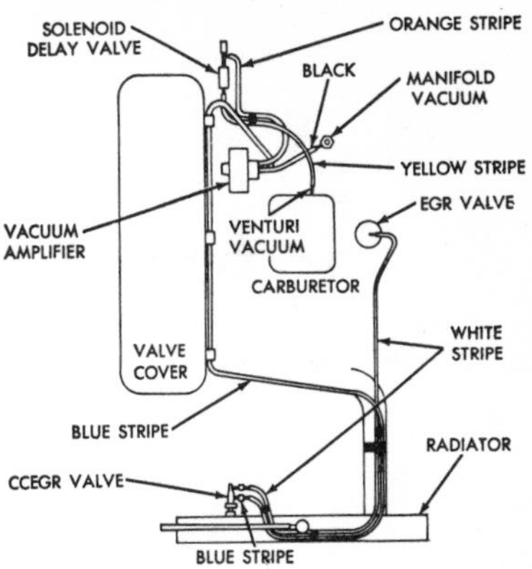

Fig. 20 *EGR System vacuum hose routing.* 1974 *Chrysler* V8-318 (*venturi system*), *California*

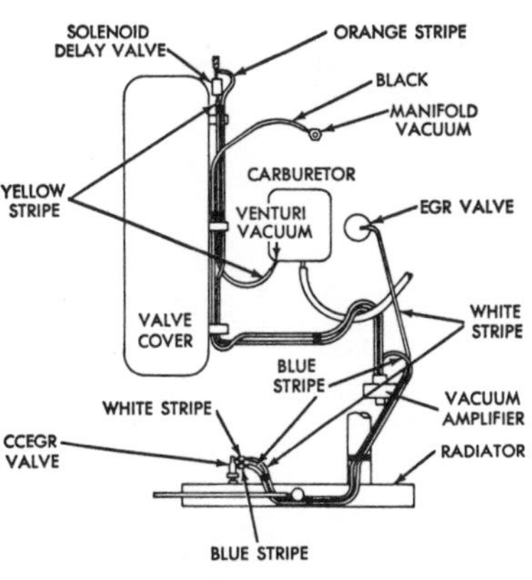

Fig. 21 *EGR system vacuum hose routing.* 1974 *Chrysler* V8-360 (*venturi system*), *California*

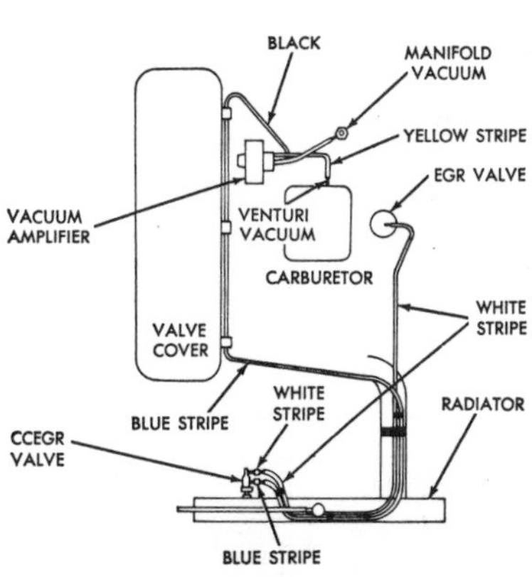

Fig. 22 *EGR system vacuum hose routing.* 1974 *Chrysler* V8-360 (*venturi system*) *exc. California*

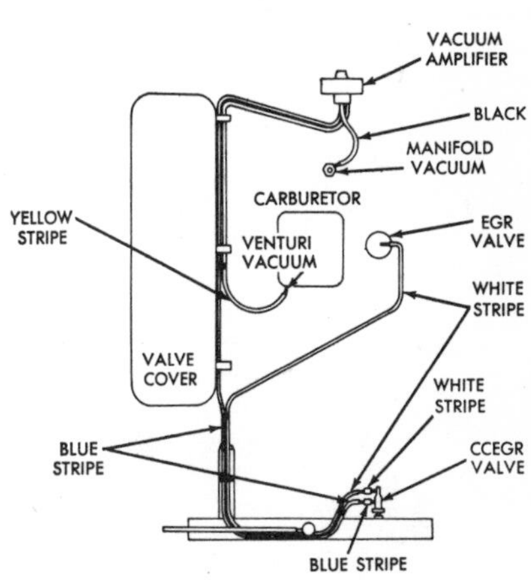

Fig. 23 *EGR System vacuum hose routing.* 1974 *Chrysler* V8-400, 440 (*venturi system*) *exc. California*

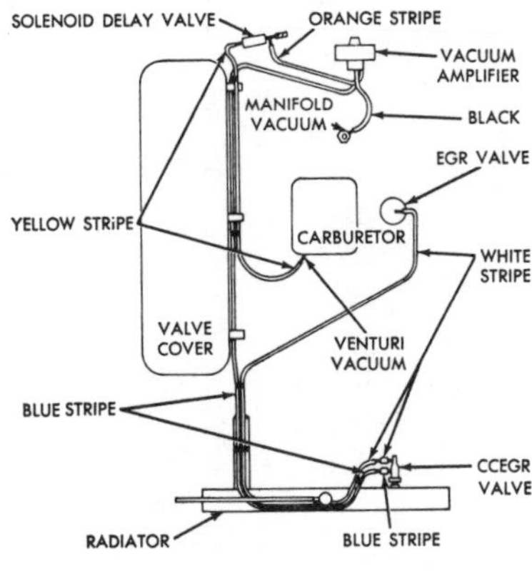

Fig. 24 *EGR system vacuum hose routing.* 1974 *Chrysler* V8-400, 440 (*venturi system*), *California*

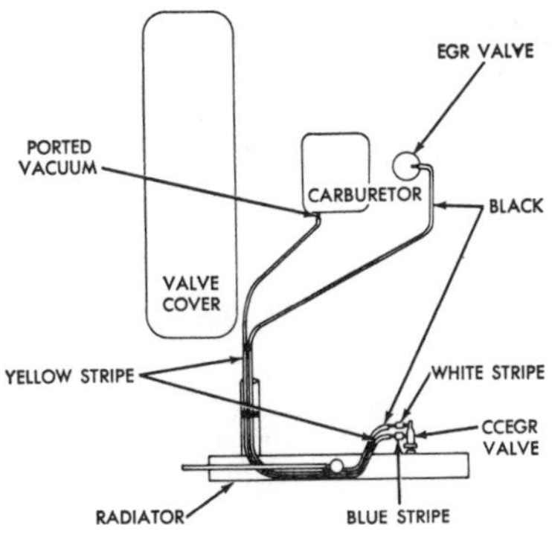

Fig. 25 *EGR system vacuum hose routing.* 1974 *Chrysler* V8-400, 440 (*ported system*), *exc. California*

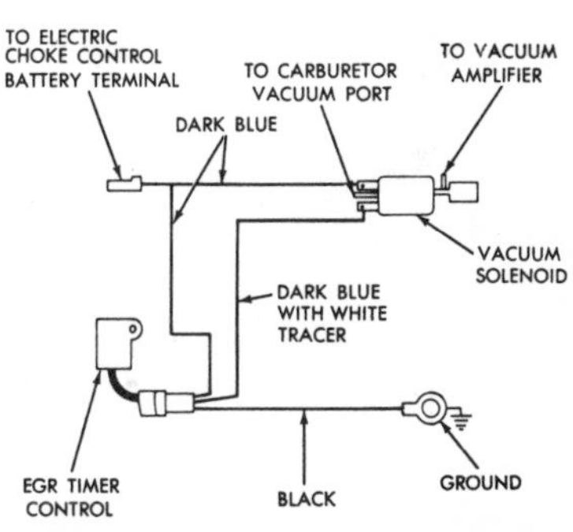

Fig. 26 *EGR Time Delay Valve system wiring.* 1974 *Chrysler*

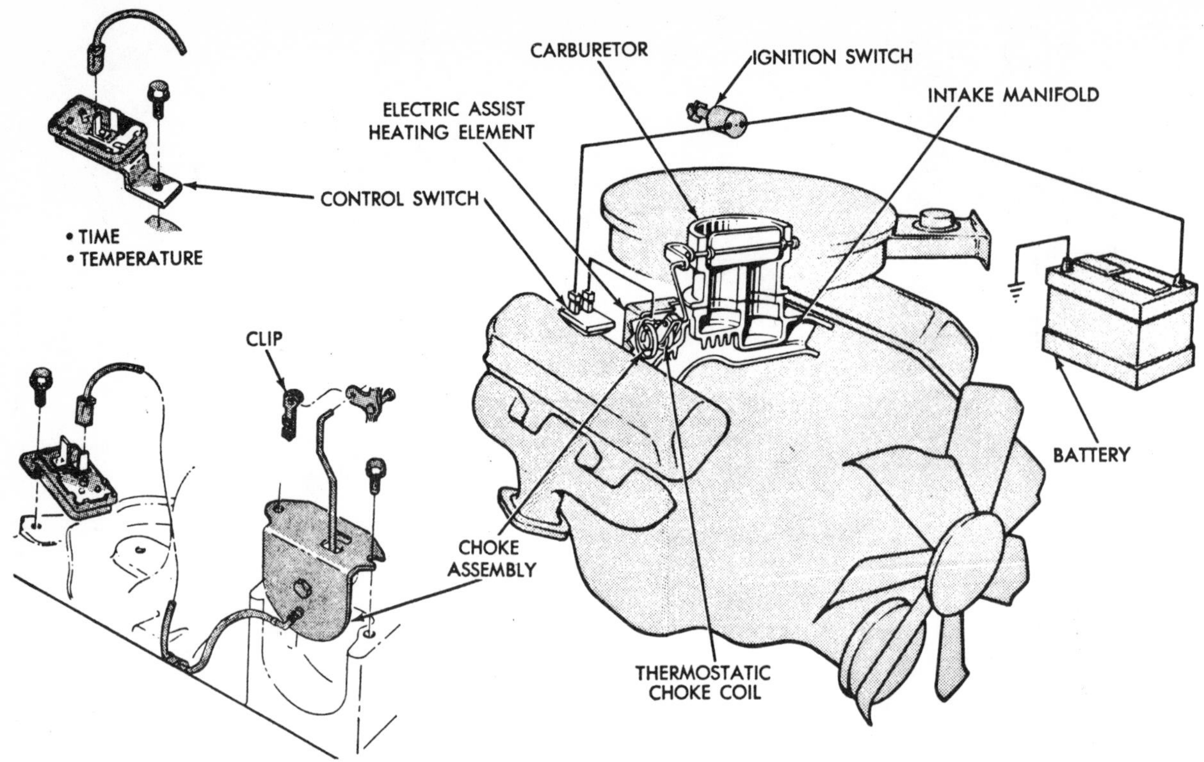

Fig. 27 Electric assist choke. 1973-74 Chrysler

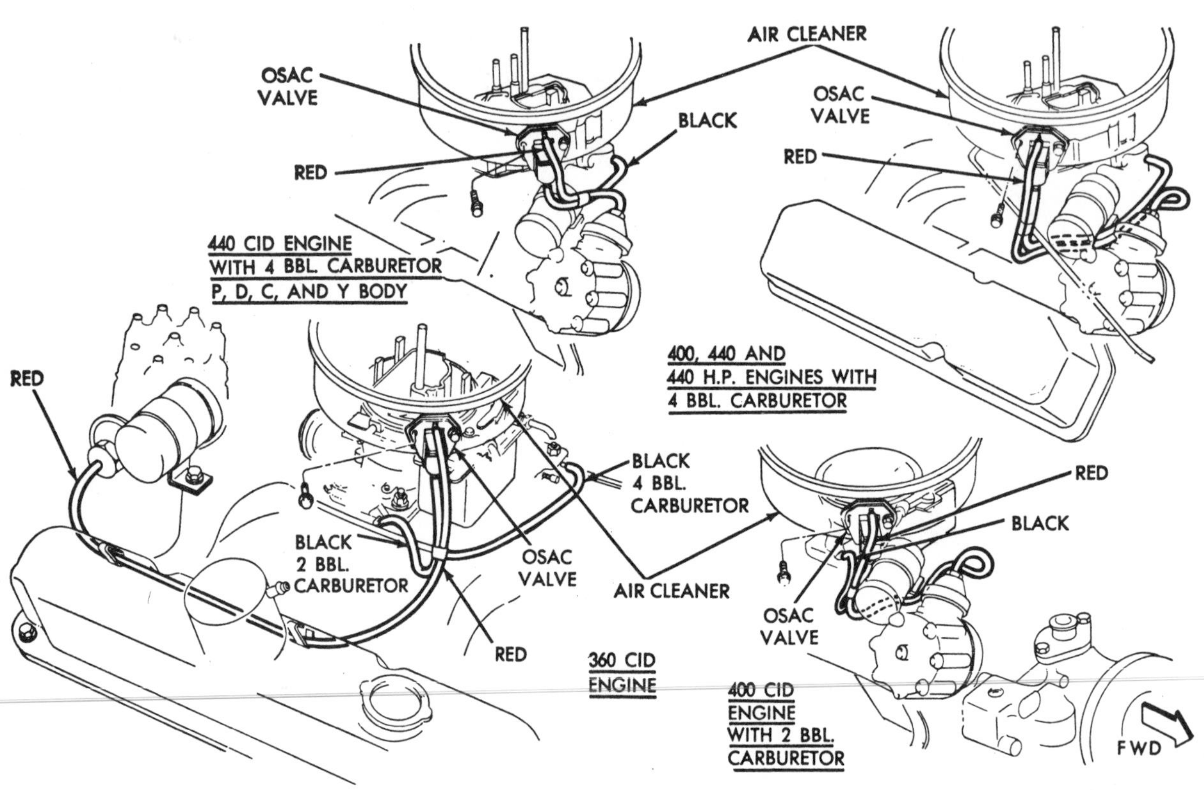

Fig. 28 OSAC valve vacuum hose routing. 1974 Chrysler V8-360, 400, 440

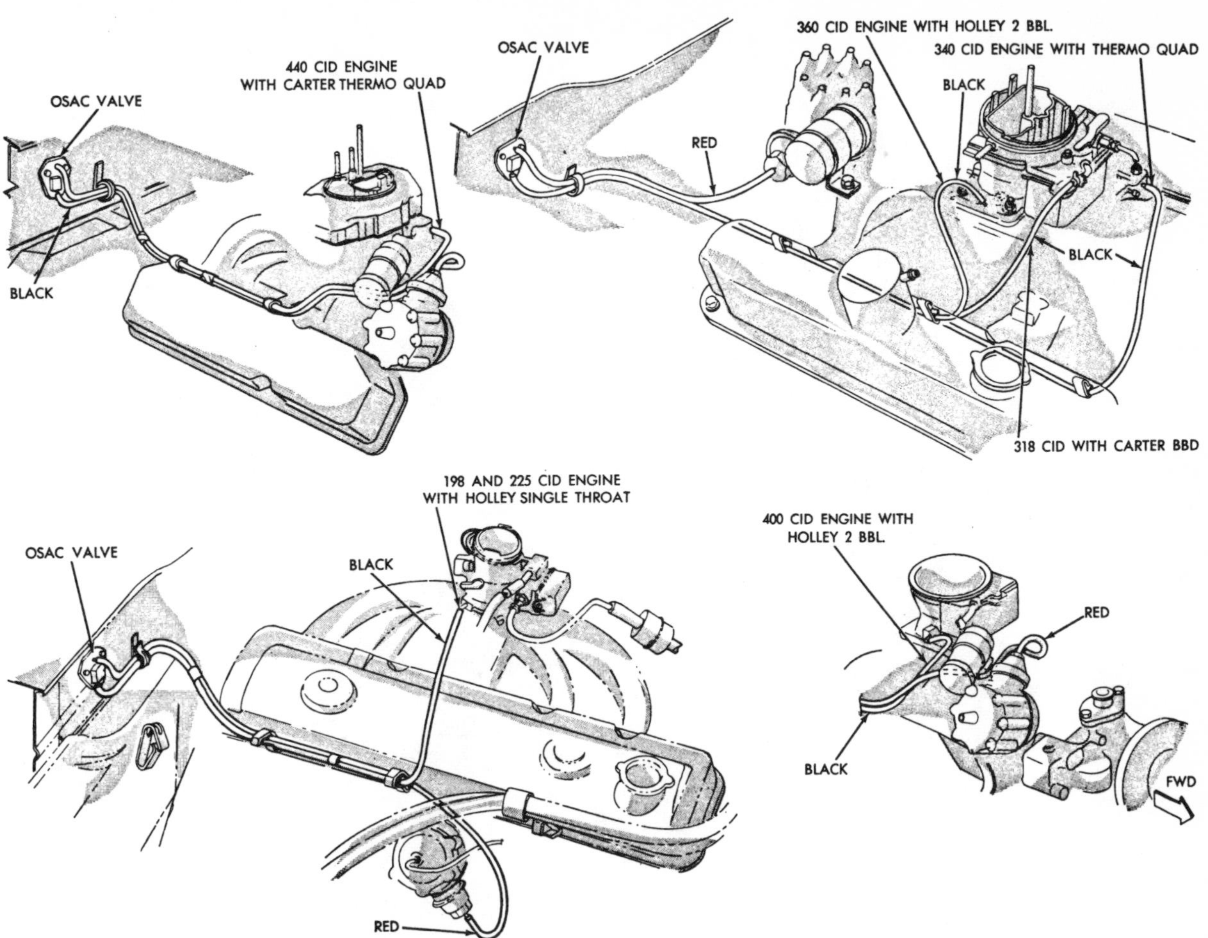

Fig. 29 OSAC valve vacuum hose routing. 1973 Chrysler

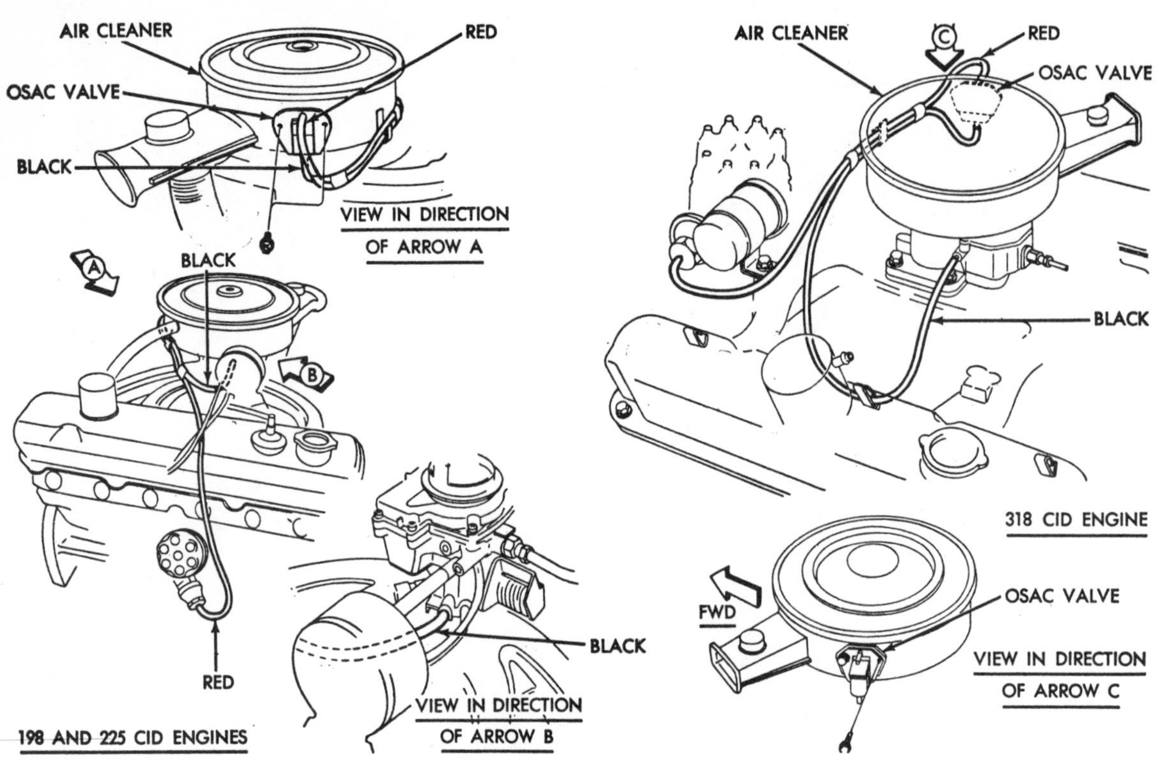

Fig. 30 *OSAC valve vacuum hose routing.* 1974 *Chrysler* 6-198, 225 *and* V8-318

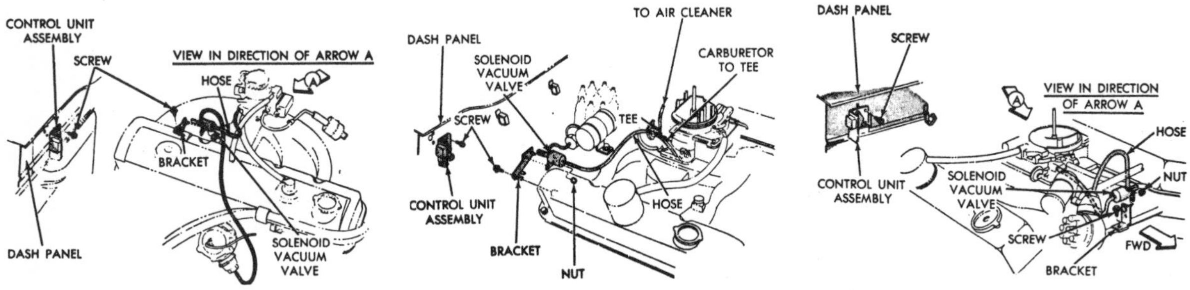

Fig. 31 *Solenoid vacuum hose routing.* 1971-72 *Chrysler six cylinder*

Fig. 32 *Solenoid vacuum hose routing.* 1971-72 *Chrysler* V8-318, 340, 360

Fig. 33 *Solenoid vacuum hose routing.* 1971-72 *Chrysler* V8-383, 400, 440

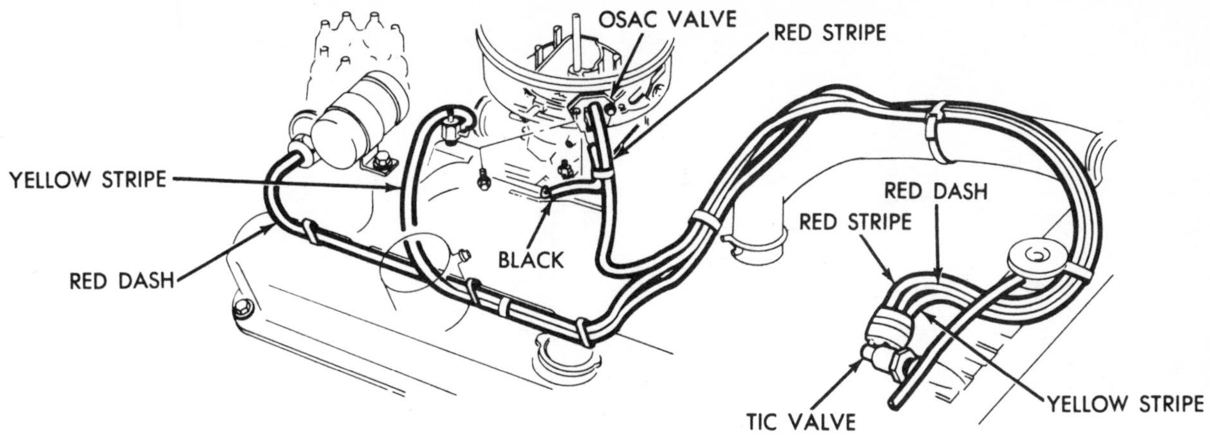

Fig. 34 Thermal Ignition Control (TIC) Valve Hose Routing. 1975 Chrysler Corp. V8-360 2-*bbl*

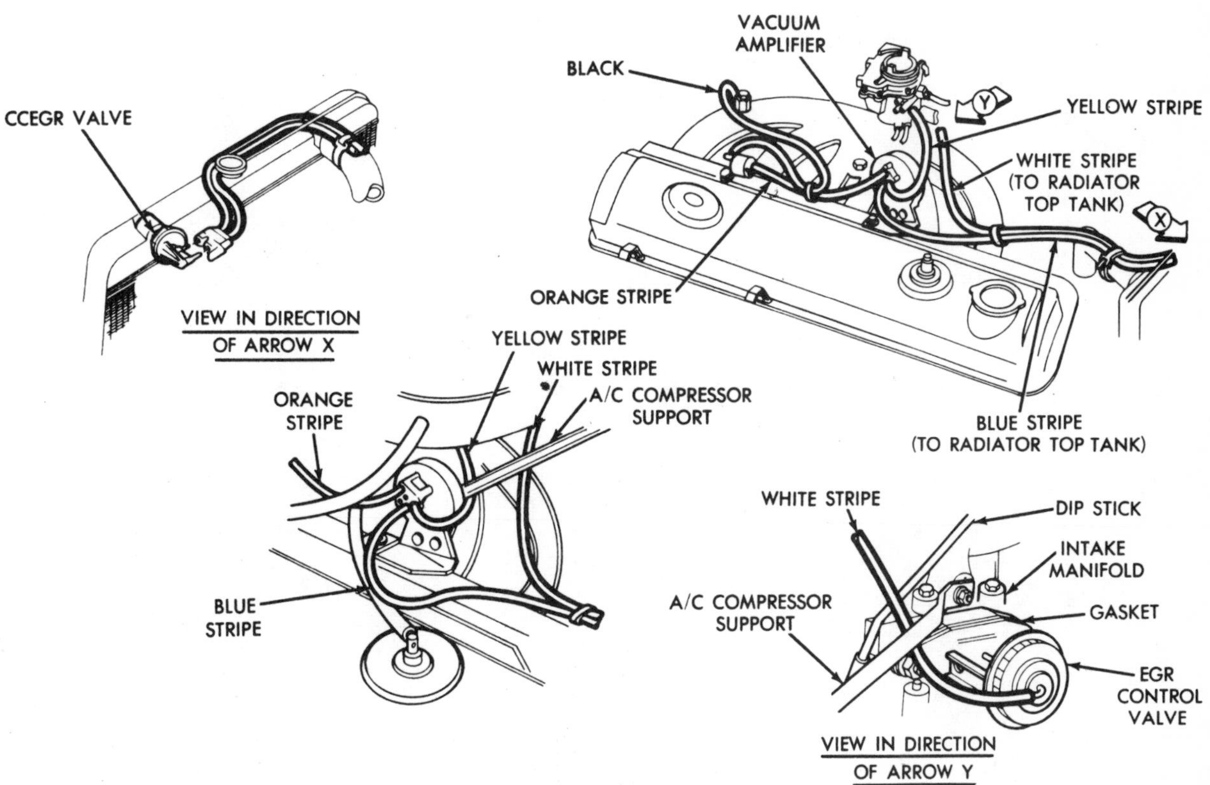

Fig. 35 EGR Vacuum Hose Routing. 1975 *Chrysler Corp.* 6-225 *with Manual Transmission*

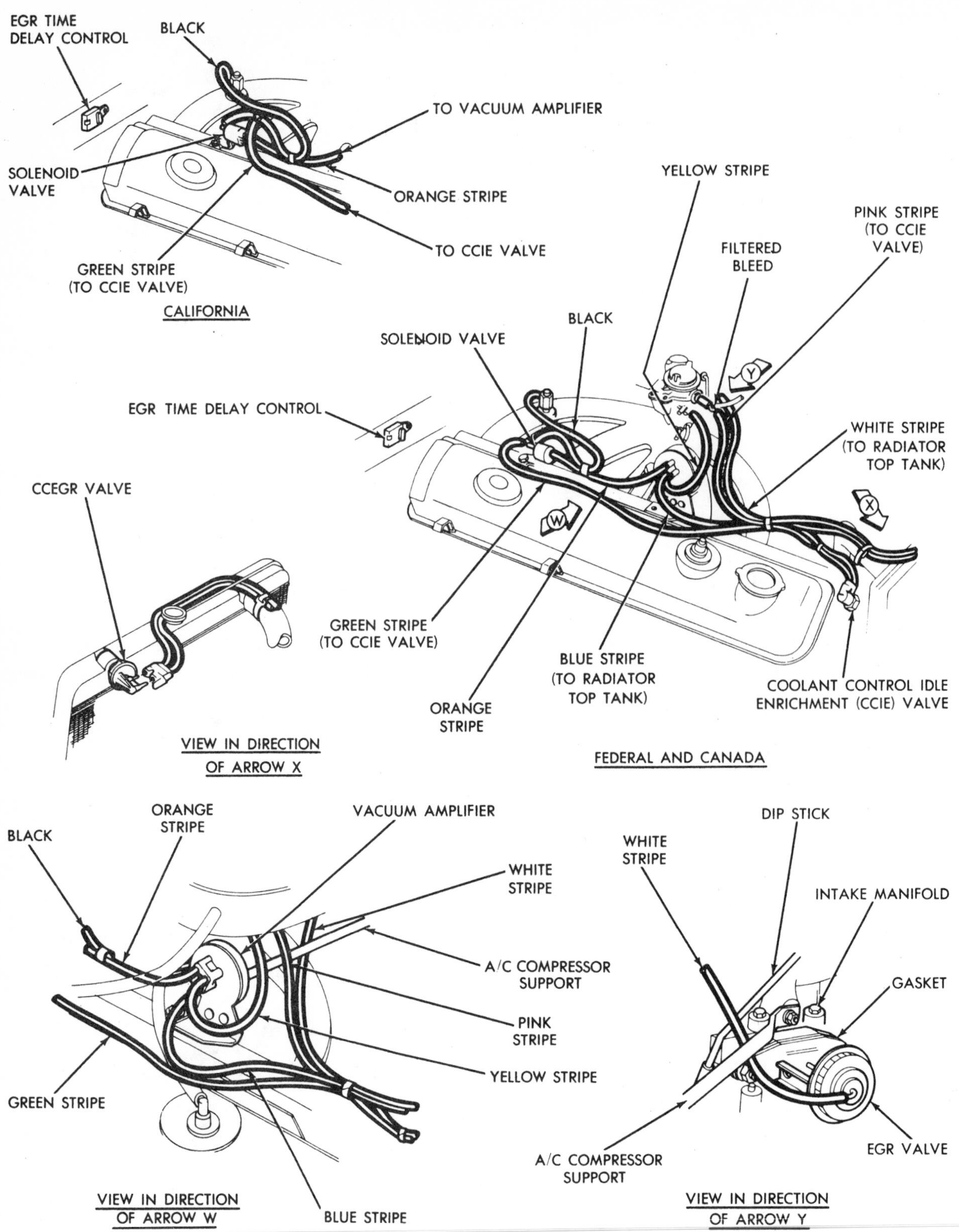

Fig. 36 EGR Vacuum Hose Routing for 225 CID Engine with Automatic Transmission

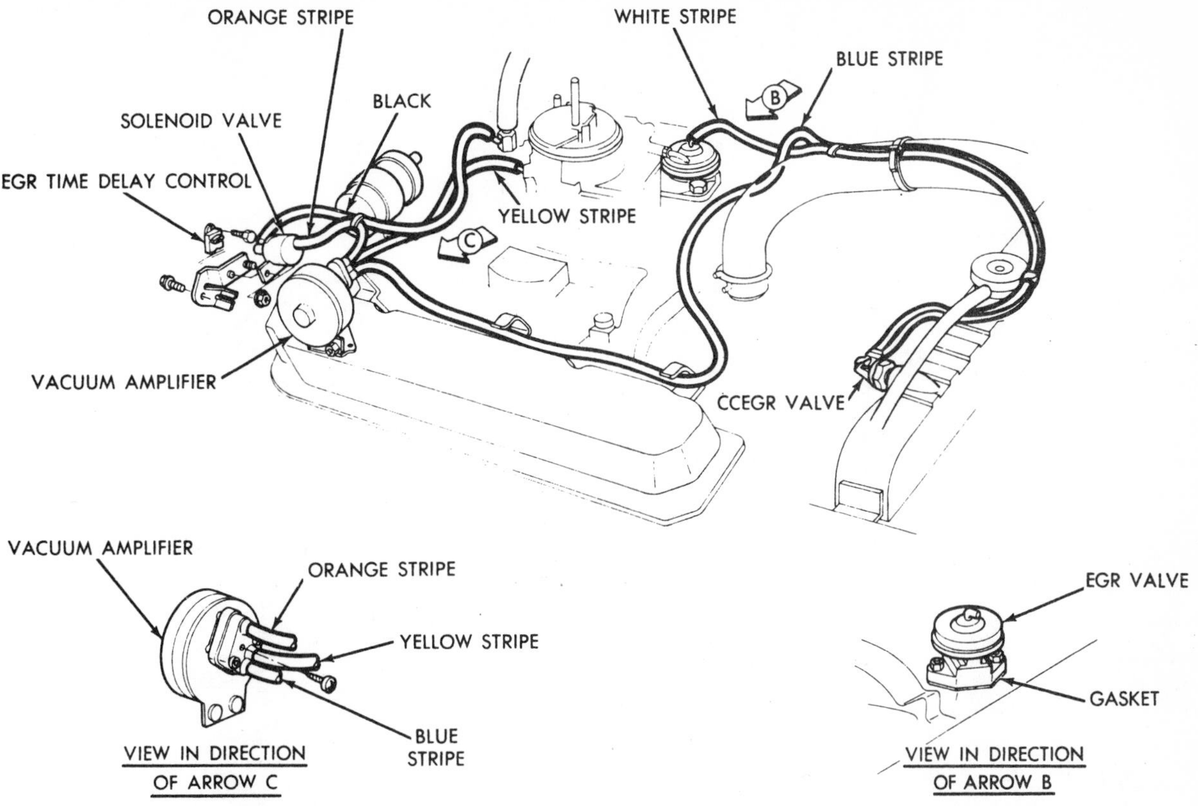

Fig. 37 EGR Vacuum Hose Routing for 318 *CID Engine with Manual Transmission (Federal and Canadian Requirement)*

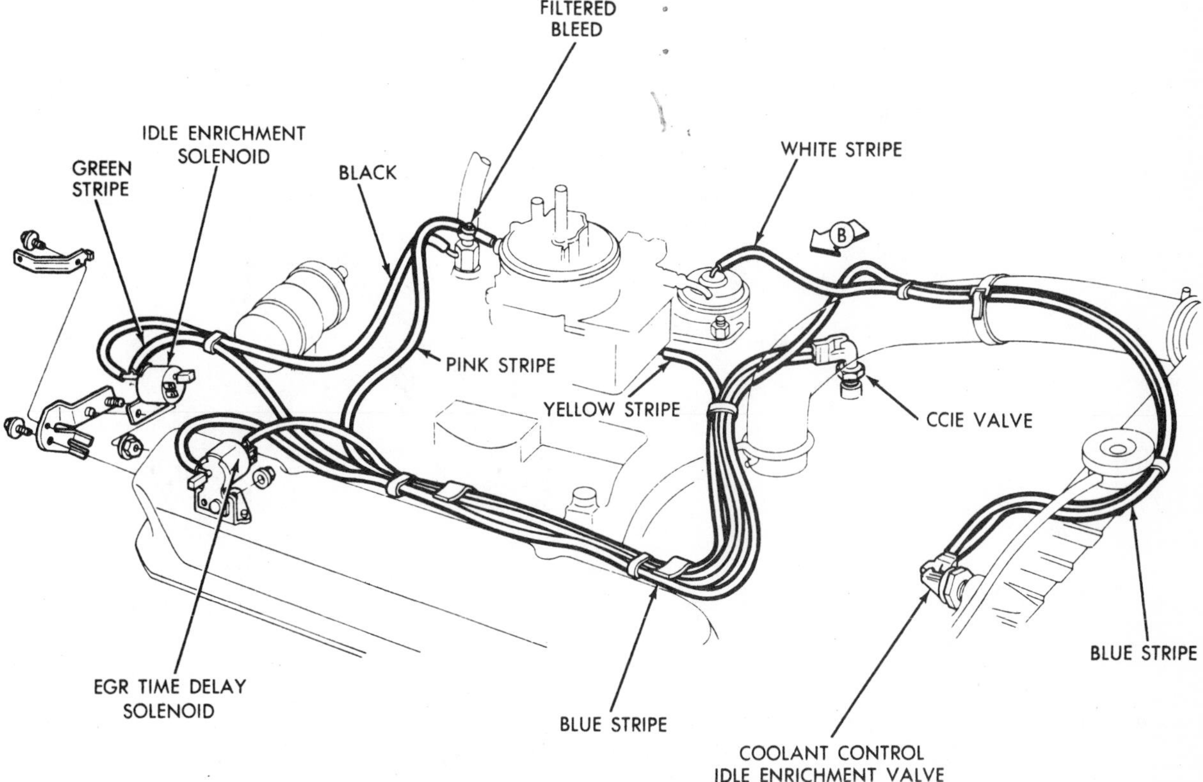

Fig. 38 *EGR Vacuum Hose Routing for* 318 *CID Engine with Automatic Transmission (Federal Requirement)*

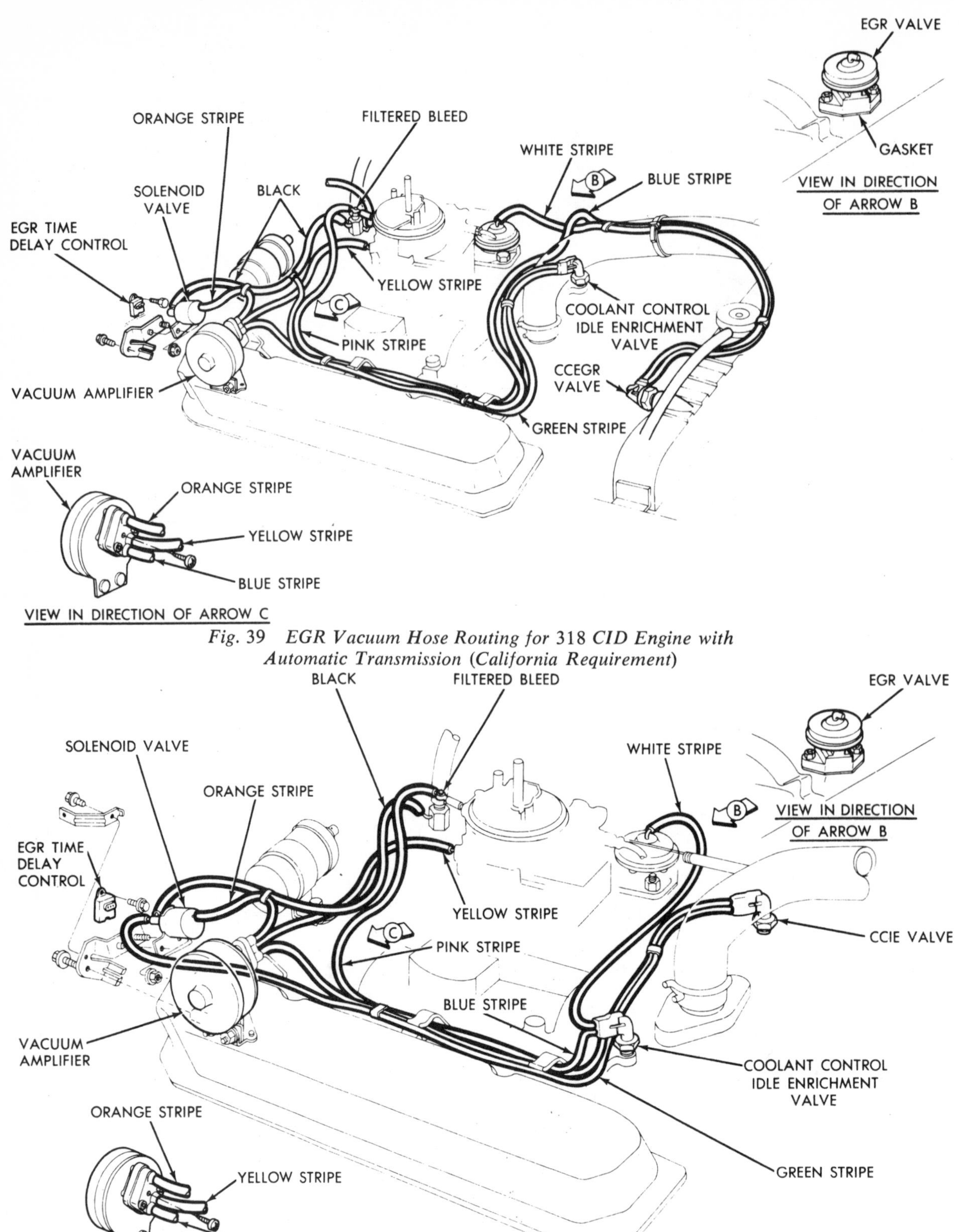

Fig. 39 EGR Vacuum Hose Routing for 318 CID Engine with Automatic Transmission (California Requirement)

Fig. 40 EGR Vacuum Hose Routing for 360 CID Engine with 2BBL Carburetor and Automatic Transmission (Federal and Canadian Requirement)

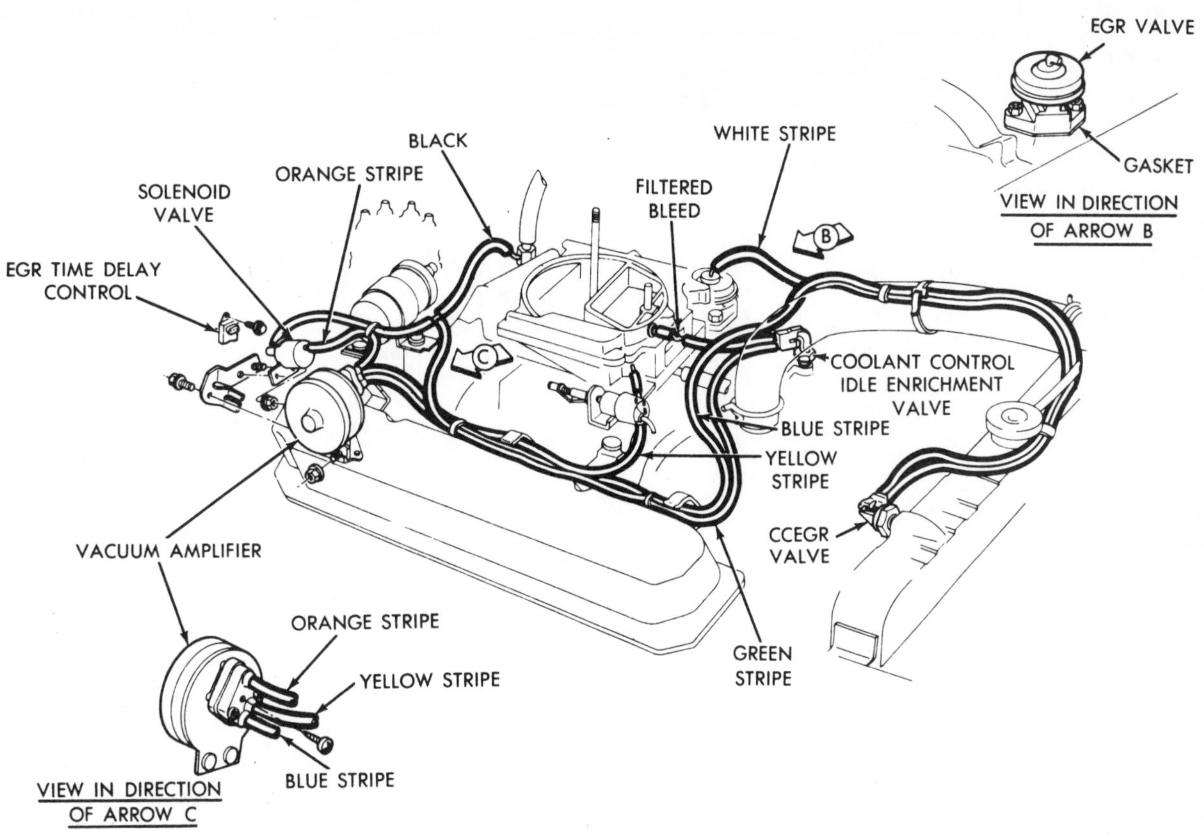

Fig. 41 EGR Vacuum Hose Routing for 360 *CID Engine with* 4*BBL Carburetor and Automatic Transmission (California Requirement)*

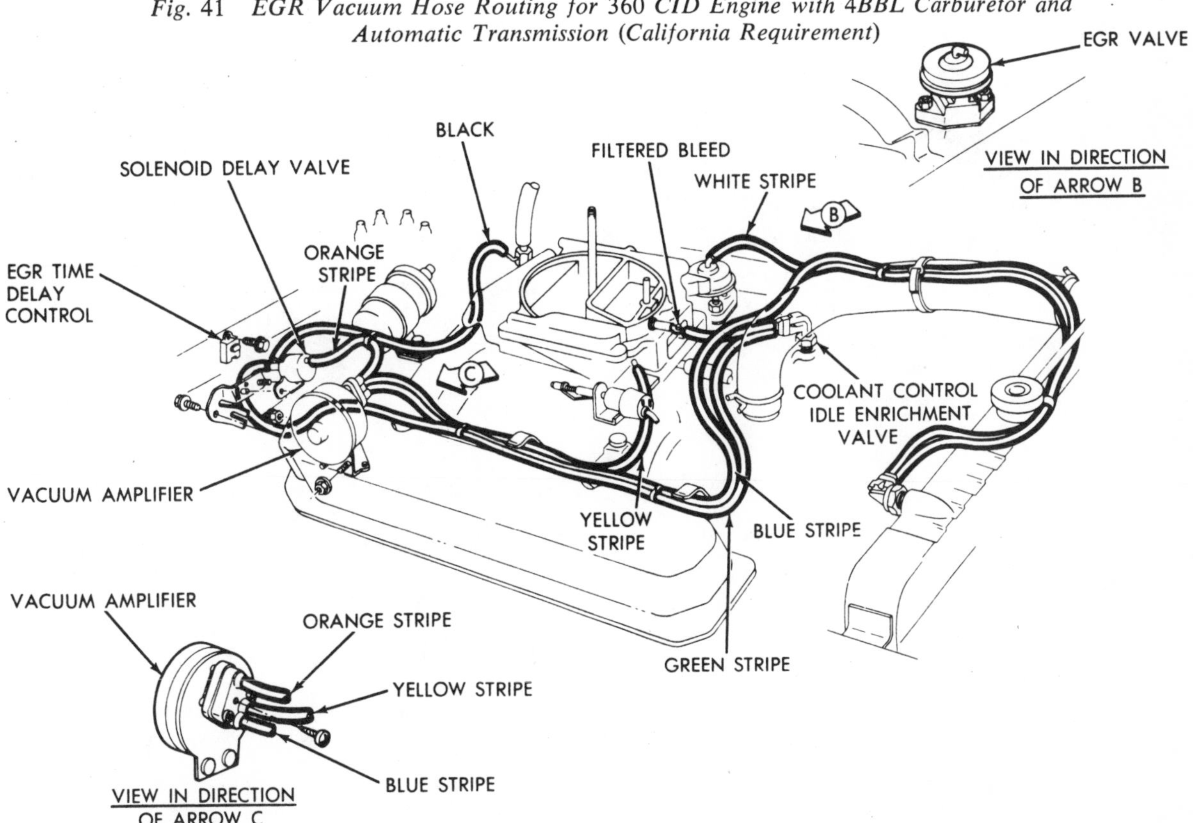

Fig. 42 EGR Vacuum Hose Routing for 360 *CID Hi Performance Engine (Federal and Canadian Requirement)*

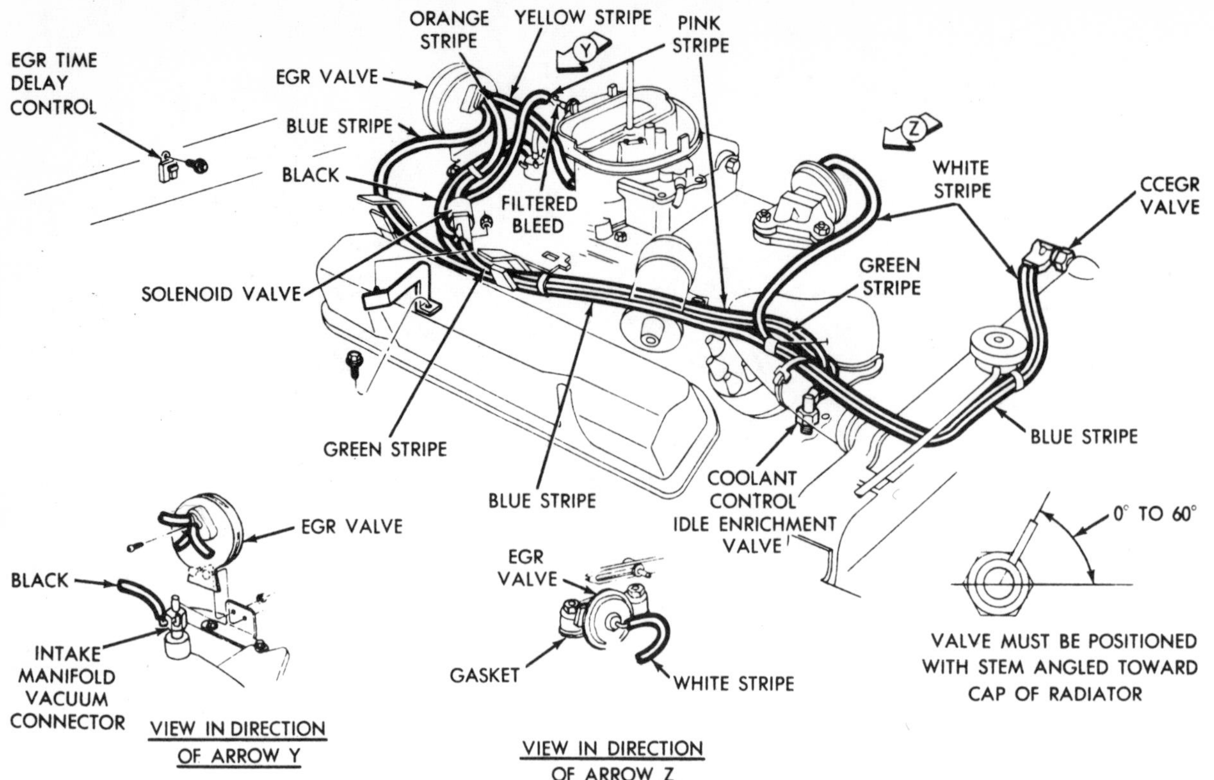

Fig. 43 EGR Vacuum Hose Routing for 400 CID Engine with 2BBL Carburetor (Federal Requirement)

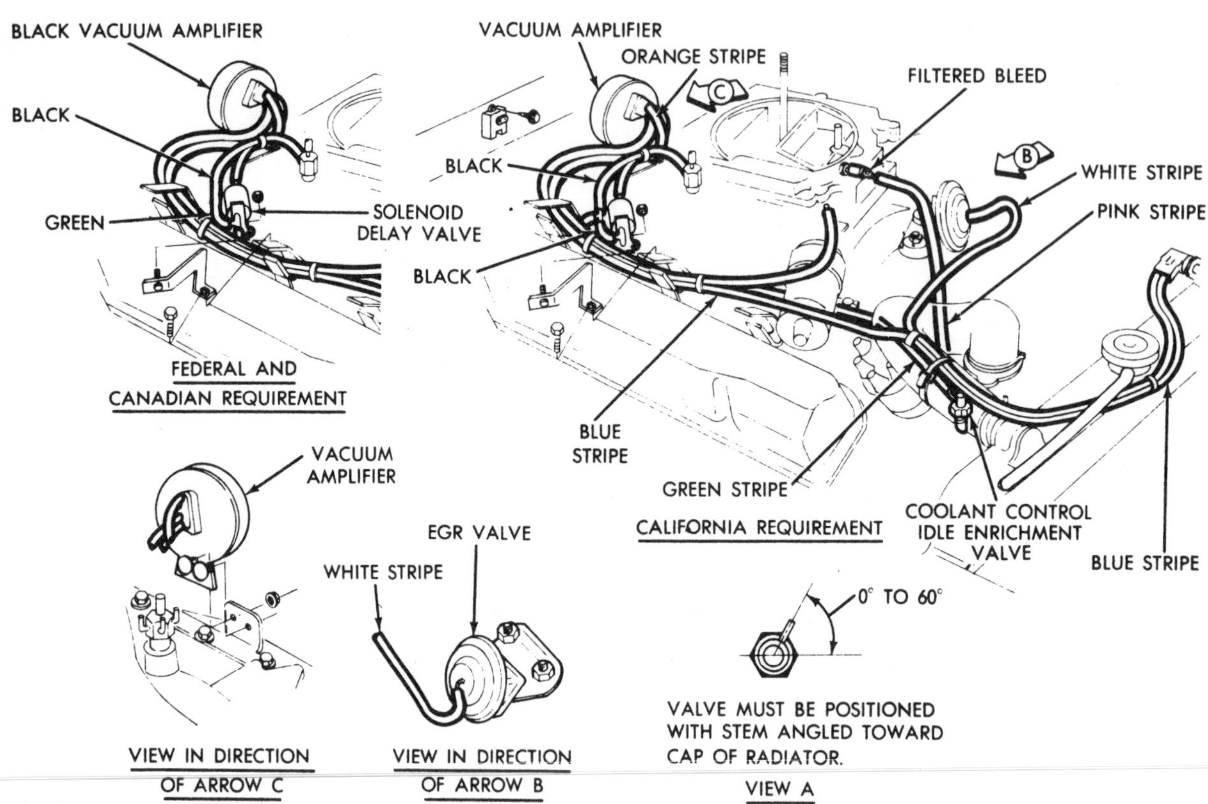

Fig. 44 EGR Vacuum Hose Routing for 400 and 440 CID Engines with 4 BBL Carburetor

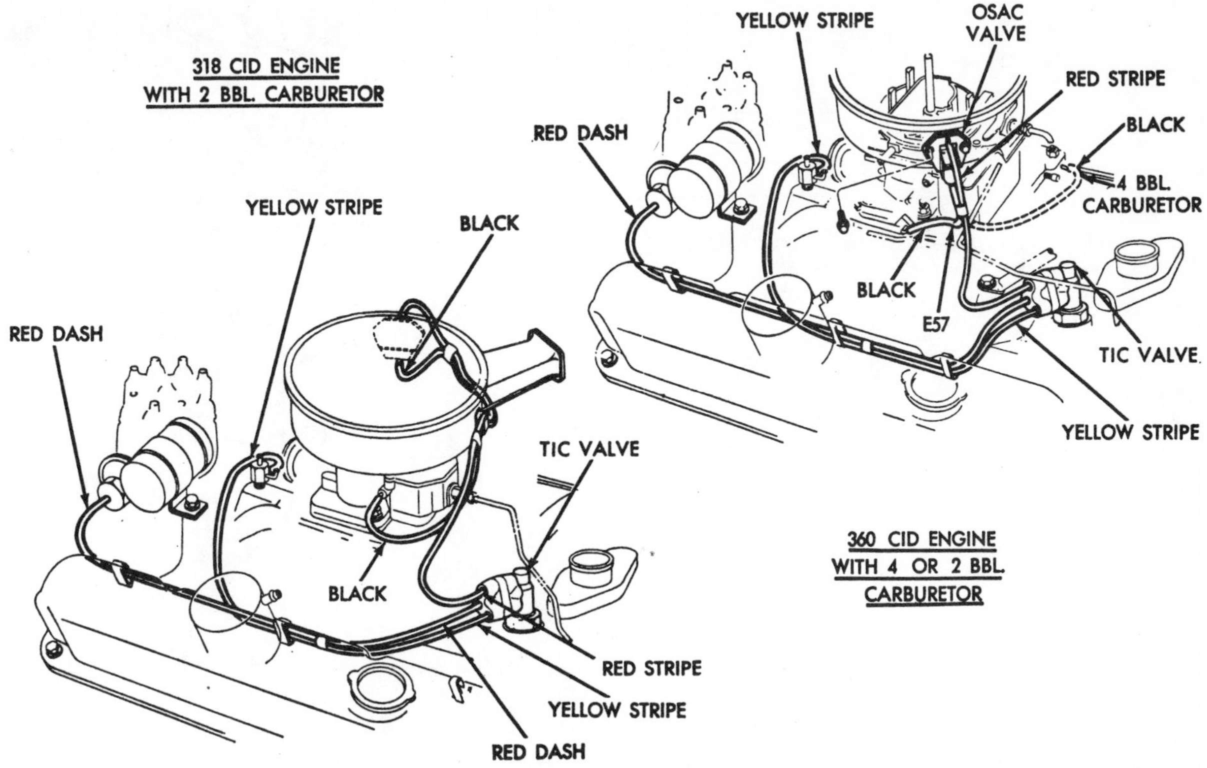

Fig. 45 *TIC valve vacuum hose routing.* 1974 *Chrysler* V8-318, 360

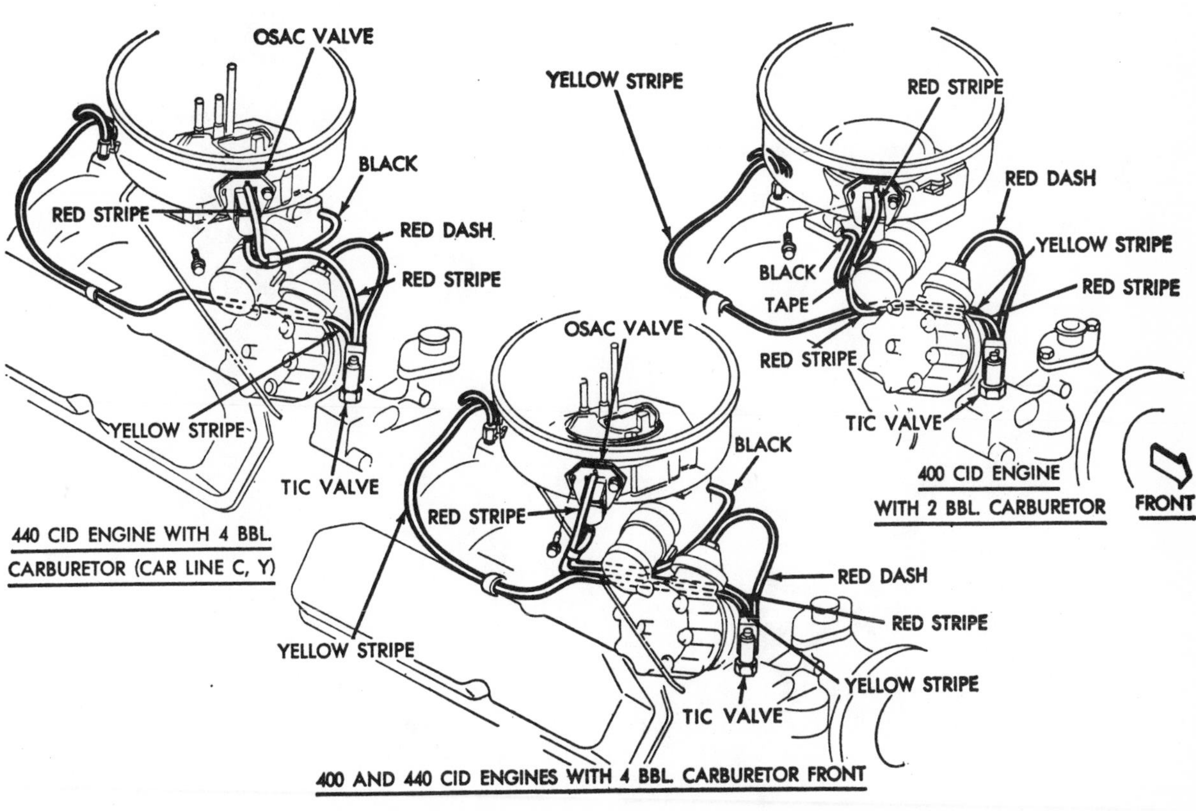

Fig. 46 *TIC valve vacuum hose routing.* 1974 *Chrysler* V8-400, 440

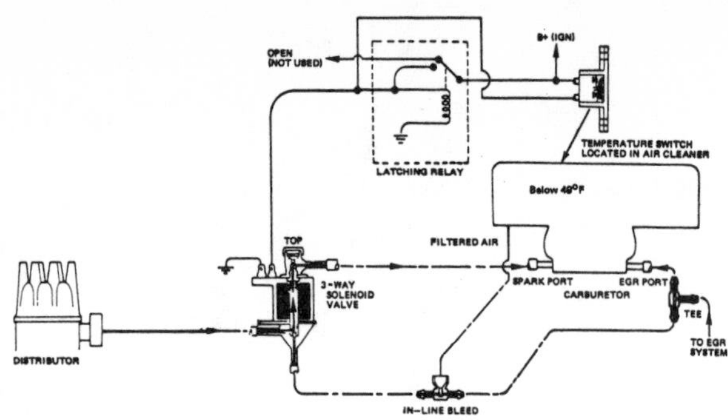

Fig. 47 CTAV system wiring. 1973-74 *Ford*

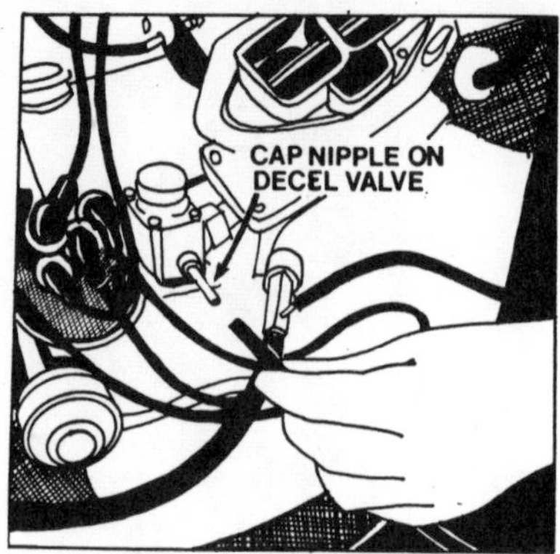

Fig. 48 Decel valve. Ford 2000*cc &* 2800*cc engines shown*

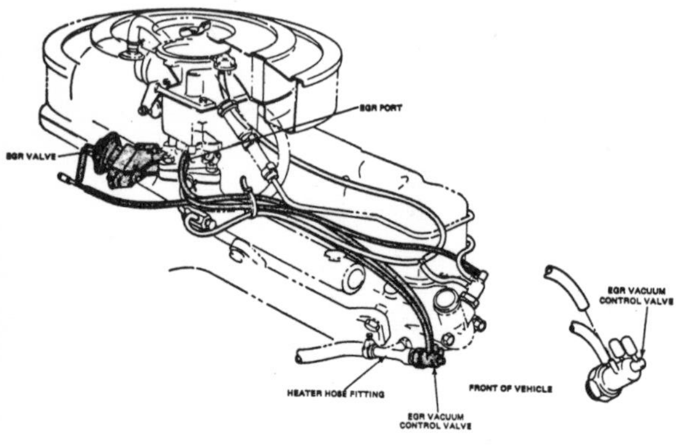

Fig. 49 *EGR system vacuum hose routing.* 1973 *Ford* 6-200

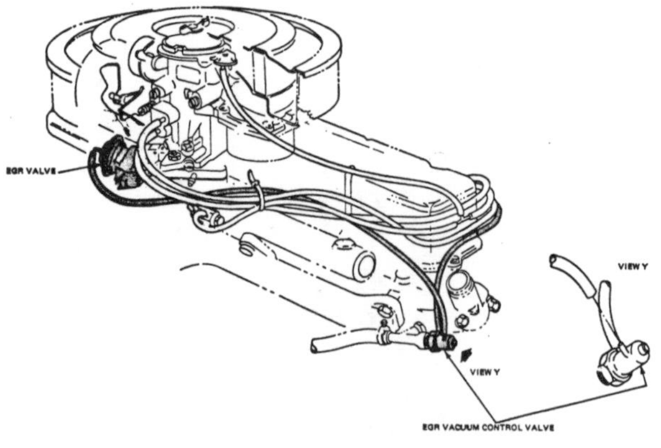

Fig. 50 *EGR system vacuum hose routing.* 1973 *Ford* 6-250 *with manual transmission*

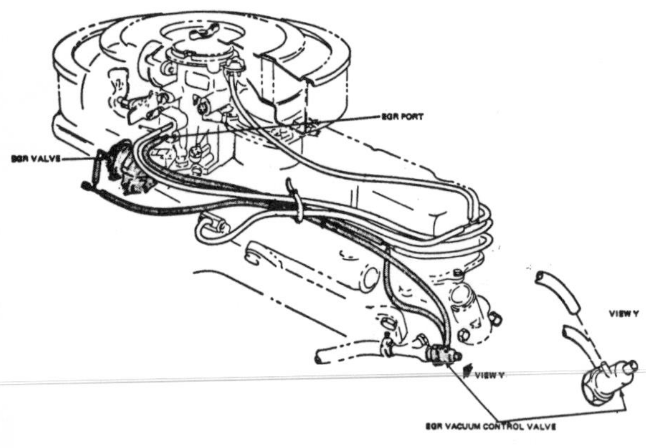

Fig. 51 *EGR system vacuum hose routing.* 1973 *Ford* 6-250 *with automatic transmission*

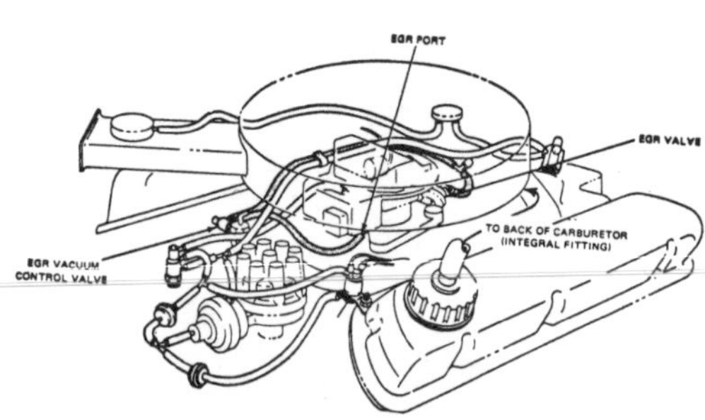

Fig. 52 *EGR system vacuum hose routing.* 1973 *Ford* V8-302

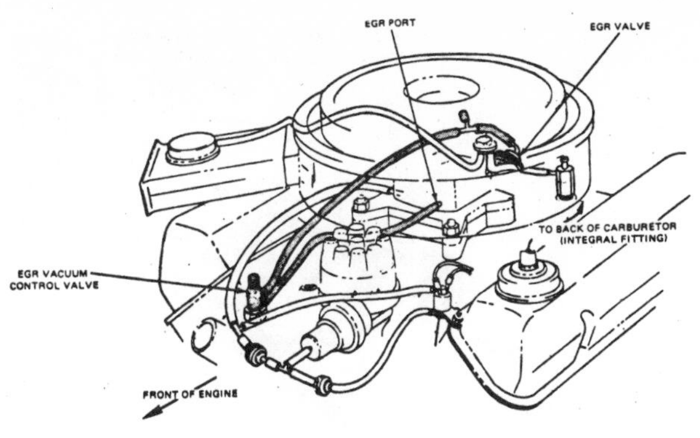

Fig. 53 EGR system vacuum hose routing. 1973 Ford V8-351W

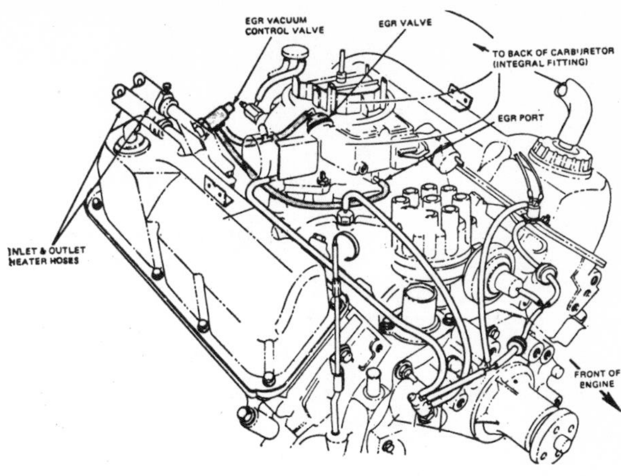

Fig. 54 EGR system vacuum hose routing. 1973 Ford V8-351C with air conditioning

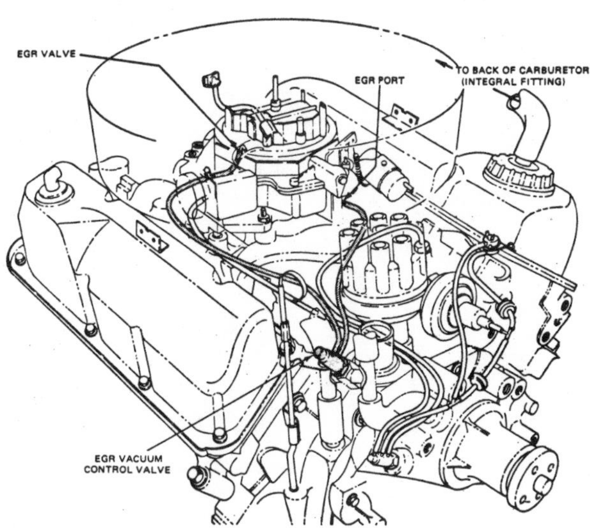

Fig. 55 EGR system vacuum hose routing. 1973 Ford V8-351C, 400 and V8-351 CJ with air conditioning

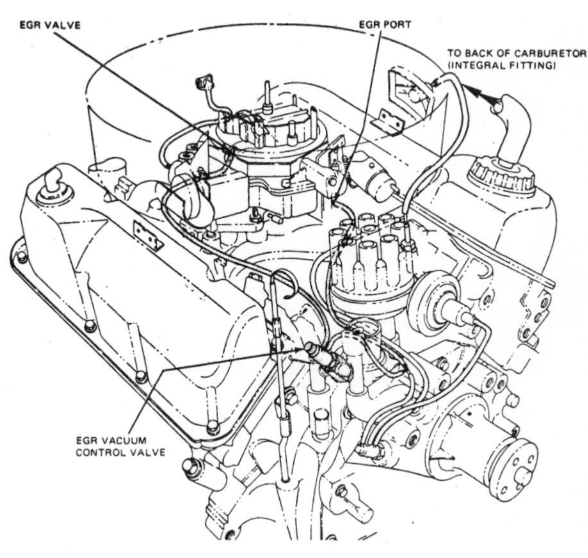

Fig. 56 EGR system vacuum hose routing. 1973 V8-351C, 400 without air conditioning

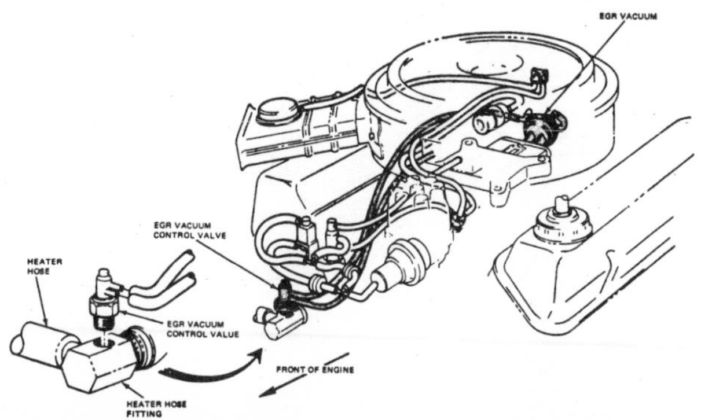

← *Fig. 57 EGR system vacuum hose routing. 1973 V8-429, 460*

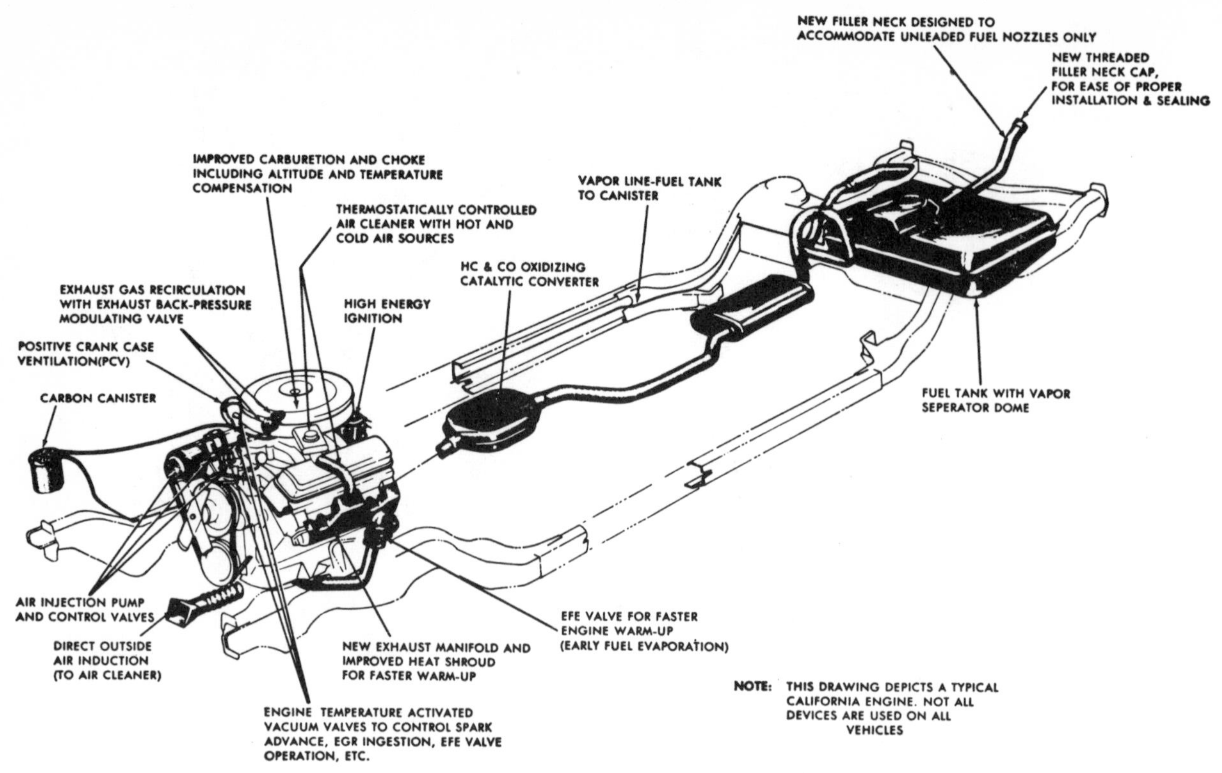

Fig. 58 Emission Control System. 1975 General Motors (typical)

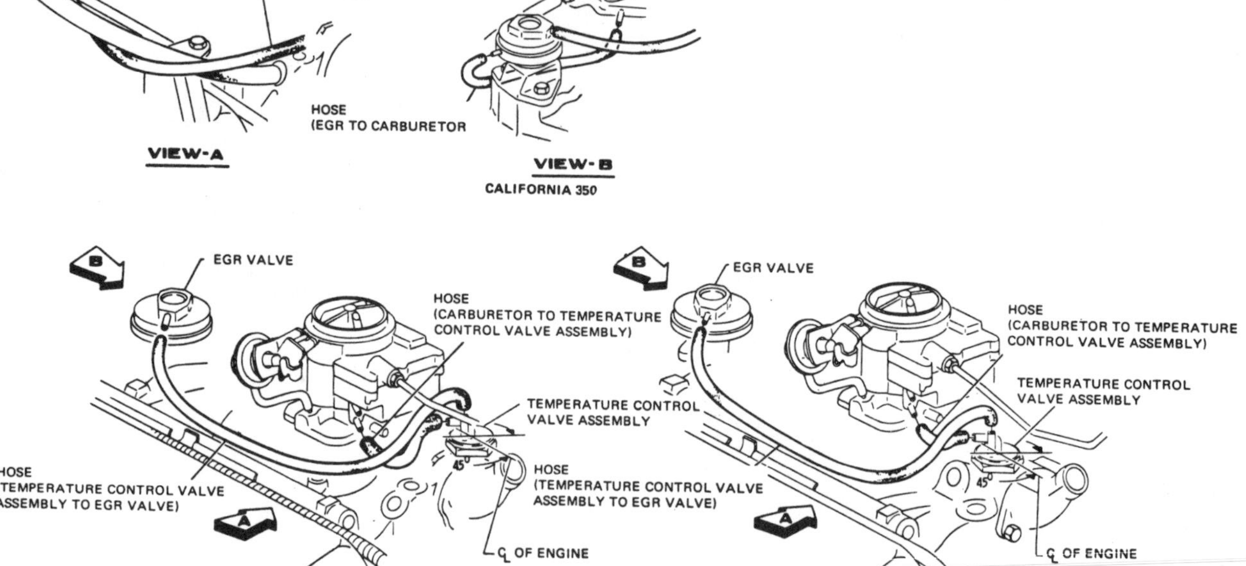

Fig. 59 EGR system vacuum hose routing. 1973-74 Buick 2 barrel carburetors

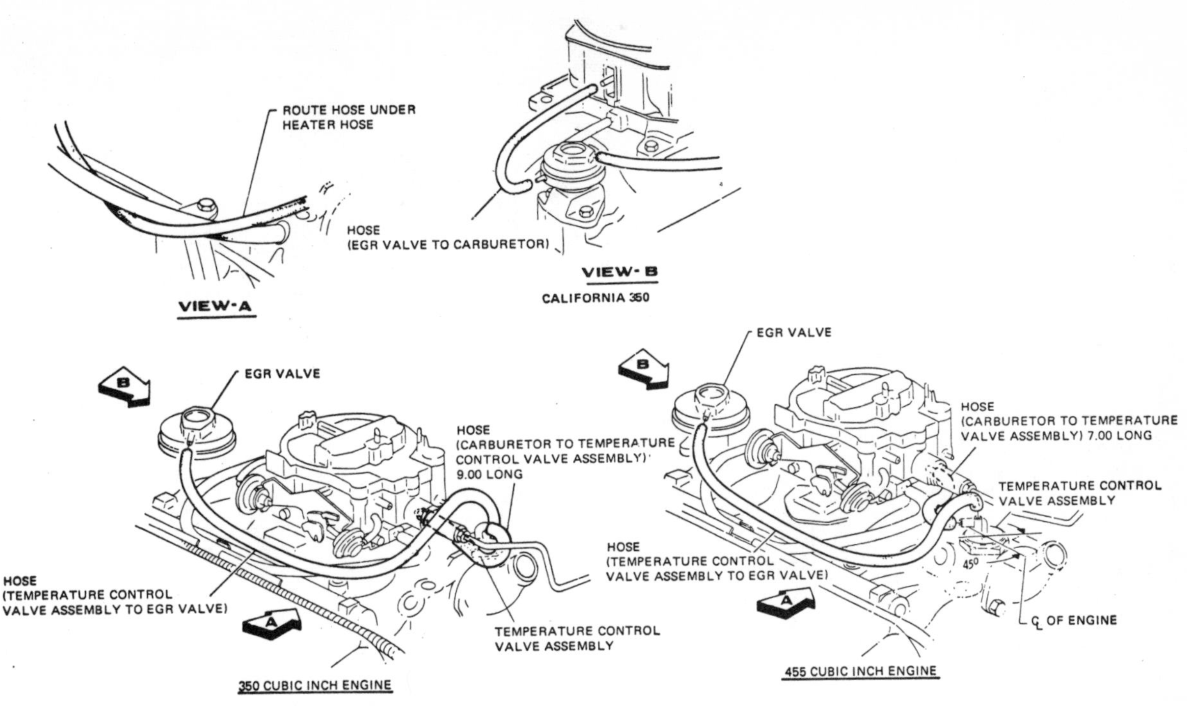

Fig. 60 EGR system vacuum hose routing. 1973-74 *Buick* 4 *barrel carburetors*

Fig. 62 EGR valve mounting. 1973-74 *Chevrolet Vega*

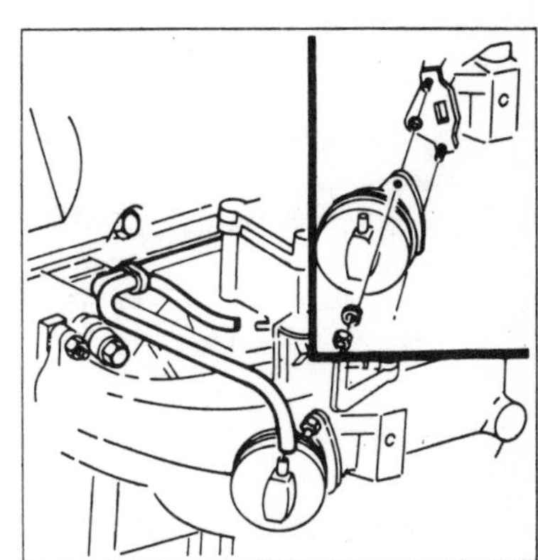

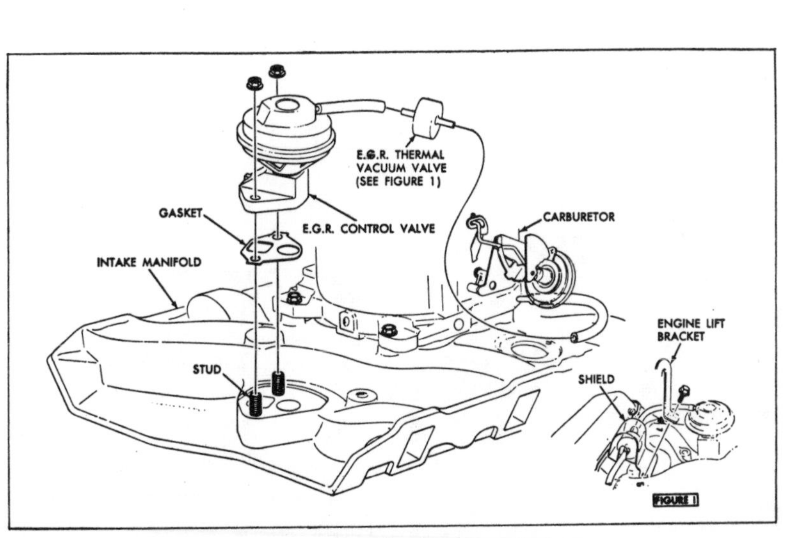

Fig. 61 EGR valve mounting. 1973-74 *Cadillac*

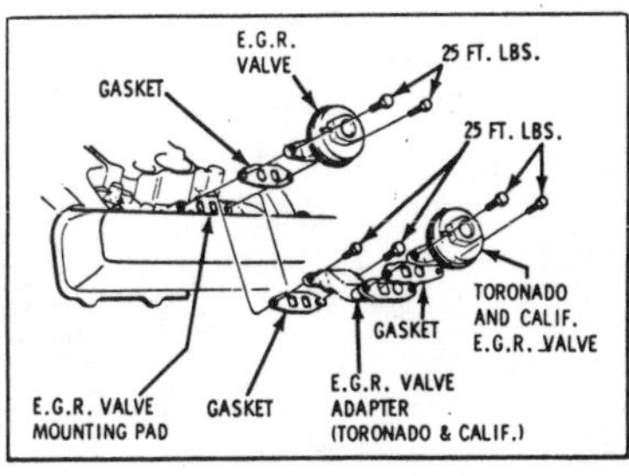

Fig. 63 EGR valve mounting. 1973-74 *Oldsmobile*

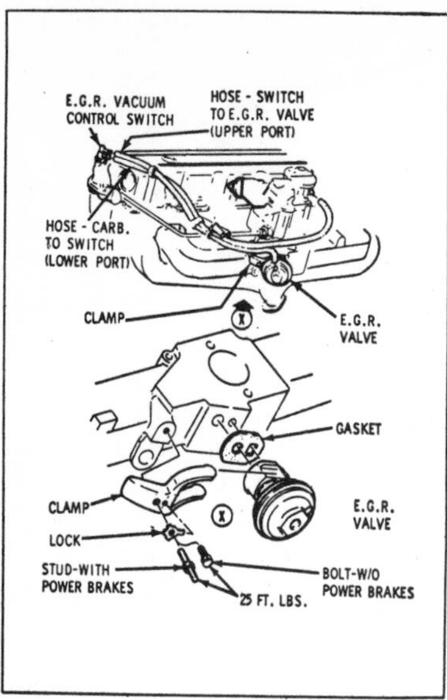

Fig. 64 EGR valve mounting General Motors 6 cylinder (typical).

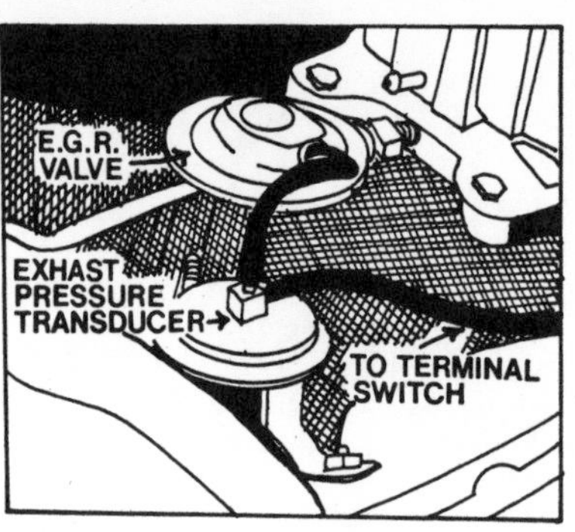

Fig. 65 Exhaust back pressure transducer valve. 1974 Cadillac

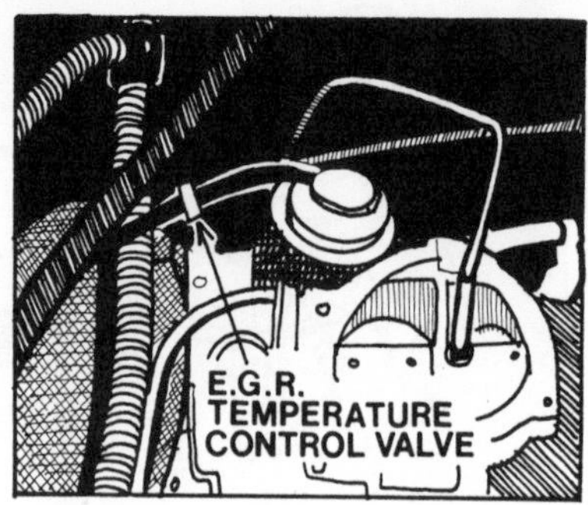

Fig. 66 EGR temperature control valve. 1973-74 Buick

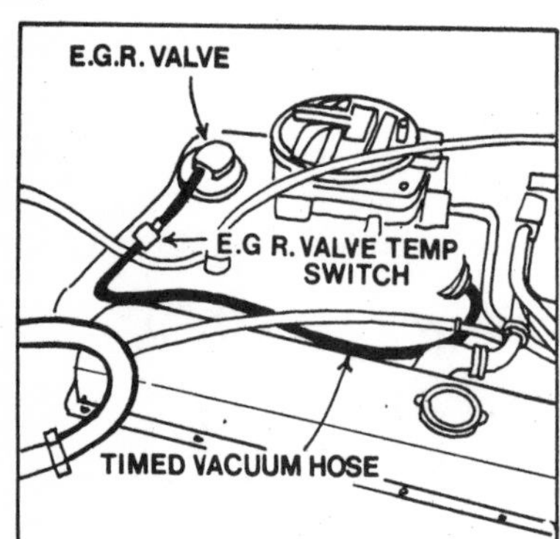

Fig. 67 EGR temperature control switch. 1973-74 Cadillac

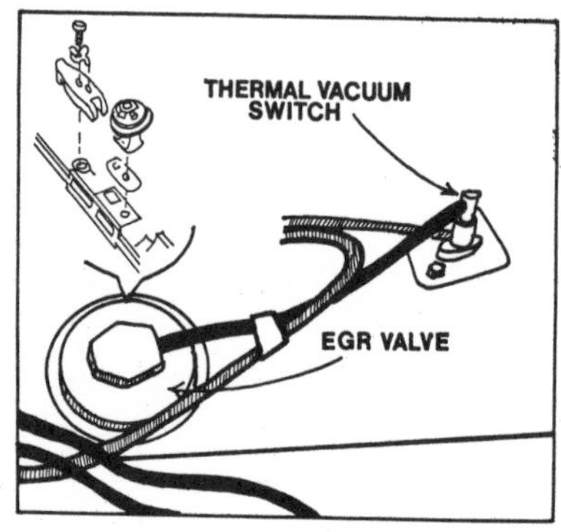

Fig. 68 EGR & TVS location. 1973-74 Chevrolet small V8 engines

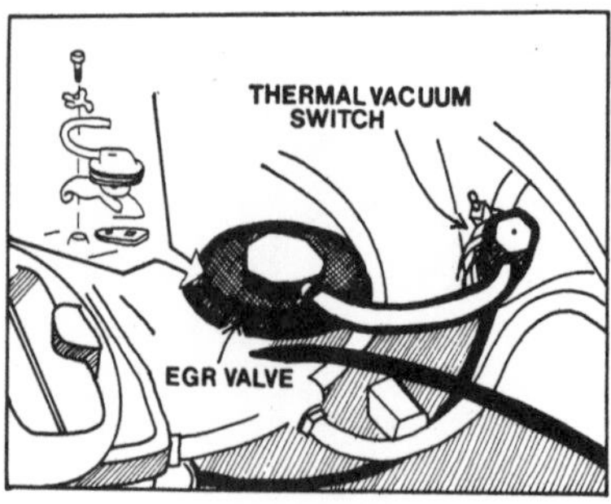

Fig. 69 EGR & TVS location. 1973-74 Chevrolet large V8 engines

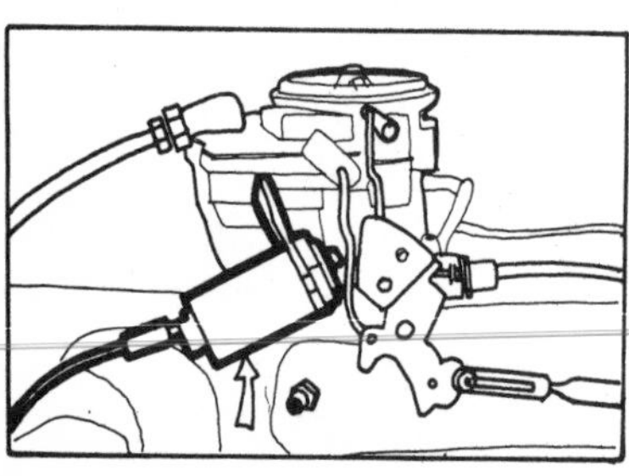

Fig. 70 Idle stop solenoid. General Motors (typical)

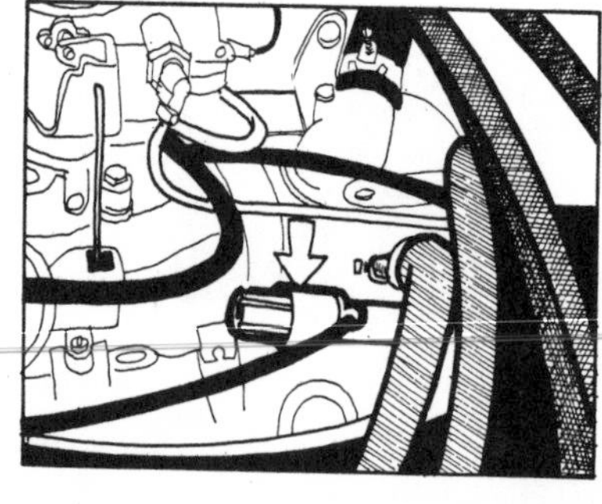

Fig. 71 Vacuum advance solenoid. 1972-74 Chevrolet small V8

Fig. 72 Vacuum advance solenoid. 1972-74 Chevrolet large V8

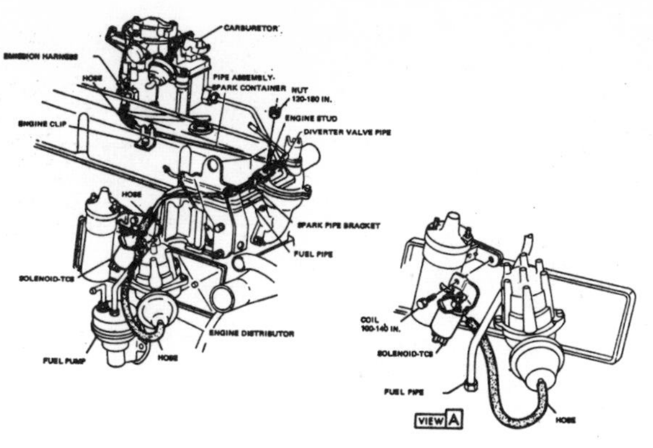

Fig. 73 TCS vacuum hose routing. General Motors 6 cylinder (typical)

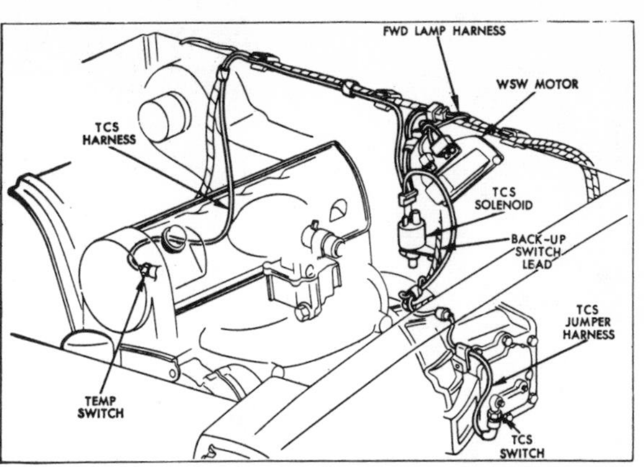

Fig. 75 TCS wiring. 1973-74 Chevrolet Vega

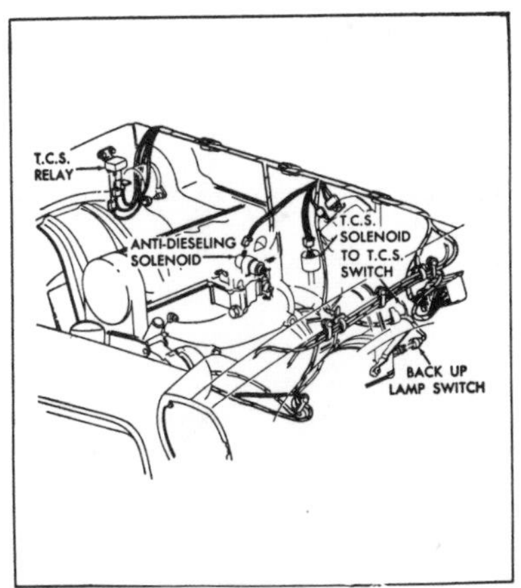

Fig. 74 TCS wiring. 1971-72 Chevrolet Vega

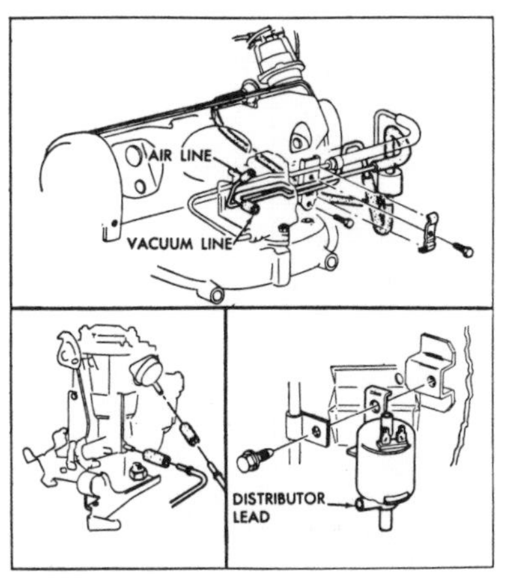

Fig. 76 TCS vacuum hose routing. 1971-72 Chevrolet Vega

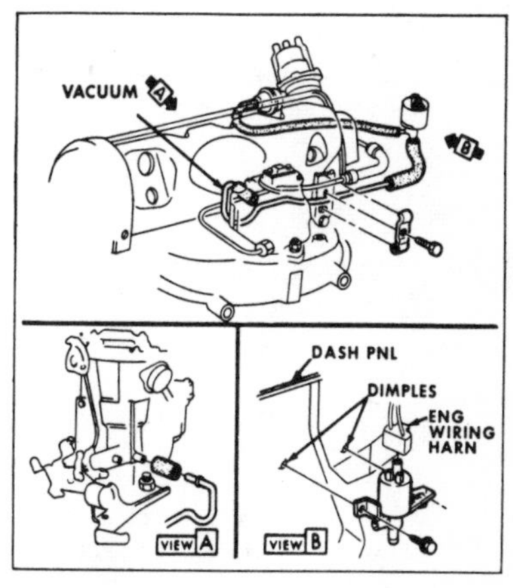

Fig. 77 TCS vacuum hose routing. 1973-74 Chevrolet Vega

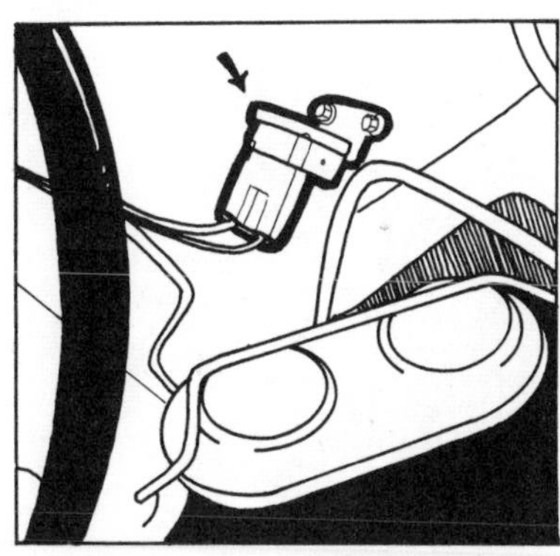

Fig. 78 TCS location. 1971-74 Chevrolet Vega

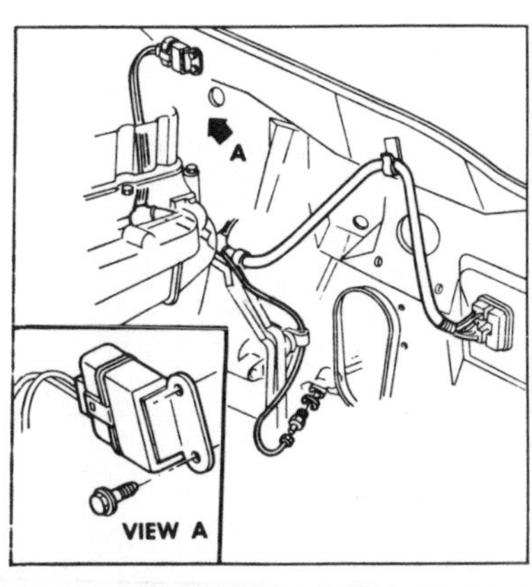

Fig. 79 TCS time relay location. 1971-74 Chevrolet (typical)

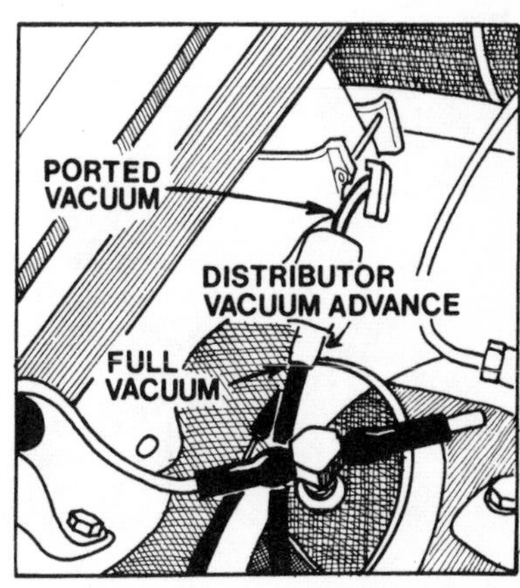

Fig. 80 Thermo Override Switch. 1973-74 Chevrolet Corvette

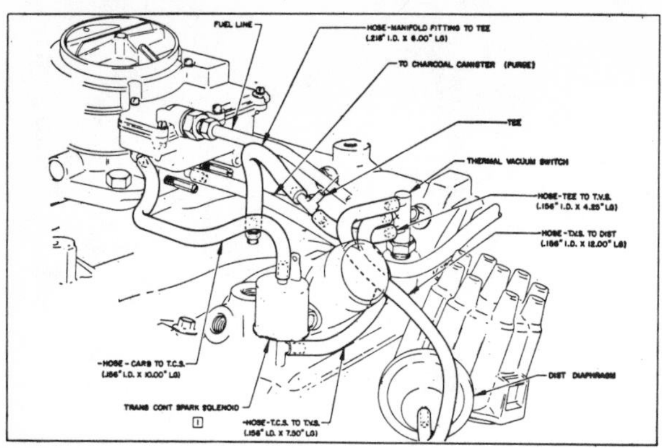

Fig. 81 *Vacuum hose routing.* 1971 *Buick Le Sabre* V8-350 2 *bar. carb. with A/C or HD cooling system*

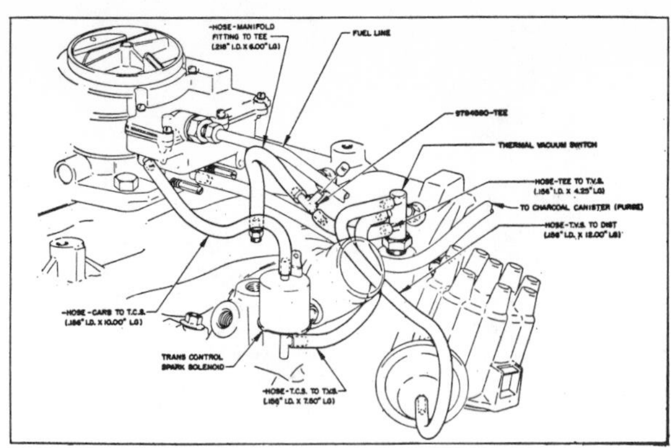

Fig. 82 *Vacuum hose routing.* 1971 *Buick Skylark* V8-350 2 *bar. carb. with HD cooling system*

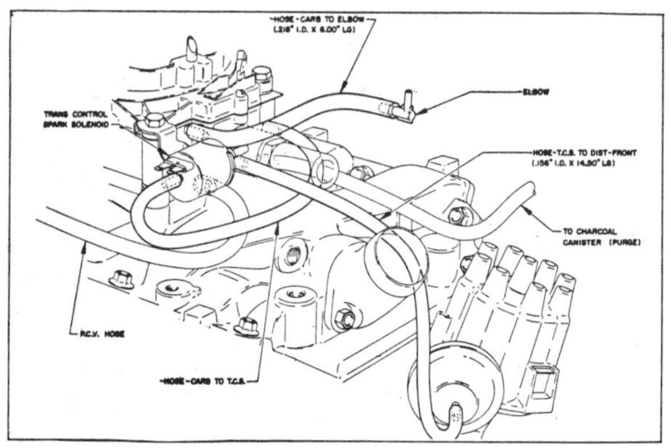

Fig. 83 *Vacuum hose routing.* 1971 *Buick Skylark* V8-350 4 *bar. carb. except HD cooling system or A/C*

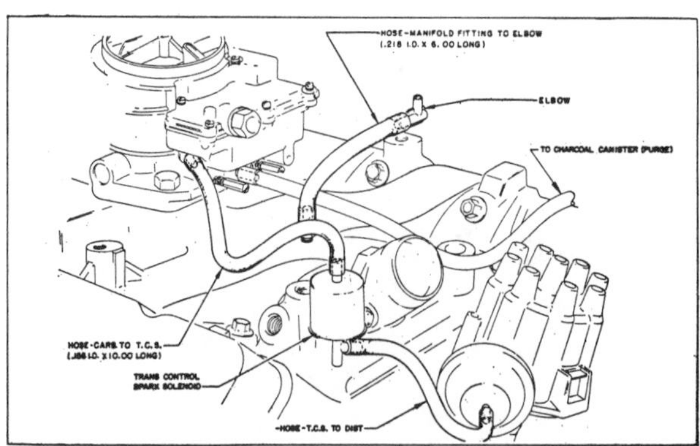

Fig. 84 *Vacuum hose houting.* 1971 *Buick Le Sabre* V8-350 2 *bar. carb. except A/C or HD cooling system and Skylark* V8-350 2 *bar. carb. except HD cooling system*

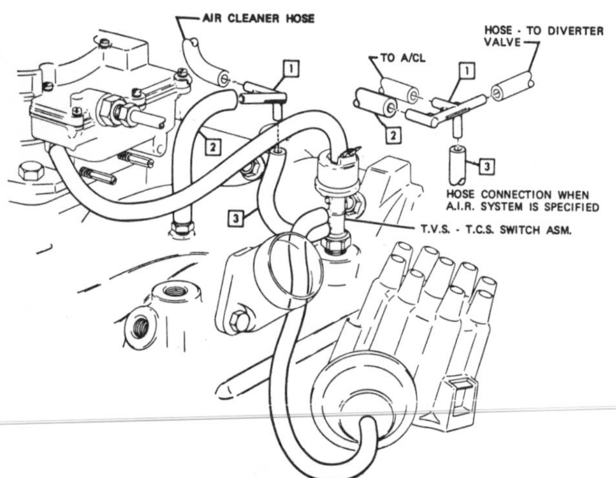

Fig. 85 *Vacuum hose routing.* 1972 *Buick* V8-350 2 *bar. carb. with A/C*

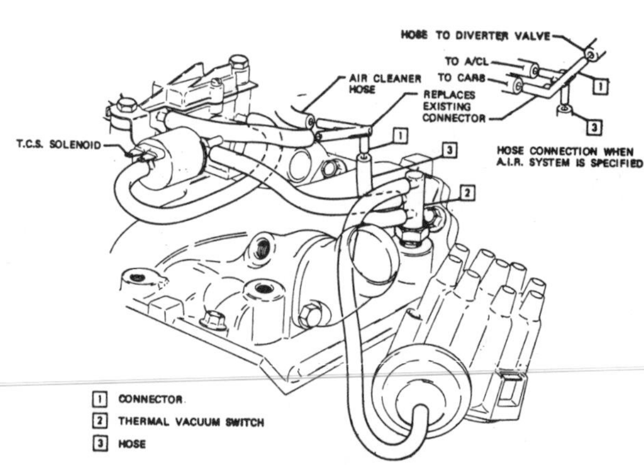

Fig. 86 *Vacuum hose routing.* 1972 *Buick* V8-350 4 *bar. carb. with HD cooling system* except *A/C*

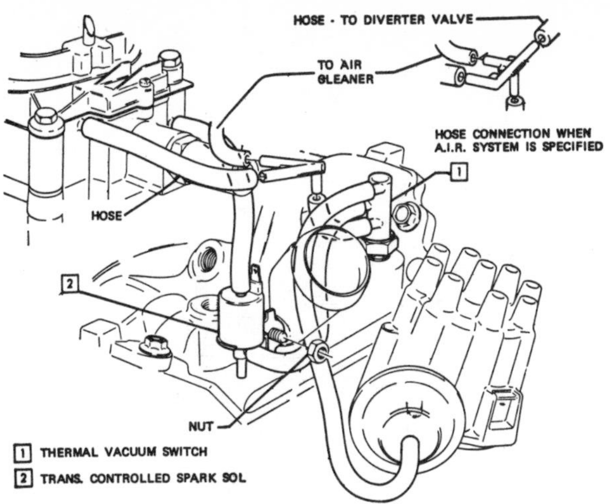

Fig. 87 *Vacuum hose routing.* 1972 *Buick* V8-350 *4 bar. carb. with A/C*

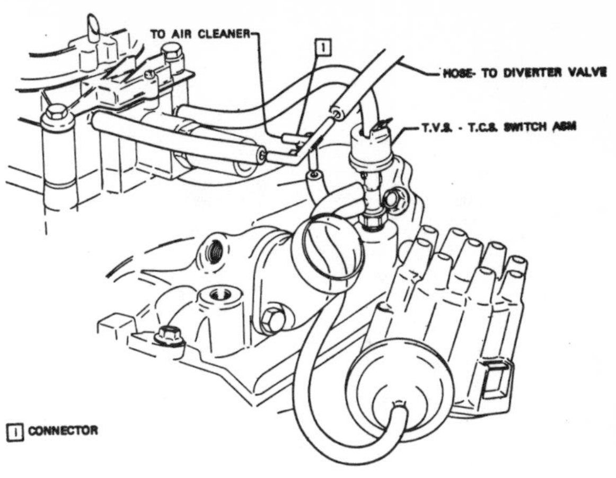

Fig. 88 *Vacuum hose routing.* 1972 *Buick Centurion, Electra, Estate Wagon, Le Sabre and Riviera* V8-455 *with A/C*

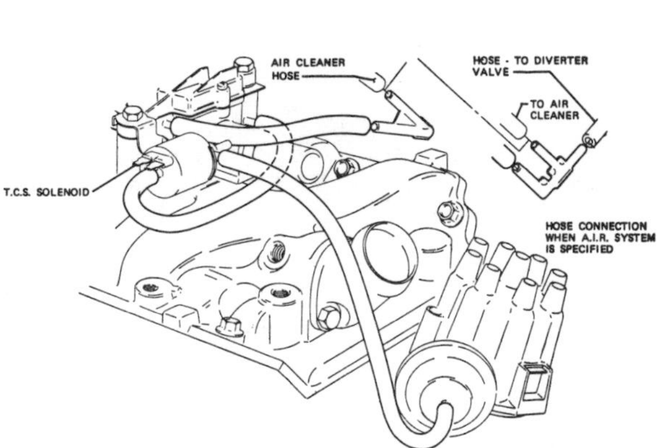

Fig. 89 *Vacuum hose routing.* 1972 *Buick Le Sabre and Skylark except A/C and HD cooling system*

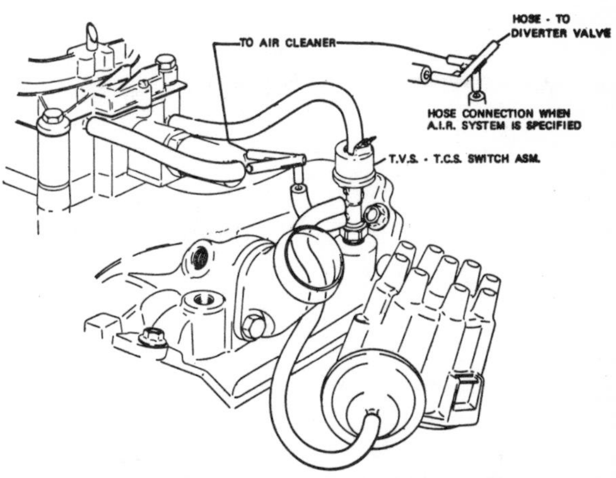

Fig. 90 *Vacuum hose routing.* 1972 *Buick Le Sabre & Skylark* V8-350 4 *bar. carb. with A/C*

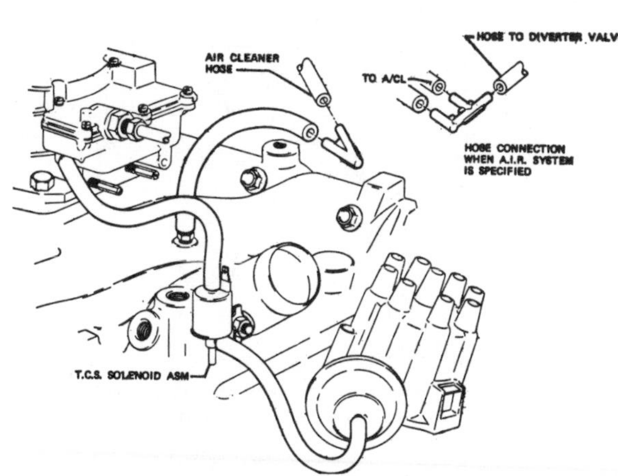

Fig. 91 *Vacuum hose routing.* 1972 *Buick* V8-350 *2 bar. carb. except A/C or HD cooling system*

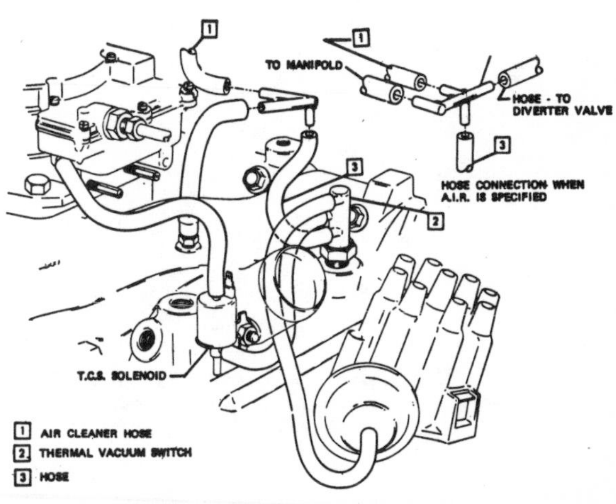

Fig. 92 *Vacuum hose routing.* 1972 *Buick* V8-350 *2 bar. carb. with HD cooling system except A/C*

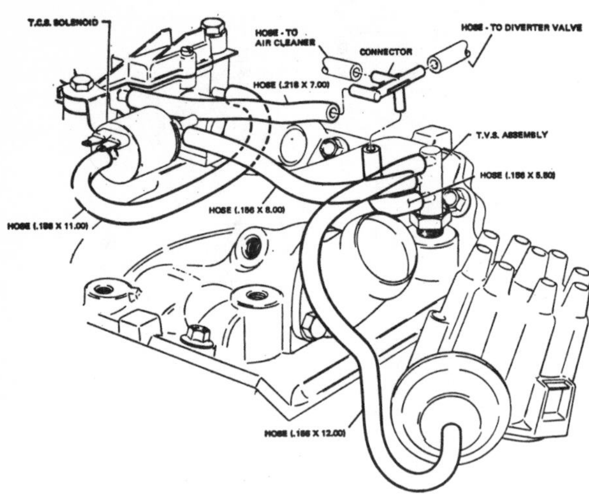

Fig. 93 *Vacuum hose routing.* 1973 *Buick* V8-455 *Stage* 1 *with automatic transmission*

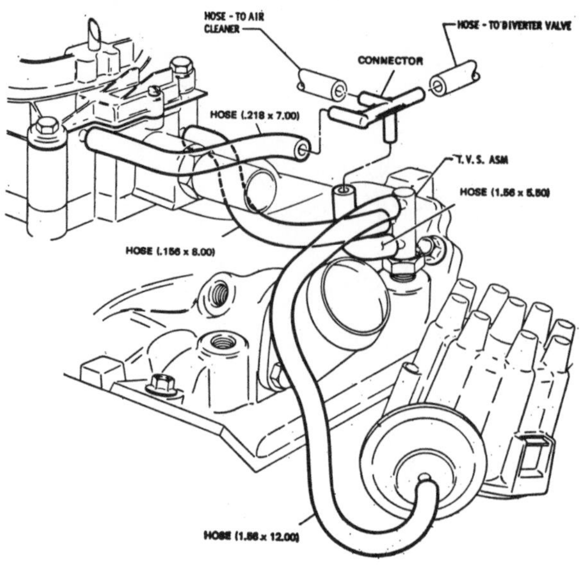

Fig. 94 *Vacuum hose routing.* 1973 *Buick* V8-350 4 *bar. carb. with A/C and automatic transmission and all* V8-455 *with automatic transmission except Stage* 1

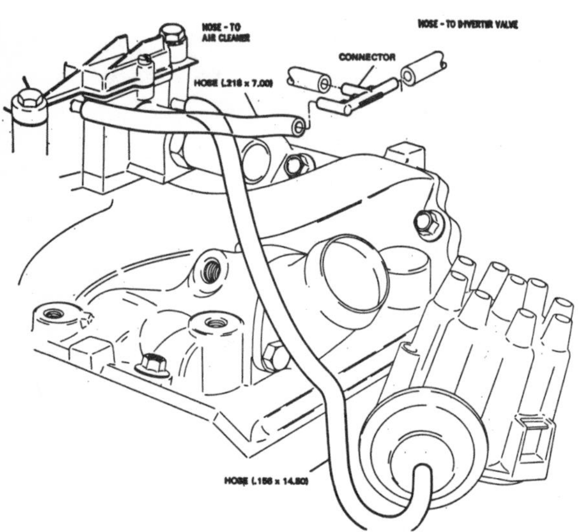

Fig. 95 *Vacuum hose routing.* 1973 *Buick* V8-350 4 *bar. carb. except A/C or automatic transmission*

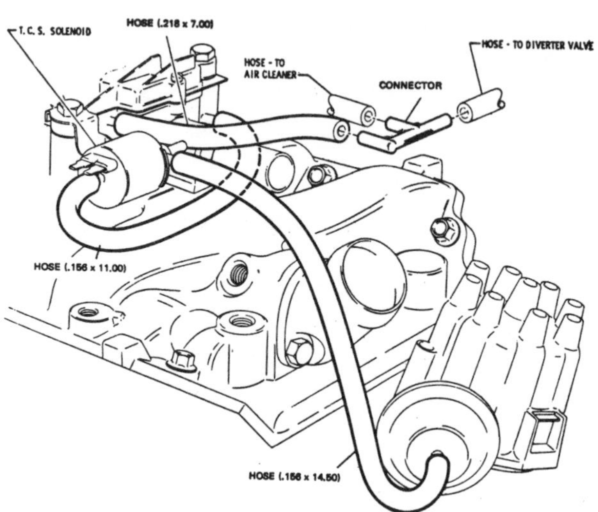

Fig. 96 *Vacuum hose routing.* 1973 *Buick* V8-350 4 *bar. with manual transmission*

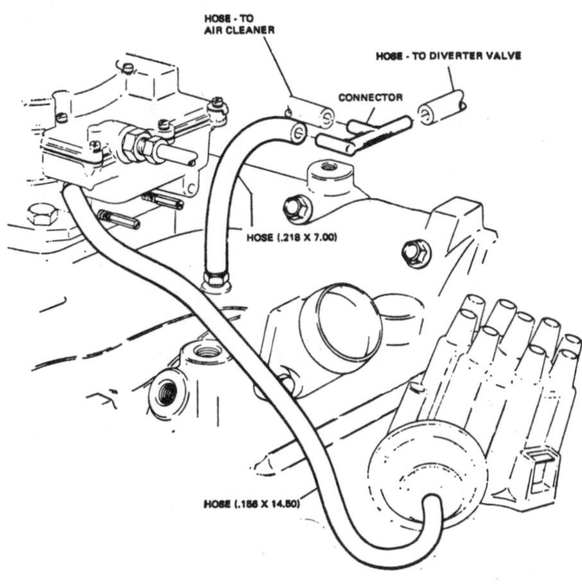

Fig. 97 Vacuum hose routing. 1973-74 *Buick* V8-350 2 *bar. carb. except A/C and automatic transmission*

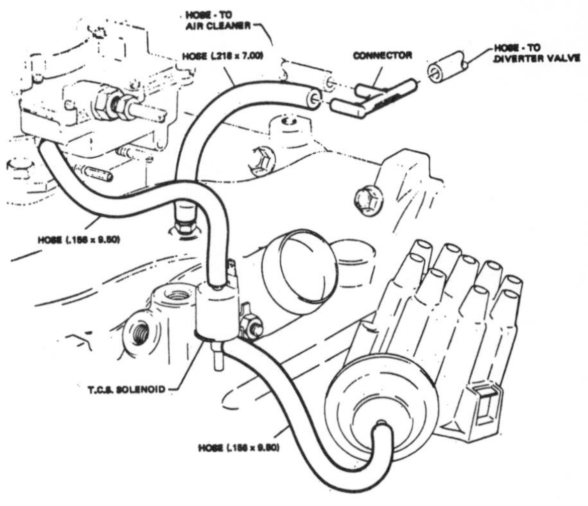

Fig. 98 *Vacuum hose routing.* 1972-73 *Buick* V8-350 2 *bar. carb. with manual transmission*

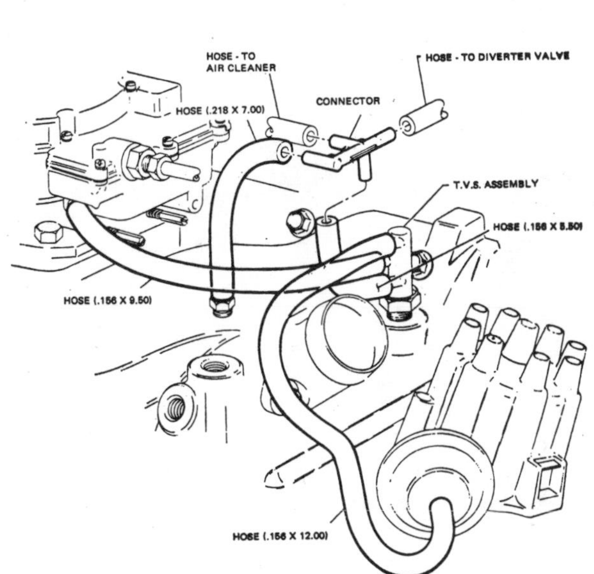

Fig. 99 *Vacuum hose routing.* 1973-74 *Buick* V8-350 2 *bar. carb. with A/C and HD cooling system*

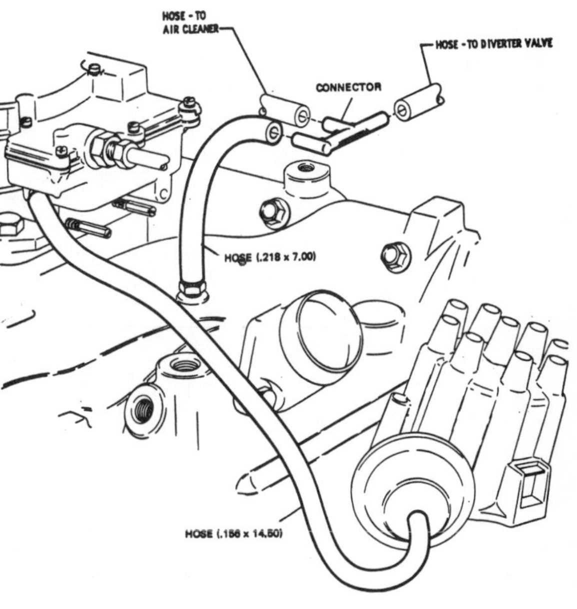

Fig. 100 *Vacuum hose routing.* 1973-74 *Buick* V8-350 2 *bar. carb. except A/C or HD cooling system*

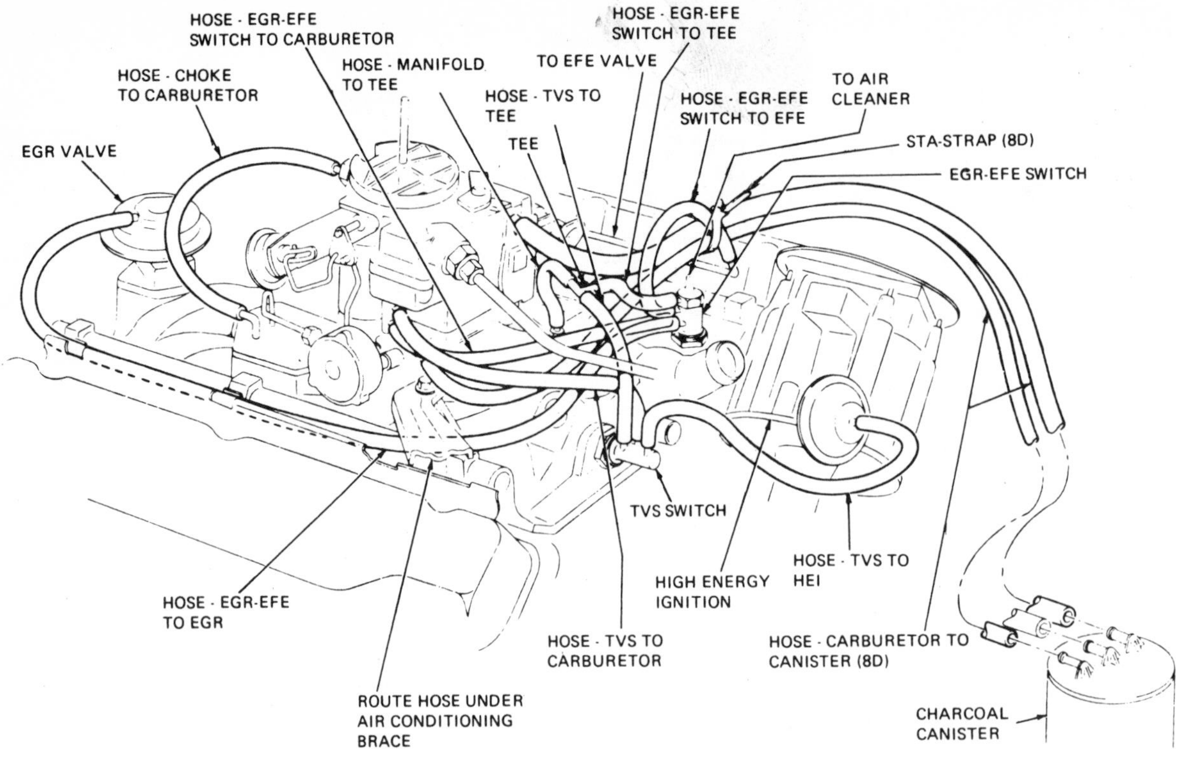

Fig. 101 *Vacuum hose routing.* 1975 *Buick intermediates,* V8-350 2-*bbl. w/o A.I.R.*

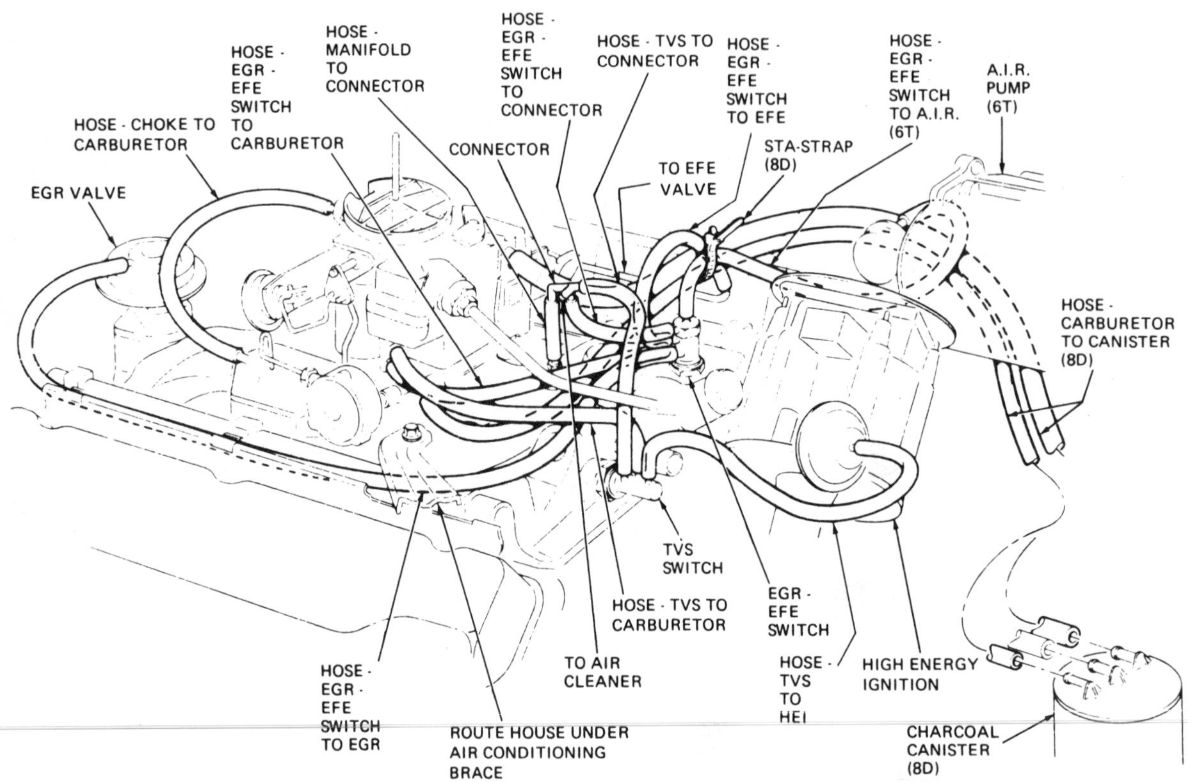

Fig. 102 *Vacuum hose routing.* 1975 *Buick intermediates* V8-350 2-*bbl. and A.I.R.*

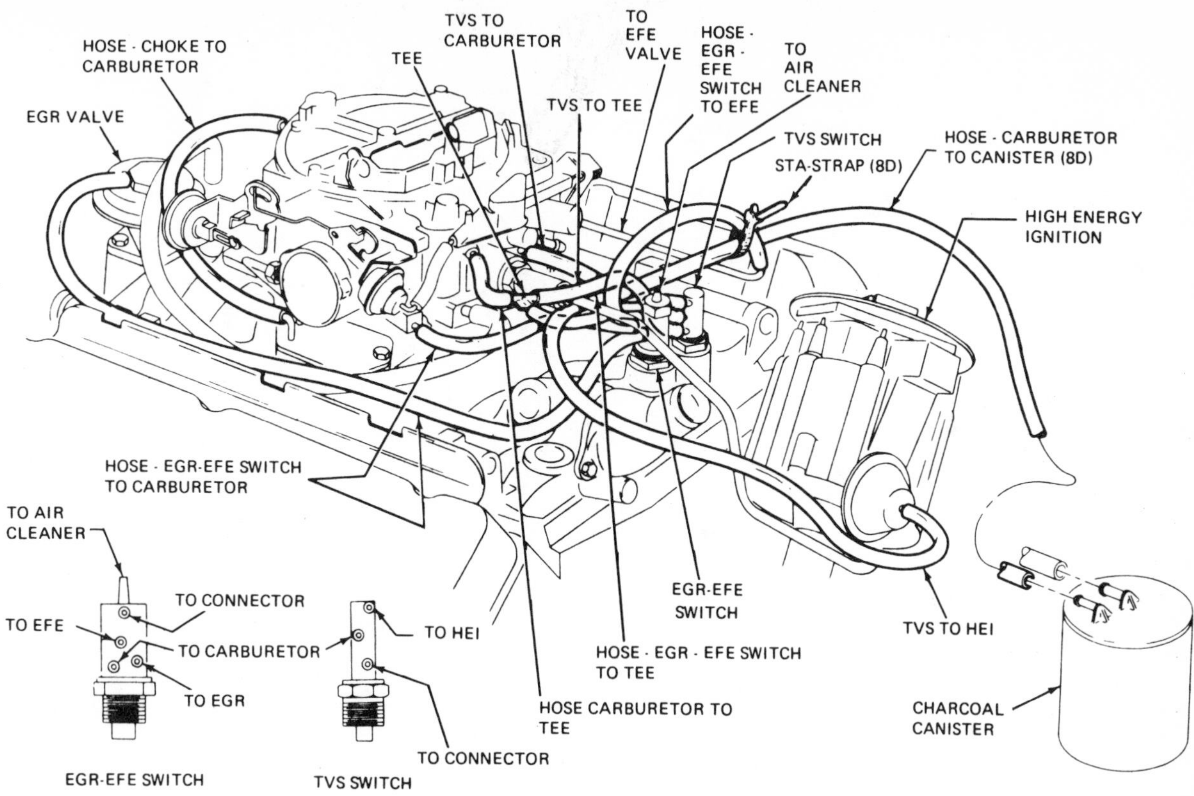

Fig. 103 *Vacuum hose routing.* 1975 *Buick full-size* V8-455 4-*bbl. w/o A.I.R.*

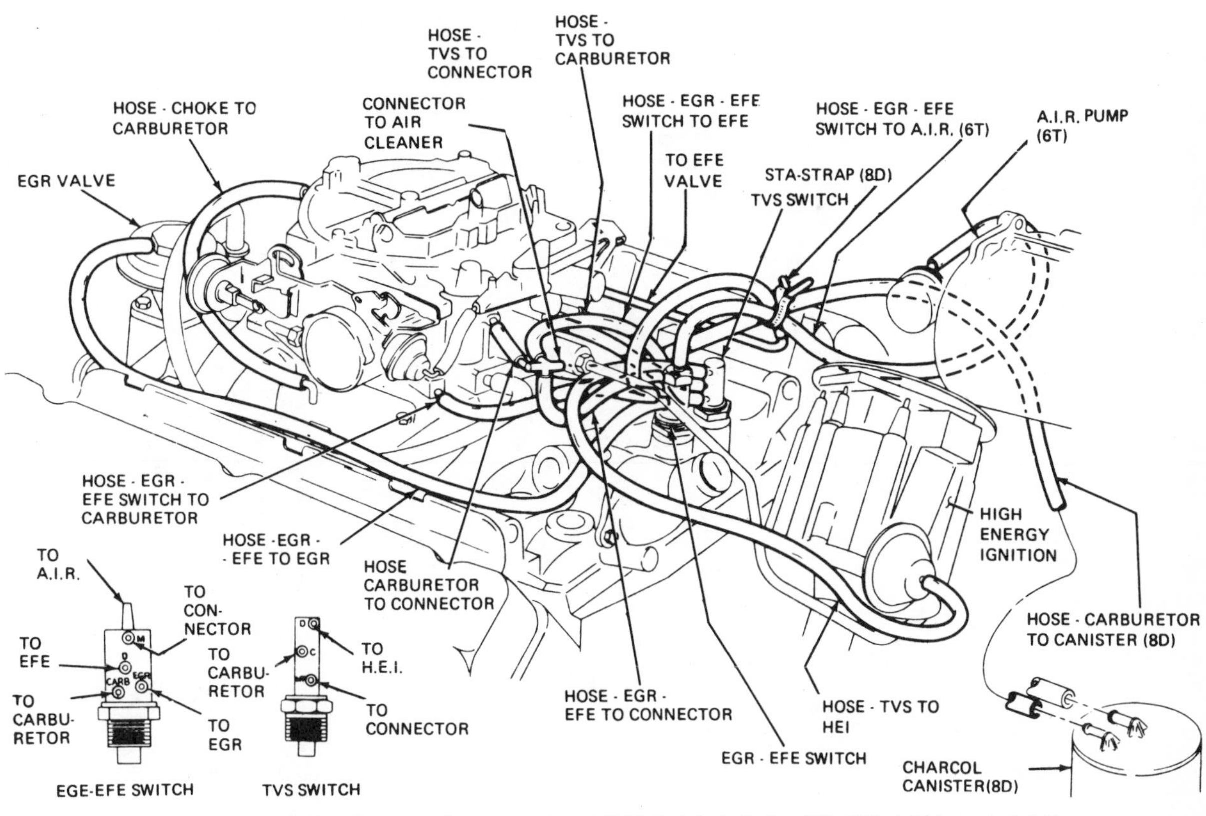

Fig. 104 *Vacuum hose routing.* 1975 *Buick full-size* V8-455 4-*bbl. and A.I.R.*

TO AIR CLEANER
TO E.F.E.
E.G.R. VALVE
TO AIR CLEANER
DIVERTER VALVE
HIGH ENERGY IGNITION
EGR-EFE SWITCH
TVS SWITCH
CHARCOAL CANISTER

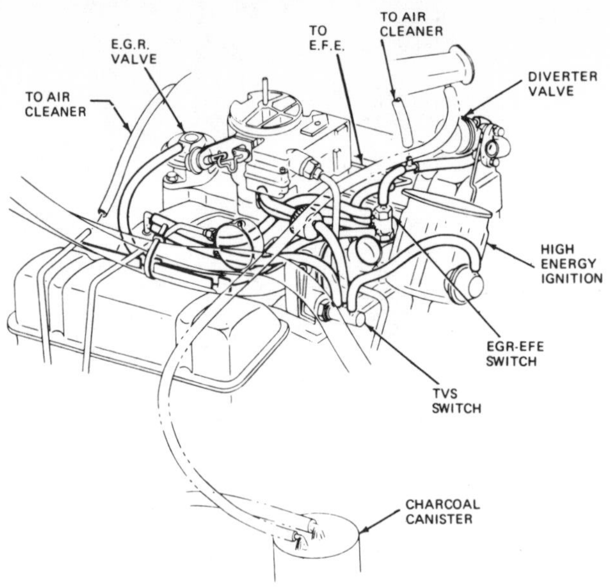

Fig. 105 *Vacuum Hose Routing with A.I.R. Buick Skyhawk* V6

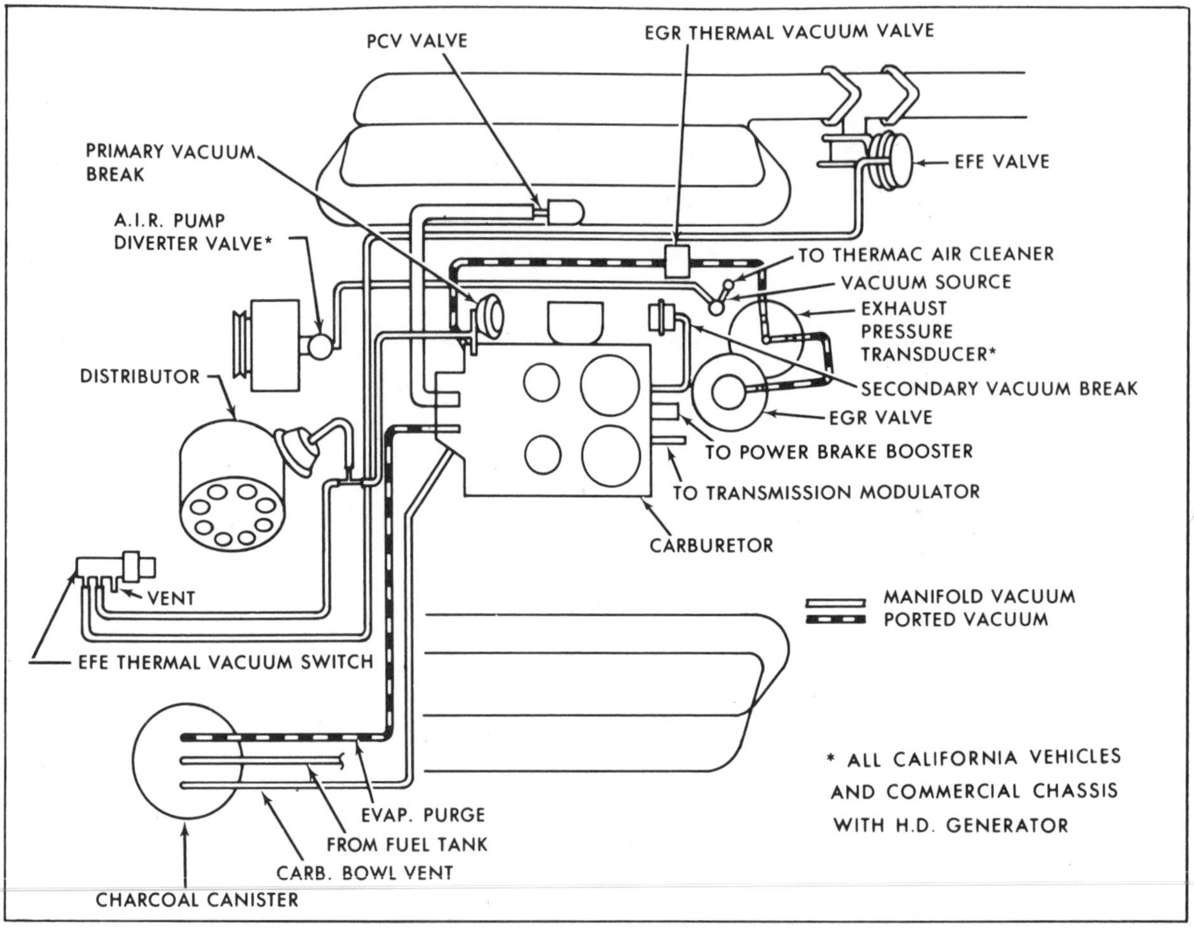

PCV VALVE
EGR THERMAL VACUUM VALVE
PRIMARY VACUUM BREAK
EFE VALVE
A.I.R. PUMP DIVERTER VALVE*
TO THERMAC AIR CLEANER
VACUUM SOURCE
EXHAUST PRESSURE TRANSDUCER*
DISTRIBUTOR
SECONDARY VACUUM BREAK
EGR VALVE
TO POWER BRAKE BOOSTER
TO TRANSMISSION MODULATOR
CARBURETOR
VENT
MANIFOLD VACUUM
PORTED VACUUM
EFE THERMAL VACUUM SWITCH
* ALL CALIFORNIA VEHICLES AND COMMERCIAL CHASSIS WITH H.D. GENERATOR
EVAP. PURGE
FROM FUEL TANK
CARB. BOWL VENT
CHARCOAL CANISTER

Fig. 106 *Vacuum Hose Routing.* 1975 *Cadillac*

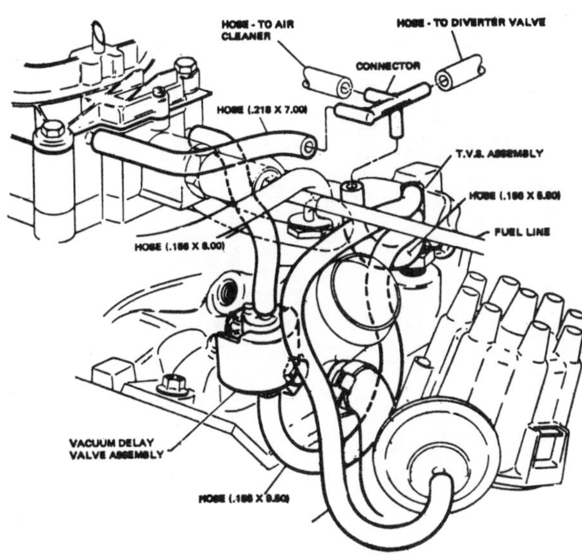

Fig. 107 *Vacuum hose routing.* 1973-74 *Buick* V8-350 4 *bar. carb.*

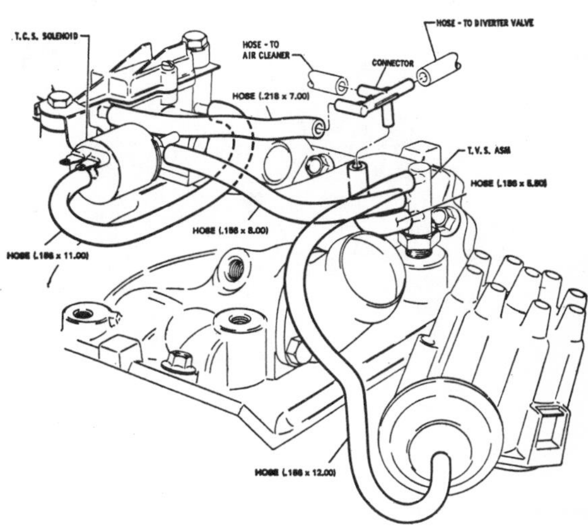

Fig. 108 *Vacuum hose routing.* 1972-74 *Buick Intermediate models with Stage* 1 *engine*

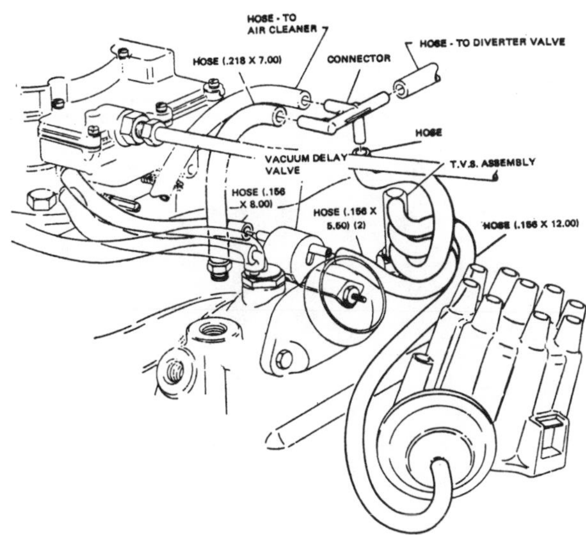

Fig. 109 *Vacuum hose routing.* 1974 *Buick intermediate models and Le Sabre with* V8-455 2 *bar. carb.*

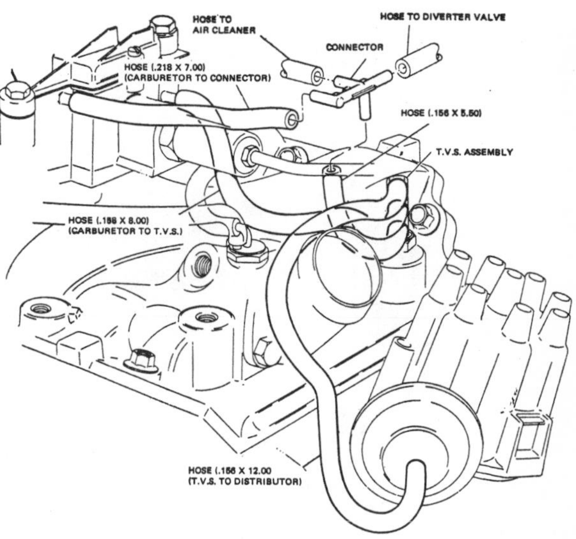

Fig. 110 *Vacuum hose routing.* 1974 *Buick except intermediate models with* V8-455 *Stage* 1

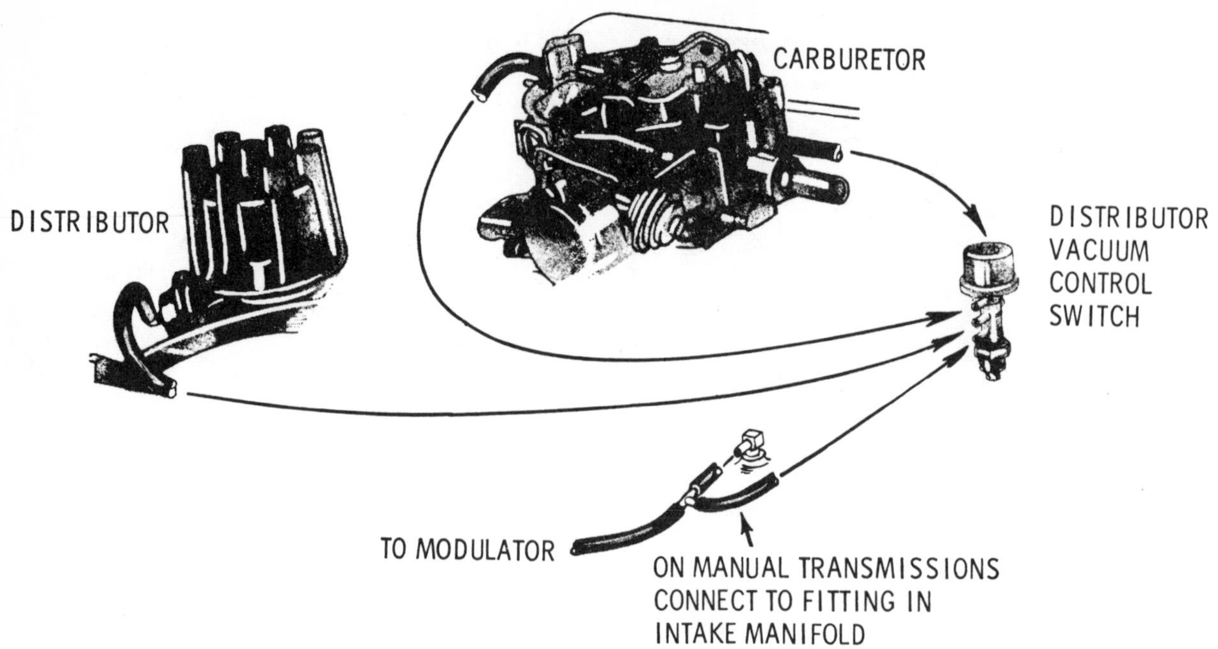

Fig. 111 *Vacuum hose routing.* 1971-72 *Oldsmobile except Toronado and* V8-350 *with manual transmission*

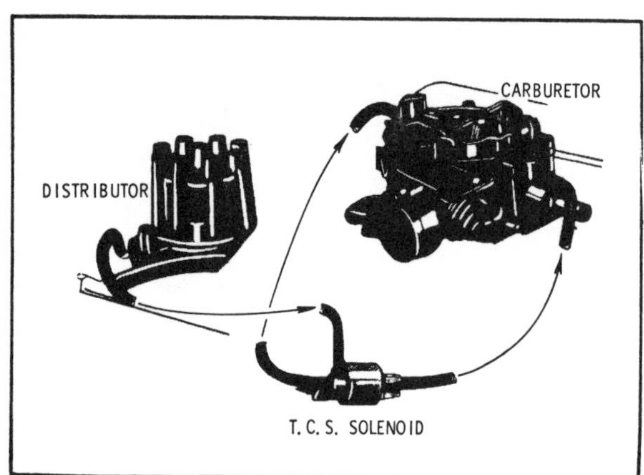

Fig. 112 *Vacuum hose routing. Oldsmobile,* 1971 *without A/C and* 1972 *with* 4 *bar. carb. and manual transmission*

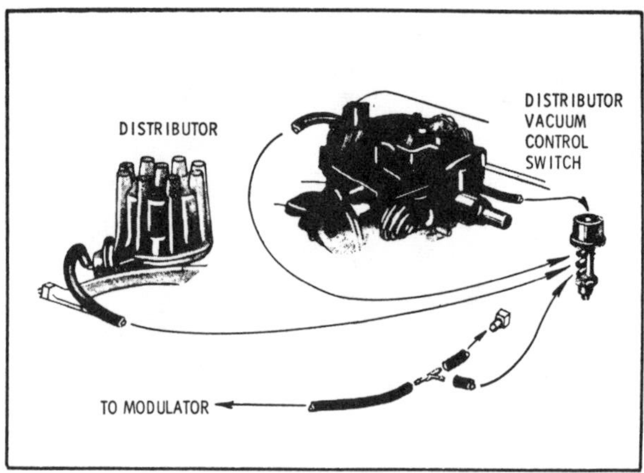

Fig. 113 *Vacuum hose routing.* 1971-72 *Oldsmobile Toronado*

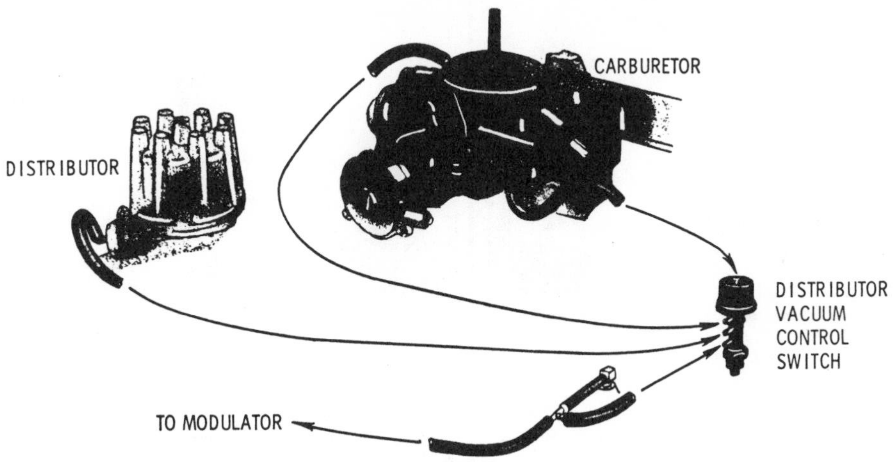

Fig. 114 *Vacuum hose routing. Oldsmobile,* 1971 *intermediate models with* V8-455, *full size models with* V8-455 *and A/C and all* 1971-72 V8-350 *with A/C*

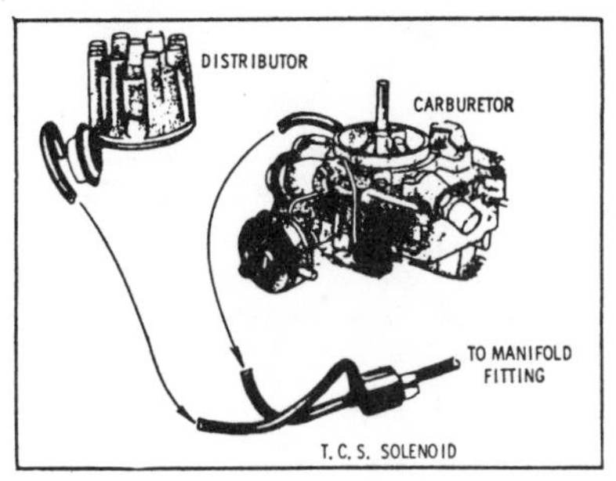

Fig. 115 *Vacuum hose routing. Oldsmobile,* 1971 *without A/C and* 1972 V8-350 *with manual transmission and no A/C*

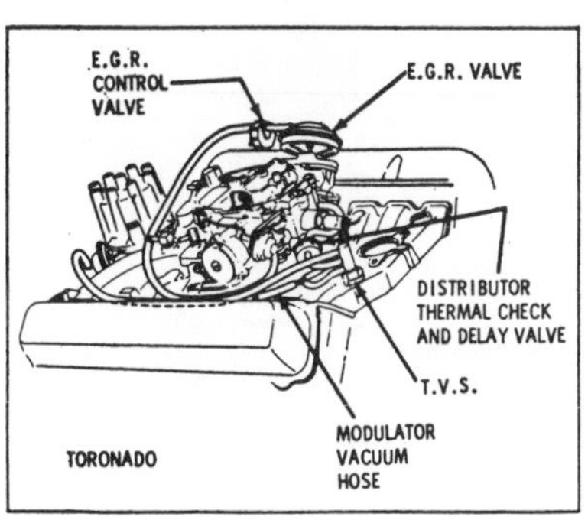

Fig. 117 *Vacuum hose routing.* 1973 *Oldsmobile Toronado*

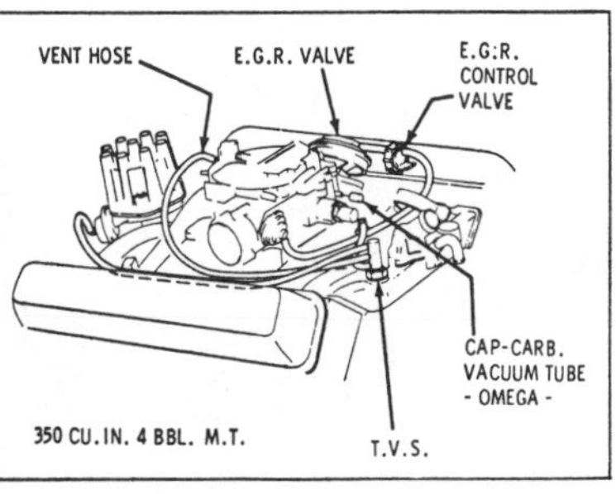

Fig. 118 *Vacuum hose routing.* 1973 *Oldsmobile with* 2 *bar. carb.*

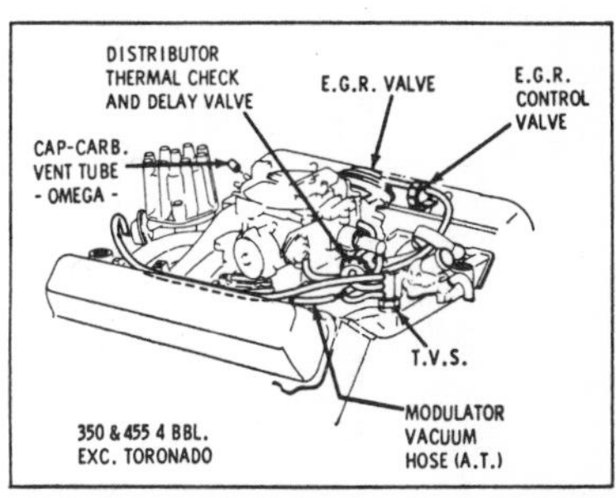

Fig. 116 *Vacuum hose routing. Oldsmobile with* 4 *bar. carb. except Toronado and* V8-350 *with manual transmission*

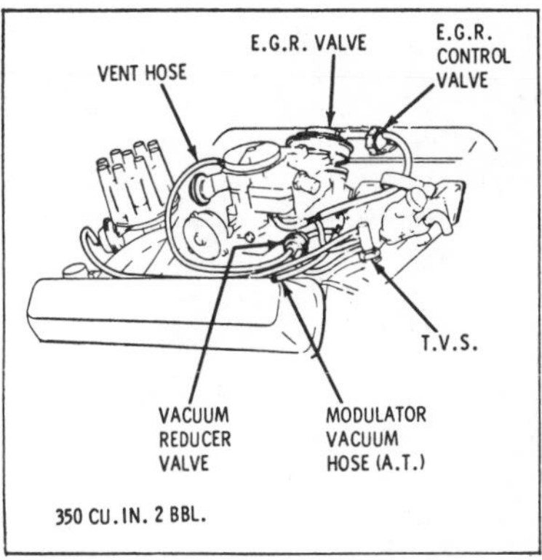

Fig. 119 *Vacuum hose routing.* 1973 *Oldsmobile* V8-350 4 *bar. carb.*

ALL 4 BBL CARBURETORS — NON CALIFORNIA

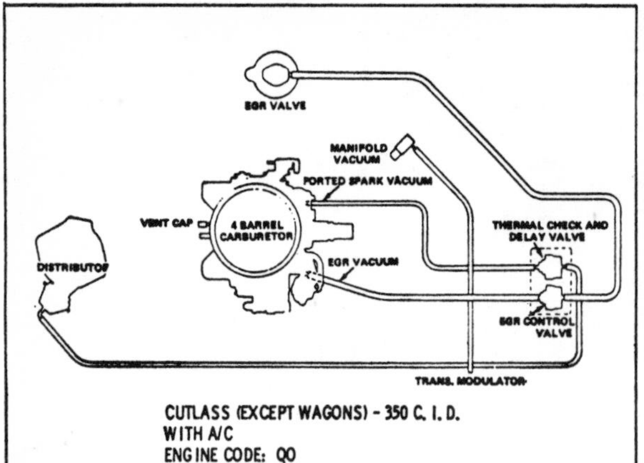

CUTLASS (EXCEPT WAGONS) - 350 C. I. D.
WITH A/C
ENGINE CODE: QO

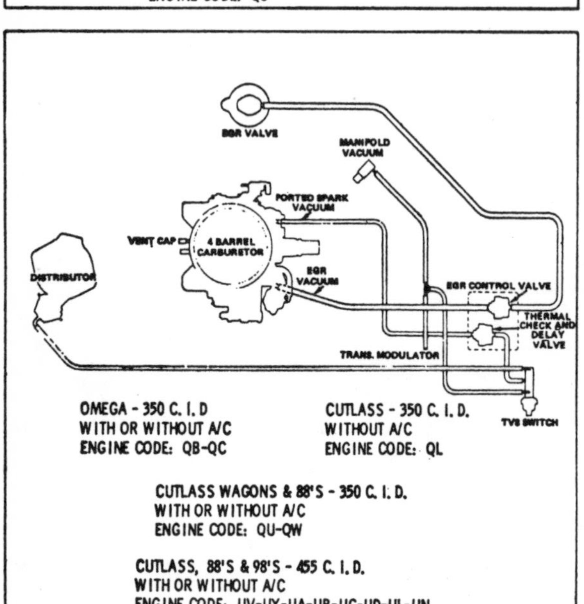

OMEGA - 350 C. I. D
WITH OR WITHOUT A/C
ENGINE CODE: QB-QC

CUTLASS - 350 C. I. D.
WITHOUT A/C
ENGINE CODE: QL

CUTLASS WAGONS & 88'S - 350 C. I. D.
WITH OR WITHOUT A/C
ENGINE CODE: QU-QW

CUTLASS, 88'S & 98'S - 455 C. I. D.
WITH OR WITHOUT A/C
ENGINE CODE: UV-UX-UA-UB-UC-UD-UL-UN

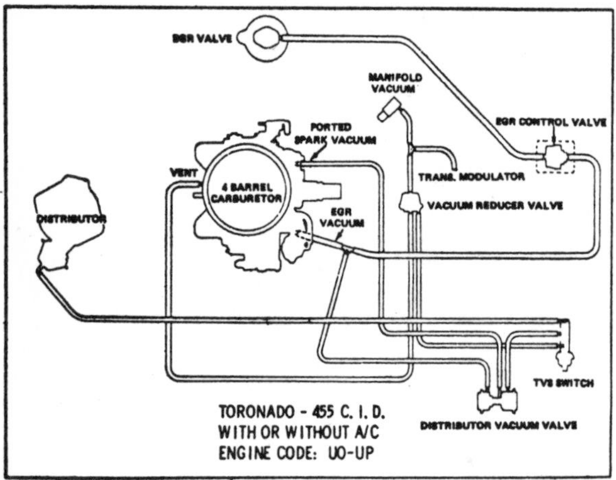

TORONADO - 455 C. I. D.
WITH OR WITHOUT A/C
ENGINE CODE: UO-UP

ALL 4 BBL CARBURETORS — CALIFORNIA

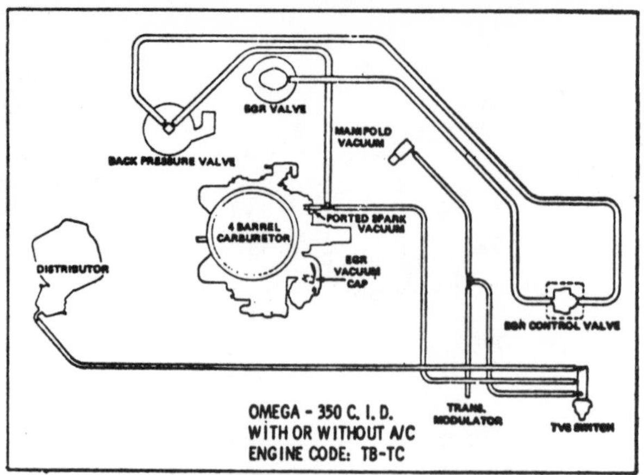

OMEGA - 350 C. I. D.
WITH OR WITHOUT A/C
ENGINE CODE: TB-TC

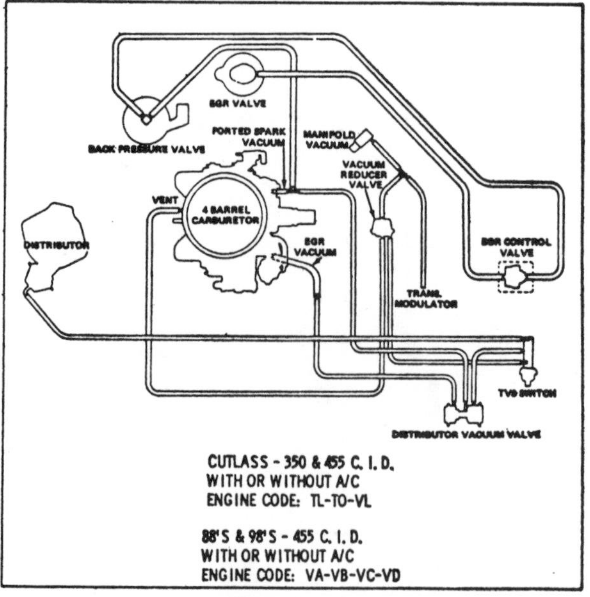

CUTLASS - 350 & 455 C. I. D.
WITH OR WITHOUT A/C
ENGINE CODE: TL-TO-VL

88'S & 98'S - 455 C. I. D.
WITH OR WITHOUT A/C
ENGINE CODE: VA-VB-VC-VD

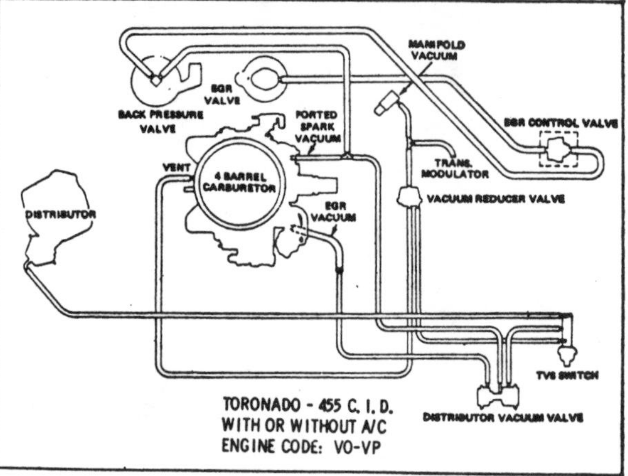

TORONADO - 455 C. I. D.
WITH OR WITHOUT A/C
ENGINE CODE: VO-VP

Fig. 120 *Vacuum hose routing.* 1974 *Oldsmobile*

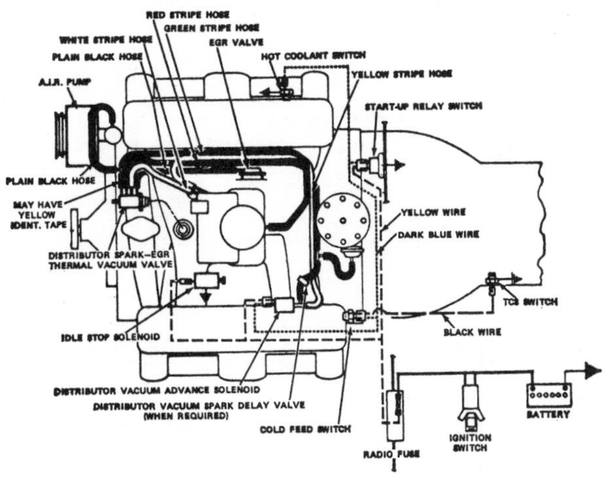

Fig. 121 *Vacuum and wiring.* 1974 *Pontiac with* 2 *bar. carb. and Air Injection Reactor*

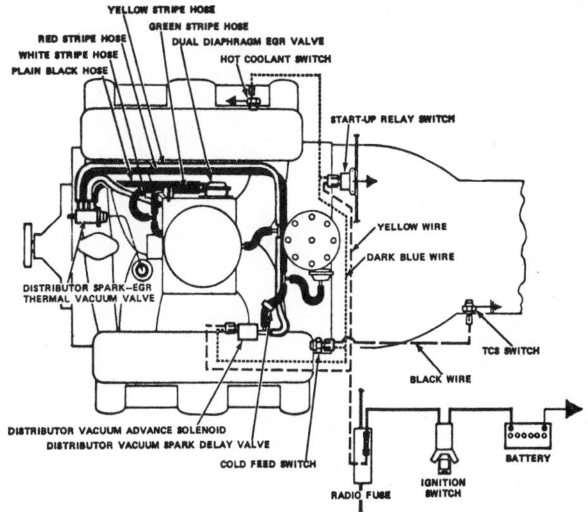

Fig. 122 *Vacuum and wiring.* 1974 *Pontiac with* 2 *bar. carb., automatic transmission and vacuum bias valve*

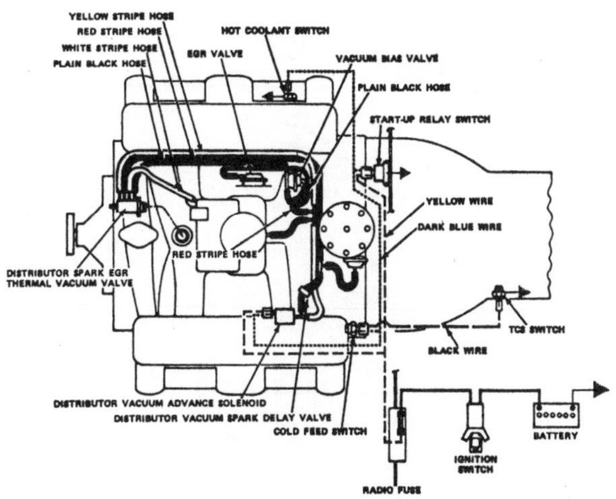

Fig. 123 *Vacuum and wiring.* 1974 *Pontiac with* 4 *bar. carb. and automatic transmission with dual diaphragm*

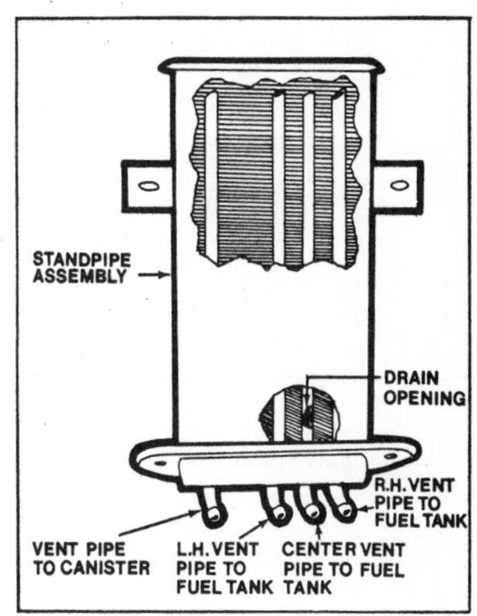

Fig. 124 *Vapor separator. General Motors (typical)*

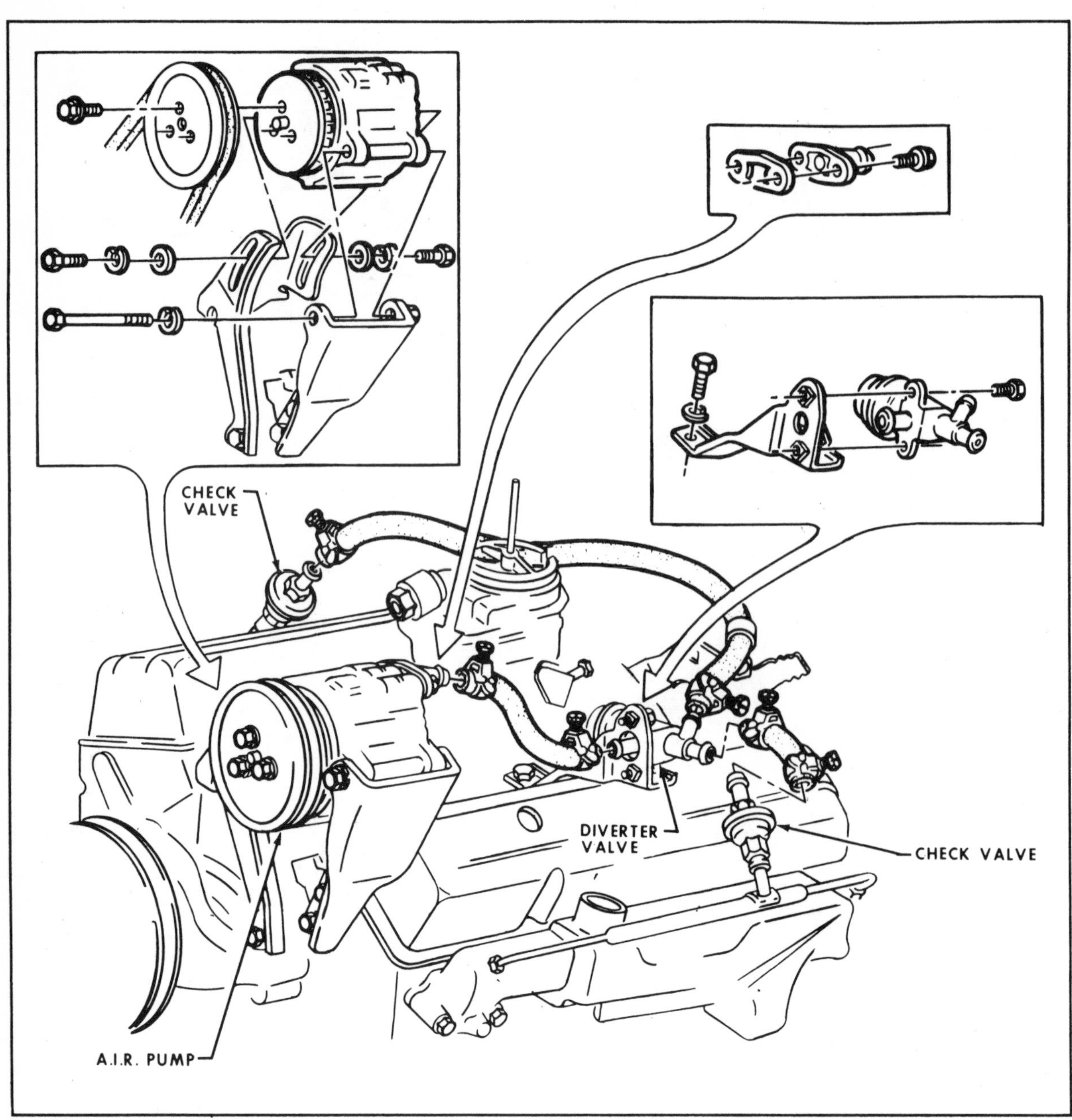

Fig. 125 Air Injection Reactor System, Chevrolet V8s (*typical*)

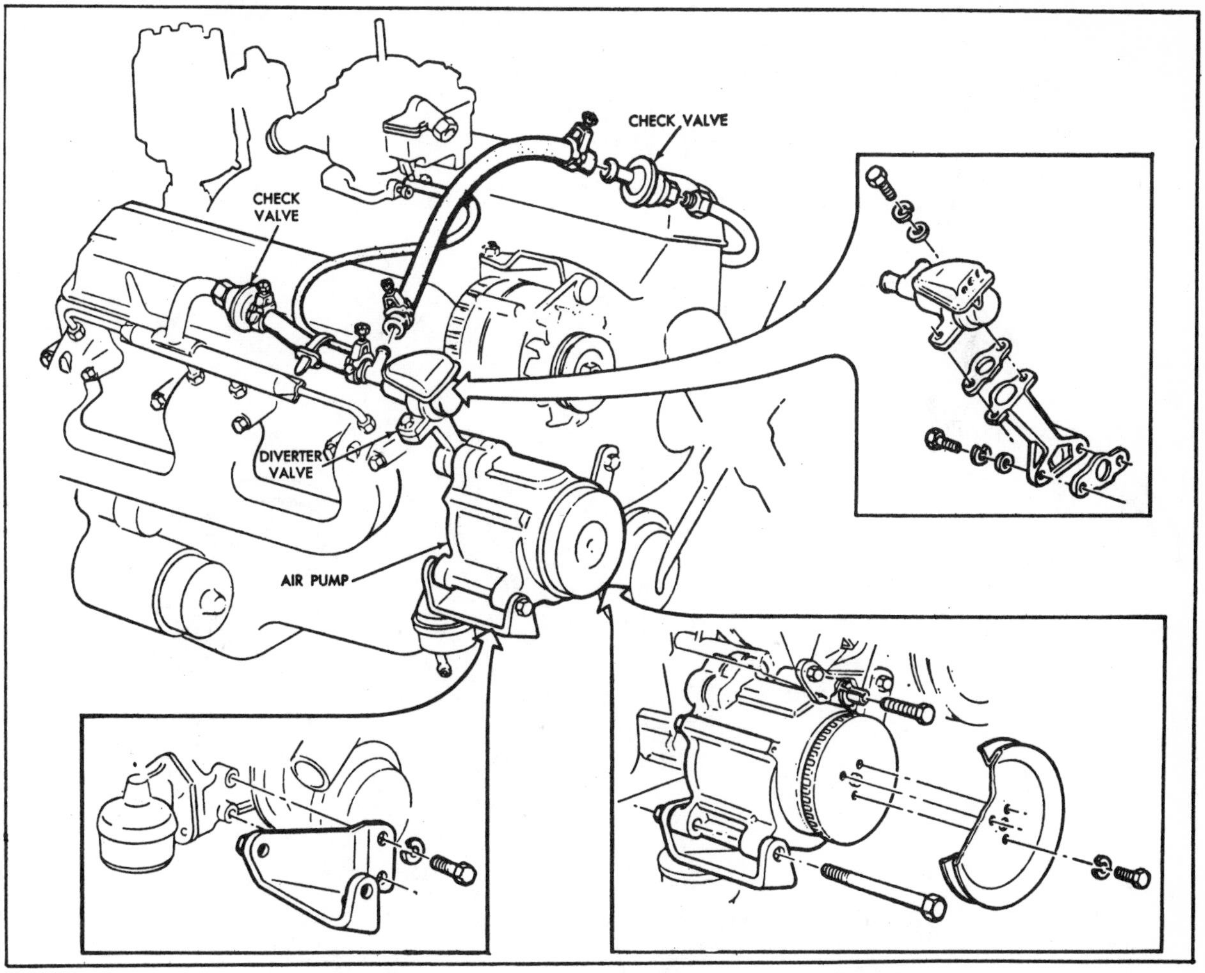

Fig. 126 *Air Injector Reactor components.* 1971-74 *Chevrolet* V8

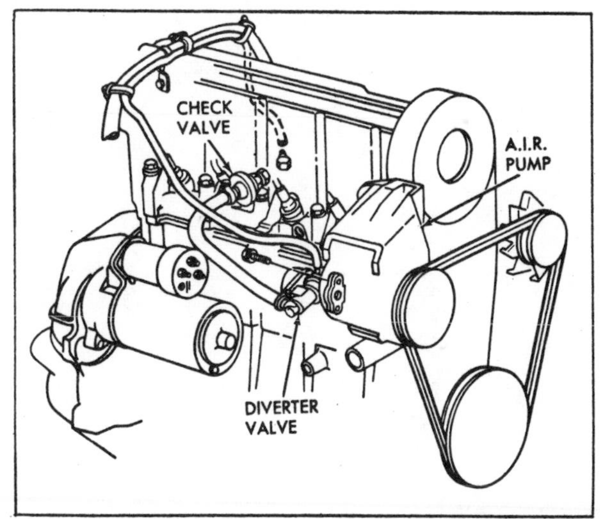

→

Fig. 127 *Air Injector Reactor components. Chevrolet Vega & Pontiac Astre*

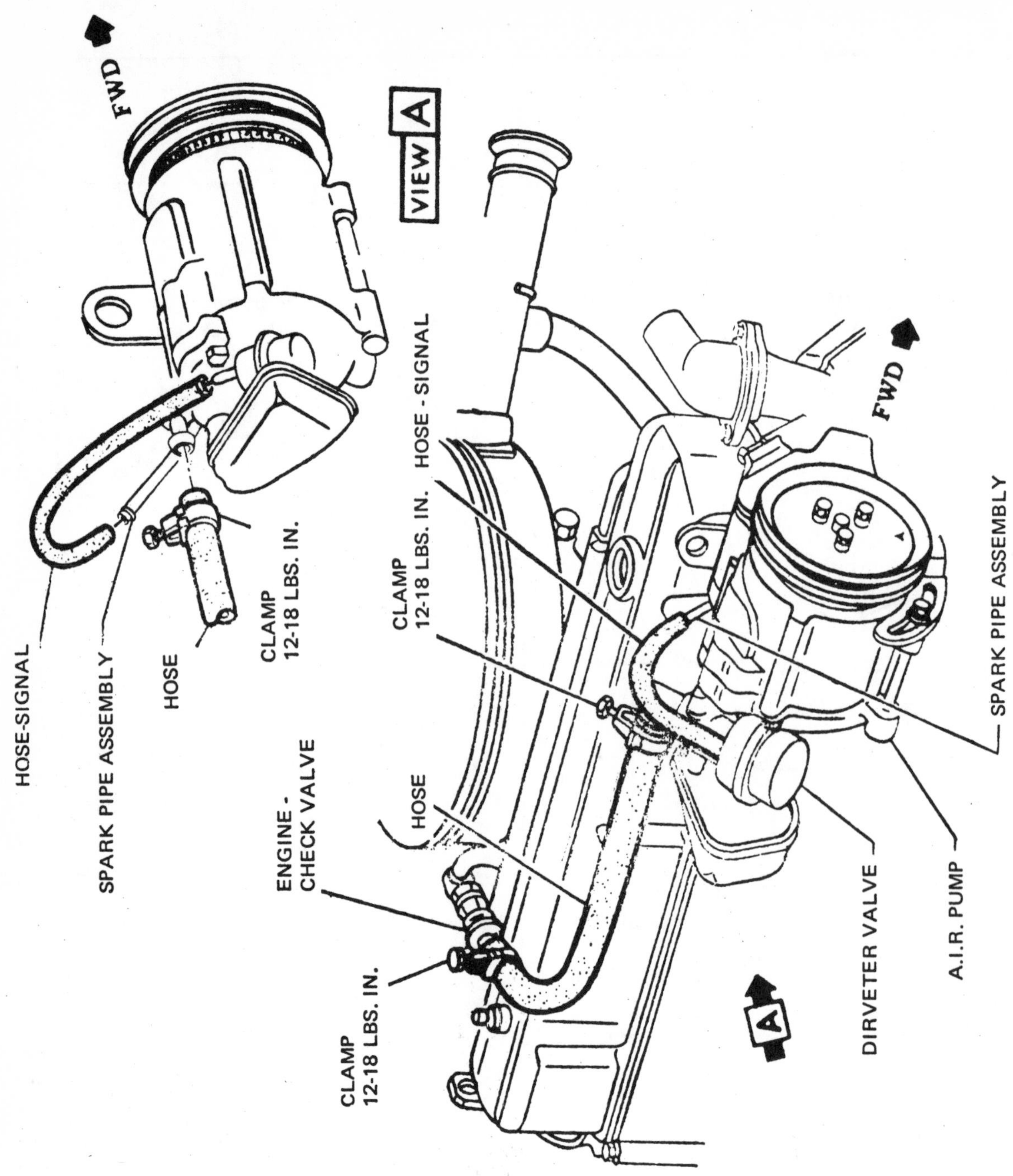

Fig. 128 Air Injector Reactor components. General Motors 6 cylinder (typical)

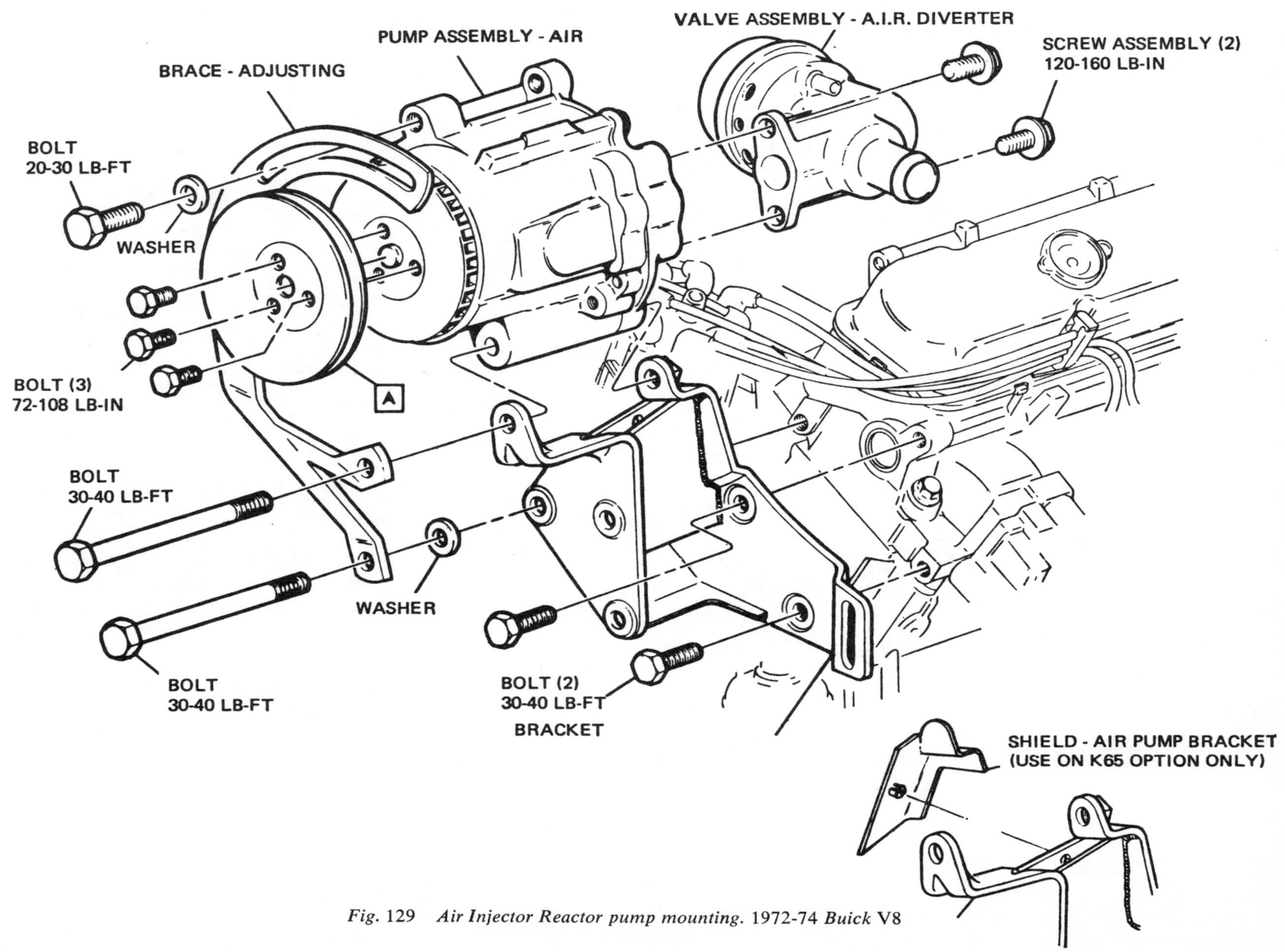

Fig. 129 *Air Injector Reactor pump mounting.* 1972-74 *Buick* V8

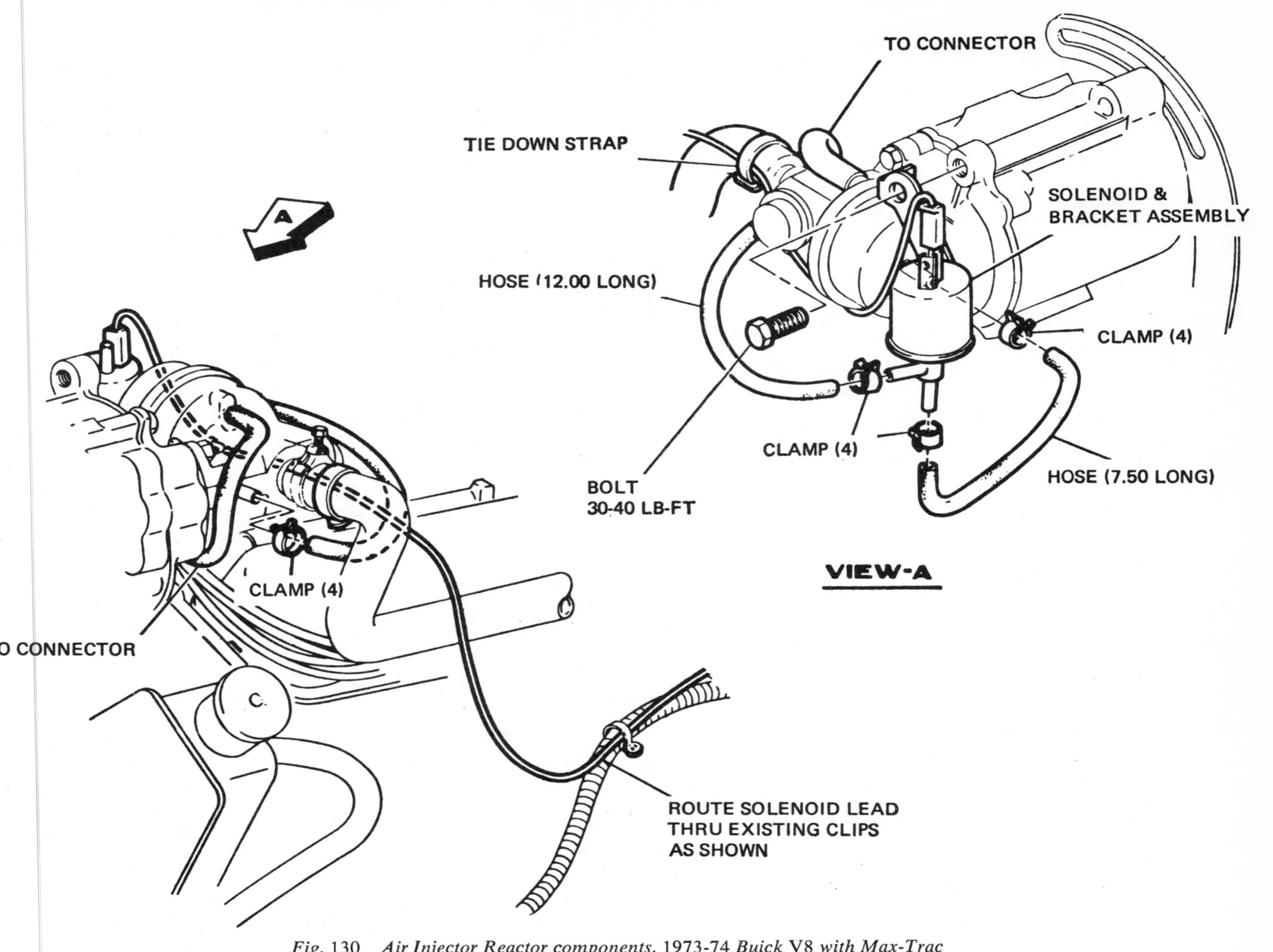

Fig. 130 *Air Injector Reactor components.* 1973-74 *Buick* V8 *with Max-Trac*

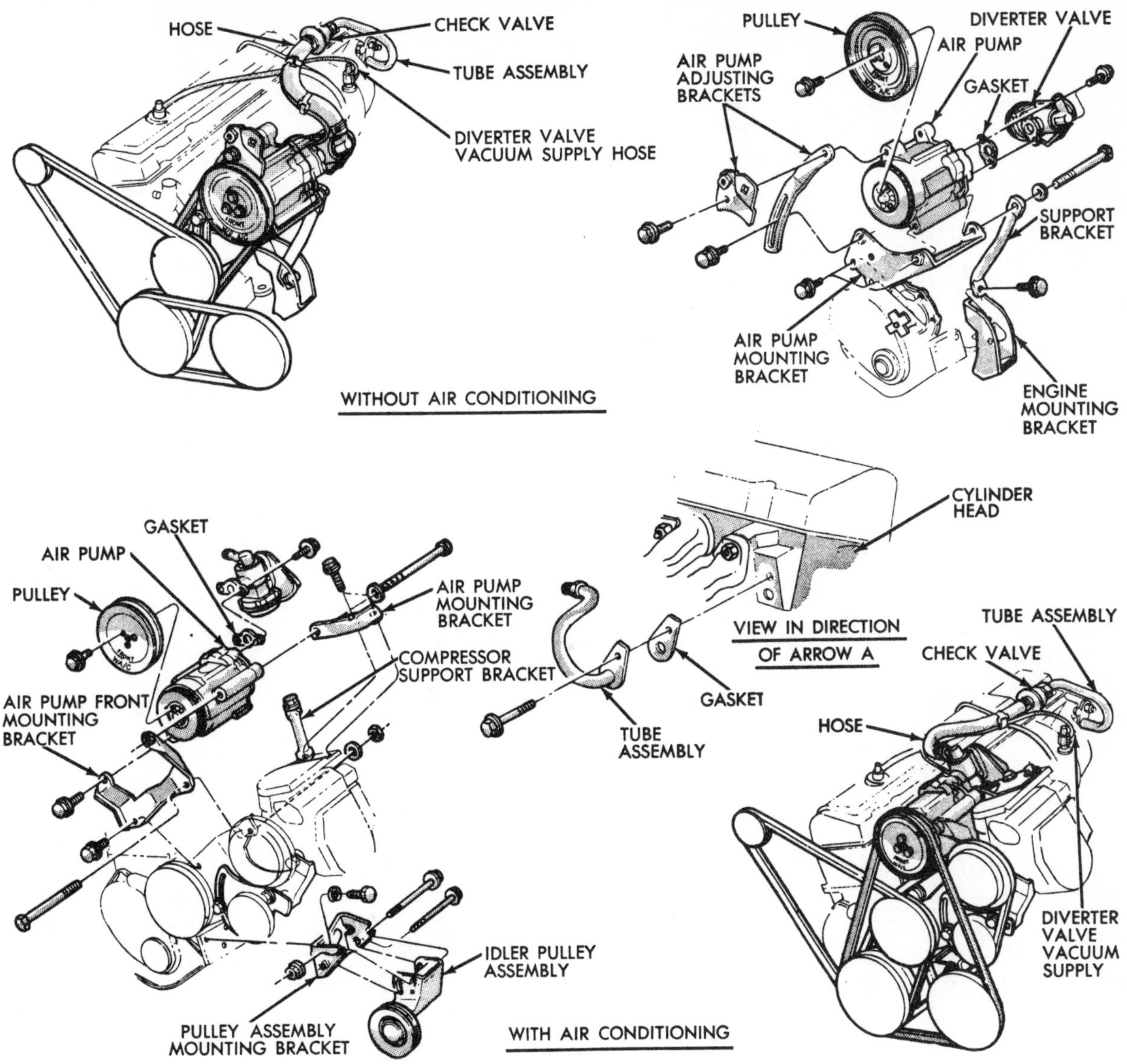
HOSE
CHECK VALVE
TUBE ASSEMBLY
DIVERTER VALVE VACUUM SUPPLY HOSE
WITHOUT AIR CONDITIONING
PULLEY
DIVERTER VALVE
AIR PUMP
AIR PUMP ADJUSTING BRACKETS
GASKET
SUPPORT BRACKET
AIR PUMP MOUNTING BRACKET
ENGINE MOUNTING BRACKET
CYLINDER HEAD
GASKET
AIR PUMP
PULLEY
AIR PUMP MOUNTING BRACKET
COMPRESSOR SUPPORT BRACKET
AIR PUMP FRONT MOUNTING BRACKET
VIEW IN DIRECTION OF ARROW A
GASKET
TUBE ASSEMBLY
TUBE ASSEMBLY
CHECK VALVE
HOSE
DIVERTER VALVE VACUUM SUPPLY
IDLER PULLEY ASSEMBLY
PULLEY ASSEMBLY MOUNTING BRACKET
WITH AIR CONDITIONING

Fig. 131 *Air Injection System.* 1972-74 *Chrysler* 6 *cylinder*

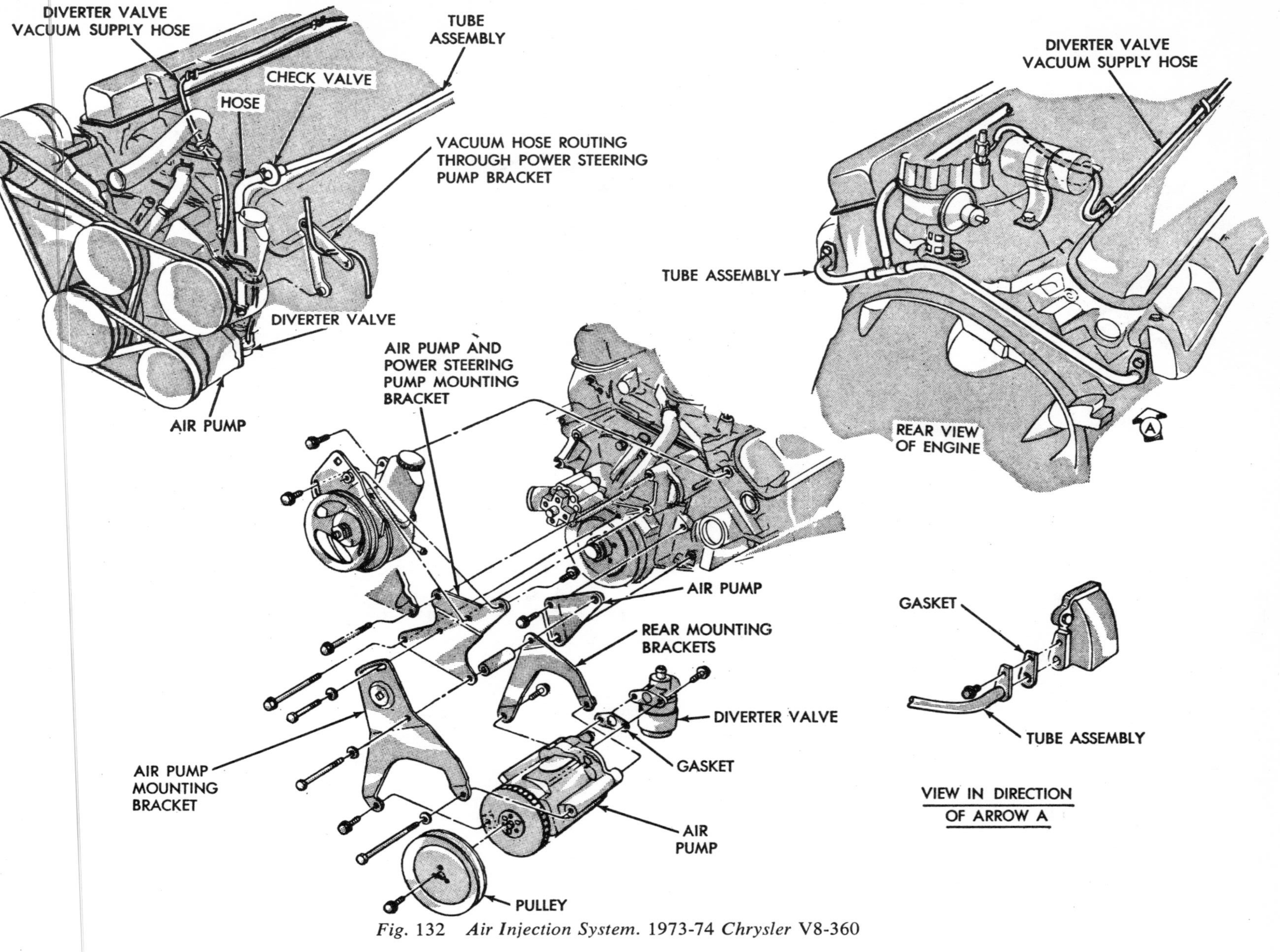

Fig. 132 *Air Injection System.* 1973-74 *Chrysler* V8-360

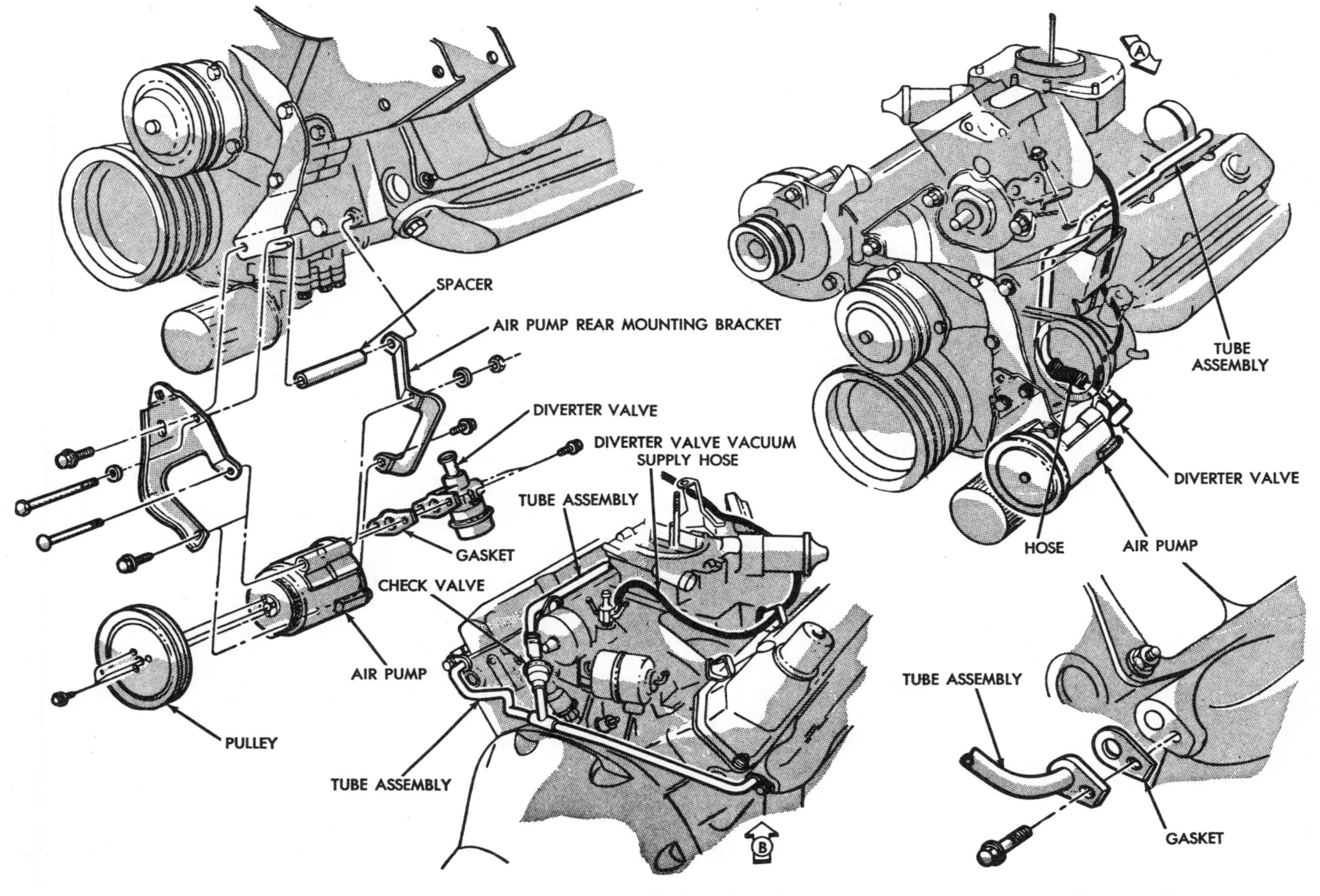

Fig. 133 *Air Injection System.* 1973-74 *Chrysler* V8-440

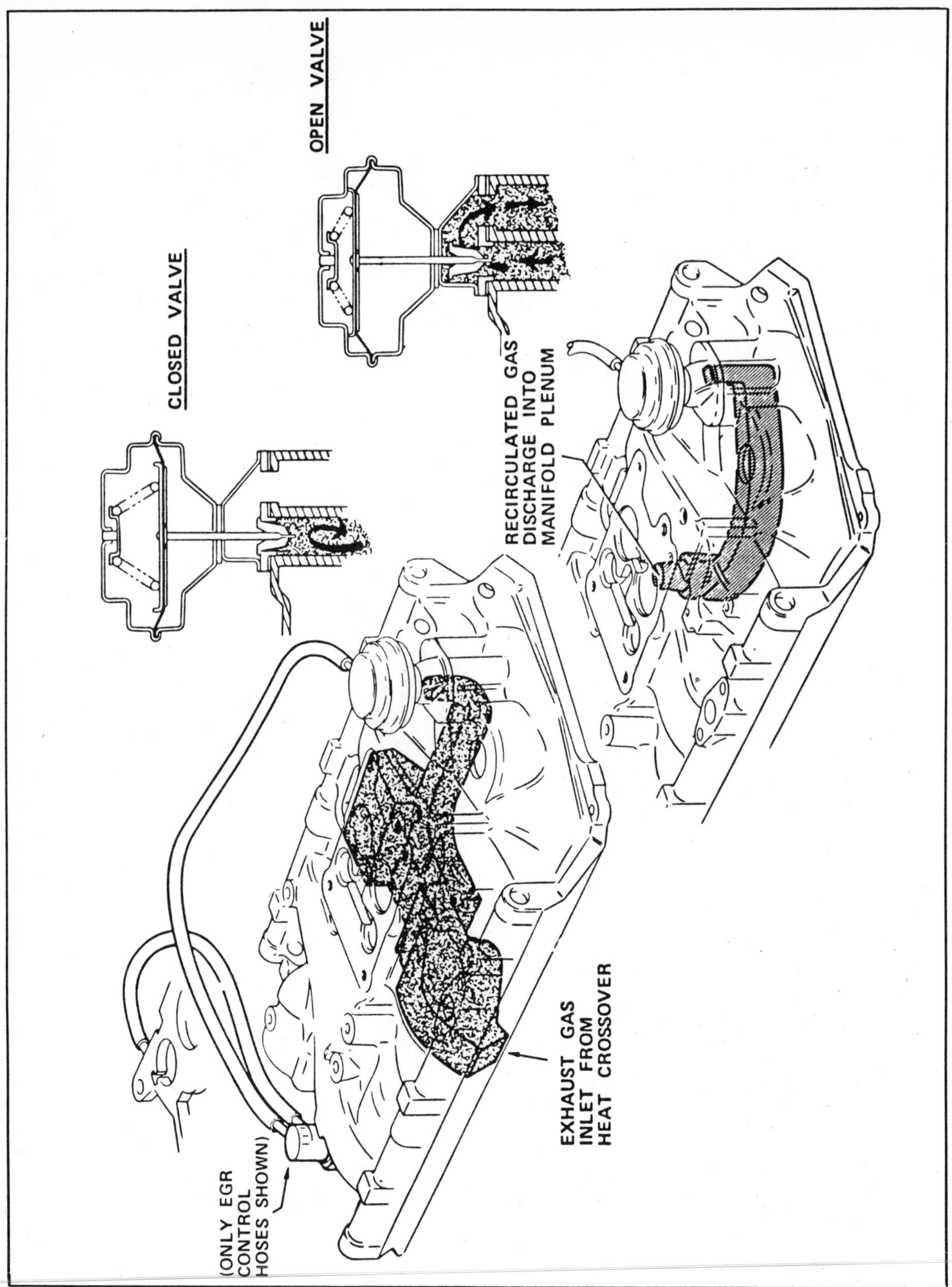

Fig. 134 *Vacuum Modulated E.G.R.* 1975 V8-350 *Apollo, Omega & Ventura* (*typical*)

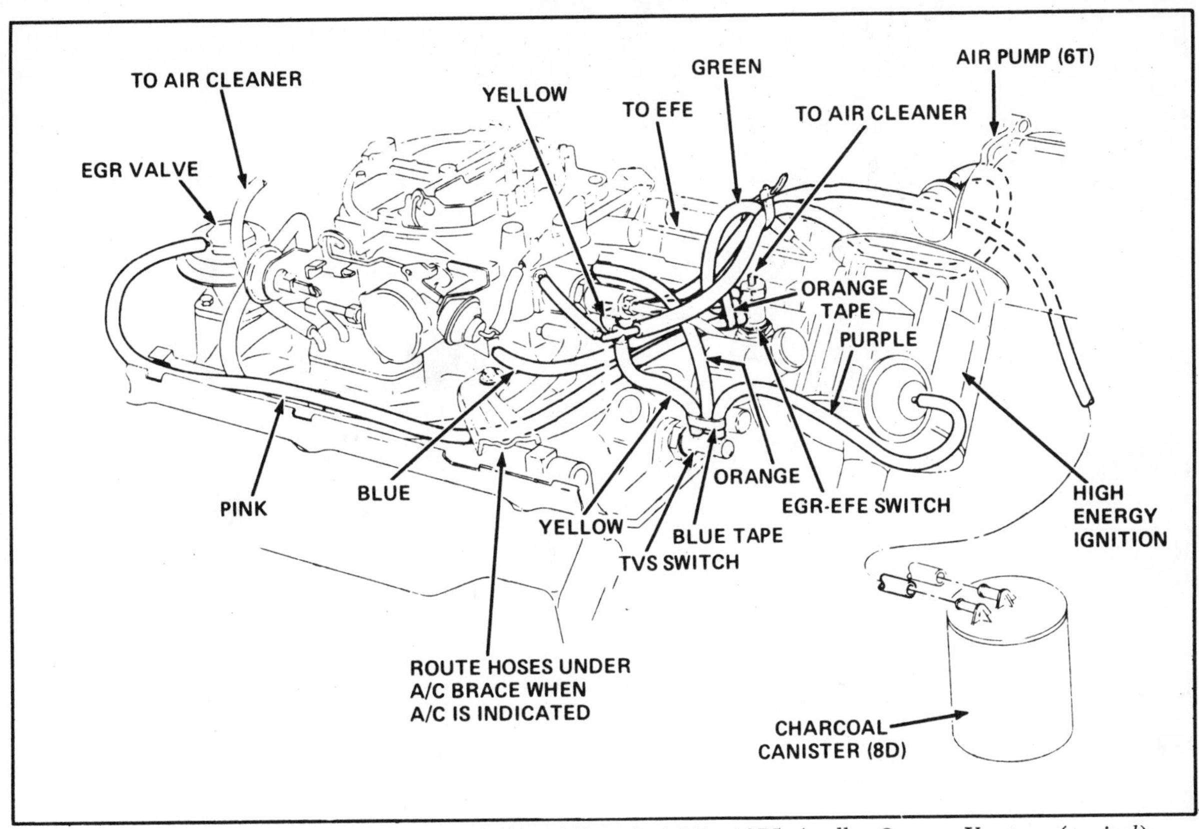

Fig. 135 *Vacuum Hose Routing.* V8-350 4-*bbl with A.I.R.*, 1975 *Apollo, Omega, Ventura* (*typical*)

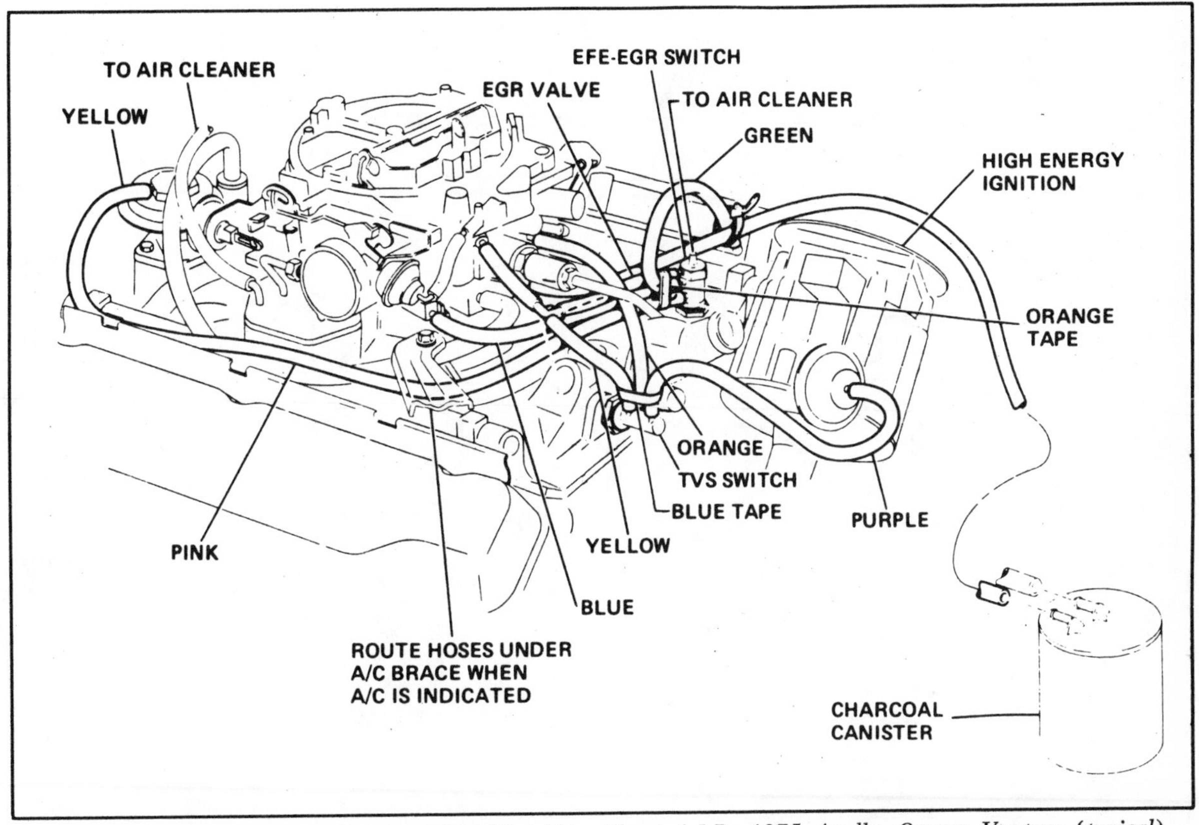

Fig. 136 *Vacuum Hose Routing.* V8-350 4-*bbl without A.I.R.*, 1975 *Apollo, Omega, Ventura* (*typical*)

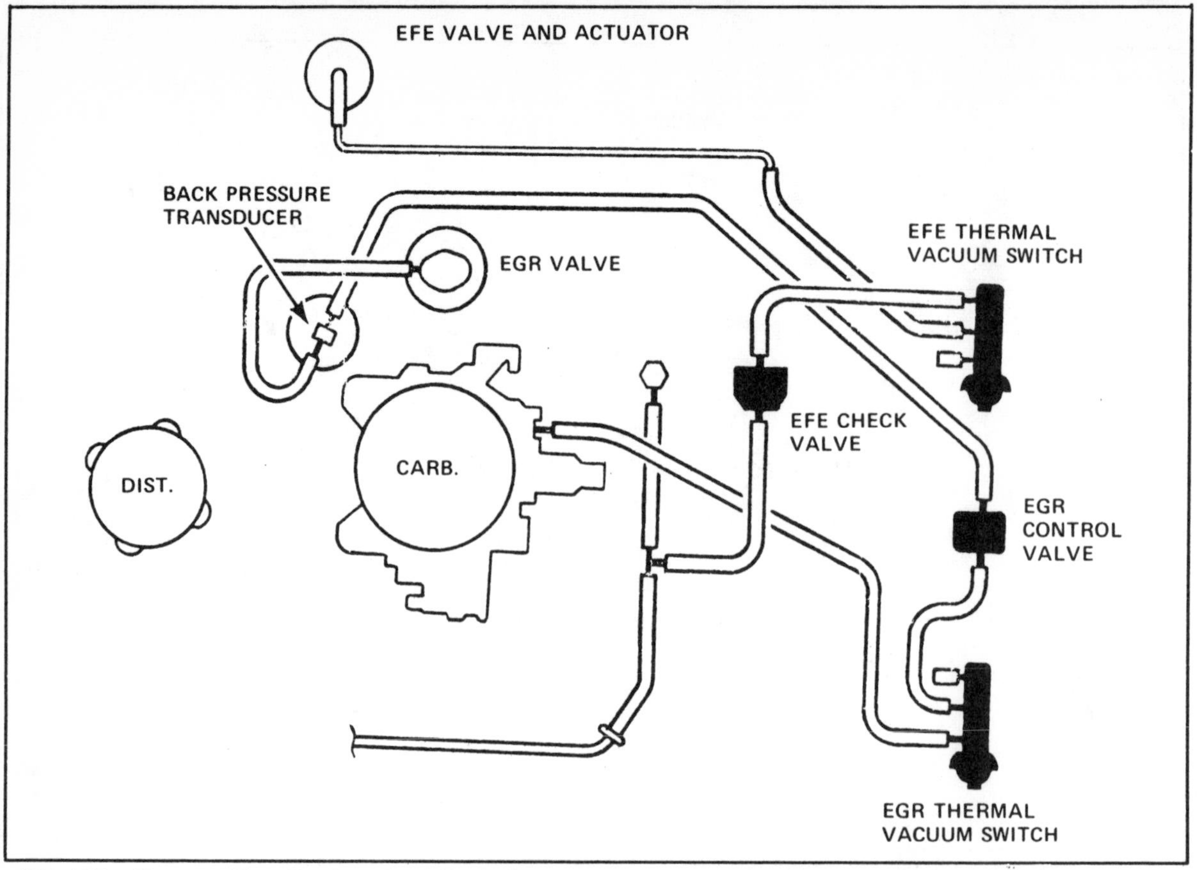

EFE VALVE AND ACTUATOR
BACK PRESSURE TRANSDUCER
EGR VALVE
EFE THERMAL VACUUM SWITCH
EFE CHECK VALVE
CARB.
DIST.
EGR CONTROL VALVE
EGR THERMAL VACUUM SWITCH

Fig. 137 *Vacuum Hose Routing.* V8-260 1975 *Apollo, Omega, Ventura w/auto. trans.* (*Calif. only*) (*typical*)

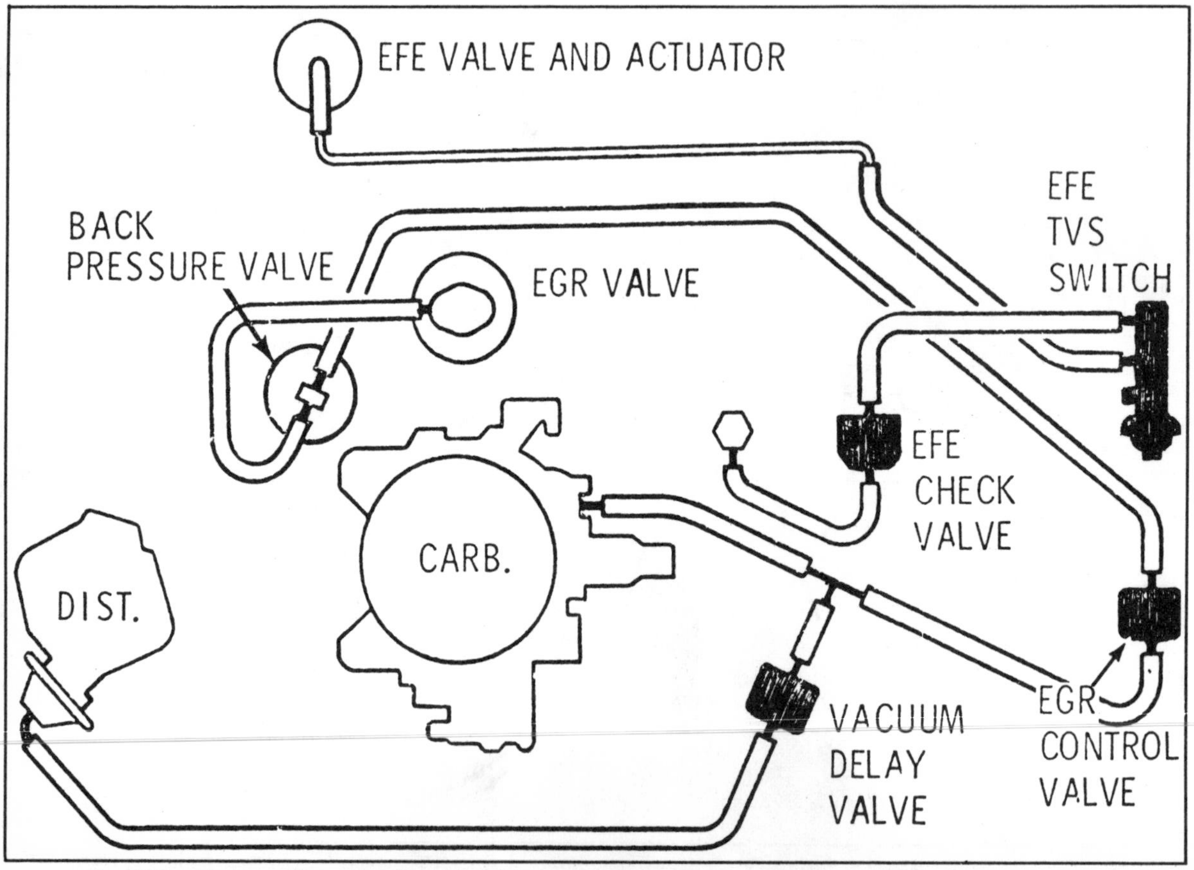

EFE VALVE AND ACTUATOR
BACK PRESSURE VALVE
EGR VALVE
EFE TVS SWITCH
EFE CHECK VALVE
CARB.
DIST.
VACUUM DELAY VALVE
EGR CONTROL VALVE

Fig. 138 *Vacuum Hose Routing.* V8-260 1975 *Apollo, Omega, Ventura w/manual trans.* (*typical*)

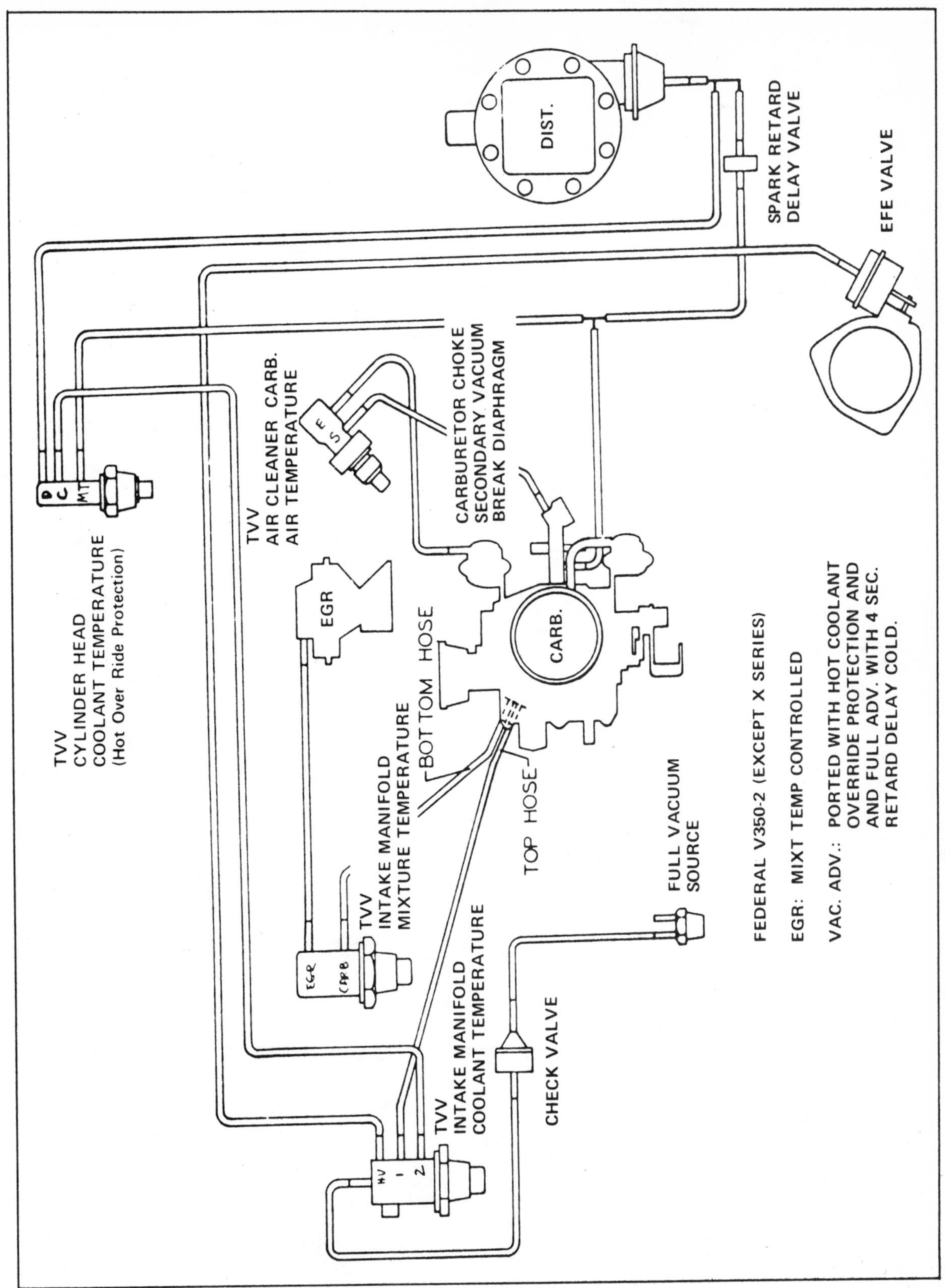

Fig. 139 *Vacuum Hose Routing.* V8-350 2-*bbl Pontiac exc. Ventura—All Federal*

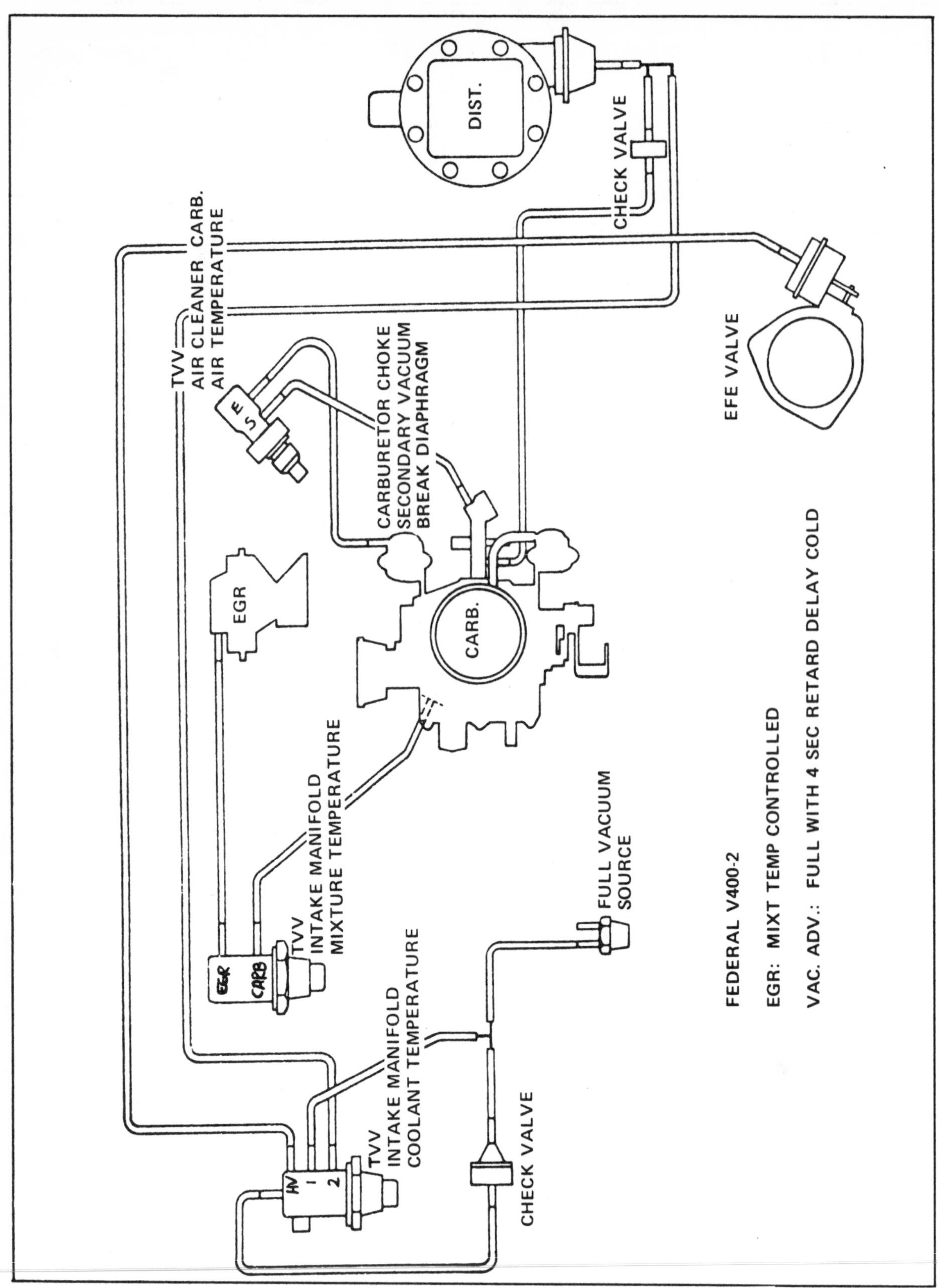

Fig. 140 Vacuum Hose Routing. V8-400 *Pontiac—All Federal*

CARBURETORS

This section contains information on carburetors used on 1974-75 models. For information on carburetors used on earlier models, refer to page 219 of your Emission Control Manual Volume I.

CONTENTS

Carter Carburetors

CARTER YF ADJUSTMENT SPECIFICATIONS

See Tuneup Chart in specifications chapter for hot idle speed.

Carb. Model	Idle Mixture Screw Setting	Float Level	Float Drop	Idle Vent Setting	Fast Idle Cam Setting	Dechoke or Unloader Setting	Pulldown Setting	Vacuum Break Setting	Choke Setting
AMERICAN MOTORS 1973–74									
6423	①	15/32	1 3/8	—	.190	.275	.215	—	1 Rich
6431	①	15/32	1 3/8	—	.190	.275	.215	—	1 Rich
1974									
6510	①	15/32	1 3/8	—	.190	.275	.215	—	1 Rich
5511	①	15/32	1 3/8	—	.190	.275	.215	—	1 Rich
7000	①	15/32	1 3/8	—	.190	.275	.215	—	1 Rich
7001	①	15/32	1 3/8	—	.190	.275	.215	—	1 Rich
7028	①	15/32	1 3/8	—	.190	.275	.215	—	1 Rich
7029	①	15/32	1 3/8	—	.190	.275	.215	—	1 Rich
1975									
7039	①	15/32	1 3/8	—	.180②	.275	.205	—	1 Rich
7041	①	15/32	1 3/8	—	.180②	.275	.205	—	1 Rich
7061	①	15/32	1 3/8	—	.180②	.275	.205	—	1 Rich
7062	①	15/32	1 3/8	—	.180②	.275	.205	—	1 Rich
7074	①	15/32	1 3/8	—	.180②	.275	.205	—	1 Rich

①—Air/fuel ratio or idle CO% rating is found in Tuneup Specification tables in specifications chapters.
②—1600 rpm hot on 2nd step of cam with TCS solenoid & EGR disconnected.

Carb. Model	Idle Mixture Screw Setting	Float Level	Float Drop	Idle Vent Setting	Fast Idle Cam Setting	Dechoke or Unloader Setting	Pulldown Setting	Vacuum Break Setting	Choke Setting
FORD 1974									
D4DE-ABA	②	3/8	—	—	.140	.250	.200	—	Index
D4DE-EA	②	3/8	—	—	.170	.250	.230	—	Index
D4DE-JA	②	3/8	—	—	.140	.250	.200	—	1 Rich
D4DE-JB	②	3/8	—	—	.140	.250	.200	—	Index
D4DE-KA	②	3/8	—	—	.140	.250	.200	—	1 Rich
D4DE-KB	②	3/8	—	—	.140	.250	.200	—	Index

②—Air/fuel ratio or idle CO% rating is found in Tuneup Specification tables in specifications chapters.

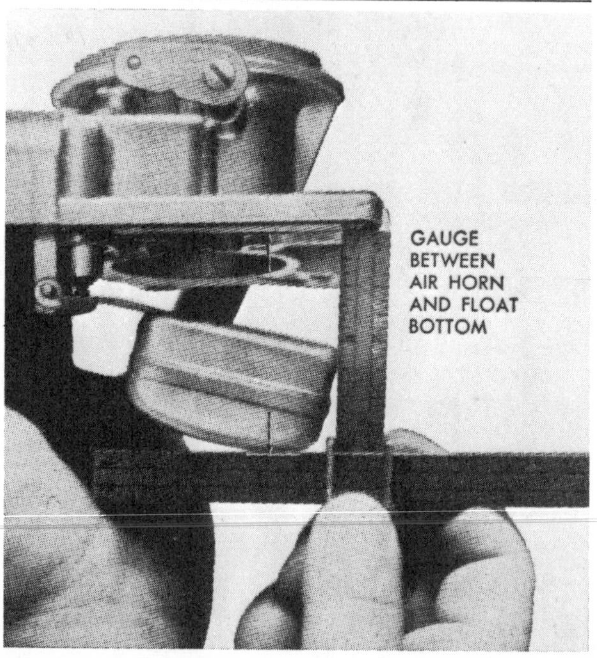

Fig. 1 YF float drop adjustment

MODEL YF ADJUSTMENTS

Float Drop Adjustment

Fig. 1

Hold the air horn upright and measure maximum clearance from top of float to bottom of air horn with float drop gauge. Bend tab at the end of the float arm to obtain specified setting listed under YF Adjustment Specifications.

Clearance on 1969-70 Ford units is measured between the throttle valve and the throttle bore (side opposite idle port). Clearance on 1971-74 Ford and 1974 American Motors units is measured between the lower edge of the choke plate and the carburetor bore.

The 1970-73 American Motors units have engine fast idle rpm settings in place of specified carburetor to choke plate clearance. Refer to *YF Specifications Chart*. Adjustment is the same as above.

NOTE: On 1974 American Motors models, the choke unloader adjustment has been eliminated. It is only necessary to check for full throttle opening when the throttle is operated from inside the vehicle.

All Other 1974 Units

Adjustments are the same as on 1970-73 models. For service procedures, refer to the Emission Control Manual.

CARTER RBS ADJUSTMENT SPECIFICATIONS

See Tuneup Chart in specifications chapter for hot idle speed.

Carb. Model	Idle Mixture Screw Setting	Float Level	Step-Up Rod	Accel. Pump Stroke	Fast Idle Linkage	Fast Idle Throttle Plate Setting	Dechoke Setting	Pulldown Setting	Dashpot Setting	Choke Setting
FORD ENGINES 1974										
D4DE-AAA	①	9/16	—	—	.115②	—	.250	.190	—	1 Lean
D4DE-AB	①	9/16	—	—	.115②	—	.250	.190	—	Index
D4DE-BB	①	9/16	—	—	.115②	—	.250	.300	—	Index
D4DE-SB	①	9/16	—	—	.115②	—	.250	.300	—	Index
D4DE-TA	①	9/16	—	—	.115②	—	.250	.190	—	Index

①—Air/fuel ratio or idle CO% rating is found in Tuneup Specification tables in specifications chapters.
②—At kickdown.

MODEL RBS ADJUSTMENTS

This carburetor incorporates a single aluminum casting with a pressed steel bowl. Adjustments are readily accessible and most calibration points are located in the single casting.

Fuel pickups are located near the centerline of the carburetor bore to gain the benefits of a concentric bowl carburetor, yet so located that engine heat being radiated through the bore is conducted through the casting but is not readily conducted to the fuel in the bowl. Two internal vapor vents allow rapid fuel vapor dissipation to help provide smooth idle conditions and to minimize hard starting when the engine is hot. An external vent, mechanically controlled by the throttle, is also used on 1974 California units.

A diaphragm-controlled stepup type metering rod controls the fuel supply. The accelerator pump is spring actuated.

The carburetor is equipped with a vacuum piston automatic choke. On 1974 California units, an electric assist choke is used to open the choke plate within 1-1½ minutes after the underhood temperatures reach approximately 60° F. For service procedures, refer to the Emission Control System

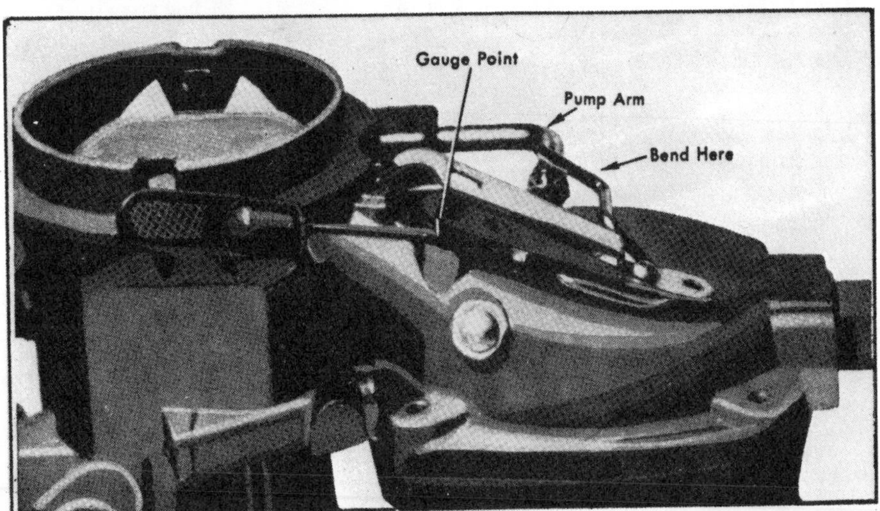

Fig. 2 Bowl vent adjustment

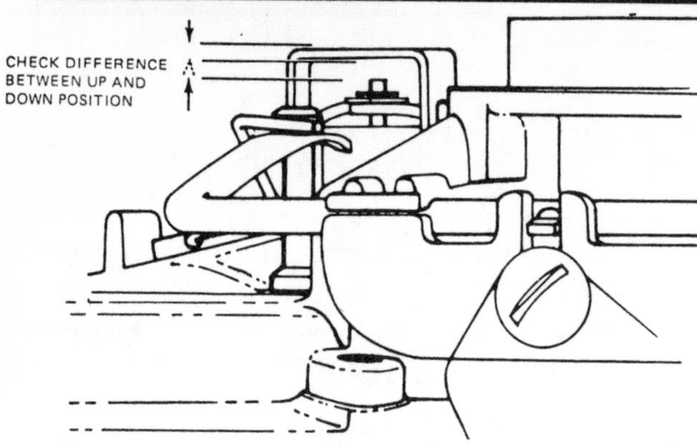

Fig. 3 Bowl vent adjustment. 1974 *California units*

chapter in the Emission Control Manual.

The 1973-74 RBS unit incorporates an Exhaust Gas Recirculation port. The EGR port connects to the primary bore and allows a metered amount of exhaust gas to be fed into the fuel/air mixture.

The carburetor model number is stamped on the side of the flange near the throttle lever.

Bowl Vent Adjustment

1974 California Units

With the accelerator pump properly adjusted, place the throttle at curb idle position on the extended solenoid. Measure the direction between the top of the vent guard and the top of the vent valve stem. Then open the throttle until the vent valve seats and measure the same distance again. The difference between the two measurements is the vent opening, Fig. 3. Refer to Carter RBS Specification Chart. Adjust it by bending the link at the accelerator pump arm contact point.

All Other 1974 Units

Adjustments are the same as for 1970-1973 models. For service procedures refer to the Emission Control Manual.

Fast Idle Cam Adjustment

1971-74 Units

Position the fast idle screw on the kickdown step of the fast idle cam against the shoulder of the high step. Adjust it by bending the choke plate connecting rod to obtain the specified clearance between the lower edge of the choke plate and the carburetor bore.

Dechoke Clearance

1970-74 Ford Units

Hold the throttle lever at the wide open position and close the choke plate as far as possible without forcing it. The dechoke clearance on the 1970 units is measured between the upper edge of the choke plate and the inner wall of the main body. While clearance on 1971-74 units is measured between the lower edge of the choke plate and the inner wall of the main body.

CARTER BBD ADJUSTMENT SPECIFICATIONS

See Tuneup Chart in specifications chapter for hot idle speed.

Carb. Model	Initial Idle Mix. Screws Turns Open	Float Level	Pump Travel Inch	Bowl Vent Drill Size	Choke Unloader Drill Size	Choke Vacuum Kick Drill Size	Fast Idle Cam Position Drill Size	Automatic Choke Setting
CHRYSLER, DODGE & PLYMOUTH								
1974								
6464S	①	¼	½③	—	.325	.150	.095	Fixed
6465S	①	¼	½③	—	.325	.110	.095	Fixed
6466S④	①	¼	½③	—	.325	.150	.095	Fixed
6467S④	①	¼	½③	—	.325	.110	.095	Fixed
1975								
800S	①	¼	½③	—	.280	.130	.070	Fixed
8001S	①	¼	½③	—	.310	.110	.070	Fixed
8003S	①	¼	½③	—	.310	.110	.070	Fixed
8062S	①	¼	½③	—	.310	.110	.070	Fixed
8064S	①	¼	½③	—	.310	.070	.070	Fixed
8066S	①	¼	½③	—	.280	.130	.070	Fixed

①—Air/fuel ratio or idle CO% rating is found in Tuneup Specification tables in specifications chapters.

③—At idle.

④—With California Emission package.

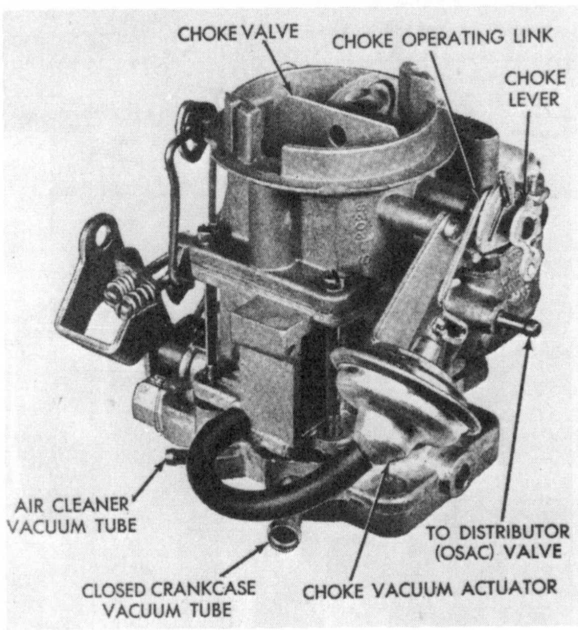

Fig. 4

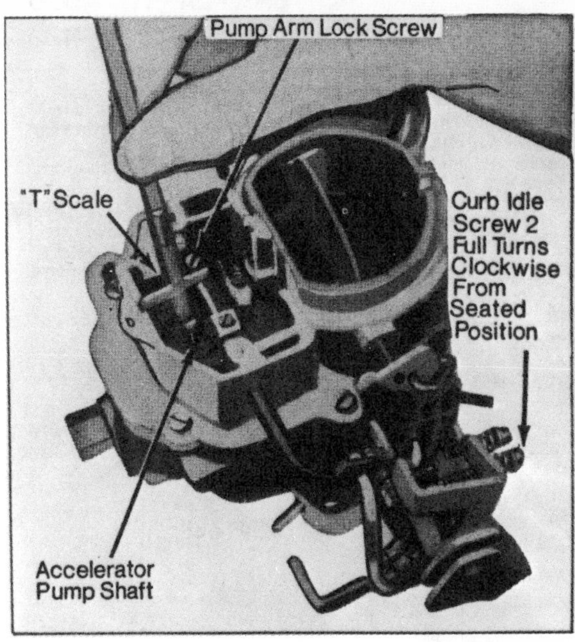

Fig. 5

MODEL BBD ADJUSTMENTS

Automatic Choke Adjustment

Note that the 1973-74 ECS equipped unit incorporates a Canister Purge Port.

The carburetors illustrated in Fig. 4 are used on the larger V8 engines. The one on the right is a standard model while the one at the left is used with CAP or CAS equipment. Note that the CAP model incorporates a dashpot for use with manual shift transmissions only. Also, on 1973-74 Chrysler units, an electric choke system is incorporated to open the choke at approximately 63°. For service information refer to the Emission Control System chapter in the Emission Control Manual.

Accelerator Pump

1974 1¼-inch Bore Units

1. Back off the curb idle adjusting screw, completely closing the throttle valve. Then open the choke valve, allowing the throttle valves to seat in the bores. Make sure that the accelerator pump S link is located in the outer hole or the pump arm.
2. Turn the curb idle adjusting screw until the screw contacts. Stop. Then rotate the screw two additional turns.
3. Measure the distance between the air horn surface and the top of the accelerator pump shaft. Refer to BBD Specifications Chart.
4. Adjust it by loosening the pump arm adjusting screw and rotating the sleeve until the proper dimension is obtained. Tighten the adjusting screw.

Choke Vacuum Kick Adjustment

Refer to the Emission Control Manual for procedures. When using an auxiliary vacuum source, disconnect the vacuum hose from the carburetor and connect it to the hose from the vacuum supply with a small length of tube to act as a fitting. Removal of the hose from the diaphragm may require forces which damage the system. On all 1969-72 units, apply a vacuum of 10 or more inches of mercury. On all 1973-74 units, apply a vacuum of 15 or more inches of mercury.

CARTER TQ ADJUSTMENT SPECIFICATIONS

See Tuneup Chart in specifications chapters for hot idle speeds.

Carb. Model	Air/Fuel Ratio	Float Setting	Secondary Throttle Linkage	Secondary Air Valve Opening	Secondary Air Valve Spring	Pump Travel	Choke Control Lever (On Car)	Choke Unloader	Fast Idle rpm	Choke Setting
CHRYSLER, DODGE, IMPERIAL & PLYMOUTH										
1974										
6452S	①	⑤	②	½	1¼ Turn	35/64	3⅜③	.310	1900	Fixed
6453S	①	⑤	②	½	1¼ Turn	31/64	3⅜③	.310	1900	Fixed
6454S④	①	⑤	②	½	1¼ Turn	35/64	3⅜③	.310	1900	Fixed
6455S④	①	⑤	②	½	1¼ Turn	31/64	3⅜③	.310	1900	Fixed
6456S	①	⑤	②	½	1¼ Turn	35/64	3⅜③	.310	1700	Fixed
6457S④	①	⑤	②	½	1¼ Turn	31/64	3⅜③	.310	1800	Fixed
6459S④	①	⑤	②	½	1¼ Turn	31/64	3⅜③	.310	1800	Fixed
6460S	①	⑤	②	½	1¼ Turn	31/64	3⅜③	.310	1700	Fixed
6461S④	①	⑤	②	½	1¼ Turn	31/64	3⅜③	.310	1700	Fixed
6462S	①	⑤	②	½	1¼ Turn	31/64	3⅜③	.310	1700	Fixed
6463S④	①	⑤	②	½	1¼ Turn	31/64	3⅜③	.310	1700	Fixed
6487S⑥	①	⑤	②	½	1¼ Turn	35/64	3⅜③	.310	2000	Fixed
6488S④	①	⑤	②	½	1¼ Turn	35/64	3⅜③	.310	1800	Fixed
6489S	①	⑤	②	½	1¼ Turn	31/64	3⅜③	.310	2000	Fixed
6496S	①	⑤	②	½	1¼ Turn	31/64	3⅜③	.310	2000	Fixed
6498S⑤	①	29/32	②	33/64	1¼ Turn	31/64	3⅜③	.310	1900	Fixed
6499S④	①	29/32	②	33/64	1¼ Turn	35/64	3⅜③	.310	1900	Fixed
1975										
9002S	①	29/32	②	½	1¼ Turn	35/64	3⅜	.310	1600	Fixed
9004S	①	29/32	②	½	1¼ Turn	35/64	3⅜	.310	1600	Fixed
9008S	①	29/32	②	½	1¼ Turn	35/64	3⅜	.310	1800	Fixed
9009S	①	29/32	②	½	1¼ Turn	35/64	3⅜	.310	1600	Fixed
9010S	①	29/32	②	½	1¼ Turn	35/64	3⅜	.310	1600	Fixed
9011S	①	29/32	②	½	1¼ Turn	35/64	3⅜	.310	1600	Fixed
9012S	①	29/32	②	½	1¼ Turn	35/64	3⅜	.310	1800	Fixed
9046S	①	29/32	②	½	1¼ Turn	35/64	3⅜	.310	1800	Fixed
9050S	①	29/32	②	½	1¼ Turn	35/64	3⅜	.310	1600	Fixed
9051S	①	29/32	②	½	1¼ Turn	35/64	3⅜	.310	1600	Fixed
9052S	①	29/32	②	½	1¼ Turn	35/64	3⅜	.310	1800	Fixed
9053S	①	39/32	②	½	1¼ Turn	35/64	3⅜	.310	1800	Fixed

①—For Air/fuel ratio and idle CO%, see Tuneup charts in specifications chapters.
②—Adjust link so primary and secondary stops both contact at same time.
③—Off car.
④—With California Emission package.
⑤—Brass float, 1 inch; cellular plastic float, 29/32 inch.
⑥—Except California.

Carb. Model	Air/Fuel Ratio	Float Setting	Secondary Throttle Linkage	Secondary Air Valve Opening	Secondary Air Valve Spring	Pump Travel	Choke Control Lever (On Car)	Choke Unloader	Fast Idle rpm	Choke Setting
FORD & MERCURY										
1974										
D4AE-BB, BC	①	1 1/16	②	.468	—	5/16③	—	.250	1250	Index

①—For Air/fuel ratio and idle CO%, see Tuneup charts in specifications chapters.
②—Adjust link so primary and secondary stops both contact at same time.
③—Measured bottom of S link to top of bowl cover.

MODEL TQ ADJUSTMENTS

The TQ (Thermo-Quad) carburetor is unique in design in that it has a black main body or fuel bowl of molded phenolic resin. This acts as an effective heat insulator. Fuel is kept cooler by about 20 degrees Fahrenheit than in carburetors of all metal design. Another reason for the lower operating temperatures is its suspended design metering system. All calibration points with the exception of the idle adjusting screws, are in the upper aluminum casting or air horn and are in effect suspended in cavities in the plastic main body.

Some 1974 units incorporate cellular plastic floats. Note that the float level settings are different. Refer to the TQ Specifications Chart.

Fast Idle Cam & Linkage

Fig. 6

With the fast idle adjusting screw on the second

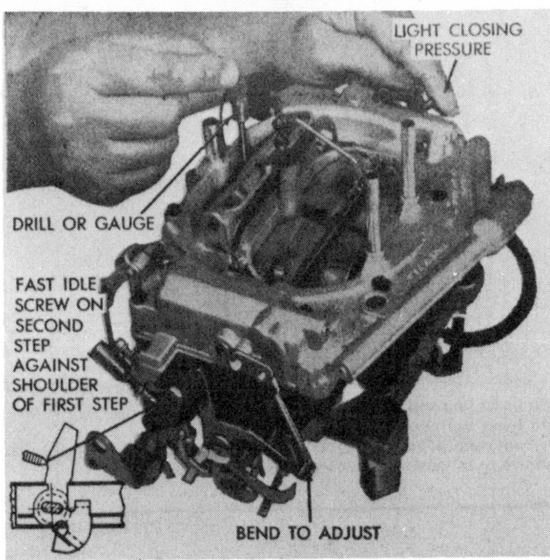

Fig. 6 TQ fast idle cam & linkage adjustment

step of the fast idle cam, move the choke valve toward the closed position with light pressure on the choke control lever. The clearance between the choke valve lower edge and the air horn wall should be .110-inch on all 1971-73 units, .100-inch on 1974 Chrysler units and .099-inch on 1974 Ford units. Adjust it by bending the fast idle connector rod at an angle.

Secondary Throttle Lockout

Fig. 8

Move the choke control lever to the open choke position. Measure the clearance between the lockout lever and stop. Clearance should be .010-.030-inch on all 1971-73 units and .060-.090-inch on 1974 units. Adjust it by bending the tang on the fast idle control lever.

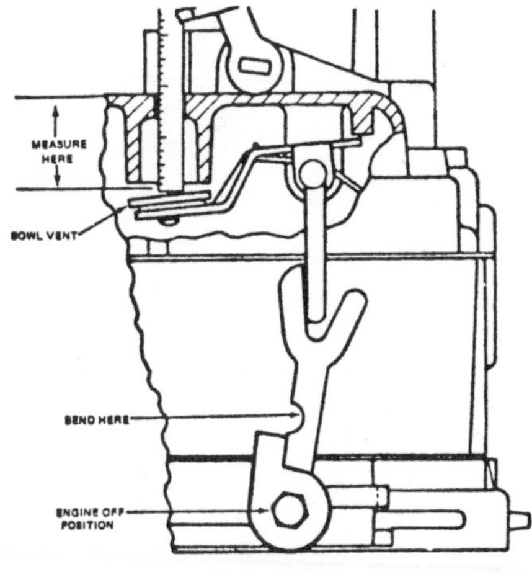

Fig. 7 TQ bowl vent valve adjustment

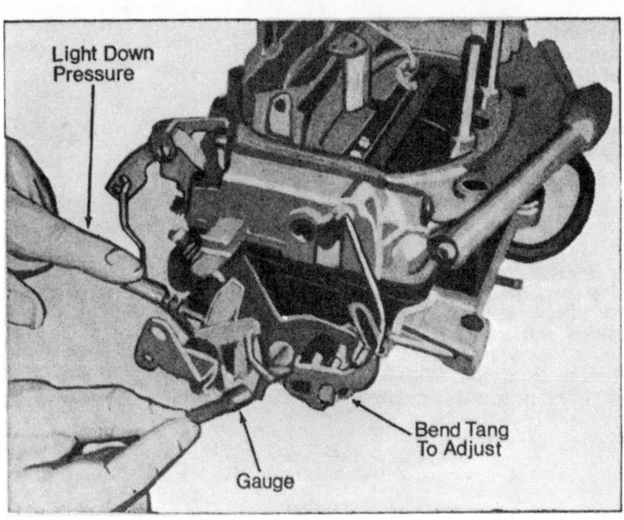

Fig. 8 TQ secondary throttle lockout

Bowl Vent Valve Adjustment

Fig. 7

Remove the bowl vent valve checking hole plug in the bowl cover. With the throttle valves at curb idle, insert a narrow ruler down through the hole. Allow the ruler to rest lightly on top of the valve. The dimension should be .850-inch on all 1971-73 units, .812-inch on 1974 Chrysler units and .900-inch on 1974 Ford units. Adjust it by bending the bowl vent operating lever at the notch. Install a new plug.

Fast Idle Speed Cam

NOTE: On 1974 Chrysler units, remove the air cleaner and plug the vacuum fittings to the heated air control and OSAC valves. On 1974 Ford units, remove the air cleaner, disconnect the vacuum hoses at the carburetor spark port and distributor primary diaphragm. Then install a jumper hose between the two disconnected hoses. Disconnect and plug the EGR vacuum line.

All Other 1974 Units

Adjustments are the same as for 1970-73 models. For service procedures, refer to the Emission Control Manual.

Service Bulletins

1. If a stumble or a lag is encountered on acceleration on 1973 Chrysler Corp. cars with V8-340, 400, 440 engines with a Carter Thermo-Quad carburetor, it may be caused by an undersize accelerating pump plunger cup. This can be verified by checking the discharge from

Fig. 9

the accelerating pump discharge jets.

If the condition is considered to be caused by a deficiency in the pump circuit, the plunger should be replaced. A kit #3780111 is available for this purpose and consists of a plunger and check valve seat. The seat must be replaced because it becomes damaged during removal of the plunger.

2. When installing the bowl cover on the Carter TQ carburetors, it is important that the float lever pins are correctly positioned—centered in their supports. If the pins are not properly placed, they may be trapped between the gasket surfaces. When the bowl cover screws are tightended, the bowl will crack.

Ford Autolite/Motorcraft Carburetors

MODEL 2100, 6200-2V CARB. ADJUSTMENT SPECIFICATIONS

See Tuneup Chart in specifications chapters for hot idle speeds.

Carb. Model (Code 9510) ①	Idle Mixture Turns Open	Float Level (Dry)	Fuel Level (Wet)	Pump Setting Hole No. ④	Choke Plate Clearance (Pulldown)	Fast Idle Cam Linkage Clearance	Fast Idle Speed (Hot Engine)	Dechoke Clearance ②	Dashpot Setting	Choke Setting
AMERICAN MOTORS 1974										
4DA2	③	13/32	25/32	Inboard	.140	.130	1600	.250	.140	1 Rich
4DA2-E	③	13/32	25/32	Inboard	.140	.130	1600	.250	.140	1 Rich
4DM2	③	13/32	25/32	Inboard	.130	.130	1600	.250	.140	2 Rich
4RA2	③	13/32	25/32	Inboard	.140	.130	1600	.250	.140	1 Rich
4RAC2	③	13/32	25/32	Inboard	.140	.130	1600	.250	.140	1 Rich
1975										
5DAZ	③	13/32	3/4	—	.140	.130	1600⑦	.250	—	1 Rich
5DMS	③	13/32	3/4	—	.130	.130	1600⑦	.250	.093	2 Rich
5RAS	③	13/32	3/4	—	.140	.130	1600⑦	.250	—	1 Rich
FORD & MERCURY 1974										
D4AE-DA	③	7/16	13/16	No. 2A	—	—	—	—	—	1 Rich
D4AE-EA	③	7/16	13/16	No. 2A	—	—	—	—	—	3 Rich
D4AE-FA	③	7/16	13/16	No. 3A	—	—	—	—	—	3 Rich
D4AE-GA	③	7/16	13/16	No. 3A	—	—	—	—	—	3 Rich
D4AE-HB	③	7/16	13/16	No. 3A	—	—	—	—	—	3 Rich
D4AE-KA	③	7/16	13/16	No. 2A	—	—	—	—	—	3 Rich
D4DE-RB	③	7/16	13/16	No. 2	—	—	—	—	—	3 Rich
D4DE-LA	③	7/16	13/16	No. 2	—	—	—	—	—	3 Rich
D4DE-NB	③	7/16	13/16	No. 2	—	—	—	—	—	3 Rich

(continued)

MODEL 2100, 6200-2V CARB. ADJUSTMENT SPECIFICATIONS—Continued

See Tuneup Chart in specifications chapters for hot idle speeds.

Carb. Model (Code 9510) ①	Idle Mixture Turns Open	Float Level (Dry)	Fuel Level (Wet)	Pump Setting Hole No. ④	Choke Plate Clearance (Pulldown)	Fast Idle Cam Linkage Clearance	Fast Idle Speed (Hot Engine)	Dechoke Clearance ②	Dashpot Setting	Choke Setting
1974										
D4DE-PA	③	7/16	13/16	No. 2	—	—	—	—	—	3 Rich
D4DE-VA	③	7/16	13/16	No. 2A	—	—	—	—	—	3 Rich
D4OE-CA	③	7/16	13/16	No. 2	—	—	—	—	—	3 Rich
D4OE-EA	③	7/16	13/16	No. 2	—	—	—	—	—	3 Rich
D4OE-FA	③	7/16	13/16	No. 2A	—	—	—	—	—	3 Rich
D4OE-PA	③	7/16	13/16	No. 2A	—	—	—	—	—	3 Rich
D4ME-BA	③	7/16	13/16	No. 3A	—	—	—	—	—	3 Rich
D4ME-CA	③	7/16	13/16	No. 3A	—	—	—	—	—	3 Rich

①—Stamped on left side of fuel bowl or on tag attached to bowl cover.
②—Minimum clearance between choke plate and air horn wall with throttle plates wide open.
③—Air/fuel ratio or idle CO% rating is found in Tuneup Specification tables in specifications chapters.
④—With link in inboard hole in pump lever.
⑦—Hot on 2nd step of cam with TCS solenoid & EGR disconnected.

2100, 6200-2V & 4100-4V ADJUSTMENTS

Models 2100, 6200-2V,

Figs. 10 thru 12

These carburetors have two main bodies—the air horn and the throttle body. The air horn assembly, which serves as a cover for the throttle body, contains the choke plate and vents for the fuel bowl. On all 1969 units and 1972 Ford units, an external bowl vent valve is used.

A choke modulator assembly is incorporated in the 1970-74 units, Fig. 13. While a staged choke system is an added feature used on 1972 Ford installations, Fig. 11. This system, through the use of a bimetal sensor and a series of diaphragms, pulls open the choke plate within 15-60 seconds. The system operates only during times when underhood temperatures are above approximately 60 degrees F. The 1973 units have an additional port for the Exhaust Gas Recirculation (EGR) system, Fig. 12. On 1973-74 Ford units an electric choke system is incorporated which opens the choke plate within 1-1½ minutes when underhood temperatures are above approximately 55° to 60°. For service information refer to the Emission Control System chapter in the Emission Control Manual.

The throttle plate, accelerating pump, power valve and fuel bowl are in the throttle body. The

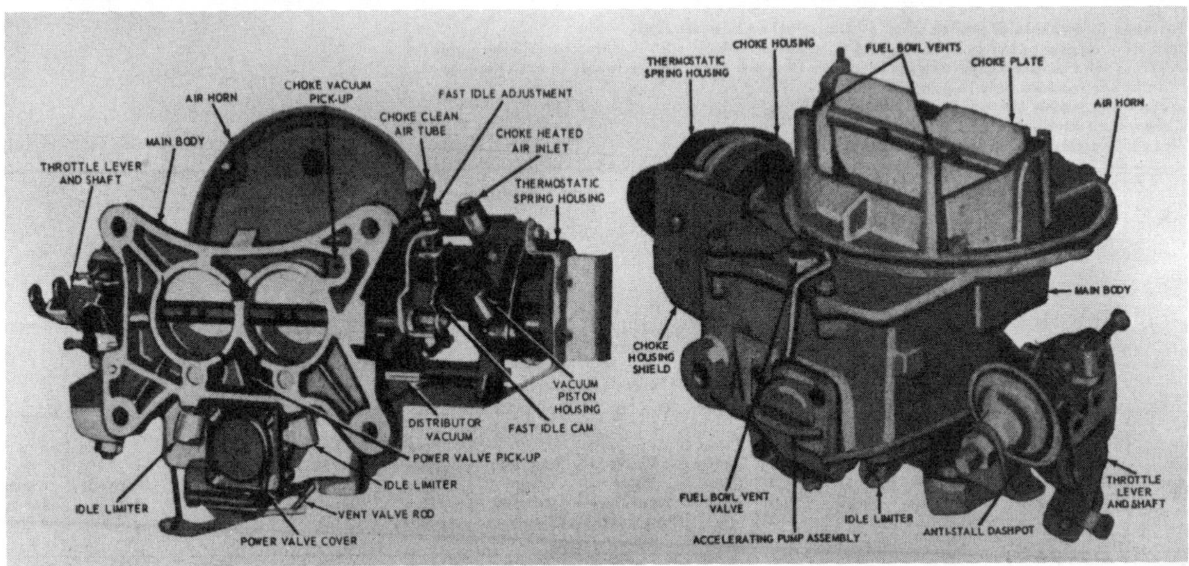

Fig. 10 Typical Autolite/Motorcraft 2100, 6200 *carburetor.* 1969

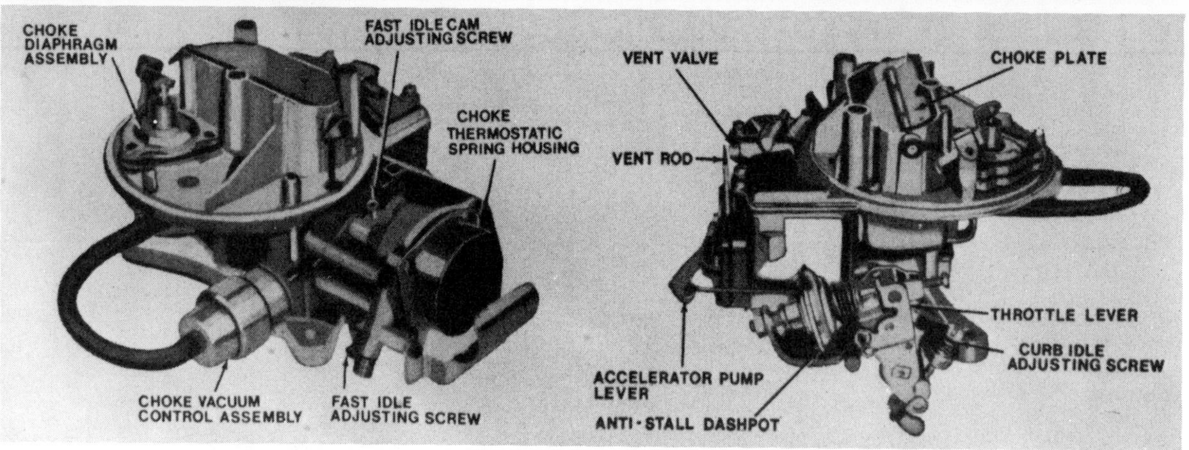

Fig. 11 *Typical Autolite/Motorcraft* 2100 *carburetor.* 1970-72

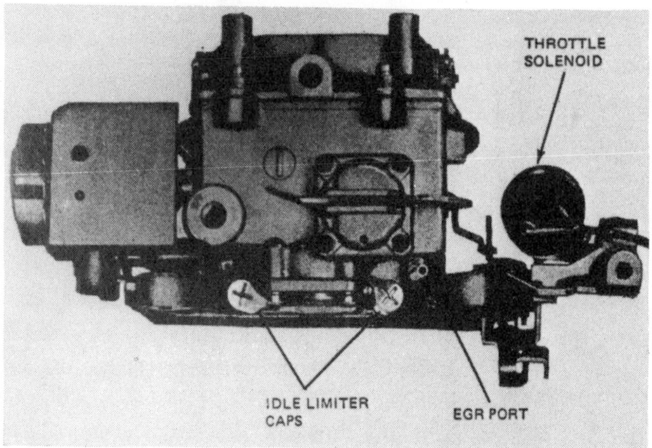

Fig. 12 *Autolite/Motorcraft* 2100 *carburetor.* 1973-74

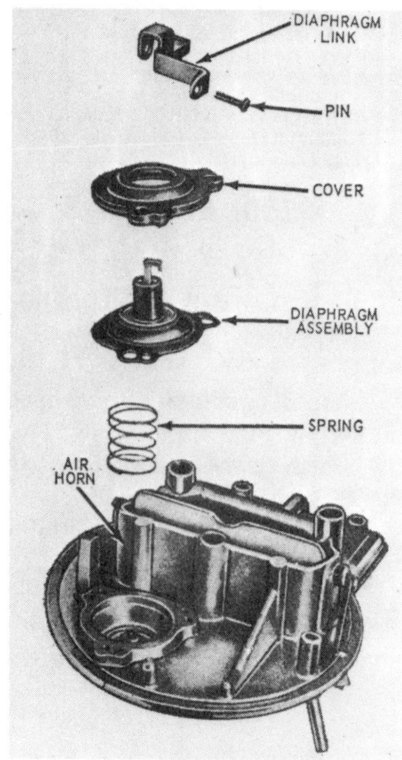

Fig. 13 *Autolite/Motorcraft* 2100 *choke diaphragm assembly*

choke housing is attached to the throttle body.

The two bodies each contain a main and a booster venturi, main fuel discharge, accelerating pump discharge, idle fuel discharge, and a throttle plate. An antistall dashpot is attached to the carburetor when the vehicle is equipped with an automatic transmission.

Choke Plate Clearance (Pulldown) Adjustment

1971-74 American Motors Units

1. Loosen the choke cover retaining screws. Rotate the choke cover ¼ turn counterclockwise (rich) from the index and tighten the retaining screws. Disconnect the choke heat inlet tube.
2. Align the fast idle speed adjusting screw with the second step of the fast idle cam, Fig. 15.
3. Start the engine without moving the accelerator linkage. Turn the fast idle cam lever adjusting screw out counterclockwise 3 full turns.
4. Measure the clearance between the lower edge of the choke valve and the air horn wall. Refer to the *2100 Specifications Chart* for the correct setting. Adjust it by grasping the modulator arm securely with a pair of pliers at point A and twisting the arm at point B with a second pair of pliers. Twist toward the front of the carburetor to increase clearance and toward the rear to decrease clearance, Fig. 16.

CAUTION: Use extreme care while twisting the modulator arm to avoid damaging the nylon piston rod of the modulator assembly.

NOTE: Connect the choke heat tube. Turn the fast idle cam lever adjusting screw in (clockwise) 3 full turns. Do not reset the choke cover until the

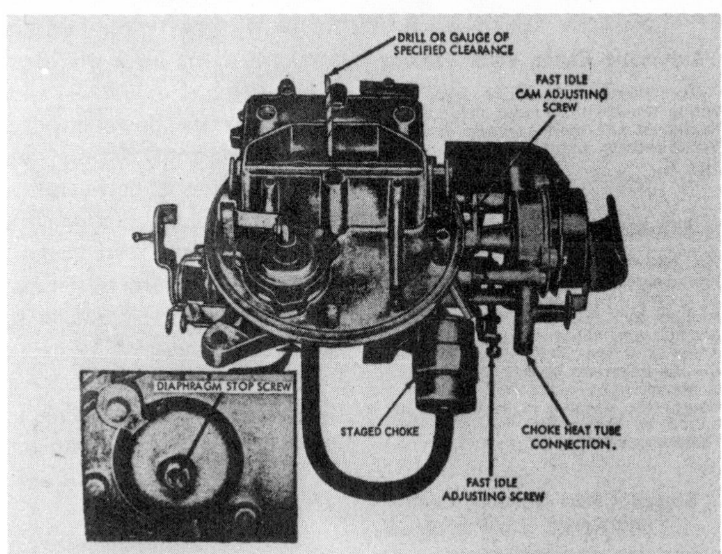

Fig. 14 *Choke plate pulldown clearance* 2100. 1970 *American Motors and* 1970-74 *Ford*

fast idle cam linkage adjustment has been performed.

1973-74 Ford Units

Since the choke plate pulldown is set in production by means of an air/fuel meter, no specific clearance is indicated for pulldown adjustment. If the vehicle shows indication of leanness during cold starting, decrease the clearance between the choke plate and the air horn wall by 0.020-inch. If the engine shows signs of an overrich condition during cold starting, increase the pulldown clearance by 0.020-inch. If additional adjustment is required always make the adjustments in steps of 0.020-inch. If the original pulldown adjustment is lost, set the clearance between the choke plate and the air horn to 0.160-inch. Then adjust as required in steps of 0.020-inch, Fig. 14.

Fig. 16 *Choke plate pulldown clearance* 2100. 1971-74 *American Motors*

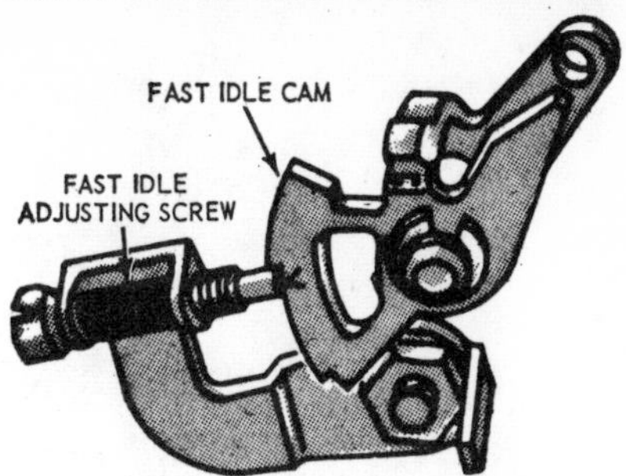

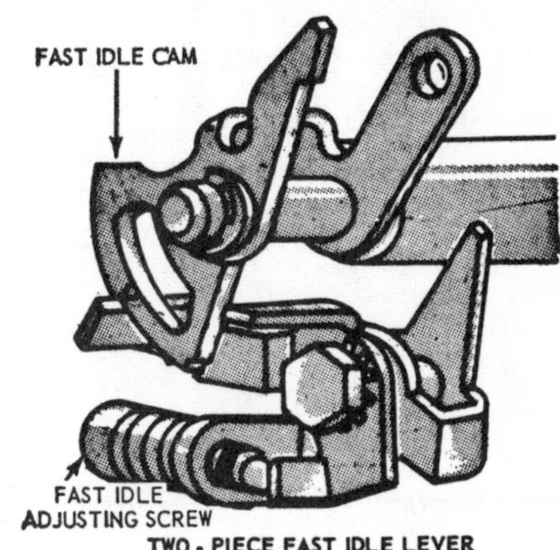

Fig. 15 *Autolite/Motorcraft fast idle adjustment* 2100

Fast Idle Cam Clearance

1969-74 Units

1. Loosen the choke thermostatic spring housing retainer screws and set the housing 90 degrees in the rich direction.
2. Position the fast idle speed screw at the kick-down step of the fast idle cam. The kickdown step is identified on most units by a V stamped

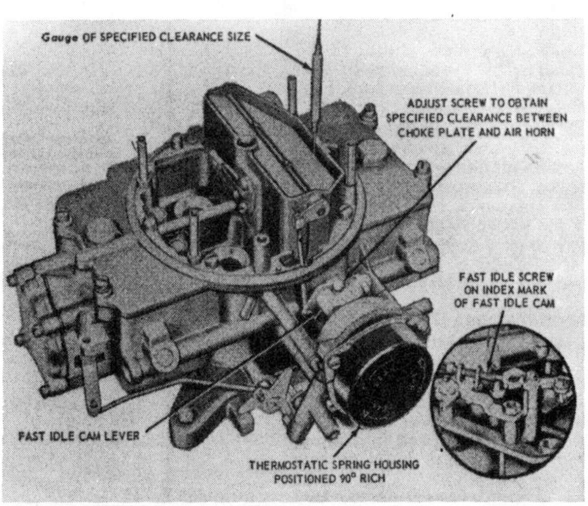

Fig. 17 *Vacuum piston type choke fast idle cam linkage adjustment.* 2100, 6200, 4100

Fig. 18 Automatic choke adjustment. 2100, 6200, 4100

on the cam, Fig. 15. When a two-piece fast idle lever is used, a tang on the top lever will align with the V mark on the cam, Fig. 15.

3. Be sure the cam is at the kickdown position while checking or adjusting the fast idle cam clearance. Check the clearance between the lower edge of the choke plate and the air horn wall, Fig. 17. Refer to *2100 Specifications Chart*. Adjust the clearance by turning the fast idle cam clearance adjusting screw clockwise to increase, and counterclockwise to decrease the clearance.
4. Set the choke thermostatic spring housing to specifications, Fig. 18. Adjust the antistall dashpot, idle speed and fuel mixture.

MODEL 4300-4V ADJUSTMENT SPECIFICATIONS

See Tuneup Chart in specifications chapters for hot idle speeds.

Carb. Model (Code 9510) ①	Idle Mixture Turns Open	Float Level (Dry)	Pump Setting (Hole No.)	Choke Plate Clearance (Pulldown)	Fast Idle Cam Linkage Setting	Fast Idle Speed (Hot Engine)	Auxiliary Inlet Valve Setting	Dechoke Clearance	Dashpot Setting	Choke Setting
AMERICAN MOTORS 1974										
4TA4	②	13/16	Center	.170	.160	1600	.050	.325	9/64	2 Rich
4TA4 Police	②	25/32	Center	.170	.160	1600	.030	Preset	9/64	2 Rich
4TM4	②	13/16	Center	.170	.160	1600	.050	.325	9/64	2 Rich
1975										
5TA4-P③	②	29/32	—	.140	.160	1600④	—	.325	—	2 Rich

①—Tag attached to bowl cover.
②—Air/fuel ratio or idle CO% rating is found in Tuneup Specification tables in specifications chapters.
③—Model 4350.
④—Hot on 2nd step of cam with TCS solenoid & EGR disconnected.

Carb. Model (Code 9510) ①	Idle Mixture Turns Open	Float Level (Dry)	Pump Setting (Hole No.)	Choke Plate Clearance (Pulldown)	Fast Idle Cam Linkage Setting	Fast Idle Speed (Hot Engine)	Auxiliary Inlet Valve Setting	Dechoke Clearance	Dashpot Setting	Choke Setting
FORD AND MERCURY ENGINES 1974										
D4AE-AA	⑤	3/4	#1	.230	.200	—	1/16	—	—	Index
D4AE-NA	⑤	3/4	#1	.220	.200	—	1/16	—	—	Index
D4OE-AA	⑤	13/16	#1	.180	.180	—	1/32	—	—	Index
D4OE-BA	⑤	13/16	#1	.170	.170	—	1/32	—	—	Index
D4TE-ATA	⑤	13/16	#1	.220	.180	—	1/16	—	—	Index
D4VE-AB	⑤	3/4	#1	.220	.200	—	1/16	—	—	Index

①—Tag attached to bowl cover.
③—8-390 with Imco 2 Rich, with Thermactor 1 rich.
④—8-428 with Imco Index, with Thermactor 1 rich.
⑤—Air/fuel ratio or idle CO% rating is found in Tuneup Specification tables in specifications chapters.

MODEL 4300-4V ADJUSTMENTS

The automatic choke system consists of a standard bimetal thermostat. On 1972 Ford units a staged choke release system is used which opens the choke plate within 15-60 seconds when underhood temperatures are above 60°, Figs. 19 and 20. On 1973-74 Ford units an electric choke system is incorporated which opens the choke within 1-1½ minutes when underhood temperatures are above approximately 55° to 60°. On 1973-74 American Motors units, an electric choke system is also incorporated which opens the choke when underhood temperatures are above approximately 95°. For service information refer to the Emission Control System chapter in the Emission Control Manual.

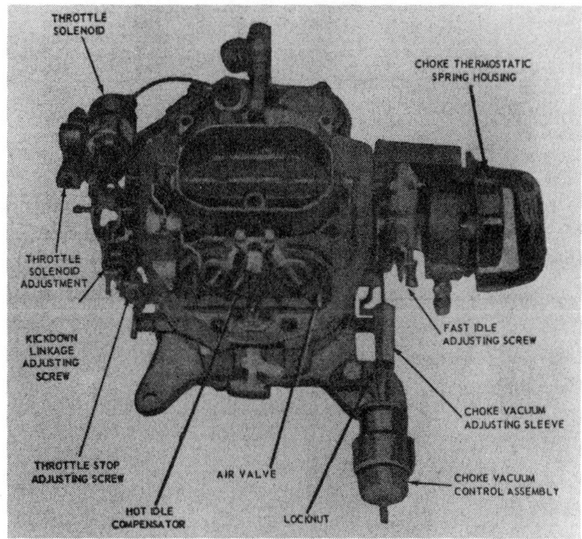

Fig. 19 4300A-4V *carburetor with staged choke.* 1972

Auxiliary Valve Setting

1969-74 Ford and 1973-74 American Motors Units

1. Turn the air horn assembly upright allowing the float to hang freely.
2. Push up on the float until the primary fuel inlet needle lightly contacts its seat.
3. While holding the float in this position, measure the clearance between the float level auxiliary tab and the auxiliary inlet valve plunger.
4. Adjust by bending the tab. Refer to *4300 Specifications Chart.*

NOTE: *IMPORTANT:* To measure this clearance on a police fleet carburetor with a semi-articulating float, the float assembly must be positioned so that the bottom of both pontoons are the same distance from the gasket surface of the air horn when the primary fuel inlet is seated.

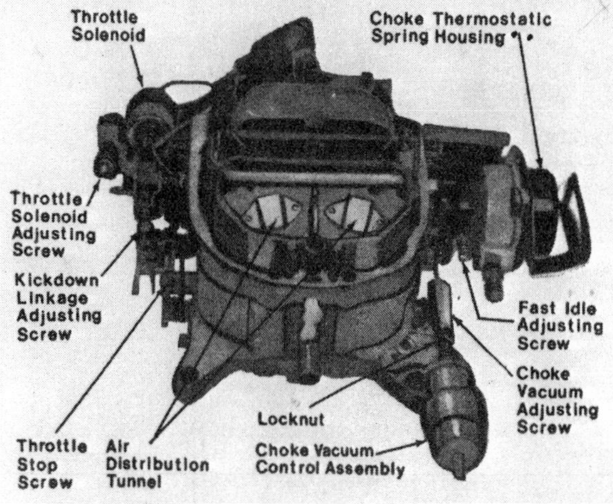

Fig. 20 4300D-4V *carburetor with staged choke.* 1972

MODEL 5200 ADJUSTMENT SPECIFICATIONS

See Tuneup Chart in specifications chapters for hot idle speeds.

Carb. Model (9510) ①	Idle Mixture Turns Open	Float Level	Pump Setting (Hole)	Choke Pulldown	Dechoke Clearance	Fast Idle Speed	Fast Idle Cam Clearance	Dashpot Setting	Choke Setting
1974									
D42E-AA	②	.460	#2	.280	.255	—	.1575	—	Index
D42E-AC	②	.460	#2	.280	.255	—	.158	—	Index
D42E-BA	②	.460	#2	.280	.255	—	.1575	—	1 Rich
D42E-CB	②	.460	#2	.280	.255	—	.1575	—	Index
D42E-CD	②	.460	#2	.280	.255	—	.158	—	Index
D42E-DB	②	.460	#2	.280	.255	—	.1575	—	1 Rich
D42F-EA	②	.460	#2	.236	.255	—	.1575	—	Index
D42E-EB	②	.460	#2	.236	.255	—	.158	—	Index
D42F-FA	②	.460	#2	.236	.255	—	.1575	—	Index
D42F-GA	②	.460	#2	.236	.255	—	.1575	—	Index
D42E-KA	②	.460	#2	.280	.255	—	.158	—	1 Rich
D4ZE-AA	②	.430	#2	.195	.256	—	.195	—	1 Rich
D4ZE-BA	②	.430	#2	.195	.256	—	.195	—	1 Rich
D4ZE-BC	②	.435	#2	.195	.255	—	.195	—	1 Rich
D4ZE-CA	②	.430	#2	.195	.256	—	.195	—	1 Rich
D4ZE-DA	②	.430	#2	.195	.256	—	.195	—	1 Rich
D4ZE-DC	②	.435	#2	.195	.255	—	.195	—	1 Rich

①—Tag attached to carburetor.
②—Air/fuel ratio or idle CO% rating is found in Tuneup Specification tables in specifications chapters.

THE 1974 ADJUSTMENT PROCEDURES ARE THE SAME AS IN PREVIOUS YEARS. SEE THE EMISSION CONTROL MANUAL, VOLUME I.

GM Delco/Rochester Carburetors

MODEL 2GC, 2GV CARBURETOR ADJUSTMENT SPECIFICATIONS

See Tuneup Chart in specifications chapters for hot idle speeds.
★Located on tag attached to or stamped on carburetor.

Carb. Part No. ★	Float Level	Float Drop	Pump Rod	Idle Vent	Intermediate Choke Rod	Vacuum Break	Automatic Choke	Choke Rod	Choke Unloader	Fast Idle Speed
BUICK 1974										
7044141	15/32	1 9/32	1 15/32	—	—	.160⑥	—	.080	.180	—
7044142	15/32	1 9/32	1 15/32	—	—	.140⑤	—	.080	.180	—
7044144	15/32	1 9/32	1 15/32	—	—	.140⑤	—	.080	.180	—
7044442	15/32	1 9/32	1 15/32	—	—	.140⑤	—	.080	.180	—
7044444	15/32	1 9/32	1 15/32	—	—	.140⑤	—	.080	.180	—
1975										
7045140	15/32	1 9/32	—	—	—	.140⑤	—	.080	.180	—
7045143	15/32	1 9/32	—	—	—	.140⑤	—	.080	.180	—
7045145	15/32	1 9/32	—	—	—	.120⑤	—	.080	.140	—
7045146	15/32	1 9/32	—	—	—	.120⑤	—	.080	.140	—
7045147	15/32	1 9/32	—	—	—	.120⑤	—	.080	.140	—
7045148	15/32	1 9/32	—	—	—	.120⑤	—	.080	.140	—
7045149	15/32	1 9/32	—	—	—	.120⑤	—	.080	.140	—
7045150	15/32	1 9/32	—	—	—	.120⑤	—	.080	.180	—
7045446	15/32	1 9/32	—	—	—	.120⑤	—	.080	.140	—
7045447	15/32	1 9/32	—	—	—	.140⑤	—	.080	.180	—
7045448	15/32	1 9/32	—	—	—	.120⑤	—	.080	.140	—
7045449	15/32	1 9/32	—	—	—	.120⑤	—	.080	.140	—
7045450	15/32	1 9/32	—	—	—	.120	—	.080	.180	—
7045451	15/32	1 9/32	—	—	—	.140	—	.080	.180	—
7045452	15/32	1 9/32	—	—	—	.120	—	.080	.140	—
7045453	15/32	1 9/32	—	—	—	.140	—	.080	.180	—

①—Rod is installed in lower of two lever holes.
②—At slow idle rpm vent valve should be open to specified dimension.
③—Holes in lever are marked ALT or STD. Install in proper hole.
④—Secondary adjustment .140″.
⑤—Secondary adjustment .120″.
⑥—Secondary adjustment .130″.

Carb. Part No. ★	Float Level	Float Drop	Pump Rod	Idle Vent	Intermediate Choke Rod	Vacuum Break	Automatic Choke	Choke Rod	Choke Unloader	Fast Idle Speed
CHECKER MOTORS 1974										
7044114	19/32	1 9/32	1 9/16	—	—	.130	—	.245	.325	1600

Carb. Part No. ★	Float Level	Float Drop	Pump Rod	Idle Vent	Intermediate Choke Rod	Vacuum Break	Automatic Choke	Choke Rod	Choke Unloader	Fast Idle Speed
CHEVROLET ENGINES 1974										
7044111	19/32	1 9/32	1 21/32	—	—	.140	—	.200	.250	1600
7044112	19/32	1 9/32	1 9/16	—	—	.130	—	.245	.325	1600
7044113	19/32	1 9/32	1 21/32	—	—	.140	—	.200	.250	1600
7044114	19/32	1 9/32	1 9/16	—	—	.130	—	.245	.325	1600
7044115	19/32	1 9/32	1 21/32	—	—	.140	—	.200	.250	1600
7044116	19/32	1 9/32	1 9/16	—	—	.130	—	.245	.325	1600
7044117	19/32	1 9/32	1 9/16	—	—	.140	—	.245	.325	1600
7044118	19/32	1 9/32	1 9/16	—	—	.130	—	.245	.325	1600
7044120	19/32	1 9/32	1 21/32	—	—	.130	—	.200	.250	1600
7044123	19/32	1 9/32	1 21/32	—	—	.140	—	.200	.250	1600
7044124	19/32	1 9/32	1 9/16	—	—	.130	—	.245	.325	1600
7044126	19/32	1 9/32	1 21/32	—	—	.140	—	.200	.250	1600
7044127	19/32	1 9/32	1 9/16	—	—	.130	—	.245	.325	1700
7044129	19/32	1 9/32	1 21/32	—	—	.140	—	.200	.250	1600

(continued)

MODEL 2GC, 2GV CARBURETOR ADJUSTMENT SPECIFICATIONS—Continued

See Tuneup Chart in specifications chapters for hot idle speeds.
★Located on tag attached to or stamped on carburetor.

CHEVROLET ENGINES—continued
1975

Carb. Part No. ★	Float Level	Float Drop	Pump Rod	Idle Vent	Intermediate Choke Rod	Vacuum Break	Automatic Choke	Choke Rod	Choke Unloader	Fast Idle Speed
7045101	19/32	1 7/32	1 19/32	—	—	.130	—	.375	.350	—
7045102	19/32	1 7/32	1 19/32	—	—	.130	—	—	.350	—
7045103	19/32	31/32	1 5/8	—	—	.130	—	.380	.350	—
7045105	19/32	1 7/32	1 19/32	—	—	.130	—	.375	.350	—
7045106	19/32	1 7/32	1 19/32	—	—	.130	—	.380	.350	—
7045111	21/32	31/32	1 5/8	—	—	.130	—	.400	.350	—
7045112	21/32	31/32	1 5/8	—	—	.130	—	.400	.350	—
7045114	21/32	31/32	1 5/8	—	—	.130	—	.400	.350	—
7045115	21/32	31/32	1 5/8	—	—	.130	—	.400	.350	—
7045123	21/32	31/32	1 5/8	—	—	.130	—	.400	.350	—
7045124	21/32	31/32	1 5/8	—	—	.130	—	.400	.350	—
7045401	21/32	1 7/32	1 19/32	—	—	.130	—	.380	.350	—
7045402	21/32	1 7/32	1 19/32	—	—	.130	—	.375	.350	—
7045405	21/32	1 7/32	1 19/32	—	—	.130	—	.380	.350	—
7045406	21/32	1 7/32	1 19/32	—	—	.130	—	.380	.350	—
7045407	19/32	1 7/32	1 5/8	—	—	.130	—	.380	.350	—
7045408	19/32	1 7/32	1 19/32	—	—	.130	—	.380	.350	—
7045410	21/32	31/32	1 5/8	—	—	.130	—	.400	.350	—
7045412	21/32	31/32	1 19/32	—	—	.130	—	.400	.350	—

②—Gauge from lip at toe of float to air horn gasket.

③—At slow idle rpm vent valve should be opened to specified dimension.

OLDSMOBILE
1974

Carb. Part No. ★	Float Level	Float Drop	Pump Rod	Idle Vent	Intermediate Choke Rod	Vacuum Break	Automatic Choke	Choke Rod	Choke Unloader	Fast Idle Speed
7044159④	15/32	1 9/32	1 11/32	—	—	.200	On Index	.160	.250	900③
7044162④	15/32	1 9/32	1 11/32	—	—	.250	On Index	.160	.250	1000③

②—At slow idle rpm vent valve should open to specified dimension.

③—On low step of cam.
④—California.

PONTIAC
1973–74

Carb. Part No. ★	Float Level	Float Drop	Pump Rod	Idle Vent	Intermediate Choke Rod	Vacuum Break	Automatic Choke	Choke Rod	Choke Unloader	Fast Idle Speed
7043060	21/32	1 9/32	1 11/32	—	—	.160	1 Lean	.085	.180	—
7043062	21/32	1 9/32	1 5/16	—	—	.170	1 Lean	.085	.180	—
7043070	23/32	1 9/32	1 11/32	—	—	.160	1 Lean	.085	.180	—
7043071	23/32	1 9/32	1 5/16	—	—	.200	1 Lean	.085	.180	—
7043072	23/32	1 9/32	1 5/16	—	—	.170	1 Lean	.085	.180	—

1974

Carb. Part No. ★	Float Level	Float Drop	Pump Rod	Idle Vent	Intermediate Choke Rod	Vacuum Break	Automatic Choke	Choke Rod	Choke Unloader	Fast Idle Speed
7044063	21/32	1 9/32	1 5/16	—	—	.160	1 Lean	.085	.180	—
7044066	21/32	1 9/32	1 11/32	—	—	.180	1 Lean	.085	.180	—
7044067	21/32	1 9/32	1 11/32	—	—	.180	1 Lean	.085	.180	—

1975

Carb. Part No. ★	Float Level	Float Drop	Pump Rod	Idle Vent	Intermediate Choke Rod	Vacuum Break	Automatic Choke	Choke Rod	Choke Unloader	Fast Idle Speed
7045143	15/32	—	1 13/16	.025	—	.140②	—	.080	.180	—
7045160	9/16	1 7/32	1 3/4	.025	—	.145③	—	.085	.180	—
7045162	9/16	1 7/32	1 13/16	.025	—	.145④	—	.085	.180	—
7045171	9/16	1 7/32	1 13/16	.025	—	.145④	—	.085	.180	—

①—With choke valve closed, pull upward on choke rod to the limit of its travel. The end of rod should fit the gauge notch on the choke lever.

②—Rear .120".
③—Rear .265".
④—Rear .260".

THE 1974 ADJUSTMENT PROCEDURES ARE THE SAME AS IN PREVIOUS YEARS. SEE THE EMISSION CONTROL MANUAL, VOLUME I.

QUADRAJET 4MC & 4MV ADJUSTMENT SPECIFICATIONS

See Tuneup Chart in specifications chapters for hot idle speeds.

Carb. Model	Float Level	Pump Rod Hole	Pump Rod Adj.	Idle Vent	Air Valve	Fast Idle (Bench)	Choke Rod	Vacuum Break	Air Valve Dash-pot	Choke Unloader	Air Valve Lockout	Secondary Metering Rods	Air Valve Spring Windup
BUICK 1974													
7044240	13/32	Inner	1/4	—	—	2	.130	.215⑤	.030	.325	.015	53/64	7/16
7044241	13/32	Inner	1/4	—	—	2	.130	.215⑥	.030	.325	.015	53/64	7/16
7044242	13/32	Inner	1/4	—	—	2	.130	.200⑦	.030	.325	.015	53/64	7/16
7044244	15/32	Outer	3/8	—	—	2	.130	.170①	.030	.325	.015	53/64	11/16
7044246	15/32	Outer	3/8	—	—	2	.130	.170①	.030	.325	.015	53/64	11/16
7044540	13/32	Inner	1/4	—	—	2	.130	.215⑤	.030	.325	.015	53/64	7/16
7044544	15/32	Outer	3/8	—	—	2	.130	.170①	.030	.325	.015	53/64	11/16
7044546	15/32	Outer	3/8	—	—	2	.130	.170①	.030	.325	.015	53/64	11/16
7044547	15/32	Outer	3/8	—	—	2	.130	.170①	.030	.325	.015	53/64	11/16
7044549	15/32	Outer	3/8	—	—	2	.130	.170①	.030	.325	.015	53/64	11/16
7044551	13/32	Inner	1/4	—	—	2	.130	.215⑤	.030	.325	.015	53/64	7/16
1975													
7045240	7/16	Inner	9/32	—	—	—	.095	.135⑧	—	.240	.015	—	7/16
7045241	5/16	Outer	15/32	—	—	—	.095	.135⑨	—	.240	.015	—	3/4
7045244	5/16	Outer	15/32	—	—	—	.095	.130⑨	—	.240	.015	—	3/4
7045246	5/16	Outer	15/32	—	—	—	.095	.130⑨	—	.240	.015	—	3/4
7045544	5/16	Outer	15/32	—	—	—	.095	.145⑩	—	.240	.015	—	3/4
7045546	5/16	Outer	15/32	—	—	—	.095	.145⑩	—	.240	.015	—	3/4
7045548	7/16	Inner	9/32	—	—	—	.095	.135⑧	—	.240	.015	—	7/16
7045549	7/16	Inner	9/32	—	—	—	.095	.135⑧	—	.240	.015	—	7/16
7045551	7/16	Inner	9/32	—	—	—	.095	.135⑧	—	.240	.015	—	7/16
7045553	5/16	Outer	15/32	—	—	—	.095	.145⑨	—	.240	.015	—	3/4
7045554	5/16	Outer	15/32	—	—	—	.095	.145⑩	—	.240	.015	—	3/4

①—Secondary adjustment .150″.
②—Early 3/8″; late 7/16″.
③—Early, inner; late, outer.
④—Early 9/32″; late 13/32″.
⑤—Secondary adjustment .160″.
⑥—Secondary adjustment .195″.
⑦—Secondary adjustment .180″.
⑧—Rear .120.
⑨—Rear .115.
⑩—Rear .130.

Carb. Model	Float Level	Pump Rod Hole	Pump Rod Adj.	Idle Vent	Air Valve	Fast Idle (Bench)	Choke Rod	Vacuum Break	Air Valve Dash-pot	Choke Unloader	Air Valve Lockout	Secondary Metering Rods	Air Valve Spring Windup
CADILLAC 1974													
7044230	.250	Inner	.250	—	—	②	.110	.185	.030	.312	.015	.840	④
7044232	.360	Inner	.250	—	—	②	.110	.200	.030	.312	.015	.840	④
7044233	.290	Outer	.344	—	—	②	.110	.185	.030	.312	.015	.840	3/8
7044234	.250	Inner	.344	—	—	②	.110	.185	.030	.312	.015	.840	7/16
7044235	.360	Inner	.344	—	—	②	.110	.200	.030	.312	.015	.840	9/16
7047430	.250	Inner	—	—	—	②	.110	.185	—	.310	.015	—	—
7047431	.250	Inner	—	—	—	②	.110	.185	—	.310	.015	—	—
7047432	.360	Inner	—	—	—	②	.110	.200	—	.310	.015	—	—
7047433	.290	Outer	—	—	—	②	.110	.185	—	.310	.015	—	—
7047434	.360	Inner	—	—	—	②	.110	.200	—	.310	.015	—	—
7044530	.250	Inner	.250	—	—	②	.110	.185	.030	.312	.015	.840	3/8
7044532	.360	Inner	.250	—	—	②	.110	.200	.030	.312	.015	.840	1/2
17050631	.360	Outer	—	—	—	②	.110	.200	—	.310	.015	—	—
17050632	.250	Outer	—	—	—	②	.110	.185	—	.310	.015	—	—
1975													
7045230	15/32	Outer	3/8	.075	—	2 Turns	.080	⑤	.030	.215	.015	—	7/16
7045530	15/32	Outer	3/8	.075	—	2 1/4 Turns	.080	.230	.030	.215	.015	—	1/4

①—1925 rpm on engine.
②—1200–1250 rpm on second step and A/C. off.
③—Exc. Calif., Inner; California, Outer.
④—Up to 4000 ft. altitude, 1/2 turn. Above 4000 ft. altitude, 9/16 turn for Eldorado, 7/16 turn for all others exc. commercial vehicles and 3/8 for commercial vehicles.
⑤—Front .160″, rear .130″.

(continued)

QUADRAJET 4MC & 4MV ADJUSTMENT SPECIFICATIONS—Continued

See Tuneup Chart in specifications chapters for hot idle speeds.

Carb. Model	Float Level	Pump Rod		Idle Vent	Air Valve	Fast Idle (Bench)	Choke Rod	Vacuum Break	Air Valve Dash-pot	Choke Unloader	Air Valve Lockout	Secondary Metering Rods	Air Valve Valve Spring Windup
		Hole	Adj.										
CHECKER MOTORS 1974													
7044502	1/4	Inner	—	—	—	—	.430	.230	—	.450	—	—	7/8
CHEVROLET ENGINES 1974													
7044201	3/8	Inner	13/32	—	—	2 Turns	.430	.250	.015	.450	—	—	7/16
7044202	1/4	Inner	13/32	—	—	2 Turns	.430	.230	.015	.450	—	—	7/8
7044203	1/4	Inner	13/32	—	—	2 Turns	.430	.230	.015	.450	—	—	7/8
7044206	1/4	Inner	13/32	—	—	2 Turns	.430	.230	.015	.450	—	—	7/8
7044207	1/4	Inner	13/32	—	—	2 Turns	.430	.230	.015	.450	—	—	7/8
7044208	1/4	Inner	13/32	—	—	2 Turns	.430	.230	.015	.450	—	—	1 Turn
7044209	1/4	Inner	13/32	—	—	2 Turns	.430	.230	.015	.450	—	—	1 Turn
7044210	1/4	Inner	13/32	—	—	2 Turns	.430	.230	.015	.450	—	—	1 Turn
7044211	1/4	Inner	13/32	—	—	2 Turns	.430	.230	.015	.450	—	—	1 Turn
7044221	3/8	Inner	13/32	—	—	2 Turns	.430	.250	.015	.450	—	—	7/16
7044223	3/8	Inner	13/32	—	—	2 Turns	.430	.250	.015	.450	—	—	7/16
7044225	3/8	Inner	13/32	—	—	2 Turns	.430	.250	.015	.450	—	—	7/16
7044500	3/8	Inner	—	—	—	2 Turns	.430	.250	.015	.450	—	—	7/16
7044502	1/4	Inner	13/32	—	—	2 Turns	.430	.230	.015	.450	—	—	7/8
7044503	1/4	Inner	13/32	—	—	2 Turns	.430	.230	.015	.450	—	—	7/8
7044505	3/8	Inner	—	—	—	2 Turns	.430	.250	.015	.450	—	—	7/16
7044506	1/4	Inner	13/32	—	—	2 Turns	.430	.230	.015	.450	—	—	7/8
7044507	1/4	Inner	13/32	—	—	2 Turns	.430	.230	.015	.450	—	—	7/8
7044508	3/8	Inner	13/32	—	—	2 Turns	.430	.250	.015	.450	—	—	7/16
7044509	1/4	Inner	13/32	—	—	2 Turns	.430	.230	.015	.450	—	—	7/8
1975													
7045200	17/32	Inner	.275	—	—	—	.300	①	.015	.325	—	—	9/16
7045202	15/32	Inner	.275	—	—	—	.300	②	.015	.325	—	—	7/8
7045203	15/32	Inner	.275	—	—	—	.300	②	.015	.325	—	—	7/8
7045204	15/32	Inner	.275	—	—	—	.325	①	.015	.325	—	—	7/8
7045206	15/32	Inner	.275	—	—	—	.300	②	.015	.325	—	—	7/8
7045207	15/32	Inner	.275	—	—	—	.300	②	.015	.325	—	—	7/8
7045208	15/32	Inner	.275	—	—	—	.300	②	.015	.325	—	—	7/8
7045209	15/32	Inner	.275	—	—	—	.300	②	.015	.325	—	—	7/8
7045210	15/32	Inner	.275	—	—	—	.300	②	.015	.325	—	—	7/8
7045211	15/32	Inner	.275	—	—	—	.300	②	.015	.325	—	—	7/8
7045218	15/32	Inner	.275	—	—	—	.325	①	.015	.375	—	—	9/16
7045222	15/32	Inner	.275	—	—	—	.300	②	.015	.325	—	—	7/8
7045223	15/32	Inner	.275	—	—	—	.300	②	.015	.325	—	—	7/8
7045224	15/32	Inner	.275	—	—	—	.325	②	.015	.325	—	—	3/4
7045228	15/32	Inner	.275	—	—	—	.325	②	.015	.325	—	—	3/4
7045501	15/32	Inner	.275	—	—	—	.325	②	.015	.325	—	—	9/16
7045502	15/32	Inner	.275	—	—	—	.300	②	.015	.325	—	—	7/8
7045503	15/32	Inner	.275	—	—	—	.300	②	.015	.325	—	—	7/8
7045504	15/32	Inner	.275	—	—	—	.300	②	.015	.375	—	—	7/8
7045506	15/32	Inner	.275	—	—	—	.300	②	.015	.325	—	—	7/8
7045507	15/32	Inner	.275	—	—	—	.300	②	.015	.325	—	—	7/8
7045509	15/32	Inner	.275	—	—	—	.300	②	.015	.325	—	—	7/8
7045510	15/32	Inner	.275	—	—	—	.325	②	.015	.325	—	—	7/8
7045512	15/32	Inner	.275	—	—	—	.325	②	.015	.325	—	—	7/8
7045514	15/32	Inner	.275	—	—	—	.300	②	.015	.375	—	—	7/8

①—Front .200, Rear .550.

②—Front .180, Rear .170.

(continued)

QUADRAJET 4MC & 4MV ADJUSTMENT SPECIFICATIONS—Continued

See Tuneup Chart in specifications chapters for hot idle speeds.

Carb. Model	Float Level	Pump Rod		Idle Vent	Air Valve	Fast Idle (Bench)	Choke Rod	Vacuum Break	Air Valve Dash-pot	Choke Unloader	Air Valve Lockout	Secondary Metering Rods	Air Valve Valve Spring Windup
		Hole	Adj.										
OLDSMOBILE 1973–74													
7043250	¼	Inner	—	—	—	2 Turns	.230	.200	—	.300	.035	—	½
7043251	¼	Inner	—	—	—	2 Turns	.230	.200	—	.300	.035	—	¾
7043252	¼	Inner	—	—	—	2 Turns	.230	.200	—	.300	.035	—	¾
7043255	¼	Inner	—	—	—	2 Turns	.230	.200	—	.300	.035	—	½
7043256	¼	Inner	—	—	—	2 Turns	.230	.200	—	.300	.035	—	½
7043250	¼	Inner	⅜	—	—	—	.230	.200	.030	.300	.035	.070	½
7043251	¼	Inner	⅜	—	—	—	.230	.200	.030	.300	.035	.070	¾
7043252	¼	Inner	⅜	—	—	—	.230	.200	.030	.300	.035	.070	¾
7043255	¼	Inner	⅜	—	—	—	.230	.200	.030	.300	.035	.070	½
7043256	¼	Inner	⅜	—	—	—	.230	.200	.030	.300	.035	.070	½
7043259	¼	Inner	⅜	—	—	—	.230	.200	.030	.300	.035	.070	—
1974													
7044152	—	—	—	—	—	—	—	.200	—	—	—	—	—
7044557	¼	Inner	⅜	—	—	2 Turns	.230	.200	.030	.300	.035	.070	¾
7044558	¼	Inner	⅜	—	—	2 Turns	.230	.200	.030	.300	.035	.070	¾
7044559	¼	Inner	⅜	—	—	2 Turns	.230	.275	.030	.275	.035	.070	¾
1975													
7045183	15/32	Inner	9/32	.025	—	—	.135	.190①	.030	.230	.015⑥	—	½
7045184	15/32	Inner	9/32	.025	—	—	.135	.190①	.030	.230	.015⑥	—	¾
7045185	15/32	Inner	9/32	.025	—	—	.135	.190①	.030	.230	.015⑥	—	¾
7045246	5/16	Outer	⅜	.025	—	—	.095	.130②	.015	.240	.015⑥	—	¾
7045250	15/32	Inner	9/32	.025	—	—	.170	.245③	.030	.300	.015⑥	—	½
7045251	15/32	Inner	9/32	.025	—	—	—	.190①	.030	.230	.015⑥	—	¾
7045264	½	Inner	9/32	.025	—	—	.130	.150⑤	.030	.230	.015⑥	—	½
7045483	15/32	Inner	9/32	.025	—	—	.160	.275①	.030	.230	.015⑥	—	½
7045484	15/32	Inner	9/32	.025	—	—	.135	.190①	.030	.230	.015⑥	—	¾
7045485	15/32	Inner	9/32	.025	—	—	.160	.275③	.030	.230	.015⑥	—	¾
7045546	5/16	Outer	⅜	.025	—	—	.095	.145④	.030	.240	.015⑥	—	¾
7045550	15/32	Inner	9/32	.025	—	—	.160	.275③	.030	.230	.015⑥	—	½
7045551	15/32	Inner	9/32	.025	—	—	.135	.190①	.030	.230	.015⑥	—	¾
7045553	15/32	Inner	9/32	.025	—	—	.135	.150⑤	.030	.230	.015⑥	—	½
7045554	15/32	Inner	9/32	.025	—	—	.160	.275③	.030	.230	.015⑥	—	½
7045557	½	Inner	9/32	.025	—	—	.130	.150⑤	.030	.240	.015⑥	—	¾
7045559	5/16	Outer	⅜	.025	—	—	.095	.145④	.030	.240	.015⑥	—	¾

①—Rear adjustment .140″.
②—Rear adjustment .115″.
③—Rear adjustment .180″.
④—Rear adjustment .130″.
⑤—Rear adjustment .260″.
⑥—Secondary lockout.

Carb. Model	Float Level	Pump Rod Hole	Pump Rod Adj.	Idle Vent	Air Valve	Fast Idle (Bench)	Choke Rod	Vacuum Break	Air Valve Dash-pot	Choke Unloader	Air Valve Lockout	Secondary Metering Rods	Air Valve Valve Spring Windup
PONTIAC 1974													
7043263	13/32	Inner	.410	—	—	—	.205	.290	.025	.310	.015	—	⅝
7044262	13/32	Inner	.410	—	—	2 Turns	.200	.260	.025	.300	.010	—	⅜
7044266	13/32	Inner	.410	—	—	2 Turns	.200	.260	.025	.300	.010	—	½
7044267	13/32	Inner	.410	—	—	—	.205	.260	.025	.310	.015	—	⅜
7044268	13/32	Inner	.410	—	—	2 Turns	.200	.260	.025	.300	.010	—	½
7044269	13/32	Inner	.410	—	—	2 Turns	.200	.290	.025	.300	.010	—	½
7044270	13/32	Inner	.410	—	—	2 Turns	.200	.290	.025	.300	.010	—	¾
7044272	13/32	Outer	.315	—	—	2 Turns	.200	.290	.025	.300	.010	—	⅜
7044273	13/32	Inner	.410	—	—	2 Turns	.200	.290	.025	.300	.010	—	¾
7044274	13/32	Outer	.315	—	—	2 Turns	.200	.290	.025	.300	.010	—	9/16
7044278	25/64	Inner	.410	—	—	2 Turns	.200	.260	.025	.310	.015	—	¾
7044280	25/64	Inner	.410	—	—	2 Turns	.200	.260	.025	.310	.015	—	½

(continued)

QUADRAJET 4MC & 4MV ADJUSTMENT SPECIFICATIONS—Continued

See Tuneup Chart in specifications chapters for hot idle speeds.

Carb. Model	Float Level	Pump Rod Hole	Pump Rod Adj.	Idle Vent	Air Valve	Fast idle (Bench)	Choke Rod	Vacuum Break	Air Valve Dash-pot	Choke Unloader	Air Valve Lockout	Secondary Metering Rods	Air Valve Valve Spring Windup
PONTIAC—continued													
1974													
7044560	13/32	Inner	.410	—	—	2 Turns	.200	.260	.025	.300	.010	—	3/8
7044567	13/32	Outer	.315	—	—	2 Turns	.200	.290	.025	.300	.010	—	9/16
7044568	13/32	Inner	.410	—	—	2 Turns	.200	.260	.025	.300	.010	—	1/2
7044569	13/32	Inner	.410	—	—	2 Turns	.200	.260	.025	.300	.010	—	1/2
7044570	13/32	Outer	.315	—	—	2 Turns	.200	.290	.025	.300	.010	—	3/8
7044572	13/32	Inner	.410	—	—	2 Turns	.200	.260	.025	.300	.010	—	1/2
1975													
7045246	5/16	Outer	15/32	.025	—	—	.095	.130①	.015	.240	.015	—	3/4
7045260	1/2	Inner	9/32	—	—	—	.130	.150④	.030	.230	—	—	1/2
7045262	1/2	Inner	9/32	—	—	—	.130	.150④	.030	.230	—	—	1/2
7045263	1/2	Inner	9/32	—	—	—	.130	.150④	.030	.230	—	—	1/2
7045264	1/2	Inner	9/32	—	—	—	.130	.150④	.030	.230	—	—	1/2
7045266	1/2	Inner	9/32	—	—	—	.130	.150④	.030	.230	—	—	1/2
7045268	1/2	Inner	9/32	—	—	—	.130	.150④	.030	.230	—	—	.375
7045269	1/2	Inner	9/32	—	—	—	.130	.160③	.030	.230	—	—	1/2
7045274	1/2	Inner	9/32	—	—	—	.130	.150④	.030	.230	—	—	1/2
7045546	5/16	Outer	15/32	.025	—	—	.095	.145②	.015	.240	.015	—	3/4
7045562	1/2	Inner	9/32	—	—	—	.130	.150④	.030	.230	—	—	1/2
7045564	1/2	Inner	9/32	—	—	—	.130	.150④	.030	.230	—	—	1/2
7045566	1/2	Inner	9/32	—	—	—	.130	.150④	.030	.230	—	—	1/2
7045568	1/2	Inner	9/32	—	—	—	.130	.150④	.030	.230	—	—	1/2
7045569	1/2	Inner	9/32	—	—	—	—	.145②	.030	.230	—	—	1/2
7045571	1/2	Inner	9/32	—	—	—	—	.160③	.030	.230	—	—	3/4
7045572	5/16	Outer	15/32	.025	—	—	.095	.145④	.015	.240	.015	—	1/2
7045573	1/2	Inner	9/32	—	—	—	—	.160③	.015	.230	—	—	1/2
7045575	5/16	Outer	15/16	.025	—	—	.095	.150④	.015	.230	—	—	.375

①—Rear .115″.
②—Rear .130″.
③—Rear .265″.
④—Rear .260″.

QUADRAJET 4MV, 4MC ADJUSTMENTS

Choke Coil Rod Adjustment

1973-74 Buick, 1969-74 Cadillac & Chevrolet, 1970-71 Ford, Fig. 21

1. Remove the choke coil assembly to disengage the choke rod from the vacuum break lever.
2. Reinstall the coil assembly but do not install the rod into the lever.
3. With choke valve completely closed, fast idle cam in cold start position, and vacuum break lever in maximum upward position, pull the choke rod upward to the end of travel. The upper end of the rod should be positioned in gauging notch, Fig. 21. Bend choke rod to adjust and reassemble the coil assembly, rod and lever.

1970-74 Oldsmobile & 1973-74 Pontiac, Fig. 22

Place the fast idle cam follower on the highest step of the fast idle cam. Rotate the choke cover and coil assembly counterclockwise until the choke valve just closes and the index point on the cover aligns with the center index point on the choke housing.

1969 Oldsmobile and 1969-72 Pontiac

With fast idle adjusted and cam follower on second step and against high step of cam, close choke and check the dimension between the lower edge of the choke valve and the inner wall of the main body. Bend choke rod to adjust.

1969-72 Buick, Fig. 21

With the choke valve completely closed and the

choke rod in the bottom of the choke lever slot, pull or push choke coil rod to end of travel. Rod should be positioned as shown. Bend choke coil rod to adjust.

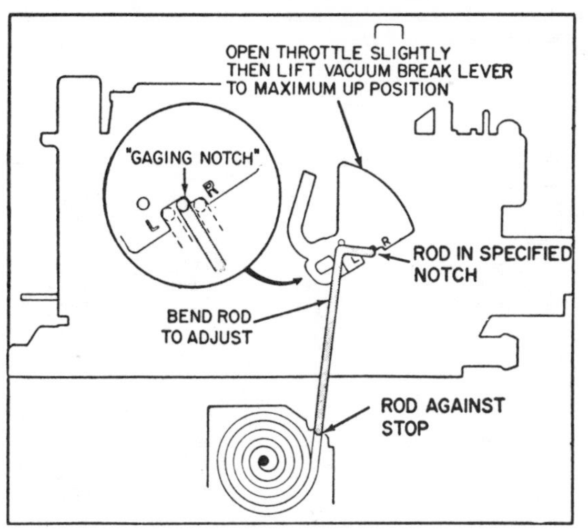

Fig. 21 *Choke coil adjustment. Typical*

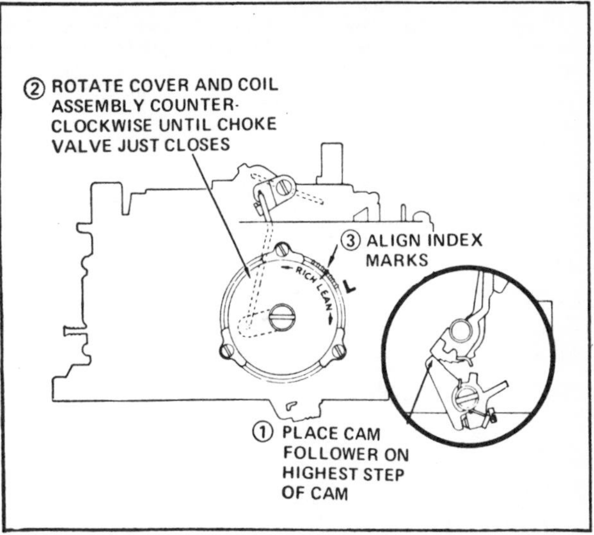

Fig. 22 4MC *choke coil adjustment*

SERVICE BULLETIN

Rochester Quadrajet

Delco/Rochester advises the possibility exists that the wrong throttle body to float bowl gaskets are being used by servicemen on 1970 and later Quadrajet carburetors. When this wrong substitution is made, vacuum leaks occur and cause rough idle due to air bypassing the primary throttle valves through the canister purge passage in the throttle body because the gasket will not seal this passage.

The difference between the throttle body to bowl gaskets is shown in Fig. 23.

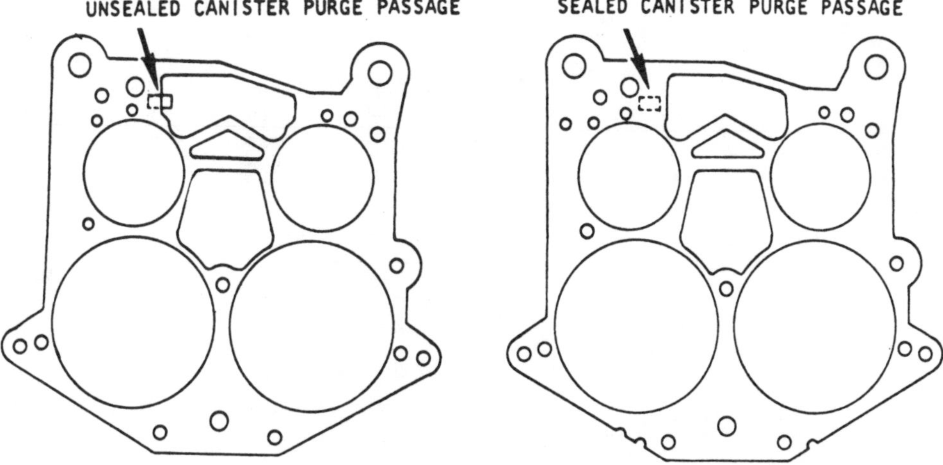

Fig. 23 *Delco/Rochester Quadrajet throttle body to float bowl gaskets*

MONOJET M, MV ADJUSTMENT SPECIFICATIONS

See Tuneup Chart in specifications chapters for hot idle speeds.

Carb. Part No. ①	Initial Idle Mix Screw Turns Open	Float Level	Metering Rod	Idle Vent	Fast Idle Off Car	Choke Rod	Vacuum Break	Unloader	Fast Idle rpm
BUICK									
1974									
7044014	—	11/32	.080	—	—	.230	.275	.500	1800
7044017	—	11/32	.080	—	—	.275	.350	.500	1800
1975									
7045012	—	11/32	.080	—	—	.160	.200⑦	.275	—
7045013	—	11/32	.080	—	—	.275	.350⑧	.275	—
7045314	—	11/32	.080	—	—	.230	.275⑧	.275	—
CHECKER MOTORS									
1974									
7044014	—	19/64	.079	—	—	.230	.275	.500	1800
7044314	—	19/64	.073	—	—	.245	.300	.500	1800
CHEVROLET									
1974									
7044014	—	11/32	.080	—	—	.230	.275	.500	1800
7044017	—	11/32	.080	—	—	.275	.350	.500	1800
7044023	—	1/8	—	—	—	.080	.130	.375	2000
7044024	—	1/8	—	—	—	.080	.130	.375	2200
7044033	—	1/8	—	—	—	.080	.130	.375	2000
7044034	—	1/8	—	—	—	.080	.130	.375	2200
7044314	—	11/32	.080	—	—	.245	.300	.500	1800
7044323	—	1/8	—	—	—	.080	.130	.375	2000
7044324	—	1/8	—	—	—	.080	.130	.375	2200
7044333	—	1/8	—	—	—	.080	.130	.375	2000
7044334	—	1/8	—	—	—	.080	.130	.375	2200
7044336	—	1/8	—	—	—	.245	.300	.500	1800
7044337	—	1/8	.080	—	—	.080	.130	.375	2000
7044339	—	11/32	—	—	—	.245	.300	.500	1800
7044340	—	1/8	.080	—	—	.080	.130	.375	2200
1975									
7045012	—	11/32	.080	—	—	.160	.200⑦	.215	—
7045013	—	11/32	.080	—	—	.275	.350⑧	.275	—
7045018	—	1/8	.080	—	—	.230	.275⑧	.275	—
7045024	—	1/8	—	—	—	.080	.100⑨	.375	—
7045025	—	1/8	—	—	—	.080	.100⑨	.375	—
7045027	—	1/8	—	—	—	.075	.350⑧	.375	—
7045028	—	1/8	—	—	—	.080	.100⑨	.375	—
7045029	—	1/8	—	—	—	.080	.100⑨	.375	—
7045038	—	11/32	.084	—	—	.080	.100⑧	.375	—
7045314	—	11/32	.080	—	—	.230	.275⑧	.275	—
OLDSMOBILE									
1974									
7044014	⑥	11/32	.080	—	—	.230	.275	.500	1800
7044017	⑥	11/32	.080	—	—	.275	.350	.500	1800
7044314	⑥	11/32	.080	—	—	.245	.300	.500	1800
1975									
7045012	⑥	11/32	.080	—	—	.160	.200⑦	.275	—
7045013	⑥	11/32	.080	—	—	.275	.350⑧	.275	—
7045314	⑥	11/32	.080	—	—	.230	.275⑧	.275	—

(continued)

MONOJET M, MV ADJUSTMENT SPECIFICATIONS—Continued

See Tuneup Chart in specifications chapters for hot idle speeds.

Carb. Part No. ①	Initial Idle Mix Screw Turns Open	Float Level	Metering Rod	Idle Vent	Fast Idle Off Car	Choke Rod	Vacuum Break	Unloader	Fast Idle rpm
PONTIAC									
1974									
7044017	⑥	11/32	.080	—	—	.275	.350	.500	1800
7044041	⑥	11/32	.079	—	—	.230	.275	.500	1800
7044314	⑥	11/32	.080	—	—	.245	.300	.500	1800
1975									
7045012	⑥	11/32	.080	—	—	.160	.200⑥	.275	—
7045013	⑥	11/32	.080	—	—	.275	.350⑦	.275	—
7045314	⑥	11/32	.080	—	—	.230	.275⑦	.275	—

①—On tag attached to carburetor.
②—20 rpm above slow idle speed.
③—Turns in from slow idle position.
④—On low step of cam.
⑤—On high step of cam.
⑥—Air/fuel ratio or idle CO% rating is found in Tuneup Specification tables in specifications chapters.
⑦—Rear .215.
⑧—Rear .312.
⑨—Rear .450.

MONOJET M & MV ADJUSTMENTS

Vacuum Break Adjustment

1969-71 All and 1971-74 Chevrolet Vega, Fig. 24

1. Open the throttle valve so that the cam follower on the throttle lever will clear the highest step on fast idle cam.
2. Rotate the choke valve to the closed position. If the thermostatic coil is warm, hold the choke valve closed with a rubber band or spring attached between choke shaft lever and the stationary part of carburetor.
3. Grasp the vacuum break plunger rod with needle nose pliers and push straight inward until the diaphragm seats.
4. With specified drill size, measure the clearance between the lower edge of the choke valve and the inside air horn wall at center of valve as shown.
5. Bend the end of vacuum break lever at the point shown to adjust.

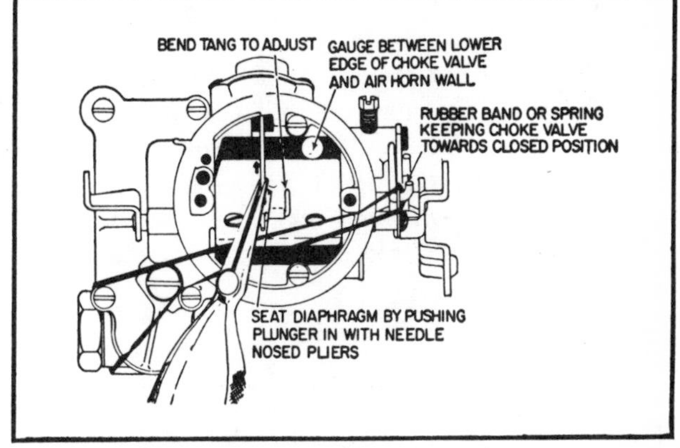

Fig. 24 Monojet vacuum break adjustment. 1969-71 *All &* 1971-74 *Chevrolet Vega*

1972-74 All Exc. Chverolet Vega, Fig. 25

1. Apply outside vacuum to vacuum break diaphragm until the plunger is fully seated.
2. With the diaphragm in seated position, push the choke valve to the closed choke position. The vacuum break rod should be at the end of slot in the diaphragm plunger and spring loaded plunger fully compressed.
3. Measure the clearance between the lower edge of the choke valve and the inside air horn wall.
4. If clearance is not as specified, adjust by bending vacuum break rod at point shown.

Unloader Adjustment

Fig. 26

1. Hold the choke valve in the closed position by applying a light force to choke coil lever.
2. Rotate the throttle lever to wide open throttle valve position.
3. Bend unloader tang on the throttle lever to obtain specified dimension between lower edge of choke valve (at center) and the air horn wall.

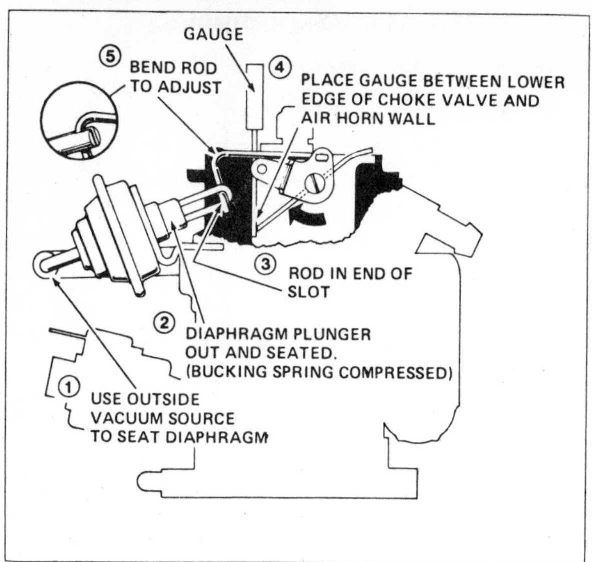

Fig. 25 Monojet vacuum break adjustment. 1972-74 *All exc. Chevrolet Vega*

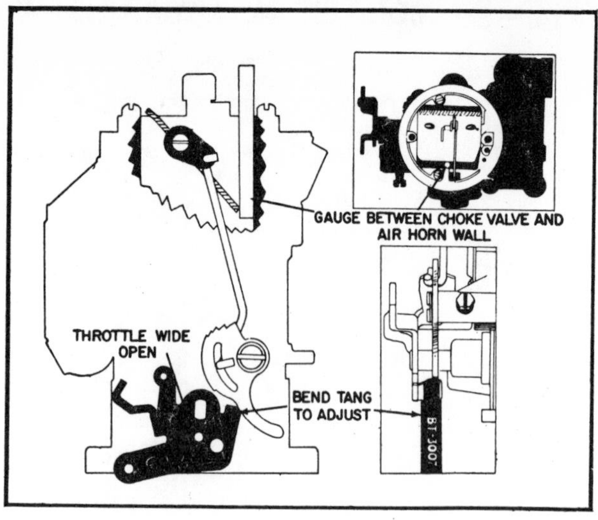

Fig. 26 Monojet unloader adjustment

5. Connect the coil rod to the choke lever and install retaining clip.

Choke Coil Adjustment

1969-71 All Exc. Chevrolet Vega, Fig. 27

1. Hold choke valve closed.
2. Pull upward on the coil rod to end of travel.
3. The bottom of the rod end which slides into hole in choke lever should be even with top of hole. *On Pontiac applications rod should be adjusted to fit in notch in top of choke lever.*
4. Bend choke coil rod at point shown to adjust.

1971-74 Chevrolet Vega and All 1972-74, Fig. 28

1. On Vega models, hold the choke valve open. On all other models, hold the choke valve closed.
2. With thermostatic coil rod disconnected from the upper lever, push downward on the rod to the end of travel.
   NOTE: On 1972 California Vega applications, a swivel is used on end of choke coil rod. Turn swivel up or down on rod until top of pin on swivel is even with bottom of hole in lever.
3. Bend choke coil rod at point shown to adjust.

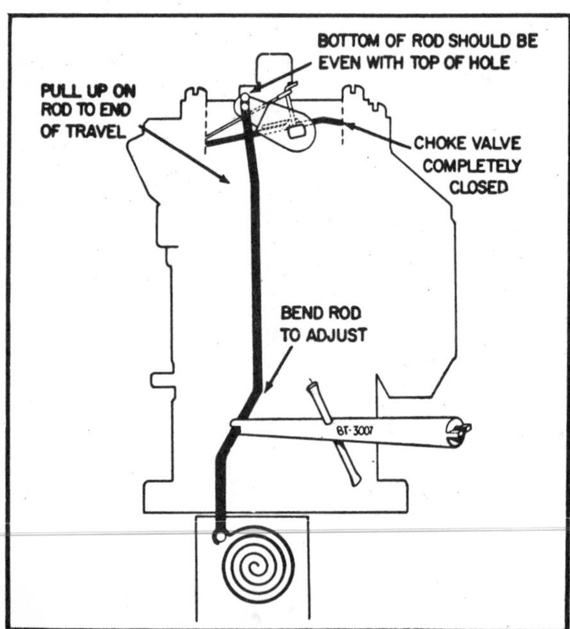

Fig. 27 Monojet choke coil adjustment. Typical

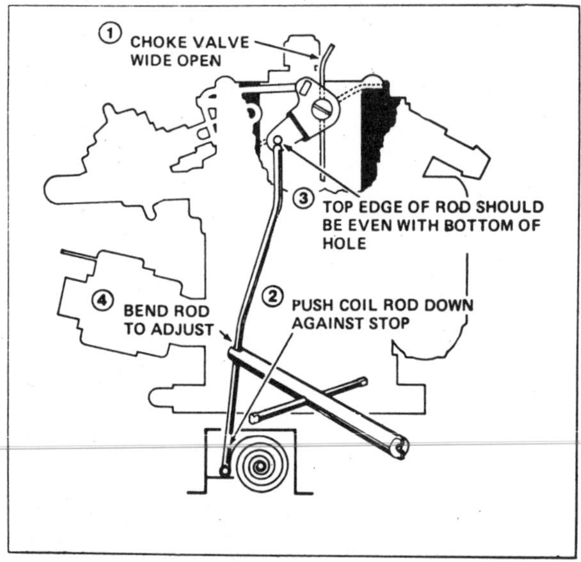

Fig. 28 Monojet choke coil adjustment. Typical

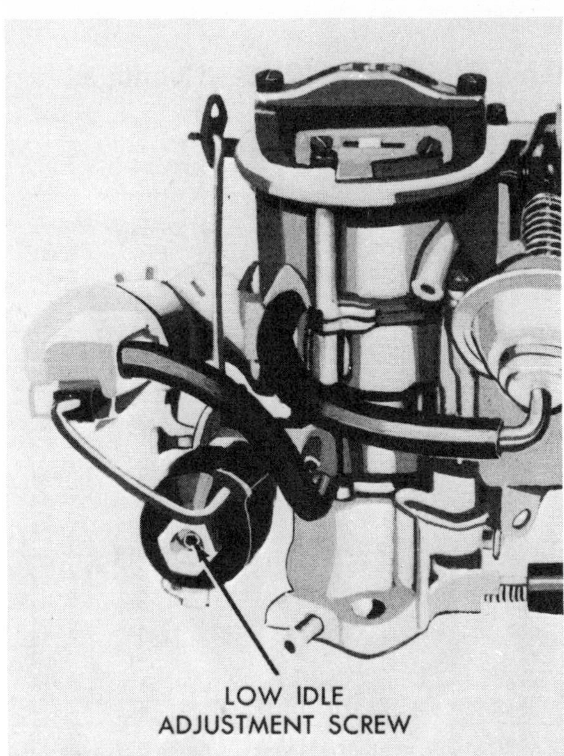

Low Idle Speed Adjustment

Fig. 29

1. Adjust the curb idle speed.
2. Adjust the low idle speed by turning the allen head screw located in the end of the idle stop solenoid, Fig. 29.

NOTE: When making the low idle adjustment, clockwise rotation of the screw should never be continued after the screw is bottomed out against the armature. Increased rotation will result in raising the solenoid cover up through the staked housing.

Fig. 29 Monojet low idle speed adjustment, 1972-73 *Chevrolet*

Holley Carburetors

ONE & TWO BARREL CARB. ADJUSTMENT SPECIFICATIONS

See Tuneup Chart in specifications chapter for hot idle speeds.

Carb. Part No.①	Carb. Model	Idle Mixture Turns Open	Float Level (Dry)	Fuel Level (Wet)	Pump Setting	Bowl Vent Clearance	Fast Idle		Choke Unloader Clearance	Vacuum Kick Drill Size	Cam Position Drill Size	Choke Setting
							Bench	On Car				
CHRYSLER ENGINES 1974												
R-6721A	1945	⑱	1/32	—	11/16	—	.080	1600	.250	.140	.080	Fixed
R-6722A	1945	⑱	1/32	—	13/16	—	.080	1800	.250	.090	.080	Fixed
R-6723A	1945	⑱	1/32	—	11/16	—	.080	1600	.250	.140	.080	Fixed
R-6724A	1945	⑱	1/32	—	3/4	—	.080	1800	.250	.080	.080	Fixed
R-6725A⑨	1945	⑱	1/32	—	11/16	—	.080	1600	.250	.140	.080	Fixed
R-6726A⑨	1945	⑱	1/32	—	3/4	—	.080	1800	.250	.090	.080	Fixed
R-6731A	2245	⑱	.180	—	..255	.015	.110	1800	.170	.150	.110	Fixed
R-6737A	2245	⑱	.180	—	.255	.015	.110	1600	.170	.150	.110	Fixed

(continued)

ONE & TWO BARREL CARB. ADJUSTMENT SPECIFICATIONS—Continued

See Tuneup Chart in specifications chapter for hot idle speeds.

Carb. Part No.①	Carb. Model	Idle Mixture Turns Open	Float Level (Dry)	Fuel Level (Wet)	Pump Setting	Bowl Vent Clearance	Fast Idle		Choke Unloader Clearance	Vacuum Kick Drill Size	Cam Position Drill Size	Choke Setting
							Bench	On Car				
CHRYSLER ENGINES—continued 1975												
R-7017A	1945	⑱	3/64	—	—	—	.080	1600	.250	.130	.080	Fixed
R-7018A	1945	⑱	3/64	—	—	—	.080	1700	.250	.090	.080	Fixed
R-7019A	1945	⑱	3/64	—	—	—	.080	1600	.250	.130	.080	Fixed
R-7020A	1945	⑱	3/64	—	—	—	.080	1700	.250	.090	.080	Fixed
R-7027A	2245	⑱	3/16	—	1/4	.015	.110	1600	.170	.150	.110	Fixed
R-7029A	1945	⑱	3/64	—	—	—	.080	1600	.250	.130	.080	Fixed
R-7210A	1945	⑱	3/64	—	—	—	.080	1700	.250	.090	.080	Fixed
R-7211A	2245	⑱	3/16	—	1/4	.015	.110	1600	.170	.150	.110	Fixed
R-7226A	2245	⑱	3/16	—	1/4	.015	.110	1600	.170	.150	.110	Fixed
R-7329A	1945	⑱	3/64	—	—	—	.080	1700	.250	.130	.080	Fixed

①—Located on tag attached to carburetor or on casting.

⑱—Air/fuel ratio or idle CO% rating is found in Tuneup chart in specifications chapters.

ONE & TWO BARREL CARBURETOR ADJUSTMENTS

Model 1945

This single barrel carburetor Fig. 30, utilizes dual cellular plastic floats to control the fuel level, thus permitting high angularity operation during the most severe operating conditions. Also, the float construction eliminates the possibility of a malfunction due to a punctured float.

On 1974 Chrysler units, an electric choke system is incorporated to open the choke at approximately 60 degrees F. For service information, refer to the Emission Control System chapter.

The accelerator pump is of the piston type and is operated by a rod and a link connected to the throttle lever.

The power enrichment system on all units consists of a power valve installed near the center of the carburetor body and a vacuum piston located in the bowl cover. On 1974 California units, in addition to the vacuum operated enrichment system, a spring loaded mechanical modulator rod opens the power valve at 80 degrees of throttle opening regardless of engine vacuum.

Dry Float Setting, Fig. 31

Hold float fulcrum retaining pin in position and invert carburetor bowl. Place a straight edge across surface of bowl, contracting float toes. Remove the straight edge and measure distance float dropped from surface of fuel bowl. Refer to Holley Specifications Chart. Adjust by bending float tang to obtain proper dimension.

Fast Idle Cam Position Adjustment, Fig. 32

With fast idle speed adjusting screw contacting second highest step on fast idle cam, move the choke valve toward closed position with light pressure on the choke shaft lever. Insert specified gauge between the top of choke valve and the wall of air horn. Refer to *Holley Specifications Chart.* An adjustment will be necessary if a slight drag is not obtained as drill shank is being removed. Adjust by bending fast idle link at lower angle, until correct valve opening has been obtained.

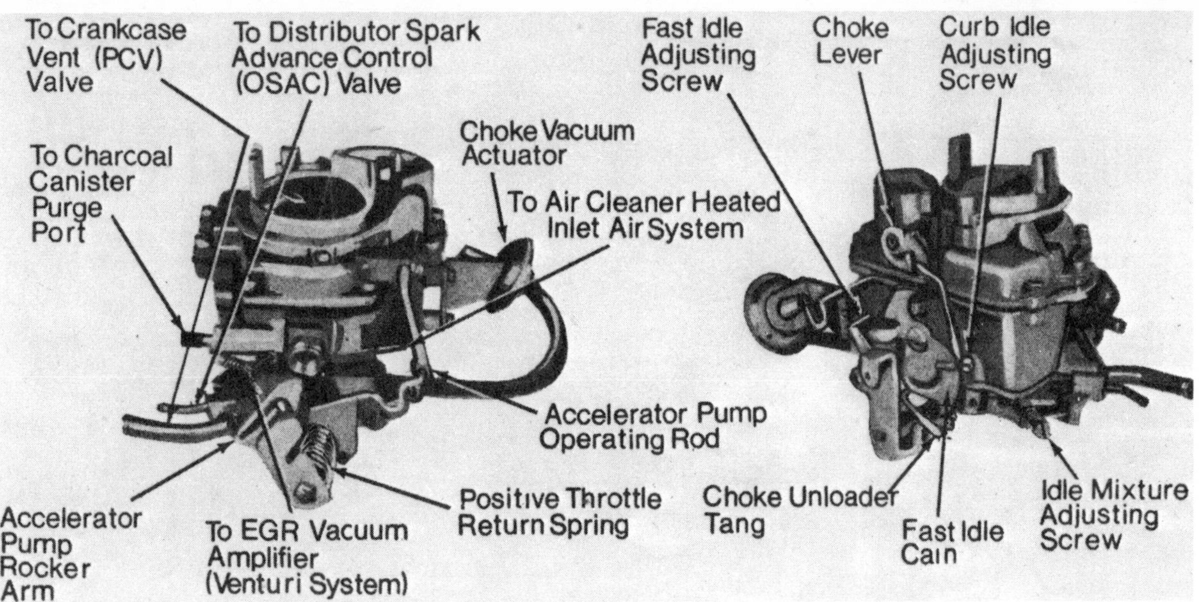

Fig. 30 *Holley model* 1945 *single barrel carburetor*

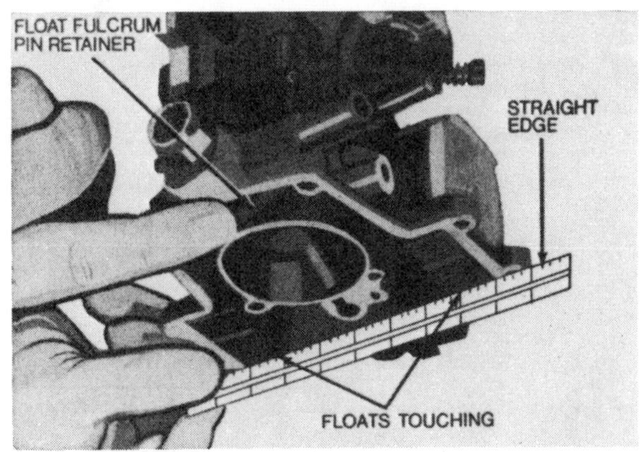

Fig. 31 *Measuring float level.* 1945 *carburetor*

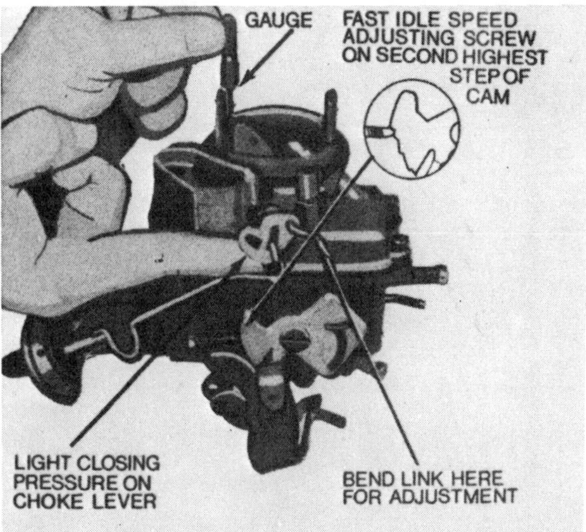

Fig. 32 *Fast idle cam position adjustment.* 1945 *carburetor*

Models 2210 & 2245

This carburetor, Fig. 33, is a two-barrel unit but can be considered as two carburetors built side by side into one unit, utilizing the same fuel and air inlets. Each throat of the carburetor has its own throttle valve and main metering systems and are supplemented by the float, accelerating, idle and power systems. The 1970 version is equipped with a distributor ground switch, Fig. 33, which retards the distributor when the carburetor is at curb idle, resulting in better emission control. The 1971 version is equipped with a hot idle compensator valve which is a thermostatically operated air bleed to relieve an overrich condition at idle. Fig. 33. The 1971-74 units have incorporated a bowl vent valve tube which works in conjunction with the vent valve. The 1973 unit has an extra port for use with the (EGR) Exhaust Gas Recirculation system. On 1973-74 Chrysler units, an electric choke system is incorporated to open choke at approximately 60° to 63°. For service information refer to the Emission Control System chapter.

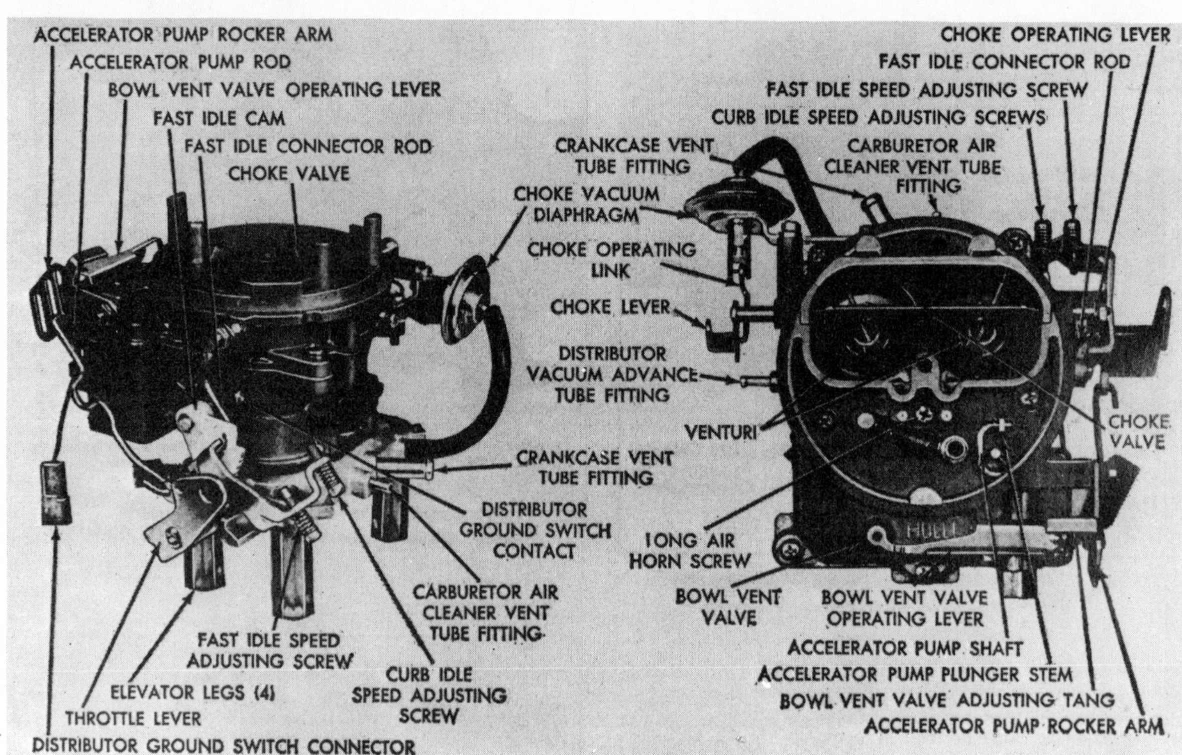
ACCELERATOR PUMP ROCKER ARM
ACCELERATOR PUMP ROD
BOWL VENT VALVE OPERATING LEVER
FAST IDLE CAM
FAST IDLE CONNECTOR ROD
CHOKE VALVE
CRANKCASE VENT TUBE FITTING
CHOKE VACUUM DIAPHRAGM
CHOKE OPERATING LINK
CHOKE LEVER
DISTRIBUTOR VACUUM ADVANCE TUBE FITTING
VENTURI
CRANKCASE VENT TUBE FITTING
DISTRIBUTOR GROUND SWITCH CONTACT
LONG AIR HORN SCREW
CARBURETOR AIR CLEANER VENT TUBE FITTING
FAST IDLE SPEED ADJUSTING SCREW
CURB IDLE SPEED ADJUSTING SCREW
ELEVATOR LEGS (4)
THROTTLE LEVER
DISTRIBUTOR GROUND SWITCH CONNECTOR
CHOKE OPERATING LEVER
FAST IDLE CONNECTOR ROD
FAST IDLE SPEED ADJUSTING SCREW
CURB IDLE SPEED ADJUSTING SCREWS
CARBURETOR AIR CLEANER VENT TUBE FITTING
CHOKE VALVE
BOWL VENT VALVE
BOWL VENT VALVE OPERATING LEVER
ACCELERATOR PUMP SHAFT
ACCELERATOR PUMP PLUNGER STEM
BOWL VENT VALVE ADJUSTING TANG
ACCELERATOR PUMP ROCKER ARM

Fig. 33 Holley models 2210 & 2245 two-barrel carburetors

5210 CARB. ADJUSTMENT SPECIFICATIONS

See Tuneup Chart in specifications chapter for hot idle speeds, air/fuel ratio and idle CO% rating.

Carb. Part No.	Carb. Model	Float Level (Dry)	Float Drop	Pump Position	Fast Idle Cam Index	Vacuum Plate Pulldown	Fast Idle Setting	Choke Setting
CHEVROLET VEGA & PONTIAC ASTRE								
1973								
R-6477A	5210	.420	1″	#3	.140	.300	2000	1 Rich
R-6478A	5210	.420	1″	#2	.140	.300	2200	2 Rich
R-6580A	5210	.420	1″	#2	.140	.300	2200	2 Rich
R-6581A	5210	.420	1″	#3	.140	.300	2000	1 Rich
1974								
338168	5210-C	.420	1″	#2	.140	.400	2200	3½ Rich
338170	5210-C	.420	1″	#2	.140	.400	2200	3½ Rich
338179	5210-C	.420	1″	#3	.140	.300	2000	2½ Rich
338181	5210-C	.420	1″	#3	.140	.300	2000	2½ Rich
1975								
348659	5210-C	.420	1″	—	—	.325	1600	3 Rich
348660	5210-C	.420	1″	#2	.110	.300	1600	4 Rich
348661	5210-C	.420	1″	—	—	.275	1600	3 Rich
348662	5210-C	.420	1″	#2	.110	.275	1600	4 Rich
348663	5210-C	.420	1″	—	—	.325	1600	3 Rich
348664	5210-C	.420	1″	#2	.110	.300	1600	4 Rich
348665	5210-C	.420	1″	—	—	.275	1600	3 Rich
348666	5210-C	.420	1″	#2	.110	.275	1600	4 Rich

OTHER 1974 ADJUSTMENT PROCEDURES ARE THE SAME AS IN PREVIOUS YEARS. SEE THE EMISSION CONTROL MANUAL, VOLUME I.

NOTES

DISTRIBUTORS

CONTENTS

This section contains information on electronic ignition systems used on 1974 and 1975 models. For information on distributors and ignition systems used on earlier models, refer to page 407 of your Emission Control Manual, Volume I.

ELECTRONIC IGNITION SYSTEMS

General Motors, Ford Motor Company and American Motors all recently introduced new electronic ignition systems. Ford's system went into use at the end of the '73 model year. GM introduced theirs with the '74s. American Motors started using their electronic ignition system on their '75 models. All 1975 cars made in the United States have an electronic ignition system as standard equipment.

The information here will update your Motor Emission Control Manual, Volume I, Electronic Ignitions section, which begins on page 421.

AMERICAN MOTORS BREAKERLESS INDUCTIVE DISCHARGE (BID) IGNITION SYSTEM

Description

The BID ignition system incorporates four major units—an electronic control unit, ignition coil, distributor and high tension wires, Fig. 1. The electronic control unit is a solid-state, moisture resistant module with the components sealed in a potting compound to resist vibration and environmental conditions. Since the control unit has an internal current regulator, a resistance wire or ballast resistor is not necessary in the primary circuit.

Battery voltage is applied to the ignition coil positive terminal when the ignition switch is in the ON or START position. Therefore, an ignition system bypass is not required in this system. The primary coil circuit is electronically regulated by this unit.

The ignition coil is of standard construction and requires no special service. The function of the ignition coil in the BID ignition system is the same as for conventional ignition systems.

The distributor is conventional except that the contact points, the condenser and the cam are replaced by a sensor and a trigger wheel. Since no wearing occurs between the trigger wheel and the sensor, dwell angle remains constant and requires no adjustment. The sensor is a small coil of fine wire which receives an alternating current signal from the electronic control unit. The sensor develops an electromagnetic field which detects the presence of metal, the metal being the leading edges of the trigger wheel teeth.

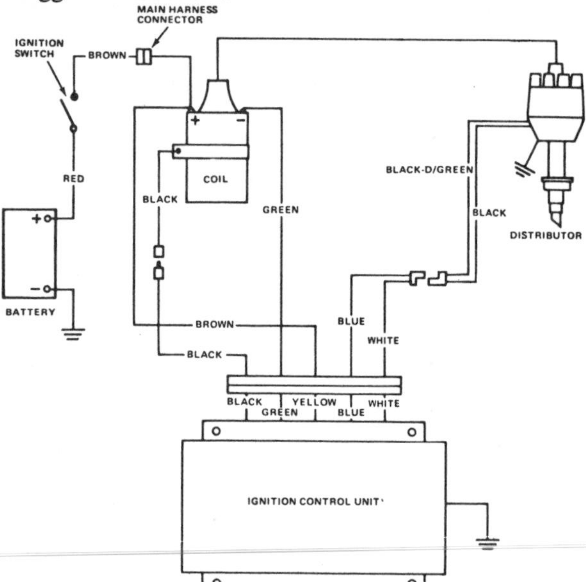

Fig. 1 BID ignition system wiring

Operation

When the ignition switch is placed in the START or RUN position, the control unit is activated. An oscillator within the control unit excites the sensor coil, in turn developing the electromagnetic field. When a leading edge of a trigger wheel tooth enters the electromagnetic field, the tooth reduces the sensor oscillation strength to a predetermined level, in turn activating the demodulator circuit. The demodulator circuit controls a power transistor located in series with the coil primary circuit. The power transistor switches the coil primary circuit off, thereby inducing a high voltage in the coil secondary winding. The high voltage is then delivered to the spark plugs through the distributor rotor, cap and high tension wires.

Troubleshooting

Ensure that all of the electrical connections are correct before proceeding with the following checks.

1. Disconnect the coil wire from the distributor. Hold the wire approximately ½ inch from a suitable ground and crank the engine, Fig. 2. If a spark jumps between the coil wire and the ground, the system is satisfactory.
2. If no spark occurs in step No. 1, connect a No. 57 test lamp between the coil positive terminal and the ground, Fig. 3. Turn the ignition switch to ON and START positions. If the test lamp does not light in both of these positions, check the ignition switch and the wiring between the battery and the ignition coil.
3. If the test lamp lights in both the ignition switch positions, connect the test lamp across the ignition coil terminals. Disconnect the distributor connector and turn the ignition switch to the ON position, Fig. 4. If the test lamp does not light, check the electronic control unit for proper ground.

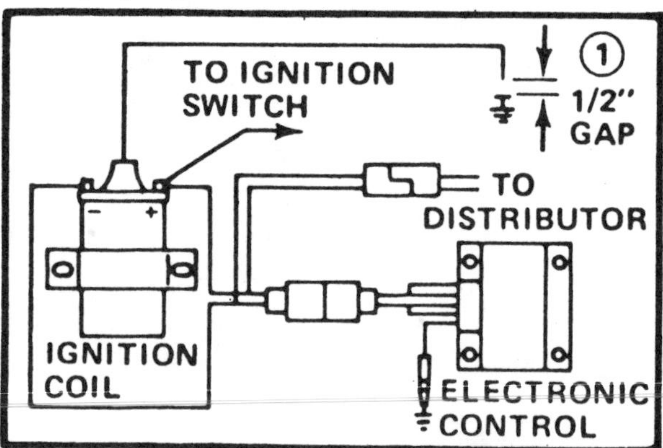

Fig. 2 Checking spark at coil wire

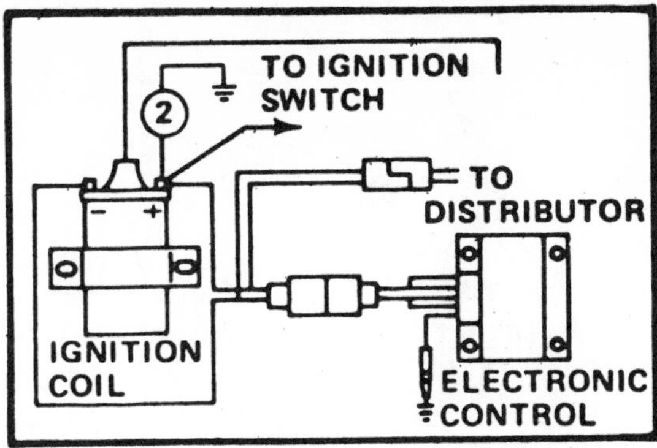

Fig. 3 Checking battery to ignition coil wiring

4. If the test lamp lights in step No. 3, connect a jumper wire across the electronic control lead terminals, Fig. 5. If the test lamp remains lit, replace the electronic control unit.
5. If the test lamp goes out in step No. 4, remove the test lamp and hold the coil wire approximately ½-inch from a suitable ground. Intermittently short the electronic control lead terminals and check for a spark at the coil wire gap, Fig. 6. If no spark occurs, replace the ignition coil. If a spark occurs, then the sensor is faulty and must be replaced.

Component Replacement

1. Place the distributor in a suitable holding fixture and remove the cap, rotor and dust shield, Fig. 7.
2. Using a small gear puller, remove the trigger wheel. Be sure that the puller jaws are gripping the trigger wheel inner shoulder to prevent trigger wheel damage. Use a thick, flat washer or nut as a spacer and do not press against the small center shaft.
3. Loosen the sensor locking screw approximately three turns. Lift the sensor lead grommet from

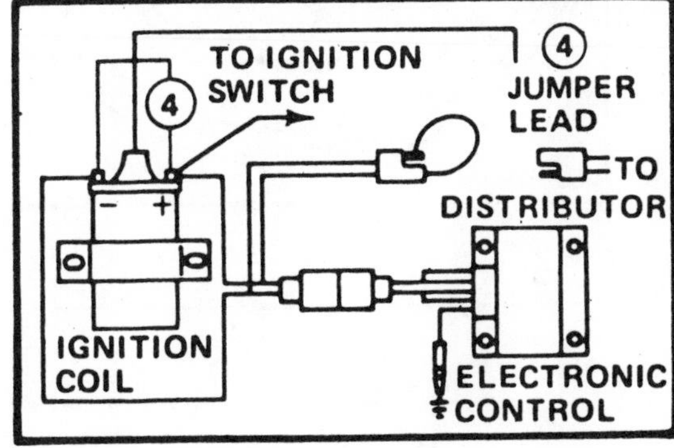

Fig. 5 Checking electronic control unit with test lamp & jumper wire

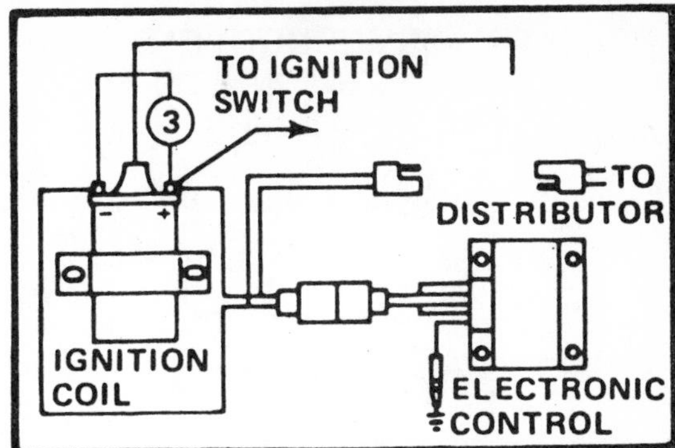

Fig. 4 Checking electronic control unit with test lamp

the distributor bowl and pull the sensor leads from the slot around the sensor spring pivot pin. Release the sensor spring and make sure that the spring clears the sensor leads. Slide the sensor from the bracket.

The sensor locking screw utilizes a tamper-proof head design and requires tool No. J-25097 for removal. However, if a special tool is not available, use a small needlenose plier to remove the screw. The service (replacement) sensor has a standard slotted head screw.

4. If a vacuum control unit is to be replaced, remove the retaining screw and the vacuum unit.
5. Install the new vacuum control unit and assemble the sensor, sensor guide, flat washer and the retaining screw.

   Install the retaining screw far enough to hold the assembly together but make sure that it does not protrude past the bottom of the sensor.
6. If the vacuum control has been replaced and the original sensor is being used, replace the special head screw with the standard slotted head screw.
7. Install the sensor assembly on the vacuum chamber bracket. Make sure that the tip of the

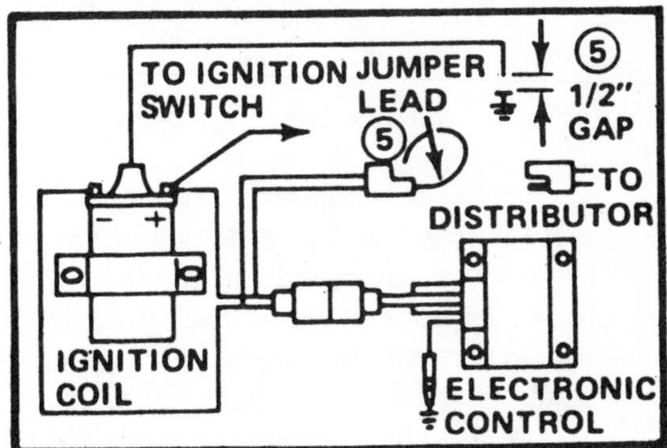

Fig. 6 Checking spark at coil wire with electronic control leads shorted

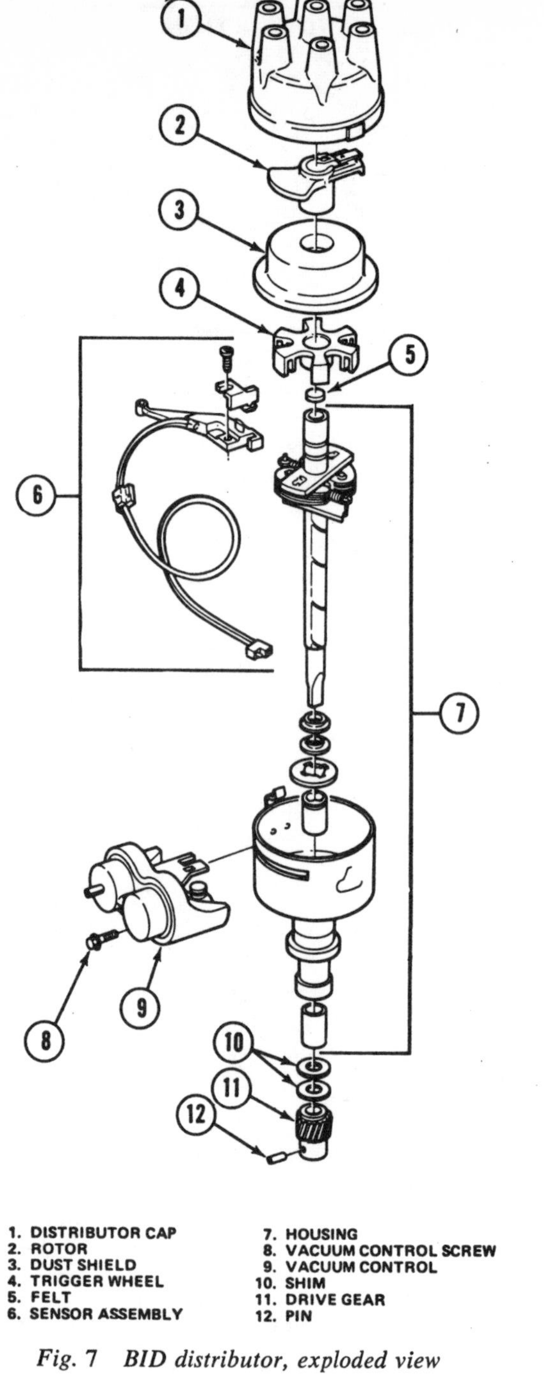

Fig. 7 BID distributor, exploded view

sensor is located properly in the summing bar. Place the sensor spring on the sensor and route the sensor leads around the spring pivot pin, Fig. 8. Install the sensor lead grommet and position the leads away from the trigger wheel.

8. Install the sensor positioning gauge over the yoke. Make sure that the gauge is against the flat of the shaft. Move the sensor sideways until the gauge can be positioned. Snug down the

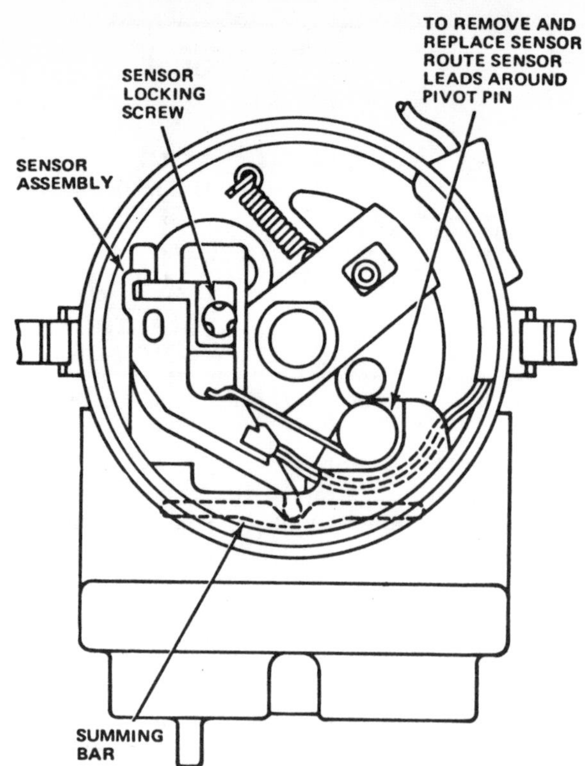

Fig. 8 Sensor installation

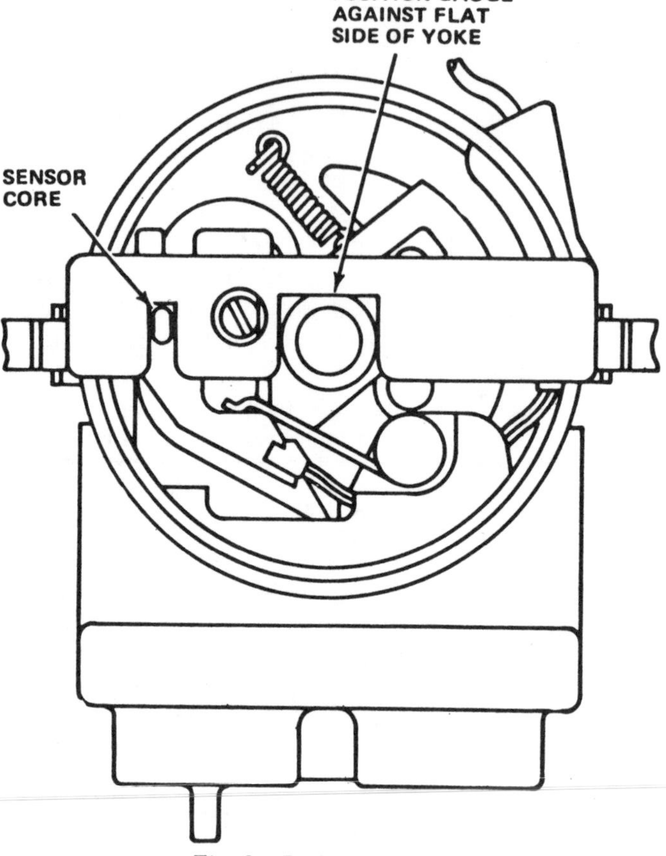

Fig. 9 Positioning sensor

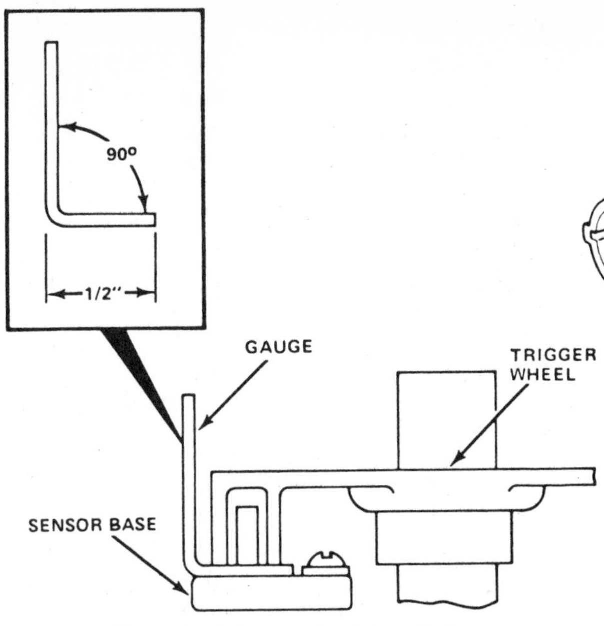

Fig. 10 Trigger wheel installation

retaining screw and check the sensor position by removing and installing the gauge, Fig. 9. When the gauge can be removed and replaced without any sensor side movement, the sensor is positioned properly. Tighten the retaining screw and check the sensor position.

9. Place the trigger wheel on the yoke and check if the sensor core is positioned approximately in the center of the trigger wheel legs. Bend a .050-inch gauge wire to the dimension specified in Fig. 10. Place it between the trigger wheel legs and the sensor base. Press the trigger wheel onto the yoke until the legs contract the gauge wire.
10. Apply 3 to 5 drops of light engine oil to the felt wick on top of the yoke. Then install the dust shield, rotor and cap.

FORD SYSTEM

1973-74 Breakerless (B/L) Solid State Ignition System

The B/L ignition system does not use ignition points and is controlled by an electronic module. Also, a new oil filled coil is incorporated. A total diagnosis of this system requires only a volt-ohmmeter tester.

The electronic module, Fig. 11, is the brain of this system and is well protected from outside elements such as heat and shock. The heat sink containing all the electronic devices is sealed in a mixture of epoxy and sand. This module cannot be disassembled and must be replaced if malfunctioning.

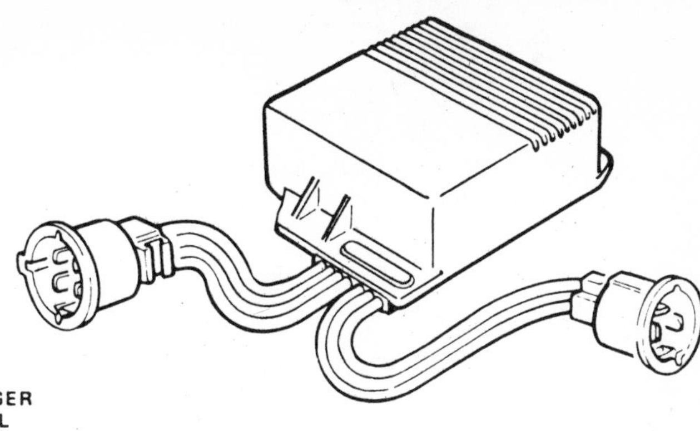

Fig. 11 Ford electronic module

The conventional ignition coils are not to be used with this system. The proper coil is easily identified as it is all blue and terminals are labeled differently from conventional ignition coils—BAT (battery) and DEC (Distributor Electronic Control), Fig. 12.

The ignition switch energizes the module through the white wire while the engine is cranking and through the red wire when the engine is running.

The B/L ignition system is protected against electrical current produced during normal vehicle operation and against reverse polarity or high voltage accidentally applied if the vehicle is jump started.

NOTE: The ignition system will be damaged if other than volt-ohm test procedures are used to check alternator output.

CAUTION: Do not use the volt-amp test procedure or any other test that utilizes a knife switch on the battery terminal.

The interval between the time that the module activates the primary ignition circuit and the time the distributor signal turns it off varies with engine speed. Consequently, a dwell measurement is insignificant.

System Diagnosis

If the ignition system is suspected of a malfunction, inspect for loose connections and check the

Fig. 12 Ford electronic ignition coil identification

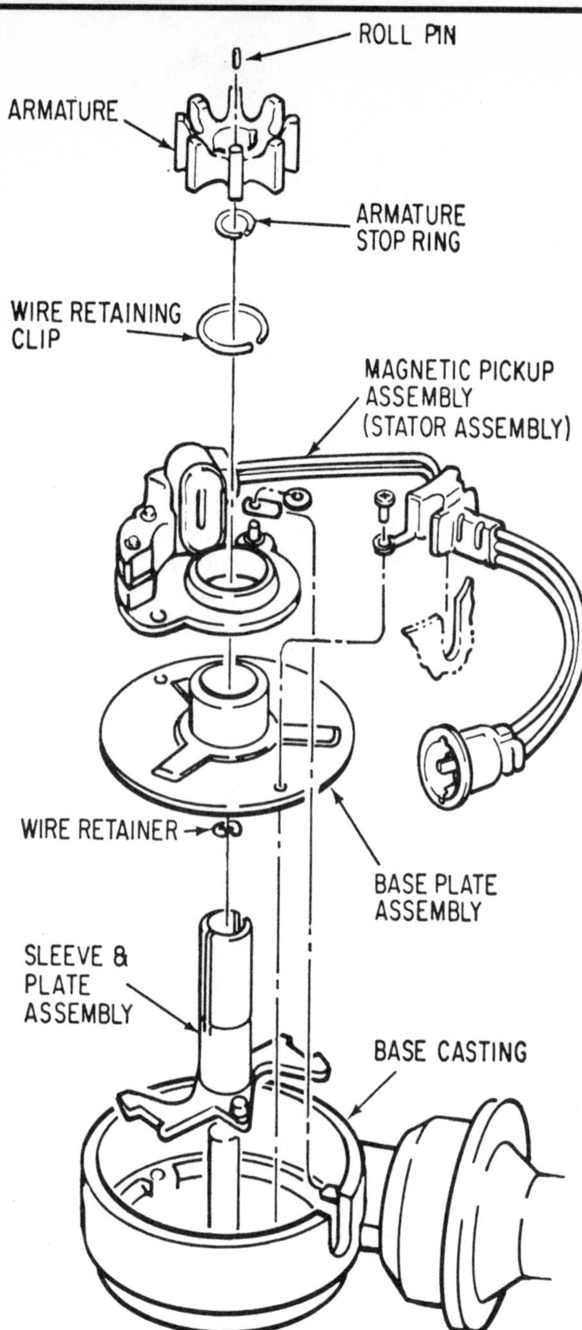

Fig. 13 Ford breakerless (B/L) distributor

Distributor Section beginning on page 407 of your Emission Control Manual. The secondary circuit is identical to that of a conventional ignition system.

If no spark is observed during the above test, check the ignition coil high tension wire. Replace it if it is damaged. If no damage is observed at the coil wire, disconnect the 3-way and 4-way connectors at the electronic module and make tests at the harness connectors. Do not make tests at the module terminals.

Voltage Tests At Harness Connectors, Fig. 15

If all of the following tests comply with the specifications, replace the module.

Key On

1. Check for battery voltage between pin No. 3 and engine ground. If the voltage is less than specified, the voltage feed wire to the module is damaged and must be repaired.
2. Check for battery voltage between pin No. 5 and engine ground. If the voltage is less than specified, proceed as follows.
   (*a*) Without disconnecting the coil, connect the voltmeter between the coil BAT terminal and engine ground.
   (*b*) Connect a jumper wire between the coil DEC terminal and engine ground.
   (*c*) With all the lights and accessories off, turn on the ignition switch.
   (*d*) A satisfactory primary circuit between the battery and the coil will register between 4.9 and 7.9 volts.
   (*e*) If less than 4.9 volts register on the voltmeter, check for worn primary circuit insulation, broken wire strands or loose and corroded terminals.
   (*f*) If a greater than 7.9 voltage is registered on the voltmeter, check the resistance wire and replace it if necessary.

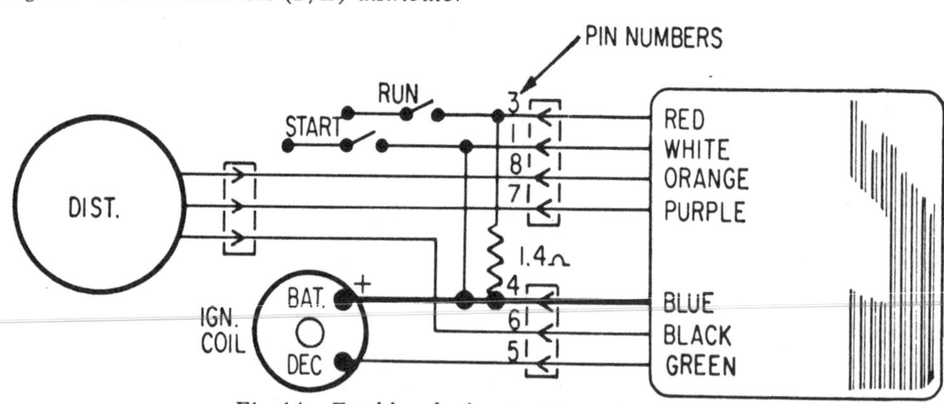

Fig. 14 Ford breakerless ignition primary circuit

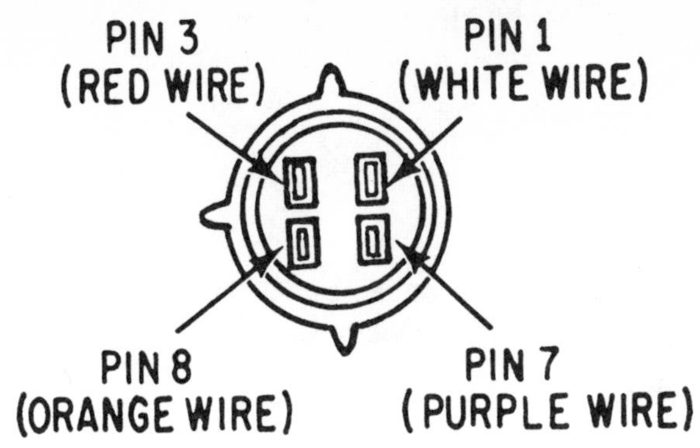

PIN 6
(BLACK WIRE)

PIN 5
(GREEN WIRE)
PIN4
(BLUE WIRE)

Fig. 15 Ford breakerless ignition female harness connectors (system test points)

Cranking Engine

1. Check for 8 to 12 volts between pin No. 1 and engine ground. If the voltage is not within specifications, the voltage feed wire to the module is damaged.
2. Check for 8 to 12 volts between pin No. 5 and engine ground. If the voltage is not within specifications, the ignition bypass circuit is open or grounded between the starter solenoid or the ignition switch and pin No. 5.
3. Check for ½ volt oscillation—using the 2.5 volt scale—between pin No. 7 and pin No. 8. If the voltmeter does not register this oscillation, proceed as follows.

   Perform the same test at the 3-wire pigtail—with the distributor disconnected—in turn eliminating the orange and purple wires as a cause of malfunction. If no oscillation is present at the pigtail, visually inspect the distributor components. Make sure that the toothed armature is not damaged, that it is tight on the sleeve and secured properly with the alignment pin, Fig. 13. If the armature is not damaged and is rotating properly when cranking the engine and the voltmeter is not oscillating, then replace the magnetic pickup (stator assembly).

Resistance Test At Harness Connectors, Fig. 15

Key Off

1. Check for resistances of 400 to 800 ohms between pin No. 7 and No. 8, 0 ohms between pin No. 6 and engine ground and for 70,000 ohms or more between ground and either pin No. 7 or pin No. 8. If any of these values do not comply with the specifications then proceed as follows.

   Perform the same test at the 3-wire pigtail—with the distributor disconnected—in turn eliminating the orange and purple wires as a cause of malfunction.

   If any of the above checks do not comply with the specifications, the magnetic pickup assembly (stator assembly) is not functioning and must be replaced.
2. Check for a resistance of 7000 to 13,000 ohms between pin No. 3 and coil secondary. Check for a resistance of 1.0 to 2.0 ohms between pin No. 5 and pin No. 4. If either check is not within the specifications, diagnose the coil separately from the rest of the system. Coil primary resistance must be within 1.0 to 2.0 ohms and coil secondary resistance must be within 7000 to 13,000 ohms.
3. Check for a resistance of more than 4.0 ohms between pin No. 5 and engine ground. If the resistance is less than specified, locate the short to the ground either at the coil DEC terminal or in the green wire, Fig. 4.
4. If a resistance of 1.0 to 2.0 ohms is not obtained between pins No. 3 and No. 4, replace the primary resistance wire.

System Diagnosis

The distributor shaft and the armature rotation, Fig. 13, causes the armature poles to pass by the core of the magnetic pickup assembly. This in turn cuts the magnetic field and signals the electronic module, Fig. 4, through the orange and purple wires, to break the primary ignition current. This induces secondary voltage in the coil to fire the spark plugs. The coil is then energized again by the primary circuit and is ready for the next spark cycle. This primary circuit is controlled by a timing circuit in the module.

Voltage Tests At Harness Connectors, Fig. 15

If all of the following tests comply with the specifications, replace the module.

Key On

1. Check for battery voltage between pin No. 3 and engine ground. If the voltage is less than specified, the voltage feed wire to the module is damaged and must be repaired.
2. Check for battery voltage between pin No. 5 and engine ground. If the voltage is less than specified proceed as follows:
   (*a*) Without disconnecting the coil, connect voltmeter between coil BAT terminal and engine ground.
   (*b*) Connect a jumper wire between the coil DEC terminal and engine ground.
   (*c*) With all lights and accessories off, turn on the ignition switch.
   (*d*) A satisfactory primary circuit between the battery and the coil will register 4.9 to 7.9 volts.
   (*e*) If less than 4.9 volts register on voltmeter, check for worn primary circuit insulation, broken wire strands or loose, corroded terminals.
   (*f*) If a greater than a 7.9 voltage is registered on the voltmeter, check and replace, if necessary, the resistance wire.

Cranking Engine

1. Check for 8 to 12 volts between pin No. 1 and engine ground. If voltage is not within specifications, the voltage feed wire to the module is damaged.
2. Check for 8 to 12 volts between pin No. 5 and ground. If voltage is not within specifications, the ignition bypass circuit is open or grounded between starter solenoid or ignition switch and pin No. 5. Also check primary connections at the coil.
3. Check for ½ volt oscillation (using the 2.5 volt scale) between pin No. 7 and pin No. 8. If the voltmeter does not register this oscillation proceed as follows:
   Perform the same test at the 3-wire pigtail (with the distributor disconnected), in turn eliminating the orange and purple wires as a cause of malfunction. If no oscillation is present at pigtail, visually inspect distributor components. Make sure that the toothed armature is not damaged, is tight on the sleeve and secured properly with the alignment pin, Fig. 13. If the armature is not damaged and is rotating properly when cranking the engine and voltmeter is not oscillating, replace the magnetic pickup (stator assembly).

Resistance Test At Harness Connectors, Fig. 15

Key Off

1. Check for resistances of: 400 to 800 ohms between pin No. 7 and No. 8, 0 ohms between pin No. 6 and engine ground and for 70,000 ohms or more between ground and either pin No. 7 or pin No. 8. If any of these values do not comply with specifications proceed as follows:
   Perform the same test at the 3-wire pigtail (with the distributor disconnected), in turn eliminating the orange and purple wires as a cause of malfunction.
   If any of the above checks do not comply with specifications, the magnetic pickup assembly (stator assembly) is not functioning and must be replaced.
2. Check for a resistance of 7000 to 13,000 ohms between pin No. 3 and coil secondary. Also check for a resistance of 1.0 to 2.0 ohms between pin No. 5 and pin No. 4. If either check is not within specifications, diagnose coil separately from rest of system. Coil primary resistance must be within 1.0 to 2.0 ohms and coil secondary resistance must be within 7000 to 13,000 ohms.
3. Check for a resistance of more than 4.0 ohms between pin No. 5 and engine ground. If resistance is less than specified, locate the short to ground either at the coil DEC terminal or in the green wire, Fig. 14.
4. If a resistance of 1.0 to 2.0 ohms is not obtained between pins No. 3 and No. 4, replace the primary resistance wire.

HIGH ENERGY IGNITION SYSTEM (H.E.I.)

The H.E.I. system utilizes an all-electronic module, pickup coil and timer core in place of the conventional ignition points and condenser. The condenser is used for noise suppression only. Point pitting and rubbing block wear resulting in retarded ignition timing is eliminated.

NOTE: H.E.I. components are not interchangeable with Unit Distributor Components.

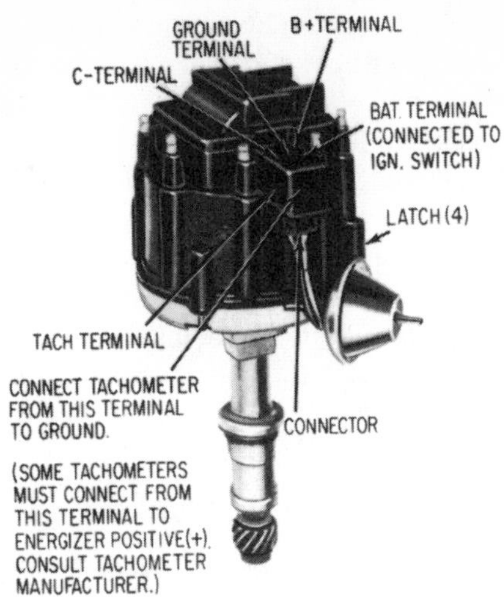

Fig. 16 H.E.I. distributor external components

Since the coil is part of the H.E.I. distributor there is no need for distributor-to-coil primary—breaker points to coil negative lead—or secondary lead—high voltage lead.

The main features of the H.E.I. system differentiating this system from the Unit Ignition system are shown in Figs. 16 and 17.

The magnetic pickup consists of a rotating timer core attached to the distributor shaft, a stationary pole piece, a permanent magnet and a pickup coil.

When the distributor shaft rotates, the teeth of the timer core line up and pass the teeth of the pole piece inducing voltage in the pickup coil. This in turn signals the all-electronic module to open the ignition coil primary circuit. Maximum inductance occurs at the moment the timer core teeth are lined up with the teeth on the pole piece. At the instant the timer core teeth start to pass the pole teeth, the primary current decreases and a high voltage is induced in the ignition coil secondary winding. The voltage is directed through the rotor and high voltage leads to fire the spark plugs. Since this is a full 12-volt system, it does not require a resistance wire.

The vacuum diaphragm is connected by linkage to the pole piece. When the diaphragm moves against spring pressure, it rotates the pole piece. This allows the poles to advance relative to the timer core. The timer core is rotated about the shaft by conventional advance weights, thus providing centrifugal advance.

CAUTION: Never connect to ground the TACH terminal, Fig. 16, of the distributor connector. This will damage the electronic circuitry of the module.

A convenient tachometer connection is incorporated in the wiring connector on the side of the distributor, Fig. 16. However, due to its transistorized design, the high energy ignition system will not trigger some models of engine tachometers.

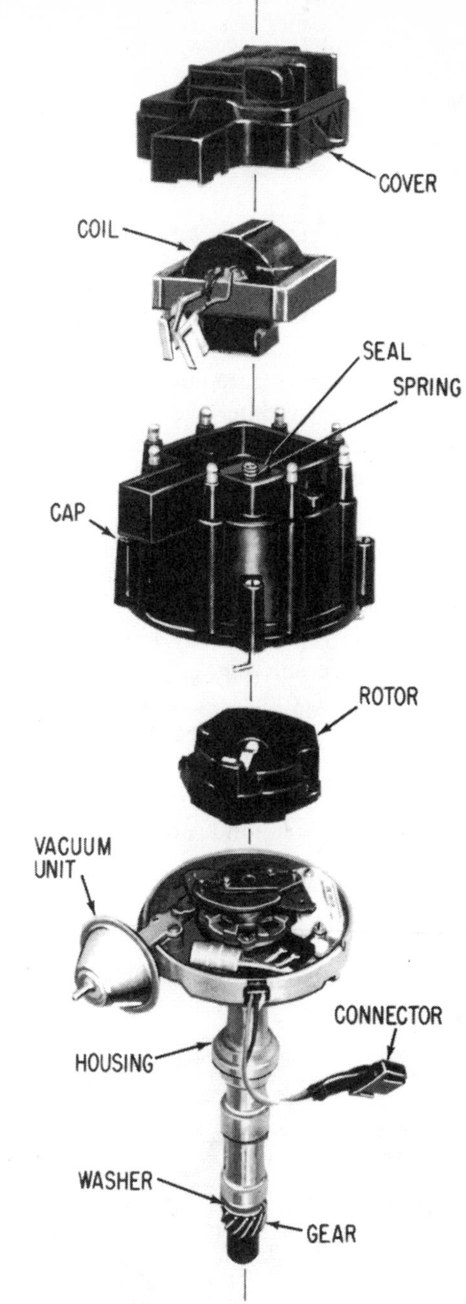

Fig. 17 H.E.I. distributor internal components

NOTE: When using a timing light to adjust ignition timing, the connection should be made at the No. 1 spark plug. Forcing foreign objects through the boot at the No. 1 terminal of the distributor cap will damage the boot and could cause engine misfiring.

The spark plug boot has been designed to form a tight seal around the spark plug and should be twisted ½ turn before removal.

System Diagnosis

With the wiring connector properly attached to the connector at the side of the distributor cap and all the spark plug leads properly connected at the plugs and at the distributor terminals, proceed as follows.

Engine Will Not Start

1. Connect the voltmeter between BAT terminal lead on the distributor connector and ground. Turn on the ignition switch.
2. If the voltage is zero, then there is an open circuit between either the distributor and the bulkhead connector, the bulkhead connector and the ignition switch, or the ignition switch and the starter solenoid. Make the required repairs.
3. If reading is battery voltage, hold one spark plug lead with insulated pliers approximately ¼-inch away from a dry area of the engine block and crank the engine. If a spark is visible, the distributor has been eliminated as a source of trouble. Check the spark plugs and the fuel system.
4. If there is no visible spark perform the Component Checkout and proceed as described further on.

Engine Starts But Runs Rough

1. Check for proper fuel delivery to the carburetor.
2. Check all vacuum hoses for leakage.
3. Visually inspect and listen for sparks jumping to ground.
4. Check ignition timing.
5. Check the centrifugal advance mechanism for proper operation.
6. Remove spark plugs and check for unusual defects such as very wide gap, abnormal fouling, cracked insulators (inside and out), etc.
7. If no defects are found, perform the Component Checkout procedure as described below.

Component Checkout

1. Remove the cap and coil assembly.
2. Inspect the cap, coil and rotor for spark arc-over.
3. Connect the ohmmeter, Fig. 18, step 1. If the ohmmeter reading is other than zero or very near to zero, the ignition coil must be replaced.
4. If no reading was obtained on the ohmmeter in step 1, reconnect the ohmmeter, Fig. 18, step 2. If the ohmmeter reading is infinite on the high scale, the ignition coil must be replaced.
5. Connect an external vacuum source to the

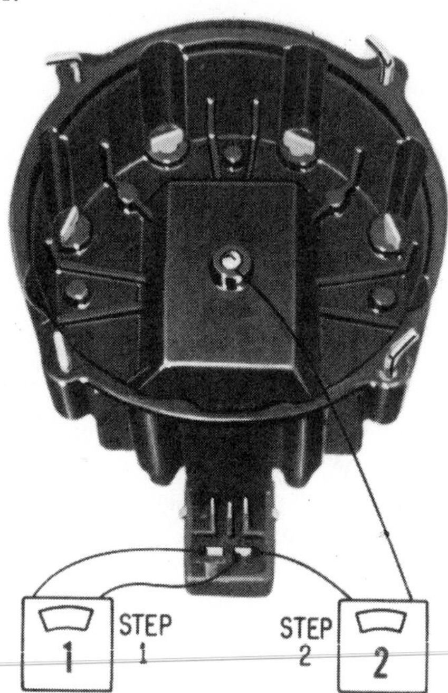

Fig. 18 *H.E.I. distributor ignition coil ohmmeter test*

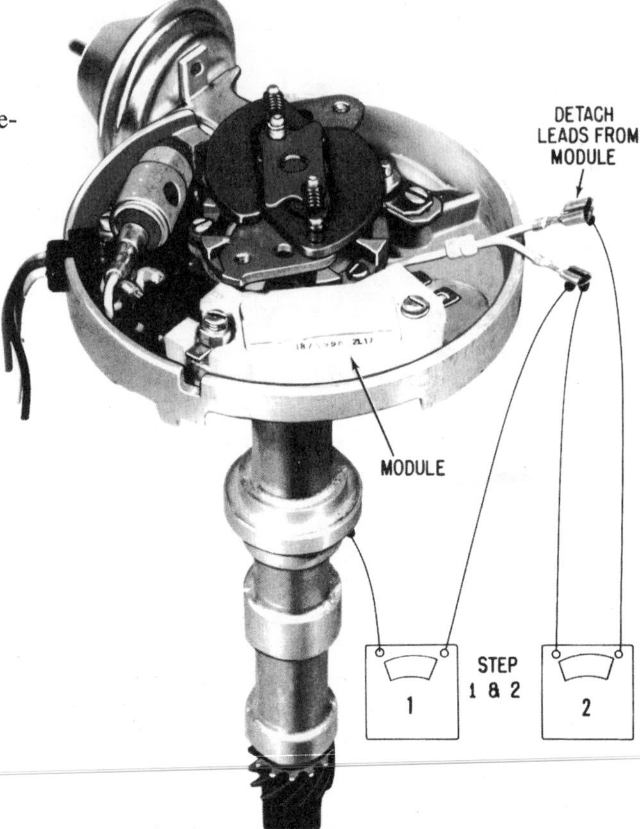

Fig. 19 *Distributor pickup coil ohmmeter test*

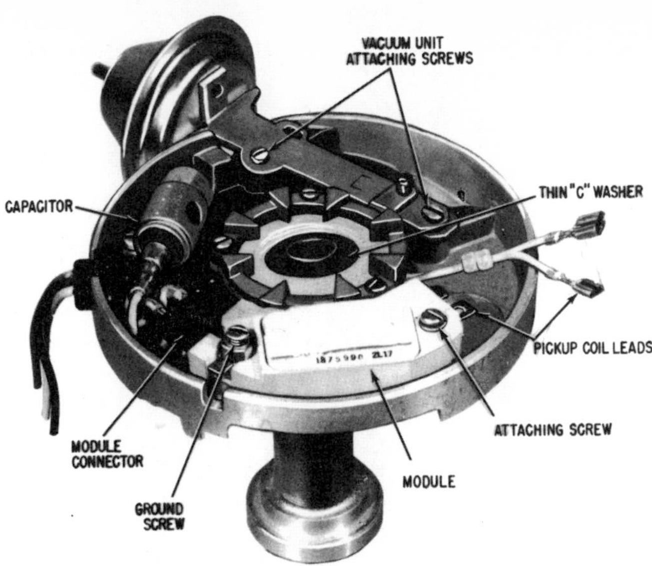

Fig. 20 H.E.I. distributor component replacement

vacuum advance unit. Replace the vacuum unit if it is inoperative.

6. If the vacuum unit is operating properly, connect the ohmeter, Fig. 19, step 1, If the ohmmeter reading on the middle scale is not infinite at all times, then the pickup coil must be replaced.
7. With the ohmeter connected, Fig. 19, step 2, the reading must be within 650 to 850 ohms at all times. If it is not, replace the pickup coil.

Components Replace

Ignition Coil Replacement, Fig. 17

1. Remove the screws holding the distributor cover to the distributor cap and remove the distributor cover.
2. Remove the four screws holding the coil to the cap.
3. Remove the harness connector and the battery wire from the side of the distributor cap.
4. Push the coil leads out of position in the cap and remove the coil.
5. Reverse the procedure to install.

Module Replacement, Fig. 20

1. Disconnect the wiring harness connector at the side of the distributor cap and remove the distributor.
2. Remove the rotor and disconnect the wires from the module terminals.
3. Remove the two mounting screws and remove the module.
   CAUTION: At installation, coat the bottom of the new module with dielectric lubricant (this is furnished with the new module) to aid in heat transfer into the distributor housing. Failure to apply the lubricant will cause excessive heat at the module and premature module failure.
4. Reverse the procedure to install.

Pole Piece, Magnet or Pickup Coil Replacement, Fig. 20

Removal

1. With the distributor removed, disconnect the wires at the module terminals.
2. Remove the roll pin from the drive gear by driving it out with a 1/8-inch diameter drift punch.
3. Remove the gear, shim and the tanged washer from the distributor shaft. Remove any burrs that may have been caused by removal of the pin.
4. Remove the distributor shaft from the housing.
5. Remove the washer from the upper end of the distributor housing.
   NOTE: The bushings in the housing are not serviceable.
6. Remove the three screws securing the pole piece to the housing and remove the pole piece, magnet and pickup coil.

Installation

1. Install the pickup coil, magnet and pole piece and loosely install the three screws holding the pole piece.
2. With the washer installed at the top of the housing, install the distributor shaft and rotate to check for proper clearance between the pole piece teeth and the timer core teeth.
3. If necessary, realign the pole piece to provide adequate clearance and secure it properly.
4. Install the tanged washer, shim and drive gear—teeth up—to the bottom of the shaft. Align the drive gear and install a new roll pin.

NOTES

IMPORTED CARS

CONTENTS

All sections include general specifications, tuneup and distributor specifications, and descriptive and servicing information on emission control systems for 1974 models. For information on earlier models, check your Emission Control Manual, Volume I, page 434.

AUDI

GENERAL ENGINE SPECIFICATIONS

Model or Engine	Bore & Stroke, Inches (mm)	Piston Displacement, Cubic Inches (cc)	Compression Ratio	Maximum Brake HP @ rpm	Maximum Torque Ft. Lbs. @ rpm	Normal Oil Pressure Pounds
1974						
100LS	3.31 x 3.32 (84.0 x 84.4)	114 (1875)	8.2	91 @ 5200	111 @ 3500	14–85
Fox	3.01 x 3.15 (76.5 x 80.0)	89.7 (1471)	8.2	75 @ 5800	81.5 @ 4000	28
1975						
100LS	3.31 x 3.32 (84.0 x 84.4)	114 (1875)	8.0	95 @ 5500	108.7 @ 3200	14–88
Fox	3.13 x 3.15 (79.7 x 80.0)	97 (1588)	8.2	81 @ 5800	90.4 @ 3300	28

TUNEUP SPECIFICATIONS

Car Model or Engine	Spark Plugs		Distributor		Firing Order	Ignition Timing		Hot Idle Speed rpm
	Type	Gap, Inch	Point Gap, Inch	Dwell Angle Degrees		Degrees	Mark Location	
1974								
Fox	Champion N8Y	.028	.016	47–53	1-3-4-2	TDC	Flywheel①	850–1000
100LS	Champion N7Y	.035–.040	.016	47–53	1-4-3-2	8 ATDC	Pulley①	850–1000

①—Timed at No. 1 cylinder, front of engine.

DISTRIBUTOR SPECIFICATIONS

Model or Engine	Distributor Part No.	Point Gap, Inch	Dwell Angle Deg.	Spring Tension, Oz.	Centrifugal Advance			Vacuum Advance		
					Start @ rpm	Int.	Full @ rpm	Inches of Vacuum to Start Plunger	Int.	Full Advance Dist. Deg. @ Vacuum
1974										
Fox	—	.016	47–53	—	—	—	—	—	—	—
100	—	—	—	—	—	—	—	—	—	—

Emission Controls

EVAPORATIVE EMISSION SYSTEM

Description

This system (Figs. 1 & 2), is designed to prevent fuel vapors from being emitted into the atmosphere. It consists of a non-vented fuel tank filler cap, fuel tank, expansion tank, an activated carbon canister, and a series of vent lines connecting the various components to the carburetor air cleaner.

Operation

Expanded fuel, caused by high ambient temperatures, is collected in the expansion tank. This fuel will be returned to the main tank by venting action as fuel is used from the main tank. Fuel vapors produced in the main tank or expansion tank pass through a vent line to a carbon canister (located in the engine compartment) where they are adsorbed by activated charcoal. A second vent line connects

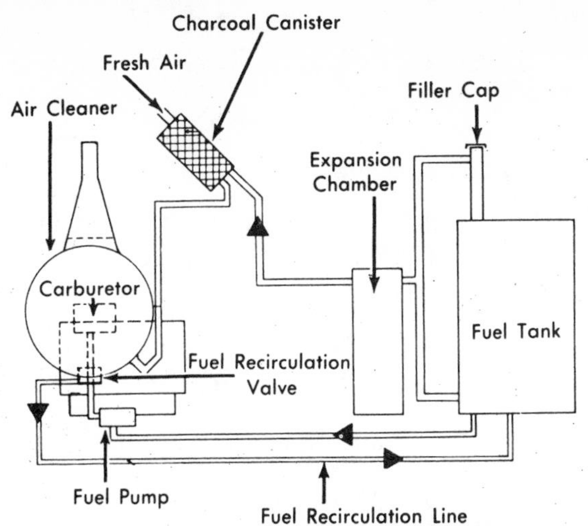

Fig. 1 *Evaporative emission control system. 100 LS models*

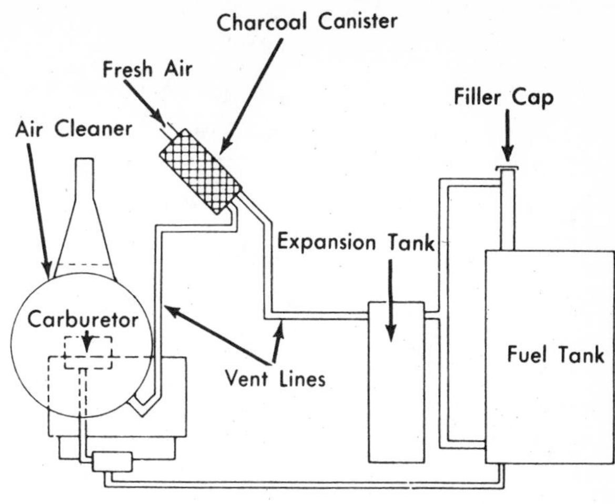

Fig. 2 *Evaporative emission control system. Fox models*

the carbon canister to the carburetor air cleaner. When the engine is running, the intake manifold vacuum draws fresh air through the carbon canister. This fresh air mixes with the fuel vapors and is drawn into the carburetor where it enters the combustion system and is burned. This action purges the activated charcoal and renews its storage capacity.

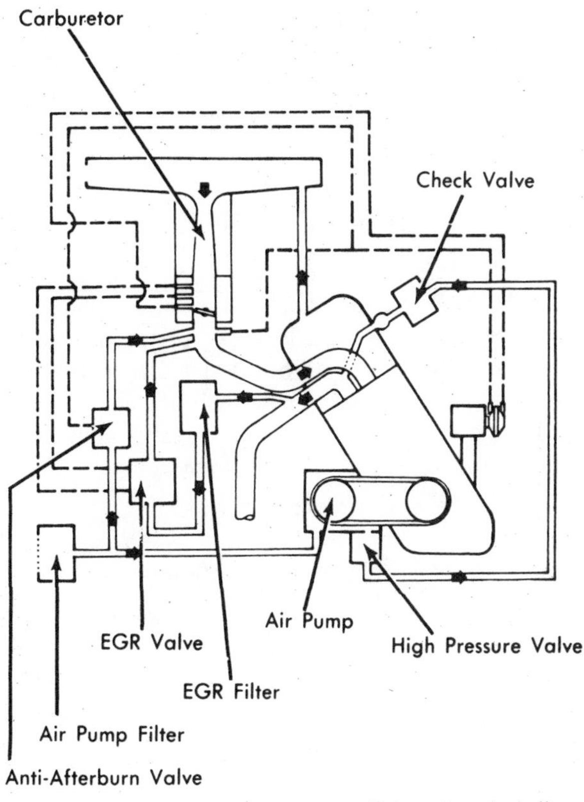

Fig. 3 *Exhaust emission control systems. Fox models*

EXHAUST GAS RECIRCULATION SYSTEM

Description

This system is designed to reduce NOx emissions by recirculating a limited amount of exhaust gas through intake system during partial load operation. Components of system are an exhaust gas filter, a vacuum controlled exhaust gas recirculation valve, and various connecting hoses, Figs. 3 & 4.

Operation

Vacuum connection on carburetor opens at a throttle opening of 18°. Vacuum operates exhaust gas recirculation valve allowing a limited amount of exhaust gas to pass through the filter, the EGR valve and into the intake manifold. At full throttle, exhaust gas recirculation is eliminated as the EGR valve closes due to the small amount of vacuum present in the vacuum line. Impurities are filtered out of exhaust gases by an exhaust gas filter.

AIR INJECTION SYSTEM

California Models Only

Description

This system is designed to reduce CO and HC emissions by injecting fresh air into exhaust port area. Components of this system are an air pump, control valve, check valve, anti-backfire valve, high pressure valve, and injection ports drilled in the cylinder head.

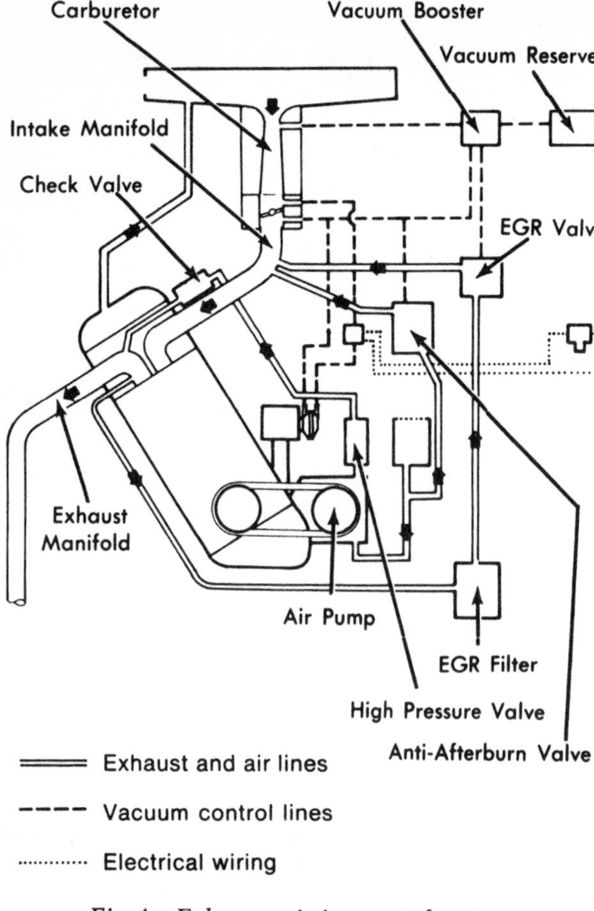

Fig. 4 Exhaust emission control system. 100 LS models

Operation

Fresh air is drawn into the air pump through a filter, then pumped through high pressure valve and check valve. From check valve air enters a drilled passage in the intake manifold and is distributed by a cast manifold in the cylinder head to the exhaust port area by drilled passages in the cylinder head. With high vacuum, the anti-backfire valve routes this air to the intake manifold where it mixes with the air/fuel mixture and prevents an over rich mixture. This leaner mixture prevents backfiring during deceleration.

FUEL RECIRCULATION SYSTEM

100 LS Models Only

Description & Operation

This system is used to send any over supply of fuel to the return by a fuel recirculation valve. This keeps emissions down during idle.

GENERAL SERVICE

Evaporative Emission System

Should any of the components of the system become damaged or fail to operate properly, they should be replaced. When inspecting or repairing the system, check all clips and hose connections for tightness. Make sure that no fuel can pass into the activated carbon canister.

Exhaust Gas Recirculation System

Remove the EGR valve and visually inspect for deposits. Check that diaphragm plunger moves freely. Connect the EGR valve to vacuum source and apply vacuum. Diaphragm plunger should lift off seat. Disconnect vacuum line. Diaphragm plunger must return to valve seat. Replace copper seal on the valve holder side and reinstall the valve. Check the entire system (lines, filter, connections) for leaks, deposits and restrictions.

Air Injection System

Check all hoses and connections for deterioration or leaks. Remove the check valve air supply hose and listen for exhaust gas leakage. Then remove the large hose from the anti-backfire valve to the air pump. With finger placed over the open end of hose (not valve), accelerate the engine and allow the throttle to close rapidly. Valve is operating properly if a momentary rushing noise is audible.

Fuel Recirculation System

Inspect all hoses for deterioration or leaks and replace or repair as necessary.

BMW

GENERAL ENGINE SPECIFICATIONS

Model or Engine	Bore & Stroke, Inches (mm)	Piston Displacement, Cubic Inches (cc)	Compression Ratio	Maximum Brake HP @ rpm	Maximum Torque Ft. Lbs. @ rpm	Normal Oil Pressure Pounds
1974						
2002	3.50 x 3.15 (89 x 80)	121 (1990)	8.3	98 @ 5500	106 @ 3500	71
2002 tii	3.50 x 3.15 (89 x 80)	121 (1990)	9.0	125 @ 5500	127 @ 4000	71
Bavaria/3.0S	3.50 x 3.15 (89 x 80)	182 (2985)	8.3	170 @ 5800	185 @ 3500	71
3.0CS	3.50 x 3.15 (89 x 80)	182 (2985)	8.3	170 @ 5800	185 @ 3500	71

TUNEUP SPECIFICATIONS

Car Model or Engine	Spark Plugs		Distributor		Firing Order	Ignition Timing		Hot Idle Speed, rpm
	Type	Gap, Inch	Point Gap, Inch	Dwell Angle, Degrees		Degrees BTDC	Mark Location	
1974								
2002	Bosch WG135T30	.028	.016	59–65	1-3-4-2	25 @ 1500①	Flywheel	850–950
2002 Tii	Bosch W175T30	.024–.028	.024	59–61	1-3-4-2	25 @ 2700②	Flywheel	850–1000
Bavaria & 3.0 CS	Bosch WG135T30	.028	—	35–41	1-5-3 6-2-4	22 @ 1700③	Flywheel	900–1000

①—Timed at No. 1 cyl., front of engine. Disconnect vacuum hose & align ball on flywheel with the pointer at 1400 rpm.

②—Timed at No. 1 cyl., front of engine. Disconnect vacuum hose & align ball on flywheel with the pointer at 2200 rpm.

③—Timed at No. 1 cyl., front of engine. Disconnect vacuum hose & align ball on flywheel with the pointer at 1700 rpm.

DISTRIBUTOR SPECIFICATIONS

Model or Engine	Distributor Part No.	Point Gap, Inch	Dwell Angle, Deg.	Spring Tension, Oz.	Centrifugal Advance			Vacuum Advance		
					Start @ rpm	Int.	Full @ rpm	Inches of Vacuum to Start Plunger	Int.	Full Adv. Dist. Deg. @ Vacuum
1974										
2002	0231-180-003	.016	59–65	—	1000	23–27 @ 2000	42–46 @ 4000	4.7–5.9	—	8–12 @ 7.7
2002 Tii	0231-180-013	.024	59–65	—	1000	17–22 @ 2000	27–31 @ 3500	①	—	①
Bavaria & 3.0 CS	0231-162-001	—	35–41	—	1000	22–26 @ 2000	31–35 @ 3500	②	—	②

①—1.97–2.99 retard.
②—6.1–9.05 retard.

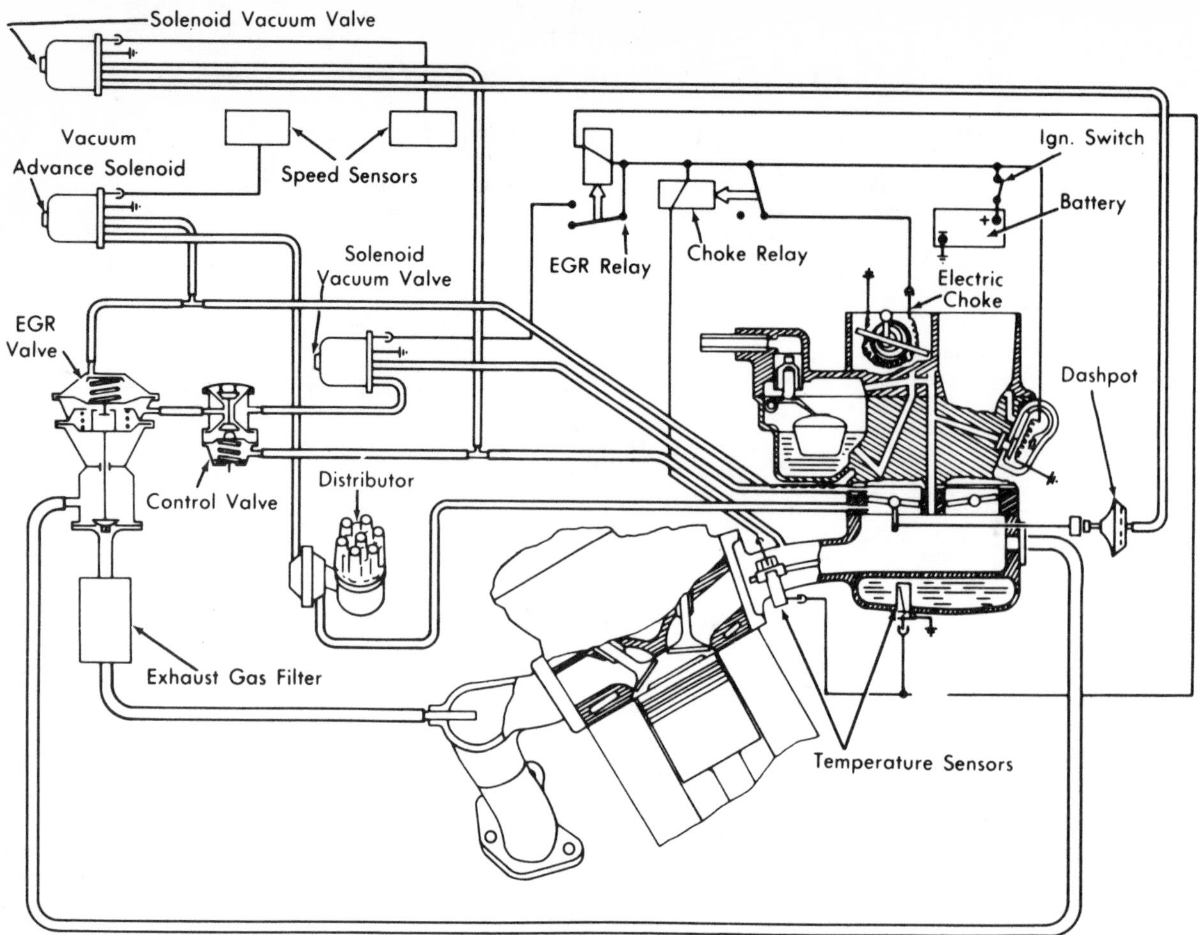

BMW 6 CYL. EXHAUST EMISSION CONTROL SYSTEM

Emission Controls

1974 Models

IGNITION TIMING

In the Tuneup Specification table on page 442 of your Emission Control Manual, Volume I, timing figures given are for static timing. Actually, engines should be timed dynamically, at the proper rpm, as indicated in the specification chart above.

EVAPORATIVE EMISSION CONTROL SYSTEM

Description

This consists of a purge system leading from the fuel tank to the hose of crankcase ventilation system. Located between fuel tank and crankcase ventilation system is a vapor storage tank and an activated carbon canister. Fuel evaporation emissions are prevented from entering the atmosphere by means of a sealed filler cap on the fuel tank. The fuel tank has no direct vent to the atmosphere. An excess fuel return valve is also used, located in the fuel supply line near the carburetor. A fuel return line connects this valve to the fuel tank, Fig. 1.

Operation

When the engine is off, fuel vapors are collected in the vapor storage tank. Some vapors are condensed in the storage tank and flow back into the fuel tank. Excess vapors continue to the carbon canister, where they are adsorbed. When the engine is started, the air flow in the air cleaner causes a low vacuum at purge line and vapor is drawn from the canister and the storage tank, mixed with fresh air, and burned in the engine. As fuel is drawn from the fuel tank, flow through the control system is reversed and air is drawn into the storage tank. The activated carbon canister is equipped with a screen in its bottom surface to permit fresh air to be drawn in to purge the carbon. The vapor storage tank also allows for fuel expansion of a completely filled fuel tank. Excess fuel return valve (Fig. 2) returns ex-

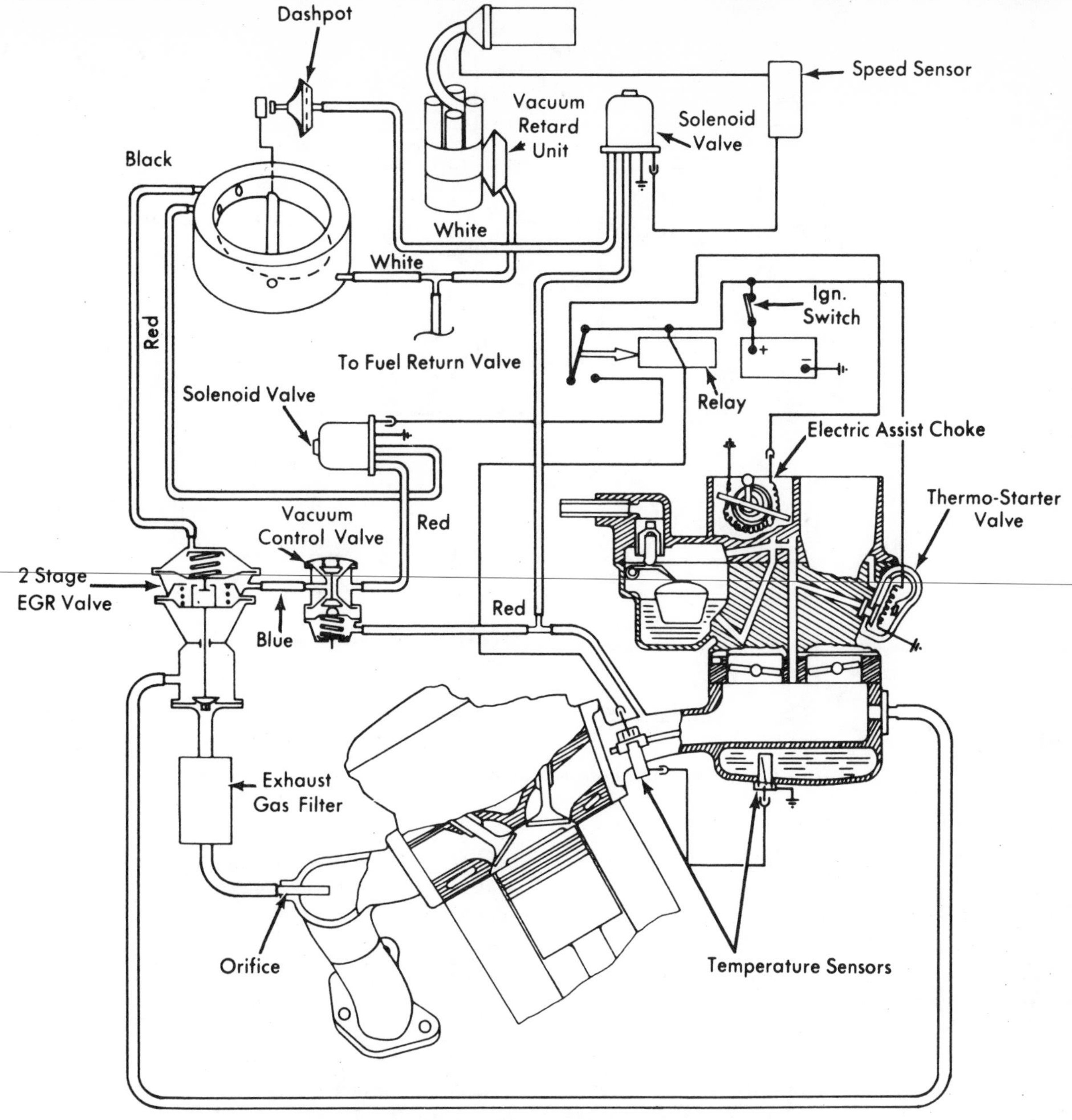

BMW 2002 EXHAUST EMISSION CONTROL SYSTEM

cess fuel from the carburetor back to the fuel tank. This circulation of fuel has a cooling effect on the fuel system and prevents vapor locks.

EXHAUST GAS RECIRCULATION VALVE

2002 & 3.0 Engines

Description

This system recirculates a small amount of exhaust gases during low engine loads, a larger amount during high load and acceleration conditions and provides no recirculation at wide open throttle or idle to assure maximum performance and a smooth idle. This complete modulation assures good engine performance at partial load coupled with effective NOx reduction.

EGR Valve

This dual-diaphragm EGR valve operates in two stages. When vacuum is about 3.15-inch Hg, it is applied to the upper diaphragm which partially lifts the valve disc from its seat and allows a small amount of exhaust gas flow. This first stage is controlled by the throttle valve of the carburetor and begins to open at about 2500 rpm. The second stage of the EGR valve is controlled by a vacuum control valve which senses absolute pressure in the intake manifold. When the second stage is opened,

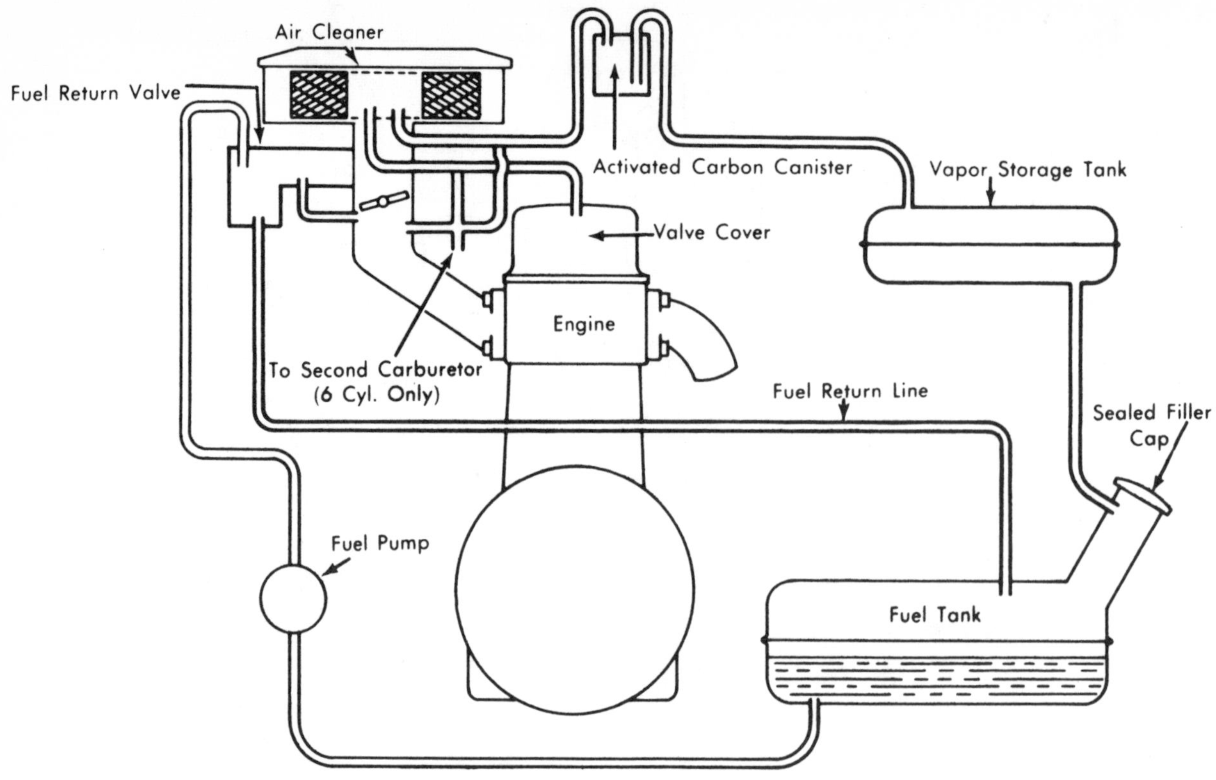

Fig. 1 *Evaporative emission control system. Typical*

the valve disc is lifted completely from its seat, allowing a completely unobstructed exhaust gas flow.

When manifold vacuum is high, a vacuum control valve closes off vacuum to EGR valve. During periods of low manifold vacuum, such as acceleration, the control valve opens allowing vacuum to operate second stage of EGR valve and allow additional exhaust gas recirculation.

The temperature controlled vacuum solenoid valve is controlled by the same two temperature sensors used for the electric assist choke system on 2002 engines and by the sensor mounted in the intake manifold water passage on 3.0 engines. When ambient temperature is below 63° or coolant temperature is below 113°, solenoid closes vacuum flow to vacuum control valve. This prevents the second stage of the EGR valve from operating when the engine is cold which results in improved cold driveability.

DASHPOT SYSTEM

2002 & 3.0 Engines

To help control emissions during deceleration, the throttle plate is held slightly open by means of a vacuum operated diaphragm unit, or dashpot. At a speed of over 1750 ± 100 rpm for 2002 engines or 1920 ± 100 rpm for 3.0 engines, the speed sensor actuates a vacuum solenoid valve to vent vacuum diaphragm unit to atmosphere. A spring in the vacuum unit then causes the carburetor linkage to open slightly. As engine speed drops below 1650 ± 100 rpm for 2002 engines or 1800 ± 100 rpm for 3.0 engines, the speed sensor interrupts the flow of current to the valve. This allows intake manifold vacuum to retract the plunger of the vacuum unit and return the throttle to idle position.

VACUUM RETARD UNIT

2002 & 2002 Tii Engines

No vacuum advance is used on these engines. In its place a vacuum retard unit is used which is controlled by a special vacuum port in the carburetor. This port is positioned to allow vacuum retard at idle and cold fast idle speeds only. This allows a larger throttle opening which reduces exhaust emissions.

DUAL VACUUM ADVANCE UNIT

3.0 Engine

The distributor is equipped with both a vacuum retard and an advance unit. The retard unit receives its vacuum from a special port in the carburetor throttle body. This port is positioned to provide vacuum retard with throttle at idle position and when throttle is held open by dashpot. As the throttle is opened beyond this point, the ignition retard is gradually deactivated. Thus, timing is retarded during idle and deceleration to reduce exhaust emissions. The vacuum advance unit is controlled by a speed sensor which operates a solenoid vacuum valve. In order to maintain low NOx levels, this system supplies vacuum advance only when engine speed exceeds 2500 rpm.

COOLANT TEMPERATURE AND ELECTRICALLY ASSIST CHOKE

2002 & 3.0 Engines

The position of the choke plate is controlled by a bi-metal spring which responds to coolant temperature and an electrical heating coil. Cut-in point of the heating element is controlled by two temperature sensors. One sensor is located on the intake manifold and senses heat radiation from the cylinder head and the engine block. At ambient temperatures above 63° F, the switch applies power

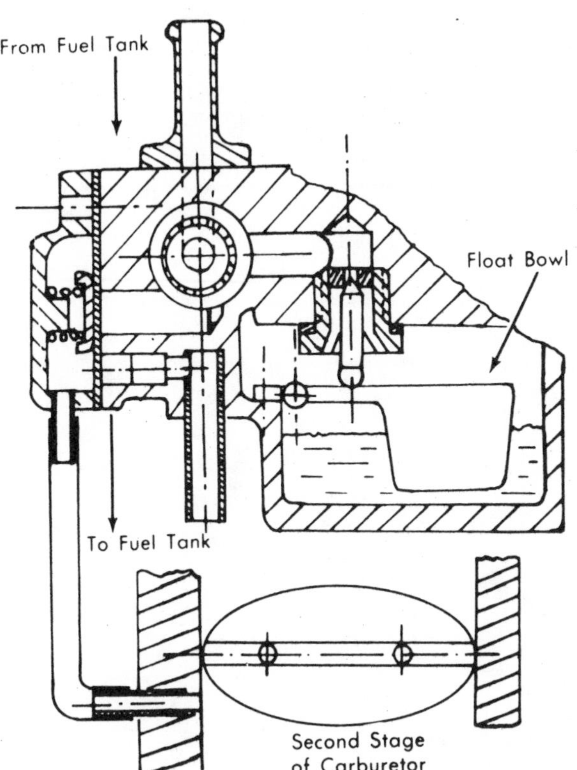

Fig. 2 Fuel return valve

to the choke heater. The second sensor is located in water jacket of the intake manifold heating system and at coolant temperatures above 113° F, the switch applies power to the choke heater. These switches operate so that power is applied to electric choke only when ambient temperature is above 63° and coolant temperature is above 113°. This allows the choke to operate normally at low temperatures but allows fast operation at higher temperatures to prevent an over rich mixture which reduces exhaust emissions.

VACUUM LIMITER VALVE

2002 Tii Engine

This valve controls exhaust emissions during deceleration and is attached into a hose connected between the air cleaner and the intake manifold. The valve is controlled by a vacuum line which is connected to the vacuum line between the intake manifold and the vacuum retard unit of the distributor. When the intake manifold vacuum is high during deceleration the valve opens and allows additional air from the air cleaner to enter the intake manifold. At the same time the fuel injection pump is calibrated to provide a small amount of additional fuel which provides a combustible mixture.

GENERAL SERVICE

Exhaust Gas Recirculation System

Testing

Connect the infra-red exhaust gas analyzer and allow the engine to idle. Lift the diaphragm of the EGR valve with finger or dull tool, using care not to damage the diaphragm. Idle speed must drop about 500 rpm and CO reading remain steady or increase slightly. If CO reading decreases, or if engine stalls, air leaks exist in system. Remove black vacuum hose from carburetor and connect to secondary venting hose of the crankcase ventilation system and plug the loose end of the secondary venting hose. The first stage of EGR valve must open and rpm should drop about 150-200 rpm. Now, remove the red vacuum hose from the carburetor and connect to secondary venting hose. Remove the white vacuum hose from the control valve on firewall. Again rpm should decrease 150-200. If either test fails, the valve is defective and must be replaced.

Cleaning

If tests indicate that the EGR valve requires cleaning, remove major deposits from the valve using a suitable tool. If sharp tools are used, use care not to damage the diaphragm or scratch the valve. Complete the cleaning operation using a suitable solvent and brush.

Dashpot System

Testing

Step on accelerator and release quickly. Rpm must return to idle with a certain delay. If not, adjust the dashpot.

Adjusting

With the vacuum hose removed from dashpot, idle speed must increase to 1400-1500 rpm for 2002 engines and 1700 ± 50 rpm for 3.0 engines. If necessary, adjust by turning dashpot in the bracket. Reinstall the vacuum hose and test dashpot system.

Vacuum Advance Solenoid

Testing

Remove the vacuum hose from advance side of distributor. Start the engine and increase speed to 2500 ± 50 rpm. Vacuum should be felt at disconnected end of vacuum advance hose. If no vacuum is felt, remove electrical connector from vacuum solenoid and connect a voltmeter. Voltmeter should read 12 volts below 2200 ± 100 rpm. If not, the speed sensor is defective. Test the vacuum solenoid valve as previously described.

Vacuum Control Valve

Testing

Ensure that all vacuum connections are correct. Remove the red vacuum hose from the carburetor and connect to vacuum source. Engine speed should not decrease. Disconnect blue vacuum hose from second stage of EGR valve and feel for vacuum. If vacuum is present, the valve is defective. With engine at idle, blow through blue hose, air should flow freely.

NOTE: *Do not use pressurized air.* Reconnect vacuum hoses and disconnect the white vacuum hose from dashpot. Turn dashpot until plunger is free of throttle lever and reconnect the vacuum hose. Remove the white vacuum hose from the carburetor and connect to secondary venting hose and plug loose end of secondary vent hose. Start the engine and detach the white hose from the intake manifold to control valve. A considerable speed drop must occur and the blue hose connected to the EGR valve must be under vacuum. If not, replace the control valve.

Vacuum Solenoid

Ensure that the valve is open to vacuum flow when de-energized. Connect the solenoid to 12 volt power source. The valve should close.

BRITISH LEYLAND

AUSTIN & MG/MIDGET
GENERAL ENGINE SPECIFICATIONS

Model or Engine	Bore & Stroke, Inches (mm)	Piston Displacement Cubic Inches (cc)	Compression Ratio	Maximum Brake HP @ rpm	Maximum Torque Ft. Lbs. @ rpm	Normal Oil Pressure Pounds
1974						
Austin Marina MGB	3.16 x 3.50 (80.3 x 89.0)	109.8 (1798)	8.0	81 @ 5400	97 @ 2900	15–50
Midget	2.78 x 3.20 (71 x 81)	77.9 (1275)	8.0	55 @ 5500	67 @ 3200	15–50

TUNEUP SPECIFICATIONS

Car Model or Engine	Spark Plugs		Distributor		Firing Order	Ignition Timing		Hot Idle Speed rpm
	Type	Gap, Inch	Point Gap, Inch	Dwell Angle, Degrees		Degrees BTDC	Mark Location	
1974								
MGB-GT	Champion N9Y	.025	.014–.016	57–63	1-3-4-2	6 (Static) 11 (Strobo)	①	850
Midget	Champion N9Y	.025	.014–.016	57–63	1-3-4-2	TDC (Static) 9 (Strobo)	①	1000
Austin Marina	Champion N9Y	.035	.014–.016	57–63	1-3-4-2	6 (Static) 12 (Strobo)	①	850

①—Pointer on timing case, notch on crankcase pulley.

DISTRIBUTOR SPECIFICATIONS

Model or Engine	Distributor Part No.	Point Gap, Inch	Dwell Angle, Deg.	Spring Tension, Oz.	Centrifugal Advance			Vacuum Advance		
					Start @ rpm	Int.	Full @ rpm	Inches of Vacuum to Start Plunger	Int.	Full Advance Dist. Deg. @ Vacuum
1974										
MGB-GT	—	.014–.016	57–63	18–24	—	—	—	—	—	—
Midget	—	.014–.016	57–63	18–24	—	—	—	—	—	—
Austin Marina	—	.014–.016	57–63	18–24	—	—	—	—	—	—

JAGUAR
GENERAL ENGINE SPECIFICATIONS

Model or Engine	Bore & Stroke, Inches (mm)	Piston Displacement, Cubic Inches (cc)	Compression Ratio	Maximum Brake HP @ rpm	Maximum Torque Ft. Lbs. @ rpm	Normal Oil Pressure Pounds
1974						
E-Type V12 (5.3)	3.54 x 2.76 (90.0 x 70.2)	326 (5343)	7.8	255 @ 6000	288 @ 3500	80
XJ6 4.2	3.63 x 4.17 (92.1 x 105.7)	258.43 (4235)	8.0	186 @ 4500	240 @ 3750	40
XJ12L (5.3)	3.54 x 2.76 (90.0 x 70.2)	326 (5343)	7.8	250 @ 6000	283 @ 3500	80

TUNEUP SPECIFICATIONS

Car Model or Engine	Spark Plugs		Distributor		Firing Order	Ignition Timing		Hot Idle Speed, rpm
	Type	Gap, Inch	Point Gap, Inch	Dwell Angle, Degrees		Degrees BTDC	Mark Location	
1974								
XJ6	Champion N11Y	.025	.014–.016	35	1-5-3 6-2-4	8	Damper	750
XJ12	Champion N10Y	.025	.020–.022	22–27	1A-6B-5A-2B① 3A-4B-6A-1B 2A-5B-4A-3B	10	Damper	750
E-Type V12	Champion N10Y	.025	.020–.022	22–27	1A-6B-5A-2B 3A-4B-6A-1B 2A-5B-4A-3B	10	Damper	650②

①—B-position on driver's side ②—Manual trans. 750 w/auto trans.

DISTRIBUTOR SPECIFICATIONS

Model or Engine	Distributor Part No.	Point Gap, Inch	Dwell Angle, Deg.	Spring Tension, Oz.	Centrifugal Advance			Vacuum Advance		
					Start @ rpm	Int.	Full @ rpm	Inches of Vacuum to Start Plunger	Int.	Full Advance Dist. Deg. @ Vacuum
1974										
XJ-6 4.2	—	.014–.016	35	—	—	—	—	—	—	—
XJ-12 5.3	—	.020–.022	22–27	—	—	—	—	—	—	—
E-Type V12 (5.3)	—	.020–.022	22–27	—	—	—	—	—	—	—

TRIUMPH

GENERAL ENGINE SPECIFICATIONS

Model or Engine	Bore & Stroke, Inches (mm)	Piston Displacement, Cubic Inches (cc)	Compression Ratio	Maximum Brake HP @ rpm	Maximum Torque Ft. Lbs. @ rpm	Normal Oil Pressure Pounds
1974						
TR6	2.94 x 3.74 (74.7 x 95)	152 (2498)	7.7	106 @ 4900	133 @ 3000	60
Spitfire	2.89 x 3.45 (73.7 x 87.5)	91 (1493)	8.0	57 @ 4000	90 @ 2500	40–60
GT6Mk. 3	2.94 x 2.99 (74.7 x 76)	122 (1998)	8.0	79 @ 4900	97 @ 2900	45–55

TUNEUP SPECIFICATIONS

Car Model or Engine	Spark Plugs		Distributor		Firing Order	Ignition Timing		Hot Idle Speed, rpm
	Type	Gap, Inch	Point Gap, Inch	Dwell Angle, Degrees		Degrees BTDC	Mark Location	
1974								
TR6	Champion N9Y	.025	.014–.016	34–37	1-5-3-6-2-4	10	Crankshaft pulley	800–850
Spitfire	Champion N9Y	.025	.014–.016	38–40	1-3-4-2	10	Crankshaft pulley	800–850

DISTRIBUTOR SPECIFICATIONS

Model or Engine	Distributor Part No.	Point Gap, Inch	Dwell Angle, Deg.	Spring Tension, Oz.	Centrifugal Advance			Vacuum Advance		
					Start @ rpm	Int.	Full @ rpm	Inches of Vacuum to Start Plunger	Int.	Full Advance Dist. Deg. @ Vacuum
1974										
TR6	—	.014–.016	34–37	18–24	—	—	—	—	—	—
Spitfire	—	.014–.016	38–40	17–21	—	—	—	—	—	—

Emission Controls

1974 MODELS THERMOSTATICALLY CONTROLLED AIR CLEANER

Exc. Triumph, MG & MGB

The air intake temperature control system is designed to maintain the air temperature entering the carburetors at approximately 105° F. A temperature sensor controls a flap valve which regulates the amount of air entering from the hot and cold air inlet, maintaining the correct air temperature under all engine temperature conditions, Fig. 1.

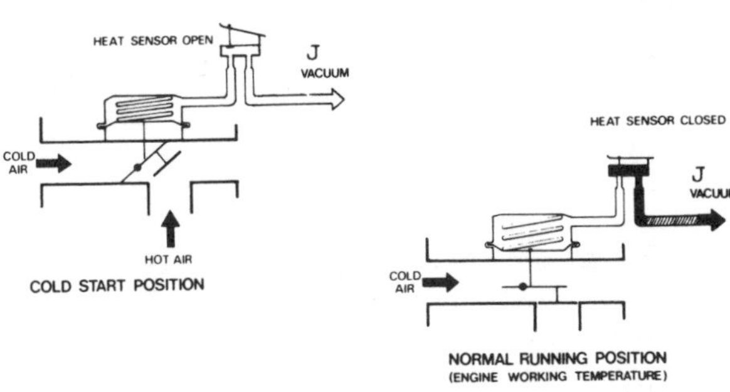

Fig. 1 Air intake temperature control system

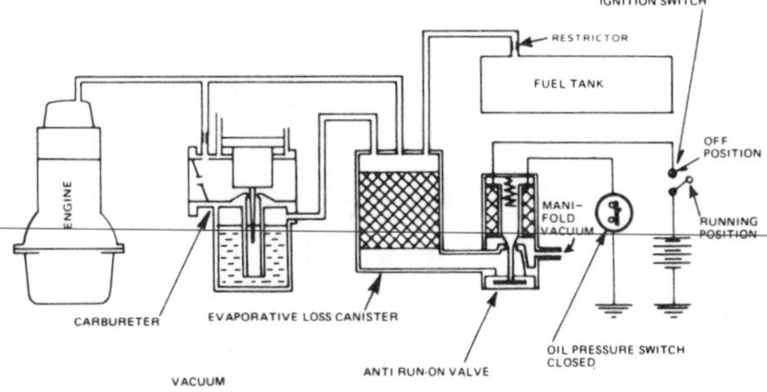

Fig. 2 Engine run condition

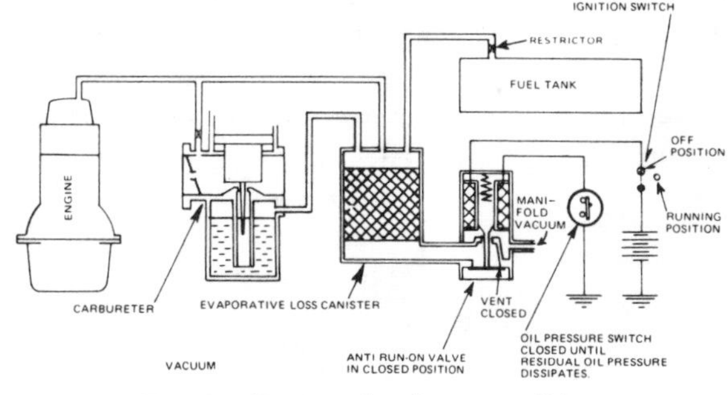

Fig. 3 Engine shutdown condition

EVAPORATIVE EMISSION CONTROL

This is designed to prevent fuel vapors from venting to the atmosphere. Fuel vapors from the fuel tank and carburetor float bowls are vented to and stored in the carbon canister while the engine is stationary. With the engine running, the fuel vapors are drawn into the low depression areas of the carburetors via the crankcase emission system, Figs. 2 & 3.

If the car is parked with a full fuel tank in high ambient temperatures, fuel expands and is displaced into an expansion tank as a liquid. Vapors from the liquid fuel travel to the carbon canister and are stored by the carbon until the engine is started and the system purged.

Anti Run-On Valve

To prevent a tendency to run-on after the ignition is switched off when using 91 octane fuel, an anti-run-on valve is fitted into the carbon canister vent line. When the ignition is switched OFF, a voltage is applied to the anti-run-on valve solenoid. The solenoid closes the canister vent and simultaneously allows a vacuum to apply a depression to the top of the float chamber, which equals the depression already present in the carburetor low depression area, thus preventing fuel flow across the mixture needles. As the oil pressure drops, an oil pressure switch breaks the circuit and de-energizes the solenoid, ready for restarting.

NOTE: Triumph vehicles include a carburetor vent valve.

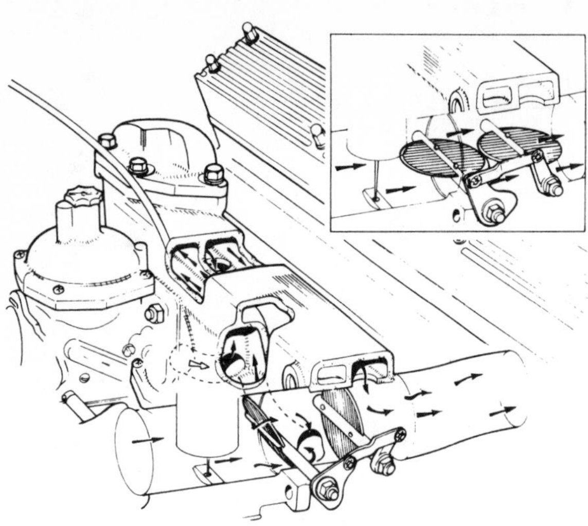

Fig. 4 Duplex manifold system

Duplex Manifold System

XJ6 Models

The duplex or secondary manifold is water heated to preheat the mixture before it enters the combustion chamber, and contains a throttle plate which is mounted directly behind and interconnected with the carburetor throttle (primary) plate. The secondary throttle plate remains closed for approximately the first 20° of movement of the primary throttle plate, thereby routing the incoming mixture through the preheated secondary manifold.

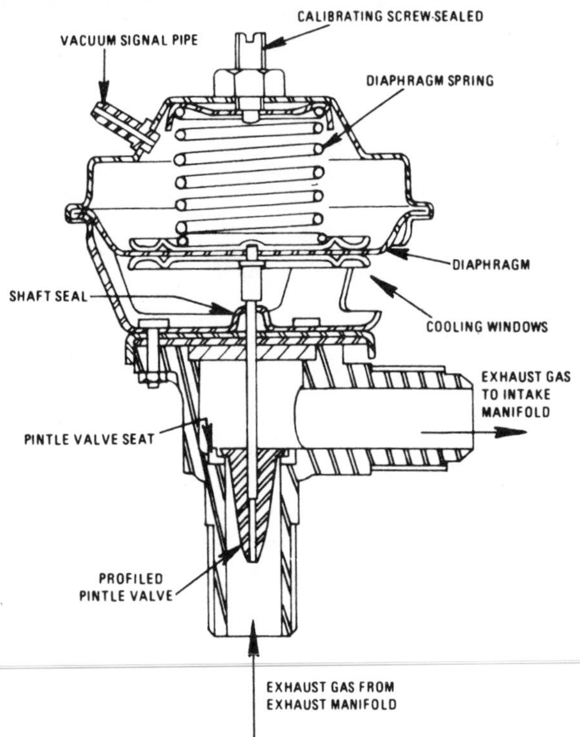

Fig. 5 EGR vacuum controlled metering valve

At full throttle, both throttle plates are fully open, Fig. 4.

Exhaust Gas Recirculation System

Jaguar & Triumph

This is used to reduce emissions of oxides of nitrogen by tapping exhaust gases from the exhaust manifolds and feeding them directly into each carburetor low depression area through restrictor drillings in the exhaust manifold. Later 1974 vehicles are the same as 1973 except for the addition of a vacuum controlled metering valve, Fig. 5.

An EGR cut out is also fitted to Triumph vehicles the function of which is to cut the signal to the EGR Valve by opening an air bleed into the vacuum line when the choke is in use.

Thermostatic Vacuum Switch

Jaguar & Triumph

This is fitted as an engine protection device to prevent overheating. It cuts out ignition retard to distributor at 220° F. Simultaneously, air at atmosphere pressure is also allowed to enter behind each carburetor bypass valve to keep the valves closed.

Solenoid Valve

V12 With Automatic Transmission

This is a three-way valve which changes the vacuum source from a high vacuum at the inlet manifold (desired at low speed up to 35 mph), to a reduced vacuum source at the left hand rear carburetor throttle edge (desired above 35 mph).

Transmission Pressure Switch

Jaguar

Controlled by transmission governor pressure at 35 mph provides the electrical signal to activate the solenoid valve.

Thermostatic Switch

XJ-6, 12, Series III, TR6 & Spitfire

Fitted into the engine cooling system outlet pipe, it energizes the solenoid valve until the coolant reaches approximately 185° F and ensures the ignition remain retarded at all engine speeds during engine warmup, thereby reducing emissions and assisting the engine warmup rate, Fig. 6.

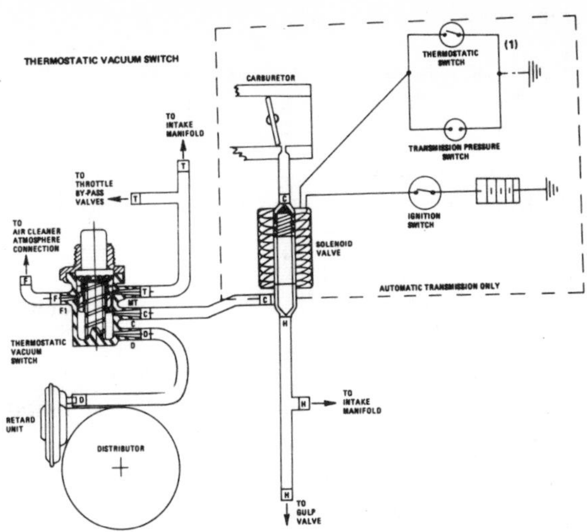

Fig. 6 Diagrammatic layout, XJ-12 series

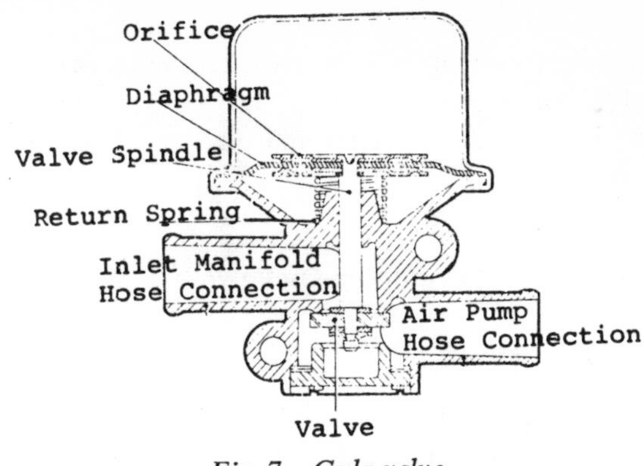

Fig. 7 Gulp valve

to maintain the required pressure in the supply half of the system.

Air Injection System

Exc. Triumph

An air delivery pump supplies air under pressure through a non-return valve to the exhaust ports just above the exhaust valve heads. This air combines with the exhaust gases to continue the oxidation process in the exhaust system. The non-return valve prevents reverse flow in the air injection rails when exhaust gas pressure exceeds air supply pressure.

Gulp Valve

Exc. Triumph

The gulp valve, Fig. 7, provides a quantity of air to the inlet manifolds under conditions of high manifold vacuum, such as sudden throttle closure. This additional air compensates for the temporarily overrich mixture caused by evaporation of the residual fuel on the induction manifold walls to form a weaker mixture that will burn in the cylinders. The gulp valve is actuated by manifold depression via a rubber pipe connected to the intake manifold.

Fuel Recirculation System

Jaguar

With the ignition ON, the recirculating type of fuel system continuously supplies fuel from the tank to the carburetors and recirculates the excess fuel to the tank. A non-return and pressure regulating valve is located in the return line to the tank to maintain the required pressure in the supply half of the system.

XJ-12

In addition to the above system, the XJ-12 incorporates a second fuel pump for supply and two solenoid valves in the recirculation return lines to ensure that fuel is recirculated to the same tank from which it was pumped.

For example, when the left tank is selected for fuel supply, the pump on the right side of the vehicle is energized along with the solenoid on the left side. The solenoid on the right side is closed, as it is not energized, and ensures that fuel from the left tank is recirculated from the engine to the left tank.

Positive Crankcase Ventilation

While the engine is running, vapors from the crankcase are drawn through a filter/flame trap and a branched pipe system into the low depression area of each carburetor and recycled through the engine induction system. With the engine at rest, the vapors are vented to the carbon canister and stored.

GENERAL SERVICE

Thermostatically Controlled Air Cleaner

Checking Flap Control Valve

Disconnect the vacuum line and apply a minimum vacuum of 9 in. HG. Check that flap moves to fully closed (HOT) position. Replace if operation is outside limits.

Checking Temperature Sensor

Disconnect sensor vacuum supply line, apply a minimum vacuum of 9 in. HG and check that flap valve has moved flap to closed (HOT) position and holds in that position until vacuum is released.

Anti-Run-On Valve

Test Procedure

With engine running, supply a hot feed to the solenoid. The engine should stop. If not, check vacuum supply and/or oil pressure switch function, or solenoid feed line or line fuse.

Duplex Manifold System

Secondary Throttle Adjustment

1. Loosen screw until it clears the manifold.
2. Adjust the screw until it just contacts the manifold, then adjust a further ½ turn clockwise.

Exhaust Gas Recirculation System

Decarbonize Inlet Drillings

1. Remove the blanking plug from carburetor mounting flanges.
2. Hold the throttle open.
3. Remove the carbon deposits with a mild steel rod 8 inches long, ⅛-inch diameter.
4. Refit blanking screws.

Decarbonize Restrictors and Y Pieces

1. Unscrew the union nut securing the outlet pipe to the adapter.
2. Remove the carburetors.
3. Remove the restrictor from adapter.
4. Clean Y piece, pipes and restrictors with wire brush and forced air.
5. Refit the carburetor. Use new gasket and seals, etc.

A similar arrangement is fitted to the XJ-6. However, restrictor sizes are different from those of the V-12s.

Solenoid Valve

Solenoid Valve Test

1. Make sure ignition is switched off.
2. Disconnect vacuum pipes from valve.
3. Connect a suitable length of hose to thermostatic switch port.
4. Blow down hose. Air should emit from throttle edge tapping port.
5. Switch on ignition.
6. Blow down hose, air should emit from adjacent port.
7. Should valve fail test 4 the switch is defective and must be replaced. Failure of test 6 indicates defective valve or electrical feed.
8. Detach the test hose and refit service hoses.

Air Injection System

Testing

1. Check belt tension
   E Type V12
   XJ-12 4-lb. load—.25-inch deflection at belt mid point.
   XJ-6 2.2-lb. load—.15-inch deflection at belt mid point.
2. Disconnect delivery pipe at check valve and check for air delivery from pump with engine running. If there is no air delivery, replace the pump.
3. Remove the check valve and blow through it from each connection. Air should only pass through the valve when blown from supply hose connection. If air passes when blown from the manifold connection, replace the check valve.
4. Reconnect the air pump and the check valve. Remove the air injection tubes. With the engine running, check for air delivery from all tubes. Check air injection tube passages in the head for obstructions.

Gulp Valve

Testing

Remove the air supply hose and connect a vacuum gauge to the air supply connection of the gulp valve. With the engine idling, zero vacuum should be registered. Replace the gulp valve if a reading is obtained. By opening and closing the throttle rapidly, the gauge should register a vacuum and retain reading until the line is disconnected. If the gauge fails to respond and vacuum is available at the sensing tube, replace the gulp valve.

CAPRI

GENERAL ENGINE SPECIFICATIONS

Model or Engine	Bore & Stroke, Inches (mm)	Piston Displacement Cubic Inches (cc)	Compression Ratio	Maximum Brake HP @ rpm	Maximum Torque Ft. Lbs. @ rpm	Normal Oil Pressure Pounds
1974						
2000cc	3.575 x 3.029 (91.0 x 77.0)	122 (1993)	8.2	85 @ 5600	98 @ 3800	45–65
2800 V-6	3.66 x 2.70 (93.0 x 68.5)	171 (2792)	8.2	119 @ 5200	147 @ 2800	40

TUNEUP SPECIFICATIONS

Car Model or Engine	Spark Plugs		Distributor		Firing Order	Ignition Timing		Hot Idle Speed, rpm
	Type	Gap, Inch	Point Gap, Inch	Dwell Angle, Degrees		Degrees BTDC	Mark Location	
1974								
2000cc Man.	BF-42	.028–.032	.023–.027	37–41	1-3-4-2	0	Pulley	800–960
2000cc Auto.	BF-42	.028–.032	.023–.027	37–41	1-3-4-2	0	Pulley	800–1600
2800	AG-32A	.032–.036	.023–.027	37–41	1-4-2-5-3-6	0	Pulley	800–1300

DISTRIBUTOR SPECIFICATIONS

Model or Engine	Distributor Part No.	Point Gap, Inch	Dwell Angle, Deg.	Spring Tension, Oz.	Centrifugal Advance			Vacuum Advance		
					Start @ rpm	Int.	Full @ rpm	Inches of Vacuum to Start Plunger	Int.	Full Advance Dist. Deg. @ Vacuum
1974										
2000cc Manual	Bosch 74 HF-12100-CA	.023–.027	37–41	—	0 @ 800–960	15 @ 1900–2200	22–26 @ 4500	3.78	6.5–7.0 3.5–7.5	4–8 @ 11.8–13.2
2000cc Auto.	Bosch 74HF-12100-CA	.023–.027	37–41	—	0 @ 800–1660	15 @ 2500–3050	20–24 @ 3850	8.50	14.1–14.6 7.5–17.5	4–8 @ 10.23–12.09
2800 V-6 Manual	Bosch 74 TF-12100-NA	.023–.027	37–41	—	0 @ 800–1300	15 @ 2500–3050	16–20 @ 3200	4.10	6.48–6.80 4–8	10–14 @ 13.8–14.9
2800 V-6 Auto.	Bosch 74 TF-12100-RA	.023–.027	37–41	—	0 @ 800–1300	15 @ 2500–3050	16–20 @ 3200	4.10	6.48–6.80 4–8	4–8 @ 10.63–12.17

Emission Controls

EMISSION CONTROL SYSTEM COMPONENT APPLICATION

	DUAL DIAPHRAGM DISTRIBUTOR	EGR & EGR PVS	DECEL VALVE	DECEL VALVE PVS	VACUUM RESERVOIR	THERMACTOR
2000 cc MANUAL	YES	YES	YES	YES	NO	CALIFORNIA ONLY
2000 cc AUTOMATIC	YES	YES	NO	NO	CALIFORNIA ONLY	CALIFORNIA ONLY

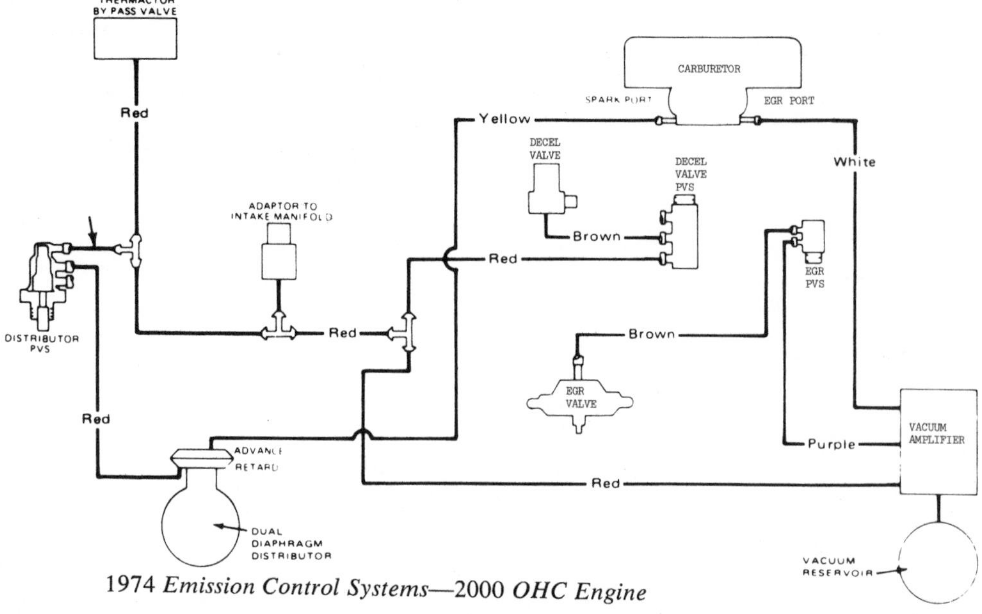

1974 *Emission Control Systems*—2000 *OHC Engine*

EMISSION CONTROL SYSTEM COMPONENT APPLICATION

	DUAL DIAPHRAGM DISTRIBUTOR	EGR	EGR PVS	DECEL VALVE	DECEL VALVE PVS	VACUUM RESERVOIR	THERMACTOR
2800 cc MANUAL	CALIFORNIA ONLY *	YES	NO	YES	NO	CALIFORNIA ONLY	YES
2800 cc AUTOMATIC	CALIFORNIA ONLY *	YES	NO	NO	NO	CALIFORNIA ONLY	YES

*VEHICLES SOLD OUTSIDE CALIFORNIA WILL BE FITTED WITH A COMMON DUAL DIAPHRAGM DISTRIBUTOR BUT THE SECONDARY (RETARD) DIAPHRAGM WILL BE OPEN TO ATMOSPHERE

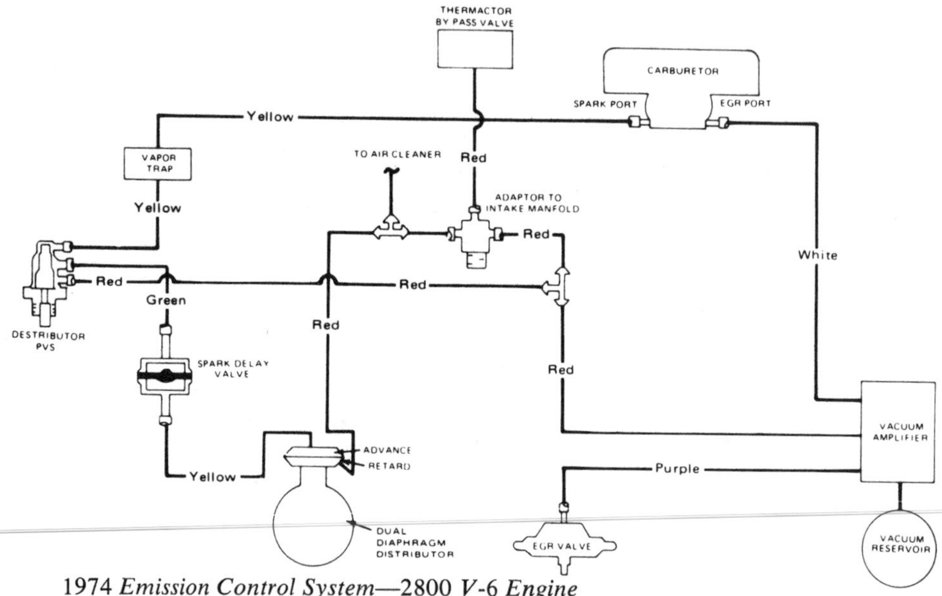

1974 *Emission Control System*—2800 *V-6 Engine*

1974 MODELS

Electric Assisted Choke

All Capri passenger cars use an electrically heated choke thermostatic spring housing as an aid to fast choke release for better emission characteristics during engine warmup.

The electric assist heater used on the Capri 5200 2V carburetor (Fig. 1) is a constant temperature PTC (positive temperature coefficient) unit. It is powered from the center tap of the alternator. The heater is installed between the choke thermostatic spring and the choke casting, and heats when the engine is running.

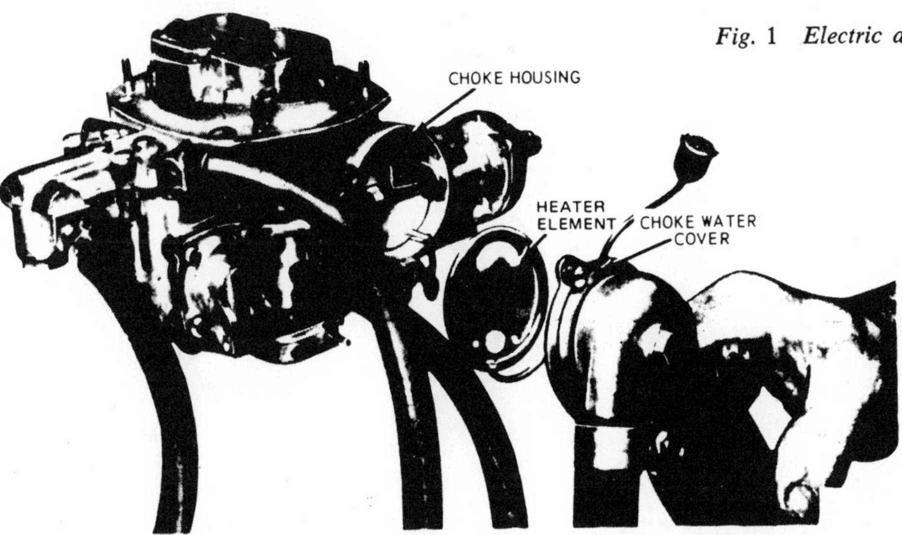

Fig. 1 Electric assist choke

Deceleration Valve System

Deceleration valves are used to provide enriched mixture on engine deceleration. When this occurs with a closed throttle, the valve provides momentary fuel/air flow, bypassing the carburetor.

NOTE: Two valves are used for 1974. One is modified for control by a temperature-sensitive PVS valve, while the other is retained from 1973 (Fig. 2).

PVS (Ported Vacuum Switch)

These switches are used in several places in the emission systems. Used with two or three ports, the valves can turn vacuum on and off or switch between two vacuum sources for a third delivery point (Fig. 3).

All PVS valves have an opening and closing temperature. When closed, the typical 3-port PVS provides a path through the center and bottom holes. In the case of the PVS used to provide engine speed increase during prolonged idle periods, this provides carburetor spark port vacuum to the distributor vacuum advance diaphragm. If the engine should overheat while idling, the PVS switches port sources and connects the distributor to full intake manifold vacuum. This increases the engine speed until cooldown occurs. When the engine temperature drops, the PVS once again connects the distributor to the spark port.

Spark Delay Valves (SDV)

Basically, the spark delay valve works to slow air flow in the vacuum lines, thus providing closer control on vacuum-operated equipment.

NOTE: All 1974 SDVs have an internal, sintered orifice and filter pack and cannot be installed on pre-1974 systems (Fig. 4).

Exhaust Gas Recirculation System (EGR)

The Exhaust Gas Recirculation System (EGR) is designed to reintroduce small amounts of exhaust gas into the combustion cycle, reducing combustion temperatures and thus reducing the generation of oxides of nitrogen (NO_X). The amount of exhaust gas reintroduced and the timing of the cycle are controlled by various factors such as engine vacuum, temperature, and on some vehicles, vehicle speed.

EGR Valve

The EGR valve (Fig. 5) is a vacuum-operated unit that attaches to a spacer that fits under the carburetor. This valve can only be cleaned with sandblast equipment, or replaced. When the valve is open, exhaust gas is permitted to enter the intake manifold passages. When the valve is closed, internal or external sealing takes place, preventing the flow of exhaust gases into the intake passages.

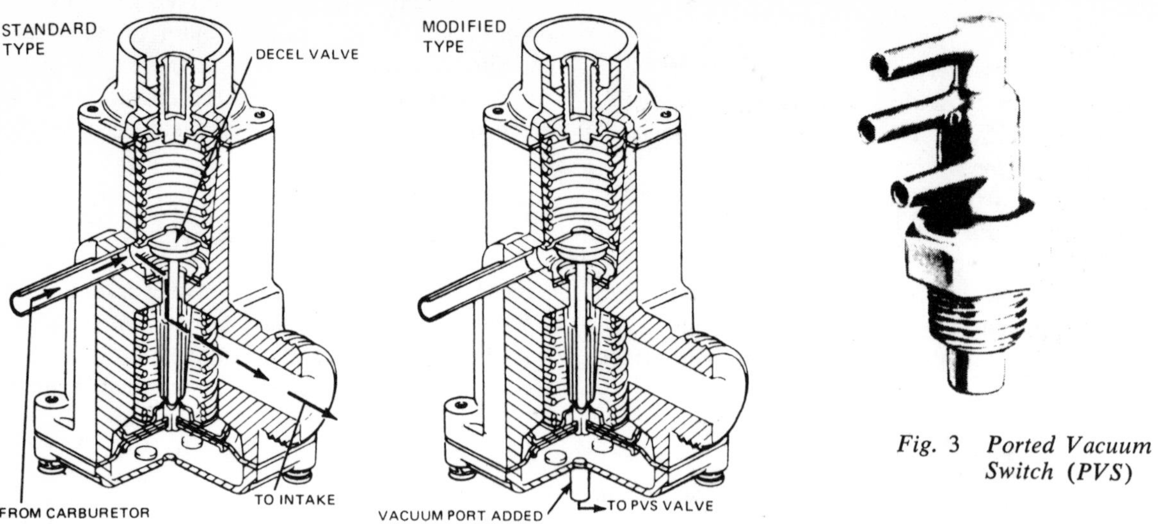

Fig. 2 Typical 1974 Deceleration Valves

Fig. 3 Ported Vacuum Switch (PVS)

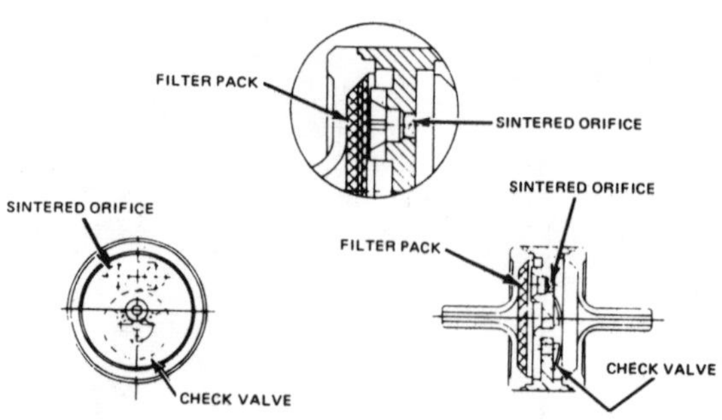

Fig. 4 Spark Delay Valve (SDV)

Venturi Vacuum Amplifier

The EGR venturi vacuum amplifier (Fig. 6) uses a relatively weak venturi vacuum signal in the throat of the carburetor to shape a strong intake manifold vacuum signal to operate the EGR valve. In other words, the intake manifold vacuum operates the EGR valve, under the control of the carburetor venturi vacuum. This makes it possible to achieve an accurate, repeatable and almost exact proportion between venturi air flow and EGR flow. Thus, it assists in controlling oxides of nitrogen emissions with minimal sacrifice in vehicle driveability.

The amplifier features a vacuum reservoir and check valve to maintain adequate vacuum supply regardless of variations in engine manifold vacuum (Fig. 7).

A relief valve is also used to dump or cancel the output EGR signal whenever the venturi vacuum signal is equal to, or greater than, the intake manifold vacuum. This allows the EGR valve to close at or near wide open throttle acceleration, when maximum power is required from the engine.

For some engine applications, the amplifier is calibrated with a 2-inch Hg output bias. In other words, when the venturi vacuum signal is at zero, the output signal already reads 2 inches Hg. This feature permits a rapid system response in overcoming the EGR valve spring closing force.

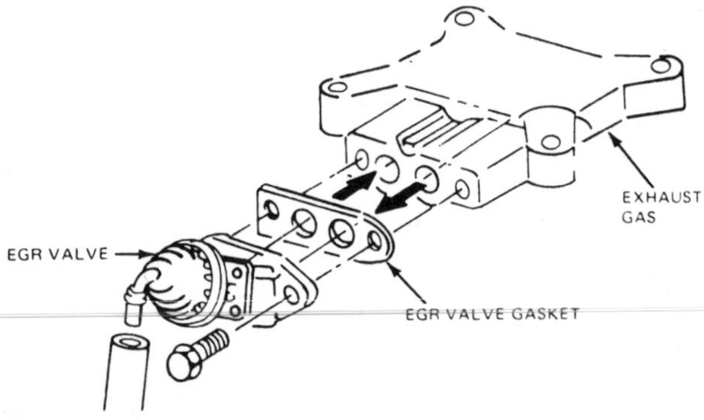

Fig. 5 Spacer Entry EGR System

EGR/CSC System

The EGR/CSC System (Fig. 8) regulates both distributor spark advance and EGR valve operation according to coolant temperature, by sequentially switching vacuum signals.

The major EGR/CSC system components are:

1. 95° F EGR—PVS valve
2. Spark Delay Valve (SDV)
3. Vacuum Check Valve

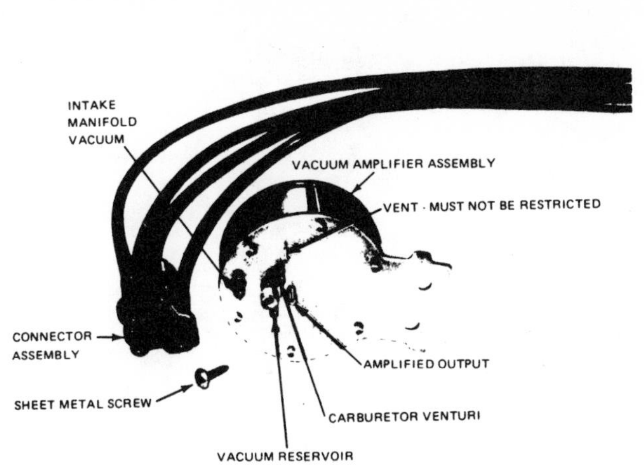

Fig. 6 Venturi Vacuum Amplifier

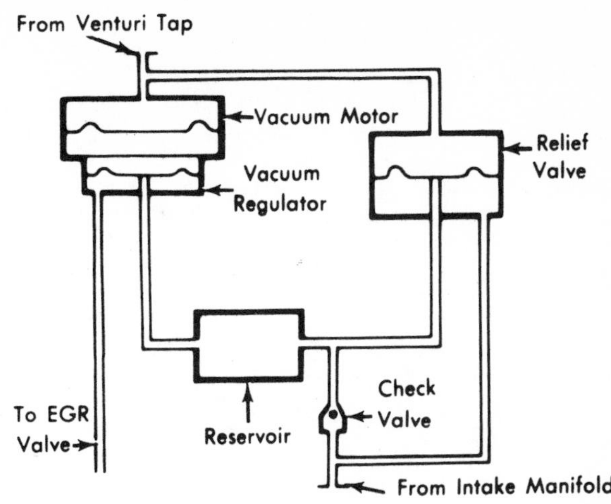

Fig. 7 Vacuum Amplifier System

When the engine coolant temperature is below 82° F, the EGR—PVS valve admits carburetor EGR port vacuum (occurring at about 2500 rpm) directly to the distributor advance diaphragm, through the one-way check valve (Fig. 9).

At the same time, the EGR—PVS valve shuts off carburetor EGR vacuum to the EGR valve and transmission diaphragm.

When engine coolant temperature is 95° F and above, the EGR—PVS valve is actuated and directs carburetor EGR vacuum to the EGR valve and transmission instead of the distributor (Fig. 10).

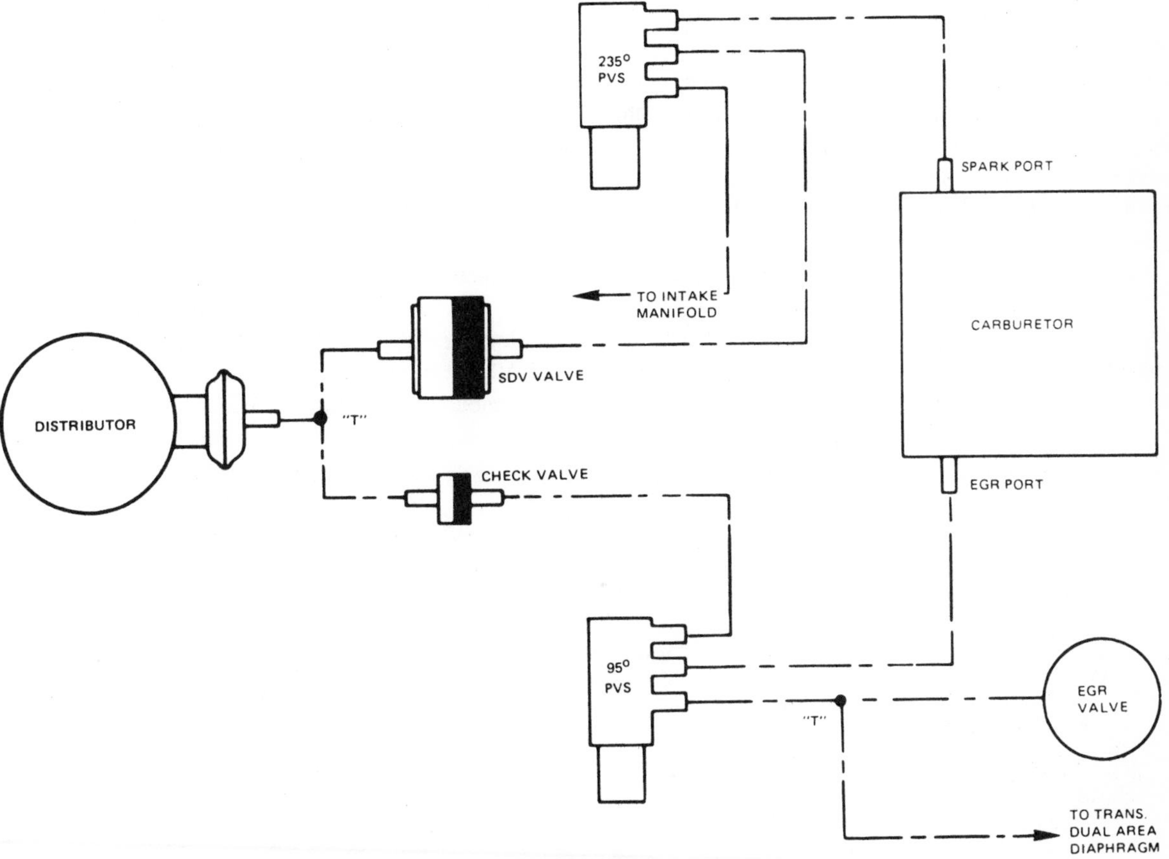

Fig. 8 Schematic of EGR/CSC System

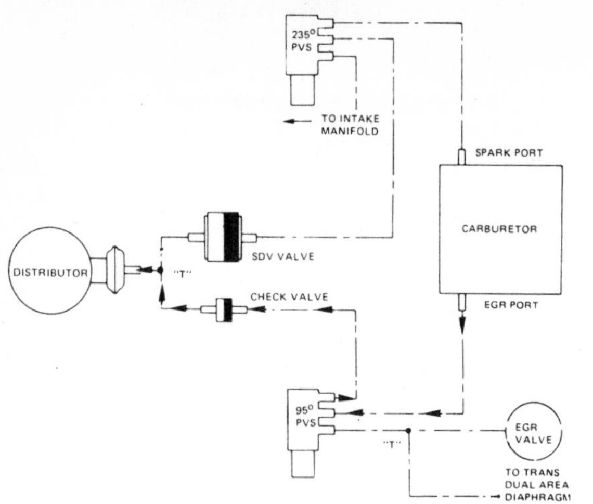

Fig. 9 EGR/CSC System Operation—Below 82° *F.*

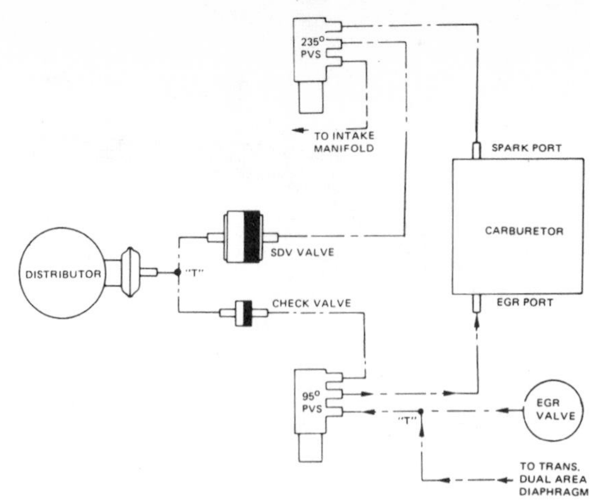

Fig. 10 *EGR/CSC System Operation—Above* 95° *F.*

At temperatures between 82° F and 95° F, the EGR—PVS valve may be open, closed or in mid-position.

The SDV valve delays carburetor spark vacuum to the distributor advance diaphragm by restricting the vacuum signal through the SDV valve for a predetermined time. During normal acceleration, little or no vacuum is admitted to the distributor advance diaphragm until acceleration is completed, because of (1) the time delay of the SDV valve and (2) the rerouting of EGR port vacuum, if the engine coolant temperature is 95° F or higher.

The check valve blocks off vacuum signal from the SDV valve to the EGR—PVS valve so that carburetor spark vacuum will not be dissipated when the EGR—PVS valve is actuated above 95° F.

The 235° F PVS valve is not part of the EGR/CSC system, but is connected to the distributor vacuum advance to prevent engine overheating while idling as on previous models. At idle speeds, no vacuum is generated at either the carburetor spark port or EGR port and engine timing is fully retarded. When engine coolant temperature reaches 235° F, however, the valve is actuated to admit intake manifold vacuum to the distributor advance diaphragm. This advances engine timing and speeds up the engine. The increase in coolant flow and fan speed lowers engine temperature.

TESTING AND ADJUSTMENT

Deceleration Valves—High Idle Speed

Excessively high engine idle can be caused by a hanging valve or maladjustment. Check as follows.

1. Attach the tachometer to the engine.
2. Operate the engine for twenty minutes at 1200 rpm to stabilize engine temperature.
3. Disconnect the rubber hose between the decel valve and carburetor at the decel valve end and cap the nipple on the valve.
4. Verify that ignition timing, idle speed and carburetor mixtures are set to specifications.

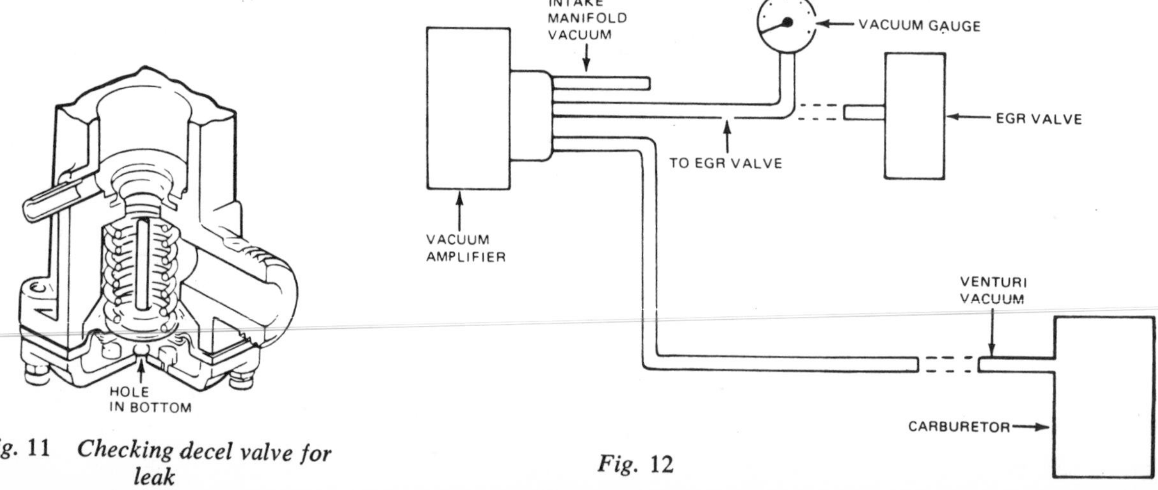

Fig. 11 *Checking decel valve for leak*

Fig. 12

5. Increase engine speed to 3000 rpm and hold for approximately 5 seconds. Then release the throttle. If the engine does not return to normal idle speed, check for throttle linkage hangups and correct them, if necessary, before continuing.
6. Remove the cap from the decel valve nipple and tee a vacuum gauge into the hose between the decel valve and the carburetor.
7. Increase engine speed to 3000 rpm and hold for approximately 5 seconds. Release the throttle and measure the time required for the vacuum reading to drop to zero. This should take from 2 to 5 seconds.
8. If the valve is not within specifications, adjust as required to meet specifications (2 to 5 seconds).
9. Turning the adjusting screw inward reduces the time the valve is open; turning it outward increases the open time. If the valve cannot be adjusted within limits of the adjusting screw, replace the valve.

If the valve closes sooner than specified, engine deceleration will be too lean. If the valve stays open longer than 5 seconds, excessive engine speed will be experienced.

The deceleration valve should be checked and adjusted, if necessary, any time the engine idle speed or fuel mixture has been adjusted. This will assure that factory specifications are met for this system.

Excessive initial timing and/or an overly rich mixture can cause a properly functioning valve to hang open. Obviously, any adjustment that affects manifold vacuum also affects the decel valve opening and closing points. The higher the vacuum, the sooner the valve opens and the later it closes. When checking the decel valve, idle vacuum should not exceed 18.5 inches Hg for engines with dual-diaphragm distributors, or 19.5 inches Hg with a single diaphragm distributor.

Deceleration Valve—Rough Idle

Rough idle or excessively lean air/fuel mixture can be caused by a ruptured or leaking decel valve diaphragm. Check as follows.

1. To check for a vacuum leak, place a finger over the small hole in the bottom of the decel valve (Fig. 11).
2. Improvement of idle quality and/or significant change in idle speed indicates the diaphragm is leaking and should be replaced.

Automatic Choke Operation

Conventional Choke

1. Remove the air cleaner assembly.
2. Check the choke plate and choke linkage to ensure free operation without sticking or binding.
3. Check whether the thermostatic spring housing is set to specification given on the Emission Certification Label.
4. If the thermostatic spring housing is not set to specifications, loosen the clamp screws that attach the thermostatic spring housing to the choke housing.
5. Set the thermostatic spring housing to the specified index mark.
6. Tighten the clamp screws.
7. Replace the air cleaner.

Electric Assist Choke

1. With the engine off, remove the air cleaner. Verify that the holddown wingnuts have not been overtorqued, thus causing the A/C housing to interfere with the choke plate operation.
2. Check the following for freedom of operation —choke plate, all linkages, fast idle cam, etc.
3. If a delay valve is used, use delay valve diagnostic procedure and verify integrity of the delay valve.
4. With the engine operating, disconnect the stator lead at the choke cap lead connector and connect a 0.3 amp ammeter between the choke cap terminal and the stator lead.
5. Start the engine and operate for approximately 5 minutes. Current flow must be .3 to .75 amps at 5 minutes.
6. If no current draw is noted, verify that the alternator is functioning properly. The electric choke is out of specifications if the above conditions are not met and the choke cap should be replaced.
7. Verify that engine coolant is flowing through the choke housing. Housing should be hot. If not, check hoses for restriction.

Carburetor

NOTE: Most carburetor adjustments are factory set, and based on guidelines determined for reduced engine emission. When making carburetor adjustments affecting the idle mixture or speeds, always readjust the fuel deceleration valve if so equipped.

Following are the methods for making adjustments designed to allow conformation to factory specifications for emission levels for 1974.

Adjust Idle Fuel Mixture

With the engine at operating temperature (on fast idle step minimum of 20 minutes), tachometer connected, ignition timing, curb idle speed to specifications and idle fuel limiters fully counterclockwise—remove the air cleaner for easy access to idle mixture screws.

1. If recommended exhaust analyzer is available, perform an Idle CO check reading to verify that the exhaust emissions are within specifications (see specifications chart).
2. If CO is not within specifications, readjust CO to specifications.
3. If recommended exhaust gas analyzer is not available, use alternate idle fuel mixture adjusting procedure to adjust idle fuel mixture.

Idle CO Check and Adjusting Procedure—Exhaust Gas Analyzer

The following Idle CO adjusting procedure is recommended using the Rotunda CO meter No. BRE 42-721 or the Sun Meter No. EET-910 (or other equivalent).

1. Turn on the CO analyzer, and adjust the zero deflection and span setting as recommended by the manufacturer.
2. Allow analyzer to warm up for the specified time recommended in the manufacturer's instruction manual.
3. Before inserting the probe into the exhaust pipe, recheck the zero deflection and span settings and readjust, if necessary.

   Frequent checks of the meter against a known calibrated gas are recommended to verify the integrity of the equipment.

   Engine temperatures must be normalized for accurate reading. Operate the engine at fast idle speed for a minimum of 20 minutes.
4. Place the heater temperature control lever in the maximum heat position during the reading and setting periods. It is not necessary to operate the heater motor.
5. Engine timing and idle speed must be to specifications, idle limiters in maximum counterclockwise position, all vacuum hoses must be connected. Disconnect the thermactor air supply hose at the check valve.
6. The evaporative emission purge line to the air cleaner must be disconnected on all vehicles. For a valid reading, the air cleaner must be in position when readings are taken.

Reading and Setting Idle CO

1. Insert the probe of the prepared CO analyzer into the tail pipe according to the manufacturer's instructions.
2. Increase engine speed slightly and allow throttle to return to normal closed position. If equipped with automatic transmission, place selector lever to Drive.
3. Observe reading on the analyzer meter after allowing at least 10 seconds for stabilization of the instrument. All readings must be completed within 30 seconds on 4-cylinder and 60 seconds on 6-cylinder engines to preclude erroneous readings due to engine overheating.
4. If the reading in Step 3 is not within specifications, remove the probe and recheck the instrument calibration and adjust if required. Repeat Step 2 and 3 after stabilization of engine temperatures.
5. If the reading is still not within specifications remove the air cleaner and the limiter caps. Adjust the idle mixture screws as required to provide for correct CO reading. Correct idle speed immediately, if necessary, to maintain specified rpm. Install the air cleaner. Restabilize engine temperature by operating at a fast idle speed.
6. Repeat Steps 2 thru 5 until correct CO and idle speed are obtained.
7. Install service (blue) limiter cap(s) on the idle mixture screws so that they are against the stop(s) and it is not possible to turn them counterclockwise. Pre-soaking the limiter cap(s) in hot water will soften material and reduce effort required to install the caps on the screw head.
8. Recheck and verify that CO readings were not changed while installing the limiter cap(s).
9. Remove all test equipment and refit the evaporative emission hose to the air cleaner.

Spark Delay Valve (SDV) Function—All Systems

1. Set the distributor tester vacuum gauge to 10 inches Hg. Connect the black side of delay valve to the vacuum source. Connect the 24-inch section of vacuum hose to the gauge and to the colored side of delay valve. Apply vacuum and observe time in seconds for gauge to reach 8 inches Hg with a 10-inch Hg vacuum source.
2. To inspect the delay valve for excessive restriction, the minimum and maximum time for

the valve to reach 8 inches Hg should be as shown.

When checking the delay valve, care must be exercised to prevent oil or dirt from getting into the valve, as this will impair the functioning of the valve.

EGR System Function—Checking EGR Valve On Vehicle

Check all vacuum hoses in the system to be sure they are open and not broken, split or cracked and fit snugly onto connectors. Remove the EGR vacuum supply hose from the EGR valve and hook a vacuum hose from the EGR valve to an external gauge (in increments of 1-inch Hg with 0.10-inch Hg graduations) variable vacuum source with minimum 10-inch Hg capacity.

1. Start the engine and stabilize temperatures.
2. Gradually apply vacuum to the EGR valve and simultaneously observe the movement of the EGR valve stem.

   The stem should visually be observed to start to move within ½ to 1.0-inch Hg of the diaphragm signal vacuum as shown on the EGR valve chart.

   If the valve does not meet start-to-open specification, replace it.
3. With engine at idle, apply vacuum to the EGR valve to at least 8 inches Hg. Engine should roughen, rpm should decrease and/or stop completely. If idle quality doesn't change, there is no EGR flow and something is plugging the EGR system.
4. Repeat the cleaning procedure to determine the problem.
5. With engine off, apply 8 inches Hg for a minimum of 30 seconds. Replace the EGR valve if not within specifications.
6. Restart the engine and stabilize temperatures. If the engine idle quality is not acceptable after completion of the cleaning process, the EGR valve may not be sealing properly. If this condition is encountered, install a new EGR valve and a new gasket.
7. Recheck the idle condition of the engine. If there is no improvement in idle quality the problem is elsewhere. The original EGR valve should be reinstalled and further engine diagnosis, shown in Fig. 14, should be performed to determine the offending component. If there is improvement in idle quality, change the EGR valve.

Carburetor EGR Port(s)

To check the carburetor EGR port (or ports if more than one), perform the following steps.

1. Attach a vacuum gauge directly to the EGR source on the carburetor using a suitable hose.
2. With the engine running, open the carburetor throttle quickly and momentarily to at least the ½ open position. Avoid overspeeding.
3. Observe the vacuum gauge for a quick rise and fall as the throttle is opened and closed. If a vacuum is evident, the EGR port is open. If no vacuum is evident, the EGR port in the carburetor is plugged or restricted and should be cleaned.

Venturi Vacuum Amplifier System

The amplifiers have built-in calibrations, and no external adjustments are required. If the amplifier tests reveal it is malfunctioning, replace the amplifier. All connections are located on one side of the amplifier. A vacuum connector and hose assembly is used to insure that proper connections are made at the amplifier. The amplifier is retained with a sheet metal screw.

1. Operate the engine until normal operating temperatures are reached.
2. Before the vacuum amplifier is checked, inspect all other basic components of the EGR system—EGR valve, EGR/PVS valve, hoses, routing, etc.
3. Check the vacuum amplifier connections for proper routing and installation.
4. Remove the hose at the EGR valve (Fig. 15).
5. Connect vacuum gauge to EGR hose. Gauge must read in increments of at least 1 inch Hg graduation.
6. Remove the hose at carburetor venturi (leave off).
7. With engine at curb idle speed, the vacuum gauge reading should be within ± 0.3 inch Hg of specified bias value as shown in amplifier specifications for other than zero bias. Zero bias may read from 0 to 0.5-inch Hg. If out of specification, replace the amplifier.
8. Depress the accelerator and release it after the engine has reached 1500 to 2000 rpm. After engine has returned to idle, the vacuum must return to bias noted in Step 7. If the bias has changed, replace the amplifier. Also, if vacuum shows a marked increase (greater than 1-inch Hg) during acceleration period, the amplifier should be replaced.
9. Hook up venturi hose at the carburetor with

the engine at curb idle rpm. If a sizeable increase in output vacuum is observed, (more than 0.5-inch Hg above Step 7), check idle speed. High idle speed could increase output vacuum due to venturi vacuum increase. See engine decal for correct idle specifications.

10. Check amplifier reservoir and connections as follows. Disconnect the external reservoir hose at the amplifier and cap or plug. Depress the accelerator rapidly to 1500 to 2000 rpm. The vacuum should increase to 4-inch Hg or more. If out of specifications, replace the amplifier.

EGR Valve Removal

Remove the EGR valve for cleaning. Do not strike or pry on the valve diaphragm housing or supports, as this may damage the valve operating mechanism and/or change the valve calibration. Check the orifice hole in the EGR valve body for deposits. A small hand drill may be used to clean the hole if plugged. Extreme care must be taken to avoid enlarging the hole or damaging the surface of the orifice plate.

Valves Which Cannot Be Disassembled

Valves which are riveted or otherwise permanently assembled should be replaced if highly contaminated. They cannot be cleaned.

Valves Which Can Be Disassembled

Separate the diaphragm section from the main mounting body. Clean the valve plates, stem and mounting plate, using a small power driven rotary type wire brush. Take care not to damage the parts. Remove deposits between the stem and the valve disc by using a steel blade or shim approximately 0.028-inch thick in a sawing motion around the stem shoulder at both sides of the disc.

The poppet must wobble and move axially before reassembly.

Clean the cavity and passages in the main body of the valve with a power driven rotary wire brush. If the orifice plate has a hole less than 0.450-inch, it must be removed for cleaning. Remove all loosened debris using shop compressed air. Reassemble the diaphragm section on the main body using a new gasket between them. Torque the attaching screws to specification. Clean the orifice plate and the counterbore in the valve body. Reinstall the orifice plate using a small amount of contact cement to retain the plate in place during assembly of the valve to the carburetor spacer. Apply cement only to outer edges of orifice plate to avoid restriction of orifice.

Cleaning EGR Supply Passages and Carburetor Spacer

Remove the carburetor and the carburetor spacer. Clean the supply tube with a small power driven rotary type wire brush or blast cleaning equipment. Clean the exhaust gas passages in the spacer using a suitable wire brush and/or scraper. The machined holes in the spacer can be cleaned by using a suitable round wire brush. Hard encrusted material should be probed loose first, then brushed out.

EGR Valve Inspection and Off Vehicle Test

After cleaning the valve, connect a vacuum hose from the EGR valve to an externally gauged variable vacuum source with minimum 10-in. Hg capacity. Start at low vacuum (less than 2-in. Hg) and increase vacuum steadily up to 10 inches. The valve stem must move smoothly without apparent sticking, binding, or chattering action. The valve should not be noisy or exhibit excessive vibration due to this operation. If erratic motion or vibration is detected, replace the valve. The valve stem may cease to move above 7-in. Hg of applied vacuum. This is not cause for replacement. Remove vacuum and, using a felt tip pencil, mark stem position closest to the valve main body. Reinstall the valve and related components on engine using new gaskets. Perform the EGR On Vehicle test outlined under Testing EGR System Function to fully determine whether the EGR valve should be replaced.

COLT

GENERAL ENGINE SPECIFICATIONS

Model or Engine	Bore & Stroke, Inches (mm)	Piston Displacement Cubic Inches (cc)	Compression Ratio	Maximum Brake HP @ rpm	Maximum Torque Ft. Lbs. @ rpm	Normal Oil Pressure, Pounds
1974						
1600	3.03 x 3.39 (76.9 x 36.0)	97.5 (1597)	8.5	83 @ 5600	89 @ 3600	57–71
2000	3.31 x 3.54 (84.13 x 89.9)	121.7 (2000)	8.5	94 @ 5500	108 @ 3600	57–71

TUNEUP SPECIFICATIONS

Car Model or Engine	Spark Plugs		Distributor		Firing Order	Ignition Timing		Hot Idle Speed, rpm
	Type	Gap, Inch	Point Gap, Inch	Dwell Angle Degrees		Degrees BTDC	Mark Location	
1974								
1600 Auto	N9Y	.028–.031	.018–.021	49–55	1-3-4-2	0*	Pulley	850
1600 Std	N9Y	.028–.031	.018–.021	49–55	1-3-4-2	0	Pulley	850
2000 Auto	N9Y	.028–.031	.018–.021	49–55	1-3-4-2	3	Pulley	850

*W/O EGR—3 BTDC/850 rpm.

DISTRIBUTOR SPECIFICATIONS

Model or Engine	Distributor Part No.	Point Gap, Inch	Dwell Angle Deg.	Spring Tension, oz.	Centrifugal Advance			Vacuum Advance		
					Start @ rpm	Int.	Full @ rpm	Inches of Vacuum to Start Plunger	Int.	Full Adv. Dist. Deg. @ Vacuum
1974										
1600	T3T03871	.018–.021	49–55	17.6–22.4	−0.3 @ 500	6.2 @ 1000	14 @ 3050	6.7	5.2 @ 11.81	8.5 @ 15.75
2000	T3T13671	.018–.021	49–55	17.6–22.4	0 @ 500	7 @ 1400	10 @ 2500	8.7	5.25 @ 13.78	8.5 @ 17.72

Emission Controls

1974 MODELS CLEANER AIR SYSTEM

Description, Figs. 1 and 2

As ambient temperatures become colder and the air becomes denser, the air-fuel mixture becomes leaner. The result is lowered engine output. If the air-fuel mixture is enriched to overcome this problem, the amount of carbon monoxide and hydrocarbons is increased. To cope with this problem, the air intake is thermostatically controlled by a bimetal within the air cleaner snorkel. This bimetal regulates a control valve which responds to underhood temperatures and controls the air which flows through two circuits. When the underhood temperature is 41° F or lower, the air flow will be preheated via a hot air pipe. When the underhood temperature is between approx-

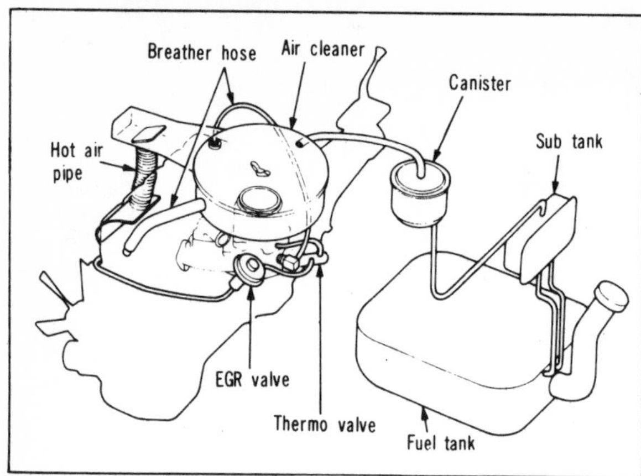

Fig. 1 Cleaner air system

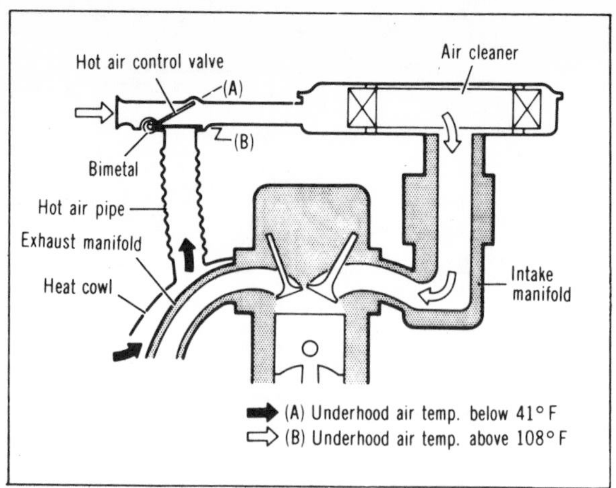

Fig. 2 Thermostatically controlled air cleaner

imately 41° F to 108° F, the air flow will be through the hot air pipe and the air cleaner snorkel. When the underhood temperature is above 108° F, the air flow will be through the snorkel.

This system permits leaner carburetor settings with a reduction in hydrocarbons and carbon monoxide emissions. This system also improves engine warmup characteristics and minimizes carburetor icing.

The system, which is basically the same as in previous years, has been slightly modified.

General Service

Every 12,000 miles or 1 year, perform the following:

1. Check the case and cover for deformation or damage and replace as necessary.
2. Check seal washers and packing for damage and air tightness. Correct or replace as necessary.
3. Check the air filter for excessive dirt, obstructions, damage, etc. Clean the filter by blowing compressed air from inside out or replace it if necessary. Every 24,000 miles or 2 years, replace the filter.
   NOTE: When reinstalling the air filter, make certain that the oil stained portion at the blowby gas suction port is positioned so that the oil stained area will not be enlarged.
4. Using the description provided, visually confirm the operation of hot air control valve located within the snorkel.

POSITIVE CRANKCASE VENTILATION SYSTEM

Description, Fig. 3

The positive crankcase ventilation (PCV) system

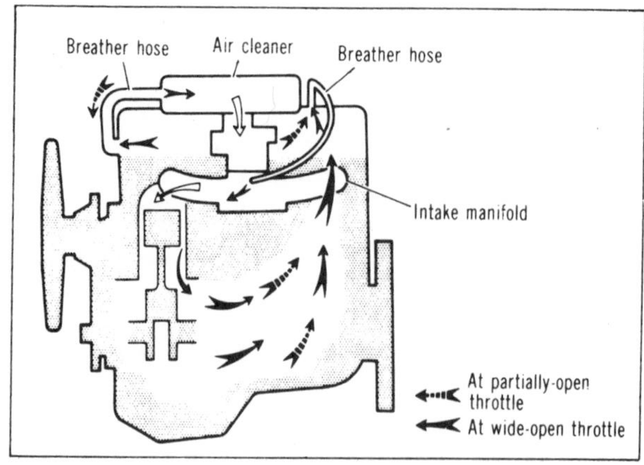

Fig. 3 Positive crankcase ventilation system

is used to prevent the discharge of harmful carbon monoxide and hydrocarbons into the atmosphere. When the engine is operating, the blowby gases and vapors within the crankcase are routed through a PCV valve and into the combustion chamber where they are burned.

General Service

Every 24,000 miles or 2 years, check the crankcase ventilation hoses and jet for obstructions or damage. Clean or replace hoses and jet as necessary.

EXHAUST GAS RECIRCULATION

Description, Fig. 4

All California vehicles use the exhaust gas recirculation (EGR) system. This system allows a small amount of exhaust gases to be drawn into the combustion chamber to reduce oxides of

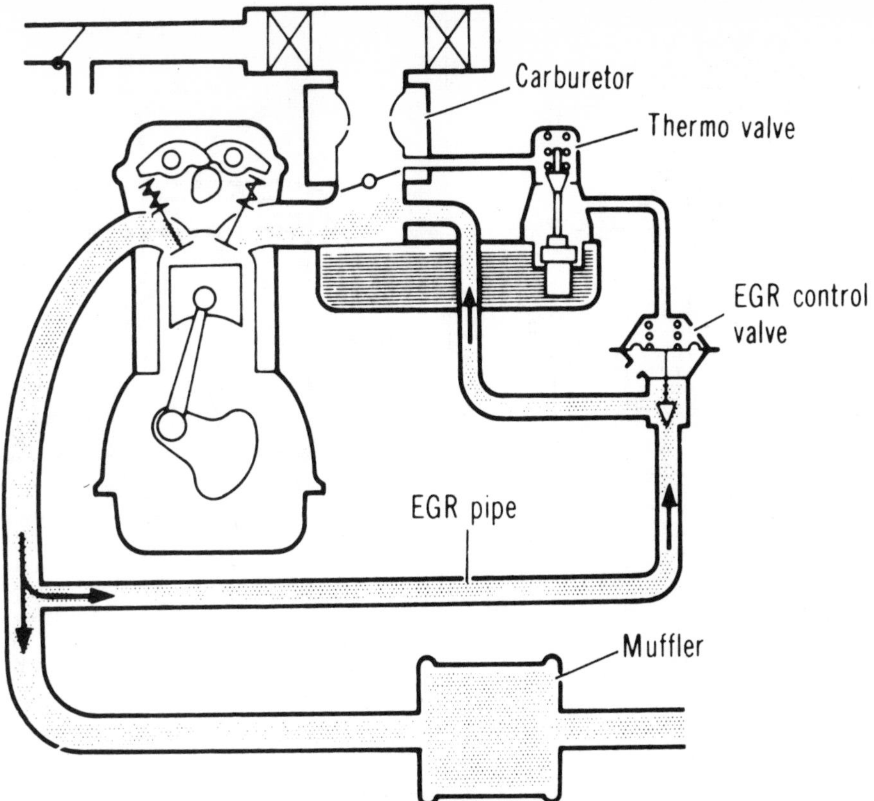

Fig. 4 Exhaust gas recirculation system

nitrogen. The EGR valve is activated by vacuum and the vacuum is controlled by a thermo valve, Fig. 5, located in the vacuum passage. This thermo valve senses intake manifold coolant temperature and controls the ON-OFF motion of the EGR valve. To maintain satisfactory startup and driveability during warmup, the EGR valve remains closed until the coolant is above 140° F. Fig. 6 shows the construction of the EGR valve.

General Service

The EGR valve may be removed by disconnecting the vacuum hose and pipe from the valve. When

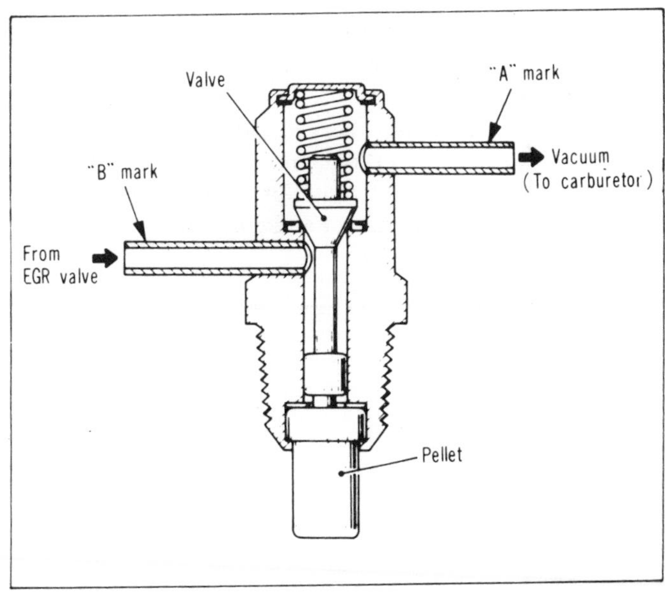

Fig. 5 Thermo valve

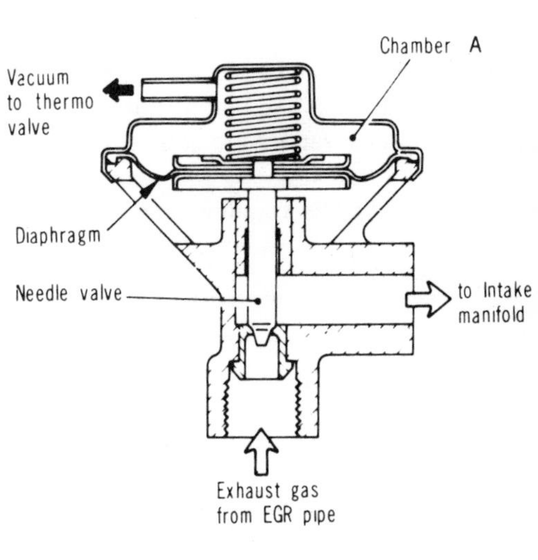

Fig. 6 EGR valve

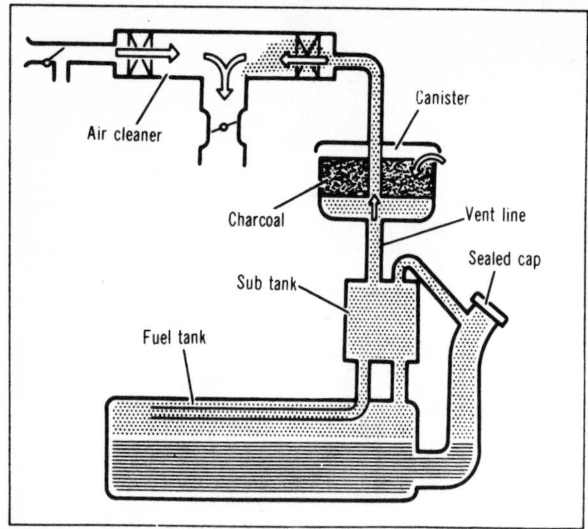

Fig. 7 Evaporation control system

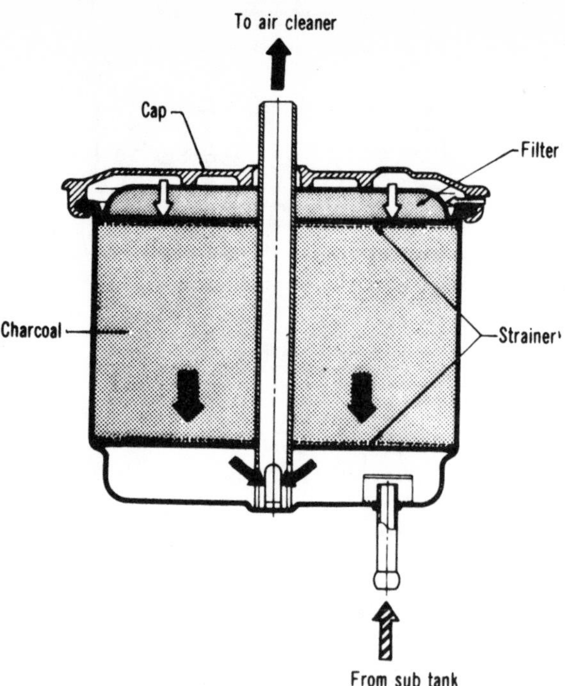

Fig. 8 Charcoal canister

installing the valve, make certain that the pipe is on correctly and torque nut to 22-25 ft. lbs.

Every 12,000 miles or 1 year, visually inspect the EGR valve for deposits. Remove the deposits with compressed air or solvent as necessary. Check the vacuum hoses for cracks and deterioration. Replace as necessary.

Also, during the same period, confirm the operation of the thermo valve by increasing engine speed to 2000-3000. The EGR valve should remain closed if the engine coolant is 140° or lower and should be opened if the engine is warmer.

EVAPORATIVE CONTROL SYSTEM

Description, Fig. 7

This system prevents hydrocarbons from escaping into the atmosphere due to normal fuel vaporization. Gasoline vapors are routed to an activated charcoal canister, Fig. 8, for temporary storage. When the engine is running, outside air is drawn through the canister thereby purging the vapors. The air vapor mixture is then drawn into the engine through the air cleaner.

The subtank is designed to momentarily reduce any overflow of gasoline in the fuel tank caused by temperature rise. It also prevents raw fuel from entering the vapor line under extreme cornering conditions.

General Service

1. Every 12,000 miles or 1 year, disconnect fuel vapor vent line and blow compressed air through it to ensure that no obstructions exist.
2. At the same interval, clean the area around air suction port of canister.
3. Every 24,000 miles or 2 years, replace the filter and all rubber and vinyl hoses.

DATSUN

GENERAL ENGINE SPECIFICATIONS

Model or Engine	Bore & Stroke, Inches (mm)	Piston Displacement, Cubic Inches (cc)	Compression Ratio	Maximum Brake HP @ rpm	Maximum Torque Ft. Lbs. @ rpm	Normal Oil Pressure, Pounds
1974						
B210	2.87 x 3.03 (73.0 x 77.0)	78.6 (1288)	8.5	67 @ 6000	71 @ 3600	43–50
610	3.35 x 3.39 (85.0 x 86.0)	119 (1952)	8.5	97 @ 5600	102 @ 3200	11–40 Idling
710	3.35 x 3.07 (85.0 x 78.0)	108 (1770)	8.5	93 @ 6000	99 @ 3200	11–40
260Z	3.27 x 3.11 (83.0 x 79.0)	157 (2565)	8.8	139 @ 5200	137 @ 4400	11–40

TUNEUP SPECIFICATIONS

Car Model or Engine	Spark Plugs		Distributor		Firing Order	Ignition Timing		Hot Idle Speed, rpm
	Type	Gap, Inch	Point Gap, Inch	Dwell Angle, Degrees		Degrees BTDC	Mark Location	
1974								
B210 (A13)	NGK BP-5ES Hitachi L46PW	.031–.035	.0177–.0217	49–55	1-3-4-2	5	Pulley	800①
610 (L20B)	Hitachi CGR-600 Hanshin HR-15-1	.028–.031	.0177–.0217	49–55	1-3-4-2	12	Pulley	750①
710 (L18)	Hanshin HS-IS-1	.028–.031	.0177–.0217	49–55	1-3-4-2	12	Pulley	800①
260Z (L26)	NGK BP-6ES	.031–.035	.0118–.0157	—	1-5-3-6-2-4	②	Pulley	750①

①—Auto trans., 650 in D.
②—Man. trans., 8° ATDC (retarded); Auto. Trans.; 15° BTDC (advanced).

DISTRIBUTOR SPECIFICATIONS

Model or Engine	Distributor Part No.	Point Gaps, Inch	Dwell Angle Deg.	Spring Tension, oz.	Centrifugal Advance			Vacuum Advance		
					Start @ rpm	Int.	Full @ rpm	Inches of Vacuum to Start Plunger	Int.	Full Advance Dist. Deg. @ Vacuum
1974										
B-210 (A13)	D4A2-02	.0177–.0217	49–55	17.6–22.4	0 @ 550	3.75 @ 750	13.5 @ 1975	5.91	—	6.5 @ 9.65
610 (L20B)	D4A2-01	.0177–.0217	49–55	17.6–22.88	0 @ 550	—	10 @ 2150	5.91	—	3.5 @ 9.84
710 (L18)	D4A2-01	.0177-.0217	49–55	17.6–22.88	0 @ 550	—	10 @ 2150	5.91	—	3.5 @ 9.84
260Z (L26) Std	D6F3-01	.0118–.0157	—	—	0 @ 500	—	13 @ 1600	11.8	—	6 @ 18.7
260Z (L26) Auto	D6F3-02	.0018–.0157	—	—	0 @ 500	—	13 @ 1600	11.8	—	6 @ 18.7

Emission Controls

1974 MODELS EXHAUST GAS RECIRCULATION

Description, Figs. 1 & 2, 260Z, 610, 710, B210

The exhaust gas recirculation system allows a small amount of exhaust gases to be drawn into the combustion where it reduces the combustion chamber temperatures and reduces NOx produced during the combustion process.

The EGR system used on 610 and 710 models consists of the EGR control valve, solenoid valve, coolant temperature sensor, modulator, EGR passages and vacuum hoses, Fig. 3.

The EGR system used on 260Z models consists

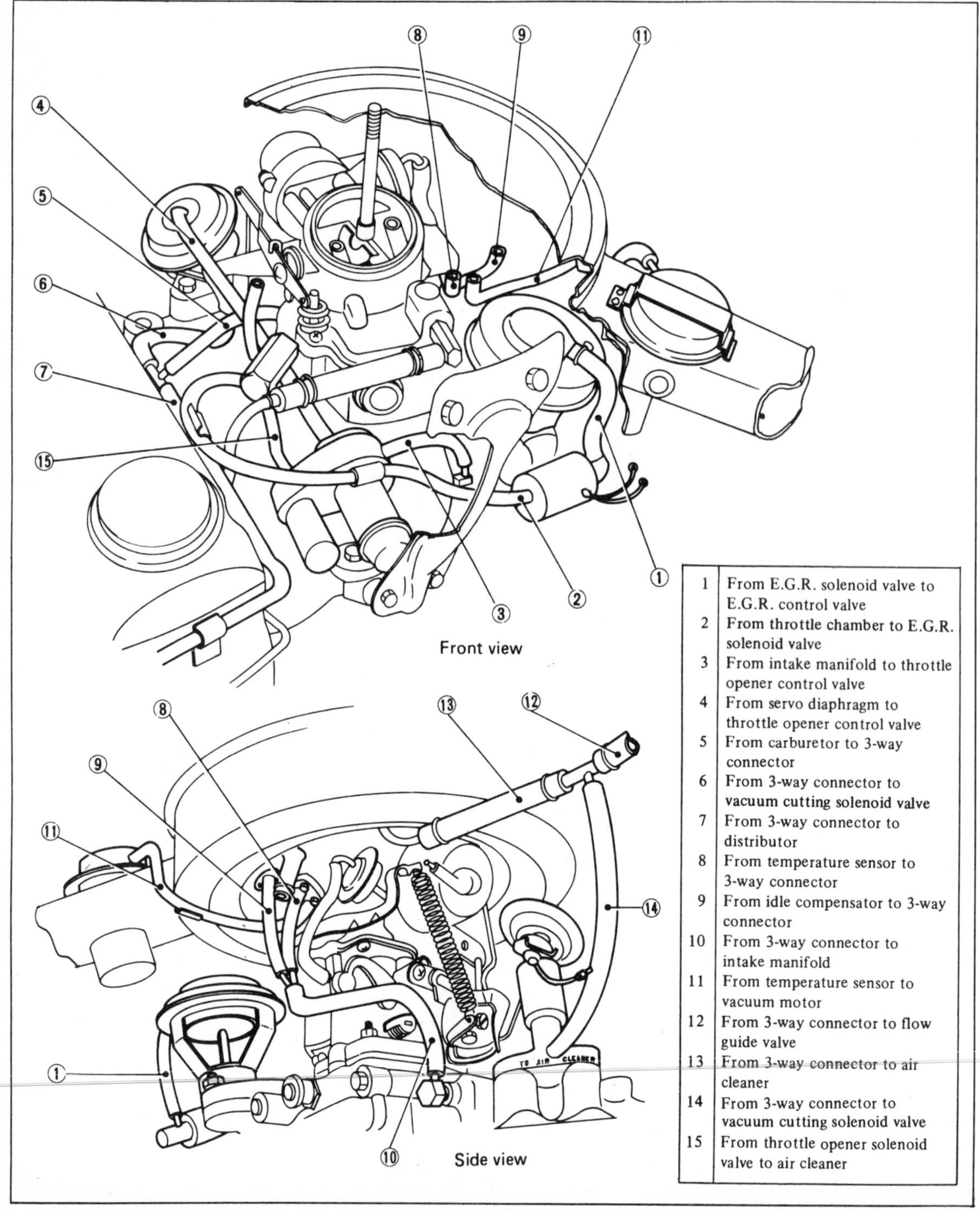

of the balance tube, control valve, solenoid valve, thermovalve, EGR tube, vacuum hose and water hose, Fig. 4.

Operation

When the EGR control valve opens, exhaust gases from the exhaust manifold are admitted into the chamber of the adapter which is installed on the EGR control valve. The gases proceed through the EGR tube, are measured by the EGR control valve and are then drawn into the intake manifold.

Because the engine runs unsteadily with exhaust gases recirculating while the engine is at low temperatures, it is necessary to cut exhaust gases from recirculating for a few minutes after starting. Therefore, a drop in performance during warmup is prevented by electrically opening and closing the vacuum passage for the EGR control valve with the water temperature sensor and through the modu-

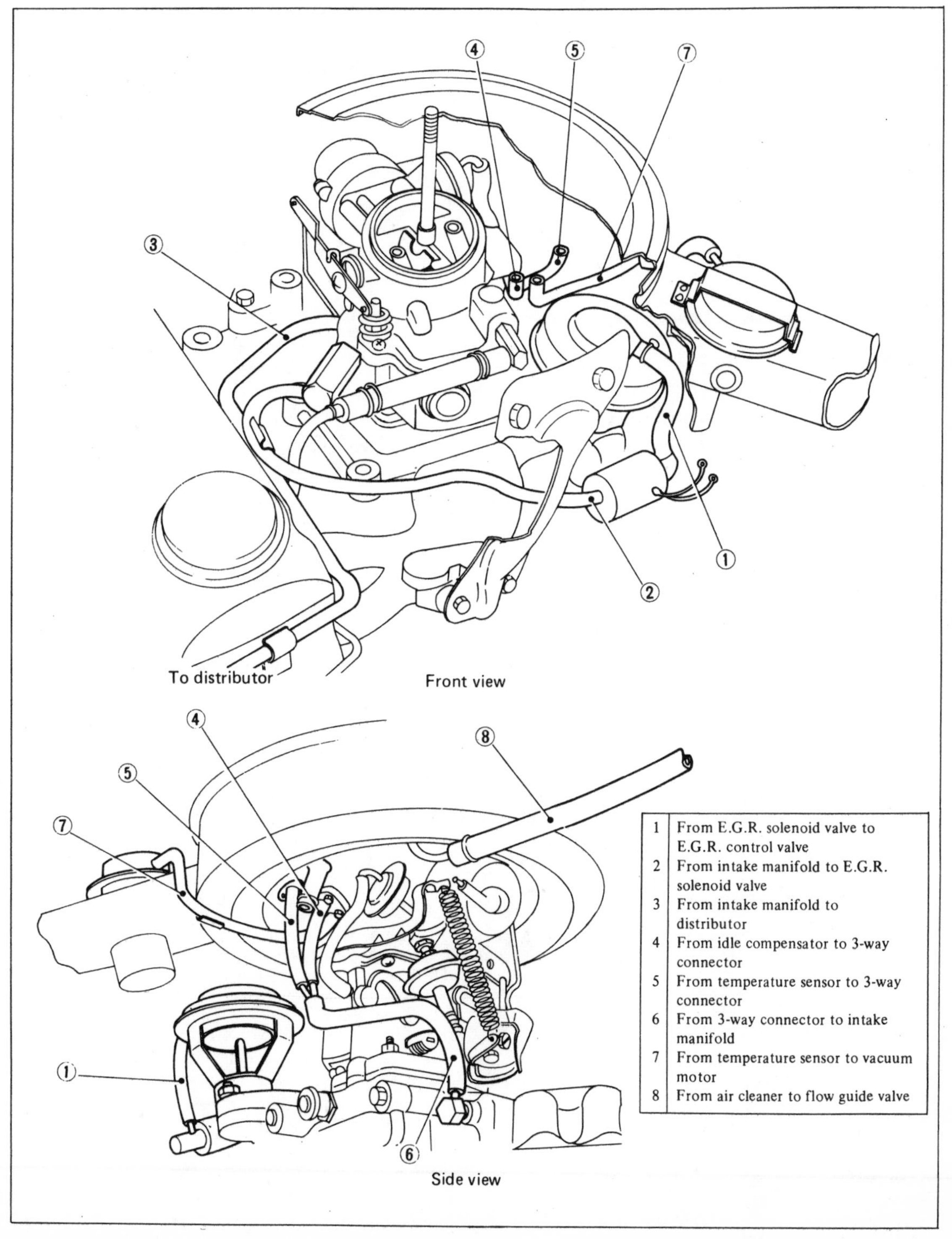

1	From E.G.R. solenoid valve to E.G.R. control valve
2	From intake manifold to E.G.R. solenoid valve
3	From intake manifold to distributor
4	From idle compensator to 3-way connector
5	From temperature sensor to 3-way connector
6	From 3-way connector to intake manifold
7	From temperature sensor to vacuum motor
8	From air cleaner to flow guide valve

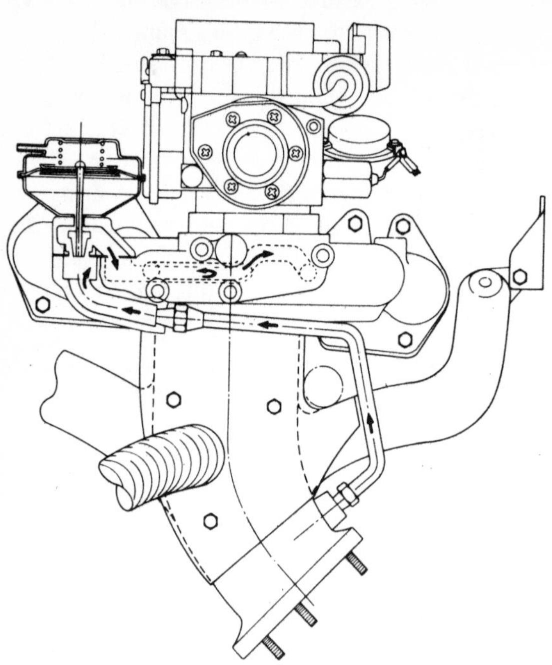

Fig. 1 EGR control system. Except 260Z

lator. Further, to insure the engine performance at high speeds under full load and to improve idling stability, the recirculating exhaust gases are cut off in proportion to the opening of the carburetor.

AIR INJECTION SYSTEM

260Z & 610

Description, Fig. 5

The air injection pump receives clean air through a hose connected to a fitting attached to the carburetor air cleaner.

This rotary vane type pump has been designed to draw air in and compress it to produce maximum air flow with quiet operation. A fresh air line from the air injection pump is routed to a check valve, which prevents exhaust gas from entering the air pump in the event exhaust manifold pressure is greater than air injection pressure, or in the case of an inoperative pump. The compressed fresh air is injected through an injection nozzle to the exhaust ports.

An anti-backfire valve has been installed to eliminate popping in the exhaust system when the throttle is closed during high speed coasting. Controls which have been incorporated to assure reliable system operation include an anti-backfire valve and a check valve.

Air pump, Figs. 6 & 7

The air pump on all models is a two-vane type except for the 260Z. It is a three-vane type on the 260Z. It is a positive displacement vane which requires no lubricating service.

The die-cast aluminum air pump assembly attached to the front of the engine is driven by an air pump drive belt. A rotor shaft, drive hub, relief valve and inlet and outlet tubes are visible on the pump exterior. A rotor, vanes, carbon shoes, and shoe springs make up the rotating unit of the pump. The rotor located in the center of the pump is belt-driven. The vanes rotate freely around the off-center pivot pin and follow the circular-shaped pump bore. In the two-vane type, the vanes form two chambers in the housing. Each vane completes

Fig. 2

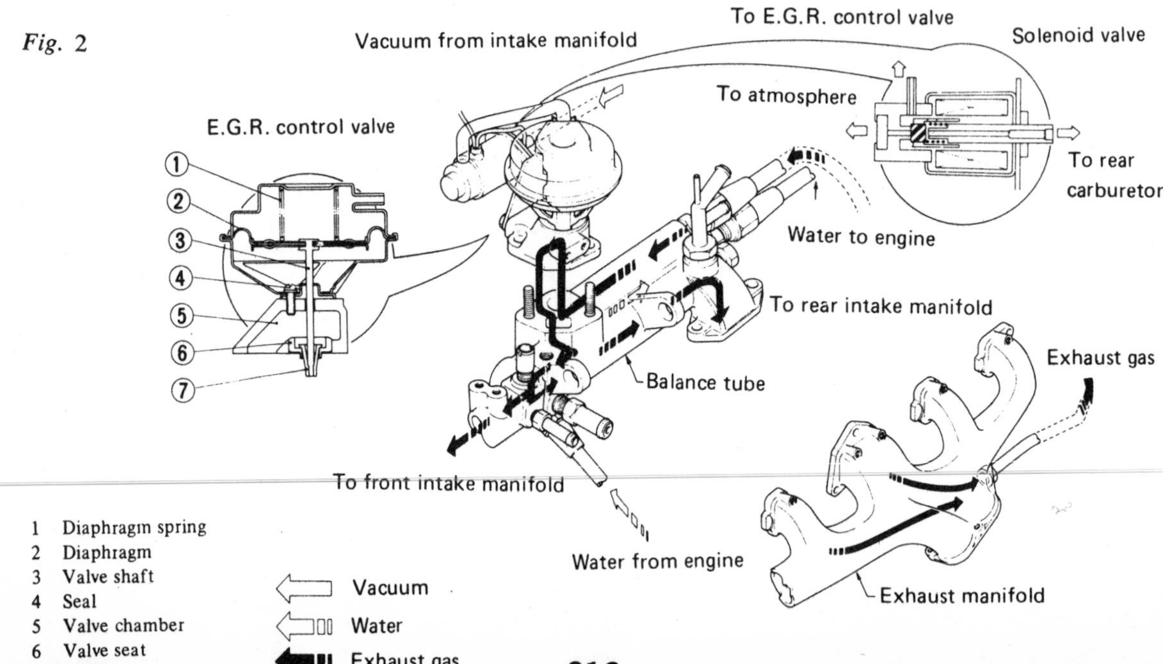

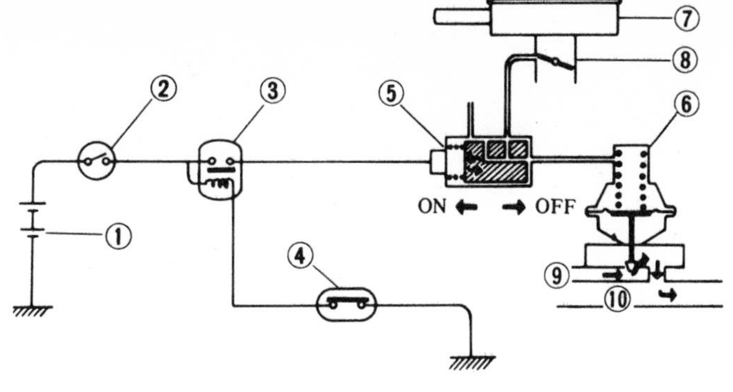

1 Battery
2 Ignition key
3 E.G.R. control relay
4 Water temperature switch
5 E.G.R. solenoid valve
6 E.G.R. control valve
7 Air cleaner
8 Throttle valve
9 Exhaust passage
10 Intake manifold

E.G.R.	Switch operating temperature		Water temperature switch	Relay	E.G.R. solenoid valve	E.G.R. control valve
Actuated	31 to * 41°C (88 to 106°F)	Above	ON	OFF	OFF	Open
Not actuated		Below	OFF	ON	ON	Close

Note *: **The water temperature switch is designed to operate at a coolant temperature somewhere between 31°C (88°F) and 41°C (106°F). Operating points vary slightly with individual characteristics.**

Fig. 3 *EGR system,* 610 *and* 710

a pumping cycle in every revolution of the rotor. Air is drawn into the inlet cavity through a tube connected to the air cleaner. Air is sealed between the vanes and moved into a smaller cavity—the compression area.

After compression, the vanes pass the outlet cavity. Subsequently they pass the stripper, a section of the housing that separates the outlet and inlet cavities. Continuing the cycle, the vanes again enter the inlet cavity to repeat the pumping cycle. The relief valve, located in the outlet cavity, consists of a preloaded spring, seat, and pressure-setting plug. Its function is to relieve the outlet air flow when the pressure exceeds a preset value.

Carbon shoes support the vanes from slots in the rotor. The shoes are designed to permit sliding of the vanes and to seal the rotor interior from the air cavities. Leaf springs which are behind the follower side of the shoes compensate for shoe wear and vane operating sound. The rotor is further sealed by flexible carbon seals. The plates also seal off the housing and end cover to confine the air to the pump cavities.

The rotor is a steel ring bolted to the rotor end. This ring prevents the rotor from spreading at high speed, and also positions and holds the rear bearing and the carbon seal.

The front and rear bearings which support the rotor are of two types. The front bearing uses ball bearings and the rear bearing uses needle bearings. The vane uses needle bearings. All the bearings have been greased.

In addition to the air injection system, certain controls have been incorporated to assure reliable system operation.

Anti-backfire valve, Fig. 8

This valve is controlled by the intake manifold vacuum to prevent exhaust system backfire at the initial period of deceleration.

At that time, the mixture in the intake manifold is too rich to ignite and burn in the combustion chamber and burns easily in the exhaust system with injected air in the exhaust manifold.

The anti-backfire valve provides a supply of air to the intake manifold, thereby making the air-fuel mixture leaner and preventing backfire.

The inlet of the anti-backfire valve is installed on the middle portion of the hose connecting the air pump and check valve and the outlet of it is connected to the intake manifold.

If the valve does not work properly, the extremely rich air-fuel mixture will go through the combustion chambers and meet high-temperature and injected air which ignites the mixture and results in backfiring.

Check valve, Fig. 9

A check valve is located in the air pump discharge lines. The valve prevents the backflow of exhaust gas. Backflow of exhaust gas occurs in one of the following cases.

1. When air pump drive belt fails.
2. When relief valve spring fails.

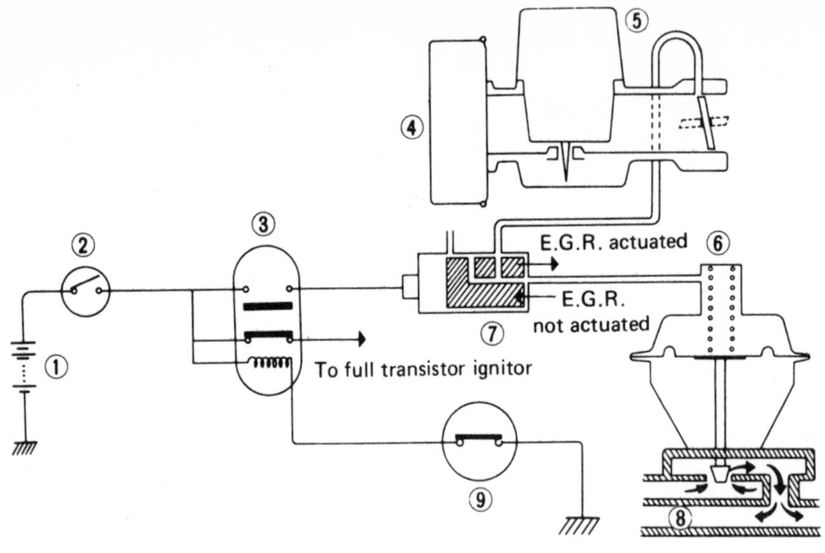

1 Battery
2 Ignition switch
3 Relay
4 Air cleaner
5 Carburetor
6 E.G.R. control valve
7 E.G.R. solenoid valve
8 Balance tube
9 Water temperature switch

E.G.R.	Switch operating temperature		Water temp. SW.	Relay	E.G.R. solenoid valve	E.G.R. control valve
Not actuated	* 31 to 41°C (88 to 106°F)	Below	OFF	ON	ON	CLOSE
Actuated		Above	ON	OFF	OFF	OPEN

Fig. 4 *EGR schematic.* 260Z

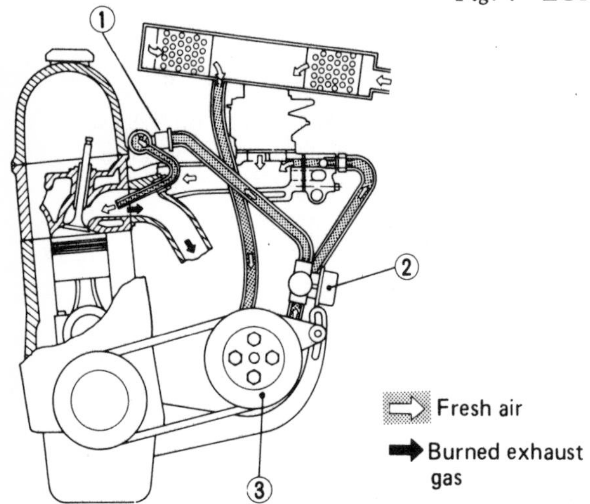

1 Check valve
2 Anti-backfire valve
3 Air pump

Fig. 5 *Air injection system.* 260Z *and* 610

Air pump relief valve

The air pump relief valve is mounted in the discharge cavity of the air pump and accomplishes the following functions without affecting effectiveness of the exhaust emission control system.

1. Minimizes exhaust gas temperature rise.
2. Minimizes horsepower losses resulting from air injection into the exhaust system.
3. Protects pump from excessive back pressure.

Air injection into each exhaust port, Fig. 10

Fresh air from the air pump is injected into the individual exhaust ports of the cylinder head located near the exhaust valve.

Pressurized air is transmitted through hoses and air distribution manifold.

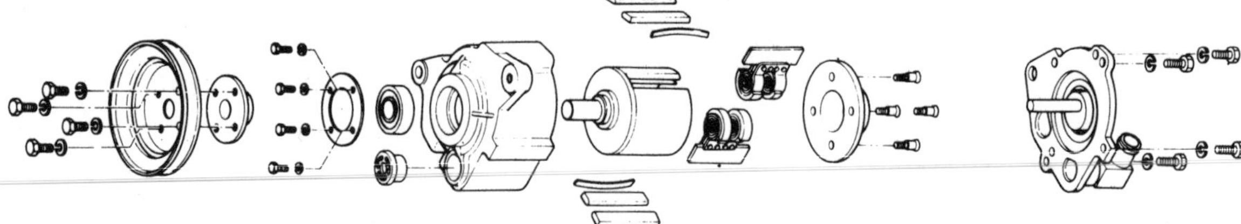

Fig. 6 *Air pump, two vane type, used on* 610

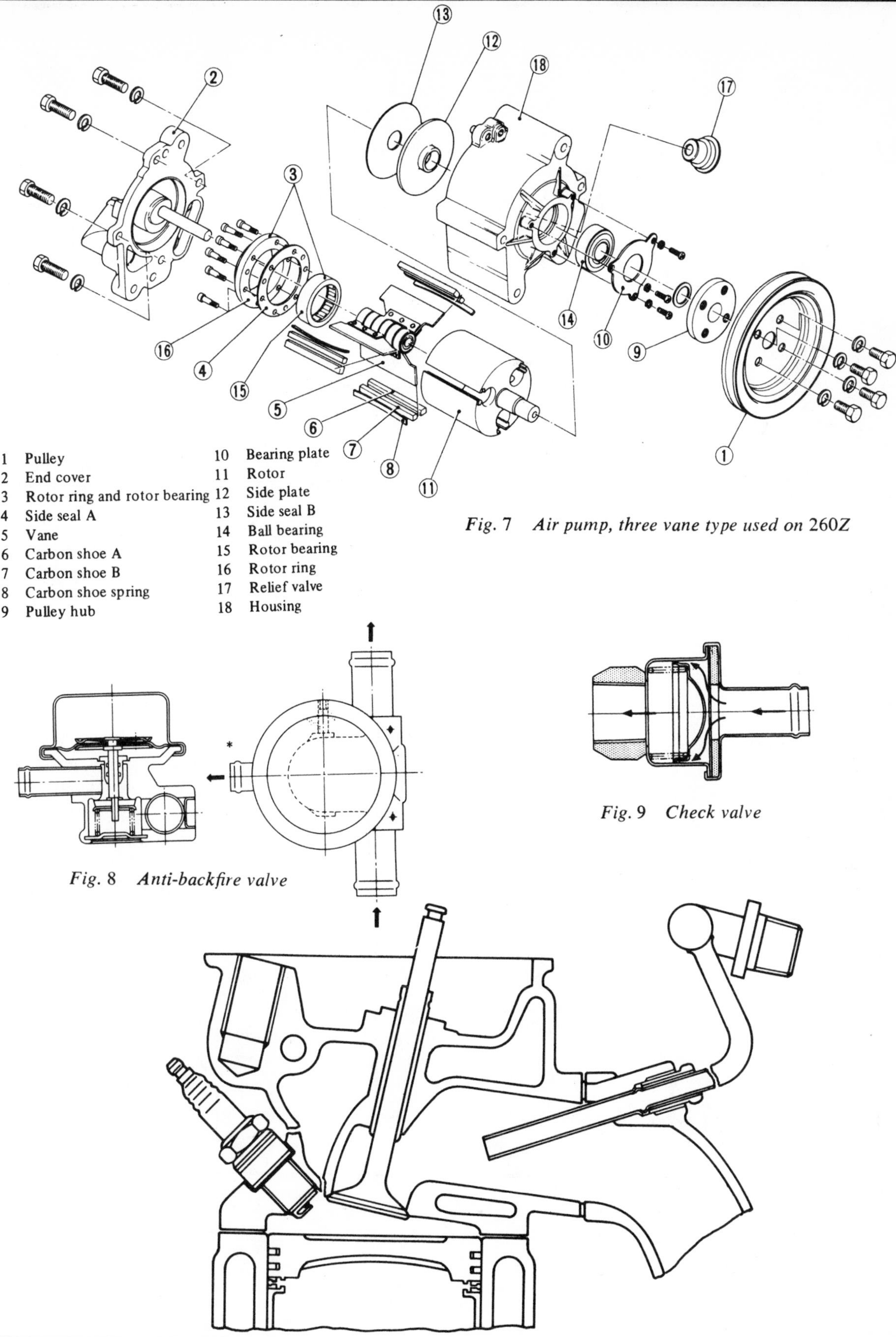

Fig. 7 Air pump, three vane type used on 260Z

Fig. 8 Anti-backfire valve

Fig. 9 Check valve

Fig. 10 Air injection nozzles

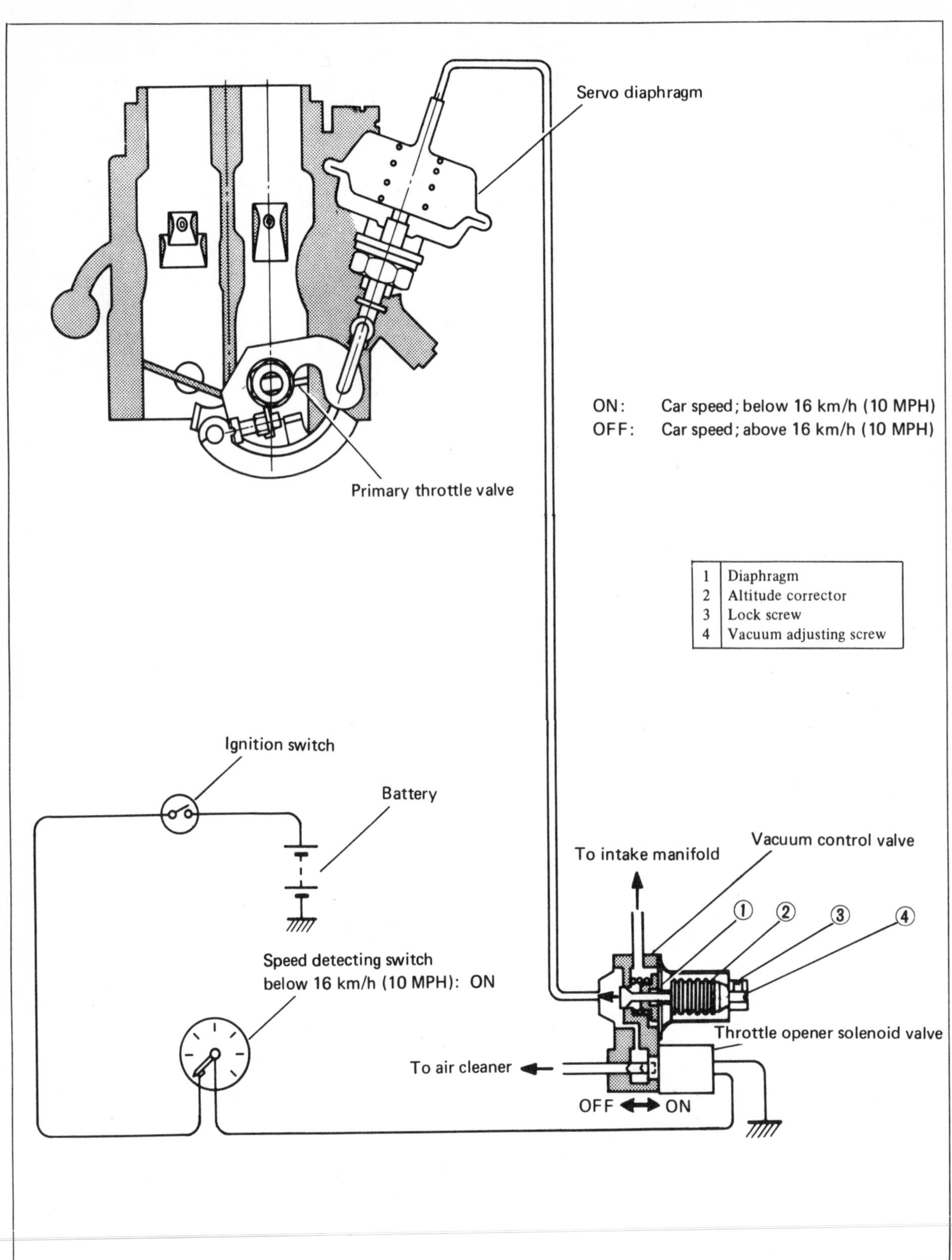

Fig. 11 *Schematic of throttle opener system. B*-210

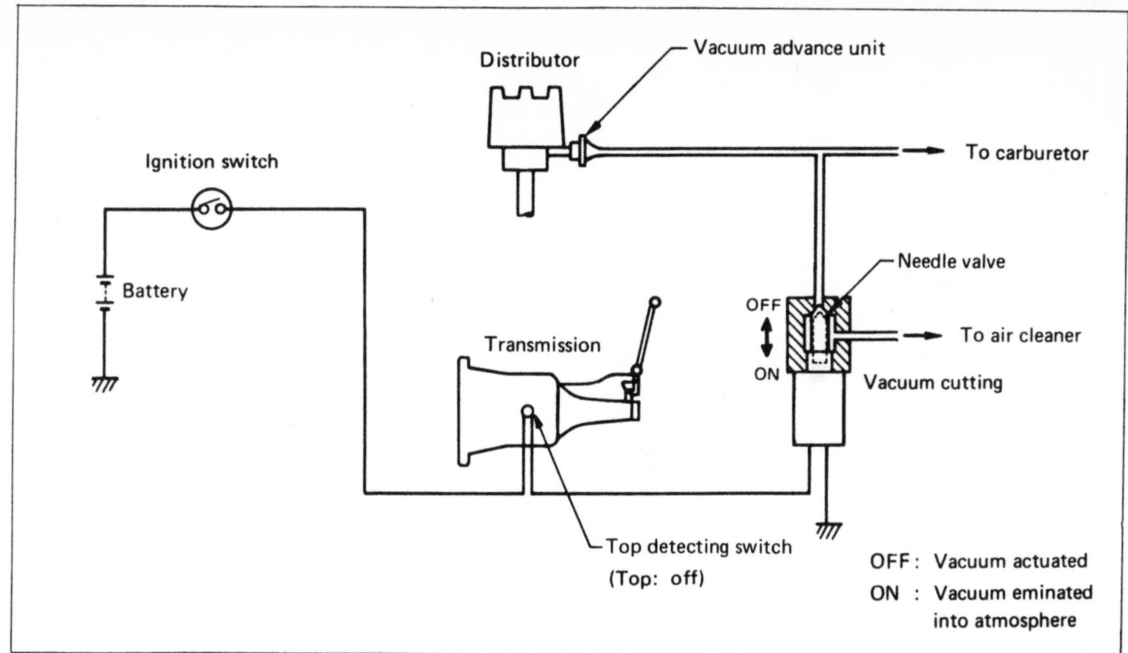

Fig. 12 *Schematic of transmission controlled vacuum advance*

THROTTLE OPENER CONTROL SYSTEM

B210

Description, Manual Trans. Only

The function of the throttle opener is to open the throttle valve of the carburetor slightly in car deceleration. During deceleration, manifold vacuum rises. Therefore the quantity of mixture in the engine is not sufficient to allow normal combustion. A great amount of unburned HC is emitted. The carburetor equipped with the throttle opener supplies the engine with an adequate charge of combustible mixture to keep proper combustion during deceleration, resulting in a remarkable reduction of HC emission.

The operation of the throttle opener is as follows. A schematic drawing of the system is shown in Fig. 11.

At the moment when the manifold vacuum increases as occurs upon deceleration, the control valve opens to transfer the manifold vacuum to the servo diaphragm chamber and the throttle valve of the carburetor opens slightly. As the car speed decreases (above 10 mph) the manifold vacuum lowers to the predetermined value. The vacuum control valve begins to close gradually, keeping the manifold vacuum at the predetermined constant value.

As a result, both low HC emission and normal engine brake during deceleration are obtained.

The altitude corrector is provided with a slight preload to compensate the variation of the atmospheric pressure.

Throttle opener solenoid valve

The throttle opener solenoid valve is actuated and the servo diaphragm chamber is open to the atmosphere when the car is running at speeds below 10 mph. In this case the servo diaphragm does not operate.

When car speed exceeds 10 mph, the throttle opener solenoid valve becomes inoperative and the intake manifold is communicated to the servo diaphragm chamber. However, the servo diaphragm does not usually operate because the operating pressure of the vacuum control valve is higher than the intake manifold vacuum in continuous driving.

The servo diaphragm operates only when the car is running at speeds over 10 mph and the intake manifold vacuum pressure is higher than the operating pressure of the vacuum control valve.

TRANSMISSION CONTROLLED VACUUM ADVANCE SYSTEM

Description, Fig. 12 (Manual Trans. Only)

This system provides the vacuum advance only when the gear is in the top (4th) position, and retarded spark timing at the other positions for complete combustion.

When electric current flows through the vacuum cutoff solenoid valve, the needle valve opens and

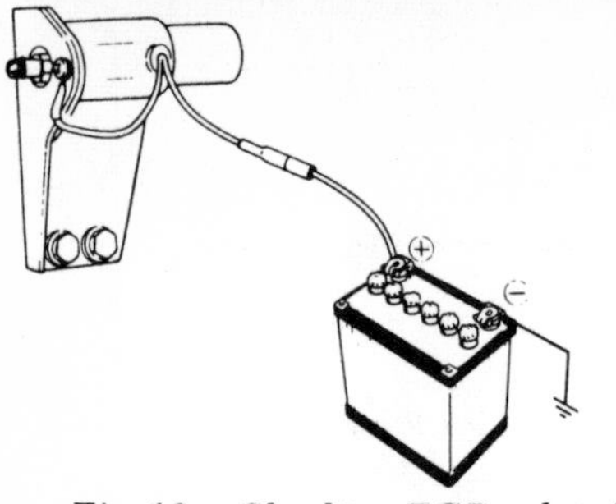

Fig. 13 Checking EGR solenoid

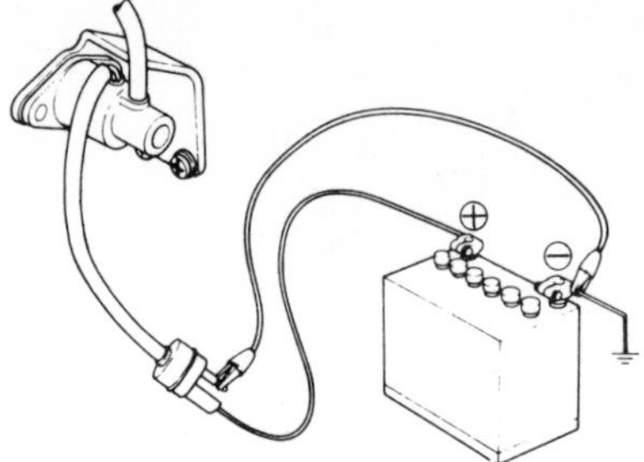

Fig. 14 Checking EGR solenoid

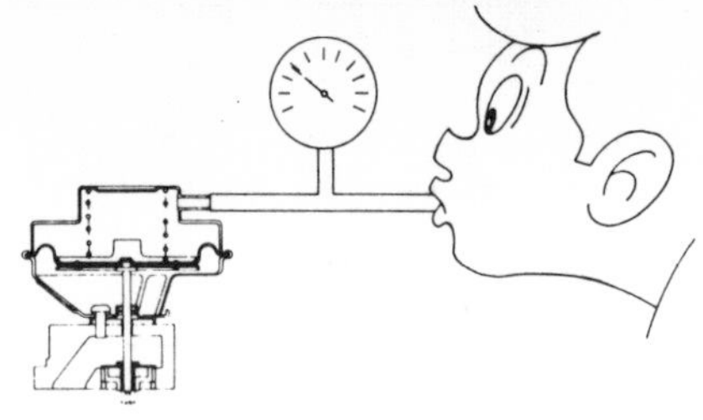

Fig. 15 Checking EGR control valve

introduces air from the air cleaner into the vacuum advance unit of the distributor through the vacuum hose. The vacuum advance is eliminated. When the vacuum cutoff solenoid valve is de-energized, the needle valve closes and the vacuum created by the carburetor is introduced into the vacuum advance unit of the distributor to provide usual vacuum advance.

The top detecting switch, located on the transmission case, operates so as to interrupt the flow of electric current when the gear is placed into TOP, but allows it to flow in the other gear positions.

GENERAL SERVICE

EGR SYSTEM

Checking & Inspection Except 260Z

1. Visually inspect the entire EGR control system. Clean it for ease of inspection if it is contaminated with oil. Replace rubber hoses if they are found to be cracked or broken.
2. When it becomes necessary to inspect the EGR control valve, check to be sure that the EGR solenoid valve is properly wired.
3. Increase the engine speed from idling to 3000 to 3500 rpm, noting if plate of EGR control valve diaphragm and valve shaft move upwards as speed is increased.
4. Disconnect EGR solenoid valve harness, and connect it directly to the battery to apply battery voltage (12V) to EGR solenoid valve, Figs. 13 & 14. Race the engine again without disturbing the above setup.
   NOTE: The EGR control valve should be kept stationary.
5. With engine running at idling speed, push up the EGR control valve diaphragm by manually pressing the bottom dish. It is normal if the engine loses stability.

260Z

1. Visually inspect the entire EGR control system. Clean it for ease of inspection if it is contaminated with oil. Replace the tube and the like if they are found to be cracked or broken.
2. When it becomes necessary to inspect the EGR control valve, check to be sure that the EGR solenoid valve is properly wired.
3. Increase the engine speed from idling to 3000 to 3500 rpm, noting if the plate of the EGR control valve diaphragm and valve shaft move upwards as speed is increased.
4. Disconnect the EGR solenoid valve harness, and connect it directly to the battery to apply the battery voltage (12V) to EGR solenoid valve. Race the engine again without disturbing the above setup.
   The EGR control valve should be kept stationary.
5. With the engine running at idling speed, push up the EGR control valve diaphragm by manually pressing the bottom dish. It is normal if the engine loses stability.

Checking EGR Valve

1. Remove the EGR control valve from the engine.
2. Apply a vacuum of −120 to −130 mm Hg (−4.72 to −5.12 in Hg) to the EGR control valve. The vacuum application can easily be made by the method illustrated in Fig. 15.
   It is correct if the valve moves into the full-up position.
   The EGR control valve should stay uplifted for more than 30 seconds after the vacuum is stopped.
3. Visually inspect the EGR control valve for signs of damage, wrinkle or other deformations.
4. Clean the EGR control valve seat with a brush and compressed air as shown in Fig. 16, to eliminate clogging of the EGR control valve.

Checking EGR Solenoid Valve

Check EGR solenoid valve as instructed below. An ohmmeter and battery are required.

1. Check the EGR solenoid valve for proper conduction.

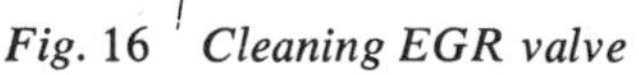

Fig. 16 Cleaning EGR valve

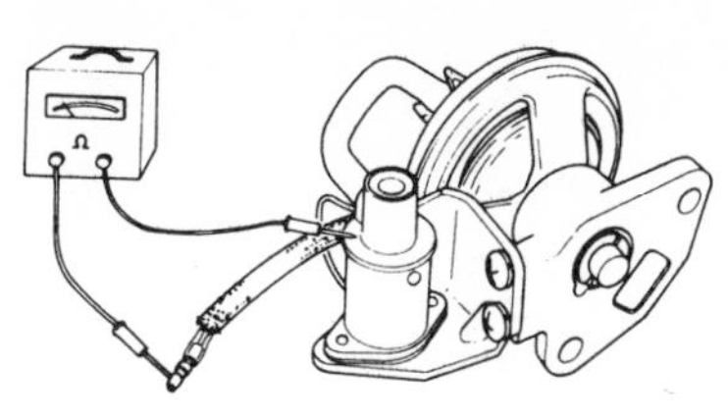

Fig. 17 Checking EGR solenoid

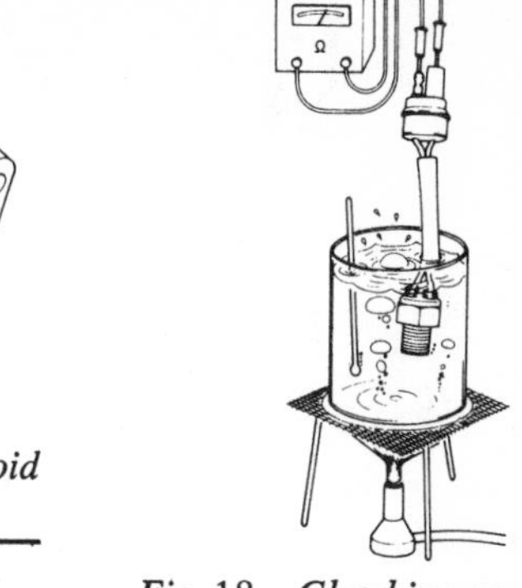

Fig. 18 Checking coolant temperature switch

Test No.	Water temperature °C (°F)	Resistance value Ω
1	15 to 25 (59 to 77)	2,300 to 3,700
2	45 to 55 (113 to 131)	650 to 980

Fig. 19 Resistance values for checking coolant temperature switch. 610

If the ohmmeter pointer does not deflect, it is considered as broken and needs to be replaced.

2. If the ohmmeter pointer deflects in step 1 above, check the EGR solenoid valve to ensure that it clicks when intermittently electrified as shown in Fig. 17.

   If a click is heard, the EGR solenoid valve is normal.
3. The EGR solenoid valve is considered as sticking and must be replaced when it does not click in step 2 above.

Checking Coolant Temperature Switch—Except 610 Models

1. A thermometer and ohmmeter are needed for checking water temperature switch, Fig. 18.
2. The following is the procedure for checking OFF of water temperature switch.

   Starting from water temperature at 25° C (77° F) and below, check continuity of water temperature switch and ensure that a reading is infinite, that is, switch is open.
3. The following is the procedure for checking ON of water temperature switch.

   Increasing water temperature from about 25° C (77° F), make continuity check of water temperature switch. Operation is normal if an ohmmeter reading drops to zero at water temperature somewhere between 31 to 41° C (88 to 106° F) and remains zero at about 41° F (106° F).
4. If steps 2 and 3 above are satisfactorily completed then the switch is good.

610 Models

Required instruments are an ohmmeter and a thermometer, Fig. 18.

The water temperature sensor under test is good if the test results conform to the normal temperature-resistance relationships given in the table above, Fig. 19.

When the obtained resistance value is not held within the specified range, replace the sensor.

NOTES:

1. Choose test No. 1 or No. 2. It is not necessary to test both temperature ranges.
2. In test No. 1 the sensor may be heated dry in the atmosphere.

Operation of the modulator is normal if the EGR lamp goes on and off properly in the above test.

If the EGR lamp fails to go on and off correctly, replace the modulator.

Air Injection System

Checking secondary air injection system hoses

Check air system hoses and fittings for loose connections, cracks or deterioration. Retighten or replace if necessary.

Checking air system manifold

Check the air gallery pipe and injection nozzles for loose connections and cracks. Retighten or replace if necessary.

It is very difficult to remove the air gallery from the exhaust manifold without bending the pipe,

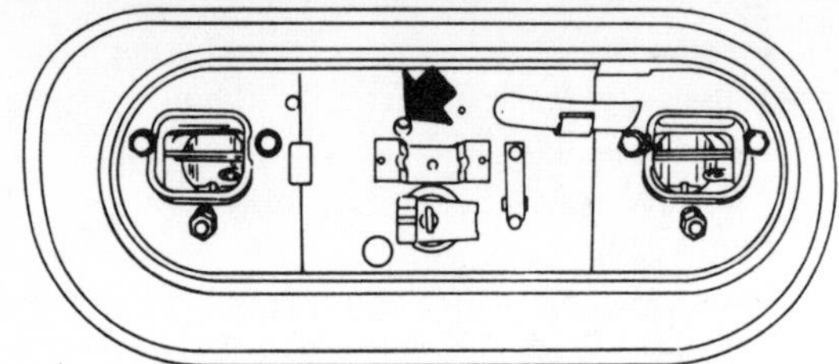

Fig. 20 Air inlet hole of anti-backfire valve. 260Z

which could result in fractures or leakage. Therefore, removal of the air gallery pipe and injection nozzles should be undertaken only when they are damaged.

1. Lubricate the connecting portion of the air injection nozzle and air gallery with engine oil.
2. Hold the air injection nozzle hexagon head with a wrench and unfasten flare screw connecting air gallery to injection nozzle. Remove the air gallery.

   NOTES:

   Apply engine oil to screws several times during above work.

   Be careful not to damage other parts.
3. Unfasten the air injection nozzle from the cylinder head applying engine oil to the threaded portion.
4. Check the air gallery and the nozzle for fractures or leakage. Clean the air injection nozzle with a wire brush.
5. At the time of installation, assemble the nozzle seat on the injection nozzle and tighten the air gallery flange screw to a torque of 36 to 43 ft-lbs.
6. With the engine running, check the cylinder head, air injection nozzle and air gallery for leaks.

Checking control valves and air pump

The following procedures are recommended for checking and/or ascertaining that the various components of the exhaust emission control system are operating properly.

The engine and all components must be at normal operating temperatures when the tests are performed. Prior to performing any extensive diagnosis of the exhaust control system, it must be determined that the engine as a unit is functioning properly.

Testing check valve

This test can be performed at the same time as the air pump test.

1. Operate the engine until it reaches normal operating temperature.
2. Inspect all hoses and hose connectors for obvious leaks. Correct them, if necessary, before checking the valve operation.
3. Visually inspect the position of the valve plate inside the valve body. It should be lightly positioned against the valve seat away from the air distributor manifold.
4. Insert a probe into the valve connection on the check valve and depress the valve plate. It should freely return to the original position, against the valve seat, when released.
5. Leave the hose disconnected and start the engine. Slowly increase engine speed to 1500 rpm and watch for exhaust gas leakage at the check valve. There should be no exhaust leakage. The valve may flutter or vibrate at idle speed. This is due to exhaust pulsations in the manifold.
6. If the check valve does not meet the recommended conditions, replace it.

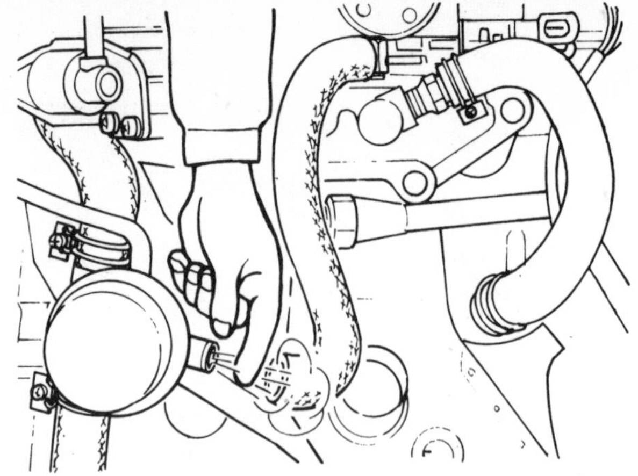

Fig. 21 Testing anti-backfire valve. 610

Testing anti-backfire valve

260Z Models

1. Operate the engine until it reaches manual operating temperature.
2. Inspect the inlet and outlet hoses of the valve and the hose connections for obvious leaks. Correct them if necessary.
3. Remove the air cleaner cover.
4. Place a finger on the inlet hole of valve. Do not shut inlet hole off, Fig. 20.
5. Raise engine speed to 3000 to 3500 rpm from idle speed gradually by the manual operation of throttle valve linkage.
6. Release the linkage suddenly. If the air flow through the valve inlet is felt at this time, the valve is correct for operation.
7. If the air flow through the valve inlet is not felt, or constant gulping of air is observed, replace the valve with a new one.

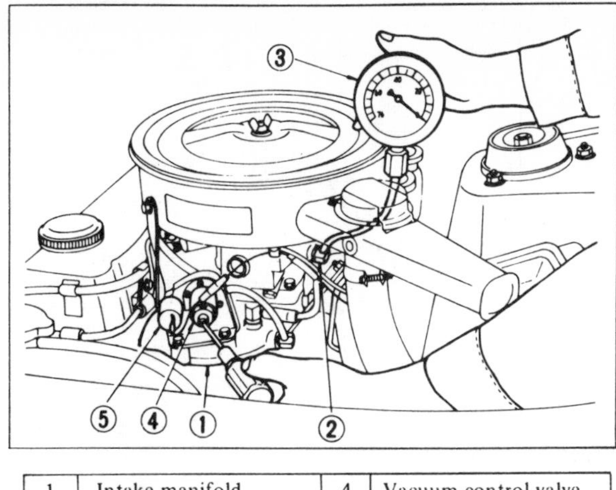

1	Intake manifold	4	Vacuum control valve
2	Connector	5	Throttle opener solenoid
3	Vacuum gauge		

Fig. 22 Adjusting throttle opener

NOTES:

The anti-backfire valve cannot be disassembled.

The anti-backfire valve must be installed with its diaphragm chamber upward.

610 Models

1. Operate the engine until it reaches normal operating temperature.
2. Inspect all hoses and hose connections for obvious leaks, and correct them if necessary before checking the anti-backfire valve operation.
3. Disconnect the air hose to intake manifold at anti-backfire valve. Insert a suitable plug in the hose and fasten it securely.
4. Open and close the throttle valve rapidly. If air flow is felt for one to two seconds by a finger at the anti-backfire valve outlet to the intake manifold, the valve is functioning properly, Fig. 21.

   If the air flow is not felt or the air flow is felt continuously for more than two seconds, the valve should be replaced.
5. Connect the air hose to the intake manifold and disconnect the air inlet hose from the air pump at the anti-backfire valve. If engine idle speed changes excessively, valve function is not correct and the valve should be replaced.

NOTE: It is not abnormal for there to be afterburning if the engine is raced while the car is stationary.

Testing air pump

1. Operate the engine until it reaches normal operating temperature.
2. Inspect all hoses, hose connections and air gallery for leaks and correct them if necessary before checking the air injection pump.
3. Check the air injection pump belt tension and adjust it to specifications if necessary.
4. Disconnect the air supply hose at the check valve.
5. Insert the open pipe end of Air Pump Test Gauge Adapter ST19870000 in the air supply hose. Clamp hose securely to adapter to prevent it from blowing out. Position the adapter and the test gauge so that the air blast emitted through the drilled pipe plug will be harmlessly dissipated.
6. Connect a tachometer. With engine speed at 1500 rpm for 260Z models and 2600 rpm for 610 models, observe the pressure produced at the test gauge. Air pressure should be .63 inches Hg or more for 260Z models and 1.73 inches Hg or more for 610 models.
7. If the air pressure does not meet the above specifications, proceed as follows:

   Repeat steps 2 and 3 above.

   Check the air cleaner on 260Z models.

   On 610 models, disconnect the air supply hose at the anti-backfire valve. Then plug the air hose opening and repeat the pressure test.
8. With engine speed at 1500 rpm, close the hole of the test gauge by finger. If a leaking sound is heard or leaking air is felt by the finger at the relief valve, the relief valve is malfunctioning. The relief valve should be replaced or repaired.
9. If the air injection pump does not meet the minimum requirement of the pressure test, it should be replaced.

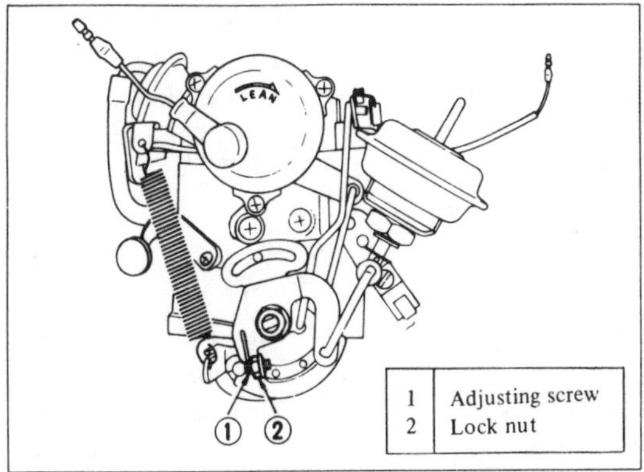

1	Adjusting screw
2	Lock nut

Fig. 23 Servo diaphragm adjusting screw

Checking and Adjusting Throttle Opener

B210 Models

1. Warm the engine up until it reaches operating temperature. Make sure that the automatic

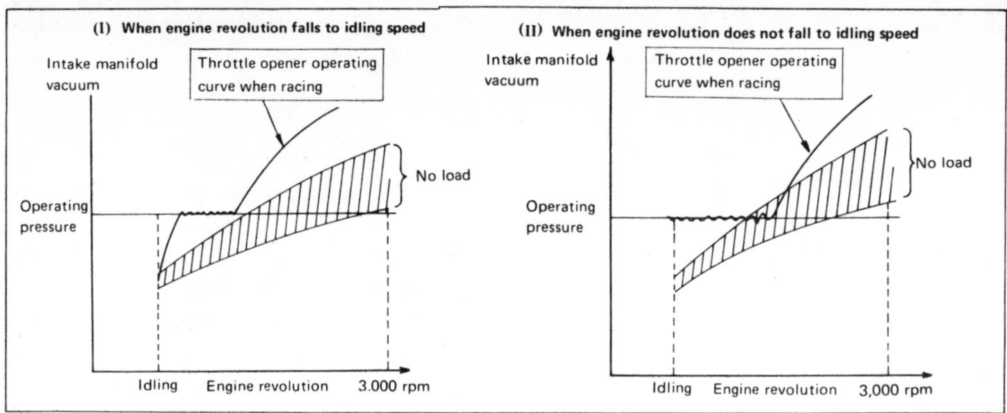

Fig. 24 Characteristic curves of throttle opener

choke valve is fully open.

2. Disconnect the vacuum hose between the intake manifold and the automatic temperature controlled air cleaner. Install a vacuum gauge to the intake manifold connector as shown, Fig. 22.
3. Disconnect the throttle opener solenoid and vacuum cutoff valve solenoid harness and free solenoids.
4. Check the engine idling. Adjust if necessary to 800 rpm.
5. Connect the servo diaphragm vacuum hose directly to the intake manifold connector. Do not route through the vacuum control valve.
6. With the vacuum pressure in the intake manifold, the servo diaphragm operates, and thus, the primary throttle valve is opened. When the servo diaphragm operates normally, the engine speed rises reaching 1650 to 1850 rpm. When the engine speed is not within this range, turn the adjusting screw as necessary, Fig. 23.
7. When the engine speed is lower than the prescribed range, turn the adjusting screw clockwise.
8. When the engine speed is higher than the prescribed range, turn the adjusting screw counterclockwise.
9. Upon completion of the adjustment, set the adjusting screw lock nut securely, making sure that engine speed is in the prescribed range.
10. Disconnect the servo diaphragm vacuum hose from the intake manifold, and connect it to the vacuum control valve. Connect the vacuum hose of the control valve to the intake manifold (normal piping).
11. Place the shift lever in neutral for manual transmission. Raise the engine speed up to approximately 3000 rpm under no-load, and close the throttle valve by releasing it.
    Examine the engine speed to see whether it falls to idling speed.
12. When engine revolution falls to idling speed, Fig. 24.

    The primary throttle valve is opened by the link connected to it. When the engine speed is increased to approximately 3000 rpm and lowered naturally from this speed, change in the servo diaphragm link stroke, manifold vacuum, and engine speed are as shown in Fig. 25. As the engine speed lowers, vacuum pressure generated in the intake manifold also lowers. However, dropping of vacuum pressure in the intake manifold is suspended for a few seconds by operating the servo diaphragm and the vacuum control valve. (In the graph shown, the curve is comparatively flat.) Thus, HC emission emitted under these conditions is controlled by these devices.

    Operating pressure changes depending on altitude, and thus, servo diaphragm and control valve operations are adjusted in coincidence with the altitude at which the car is driven automatically. The graph shown in Fig. 26 indicates the change in operating depression for changes in atmospheric pressure and altitude.
13. When engine revolution does not fall to idling speed, Fig. 24.

    The engine revolution does not fall to idling speed because the operating pressure comes, as shown in Fig. 24 (II), in the vacuum range under no-load condition, and the servo diaphragm is actuated thereby to open the throttle valve.

    In such a case, when checking for proper operating pressure setting it is necessary to reduce the vacuum pressure of the intake manifold lower than the operating pressure of the throttle opener.

    Any one of the three methods shown in Fig. 27 is usually used for the testing.

    In this case it is necessary to labor the engine

on the road, on the chassis dynamometer, or with the rear axle housing lifted off the ground with a stand. The car should then be accelerated from 40 to 50 mph in high gear. After the above procedure has been completed, the accelerator pedal is released.

During the testing, measure the throttle opener operating pressure to see whether or not it is in the predetermined value. See Fig. 27. Adjustment is exactly the same as with the engine at idle.

When atmospheric pressure is known, operating pressure is found by following the allow line A. When altitude is known, operating pressure is found by following the arrow line B. Turn the adjusting screw of the vacuum control valve, Fig. 28. Adjust the vacuum control valve so that vacuum pressure in the intake manifold is suspended for a few seconds at the value of operating pressure found as described in step 1 above while the engine speed decreases from 3000 to 1000 rpm.

NOTES:

1. When turning the vacuum adjusting screw, do not depress the screw with a screwdriver.
2. When measuring operating pressure, be sure to tighten the lock screw of the vacuum control valve first.
3. When the servo diaphragm does not draw the link or operating pressure is high vacuum, turn the vacuum adjusting screw clockwise. When the servo diaphragm draws the link at idling speed or operating pressure is low vacuum, turn the vacuum adjusting screw counterclockwise.

Set lock screw stationarily, repeat the above described adjustment, and make sure that the operating pressure is correct and that the engine speed settles down at the rated idling speed.

Checking Transmission Controlled Spark Electrical System

B210 Models

Pull off the vacuum hose from the distributor. If vacuum is felt through this vacuum hose at the top gear position and is not felt at the other positions, it is satisfactory.

CAUTION: Lock the front and rear wheels by fully pulling the parking brake lever before conducting this test.

If any deficiency is found by the check mentioned above, either of the following conditions may be the cause.

1. Loose connection or broken harness and fuse.
2. Air leakage resulting from loose connection of vacuum tube.
3. Malfunction of TOP switch.
4. Malfunction of vacuum cutoff solenoid valve.

Checking top detecting switch

NOTE: An ohmmeter is needed for checking the top detecting switch.

1. Make sure of insulation between lead wire terminal of transmission switch and switch body.
2. Disconnect lead wires from the switch, and connect the ohmmeter as illustrated in Fig. 29.
3. Ohmmeter should indicate infinity (∞) when shift lever is in Top gear position, and zero at

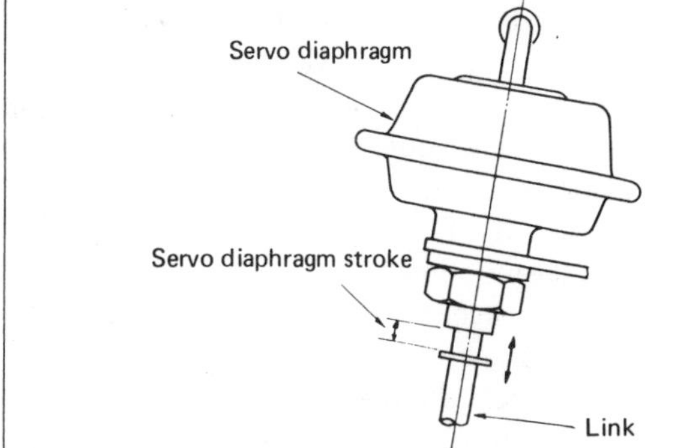

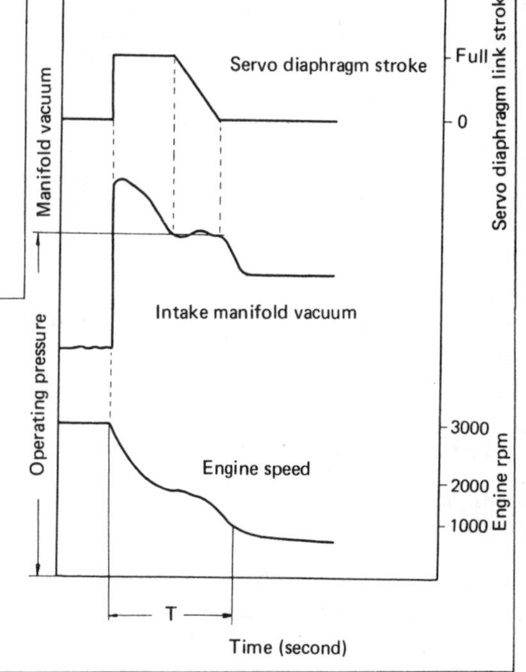

Fig. 25 Changes in servo diaphragm link, stroke, intake manifold vacuum and engine speed

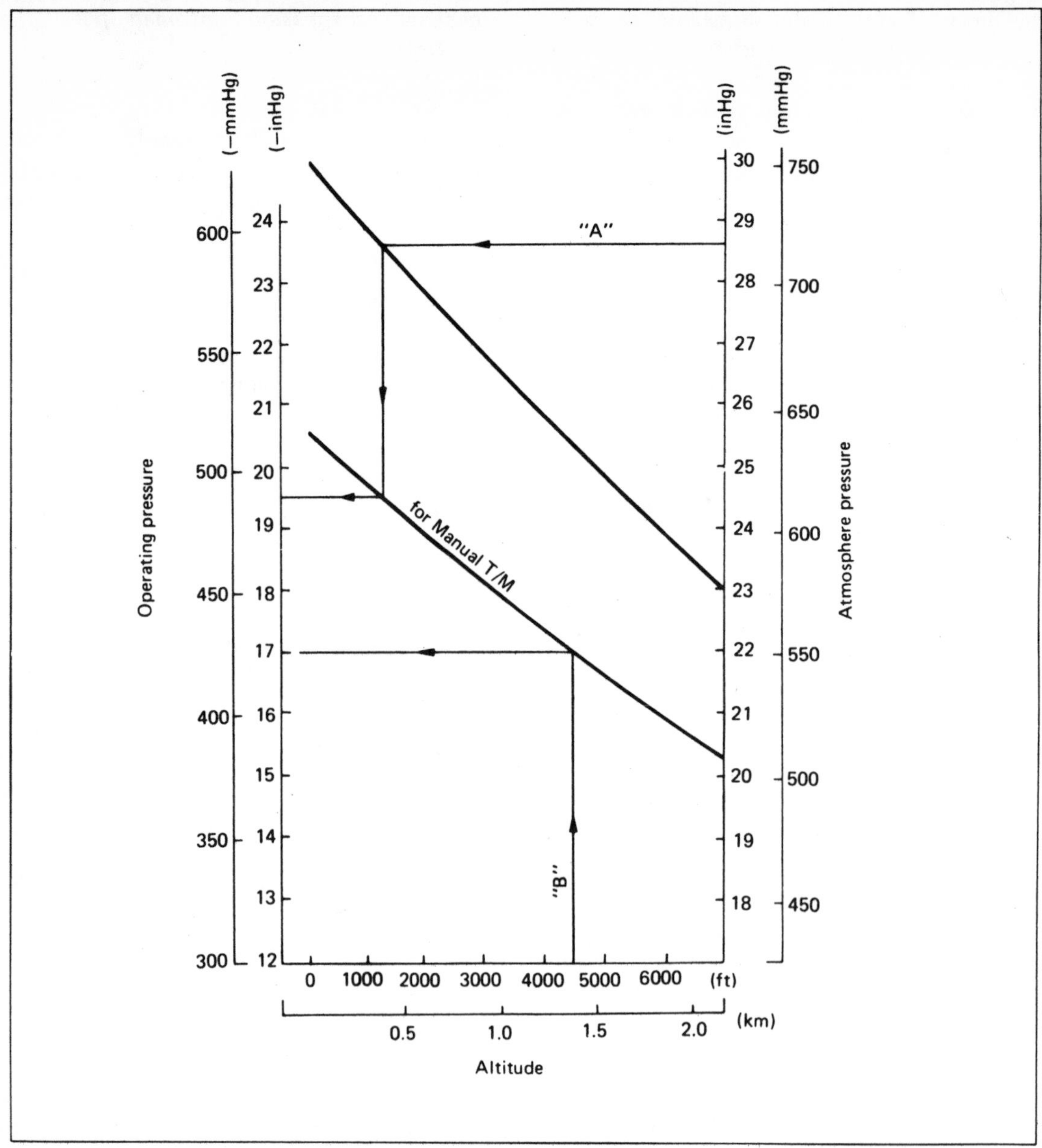

Fig. 26 Changes in operating pressure for changes in atmospheric pressure and altitude.

the other gear positions including Neutral position.

4. If it does not work properly in step 3, replace the switch with a new one.

Temperature Controlled Air Cleaner

Checking hot air control valve
Inspection

Among the possible problems with this device, the most frequent is the permanent opening of the valve.

This problem is not noticeable in warm weather but in cold weather it appears as poor performance of the engine—such as tardy acceleration, hesitation or engine stall. In such a case, inspect this device first before checking the carburetor.

Another problem which may arise is that the underhood air is kept closed by the valve regardless of the temperature of the suction air around the sensor while the engine is running. This would manifest itself in the form of extremely excessive fuel consumption or a decrease in power.

The inspection of this device should be carried out as follows.

1. Inspect whether the vacuum hoses are connected to the correct positions.
2. Inspect the hoses for cracks, distortion or plugging.

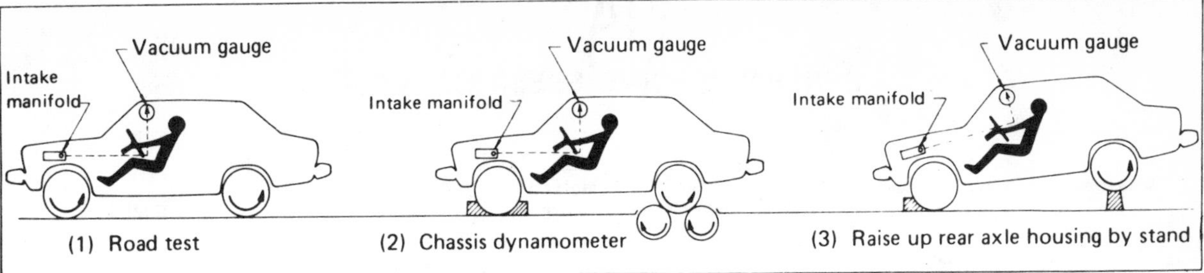

Fig. 27 Testing operating pressure of throttle opener when engine rpm fails to return to idle.

Checking of vacuum motor

1. With engine shut down, inspect the position of the valve (placing a mirror at the end of inlet pipe for inspection). The correct condition of the valve is that it keeps the inlet of underhood air open and that of hot air closed. Otherwise, inspect the linkage of the valve.
2. Disconnect the hose at the vacuum motor inlet, and directly apply the vacuum of the manifold to the vacuum motor by connecting another hose. Sucking by mouth may be substituted for this process. If the underhood air inlet is closed by the valve, the valve is in good condition. Inspect the linkage if found otherwise. When no problem is found in the linkage, it signifies a problem in the vacuum motor.
3. The valve is in the correct condition if it keeps the underhood air inlet closed when the passage in the hose is stopped by twisting or clamping it while applying the vacuum. If this is not the case, it is an indication of leakage in the vacuum motor.
4. When a problem is found in the vacuum motor through this check, replace the air cleaner assembly.

Checking of sensor

1. Perform the engine test by keeping the temperature around the sensor below 30° C (86° F). Make sure that the engine is cooled down before the test is conducted.

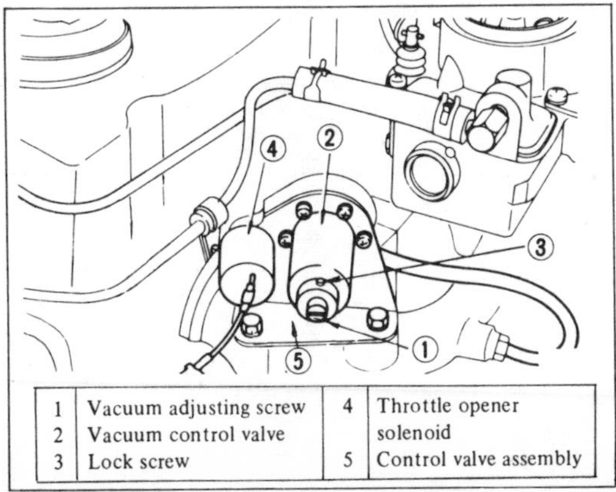

1	Vacuum adjusting screw	4	Throttle opener solenoid
2	Vacuum control valve		
3	Lock screw	5	Control valve assembly

Fig. 28 Vacuum control valve

2. Before starting the engine, make certain that the valve on the underhood air side fully opens.
3. Start the engine and operate it at idling speed. The valve is in good condition if the underhood air side fully closes immediately after starting.
4. Carefully watch the valve to ascertain that it gradually begins to open as the engine warms up. But when the ambient temperature is low it takes considerable length of time for the valve to begin to open. In some cases it barely opens. This should not be regarded as a problem.

   If the valve does not operate satisfactorily or if the condition of the valve is questionable, conduct the following test.
5. Remove the air cleaner cover, and put a thermister or a small thermometer as close to the sensor as possible with adhesive tape. Install the air cleaner cover again.
6. Start the engine and continue idling as described above. When several minutes have passed and with the valve partially opened, read the thermister indication. It is correct if the reading falls between 38° C (100° F) and 55° C (130° F). If the reading does not fall within these limits, replace the sensor.

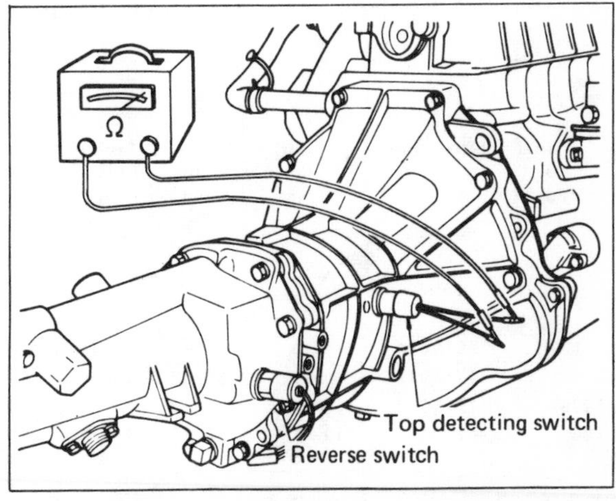

Fig. 29 Checking top detecting switch

FIAT

GENERAL ENGINE SPECIFICATIONS

Model or Engine	Bore & Stroke, Inches (mm)	Piston Displacement, Cubic Inches (cc)	Compression Ratio	Maximum Brake HP @ rpm	Maximum Torque Ft. Lbs. @ rpm	Normal Oil Pressure, Pounds
1974						
X1/9	3.38 x 2.19 (86 x 55.5)	79 (1290)	8.5	66 @ 6200	68 @ 3600	50–71
128	3.38 x 2.19 (86 x 55.5)	79 (1290)	8.5	66 @ 6200	68 @ 3600	50–71
128SL	3.38 x 2.19 (86 x 55.5)	79 (1290)	8.5	66 @ 6200	68 @ 3600	50–71
124TC	3.16 x 3.12 (80 x 79.2)	97 (1592)	8.0	78 @ 6000	85 @ 3600	64–87
124 Sport Coupe	3.30 x 3.12 (84 x 79.2)	107 (1756)	8.0	92 @ 6200	92 @ 3000	64–86
124 Sport Spider	3.30 x 3.12 (84 x 79.2)	107 (1756)	8.0	92 @ 6200	92 @ 3000	64–86

TUNEUP SPECIFICATIONS

Car Model or Engine	Spark Plugs		Distributor		Firing Order	Ignition Timing		Hot Idle Speed, rpm
	Type	Gap, Inch	Point Gap, Inch	Dwell Angle, Degrees		Degrees BTDC	Mark Location	
1974								
X1/9	Champ. N9-Y	.020–.024	55	—	1-3-4-2	0①	Pulley	800–900
All 128	Champ. N9-Y	.020–.024	52–58	.014	1-3-4-2	0①	Pulley	800–900
All 124	Champ. N7-Y	.020–.024	52–58	.013	1-3-4-2	0②	Pulley	700–750 Auto 800–900 Std

①—Timed at No. 1 cylinder, right side of vehicle.
②—Timed at No. 1 cylinder, front of engine.

DISTRIBUTOR SPECIFICATIONS

Model or Engine	Distributor Part No.	Point Gap, Inch	Dwell Angle, Deg.	Spring Tension, Oz.	Centrifugal Advance			Vacuum Advance		
					Start @ rpm	Int.	Full @ rpm	Inches of Vacuum to Start Plunger	Int.	Full Advance Dist. Deg. @ Vacuum
1974										
X 1/9	4315012	.016	55	14–16	800–1200	10.5 @ 1500	29 @ 4700	—	—	—
128	4315012	.016	52–58	14–16	800–1200	10.5 @ 1500	29 @ 4700	—	—	—
128SL	4315011	.016	52–58	14–16	850–1150	10 @ 1100	28 @ 4800	3.9	—	③
124	4293052	.012–.019② .016①	52–58	18–21	850–1150	20.5 @ 2000	36 @ 3600	—	—	—

①—Trailing set. ②—Leading Set. ③—10° retard @ 9.8.

Emission Controls

1974 MODELS

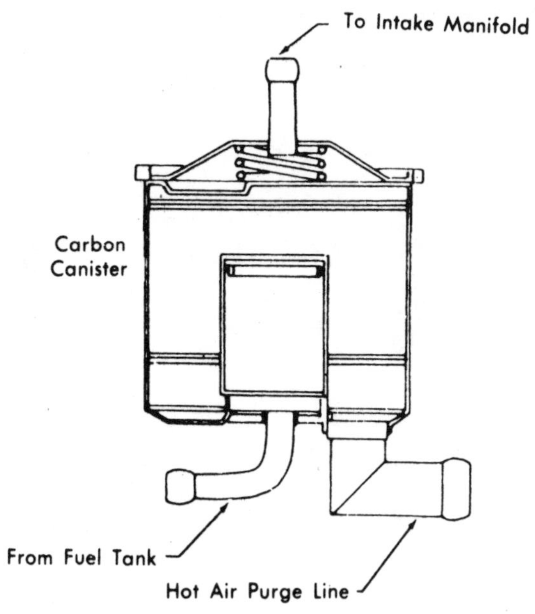

Fig. 1 Activated carbon canister

AIR INJECTION SYSTEM

All Models, Figs. 2 & 3

Description & Operation

The air pump forces air through the diverter valve, the check valve and injection nozzles to exhaust valve area. The diverter valve is controlled by vacuum from the intake manifold. The diverter valve directs air to injection nozzles under all running conditions except when decelerating with fully closed throttle, at which time the diverter valve diverts air to the atmosphere. The check valve prevents back pressure from the exhaust manifold from damaging the air pump. The air pump is equipped with a pressure relief valve to prevent air pump damage if the hoses become clogged.

EVAPORATIVE EMISSION CONTROL

Description

The fuel evaporation system consists of a fuel tank with a sealed filler cap, vapor separator, 3-way check valve and a charcoal canister, Fig. 1.

Operation

Fuel vapors from the fuel tank enter the vapor separator, where any condensed liquid is returned to the fuel tank. From the vapor separator, vapors travel through a 3-way check valve. The check valve routes the vapors either to the carbon canister, or to the atmosphere if there is excessive pressure in the fuel tank. The check valve also allows the air to enter the fuel tank. The vapors then travel to the carbon canister where they are stored until the engine is started. When the engine is running the vacuum from the intake manifold (and on X1/9 heat from exhaust manifold) purges the charcoal canister and burns vapors in the combustion chamber.

EXHAUST GAS RECIRCULATION

124 Models, Fig. 2

Description & Operation

This system is controlled by the thermovalve

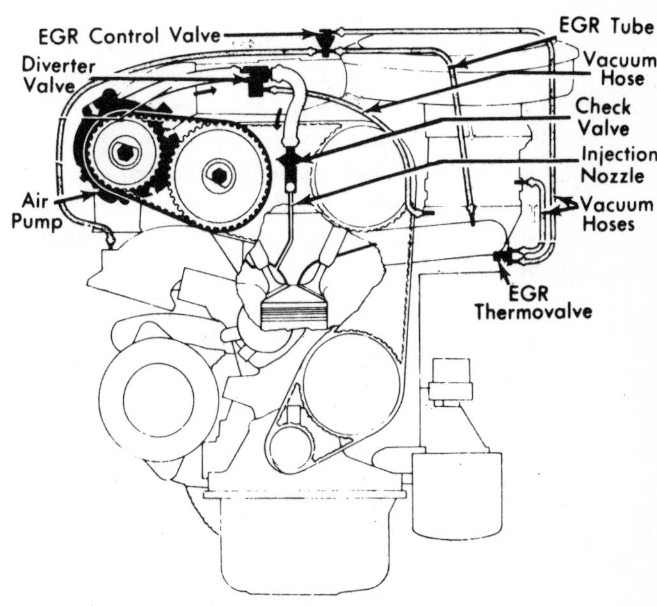

Fig. 2 124 exhaust emission control system

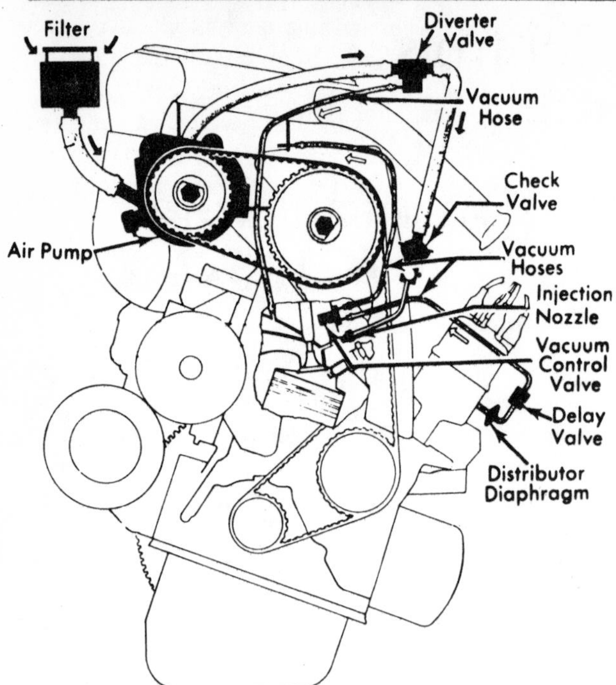

Fig. 3 X1/9 *and* 128 *exhaust emission control system*

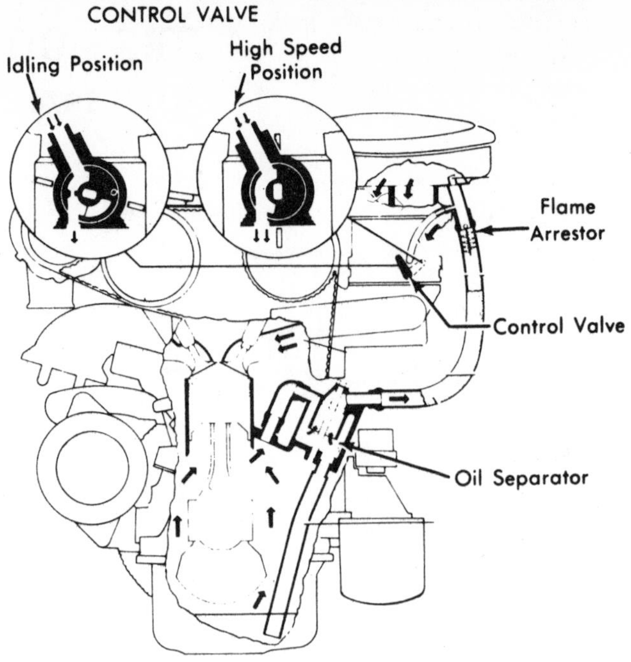

located in the intake manifold water passage. With the engine at operating temperature, the thermovalve opens the vacuum passage from the carburetor to the EGR control valve. Vacuum opens the control valve allowing a small amount of exhaust gas from the exhaust manifold to enter the intake manifold to reduce NOx emissions.

IGNITION TIMING RETARD

128 & X1/9 Models

Description & Operation

When the engine is cold, the thermovalve closes cutting off vacuum to the distributor diaphragm. With this, ignition timing is advanced to 10° BTDC. When engine temperature reaches 65° F, the thermovalve allows vacuum to the delay valve. The delay valve slows vacuum for seven seconds, after which full vacuum retards timing 10°. Timing is then at TDC.

POSITIVE CRANKCASE VENTILATION

Description

This system consists of a sealed oil filler cap, a connecting hose located between carburetor air cleaner and oil separator, and a control valve located on the carburetor, Figs. 4 & 5.

Operation

During idle and part throttle operation, crank-

CONTROL VALVE
Idling Position
High Speed Position
Flame Arrestor
Control Valve
Oil Separator

Fig. 4 124 *crankcase ventilation system*

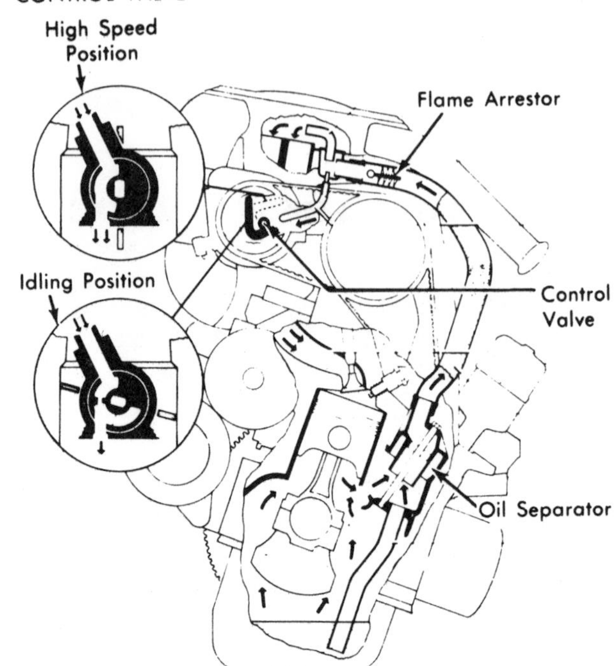

Fig. 5 X1/9 *and* 128 *crankcase ventilation system*

case fumes and vapors pass through oil separator and connecting hose to the carburetor air cleaner where they are drawn into the intake manifold and enter combustion system to be burned. As the carburetor throttle is opened wider the control valve, in the carburetor, is actuated. This action opens the vacuum line allowing fumes and vapors to enter into base of carburetor where they are drawn into combustion chamber and burned. A flame arrestor is located within the main connecting hose. Should a backfire occur, the flame arrestor would prevent damage to engine.

GENERAL SERVICE

Ignition Timing Retard

Adjustment

With the engine at normal operating temperature, set idle to 800 rpm and timing to TDC. Disconnect and plug vacuum hose from retard diaphragm to avoid vacuum leaks. Timing should be 10° BTDC. If advance is more than the specified amount and engine rpm is higher than 800 rpm, temporarily readjust idle speed to 800 rpm. Advance should be to specification with readjusted idle. Reconnect the vacuum hose and observe that timing is retarded to TDC. Readjust idle to recommended 850 rpm.

POSITIVE CRANKCASE VENTILATION

Every 3000 miles, clean the carburetor air cleaner. Replace it every 6000 miles. Every 12,000 miles, clean all components and inspect for damage. Replace all parts as necessary.

MAZDA

GENERAL ENGINE SPECIFICATIONS

Model or Engine	Bore & Stroke, Inches (mm)	Piston Displacement, Cubic Inches (cc)	Compression Ratio	Maximum Brake HP @ rpm	Maximum Torque Ft. Lbs. @ rpm	Normal Oil Pressure, Pounds
1974						
808	3.07 x 3.27 (78 x 83)	96.8 (1586)	8.6	70 @ 5000	82 @ 3500	50–64
RX-2	Rotary	69.8 (1146)	9.4	97 @ 6500	98 @ 4000	71
RX-3	Rotary	69.8 (1146)	9.4	90 @ 6000	96 @ 400	71
RX-4	Rotary	80 (1308)	9.2	110 @ 6000	117 @ 3500	71
1975						
808	78.0 x 83.0	96.8 (1586)	8.6	64 @ 5000	78 @ 3000①	50–64
RX-3	Rotary	69.8 (1146)	9.4	90 @ 6000	96 @ 4000	71
RX-4	Rotary	80 (1308)	9.2	110 @ 6000	117 @ 3500	71

①—California 77 @ 3000.

TUNEUP SPECIFICATIONS

Car Model or Engine	Spark Plugs		Distributor		Firing Order	Ignition Timing		Hot Idle Speed rpm
	Type	Gap, Inch	Point Gap, Inch	Dwell Angle, Degrees		Degrees BTDC	Mark Location	
1974								
808 Auto	NGK BP-6ES	.031	.020	49–55	1-3-4-2	8 advance 4 retard	Pulley	800–850
808 Std	NGK BP-6ES	.031	.020	49–55	1-3-4-2	5	Pulley	800–850
RX2-3	NGK B-7EM	.024–.028	.016–.020	55–61	1-2	lead 5 ATC trail 10 ATDC	①	700
RX-4	NGK B-7EM	.024–.028	.016–.020	55–61	1-2	lead 5 ATC trail 5 ATDC	①	700

①—Eccentric shaft pulley.

DISTRIBUTOR SPECIFICATIONS

Model or Engine	Distributor Part No.	Point Gap, Inch	Dwell Angle, Deg.	Spring Tension, Oz.	Centrifugal Advance			Vacuum Advance		
					Start @ rpm	Int.	Full @ rpm	Inches of Vacuum to Start Plunger	Int.	Full Advance Dist. Deg. @ Vacuum
1974										
808 Std.	—	.020	49–55	20	0 @ 550	—	11 @ 2000	0 @ 12.6	—	7.5 @ 21.65
808 Auto	—	.020	49–55	20	0 @ 1000	—	11 @ 2100	0 @ 9.45	—	7.5 @ 18.31
RX2-3	—	.018–.002	55–61	18–23	Leading 0 @ 500	—	7.5 @ 1500	Trailing 0 @ 3.94	—	8.5 @ 15.75
RX4	—	.016–.020	55–61	18–23	Leading 0 @ 500	—	10 @ 2000	0 @ 3.94	—	15 @① 15.75

①—13 @ 15.7 w/automatic.

Emission Controls

1974 MODELS

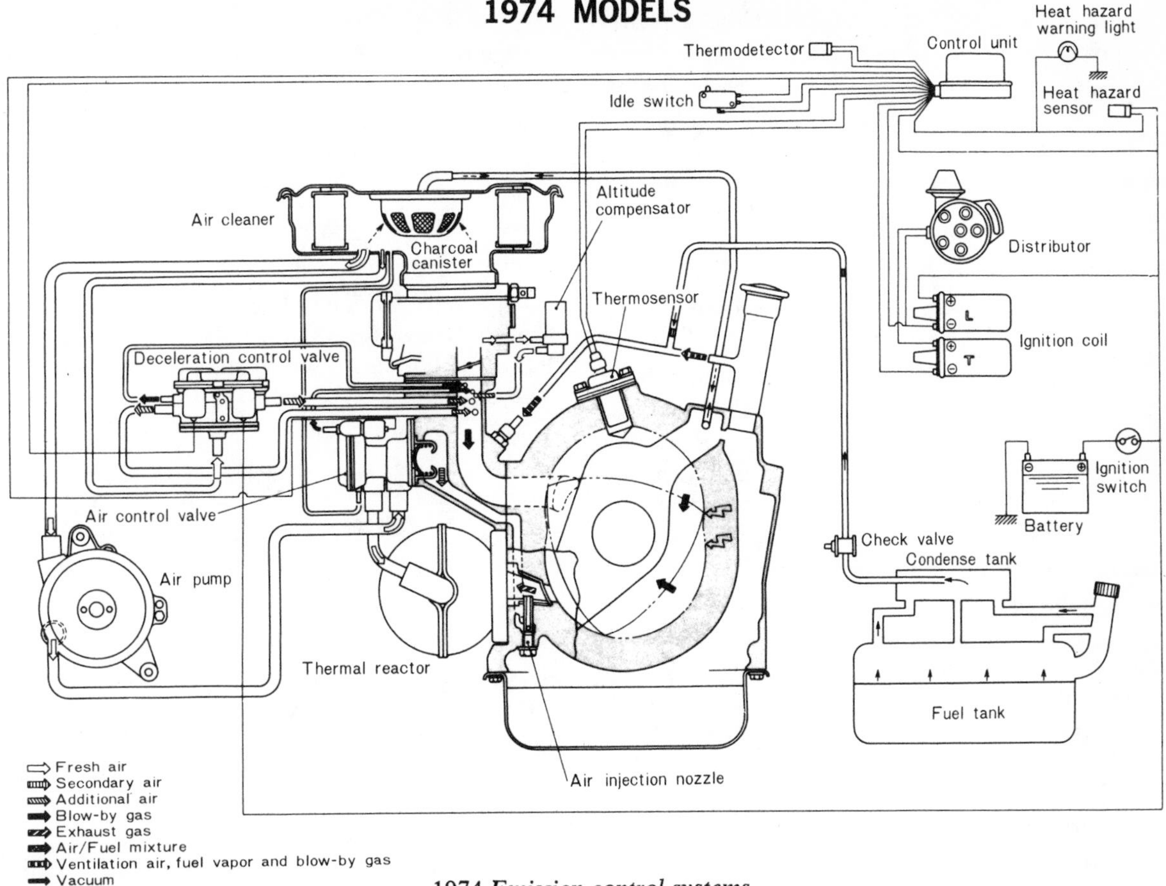

1974 *Emission control systems*

Description

This system is comprised of an exhaust emission control system which reduces harmful composites in the exhaust gas, a positive crankcase ventilation system which channels the blow-by gas from the crankcase into the combustion chamber to burn it up, and an evaporative emission control system which stores the fuel vapor from the fuel system and leads it to the combustion chamber.

THROTTLE OPENER SYSTEM

808 Models

Description

The throttle opener system is composed of a servo diaphragm connected to a throttle lever, and a vacuum control valve which controls the intake manifold vacuum led to the servo diaphragm. This system reduces hydrocarbons during deceleration.

During deceleration, the air fuel mixture entering the engine is not sufficient, making normal combustion impossible and causing a large amount of hydrocarbons to be emitted out into the atmosphere. The throttle opener system takes advantage of the intake manifold vacuum during deceleration to slightly open the primary throttle valve in the coasting condition (to an opening of 1400 ± 100 rpm when unloaded) so that an optimum amount of combustible mixture is fed to the engine to continue proper combustion. This arrangement brings about a large reduction of hydrocarbons during deceleration.

Vacuum Control Valve

The vacuum control valve detects the intake manifold vacuum that acts on the servo diaphragm in order to open the primary throttle valve during deceleration. A small hole fitted on the valve leads the air onto the servo diaphragm after the valve is closed to return the throttle valve back.

The vacuum control valve consists of a diaphragm, diaphragm return spring, valve attached to the diaphragm, altitude corrector, etc., and has a cross section as shown.

A high vacuum that develops in the intake manifold during deceleration is channeled to the diaphragm chamber. Vacuum in the diaphragm chamber overcomes the force of the diaphragm return spring and opens the valve. Vacuum then passes between the valve and valve seat to the servo diaphragm chamber. This causes the servo diaphragm to open the primary throttle valve to a specified opening.

As the vehicle speed falls, the intake manifold vacuum also decreases, so that the primary throttle valve linked to the servo diaphragm returns gradually to the opening of idling. The vacuum control valve is also closed by the force of the diaphragm return spring. Therefore, as soon as the vacuum ceases to act on the servo diaphragm chamber, the atmospheric pressure comes through the air passage into the servo diaphragm chamber and fills it, thus completely returning the primary throttle valve to the opening of idling. The diaphragm return spring of the vacuum control valve is set to start operating when the intake manifold vacuum becomes 22.0 in. Hg, so the vacuum control valve does not work except during deceleration.

The altitude corrector in the vacuum control valve prevents the vacuum control valve from showing varied responses due to difference in atmospheric pressure—altitude. The altitude corrector (bellows) contracts according to the change in atmospheric pressure, thus adjusting the diaphragm return spring to proper tension so that the vacuum control valve operates in accordance with the change in atmospheric pressure.

Servo Diaphragm

The servo diaphragm, connected to the primary throttle lever of the carburetor, responds to the intake manifold vacuum controlled by the vacuum control valve to open the primary throttle valve to a specified opening.

ACCELERATOR SWITCH & THERMOSENSOR

808 Models with Auto. Trans.

The accelerator switch attached on the accelerator linkage and the thermosensor attached on the intake manifold control the ignition timing. The accelerator switch closes the retard circuit when the accelerator pedal is depressed ¾-way, while it opens the retard circuit when the accelerator pedal is depressed ¾-way. The thermosensor closes the retard circuit when the temperature of the cooling water in the engine rises above 122-140° F, while it opens the retard circuit when the temperature of the cooling water is below 122-140° F. Only at the time both the accelerator switch and the thermosensor close, the ignition timing is retarded from 8° BTDC to 4° BTDC.

POSITIVE CRANKCASE VENTILATION SYSTEM

Description & Operation

The positive crankcase ventilation system channels blow-by gases into the intake manifold to burn it up in the combustion chamber and helps to control air pollution caused by crankcase blow-by gas. The air and blow-by gases flow in the ventilation system as shown in Fig. 1.

EVAPORATIVE EMISSION CONTROL SYSTEM

Description, Fig. 2

The evaporative emission control system seals the fuel system completely and prevents emission of the fuel vapor generated by the ambient temperature around the fuel tank when the car is running or standing. The fuel vapor rising from the surface of the fuel in the fuel tank due to the high ambient temperature is channeled into the condense tank and condensed fuel is fed back to the fuel tank. The fuel vapor that has not condensed in the condense tank is led into the carbon canister. The active carbon in the canister absorbs the fuel vapors and stores them. During periods of engine operation, the fuel vapor stored in the carbon canister is purged from the active carbon by fresh air drawn from the inlet hole at the bottom of the canister, and sucked into the air cleaner. Then the fuel vapor in the air cleaner is led into the combustion chamber through the intake manifold and burnt up.

Operation

Condense Tank, Fig. 3

The condense tank is installed near the fuel tank and condenses the fuel vapor coming from the fuel tank and returns it to the fuel tank.

Check Valve

The check valve located between the condense tank and the canister works appropriately when the conditions mentioned below take place, relating to the completely sealed ventilation type fuel system.

1. When the evaporative system is normal, the flow of fuel vapor and ventilation during engine operation are as shown in Fig. 4.

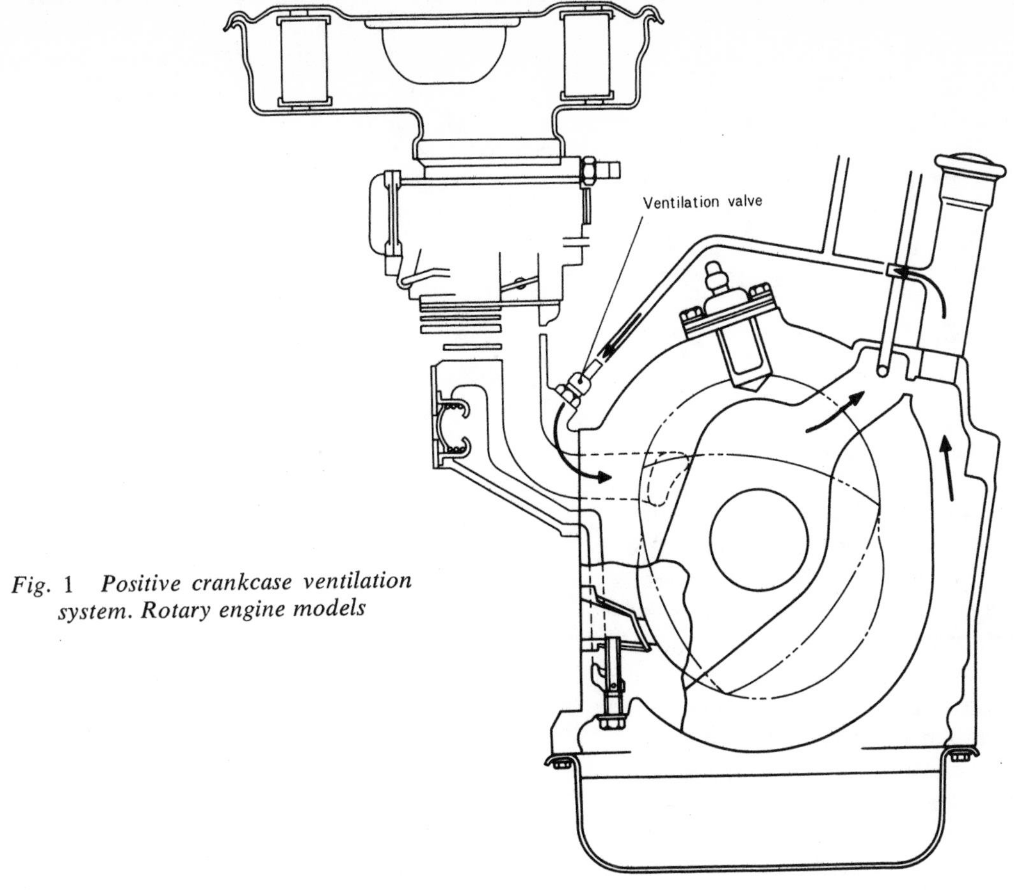

Fig. 1 Positive crankcase ventilation system. Rotary engine models

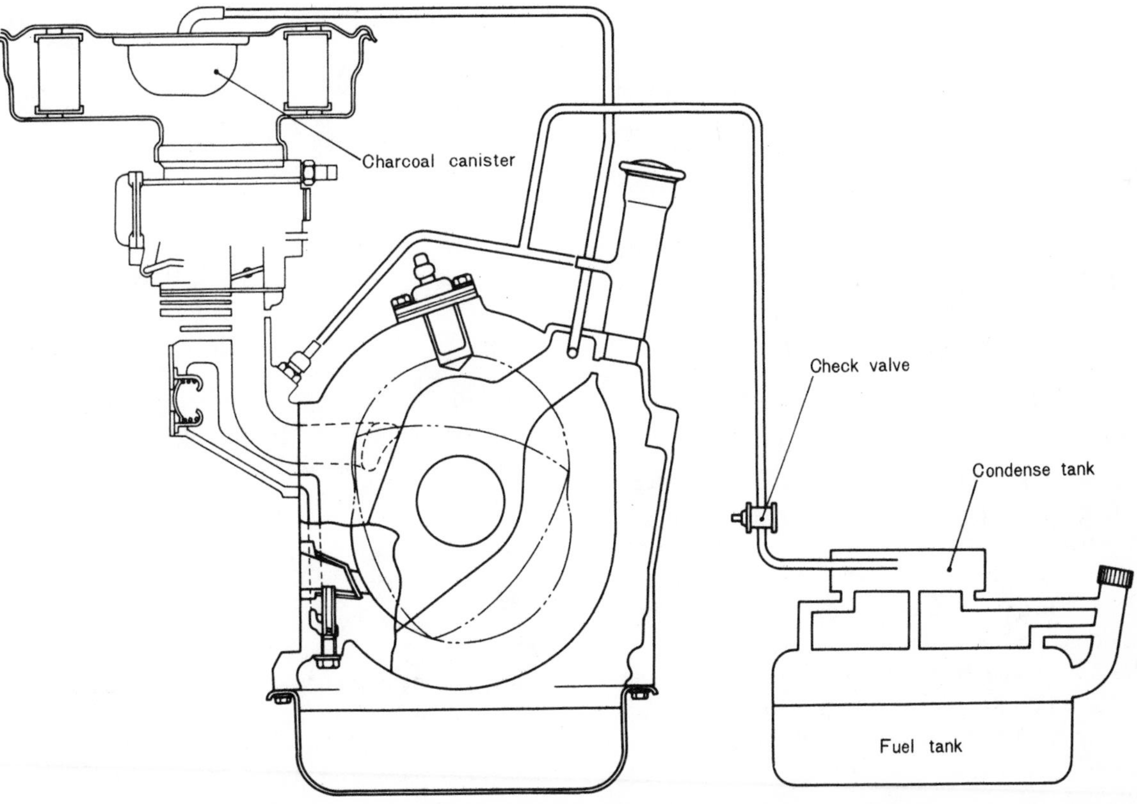

Fig. 2 Evaporative emission control system. Rotary engine models

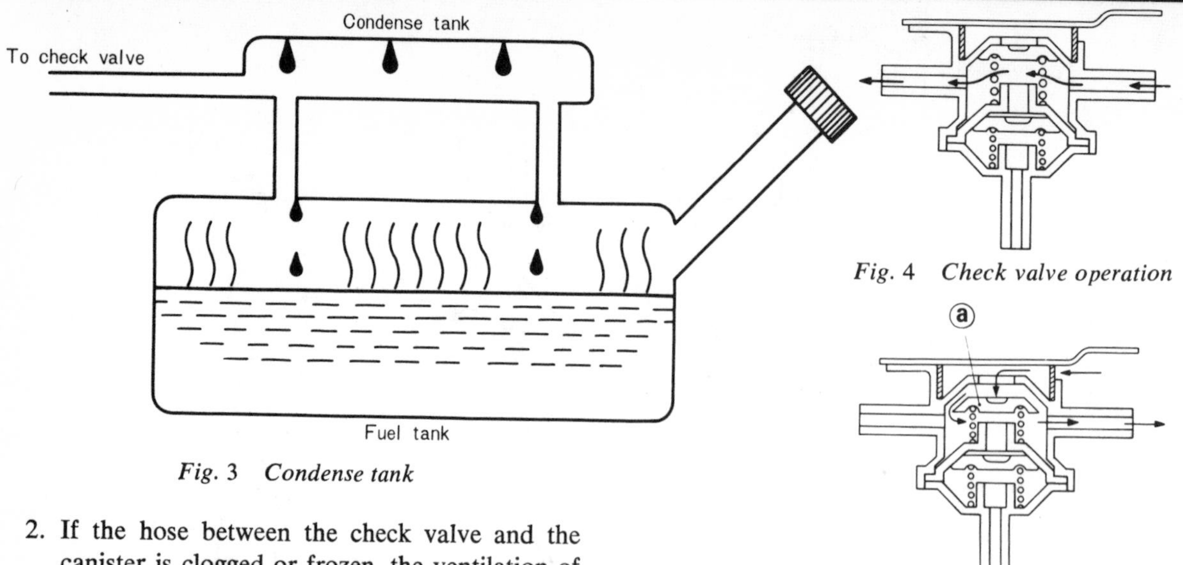

Fig. 3 Condense tank

Fig. 4 Check valve operation

Fig. 5 Check valve operation

2. If the hose between the check valve and the canister is clogged or frozen, the ventilation of the fuel system would not work at all and as a result, the fuel supply to the engine will be cut off. Therefore, when the evaporative line is clogged, the valve, Fig. 5, is opened by the negative pressure in the fuel tank and the ventilation passage to the atmosphere is opened.
3. When the fuel vapor in the fuel tank is expanded due to intense heat, the pressure in the fuel tank will increase. In order to prevent the increase of the pressure in the fuel tank, the valve, is opened to release the pressure to the atmosphere.

Canister

The canister which is installed in the engine room on 808 models and within the air cleaner housing on rotary engine models absorbs the fuel vapor generated in the fuel tank with the active carbon and stores them.

AIR INJECTION SYSTEM, THERMAL REACTOR & SECONDARY AIR CONTROL SYSTEM

Rotary Engine Models, Fig. 6

Description

The air injection and thermal reactor system, consisting of a thermal reactor, an air pump, a check valve, air injection nozzles and an air control valve, injects into the exhaust ports secondary air necessary for oxidation of hydrocarbon and carbon monoxide contained in the exhaust gas.

The air sucked from the air cleaner by the air pump is sent into the air control valve. The air (secondary air) from the air control valve ordinarily flows into the exhaust ports through the check valve and the air injection nozzles. However, under the conditions mentioned below, the flow of the secondary air into the exhaust ports is stopped by the ignition and air flow control system as well as protective system (operation of air cut valve), and the air (cooling air) flows into the thermal reactor cooling air jacket to properly maintain the temperature of the reactor.

1. When the engine speed is over 4000 rpm (in case of automatic transmission, 4800 rpm when engine is cold and 3400 rpm when engine is hot). Operation of ignition and air flow control system.
2. When the engine speed is over 1200 rpm during deceleration (1400 rpm in case of automatic transmission). Operation of ignition and air flow control system.
3. When running under full load (throttle valve is nearly wide open).
4. When the floor temperature is over approximately 120° C (248° F). Operation of protective system.

The timing of supplying the secondary air into the exhaust ports and the cooling air into the thermal reactor cooling air jacket is controlled in accordance with the operating conditions of the vehicle.

Operation

Air Pump

The air pump is a vane type driven by the V-belt mounted on the eccentric shaft pulley. The air pump sucks fresh filtered air from the air cleaner, compresses the air and injects it through the air control valve, check valve and air injection nozzles into the exhaust ports adjacent to the thermal reactor.

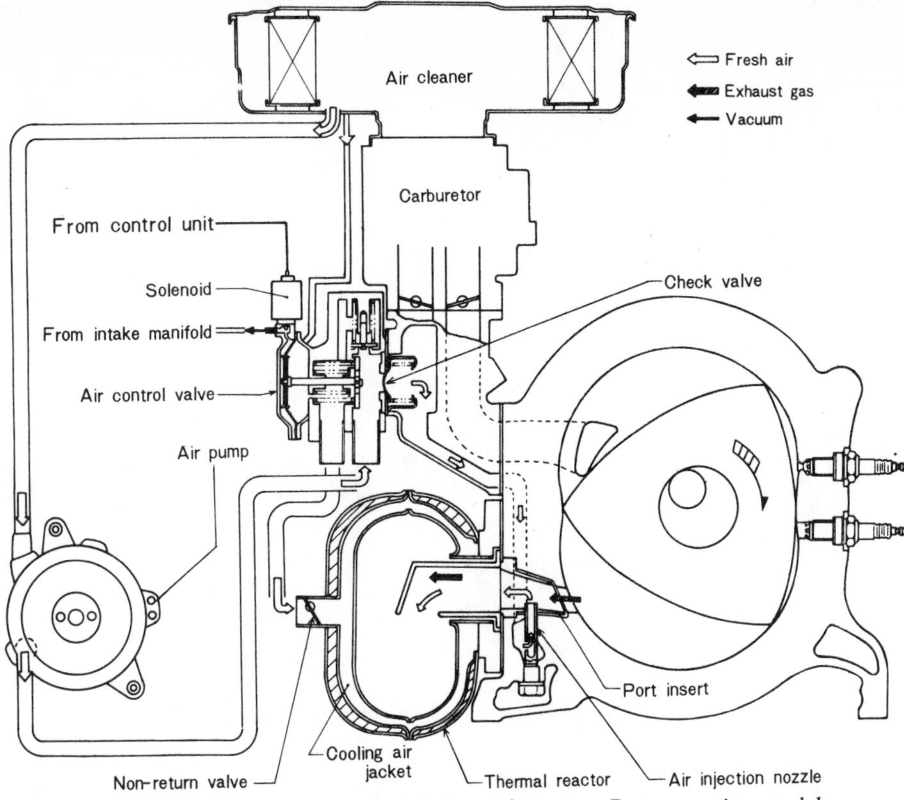

Fig. 6 Air injection system and thermal reactor. Rotary engine models

Check Valve, Fig. 7

The check valve opens and closes according to the pressure difference between secondary air and exhaust gas to prevent exhaust gas from backflowing into the air injection system and scorching the air pump, hoses, etc. When the pressure of secondary air in the air injection system exceeds the exhaust gas pressure, the secondary air opens the check valve and flows through the air injection nozzles into the exhaust ports.

When the secondary air pressure drops lower than the exhaust gas pressure due to failure of the air pump belt, breaking of the secondary air hose, etc., the check valve closes to prevent the backflow of the exhaust gas into the air injection system.

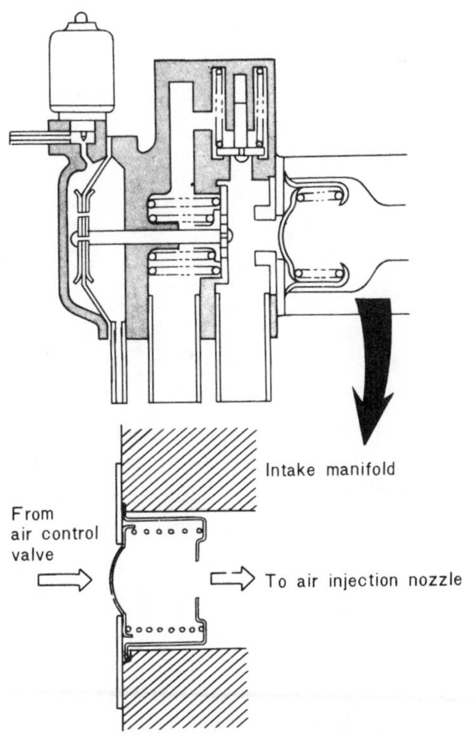

Fig. 7 Check valve operation

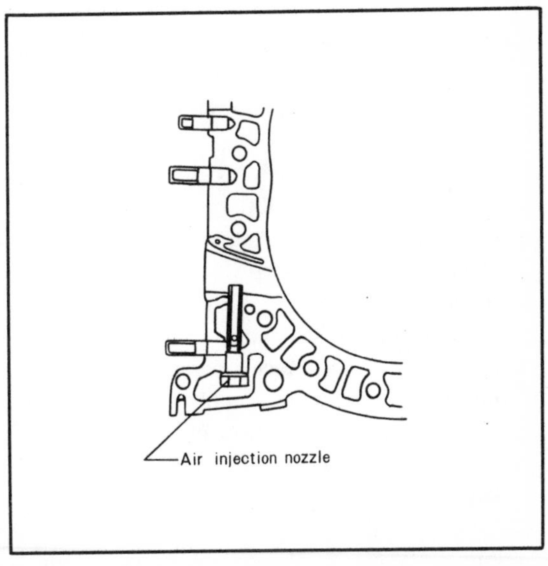

Fig. 8 Air injection nozzles

Air Injection Nozzles, Fig. 8

The air injection nozzles are attached to each of the front and rear rotor housings. The secondary air channeled via the air pump and the check valve is injected through the nozzles into the exhaust ports adjacent to the thermal reactor.

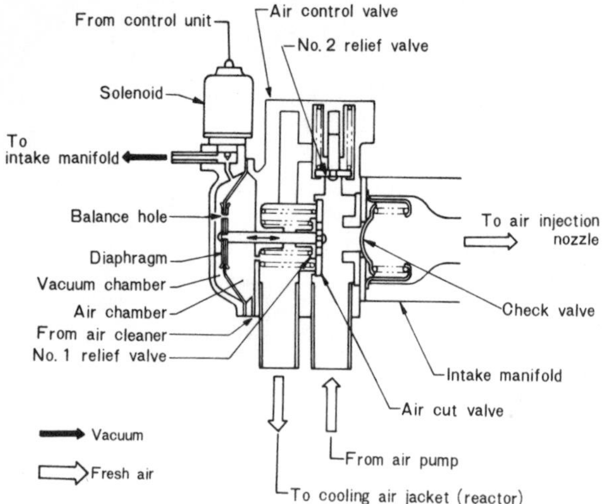

Fig. 9 Crossection of air control valve

Air Control Valve, Fig. 9

The air control valve, consisting of an air cut valve, a No. 1 relief valve and a No. 2 relief valve, has the following functions.

1. When the air cut valve is not operating, it becomes the passage of the secondary air from the air pump into the exhaust ports through the check valve and air injection nozzles. Operation of air control valve.
2. When the engine speed is over 4000 rpm (in case of automatic transmission, 3400 rpm when the engine is hot and 4800 rpm when it is cold), the supply of the secondary air into the exhaust ports stops and the secondary air (cooling air) flows into the thermal reactor cooling air jacket to cool the reactor to properly maintain the temperature of the reactor. Operation of air cut valve.
3. When the engine speed is over 1200 rpm during deceleration (1400 rpm in case of automatic transmission), supply of the secondary air into the exhaust ports stops and the secondary air (cooling air) flows to the thermal reactor cooling air jacket. The secondary air cutting in this instance prevents excessive supply of the secondary air into the exhaust ports and deteriorated reaction efficiency of the exhaust gas in the reactor. Operation of air cut valve.
4. When the air pressure in the air injection system is excessive, the supply of the secondary air into the exhaust ports is adjusted properly and the excessive secondary air (cooling air) is relieved to the thermal reactor cooling air jacket to cool the reactor. Operation of No. 1 relief valve and No. 2 relief valve.

The air cut valve opens and closes according to the difference of pressure between the vacuum chamber and the air chamber. This valve, which is connected to the diaphragm, is closed during normal operation by the intake manifold vacuum.

When the engine speed exceeds 4000 rpm (in case of automatic transmission 3400 rpm warm, 4800 rpm cold), the control unit actuates the solenoid to close the vacuum sensing. This equalizes the pressures in the two chambers. The spring force causes the valve to open and the air in the air injection system is channeled to the thermal reactor cooling air jacket before being expelled to the atmosphere. At the same time, the air cut valve closes the secondary air passage to cut secondary air supply into the exhaust ports.

During deceleration with the accelerator pedal released completely when the engine speed is over 1200 rpm (1400 rpm in case of automatic transmission), the solenoid of the air control valve closes the vacuum sensing between the intake manifold and the air control valve by means of the low speed switch in the control unit and the idle switch. Consequently, the spring force causes the valve to open and the air in the air injection system is channeled to the thermal reactor cooling air jacket before being expelled to the atmosphere. At the same time, the air cut valve closes the secondary air passage to cut secondary air supply into the exhaust ports.

When the engine is running with full load, the difference of pressure between the vacuum chamber and the air chamber of the air control valve diminishes because the intake manifold vacuum which is led to the vacuum chamber decreases. Consequently, the spring force causes the valve to open and the air in the air injection system is channeled to the thermal reactor cooling air jacket before being expelled to the atmosphere. At the same time, the air cut valve closes the secondary air passage to cut secondary air supply into the exhaust ports. The No. 1 relief valve is opened and closed in accordance with air pressure in the air injection system and the force of the return spring. When the air pressure in the air injection system increases, the No. 1 relief

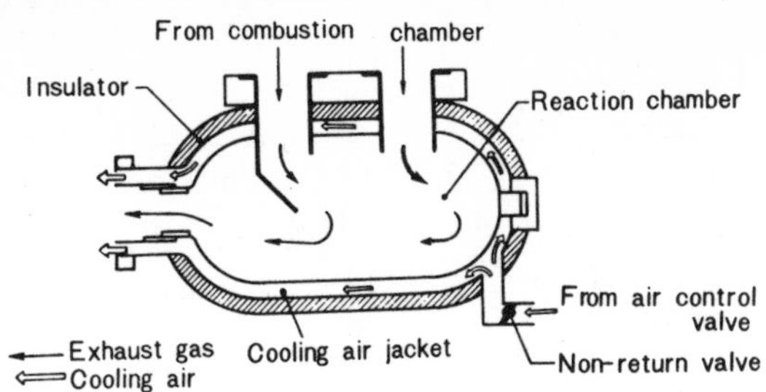

Fig. 10 Thermal reactor air flow

valve is opened and the air is led to the thermal reactor cooling air jacket to cool it before being expelled to the atmosphere. Thus the secondary air flow rate is being controlled. When the air pressure decreases, the spring closes the valve.

The No. 2 relief valve is opened and closed in accordance with air pressure in the air injection system and the force of the return spring. When the air pressure in the air injection system exceeds the specified value, the No. 2 relief valve is opened and the air is led to the thermal reactor cooling air jacket to cool it before being expelled to the atmosphere. Thus the secondary air flow rate is controlled. When the air pressure decreases, the spring closes the valve.

Thermal Reactor

The thermal reactor is mounted just outside the exhaust ports. It oxidizes the unburned exhaust gas expelled from the engine, to reduce the noxious components such as hydrocarbon and carbon monoxide. When the engine speed is high or during deceleration or full load running, the air control valve feeds fresh air from the air pump to the thermal reactor cooling air jacket to properly maintain the temperature of the reactor. The non-return valve which prevents backflow of exhaust gas from the reactor is attached at the air inlet of the reactor.

Ignition and Air Flow Control System, Fig. 10

The ignition and air flow control system consists of a thermosensor, a thermodetector, an idle switch and a control unit including high speed switch, low speed switch, thermoswitch and trailing ignition switch. This system ignites and cuts the trailing spark plug to suit engine temperature and engine speed in order to enhance the reactivity of the thermal reactor when the engine is cold. This system has an additional function of regulating the air control valve and the deceleration control valve.

The operating time of the ignition and air flow control system is shown by the following table, Fig. 11 and 12.

Thermosensor

The thermosensor, which is placed in the cooling water passage, detects the water temperature and sends the signal to the control unit.

When the water temperature rises to the specified value, the thermoswitch and the trailing ignition switch in the control unit close by means of the thermosensor. The electric current then flows to the

Fig. 11 Operating mode of air flow control system

Secondary Air Injection Cut

Manual transmission

Operating time	Parts that operate coordinately
When engine speed is over 4,000 rpm	solenoid of air control valve, air cut valve, high speed switch
During deceleration when engine speed is over 1,200 rpm	solenoid of air control valve, air cut valve, low speed switch, idle switch
When running under full load (throttle valve is nearly wide open)	air cut valve
When floor temperature is over approximately 120°C (248°F) (Protective system)	heat hazard sensor, control unit, solenoid of air control valve, air cut valve

Automatic transmission

Operating time	Parts that operate coordinately
When engine speed is over the specified value 4,800 rpm when cold 3,400 rpm when hot	solenoid of air control valve, air cut valve, high speed switch, thermosensor, thermoswitch (the last two parts when engine is hot)
During deceleration when engine speed is 1,400 rpm	solenoid of air control valve, air cut valve, low speed switch, idle switch
When running with full load (throttle valve is nearly wide open)	air cut valve
When floor temperature is over approximately 120°C (248°F) (Protective system)	heat hazard sensor, control unit, solenoid of air control valve, air cut valve

Control of Trailing Spark Plug Ignition

Manual transmission

Operating time	Parts that operate coordinately
1. Trailing spark plug does not ignite. (Only leading spark plug ignites.)	
During cruising and acceleration (deceleration excluded) when engine speed is 1,200 ~ 4,000 rpm at cold condition	low speed switch, high speed switch, idle switch, trailing ignition switch
2. Trailing spark plug ignites. (Both leading and trailing spark plugs ignite.)	
When engine is hot	thermosensor, thermoswitch, trailing ignition switch
During cruising, acceleration and deceleration when engine speed is below 1,200 rpm or over 4,000 rpm at cold condition	low speed switch, high speed switch, trailing ignition switch, idle switch

Automatic transmission

Operating time	Parts that operate coordinately
1. Trailing spark plug does not ignite. (Only leading spark plug ignites.)	
During cruising and acceleration (deceleration excluded) when engine speed is 1,400 ~ 4,800 rpm at cold condition	low speed switch, high speed switch, idle switch, trailing ignition switch
2. Trailing spark plug ignites. (Both leading and trailing spark plugs ignite.)	
When engine is hot	thermosensor, thermoswitch, trailing ignition switch
During cruising, acceleration and deceleration when engine speed is below 1,400 rpm or over 4,800 rpm at cold condition	low speed switch, high speed switch, trailing ignition switch, idle switch

Fig. 12 Operating mode of trailing spark plug ignition

trailing side ignition coil and the trailing spark plug is ignited. In case of automatic transmission, the opening/closing time of the high speed switch in the control unit goes from 4800 rpm when the engine is cold to 3400 rpm when it is hot. Consequently, when the engine speed is over 3400 rpm hot, the high speed switch closes and the electric current flows to the solenoid of the air control valve and the solenoid cuts the vacuum sensing between the intake manifold and the air chamber of the air control valve. The air cut valve of the air control valve then stops the supply of the secondary air into the exhaust ports by means of the spring force. The secondary air flows into the thermal reactor cooling air jacket to cool the reactor.

Thermodetector

The thermodetector which detects the ambient temperature corrects the operating temperature of the thermosensor to resume the ignition of the trailing spark plug after the minimum time required for the thermal reactor warmup.

Control Unit

In the control unit are the thermoswitch, trailing ignition switch, low speed switch and high speed switch. The functions are as follows. Refer to Fig. 13.

1. In the whole hot operating range, the thermoswitch and the trailing ignition switch close and the electric current flows to the trailing side ignition coil and the trailing spark plug is ignited. Operation of the thermoswitch and trailing ignition switch.
2. When the engine speed is over 3400 rpm hot, the thermoswitch and the high speed switch close and the electric current flows to the solenoid of the air control valve. Consequently, the solenoid cuts the vacuum sensing between the intake manifold and the vacuum chamber. This actuated the air cut valve to stop the supply of the secondary air into the exhaust ports and the air flows into the thermal reactor cooling air jacket (only in case of automatic transmission). Operation of thermoswitch and high speed switch.
3. When the engine speed is over 4000 rpm (in case of automatic transmission, 4800 rpm cold and 3400 rpm hot), the high speed switch closes and the electric current flows to the solenoid of the air control valve. The solenoid consequently cuts the vacuum sensing between the intake manifold and the vacuum chamber of the air control valve. This actuates the air cut valve to stop the supply of the secondary air into the exhaust ports and the air flows to the thermal reactor cooling air jacket. Operation

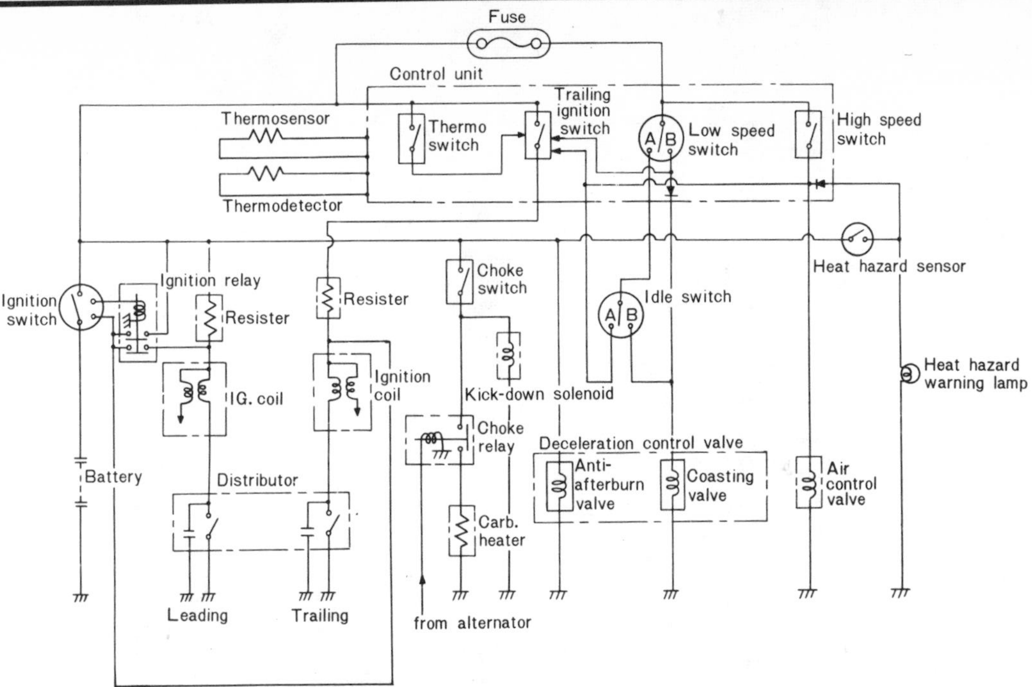

Fig. 13 *Control unit wiring schematic*

of high speed switch.

4. Whether cold or hot, when the engine speed is over 1200 rpm (1400 rpm in case of automatic transmission), point [A] of the low speed switch closes and the electric current flows to the idle switch, during deceleration when the accelerator pedal is relieved completely, point [A] of the idle switch closes, and so the electric current from the low speed switch flows to the solenoid of the air control valve. The solenoid then closes the vacuum sensing between the intake manifold and the air control valve. This actuates the air cut valve to stop the supply of the secondary air into the exhaust port and the air flows into the thermal reactor cooling air jacket. At the same time, since the electric current to the solenoid of the coasting valve stops, the solenoid opens the atmospheric pressure sensing line. This actuates the coasting valve and the fresh air from the air cleaner enters the intake manifold and prevents afterburn. Operation of low speed switch.
5. When the engine speed is below 1200 rpm (1400 rpm in case of automatic transmission), point [B] of the low speed switch closes. The electric current flows to the trailing side ignition coil through the trailing ignition switch, and ignites the trailing spark plug. Operation of low speed switch and trailing ignition switch.

Idle Switch

The idle switch detects the deceleration condition of the car. It sends the decelerating condition signal to the control unit and the coasting valve.

The functions are as follows. (Refer to Fig. 13).

1. While deceleration (with the accelerator pedal released) when the engine speed is over 1200 rpm (1400 rpm in case of automatic transmission), point [A] of the idle switch closes and the electric current flows to the air control valve solenoid from the low speed switch. The solenoid consequently cuts the vacuum sensing between the intake manifold and the vacuum chamber of the air control valve. This actuates the air cut valve to stop the supply of the secondary air into the exhaust ports and the air flows to the thermal reactor cooling air jacket.
2. At the same time, since the electric current to the solenoid of the coasting valve stops, the solenoid opens the atmospheric pressure sensing line. This actuates the coasting valve and the fresh air from the air cleaner enters the intake manifold and prevents afterburn.
3. When the point [B] of the low speed switch and point [A] of the idle switch are closed, the electric current flows to the trailing side ignition coil through the trailing ignition switch, and ignites the trailing spark plug.

Additional Air Control System, Fig. 14

The additional air control system consists of the deceleration control valve and the altitude compensator. During deceleration and gear shifting and immediately after turning off the ignition switch,

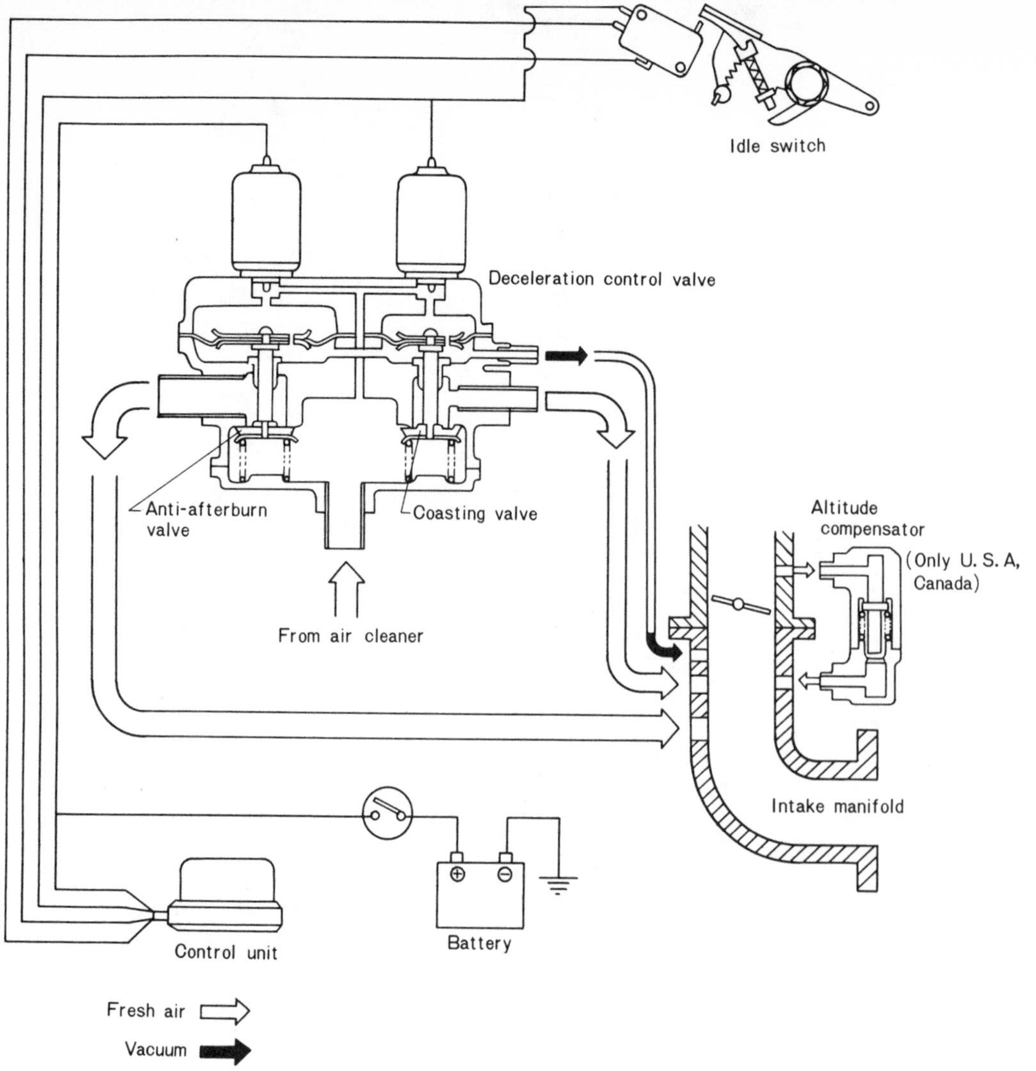

Fig. 14 *Additional air control system*

the additional air control system sends the fresh air from the air cleaner to the intake manifold and adjusts the excessively rich fuel air mixture preventing afterburn and reducing emissions during deceleration. (Operation of deceleration control valve.) In order to adjust the excessively rich fuel air mixture in running in the highland area, the air is supplied to the intake manifold to improve the combustion.

Deceleration Control Valve, Fig. 15

The deceleration control valve consists of an anti-afterburn valve and the coasting valve. The functions are as follows.

1. When the engine speed is over 1200 rpm (1400 rpm in case of automatic transmission), and during deceleration when the accelerator pedal is relieved completely, the deceleration control valve sends the fresh air from the air cleaner to the intake manifold. Operation of coasting valve.
2. Immediately after deceleration and during gear shifting the deceleration control valve sends the fresh air from the air cleaner to the intake manifold. Operation of anti-afterburn valve.
3. Immediately after turning off the ignition switch, the deceleration control valve sends the fresh air from the air cleaner to the intake manifold. Operation of anti-afterburn valve and coasting valve.

The anti-afterburn valve operates by pressure difference between the vacuum chamber and the air chamber and the spring force. The balance hole in the diaphragm connects the vacuum chamber and the air chamber to control the duration of valve opening.

The intake manifold vacuum rises during deceleration and gear shifting, and the pres-

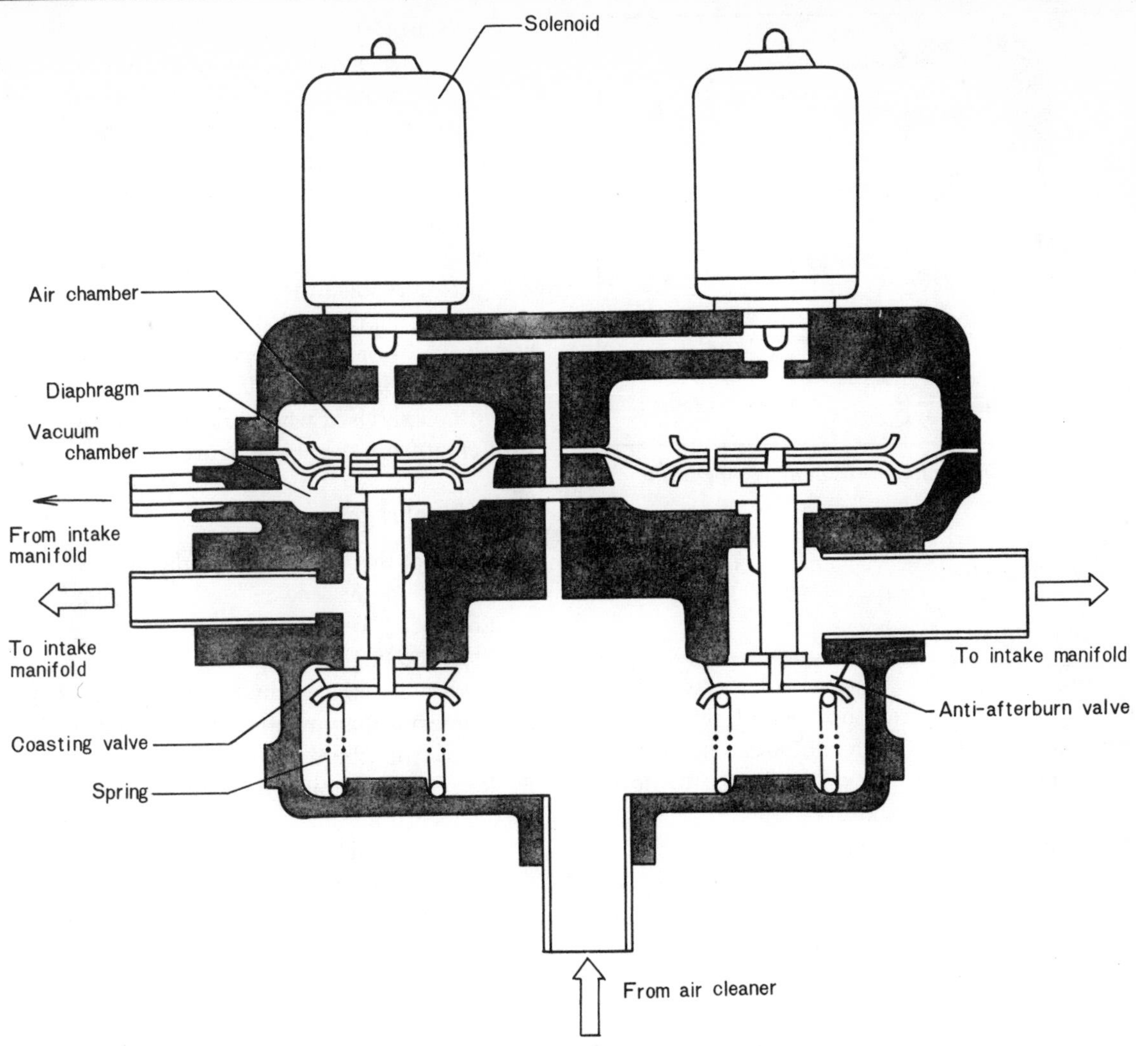

Fig. 15 Crossection of deceleration control valve

sure difference between the two chambers opens the valve connected to the diaphragm, so that fresh air from the air cleaner is led into the intake manifold to correct overrich mixture, thus preventing afterburn. When the balance hole equalizes pressure difference, the valve is closed to shut off air. When the ignition switch is turned on, the solenoid shuts the atmospheric pressure sensing line leading to the air chamber. When the engine is switched off the solenoid opens the sensing lines, and due to the resulting pressure difference between the vacuum chamber and the air chamber, the valve connected to the diaphragm is opened. Fresh air is led from the air cleaner into the intake manifold to prevent afterburn. The coasting valve operates by pressure difference between the vacuum chamber and the air chamber and the spring force. The rise of intake manifold vacuum during deceleration and gear shifting causes the valve to open. Air from the air cleaner is supplied into the intake manifold to prevent afterburn and to keep the thermal reactor operating.

During deceleration when the engine speed is above 1200 rpm (1400 rpm for automatic transmission), the control unit and the idle switch command solenoid to open the atmospheric pressure sensing line leading to the air chamber, and due to resulting pressure difference between the vacuum chamber and the air chamber, the valve connected to the diaphragm is opened. Fresh air is led from the air cleaner into the intake manifold to prevent afterburn. When the ignition switch is turned on, the solenoid shuts the atmospheric pressure sensing line leading to the air chamber. When the engine is switched off the solenoid opens the sensing line, and due to the resulting pressure difference between the vacuum chamber and the air chamber, the valve connected to the diaphragm is opened. Fresh air is led from

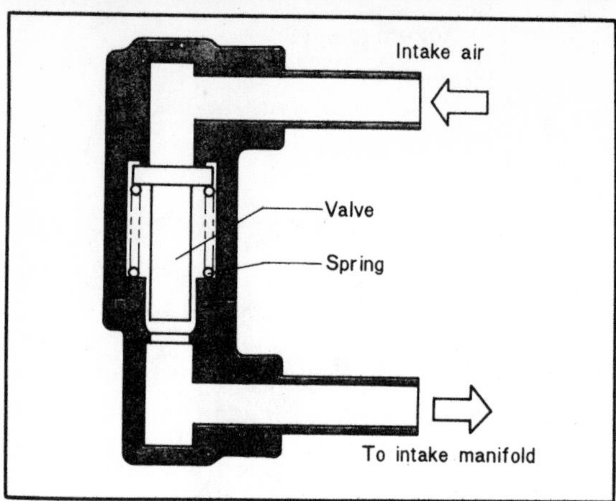

Fig. 16 *Crossection of altitude compensator*

the air cleaner into the intake manifold to prevent afterburn.

Altitude Compensator, Fig. 16

In order to prevent the fuel/air mixture from becoming excessively rich because of the low atmospheric pressure in high altitudes, the altitude compensator sends the air to the intake manifold and adjusts the fuel air mixture.

In high altitudes, especially during idling, part of the inhaled air is controlled by the altitude compensator and enters the intake manifold directly. This enables the overrich mixture to be properly adjusted. The hoses for altitude compensator are blue for identification.

Kickdown Control System (Auto. Trans.)

As well as the normal kickdown operation for the transmission shifting, the kickdown solenoid is energized to cause the kickdown when the choke system is in operating condition (the choke switch is closed) for semiautomatic choke system or when the engine water temperature is cold (the water temperature switch is closed) for full-automatic choke system.

GENERAL SERVICE THROTTLE OPENER SYSTEM

808 Models

Vacuum Control Valve

1. Remove the intake manifold suction hole plug and install a vacuum gauge. The vacuum gauge tube must have 0.12 in. inner diameter and the length of the vacuum gauge tube must be within 6.6 ft.
2. Start the engine.
3. Raise the engine speed to about 3000 rpm, then drop it suddenly.
4. Read the vacuum gauge needle. When the gauge needle, after registering its highest value above 22.0 in. Hg, descends to the vicinity of 22.0 in. Hg, if it comes to a rest for a few seconds (operating depression) and then starts to fall gradually until it indicates the idle vacuum, then the vacuum control valve is normal. Adjust or replace the vacuum control valve (operating depression) if necessary.

NOTE: The operating depression is set under the atmospheric pressure of 29.92 in. Hg, so precaution should be exercised when the atmospheric pressure is different from the above figure.

Servo Diaphragm

1. Connect the tachometer to the engine.
2. Warm up the engine sufficiently, and set the idle speed to 800-850 rpm.
3. Stop the engine.
4. Disconnect the vacuum sensing tube between the servo diaphragm and the vacuum control valve from the servo diaphragm.
5. Remove the intake manifold suction hole plug.
6. Connect the intake manifold and the servo diaphragm with a suitable test tube so that the intake manifold vacuum can be led directly to the servo diaphragm.
7. Remove the vacuum sensing tube between the carburetor and the distributor vacuum control unit.
8. Start the engine and read the engine speed. If the engine speed is 1400 ± 100 rpm, the servo diaphragm is normal. If the engine speed is not 1400 ± 100 rpm, adjust the engine speed to 1400 ± 100 rpm using the throttle opener adjusting screw. If the engine speed remains the usual idle speed (800 rpm) even after the throttle opener has been adjusted, the servo diaphragm is defective.
9. After checking the servo diaphragm, remove the test tube from the intake manifold and servo diaphragm, then connect the disconnected vacuum sensing tube to the servo diaphragm.

Throttle Opener Adjustment

1. Connect a tachometer to the engine.
2. Start the engine and set the idle speed to 800-850 rpm.
3. Stop the engine.
4. Disconnect the vacuum sensing tube between the servo diaphragm and the vacuum control valve from the servo diaphragm.

5. Remove the intake manifold suction hole plug.
6. Attach a suitable test tube between the intake manifold and servo diaphragm to lead the intake manifold vacuum directly to the servo diaphragm.
7. Start the engine and read the engine speed. If the engine speed is above or below 1400 ± 100 rpm, adjust the engine speed to 1400 rpm using the throttle opener adjusting screw. When the engine speed is lower than the specified value, turn the adjusting screw clockwise. When it is higher, turn the adjusting screw counterclockwise.
8. Stop the engine.
9. Perform the operations of steps 4-6 in reverse sequence.
10. Attach a vacuum gauge to the intake manifold.
11. Start the engine.
12. Raise the engine speed to about 3000 rpm and drop it suddenly.
13. Operate the vacuum control valve adjusting screw so that while the engine speed descends from 3000 rpm to 1000 rpm, the vacuum gauge needle will indicate a value of 22.0 in. Hg and the gauge needle remains stationary for a few seconds.

Accelerator Switch Adjustment

808 Models with Auto. Trans.

1. Loosen the lock nut and adjusting screw of the accelerator switch.
2. Fully depress the accelerator pedal and gradually tighten the adjusting screw until the accelerator switch clicks. Then further tighten it by 2½ turns.
3. Tighten the lock nut.

Thermosensor

808 Models with Auto. Trans.

To inspect the thermosensor, connect a test light to the thermosensor, and place it in water with a thermometer and gradually heat the water. Check the water temperature when the light starts to go on. If the light does not go on at the temperature of 122-140° F, replace the thermosensor.

POSITIVE CRANKCASE VENTILATION SYSTEM

Checking Ventilation Valve Rotary Engine Models Only

1. Check to see that the air cleaner element is not clogged.
2. Install a vacuum gauge.
3. Start the engine. When the engine speed is raised to 2500-3000 rpm, the vacuum reading must be under 60 mm-Hg.

EVAPORATIVE EMISSION SYSTEM

Checking evaporative line

1. Disconnect the evaporative hose from the T joint which is connected to the ventilation hose on rotary engine models, and from the canister which is connected to the check valve on 808 models.
2. Connect the disconnected hose to the U-type manometer.
3. Apply compressed air gradually into the manometer and the difference of water level should be 14.0 inches. After that, blind the inlet of the manometer.
4. Leave the manometer for five minutes, with the inlet blind. Then, if the difference of water level is over 13.5 inches, the evaporative line will be in good condition. If the difference is not within the specifications, inspect the following parts. If there is any defect, repair or replace as necessary.
   Leaky or loose hoses.
   Leaky condense tank.
   Leaky fuel tank.
   Leaky or loose fuel line.
   Leaky filler cap.
   Leaky fuel gauge unit.

Charcoal Canister

Rotary Engine Models

1. Check to see that the air cleaner element is not clogged.
2. Visually check the adhering condition of oil. When the whole surface is damp with oil, measure the ventilation resistance.
3. Attach a vacuum gauge. Check to see that when the engine speed is raised to 2500-3000 rpm, the vacuum gauge reads under 60 mm-Hg.

NOTE: The charcoal canister and air cleaner cover should be replaced as an assembly only.

Check Valve

1. Remove the check valve.
2. Cover one end of the check valve by hand, and install the pressure gauge to the other end.
3. Breathe in and out of the check valve with pressure of about 7.1 lb/in². If the valve op-

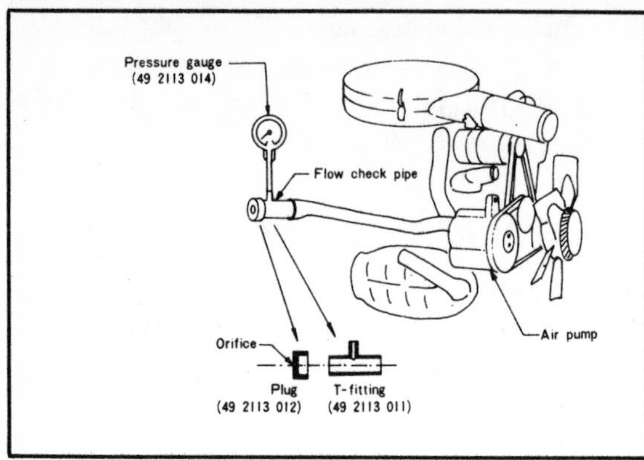

Fig. 17 Checking air pump

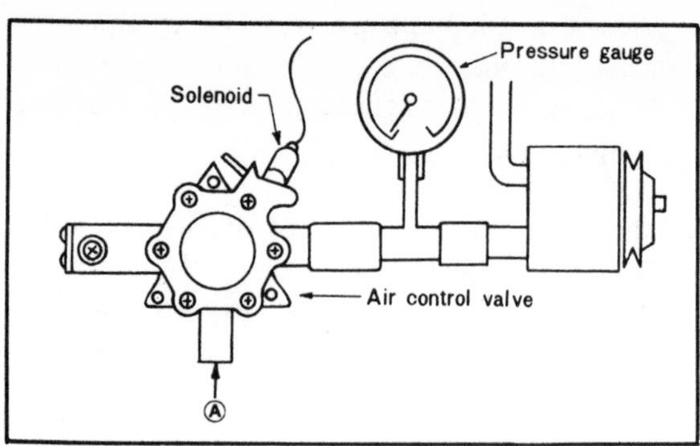

Fig. 18 Checking air control valve

erates it is satisfactory. If not, replace it with a new one.

AIR INJECTION SYSTEM

Rotary Engine Models

Air Pump

1. Check to see that the air pump V belt tension is proper.
2. Check to see that air hoses are free of air leaks.
3. Attach the air pump gauge set, Fig. 17.
4. Run the engine at idle speed (manual transmission—900 rpm, automatic transmission—750 rpm in D range). If the pressure gauge reading is more than 0.68 lb/in² for manual transmission or 0.48 lb/in² for automatic transmission, the air pump is normal.

Check Valve

1. Disconnect the air hose (air pump-air control valve) from the air control valve.
2. Run the engine at idle speed.
3. Hold a finger over the inlet of the air control valve (the inlet from which the air hose is removed). If exhaust gas flow is felt, replace the check valve, spring and gasket.

Thermal Reactor

1. Check to see that the thermal reactor is not damaged or cracked.
2. Remove the air hose leading to the air control valve and check to see that the non-return valve works smoothly.
3. Start the engine and keep it running at idle speed.
4. Make sure that most exhaust gas is not released from the tail of cooling air pipe.

Air Control Valve

1. Check the air pump according to the procedures described previously.
2. Attach the connector of the solenoid terminal to the battery and check the operation of the solenoid. If the clicking sound is audible, the solenoid is normal.
3. Attach the pressure gauge as shown in Fig. 18.
4. Remove the air hose from outlet [A] of the air control valve.
5. Start the engine and keep it running at idle speed (900 rpm for manual transmission, 750 rpm in D range for automatic transmission). Check to see that there is no air leak from outlet [A] of the air control valve.

Manual transmission

Make sure that the pressure gauge reads 1.2-2.8 lb/in² when the engine speed is 3500 rpm and that there is air leak from outlet [A].

Automatic transmission

Make sure that the pressure gauge reads 1.2-2.6 lb/in² when the engine speed is 3000 rpm and that there is air leak from outlet [A].

6. Connect the solenoid terminal to the battery. Make sure that the pressure gauge reads 0-0.75 lb/in² and that air flows from outlet [A] of the air control valve.
7. Simple checking of air control valve (check every valve incorporated). When the No. 1 relief valve, No. 2 relief valve or the air cut valve is faulty, the air sent from the air pump during idling flows into the air cooling pipe.

Thermosensor

1. Make sure that there is no boot breakage.
2. Connect the ohmmeter as shown in Fig. 19,

and check the resistance. The readings as shown below indicate that the thermosensor is normal.

Over 7 kilo-ohms before warmup. (When ambient and water temperatures are under 30° C (86° F).

Under 2.3 kilo-ohms after warmup. (When temperature is over 70° C (156° F).

Thermodetector

Connect the ohmmeter to the terminals of the thermodetector and check the resistance. If the ohmmeter readings are within the range shown in Fig. 20, the thermodetector is normal.

Control Unit

1. Make sure that the fuse of the control unit is in good condition.
2. Disconnect the couplers of the thermosensor and idle switch. Check the following points.

   Connect a timing light to the high tension cord of the trailing side distributor. Check to see that the timing light does not go on when the engine speed is under 3600-4400 rpm (automatic transmission: 4320-5280 rpm), and goes on when the engine speed is raised to more than 3600-4400 rpm (automatic transmission: 4320-5280 rpm).

   Connect an ammeter to the air control valve solenoid. Check to see that the current does not flow to the solenoid when the engine speed is under 3600-4400 rpm (automatic transmission: 4320-5280 rpm), and there is flow to the solenoid when the engine speed is above 3600-4400 rpm (automatic transmission: 4320-5280 rpm).
3. With the thermosensor connector terminal short-circuited, check the following points.

   Connect the timing light to the high tension cord of the trailing side distributor and check to see that the timing light goes on in the whole range of revolution including under 3600-4400 rpm (automatic transmission: 4320-5280 rpm).

   Only automatic transmission:

   Connect an ammeter to the air control valve solenoid. Check to see that the current does not flow to the solenoid when the engine speed is under 3060-3740 rpm, and there is flow to the solenoid when the engine speed is above 3060-3740 rpm.
4. Connect the thermosensor coupler as before. With the idle switch coupler removed, check the following points.

   Connect an ammeter to the coasting valve solenoid and check to see that there is current flow to the ammeter when idling.

   Disconnect the hose (air cleaner-deceleration control valve) from the deceleration control valve and plug the air suction port of the deceleration control valve.

   When the engine speed is gradually lowered from 2000-3000 rpm, the current begins to flow at 1100-1450 rpm (automatic transmission: 1250-1650 rpm).
5. Connect the idle switch coupler as before.
6. Connect the hose to the deceleration control valve.

Deceleration Control Valve

1. Disconnect the hose (air cleaner-deceleration control valve) from the air cleaner.
2. Run the engine at idle speed.
3. Make sure that air is not sucked in through the air suction hose of the deceleration control valve.
4. Stop the engine.
5. Disconnect the hose (coasting valve-intake manifold) from the deceleration control valve and plug the air suction port of the deceleration control valve (coasting valve).

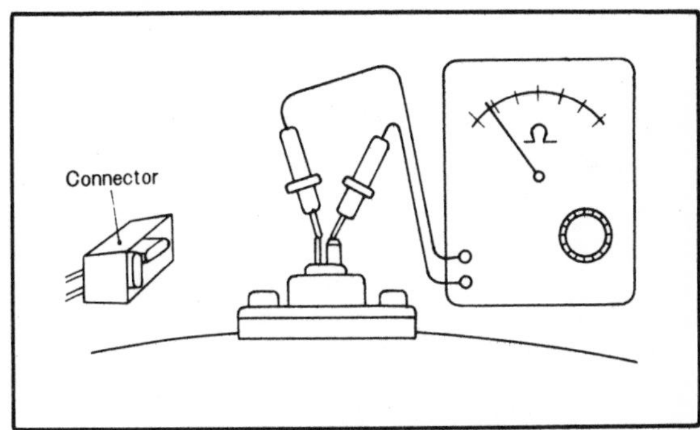

Fig. 19 Checking thermosensor

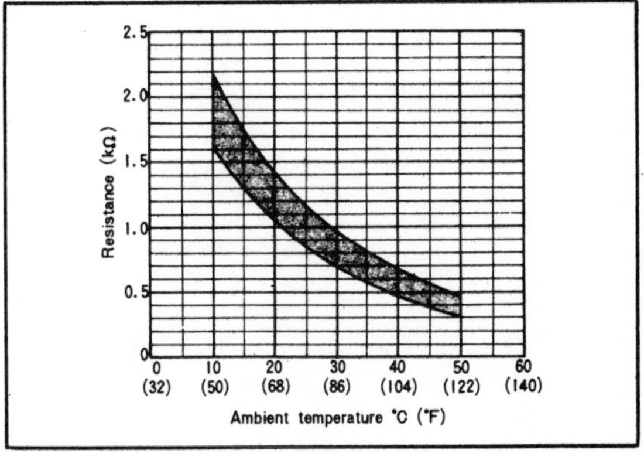

Fig. 20 Checking resistance of thermodetector

6. Run the engine at idle speed.
7. Disconnect the solenoid terminal for the anti-afterburn valve at the quick disconnect.
8. Hold your hand over the opening of the air suction hose for the deceleration control valve. If vacuum is felt, the deceleration control valve (anti-afterburn valve) is normal.
9. Stop the engine.
10. Connect the solenoid terminal at the quick disconnect.
11. Connect the hose to the deceleration control valve (coasting valve).
12. Disconnect the hose (anti-afterburn valve-intake manifold) from the deceleration control valve and plug the air suction port of the deceleration control valve (anti-afterburn valve).
13. Run the engine at idle speed.
14. Disconnect the solenoid terminal for the coasting valve at the quick disconnect.
15. Hold your hand over the opening of the air suction hose for the deceleration control valve. If vacuum is felt, the deceleration control valve (coasting valve) is normal.
16. Stop the engine.
17. Connect the solenoid terminal at the quick disconnect.
18. Connect the hoses to the air cleaner and deceleration control valve (anti-afterburn valve).

Altitude Compensator

1. Disconnect the air inlet hose from the altitude compensator.
2. Run the engine at idle speed.
3. Hold a finger over the inlet of the altitude compensator (the inlet from which the air inlet hose is removed). At this moment, a decrease in the number of engine revolutions indicates the altitude compensator is in good condition. When the inspection is carried out in areas of high elevation there will be a further decrease in the number of engine revolutions.

MERCEDES

GENERAL ENGINE SPECIFICATIONS

Model or Engine	Bore & Stroke, Inches (mm)	Piston Displacement Cubic Inches	Compression Ratio	Maximum Brake HP @ rpm	Maximum Torque Ft. Lbs. @ rpm	Normal Oil Pressure Pounds
1974						
240D	3.58 x 3.64 (90.9 x 92.5)	146.7	21.0	62 @ 4000	97 @ 2400	28–85
230	3.69 x 3.29 (93.7 x 83.9)	140.8	8.0	95 @ 4800	128 @ 2500	28–85
280 280C	3.39 x 3.10 (86.0 x 78.8)	167.6	8.0	130 @ 5000①	150 @ ②3500	28–85
450	3.62 x 3.35 (92.0 x 85.0)	275.8	8.0	190 @ 4750③	240 @ 3000④	28–85
1975						
240D	3.58 x 3.64 (90.9 x 92.5)	146.7	21.0	62 @ 4000	97 @ 2400	28–85
300D	3.58 x 3.64 (90.9 x 92.5)	183.4	21.0	77 @ 4000	115 @ 2400	28–85
230	3.69 x 3.29 (93.7 x 83.9)	140.8	8.0	93 @ 4800①	125 @ 2500②	28–85
280 280C 280S	3.39 x 3.10 (86.0 x 78.8)	167.6	8.0	120 @ 4800	143 @ 2800	28–85
450 SE, SEL, SLC	3.62 x 3.35 (92.0 x 85.0)	275.8	8.0	180 @ 4750	220 @ 3000	28–85

①—California 123 @ 5000.
②—California 143 @ 3600.
③—California 180 @ 4750.
④—California 232 @ 3000.

TUNEUP SPECIFICATIONS

Car Model or Engine	Spark Plugs		Distributor		Firing Order	Ignition Timing		Hot Idle Speed rpm
	Type	Gap, Inch	Point Gap, Inch	Dwell Angle Degrees		Degrees BTDC	Mark Location	
1974								
240D	—	—	—	—	1-3-4-2	24①	—	—
230	Bosch W175T30	.024	—	46–48	1-3-4-2	10	Pulley	750–800 Std & Auto
280	Bosch W175T30	.024	—	33–35	1-3-4-2	4	Pulley	750–950 Auto
450	Bosch W175T30	.024	—	29–31	15486372	5	Pulley	700–800 Auto

①—California 85 @ 4500.
②—California 122 @ 2500.
①—California 85 @ 4500.
②—California 122 @ 2500.

DISTRIBUTOR SPECIFICATIONS

Model or Engine	Distributor Part No.	Point Gap, Inch	Dwell Angle Deg.	Spring Tension, Oz.	Centrifugal Advance			Vacuum Advance		
					Start @ rpm	Int.	Full @ rpm	Inches of Vacuum to start Plunger	Int.	Full Advance Dist. Deg. @ Vacuum
1974										
230	0-231-170-137	—	46–48	—	15–20 @ 1500	27–32 @ 3000	42–48 @ 4500	—	—	—
280	0-231-310-002	—	33–35	—	13–17 @ 1500	31–35 @ 3000	37–41 @ 4500	—	—	—
450	0-231-403-006 0-231-403-007	— —	29–31	—	11–15 @ 1500	18–22 @ 3000	—	—	—	—

Emission Controls

1974 MODELS

EVAPORATIVE EMISSION CONTROL

The fuel evaporation control system which serves to prevent fuel vapors from escaping from the fuel system into the atmosphere remains unchanged in its well known arrangement.

Vacuum Switch-over Valves

230, 280 & 280C

In order to distinguish between the function of the individual valves, the filter caps have been colorcoded according to valve function, Fig. 1.

White cap = Valve for retarded ignition
Grey cap = Valve for throttle valve lift
Brown cap = Valve for EGR

NOTE: The vacuum ports on these valves must not be interchanged when installing the valves. The vacuum source line must always be connected to the center port of the switch-over valve.

It does not matter whether the port used is on the bottom or top of the valve.

Ignition Change-over

280, 280C

The vacuum retard unit is controlled by switch-over valve, Fig. 2. The switch-over valve is electrically controlled over two relays by the 17° C (62° F) temperature switch in the oil filter housing, the 100° C (212° F) temperature switch in the sensor box on the cylinder head, Fig. 3, the rpm relay, the oil pressure switch on the transmission and the vacuum switch.

The ignition timing will be retarded with the engine at operating temperature (over 17° C/62° F oil temperature and below 100° C/212° F cooling water temperature) and up to engine speed of 3400 rpm, and with A/C switched off. Both temperature switches and the rpm-switch are open, breaking the electrical contact to the switch-over valve. The vacuum retard unit of the distributor is connected to the intake manifold vacuum.

Retarded ignition will be cancelled if any of the following conditions are met. The switch-over valve will open the vacuum-retard unit on the distributor to the atmosphere and will cancel retarded ignition.

If ignition retard is cancelled, the ignition timing is advanced by 9–13 degrees.

1. Below 17° C (62° F) oil temperature. The temperature switch is closed, making contact over relay boxes to the switch-over valve, Fig. 4.
2. Above 100° C (212° F) cooling water temperature. The temperature switch is closed, Fig. 3.

The switch-over valve receives electrical cur-

Part No.	Color	De-energized (Dead)	Energized (Live)	Operation
001 540 04 97 001 540 07 97	white grey	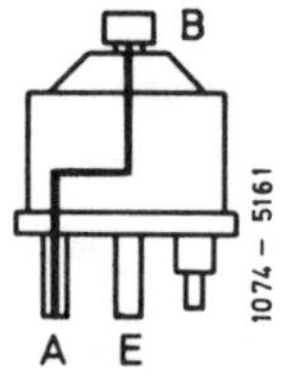 B; A E; 1074 - 5161	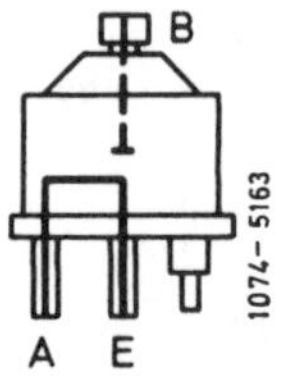 B; A E; 1074 - 5163	De-energized = Vacuum supply port E is connected to port A. Port B. is closed to atmosphere. Energized = Port A is open to port B (atmosphere). Vacuum supply port E is closed.
001 540 11 97	brown	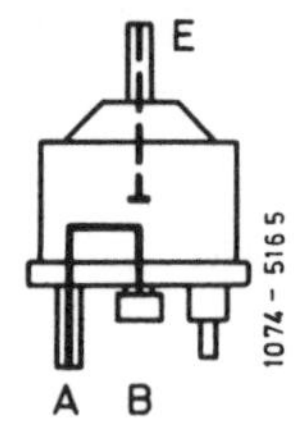 E; A B; 1074 - 5165	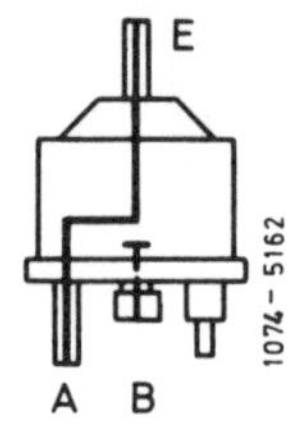 E; A B; 1074 - 5162	De-energized = Port A is connected to port B (atmosphere). Vacuum supply port E is closed. Energized = Vacuum supply port E is connected to port A. Port B (atmosphere) is closed.

A = Port connected to vacuum unit
B = Port connected to atmosphere
E = Port connected to vacuum source

Fig. 1 Vacuum switchover valve identification. 230 & 280 models

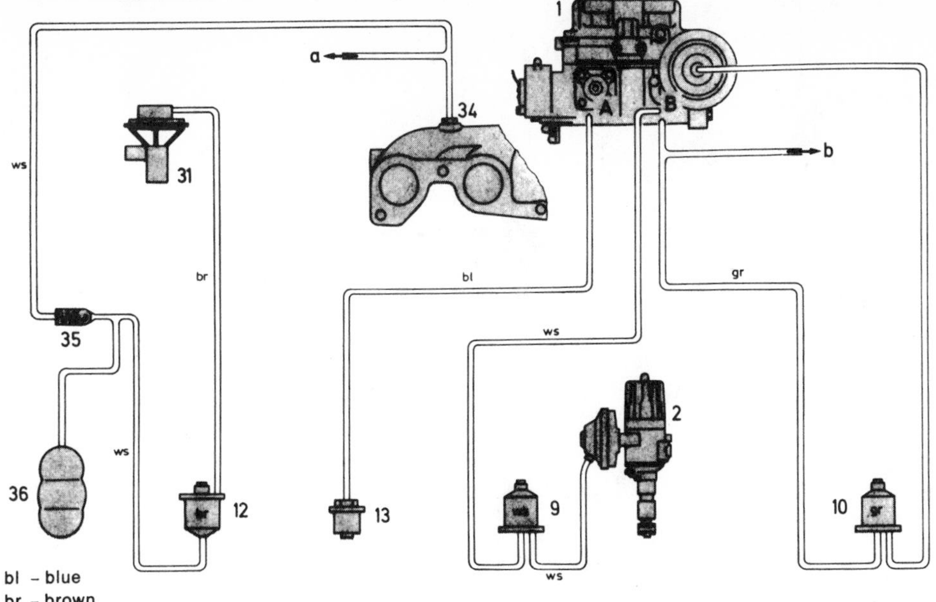

9 Switch-over valve, ignition
10 Switch-over valve, throttle valve lift
12 Switch-over valve, EGR
13 Vacuum switch
31 EGR valve
34 Vacuum connection at intake manifold
35 Check valve
36 Vacuum tank
a Vacuum connection, air conditioner
b Vacuum connection, fuel return valve
A Connection, vacuum switch
B Connection, ignition change-over
C Connection, throttle valve lift and fuel return valve

bl - blue
br - brown
gr - grey
ws - white

Fig. 2 Vacuum schematic of ignition changeover. 280 *models*

rent over relay boxes.

3. With engine speed above 3400 rpm, oil temperature above 17° C (62° F) and cooling water temperature below 100° C (212° F).

   Both temperature switches are open. Rpm switch 3000/3400 rpm in relay is closed making positive contact over the relay box to the switch-over valve.

4. When transmission shifts into fourth gear.

   The oil pressure switch on the automatic transmission is closed making contact over the relay box to the switch-over valve.

5. For rpm stabilization with air conditioner compressor operating.

   The power supply for the electrical clutch on the A/C compressor will also connect the switch-over valve to power. The switch-over valve opens the vacuum retard unit on the distributor to the atmosphere.

6. With the engine under load and the intake

Fig. 3 Temperature switch. 280 *models*

1 Pick up, telethermometer
8 100° C (212° F) temperature switch
32 65° C (149° F) temperature switch

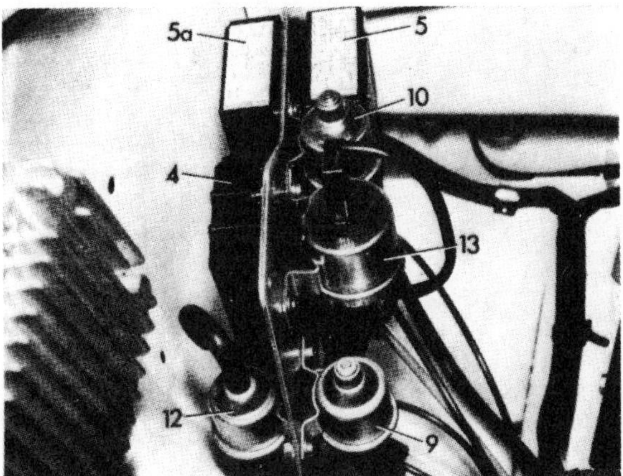

Fig. 4 RPM switch, vacuum switch, switchover valves and relay boxes. 280 *models*

4 RPM-relay with two rpm-switches 1800/2000 rpm and 3000/3400 rpm
5 Relay box (001 542 14 19) 8-prong plug
5a Relay box (001 542 12 19) 12-prong plug
9 Switch-over valve, ignition
10 Switch-over valve, throttle valve lift
12 Switch-over valve, exhaust gas recirculation
13 Vacuum switch

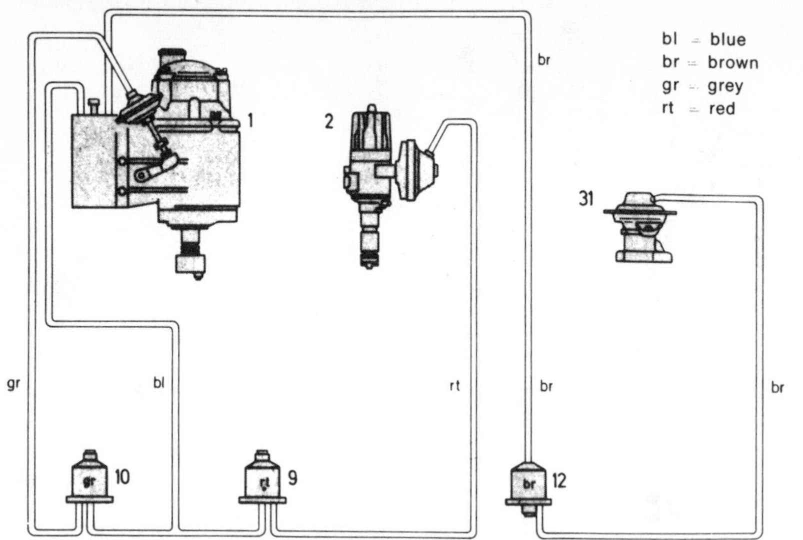

Fig. 5 Vacuum schematic of ignition changeover. 230 models

manifold vacuum less than 6 in. Hg.

The vacuum switch, Fig. 4, is open, making contact to the switch-over valve over relay boxes.

Throttle Valve Lift

With the engine at operating temperature (over 17° C/62° F oil temperature and below 100° C/ 212° F cooling water temperature) and with the engine speed above 2000 rpm, the throttle valve lift is in effect during deceleration.

Both temperature switches are open. The rpm switch, 1800/2000 rpm in relay is closed, energizing the switch-over valve over the relay box and opening the vacuum governor on the carburetor to the atmosphere. The compression spring on the vacuum governor pushes the adjusting screw against the throttle valve lever preventing the throttle from returning to the idle speed position.

Throttle valve lift is cancelled during deceleration if any of the following conditions are met. The electrical connection to the switch-over valve is interrupted and the intake manifold vacuum is connected to the vacuum governor. The throttle valve will return to its idle position.

1. Oil temperature is below 17° C (62° F).

   The 17° C (62° F) temperature switch is closed.
2. Above 100° C (212° F) cooling water temperature.

   The 100° C (212° F) temperature switch is closed.
3. Engine speed is below 1800 rpm.

   The rpm-switch 1800/2000 rpm in rpm-relay is open.

230

With the engine at normal operating tempera-

Fig. 6 Temperature switch. 230 models

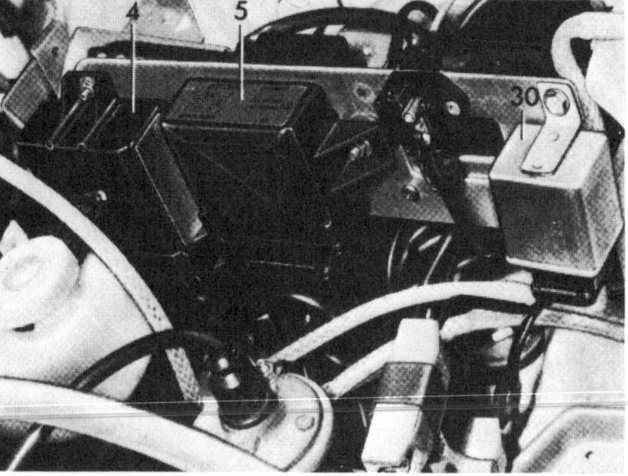

Fig. 7 RPM relay (4), relay box (5) and delay relay (30). 230 models

ture, the ignition timing is controlled up to 2000 rpm engine speed solely by the centrifugal advance mechanism.

The vacuum advance unit on the ignition distributor is controlled by a switch-over valve, Fig. 5.

1. At oil temperature below 25° C (77° F).

   The 25° C (77° F) temperature switch is closed. The 1800/2000 rpm switch in relay is open. The switch-over valve is de-energized. Vacuum advance is effective.
2. Oil temperatures are above 25° C (77° F) and engine speeds above approximately 2000 rpm.

The 25° C (77° F) temperature switch (Fig. 6), is open. The rpm switch is closed. The switch-over valve is de-energized. Vacuum advance is effective.

Under certain conditions during deceleration, the throttle valve is held slightly open by the vacuum governor on the carburetor.

The vacuum governor on the carburetor is controlled by the 25° C (77° F) temperature switch, the switch-over valve, Fig. 5, and the rpm relay Fig. 7.

Throttle valve lift takes place during deceleration at oil temperatures above 25° C (77° F) with temperature switch open. The 1800/2000 rpm switch in relay is closed. The switch-over valve is energized and interrupts the connection between the intake manifold and the vacuum governor which is then connected to the atmosphere.

The compression spring on the vacuum governor pushes the adjusting screw against the throttle valve lever preventing the throttle from returning to the idle speed position.

Throttle lift does not take place during deceleration:

1. The oil temperature is below 25° C (77° F).
2. The 25° C (77° F) temperature switch is closed.

At oil temperatures above 25° C (77° F) and engine speeds below 1800 rpm.

The 1800/2000 rpm switch in relay is open.

If any of the above conditions are met, the switch-over valve is de-energized and the vacuum connection from the intake manifold to the vacuum governor is restored. The throttle valve will then return to its idle position.

450 SE, SEL, SL & SLC

The ignition will be retarded at idle and during deceleration, and with coolant temperatures below 100° C (212° F) and air conditioning switched off (vacuum retard effective on distributor), Fig. 8.

A switch-over valve is incorporated in the vacuum line between the intake manifold and the distributor vacuum cell.

With the switch-over valve not activated, the vacuum arrives at the diaphragm of the vacuum cell at the distributor from the throttle valve via the switch-over valve.

Ignition retard is cancelled.

1. Coolant temperatures are above 100° C (212° F).

   The 100° C (212° F) temperature switch in the thermostat housing is closed and activates the switch-over valve via relay. The valve switches and the diaphragm of the vacuum retard unit is connected to atmosphere.

   The ignition timing will be advanced approximately 12° by the spring in the vacuum retard unit.
2. When switching on the air conditioning, the switch-over valve is also activated. Ignition retard is cancelled.

EXHAUST GAS RECIRCULATION

By means of the EGR valve, a portion of the exhaust gas is recirculated from the exhaust manifold into the intake manifold.

The EGR valve is controlled by the venturi vacuum and is dependent on the throttle valve position, the oil temperature and engine rpm.

Operation

280 & 280C

With the engine at operating temperature (over 17° C/62° F oil temperature, over 65° C/149° F cooling water temperature, below 100° C/212° F cooling water temperature) the intake manifold vacuum less than 6 in. Hg and an engine speed up to 3400 rpm, exhaust gas is recirculated into the intake manifold.

The 17° C (62° F) temperature switch, the 100° C (212° F) temperature switch and the vacuum switch are open, the 65° C (149° F) temis energized, opening the vacuum connection from the vacuum tank under the right fender to the EGR valve. The EGR valve opens.

Exhaust gas recirculation is cancelled if any of the following conditions are met. The electrical connection to the switch-over valve is interrupted and the vacuum unit of the EGR valve is open to atmosphere.

1. The oil temperature is below 17° C (62° F). The 17° C (62° F) temperature switch is closed.
2. The cooling water temperature is below 65° C (149° F).

The 65° C (149° F) temperature switch is open.

3. Intake manifold vacuum is more than 6 in. Hg.
   The vacuum switch is closed.
4. Engine speed is above 3400 rpm.
   The rpm-switch 3000/3400 in rpm relay is closed.

230

EGR takes place above 25° C (77° F) oil temperature up to an engine speed of 3600 rpm. The 25° C (77° F) temperature switch, Fig. 5, is open. The 3400/3600 rpm switch in relay is closed. The switch-over valve, Fig. 6 is energized and venturi vacuum from the carburetor reaches the EGR valve, Fig. 5, via the switch-over valve.

At sufficient vacuum, the EGR valve will begin to open.

There is no EGR.

1. Oil temperature is below 25° C (77° F).
   The 25° C (77° F) temperature switch is closed.
2. Engine speed is above 3600 rpm.

The 3400/3600 rpm switch in relay is open.

The switch-over valve, Fig. 12, is de-energized by the relay box, Fig. 7. The vacuum connection to the EGR valve is interrupted.

AIR INJECTION SYSTEM

This system is used on 280 and 450 California models. It consists of an anti-backfire valve on 280 models, diverter valve, diverter control valve on 450 models, check valve, air injection nozzles and thermal reactors, Fig. 9, on 280 models, which are used in place of exhaust manifolds.

280 Operation, Fig. 10

Air is injected into the exhaust ports up to an engine speed of 3450 rpm. The oxygen in the air is mixed with the exhaust gas and allows afterburning in the reactor.

At engine speeds above 3450 rpm and during the transition to deceleration, the air is diverted from the exhaust ports to the air filter.

The direction of air flow is controlled by the anti-backfire valve.

The anti-backfire valve has the function to control the air injection to the reactors or the air discharge to the air filter.

In addition, the anti-backfire valve has to prevent backfiring during the transition to deceleration and when the engine is turned off.

The control of the valve establishes four different operating modes.

1. Air injection under operating conditions up to an engine speed of 3450 rpm.
   The lower diaphragm chamber of the anti-backfire valve is connected with a white vacuum line directly to the carburetor. The vacuum connection on the carburetor is located below the throttle valve. When the engine is operating, the air in the lower diaphragm chamber is evacuated. At the same time, the air in the upper diaphragm chamber is drawn out through the compensating orifice if the switch-over valve has closed the vent line. The compression spring lifts the valve stem and the port for the air injection.
2. Air discharge during transition to decelerating below 3450 rpm.

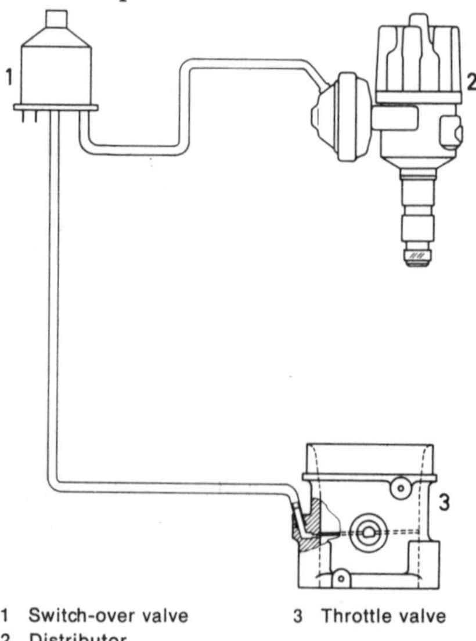

1 Switch-over valve
2 Distributor
3 Throttle valve

Fig. 8 Vacuum schematic of ignition changeover. 450 models

Due to the high vacuum when decelerating, the balance of both diaphragm chambers is disturbed. A high vacuum is drawn on the lower diaphragm chamber and the balance between the upper and lower chamber can only be restored slowly through the compensating orifice. The diaphragm is pulled downwards, closing the port for the air injection. The air from the pump is discharged through the port to the air filter. Thereby, backfiring in the reactor is avoided.

3. Air discharge under operating conditions above 3450 rpm.
   At engine speeds above 3450 rpm, the rpm switch in the relay box breaks the electrical contact to the switch-over valve. The switch-over valve connects the upper diaphragm chamber to the atmosphere. The atmospheric pressure overpowers the spring, closing the

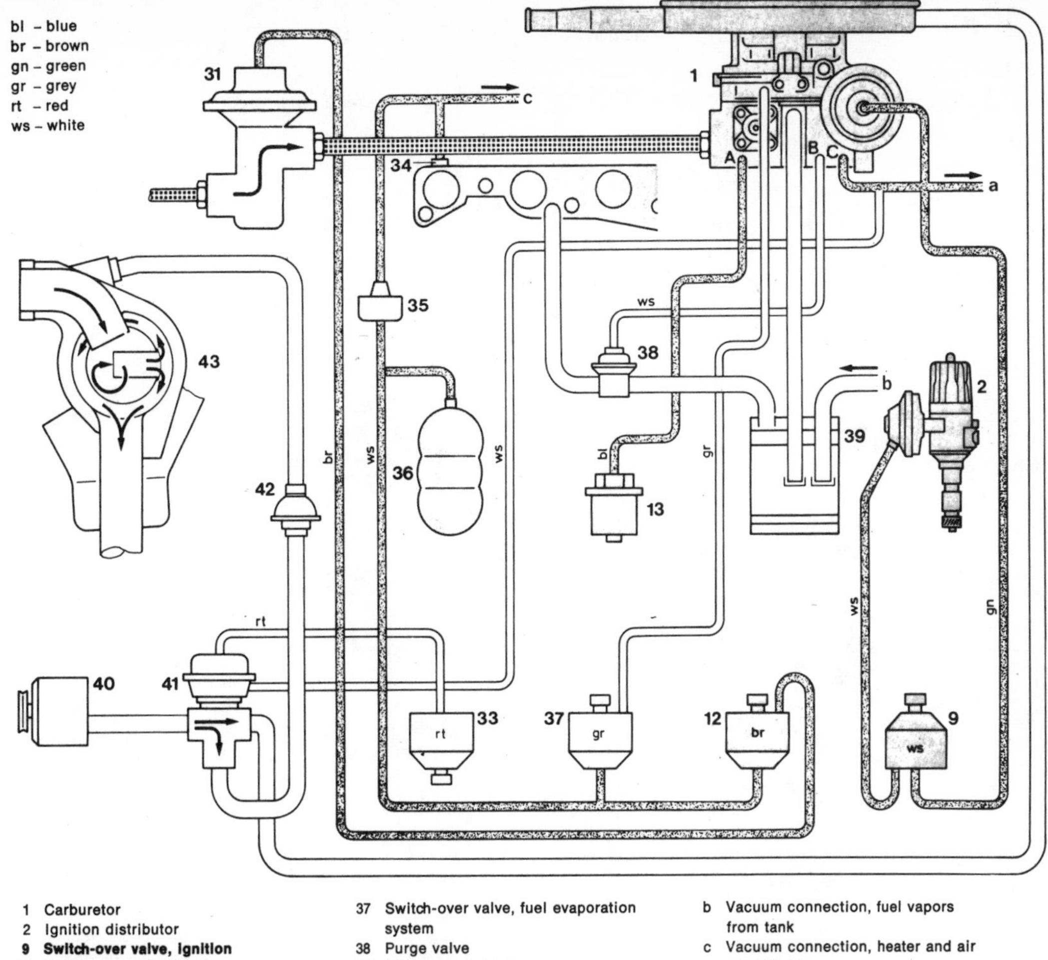

1 Carburetor
2 Ignition distributor
9 Switch-over valve, ignition
12 Switch-over valve, EGR
13 Vacuum switch
31 Exhaust gas recirculation valve
33 Switch-over valve, air injection
34 Vacuum connection, intake manifold
35 Check valve
36 Vacuum tank in right fender
37 Switch-over valve, fuel evaporation system
38 Purge valve
39 Charcoal canister
40 Air pump
41 Anti-backfire valve
42 Check valve
43 Reactor
a Vacuum connection, fuel return valve
b Vacuum connection, fuel vapors from tank
c Vacuum connection, heater and air conditioner
A Connection, vacuum switch
B Connection, evaporation control valve
C Connection, fuel return valve, anti-backfire valve, ignition change-over, and vacuum governor

Fig. 10 *AIR, EGR, ignition changeover and evaporative emission control systems,* 280 *models*

port for the air injection and opening the port to discharge the air into the air filter.

4. Air discharge while engine comes to a stop

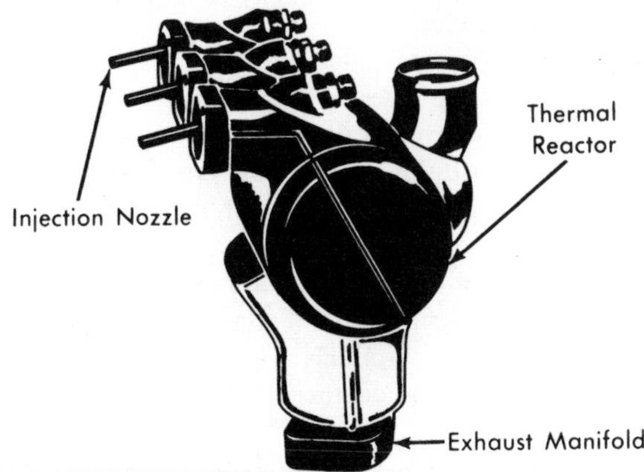

Fig. 9 *Thermal reactor,* 280 *models*

when ignition is turned off.

When the ignition is turned off, the switch-over valve is de-energized and the upper diaphragm chamber is connected to atmosphere. The atmospheric pressure closes the port for the air injection and opens discharge port.

450, Fig. 11

The air supplied by the air pump is routed to the diverter valve and from there either via a check valve to the cylinder heads or is discharged via a muffler. Air injection and/or discharge is controlled by a diverter control valve which is directly connected to manifold vacuum and will pass vacuum during coasting on to the diverter valve at a vacuum of more than 15.75 in.Hg so that the air can be discharged via the muffler.

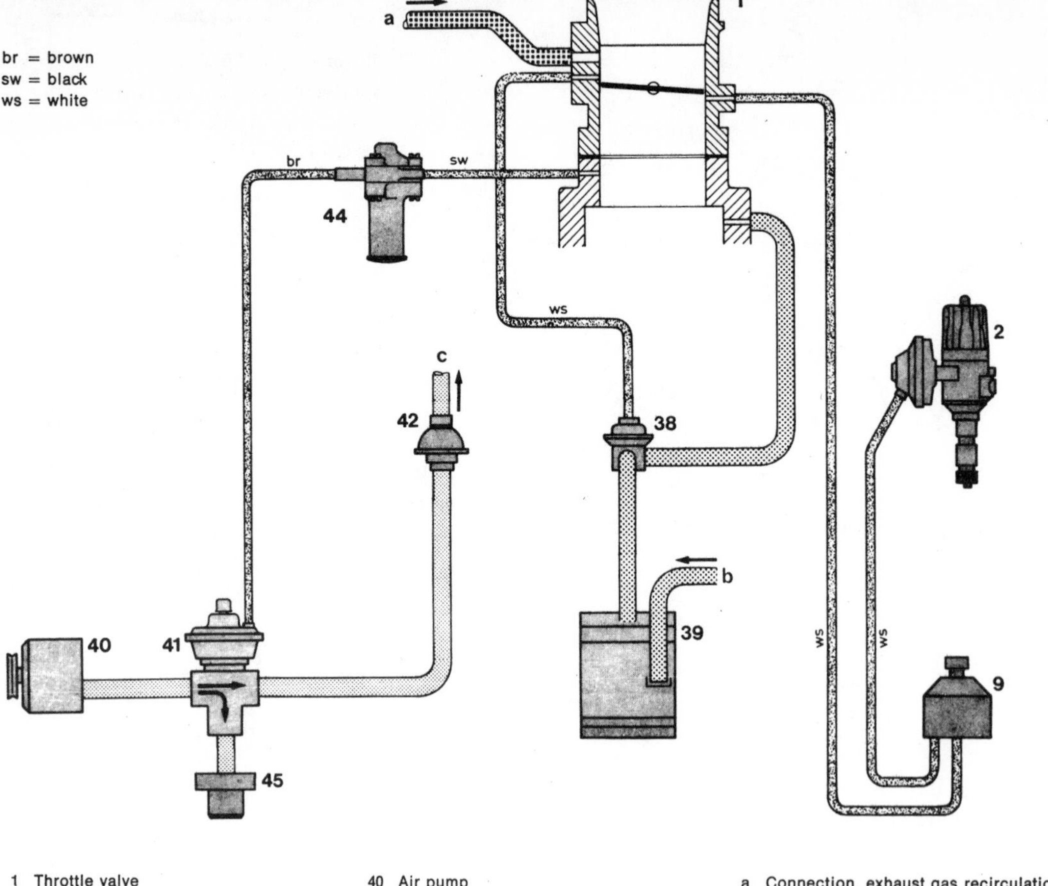

1 Throttle valve
2 Ignition distributor
9 Switch-over valve, ignition
38 Purge valve
39 Charcoal canister
40 Air pump
41 Diverter valve
42 Check valve
44 Diverter control valve
45 Muffler
a Connection, exhaust gas recirculation (EGR)
b Connection, fuel vapors from tank
c Connection, air injection line to cylinder head

Fig. 11 *Air injector reactor system.* 450 *California models*

The diverter control valve is connected directly to the intake manifold. The chamber above the diaphragm is being evacuated by manifold vacuum. At a vacuum of more than 15.75 in. Hg the diaphragm will be pulled upwards against the fixed force of the spring and by atmospheric pressure. This will open the passage indicated by the arrows and will pass vacuum to the diverter valve.

General Service

230, Fig. 12

With the following tests ignition change-over, EGR, and throttle valve lift are checked.

The following functional tests should be performed in the sequence listed and with the engine at operating temperature.

Run engine to operating temperature at idle.

Test No. 1

Disconnect the plug of line to the 25° C (77° F) temperature switch (14) in the oil filter housing and connect to ground.

Result

Engine rpm should increase (ignition vacuum advance is effective).

If engine rpm does not increase.

1. Check vacuum lines for condition and correct connection.

   The blue vacuum line from the carburetor should be connected to the center port of the red switch-over valve. The red vacuum line to the distributor should be connected to the outer port of the switch-over valve.
2. Check switch-over valve.

   Disconnect the plug from relay box, Fig. 7. Turn the ignition on. Connect terminals 8 and 1, as well as terminals 4 and 3. The red switch-over valve should then click audibly. This can also be felt.

   If tests 1 and 2 reveal no problem, replace the relay box.

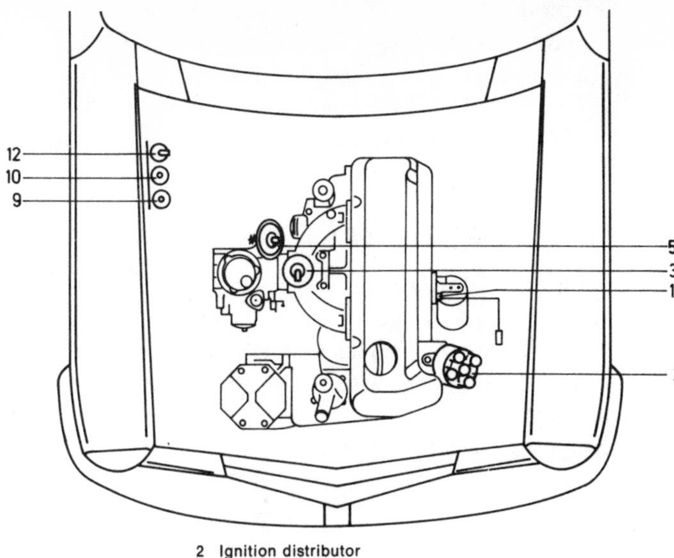

2 Ignition distributor
9 Switch-over valve, ignition
10 Switch-over valve, throttle valve lift
12 Switch-over valve, EGR
14 25° C (77° F) temperature switch
31 EGR valve
51 Vacuum governor

Fig. 12 *Component location,* 230 *models*

Test No. 2

Increase engine speed to approximately 2500 rpm and then remove the red vacuum line at the distributor.

Result

Engine rpm should drop slightly (ignition vacuum advance is cancelled).

If engine speed does not decrease:

Check rpm switch 1800/2000 rpm in rpm relay, Fig. 7.

> **CAUTION:** When testing electronic rpm switches, use only voltmeter. Use of a test light may damage rpm switches.
>
> Remove the plug from the red switch-over valve. Connect the test cable to the valve and reconnect plug.
>
> Connect the voltmeter to the test cable.
>
> When increasing engine speed, the voltmeter should read 13 volts up to approximately 2000 rpm. The reading should drop to zero volts above 2000 rpm. When decreasing engine speed, voltmeter should read approximately 13 volts when speed drops below approximately 1800 rpm.
>
> **NOTE:** Less than 11 volts with voltage on indicates excessive resistance.
>
> Replace rpm-relay or relay box, Fig. 7.

Test No. 3

Place your hand on the brown EGR switch-over valve. It may be necessary to remove the switch-over valve from the panel to isolate it from the operation of the other valves. Increase engine speed.

Result

At approximately 3600 rpm, the switch-over valve should switch.

If the brown switch-over valve does not function at the specified rpm

1. Test switch-over valve.

   Remove the plug from the rpm-relay. Connect terminals 2 and 5. With the ignition turned on, the switch-over valve should click audibly. This can also be felt.
2. Test the rpm-switch 3400/3600 rpm in rpm relay.

> **CAUTION:** When testing electronic rpm-switches, use only voltmeter. Use of a test light may damage rpm switches.
>
> Remove the plug from brown switch-over valve. Connect test cable to the valve and reconnect the plug.
>
> Connect the voltmeter to the test cable.
>
> Start the engine and increase the engine speed. Up to approximately 3600 rpm, the voltmeter should indicate about 13 volts. Above 3600 rpm, the voltmeter should go back to zero volts.
>
> If no voltage is measured at the plug below 3600 rpm, replace the rpm-relay, Fig. 7.

Test No. 4

Connect the EGR valve directly to the intake manifold vacuum (use the blue vacuum line).

Result

The engine should run poorly or stall (EGR valve is open).

If the engine speed does not change

1. Test the EGR valve.

   Remove the EGR valve and connect it to the vacuum. Check whether the valve stem lifts from its seat.
2. Clean the EGR bores in the intake manifold.

   With a 10 mm drill, remove exhaust deposits from the distribution tube and clean out with compressed air. If necessary, remove the intake manifold.

Test No. 5

Connect a tachometer, increase engine speed to approximately 2500 rpm, and release the throttle slowly. At the same time, observe the vacuum governor on the carburetor.

Result

The vacuum governor should pop out above approximately 2000 rpm and retract below approximately 1800 rpm.

If the vacuum throttle control does not move

1. Check vacuum lines.

   The blue vacuum line should be connected to the center port of the gray switch-over valve. The gray vacuum line to the vacuum governor should be connected to the outer port of the switch-over valve.

2. Test switch-over valve.

   Remove the plug from the relay box, Fig. 7. Connect terminals 2 and 8. When the ignition is turned on, the switch-over valve should click (this can also be felt at the valve).

   If the vacuum lines and the switch-over valve are functioning properly, then the relay box must be replaced.

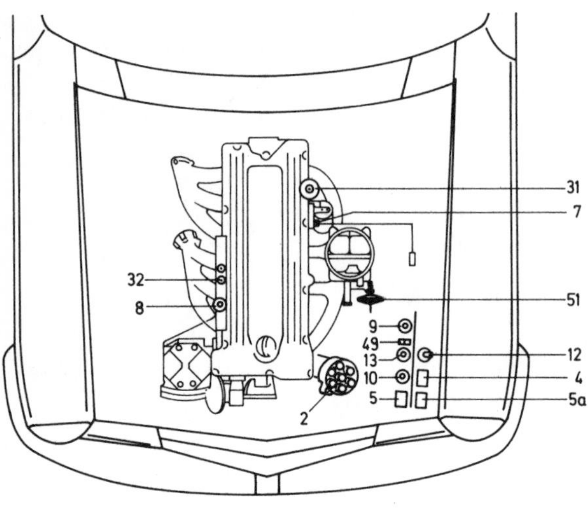

Fig. 13 Component location, 280 except California models

3. Test the 25° C (77° F) temperature switch.

   Remove the plug from the relay box, Fig. 7, and connect a test light to terminals 5 and 8. The test light should not go on above 25° C (77° F) oil temperature.

280 Exc. California, Fig. 13

With the following tests ignition change-over, EGR, and throttle valve lift are checked.

The following functional tests are to be made in the specified sequence with the engine at operating temperature.

Run the engine at idle.

Test No. 1

Disconnect the plug of line to 17° C (62° F) temperature switch in the oil filter housing and connect to ground.

Result

Engine speed should increase (ignition retard is cancelled).

If engine speed does not increase

1. Check vacuum lines.

   Check the white vacuum lines from the carburetor to the switch-over valve and from switch-over valve to ignition distributor for condition and correct connection. The vacuum line from the carburetor must be connected to the center port of the switch-over valve.

2. Check switch-over valve.

   Disconnect the plug from relay boxes. Connect terminals 8 and 9 of plug of relay box with a jumper cable. With ignition turned on, the switch-over valve must click audibly. This can also be felt.

Test No. 2

Unplug 100° C (212° F) temperature switch and connect to ground.

Result

Engine speed should increase (ignition retard is cancelled). Auxiliary fan should run.

If engine speed does not increase

Check wire connection.

Unplug 100° C (212° F) temperature switch and connect the voltmeter between plug and ground. Pull the plug on the relay box and connect terminals 8 and 4. With ignition turned on, the voltmeter should indicate approximately 13 volts.

If voltmeter indicates 13 volts, replace relay box.

Test No. 3

Turn on air conditioner.

Result

Engine speed should not drop (ignition retard is cancelled).

If engine speed decreases

Test voltage.

Disconnect the plug from the relay box. Connect the voltmeter to terminals 2 and 3. With the engine running and the air conditioner switched on, the voltmeter should indicate approximately 13 volts.

If the voltmeter reading is approximately 13 volts, the relay box has to be replaced.

If no voltage reading is obtained, the wiring of the air conditioner has to be checked.

Test No. 4

Remove the vacuum line on top of the switch-over valve. Remove the blue vacuum line on the vacuum switch.

Result

Engine speed should increase (ignition retard is cancelled).

If engine speed does not increase

Check vacuum switch.

Disconnect the plug from relay box and connect the voltmeter to terminals 7 and 8. With engine running at idle speed, the voltmeter should read approximately 13 volts.

When disconnecting the vacuum line from the vacuum switch, the voltmeter should read zero volts.

If voltage values are as indicated, replace relay box.

Test No. 5

Disconnect the plug from the connection at the relay support and ground male terminal 2 (wire color brown/white).

Result

Engine speed should increase (ignition retard is cancelled).

If engine speed does not increase, the relay box has to be replaced.

Test No. 6

Remove the blue vacuum line from the vacuum switch.

Result

Engine should run poorly or stall (EGR valve is open).

If engine speed does not change

1. Check 65° C (149° F) temperature switch.

   Disconnect plug from relay box and connect voltmeter to terminals 8 and 6. Above 65° C (149° F) cooling water temperature, the voltmeter should read approximately 13 volts.
2. Check switch-over valve.

   Disconnect plug from relay box and connect terminals 8 and 5. When ignition is turned on, the switch-over valve must click audibly. This can also be felt.
3. Check EGR valve.

   In order to check the EGR valve vacuum must be directly connected to the valve.

   Run the engine at idle speed. Pull off both vacuum lines from switch-over valve and connect both lines together. The engine should run poorly or stall.

   If tests 1, 2, and 3 locate no problems, replace the relay box.

Test No. 7

Remove the vacuum line from the top of the switch-over valve. Remove the blue vacuum line on the vacuum switch. Place your hand on the brown EGR switch-over valve. Increase the engine speed.

Result

At approximately 3400 rpm, the switch-over valve should click.

If the switch-over valve does not click, replace rpm relay.

Test No. 8

Increase engine speed to approximately 2500 rpm and release the throttle slowly. At the same time observe the vacuum governor on the carburetor.

Result

The vacuum governor should pop out above 2000 rpm and should return below 1800 rpm.

If vacuum governor does not operate

1. Check vacuum lines.

   Check condition and correct connection of

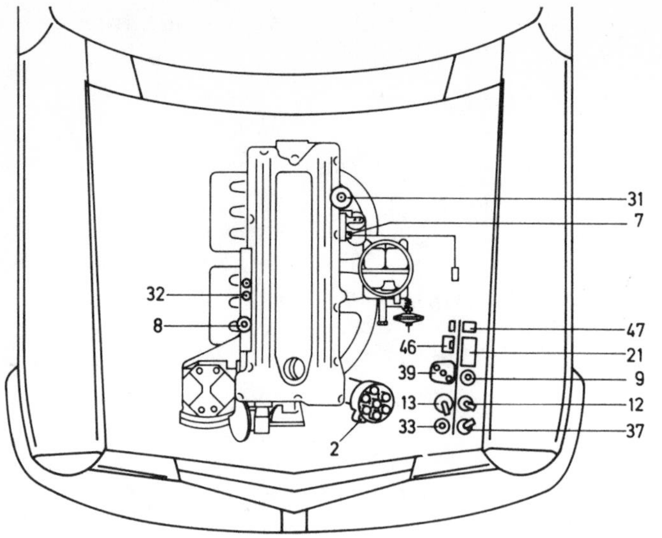

2 Ignition distributor
7 17° C (62° F) temperature switch
8 100° C (212° F) temperature switch
9 Switch-over valve, ignition
12 Switch-over valve, EGR
13 Vacuum switch
21 Relay box
31 EGR valve
32 65° C (149° F) temperature switch
33 Switch-over valve, air injection
37 Switch-over valve, fuel evaporation system
39 Charcoal canister
46 Resistor for automatic choke
47 Relay for resistor, automatic choke

Fig. 14 *Component location,* 280 *California models*

lines. The gray vacuum line from the base of the carburetor must be connected to the center port of the switch-over valve.

2. Check switch-over valve.

Disconnect the plug from the relay box and connect terminals 7 and 8.

When the ignition is turned on, the switch-over valve must click audibly. This can also be felt.

CAUTION: When testing electronic rpm switches, use only voltmeter. Use of a test light may damage the rpm switches.

Pull the plug from the gray switch-over valve. Connect the test cable to the valve and reconnect plug. Connect voltmeter to test cable. Start engine and increase engine speed. Above approximately 2000 rpm, the voltmeter should read 13 volts.

When reducing the engine speed, the voltmeter should drop to zero volts at approximately 1800 rpm.

If no voltage is available at the plug of the switch-over valve above 2000 rpm, repeat the same test without the relay box. Remove

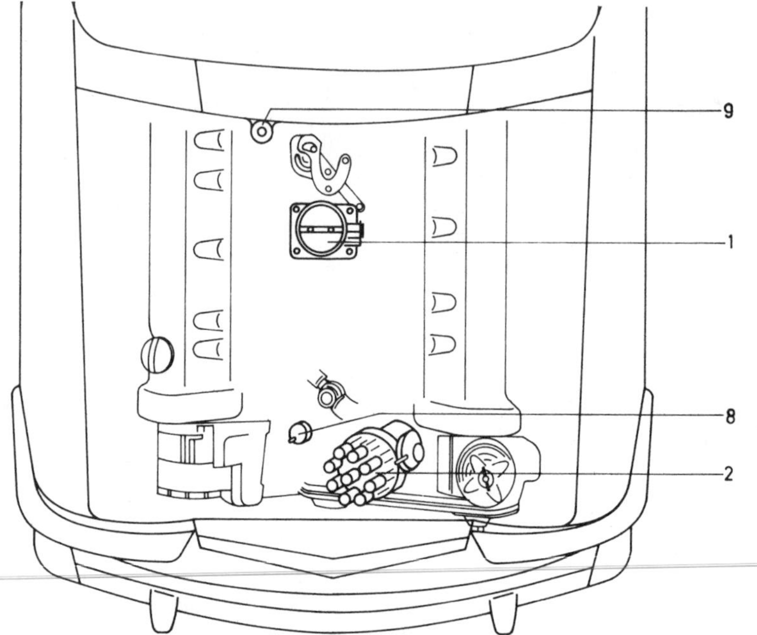

1 Throttle valve
2 Ignition distributor
3 Throttle valve housing
8 100° C (212° F) temperature switch
9 Switch-over valve, ignition

Fig. 15 *Component location,* 450 *except California models*

the plug from the relay box and connect the voltmeter to terminals 2 and 3.

If a voltage of approximately 13 volts is measured at an engine speed above 2000 rpm, replace the relay box.

If no voltage is measured above 2000 rpm, replace the rpm relay.

Test No. 9

Unplug 100° C (212° F) temperature switch and connect to ground. Increase engine speed above 2000 rpm. Observe the vacuum governor.

Result

The vacuum governor should not pop out.

If the vacuum governor does pop out, the relay box has to be replaced.

280 California

With the following tests ignition change-over, EGR, air injection, choke cover heater and fuel evaporation system in the engine compartment are checked.

The following functional tests are to be made in the specified sequence with the engine at operating temperature.

Run engine at idle.

Test No. 1

Disconnect the plug of the line to 17° C (62° F) temperature switch in the oil filter housing and connect to ground.

Result

Engine speed should increase (ignition retard is cancelled).

If engine speed does not increase

1. Check vacuum lines.

   The green vacuum line from the carburetor to the switch-over valve should be connected to the center port. The white vacuum line should be connected to the outside port of the switch-over valve and lead to the ignition distributor.
2. Check switch-over valve.

   Disconnect plug from the relay box. Connect terminals 2 and 10. When the ignition is turned on, the switch-over valve should click audibly. This can also be felt.

   If the switch-over valve clicks, replace relay box.

Test No. 2

Unplug 100° C (212° F) temperature switch and connect to ground.

Result

Engine speed should increase (ignition retard is cancelled). Auxiliary fan should run.

If the engine speed does not increase, replace relay box.

Test No. 3

Turn on the air conditioner.

Result

Engine speed should not drop (ignition retard is cancelled).

If engine speed decreases

Check voltage at relay box.

Remove the plug of relay box and connect the voltmeter to terminals 8 and 3 of plug. With air conditioning in operation, voltmeter should read approximately 13 volts. If the voltmeter reads 13 volts, replace relay box.

If it reads zero volts, check the electrical circuit of air conditioner.

Test No. 4

Remove vacuum line from top of switch-over valve.

Remove blue vacuum line from vacuum switch.

Result

Engine speed should increase (ignition retard is cancelled).

If engine speed does not increase

1. Check vacuum switch.

   Disconnect the plug from relay box. Connect the voltmeter to terminal 11 and 2. With the engine running, the voltmeter should read approximately 13 volts.

   Remove the vacuum line from vacuum switch. The voltmeter should read zero volts.

   If both readings are correct, replace relay box.
2. Check 65° C (149° F) temperature switch.

   Remove plug from 65° C (149° F) temperature switch and connect voltmeter between plug and 65° C (149° F) temperature switch. Disconnect plug from relay box. Connect terminals 2 and 9.

   With the ignition turned on and at a cooling water temperature above 65° C (149° F), the voltmeter should read approximately 13 volts.

Test No. 5

Remove blue vacuum line from vacuum switch.

Result

Engine should run poorly or stall (EGR valve is open).

If engine speed does not change

1. Check vacuum lines.

   The white vacuum line from the vacuum tank under the right fender should be connected to the center port on top of the switch-over valve. The brown vacuum line to the EGR valve should be connected to the outside port on the bottom of the switch-over valve.

2. Check switch-over valve.

   Disconnect plug from relay box and connect terminals 2 and 12. With the ignition turned on, the switch-over valve should click noticeably. This can also be felt.

3. Check EGR valve.

   Unplug the brown vacuum line at the connection on the fire wall and connect to the vacuum line for air conditioner. Run the engine at idle speed. The engine should run poorly or stall.

Test No. 6

Disconnect center air hose on air filter.

Result

There should be air flow present.

If no airflow is present, disconnect center air hose at air filter. If an airflow is present here

1. Check vacuum lines.

   The white vacuum line from the carburetor should be connected to the center port at the anti-backfire valve. The red vacuum line should be connected from the outer port of the anti-backfire valve to the switch-over valve.

2. Check switch-over valve.

   Disconnect plug from relay box and connect terminals 2 and 1. With the ignition turned on, the switch-over valve should click noticeably. This can also be felt.

   If the above parts are in proper operating condition and air is still being discharged while the engine is idling, the anti-backfire valve has to be replaced.

Test No. 7

Increase engine speed slowly to above 3450 rpm.

Result

The air flow in the air injection hose should stop at approximately 3450 rpm.

If air flow does not stop above approximately 3450 rpm

Check rpm-switch 3250/3450 rpm in relay box

CAUTION: When testing electronic rpm-switches, use only voltmeter. Use of a test light may damage rpm-switches.

Disconnect the plug from the red switch-over valve and connect the test cable. Reconnect the plug to the switch-over valve and connect the voltmeter to the test cable. Start the engine and increase engine speed to approximately 2450 rpm. The voltmeter should read approximately 13 volts.

Test No. 8

Disconnect the plug of the line to 17° C (62° F) temperature switch in the oil filter housing and connect to ground.

Result

The relay for the resistor for the automatic choke will click noticeably.

If the relay for the resistor for the automatic choke does not switch

1. Check relay in relay box.

   Disconnect the plug from the relay for the resistor for automatic choke and connect the voltmeter to terminals 1 and 3. Unplug connection of line to 17° C (62° F) temperature switch and connect to ground. With the ignition turned on, the voltmeter should read approximately 13 volts. If no voltage is indicated, the relay box has to be replaced.

2. Check relay for resistor for automatic choke.

   Connect voltmeter to the exit of the resistor (upper terminal) and to ground. With the ignition on, the voltmeter should indicate approximately 13 volts. In case no voltage is indicated, relay should be replaced.

   Unplug the connection of line to 17° C (62° F) temperature switch and connect to ground. The voltmeter should indicate approximately 5 volts.

   In case no voltage is indicated, replace the resistor. In case a voltage of approximately 13 volts is now indicated, replace the choke cover with heating element.

Test No. 9

Turn off the engine. Disconnect the gray vacuum line of the float chamber vent valve at the connection on the carburetor.

Result

There should be no vacuum present. Reconnect the vacuum line.

If there is vacuum present

1. Check vacuum lines.

   The white vacuum line from the vacuum tank should be connected to the center port on top of switch-over valve. The gray vacuum line to the float chamber vent valve should be connected to the side port on the bottom of the switch-over valve.

2. Check switch-over valve.

   Disconnect the plug from switch-over valve and connect the voltmeter. When the ignition is turned on, the voltmeter should read approximately 13 volts. If voltage is present, reconnect plug. The switch-over valve should click audibly. This can also be felt.

Test No. 10

Start engine and again remove vacuum line.

Result

Vacuum should be present (hissing sound).

If there is no vacuum present

Check float chamber vent valve for leaks.

Unscrew float chamber vent valve. With the vacuum line connected, turn the ignition on and off. The valve stem should move in and out. If not, replace the diaphragm of vent valve.

Test No. 11

Remove the thin center hose on the charcoal canister and close the hose opening with your finger. Increase engine speed slowly to more than 2000 rpm.

Result

During idle, a slight vacuum should be present. The vacuum should increase with rising engine speed.

If no vacuum is present at idle

1. Check vacuum hose to intake manifold.

   Disconnect hose to the charcoal canister at the purge valve. With compressed air, blow out purge valve and hose towards the intake manifold. If necessary, replace purge valve.

   If the vacuum does not increase at higher engine speeds.

2. Check vacuum at purge valve.

   Disconnect the white vacuum line at purge valve. Connect the vacuum gauge or close hose end with finger. Increase engine speed slowly. At idle, no vacuum should be present. With higher engine speeds, the vacuum should increase.

   If there is vacuum present, replace the purge valve.

   If no vacuum is present, blow out the vacuum line towards carburetor with compressed air.

450 Exc. California

With this test ignition change-over is checked. Run the engine at idle.

Test No. 1

Unplug 100° C (212° F) temperature switch and connect to ground.

Result

Engine speed should increase (ignition retard is cancelled). On model 116 the auxiliary fan should operate.

If engine speed does not increase

1. Check vacuum lines.

   The white vacuum line from the throttle valve housing should be connected to the center port of the switch-over valve. The other white line from the outside port of the switch-over valve should be connected to the vacuum retard unit on the distributor.

2. Check switch-over valve.

   Disconnect the plug from the relay and connect terminals 3 and 4. With the ignition on, the switch-over valve should click audibly. This can also be felt.

   If switch-over valve switches, replace the relay.

   If the auxiliary fan does not operate (model 116 only)

3. Check auxiliary fan.

   Disconnect the plug of relay. Connect terminals 1 and 3. With the ignition on, the auxiliary fan should run.

4. Check relay.

   Remove the plug from relay. Connect terminals 3 and 5. Remove the plug from 100° C

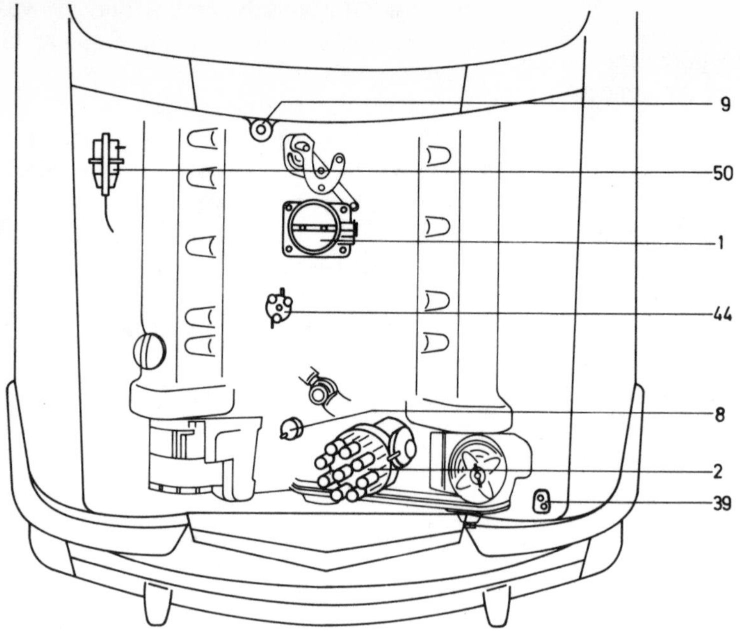

Fig. 16 Components location. 450 California models

(212° F) temperature switch and connect to ground.

With the ignition on, the auxiliary fan should run.

Test No. 2

Switch on air conditioning.

Result

Engine speed should increase slightly (ignition retard is cancelled).

If the engine speed does not increase, check whether air conditioning is functioning.

If air conditioning is functioning, replace the relay.

If air conditioning is not functioning, the problem is in the electrical circuit of air conditioning.

450 California, Fig. 16

With the following tests ignition change-over, EGR, CO values, and the fuel evaporation system in the engine compartment are checked.

The following functional tests should be performed in the sequence listed and with the engine at operating temperatures.

Test No. 1

Unplug 100° C (212° F) temperature switch and connect to ground.

Result

Engine speed should increase (ignition retard is cancelled). On model 116 the auxiliary fan should run.

If engine speed does not increase

1. Check vacuum lines.

   The white vacuum line from the throttle valve housing should be connected to the center port of the switch-over valve. The other white line from the outside port of the switch-over valve should be connected to the vacuum retard unit on the distributor.
2. Check switch-over valve.

   Disconnect plug from relay and connect terminals 3 and 4. With the ignition on, the switch-over valve should click audibly. This can also be felt.

   If the switch-over valve switches, replace the relay.

   If the auxiliary fan does not operate (model 116 only)
3. Check auxiliary fan.

   Disconnect the plug of the relay. Connect terminals 1 and 3. With the ignition on, the auxiliary fan should run.
4. Check relay.

   Remove the plug from the relay. Connect terminals 3 and 5. Remove plug from 100° C (212° F) temperature switch and connect to ground.

   With the ignition on, the auxiliary fan should run.

Test No. 2

Switch on air conditioning.

Result

Engine speed should increase slightly (ignition retard is cancelled).

If the engine speed does not increase, check whether air conditioning is functioning.

If air conditioning is functioning, replace the relay.

If air conditioning is not functioning, the problem is in the electrical circuit of air conditioning.

Test No. 3

Remove air filter top cover and check whether exhaust gas is emitted from the recirculation line in the throttle valve housing.

If no exhaust is emitted into the throttle valve housing, clean throttle housing and the EGR line.

Test No. 4

Remove the air filter housing and put aside without unplugging the warm air sensor. Disconnect the brown vacuum line at diverter control valve. Increase engine speed to above 2000 rpm. Release throttle linkage.

Result

Vacuum should be present at the port of the diverter control valve only when the throttle linkage is released (hissing noise).

If no vacuum is available at the diverter control valve, the valve should be replaced.

Test No. 5

Test CO values with CO tester.

Result

Should be maximum 1.0% CO with air injection.

If the CO measurements do not differ for measurements with and without air injection

1. Check brown vacuum line.

   The brown vacuum line from the diverter control valve to the diverter valve should be checked for tightness.

3. Check diverter valve.

   Remove muffler. With the engine running and the warm air sensor disconnected at the air filter, air should be discharged from the muffler hose.

Test No. 5a

Test CO values with CO tester without air injection.

For this test, remove the air filter housing and put aside without unplugging the warm air sensor.

Disconnect the brown vacuum line at the diverter control valve and connect this line to vacuum supply line for cruise control actuator.

Result

More than 1.0% CO without air injection.

Test No. 6

Remove the thin hose on the charcoal canister and close the hose opening with your finger. Increase engine speed slowly to more than 2000 rpm.

Result

During idle, a slight vacuum should be present. The vacuum should increase with rising engine speed.

If no vacuum is present at idle

1. Check vacuum hose to intake manifold.

   Disconnect the hose to the charcoal canister at the purge valve. With compressed air, blow out purge valve and hose towards the intake manifold. If necessary, replace purge valve.

   If the vacuum does not increase at higher engine speeds

2. Check vacuum at purge valve.

   Disconnect white vacuum line at purge valve. Connect the vacuum gauge or close hose end with finger. Increase engine speed slowly. At idle, no vacuum should be present. With higher engine speeds, the vacuum should increase.

   If there is vacuum present, replace purge valve.

   If no vacuum is present, blow out the vacuum line towards connection at throttle valve housing with compressed air. If necessary, clean the throttle valve housing.

AIR INJECTION SYSTEM

Testing

280

Disconnect the center air hose on the air filter. Air flow should be present. Increase engine speed slowly to above 3450 rpm. Air flow should stop at approximately 3450 rpm.

450

Test CO levels with a suitable exhaust gas analyzer. With air injection connected, CO level should be a maximum of 1%. With air injection disconnected, CO level should be more than 1%.

OPEL

GENERAL ENGINE SPECIFICATIONS

Model or Engine	Bore & Stroke, Inches (mm)	Piston Displacement, Cubic Inches (cc)	Compression Ratio	Maximum Brake HP @ rpm	Maximum Torque Ft. Lbs. @ rpm	Normal Oil Pressure, Pounds
1974						
All	3.66 x 2.75 (92.9 x 69.8)	115.8 (1897)	7.6	75 @ 4800	92 @ 2800	28

TUNEUP SPECIFICATIONS

Car Model or Engine	Spark Plugs		Distributor		Firing Order	Ignition Timing		Hot Idle Speed, rpm
	Type	Gap, Inch	Point Gap, Inch	Dwell Angle, Degrees		Degrees BTDC	Mark Location	
1974								
1900 Std	AC42FS	.030	.016	47–53	1-3-4-2	①	Flywheel	850–900
1900 Auto	AC42FS	.030	.016	47–53	1-3-4-2	①	Flywheel	800–850
①—Align timing marks w/dist. retard hose disconnected & plugged.								
1975								
All	AC42FS	.030	.016	47–53	1-3-4-2	①	Flywheel	800–900

DISTRIBUTOR SPECIFICATIONS

Model or Engine	Distributor Part No.	Point Gap, Inch	Dwell Angle, Deg.	Spring Tension, Oz.	Centrifugal Advance			Vacuum Advance		
					Start @ rpm	Int.	Full @ rpm	Inches of Vacuum to Start Plunger	Int.	Full Advance Dist. Deg. @ Vacuum
1974-75										
1900	Bosch	.016	47–53	14–19	1000–1200	7.5–15 @ 1400	28–32 @ 3600	–5 @ 2.9–4.1	—	1–5 @ 4.5–5.0
	Delco Remy	.016	47–53	16.6–20.5	1000–2000	7.5–14.5 @ 1400	26–34 @ 3600	–5 @ 2.8–4.0	—	1–4 @ 4.3–4.9

Emission Controls

1974 MODELS

EVAPORATIVE EMISSION CONTROL

Description

This system consists of the following components—a non-vented filler cap, an activated carbon canister incorporating an oiled foam filter in its base, a fuel tank having a special overfill protection and venting provisions to eliminate liquid fuel being supplied to the engine through the vapor line and various connecting hoses between these components, Fig. 1.

Operation

When the engine is not running, fuel vapors formed in the fuel tank pass through a vent hose into the carbon canister where they are adsorbed by activated carbon. When the engine is running, the intake manifold vacuum draws fresh air through the oiled foam filter and over the activated carbon. This action purges the canister and renews its storage capacity. The fresh air and fuel vapors, from the canister, are drawn through a hose to the intake manifold where they enter the combustion system and are burned. The fuel tank overfill protection de-

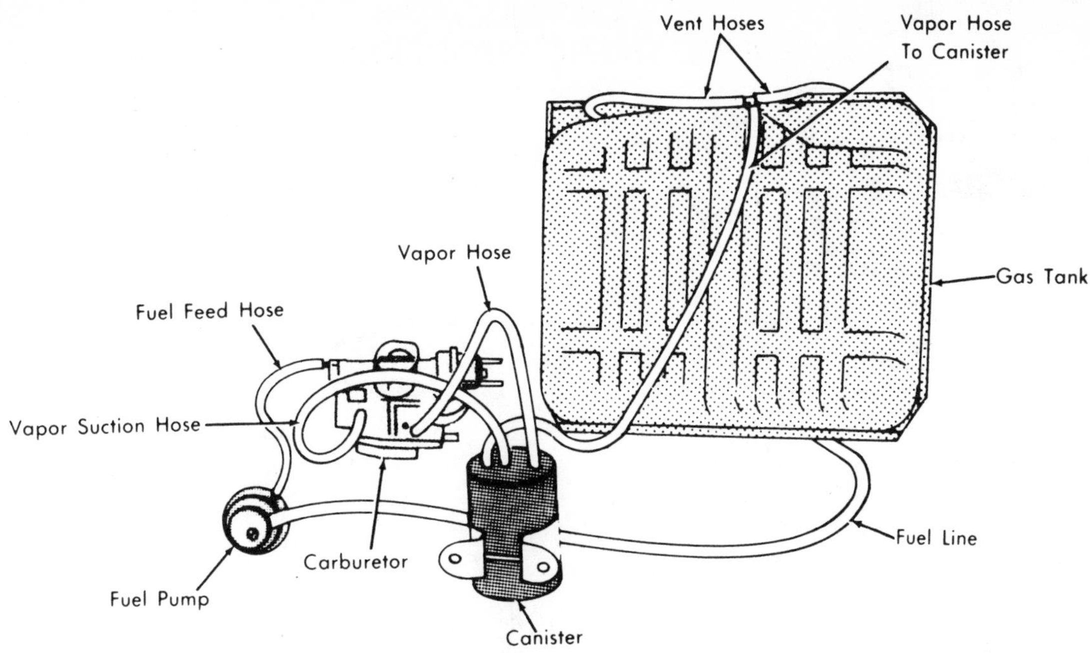

Fig. 1 Evaporative emission control system

vice prevents the fuel tank from being overfilled. When the fuel tank is filled a small volume of air space is left in the fuel tank to allow for thermal expansion of fuel.

EXHAUST GAS RECIRCULATION

California Models, Fig. 2

This system consists of a pipe connected to the exhaust system, two in-line control valves, a pipe from control valves to intake manifold, a vacuum hose connected between regulating valve and intake manifold, and a second vacuum hose connected from shut-off valve to a ported vacuum port on carburetor. Shut-off valve vacuum source varies with throttle opening and valve begins to open when 2.8-inch of vacuum is applied. Regulating valve is operated by manifold vacuum which varies with engine load and is fully open between 3.5 and 9.8-inch of vacuum. This valve closes to a small flow when vacuum is above 11.8-inch. The effect of these two valves is to provide no exhaust gas recirculation at idle, a little recirculation at low engine loads and a maximum recirculation flow at higher load conditions.

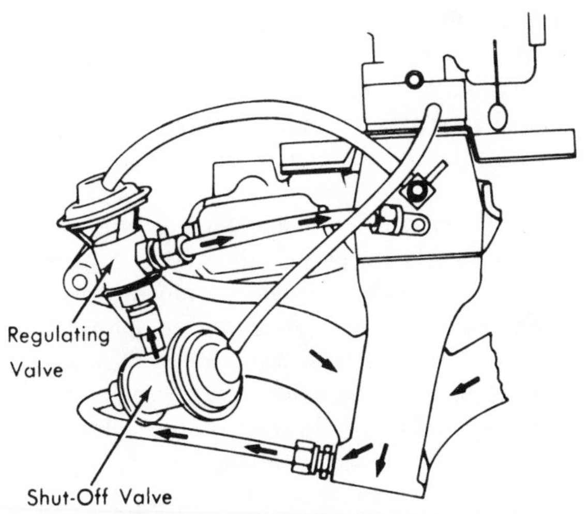

Fig. 2 Exhaust gas recirculation system. California models

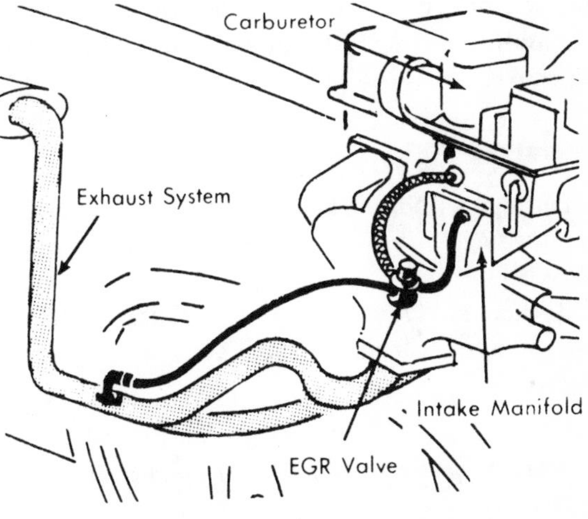

Fig. 3 Exhaust gas recirculation system. Exc. California models

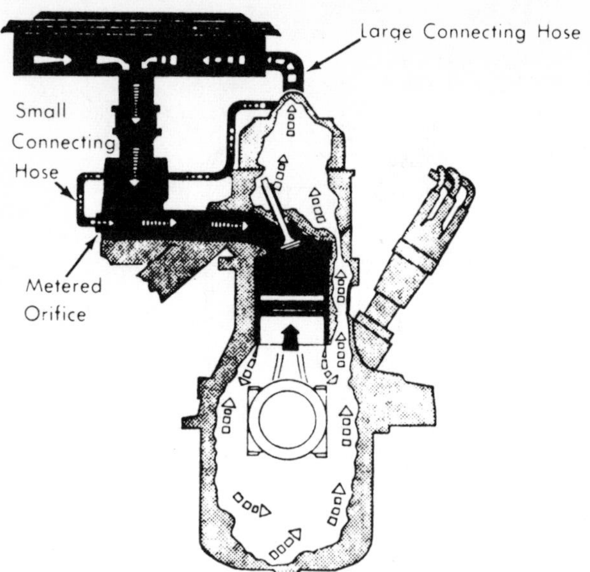

Fig. 4 Positive crankcase ventilation system

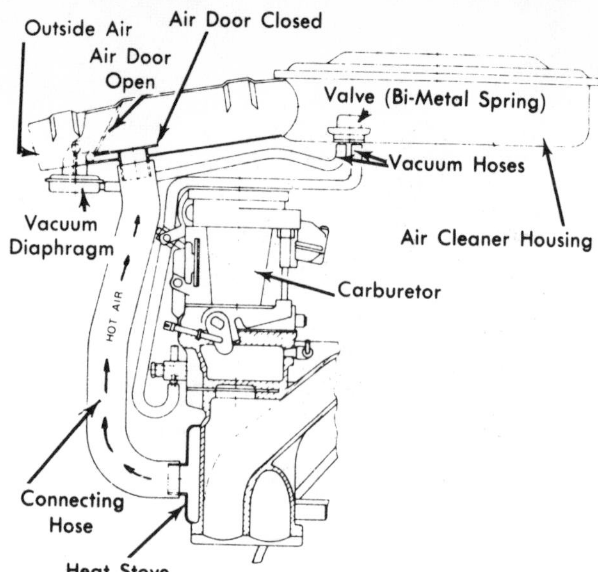

Fig. 5 Thermostatically controlled air cleaner

Exc. California Models, Fig. 3

This system consists of a pipe connected to the exhaust system, an EGR valve, a pipe from the valve to the intake manifold and a vacuum hose connected from the EGR valve to the base of the carburetor. The system does not receive sufficient vacuum at idle to operate, but will operate during acceleration and part throttle providing sufficient intake manifold vacuum is present. As a result, no exhaust gas recirculation occurs during period of idle and low intake manifold vacuum.

POSITIVE CRANKCASE VENTILATION

Description

The closed crankcase ventilation system consists of one large hose connected from air cleaner to rocker arm cover. A small hose, incorporating a metered orifice, connects intake manifold to rocker arm cover. A sealed oil filler cap is also used, Fig. 4.

Operation

During periods of low intake manifold vacuum, crankcase gases are drawn into air cleaner through a large connecting hose. During periods of high manifold vacuum, crankcase gases are drawn into intake manifold through a small connecting hose and metered orifice.

THERMOSTATICALLY CONTROLLED AIR CLEANER

The carburetor air intake system consists of a heat stove, a corrugated paper heated air pipe and an air cleaner incorporating a temperature controlled door operated by vacuum through a temperature sensor, Fig. 5. Operation is as follows.

1. Heat stove is a sheet metal cover, shaped and bolted onto exhaust manifold.
2. Temperature controlled air cleaner is designed to mix this heated air with cold air from engine compartment so that carburetor air temperature averages 95°. Mixing is done by an air door located in snorkel. Most of the time the door will be partially open. When underhood temperature reaches about 110°, door will close, not allowing any more warm air from manifold to enter air cleaner.
3. Temperature door is moved by a diaphragm type vacuum motor. When there is no vacuum present in the motor, the diaphragm spring forces the door closed. Whenever the engine is running, the amount of vacuum present in vacuum motor depends on the temperature sensor in the air cleaner which is located in the vacuum line between intake manifold and vacuum motor.
4. Inside sensor, a bi-metal temperature sensing spring starts to open a valve to bleed more air into vacuum line whenever temperature in air cleaner rises above 95°, sensing spring starts to close the air bleed in vacuum line, allowing more manifold vacuum to reach vacuum motor. Whenever there is 9 inches or more of vacuum in vacuum motor, diaphragm spring is compressed and door is opened.
5. When starting a cold engine (air temperature under 85°), the air door will open immediately.

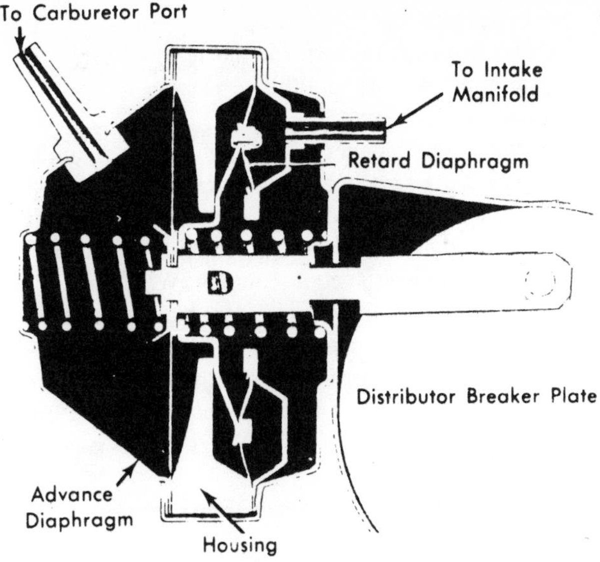

Fig. 6 Dual diaphragm unit

This is because the air bleed valve in sensor is closed so that full manifold vacuum is applied in the vacuum motor. As soon as the air cleaner starts receiving hot air from the heat stove, the sensor will cause the air door to close partially, mixing cold and hot air as necessary to regulate air cleaner temperature within 15° of the ideal 95° air inlet temperature.

6. While air cleaner temperature is being regulated, accelerating the engine hard will cause vacuum level in intake manifold and in vacuum motor to drop. Whenever vacuum drops below 5 inches, diaphragm spring will close the air door in order to get the maximum outside air flow required for maximum acceleration.

DUAL VACUUM ADVANCE UNIT

The dual vacuum advance unit, Fig. 6, operates as follows:

The advance side of the unit is supplied with vacuum from a port in the primary barrel of the carburetor, located just above the throttle valve. This port does not supply vacuum during idling or during closed throttle deceleration. It supplies full vacuum—to advance timing—at all speeds when the throttle valve is opened enough to uncover the port.

The retard side of the unit is supplied with an intake manifold vacuum through a line connected directly to the intake manifold. During idling and deceleration—when there is no vacuum to advance side of unit—the retard side of unit will cause the timing to be retarded about 5°. However, during part throttle operation, when vacuum is supplied to advance side of unit, advance side will overpower retard unit and retard unit will have no effect on timing.

GENERAL SERVICE

Evaporative Emission System

Every 12,000 miles, replace the foam filter assembly.

Exhaust Gas Recirculation System

Every 12,000 miles, check EGR system as follows:

With engine at normal operating temperature, connect a tachometer and note idle rpm. Disconnect the vacuum hose at the intake manifold that goes to the air cleaner. On non-California models, connect the vacuum line from the EGR valve to the intake manifold fitting. On California models, leave the regulating valve connected to the intake manifold source but connect the vacuum hose of the shut-off valve to the intake manifold fitting. When the hose is connected to the intake manifold idle speed should decrease between 100-240 rpm (non-California models) or 270-300 rpm (California models). If idle speed does not decrease the amount indicated, remove the EGR valve(s) and fitting on the intake manifold and clean it. Reconnect the vacuum hoses to their proper places.

Positive Crankcase Ventilation System

Every 12,000 miles, check the hoses and metered orifices and clean them if necessary. Under more severe conditions, perform this operation every 6000 miles.

THERMOSTATICALLY CONTROLLED AIR CLEANER

Testing

Vacuum Motor

Check all hoses for damage. With the engine OFF, observe the position of damper door through the snorkel. The door should be in such a position that the heat stove passage is covered. If not, check for binds in the linkage. Apply at least 9 inches of vacuum to diaphragm assembly through the hose disconnected at sensor unit. The damper door should completely close snorkel passage when vacuum is applied. With vacuum applied, clamp hose to trap vacuum in diaphragm assembly. Snorkel passage should remain closed. If not, there is a leak in the diaphragm assembly.

Sensor

Test with the engine cold (engine compartment temperature below 85°). Observe air door before starting the engine. It should be closed. Start the engine and allow it to idle. Immediately after starting engine, air door should open. As the engine warms ups, the air door should start to close and the air cleaner should become warm to the hand.

If correct operation of air cleaner is in doubt, proceed to the thermometer test.

NOTE: In order to perform the following test, the engine must be cold and the air cleaner temperature below 85° F.

Remove air cleaner cover and install a suitable temperature gauge as close as possible to the sensor. Reinstall air cleaner cover (do not install wing nut). Start the engine. The air door should open immediately if engine is cool enough. When air door starts to close, remove air cleaner cover and read the temperature gauge. It must read 95 ± 15°. If air door does not start to close at temperature indicated, the temperature sensor is defective and must be replaced.

PEUGEOT

GENERAL ENGINE SPECIFICATIONS

Model or Engine	Bore & Stroke, Inches (mm)	Piston Displacement, Cubic Inches (cc)	Compression Ratio	Maximum Brake HP @ rpm	Maximum Torque Ft. Lbs. @ rpm	Normal Oil Pressure, Pounds
1974						
504	3.46 x 3.20 (88 x 81)	120.3 (1971)	7.6	82 @ 5200	105 @ 3000	45
504D	3.54 x 3.27 (90 x 83)	129 (2112)	22.2	62 @ 4500	88 @ 2000	—

TUNEUP SPECIFICATIONS

Car Model or Engine	Spark Plugs		Distributor		Firing Order	Ignition Timing		Hot Idle Speed rpm
	Type	Gap, Inch	Point Gap, Inch	Dwell Angle, Degrees		Degrees, BTDC	Mark Location	
1974								
504	—	.025	.016	55	1-3-4-2	5	Pulley	—
504D	—	—	—	—	—	—	—	—

DISTRIBUTOR SPECIFICATIONS

Model or Engine	Distributor Part No.	Point Gap, Inch	Dwell Angle Deg.	Spring Tension, oz.	Centrifugal Advance			Vacuum Advance		
					Start @ rpm	Int.	Full @ rpm	Inches of Vacuum to Start Plunger	Int.	Full Adv. Dist. Deg. @ Vacuum
1974										
504	—	.016	55–59	—	1400	10 @ 3000	16 @ 3900	—	—	—
504D	—	.016	—	—	1400	10 @ 3000	16 @ 3900	—	—	—

Emission Controls

1974 MODELS

POSITIVE CRANKCASE VENTILATION

Description

This system consists of a sealed oil filter cap, a connecting hose which incorporates a PCV valve and is located between the oil filter cap and the carburetor air intake, and a second hose (vacuum line) connected between the first hose and intake manifold. Located in this second hose is a metered orifice, Fig. 1. A metal strainer is fitted in the oil filler tube to trap liquid condensate.

Operation

During idle or periods of deceleration, when the carburetor throttle valve is closed, crankcase fumes enter directly into the intake manifold through a vacuum line. The metered orifice—located in vacuum line—controls the flow of fumes from the crankcase and prevents the idle from being disturbed. During normal operation, when the carburetor throttle valve is open, intake manifold vacuum in vacuum line decreases and crankcase fumes are drawn directly through the PCV valve into the carburetor air intake. During periods of partial throttle operation, crankcase fumes may enter through both systems, at the same time. Crankcase fumes then enter the combustion system where they are burned.

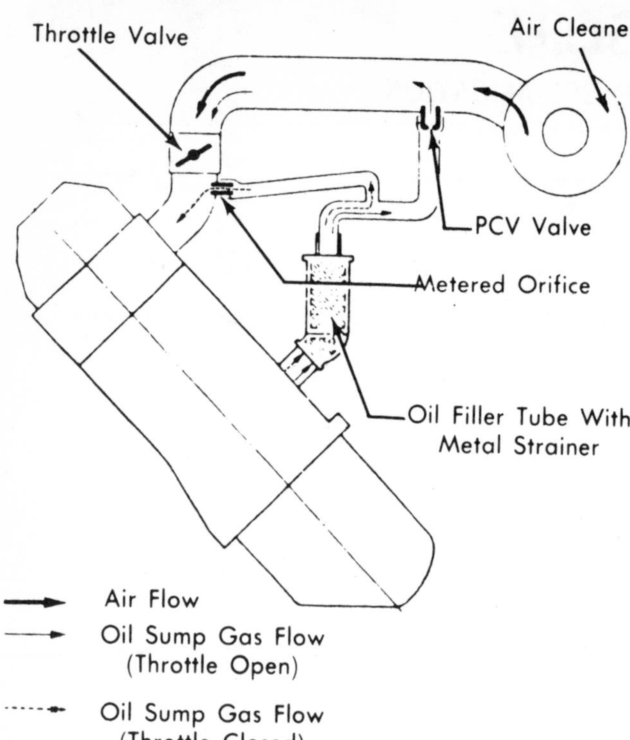

Fig. 1 Crankcase ventilation system

EVAPORATIVE EMISSION CONTROL

Description

This system, Fig. 2, is designed to prevent fuel vapors from entering the atmosphere. The system incorporates a sealed fuel tank, a separator (expansion tank), an activated charcoal canister and ventilation lines which connect the various components and terminate at the intake manifold.

Operation

When the engine is stopped, fuel vapors from the fuel tank pass through a vent line to the separator. Any liquid fuel entering the separator is returned to the fuel tank through a vent line. The fuel vapors then pass through a vent line to the canister where they are adsorbed by activated charcoal. When the engine is running, intake manifold vacuum passes through the vent line to the charcoal canister. Fresh air is drawn into the canister, it mixes with the fuel vapors and is drawn into the intake manifold where it enters the combustion system and is burned. This action cleanses the activated charcoal and renews its storage capacity.

GENERAL SERVICE

Positive Crankcase Ventilation

Every 9000 miles inspect and clean the PCV valve, metered orifice and all hoses.

Evaporative Emission System

No maintenance is generally required, but all components should be checked for proper operation and replaced as required.

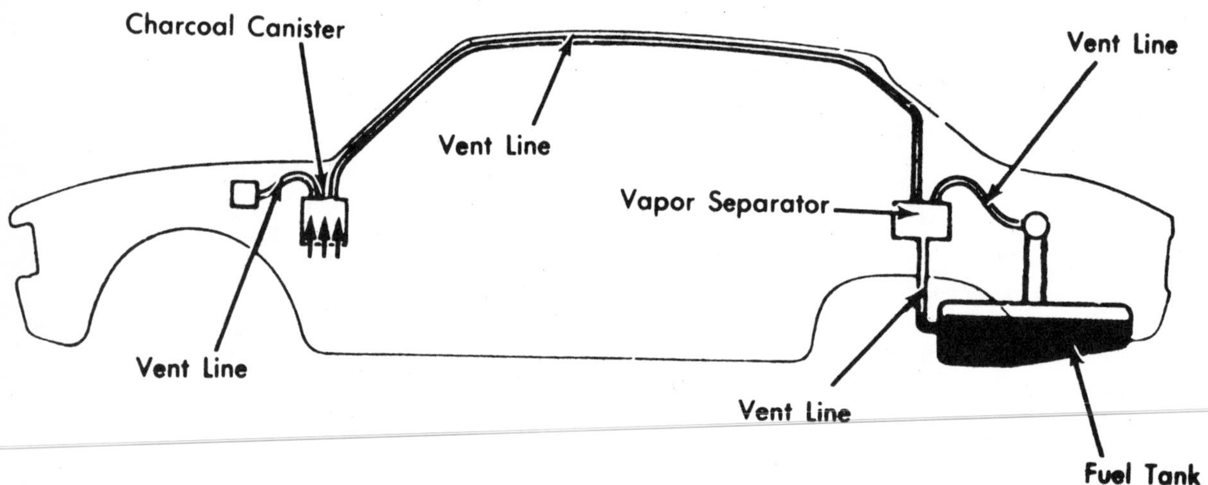

Fig. 2 Evaporative emission control system

PORSCHE

GENERAL ENGINE SPECIFICATIONS

Model or Engine	Bore & Stroke, Inches (mm)	Piston Displacement, Cubic Inches (cc)	Compression Ratio	Maximum Brake HP @ rpm	Maximum Torque Ft. Lbs. @ rpm	Normal Oil Pressure Pounds
1974						
914	3.66 x 2.59 (93.0 x 66.0)	110 (1795)	7.3	72 @ 4800	94 @ 3400	28–42
914 2 liter	3.70 x 2.80 (94.0 x 71.0)	120 (1971)	7.6	91 @ 4900	109 @ 3000	28–42
911	3.54 x 2.77 (90.0 x 70.4)	162 (2653)	8.0	143 @ 5700	168 @ 3800	29–90
911S & Carrera	3.54 x 2.77 (90.0 x 70.4)	162 (2653)	8.5	167 @ 6800	168 @ 4000	29–90
1975						
914 1.8	3.66 x 2.59 (93.0 x 66.0)	109.5 (1795)	7.3	73 @ 4900	189 @ 4000	28–42
914 2.0	3.70 x 2.79 (94.0 x 71.0)	120.3 (1971)	7.6	84 @ 4900	97 @ 4000	28–42
911S & Carrera	3.54 x 2.77 (90.0 x 70.4)	163.97 (2687)	8.5	157 @ 5800①	166 @ 4000	29–90

①—California 152.

TUNEUP SPECIFICATIONS

Car Model or Engine	Spark Plugs		Distributor		Firing Order	Ignition Timing		Hot Idle Speed, rpm
	Type	Gap, Inch	Point Gap, Inch	Dwell Angle, Degrees		Degrees BTDC	Mark Location	
1974								
911	Bosch W215-P21	.022	.016	34–40	1-6-2-4-3-5	5 ATDC①	Pulley	—
911S Carrera	Bosch W235-P21	.022	.016	34–40①	1-6-2-4-3-5	5 ATDC①	Pulley	—
914 1.8	Bosch W175-T2	.028	.016	44–50	1-4-3-2	27②	Pulley	—
914 2.0	Bosch W175-T2	.028	.016	44–50	1-4-3-2	27②	Pulley	—

①—Timed at No. 1 cylinder, left rear of engine. ②—At 3500 rpm.

DISTRIBUTOR SPECIFICATIONS

Model or Engine	Distributor Part No.	Point Gap, Inch	Dwell Angle Deg.	Spring Tension, Oz.	Centrifugal Advance			Vacuum Advance		
					Start @ rpm	Int.	Full @ rpm	Inches of Vacuum to Start Plunger	Int.	Full Advance Dist. Deg. @ Vacuum
1974										
911-Carrera	Bosch	.016	35–41	—	0 @ 1020	9.5 @ 2000	15.8 @ 6000	—	—	—
911-Carrera	Marelli	.016	34–40	23–28	0 @ 1380	7.8 @ 2150	14.2 @ 6300	—	—	—

Emission Controls

THERMOSTATICALLY CONTROLLED AIR CLEANER

911 Models, Fig. 1

Description & Operation

The fresh air flap is controlled by the accelerator linkage and starts to open at a throttle valve angle of 20°. At about 60° angle, the flap is opened completely and closes off the warm air channel. The thermostat causes the warm air flap to begin closing at 104° F and flap is completely closed at 131° F. During normal running, the warm air flap fluctuates according to the temperature of the preheated air and the throttle opening. The intake air therefore maintains itself at about 100° F.

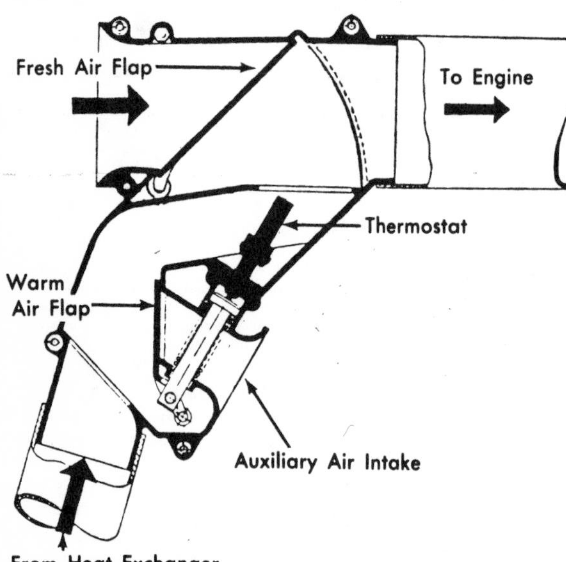

Fig. 1 Thermostatically controlled air cleaner. 911 models

914 Models, Fig. 2

Description & Operation

During load dependent control function, if the throttle flap is closed or only slightly open, with the engine running, the high vacuum moves the diaphragm and releases the hot air supply by means of the regulating flap. If the vacuum drops when accelerating, the diaphragm adjusts the regulating flap so that the hot air of the intake air decreases until the engine finally receives cold air only.

During temperature control function, the bi-metal valve remains closed as long as the intake air has a temperature of less than about 132° F. At this time, unrestricted vacuum is applied in the diaphragm

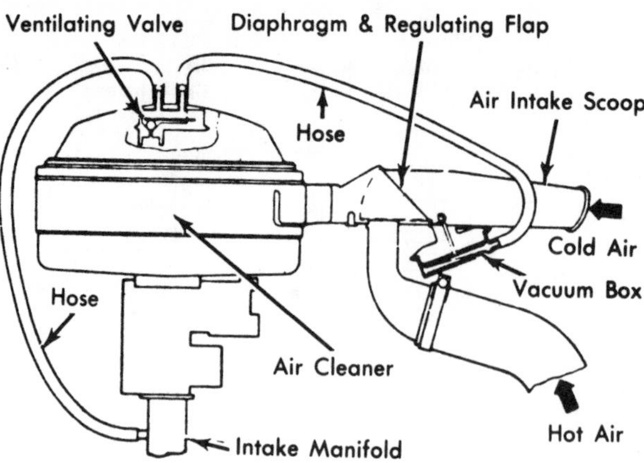

Fig. 2 Thermostatically controlled air cleaner. 914 models

box. Hot air is fed to the air intake by diaphragm and the hot air regulating flap. If the temperature reaches 132° F, the valve opens and outside air flowing in reduces the vacuum. The regulating flap in the air intake manifold then shuts off the hot air supply independent of the throttle valve setting. This provides temperature regulation of the intake air during all operating conditions.

ENGINE OVERRUN SYSTEM

914 Models, Fig. 3

Description & Operation

At high engine speeds and with the throttle closed (deceleration), vacuum is present in the intake air distributor. In this condition, the pneumatic valve will open so that air can pass through the hose from the air cleaner to the intake air distributor. The air/fuel mixture is thus leaned out with this additional air to provide a more complete combustion during engine overrun (deceleration) conditions.

During deceleration, the mixture becomes too rich for proper combustion. To keep the CO content low during this condition, additional air is conveyed to the air intake distributor.

EVAPORATIVE EMISSION CONTROL

Description

This system, (Figs. 4 & 5), is designed to prevent fuel vapors from the vehicle's fuel system from

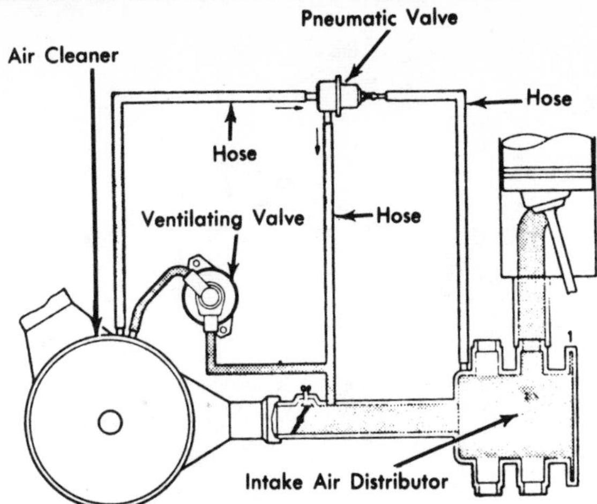

Fig. 3 Engine overrun system. 914 models

entering the atmosphere. The system consists of a sealed fuel tank filler cap, an expansion tank, vent tank, carbon canister and a series of hoses. One connects the carbon canister to the air cleaner and the other connects the carbon canister to the engine cooling system blower assembly.

Operation

Excess fuel from expansion or from parking on a steep angle is collected in the expansion tank. This fuel will return to the main tank when the engine is running and the fuel system is purged.

Fuel vapors, due to the system being sealed, are stored in the vent tank. When pressure is created in the fuel system due to heat, vapors are forced to the carbon canister where they are absorbed by activated carbon. When the engine is running, air from the engine's cooling blower assembly is forced into the carbon canister. This air forces vapors in the activated carbon into the air cleaner where they are drawn into the carburetor and the engines combustion system. Air from the engine's blower system is also used to compensate for fuel being drawn from the main tank when the engine is running.

POSITIVE VENTILATION SYSTEM

911 Models, Fig. 6

Description & Operation

Components of system consist of a connecting hose located between crankcase and oil tank, and a second hose connecting oil tank to engine air cleaner. Vapors and gases produced in the crankcase are vented through the connecting hose to oil tank. From oil tank, vapors and gases pass through a second connecting hose to engine air cleaner where they are drawn into the combustion chambers and burned.

914 Models, Fig. 7

Description & Operation

Components of system consist of connecting hoses between air cleaner and cylinder head covers, an oil breather with a regulator valve incorporated

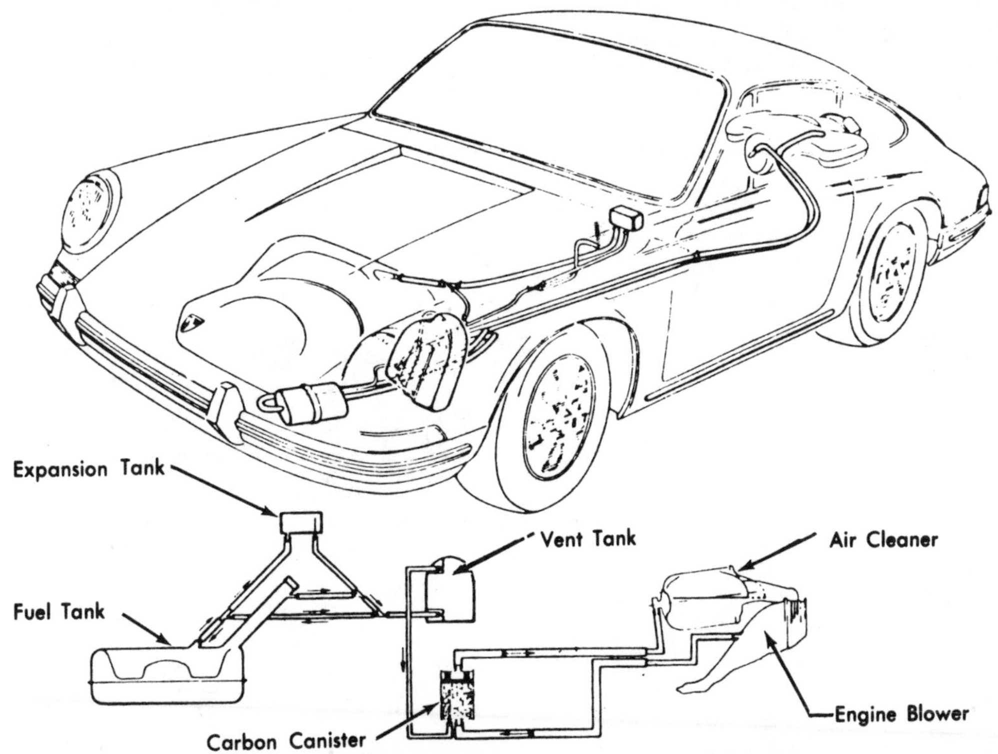

Fig. 4 Evaporative emission control system. 911 models

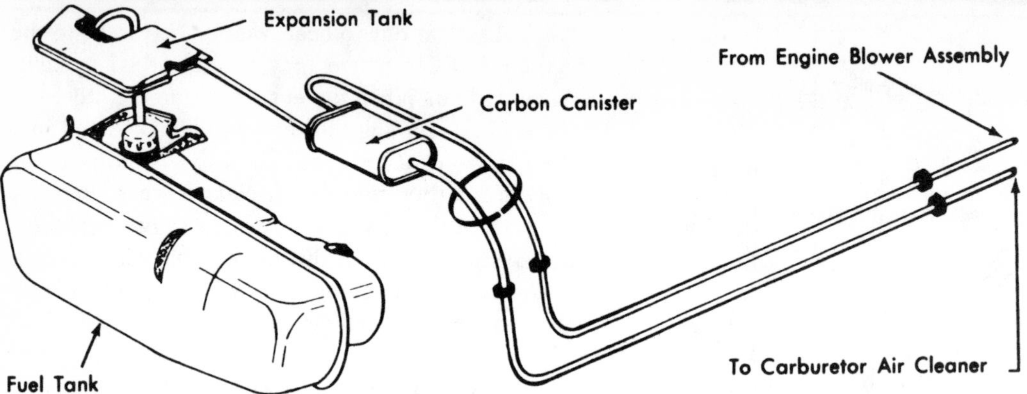

Fig. 5 Evaporative emission control system. 914 *models*

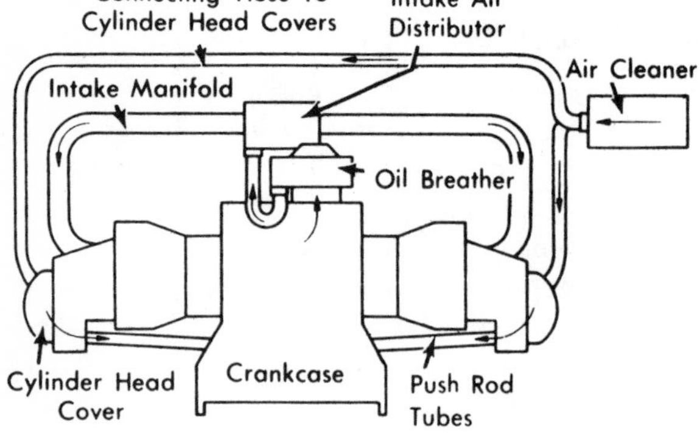

Fig. 7 *Positive crankcase ventilation system.* 914 *models*

and a connecting hose from oil breather to intake air distributor. Vapors and gases produced in the crankcase are mixed with fresh air from air cleaner and flow through oil breather into intake air distributor. From intake air distributor, fumes pass into combustion chambers and are burned. Regulator valve controls flow of vapors and gases into engine.

EVAPORATIVE EMISSION SYSTEM

General Service

Every 10,000 miles or 1 year inspect the entire system and check for proper operation. Every 50,000 miles, replace the charcoal canister.

Engine Overrun

A complete maintenance and inspection should be carried out at least once a year. Inspect all components for proper operation and check all hoses for deterioration.

Remove the hose between the valve and the air cleaner at the air cleaner. Start the engine and increase speed to 3000 rpm. Quickly close the throttle. Air should be drawn into the hose at the suction end. If no suction effect is detected, replace the valve.

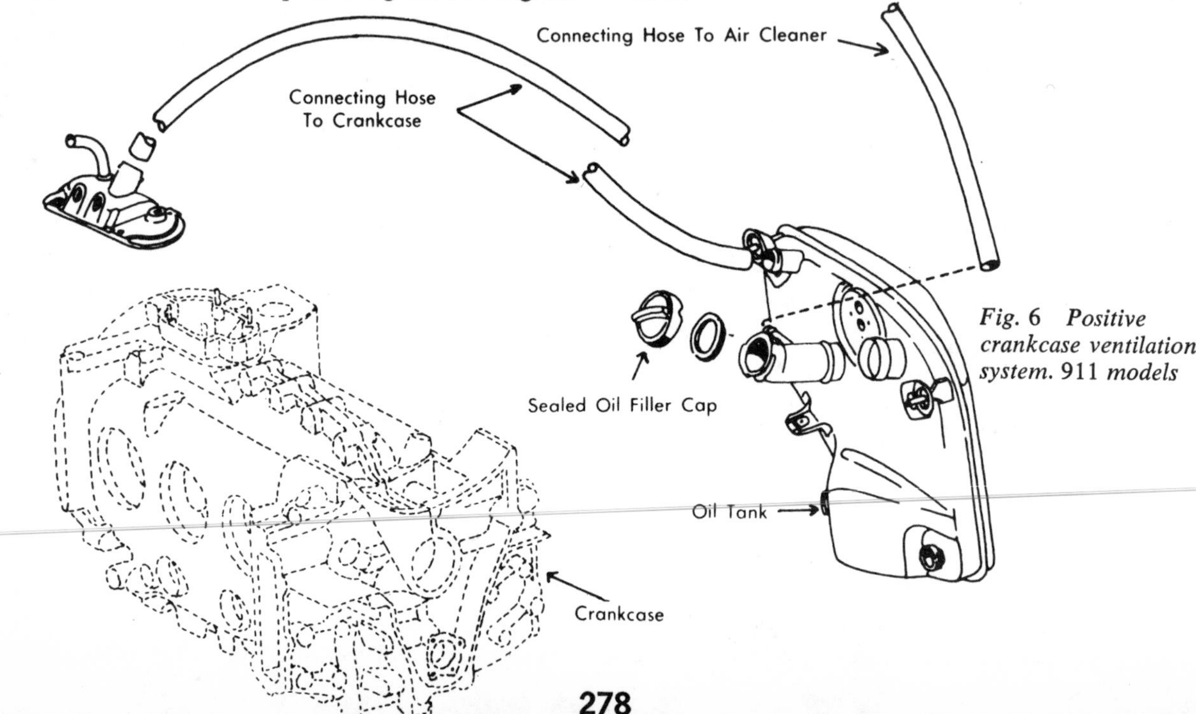

Fig. 6 *Positive crankcase ventilation system.* 911 *models*

RENAULT

GENERAL ENGINE SPECIFICATIONS

Model or Engine	Bore & Stroke Inches (mm)	Piston Displacement, Cubic Inches (cc)	Compression Ratio	Maximum Brake HP @ rpm	Maximum Torque Ft. Lbs. @ rpm	Normal Oil Pressure, Pounds
1974						
R12	3.11 x 3.31 (79 x 84)	101 (1647)	7.5	65 @ 5000	88 @ 2500	60–80
R15, R17	3.11 x 3.31 (79 x 84)	101 (1647)	7.5	65 @ 5000	88 @ 2500	60–80
Gordini 17	3.03 x 3.31 (77 x 84)	95.5 (1595)	9.0	107 @ 6000	96 @ 4500	60–80

TUNEUP SPECIFICATIONS

Car Model or Engine	Spark Plugs		Distributor		Firing Order	Ignition Timing		Hot Idle Speed, rpm
	Type	Gap, Inch	Point Gap, Inch	Dwell Angle, Degrees		Degrees BTDC	Mark Location	
1974								
R-12	Champion N-5	.025–.028	.016–.020	52–58	1-3-4-2	10	—	Auto.825–875 Std.625–675①
R-15	Champion N-5	.025–.028	.016–.020	52–58	1-3-4-2	10	—	Auto.825–875 Std.625–675①
R-17TL	Champion N-5	.025–.028	.016–.020	52–58	1-3-4-2	10	—	Auto.825–875 Std.625–675①
R-17G	Champion N—3	.025–.028	.016–.020	54–60	1-3-4-2	TDC ± 1	—	1000

①—In drive.

DISTRIBUTOR SPECIFICATIONS

Model or Engine	Distributor Part No.	Point Gap, Inch	Dwell Angle, Deg.	Spring Tension, Oz.	Centrifugal Advance			Vacuum Advance		
					Start @ rpm	Int.	Full @ rpm	Inches of Vacuum to Start Plunger	Int.	Full Advance Dist. Deg. @ Vacuum
1974										
R-12	7700574809①	.016–.020	52–58	12–16	0–2 @ 1000	10–14 @ 2000	30–34 @ 4500	—	—	16.4–20.4 @ 2②
R-15	7700574809③	.016–.020	52–58	12–16	0–2 @ 1000	10–14 @ 2000	30–34 @ 4500	—	—	16.4–20.4 @ 2②
R-17TL	7700574809	.016–.020	52–58	12–16	0–2 @ 1000	10–14 @ 2000	30–34 @ 4500	—	—	—
R-17G	7700552516	.016–.020	54–60	12–16	6.3 @ 1000	12.7 @ 2000	16 @ 2500	—	—	—

①—Automatic—7700559147 ②—Automatic only. ③—Automatic—7700559147 ④—7° retard @ 12

Emission Controls

1974 MODELS

EVAPORATIVE EMISSION CONTROL SYSTEM

Description

This system, Fig. 1, is designed to prevent fuel vapors from being emitted into the atmosphere. Components of the system are a non-vented fuel tank filler cap, an expansion tank, a carbon canister filled with activated charcoal, a control valve (built into the carburetor float chamber), and a series of ventilation lines which are used to connect the various components.

Operation

Expanded fuel (caused by high ambient temperatures) and fuel vapors pass from the fuel tank to the expansion tank. Any liquid fuel entering the

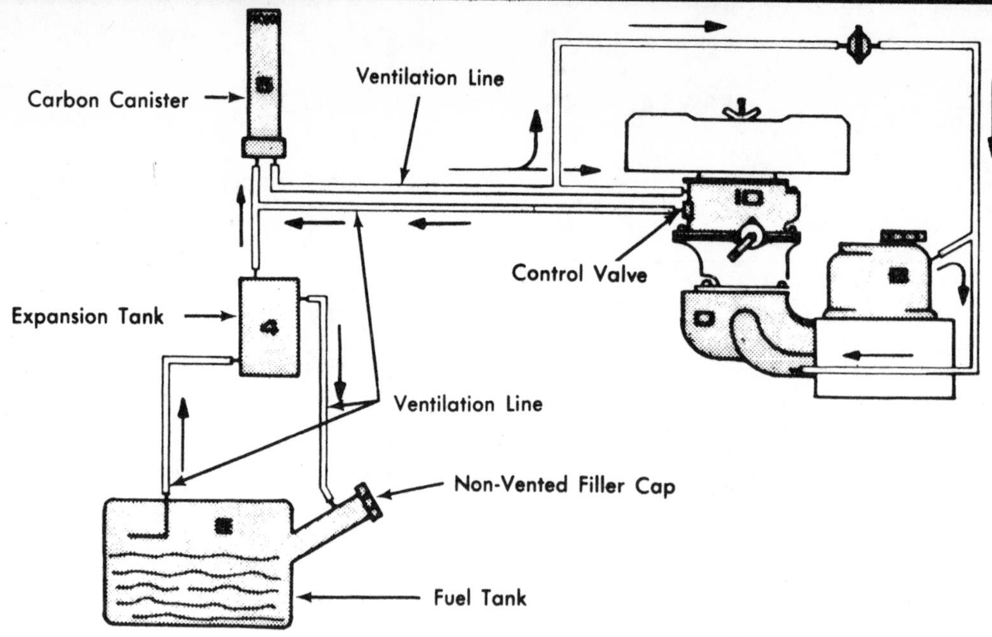

Fig. 1 Evaporative emission control system. (typical)

expansion tank is returned to the main fuel tank as the fuel level lowers during normal engine operation. Fuel vapors pass from the expansion tank through a ventilation line to the carbon canister where they are adsorbed by activated charcoal. High ambient temperatures will also cause fuel in the carburetor float chamber to expand. When the engine is not running, the carburetor float chamber control valve is open to the carbon canister and fuel vapors from the float chamber pass to the canister where they are adsorbed by activated charcoal. A ventilation line is connected between the carbon canister and the carburetor. When the engine is running, intake manifold vacuum, acting on this vent line, causes fresh air to be drawn into the canister. This fresh air mixes with the fuel vapors and together they are drawn into the carburetor and intake manifold where they enter the com-

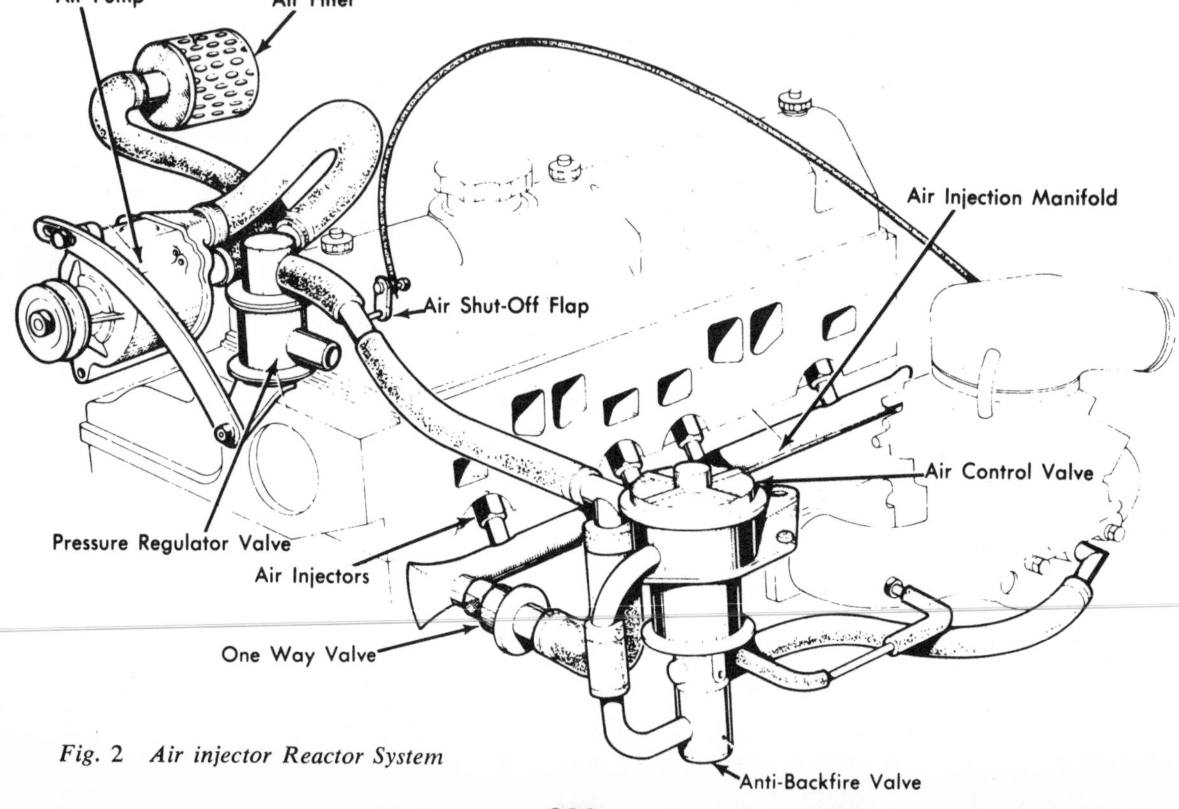

Fig. 2 Air injector Reactor System

bustion system and are burned. This action cleanses the charcoal and renews its storage capacity.

AIR INJECTION SYSTEM

Description

This system, Fig. 2, consists of an air pump, filter, pressure regulator valve, air shut off flap, air control valve, anti-backfire valve and manifold air injectors. EGR system consists of a choke controlled switch, solenoid valve, EGR valve, micro switch and micro switch control cam. Carburetors are Weber 32 DIR 37 (manual transmissions) and 32 DIR 38 (automatic transmissions). Carburetors are equipped with a fuel shut off valve. Operation of the system is as follows:

Air Pump

The air pump is a two vane rotary pump which draws air through a filter. When the engine speed increases, the volume of air from the pump also increases.

Air Control Valve

This is located on top of the anti-backfire valve. The valve remains closed at starting and idling. As engine speed increases, air pressure increases causing the diaphragm to pull the plunger upward. This allows air to enter the intake manifold.

Anti-Backfire Valve

The anti-backfire valve is located under the air control valve. Operated by vacuum from the intake manifold, the valve allows air to enter the intake manifold upon deceleration. Additional air leans air/fuel ratio which reduces level of emissions during deceleration.

Pressure Regulator

This is located on the discharge line of the pump and limits air pressure to a maximum of 4.27 psi at 3000 rpm.

Air Shut Off Flap

This device is operated by the choke cable. The flap prevents air from flowing to the intake manifold when the choke is in operation. With the engine running and the choke operational, air exits by the pressure regulator valve.

One-Way Valve

The one-way valve is located on the air manifold supply line. This valve prevents exhaust gases from flowing back into the pump where it would cause damage.

Manifold & Air Injectors

These direct the air in the exhaust ports to the exhaust valve heads.

Carburetor

Both carburetors (32 DIR 37 & 32 DIR 38) are equipped with a fuel shut off valve on the idle jet of the primary barrel. This electrically actuated valve cuts off idle fuel circuit when the ignition is turned off.

Filter

The filter is a throw away-type pleated paper filter located in a hose on the intake side of pump.

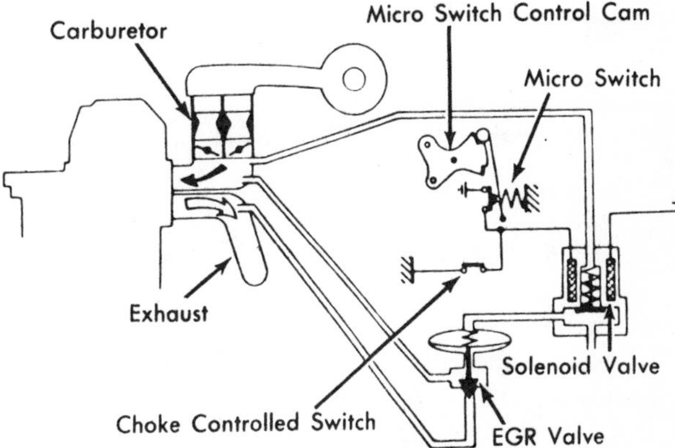

Fig. 3 Exhaust gas recirculation system. With auto. trans. exc. California

EXHAUST GAS RECIRCULATION SYSTEM

Models With Auto. Trans. Exc. California, Fig. 3

With the choke control knob pulled out no gas recirculation takes place. With the knob pushed in a micro switch, controlled by the throttle position, controls the exhaust gas recirculation. At idle or full throttle, the micro switch is closed allowing no exhaust recirculation. When the throttle is at intermediate speeds, the micro switch is open allowing vacuum to EGR valve. This allows exhaust gas to recirculate into the intake manifold.

California Models with Auto. Trans., Fig. 4.

This system operates the same as above, but uses a progressive EGR valve. The vacuum for the control valve is taken from venturi of the primary barrel of the carburetor. This vacuum regulates the amount of opening of EGR valve in relation to

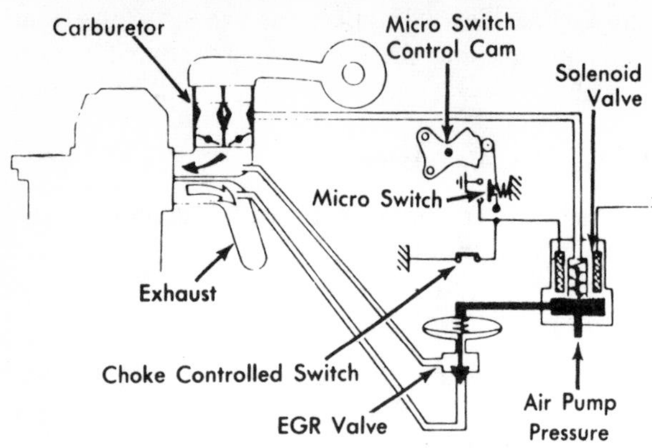

Fig. 4 Exhaust gas recirculation system. California models with auto. trans.

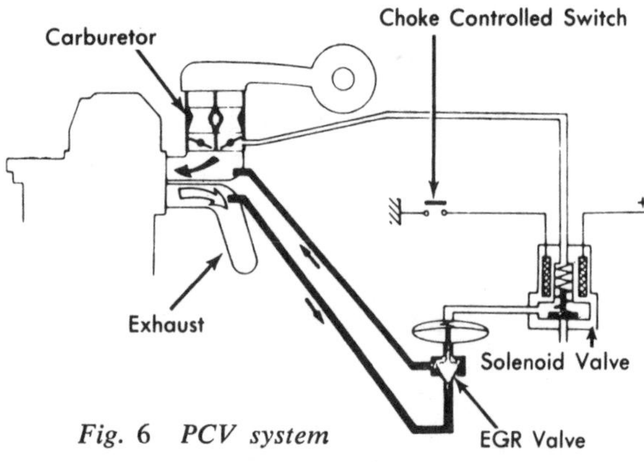

Fig. 6 PCV system

engine speed. When the choke control knob is pulled out, the EGR valve diaphragm is subject to pressure from the air pump and not just vented to atmosphere as in the above system.

California Models with Manual Trans., Fig. 5.

With the choke control knob pulled out, the current passes through the solenoid valve. This vents the EGR valve to the atmosphere not allowing exhaust gases to recirculate. When the control knob is pushed fully in the solenoid valve switch is open allowing no current to solenoid valve. This allows vacuum to open EGR valve and permits exhaust gas recirculation.

POSITIVE CRANKCASE VENTILATION SYSTEM

Description

The system (Fig. 6) consists of a non-vented oil filler cap, a PCV valve controlled by intake manifold vacuum, appropriate hose connections between crankcase and intake manifold, and between carburetor and crankcase, and a flame arrestor mounted in the connecting hose.

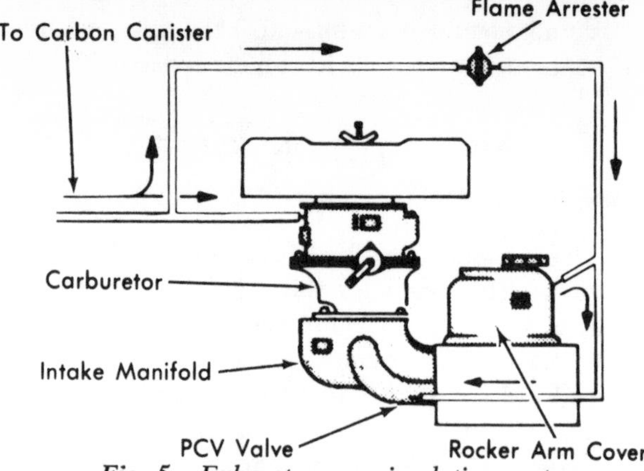

Fig. 5 Exhaust gas recirculation system. California models with manual trans.

Operation

Crankcase fumes and vapors are drawn through the rocker arm cover and PCV valve into the intake manifold where they combine with the air/fuel mixture and enter the combustion system to be burned. The PCV valve is designed to remain closed when the engine is not running, preventing an accumulation of hydrocarbon laden fumes from collecting in intake manifold which could result in hard starting. When engine is started, manifold vacuum pulls valve open against spring pressure and as long as there is vacuum the valve floats, permitting crankcase fumes to enter intake manifold. A flame arrestor is interconnected in the ventilation hose. Should a backfire occur, the flame arrestor would prevent fumes which may have been ignited from entering the carburetor. During certain engine operations, where intake manifold vacuum is low preventing PCV valve from opening, crankcase fumes will pass through the connecting hose to the carburetor where they enter the combustion system.

GENERAL SERVICE

Evaporative Emission Control System

Every 9000 miles, clean the charcoal canister filter located at the intake of the canister.

Exhaust Gas Recirculation

Every 12,000 miles check the operation of the EGR system. Carbon deposits on the EGR valve can be removed using a wire brush or scraper.

TESTING

California Models with Manual Transmission

Check when the engine is hot and idling with the choke pushed fully in. Apply vacuum to open EGR valve. The engine should begin to idle rough.

All Models with Automatic Transmission

Check when the engine is hot and idling with the choke pushed in. Move the micro switch actuating blade away from the control cam to cut off the current to solenoid valve. Engine should begin to run rough.

AIR INJECTION SYSTEM

Every 12,000 miles, replace the filter element in the air pump. If the pump is found to be defective, replace it.

Component Tests & Adjustments

Air Shut Off Flap

The choke cable must be adjusted properly before an adjustment can be made on the air shut-off flap. With the choke cable adjusted, pull the choke control knob all the way out and move the air shut-off flap actuating lever as far as it will go toward the pressure regulator valve side. Then tighten the set screw securing the cable to air shut-off flap actuating lever.

One Way Valve

Remove the valve and blow through it in the direction of air flow. There should be no restriction. Blow in opposite direction. There should be no air flow. If incorrect operation is found, replace the valve.

Anti-Backfire Valve

Disconnect the hose between the valve and the intake manifold. Accelerate the engine and release the pedal. When engine is decelerating, air is blown for approximately five seconds through the outlet side of valve. If time is incorrect, replace the valve.

Air Pressure

Remove the air shut-off flap and install a suitable pressure gauge adaptor in its place. Connect the air pressure gauge. Run engine at 3000 rpm, maximum pressure should be 4.27 psi.

Positive Crankcase Ventilation System

Every 6000 miles, clean the flame arrestor. Every 12,000 miles, replace the PCV valve and inspect and clean all hoses and fittings. Replace parts as necessary to insure proper operation of the system.

SAAB

GENERAL ENGINE SPECIFICATIONS

Model or Engine	Bore & Stroke, Inches (mm)	Piston Displacement, Cubic Inches (cc)	Compression Ratio	Maximum Brake HP @ rpm	Maximum Torque Ft. Lbs. @ rpm	Normal Oil Pressure, Pounds
1974						
99 LE, EMS	3.54 x 3.07 (90 x 78)	121 (1985)	8.7	110 @ 5500	123 @ 3700	54–60
Sonnett III	3.54 x 2.63 (90 x 66.8)	103.6 (1698)	8.0	65 @ 4700	85 @ 2500	47–55
1975						
All 99 exc. Cal.	3.54 x 3.07 (90 x 78)	121 (1985)	8.7	115 @ 5500	123 @ 3500	54–60
All 99 Calif.	3.54 x 3.07 (90 x 78)	121 (1985)	8.7	110 @ 5500	119 @ 3500	54–60

TUNEUP SPECIFICATIONS

Car Model or Engine	Spark Plugs		Distributor		Firing Order	Ignition Timing		Hot Idle Speed, rpm
	Type	Gap, Inch	Point Gap, Inch	Dwell Angle, Degrees		Degrees BTDC	Mark Location	
1974								
99C	Champion N8Y	.024–.028	.014	48–52	1-3-4-2	14	Flywheel	800
99E	Champion N8Y	.024–.028	.014	48–52	1-3-4-2	12	Flywheel	800–850
Sonett III	Champion N11Y	.024–.028	.012–.016	48–52	1-3-4-2	4	Flywheel	900
1975								
All 99	Champion N8Y	.024–.028	.014	48–52	1-3-4-2	14①	Flywheel	825–925

①—@800 rpm.

DISTRIBUTOR SPECIFICATIONS

Model or Engine	Distributor Part No.	Point Gap, Inch	Dwell Angle, Deg.	Spring Tension, oz.	Centrifugal Advance			Vacuum Advance		
					Start @ rpm	Int.	Full @ rpm	Inches of Vacuum to Start Plunger	Int.	Full Advance Dist. Deg. @ Vacuum
1974										
99	7992196	.012–.016	48–52	15–21	1 @ 500	5 @ 800	13.5 @ 2400	3.5	5 @ 1500	8.5 @ 21
Sonett III	0231-146-084	.012–.016	48–52	14–19	1 @ 500	5 @ 800	13.5 @ 2400	3.5	—	8.5 @ 11

Emission Controls

1974 MODELS

EVAPORATIVE EMISSION CONTROL SYSTEM

Description

This system controls the emission of fuel vapors into the atmosphere. The system is sealed to outside air by a sealed filler cap. A charcoal canister is provided to adsorb fuel vapors. The fuel tank is located between the rear wheels of the car while the charcoal canister is located in the engine compartment, Figs. 1 and 2.

Operation

When the engine is not running, vapors created in the fuel system travel through pipes to the charcoal canister and are adsorbed and stored in the charcoal element.

When the engine is running, vapors stored in the charcoal canister are purged by fresh air from the engine air cleaner which is drawn in through the canister filter in the bottom of the canister. Fuel vapors are then drawn into the engine to be burned with the regular air/fuel mixture.

DECELERATION VALVE

V4 Engine

The deceleration valve assembly (Fig. 3), is connected to the intake manifold. The valve body contains a spring loaded diaphragm which is held in place by the bottom cover. The diaphragm is subjected to manifold vacuum on the top side and to atmospheric pressure on the underside by a bleed hole in the cover. During periods of deceleration, intake manifold vacuum is sufficient for the diaphragm to overcome the spring loading and lift the deceleration valve off its seat. With the valve open, the vacuum draws a metered amount of air and fuel from the fuel pickup tube and the air bleed which flows from the outlet tube through the deceleration valve and into the manifold. This additional air/fuel mixture, coupled with other engine modifications, provides improved combustion. The air/fuel supply needed for combustion is fed to the engine through a hose which connects the deceleration valve to the deceleration section of the carburetor.

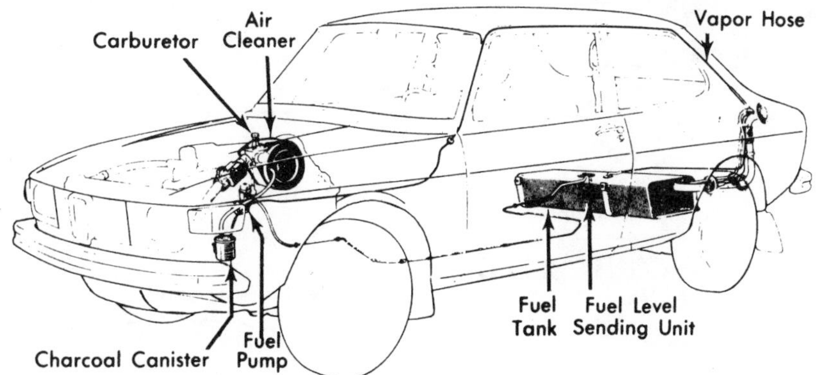

Fig. 1 Evaporative emission control system. 99 models

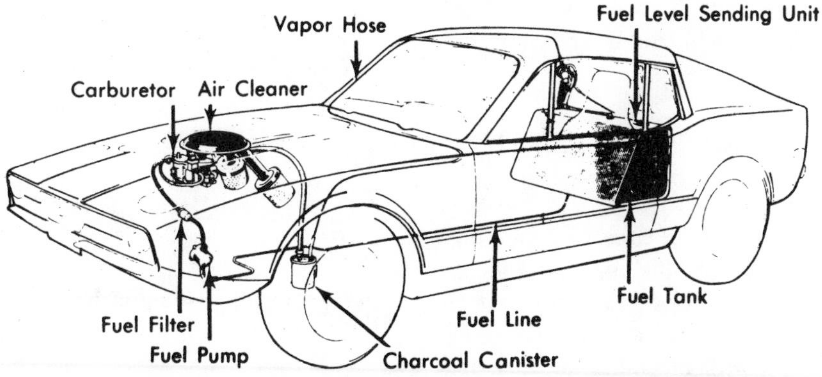

Fig. 2 Evaporative emission control system. Sonett III

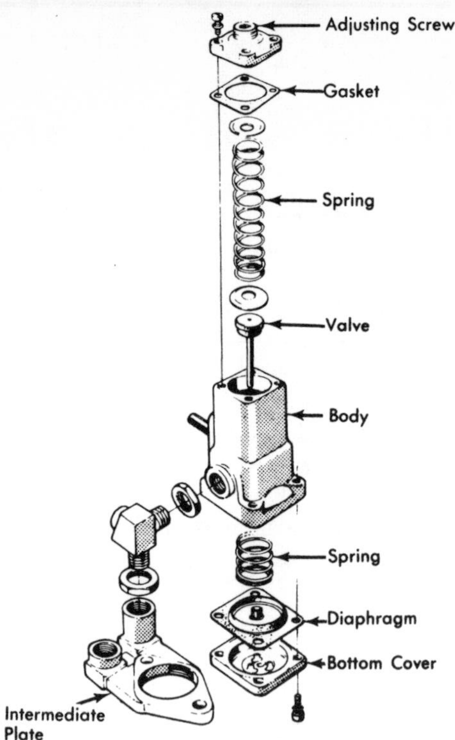

Fig. 3 Exploded view of deceleration valve

THERMOSTATICALLY CONTROLLED AIR CLEANER

V4 Engine

The air cleaner incorporates a valve assembly, which comprises a metal box fed by two air inlets, one for normal cold air intake and the other forming a hot air intake from a separate heat stove around the exhaust pipe. Enclosed in the box is a spring-loaded flap valve which pivots to control the proportions of hot and cold air entering the engine. A thermostatic bulb is connected through a spring linkage to the flap valve. As the engine warms up, air is drawn through hot air intake over the thermostatic bulb and into the air cleaner. When the air temperature reaches approximately 90° F, the thermostatic bulb expands and begins to force the flap valve down. This allows cold air to enter and mix with the hot air. Hot air intake is completely closed when intake air temperature reaches 95°-105° F.

POSITIVE CRANKCASE VENTILATION

Description

This system (Figs. 4 and 5), circulates filtered air from the air cleaner through the engine crankcase. Blow-by gases are drawn out of the crankcase up through the valve cover and hose to the intake manifold for burning with incoming air/fuel mixture. System components consist of a flame guard, hoses and flow control valve. Saab 99 engines use an oil trap between the crankcase and the air filter, and another oil trap in the camshaft cover.

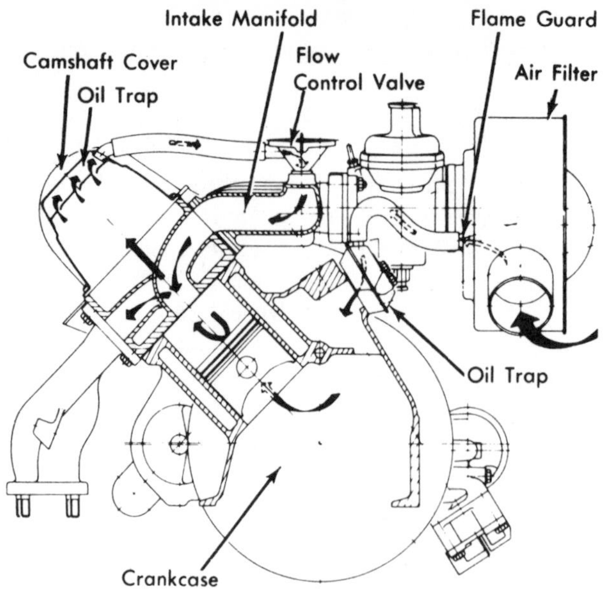

Fig. 4

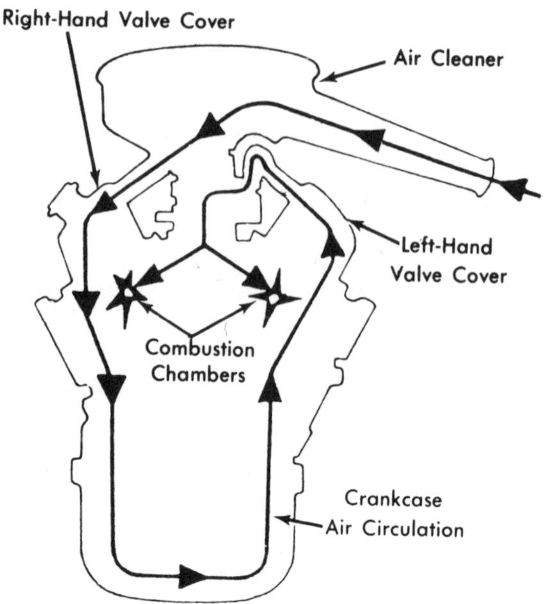

Fig. 5 Positive crankcase ventilation. V4 engine

GENERAL SERVICE

Deceleration Valve

Testing

NOTE: Air cleaner must be installed for this test.

1. With the engine idling at normal operating temperature, disconnect the hose between the

carburetor and the deceleration valve and check for vacuum passing through the valve. If vacuum is present, the adjusting screw on the deceleration valve has to be screwed in further until the valve is closed. Reconnect the hose between the carburetor and the deceleration valve.

2. Connect a tachometer and adjust idling speed to 900 rpm. Open the throttle to obtain 3000 rpm. Release the throttle and measure the time required for the engine speed to drop from 3000 rpm to idle. If deceleration valve is correctly adjusted, time should be between 7-8 seconds. If it is not between 7-8 seconds, the valve must be adjusted.

Adjusting

If the required time for the engine to decelerate from 3000 rpm to idle is more than 7-8 seconds, the deceleration valve adjusting screw should be turned clockwise. If required time is less than 7-8 seconds the adjusting screw should be turned counterclockwise until the desired time is reached.

Thermostatically Controlled Air Cleaner

Testing

1. Remove the front hose. With the valve assembly in position, engine cold, and an ambient temperature in the engine compartment of 85° F or less, the flap valve should be in the forward position shutting off cold air intake.
2. Start the engine and run at fast idle 2-6 minutes. When ambient temperature reaches 50°-70° F the valve plate should move towards the middle or back position. If not, remove the unit and check for possible wear or breakage of valve or linkage.

Positive Crankcase Ventilation

Every 12,000 miles check the system for proper operation. If necessary, clean the system components in a suitable solvent. Replace the parts as necessary to maintain proper operation.

TOYOTA

GENERAL ENGINE SPECIFICATIONS

Model or Engine	Bore & Stroke, Inches (mm)	Piston Displacement, Cubic Inches (cc)	Compression Ratio	Maximum Brake HP @ rpm	Maximum Torque Ft. Lbs. @ rpm	Normal Oil Pressure, Pounds
1974						
Corolla 1200	2.95 x 2.60 (75 x 66)	71.2 (1166)	9.0	65 @ 6000	67 @ 3800	51–63
Corolla 1600	3.35 x 2.76 (85 x 70)	96.9 (1588)	8.5	88 @ 6000	91 @ 3800	57–71
Corona, Celica	3.48 x 3.15 (88.5 x 80)	120 (1968)	8.5	97 @ 5500	106 @ 3600	57–71
Mark II	3.15 x 3.35 (80 x 85)	156.4 (2563)	8.5	122 @ 5200	141 @ 3600	57–71

TUNEUP SPECIFICATIONS

Car Model or Engine	Spark Plugs		Distributor		Firing Order	Ignition Timing		Hot Idle Speed, rpm
	Type	Gap, Inch	Point Gap, Inch	Dwell Angle, Degrees		Degrees BTDC	Mark Location	
1974								
Corolla 1200	①	.030	.016–.020	50–54	1-3-4-2	5	Timing cover	600
Corolla 1600	①	.030	.016–.020	50–54	1-3-4-2	5	Timing cover	750
Corona, Celica	①	.028–.032	.016–.020	50–54	1-3-4-2	7	Timing cover	650
Mark II	①	.030	.016–.020	39–43	1-5-3-6-2-4	5	Timing cover	750

①—Either Denso W20EP or NGK BP6ES.

DISTRIBUTOR SPECIFICATIONS

Model or Engine	Distributor Part No.	Point Gap, Inch	Dwell Angle, Deg.	Spring Tension, Oz.	Centrifugal Advance			Vacuum Advance		
					Start @ rpm	Int.	Full @ rpm	Inches of Vacuum to Start Plunger	Int.	Full Advance Dist. Deg. @ Vacuum
1974										
Corolla 1200	—	.016–.020	50–54	14–19	0 @ 1300	—	14 @ 4200	4.33	6 @ 7.87	9 @ 9.84
Corolla 1600	—	.016–.020	50–54	14–19	0 @ 1000	8.5 @ 2000	16.5 @ 4600	3.15	3 @ 4.06	7 @ 5.51
Corona, Celica	—	.016–.020	50–54	14–19	0 @ 1200	10 @ 2700	13 @ 5200	3.15	4.7 @ 4.72	7.5 @ 5.91
Mark II	—	.016–.020	39–43	14–19	0 @ 1500	6 @ 2400	14 @ 3600	3.54	5.7 @ 7.00	8.5 @ 9.45

Emission Controls

1974 MODELS

EVAPORATIVE EMISSION CONTROL SYSTEM

Description

This system is designed to prevent fuel vapors from escaping into the atmosphere by use of one or more of the following components—a fuel tank with a sealed filler cap, fuel and vapor separator, check valve, charcoal canister, vacuum switching valve and either a connection at intake manifold or at the carburetor.

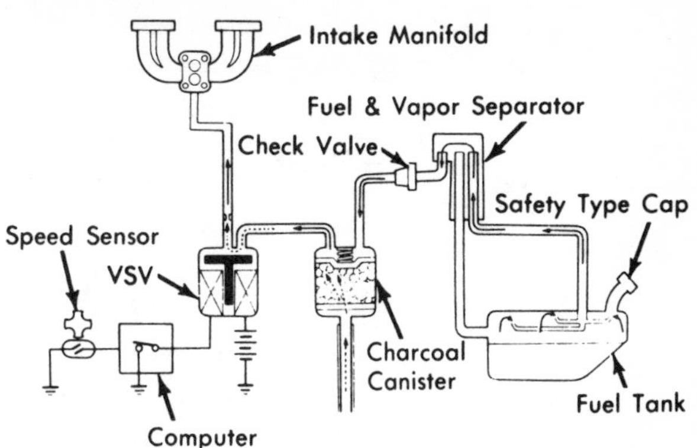

Fig. 2 Evaporative emission control system. With vapor separator, (Exc. California)

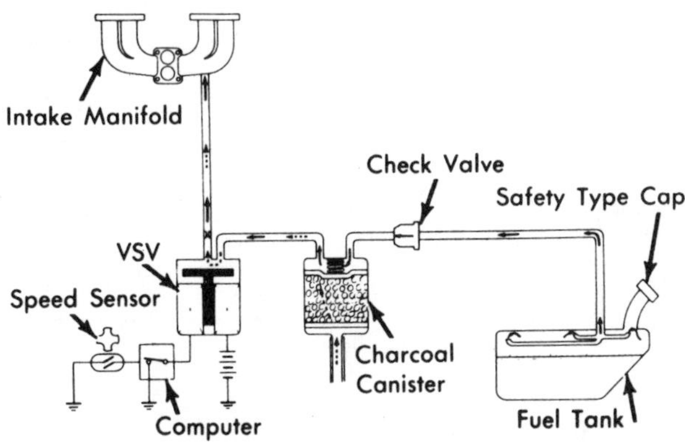

Fig. 1 Evaporative emission control system. Without vapor separator, (Exc. California)

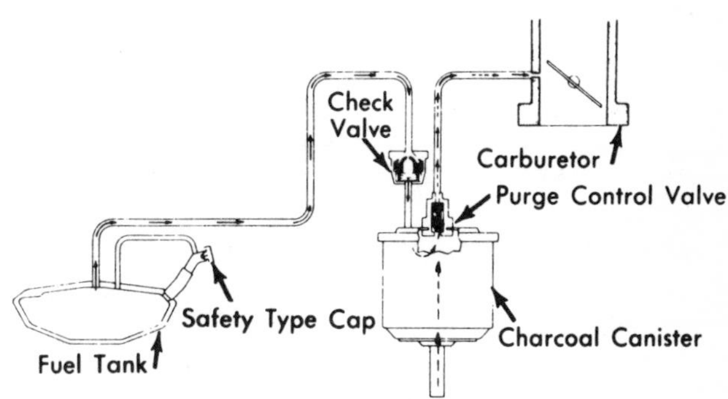

Fig. 2A Evaporative emission control system. 4M engine (California)

Operation

All Models Exc. California with 4M Engine, Figs. 1 & 2

These models use a vacuum switching valve which is controlled by a speed sensor and computer. The vapor line is routed from the charcoal canister to the vacuum switching valve and then to the intake manifold. At approximately 15 mph the vacuum switching valve is opened allowing fuel vapors to be drawn from the charcoal canister into the combustion chamber where they are burned.

California Models with 4M Engine, Fig. 2A

These models do not use a vacuum switching valve but route the fuel vapor line from the charcoal canister directly to the carburetor, just above the throttle plate. With the throttle plate closed no vacuum is created in the charcoal canister line and the purge valve remains closed. When the throttle plate is opened, the vacuum created opens the purge valve and draws vapor from the charcoal canister into the carburetor where it mixes with the air and fuel mixture which is then burned in the combustion chamber.

EXHAUST GAS RECIRCULATION

Description

California Models with 18R-C, 4M & F Engines

This system consists of an EGR valve, EGR valve sensor and tubes. It is controlled by a vacuum switching valve, speed sensor and thermo sensor.

Operation

18R-C & F Engines, Fig. 3

The EGR system is on when the speed sensor and all temperature sensors are in the ON range. When all speed and temperature sensors are on, the computer operates the vacuum switching valve which allows the vacuum from the carburetor to open the EGR valve allowing exhaust gases to enter

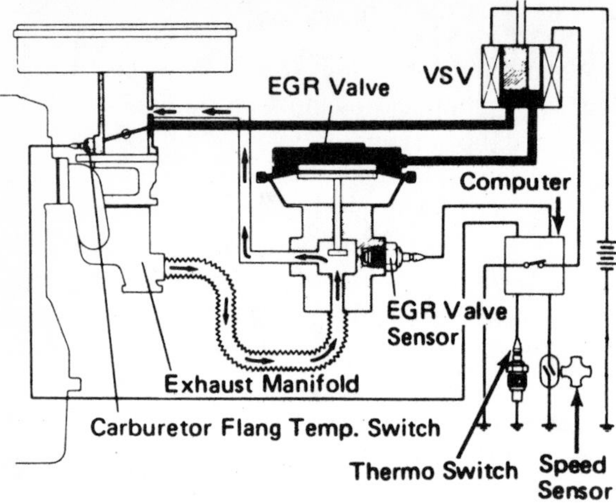

Fig. 3 Exhaust gas recirculation system. Models with 18R-C engine

the carburetor above the throttle plate. When any one of the speed or temperature sensors are in the OFF range, the EGR system is shut off.

4M Engine

The EGR system is in operation when the speed sensor and engine coolant temperature sensors are in the ON range (for speed and temperature see appropriate table). When speed and temperature sensors are on, the computer operates the vacuum switching valve, which provides vacuum to the EGR vacuum control valve. This valve allows vacuum to chamber A and atmospheric pressure to chamber B, Fig. 4, on the EGR valve, which allows the exhaust gases to the engine intake manifold. When either sensor is in the OFF range, the EGR system is off.

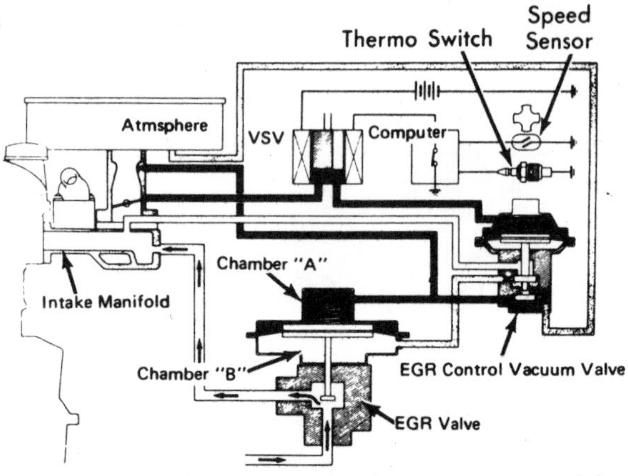

Fig. 4 Exhaust gas recirculation system. Models with 4M engine

TRANSMISSION CONTROLLED SPARK

Description

This system controls the vacuum advance or the vacuum retard and consists of computer, vacuum switching valve, speed sensor, thermo switch and vacuum control diaphragm on the distributor.

Operation

1. When the engine coolant temperature is between approximately 140-212° F, and the speed is under 36 mph (3K-C engine), 41 mph (2T-C & F engines), or 62 mph (18R-C & 4M engines), the temperature and speed sensors close circuits to the computer. In turn, the circuit to vacuum switching valve coil is closed and the coil is energized. This turns on the vacuum switching valve. Refer to chart for correct temperatures and speeds.

Control Sensors Operating Range

Application	Thermo Sensor On	Speed Sensor On
3K-C	140–212°F	11–36 mph
2T-C (Fed.)	140–221°F	31–41 mph
2T-C (Calif.)		
Man. Trans.	140–221°F	16–41 mph
Auto. Trans.	140–221°F	24–65 mph
18R-C (Fed.)	140–217°F	16–62 mph
18R-C (Calif.)	140–217°F	11–41 mph
4M (Fed.)	140–221°F	16–62 mph
4M (Calif.)	140–221°F	16–65 mph
F (Fed.)	140–208°F	①13–41 mph
F (Calif.)	113–217°F	①13–41 mph

①—Acceleration figures shown, deceleration figures are—Federal—31–9 mph and Calif.—26–9 mph.

2. On Land Cruiser models (F engine), the vacuum switching valve provides vacuum to act on the distributor retard diaphragm and ignition is thus retarded.
3. On all other engines (except 4M), when the vacuum switching valve is turned on, it cuts off all vacuum to the vacuum advance unit of the distributor. Only centrifugal advance is provided. On 4M engines, the vacuum switching valve applies vacuum to the retard side of distributor and allows atmosphere to the advance side which retards ignition timing.

Throttle Positioner RPM

Application	①Rpm Setting
3K-C	1500
2T-C & 18R-C	1400
4M	
Man. Trans.	1300
Auto. Trans.	1200
F	1200

①—Set in Neutral.

THROTTLE POSITIONER

Description

This system consists of a diaphragm-type vacuum actuator which is linked to the carburetor throttle linkage. The actuator is controlled by a vacuum switching valve and prevents complete throttle closing under certain deceleration conditions.

Operation

1. The positioner is controlled through the speed sensor by vacuum switching valve. At low speeds the valve allows atmospheric air to the diaphragm of throttle positioner. This sets the throttle positioner so that when the throttle is released, the throttle valve contacts the positioner and holds the throttle in a slightly opened position. Refer to chart for operating speeds.

Throttle Positioner Operating Range

Application	①On	②Off
3K-C & 2T-C	15 ± 4 mph	11 ± 2 mph
18R-C	③15 ± 4 mph	11 ± 2 mph
4M (Fed.)	15 ± 4 mph	11 ± 2 mph
4M (Calif.)	15 ± 5 mph	11 ± 3 mph
F (Fed.)	13 ± 2 mph	9 ± 4 mph
F (Calif.)	13 ± 3 mph	9 ± 4 mph

①—Upon acceleration system turns on.
②—Upon deceleration system turns off.
③—Preferred setting 13 mph.

2. When the vehicle speed decreases to about 10 mph (for specific engine speeds see Throttle Positioner Operating Range table), the vacuum switching valve, because of signals from the speed sensor, allows vacuum to the diaphragm of the throttle positioner. This releases the throttle positioner lever from its set position and allows the throttle valve to return to normal idling position.

AUXILIARY ACCELERATION PUMP

Description

This system consists of a warm up sensing valve, vacuum lines and a second accelerator pump diaphragm on the carburetor. The system is controlled by water temperature at the warm up sensing valve.

Operation

This system operates when engine coolant temperature is below 117.5° F when a warm-up sensing valve opens allowing vacuum to auxiliary acceleration pump diaphragm which injects additional fuel into carburetor.

MIXTURE CONTROL SYSTEM

Description

This system consists of a mixture control valve connected to intake manifold and to vacuum switching valve. The unit is controlled by vacuum switching valve, computer and speed sensor. The mixture control valve allows fresh air to pass into the intake manifold during deceleration from high or intermediate speeds. The valve serves to control air/fuel ratio during these periods.

Operation

When idling or at low speed, the speed sensor signals the computer to cut off vacuum to switching valve and no vacuum is allowed to the mixture control valve. During normal running at intermediate and high speed, the vacuum switching valve receives signals from the speed sensor which allows vacuum to reach the mixture control diaphragm. This vacuum is not high enough to activate the valve at this time. When the throttle is released suddenly, additional vacuum is created. This causes the control valve to open momentarily and allows fresh air to be drawn through the mixture control valve and into the intake manifold.

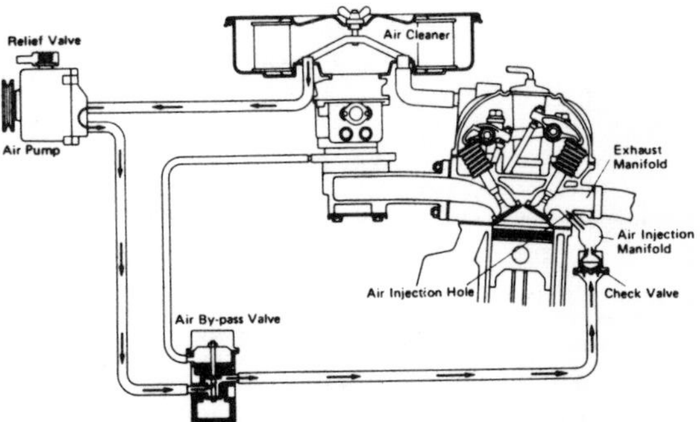

Fig. 5 Air injection reactor system. California 2TC engine

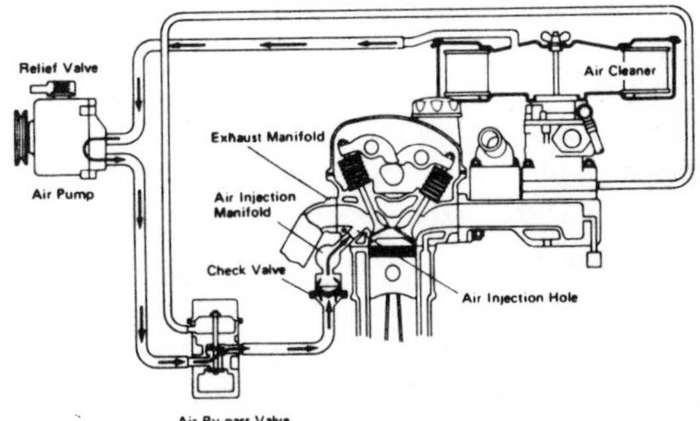

Fig. 6 Air injection reactor system. 4M engine

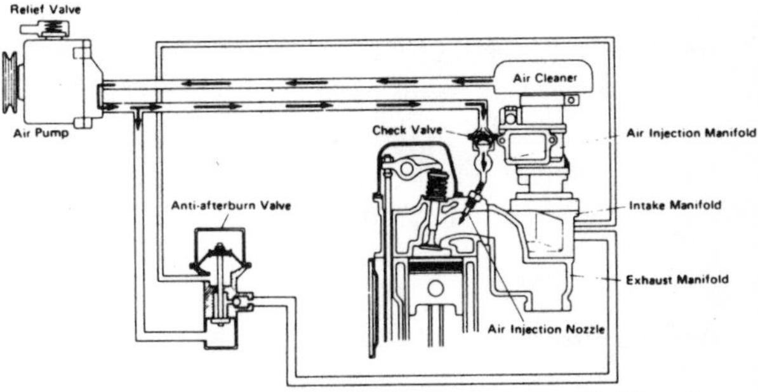

Fig. 7 Air injection reactor system. California F engine

AIR INJECTION SYSTEM

Description

This system, Figs. 5 thru 8, consists of an air pump, a by-pass valve (anti-afterburn valve on F

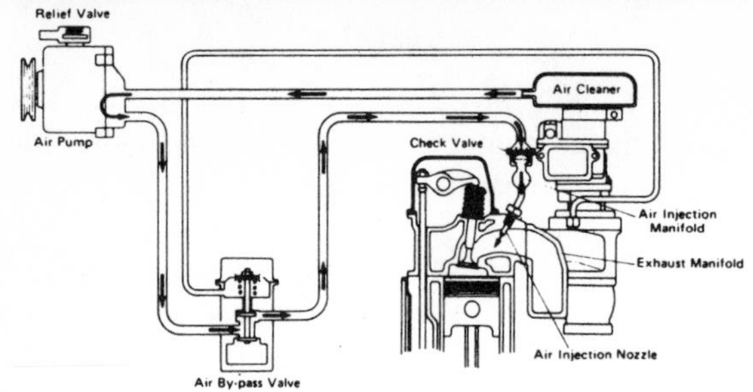

Fig. 8 Air injection reactor system. Exc. California F engine

engine in California), a check valve, an air distribution manifold, an injection nozzle for each cylinder exhaust port, a vacuum sensing hose and air supply hoses connecting the system.

Operation

Air under pressure from the air pump flows through a check valve to the air distribution manifold where it enters the exhaust manifold through air injection nozzles. A check valve is used to prevent a back flow of exhaust gas from entering the air pump when exhaust pressure exceeds air pump delivery pressure. During periods of engine deceleration, air is diverted to the atmosphere through a by-pass valve to prevent engine popping. Operation of individual components is as follows.

Air Pump

The pump consists of a pulley, housing, rotor subassembly, two vane assemblies, four carbon shoes, two shoe springs, front and rear carbon seals, rear rotor ring, ring bearing and housing cover sub-assembly. Pump is driven by crankshaft pulley by means of a V belt. One end of the vane is pivoted to a needle bearing case which is supported on the pivot shaft. The opposite end of the vane protrudes from an opening in the rotor into the air chamber. The space enclosed by rotor, vanes and housing changes as rotor rotates. The air intake volume increases as the rotor rotates. This air is then compressed into the exhaust chamber. A relief valve installed on the pump relieves excess air pressure in the pump, preventing damage to the system.

Anti-Afterburn Valve, Fig. 9

An anti-afterburn valve is provided to prevent afterburn in the system. At sudden deceleration, the valve causes air delivered from the air pump to enter the intake manifold. The anti-afterburn valve is connected to the intake manifold by a vacuum hose, which supplies the vacuum to operate the valve.

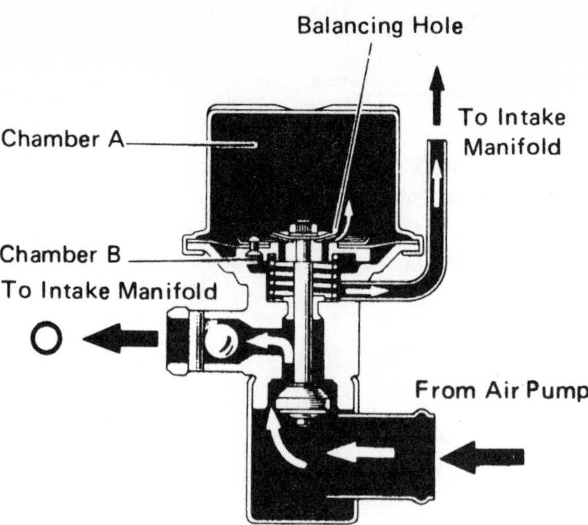

Fig. 9 Anti-afterburn valve

By-Pass Valve, Fig. 10

A by-pass valve is provided to prevent afterburn in the system. At sudden deceleration, the valve causes air delivered from the air pump to escape into the atmosphere instead of being delivered to the air injection nozzles. The by-pass valve is connected to the intake manifold by a vacuum sensing hose, which supplies vacuum to operate the valve.

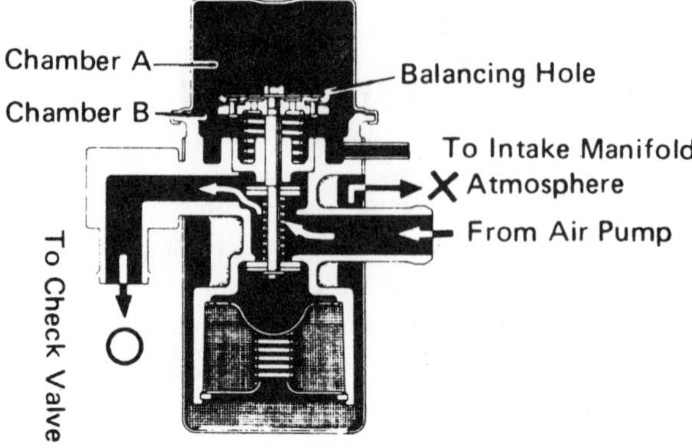

Fig. 10

Check Valve

A valve is provided in the system to stop exhaust gases from flowing back into the air pump. When the pressure of air from the air pump is greater than that of exhaust gas it opens the valve and is injected into the exhaust manifold. If the exhaust gas pressure should exceed the air pump pressure, the valve closes preventing gas from entering the air pump.

Air Injection Manifold & Nozzles

The manifold and nozzle assembly allows even distribution of air into the exhaust port of each cylinder. The nozzle is fixed in place at each exhaust port and is connected to air injection mani-

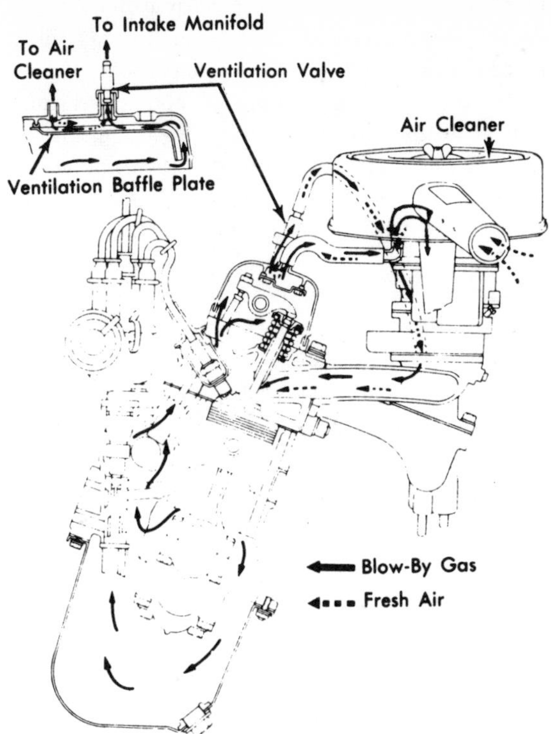

Fig. 11 *Crankcase ventilation system.* 3*KC engine*

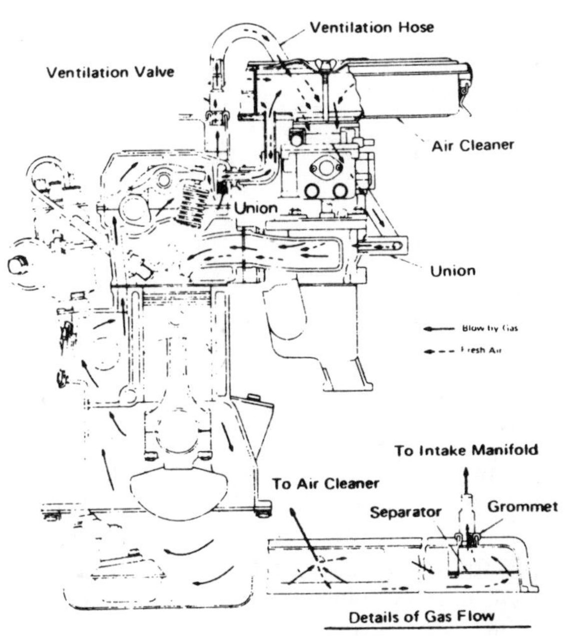

Fig. 12 *Crankcase ventilation system.* 18*R-C engine*

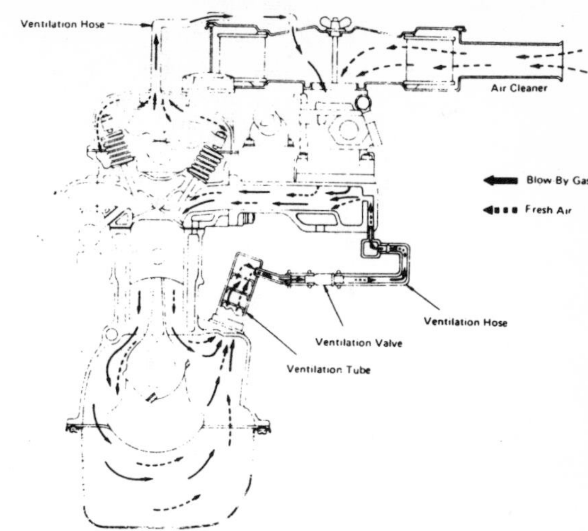

Fig. 13 *Crankcase ventilation system.* 4*M engine*

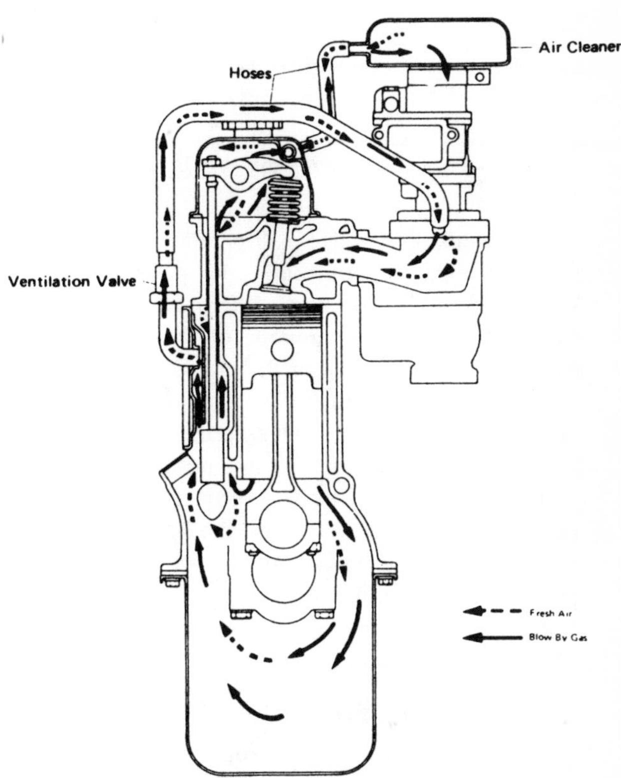

Fig. 14 *Crankcase ventilation system. F engine*

fold by means of a screw on each end of the manifold branches.

POSITIVE CRANKCASE VENTILATION

Description

This system, Figs. 11 thru 15, consists of a hose connecting the air cleaner and crankcase and a hose connecting the crankcase and intake manifold with a ventilation valve located in it.

Operation

Air enters the system from the air cleaner to the cylinder head cover. Fresh air mixes with crankcase fumes and enters ventilation tube into ventilation valve. Ventilation valve regulates the amount of air flow to meet the change in operating conditions. The air is then drawn into the intake manifold, through a connecting hose, where it enters the combustion system and is burned.

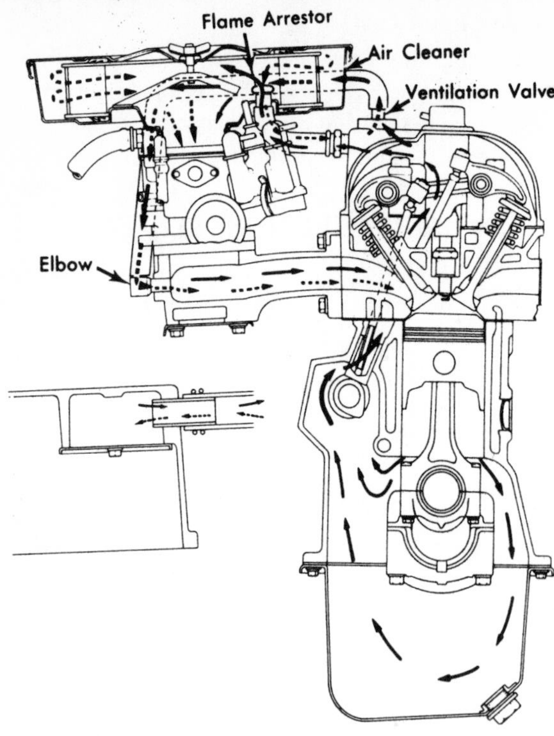

Fig. 15 *Crankcase ventilation system.* 2*T-C engine*

The ventilation valve is operated by pressure difference between crankcase and intake manifold. When there is no pressure difference (engine not running) or when the pressure of the intake manifold is greater than that of the crankcase, the valve is closed. During engine idle, high intake manifold vacuum overcomes the valve spring and the valve is pulled toward the intake manifold side by vacuum. This causes air to pass through the restricted passage between the valve and the housing. During normal engine operation, the valve remains in a position where spring pressure and intake manifold vacuum balance. The amount of air flow then depends on the position of valve.

GENERAL SERVICE

Transmission Controlled Spark

Testing Vacuum System

Disconnect the vacuum sensing hose from the distributor and connect the vacuum gauge in its place. The vacuum gauge must be placed so that it can be read by the driver. Road test the vehicle. Place it on a dynamometer or raise the wheels and bring the vehicle (speedometer) to various speeds of TCS operation. Observe the vacuum gauge readings. Maximum vacuum readings indicate OFF condition of TCS.

Testing Electrical System

1. Pull off vacuum switching valve connector and plug in special checker connector in its place. Attach ground connector to vehicle body and place checker on instrument panel.
2. Turn the ignition switch on and push the button on the side of checker. All three lamps will light if checker is in normal operating condition.
3. Running test on TCS system must be done at TCS operating speeds and temperatures. To achieve speeds required for tests, either road test, place vehicle on a chassis dynamometer, or raise up rear wheels under the axle housing. The TCS system is on whenever TCS indicator lamp on checker lights up.

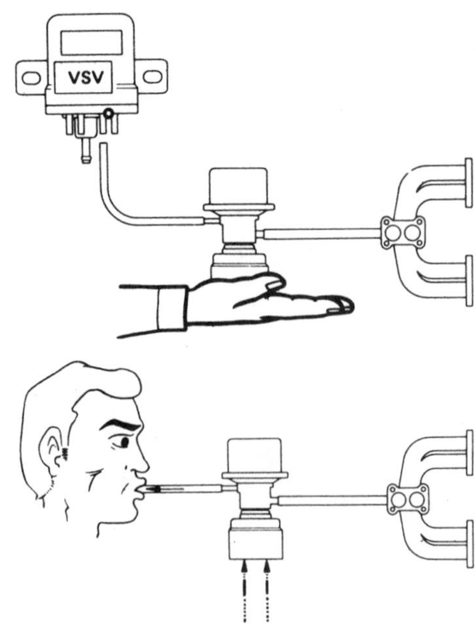

Fig. 16 *Checking mixture control valve*

Mixture Control Valve

Testing, Fig. 16

1. Disconnect the vacuum hose between MC valve and VSV, at VSV, and start the engine. Place hand over MC valve intake port and check for vacuum. If vacuum is felt, valve is defective. Then draw air through disconnected vacuum hose. Air should momentarily flow through MC valve.
2. With MC valve vacuum line still disconnected from VSV, connect a vacuum gauge to VSV so that the gauge is visible to the driver. Road test the vehicle, place on dynamometer or raise rear wheels and increase speedometer speed to above 41 ± 2 mph. At this point vacuum should be indicated on gauge. Decrease speedometer speed to 31 ± 5 mph. Vacuum should drop to zero.

Throttle Positioner

Testing

With the vehicle on the dynamometer, rear wheels raised, or while road testing vehicle, connect a vacuum gauge to the throttle positioner vacuum port on VSV. Raise vehicle speed slowly. The throttle positioner should turn on (no vacuum indicated on vacuum gauge) at about 15 mph. Raise vehicle speed to above 25 mph and decelerate to about 10 mph. Throttle positioner should turn off (vacuum reading on vacuum gauge).

Adjusting

With engine warmed, pull off the thermo sensor connector and adjust engine idling to specified rpm. See Tuneup Charts. Disconnect vacuum hose from throttle positioner and set throttle positioner to ON position. Using throttle positioner adjusting screw, set rpm to speed specified in the following table. Reconnect the vacuum hose and thermo sensor connector.

Speed Sensor

Testing

Disconnect the speedometer cable at the transmission. Disconnect the computer and connect

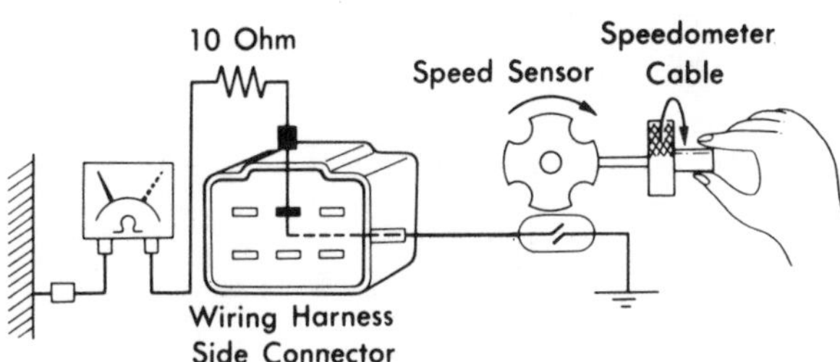

Fig. 17 Checking speed sensor

ohmmeter as shown in Fig. 17. Turn the cable by hand and count the number of on/off cycles. The number should be four for every one revolution of the speedometer cable.

Thermo Sensor

Connect the ohmmeter to the terminal of the sensor and to the body of the sensor. With temperature below 140° F or above 212° F thermo sensor should show conductivity. With temperature between 140° F and 212° F thermo sensor should show no conductivity.

Vacuum Switching Valve

Short Circuit Test

Unplug the valve connector and with a circuit tester check for shorting between various terminals and vacuum switching valve body. If any shorting is detected, the valve should be replaced.

Open Circuit Test

Unplug the valve connector and measure the resistances between positive (+) terminal and other terminals using a circuit tester. Replace valve if resistance is not to specified value.

AIR INJECTION SYSTEM

Every 6000 miles or 6 months, check system for proper operation. Clean or replace parts as necessary.

Component Testing

Air Pump

Disconnect the air outlet hose from the pump and install special tester 09258-60010 into the outlet. Make certain that the drive belt is correctly adjusted. Start the engine and raise the rpm as specified below. Check for discharge pressure.

Model	RPM	Discharge Pressure (Minimum)
2TC	1950	2.1 psi
4M	1350	2.1 psi
F	1000	2.1 psi

Make certain that the tester is not leaking at the connector. Observe the reading. The needle should be in the green area. If it is in the red area, check the relief valve and replace it if it is leaking. If not, the pump should be removed and inspected and repaired as necessary.

Pressure Relief Valve

Check the air pump discharge pressure just as air starts to come out from the relief valve discharge hole. Pressure should be 2.8-5 psi.

Anti-Afterburn Valve

At idle, remove the hose to the intake manifold. No air should be felt. Raise engine speed. Air should be felt for a short time. If the valve does not perform as specified it is defective and should be replaced.

By-Pass Valve

Check the by-pass valve for leakage at idle. Replace the valve if leakage exists. Increase engine speed and close the throttle suddenly. If air exhausts through valve at the instant the throttle is closed, the valve is satisfactory.

POSITIVE CRANKCASE VENTILATION

Every 12,000 miles, check and clean the PCV system. Every 24,000 miles or two years, replace the PCV valve. Every 3000 miles clean the air cleaner element and replace it every 18,000 miles.

VOLKSWAGEN

MODEL IDENTIFICATION

Type 1—Beetle, Super Beetle, Karmann Ghia   Type 2—Station Bus   Type 4—412
Type 32/33—Dasher

GENERAL ENGINE SPECIFICATIONS

Model or Engine	Bore & Stroke, Inches (mm)	Piston Displacement, Cubic Inches (cc)	Compression Ratio	Maximum Brake HP @ rpm	Maximum Torque Ft. Lbs. @ rpm	Normal Oil Pressure, Pounds
1974						
Type 1	3.37 x 2.72 (83 x 69)	96.6 (1584)	7.3	46 @ 4000	72 @ 2800	28
Type 2	3.66 x 2.59 (93 x 66)	109.5 (1795)	7.3	65 @ 4200	91 @ 3000	28
Type 4	3.54 x 2.59 (90.6 x 66)	102.5 (1679)	8.2	76 @ 4900	95 @ 2700	28
Dasher	3.01 x 3.15 (76.5 x 80.0)	89.75 (1470)	8.2	75 @ 6000	79 @ 4000	28

TUNEUP SPECIFICATIONS

Car Model or Engine	Spark Plugs: Type	Spark Plugs: Gap, Inch	Distributor: Point Gap, Inch	Distributor: Dwell Angle, Degrees	Firing Order	Ignition Timing: Degrees BTDC	Ignition Timing: Mark Location	Hot Idle Speed, rpm
1974								
Type 1	Bosch① W145TI	.028	.016–.020	44–50	1-4-3-2	7.5②	Fig. B	800–900 Std. 900–1000 Auto
Type 4	Bosch① W145TI	.028	.016	44–50	1-4-3-2	27 @ 3500		800–1000
Dasher	Bosch① W145TI	.028	.015	47–53	1-3-4-2	30 @ 3000③		850–1000

①—or Champion L-88-A.
②—Vac. disconnected @ 800–900 rpm. Cal. M/T −5° ATDC w/vac. connected.
③—Vac. disconnected.

DISTRIBUTOR SPECIFICATIONS

Model or Engine	Distributor Part No.	Point Gap, Inch	Dwell Angle, Deg.	Spring Tension, Oz.	Centrifugal Advance: Start @ rpm	Centrifugal Advance: Int.	Centrifugal Advance: Full @ rpm	Vacuum Advance: Inches of Vacuum to Start Plunger	Vacuum Advance: Int.	Vacuum Advance: Full Advance Dist. Deg. @ Vacuum
1974										
Type 1-Man.①	VW 043-905-205	.016	44–50	—	1050–1250	7–12 @ 1600	20–25 @ 3800	2.2–3.9	—	8–12 @ 7.9
Type 1-Auto.②	VW 043-905-205A	.016	44–50	—	1050–1200	12–14 @ 1600	22–25 @ 3900	2.4–3.9	—	8–12 @ 7.9
Type 4-Man. 1700	VW 022-905-205H	.016	44–50	—	800	—	14½ @ 1200	5.4–7	—	5–9 @ 8
Type 4-Auto. 1800	VW 022-905-205S	.016	44–50	—	1000–1200	9–14 @ 1600	21–25 @ 3400	3.2–4.3	—	8–12 @ 7.9
Dasher③	VW 055-905-205	.016	44–50	—	1050–1350	16–20 @ 2200–2300	26–30 @ 5000	8.3–9.4④	—	11–14 @ 13.1 13.7⑤
Dasher⑥	VW 056-905-205C	.016	47–53	—	1100–1400	15–20 @ 2100–2200	26–30 @ 5000	7.9–9.4⑦	—	11–15 @ 13.7⑧

①—Except Calif.
②—Manual-Calif.
③—Except Calif.
④—Retard 6.3–8.4.
⑤—Retard 8–9° @ 9.4–11.6.
⑥—California.
⑦—Retard 5.9–7.4.
⑧—Retard 8–9° @ 9.8–11.8.

Emission Controls

1974 MODELS

POSITIVE CRANKCASE VENTILATION

Description

Through the use of this system harmful emissions from the engine crankcase are not permitted to reach the outside air. These emissions are recirculated to the intake air system and then burned in the combustion chamber.

Operation

Exc. Dasher & Fuel Injected Engines, Fig. 1 & 2

Harmful pollutants in the engine crankcase are recirculated from the crankcase breather through a rubber hose to the air cleaner. These pollutants mix with the air/fuel mixture in the carburetor and are later burned in the engine.

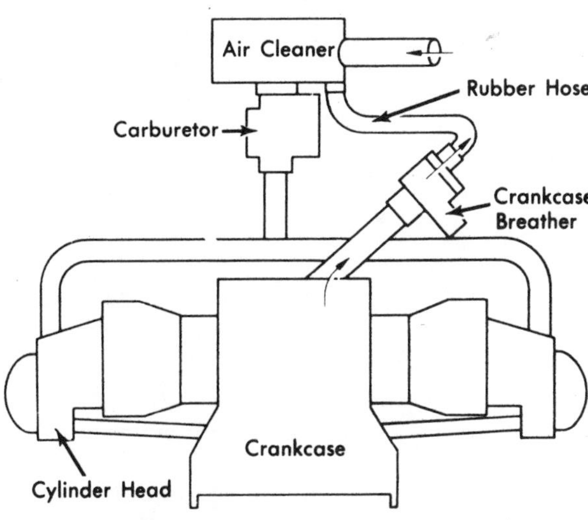

Fig. 1 Crankcase ventilation system, Beetle, Karmann Ghia, Thing

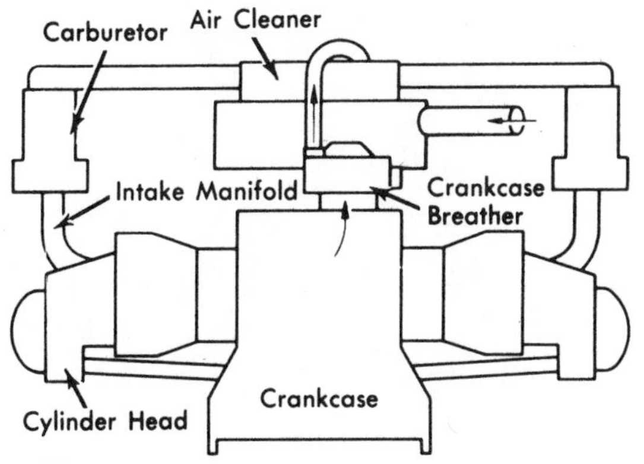

Fig. 2 Crankcase ventilation system, all vans

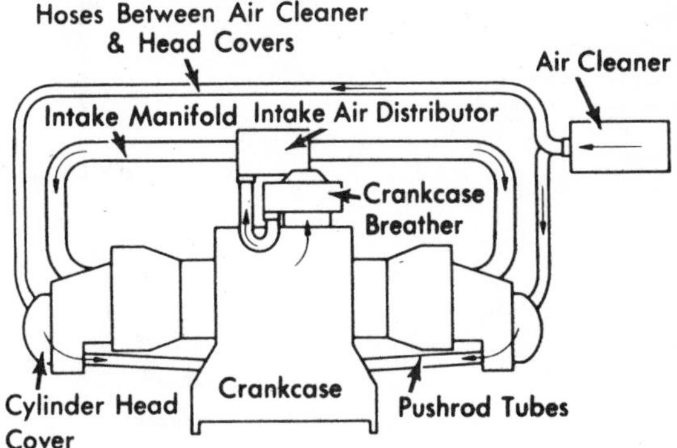

Fig. 3 Crankcase ventilation system, all with fuel injection

Fuel Injected Engines, Fig. 3

Fresh air coming from the air cleaner passes through the cylinder head covers and push rod tubes into the engine crankcase. Here the fresh air is mixed with the crankcase pollutants and recirculated via the crankcase breather and the intake air distributor to the combustion chamber, where they are burned. A regulator valve between the crankcase breather and the intake air distributor controls the flow of the recirculated fresh air/emission mixture to the engine.

AIR INJECTION SYSTEM

Dasher & Van Models

Description, Fig. 4

This system used on California models is designed to reduce HC and CO emissions by injecting air into the exhaust port. This system consists of an air pump, control valve, check valve, anti-backfire valve, high pressure valve and the injection ports drilled into the cylinder heads.

Operation

The air pump forces air through the filter, through the high pressure valve and through the check valve. Air from the check valve then passes through the drilled passages in the cylinder heads and into the exhaust ports. Under high manifold vacuum conditions, the anti-backfire valve routes this air to the intake manifold and mixes with the incoming air/fuel mixture to prevent an overrich mixture. This leaner mixture prevents backfiring upon deceleration.

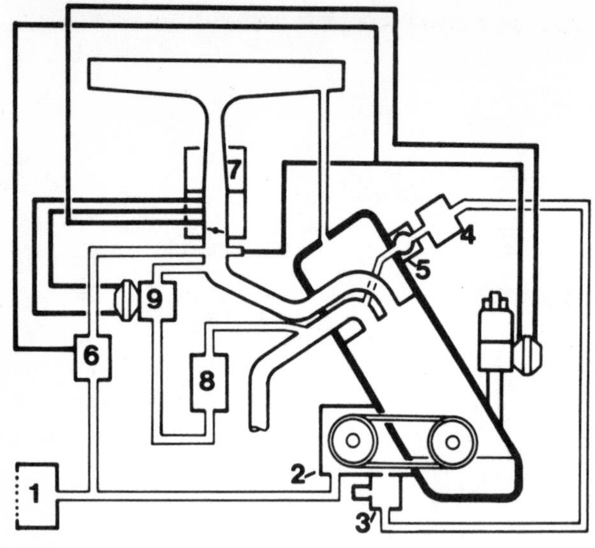

1 Air pump filter
2 Air pump
3 Relief valve
4 Check valve
5 Air manifold
6 Anti-backfire valve
7 Carburetor
8 EGR filter
9 EGR valve

Fig. 4 Air injection system, Dasher

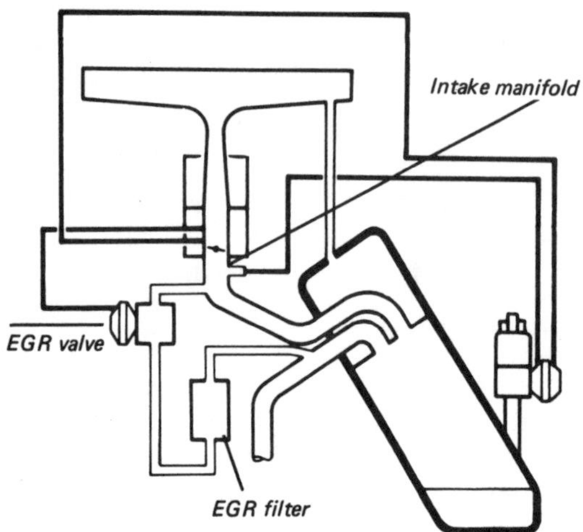

Fig. 5 EGR system, Dasher

EXHAUST GAS RECIRCULATION

All Models Exc. 412 with Man. Trans.

Description

Exhaust gas from the exhaust manifold passes through a filter where it is cleaned. The vacuum operated EGR valve controls the amount of this exhaust gas which is allowed into the intake manifold. The addition of exhaust gas reduces the formation of Oxides of Nitrogen (NOx) in the exhaust, Fig. 5.

Operation

The vacuum operated EGR valve allows a metered amount of exhaust gases to pass through the filter, the EGR valve and into the intake manifold. During full throttle, EGR is cancelled due to the small amount of vacuum present in the intake manifold.

EVAPORATIVE EMISSION CONTROL SYSTEM

Description

This system (Figs. 6 & 7) is designed to prevent fuel vapors from being emitted into the atmosphere. The system consists of a non-vented fuel tank filler cap, an expansion chamber, an activated charcoal canister, and a series of vent lines which interconnect the components between the fuel tank and the carburetor air cleaner. A pressure line, used to purge the system, is connected between the engine blower assembly and the charcoal canister.

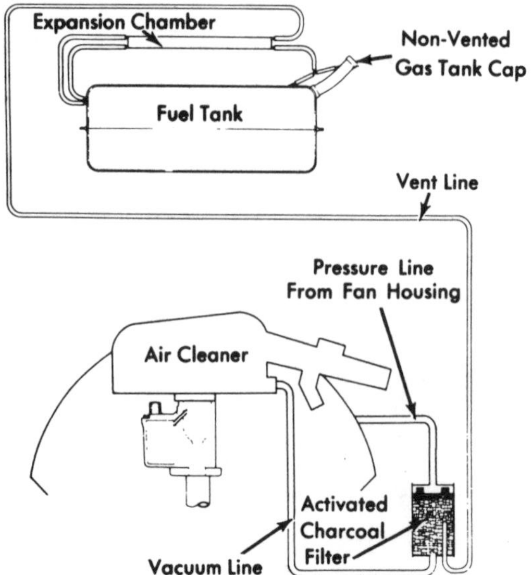

Fig. 6 Evaporative system, all except Dasher

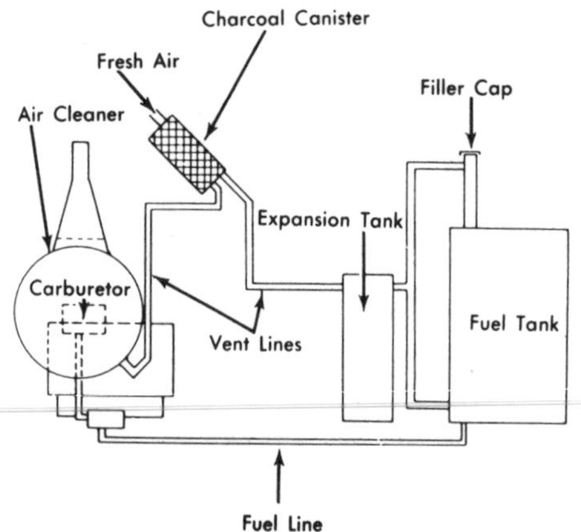

Fig. 7 Evaporative system, Dasher

Adjusting & Checking California Version

Idle Adjustments

1. Engine at operating temperature.
2. Disconnect hose between air pump and air manifold at pump, plug the hose.
3. Adjust ignition timing to 3° ATDC with the vacuum hoses connected.
4. Adjust idle speed to 925 ± 75 RPM with idle speed adjusting screw.
5. Adjust CO with idle mixture adjusting screw to 1.5%.
6. Reconnect air pump hose.
7. CO should now be below 1%.

Checking EGR Valves

1. Disconnect vacuum lines from EGR valve.
2. Disconnect vacuum at ignition distributor vacuum unit and extend hose.
3. Start engine and idle.
4. Connect extended vacuum hose to each EGR valve vacuum connection.
5. Engine should run rough or stall.
   At the right connection (installed position) engine is less affected than at the left connection.
6. If idle is steady during both connections, the exhaust line is blocked or the EGR valve is defective.
   If idle is steady during only one connection, the EGR valve is defective.

Checking Air Pump System

1. Remove air manifold, clean.
2. With compressed air blow into anti-backfire valve in direction of airflow only.
3. Clean or replace air pump filter.
4. Start engine. Exhaust gas should flow equally from air inlets.
5. If the air outlet of the relief valve is blocked with your thumb and the engine is idling, only slight pressure should be developed.

Anti-backfire Valve

1. Disconnect line from air pump filter to anti-backfire valve.
2. With running engine, momentarily disconnect vacuum line from anti-backfire valve. The anti-backfire valve should draw in air noticeably.
3. Replace anti-backfire valve when warm engine backfires.

EGR Valve

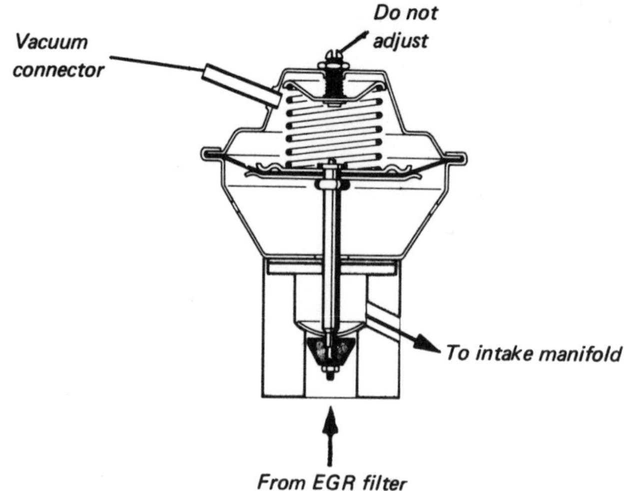

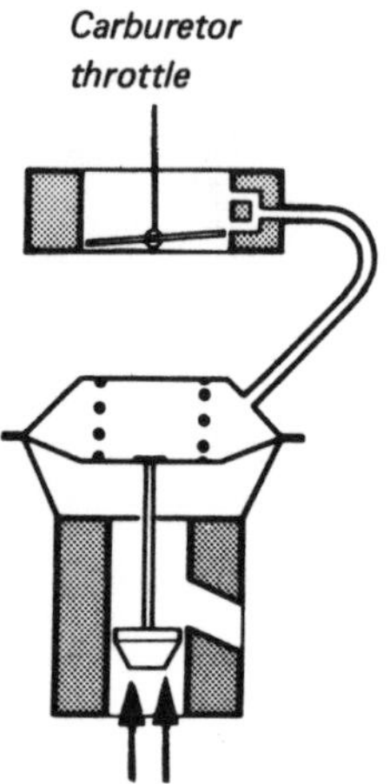

Idle

- Closed throttle – no vacuum at bypass drillings
- No exhaust gas recirculation

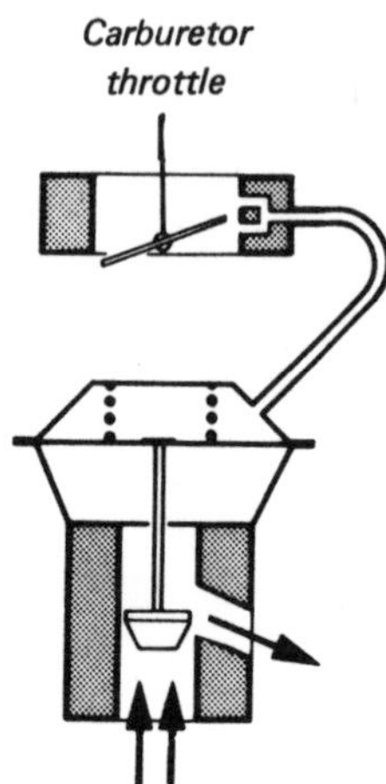

Slight Throttle

- Throttle open
- Slight vacuum
- Partial exhaust gas recirculation

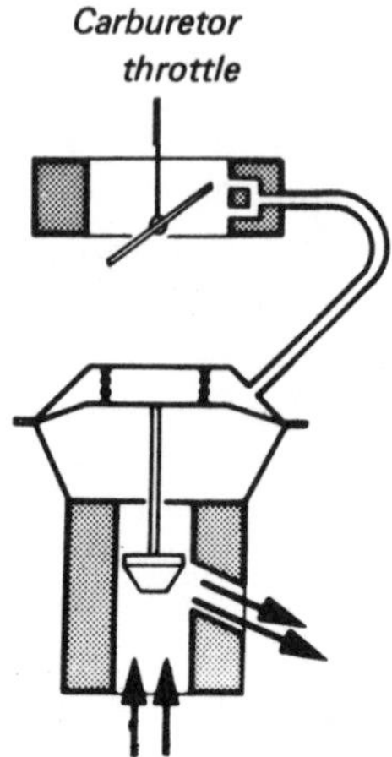

More Throttle

- Throttle open
- More vacuum
- Full exhaust gas recirculation

Operation

Fuel tank venting

An expansion chamber for the tank and vent lines are parts of the fuel tank vent system. These components prevent fuel from escaping to the outside at extremely high outside temperatures and when the car is driven or parked at an incline or in any other non-level position.

Activated charcoal filter

Vapors from the fuel tank are trapped in a container filled with activated charcoal. The filter is connected to the fuel tank vent system that we described above. The illustration shows how it works.

Fuel vapors pass through the filter and deposit hydrocarbons on the surface of the charcoal filter element. When the engine is running, fresh air diverted from the cooling fan of the engine cleans the filter and routes these hydrocarbons back to the engine where they are burned during normal combustion.

GENERAL SERVICE

Every 10,000 miles or yearly check the air injection system components for proper operation. Clean the air pump filter. Every 18,000 miles or 2 years, replace the air pump filter.

Every 24,000 miles or 2 years, check the EGR valve for proper operation by running the engine and visually checking whether the pin moves in and out in proportion to engine speed. Check for leaks and general condition of hoses. Replace the exhaust gas filter.

Every 30,000 miles, replace the activated charcoal filter. Inspect the system for damaged, deteriorated or loose hose connections. Replace or repair as necessary.

Air Injection System, Dasher

Checking EGR Valves

1. Disconnect the vacuum lines from the EGR valve.
2. Disconnect vacuum at distributor vacuum unit and extend the hose.
3. Start the engine and idle.
4. Connect the extended vacuum hose to each EGR valve vacuum connection.
5. The engine should run rough or stall.

   At the right connection (installed position) the engine is less affected than at the left connection.
6. If idle is steady during both connections, the exhaust line is blocked or the EGR valve is defective. If idle is steady during only one connection, the EGR valve is defective.

Checking Air Pump System

1. Remove air manifold and clean it.
2. With compressed air, blow into the anti-backfire valve in the direction of airflow only.
3. Clean or replace the air pump filter.
4. Start the engine. Exhaust gas should flow equally from air inlets.
5. If the air outlet of the relief valve is blocked with your thumb and the engine is idling, only slight pressure should be developed.

Anti-backfire Valve

1. Disconnect the line from the air pump filter to the anti-backfire valve.
2. With the engine running, momentarily disconnect the vacuum line from anti-backfire valve. The anti-backfire valve should draw in air noticeably.
3. Replace the anti-backfire valve when warm engine backfires.

VOLVO

VEHICLE IDENTIFICATION

Year	Engine Type	Output BHP	Vehicle Series
1974	B20F	109	140
	B30F	138	160

GENERAL ENGINE SPECIFICATIONS

Model or Engine	Bore & Stroke, Inches (mm)	Piston Displacement, Cubic Inches (cc)	Compression Ratio	Maximum Brake HP @ rpm	Maximum Torque Ft. Lbs. @ rpm	Normal Oil Pressure, Pounds
1974						
B20F	3.50 x 3.15 (88.9 x 88.0)	121 (1986)	8.7	109 @ 6000	115 @ 3500	35–85
B30F	3.50 x 3.15 (88.9 x 88.0)	182 (2979)	8.7	138 @ 5500	154 @ 3500	36–85
1975						
240	3.50 x 3.15 (88.9 x 88.0)	121 (1986)	8.7	98 @ 6000①	110 @ 3500①	35–85
164	3.50 x 3.15 (88.9 x 88.0)	182 (2979)	8.7	130 @ 5250②	150 @ 4000②	35–85

①—94 @ 6000 Calif. 105 @ 3500 Calif.
②—125 @ 5250 Calif. 145 @ 4000 Calif.

TUNEUP SPECIFICATIONS

Car Model or Engine	Spark Plugs: Type	Spark Plugs: Gap, Inch	Distributor: Point Gap, Inch	Distributor: Dwell Angle, Degrees	Firing Order	Ignition Timing: Degrees BTDC	Ignition Timing: Mark Location	Hot Idle Speed rpm
1974-75								
B20F	Bosch W200T35	.028–.032	.014	59–65	1-3-4-2	10	Pulley	800 Std. 700 Auto.
B30F	Bosch W200T35	.028–.032	.010	39–45	1-5-3-6-2-4	10	Pulley	800 Std. 700 Auto.

DISTRIBUTOR SPECIFICATIONS

Model or Engine	Distributor Part No.	Point Gap, Inch	Dwell Angle, Deg.	Spring Tension, oz.	Centrifugal Advance: Start @ rpm	Centrifugal Advance: Int.	Centrifugal Advance: Full @ rpm	Vacuum Advance: Inches of Vacuum to Start Plunger	Vacuum Advance: Int.	Vacuum Advance: Full Advance Dist. Deg. @ Vacuum
1974-75										
B20F	462552-1	.014	59–65	18–22	840–1060	5 @ 1660–1960	12 @ 4500	1.2–4.3	①	②
B30F	461527-4	.010	39–45	18–22	850–1150	5 @ 1500–1800	10½ @ 3180	1.2–4.3	③	④

①—3° retard @ 3.1–5.
②—5° retard @ 5.1.
③—2° retard @ 2.5–4.7.
④—4-6° retard @ 5.1.

Emission Controls

1974 MODELS

EVAPORATIVE EMISSION CONTROL SYSTEM

Description

This system is designed to prevent fuel vapor emission from the fuel system being discharged into the atmosphere. The fuel system is completely sealed and vented only through a carbon canister which absorbs fuel vapors, Fig. 1. This system consists of the following components.

Fuel Tank & Filler Cap

The tank is fitted with a sealed filler cap and is vented by two vent lines, one from the filler neck and the other from the top of the tank to a balance valve.

Expansion Tank

This tank is located inside the fuel tank and stores fuel expansion caused by high ambient temperature with a full tank.

Charcoal Canister

The canister is filled with activated carbon and has a replaceable foam filter in the bottom of the canister. The vent line from the expansion tank is connected to the canister and fuel vapors from the tank are adsorbed by the carbon when the engine is not running. Another vent line on the canister connects to the air intake of the fuel injection inlet

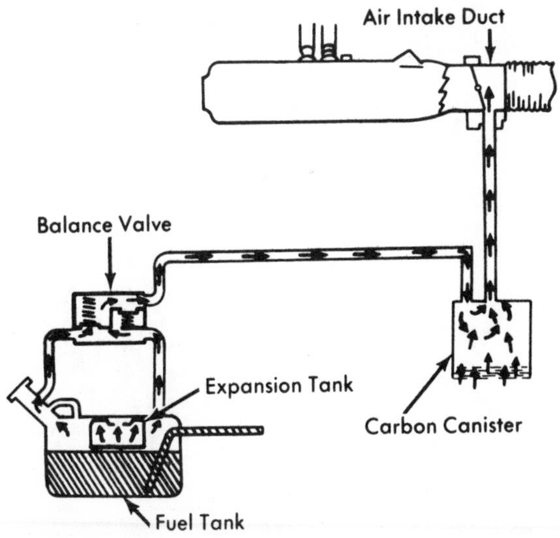

Fig. 1 Evaporative emission control system

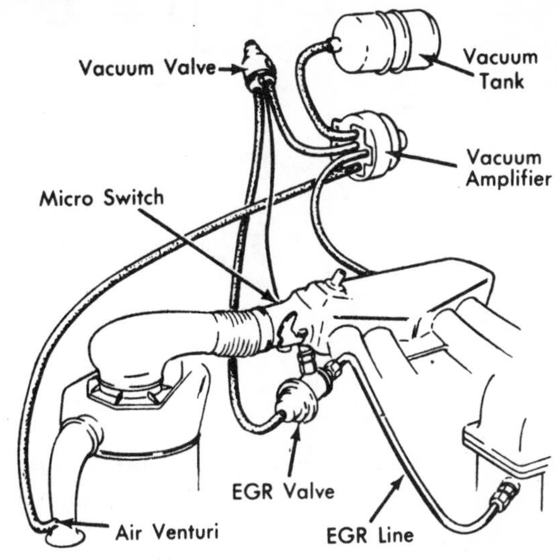

Fig. 2 EGR system with vacuum amplifier, 140 *series*

duct. When the engine is running faster than idle, fuel vapors and air drawn in through the bottom of the canister will be drawn into the engine and burned. This purging action renews the adsorbing capacity of the carbon.

EXHAUST GAS RECIRCULATION SYSTEM

140 Series with B20E & B20F Engines

Operation

The vacuum Amplified EGR system (Fig. 2), uses two vacuum sources, venturi vacuum and manifold vacuum. The system uses venturi vacuum at the air cleaner as a measure of total air flow. This weak venturi signal of vacuum controls the vacuum amplifier to regulate the EGR valve. The amplifier receives two signals, a weak venturi signal to be amplified and a strong manifold vacuum for its power source. The system has a vacuum tank and check valve to maintain an adequate vacuum source regardless of variations in the manifold vacuum. The EGR valve is only open between idle and full throttle.

140 Series with B20B Engine
160 Series with B30E & B30F Engines &
164 Series with B30A

Operation

With the unamplified system, exhaust gas recirculation occurs only when the throttle is between

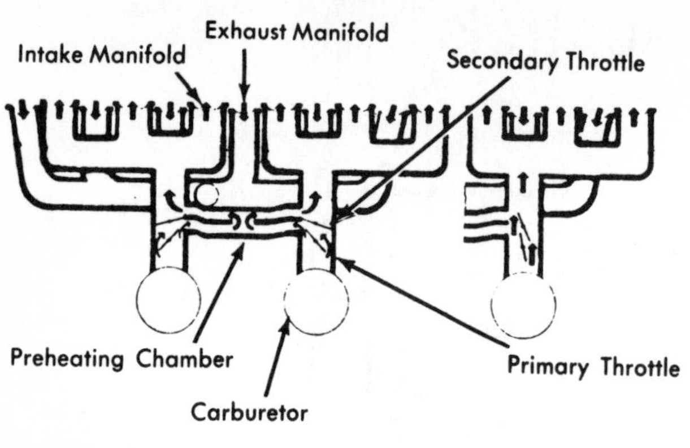

Fig. 3 Dual manifold system

idle and full throttle position. When the throttle is closed, the opening for the EGR valve vacuum line is in front of the throttle and no vacuum is supplied to the valve. Hence, no recirculation takes place. When the throttle is partly opened it places the vacuum line opening behind the throttle valve, resulting in a vacuum. This vacuum now opens the EGR valve and allows recirculation to take place. When the throttle is fully opened, no vacuum is created, thus closing the EGR valve and stopping recirculation.

DUAL MANIFOLD

140 Series with B20B Engine & 164 Series with B30A Engine

Operation

The intake manifold is fitted with a secondary throttle plate at each carburetor, Fig. 3. When the engine is idling and during normal driving, the secondary throttle plates are closed. This forces air/fuel mixture through a central preheating chamber where a completely evaporated mixture is obtained. During high speed or heavy load driving (wide open throttle), secondary throttle plates open to allow air/fuel mixture to enter directly into the cylinders without going through the preheating chamber.

THERMOSTATICALLY CONTROLLED AIR CLEANER

140 Series with B20B Engine & 164 Series with B30A Engine

Operation

The constant temperature air cleaner consists of a housing incorporating a preset thermostat. The thermostat is connected to a valve which controls air intake from both hot and cold air intake tubes. Air supplied to the carburetors is maintained at a constant temperature of approximately 90° F (140 series) or 87 ± 9° F (164 series).

DISTRIBUTOR

140 & 160 Series, Fig. 4

Operation

The B30A 6-cylinder engine is equipped with a dual diaphragm vacuum unit. However, the advance side of the unit is disconnected and plugged. The B20B 4-cylinder engine is equipped with a distributor having a retard unit only. This unit retards timing about 3° during idling or engine braking to reduce emissions in these modes. Some

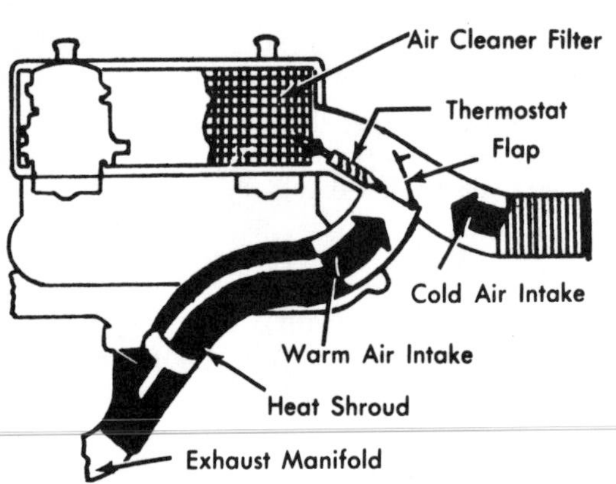

Fig. 4 Thermostatically controlled air cleaner

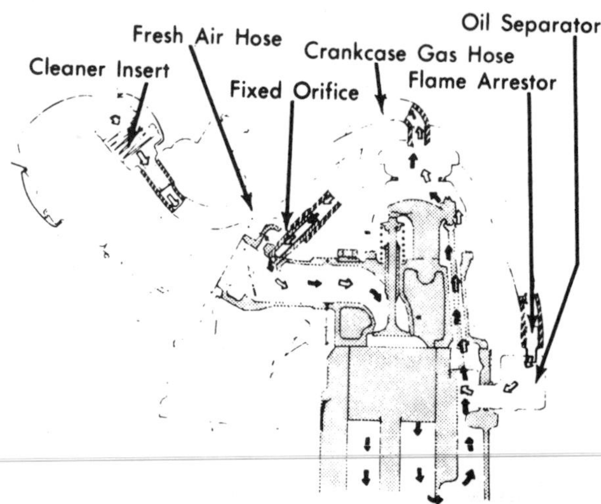

Fig. 5 Positive crankcase ventilation system, 140 series

early B20B 4-cylinder engines with automatic transmission are equipped with a plastic bottle on hose between the carburetor and the distributor. The function of this bottle is to delay, for about 6 seconds, the operation of the vacuum retard unit. This bottle is mounted on the firewall near the ignition coil.

POSITIVE CRANKCASE VENTILATION

140 Series

Description

The crankcase ventilation system consists of two hoses, flame arrestor, fixed orifice and oil separator. The fresh air hose connects the air cleaner to the crankcase. The crankcase gas hose connects the rocker arm cover to the intake manifold.

160 Series

The crankcase ventilation system consists of two hoses, flame arrestor, fixed orifice and an oil separator. The fresh air hose connects the air cleaner to the rocker arm cover. The crankcase gas hose connects the crankcase to the intake manifold.

All Fuel Injection Models

The crankcase ventilation system consists of two hoses, flame trap and an oil trap. The fresh air hose connects the air cleaner to the crankcase. The crankcase gas hose connects the crankcase to the intake manifold.

140 Series, Fig. 5

Operation

Fresh air is drawn into the crankcase through the crankcase gas hose, flame arrestor and oil separator. Crankcase gases are drawn into the intake manifold through the crankcase gas hose and the fixed orifice.

160 Series, Fig. 6

Fresh air is drawn through the fresh air hose and the flame arrestor into the rocker arm cover and is directed by a baffle into the crankcase. Crankcase gases are drawn into the intake manifold through the oil separator and the crankcase gas hose.

Models with Fuel Injection, Fig. 7

Fresh air is drawn into the crankcase through the fresh air hose, flame and oil trap. Crankcase gas is drawn into the intake manifold through the crankcase gas hose.

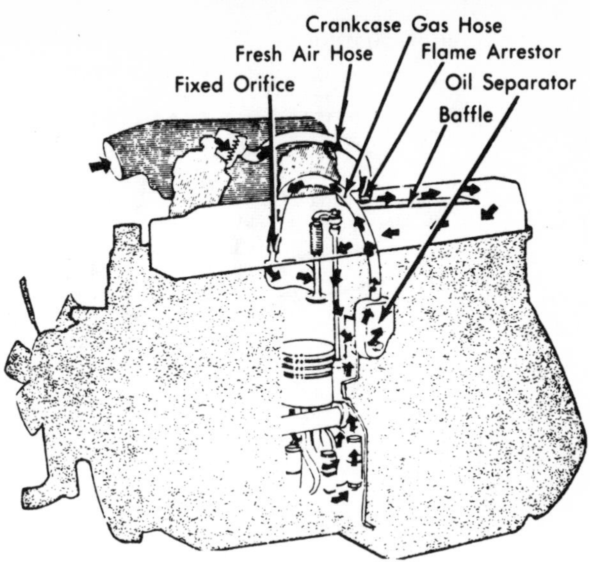

Fig. 6 Positive crankcase ventilation system, 164 series

GENERAL SERVICE

Exhaust Gas Recirculation

Every 12,000 miles, inspect the system for loose, cracked or deteriorated hoses. Replace or repair as necessary. Clean all hoses and pipes. Every 25,000 miles, replace the EGR valve.

Positive Crankcase Ventilation

Periodically inspect the system for deteriorated or leaking hoses. The calibrated orifice located on the intake manifold should be cleaned every 12,000 miles.

Exhaust Gas Recirculation

Every 12,000 miles, inspect the system for deteriorated or leaking hose. Every 25,000 miles, replace the EGR valve.

Testing

EGR Valve

With the engine running, remove the EGR valve vacuum hose at the intake manifold and apply vacuum to the hose. The engine should stop or run erratically. If not, valve is defective and should be cleaned or replaced.

EGR System

1. With the ignition on but the engine not running,

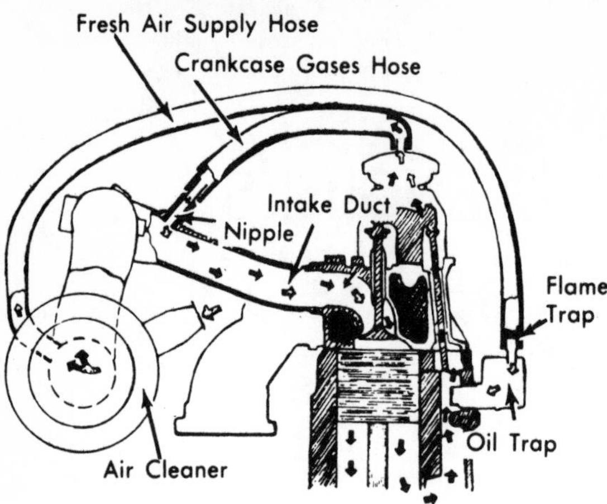

Fig. 7 Positive crankcase ventilation system, fuel injected models

disconnect the wire at micro switch and connect a test light to the wire and the micro switch terminal.

2. Insert a .035-inch thickness gauge between the throttle adjustment screw and stop. Open and close the throttle by hand. The test light should light. Replace .035-inch gauge with one .050-inch thick and repeat the test. The test light should not light. If the micro switch fails this test it should be replaced or adjusted as necessary.
3. Start the engine and remove the vacuum line from the vacuum amplifier at the venturi marked 1. Connect the external vacuum source to the venturi marked 1. The vacuum should hold and the idle should not change. Disconnect the micro switch wire. The EGR valve should open and idle should be erratic. Reconnect the micro switch wire and vacuum line. Increase the engine rpm and make sure the EGR valve opens. If the vacuum amplifier or EGR valve fails these tests it is defective and should be replaced.

TRUCK AND DIESEL ENGINES

SPECIFICATIONS

TRUCK ENGINES

DIESEL ENGINES

AUTOCAR

MODEL INDEX & ENGINE APPLICATION

ENGINE IDENTIFICATION—The Autocar Service Parts Identification Plate is located inside the truck cab. Stamped on the plate is the model of the engine, transmission, auxiliary transmission, rear axle and front axle. This data represents only the equipment on the vehicle as shipped from the factory. Prior to Autocar's assimilation by The White Motor Company, identification plates were attached to engines and transmissions.

Gasoline Engines

Model	Engine Make	Basic Engine Model ②	Crank-case Refill Capacity, Qts.	Cooling System Capacity, Qts.
C65, D, T	White	390A	15	①
C65, D, T	White	490A	16	①
C5564	White	6-185A	8	①
C5566	White	6-185A	8	①
C5764-OH	White	6-185A	8	①
C5766-OH	White	6-185A	8	①
C6564	White	390A	16	①
C6564, T	White	490A	16	①
C6764	White	390A	16	①
C6764	White	490A	16	①
C85, T	White	490A	16	①
C87	White	390A	16	①
C87, D-OH	White	490A	16	①
C9564	White	490A	16	①
C9764, S OH	White	490A	16	①
C10364	White	390A	16	①
C10364S OH	White	490A	16	①

Diesel Engines

Model	Engine Make	Basic Engine Model ②	Crank-case Refill Capacity, Qts.	Cooling System Capacity, Qts.
A75T	Cummins	NH-195	28	①
A75T	Cummins	NH-220	28	①
A7564T	Cummins	NH-195	28	①
A7564T	Cummins	NH-220	28	①
A102T	Cummins	NH-195	28	①
A102T	Cummins	NH-220	28	①
A10264	Cummins	NH-195	28	①
A10264	Cummins	NH-220	28	①
A10464LS	Cummins	NH-220	28	①
CK64	Cummins	NH-230		①
DC65, T, TL	Cummins	JT		①
DCU70, T, TL	Cummins	NH-195	28	①
DCU70, T, TL	Cummins	HRF	28	①
DCU7064T, TL	Cummins	NH-195	28	①
DCU7064T, TL	Cummins	HRF	28	①
DCU72T, TL	Cummins	V8-265	20	①
DCV7264T, TL	Cummins	V8-265	20	①
DCV73T, TL	Cummins	V8-265	20	①
DCV7364T, TL	Cummins	V8-265	20	①
DC74T	Cummins	NH-195	28	①
DC74T	Cummins	NH-220	28	①
DC75T	Cummins	NH-195	28	①
DC75T	Cummins	NH-220	28	①
DC75TL	Cummins	NH-195	28	①
DC75TL	Cummins	NH-220	28	①
DCU75T	Cummins	NH-195	28	①
DCU75T	Cummins	NH-220	28	①
DC85	Cummins	NH-195	28	①
DC85	Cummins	NH-220	28	①
DC87, D	Cummins	HRB	28	①
DC87, D	Cummins	HRF	28	①
DC87T	Cummins	HN-230		①
DC102, T, TL	Cummins	HRB	28	①
DC102, T, TL	Cummins	NH-220	28	①
DC103D	Cummins	NH-220	28	①
DC103T	Cummins	NH-195	28	①
DC103T	Cummins	NH-220	28	①
DC6564	Cummins	JT		①
DC6764	Cummins	JT		①
DC7366	Cummins	NH-230		①
DC7564, T, TL	Cummins	NH-195	28	①
DC7564, T, TL	Cummins	NH-220	28	①
DC9364	Cummins	NH-230		①
DC9564	Cummins	NH-195	28	①
DC9564	Cummins	NH-220	28	①
DC9564TMS	Cummins	NH-250	28	①
DC9764S	Cummins	HRB	28	①
DC9964 OHNES	Cummins	NH-195	28	①
DC9964 OHNES	Cummins	HRF	28	①
DC9964	Cummins	NH-230		①
DC9966	Cummins	NH-230		①
DC10264, L	Cummins	NH-195	28	①
DC10264, L	Cummins	NH-220	28	①
DC10364S OH	Cummins	HRB	28	①
DC10364S OH	Cummins	NH-195	28	①
DC10364S	Cummins	NH-220	28	①
DC10364	Cummins	NH-230		①
DC10366	Cummins	NH-230		①
DC10464LS	Cummins	NH-220	28	①
DC10464LS	Cummins	NH-220	28	①
DC20364S OH	Cummins	NH-220	28	①
S42, A42	Cummins	NH-230		①
S64, A64	Cummins	NH-230		①
60DF	Cummins	C-160		①
80DF	Cummins	C-160		①

①—Cooling system capacity varies depending on engine and radiator installed.
②—Optional engines available in most Diesel models.

BROCKWAY

BROCKWAY SPECIFICATIONS ARE SAME AS PREVIOUS YEARS.
CHECK PAGE 556 OF YOUR EMISSION CONTROL MANUAL, VOLUME I.

CHEVROLET

TRUCK MODELS & ENGINE APPLICATION

IDENTIFICATION PLATE: Located inside of driver's compartment. Engine identification and other unit data on plate represents only the equipment in the vehicle when shipped from the factory.

Model	Year	Engine Make	Standard Engine Model	Crank-case Refill Capacity Qts.	Cooling System Capacity, Qts.
BLAZER					
6 Cyl.	1974-75	Own	6-250	4	15
V8	1974-75	Own	V8-350	4	18
EL CAMINO					
1AC80, AD80	1974-75	Own	V8-350	4	18
VEGA					
1HV05	1974-75	Own	4-140	4	—
CONVENTIONAL GASOLINE					
C10	1974-75	Own	6-250	4	15
C10	1974-75	Own	V8-350	4	18
C20	1974-75	Own	6-250	4	15
C20	1974-75	Own	V8-350	4	18
C30	1974-75	Own	6-250	4	15
C30	1974-75	Own	V8-350	4	18
CE60	1974	Own	V8-350	4	21
CM60	1973-74	Own	V6-305	8	36
CS60	1974	Own	6-292	5	17
HM80	1973-74	Own	V6-432	10	37
CE65	1973-74	Own	V8-366	6	33
CM65	1973-74	Own	V6-379	10	34.5
FOUR-WHEEL DRIVE					
K10	1974-75	Own	6-250	4	15
K10	1974-75	Own	V8-350	4	18
K20	1974-75	Own	6-250	4	15
K20	1974-75	Own	V8-350	4	18
TANDEM SERIES					
ME65	1973-74	Own	V8-366	6	33.1
MM65	1974	Own	V6-432	10	36
JM80	1973-74	Own	V6-432	10	37
STEP-VAN & FORWARD CONTROL SERIES					
G10	1974	Own	6-250	4	13
G10	1974	Own	V8-350	4	16
P10	1974	Own	6-250	4	13
G20	1974	Own	6-250	4	13
G20	1974	Own	V8-350	4	16
P20	1974	Own	6-250	4	13

Model	Year	Engine Make	Basic Engine Model	Crank-case Refill Capacity, Qts.	Cooling System Capacity, Qts.
P20	1974	Own	V8-250	4	17
G30	1974	Own	6-250	4	13
G30	1974	Own	V8-350	4	16
P30	1974	Own	6-250	4	13
P30	1974	Own	V8-350	4	17
TILT CAB SERIES					
TE60	1973-74	Own	V8-350	4	28.1
TE65	1974	Own	V8-366	6	35
TM60	1974	Own	V6-305	8	46.6
TM65	1973-74	Own	V6-379	8	45
TM80	1974	Own	V6-432	10	47
WM80	1973-74	Own	V6-432	10	47
SCHOOL BUS SERIES					
SS60	1974	Own	6-292	5	17
SM60	1973-74	Own	V6-305	8	36
SE60	1973-74	Own	V8-350	4	20
SG60	1973-74	GMC	DH478	10	29
CONVENTIONAL DIESELS					
CG60	1974	GMC	DH478	10	29
HV70	1972-74	Detroit	6V-53N	14	36.5
HC90	1973-74	Cum'ins	NTC290	—	61.5
HH90	1974	Detroit	8V-71	24	80
HN90	1973-74	Cum'ins	NHC250	24	52.9
TILT DIESELS					
TG60	1973-74	GMC	DH478	11	38.3
TV70	1973-74	Detroit	6V-53N	14	31.5
WV70	1972-74	Detroit	6V-53N	16	31.5
FB90	1972-74	Cum'ins	V8-903	26	61
F190	1972-74	Detroit	6-71N	19	51.2
FC90	1974	Cum'ins	NTC-290	—	55
FH90	1972-74	Detroit	8V-71N	24	73
FN90	1972-74	Cum'ins	NHC-250	20	53
D190	1972-74	Detroit	6-71N	19	51.2
DN90	1972-74	Cum'ins	NHC-250	20	53
DC90	1974	Cum'ins	NTC-290	—	55
DH90	1972-74	Detroit	8V-71NE	24	73
DB90	1972-74	Cum'ins	V8-903	26	61
DP90	1972-74	Detroit	12V-71	38	98

GENERAL ENGINE SPECIFICATIONS

Engine Model	Carb. Type	Bore & Stroke	Comp. Ratio	Horsepower @ rpm	Torque Lbs. Ft. @ rpm	Governed Speed Rpm No Load	Normal Oil Pressure Lbs.
1974							
4-140③	2 Bore	3.50 x 3.62	8.2	75 @ 5000	88 @ 3000	—	64
4-140③	1 Bore	3.50 x 3.62	8.0	75 @ 4400	115 @ 2400	—	40
4-140③	2 Bore	3.50 x 3.62	8.0	85 @ 4400	122 @ 2400	—	40
6-250③	1 Bore	3.87 x 3.53	8.25	100 @ 3600	175 @ 1800	—	40–60
6-292③	1 Bore	3.87 x 4.12	8.0	120 @ 3600	215 @ 2000	—	40–60
V6-305C③	2 Bore	4.250 x 3.58	—	148 @ 4000	238 @ 1600	—	57
V8-350③	2 Bore	4.00 x 3.48	8.5	145 @ 3800	250 @ 2200	—	40
V8-350③	4 Bore	4.00 x 3.48	8.5	160 @ 3800	255 @ 2400	—	40
V8-350③	4 Bore	4.00 x 3.48	8.5	160 @ 3800	245 @ 2400	—	40
V8-366③	4 Bore	3.937 x 3.76	—	200 @ 4000	310 @ 2800	—	40–55
V6-379③	2 Bore	3.562 x 3.86	—	170 @ 3600	280 @ 1600	—	57
V8-400③	2 Bore	4.126 x 3.76	8.5	150 @ 3200	290 @ 2000	—	40
V8-400③	4 Bore	4.126 x 3.76	8.5	180 @ 3800	290 @ 2400	—	40
V6-432③	2 Bore	4.875 x 3.86	—	190 @ 3200	331 @ 1600	—	60
V8-427③	4 Bore	4.25 x 3.76	—	230 @ 4000	360 @ 2800	—	40–55
V8-454③	4 Bore	4.25 x 4.00	8.25	230 @ 4000	350 @ 2800	—	40
V8-454③	4 Bore	4.25 x 4.00	8.25	245 @ 4000	365 @ 2800	—	40
V8-454③	4 Bore	4.25 x 4.00	8.25	235 @ 4000	360 @ 2800	—	40
V6-478③	2 Bore	5.125 x 3.86	—	192 @ 3200	371 @ 1400	—	60
1975							
4-140③	1 Bore	3.50 x 3.625	8.0	78 @ 4200	120 @ 2000	—	40
4-140③	2 Bore	3.50 x 3.625	8.0	87 @ 4400	122 @ 2800	—	40
6-250③	1 Bore	3.875 x 3.53	8.25	105 @ 3800	185 @ 2100	—	40–60
6-292③	1 Bore	3.875 x 4.12	8.0	120 @ 3600	215 @ 2000	—	40–60
6-292③	1 Bore	3.875 x 4.12	8.0	130 @ 3600	225 @ 2000	4000	40–60
8-350③	2 Bore	4.00 x 3.48	8.5	145 @ 3800	250 @ 2200	—	40
8-350③	4 Bore	4.00 x 3.48	8.5	160 @ 3800	250 @ 2400	—	40
8-350③	4 Bore	4.00 x 3.48	8.5	160 @ 4000	265 @ 2400	—	40
8-366③	4 Bore	3.937 x 3.76	8.0	195 @ 4000	290 @ 2800	4000	40–55
8-366③	4 Bore	3.937 x 3.76	8.0	200 @ 4000	305 @ 2800	4000	40–55
8-400③	4 Bore	4.126 x 3.76	8.5	175 @ 3600	290 @ 2800	—	40
8-427③	4 Bore	4.25 x 3.76	7.8	220 @ 4000	360 @ 2400	4000	40–55
8-454③	4 Bore	4.25 x 4.00	8.15	215 @ 4000	350 @ 2400	—	40
8-454③	4 Bore	4.25 x 4.00	8.15	245 @ 4000	355 @ 3000	—	40
8-454 Calif. H.D.③	4 Bore	4.25 x 4.00	8.15	245 @ 4000	375 @ 3000	—	40

③—Ratings are NET—as installed in vehicle.

TUNEUP SPECIFICATIONS

★When using a timing light, disconnect vacuum hose or tube of distributor and plug opening in hose or tube so idle speed will not be affected.

▲Before removing wires from distributor cap, determine location of No. 1 wire in cap, as distributor position may have been altered from that shown at the end of this chart.

Engine	Spark Plug		Distributor		Firing Order ▲	Ignition Timing★		Hot Idle Speed		Comp. Press. Lbs. ②	Fuel Pump Press. Lbs.
	Type AC	Gap Inch	Point Gap Inch (New)	Dwell Angle Deg.		Deg. BTDC ①	Mark Location	Std. Trans.	Auto. Trans.		
1974											
4-140	R42TS	.035	.019	31–34	(46)	(34)	Damper	700	750D	140	3–4½
6-250 Light Duty	R46T	.035	.019	31–34	(47)	8	Damper	850	600D	130	3½–4½
6-250 Heavy Duty	R46T	.035	.019	31–34	(47)	6	Damper	600	600	130	3½–4½
6-292	R44T	.035	.019	31–34	(47)	8	Damper	600	600	130	3½–4½

(continued)

TUNEUP SPECIFICATIONS—Continued

★When using a timing light, disconnect vacuum hose or tube at distributor and plug opening in hose or tube so Idle speed will not be affected.

▲Before removing wires from distributor cap, determine location of the No. 1 wire in cap, as distributor position may have been altered from that shown at the end of this chart.

Engine	Spark Plug		Distributor		Firing Order ▲	Ignition Timing★		Hot Idle Speed		Comp. Press. psi ②	Fuel Pump Press. Lbs.
	Type	Gap Inch	Point Gap Inch (New)	Dwell Angle Deg.		Deg. BTDC ①	Mark Locations	Std. Trans.	Auto.		
1974											
V8-350, 145 H.P.	R44T	.035	.019	29–31	㊽	㊱	Damper	900	600D	150	7–8½
V8-350 Light Duty	R44T	.035	.019	29–31	㊽	8	Damper	900	600D	150	7–8½
V8-350 Light Duty	R44T	.035	.019	29–31	㊽	㊲	Damper	900	600D	150	7–8½
V8-350 Light Duty, Calif.	R44T	.035	.019	29–31	㊽	㊳	Damper	900	600D	150	7–8½
V8-350 Heavy Duty	R44T	.035	.019	29–31	㊽	4	Damper	600	600	150	7–8½
V8-454 Light Duty	R44T	.035	.019	29–31	㊽	10	Damper	800	600D	150	7–8½
V8-454 Heavy Duty	R44T	.035	.019	29–31	㊽	8	Damper	700	700	150	7–8½
1975											
4-140㊸	R43TSX	.060	—	—	㊻	㊺	Damper	1200	750D	140	3–4½
4-140㊹	R43TSX	.060	—	—	㊻	㉞	Damper	700	600D	140	3–4½
6-250	R46TX	.060	—	—	㊼	10	Damper	900	550D	130	3½–4½
6-292	R44TX	.060	—	—	㊼	8	Damper	600	600	130	3½–4½
8-350 Light Duty	R44TX	.060	—	—	㊽	6	Damper	800	600D	150	7–8½
8-350 Heavy Duty㉜	R44TX	.060	—	—	㊽	8	Damper	600	600	150	7–8½
8-350 Heavy Duty㊶	R44TX	.060	—	—	㊽	2	Damper	700	700	150	7–8½
8-400 Heavy Duty㉜	R44TX	.060	—	—	㊽	4	Damper	700	700	150	7–8½
8-400 Heavy Duty㊶	R44TX	.060	—	—	㊽	2	Damper	700	700	150	7–8½
8-454 Light Duty	R44TX	.060	—	—	㊽	16	Damper	—	650D	150	7–8½
8-454 Heavy Duty㉜	R44TX	.060	—	—	㊽	8	Damper	700	700	150	7–8½
8-454 Heavy Duty㊶	R44TX	.060	—	—	㊽	8	Damper	600	600	150	7–8½

①—Before top dead center.

②—Plus or minus 20 psi.

㉜—Exc. California.

㉞—Synchromesh Trans., 10° BTDC; Auto. Trans., 12° BTDC.

㊱—Auto. Trans. 8° BTDC. Std. Trans. 0° TDC.

㊲—C, K 10 & 20, Suburbans and G 20 & 30 Sportvans. Auto. Trans. 12°, Man. Trans. exc. Suburban 8°, Man. Trans. Suburban 6°.

㊳—Auto. Trans. exc. Suburban 8°, Auto. Trans. Suburban 6°, Man. Trans. 4°.

㊴—Exc. Calif., 550 rpm.; Calif., 750 rpm.

㊶—California.

㊸—1 Barrel Carb.

㊹—2 Barrel Carb.

㊻—Cylinder numbering from front to rear, firing order 1-3-4-2.

㊼—Cylinder numbering from front to rear, firing order 1-5-3-6-2-4.

㊽—Cylinder numbering from front to rear, left bank 1-3-5-7; right bank 2-4-6-8, firing order 1-8-4-3-6-5-7-2.

DISTRIBUTOR SPECIFICATIONS

Model	Distributor Number	Rotation ①	Breaker Gap (New)	Dwell Angle Deg.	Breaker Arm Spring Tension	Centrifugal Advance Degrees @ rpm of Distributor		Vacuum Advance	
						Advance Starts	Full Advance	Inches of Vacuum To Start Plunger	Max. Adv. Dist. Deg. @ Vacuum
1974									
4-140	1110496	C	.019	31–34	19–23	0 @ 800	11 @ 2400	7	12 @ 15
6-250, 10 Ser. Exc. G	1110499	C	.019	31–34	19–23	0 @ 550	12 @ 2050	7	12 @ 15½
6-250, 10 Ser. G	1110500	C	.019	31–34	19–23	0 @ 500	12 @ 2050	7	12 @ 15½
6-250, 20–30 Ser. Exc. G	1110520	C	.019	31–34	19–23	0 @ 550	12 @ 2050	13	5 @ 13½
6-250, 20–30 Ser. G	1110525	C	.019	31–34	19–23	0 @ 550	12 @ 2050	13	5 @ 13½
6-292, 20–30 Ser.	1110518	C	.019	31–34	19–23	0 @ 500	12 @ 2100	10	5 @ 13½
8-350, C, K10, Suburban	1112093	C	.019	29–31	19–23	0 @ 550	9 @ 2100	6	7½ @ 14
8-350, G10-30	1112847	C	.019	29–31	19–23	0 @ 550	9 @ 2100	3	7 @ 8½
8-350 Auto. Trans. (Calif.)④	1112847	C	.019	29–31	19–23	0 @ 550	9 @ 2100	3	7 @ 8
8-350, C, K, G	1112543	C	.019	29–31	19–23	0 @ 500	11 @ 2100	6	7½ @ 14
8-350 Auto. Trans.③	1112848	C	.019	29–31	19–23	0 @ 450	7 @ 2100	3	7 @ 8½
8-350 Std. Trans.③	1112844	C	.019	29–31	19–23	0 @ 500	10 @ 2100	3	7 @ 8½
8-350 Std. Trans.⑤	1112844	C	.019	29–31	19–23	0 @ 500	10 @ 2100	3	7 @ 8½
8-350 Std. Trans.⑥	1112849	C	.019	29–31	19–23	0 @ 500	11 @ 2100	3	7 @ 8½
8-350 G, P-30	1112097	C	.019	29–31	19–23	0 @ 600	11 @ 2100	8	5 @ 13½
8-454 C, K-10	1112113	C	.019	29–31	19–23	0 @ 550	9 @ 2100	6	10 @ 15.7
8-454 C, K, Suburban	1112504	C	.019	29–31	19–23	0 @ 550	9 @ 2100	8	8 @ 16
8-454 C, K20-30	1112105	C	.019	29–31	19–23	0 @ 550	10 @ 2100	6	12 @ 14.3
1975									
4-140	1112862	C	—	—	—	0 @ 810	11 @ 2400	5	12 @ 12
6-250	1112863	C	—	—	—	0 @ 550	8 @ 2100	4	9 @ 12
6-250 Calif.	1110650	C	—	—	—	0 @ 550	8 @ 2100	4	7 @ 12
6-292	1112887	C	—	—	—	0 @ 550	12 @ 2100	10	5 @ 13
8-350	1112880	C	—	—	—	0 @ 600	11 @ 2100	4	9 @ 12
8-350	1112888	C	—	—	—	0 @ 550	8 @ 2100	4	9 @ 12
8-350	1112940	C	—	—	—	0 @ 600	10 @ 2100	8	7½ @ 15½
8-350, 400 Calif.	1112884	C	—	—	—	0 @ 575	11 @ 2100	8	5 @ 13
8-400	1112941	C	—	—	—	0 @ 500	9½ @ 1725	8	5 @ 13
8-454 L.D.⑦	1112886	C	—	—	—	0 @ 900	6 @ 2100	4	9 @ 7
8-454 L.D.⑧	1112943	C	—	—	—	0 @ 550	9 @ 2100	6	10 @ 15
8-454 H.D.	1112869	C	—	—	—	0 @ 550	10 @ 2100	6	10 @ 15
8-454 H.D.	1112494	C	—	—	—	0 @ 550	10 @ 2100	10	7 @ 17

①—As viewed from top; C, clockwise; CC, counterclockwise.
②—Set with vacuum line disconnected.
③—C-K 10, C-K 20 Suburban, G 10-20 G 30 Sport Van.
④—C, K 10-20, Exc. Suburban.
⑤—C10 Suburban (Calif.)
⑥—C, K10, Exc. Suburban G10-30.
⑦—With catalyst converter.
⑧—Without catalyst converter.

CHEVROLET LUV

ENGINE APPLICATION

Year	Engine Make	Standard Engine Model	Crankcase Refill Capacity, Qts.	Cooling System Capacity, Qts.
1972–75	ISUZU	4-110	4.2①	6.0

①—Add one quart for oil filter.

GENERAL ENGINE SPECIFICATIONS

Engine Model	Carb. Type	Bore & Stroke, Inches	Comp. Ratio	Horsepower @ rpm	Torque Lbs. Ft. @ rpm	Normal Oil Pressure, Lbs.
1972-75						
4-110	2 Bore	3.31 x 3.23	8.2	75 @ 5000	88 @ 3000	57

TUNEUP SPECIFICATIONS

★When using a timing light, disconnect vacuum hose or tube at distributor and plug opening in hose or tube so idle speed will not be affected.

▲Before removing wires from distributor cap, determine location of No. 1 wire in cap, as distributor position may have been altered from that shown at the end of this chart.

Engine	Spark Plug		Distributor		Firing Order ▲	Ignition Timing★		Hot Idle Speed	Comp. Press. Lbs.	Fuel Pump Press. Lbs.
	Type	Gap Inch	Point Gap Inch	Dwell Angle Deg.		Deg. BTDC①	Mark Location			
1974										
4-110	NGK BP-6ES	.035	.020	49–55	④	12	Damper	700	163②	3¾
1975										
4-110	NGK BP-6ES	.030	.020	49–55	④	12	Damper	700	163②	4½

①—Before Top Dead Center.
②—Variance per cylinder not to exceed 8.5 lbs.
④—Front to rear, 1-3-4-2.

DISTRIBUTOR SPECIFICATIONS

Model	Distributor Number	Rotation ①	Breaker Gap	Dwell Angle Deg.	Breaker Arm Spring Tension	Centrifugal Advance Deg. @ rpm of Distributor		Vacuum Advance	
						Advance Starts	Full Advance	Inches of Vacuum To Start Plunger	Max. Adv. Dist. Deg. @ Vacuum
1974									
4-110	D417-62	CC	.020	49–55	1.1–1.43	—	—	—	—
1975									
4-110	D417-64	CC	.020	49–55	1.1–1.43	—	—	—	—
1975③									
4-110	D417-62	CC	.020	49–55	1.1–1.43	—	—	—	—

①—As viewed from top.
③—California.

DIAMOND REO

MODEL INDEX & ENGINE APPLICATION

Models	Year	Engine Make	Standard Engine Model	Crank-case Refill Capacity, Qts.	Cooling System Capacity, Qts.
CONVENTIONAL TRUCKS					
DC-10142	1974	Own	6-200		
DC-10142D	1974	Cummins	V8-210		
DC-10144	1974	Own	6-200		
DC-10144D	1974	Cummins	V8-210		
CONVENTIONAL TANDEMS					
DC-10164	1974	Own	6-200		
DC-10164D	1974	Cummins	V8-210		
DC-10166	1974	Own	6-200		
DC10166D	1974	Cummins	V8-210		
CONVENTIONAL DIESEL					
C-11664DFLW	1973–74	Cummins	NTC-350		
C-11664DFW	1973–74	Cummins	NTC-350		

Models	Year	Engine Make	Standard Engine Model	Crank-case Refill Capacity, Qts.	Cooling System Capacity, Qts.
90″ BBC DIESEL					
C-9242D	1974	Cummins	NTC-290		
C-9242DL	1974	Cummins	NTC-290		
C-9264D	1974	Cummins	NTC-290		
C-9264DL	1974	Cummins	NTC-290		
TILT C.O.E. DIESEL					
CO-5442D	1974	Cummins	NTC-290		
CO-5442DL	1974	Cummins	NTC-290		
CO-5464D	1974	Cummins	NTC-290		
CO-5464DL	1974	Cummins	NTC-290		
CO-5464DW	1973–74	Cummins	NTC-350		
CO-5464DLW	1973–74	Cummins	NTC-350		
CO-8842D	1974	Cummins	NTC-290		
CO-8842DL	1974	Cummins	NTC-290		
CO-8864D	1974	Cummins	NTC-290		
CO-8864DL	1974	Cummins	NTC-290		
CO-8864DW	1973–74	Cummins	NTC-350		
CO-8864DLW	1973–74	Cummins	NTC-350		

GENERAL ENGINE SPECIFICATIONS

Engine Model	Number Cylinders & Valve Location	Bore & Stroke	Piston Displ. Cu. In.	Comp. Ratio	Horsepower @ rpm	Torque Lbs. Ft. @ rpm	Governed Speed Rpm No Load	Normal Oil Pressure Psi
1974								
6-200	6 In Head	4¼ x 4.7	400	7.5	172 @ 3200	345	3200	35
8-250	8 In Head	4¼ x 4⅛	468	7.5	228 @ 3400	404	3400	35

TUNEUP & VALVE SPECIFICATIONS

Engine Model	Firing Order	Spark Plug		Ignition Timing		Valve Angles		Valve Lash		Minimum Valve Spring Pressure Lbs. @ Inch Length
		Type	Gap	Deg. BTDC	Location	Seat	Face	Intake	Exhaust	
1970-74⑦										
200	153624	16	.025	6	Damper①	30	29½	.023C	.023C	64 @ 1.78⑤

①—1964 and later engines include flywheel timing marks visible through an opening on left side of flywheel housing. Either may be used depending on ease of viewing.

⑤—Exhaust springs 63.5 @ 1.583″.

⑦—1973 Calif. & all 1974, electronic ignition.

DISTRIBUTOR SPECIFICATIONS

ALL SPECIFICATIONS ARE SAME AS PREVIOUS YEARS.
SEE PAGE 578 OF EMISSION CONTROL MANUAL, VOLUME I.

DIVCO

ALL SPECIFICATIONS ARE SAME AS PREVIOUS YEARS.
SEE PAGES 579-581 OF EMISSION CONTROL MANUAL, VOLUME I.

DODGE AND PLYMOUTH

MODEL INDEX & ENGINE APPLICATION

ENGINE NUMBER LOCATION: The engine serial number location is located on a machined surface on the cylinder block.
The engine serial number prefix denotes the series letter, followed by engine model, followed by serial number.

Model	Year	Engine Make	Standard Engine Model	Crank-case Refill Capacity, Qts.	Cooling System Capacity, Qts.
Compact And Sportsman					
B100	1971–75	Own	6-225	5	13
B100	1973–75	Own	V8-318	5	17
B200	1971–75	Own	6-225	5	13
B200	1971–75	Own	V8-318	5	18
B300	1973–75	Own	V8-318	5	17
Dodge Ramcharger					
AW100	1974–75	Own	V8-318	5	17
AD100	1975	Own	V8-318	5	17
Plymouth Trial Duster					
PW100	1974	Own	V8-318	5	17
Plymouth Voyager					
PB100	1974	Own	6-225	5	13
PB200	1974	Own	6-225	5	13
PB300	1974	Own	6-225	5	13
Tradesman					
B100	1972–75	Own	6-225	5	13
B100	1971–75	Own	V8-318	5	18
B200	1972–75	Own	6-225	5	13
B200	1971–75	Own	V8-318	5	18
B300	1971–75	Own	6-225	5	13
B300	1971–75	Own	V8-318	5	18
Conventional Cab					
D100	1969–75	Own	6-225	5	13
D100	1973–75	Own	V8-318	5	17
W100	1969–75	Own	6-225	5	13
W100	1973–75	Own	V8-318	5	17
D200	1969–75	Own	6-225	5	13
D200	1973–75	Own	V8-318	5	17
W200	1969–75	Own	6-225	5	13
W200	1973–75	Own	V8-318	5	17
D300	1969–75	Own	6-225	5	14
D300	1973–75	Own	V8-318	5	17
W300	1969–75	Own	6-225	5	14
D500	1969–75	Own	6-225	5	14
D500	1973–75	Own	V8-318	6	19
D600	1973–75	Own	V8-318	6	19
W600	1972–75	Own	V8-318	6	19
D700	1975	Own	V8-361	—	—
D800	1969–75	Own	V8-361	8	26
LCF Cab					
C800	1969–75	Own	V8-361	8	27
CN800	1974	Cat.	1100	—	—
CNT800	1974	Cat.	1100	—	—
CN800	1975	Cummins	V555	—	—
CNT800	1975	Cummins	V555	—	—
CT800	1969–75	Own	V8-361	8	27
CT900	1969–73	Own	V8-413	8	28
CN900	1969–75	Cummins	NH-230	20	41
CNT900	1969–75	Cummins	NH-230	20	41
CN950	1974–75	Cummins	Super 250	28	45½
CNT950	1974–75	Cummins	Super 250	28	45½
C1000	1969–73	Own	V8-413	8	28
Tilt Cab					
LS1000	1972–75	Cummins	NH-230	20	44
LT1000	1972–75	Cummins	NH-230	20	44
Motor Home					
M300	1975	Own	V8-318	—	—
MB300	1972–74	Own	V8-360	5	16
MB300	1973–74	Own	V8-318	5	17
RM300	1974	Own	V8-318	—	—
MBL300	1975	Own	V8-318	—	—
MBH300	1975	Own	V8-360	—	—

(continued)

Model	Year	Engine Make	Standard Engine Model	Crank-case Refill Capacity, Qts.	Cooling System Capacity, Qts.
RM350	1974	Own	V8-318	—	—
RM400	1974	Own	V8-440	—	—
M400	1975	Own	V8-318	—	—
M500	1975	Own	V8-440	—	—
School Bus					
S600	1973–75	Own	V8-318	6	19
S700	1975	Own	V8-361	—	—
Kary Van					
CB300	1974–75	Own	6-225	—	—
CB300	1974–75	Own	V8-318	—	—
D500	1974–75	Own	V8-318	—	—
D600	1974–75	Own	V8-318	—	—
D700	1975	Own	V8-361	—	—

GENERAL ENGINE SPECIFICATIONS

Engine Code	Engine Model	Carb. Type	Bore & Stroke	Comp. Ratio	Horsepower @ rpm	Torque Lbs. Ft. @ rpm	Governed Speed Rpm	Normal Oil Pressure Lbs.
1974								
225-1	6-225②	1 Bore	3.40 x 4.125	8.4	105 @ 4000	180 @ 2000	3600	50
225-1	6-225③	1 Bore	3.40 x 4.125	8.4	110 @ 4000	175 @ 2000	3600	50
318-1	V8-318②	2 Bore	3.91 x 3.31	8.6	155 @ 4000	255 @ 2400	3800	50–70
318-1	V8-318③	2 Bore	3.91 x 3.31	8.6	150 @ 4000	235 @ 2400	3800	50–70
318-3	V8-318	2 Bore	3.91 x 3.31	7.8	140 @ 4000	250 @ 2000	3700	60–80
360	V8-360②④	2 Bore	4.00 x 3.58	8.4	185 @ 4000	295 @ 2400	3900	50–70
360	V8-360②⑤	2 Bore	4.00 x 3.58	8.4	210 @ 4000	285 @ 2400	3900	50–70
360	V8-360③	2 Bore	4.00 x 3.58	8.4	175 @ 4000	285 @ 2400	3900	50–70
361-3	V8-361	2 Bore	4.12 x 3.38	7.49	140 @ 3600	260 @ 2000	3600	60–80
361-4	V8-361	2 Bore	4.12 x 3.38	7.48	155 @ 3200	295 @ 2000	3600	60–80
400	V8-400②	2 Bore	4.342 x 3.38	8.2	185 @ 4000	305 @ 2400	—	45–65
400	V8-400③	2 Bore	4.342 x 3.38	8.2	175 @ 4000	305 @ 2400	—	45–65
413-2	V8-413	2 Bore	4.188 x 3.75	7.54	165 @ 3200	325 @ 2000	3600	60–80
413-3	V8-413	4 Bore	4.188 x 3.75	7.54	180 @ 3200	335 @ 2000	3600	60–80
440-1	V8-440②④	4 Bore	4.32 x 3.75	8.12	230 @ 4000	350 @ 3200	—	45–65
440-1	V8-440②⑤	4 Bore	4.32 x 3.75	8.12	225 @ 4000	345 @ 3200	—	45–65
440-3	V8-440③	4 Bore	4.32 x 3.75	8.2	235 @ 4000	340 @ 2400	—	45–65
1975								
225-1	6-225②	1 Bore	3.40 x 4.125	8.4	95 @ 3600	175 @ 2000	3800	30–80
225-1	6-225③	1 Bore	3.40 x 4.125	8.4	105 @ 3600	175 @ 2000	3800	30–80
318-1	V8-318②	2 Bore	3.91 x 3.31	8.58	150 @ 4000	255 @ 2000	3900	30–80
318-1	V8-318③④	2 Bore	3.91 x 3.31	8.58	150 @ 4000	230 @ 2400	3900	30–80
318-1	V8-318③⑤	2 Bore	3.91 x 3.31	8.58	155 @ 4000	245 @ 2000	3900	30–80
318-3	V8-318	2 Bore	3.91 x 3.31	7.8	140 @ 4000	250 @ 2000	3800	30–80
360	V8-360	2 Bore	4.00 x 3.58	8.4	175 @ 4000	285 @ 2400	3800	30–80
361	V8-361	2 Bore	4.12 x 3.375	7.98	155 @ 3200	295 @ 2000	3800	30–80
413	V8-413	4 Bore	4.188 x 3.75	7.54	180 @ 3200	335 @ 2000	3800	30–80
440	V8-440	4 Bore	4.32 x 3.75	8.2	235 @ 4000	340 @ 2400	—	30–80

②—Light duty.
③—Heavy duty.
④—Exc. Calif.
⑤—Calif.

TUNEUP SPECIFICATIONS

★When using a timing light, disconnect vacuum tube or hose at distributor and plug opening in hose or tube so idle speed will not be affected.

▲Before removing wires from distributor cap, determine location of No. 1 wire in cap, as distributor position may have been altered from that shown at the end of this chart.

Engine	Spark Plug		Distributor		Firing Order ▲	Ignition Timing★		Hot Idle Speed		Comp. Press. Lbs. ②	Fuel Pump. Press. Lbs.
	Type	Gap Inch	Point Gap Inch	Dwell Angle Deg.		Deg. BTDC ①	Mark	Std. Trans.	Auto. Trans.		
1974											
6-225⑰	N11Y	.035	—	—	Fig. A	TDC⑲	Damper	800	750	100	3½–5
8-318-1⑰	N11Y	.035	—	—	Fig. C	TDC⑳	Damper	750	750	100	5–7
8-318-3⑰	E10	.035	—	—	Fig. C	TDC	Damper	700	700	100	5–7
8-360⑰	N12Y	.035	—	—	Fig. C	5㉑	Damper	750	750	100	5–7
8-361-3⑰	N6	.035	—	—	Fig. B	2½	Damper	700	700	100	6–7½
8-361-4⑰	N6	.035	—	—	Fig. B	2½	Damper	700	700	100	6–7½
8-400⑰㉒	J13Y	.035	—	—	Fig. B	7½	Damper	750	750	100	5–7
8-400⑰㉒	J11Y	.035	—	—	Fig. B	2½	Damper	750	750	100	5–7
8-413-2⑰	N6	.035	—	—	⑯	2½	Damper	700	—	100	6–7½
8-413-3⑰	N6	.035	—	—	⑯	5	Damper	700	—	100	6–7½
8-440⑰㉒	J11Y	.035	—	—	Fig. B	10㉔	Damper	700	700	100	5–7
8-440-1⑰	J11Y	.035	—	—	Fig. B	7½	Damper	700	700	100	5–7
8-440-3⑰	BL9Y	.035	—	—	Fig. B	7½	Damper	700	700	100	5–7
8-478⑩	UJ6	.035	.016	28–32	—	10	Damper	—	—	120	—
8-549⑩	UJ6	.035	.016	28–32	—	7	Damper	—	—	120	—
1975											
6-225-1	BL11Y	.035	—	—	—	—	—	—	—	—	—
8-318-1	N11Y	.035	—	—	—	—	—	—	—	—	—
8-318-3	F10	.035	—	—	—	—	—	—	—	—	—
8-360	N12Y	.035	—	—	—	—	—	—	—	—	—
8-361	N6	.035	—	—	—	—	—	—	—	—	—
8-413	N6	.035	—	—	—	—	—	—	—	—	—
8-440	J11Y	.035	—	—	—	—	—	—	—	—	—

①—Before top dead center.
②—Plus or minus 20 psi.
⑩—See International chapter for service on this engine.
⑯—To determine proper firing order diagram it is necessary to observe rotor rotation. Use Fig. B if rotation is counterclockwise and Fig. D if clockwise. This is caused by the fact that some engines use timing gears while others use a timing chain.
⑰—With Electronic Ignition.
⑲—Distributor #3755056, timing 2½°.
⑳—Distributor #3755201, timing 2½°.
㉑—Distributor #3755821, timing 2½°.
㉒—Light Duty.
㉔—California 5°.

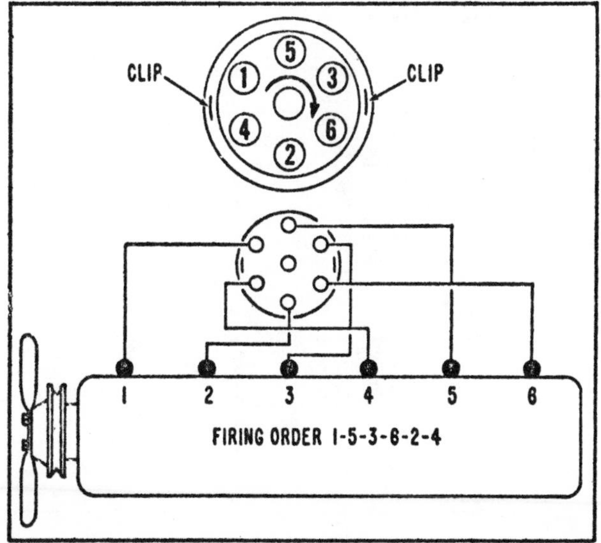

Fig. A

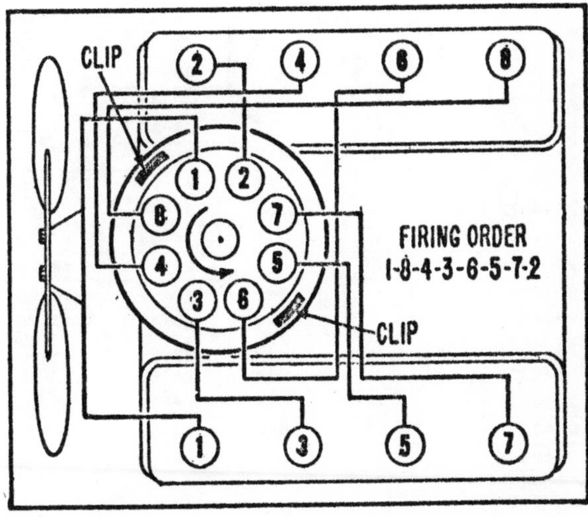

Fig. B

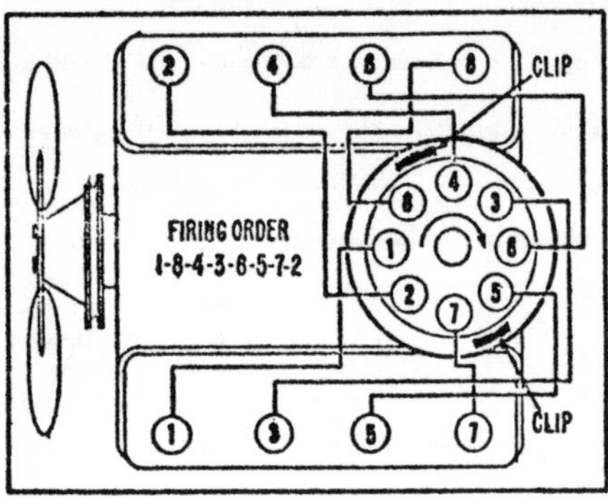

Fig. C

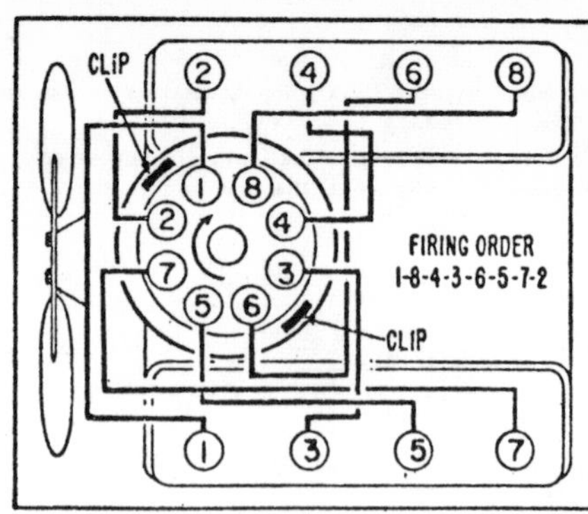

Fig. D

DISTRIBUTOR SPECIFICATIONS

Distributor Part No. ①	Rotation ②	Breaker Gap	Dwell Angle Deg.	Breaker Arm Spring Tension	Centrifugal Advance Degrees @ rpm of Distributor		Vacuum Advance	
					Advance Starts	Full Advance	Inches of Vacuum To Start Plunger	Max. Adv. Dist. Deg. @ Vacuum
AY-4102A-1	C	.020	36–42	17–20	1 @ 450	8 @ 1800	—	—
IBP-4003R	C	.020	27–32	17–20	1 @ 450	9 @ 2000	7.1	12 @ 12.4
IBP-4006D	CC	.017	27–32	17–20	2 @ 425	13 @ 1750	7.2	14 @ 15
IBP-4008	CC	.017	27–32	17–20	2 @ 425	13 @ 1950	7.1	14 @ 15
IBP-4008A	CC	.017	27–32	17–20	1 @ 440	13 @ 2100	7.1	14 @ 15
IBR-4001A	C	.020	36–42	17–20	1 @ 450	8 @ 1800	6.8	10 @ 16
IBR-4002A	C	.020	36–42	17–20	1 @ 440	8 @ 1550	5.3	10 @ 16
IBR-4002B	C	.020	36–42	17–20	1 @ 440	8 @ 1550	4.5	12 @ 16
1889750	C	.020	40–45	17–21	1 @ 475	12 @ 1925	4.7	12 @ 14
2095270	C	.020	40–45	17–21	1 @ 450	11 @ 2200	4.9	10 @ 12
2095843	C	.017	27–32	17–21	1 @ 600	9 @ 2000	6	11 @ 12
2095844	CC	.017	27–32	17–21	2 @ 425	14 @ 1750	7	11 @ 12
2095845	CC	.017	27–32	17–21	2 @ 425	14 @ 1950	6	11 @ 12
2095846	CC	.017	27–32	17–21	1 @ 440	14 @ 2100	6	11 @ 12
2095957	C	.020	36–42	17–21	2 @ 440	8 @ 1550	5	12 @ 16
2095974	C	.020	40–45	17–21	2 @ 475	14 @ 2200	6	12 @ 12
2095976	C	.020	40–45	17–21	1 @ 475	12 @ 2300	6	7 @ 13
2098665	C	.020	40–45	17–20	1 @ 525	14 @ 2200	8.5	8 @ 10
2098670	C	.020	40–45	17–20	1 @ 560	12 @ 2500	10.5	7 @ 13
2098604	CC	.017	28–33	17–20	2 @ 425	13 @ 1600	9.2	11 @ 12
2098675	C	.020	40–45	17–20	4 @ 475	14 @ 2200	8.5	8 @ 10
2098687	CC	.017	28–33	17–20	2 @ 425	13 @ 2000	9.2	11 @ 12
2098692	C	.020	40–45	17–20	1 @ 540	10 @ 2000	8.5	8 @ 10
2444254	C	.020	40–45	17–20	1 @ 560	12 @ 2500	10.5	7 @ 13
2444255	C	.020	40–45	17–20	1 @ 525	14 @ 2200	9.2	11 @ 12
2444256	C	.020	40–45	17–20	3 @ 475	14 @ 2200	8.5	8 @ 10
2444258	C	.017	28–32	17–20	1 @ 480	11 @ 2300	9	12 @ 16
2444275	CC	.017	28–33	17–20	4 @ 425	13 @ 1600	9.2	11 @ 12
2444276	CC	.017	28–33	17–20	3 @ 425	13 @ 2000	9.2	11 @ 12
2444277	C	.020	36–42	17–21	1 @ 440	8 @ 1550	10	12 @ 16
2444291	C	.017	28–33	17–20	1 @ 450	6 @ 2000	9.2	11 @ 12
2444292	CC	.017	28–33	17–20	2 @ 425	14 @ 1750	9.2	11 @ 12
2444295	C	.020	40–45	17–20	1 @ 540	9 @ 2000	8.5	8 @ 10
2444648	C	.020	40–45	17–20	1 @ 475	12 @ 2200	6	7 @ 13
2444671	C	.020	40–45	17–20	1 @ 475	12 @ 2500	6	8 @ 10
2642234	C	.017	28–32	17–20	1 @ 450	12 @ 1750	6.5	13 @ 13
2642238	C	.017	28–32	17–20	1 @ 475	10 @ 1750	6.5	13 @ 13
2642244	CC	.017	28–32	17–20	1 @ 450	12 @ 2150	6	11 @ 13
2642346	C	.017	28–32	17–20	3 @ 500	17 @ 1900	8	13 @ 15

(continued)

Distributor Part No. ①	Rotation ②	Breaker Gap	Dwell Angle Deg.	Breaker Arm Spring Tension	Centrifugal Advance Degrees @ rpm of Distributor		Vacuum Advance	
					Advance Starts	Full Advance	Inches of Vacuum To Start Plunger	Max. Adv. Dist. Deg. @ Vacuum

DISTRIBUTOR SPECIFICATIONS—Continued

2642349	C	.020	40–45	17–20	2 @ 500	20 @ 2500	6	11 @ 12
2642352	C	.020	40–45	17–20	3 @ 475	20 @ 2500	6	8 @ 10
2642354	C	.020	40–45	17–20	2 @ 500	17 @ 2200	6	7 @ 13
2642356	C	.017	28–32	17–20	4 @ 500	17 @ 1500	6	13 @ 13
2642371	C	.017	28–32	17–20	2 @ 475	14 @ 2000	6	11 @ 12
2642373	CC	.017	28–32	17–20	4 @ 500	20 @ 2200	5.5	14 @ 14
2642531	CC	.017	28–32	17–20	2 @ 550	17 @ 2200	6	14 @ 16
2642718	C	.017	28–32	17–20	2 @ 525	11 @ 2350	8	13 @ 15
2642721	C	.017	28–32	17–20	1 @ 475	13 @ 2250	8	13 @ 15
2642724	C	.017	28–32	17–20	2 @ 475	19 @ 2350	8	13 @ 16
2642727	CC	.017	28–32	17–20	1 @ 450	11 @ 2150	10	13 @ 16
2642752	C	.020	40–45	17–20	1 @ 475	9 @ 2250	6	8 @ 10
2642792	C	.020	40–45	17–20	1 @ 500	13 @ 2400	8	7 @ 16
2642795	C	.020	40–45	17–20	2 @ 475	13 @ 2400	6	7 @ 10
2642810	CC	.017	28–32	17–20	2 @ 550	15 @ 2200	12	14 @ 16
2642949	CC	.017	28–32	17–20	3 @ 525	15 @ 2300	12	14 @ 16
2875206	C	.020	40–45	17–20	0 @ 425	21 @ 2200	6	7 @ 13
2875338	C	.017	28–33	17–20	1 @ 475	14 @ 2250	8	13 @ 15
2875340	C	.017	28–33	17–20	0 @ 425	12 @ 2350	8	13 @ 15
2875342	C	.017	28–33	17–20	0 @ 425	19 @ 2350	9	10 @ 15
2875346	CC	.017	28–32	17–20	0 @ 350	14 @ 1750	7	11 @ 12
2875348	CC	.017	28–33	17–20	0 @ 350	13 @ 1600	7	11 @ 12
2875350	CC	.017	28–33	17–20	0 @ 350	13 @ 2000	7	11 @ 12
2875352	CC	.017	28–33	17–20	0 @ 425	19 @ 2200	6.5	10 @ 13
2875354	CC	.017	28–33	17–20	0 @ 425	16 @ 2250	5	8 @ 10
2875364	C	.020	40–45	17–20	0 @ 425	14 @ 2000	8	6 @ 13
2875366	C	.020	40–45	17–20	0 @ 425	14 @ 2000	6	6 @ 8
2875822	C	.020	42–47	17–20	1 @ 550	14 @ 2000	10	7.75 @ 16
2875826	C	.020	42–47	17–20	1 @ 550	14 @ 2000	7	7.75 @ 10
2875838	C	.020	42–47	17–20	1–4 @ 550	12 @ 1900	7.5	8.5 @ 10
2875796	C	.017	30–35	17–20	1 @ 550	19 @ 2400	10.5	10.75 @ 15
2875800	C	.017	30–35	17–20	1 @ 500	14 @ 2150	10.5	11 @ 15
2875804	C	.017	30–35	17–20	½–3½ @ 500	17 @ 2250	9.5	13.5 @ 15
2875653	CC	.016	28–32	17–21	1–4½ @ 500	14.5 @ 1600	7	11.5 @ 12
2875770	CC	.017	30–35	17–21	1–5 @ 500	17 @ 175C	7	11.5 @ 12
2875876	CC	.017	30–35	17–21	1–5 @ 500	17 @ 1750	7	11.5 @ 12
2875742	CC	.017	30–35	17–20	1 @ 550	23 @ 2350	8.5	13.5 @ 13.5
2875747	CC	.017	30–35	17–20	1 @ 500	19 @ 2300	8.5	13.5 @ 13.5
2875655	CC	.016	28–32	17–21	1–4½ @ 500	14.5 @ 1600	7	11.5 @ 12
2875654	CC	.016	28–32	17–21	½–3½ @ 500	14.5 @ 2000	7	11.5 @ 12
2875966	CC	.016	28–32	17–21	½–3½ @ 500	14.5 @ 2000	7½	11.5 @ 12
2959339	CC	.016	28–32	17–21	0 @ 420	12 @ 1600	7	8 @ 11¼
2959396	CC	.016	25–29	17–21	0 @ 320	8 @ 1600	5	8 @ 11.2
3438225	C	.017	30–34	17–20	1 @ 550	16 @ 2100	12	10.5 @ 15
3438227	C	.017	30–34	17–20	1 @ 550	12 @ 2100	10.5	9.75 @ 15
3438237	C	.020	41–46	17–20	0 @ 525	14 @ 1600	7	7.75 @ 10
3438255	C	.017	30–34	17–20	1 @ 550	16 @ 2100	10.5	9.75 @ 15
3498087	CC	.016	28–32	17–21	0–2 @ 340	8 @ 1600	7	8 @ 11¼
3656252	C	.020	41–46	17–20	½–4½ @ 550	14 @ 2000	10	7½ @ 15
3656257	C	.020	41–46	17–20	½–4½ @ 550	14 @ 2000	7	7½ @ 9½
3656260	C	.020	41–46	17–20	½–3½ @ 700	14 @ 2000	10	7½ @ 15
3656266	C	.020	41–46	17–20	½–3½ @ 700	14 @ 2000	7	7½ @ 9½
3656269	C	.020	41–46	17–20	1–4 @ 550	11 @ 1900	7½	8½ @ 10
3656272	C	.017	30–34	17–20	1½–5½ @ 550	16 @ 2100	10	10½ @ 15
3656275	C	.017	30–34	17–20	0–4 @ 600	16 @ 2100	10	10½ @ 15
3656287	C	.017	30–34	17–20	½–3½ @ 550	14 @ 2200	10	10½ @ 16

(continued)

Distributor Part No. ①	Rotation ②	Breaker Gap	Dwell Angle Deg.	Breaker Arm Spring Tension	Centrifugal Advance Degrees @ rpm of Distributor		Vacuum Advance	
					Advance Starts	Full Advance	Inches of Vacuum To Start Plunger	Max. Adv. Dist. Deg. @ Vacuum

DISTRIBUTOR SPECIFICATIONS—Continued

3656294	C	.017	30-34	17-20	½-4 @ 550	16 @ 2200	10	10½ @ 15
3656329	CC	.017	30-34	17-20	1-5 @ 650	14 @ 2000	10½	10½ @ 15½
3656359	CC	.017	30-35	17-20	1-6 @ 550	16 @ 1750	7	11½ @ 12
3656365	CC	.016	28-32	17-21	½-4 @ 550	14 @ 2000	7	11.5 @ 12
3656373	CC	.017	30-35	17-20	1-6 @ 550	16 @ 1750	7	11½ @ 12
3656375	CC	.016	28-32	17-21	1-6 @ 550	14 @ 1600	7	11½ @ 12
3656377	CC	.016	28-32	17-21	1-5 @ 550	14 @ 1600	7	11½ @ 12
3656379	CC	.016	28-32	17-21	½-4 @ 550	14 @ 2000	7	11.5 @ 12
3656667	C	—	—	—	0-2 @ 500	1 @ 2150	9½	10 @ 14
3656672	C	—	—	—	0-2 @ 500	14 @ 2150	10	9½ @ 14½
3656678	CC	—	—	—	0-3½ @ 500	16 @ 1700	7	10.5 @ 11½
3656762	C	—	—	—	0-2 @ 500	14 @ 2150	10	9½ @ 14½
3656763	C	—	—	—	0-3½ @ 500	16 @ 2050	9	12 @ 15
3656780	C	—	—	—	0-3½ @ 500	15½ @ 1950	9	12½ @ 15
3656791	CC	—	—	—	½-3½ @ 550	15 @ 1950	10½	10½ @ 15½
3656830	CC	—	—	—	1-5 @ 550	16 @ 1600	9½	9.5 @ 13½
3656839	CC	—	—	—	1-4 @ 550	13½ @ 1900	9½	9½ @ 13½
3656872	CC	—	—	—	1-4 @ 550	13½ @ 1900	9½	9.5 @ 13½
3656876	CC	—	—	—	1½-4½ @ 550	14½ @ 1650	7½	11.5 @ 12
3656877	CC	—	—	—	1½-4½ @ 550	14½ @ 1650	7½	11.5 @ 12
3656878	CC	—	—	—	1-3½ @ 550	14 @ 1900	9½	9.5 @ 13½
3755037	C	—	—	—	½-4½ @ 550	14 @ 2000	9½	14 @ 15
3755042	C	—	—	—	½-4½ @ 550	14 @ 2000	7¼	10 @ 11
3755056	C	—	—	—	0-3 @ 500	14 @ 2100	10½	8 @ 12
3755062	C	—	—	—	½-4½ @ 550	14 @ 2000	10	8 @ 15
3755071	C	—	—	—	½-4½ @ 550	14 @ 2000	7	7½ @ 9½
3755075	C	—	—	—	½-2½ @ 500	12 @ 1900	7	5½ @ 9½
3755150	CC	—	—	—	1½-4½ @ 560	14 @ 1950	10½	10½ @ 15½
3755157	CC	—	—	—	½-4 @ 650	12½ @ 2500	10½	10½ @ 15½
3755160	C	—	—	—	0-3½ @ 500	15½ @ 2000	9½	10 @ 14
3755201	C	—	—	—	½-3 @ 550	14 @ 2150	10	9½ @ 15
3755205	C	—	—	—	1-3½ @ 550	14 @ 1900	7½	10.5 @ 13½
3755467	C	—	—	—	½-3½ @ 550	14 @ 2000	9	10 @ 15½
3755470	C	—	—	—	½-3½ @ 550	12 @ 2000	7	10 @ 11½
3755475	C	—	—	—	½-4 @ 550	14 @ 2000	7	12 @ 12½
3755518	CC	—	—	—	½-3½ @ 650	12 @ 2000	8	11 @ 14
3755520	CC	—	—	—	1-5 @ 550	16 @ 1600	9½	9.5 @ 13½
3755522	CC	—	—	—	½-3 @ 650	10 @ 2000	8	11 @ 14
3755820	C	—	—	—	1-3½ @ 700	13½ @ 2400	9	9½ @ 13
3755821	C	—	—	—	1-4½ @ 600	16 @ 2050	9	12½ @ 15½
3755825	C	—	—	—	½-3½ @ 650	14 @ 2000	9	10 @ 15½
3755841	C	—	—	—	1-4½ @ 650	14 @ 2000	7	12 @ 12½

①—Plate on housing. ②—C: Clockwise; CC: Counter clockwise.

FORD

MODEL INDEX & ENGINE APPLICATION

Model	Year	Engine Make	Standard Engine Model	Crank-case Refill Capacity, Qts.	Cooling System Capacity, Qts.
CONVENTIONAL GASOLINE MODELS					
Bronco	1973–75	Own	6-200	6	9.2
	1975	Own	V8-302	4	14.7
Econoline	1970–74	Own	6-240	5	—
	1973–74	Own	6-300	4	14¼
Ranchero	1969–74	Own	6-250	5	10
	1974	Own	V8-302	4	15
	1975	Own	V8-351	4	15.9
F-100 (4x4)	1965–74	Own	6-240	5	14
(4x2)	1965–74	Own	6-240	4	13
	1973–75	Own	6-300	6	14½
F-150	1975	Own	6-300	5	14.4
F-250 (4x2)	1956–74	Own	6-240	4	14
(4x4)	1965–74	Own	6-240	5	14
	1975	Own	V8-360	5	22.3
F-350	1973–75	Own	6-300	6	14½③
	1975	Own	V8-389	—	29
F-500	1973–75	Own	6-300	6	19
F-600 (4x4)	1968–75	Own	6-300	6	19
	1971–75	Own	6-330	9	26
F-700	1973–75	Own	V8-361	8	25
F-750	1964–75	Own	V8-361	8	24①
TILT CAB GASOLINE MODELS					
C-600	1965–74	Own	6-300	6	23
C-700	1973–75	Own	V8-361	8	25
C-750	1964–75	Own	V8-361	8	28①
C-800	1964–75	Own	V8-361	8	28①
C-900	1970–75	Own	V8-401	9	52②
TANDEM AXLE GASOLINE MODELS					
CT-800	1964–74	Own	V8-361	8	28①
CT-900	1971–75	Own	V8-401	9	—
SCHOOL BUS MODELS					
B-500	1973–75	Own	6-300	6	19
B-600	1968–75	Own	6-300	6	19
B-700	1965–74	Own	V8-330	8	25
B-750	1964–74	Own	V8-361	8	24①
PARCEL DELIVERY GASOLINE MODELS					
P-400	1973–75	Own	6-300	5	18
P-450	1975	Own	V8-360	5	—
P-500	1973–75	Own	6-300	5	18
P-550	1975	Own	V8-390	5	—
P-600	1975	Own	6-300	5	18.1
MOTOR HOME MODELS					
M-400	1972–75	Own	V8-360	5	22
M-450	1972–74	Own	V8-360	5	22
M-500	1972–75	Own	V8-390	5	23
LOUISVILLE GASOLINE MODELS					
LN-600	1970–74	Own	6-300	6	19
	1975	Own	V8-361	8	25
LN-700	1973–75	Own	V8-361	8	25
LN-750	1970–74	Own	V8-361	8	25
	1975	Own	V8-389	—	25
L-800	1971–75	Own	V8-361	8	25.5
LN-800	1970–75	Own	V8-361	8	25.5
LT-800	1973–74	Own	V8-361	8	25½
	1975	Own	V8-389	—	25½
LNT-800	1973–74	Own	V8-361	8	25½
	1975	Own	V8-389	—	25½
LTS-800	1973–74	Own	V8-361	8	25½
	1975	Own	V8-389	—	25½
LT-880	1972–75	Own	V8-475	9	47
LNT-880	1972–75	Own	V8-475	9	47
L-900	1970–75	Own	V8-401	9	47
LN-900	1970–75	Own	V8-401	9	47
LT-900	1971–75	Own	V8-401	9	47
LNT-900	1971–75	Own	V8-401	9	47
LTS-900	1971–75	Own	V8-401	9	47
LOUISVILLE DIESEL MODELS					
LN-6000	1970–74	Cat.	V-150	12	25
LN-7000	1970–74	Cat.	V-175	12	25
	1975	Cat.	V-190	—	—
L-8000	1970–74	Cat.	V-175	12	25
	1975	Cummins	V-555	—	28
	1975	Cat.	V-225	—	40
LN-8000	1970–74	Cat.	V-175	12	25
	1975	Cummins	V-555	—	28
	1975	Cat.	V-225	—	40
LT-8000	1970–74	Cat.	V-175	12	25
	1975	Cat.	V-190	—	42
LTS-8000	1971–74	Cat.	V-175	12	25
	1975	Cat.	V-190	—	42
LNT-8000	1970–74	Cat.	V-175	12	25
	1975	Cat.	V-190	—	42
L-9000	1970–75	Cummins	NH-230	24	47
	1975	Cummins	NTC-250	—	44
LN-9000	1970–75	Cummins	NH-230	24	47
	1975	Cummins	NTC-250	—	44
LT-9000	1970–75	Cummins	NH-230	24	47
LTS-9000	1971–75	Cummins	NH-230	24	47
LNT-9000	1970–75	Cummins	NH-230	24	47
FORD DIESEL MODELS					
C-6000	1970–74	Cat.	V-150	12	25
F-6000	1970–74	Cat.	V-150	12	25
B-7000	1971–74	Cat.	V-175	12	25
C-7000	1970–74	Cat.	V-175	12	25
	1975	Cat.	V-190	—	42
F-7000	1970–74	Cat.	V-175	12	25
	1975	Cat.	V-190	—	42
C-8000	1970–74	Cat.	V-200	12	25
	1975	Cat.	V-225	10	40
CT-8000	1974	Cat.	V-200	12	25
	1975	Cat.	V-190	—	—

(continued)

MODEL INDEX & ENGINE APPLICATION—Continued

Model	Year	Engine Make	Standard Engine Model	Crank-case Refill Capac-ity, Qts.	Cooling System Capac-ity, Qts.
W-9000	1970–74	Cummins	NH-230	20	49
	1975	Cummins	NTC-290	—	49
WT-9000	1970–74	Cummins	NH-230	20	49
	1975	Cummins	NTC-290	—	49

(1)—Add 1½ qts. if equipped with Transmatic transmission.
(2)—Add 7 qts. if equipped with Transmatic transmission.
(3)—Add 2 qts. if equipped with dual rear tires.

GENERAL ENGINE SPECIFICATIONS

▲When using a timing light, disconnect vacuum tube or hose at distributor and plug opening in hose or tube so idle speed will not be affected.

Engine Code On Truck Rating Plate ▲	Engine Model	Carb. Type	Bore & Stroke	Comp. Ratio	Horsepower @ rpm	Torque Lbs. Ft. @ rpm	Governed Speed Rpm No Load	Normal Oil Pressure Lbs.
1974								
T	6-200	1 Bore	3.68 x 3.13	8.3	85 @ 3800	150 @ 1800	—	35
A	6-240	1 Bore	4.00 x 3.18	7.9	(37)	(38)	4000	40–50
L	6-250	1 Bore	3.68 x 3.91	8.0	92 @ 3200	234 @ 1600	—	35–55
B	6-300(2)	1 Bore	4.00 x 3.98	7.9	(39)	(40)	4000	40–50
B	6-300(3)	1 Bore	4.00 x 3.98	7.9	126 @ 3400	272 @ 1800	4000	40–50
(67)	V8-302	2 Bore	4.00 x 3.00	8.0	(41)	(42)	—	50–65
C	V8-330	2 Bore	3.88 x 3.50	7.4	(43)	—	3900	35–55
D	V8-330(3)	2 Bore	3.88 x 3.50	7.4	(44)	(45)	3900(34)	(68)
Q	V8-351	2 Bore	4.00 x 3.50	7.9	163 @ 4200	278 @ 2000	—	50–70
Q	V8-351	4 Bore	4.00 x 3.50	7.9	254 @ 5600	292 @ 3400	—	50–70
Y	V8-360	2 Bore	4.05 x 3.50	8.0	(46)	(47)	—	45–55
E	V8-361(3)	2 Bore	4.05 x 3.50	7.2	(48)	(49)	3800	45–70
H	V8-390	2 Bore	4.05 x 3.78	8.2	(50)	(51)	—	45–55
M	V8-390	4 Bore	4.05 x 3.78	8.2	(52)	(53)	—	45–55
F	V8-391(3)	4 Bore	4.05 x 3.79	7.2	(54)	(55)	3800	45–70
S	V8-400	2 Bore	4.00 x 4.00	8.0	171 @ 3400	329 @ 2000	—	—
H	V8-401(66)	4 Bore	4.125 x 3.75	7.3	(56)	(57)	3600(5)	52–62
J	V8-460	4 Bore	4.36 x 3.850	8.0	(58)	(59)	—	35–65
J	V8-475	4 Bore	4.50 x 3.75	7.2	(60)	(61)	—	52–62
K	V8-477(66)	4 Bore	4.50 x 3.75	7.2	(62)	(63)	3400(5)(36)	52–62
L	V8-534(66)	4 Bore	4.50 x 4.20	7.3	(64)	(65)	3200(5)	52–62
1975								
T	6-200	1 Bore	3.68 x 3.13	8.3	—	—	—	30–35
A	6-240	1 Bore	4.00 x 3.18	8.0	—	—	—	40–55
L	6-250	1 Bore	3.68 x 3.91	8.0	—	—	—	35–55
B	6-300	1 Bore	4.00 x 3.98	7.9	(69)	(70)	—	40–50
B	6-300(3)	1 Bore	4.00 x 3.98	7.9	126 @ 3400	234 @ 1600	—	40–50
G	V8-302	2 Bore	4.00 x 3.00	8.0	(71)	(72)	—	50–65
C	V8-330	2 Bore	3.87 x 3.50	7.4	137 @ 3200	272 @ 1800	—	30–55
D	V8-330(3)	2 Bore	3.87 x 3.50	7.4	137 @ 3600	250 @ 2400	—	(68)
M	V8-351	2 Bore	4.00 x 3.50	8.0	—	—	—	—
Y	V8-360	2 Bore	4.05 x 3.50	—	(73)	(74)	—	45–55
E	V8-361(3)	4 Bore	4.05 x 3.50	7.2	170 @ 3600	284 @ 2400	—	45–70
—	V8-389(3)	4 Bore	4.05 x 3.78	7.2	180 @ 3600	230 @ 2700	—	—
H	V8-390	2 Bore	4.05 x 3.78	—	157 @ 3600	291 @ 1800	—	45–55
M	V8-390	4 Bore	4.05 x 3.78	—	208 @ 4500	324 @ 2800	—	45–55
S	V8-400	2 Bore	4.00 x 4.00	8.0	—	—	—	—
H	V8-401(66)	4 Bore	4.125 x 3.75	7.3	171 @ 3400	274 @ 2800	—	52–62
J	V8-460	4 Bore	4.36 x 3.85	8.0	239 @ 4200	374 @ 2600	—	35–65
J	V8-475	4 Bore	4.50 x 3.75	7.2	203 @ 3400	341 @ 2600	—	—
K	V8-477(66)	4 Bore	4.50 x 3.75	7.2	197 @ 3200	341 @ 2600	—	52–62
L	V8-534(66)	4 Bore	4.50 x 4.20	7.3	212 @ 3000	392 @ 1800	—	52–62

GENERAL ENGINE SPECIFICATION NOTES

②—Light duty.
③—Heavy duty.
⑤—Auto. Trans. 200 rpm higher.
㉞—Auto. Trans. 100 rpm lower.
㊱—Model 475, 3600 rpm with man. trans., 3800 rpm with auto. trans.
㊲—F-100 Man. Trans. 106 @ 3800, Auto. Trans. 100 @ 3800; E-100, 200, 300 Man. Trans. 108 @ 3800; E-100 all & E-200 except Club Wagon with Auto. Trans. 102 @ 4000; E-200, 300 Club Wagon with Auto. Trans. 104 @ 4000.
㊳—F-100 Man. Trans. 178 @ 2000, Auto. Trans. 173 @ 2400; E-100, 200, 300 Man. Trans. 181 @ 2000; E-100 all, & E-200 except Club Wagon with Auto. Trans. 181 @ 2400; E-200, 300 Club Wagon with Auto. Trans. 182 @ 2400.
㊴—E-100, 200 119 @ 3400; E-300 118 @ 3400; F-100 113 @ 3400; F-250, 350 114 @ 3400; P-350, 500 117 @ 3600; F-B-500 126 @ 3400.
㊵—E-100, 200, 300 226 @ 1800; F-100 218 @ 1800; F-250, 350 222 @ 1600; P-350, 500 227 @ 1800; F-B-500 234 @ 1600.
㊶—Bronco & Ranchero Man. Trans. 144 @ 4000; Bronco Auto. Trans. 138 @ 3800; Ranchero Auto. Trans. 142 @ 4000; E-100, 200 & Club Wagons Man. Trans. 143 @ 3800, Auto. Trans. 144 @ 3600; F-100 Man. Trans. 145 @ 4000, Auto. Trans. 137 @ 3800; E-300 139 @ 3800.
㊷—Bronco & F-100 Man. Trans. 235 @ 2000; Bronco Auto. Trans. 222 @ 2600; F-100 Auto. Trans. 219 @ 2600; Ranchero Man. Trans. 239 @ 2600, Auto. Trans. 227 @ 2600; E-100, 200 & Club Wagons 238 @ 2200; E-300 229 @ 2200.
㊸—F-500 137 @ 3200; B-500 138 @ 3200.
㊹—F & LN Series Man. Trans. 137 @ 3600, C6 Auto. Trans. 135 @ 3600, Auto. Trans. except C6 131 @ 3600; B-Series Man. Trans. 138 @ 3600, C6 Auto. Trans. 136 @ 3600, Auto. Trans. except C6 132 @ 3600; C Series Man. Trans. 140 @ 3600, Auto. Trans. 128 @ 3800.
㊺—F, LN, & B Series Man. Trans. and C6 Auto. Trans. 250 @ 2400, Auto. Trans. except C6 247 @ 2400; C Series Man. Trans. 253 @ 2400, Auto. Trans. 246 @ 2400.
㊻—F-100 4 x 2 Man. Trans. 157 @ 4000, Auto. Trans. 151 @ 3800; F-100 4 x 4 Man. Trans. 153 @ 4000, Auto. Trans. 148 @ 3800; F-250,;350 @ 3600.
㊼—F-100 4 x 2 Man. Trans. 265 @ 2200, Auto. Trans. 151 @ 3800; F-100 4 x 4 Man. Trans. 262 @ 2200, Auto. Trans. 256 @ 2200; F-250, 350 263 @ 2000.
㊽—F-LN-600, 750 Man. Trans. 153 @ 3600, Auto. Trans. 147 @ 3400; B Series & CT-800 Man. Trans. 154 @ 3600; B Series & C-600, 800 Auto. Trans. 148 @ 3400; C-600, 800 Man. Trans. 156 @ 3600; L-Line 800 158 @ 3600.
㊾—F-LN-600, 750 & B Series Man. Trans. 278 @ 2400, Auto. Trans. 275 @ 2400; C-600, 800 & CT-800 Man. Trans. 279 @ 2400; C-600, 800 Auto. Trans. 273 @ 2400; L-Line 800 280 @ 2400.
㊿—F-100 Auto. Trans. 160 @ 3600; F-250, 350 159 @ 3400.
(51)—F-100 Auto. Trans. 295 @ 2000; F-250, 350 296 @ 2000.
(52)—F-250, 350 Man. Trans. 208 @ 4500, Auto. Trans. 206 @ 4600.
(53)—F-250, 350 Man. Trans. 324 @ 2800, Auto. Trans. 302 @ 2800.
(54)—F-LN-750 Man. Trans. 180 @ 3600, Auto. Trans. 174 @ 3400; B Series Man. Trans. 181 @ 3600; B Series & C-750, 800 Auto. Trans. 175 @ 3400; C-750, 800 Man. Trans. 179 @ 3600; CT-800 177 @ 3600; L-Line 800 182 @ 3600.
(55)—F-LN-750 & B Series Man. Trans. 320 @ 2400, Auto. Trans. 317 @ 2400; C-750, 800 Man. Trans. 318 @ 2400, Auto. Trans. 315 @ 2400; CT-800 317 @ 2400; L-Line 800 182 @ 3600.
(56)—L-LT-LTS 900 & CT-900 171 @ 3400; LN-LNT-900 169 @ 3400; C-900 173 @ 3400.
(57)—L-LT-LTS-900 274 @ 2800; LN-LNT-900 273 @ 2800; C-900 & CT-900 278 @ 2800.
(58)—Ranchero 216 @ 4600; F-100 238 @ 4200; F-250, 350 239 @ 4200.
(59)—Ranchero 356 @ 2600; F-100 380 @ 2600; F-250, 350 374 @ 2600.
(60)—LT-880 203 @ 3400; LTN-880 197 @ 3400.
(61)—LT-880 341 @ 2600; LTN-880 336 @ 2600.
(62)—L-LT-LTS-900 Man. Trans. 197 @ 3200, Auto. Trans. 190 @ 3200; LN-LNT-900 195 @ 3200; C-900 Man. Trans. 198 @ 3200, Auto. Trans. 194 @ 3200; CT-900 196 @ 3200.
(63)—L-LT-LTS-900 Man. Trans. 341 @ 2600, Auto. Trans. 336 @ 2600; LN-LNT-900 340 @ 2600; C-900 Man. Trans. 344 @ 2600, Auto. Trans. 338 @ 2600; CT-900 343 @ 2600.
(64)—L-LT-LTS-900 Man. Trans. 212 @ 3000, Auto. Trans. 206 @ 3000; LN-LNT-900 210 @ 3000; C-900 Man. Trans. 213 @ 3000, Auto. Trans. 210 @ 3000; CT-900 211 @ 3000.
(65)—L-LT-LTS-900 Man. Trans. 392 @ 1800, Auto. Trans. 389 @ 1800; LN-LNT-900 391 @ 1800; C-900 Man. Trans. 394 @ 1800, Auto. Trans. 391 @ 1800; CT-900 393 @ 1800.
(66)—Super Duty.
(67)—Ranchero engine code F, all except Ranchero G.
(68)—With velocity governor 35–55 p.s.i., without velocity governor 45–70 p.s.i.
(69)—E-100 103 @ 3000; E-150, 250, 350 118 @ 3400; F-100 except California 101 @ 3000 F-100 California 100 @ 3000; F-150, 250, 350 114 @ 3400; P-350, 400, 500 117 @ 3600; F-B-500 126 @ 3400.
(70)—E-100 222 @ 1800; E-150, 250, 350 226 @ 1800; F-100 except California 219 @ 1800 F-100 California 220 @ 1800; F-150, 250, 350 222 @ 1600; P-350, 400, 500 227 @ 1800; F-B-500 234 @ 1600.
(71)—F-100 except California 133 @ 3800, F-100 California 135 @ 3600; Bronco except California 125 @ 3600, Bronco California 121 @ 3400.
(72)—F-100 except California 222 @ 2000, F-100 California 221 @ 2200; Bronco except California 218 @ 2200, Bronco California 216 @ 1600.
(73)—F-100 except California 155 @ 3800, F-100 California 149 @ 4000; F-150, 250, 350 145 @ 4600.
(74)—F-100 except California 262 @ 2200, F-100 California 251 @ 2200; F-150, 250, 350 263 @ 2000.

TUNEUP SPECIFICATIONS

▲When using a timing light, disconnect vacuum tube or hose at distributor and plug opening in hose or tube so idle speed will not be affected.

Engine	Spark Plug		Distributor		Firing Order	Ignition Timing▲		Hot Idle Speed		Comp. Press. psi ②	Fuel Pump Press. Lbs.
	Type	Gap Inch	Point Gap Inch	Dwell Angle Deg.		Deg. BTDC ①	Mark Locations	Std. Trans.	Auto. Trans.		
1974											
6-200, 250	BRF-82	.034	—	—	153624	—	Damper	—	—	—	4½–5½
6-240	BRF-42	.034	—	—	153624	—	Damper	—	—	—	4–6
6-300	BRF-31	.030	—	—	153624	—	Damper	—	—	—	4–6
6-300	BRF-42	.034	—	—	163624	—	Damper	—	—	—	4–6
6-300㉓	BTRF-42	.044	—	—	153624	—	Damper	—	—	—	4–6
8-302	BRF-42	.034	—	—	15426378④	—	Damper	—	—	—	4–6
8-302㉓	BRF-42	.054	—	—	15426378④	—	Damper	—	—	—	4–6
8-330	BRF-31	.030	—	—	15426378④	—	Damper	—	—	—	5–6
8-351	ARF-42	.044	—	—	13726548④	—	Damper	—	—	—	5–7
8-360㉔	BRF-42	.044	—	—	15426378④	—	Damper	—	—	—	5–6
8-360	BRF-42	.034	—	—	15426378④	—	Damper	—	—	—	5–6
8-360㉓	BRF-42	.054	—	—	15426378④	—	Damper	—	—	—	5–6
8-361	BRF-31	.030	—	—	15426378④	—	Damper	—	—	—	5–6
8-390㉔	BRF-42	.044	—	—	15426378④	—	Damper	—	—	—	5–6
8-390	BRF-42	.034	—	—	15426378④	—	Damper	—	—	—	5–6
8-391	BRF-31	.030	—	—	15426378④	—	Damper	—	—	—	5–6
8-400	ARF-42	.044	—	—	13726548④	—	Damper	—	—	—	5–7
8-401	BRF-31	.030	—	—	15486372④	—	Damper	—	—	—	7
8-460㉔	ARF-52	.054	—	—	15426378④	—	Damper	—	—	—	5–6
8-460	ARF-42	.044	—	—	15426378④	—	Damper	—	—	—	7
8-477	BRF-31	.030	—	—	15486372④	—	Damper	—	—	—	7
8-534	BRF-31	.030	—	—	15486372④	—	Damper	—	—	—	7

TUNEUP NOTES

①—Before top dead center.
②—Plus or minus 20 lbs.
④—Cylinder numbering (front to rear): Right bank 1-2-3-4, left bank 5-6-7-8.
㉓—Breakerless ignition.
㉔—Exc. Calif.

DISTRIBUTOR SPECIFICATIONS

Engine Model	Distributor Number	Breaker Gap, In.	Dwell Angle, Deg.	Breaker Arm Spring Tension Oz.	Centrifugal Advance Deg. @ Dist. rpm		Vacuum Advance Deg. @ In. of Mercury	
					Advance Starts	Maximum Advance	Advance Starts	Maximum Advance
6-200	D3BF-12127-CA	—	—	—	¾ @ 500	12½ @ 2000	⅝ @ 5	7¼ @ 20
6-240	D3UF-12127-BA	—	—	—	¼ @ 500	10 @ 2000	½ @ 5	7¼ @ 20
6-240	D3UF-12127-PA	—	—	—	½ @ 500	10½ @ 2000	4 @ 5	5½ @ 20
6-240	D3UF-12127-RA	—	—	—	¼ @ 500	10 @ 2000	4 @ 5	5½ @ 20
6-250	D3DF-12127-FA	—	—	—	¾ @ 500	10½ @ 2000	1½ @ 5	9¼ @ 20
6-250	D3OF-12127-RA	—	—	—	¾ @ 500	10 @ 2000	2 @ 5	9¼ @ 20

(continued)

DISTRIBUTOR SPECIFICATIONS—Continued

Engine Model	Distributor Number	Breaker Gap, In.	Dwell Angle, Deg.	Breaker Arm Spring Tension Oz.	Centrifugal Advance Deg. @ Dist. rpm		Vacuum Advance Deg. @ In. of Mercury	
					Advance Starts	Maximum Advance	Advance Starts	Maximum Advance
1974								
6-250	D4DE-12127-LA	—	—	—	¾ @ 500	9½ @ 2000	¾ @ 5	9¼ @ 20
6-250	D4DE-12127-NA	—	—	—	¾ @ 500	10 @ 2000	¾ @ 5	9¼ @ 20
6-250	D4DE-12127-RA	—	—	—	¾ @ 500	10½ @ 2000	2 @ 5	9¼ @ 20
6-300	D3TF-12127-GA	—	—	—	½ @ 500	7¼ @ 2000	⅝ @ 5	9¼ @ 20
6-300	D4TE-12127-EA	—	—	—	½ @ 500	7¼ @ 2000	⅝ @ 5	9¼ @ 20
8-302	D3BF-12127-BA	—	—	—	½ @ 500	12 @ 2000	½ @ 5	11½ @ 20
8-302	D3BF-12127-DA	—	—	—	⅝ @ 500	13½ @ 2000	½ @ 5	11½ @ 20
8-302	D3OF-12127-DA	—	—	—	½ @ 500	11 @ 2000	⅝ @ 5	5¼ @ 20
8-302	D3OF-12127-HB	—	—	—	¾ @ 500	13½ @ 2000	¾ @ 5	11¼ @ 20
8-302	D3UF-12127-EA	—	—	—	⅝ @ 500	14½ @ 2000	¾ @ 5	9¼ @ 20
8-302	D3UF-12127-FA	—	—	—	¾ @ 500	14 @ 2000	¾ @ 5	13¼ @ 20
8-302	D3UF-12127-GA	—	—	—	½ @ 500	11½ @ 2000	¼ @ 5	5¼ @ 20
8-302	D3UF-12127-JA	—	—	—	¾ @ 500	10½ @ 2000	½ @ 5	7¼ @ 20
8-302	D3UF-12127-KA	—	—	—	¾ @ 500	11 @ 2000	½ @ 5	7¼ @ 20
8-302	D4BE-12127-FA	—	—	—	¼ @ 500	11½ @ 2000	¼ @ 5	5¼ @ 20
8-302	D4BF-12127-EA	—	—	—	¼ @ 500	13½ @ 2000	¼ @ 5	11½ @ 20
8-302	D4TE-12127-PA	—	—	—	¼ @ 500	11½ @ 2000	½ @ 5	11½ @ 20
8-302	D4TE-12127-VA	—	—	—	¼ @ 500	10 @ 2000	¼ @ 5	11½ @ 20
8-302	D4UE-12127-FA	—	—	—	¼ @ 500	11 @ 2000	½ @ 5	11½ @ 20
8-302	D4UE-12127-HA	—	—	—	¼ @ 500	12½ @ 2000	¾ @ 5	9½ @ 20
8-330	D3HF-12102-BA	—	—	—	½ @ 500	14 @ 2000	2 @ 5	5½ @ 20
8-330	D3TF-12127-EA	—	—	—	¾ @ 500	12½ @ 2000	⅝ @ 5	9¼ @ 20
8-330	DETF-12102-AA	—	—	—	¼ @ 500	14 @ 2000	2 @ 5	5½ @ 20
8-351C	D3ZF-12127-GA	—	—	—	½ @ 500	11 @ 2000	½ @ 5	12½ @ 20
8-351C	D4AE-12127-AA	—	—	—	¼ @ 500	10½ @ 2000	½ @ 5	12½ @ 20
8-351CJ	D3OF-12127-FA	—	—	—	½ @ 500	13 @ 2000	1½ @ 5	5¼ @ 20
8-351CJ	D3OF-12127-GA	—	—	—	½ @ 500	13½ @ 2000	1¾ @ 5	5½ @ 20
8-359	D4HE-12127-AA	—	—	—	¼ @ 500	11 @ 2000	4 @ 5	5½ @ 20
8-360	D3TF-12127-HA	—	—	—	⅝ @ 500	14 @ 2000	2 @ 5	5¼ @ 20
8-360	D3TF-12127-PA	—	—	—	¾ @ 500	17½ @ 2000	1¼ @ 5	9¼ @ 20
8-360	D3TF-12127-UA	—	—	—	¾ @ 500	17½ @ 2000	¾ @ 5	9¼ @ 20
8-360	D4TE-12127-AA	—	—	—	—	—	—	—
8-360	D4TE-12127-TA	—	—	—	½ @ 500	16½ @ 2000	5 @ 5	7¼ @ 20
8-360	D4TE-12127-YA	—	—	—	¼ @ 500	13½ @ 2000	3⅞ @ 5	5¼ @ 20
8-361	D3TF-12102-CA	—	—	—	1¼ @ 500	14 @ 2000	1¾ @ 5	5½ @ 20
8-361	D3TF-12102-FA	—	—	—	1¼ @ 500	14 @ 2000	1¾ @ 5	5½ @ 20
8-361	D4TE-12102-AA	—	—	—	1¼ @ 500	14 @ 2000	1¾ @ 5	5½ @ 20
8-390	D3TF-12127-HA	—	—	—	⅝ @ 500	14 @ 2000	2 @ 5	5½ @ 20
8-390	D3TF-12127-VA	—	—	—	¾ @ 500	11 @ 2000	½ @ 5	5½ @ 20
8-390	D3TF-12127-XA	—	—	—	½ @ 500	15¼ @ 2000	1¼ @ 5	13¼ @ 20
8-390	D4TE-12127-UA	—	—	—	¼ @ 500	10½ @ 2000	1 @ 5	7½ @ 20
8-391	D3TF-12102-BA	—	—	—	¼ @ 500	14 @ 2000	¼ @ 5	7½ @ 20
8-391	D3TF-12102-GA	—	—	—	¼ @ 500	14 @ 2000	¼ @ 5	7½ @ 20
8-400	D4OE-12127-CA	—	—	—	¼ @ 500	10½ @ 2000	2¼ @ 5	13½ @ 20
8-460	D4TE-12127-HA	—	—	—	¼ @ 500	11¼ @ 2000	⅝ @ 5	11¼ @ 20
8-460	D4TE-12127-NA	—	—	—	¼ @ 500	8½ @ 2000	¾ @ 5	9½ @ 20
8-460	D4VE-12127-CA	—	—	—	¼ @ 500	10½ @ 2000	⅝ @ 5	11¼ @ 20
8-401, 475, 477, 534	D3HF-12127-AA	—	—	—	1¼ @ 500	14 @ 2000	¼ @ 5	9½ @ 20

FORD COURIER

MODEL INDEX & ENGINE APPLICATION

Model	Year	Engine Make	Standard Engine Model	Crankcase Refill Capacity, Qts.	Cooling System Capacity Qts.
Courier	1972–74	Toyo Kogyo	4-109	4①	7½

①—Includes one quart with filter replacement.

GENERAL ENGINE SPECIFICATIONS

Engine Model	Carb. Type	Bore & Stroke	Comp. Ratio	Horsepower @ rpm	Torque Lbs. Ft. @ rpm	Normal Oil Pressure Lbs.
1972-74						
4-109.6	2 Bore	3.07 x 3.70	8.6	74 @ 5000	92 @ 3500	50–64

TUNEUP SPECIFICATIONS

▲Before removing wires from distributor cap, determine location of No. 1 wire in cap, as distributor position may have been altered from that shown at the end of this chart.

Engine	Spark Plug		Distributor		Firing Order Fig. ▲	Ignition Timing		Hot Idle Speed, Rpm	Comp. Press. Psi	Fuel Pump Press., Lbs.
	Type	Gap Inch	Point Gap Inch	Dwell Angle Deg.		Deg. BTDC ①	Mark Locations			
1972-73										
4-109	AG32A	.031	.020	49–55	1-3-4-2	5	Pulley	725	②	2.8–3.6
1974										
4-109	AG32A	.031	.020	49–55	1-3-4-2	3	Pulley	—	②	2.8–3.6

①—Before top dead center. ②—When checking compression, lowest cylinder must be within 75% of highest.

DISTRIBUTOR SPECIFICATIONS

Engine	Distributor Number	Breaker Gap, In.	Dwell Angle, Deg.	Breaker Arm Spring Tension Oz.	Centrifugal Advance Deg. @ Dist. rpm		Vacuum Advance Deg. @ In. of Mercury		
					Advance Starts	Maximum Advance	Advance Starts	Maximum Advance	Retard
1972-73									
4-109②	—	.020	49–55	17–20	0 @ 550	10.5 @ 2600	—	—	5 ATDC③
4-109①	—	.020	49–55	17–20	0 @ 600	14 @ 2200	0 @ 12.6	7.5 @ 21.7	—
1974									
4-109④	—	.020	49–55	17–20	0 @ 600	14 @ 2200	0 @ 8.7	7.5 @ 17.7	—
4-109⑤	—	.020	49–55	17–20	0 @ 660	14 @ 2200	0 @ 10.6	7.5 @ 19.7	—

①—California.
②—Except California.
③—After top dead center.
④—Manual trans.
⑤—Auto. trans.

INTERNATIONAL

MODEL INDEX & ENGINE APPLICATION

ENGINE IDENTIFICATION—Engine model takes the form of a prefix to the engine serial number. For example, a V-266 engine serial number would read V-266-000000. Engine numbers are located on machined boss on cylinder block.

Truck Model or Series	Year	Standard Engine Make	Standard Engine Model	Oil Pan Refill Capacity, Qts.	Cooling System Capacity, Qts.
SCOUT					
Scout II	1973–74	Own	6-258	4	12
LOADSTAR					
1600	1972–74	Own	V-345	10	22
1600 4 x 4	1974	Own	V-304	—	—
1700	1972–74	Own	V-345	10	22
1750	1973–74	Own	DV-550B	—	42
1850	1973–74	Own	DV-550B	—	42
1800	1964–74	Own	V-345	10	22
F-1800	1964–74	Own	V-345	10	22
F-1850	1973–74	Own	DV-550B	—	42
CARGOSTAR					
CO-1610B	1974	Own	V-345	—	—
CO-1710B	1974	Own	V-345	—	—
CO-1810B	1974	Own	V-345	—	—
CO-1850B	1974	Own	DV-550B	10	—
COF-1910B	1974	Own	VS-401	10	—
COF-1950B	1974	Own	DV-550B	10	—
FLEETSTAR					
F-2010A	1972–74	Own	RD-450	9	47.7
F-2050A	1973–74	Own	CV-550B	—	57.3
F-2070A	1973–74	Detroit①	6-71N	30	48
2010A	1969–74	Own①	RD-450	9	47.7
2050A	1973–74	Own①	DV-550B	—	57.3
2070A	1973–74	Detroit①	6-71N	30	48
TRANSTAR					
4270	1973–74	Detroit①	8V-71	27	67
4370	1973–74	Cum'ins②	NTC-290	34.5	54
F-4270	1973–74	Detroit①	8V-71	27	67
F-4370	1973–74	Cum'ins②	NTC-290	34.5	54
CO-4070B	1974	Cummins	NTC-290	—	55
COF-4070B	1974	Cummins	NTC-290	—	55

①—See Detroit Diesel section for specs.
②—See Cummins chapter for specs.

Truck Model or Series	Year	Standard Engine Make	Standard Engine Model	Oil Pan Refill Capacity, Qts.	Cooling System Capacity, Qts.
TRAVELALL					
100 4 x 2	1974	Own	V-345	—	—
100 4 x 4	1974	Own	V-392	—	—
200 4 x 2	1974	Own	V-392	—	—
200 4 x 4	1974	Own	V-392	—	—
PAYSTAR					
5050 4 x 4	1973–74	Own	DV-550B	—	—
5070 4 x 4	1974	Detroit	6-71	—	—
5050 6 x 4	1973–74	Own	DV-550B	—	—
5050 6 x 6	1973–74	Own	DV-550B	—	—
F-5070 6 x 4	1973–74	Detroit①	6-71	30	—
F-5070 6 x 6	1974	Detroit	6-71	—	—
F-5050SF 6x4	1973–74	Own	CV-550B	—	—
F-5070SF 6x4	1973–74	Detroit	6-71N	30	—
SCHOOLMASTER SERIES					
1603	1964–74	Own	V-304	9	21
1703	1964–74	Own	V-304	9	21
1803	1964–74	Own	V-345	9	21.9
METRO SERIES					
MS-1210	1974	Jeep	6-258	4	15.6
MHC-1310	1974	Own	V-392	—	24
MS-1510	1974	Own	V-345	—	15.6
MHC-1510	1974	Own	V-392	—	24
100, 110, 120, 130 SERIES					
100	1974	Jeep	6-258	4	12
100 4 x 4	1974	Own	V-304	—	17
200, 210 and 230 SERIES					
200	1974	Jeep	6-258	4	12
200 4 x 4	1974	Jeep	6-258	4	—
500 SERIES					
500	1974	Jeep	6-258	4	12

GENERAL ENGINE SPECIFICATIONS

Engine Model	Carb. Type	Bore & Stroke	Comp. Ratio	Horsepower @ rpm	Torque Lbs. Ft. @ rpm	Comp. Pressure Cranking Speed ①	Governed Speed Rpm	Normal Oil Pressure Lbs.
1973-74								
OHV-6............6-258	1 Bore	3¾ x 3.895	8.0	115 @ 3800	199 @ 2000	—	—	32
1962-74								
OHV-6...........BD-308	2 Bore	3¹³⁄₁₆ x 4½	6.5	136 @ 3200	274 @ 1800	110	3200	35–45
1973-74								
OHV-6...........RD-406	2 Bore	4⅜ x 4½	7.1	160 @ 2750	336 @ 1400	143	2750	35–45
OHV-6...........RD-450	2 Bore	4⅜ x 5	7.1	168 @ 2600	372 @ 1400	142	2600	35–45
OHV-6...........RD-501	4 Bore	4½ x 5¼	6.8	181 @ 2600	406 @ 1400	145	2600	35–45
1973-75								
OHV-V8...........V-304	2 Bore	3⅞ x 3⅞₃₂	8.2	147 @ 3900	240 @ 2400	145	—	50
1973-74								
OHV-V8...........V-304	4 Bore	3⅞ x 3⅞₃₂	8.2	153 @ 3900	246 @ 2400	145	—	50
1973-75								
OHV-V8...........V-345	2 Bore	3⅞ x 3²¹⁄₃₂	8.1	157 @ 3800	266 @ 2400	143	3800	50
OHV-V8...........V-345	4 Bore	3⅞ x 3²¹⁄₃₂	8.1	163 @ 3800	273 @ 2400	143	3800	50
1973-74								
OHV-V8...........V-392	2 Bore	4⅛ x 3²¹⁄₃₂	8.0	191 @ 3600	299 @ 2800	143	3600	50
1973-75								
OHV-V8...........V-392	4 Bore	4⅛ x 3²¹⁄₃₂	8.0	194 @ 3600	308 @ 2800	143	3600	50
1973-74								
OHV-V8②.........V-400	2 Bore	4¹¹⁄₆₄ x 3¹¹⁄₁₆	8.25	211 @ 4000	326 @ 2800	—	—	37–45
OHV-V8...........V-401	2 Bore	4⅛ x 3¾	7.7	186 @ 3400	322 @ 2400	139	3400	40–55
1975								
OHV-8..........MV-404	2 Bore	4⅛ x 3¾	8.1	188 @ 3600	311 @ 2300	—	3600	44–50
OHV-8..........MV-404	4 Bore	4⅛ x 3¾	8.1	210 @ 3600	336 @ 2800	—	3600	44–50
OHV-8..........MV-446	4 Bore	4⅛ x 4³⁄₁₆	8.1	235 @ 3600	385 @ 2600	—	3600	44–50
1973-74								
OHV-V8...........V-478	2 Bore	4½ x 3¾	7.6	209 @ 3400	384 @ 2200	140	3400	40–55
OHV-V8...........V-549	4 Bore	4½ x 4⁵⁄₁₆	7.6	227 @ 3200	446 @ 2000	140	3200	40–55

①—Plus or minus 10 lbs. ②—See V8-401 in Jeep chapter for service data.

TUNEUP & VALVE SPECIFICATIONS

★When using a timing light, disconnect vacuum tube or hose at distributor (if equipped) and plug opening in hose or tube so idle speed will not be affected.

Engine Model	Firing Order	Spark Plugs		Ignition Timing★		Valve Seat Angle, Degrees	Valve Clearance H-Hot C-Cold		Valve Spring Pressure, Lb. @ In. Length
		Type①	Gap	Timing Mark Deg. BTDC⑦	Location		Intake	Exhaust	
1975									
4-196	1342	RJ10Y	.030	TDC⑬	Damper	⑥	Zero	Zero	188 @ 1⁷⁄₆₄
1974-75									
V-345	18736542④	⑩	.030⑮	TDC⑭	Damper	45	Zero	Zero	188 @ 1²⁷⁄₆₄
V-392	18736542④	⑩	.030	TDC⑪	Damper	⑥	Zero	Zero	188 @ 1²⁷⁄₆₄
1975									
MV-404	12734568⑫	RBN4	.030	9	—	45	Zero	Zero	188 @ 1²⁷⁄₆₄
MV-446	12734568⑫	RBN4	.030	5	—	45	Zero	Zero	188 @ 1²⁷⁄₆₄

(continued)

TUNEUP NOTES

(1)—Champion
(2)—Intake 30°, exhaust 44°.
(3)—Outer spring.
(4)—Cylinder numbering (front to rear): Left bank 1-3-5-7, right bank 2-4-6-8.
(5)—Connect timing light to No. 8 spark plug.
(6)—Intake 30°, exhaust 45°.
(7)—Before top dead center.
(8)—Scout w/turbocharger 10°.
(9)—Intake 29°, exhaust 44°.
(10)—Scout and 150–500 Series RJ10Y; 1600–1800 Series RJ6.
(11)—Models with Thermo Quad Carburetor 5° BTDC; Low compression engines 5° BTDC.
(12)—Cylinder numbering (front to rear): Left bank 2-4-6-8, right bank 1-3-5-7.
(13)—Low compression engines 5° BTDC.
(14)—L.P.G. models 10° BTDC; Low compression engines 5° BTDC.
(15)—L.P.G. models .015″.

DISTRIBUTOR SPECIFICATIONS

Engine Application	Distributor		Rotation Rotor End	Point Gap Inch	Dwell Angle Deg.	Breaker Arm Spring Tension Ounces	Centrifugal Advance Deg. @ Dist. rpm		Vacuum Advance	
	Make	Model					Advance Starts	Full Advance	Inches of Vacuum to Start Advance	Max. Adv. Dist. Deg. @ Vacuum
BD, PT, RD ENGINES										
	Delco-Remy	1110429	C	.019	28–35	17–21	5 @ 400	14 @ 1000	—	—
	Delco-Remy	1112692	CC	.019	31–34	19–23	2 @ 350	12 @ 1750	—	—
FOUR-CYLINDER ENGINES										
4-152	Delco-Remy	1110266	—	.016	74–76	19–23	1 @ 350	14 @ 2100	3 to 5	7 @ 10
4-152	Holley	2274-P	—	.026	34–48	17–20	1 @ 375	14 @ 2000	2 to 5	10 @ 14
4-152	Holley	3119-P	—	.017	69–74	17–20	1 @ 600	11 @ 2000	—	—
4-196	Holley	3857-P	—	.017	42–48	17–20	1 @ 300	16 @ 1800	5 to 7	11 @ 14
4-196	Prestolite(3)	464359-C91(3)	C	.008(4)	26–32	—	5 @ 600	17.8 @ 2200	5 to 7	6 @ 15
V8 ENGINES										
V-266, 304	Prestolite	285098-C91	—	.017	25–29	17–20	1 @ 350	14 @ 2000	5 to 7	14 @ 11
V-304, 345	Prestolite	285093-C91	—	.017	25–29	17–20	1 @ 350	14 @ 2000	5 to 7	14 @ 11
V-301, 345	Prestolite	285096-C91	—	.017	25–29	17–20	1 @ 350	14 @ 2000	5 to 7	14 @ 11
(1)	Prestolite	291262-C92	—	(2)	25–29	17–21	1 @ 350	14½ @ 2000	5 to 7½	7 @ 11½
(1)	Prestolite	354206-C91	—	(2)	25–29	17–21	1 @ 350	14½ @ 2000	5 to 7½	7 @ 11½.
V-304	Prestolite(3)	467073-C91(3)	C	.008(4)	26–32	—	2 @ 600	16.8 @ 2100	5 to 7	8 @ 15
V-304, 345	Prestolite	291260-C94	—	(2)	25–29	17–21	1 @ 350	14½ @ 2000	5 to 7½	7 @ 11½
V-304, 345	Prestolite	359217-C91	—	(2)	25–29	17–21	1 @ 350	14½ @ 2000	5 to 7½	7 @ 11½
V-304, 345	Prestolite	359220-C91	—	(2)	25–29	7–21	1 @ 350	14½ @ 2000	5 to 7½	7 @ 11½
V-304, 345	Prestolite(3)	461270-C91(3)	C	.008(4)	26–32	—	2 @ 550	16.7 @ 2200	5 to 7	6 @ 15
(5)	Prestolite(3)	463333-C91(3)	C	.008(4)	26–32	—	½ @ 300	14½ @ 2000	5 to 7½	8 @ 15
(5)	Prestolite(3)	463334-C91(3)	C	.008(4)	26–32	—	½ @ 300	17 @ 1800	4¾ to 6¼	8 @ 15
(5)	Prestolite(3)	463335-C91(3)	C	.008(4)	26–32	—	½ @ 300	14½ @ 2000	5 to 7½	8 @ 15
(5)	Prestolite(3)	463336-C91(3)	C	.008(4)	26–32	—	½ @ 300	17 @ 1800	4¾ to 6¼	8 @ 15
V-345	Prestolite(3)	448685-C91(3)	C	.014(4)	22–28	—	½ @ 400	17 @ 2000	5 to 7	4 @ 11
V-345	Prestolite(3)	461271-C91(3)	C	.008(4)	26–32	—	½ @ 400	12.4 @ 2000	5 to 7	6 @ 15
V-345	Prestolite(3)	461272-C91(3)	C	.008(4)	26–32	—	½ @ 400	12.4 @ 2000	5 to 7	6 @ 15
V-345 L.P.G.	Prestolite(3)	463330-C91(3)	C	.008(4)	26–32	—	1 @ 400	12½ @ 2000	5 to 7	8 @ 15
V-345 L.P.G.	Prestolite(3)	463331-C91(3)	C	.008(4)	26–32	—	1 @ 400	12½ @ 2000	5 to 7	8 @ 15
V-345 L.P.G.	Prestolite(3)	463332-C91(3)	C	.008(4)	26–32	—	1 @ 400	12½ @ 2000	5 to 7	8 @ 15
V-392	Prestolite	285092-C91	—	.017	25–29	17–20	1 @ 350	12 @ 2000	5 to 7	14 @ 11
V-392	Prestolite	285095-C91	—	.017	25–29	17–20	1 @ 350	12 @ 2000	5 to 7	14 @ 11
V-392	Prestolite	323418-C93	—	(2)	25–29	17–21	½ @ 350	12½ @ 2000	5 to 7	7 @ 11
V-392	Prestolite	359218-C91	—	(2)	25–29	17–21	½ @ 350	12½ @ 2000	5 to 7	7 @ 11
V-392	Prestolite	359221-C91	—	(2)	25–29	17–21	½ @ 350	12½ @ 2000	5 to 7	7 @ 11
V-392	Prestolite(3)	448686-C91(3)	C	.008(4)	26–32	—	2.7 @ 400	15 @ 2200	5 to 7	6 @ 15
V-392	Prestolite(3)	461273-C91(3)	C	.008(4)	26–32	—	½ @ 400	12.4 @ 2000	5 to 7	6 @ 15
V-392	Prestolite(3)	467034-C91(3)	C	.008(4)	26–32	—	3.6 @ 650	15½ @ 2000	5 to 7	8 @ 15
V-392	Prestolite(3)	467035-C91(3)	C	.008(4)	26–32	—	3.6 @ 650	15½ @ 2000	5 to 7	8 @ 15
V-392	Prestolite(3)	519861-C91(3)	C	.008(4)	26–32	—	½ @ 400	12.4 @ 2000	5 to 7	6 @ 15
V-400	Delco-Remy	1112215	—	.016	29–31	17–21	¾ @ 400	14¼ @ 2000	4 to 6	8¼ @ 13
V-400	Delco-Remy	1112904	—	.016	29–31	17–21	¾ @ 400	14¼ @ 2000	9 to 11	6 @ 15½
MV-404	Prestolite(3)	446916-C91(3)	CC	.008(4)	26–32	—	2 @ 600	12.4 @ 1900	5 to 7	4 @ 12
MV-404	Prestolite(3)	446920-C91(3)	CC	.008(4)	26–32	—	2 @ 600	12.4 @ 1900	5 to 7	4 @ 12

(continued)

DISTRIBUTOR SPECIFICATIONS—Continued

Engine Application	Distributor Make	Distributor Model	Rotation Rotor End	Point Gap Inch	Dwell Angle Deg.	Breaker Arm Spring Tension Ounces	Centrifugal Advance Deg. @ Dist. rpm: Advance Starts	Centrifugal Advance: Full Advance	Vacuum Advance: Inches of Vacuum to Start Advance	Vacuum Advance: Max. Adv. Dist. Deg. @ Vacuum
MV-404	Prestolite③	446921-C91③	CC	.008④	26–32	—	2 @ 600	12.4 @ 1900	5 to 7	4 @ 12
MV-446	Prestolite③	446917-C91③	CC	.008④	26–32	—	2 @ 600	12.4 @ 1900	10 to 12	4 @ 15
MV-446	Prestolite③	446918-C91③	CC	.008④	26–32	—	2 @ 600	12.4 @ 1900	10 to 12	4 @ 15
V-461	Holley	1882-1	—	.016	28–32	17–20	1 @ 300	10 @ 1650	6 to 7	7 @ 11
V-401, 549	Holley	1883-1	—	.016	28–32	17–20	1 @ 350	11 @ 1600	6 to 7	7 @ 11
L.P.G.	Holley	2293	—	.016	28–32	17–20	1 @ 350	7 @ 1600	5 to 6	5 @ 10
V-401, 549	Prestolite	286686-C93	—	②	25–29	17–21	½ @ 350	8 @ 1600	5½ to 7½	7 @ 11
V-401, 549	Prestolite	359223-C91	—	②	25–29	17–21	½ @ 350	8 @ 1600	5½ to 7½	7 @ 11
V-401, 549	Prestolite	359226-C91	—	②	25–29	17–21	½ @ 350	8 @ 1600	5½ to 7½	7 @ 11
V-401, 549	Prestolite	359228-C91	—	②	25–29	17–21	½ @ 350	8 @ 1600	5½ to 7½	7 @ 11
V-401, 549	Prestolite	359230-C91	—	②	25–29	17–21	½ @ 350	8 @ 1600	5½ to 7½	7 @ 11
V-401, 549	Prestolite	359231-C91	—	②	25–29	17–21	½ @ 350	8 @ 1600	5½ to 7½	7 @ 11
V-401, 549	Prestolite	359233-C91	—	②	25–29	17–21	½ @ 350	8 @ 1600	5½ to 7½	7 @ 11
V-478	Prestolite	286684-C93	—	②	25–29	17–21	0 @ 350	12 @ 1600	5½ to 7½	7 @ 11
V-478	Prestolite	359227-C91	—	②	25–29	17–21	0 @ 350	12 @ 1600	5½ to 7½	7 @ 11
V-478	Prestolite	359229-C91	—	②	25–29	17–21	0 @ 350	12 @ 1600	5½ to 7½	7 @ 11
V-478	Prestolite	359232-C91	—	②	25–29	17–21	0 @ 350	12 @ 1600	5½ to 7½	7 @ 11

①—V-266, 304, 345.
②—New .017", used .014".
③—Electronic breakerless ignition system.
④—Clearance between end of trigger wheel tooth and sensor.
⑤—V-304, 345 & 392 low compression engines.

JEEP

GENERAL ENGINE SPECIFICATIONS

Model or Series	Engine Make	Engine Model	Bore & Stroke	Piston Displ. Cu. In.	Comp. Ratio	Horsepower @ rpm	Normal Oil Pressure Psi	Oil Pan Refill Capacity, Qts. ②	Cooling System Capacity, Qts. ①
JEEP 1972-75									
CJ Series	Amer. Mtrs.	6-232	3.750 x 3.500	232	8.0	100 @ 3600③	37–75	5	10½
1972-74									
Commando	Amer. Mtrs.	6-232	3.750 x 3.500	232	8.0	100 @ 3600③	37–75	5	10½
1972-75									
J-100 Series	Amer. Mtrs.	6-258	3.75 x 3.895	258	8.0	110 @ 3500③	37–75	5	10½
1974-75									
	Amer. Mtrs.	V8-360④	4.08 x 3.44	360	8.25	175 @ 4000	37–75	4	—
	Amer. Mtrs.	V8-360⑤	4.08 x 3.44	360	8.25	195 @ 4400	37–75	4	—
1972-75									
	Amer. Mtrs.	V8-304	3.75 x 3.440	304	8.4	150 @ 4200③	37–75	4	14
1974-75									
	Amer. Mtrs.	V8-360④	4.08 x 3.44	360	8.25	175 @ 4000	37–75	4	—
	Amer. Mtrs.	V8-360⑤	4.08 x 3.44	360	8.25	195 @ 4400	37–75	4	—
	Amer. Mtrs.	V8-401	4.16 x 3.68	401	8.25	215 @ 4200	37–75	4	—

①—With heater.
②—Add 1 qt. with filter change.
③—Ratings are NET—as installed in vehicle.
④—2 Barrel Carb.
⑤—4 Barrel Carb.

TUNEUP SPECIFICATIONS

★When using a timing light, disconnect vacuum hose or tube at distributor and plug opening in hose or tube so idle speed will not be affected.

Engine	Spark Plug		Distributor		Firing Order	Ignition Timing★		Hot Idle Speed		Comp. Press. Lbs.	Fuel Pump Press. Lbs.
	Type	Gap Inch	Point Gap Inch	Dwell Angle Deg.		Deg. BTDC ①	Mark	Std. Trans.	Auto. Trans.		
JEEP											
1974											
6-232	N12Y	.035	.016	31–34	1-5-3-6-2-4	5	Damper	600	—	140	4–5½
6-258	N12Y	.035	.016	31–34	1-5-3-6-2-4	3	Damper	600	550D⑬	150	4–5½
V8-304	N12Y	.035	.016	29–31	1-8-4-3-6-5-7-2⑥	5	Damper	750	—	140	4–6½
V8-360	N12Y	.035	.016	29–31	1-8-4-3-6-5-7-2⑥	5	Damper	750	700D⑬	140	4–6½
V8-401	N12Y	.035	.016	29–31	1-8-4-3-6-5-7-2⑥	5	Damper	650	600D⑬	140	4–6½
1975											
6-232⑭	N12Y	.035	—	—	1-5-3-6-2-4	5	Damper	700	—	140	—
6-232⑮	N12Y	.035	—	—	1-5-3-6-2-4	5	Damper	600	—	140	—
6-258⑭	N12Y	.035	—	—	1-5-3-6-2-4	3	Damper	700	—	150	—
6-258⑯	N12Y	.035	—	—	1-5-3-6-2-4	3	Damper	650	550	150	—
6-258⑭	N12Y	.035	—	—	1-5-3-6-2-4	3	Damper	600	—	150	—
V8-304	N12Y	.035	—	—	1-8-4-3-6-5-7-2⑥	5	Damper	750	—	140	—
V8-360, 401	N12Y	.035	—	—	1-8-4-3-6-5-7-2⑥	2.5	Damper	750	700	140	—
JEEP TRUCKS											
1974											
6-258	N12Y	.035	.016	31–34	1-5-3-6-2-4	3	Damper	600	550D⑬	150	4–5½
V8-304	N12Y	.035	.016	29–31	1-8-4-3-6-5-7-2⑥	5	Damper	750	—	140	4–6½
V8-360	N12Y	.035	.016	29–31	1-8-4-3-6-5-7-2⑥	5	Damper	750	700D⑬	140	4–6½
V8-401	N12Y	.035	.016	29–31	1-8-4-3-6-5-7-2⑥	5	Damper	650	700D⑬	140	4–6½
1975											
6-258⑭	N12Y	.035	—	—	1-5-3-6-2-4	3	Damper	700	—	150	—
6-258⑮	N12Y	.035	—	—	1-5-3-6-2-4	3	Damper	650	550	150	—
6-258⑯	N12Y	.035	—	—	1-5-3-6-2-4	3	Damper	600	—	150	—
V8-304	N12Y	.035	—	—	1-8-4-3-6-5-7-2⑥	5	Damper	750	—	140	—
V8-360, 401	N12Y	.035	—	—	1-8-4-3-6-5-7-2⑥	2.5	Damper	750	700	140	—

①—Before top dead center.
⑥—Cylinder numbering (front to rear): Left bank 1-3-5-7, right bank 2-4-6-8.
⑬—Disconnect TCS wires at solenoid vacuum valve.
⑭—Without EGR.
⑮—California.
⑯—With EGR.

DISTRIBUTOR SPECIFICATIONS

★NOTE: If advance is checked on the vehicle, double the rpm and degrees to get crankshaft figures.

Engine	Distributor Part No.	Rotation	Breaker Gap	Dwell Angle	Breaker Arm Spring Tension Oz.	Centrifugal Advance Degrees @ rpm of Distributor★		Vacuum Advance	
						Advance Starts	Full Advance	Inches of Vacuum To Start Plunger	Max. Adv. Dist. Deg. @ Vacuum
1974									
Six	1110529	C	.016	31–34	17–21	0–2 @ 500	14 @ 2300	5	9 @ 13
V8	1112112	C	.016	29–31	17–21	0–1¾ @ 500	14 @ 2000	5	8.25 @ 12¾
V8	1112179	C	.016	29–31	17–21	0–1 @ 400	17 @ 2200	5	8.25 @ 12¾
V8	1112215	C	.016	29–31	17–21	0–1½ @ 400	16 @ 2200	4	8.25 @ 13
1975									
Six	3224968	C	—	—	—	1 @ 500	16 @ 1500	—	—
Six	3224969	C	—	—	—	2 @ 500	16 @ 1500	—	—
V8	3224965	C	—	—	—	1 @ 400	24 @ 1500	—	—
V8	3224746	C	—	—	—	1½ @ 400	25.5 @ 1500	—	—
V8	3225295	C	—	—	—	2 @ 500	21.5 @ 1500	—	—

MACK

MODEL INDEX & ENGINE APPLICATION

B MODELS

Truck Model	Engine Model ①	Crank-case Refill Capacity, Qts.	Cooling System Capacity, Qts.
B20	EN291	8	32
B30	EN331	8	32
B34	EN401	8	34
B42, B421	EN402	8	34
B422, B4226	EN438	13	48
B426	EN402	8	34
B43	END673	15	48
B45	END475	19	48
B46	EN402	8	34
B462	EN438	13	48
B47	END465	15	48
B48, B486	EN414	8	34
B49	END475	19	48
B53, B57	END673	15	48
B61	END673P	15	48
B61	END711	19	48
B613	ENDT673	15	52
B615	END864	⑧	62
B66	EN450	13	52
B67	END673P	15	48
B673	ENDT673	15	52
B68	EN540	13	52
B70	EN707C	15	58
B72	EN707C	15	62
B73	NH②	—	52
B733	NT280②	—	54
B75	END673P	15	62
B75	END711	19	62
B753	ENDT673	15	62
B755	END864	⑧	62
B77	NHS6B②	—	54
B773	NT335②	—	54
B777	V8-265②	—	48
B80	EN707C	15	58
B81	END673P	15	54
B813, B8136	ENDT673	15	54
B815	END864	⑧	74
B83	NH②	—	56
B833	NH②	—	58
B85	NHS6B②	—	58
B853	NT280②	—	58
B87	NHRS6B②	—	58
B873	NT335②	—	58

C & DM MODELS

Truck Model	Engine Model ①	Crank-case Refill Capacity, Qts.	Cooling System Capacity, Qts.
C607	END673	15	72
C609	END707	19	73
C609	END711	19	73
C611	ENDT673	15	73
C615	END864	⑧	73
DM401	END475	15	32
DM403	END465C	15	42
DM410	EN414A	8	32
DM487	ENDT475	16	37
DM607	END673	15	44
DM6076	END673	15	52
DM609	END707	19	49
DM611	ENDT673	15	52
DM615	END864	⑧	56
DM640	EN540A	13	58
DM685	ENDT675	19	57
DM807	END673	15	62
DM809	END707	19	62
DM811	ENDT673	—	62
DM815	END864	⑧	62
DM819	ENDT864	⑧	64
DM831	NH220②	—	60
DM837	NHC250②	—	60
DM845	NTC335②	—	64
DM863	NTC335②	—	64
DM885	ENDT675	19	62

F MODELS

Truck Model	Engine Model ①	Crank-case Refill Capacity, Qts.	Cooling System Capacity, Qts.
F607	END673	15	44
F609	END707	19	⑦
F609	END711	19	⑨
F611	ENDT673	15	④
F685	ENDT675	19	55
F707	END673P	15	44
F709	END711	19	⑦
F711	ENDT673	15	⑩
F715	END864	⑧	55
F719	ENDT864	⑧	60
F723	ENDT864A	⑧	60
F731	NH220②	—	⑤
F737	NH250②	—	⑤
F741	NTO-6-B②	—	58
F743	V8-265②	—	48
F745	NT280②	—	52
F749	NHS②	—	52
F759	NHRS②	—	58
F763	NTC335②	—	54
F765	NT-380②	—	58

FL MODELS

Truck Model	Engine Model ①	Crank-case Refill Capacity, Qts.	Cooling System Capacity, Qts.
FL707	END673	15	48
FL709	END707	19	53
FL711	ENDT673	15	55
FL715	END864	⑧	59
FL719	ENDT864	⑧	59
FL731	NH220②	—	48
FL737	NHC250②	—	48
FL739	NHCT270②	—	48
FL763	NTC335②	—	54
FL675	NT380②	—	54
FL773	8V71③	—	66
FL785	ENDT675	19	55

G, H AND MB MODELS

Truck Model	Engine Model ①	Crank-case Refill Capacity, Qts.	Cooling System Capacity, Qts.
G73	NH220②	—	48
G733	NT②	—	48
G75	END673	15	56
G753	ENDT673	15	56
G773	NRT②	—	48
H67	END673	15	48
H673	ENDT673	15	52
H69	END673	15	48
H693	ENDT673	15	52
MB401	END475	15	33
MB402	EN402	8	36
MB403	END465	15	42
MB410	EN414A	8	32
MB478	ENDT475	16	37
MB605	END673	15	44
MB607	END673D	15	49
MB609	END707	—	49
MB487	ENDT475	15	38

R MODELS

Truck Model	Engine Model ①	Crank-case Refill Capacity, Qts.	Cooling System Capacity, Qts.
R401	END475	15	32
R402	EN402	8	36
R403	END465C	15	42
R410	EN414A	8	32
R487	ENDT475	15	37
R567	END465D	15	40
R607	END673P	15	⑥
R609	END707	19	⑦
R609	END711	19	⑨
R611	ENDT673	15	④
R615	END864	⑧	56
R640	EN540A	13	58
R685	ENDT675	19	57
R707	END673	15	58
R709	END707	19	60
R709	END711	19	60
R711	ENDT673	15	60
R715	END864	⑧	62
R719	ENDT864	⑧	64
R731	NH220②	—	54
R737	NHC250②	—	54
R743	V8-265②	—	50
R763	NTC335②	—	66
RD607	END673E	15	44
RD611	ENDT673	15	52
RD611	ENDT673C	15	57
RD615	END864	⑧	56
RD685	ENDT675	19	57
RD731	NH230②	—	54
RD763	NTC335②	—	66
RD773	8V71N③	—	54
RD795	ENDT865	⑪	68

(continued)

MODEL INDEX & ENGINE APPLICATION—Continued

Truck Model	Engine Model ①	Crank-case Refill Capacity, Qts.	Cooling System Capacity, Qts.
U MODELS			
U401	END475	15	32
U403	END465C	15	42
U410	EN414A	8	32
U567	END465D	15	40
U607	END673P	15	⑥
U609	END707	19	④
U609	END711	19	⑨
U611	ENDT673	15	④
U611	ENDT673	15	④
U615	END864	⑧	56
U685	ENDT675	19	57

①—Mack design unless otherwise noted.
②—Cummins engine.
③—Detroit diesel engine.
④—Radiator frontal area: 700 sq. in. 52 qts.; 1000 sq. in. 60 qts.
⑤—Radiator frontal area: 700 sq. in. 42 qts.; 1000 sq. in. 52 qts.
⑥—Radiator frontal area: 560 sq. in. 44 qts.; 1000 sq. in. 60 qts.
⑦—Radiator frontal area: 700 sq. in. 49 qts.; 1000 sq. in. 60 qts.
⑧—High level 16 qts.; low level 12 qts.
⑨—Radiator frontal area; 700 sq. in. 50 qts., 1000 sq. in. 60 qts.
⑩—Radiator frontal area; 700 sq. in. 51 qts.; 1000 sq. in. 60 qts.
⑪—High level 20 qts.; low level 16 qts.

GENERAL ENGINE SPECIFICATIONS

ENGINE IDENTIFICATION—Engine model and serial number located on right front of cylinder block by timing case cover on Magnadyne engines; on Thermodyne engines on top of right front motor leg.

Engine Model	No. Cyls. & Valve Location	Bore & Stroke	Piston Disp. Cu. In.	Com-pression Ratio	Horsepower @ rpm	Torque Lb. Ft. @ rpm	Governor		Normal Oil Pressure
							No-Load Setting Rpm	Full-Load Setting Rpm	
291	6 In Head	3¾ x 4⅜	291	6.9	107 @ 2800	232 @ 1400	2950	2800	45-60
331①	6 In Block	4 x 4⅜	331	6.9	122 @ 2800	264 @ 1400	2950	2800	45-60
401, 402	6 In Block	4 1/16 x 5 5/32	401	7.3	150 @ 2800	330 @ 1400	2950	2800	45-60
414②	8 In Head	4 3/16 x 3¾	413	7.5	214 @ 4000	—	—	—	45-65
431A	6 In Head	4⅛ x 5⅜	431	6.7	142 @ 2650	350 @ 1400	2650	2500	45-60
438	6 In Head	4 5/16 x 5	438	7.1	160 @ 2600	355 @ 1400	2750	2600	45-60
464A	6 In Head	4 7/16 x 5	464	7.5	185 @ 2800	380 @ 1400	2950	2800	45-60
464B	6 In Head	4 7/16 x 5	464	7.5	185 @ 2800	380 @ 1400	2950	2800	45-60
464B①	6 In Head	4 7/16 x 5	464	6.7	185 @ 2800	380 @ 1400	2950	2800	45-60
510A	6 In Head	4 7/16 x 5½	510	6.5	185 @ 2600	415 @ 1400	2550	2400	45-60
510B	6 In Head	4 7/16 x 5½	510	7.7	185 @ 2600	415 @ 1400	2750	2600	45-60
510C①	6 In Head	4 7/16 x 5½	510	7.7	185 @ 2600	415 @ 1400	2750	2600	45-60
540①	6 In Head	4 9/16 x 5½	540	7.2	185 @ 2400	445 @ 1300	2550	2400	45-60
707A	6 In Head	5 x 6	707	6.1	232 @ 2100	615 @ 1200	2150	2000	45-60
707B	6 In Head	5 x 6	707	6.4	232 @ 2100	615 @ 1200	2250	2100	45-60
707C	6 In Head	5 x 6	707	7.5	232 @ 2100	615 @ 1200	2250	2100	45-60
707C①	6 In Head	5 x 6	707	7.0	232 @ 2100	617 @ 1200	2250	2100	45-60

①—Latest production. ②—Chrysler industrial engine HT413. See Dodge Chapter for service procedures.

TUNEUP & VALVE SPECIFICATIONS

Engine Model	Firing Order	Spark Plugs Type⑮	Spark Plugs Gap	Ignition Timing: Timing Mark	Ignition Timing: Location	Cylinder Head Torque	Valve Face Angle	Valve Lash, Cold: Intake	Valve Lash, Cold: Exhaust	Valve Spring Pressure, Lb. @ In. Length
291	153624	D14	.030	4BTC	Flywheel	100	②	.010	.025	66 @ 2 3/4⑩
331	153624	D14	.030	4BTC	Flywheel	100	②	.010	.020	66 @ 2 3/4⑩
401, 402⑬	153624	J6	.025	3BTC	Flywheel	100	②	.010	.020	66 @ 2 3/4⑩
414⑯	18436572	—	.035	5BTC	Damper	70	45	Zero	Zero	—
431A	153624	J6	.025	10BTC	③	130④	②	.010	.025⑤	51 @ 2 21/32⑩
438①	153624	J6	.020	12BTC	Damper	130④	②	.014⑫	.030⑫	105 @ 1 11/16⑩
464A	153624	J6	.020	8BTC	Flywheel	130④	②	.010	.025	105 @ 1 11/16⑩
464B⑥	153624	J6	.020	8BTC	Flywheel	130④	②	.010	.025	105 @ 1 11/16⑩
464B⑦	153624	J6	.020	⑭	Flywheel	130④	②	.010	.025	105 @ 1 11/16⑩
510A⑧	153624	D14	.030	11BTC	Flywheel	130④	②	.010	.025⑤	105 @ 1 11/16⑩
510A⑨	153624	D14	.030	15BTC	Flywheel	130④	②	.010	.025⑤	105 @ 1 11/16⑩
510B	153624	J6	.025	8BTC	③	130④	②	.010	.025	105 @ 1 11/16⑩
510C①	153624	J6	.025	8BTC	Flywheel	130④	②	.015	.025	105 @ 1 11/16⑩
540①	153624	J6	.025	13BTC	Damper	130④	②	.014	.020	105 @ 1 11/16⑩
707A	153624	D14	.030	15BTC	③	150	②	.010	.025	110 @ 2 5/32⑩
707B	153624	D14	.030	13BTC	Flywheel	150	②	.010	.025	110 @ 2 5/32⑩
707B⑪	153624	D14	.030	16BTC	Flywheel	150	②	.018	.028	110 @ 2 5/32⑩
707C	153624	J6	.025	8BTC	Flywheel	150	②	.015	.025	110 @ 2 5/32⑩
707C①	153624	J6	.025	10BTC	Flywheel	150	②	.015	.025	110 @ 2 5/32⑩

①—Latest production.
②—Intake 30°, exhaust 45°.
③—Flywheel and vibration damper.
④—Short studs 100 lb. ft.
⑤—If engine has Invar push rods, clearance is .015" cold.
⑥—With 7.5 compression ratio.
⑦—With 6.7 compression ratio.
⑧—Using "Clearomatic" pistons.
⑨—Using "Trunk Type" pistons.
⑩—Outer spring.
⑪—Special service head, spark plugs on left side, washer necessary to locate exhaust valve rocker arm.
⑫—Disregard instruction plate on manifold which gives .012 intake and .025 exhaust. Mark suggests replacing instruction plate.
⑬—The 402 engine is identical to the 401 except that the 402 has 34 cylinder head studs instead of 32.
⑭—With "Clearomatic" pistons 11°, with "Trunk" type pistons 13°.
⑮—Champion. Normal service.
⑯—Chrysler industrial engine HT413. See Dodge Chapter for service procedures on 413 engine.

DISTRIBUTOR SPECIFICATIONS

Unit Part No. ①	Rotation ②	Cam Angle, Degrees	Breaker Gap, In.	Condenser Capacity, Mfds.	Breaker Arm Spring Tension, Oz.	Centrifugal Advance Deg. @ rpm of Dist.: Advance Starts	Centrifugal Advance: Full Advance	Vacuum Advance: Inches of Vacuum to Start Plunger Movement	Vacuum Advance: Inches of Vacuum for Full Plunger Travel	Vacuum Advance: Maximum Vacuum Advance, Dist. Degrees
1111541	CC	37	.018–.024	.20–.25	17–21	1 @ 350	8.5 @ 1100	4–6	9–11	15
1111780	CC	31–37	.022	.20–.25	17–21	1 @ 350	8.5 @ 1100	None	None	None
1111795	CC	31–37	.022	.20–.25	17–21	1 @ 275	10 @ 825	None	None	None
1111800	C	31–37	.022	.20–.25	17–21	1 @ 350	10 @ 1250	None	None	None
1111819	C	31–37	.022	.20–.25	17–21	1 @ 250	10 @ 1150	None	None	None
1111833	C	31–37	.022	.20–.25	17–21	1 @ 250	10 @ 1150	None	None	None
1111842	CC	31–37	.022	.20–.25	17–21	1 @ 275	12 @ 950	None	None	None
1111843	C	31–37	.022	.20–.25	17–21	1 @ 250	7 @ 825	None	None	None
1111844	C	31–37	.022	.20–.25	17–21	1 @ 250	7 @ 825	None	None	None
1111848	CC	31–37	.022	.20–.25	17–21	1 @ 300	9 @ 1100	None	None	None
1111849	C	31–37	.022	.20–.25	17–21	1 @ 250	8 @ 950	None	None	None
1111850	C	31–37	.022	.20–.25	17–21	1 @ 250	8 @ 950	None	None	None
1111878	C	31–37	.022	.20–.25	17–21	1 @ 250	8 @ 950	None	None	None

①—Stamped on plate riveted to housing.
②—As viewed from top; C—Clockwise. CC—Counter-clockwise.

WHITE STANDARD

MODEL INDEX & ENGINE APPLICATION

ENGINE IDENTIFICATION—White service parts identification plate is attached to the left hand cab door. Stamped on the plate is the model of the engine, transmission, auxiliary transmission, rear axle and front axle. This represents only the equipment on the vehicle when it was shipped from the factory.

Truck Model	Year	Standard Engine		Oil Pan Refill Capacity, Qts.	Cooling System Capacity, Qts.
		Make	Model		
1500 SERIES & COMPAC-VAN					
1550	1973–74	White	6-200A	—	—
1550PBT	1973–74	White	6-200A	—	—
1550T	1973–74	White	6-200A	—	—
1564	1973–74	White	6-200A	—	—
4000 SERIES					
4300	1969–74	White	6-200A	8	—
4300T	1969–74	White	6-200A	8	—
4364	1969–74	White	6-200A	8	—
C4364	1973–74	GMC	6-478M	—	—
R SERIES					
RB42T	1973–74	Cummins	250	28	—
RB64	1973–74	Cummins	250	28	—
RB64T	1973–74	Cummins	250	28	—
RC42T	1973–74	Cummins	250	28	—
RC64T	1973–74	Cummins	250	28	—

GENERAL ENGINE SPECIFICATIONS

Engine Model	No. Cyls. & Valve Location	Bore & Stroke	Piston Displacement Cubic Inch	Com-pression Ratio	Horsepower @ rpm	Torque Lb. Ft. @ rpm	Engine Governed Speed	Normal Oil Pressure, Lbs.
6-55A	6 In Block	3½ x 4¼	245	7.00	100 @ 3300	190 @ 1400	3400	40
6-110A	6 In Head	3⅝ x 4⅛	255	6.70	110 @ 3400	194 @ 1400	3400	40
116A	6 In Block	3¾ x 4½	298	6.68	110 @ 3100	230 @ 1200	3100	50–55
120A	6 In Block	3⅞ x 4½	318	6.50	114 @ 2800	250 @ 1200	3000	30–35
130A	6 In Block	4 x 4½	340	6.56	120 @ 3000	270 @ 1200	3000	30–35
6-130A	6 In Head	3⅞ x 4⅛	292	6.94	130 @ 3300	230 @ 1600	3300	40
140A	6 In Block	3⅞ x 5⅛	362	6.03	125 @ 3000	285 @ 1400	3000	30–35
6-145A	6 In Head	4⅛ x 4⅛	331	6.73	145 @ 3200	270 @ 1600	3200	40
150A	6 In Block	4 x 5⅛	386	6.45	135 @ 3000	315 @ 1300	3000	30–35
6-170A	6 In Head	4⅛ x 4⅛	331	7.50	170 @ 3400	297 @ 1600	3400	40
6-185A	6 In Head	4¼ x 4¼	362	7.50	185 @ 3400	320 @ 1200	3400	40
6-186A	6 In Head	4¼ x 4¼	362	7.50	186 @ 3400	320 @ 1200	3400	40
6-200A	6 In Head	4¼ x 4.7	400	①	200 @ 3400	365 @ 1600	3200	40
230A	6 In Block	4 x 4½	340	6.56	130 @ 3000	275 @ 1200	3000	50–55
8-235A	8 In Head	4⅛ x 4⅛	440	7.30	235 @ 3400	412 @ 2400	3400	50
250A	6 In Block	4 x 5⅛	386	6.45	145 @ 3000	328 @ 1250	3000	30–35
260A	6 In Block	4⅜ x 5	451	6.25	170 @ 3000	350 @ 1200	2800	40–45
280A	6 In Block	4⅝ x 5	504	6.00	184 @ 3000	405 @ 1200	2800	40–45
290A	6 In Block	4⅝ x 5	504	6.00	186 @ 3000	405 @ 1200	2800	40–45
370A	6 In Block	4¾ x 4¼	452	6.40	175 @ 3050	360 @ 1400	3050	40–45
380A	6 In Block	4⅝ x 5	504	6.00	185 @ 2900	405 @ 1400	2900	40–45
390A	6 In Block	4¾ x 5	531	6.40	200 @ 2900	440 @ 1400	2900	40–45
450A	6 In Block	4 x 5⅛	386	6.80	145 @ 3000	328 @ 1400	3000	50–55
460A	6 In Block	4 x 5⅛	386	6.80	159 @ 3000	336 @ 1400	3000	50–55
462A	6 In Block	4 x 5⅛	386	7.00	172 @ 3200	335 @ 1400	3200	50–55
470A	6 In Block	4½ x 5	477	6.60	200 @ 2900	395 @ 1400	2900	50–55
470G	8 In Head	4⅝ x 3½	470	8.10	250 @ 3400	312 @ 1800	3300	50–75
477A	6 In Block	4½ x 5	477	6.6	185 @ 2600	398 @ 1200	2600	50–55
490A	6 In Block	4¾ x 5	531	6.40	215 @ 2900	440 @ 1200	2900	50–55
531A	6 In Block	4¾ x 5	531	6.75	200 @ 2600	450 @ 1200	2600	50–55

①—Exec. 1972-73, 7.50; 1972-73, 8.0.

TUNEUP & VALVE SPECIFICATIONS

Engine Model	Firing Order	Spark Plugs		Ignition Timing		Valve Seat Angle, Degrees	Valve Clearance H-Hot C-Cold		Valve Spring Pressure, Lb. @ In. Length
		Type⑥	Gap	Timing Mark	Location		Intake	Exhaust	
55A	153624	J8	.028	Mark	Damper	③	.009H	.012H	140 @ 1¹³⁄₃₂
6-110A	153624	⑦	.025	DC 1-10°	Damper	30	.015H	.015H	183 @ 1¹³⁄₃₂
116A	153624	⑦	.025	①	Flywheel	45	Zero	Zero	103 @ 2¹⁄₃₂
120A	153624	⑦	.025	①	Flywheel	45	Zero	Zero	103 @ 2¹⁄₃₂
130A	153624	⑦	.025	①	Flywheel	45	Zero	Zero	103 @ 2¹⁄₃₂
6-130A	153624	⑦	.025	DC 1-10°	Damper	30	.015H	.015H	183 @ 1¹³⁄₃₂
140A	153624	⑦	.025	①	Flywheel	45	Zero	Zero	103 @ 2¹⁄₃₂
6-145A	153624	⑦	.025	DC 1-10°	Damper	30	.015H	.015H	183 @ 1¹³⁄₃₂
150A	153624	⑦	.025	①	Flywheel	45	Zero	Zero	145 @ 1.758
6-170A	153624	⑦	.025	DC 1-10°	Damper	30	.023C	.023C	183 @ 1¹³⁄₃₂
6-185A	153624	⑦	.025	DC 1-10°	Damper	30	.023C	.023C	183 @ 1¹³⁄₃₂
6-186A	153624	⑦	.025	DC 1-10°	Damper	30	.023C	.023C	183 @ 1¹³⁄₃₂
6-200A	153624	⑦	.025	DC 1-10°	Damper	30	.023C	.023C	183 @ 1¹³⁄₃₂

(continued)

TUNEUP & VALVE SPECIFICATIONS—Continued

Engine Model	Firing Order	Spark Plugs		Ignition Timing		Valve Seat Angle, Degrees	Valve Clearance H-Hot C-Cold		Valve Spring Pressure, Lb. @ In. Length
		Type⑥	Gap	Timing Mark	Location		Intake	Exhaust	
230A	153624	⑦	.025	Line	Flywheel	45	Zero	Zero	145 @ 1.758
8-235A	15486372④	⑦	.025	DC 1-10°	Damper	30	.023C	.023C	⑤
250A	153624	⑦	.025	Line	Flywheel	45	Zero	Zero	145 @ 1.758
260A	153624	⑦	.025	Line	Flywheel	45	Zero	Zero	②
280A	153624	⑦	.025	Line	Flywheel	45	Zero	Zero	②
290A	153624	⑦	.025	Line	Flywheel	45	Zero	Zero	②
370A	153624	⑦	.025	Line	Flywheel	45	Zero	Zero	180 @ 1.827
380A	153624	⑦	.025	Line	Flywheel	45	Zero	Zero	180 @ 1.827
390A	153624	⑦	.025	Line	Flywheel	45	Zero	Zero	180 @ 1.827
450A	153624	⑦	.025	Line	Flywheel	45	Zero	Zero	150 @ 1.758
460A	153624	⑦	.025	Line	Flywheel	45	Zero	Zero	150 @ 1.758
462A	153624	⑦	.025	Line	Flywheel	45	Zero	Zero	150 @ 1.758
470A	153624	⑦	.025	Line	Flywheel	45	Zero	Zero	182 @ 1.612
470G	15486372④	—	.025	6° BTC	Flywheel	30	.014H	.024H	213
477A	153624	⑦	.025	Line	Flywheel	45	Zero	Zero	182 @ 1.612
490A	153624	⑦	.025	Line	Flywheel	45	Zero	Zero	182 @ 1.612
531A	153624	⑦	.025	Line	Flywheel	45	Zero	Zero	182 @ 1.612

①—Line at bottom inspection hole or steel ball at side inspection hole.
②—Inner spring 95 @ 1.827", outer 104 @ 1.827".
③—Intake 30°, exhaust 45°.
④—Cylinder numbering (front to rear): Right bank 1-2-3-4, left bank 5-6-7-8.
⑤—Intake 183 @ 1 13/32, exhaust 183 @ 1 13/16.
⑥—Champion.
⑦—J6 for 14MM, D10 for 18MM.

DISTRIBUTOR SPECIFICATIONS

Unit Part Number ①	Rotation ②	Cam Angle, Degrees	Breaker Gap, In.	Condenser Capacity, Mfds.	Breaker Arm Spring Tension, Oz. ③	Centrifugal Advance Deg. @ rpm of Dist.		Vacuum Advance		
						Advance Starts	Full Advance	Inches of Vacuum to Start Plunger Movement	Inches of Vacuum for Full Plunger Travel	Maximum Vacuum Advance, Dist. Degrees
1110132	CC	31–37	.022	.20–.25	17–21	1 @ 425	9 @ 1600	5–7	16–18	7.5
1110195	C	31–37	.022	.20–.25	17–21	1 @ 375	9 @ 1300	None	None	None
1111790	C	31–37	.022	.20–.25	17–21	1 @ 375	9 @ 1300	4–6	13	7–8
1111866	C	38–45	.016	.20–.25	19–23	1 @ 275	15 @ 1150	None	None	None
1111905	C	38–45	.016	.20–.25	19–23	1 @ 450	15 @ 1700	None	None	None
1111922	C	38–45	.016	.18–.23	19–23	1 @ 450	13 @ 1875	None	None	None
1111923	C	38–45	.016	.18–.23	19–23	1 @ 425	12 @ 1700	None	None	None
1112254	C	35	.018–.024	.18–.23	19–23	1 @ 300	10 @ 1300	None	None	None
1112262	C	31–37	.022	.20–.35	17–21	1 @ 375	9 @ 1300	7.8–5	18.5	10
1112263	C	31–37	.022	.20–.25	17–21	1 @ 375	9 @ 1300	None	None	None
1112318	C	31–37	.022	.20–.25	17–21	1 @ 375	9 @ 1300	None	None	None
1112319	C	31–37	.022	.20–.25	17–21	1 @ 375	9 @ 1300	None	None	None
1112329	C	31–37	.022	.18–.23	19–23	2 @ 375	18 @ 1300	None	None	None
1112333	C	31–37	.022	.18–.23	19–23	2 @ 375	12 @ 1300	None	None	None

①—Stamped on plate riveted to housing.
②—As viewed from top; C—Clockwise. CC—Counterclockwise.
③—Measurement taken from center of breaker point.

DIESEL ENGINES

CATERPILLAR AUTOMOTIVE DIESEL ENGINES

GENERAL SPECIFICATIONS

Engine Model	Engine Type	Bore & Stroke	Piston Displ. Cu. In.	Comp. Ratio	Firing Order	Horsepower @ rpm	Torque Ft. Lbs. @ rpm	Governed Speed Rpm Full Load	Normal Oil Pressure Psi
1673B	Precombustion	4.5 x 5.5	525	18	1-5-3-6-2-4	245 @ 2200	645 @ 1700	2200	49
1673C	Precombustion	4.75 x 6.0	638	—	1-5-3-6-2-4	250 @ 2200	690 @ 1550	2200	49
1674	Precombustion	4.75 x 6.0	638	17.5	1-5-3-6-2-4	270 @ 2200	805 @ 1400	2200	—
1693	Precombustion	5.4 x 6.5	893	16	1-5-3-6-2-4	⑧	⑧	2000	54
3306	Precombustion	4.75 x 6.0	638	—	1-5-3-6-2-4	250 @ 2200	690 @ 1550	—	—
3406	Precombustion	5.4 x 6.5	893	—	1-5-3-6-2-4	⑦	⑦	—	—
3406	Direct	5.4 x 6.5	893	—	1-5-3-6-2-4	280 @ 2100	865 @ 1375	—	—
1140 (V150)	Direct	4.50 x 4.1	522	17.5	12734568①	150 @ 3200	277 @ 1800②	3200	70
1145 (V175)	Direct	4.50 x 4.1	522	17.5	12734568①	175 @ 3200	326 @ 1600③	3200	70
1150 (V200)	Direct	4.50 x 4.5	573	17	12734568①	200 @ 3000	403 @ 1600④	3000	70
1160 (V225)	Direct	4.50 x 5.0	636	16.5	12734568①	225 @ 2800	474 @ 1400⑤	2800	70

①—Cylinder numbering (front to rear): Right bank 1-3-5-7, left bank 2-4-6-8.

②—1972 production 309 @ 1800.

③—1972 production 354 @ 1700.

④—1972 production 436 @ 1600.

⑤—1972 production 511 @ 1400.

⑦—H.P. 280 @ 2100, torque 840 @ 1400. H.P. 325 @ 2100, torque 970 @ 1400. H.P. 360 @ 2100, torque 1080 @ 1400.

⑧—H.P. 325 @ 2100, torque 1000 @ 1490. H.P. 375 @ 2100, torque 1145 @ 1450. H.P. 380 @ 2100, torque 1275 @ 1400. H.P. 425 @ 2100, torque 1275 @ 1400.

CUMMINS DIESEL ENGINES

GENERAL SPECIFICATIONS

Engine Models	Engine Breathing	Number Cylinders	Valves Per Cylinder	Bore and Stroke	Cu. In. Displ.	Maximum Horsepower @ rpm	Firing Order		Lube Oil Pressure @ Rated rpm ⑥
							Right Hand Rotation	Left Hand Rotation	
V6-215M	Natural	6	4	5½ x 4⅛	588	215 @ 3000	1-4-2-5-3-6①	1-6-3-5-2-4①	40–75
V6(N) 215M	Natural	6	4	5½ x 4⅛	588	215 @ 3000	1-4-2-5-3-6①	1-6-3-5-2-4①	40–75
VT6(N) 280M	Turbocharged	6	4	5½ x 4⅛	588	280 @ 3000	1-4-2-5-3-6①	1-6-3-5-2-4①	40–75
V8-185C	Natural	8	4	4⅝ x 3½	470	170 @ 3000	15486372	—	40–75
V8-185HT	Natural	8	4	4⅝ x 3½	470	178 @ 3000	15486372	—	40–75
V8-185HT	Natural	8	4	4⅝ x 3½	470	185 @ 3300	15486372	—	40–75
V8-210	Natural	8	4	4⅝ x 3¾	504	210 @ 3300	15486372	—	40–75
V8-71T	Turbocharged	8	—	4¼ x 5	568	⑧	—	—	—
V8E-170	Natural	8	4	4⅝ x 3½	470	170 @ 3300	15486372②	—	40–75
V8-185	Natural	8	4	4⅝ x 3½	470	185 @ 3300	15486372②	—	40–75
V-555-210	Natural	8	4	4⅝ x 4⅛	555	210 @ 3300	15486372	—	40–75
V-555-225	Natural	8	4	4⅝ x 4⅛	555	225 @ 3300	15486372	—	40–75
V-555-240	Natural	8	4	4⅝ x 4⅛	555	240 @ 3300	15486372	—	40–75
VT-555-225	Turbocharged	8	4	4⅝ x 4⅛	555	225 @ 3300	15486372	—	40–75
VT-555-240	Turbocharged	8	4	4⅝ x 4⅛	555	240 @ 3300	15486372	—	40–75
V8E-235	Natural	8	4	5½ x 4⅛	785	235 @ 2400	15486372②	12736845②	40–75
V8R-240	Natural	8	4	5½ x 4⅛	785	240 @ 2300	15486372②	12736845②	40–75
V8-265	Natural	8	4	5½ x 4⅛	785	265 @ 2600	15486372②	12736845②	40–75
V8-300M	Natural	8	4	5½ x 4⅛	785	300 @ 3000	15486372②	12736845②	40–75

(continued)

GENERAL SPECIFICATIONS—Continued

Engine Models	Engine Breathing	Number Cylinders	Valves Per Cylinder	Bore and Stroke	Cu. In. Displ.	Maximum Horsepower @ rpm	Firing Order		Lube Oil Pressure @ Rated rpm ⑥
							Right Hand Rotation	Left Hand Rotation	
V8(N) 300M	Natural	8	4	5½ x 4⅛	785	300 @ 3000	15486372②	12736845②	40–75
VT8-370M	Turbocharged	8	4	5½ x 4⅛	785	370 @ 3000	15486372②	12736845②	40–75
VT8(N) 370M	Turbocharged	8	4	5½ x 4⅛	785	370 @ 3000	15486372②	12736845②	40–75
V8-350	Natural	8	4	5½ x 5	950	350 @ 2500	15486372②	12736845②	40–75
VT8-430	Turbocharged	8	4	5½ x 5	950	430 @ 2500	15486372②	12736845②	40–75
V8-903	Natural	8	4	5½ x 4¾	903	⑤	15486372	12736845②	30–55
V12-450	Natural	12	4	5½ x 6	1710	450 @ 2100	⑨	⑨	50–90
V12-460	Natural	12	4	5½ x 6	1710	460 @ 2100	⑨	⑨	50–90
V12-500	Natural	12	4	5½ x 6	1710	480 @ 2100	⑨	⑨	50–90
V12-525	Natural	12	4	5½ x 6	1710	500 @ 2100	⑨	⑨	50–90
VT-12-600	Turbocharged	12	4	5½ x 6	1710	600 @ 2100	⑨	⑨	50–90
VT-12-635	Turbocharged	12	4	5½ x 6	1710	635 @ 2100	⑨	⑨	50–90
VT-12-700	Turbocharged	12	4	5½ x 6	1710	700 @ 2100	⑨	⑨	50–90
VTA12-800	Turbocharged	12	4	5½ x 6	1710	800 @ 2100	⑨	⑨	50–90
NH-230	Natural	6	4	5½ x 6	855	230 @ 2100	1-5-3-6-2-4	1-4-2-6-3-5	30–70
NHD-230	Natural	6	4	5½ x 6	855	220 @ 2100	1-5-3-6-2-4	1-4-2-6-3-5	30–70
NH-250	Natural	6	4	5½ x 6	855	250 @ 2100	1-5-3-6-2-4	1-4-2-6-3-5	30–70
NHCT-270	Turbocharged	6	4	5½ x 6	855	③	1-5-3-6-2-4	1-4-2-6-3-5	30–70
NTC-335	Turbocharged	6	4	5½ x 6	855	④	1-5-3-6-2-4	1-4-2-6-3-5	30–70
NHS-6	Supercharged	6	4	5⅛ x 6	743	290 @ 2100	1-5-3-6-2-4	1-4-2-6-3-5	30–70
NHRS-6	Supercharged	6	4	5⅛ x 6	743	320 @ 2100	1-5-3-6-2-4	1-4-2-6-3-5	30–70
NT-165	Turbocharged	4	4	5⅛ x 6	495	165 @ 2000	1-2-4-3	1-3-4-2	30–70
NT-180	Turbocharged	4	4	5⅛ x 6	495	180 @ 2100	1-2-4-3	1-3-4-2	30–70
NT-200	Turbocharged	4	4	5⅛ x 6	495	200 @ 2100	1-2-4-3	1-3-4-2	30–70
NTE-235	Turbocharged	6	4	5⅛ x 6	743	235 @ 2100	1-5-3-6-2-4	1-4-2-6-3-5	30–70
NT-6	Turbocharged	6	4	5⅛ x 6	743	250 @ 2100	1-5-3-6-2-4	1-4-2-6-3-5	30–70
NTO-6	Turbocharged	6	4	5⅛ x 6	743	262 @ 2100	1-5-3-6-2-4	1-4-2-6-3-5	30–70
N-927	Nautral	6	4	5½ x 6½	927	270 @ 2100	1-5-3-6-2-4	1-4-2-6-3-5	30–70
NHC-250	Natural	6	4	5½ x 6	855	250 @ 2100	1-5-3-6-2-4	1-4-2-6-3-5	30–70
NTA-370	Turbocharged	6	4	5½ x 6	855	370 @ 2100	1-5-3-6-2-4	1-4-2-6-3-5	30–70
NTA-420	Turbocharged	6	4	5½ x 6	855	420 @ 2300	1-5-3-6-2-4	1-4-2-6-3-5	30–70
NHF-240	Natural	6	4	5½ x 6	855	250 @ 2300	1-5-3-6-2-4	1-4-2-6-3-5	30–70
NHCT-CT	—	6	4	5½ x 6	855	248 @ 1800	1-5-3-6-2-4	1-4-2-6-3-5	30–70
NHC-250	Natural	6	4	5½ x 6	855	250 @ 1800	1-5-3-6-2-4	1-4-2-6-3-5	30–70
NHF-265	Natural	6	4	5½ x 6	855	265 @ 2300	1-5-3-6-2-4	1-4-2-6-3-5	30–70
NTC-280	Turbocharged	6	4	5½ x 6	855	280 @ 2100	1-5-3-6-2-4	1-4-2-6-3-5	30–70
NHTF-295	Turbocharged	6	4	5½ x 6	855	295 @ 2300	1-5-3-6-2-4	1-4-2-6-3-5	30–70
NTF-365	Turbocharged	6	4	5½ x 6	855	365 @ 2300	1-5-3-6-2-4	1-4-2-6-3-5	30–70
N-855-C250	Natural	6	4	5½ x 6	855	250 @ 2100	1-5-3-6-2-4	1-4-2-6-3-5	30–70
NT-855-320	Turbocharged	6	4	5½ x 6	855	320 @ 2300	1-5-3-6-2-4	1-4-2-6-3-5	30–70
NTA-855-C420	Turbocharged	6	4	5½ x 6	855	420 @ 2300	1-5-3-6-2-4	1-4-2-6-3-5	30–70
NTC-350	Turbocharged	6	4	5½ x 6	855	350 @ 2100	1-5-3-6-2-4	1-4-2-6-3-5	30–70
NT-270	Turbocharged	6	4	5½ x 6	855	270 @ 2100	1-5-3-6-2-4	1-4-2-6-3-5	30–70
NT-300	Turbocharged	6	4	5½ x 6	855	300 @ 2100	1-5-3-6-2-4	1-4-2-6-3-5	30–70
NT-400	Turbocharged	6	4	5½ x 6	855	400 @ 2300	1-5-3-6-2-4	1-4-2-6-3-5	30–70
NT-280	Turbocharged	6	4	5½ x 6	855	280 @ 2100	1-5-3-6-2-4	1-4-2-6-3-5	30–70
NRT-6	Turbocharged	6	4	5⅛ x 6	743	300 @ 2100	1-5-3-6-2-4	1-4-2-6-3-5	30–70
NT-310	Turbocharged	6	4	5½ x 6	855	310 @ 2100	1-5-3-6-2-4	1-4-2-6-3-5	30–70
NRTO-6	Turbocharged	6	4	5⅛ x 6	743	335 @ 2100	1-5-3-6-2-4	1-4-2-6-3-5	30–70
NT-335	Turbocharged	6	4	5½ x 6	855	335 @ 2100	1-5-3-6-2-4	1-4-2-6-3-5	30–70
NT-350	Turbocharged	6	4	5½ x 6	855	350 @ 2100	1-5-3-6-2-4	1-4-2-6-3-5	30–70
NT-380	Turbocharged	6	4	5½ x 6	855	380 @ 2300	1-5-3-6-2-4	1-4-2-6-3-5	30–70
NTC-290	Turbocharged	6	4	5½ x 6	855	290 @ 2100	1-5-3-6-2-4	1-4-2-6-3-5	40–75
NTA-380	Turbocharged	6	4	5½ x 6	855	380 @ 2300	1-5-3-6-2-4	1-4-2-6-3-5	40–75
NTA-400	Turbocharged	6	4	5½ x 6	855	400 @ 2100	1-5-3-6-2-4	1-4-2-6-3-5	40–75
NHH-250	Natural	6	4	5½ x 6	855	250 @ 2100	1-5-3-6-2-4	1-4-2-6-3-5	40–75
NHHTC-335	Turbocharged	6	4	5½ x 6	855	335 @ 2100	1-5-3-6-2-4	1-4-2-6-3-5	40–75

(continued)

GENERAL SPECIFICATIONS—Continued

Engine Models	Engine Breathing	Number Cylinders	Valves Per Cylinder	Bore and Stroke	Cu. In. Displ.	Maximum Horsepower @ rpm	Firing Order: Right Hand Rotation	Firing Order: Left Hand Rotation	Lube Oil Pressure @ Rated rpm ⑥
Pwr. Torq. 270	Turbocharged	6	4	5½ x 6	855	270 @ 2100	1-5-3-6-2-4	1-4-2-6-3-5	40–75
NTC-270TC	Turbocharged	6	4	5½ x 6	855	250 @ 2100	1-5-3-6-2-4	1-4-2-6-3-5	40–75
Super 250	Natural	6	4	5½ x 6	927	250 @ 2100	1-5-3-6-2-4	1-4-2-6-3-5	40–75
V-352-C	Natural	6	4	4⅝ x 3½	352	130 @ 3000	1-4-2-5-3-6	—	40–75
V6-140-HT	Natural	6	4	4⅝ x 3½	352	134 @ 3000	1-4-2-5-3-6	—	40–75
V6-155	Natural	6	4	4⅝ x 3½	378	155 @ 3300	1-4-2-5-3-6	—	40–75
6-71T, 6VIT	Turbocharged	6	—	4¼ x 5	426	⑦	—	—	—
V6-140	Natural	6	4	4⅝ x 3½	352	140 @ 3300	1-4-2-5-3-6①	—	30–70
V6R-180	Natural	6	4	5½ x 4⅛	588	180 @ 2300	1-4-2-5-3-6①	1-6-3-5-2-4①	40–75
V6E-195	Natural	6	4	5½ x 4⅛	588	195 @ 2500	1-4-2-5-3-6①	1-6-3-5-2-4①	40–75
V6-200	Natural	6	4	5½ x 4⅛	588	200 @ 2600	1-4-2-5-3-6①	1-6-3-5-2-4①	40–75
C-90	Natural	4	4	4 7/16 x 5	310	90 @ 2000	1-2-4-3	1-3-4-2	40–75
C-105	Natural	4	4	4 7/16 x 5	310	105 @ 2500	1-2-4-3	1-3-4-2	40–75
C-140	Turbocharged	4	4	4 7/16 x 5	310	140 @ 2500	1-2-4-3	1-3-4-2	40–75
C-160	Natural	6	4	4 7/16 x 5	464	160 @ 2500	1-5-3-6-2-4	1-4-2-6-3-5	40–75
CF-160	Natural	6	4	4 7/16 x 5	464	160 @ 2800	1-5-3-6-2-4	1-4-2-6-3-5	40–75
CR-160	Supercharged	6	4	4 7/16 x 5	464	160 @ 2200	1-5-3-6-2-4	1-4-2-6-3-5	40–75
C-175	Turbocharged	6	4	4 7/16 x 5	464	175 @ 2500	1-5-3-6-2-4	1-4-2-6-3-5	40–75
C-180	Supercharged	6	4	4 7/16 x 5	464	180 @ 2500	1-5-3-6-2-4	1-4-2-6-3-5	40–75
C-190	Turbocharged	6	4	4 7/16 x 5	464	190 @ 2500	1-5-3-6-2-4	1-4-2-6-3-5	40–75
CS-195	Supercharged	6	4	4 7/16 x 5	464	195 @ 2600	1-5-3-6-2-4	1-4-2-6-3-5	40–75
C-200	Turbocharged	6	4	4 7/16 x 5	464	200 @ 2500	1-5-3-6-2-4	1-4-2-6-3-5	40–75
J-70	Natural	4	2	4⅛ x 5	267	70 @ 2000	1-2-4-3	1-3-4-2	40–75
J-80	Natural	4	2	4⅛ x 5	267	80 @ 2500	1-2-4-3	1-3-4-2	40–75
J-120	Turbocharged	4	2	4⅛ x 5	267	120 @ 2500	1-2-4-3	1-3-4-2	40–75
J-6	Natural	6	2	4⅛ x 5	401	100 @ 1800	1-5-3-6-2-4	1-4-2-6-3-5	40–75
JNR-100	Natural	6	4	4⅛ x 5	401	100 @ 1800	1-5-3-6-2-4	1-4-2-6-3-5	40–75
JF-6	Natural	6	2	4⅛ x 5	401	110 @ 2200	1-5-3-6-2-4	1-4-2-6-3-5	40–75
JN-130	Natural	6	4	4⅛ x 5	401	130 @ 2500	1-5-3-6-2-4	1-4-2-6-3-5	40–75
JN-6	Natural	6	4	4⅛ x 5	401	130 @ 2500	1-5-3-6-2-4	1-4-2-6-3-5	40–75
JNF-130	Natural	6	4	4⅛ x 5	401	130 @ 2800	1-5-3-6-2-4	1-4-2-6-3-5	40–75
JS-6	Supercharged	6	2	4⅛ x 5	401	160 @ 2500	1-5-3-6-2-4	1-4-2-6-3-5	40–75
JNS-6	Supercharged	6	4	4⅛ x 5	401	175 @ 2500	1-5-3-6-2-4	1-4-2-6-3-5	40–75
JT-6	Turbocharged	6	4	4⅛ x 5	401	175 @ 2500	1-5-3-6-2-4	1-4-2-6-3-5	40–75
HRC-4	Natural	4	2	5⅛ x 6	495	115 @ 1800	1-2-4-3	1-3-4-2	30–70
H-135	Natural	6	2	4⅞ x 6	672	135 @ 1800	1-5-3-6-2-4	1-4-2-6-3-5	30–70
H-6	Natural	6	2	4⅞ x 6	672	160 @ 1800	1-5-3-6-2-4	1-4-2-6-3-5	30–70
NHH-180	Natural	6	4	4⅞ x 6	672	180 @ 2100	1-5-3-6-2-4	1-4-2-6-3-5	30–70
HR-6	Natural	6	2	5⅛ x 6	743	175 @ 1800	1-5-3-6-2-4	1-4-2-6-3-5	30–70
HS-6	Supercharged	6	2	4⅞ x 6	672	210 @ 1800	1-5-3-6-2-4	1-4-2-6-3-5	30–70
HRS-6	Supercharged	6	2	5⅛ x 6	743	240 @ 1800	1-5-3-6-2-4	1-4-2-6-3-5	30–70
HRF-6	Natural	6	2	5⅛ x 6	743	190 @ 2000	1-5-3-6-2-4	1-4-2-6-3-5	30–70
HU-170	Natural	6	4	4⅞ x 6	672	170 @ 1800	1-5-3-6-2-4	1-4-2-6-3-5	30–70
HHR-6	Natural	6	2	5⅛ x 6	743	175 @ 1800	1-5-3-6-2-4	1-4-2-6-3-5	30–70
NHHE-180	Natural	6	4	5⅛ x 6	743	180 @ 1950	1-5-3-6-2-4	1-4-2-6-3-5	30–70
HHRF-6	Natural	6	2	5⅛ x 6	743	190 @ 2000	1-5-3-6-2-4	1-4-2-6-3-5	30–70
NHHE-195	Natural	6	4	5⅛ x 6	743	195 @ 1950	1-5-3-6-2-4	1-4-2-6-3-5	30–70
NHH-220	Natural	6	4	5⅛ x 6	743	220 @ 2100	1-5-3-6-2-4	1-4-2-6-3-5	30–70
NHHRS-6	Supercharged	6	4	5⅛ x 6	743	320 @ 2100	1-5-3-6-2-4	1-4-2-6-3-5	30–70
NHHT-6	Turbocharged	6	4	5⅛ x 6	743	250 @ 2100	1-5-3-6-2-4	1-4-2-6-3-5	30–70
NHHTO-6	Turbocharged	6	4	5⅛ x 6	743	262 @ 2100	1-5-3-6-2-4	1-4-2-6-3-5	30–70
NHHRTO-6	Turbocharged	6	4	5⅛ x 6	743	300 @ 2100	1-5-3-6-2-4	1-4-2-6-3-5	30–70
NHE-180	Natural	6	4	5⅛ x 6	743	180 @ 2100	1-5-3-6-2-4	1-4-2-6-3-5	30–70
NHC-4	Natural	4	4	5⅛ x 6	495	130 @ 2000	1-2-4-3	1-3-4-2	30–70
NH-135	Natural	4	4	5½ x 6	570	135 @ 2100	1-2-4-3	1-3-4-2	30–70
NH-160	Natural	4	4	5½ x 6	570	160 @ 2100	1-2-4-3	1-3-4-2	30–70
NH-180	Natural	6	4	4⅞ x 6	672	180 @ 2100	1-5-3-6-2-4	1-4-2-6-3-5	30–70

(continued)

GENERAL SPECIFICATIONS—Continued

Engine Models	Engine Breathing	Number Cylinders	Valves Per Cylinder	Bore and Stroke	Cu. In. Displ.	Maximum Horsepower @ rpm	Firing Order		Lube Oil Pressure @ Rated rpm ⑥
							Right Hand Rotation	Left Hand Rotation	
NHS-180	Natural	6	4	5⅛ x 6	743	180 @ 1950	1-5-3-6-2-4	1-4-2-6-3-5	30–70
NHE-195	Natural	6	4	5⅛ x 6	743	195 @ 1950	1-5-3-6-2-4	1-4-2-6-3-5	30–70
NH-200	Natural	6	4	5⅛ x 6	743	200 @ 1950	1-5-3-6-2-4	1-4-2-6-3-5	30–70
NH-220	Natural	6	4	5⅛ x 6	743	220 @ 2100	1-5-3-6-2-4	1-4-2-6-3-5	30–70
NHE-220	Natural	6	4	5½ x 6	855	220 @ 2100	1-5-3-6-2-4	1-4-2-6-3-5	30–70
NHE-225	Natural	6	4	5½ x 6	855	225 @ 1950	1-5-3-6-2-4	1-4-2-6-3-5	30–70

①—Engine numbering (front to rear): Right bank 1-2-3, left bank 4-5-6.
②—Engine numbering (front to rear): Right bank 1-2-3-4, left bank 5-6-7-8.
③—Custom Rated; 240, 255 or 270 H.P. @ 2100 rpm.
④—Custom Rated; 260, 280, 300, 320, 335, 350 or 355 H.P. @ 2100 rpm.
⑤—Custom Rated; 280, 300 or 320 H.P. @ 2600.
⑥—rpm @ Maximum Horsepower.
⑧—Custom Rated; 308, 335 or 350 H.P. @ 2100 rpm.
⑨—Right Hand—1L-6R-2L-5R-4L-3R-6L-1R-5L-2R-3L-4R.
Left Hand—1L-4R-3L-2R-5L-1R-6L-3R-4L-5R-2L-6R.

DETROIT DIESEL (2 cycle) ENGINES

GENERAL SPECIFICATIONS

Engine Series	Bore and Stroke	Piston Disp. Cu. In.	Comp. Ratio	Horsepower @ rpm ③	Torque @ rpm	Firing Order①		No Load Governed Speed②	Idle Speed, Rpm
						Right Hand Rotation	Left Hand Rotation		
3-53	3.875 x 4.50	159	17	81 @ 2500	200 @ 1500	1-3-2	1-2-3	④	450
3-53N	3.875 x 4.50	159	18	82 @ 2500	193 @ 1500	1-3-2	1-2-3	④	—
4-53	3.875 x 4.50	212	17	122 @ 2500	271 @ 1500	1-3-4-2	1-2-4-3	④	450
4-53⑤	3.875 x 4.5	212	21	120 @ 2500	270 @ 1800	1-3-4-2	—	④	500
4-53N	3.875 x 4.50	212	21	140 @ 2800	295 @ 1800	1-3-4-2	1-2-4-3	④	—
6V-53	3.875 x 4.50	319	17	171 @ 2500	423 @ 1500	See Below	See Below	④	450
6V-53NE	3.875 x 4.50	318	21	170 @ 2600	404 @ 1400	See Below	See Below	④	—
6V-53N	3.875 x 4.50	318	21	195 @ 2600	447 @ 1400	See Below	See Below	④	—
6V-53N⑤	3.875 x 4.5	318	21	190 @ 2800	414 @ 1800	See Below	—	④	500
3-71	4.250 x 5.00	213	17	102 @ 2100	277 @ 1400	1-3-2	1-2-3	2100	385–400
4-71	4.250 x 5.00	284	17	143 @ 2100	375 @ 1600	1-3-4-2	1-2-4-3	2150	385–400
4-71E	4.250 x 5.00	284	17	140 @ 2100	375 @ 1600	1-3-4-2	1-2-4-3	2150	385–400
4-71SE	4.250 x 5.00	284	17	140 @ 2100	375 @ 1600	1-3-4-2	1-2-4-3	2150	385–400
4-71T	4.250 x 5.00	284	17	171 @ 2300	411 @ 1600	1-3-4-2	1-2-4-3	2450	385–400
6-71	4.250 x 5.00	426	17	219 @ 2100	574 @ 1600	1-5-3-6-2-4	1-4-2-6-3-5	2150	385–400
6-71E	4.250 x 5.00	426	17	210 @ 2100	574 @ 1600	1-5-3-6-2-4	1-4-2-6-3-5	2150	385–400
6-71N	4.25 x 5.00	426	18.7	218 @ 2100	604 @ 1200	1-5-3-6-2-4	1-4-2-6-3-5	2340	400
6-71N⑤	4.25 x 5.0	426	18.7	201 @ 2100	552 @ 1200	1-5-3-6-2-4	—	2100	500
6-71N⑤	4.25 x 5.0	426	18.7	219 @ 2100	600 @ 1600	1-5-3-6-2-4	—	2100	500
6-71SE	4.250 x 5.00	426	17	210 @ 2100	574 @ 1600	1-5-3-6-2-4	1-4-2-6-3-5	2150	385–400
6-71T	4.250 x 5.00	426	17	236 @ 2100	630 @ 1600	1-5-3-6-2-4	1-4-2-6-3-5	2150	385–400
6V-71	4.250 x 5.00	426	17	210 @ 2100	565 @ 1200	See Below	See Below	2340	550
6V-71N	4.25 x 5.00	426	18.7	218 @ 2100	604 @ 1200	See Below	—	2340	550
6V-71N⑤	4.25 x 5.0	426	18.7	201 @ 2100	552 @ 1200	See Below	—	2100	500
6V-71NE	4.25 x 5.00	426	18.7	195 @ 1950	570 @ 1200	1-5-3-6-2-4	1-4-2-6-3-5	—	400–450
8V-71NE⑤	4.25 x 5.0	568	18.7	242 @ 1950	696 @ 1200	See Below	—	1960	500
8V-71N⑤	4.25 x 5.0	568	18.7	265 @ 2100	732 @ 1200	See Below	—	2100	500
8V-71N⑤	4.25 x 5.0	568	18.7	289 @ 2100	758 @ 1600	See Below	—	2100	500
8V-53N	3.875 x 4.50	424	21	247 @ 2500	575 @ 1500	—	—	—	—
8V-71NE	4.25 x 5.00	567	18.7	260 @ 1950	761 @ 1200	See Below	See Below	—	—
8V-71	4.250 x 5.00	567	17	280 @ 2100	750 @ 1200	See Below	See Below	2340	550
8V-71N	4.25 x 5.00	567	18.7	420 @ 2100	761 @ 1200	See Below	—	2340	550
12V-71	4.250 x 5.00	851	17	434 @ 2100	1130 @ 1200	See Below	See Below	2340	550
12V-71N	4.25 x 5.00	851	18.7	390 @ 2100	1205 @ 1200	See Below	See Below	—	—
12V-71N⑤	4.25 x 5.0	851	18.7	270 @ 2100	1078 @ 1200	See Below	—	2200	500

①—Rotation is determined by standing at front and looking toward rear (transmission end). If crankshaft rotates clockwise engine is right-hand or "R" model; if rotation is counterclockwise engine is left-hand or "L" model.
②—Tolerance allowed: plus O, minus 25 rpm.
③—Intermittent operation rating.
④—See unit name plate.
⑤—1974.

(continued)

FORD DIESEL ENGINES

GENERAL SPECIFICATIONS

Engine Model	Engine Code on Rating Plate	Bore & Stroke	Horsepower @ rpm	Compression		Firing Order	Engine Idle Rpm	Engine Governed Speed No Load	Oil Pan Capacity, Qts.
				Ratio	Pressure ①				
Dagenham 4-220	4	3.9375 x 4.526	70 @ 2500	16	365	1-2-4-3	500–550	2700	8②
Dagenham 6-330	E	3.9375 x 4.526	112 @ 2500	16	365	1-5-3-6-2-4	500–550	2700	12②
Dorset 4-242	J	4.1250 x 4.516	83 @ 2800	16	365	1-2-4-3	500–550	3090	8②
Dorset 6-363	W	4.1250 x 4.516	128 @ 2800	16	365	1-5-3-6-2-4	500–550	3090	12②

①—Plus or minus 20 p.s.i. ②—Including filter.

GMC TORO-FLOW DIESEL ENGINES

GENERAL SPECIFICATIONS

Engine Model	Bore & Stroke	Horsepower @ rpm	Torque Ft. Lbs. @ rpm	Firing Order	Compression Pressure @ 600 rpm	Idle Speed	Governed Speed Rpm	Normal Oil Pressure
D-351-V6	4.56 x 3.58	130 @ 3200	234 @ 2000	1-6-5-4-3-2①	500	625–650	3200	60
D-478-V6	5.125 x 3.86	150 @ 3200	275 @ 2000	1-6-5-4-3-2①	500	625–650	3200	60
DH-478-V6③	5.125 x 3.86	170 @ 3200	310 @ 2000	1-6-5-4-3-2①	500	625–650	3200	60
DH-478-V6④	5.125 x 3.86	165 @ 2800	—	1-6-5-4-3-2①	500	625–650	2800	60
D-637-V8	5.125 x 3.86	195 @ 2600	—	18436572②	500	625–650	2600	60
DH-637-V8	5.125 x 3.86	220 @ 2800	—	18436572②	500	625–650	2800	60

①—Cylinder numbering (front to rear): Left bank 1-3-5, right bank 2-4-6.
②—Cylinder numbering (front to rear): Left bank 1-3-5-7, right bank 2-4-6-8.
③—Up to serial number DH478-18604.
④—Starting with serial number DH478-18604.

INTERNATIONAL DIESEL ENGINES

GENERAL SPECIFICATIONS

Engine Model	Bore & Stroke	Horsepower @ rpm	Torque, Ft. Lbs. @ rpm	Firing Order	Compression Pressure Cranking Speed	Idle Speed No Load	Governed Speed		Oil Pan Capacity Refill Quarts
							No Load rpm	Full Load rpm	
D-301	3 13/16 x 4.39	110 @ 3000	230 @ 1600	153624	350–400	500–550	3250	3000	9
D-354③	3.875 x 5	120 @ 2800	260 @ 1450	153624	430	525	3000	2800	14④
DV-462	4 1/8 x 4 5/16	185 @ 3200	337 @ 2400	18736542①	375–425	550–600	3500	3200	10
DV-462B	4 1/8 x 4 5/16	160 @ 3000	307 @ 2000	18736542①	375–425	550–600	—	3000	10
DV-462B	4 1/8 x 4 5/16	160 @ 3000	341 @ 2000	18736542①	375–425	550–600	—	3000	10
DV-550	4 1/2 x 4 5/16	210 @ 3200	391 @ 2100	18736542①	375–425	550–600	3500	3200	10
DV-550B	4 1/2 x 4 5/16	180 @ 3000	365 @ 2000	18736542①	375–425	550–600	—	3000	10
DV-550B	4 1/2 x 4 5/16	200 @ 3000	389 @ 2000	18736542①	375–425	550–600	—	3000	10
DVT-573	4 1/2 x 4 1/2	260 @ 2600	578 @ 1800	18736542①	400–470	575–625	2850	2600	21②

①—Cylinder numbering (front to rear): Right bank 2-4-6-8, left bank 1-3-5-7.
②—Add 5 qts. with filter change.
③—Refer to Perkins Diesel chapter for servicing this engine.
④—Add one quart with filter change.

MACK DIESEL ENGINES

GENERAL SPECIFICATIONS

ENGINE IDENTIFICATION—Engine model and serial number located on top of right front motor leg.

Engine Series	No. Cyls. Bore & Stroke	Piston Displ. Cu. In.	Compression Pressure @ 1000 rpm	Firing Order	Injection Timing B.T.C.	Governed Speed No Load	Idling Speed rpm	Lube Oil Pressure
END-465, B, C	6-4 7/16 x 5	464	540	1-5-3-6-2-4	31	2800	540	75 Max.
END-475	6-4.53 x 4.92	475	540	1-5-3-6-2-4	30	2600	450	71
ENDT-475	6-4.53 x 4.92	475	590	1-5-3-6-2-4	②	2600	500	71
END-673	6-4 7/8 x 6	672	530	1-5-3-6-2-4	27	2270	540	45–60
END-673A, D	6-4 7/8 x 6	672	530	1-5-3-6-2-4	29	2270	540	—
END-673B, C	6-4 7/8 x 6	672	530	1-5-3-6-2-4	28	2270	540	—
END-673E, P	6-4 7/8 x 6	672	530	1-5-3-6-2-4	29	2270	540	45–75
ENDL-673	6-4 7/8 x 6	672	530	1-5-3-6-2-4	26	2265	550	45–60
ENDL-673E	6-4 7/8 x 6	672	575	1-5-3-6-2-4	—	—	—	—
ENDLT-673	6-4 7/8 x 6	672	575	1-5-3-6-2-4	29	2265	550	45–60
ENDT-673	6-4 7/8 x 6	672	575	1-5-3-6-2-4	29	2265	540	45–60
ENDT-673A	6-4 7/8 x 6	672	575	1-5-3-6-2-4	28	2320	540	45–60
ENDT-673B	6-4 7/8 x 6	672	460	1-5-3-6-2-4	28	2310	540	—
ENDT-673C	6-4 7/8 x 6	672	575	1-5-3-6-2-4	25	2310	540	45–75
ENDT-675	6-4 7/8 x 6	672	460	1-5-3-6-2-4	28	2270	540	45–75
ENDT-676	6-4 7/8 x 6	672	460	1-5-3-6-2-4	—	2310	550	40–94
END-707	6-5 x 6	707	530	1-5-3-6-2-4	24	2280	540	45–75
END-711	6-5 x 6	707	530	1-5-3-6-2-4	28	2270	540	45–75
END-711A	6-5 x 6	707	530	1-5-3-6-2-4	30	2270	540	45–75
ENDD-711	6-5 x 6	707	530	1-5-3-6-2-4	28	2185	540	45–75
END-864	V8-5 x 5½	864	525	①	23	2500	565	75 Max.
END-864B	V8-5 x 5½	864	525	①	20	2500	565	—
ENDD-864	V8-5 x 5½	864	—	①	23	2190	565	—
ENDT-864	V8-5 x 5½	864	485	①	—	2500	565	—
ENDDT-865	V8-5¼ x 5	866	—	—	—	—	—	40–50
ENDT-865	V8-5¼ x 5	866	485	①	31③	2650	625	40–50
ENDT-866	V8-5¼ x 5	866	485	①	31③	2430④	625	40–50

①—Cylinder numbering (front to rear): Right bank 1-2-3-4, Left bank 5-6-7-8. Firing order 1-5-4-8-6-3-7-2.
②—Bosch, 24°; C.A.V. 25°.
③—Engines manufactured after Jan. 1, 1973, 27°.
④—Engines beginning May, 1974 2500 rpm.

PERKINS DIESEL ENGINES

GENERAL SPECIFICATIONS

Engine Model	Bore & Stroke	Horsepower @ rpm	Torque, Ft. Lbs. @ rpm	Firing Order	Compression Pressure Cranking Speed	Idle Speed	Governed Speed		Oil Pan Capacity Refill, Quarts
							No Load Rpm	Full Load Rpm	
4-99	3.0 x 3.5	48 @ 4000	73	1342	20:1	625	—	—	②
4-107	3.125 x 3.5	41 @ 3000	79	1342	22:1	625	—	—	②
4-108	3.125 x 3.5	52 @ 4000	79	1342	22:1	625	—	—	②
3-152	3.6 x 5	43 @ 2400	114 @ 1350	123	17.4:1	—	—	—	③
D3-152	3.6 x 5	47 @ 2500	122 @ 1300	123	18.5:1	—	—	—	③
4-236	3.875 x 5	80 @ 2800	193	1342	16.1:1	—	—	—	7
4-248	3.975 x 5	78 @ 2300	—	1342	16.1:1	—	—	—	7
D-354	3⅞ x 5	120 @ 2800	260 @ 1450	153624	430	525	3000	2800	14①
6-354	3.875 x 5	120 @ 2800	260 @ 1450	153624	16:1	—	—	—	14½
6-372	3.975 x 5	121 @ 2500	292	153624	16:1	—	—	—	14½
V8-510	4.25 x 4.50	180 @ 2800	398 @ 1650	18754362	16.5:1	—	—	—	16¼
V8-540	4.25 x 4.75	180 @ 2600	410 @ 1650	18754362	16.5:1	—	—	—	16¼

①—Add one quart with filter change.
②—Standard sump, 4.2 qt.; Vauxhall Motors, 5.4 qt.; Chrysler, 5.15 qt.; Ford Motor Co., 5.25 qt.
③—Agricultural, 5.5 qt.; industrial, 6.5 qt.; Massey Ferguson, 5.25 qt.

RETROFIT EMISSION CONTROL SYSTEMS

This section has information on systems developed in 1974 and 1975. For information on earlier systems, refer to page 645 of your Emission Control Manual, Volume I.

RETROFIT SYSTEMS

1974

DANA RETRONOX SYSTEM

Dana recently introduced a second generation Retronox system that is much simplified from the original system as described on page 649 of your Emission Control Manual. Although the new Retronox system works in essentially the same way, the plumbing and hardware has been simplified so that installation is even easier. On the new system, the carburetor doesn't even have to be removed. A vacuum operated exhaust gas recirculation valve works with two pieces of stainless steel tubing in conjunction with an engine speed switch and solenoid vacuum. Exhaust gas is recirculated through the carburetor from an exhaust pipe outlet fitting to lower NOx levels in the exhaust.

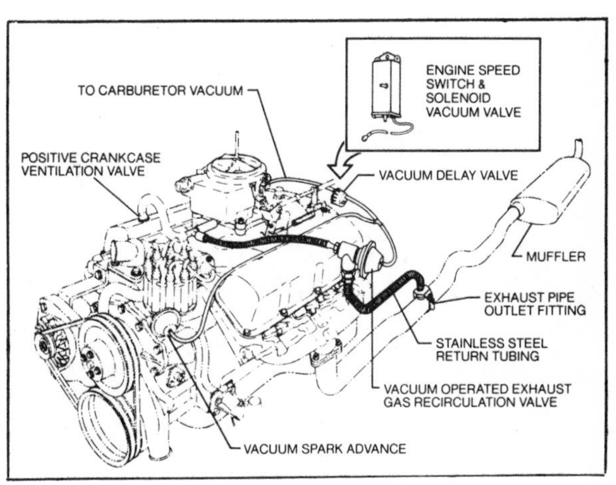

UOP CATALYTIC CONVERTER

The first retrofit catalytic converter to be approved for installation on pre-1973 vehicles is the Purzaust pellet unit. Manufactured by Universal Oil Products (UOP), the 5¾-inch diameter converter is designed for installation close to the exhaust manifold and it contains no moving parts. It is available in a variety of configurations to suit most applications. The unburned hydrocarbons and carbon monoxide from the engine's exhaust stream pass through the converter and are chemically changed into carbon dioxide and vapor.

For additional information on how a catalytic converter works see page 58 in the Emission Control Systems section.

NOTES

EMISSION CONTROL ANALYZERS AND TEST EQUIPMENT

To properly service emission control systems, it is essential that you have the proper equipment, just as you must have the proper equipment to service any other part of today's modern automobile. The following is a listing of currently available emission control analyzers and test equipment, with names and addresses of the manufacturer. For more information about any of the units listed here, please write directly to the manufacturer.

The information here was supplied by the manufacturer, as was all claims of performance and features. This listing is for your information only and does not imply an endorsement by Motor Publications.

AES I

Automotive Environmental Systems, Inc.
7300 Bolsa Avenue
Westminster, CA 92683

Constant Volume Sampler (CVS) Model 100. Features a patented stainless steel heat exchanger for low sound level and accurate temperature control for the diluted sample. The Model 100 requires little maintenance and holds a calibration through hundreds of tests.

Exhaust Analysis Console (EAC) and Data Acquisition and Control Computer (DACC). This system measures both continuous raw and dilute vehicle emissions on a modal mass basis. Catalytic efficiency, too, can be measured on a modal mass basis. Both the constant volume sampler (CVS) and the EAC and DACC have been operating for two years at the American Honda Emissions Test Lab in Gardena, California.

SHED, Model 7500. Designed for continuous use in collecting evaporative emissions from light duty motor vehicles, the SHED, or Sealed Housing for Evaporative Determinations, has been used successfully in testing programs sponsored by the EPA. The AESi SHED has a hydrocarbon leakage rate of less than 0.2% per hour, and all interior surfaces are impermeable to hydrocarbons. The ceiling provides a safety "blow out" panel made of Tedlar. Featuring an optional guillotine-type door, easy-to-clean aluminum floor, and rigid aluminum walls, which can easily be dismantled, the SHED can also be equipped with such options as refrigeration and heating systems, as well as fire detection and chemical extinguisher systems for instant fire protection.

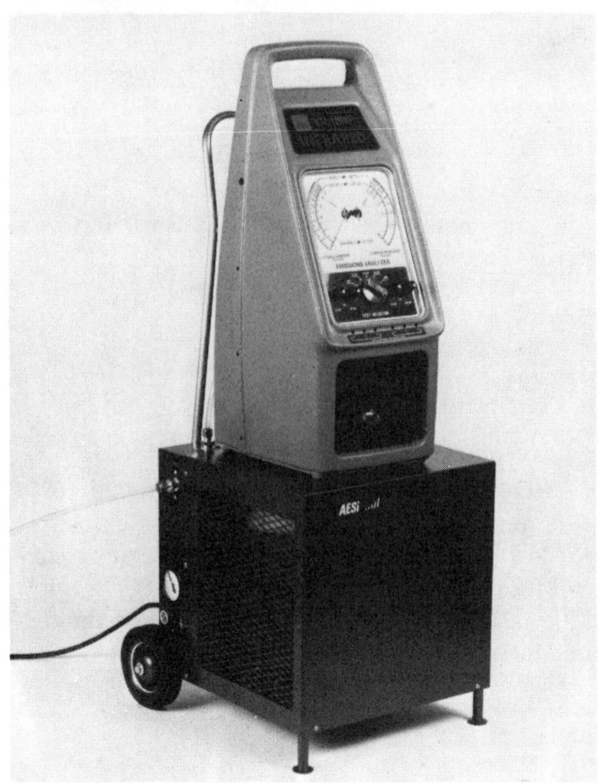

Sample Conditioning Module (SCM) Model 7900. The SCM 7900 is intended for use with all garage-type emission analyzers, and features a unique, "waterless water bath" refrigerated trap for removing moisture from the exhaust sample. This unit greatly extends the useful life and increases the accuracy of garage analyzers. It also enables garage analyzers to be used during chassis dynamometer loaded tests as well as for sampling before the catalysts on 1975 vehicles. Options available include a heavy duty filter, sample pump, sample back purge, high temperature sample probe, and push-button controlled rotary valve for selecting ambient air, sample or calibration gas.

ALLEN TEST PRODUCTS

Allen Test Products Division
The Allen Group, Inc.
2101 N. Pitcher St.
Kalamazoo, MI 49007

18-010 & 18-020 Engine Analyzer. The Allen 16-inch solid-state engine analyzer with carbon pile battery load test is available in two models—the 18-010 is the cabinet model and the 18-020 is the suspended model. The 18-010 weighs 340 pounds, the 18-020, 440 pounds. This new Allen 16-inch analyzer tests 4-, 6-, and 8-cylinder models and rotary models too. It also tests all electronic ignition systems. Both analyzers provide full test capability combined with total, programmed pushbutton function, as well as test select, crank/kill, timing light with 0-90° advance meter, secondary 20K scope, secondary 40K, vacuum/pressure, ohmmeter and AC operation.

Allen 23-070. Base cabinet for Allen 8- and 12-inch engine analyzers, includes CO/HC infra-red. The 23-080 is the CO/HC exhaust emission analyzer, and the 23-070 is the base cabinet emission analyzer. Both are designed to conform with all performance criteria established by the various state control agencies. The 23-070 features Hi-scale and Lo-scale, 8-inch meters, the NDIR method of analysis, a response of a 90% reading in a maximum of 10 seconds, zero and span drift of a maximum 2% full scale, and a warmup of 15 minutes with ambient temperature greater than 60° F.

AUTOSCAN

3641 Holdrege Ave.
Los Angeles, CA 90016

710/705 Infrared HC/CO Analyzers. These two carbon monoxide and hydrocarbon analyzers offer a high degree of accuracy, coupled with simple, foolproof operation, and were specifically designed for use with existing and forthcoming smog control laws and regulations. These two Autoscan units feature pushbutton gas calibration, unique long lasting filter, all solid-state design and separate exhaust condenser. They also provide an exclusive paper particle filter for long life, less replacement and better protection for the optical device, and a unique, self-diagnostic, self-test capability switch.

Model 4000-IR Series. An HC/CO/Engine/Electrical analyzer that features built in HC/CO infrared analysis capability. It also possesses self-diagnosis and self-service features, with modular subsystem replacement.

4030-IR HC/CO Module for Retrofit. A "building block" hydrocarbon and carbon monoxide module, designed to economically update existing Autoscan 4000 series equipment and features simple, quick, on-site module installation.

APPLIED POWER, INC.

Automotive Service Systems
Marquette Mfg. Co., Division
3800 N. Dunlap St.
St. Paul, MN 55112

Marquette Infra-Red Emissions Analyzer, No. 42-153. Analyzes engine operation through non-dispersive infra-red measurements of carbon monoxide and unburned hydrocarbons. This model also features two large, 8-inch D'Arsonval movements and day glow pointers, span gas inlet for certified calibration, 30-foot synflex pickup hose and expanded CO scale at low end for accurate low concentration readings. Available with No. 42-152 economy stand or 42-157 deluxe stand.

Marquette 42-155 I-R Emissions Analyzer, and 42-156 I-R Analyzer. Same as 42-153 analyzer, but with 42-152 or 42-157 stand, respectively. Accuracy plus or minus .25% CO, zero to ½ scale; plus or minus .5% CO ½ to full scale. Thirty-foot synflex hose with weighted shot bag to hold pickup probe in place. The gas sampler pump has 30 cu. ft./hr. rating. The aspirator features automatic water discharge. The No. 42-153 analyzer weighs 80 pounds. The deluxe stand 140 pounds, economy stand 45 pounds.

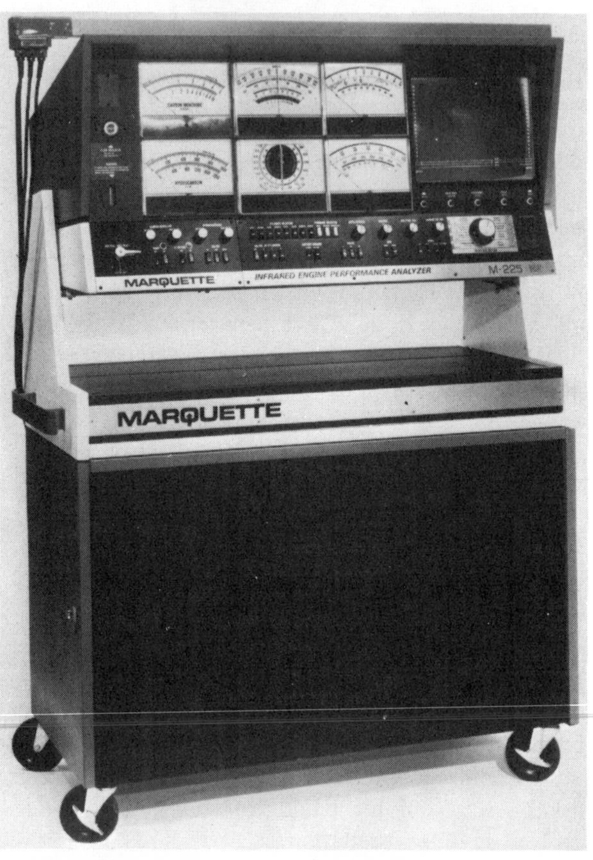

Marquette 40-222 I-R Engine Performance Analyzer. Has the total capability of engine analysis and exhaust emission analysis. This solid-state analyzer provides for all tests for measuring overall engine operation for maximum efficiency. The 40-222 is the M-222 overhead mounted engine analyzer, less track and features six large, 8-inch meters—CO meter, HC meter, tachometer-ohmmeter, volt-dwell-spark advance meter, amperes-power chek-air/fuel ratio, 15-inch oscilloscope, and 13 other features. Shipping weight 450 pounds.

BARNES ENGINEERING CO.

30 Commerce Road
Stamford, CT 06904

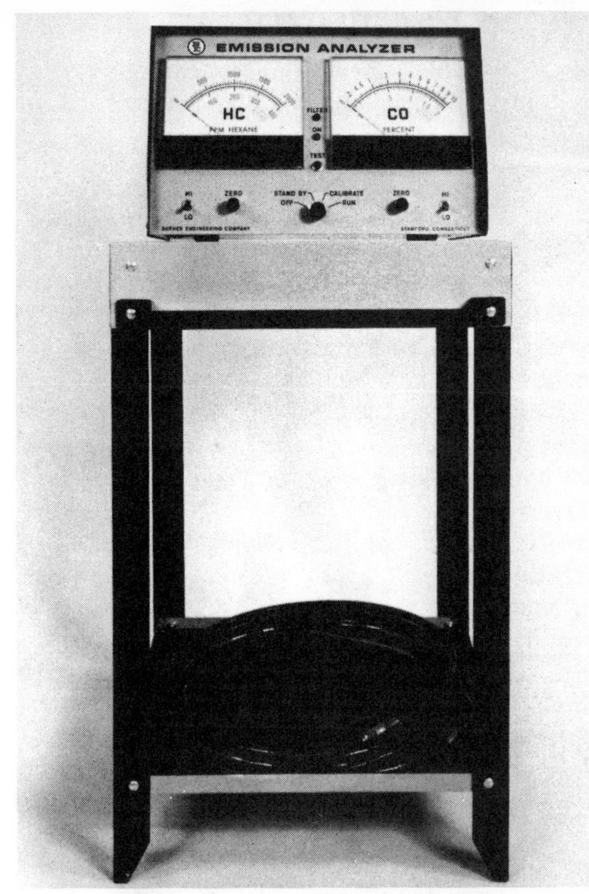

Model 1836 Emission Analyzer. Includes cart and 20-foot probe and hose assembly. **Model 8335 Emission Analyzer.** Includes linearized display, a third channel for monitoring CO2, recorder output, cart and 20-foot probe and hose assembly. Both units feature large, easy-to-read meters, separate HC and CO readouts, fast measurements, continuous accuracy, easy calibration, less than 10-minute warm-up. A roll-around cart is available for bay-to-bay use, or outside use.

CHRISTIE ELECTRIC CORP.

3410 W. 67 Street, Box 60020
Los Angeles, CA 90060

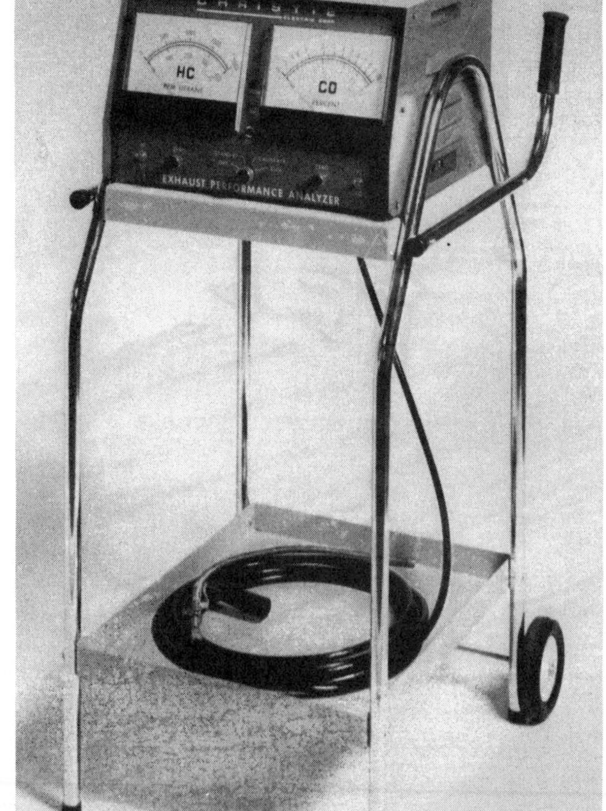

Model EA-74C. Can handle precise measurement of HC and CO exhaust emissions, checks complete engine performance. A clear-cut diagnostic chart on the analyzer interprets HC and CO meter readings, indicating if ignition, fuel or emission control systems require servicing. EA-74C features 8-inch dual scale meters; plus-or-minus 3% accuracy and a response time of 7 seconds to 90% final value.

CHRYSLER CORPORATION

Huntsville Electronics Div.
Marketing Dept, 102 Wynn Drive
Huntsville, AL 35805

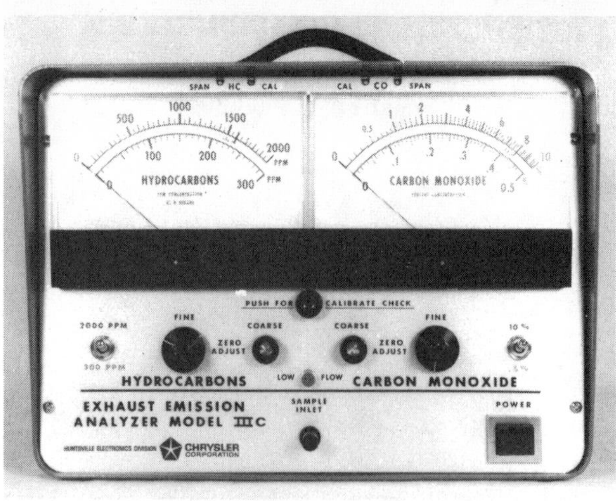

Model III-C Exhaust Emission Analyzer. Designed specifically for simplified operation in service stations and garages and is comparable in accuracy with large laboratory NDIR consoles. The III-C is primarily intended for usage on vehicles operating in the idle mode up to 2500 rpm. The III-C displays CO and HC concentrations simultaneously on the front panel meters. High and low ranges are provided to allow low gas concentration accurate readings. The III-C is designed so that zeroing of the instrument on air automatically calibrates all concentration ranges. A pushbutton check is provided to affirm proper calibration. Selected filter bandwidths are sufficiently narrow to eliminate crosstalk and water vapor response. A water trap is used to eliminate possible water blockage of the transfer line during extended operation. A front panel low-flow indicator light signals line blockage or restriction and the unit is designed to operate continuously on raw exhaust gas and thus requires no particulate filters in the gas handling system. This feature eliminates all but the most common-sense type of periodic maintenance.

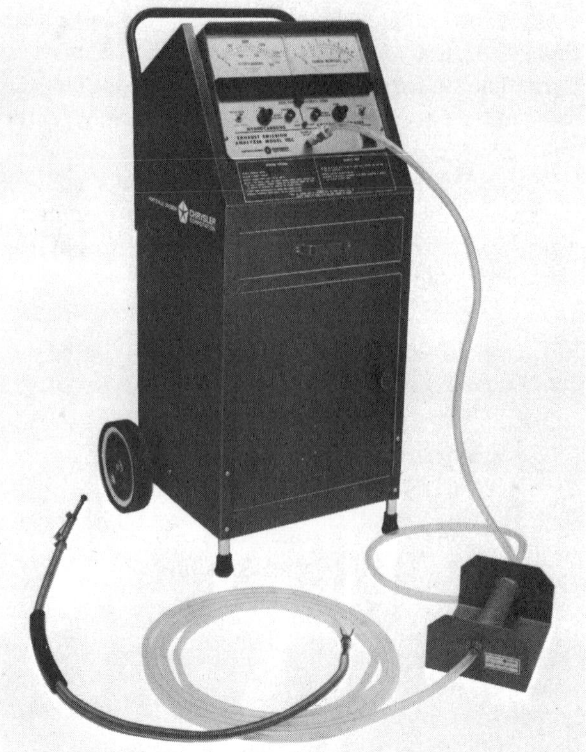

STEWART-WARNER CORP.

1826 Diversey Blvd.
Chicago, IL 60614

Infra-Red Exhaust Emission Analyzer, No. 3160-AC. The 3160 I-R Analyzer is a quite simple, accurate emission tester. Its concept has been expanded to read out 5 parts per million HC on a 400 ppm full scale and .05% CO on a 2% full scale. It also provides an adjustable meter panel, flow signal light, span gas gauge and an internal gas calibration standard, which means no altitude correction charts are required. Speed of operation is evident in the 2-step emission checkup—at both idle and 2500 rpm—and the simple, 3-step tuneup tool—adjust HC and CO at idle; check HC and CO at 2500 rpm; check for vacuum leaks.

SUN ELECTRIC CORPORATION

3011 E. Route 176
Crystal Lake, IL 60014

Model EPA-75. The basic concept of this model is to combine the accuracy of infra-red HC and CO analysis with the simplicity and reliability of all solid-state electronics. Maintenance has been reduced to the replacement of a filter when necessary. The panel of the EPA-75 includes color-coded, range-shift controls, simple, color-coded operating and calibration controls and an automatic low-flow light. The dual scales on each meter have been expanded and are easily read.

Model EET-910-I. This solid-state, non-dispersive unit can measure HC between 0-500 and 0-2000 ppm and CO between 0-2½% and 0-10%; engine speed from 0 to 3000 rpm. The EET-910-I uses an internal electromechanical span reference system, which is initially adjusted to a calibration gas. Calibration may be checked either by this electromechanical span reference system or by using a certified calibration gas. A flow indicator light indicates when filters need cleaning or changing or when sampling system becomes blocked. The EET-910-I is ready for use after five minutes warmup time with increased zero drift rate, and is virtually unaffected by fluctuations in line voltage and ambient temperature changes.

Model EET-945 & 947. These two Sun units offer engine performance evaluation and quality control testing in one package. Both models feature 7-second infra-red exhaust gas analysis, clamp-on pick-up leads, auto-ranging tachometer, pushbutton cylinder shorting, easy-reading oscilloscope, and 8-inch meters.

THERMO ELECTRON CORP.

85 First Avenue
Waltham, MA 02154

Model 8A. A portable monitor especially designed for measuring oxides of nitrogen (NO_x) in stack and exhaust emissions. Based on the chemiluminescent reaction of nitric oxide and ozone, Thermo Electron's Model 8A provides a sensitivity heretofore unavailable in a lightweight, compact and portable unit like the 8A. Designed to measure NO_x, the model 8A is unaffected by SO_2, H_2O, CO_2, O_2 and HC present in normal stack gases. The AC signal is amplified and rectified to provide an analog signal to a large display meter. The Model 8A features easy portability, high sensitivity, and is linear through the full range of measurement and is ideal for short term sampling.

Model 44. A new chemiluminescent analyzer designed specifically for automotive testing. The Model 44 uses advanced techniques to achieve superior performance, while retaining the basic simplicity and reliability of the chemiluminescent NO-NO_x monitor. This NO-NO_x analyzer offers interferencefree operation, temperature stabilized flow components; linearity to 5000 ppm with air feed to ozonator, and remote mode switching.

Model 101. An advancement in the state of the art of ambient air level analyzers. It uses a new gas titration method to calibrate O_3, NO, and NO_2, and also checks linearity.

Model 40. This new, Pulsed Fluorescent analyzer is direct, clean and specific. It's designed to measure SO_2. It requires no flames, consumable reactants, or hazardous bottled gases.

PARTS AND TIME GUIDE

The information here completely supersedes the Parts and Time Guide in Motor's Emission Control Manual, Volume I.

CONTENTS

NOTES

Parts prices are suggested retail. Parts prices and part numbers are subject to change without notice. This book contains the latest available prices and part numbers at the time of publication.

Each section contains parts and labor information for emission controls, ignition and tuneup and fuel system procedures and components.

Motor's shop time is arrived at with the cooperation of a number of representative repair shops with average equipment and operating under average working conditions. It is intended as a guide for the average shop.

Extra Time: A suitable extra charge should be made if it becomes necessary to remove any optional equipment unit such as a heater, radio, etc., in order to remove and replace or service some standard unit. Also, a suitable extra charge may be made when difficulties arise due to corrosion, rust, carbon buildup, varnish, etc.

R&R: means remove and replace the same part.

RENEW: means remove the old part and install a new one.

OVERHAUL: means to remove an assembly from a car, inspect, disassemble, repair, reassemble, install and adjust.

AMERICAN MOTORS

Time — Emission Controls (Group AB) — Time

OPERATION INDEX

AB1—POSITIVE CRANKCASE VENTILATION VALVE(P.C.V.), CLEAN OR RENEW

All Models—
Clean (0.3) 0.5
Renew (0.2) 0.3

AB2— "ENGINE MOD" SYSTEM, CHECK

Includes: Check & adjust engine idle speed & mixture & ignition timing. Check PCV valve.
1969-75 (0.4) 0.7

AB4—AIR CLEANER MOTOR, RENEW

1969-75 (0.4) 0.6

AB6—AIR PUMP, R & R OR RENEW

1969-75—
Six Cyl, (0.4) 0.7
V8 (0.4) 0.8

—NOTE—
To Renew Pump, Add (0.2) 0.2

AB9—HOSES, RENEW

1969-75—
One (0.4) 0.5
All (0.5) 0.7

AB10—ANTI-BACKFIRE VALVE, RENEW

1969-75 (0.4) 0.6

AB11—RELIEF VALVE, RENEW

1969-75—
Six Cyl. (0.5) 0.6
V8 (0.6) 0.8

AB13A—CENTRIFUGAL FILTER, RENEW

1969-75 (0.6) 0.8

AB14—AIR PUMP BELT, RENEW

1969-75 (0.2) 0.2

AB15—AIR DISTRIBUTION MANIFOLD ASS'Y, R & R OR RENEW

1968-69 (One Side)—
Exc. Below—
Right Side (0.9) 1.3
Left Side (0.7) 1.1
Ser. 10—
Right Side (1.6) 2.0
Left Side (0.5) 0.6
1970-75, Six Cyl. (0.5)
8 Cyl, Right—
Ser 01-40 (1.6) 1.8
Ser 10-80 (1.1) 1.5
Ser 70 (1.1) 1.5
8 Cyl, Left—
Ser 01-40-70 (0.9) 1.3
Ser 10-80 (0.7) 1.1

AB16—CHARCOAL CANISTER, RENEW

All Models (0.3) 0.4

AB17—SOLENOID CONTROL VALVE, RENEW

All Models (0.3) 0.4

Parts — Emission Controls — Parts

PARTS INDEX

1—EXHAUST EMISSION AIR PUMP:

1968-73 V8 ....3189720 69.50
1973 Six 3218638 70.50
1974 ....3223124 69.50
1975 ....3224465 59.75

2—EXHAUST EMISSION RELIEF VALVE:

1968-73 V8 ....4485439 2.78

3—EXHAUST EMISSION ANTI BACK-FIRE VALVE:

1969-73 V8 ....3193131 28.52
1973 Six 3218634 11.43
1974-75 Six 3223634 14.95
1974-75 V8 ....3223271 21.49

4—EXHAUST EMISSION PUMP BELT:

—NOTE—
Order By Complete Model Description.

6—DECELERATION VALVE:

1970 Six 3198319 17.44
1970 V8-390 ....3198515 19.07

7—DISTRIBUTOR THERMOSTATIC VACUUM VALVE:

1970 V8-360, 390 ....3210853 5.63
1972-75 ....3216448 7.38

8—CRANKCASE VENTILATION VALVE:

1966-69 6-232 ....3211538 1.80
1966-69 V8 ....3211538 1.80
1966-70 6-199 ....3182478 1.80
1970 6-232 (Ser. 01)—
Std. Trans. 3211538 1.80
Auto. Trans.—
Early 3182478 1.80
Late 3211538 1.80
1970 6-232 (Ser. 40)—
Early 3182478 1.80
Late 3211538 1.80
1970 6-232 (Exc. Above) 3211538 1.80
1970-75 V8 ....3211538 1.80
1971 Six (Exc. Below) 3211538 1.80
1971 6-232 (Ser. 01, 40)—
W/Auto. Trans. 3182478 1.80
1972-75 Six, Exc 3182478 1.80
Auto Trans 3211538 1.80

9—LIQUID VENT VALVE:

1970-75 (Exc. Below) 3198667 16.61
1970-73 Ser. 10, 80 ....3198666 17.66
1974-75 Ser 10,80—
4&2-Door (On Tank) 3220579 17.66
Sta Wagon 3198666 17.66

10—FUEL VAPOR CANISTER:

1971 V8 (Auto.) 3210962 22.54
1972 V8 (Auto) 3219216 32.87
1973 Six 3219216 32.87
1974 ....3219181 22.62
1975 3226809

11—FUEL VAPOR CANISTER FILTER:

1971-75 ....8120330 1.73

12—AIR CLEANER SENSOR KIT:

1972-75 V8 ....8121111 2.68
1973-75 Six 8124454 2.66

13—AIR CLEANER VACUUM CONTROL MOTOR

1972-75 V8 ....8121115 3.48

14—EXHAUST GAS RECIRCULATION VALVE

1973-75—
Stamped 881 ....3218739 17.66
Stamped 176 ....3219052 21.18
1974-75—
Stamped 470 ....3223979 27.87
Stamped 471 ....3223980 27.87
Stamped 472 ....3223981 27.87
1975 Ser 01-40 Calif 3225951
1975 (Prestolite)—
Six Exc 3224968 61.54
W/Egr 3224969 61.54
V8-304 Exc 3224965 63.46
W/Auto Trans 3224966 66.63
V8-360-401 ....3224746 63.46

Time	Tune-Up & Ignition (Group B)	Time

OPERATION INDEX

B1—TUNE-UP, MINOR

Includes: Renew points, condenser & plugs, set spark timing and adjust carburetor idle.

1968-74 Six (1.0) 1.3
1968-74 V8 (1.5) 1.7

B2—TUNE-UP, MAJOR

Includes: Check compression, clean or renew and adjust spark plugs, R & R distributor, renew points & condenser, and adjust ignition timing, carburetor and fan belts. Clean battery terminals and service air cleaner. Check coil, service manifold heat control valve and replace or clean fuel line filter.

1968-74—
Six (1.7) 2.3
V8 (2.5) 2.9
1975 Six (1.2) 1.8
1975 V8 (2.0) 2.5

—NOTE—
To Service PCV valve, Add (0.3) 0.3

B3—TUNE-UP, MAJOR & OVERHAUL CARBURETOR

1968-74 Six—
1 Barrel Carb. (3.1) 3.9
2 Barrel Carb. (3.7) 4.5
1968-74 V8—
2 Barrel Carb. (5.3) 6.0
4 Barrel Carb. (5.6) 6.4
1975 Six (2.6) 3.4
1975 V8—
2 Barrel Carb (4.8) 5.5
4 Barrel Carb (5.1) 5.9

B4—POINTS & CONDENSER RENEW

Includes: R & R distributor and set spark timing.

1968-74 (0.7) 0.9

B5—SPARK PLUGS, CLEAN & ADJUST OR RENEW

1969-75 V8 (0.5) 0.7
1969-75 Six Cyl. (0.4) 0.6

B6—COMPRESSION, TEST

1969-75 Six Cyl. (0.6) 0.7
1969-75 V8 (0.7) 0.8

B7—IGNITION TIMING, SET

All Models (0.2) 0.2

B8—DISTRIBUTOR, R & R OR RENEW

1969-75 R&R (0.4) 0.6
Renew (0.6) 0.8

B9—DISTRIBUTOR, OVERHAUL (UNIT OFF)

1969-75 (0.8) 1.1

B9A—DISTRIBUTOR, ADJUST ON STROBOSCOPE (UNIT OFF)

All Models (0.4) 0.4

B10—DISTRIBUTOR CAP, RENEW

1969-75 (0.2) 0.3

B11—IGNITION CABLE SET, RENEW

Time allowance covers installation of factory supplied sets.

Six Cyl. (0.4) 0.4
V8 (0.5) 0.5

B12—VACUUM CONTROL UNIT, RENEW

Includes: Set dwell & timing.

1969-75 Six (0.3) 0.5
1969-75 V8 (0.4) 0.6

B13—IGNITION COIL, RENEW

1969-75 (0.4) 0.4

B14—IGNITION SWITCH, RENEW

1967-69 (0.4) 0.6
1970-75—
Exc. Below (0.3) 0.5
Ser. 10-80 (0.4) 0.6

B15—ELECTRONIC IGNITION CONTROL UNIT, RENEW

1975 (0.3) 0.3

FIG. 1-TUNE-UP & IGNITION
(For Parts Identification Only)

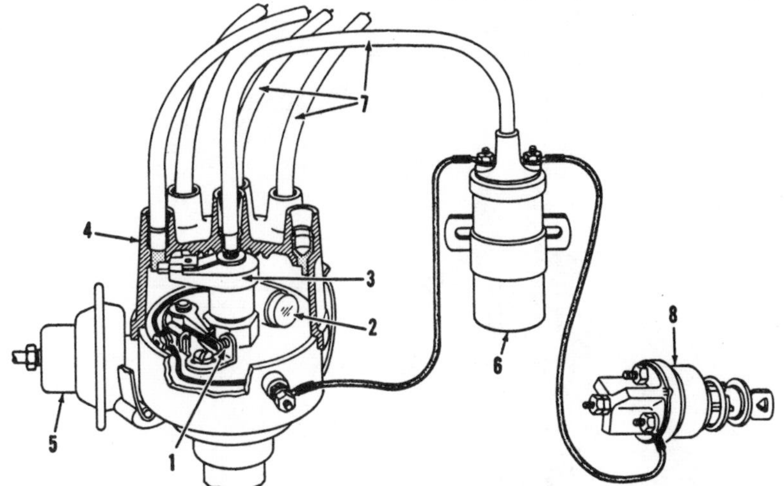

DISTRIBUTOR ASS'Y:

Application	Part No.	Price
1967-69 V8-290—		
2 Bar. Carb	3182701	47.05
4 Bar. Carb	3187537	52.86
1968-69 Six	3190890	39.67
1968-69 V8-390	3193199	50.88
1969 V8 343—		
2 Bar. Carb	3193144	44.86
4 Bar. Carb	3194669	50.95
1970 6-199	3197332	63.27
1970 Ser. 01, 40, 6-232—		
Exc. Below	3197332	63.27
Auto. Trans	3190890	39.67
1970 Ser. 10, 70, 80 (6-232)—		
Early	3197332	63.27
Late	3180070	51.42
1970 V8-304—		
Synchro-Mesh	3197232	61.85
Auto. Trans	3210193	56.77
1970 V8-360—		
2 Bar. Carb	3197232	61.85
4 Bar. Carb	3197233	61.85
1970 V8-390—		
Single Diaphram	3194669	50.95
Dual Diaphram	3197233	61.85
1971 Six	3180070	51.42
1971 V8-304	3211821	52.69
1971 V8-360	3194669	50.95
1971 V8-401	3194669	50.95
1972 Six	3215824	51.42
1972 V8-304, 360	3215825	48.05
1972 V8-401	3215826	48.96
1973 Ser 10, 80 Six—		
Std Trans	3219199	40.35
Auto Trans	3219198	51.42
1973 Ser 01,40,70 Six	3219199	40.35
1973-74 Ser 40, 70 V8-304—		
Std Trans	3217798	49.06
Auto Trans	3219197	56.75
1973-74 Ser 01, 10, 80 V8—		
304 Eng	3219197	56.75
360 Eng	3219196	57.93
1973-74 V8-401—		
Std Trans	3215826	48.96
Auto Trans	3219196	57.93

1—IGNITION POINT SET:

Application	Part No.	Price
1968-74 V8	3200197	4.11
1968-74 Six	3204202	3.27

2—CONDENSER:

Application	Part No.	Price
1968-74	3204584	1.36

3—ROTOR:

Application	Part No.	Price
1966-69 Six	4488087	1.23
1966-72 V8	8122343	2.19
1970 Six—		
Exc. Below	4488087	1.23
Ser. 01 Auto. Trans	4488087	1.23
1971 Six	4488087	1.23
1972-74 Six	4488087	1.23
1973-74 V8—		
1975 Six	8125441	2.32
1975 V8	3201799	1.78

4—DISTRIBUTOR CAP:

Application	Part No.	Price
1968-74 Six	4488091	3.72
1968-74 V8	3200192	5.49
1975 Six	8125447	4.48
1975 V8	8125443	1.86

5—VACUUM CONTROL UNIT:

Application	Part No.	Price
1966-69 Six	3204211	4.97
1967-69 V8-290	3207411	4.97
1968-69 V8-390	3208005	3.70
1969 V8-343	3207411	4.97
1970 Six—		
Exc. Below	4488072	16.61
Ser. 01 6-232 Auto. Tra	3204211	4.97
1970 V8-304—		
Synchro-Mesh	4488073	16.61
Auto. Trans	4488327	14.64
1970 V8-360	4488073	16.61
1970 V8-390—		
Exc. Below	3207411	4.97
Dual Diaph. Dist.	4488073	16.61
1971 Six	3204211	4.97
1971 V8	3207411	4.97
1972 Six	8120585	7.60
1972 V8	8120586	7.60
1973 Six	8122350	3.97
1973 V8-304—		
Std Trans	8120586	7.60
Auto Trans	8122347	4.36
1973 V8-360,401	8122347	4.36
1975 Six	8125438	10.96
1975 V8	8125437	10.96

6—IGNITION COIL:
1969-75 Exc 3208861 15.93
W/Electronic Ign. 8125028 16.50

7—IGNITION CABLE SET:
1966-69 Six 3207030 7.72
1968-72 V8 ....3209617 11.72
1970-74 Six 3207030 7.72
1973-74 V8 ....8122191 12.14
1975 Exc 8125608 5.32
V8 ....8125609 8.46

8—IGNITION SWITCH:
1969 Ser. 01, 30, 70 ....4485720 5.29
1969 Ser. 10, 80 ....3616830 4.19
1970-73—
L/Tilt Wheel 8122681 8.50
W/Tilt Wheel 3197598 8.92
1974-75—
L/Tilt Wheel 8122681 8.50
W/Tilt Wheel 3197598 8.92

Time — Fuel System & Intake Manifold (Group C) — Time

OPERATION INDEX

C1—CARBURETOR, R & R OR RENEW
1969-75 Six Cyl.—
1 Barrel (0.4) 0.6
2 Barrel (0.5) 0.7
1969-75 V8 (0.4) 0.6
—NOTE—
To Renew, Add (0.2) *0.2*

C2—CARBURETOR, R & R & OVERHAUL
1969-75 Six Cyl.—
1 Barrel (1.6) 2.1
2 Barrel (1.8) 2.7
1967-69 V8—
2 Barrel (1.9) 2.5
4 Barrel (2.2) 3.0
1970-75 V8 (1.8) 2.3

C2A—ACCELERATOR PUMP, RENEW
1969-75—
Exc. Below (0.6) 0.7
Model YF (0.6) 0.8
Model 2209 (0.5) 0.5
Model AFB (0.6) 0.8
Model 4300 (0.4) 0.5

C2B—NEEDLE & SEAT, RENEW
Includes: Check float level, idle speed and mixture.
1969-75—
Exc. Below (0.7) 1.0
Model 1931 (0.5) 0.7
Model RBS (0.6) ①0.8
Model YF (0.6) 0.8
①*Includes: R & R Carburetor*

C3A—AUTOMATIC CHOKE, OVERHAUL
1969-75 (0.6) 0.9

C3D—CHOKE HEAT TUBE (IN MANIFOLD), RENEW
1968-69—
Carb. 6200 (0.3) 0.5
AFB Carb. (0.7) 0.9
1970-75 (0.3) 0.5

C4—DASHPOT, RENEW
1969-75 (0.4) 0.5

C5—FUEL PUMP, R & R OR RENEW
1969-75 Six Cyl. (0.5) 0.7
1969-75 V8 (0.7) ①0.9
①*For Vacuum Booster & Pwr Strg Or Air Guard System, Add (0.6)* *0.6*

C6—FUEL TANK, R & R OR RENEW
1969-75—
Exc. Below (0.6) 0.9
Ser. 40 (0.7) 1.0

C7—FUEL SYSTEM, CLEAN
Includes R & R tank, blow out lines & clean or renew fuel filter.
1969-75 (1.0) 1.5

C8—INTAKE MANIFOLD GASKETS, RENEW (V8)
1969-75 (1.6) 2.3

Parts — Fuel System & Intake Manifold — Parts

PARTS INDEX

1—CARBURETOR ASS'Y (CARTER):
1969 6-199 (1 Bar)—
Synchro-Mesh 4488205 45.20
Automatic 3193884 36.81
1969 6-232 (1 Bar) 4488205 45.20
1969 6-232 (2 Bar.)—
Synchro-Mesh 3194503 55.76
Auto. Trans 3197329 61.86
1969 V8-290 (4 Bar.)—
Synchro-Mesh 3194507 76.07
Auto. Trans 3194508 76.07
1969 V8-390 (4 Bar.)—
Synchro-Mesh 4488208 91.80
Auto. Trans 3194513 75.95
1969 V8-343 (4 Bar.)—
Synchro-Mesh 3194510 76.07
Auto Trans 3194511 75.97
1970 Ser. 01, 40 6-199 (1 Bar.)—
Synchro-Mesh 3197320 37.36
Auto. Trans 8123177 37.29
1970 Ser. 01 6-232 (1 Bar.)—
Synchro-Mesh 3197320 37.36
Auto. Trans 8123177 37.29
1970 Ser. 01, 10, 80 6-232—
2 Barrel Carb—
Synchro-Mesh 3197329 61.86
Automatic 3199701 55.51
1970 Ser. 10, 70 6-232 (1 Bar.)—
Synchro-Mesh 8123177 37.29
Auto. Trans 8123177 37.29
1970 Ser. 40 6-232 (1 Bar.)—
Synchro-Mesh 3197320 37.36
Auto. Trans 8123177 37.29
1971 Ser. 01, 40 (6-232) (1 Bar)-
Synchro-Mesh 8123177 37.29
Auto. Trans 8123177 37.29
1971 Ser. 10, 70, 80 (6-232)—
1 Barrel Carb—
Synchro-Mesh 8123177 37.29
Auto. Trans 8123177 37.29
1971 6-258 (1 Bar) 8123177 37.29
1972 Six—
Synchro-Mesh 3214461 47.96
Auto. Trans (6-258) 3212940 45.91
Auto Trans (6-232) 3214463 45.91
1973-74—
YF-6299S 3219502 53.71
YF-6300S 3218901 46.50
YF-6400S 3218899 45.19
YF-6422S 3219472 49.90
YF-6401S 3219500 52.57
YF-6421S 3219469 37.36
YF-6423S 3219471 53.07
YF-6429S 3219500 52.57
YF-6424S 3219472 49.90
YF-6430S 3219501 51.95
YF-6431S 3219502 53.71
YF-6432S 3219503 53.71
YF-6510S 3220506 45.22
YF-6511S 3220505 45.22
YF-7001S 3223868 54.30
YF-7028S 3224304 66.16
YF-7029S 3224303 59.76
YF-7000S 3223867 52.97

1975—
YF-7041S 3224860 53.25
YF-7062S 3225458
YF-7039S 3224858
YF-7061S 3225457 53.50

2—CARBURETOR ASS'Y (HOLLEY):
1969 Ser 01 6-232 ....3193893 49.21

3—CARBURETOR ASS'Y (AMERICAN MOTORS):
1969 V8-290 (2 Barrel)—
Synchro-Mesh 3194505 63.07
Auto. Trans 3194506 63.07
1969 V8-343 (2 Bar.) 8121334 73.61
1970 V8-304 (2 Bar. Carb.)—
Synchro-Mesh 3197593 63.02
Auto. Trans 8121334 73.61
1970 V8-360 (2 Bar.) 8121334 73.61
1970 V8-360, 390 (4 Bar.)—
Synchro-Mesh 8122977 121.71
Auto. Trans 8122977 121.71
1971 V8-304 (2 Bar. Carb.)—
Synchro-Mesh 8121334 73.61
Auto. Trans 8121334 73.61
1971 V8-360 (2 Bar. Carb.)—
Synchro-Mesh 8121334 73.61
Auto. Trans 8121334 73.61
1971 V8-360, 401 (4 Bar.)—
Synchro-Mesh 3211106 93.37
Auto Trans (V8-360) 8122977 121.71
Auto Trans (V8-401) 8122977 121.71
1972 V8 (4-Bar)—
Synchro-Mesh 3214465 98.48
Auto. Trans.—
V8-360 ....3218802 103.90
V8-401 ....3218802 103.90
1972 V8 (2 Bar)—
V8-304 Synchro-Mesh 3214464 82.42
V8-304 Automatic 3213505 80.80
V8-360 ....3218384 86.08
1973 V8-304 (2 Bar)—
Std Trans 3218382 63.46
Auto Trans 3218383 63.46
1973 V8-360 (2 Bar) 3218384 86.08
1973 V8 (4 Bar)—
Std Trans 3218801 83.09
Auto Trans 3218802 103.90
1974 V8-304 (2 Bar)—
Synchro-Mesh 3222317 73.35
Automatic Tr 3222316 75.76
Calif 3222319 75.76
1974 V8-360 (2 Bar) 3222320 81.29
1974 V8 (4 Bar)—
Std Trans 3222323 119.56
Auto Trans 3222325 111.17

Model	Part No.	Price
1975 V8-304 Exc	3224923	81.80
W/Auto Trans	3224922	84.00
1975 V8-360	3224924	89.25
1975 4 Bar	3224925	124.50

4—CARBURETOR ZIP KIT (CARTER):

Model	Part No.	Price
1968-69 6-232 (2 Bar.)	8120521	8.63
1969 6-199 (1 Bar)	8122023	6.75
1969 V8 (4 Bar. Carb.)	4486759	8.51
1970 Six (1 Bar.)	8124351	8.31
1970 Six (2 Bar.)	4487904	6.47
1971 Six (1 Bar.)	8121138	7.22
1972 Six	8121138	7.22
1973-74 Exc	8124351	8.31
W/YF-6510&11s	8124351	8.31

5—CARBURETOR PEP KIT (HOLLEY):

Model	Part No.	Price
1969 6-232	4486727	9.45

6—CARBURETOR TUNE-UP KIT (AMERICAN MOTORS):

Model	Part No.	Price
1968-69 V8-290, 343—		
2 Barrel	4488325	11.02
1970 V8 (4 Bar.)	4487608	11.01
1970 V8 (2 Bar.)	4488325	11.02
1971-72 V8 (2 Bar.)	8121136	10.69
1971 V8 (4 Bar.)	4487608	11.01
1972 V8 (4 Bar)	8121134	8.51
1973-74	8123073	11.76

7—CARBURETOR GASKET KIT (CARTER):

Model	Part No.	Price
1967-70 6-232 (2 Bar.)	3205883	1.75
1967-69 V8 (4 Bar.)	3208350	7.40
1970-72 Six (1 Bar.)	4488046	1.92
1973-74	8122898	1.93

8—CARBURETOR GASKET KIT (HOLLEY):

Model	Part No.	Price
1969 6-232	4485959	1.35

9—CARBURETOR GASKET SET (AMERICAN MOTORS):

Model	Part No.	Price
1968-69 V8-290, 343—		
2 Barrel	4486218	2.04
1970 V8 (4 Bar.)	4487607	3.21
1970 V8 (2 Bar.)	4488324	3.20
1971-72 V8 (2 Bar.)	8120090	2.57
1971 V8 (4 Bar.)	4487607	3.21
1972 V8 (4 Bar)	8121134	8.51
1973-74	8123072	7.48
1975	8125977	

10—THERMOSTAT HOUSING ASS'Y (HOLLEY):

Model	Part No.	Price
1968-69 Six	3207276	5.51

11—THERMOSTATIC COIL & HOUSING ASS'Y (CARTER):

Model	Part No.	Price
1968-69 6-232 (2 Bar.)	4485652	7.55
1969 Six (1 Bar)—		
Synchro-Mesh (6-199)	4486596	6.24
Synchro-Mesh (6-232)	4486597	7.01
Auto Trans	3209868	6.00
1969 V8 (4 Bar. Carb.)	4486616	4.26
1970 Six (1 Bar.)	4488063	5.16
1970 Six (2 Bar.)	4487906	7.58
1971 Six (1 Bar.)	4489439	5.22
1972 Six (1 Bar)	4488063	5.16
1973-74	4488063	5.16

12—THERMOSTATIC COIL & HOUSING ASS'Y (AMERICAN MOTORS):

Model	Part No.	Price
1968-69 V8-290, 343—		
(2 Bar.)	4485448	5.51
1970 V8 (4 Bar.)	4488461	7.51
1970 V8 (2 Bar.)	4485448	5.51
1971 V8 (2 Bar.)—		
Exc. Below	4485448	5.51
V8-304 (Auto.)	8120087	6.77
1971 V8 (4 Bar.)	8120082	6.72
1972 V8 (2 Bar)	8120087	6.77
1972 V8 (4 Bar)	8121426	9.85

13—DASHPOT (CARTER):

Model	Part No.	Price
1967-69 Six	3204334	4.82
1968-69 V8 (4 Bar)	4486954	5.46
1970-71 Six (Exc Below)	8120135	7.61
1970 Six (2 Bar)	3204334	4.82
1972 Six	8120135	7.61
1973-74	8120135	7.61

15—DASHPOT (AMERICAN MOTORS):

Model	Part No.	Price
1968-69 V8-290, 343—		
(2 Bar.)	3209905	2.23
1970 V8 (4 Bar)	4488199	5.33
1970-75 V8 (2 Bar.)	3209905	2.23
1971-74 V8 (4 Bar.)	4488199	5.33

17—FUEL PUMP (NEW) (CARTER):

Model	Part No.	Price
1969 Six—		
Vacuum Wipers	3193900	23.93
Electric Wipers	3193899	13.94
1969 V8—		
Vacuum Wipers	3193986	23.93
Electric Wipers	3193985	23.93
1970 Six—		
Vacuum Wipers	3193900	23.93
Electric Wipers—		
Screwed On	3193899	13.94
Pressed On	3216577	16.21
1970 V8—		
Vacuum Wipers	3193986	23.93
Electric Wipers—		
2 Bar Carb—		
Screwed On	3193985	23.93
Pressed On	3216578	19.61
4 Bar Carb	3216578	19.61
1971-72 Six—		
Vacuum Wipers	3193900	23.93
Electric Wipers	3216577	16.21
1971-72 V8—		
Vacuum Wipers	3193986	23.93
Electric Wipers	3216578	19.61
1973 Six	3216577	16.21
1973 V8	3216578	19.61
1974 Six	3225283	11.60
1974 75 V8	8124460	16.20
1975 Six	3225283	11.60

18—FUEL TANK:

Model	Part No.	Price
1966-69 Ser. 01—		
Exc. Below	3206763	45.73
3 Seat Wagon	3206764	47.60
1967-69 Ser. 10, 50, 80—		
Exc. Below	3207934	48.46
3 Seat Wagon	8121661	41.37
1968-69 Ser. 30, 70	3208833	48.07
1970 Ser. 01—		
Exc. Below	8124101	42.37
Calif. Prod	8121512	59.91
1970 Ser. 10—		
Exc. Sta. Wagon—		
Exc. Below	3207934	48.46
Calif. Prod	4487646	62.06
Sta. Wagon (L/3 Seat)—		
Exc. Below	4487636	44.92
Calif. Prod	4487646	62.06
Sta. Wagon (W/3 Seat)—		
Exc. Below	4487637	37.38
Calif. Prod	4487647	63.36
1970 Ser. 30, 70—		
Exc. Below	4487634	47.31
Calif. Prod	4487635	69.54
1970 Ser. 40—		
Exc. Calif. Prod	4488033	44.92
Calif. Prod	4488034	52.62
1970 Ser. 80—		
Exc. Sta. Wagon—		
Exc. Below	3207934	48.46
Calif. Prod	4487646	62.06
Sta. Wagon—		
Exc. Below	4487637	37.38
Calif. Prod	4487647	63.36
1971 Ser. 01	8121512	59.91
1971-72 Ser. 10, 80—		
Exc. Below	4487646	62.06
Sta. Wagon (1971)	4487647	63.36
Sta. Wagon (1972)	8120517	64.21
1971-72 Ser. 40	4488034	52.62
1971 Ser. 70	4489223	49.01
1972 Ser 01—		
Early	8121512	59.91
Late	8121451	59.91
1972 Ser 70—		
Early	4489223	49.01
Late	8121450	49.01
1973-74 Ser 01	8121451	59.91
1973 Ser 10,80—		
Exc Below	4487646	62.06
Sta Wgn	8123103	61.59
1973-75 Ser 40	4488034	52.62
1973-74 Ser 70	8121450	49.01
1974 Ser 10&80—		
Except Below	8123350	65.19
Sta Wagon	8123103	61.59
1975 Ser 01	8125860	51.50
1975 Ser 10-85	8123350	65.19

19—INTAKE MANIFOLD TO HEAD GASKET:

Model	Part No.	Price
1969-75 Six	3183945	.87
1967-69 V8 (Set)	4488466	5.15
1970-74 V8 (Set)	4488467	5.15
1975 V8	8125869	5.41

BUICK

FULL SIZE MODELS

Time — Emission Controls (Group AB) — Time

OPERATION INDEX

AB1—POSITIVE CRANKCASE VENTILATOR (PCV) VALVE, CLEAN OR RENEW

All Models—
Renew (0.2) 0.2
Clean (0.2) 0.3

AB2—EMISSION CONTROL, CHECK (CCS)

Includes check and adjust carburetor and ignition timing

1969-75 (0.4) 0.7

AB4—AIR CLEANER MOTOR, RENEW

Includes R & R cleaner.

1969-75 (0.3) 0.5

AB5—AIR CLEANER SENSOR, RENEW

Includes R & R air cleaner.

1969-75 (0.2) 0.3

AB5A—THERMOSTATIC VACUUM SWITCH, RENEW

1969-75 (0.4) 0.5

AB6—AIR INJECTOR PUMP, R&R OR RENEW

1971-75 (0.3) 0.5

AB7—AIR PUMP DIVERTER VALVE, RENEW

1971-75 (0.2) 0.3

(Continued)

Emission Controls Time Cont'd

AB9—AIR PUMP HOSE, RENEW
1971-75 (0.2) 0.3

AB12—CHECK VALVE, RENEW
1971-75 (0.2) 0.3

AB14—AIR PUMP BELT, RENEW
1971-75 (0.2) 0.3

AB18—VAPOR CANNISTER, RENEW
1971-75 (0.2) 0.4

AB20—EXHAUST GAS RECIRCULATION VALVE, RENEW
1971-75 (0.2) 0.4

AB24—TRANS CONTROLLED SPARK SOLENOID, RENEW
1971-75 (0.2) 0.3

AB25—TRANS CONTROLLED SPARK SWITCH, RENEW
1971-75—
On Intake Manifold (0.4) 0.6
On Transmission (0.7) 0.9

Parts — Emission Controls — Parts

PARTS INDEX

1— AIR INJECTOR REACTOR PUMP:
1972-74 .... 7803943 59.95

2—CHECK VALVE:
1972 .... 5361992 4.41
1973-74 .... 4974196 4.59

3—AIR INJECTOR PUMP DRIVE BELT:
—NOTE—
Order By Complete Model Description.

4— CRANKCASE VENTILATOR VALVE:
1969-74 .... 6487503 1.23

5— DISTRIBUTOR THERMOSTATIC VACUUM SWITCH:
1968-74 .... 3024924 10.95
1975 .... 3029763 10.15

6— LIQUID VAPOR SEPARATOR:
1970—
Exc. Riviera 7028074 10.00
Riviera 1233139 21.90

7— LIQUID VAPOR CANISTER:
1970 .... 7027659 21.95
1971-74 .... 7028131 21.95

8—LIQUID VAPOR CANISTER FILTER
1970-74 .... 7026014 1.05

9—EXHAUST GAS RECIRCULATION VALVE
1972 V8-350 .... 7030642 16.85
V8-455, Std Trans 7030643 16.85
Auto Trans, Exc 7030642 16.85
Stage 1 .... 7030643 16.85
1973 V8-350, Exc 7040259 16.85
Auto Trans 7030876 16.85
1973 V8-455, Exc 7040351 16.85
Auto Trans 7040443 16.85
Stage 1 .... 7040249 16.85
1974 V8-350, Exc 7030876 16.85
Calif. 2 Bar 7041147 16.85
4 Bar 7041222 16.85
1974 V8-455, 2 Bar 7041445 16.85
4 Bar, Exc 7040443 16.85
Calif. 17050767 16.85
Hi-Perf. 17050768 16.85
1975 V8-350, 2 Bar 7043441
4 Bar 7043439

Time — Tune-Up & Ignition (Group B) — Time

OPERATION INDEX

B1—TUNE-UP, MINOR
Includes renew points, condenser & plugs, set spark timing & adjust carburetor idle. Does not include R&R distributor.
1969-74 (Exc Hi Energy Ign)—
V8-350 (1.2) 1.6
V8-430, 455 (1.4) 1.8

B2—TUNE-UP, MAJOR
Includes: Check compression, clean or renew and adjust spark plugs, renew points and condenser. Adjust ignition timing, carburetor and fan belts. Clean battery terminals and service air cleaner. Check coil and service manifold heat control valve and replace or clean fuel line filter. Does not include R & R distributor.
—NOTE—
To Service PCV Valve Add (0.2) *0.2*
1969-74 (Exc Hi Energy Ign)—
V8-350 (2.2) 2.8
V8-430, 455 (2.4) 3.0
1974-75 High Energy Ignition—
V8-350 (1.7) 2.3
V8-455 (1.9) 2.5

B3—TUNE-UP, MAJOR & OVERHAUL CARBURETOR
—NOTE—
For 1969 W/Air Cond., Add (0.2) *0.2*
To Service PCV Valve, Add (0.2) 0.2
1969-74 (Exh Hi Energy Ign)—
V8-350 (3.8) 4.5
V8-430, 455 (3.9) 4.7
1974-75 High Energy Ignition—
V8-350 (3.3) 4.0
V8-455 (3.4) 4.2

B4—POINTS & CONDENSER, RENEW
Includes set timing. Does not include R & R distributor.
1969-74 (Exc Hi Energy Ign)—
V8-350 (0.4) 0.6
V8-430, 455 (0.5) 0.8

B5—SPARK PLUGS, CLEAN & ADJUST OR RENEW
—NOTE—
To Clean, Add (0.2) *0.2*
1969-75—
V8-350, (0.4) 0.6
V8-430, 455 (0.5) 0.7

B6—COMPRESSION TEST
1969-75—
V8-350 (0.5) 0.6
V8-430, 455 (0.6) 0.7

B7—IGNITION TIMING, SET
1969-75 (0.3) 0.3

B8—DISTRIBUTOR, R & R OR RENEW
1969-75—
V8-350 (0.3) 0.3
V8-430, 455 (0.4) 0.4

B9—DISTRIBUTOR, OVERHAUL (UNIT OFF)
1969-75 (0.9) 1.1

B9A—DISTRIBUTOR, ADJUST ON STROBOSCOPE (UNIT OFF)
1969-75 (0.4) 0.4

B10—DISTRIBUTOR CAP, RENEW
1969-75 (0.3) 0.3

B11—IGNITION CABLE SET, RENEW
Time allowance covers installation of factory supplied sets only.
1969-75 (0.5) 0.6

B12—VACUUM CONTROL UNIT, RENEW
Includes: R & R distributor
1969-75—
V8-350 (0.4) 0.5
V8-430, 455 (0.5) 0.6

B13—IGNITION COIL, RENEW
1969-75 (0.4) 0.4

B14—STARTER & IGNITION SWITCH, RENEW
—NOTE—
For Air Cond., Add (0.2) *0.2*
1969-75 (0.6) 0.8

B16—STEERING & IGNITION LOCK & ACTUATOR, RENEW
1969-75—
Standard Column (1.3) 2.0
Tilt Column (1.4) 2.3

Parts | Tune-Up & Ignition | Parts

FIG.1- TUNE UP & IGNITION

(For Parts Identification Only)

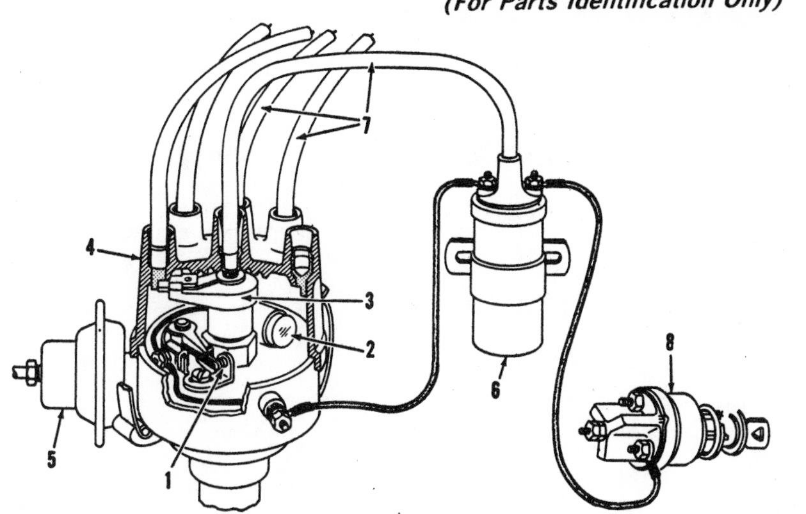

DISTRIBUTOR REWORK PACKAGE

Includes breaker plate, shield, condenser & points (use to separate points & condenser) for 1972 models w/Uni-Set.

1972 .... 1876065 5.78

DISTRIBUTOR ASS'Y:

1968-69 V8-430 .... 1111335 45.00
1968-69 V8-350—
  2 Bar. Carb. 1111964 44.15
  4 Bar. Carb 1111334 43.95
1970 V8-350—
  Exc. Below 1111986 46.35
  4 Bar. Hi-Comp. 1112006 46.40
1970 V8-455 .... 1112027 45.15
1971 V8-350 .... 1112066 45.50
1971 V8-455—
  Synchro-Mesh 1112016 45.50
  Auto Trans 1112104 45.15
1972-73 V8-350 .... 1112109 45.30
1972-73 V8-455 .... 1112110 45.15
1974 V8-350—
  Exc Below 1112541 47.10
  4 BBL Carb Hi Alt 1112861 48.10
  High Energy Ign 1112802 145.00
1974 V8-455—
  Exc Below 1112542 45.70
  GS 1112016 45.50
  High Energy Ign—
    Exc Below 1112803 145.00
    Hi-Perf 1112520 145.00
    Stage 1 .... 1112521 145.00
1975 V8-350 .... 1112896 145.00
  V8-455 .... 1112894 145.00

1— IGNITION POINT SET:

1969-74 (Exc Below) 1931988 4.40
1974 Uniset 1876600 7.25

2— CONDENSER:

1969-73 .... 1932004 1.51
1974-75 Capacitor 1876154 2.33

3— ROTOR:

1969-74, Exc 1852722 2.10
  High Energy Ign 1875943 3.08

4— DISTRIBUTOR CAP:

1969-74 Except 800061 5.95
  High Energy Ign—
    Cap 1875963 9.50
    Cover 1875960 2.73
1975 Cover 1875960 2.73

5— VACUUM CONTROL UNIT:

1969-70 .... 1116163 3.05
1971 V8-350 .... 1116163 3.05
1971-72 V8-455—
  Synchro-Mesh 1116163 3.05
  Auto Trans 1973440 3.16
1972-74 V8-350 .... 1116210 3.19
1973-74 V8-455 .... 1973440 3.16
1974 High Energy Ign—
  V8-350 .... 1973476 3.77
  V8-455 .... 1973477 3.77

6— IGNITION COIL:

1969-73 .... 1115202 13.50
1974 Exc 1115238 13.65
  High Energy Ign 1876209 23.10

7— IGNITION CABLE SET:

1969-74, Exc 8912108 16.82
  High Energy Ign.—
    V8-350 .... 8914969 36.59
    V8-455 .... 8914970 35.69
1975 V8-350 8915730
  V8-455 8915731

8— IGNITION SWITCH:

1969-73—
  Exc. Below 1990095 5.25
  W/Tilt Wheel 1990096 5.55
1974, Exc 1990098 5.70
  W/Tilt Wheel 1990099 6.20
  W/Air Bag 1990100 5.75

Time | Fuel System & Intake Manifold (Group C) | Time

OPERATION INDEX

C1—CARBURETOR, R & R OR RENEW

1969-75 (0.7) 0.9

C2—CARBURETOR, R & R & OVERHAUL

1969-75—
  2 Barrel—
    Carter (1.7) 2.4
    Rochester (1.9) 2.7
  4 Barrel—
    Carter (2.2) 3.0
    Quadrajet (1.8) 2.7
    Rochester (2.5) 3.3

C2A—ACCELERATOR PUMP, RENEW

1969-75—
  Exc. Below (0.7) 0.9
  Carter A.F.B. (1.1) 1.5
  Rochester 4MV (0.9) 1.2

—NOTE—
Does Not Include R & R Carburetor.

C2B—NEEDLE & SEAT, RENEW

1969-75—
  Exc. Below (0.6) 0.8
  Carter A.F.B. (1.0) 1.3
  Rochester 4MV (0.8) 1.1

—NOTE—
Does Not Include R & R Carburetor.

C3—AUTOMATIC CHOKE THERMOSTAT, RENEW

1969-75 (0.3) 0.5

C4—DASHPOT, RENEW

1969-75 (0.3) 0.3

C5—FUEL PUMP, R & R OR RENEW

1969-75 (Exc. Rivera)—
  L/P. Steering (0.4) 0.6
  W/P. Steering (0.5) 0.7
1969-75 Rivera (0.4) 0.7

C6—FUEL TANK, R & R OR RENEW

1969-75 (1.0) 1.4

C7—FUEL SYSTEM, CLEAN

Includes R & R tank, blow out lines & clean or renew fuel line filter.

1969-75 (1.6) 2.5

C8—INTAKE MANIFOLD GASKET, RENEW

1969-75 V8-350—
  L/Air Cond. (1.2) ②1.7
  W/Air Cond. (1.3) ②1.8
1969-75 V8-430, 455—
  L/Air Cond. (1.0) ②1.4
  W/Air Cond. (1.1) ②1.6

②*For P. Steering, Add (0.1)* *0.2*

Parts — Fuel System & Intake Manifold — Parts

PARTS INDEX

1—CARBURETOR ASS'Y (ROCHESTER):

1969 V8-350 (2 Bar. Carb.)—
Synchro-Mesh 7016941 57.25
Auto. Trans 7016940 57.25
1969 V8-350 (4 Bar. Carb.)—
Synchro-Mesh 7036754 88.45
Auto. Trans. 7036753 94.30
1969 V8-430—
Synchro-Mesh 7036752 88.45
Auto. Trans.—
Exec. Riviera 7036755 94.30
Riviera 7036755 94.30
1970 V8-350 (2 Bar. Carb.)—
Synchro-Mesh 7047043 60.00
Auto. Trans.—
L/Evap. Emission 7041349 66.80
W/Evap. Emission 7041350 66.80
1970 V8-350 (4 Bar. Carb.)—
Synchro-Mesh 7047045 103.40
Auto. Trans. 7047044 101.80
1970 V8-455 (Exc. Riviera)—
Synchro-Mesh 7047041 95.50
Auto. Trans. 7047040 97.00
1970 Riviera 7041324 103.40
1971 V8-350—
2 Bar Carb—
Except Below 7047143 69.90
Auto Trans 7047144 69.90
4 Bar Carb—
Except Below 7047145 104.35
Auto Trans 7047146 104.35
1971 V8-455 Exc 7047141 104.35
Auto Trans 7047140 104.35
1972 V8-350 (2 Bar)—
Synchro-Mesh 7047243 69.90
Auto Trans Except 7046573 69.90
Calif 7047242 69.90
1972 V8-350 (4 Bar)—
Synchro-Mesh 7047245 104.35
Auto-Trans Except 7046576 104.35
Calif 7047244 104.35
1972 V8-455 Except 7046574 104.35
Calif 7047247 104.35
1973 V8-350 (2 Bar)—
Synchro-Mesh 7047343 69.90
Auto Trans 7047342 69.90
1973 V8-350 (4 Bar)—
Synchro-Mesh 7047345 104.35
Auto Trans 7047344 104.35
1973 V8-455 Except 7047347 104.35
Stage 1 7047340 104.35
Synchro-Mesh 7047341 104.35
1974, 350 2-BBL Exc 7047442 69.90
Calif 7047445 69.90
1974, 350 4-BBL Exc 7047435 104.35
Calif 7047437 104.35
1974, 455 2-BBL 7047441 69.90
1974, 455 4-BBL Exc 7047429 104.35
Stage 1 7047439 104.35
Calif. 17050670 104.35

2—CARBURETOR OK KIT (ROCHESTER):

1968-69 V8-350—
2 Bar. Carb. 7039119 6.75
4 Bar. Carb. 7039121 9.00
1969 V8-430 7039164 9.00
1970 V8-350—
2 Bar. Carb. 7039172 7.70
4 Bar. Carb. 7039121 9.00
1970 V8-455—
Exc. Riviera 7039164 9.00
Riviera 7039189 9.00
1971 V8-350 (2 Bar. Carb.) 7039203 7.70
1971 V8-350 (4 Bar.) 7039205 9.00
1971 V8-455 7039219 9.00
1972 V8-350 (2 Bar) 7039228 7.70
1972 V8-350 (4 Bar) 7039231 9.00
1972 V8-455 7039230 9.00
1973-74 V8 (2 Bar) 7039245 7.70
1973-74 V8-350 (4 Bar) 7039247 9.00
1973-74 V8-455 (4 Bar) 7039246 9.00

3— CARBURETOR GASKET KIT (ROCHESTER):

1969 V8-350—
2 Bar. Carb. 7016840 2.75
4 Bar. Carb. 7036749 5.85
1969 V8-430 7036749 5.85
1970 V8-350—
2 Bar. Carb. 7041810 3.30
4 Bar. Carb. 7036749 5.85
1970 V8-455 7036749 5.85
1971 V8-350—
2 Bar. Carb 7041810 3.30
4 Bar. Carb. 7041695 5.05
1971 V8-455 7041695 5.05
1972 V8-350 (2 Bar) 7041969 3.30
1972 V8-350 (4 Bar) 7041977 4.90
1972 V8-455 7041977 4.90
1973-74 V8 2 Bar 7046659 3.25
4 Bar 7046663 4.90

4— CHOKE VACUUM CONTROL ASS'Y:

1968-69 V8-350—
2 Bar 7036766 3.40
4 Bar 7038237 4.05
1968-69 V8-400,430 7038237 4.05
1970 V8-455 7038237 4.05
1970 V8-350—
2 Bar. Carb.—
Synchro-Mesh 7038036 2.70
Auto. Trans. 7037911 2.70
4 Bar. Carb. 7038237 4.05
1971-74 V8, 2 Bar 7037911 2.70
4 Bar (71), V8-350 7038732 8.40
V8-455 7043720 8.40
4 Bar (72-74) 7038237 4.05
1971 V8-455 7043720 8.40

5— DASHPOT:

1968-71—
Synchro-Mesh 1385042 2.71
Auto. Trans. 1376158 2.83

6—FUEL PUMP

1967-69 V8-430 6470634 16.65
1968-71 V8-350—
Single Outlet 6417173 16.82
Dual Outlet 6470694 16.31
1969 Riviera 6417483 30.26
1970 V8-455—
Exc. Below 6470634 16.65
Riviera 6417483 30.26
1971-74 V8-455 6470634 16.65
1972-74 V8-350—
L/Air Cond 6417173 16.82
W/Air Cond 6470694 16.31

7—FUEL TANK:

1969—
Exc. Below 399730 47.30
Electra—
Early 399730 47.30
Late 1232646 49.50
Riviera 1233346 41.75
1970 Lesabre & Wildcat—
Exc. Sta. Wagon—
L/Evap. Emission 1231813 49.50
W/Evap. Emission 1233773 59.40
Sta. Wagon—
L/Evap. Emission 3972571 47.30
W/Evap. Emission 3972572 57.20
1970 Electra—
L/Evap. Emission 1233035 49.50
W/Evap. Emission 1233774 59.40
1970 Riviera—
L/Evap. Emission 1233346 41.75
W/Evap. Emission 1233337 46.15
1971-72 Lesabre 1235529 59.40
1971-72 Centurion—
Exc. Below 1235529 59.40
Estate Wagon 412259 43.95
1971-72 Electra 1235697 59.40
1971-72 Riviera 1235871 59.40
1973 Riviera 1244527 59.40
Electra 1244526 59.40
Les & Centurion 1244525 59.40
Estate Wagon 412259 43.95
1974 Les & Cent Exc 1243388 59.40
Sta Wagon 412259 43.95
1974 Electra 1244526 59.40
1974 Riviera 1244470 59.40
1975 Le Sabre 1247455
Estate Wagon 419531 45.70

8—INTAKE MANIFOLD GASKET:

1967-71 V8-430,455 1394705 4.21
1968-71 V8-350 1394953 6.55
1972-74 V8-350 1394953 6.25
1972-74 V8-455 1242283 4.21

9—ACCELERATOR PUMP

1970-74 2 Bar, Exc 7036282 4.05
V8-455 (74) 7037495 3.00
1970-74 4 Bar 7037504 3.10

10—ACCELERATOR PUMP NEEDLE & SEAT

1970-72 V8-350, 2 Bar 7035144 3.05
4 Bar 7035140 3.60
1970 V8-455, Exc 7035142 3.30
Stage 1 & Riviera 7035134 3.30
1971-72 V8-455 7035134 3.30
1973-74, 2 Bar 7035141 3.00
4 Bar, Exc 7035140 3.60
V8-455 7035134 3.30

BUICK

INTERMEDIATE AND COMPACT MODELS

Time — Emission Controls (Group AB) — Time

OPERATION INDEX

AB1—POSITIVE CRANKCASE VENTILATOR (PCV) VALVE, CLEAN OR RENEW

All Models—
Renew (0.2) 0.2
Clean (0.2) 0.3

AB2—EMISSION CONTROL, CHECK (CCS)

Includes check and adjust carburetor and ignition timing.

1969-75 (0.4) 0.7

AB4—AIR CLEANER MOTOR, RENEW

Includes R & R air cleaner.

1969-75 (0.3) 0.5

AB5—AIR CLEANER SENSOR, RENEW
Includes R & R air cleaner.
1969-75 (0.2) 0.3

AB5A—THERMOSTATIC VACUUM SWITCH, RENEW
1969-75 (0.4) 0.5

AB6—AIR INJECTOR PUMP, R & R OR RENEW
1971-75 (0.3) 0.5

AB7—AIR PUMP DIVERTER VALVE, RENEW
1971-75 (0.2) 0.3

AB9—AIR PUMP HOSE, RENEW
1971-75 (0.2) 0.3

AB12—CHECK VALVE, RENEW
1971-75 (0.2) 0.3

AB14—AIR PUMP BELT, RENEW
1971-75 (0.2) 0.3

AB18—VAPOR CANNISTER, RENEW
1971-75 (0.2) 0.4

AB20—EXHAUST GAS RECIRCULATION VALVE, RENEW
1971-75 (0.2) 0.4

AB24—TRANS CONTROLLED SPARK SOLENOID, RENEW
1971-75 (0.2) 0.3

AB25—TRANS CONTROLLED SPARK SWITCH, RENEW
1971-75—
On Intake Manifold (0.4) 0.6
On Transmission (0.3) 0.5

Parts — Emission Control — Parts

PARTS INDEX

1—AIR INJECTOR REACTOR PUMP:

1972-75, Exc	7803943	59.95
Six (74) W/AC	7803948	45.70

2—CHECK VALVE:

1972	5361992	4.41
1973-74, Exc	4974196	4.59
Six (73)	5361992	4.41
1975, 6-250	4974265	

3—AIR INJECTOR PUMP DRIVE BELT:

—NOTE—
Order By Complete Model Description.

4—CRANKCASE VENTILATOR VALVE:

1969-74 (Exc Below)	6487503	1.23
1969-70 Six	6422718	1.94
1971-72 Six	6422717	1.94
1973-74 Six (L/Nox Emiss)	6487534	1.89
1974-75, 6-250	6487936	2.20

5—DISTRIBUTOR THERMOSTATIC VACUUM SWITCH:

1968-74	3024924	10.95
1975	3029763	10.15

6—FUEL VAPOR CANISTER:

1970	7027659	21.95
1971-75 Six	7030605	26.30
1971-74 V8	7028131	21.95
1975, V8-350	7043715	21.95

7—FUEL VAPOR CANISTER FILTER

1970-74	7026014★	1.05

8—EXHAUST GAS RECIRCULATION VALVE

1972, Exc	7030643	16.85
V8-455, Auto, Exc	7030642	16.85
Stage 1	7030643	16.85
1973, Six, Exc	7035171	16.85
Auto Trans	7035169	16.85
1973, V8-350, Exc	7040259	16.85
Auto Trans	7030876	16.85
1973, V8-455, Exc	7040351	16.85
Auto Trans	7040443	16.85
Stage 1	7040249	16.85
1974, Six, Exc	7043042	16.85
Auto Trans, Exc	7043039	16.85
W/Nox Emission	7043041	16.85
1974, V8-350, Exc	7030876	16.85
Calif, 2 Bar	7041147	16.85
4 Bar	7041222	16.85
1974, V8-455, 2 Bar	7041445	16.85
4 Bar, Exc	7040443	16.85
Calif, Exc	17050767	16.85
Stage 1	7041446	16.85
1975, 6-250—		
Std Trans, Exc	7043059	
3 Speed	7043037	
Auto Trans—		
TH350	7043038	
L/Nox Emission	7043058	
L/Calif Emission	17050492	
1975, V8-350—		
2 Bar, Exc	7043440	
Sta Wag	7043441	
Air Cond	7043436	
4 Bar, Exc	7043435	
Calif	7043439	
1975, V8-455, Exc	7043437	
Calif	7043438	

Time — Tune-Up & Ignition (Group B) — Time

OPERATION INDEX

B1—TUNE-UP, MINOR
Includes renew points, condenser & plugs, set spark timing & adjust carburetor idle. Does not include R & R distributor.
1968-74 Six Cyl.—
L/Air Cond. (1.2) 1.6
W/Air Cond. (1.4) 1.8
1968-74 V8—
Exc. Below (1.2) 1.6
V8-400, 455 (1.4) 1.8

B2—TUNE-UP, MAJOR
Includes: Check compression, clean or renew and adjust spark plugs, renew points and condenser. Adjust ignition timing, carburetor and fan belts. Clean battery terminals and service air cleaner. Check coil and service manifold heat control valve and replace or clean fuel line filter. Does not include R & R distributor.

—NOTE—
To Service PCV Valve, Add (0.2) *0.2*
1968-74 Six Cyl.—
L/Air Cond. (1.7) 2.3
W/Air Cond. (1.9) 2.5
1968-74 V8—
Exc. Below (1.9) 2.5
V8-400, 455 (2.1) 2.7
1975 L6—
L/Air Cond (1.4) 2.0
W/Air Cond (1.6) 2.2
1975 V8—
L/Air Cond (1.6) 2.3
W/Air Cond (1.8) 2.5

B3—TUNE-UP, MAJOR & OVERHAUL CARBURETOR

—NOTE—
For 1968-69 W/Air Cond., Add (0.2) *0.2*
To Service PCV Valve, Add (0.2) *0.2*
1968-74 Six (3.2) 4.0
1968-74 V8-350—
2 Barrel (3.2) 4.0
4barrel (3.7) 4.5
1968-74 V8-400, 455—
Quadrajet (3.9) 4.7
1975 L6 (3.0) 3.7
1975 V8—
2 Barrel (2.9) 3.6
4 Barrel (3.4) 4.2

B4—POINTS & CONDENSER, RENEW
Includes set timing. Does not include R & R distributor.
1968-74 Six—
L/Air Cond. (0.4) 0.6
W/Air Cond. (0.6) 0.9
1968-74 V8—
Exc. Below (0.4) 0.6
V8-400, 455(0.5) 0.8

B5—SPARK PLUGS, CLEAN & ADJUST OR RENEW

—NOTE—
To Clean, Add (0.2) *0.2*
1969-75 L6—
L/Air Cond. (0.3) 0.5
W/Air Cond. (0.5) 0.7
1969-75 V8—
Exc. Below (0.4) 0.6
V8-400, 455 (0.5) 0.7

B6—COMPRESSION TEST
1969-75 Six—
L/Air Cond. (0.4) 0.5
W/Air Cond. (0.6) 0.7
1969-75 V8—
Exc. Below (0.5) 0.6
V8-400, 455 (0.6) 0.7

B7—IGNITION TIMING, SET
1969-75 (0.3) 0.3

B8—DISTRIBUTOR, R & R OR RENEW
1969-75 Six (0.4) 0.4
1969-75 V8—
V8-260, 350 (0.3) 0.3
V8-400, 455 (0.4) 0.4

B9—DISTRIBUTOR, OVERHAUL (UNIT OFF)

1969-75 (0.7) 1.1

B9A—DISTRIBUTOR, ADJUST ON STROBOSCOPE (UNIT OFF)

1969-75 (0.4) 0.4
1969-75 Exc (0.8) 1.4
Station Wagon (1.3) 1.6

B10—DISTRIBUTOR CAP, RENEW

1969-75 (0.3) 0.3

B11—IGNITION CABLE SET, RENEW

Time allowance covers installation of factory supplied sets only
1969-75 (0.5) 0.6

B12—VACUUM CONTROL UNIT, RENEW

Includes R & R distributor
1969-75—
Six, V8-260, 350 (0.4) 0.5
V8-400, 455 (0.5) 0.6

B13—IGNITION COIL, RENEW

1969-75 (0.4) 0.4

B14—STARTER & IGNITION SWITCH, RENEW

—NOTE—
For Air Cond., Add (0.2) 0.2
1969-75 (0.6) 0.8

B16—STEERING & IGNITION LOCK & ACTUATOR, RENEW

1969-75—
Standard Column (1.3) 2.0
Tilt Column (1.4) 2.3

—NOTE—
For Air Cond. On Special Models, Add (0.1) 0.2

Parts — Tune-Up & Ignition — Parts

FIG.1- TUNE-UP & IGNITION
(For Parts Identification Only)

DISTRIBUTOR REWORK PKG

Includes breaker plate, shield, condenser & points (use to separate points & condenser) for 1972 models w/Uni-Set.

1972	1876065	5.78

DISTRIBUTOR ASS'Y:

1968-69 V8-350—		
2-Barrel Carb	1111964	44.15
4-Barrel Carb	1111334	43.95
1969-71 Six—		
Std. Trans	1110465	37.80
Auto Trans	1110466	37.80
1968-69 V8-400	1111335	45.00
1969 GS-400	1112016	45.50
1970 V8-350—		
Exc. Below	1111986	46.35
4 Bar. Hi-Comp.	1112006	46.40
1970 V8-455—		
Exc. Below	1112027	45.15
Stage 1	1112016	45.50
1971 V8-350—		
Synchro-Mesh	1112006	46.40
Auto Trans	1112037	45.50
1971-72 V8-455—		
Synchro-Mesh	1112016	45.50
Auto Trans (1971)	1112104	45.15
1972-73 V8-350	1112109	45.30
1973 V8-455, Exc	1112110	45.15
Std Trans, GS	1112016	45.50
Stage 1	1112016	45.50
1973-74 6 Cyl	1110499	35.25
1974 V8-350, Exc	1112541	47.10
4 Bar Carb Hi Alt	1112861	48.10
High Energy Ign	1112802	145.00
1974 V8-455, Exc	1112542	45.70
High Energy Ign	1112803	145.00
Stage 1	1112521	145.00
Gran Sport	1112016	45.50
1975, 6-250, Exc	1112863	118.00
Auto Trans	1110650	118.00
1975, V6	1110651	151.50
V8-350	1112896	145.00
V8-455	1112894	145.00

1— IGNITION POINT SET:

1969-74 Six	1954557	3.40
V8, Exc	1931988	4.40
Uniset (1974)	1876600	7.25

2—CONDENSER:

1969-73 V8	1932004	1.51
1969-73 Six	1928111	1.51
1974-75, V8, Capacitor	1876154	2.33

3—ROTOR:

1969-73 V8	1852722	2.10
1969-74 Six	800056	1.19
1974 V8 Exc	1852722	2.10
High Energy Ign	1875943	3.08

4—DISTRIBUTOR CAP:

1968-74 V8 (Exc. Below)	800061	5.95
1968-74 Six	1971324	3.58
1974-75 High Energy Ign—		
Cap (74)	1875963	9.50
Cover (74-75)	1875960	2.73

5—VACUUM CONTROL UNIT:

1969-70 V8	1116163	3.05
1969-70 Six	1116217	3.57
1971 V8-350	1116163	3.05
1971 V8-455—		
Synchro-Mesh	1116163	3.05
Auto Trans	1973440	3.16
1972-74 V8-350, Exc	1116210	3.19
High Alt	1973440	3.16
High Energy Ign	1973476	3.77
1972-74 V8-455, Exc	1973440	3.16
Stage 1 (72)	1116210	3.19
Stage 1 (73)	1116210	3.19
Stage 1 (74)	1973476	3.77
High Energy	1973477	3.77
1973-74 Six Cyl	1973428	3.25

6—IGNITION COIL:

1969-73	1115202	13.50
1974-75 Six	1115202	13.50
1974 V8 Exc	1115238	13.65
High Energy Ign	1876209	23.10

7—IGNITION CABLE SET:

1968-69 Six Exc	2986606	7.30
AC, 1969	6292484	9.10
1969-74 V8, Exc	8912108	16.82
High Energy, V8-350	8914969	36.59
V8-455	8914970	35.69
1970-74 Six	8909903	7.54
1975, V8-350	8915730	
V8-455	8915731	

8—IGNITION SWITCH:

1969-73—		
Exc. Below	1990095	5.25
W/Tilt Wheel	1990096	5.55
1974, Exc	1990098	5.70
W/Tilt Wheel	1990099	6.20

Time — Fuel System & Intake Manifold (Group C) — Time

OPERATION INDEX

C1—CARBURETOR, R & R OR RENEW

1969-75—
Six (0.5) 0.6
V8 (0.7) 0.9

C2—CARBURETOR, R & R & OVERHAUL

1969-75—
Exc. Below (1.5) 2.2
2 Barrel (1.9) 2.7
4 Barrel (1.8) 2.9

C2A—ACCELERATOR PUMP, RENEW
1969-75—
Exc. Below (0.7) 0.9
Carter A. F. B (1.1) 1.5
Rochester 4MV (0.9) 1.2

—NOTE—
Does Not Include R & R Carburetor

C2B—NEEDLE & SEAT, RENEW
1969-75—
Exc. Below (0.6) 0.8
Carter A. F. B (1.0) 1.3
Rochester 4MV (0.8) 1.1

C3—AUTOMATIC CHOKE THERMOSTAT, RENEW
1969-75 (0.3) 0.5

C4—DASHPOT, RENEW
1969-75 (0.3) 0.3

C4A—IDLE STOP SOLENOID, RENEW
1968-71 Six (0.3) 0.3

C5—FUEL PUMP, R & R OR RENEW
1969-75—
L6 (0.3) 0.5
V8 (0.4) ①0.6
①For V8-400 W/Power Steering Add (0.1) *0.2*

C6—FUEL TANK, R & R OR RENEW
1968-74 (1.0) 1.4

C7—FUEL SYSTEM, CLEAN
Includes R & R tank, blow out lines & clean or renew fuel filter.
1969-75 Exc (1.4) 2.3
Station Wagon (1.9) 2.8

C8—INTAKE MANIFOLD GASKET, RENEW
1969-75 V8-260, 350—
L/Air Cond. (1.2) ②1.7
W/Air Cond. (1.3) ②1.8
1968-74 V8-400,455—
L/Air Cond. (1.0) 1.4
W/Air Cond. (1.1) ②1.6
②For P./Steering, Add (0.1) *0.2*

C8A—MANIFOLD GASKET, RENEW
1969-75 L6 (0.6) 1.0

Parts — Fuel System & Intake Manifold — Parts

PARTS INDEX

1—CARBURETOR ASS'Y (ROCHESTER);

Model	Part No.	Price
1969 Six—		
Std. Trans	7016947	48.75
Auto. Trans	7016902	48.75
1969 V8-350 (2 Bar. Carb.)—		
Synchro-Mesh	7016941	57.25
Auto. Trans	7016940	57.25
1969 V8-350 (4 Bar. Carb.)—		
Synchro-Mesh	7036754	88.45
Auto. Trans	7036753	94.30
1969 V8-400—		
Synchro-Mesh	7036752	88.45
Auto Trans.—		
Exc. Below	7036751	94.30
Gran Sport	7036730	89.95
1970 Six—		
Synchro-Mesh	7047015	50.70
Auto Trans	7047014	50.70
1970 V8-350 (2 Bar. Carb.)—		
Synchro-Mesh	7047043	60.00
Auto. Trans.—		
L/Evap. Emission	7041349	66.80
W/Evap. Emission	7041350	66.80
1970 V8-350 (4 Bar. Carb.)—		
Synchro-Mesh	7047045	103.40
Auto. Trans	7047044	101.80
1970 V8-455—		
Exc. Stage 1—		
Synchro-Mesh	7047041	95.50
Auto. Trans	7047040	97.00
Stage 1	7047047	103.40
1971 Six—		
Synchro-Mesh	7047117	52.35
Auto Trans	7047114	54.80
1971 V8-350 (2 Bar Carb)—		
Synchro-Mesh	7047143	69.90
Auto Trans	7047144	69.90
1971 V8-350 (4 Bar. Carb.)—		
Synchro-Mesh	7047145	104.35
Auto Trans	7047146	104.35
1971 V8-455—		
Stage 1	7047140	104.35
Exc Stage 1—		
Std. Trans	7047141	104.35
Auto Trans	7047140	104.35
1972 V8-350 (2 Bar Carb)—		
Synchro-Mesh	7047243	69.90
Auto Trans—		
Exc Calif	7046573	69.90
Calif	7047242	69.90
1972 V8-350 (4 Bar Carb)—		
Synchro-Mesh	7047245	104.35
Auto Trans—		
Exc Calif	7046576	104.35
Calif	7047244	104.35
1972 V8-455 (Exc Stage 1)—		
Exc Calif	7046574	104.35
Calif	7047247	104.35
1972 V8-455 (Stage 1)—		
Synchro-Mesh	7047241	104.35
Auto Trans—		
Exc Calif	7046575	104.35
Calif	7047240	104.35
1973 V8-350 (2 Bar Carb)—		
Century & Regal—		
Synchro-Mesh	7047343	69.90
Auto Trans	7047342	69.90
Apollo	7046928	69.90
1973 V8-350 (4 Bar. Carb.)—		
Exc Below—		
Synchro-Mesh	7047345	104.35
Auto. Trans.	7047344	104.35
Apollo	7046929	104.35
1973 V8-455—		
Synchro-Mesh	7047341	104.35
Auto. Trans.	7047347	104.35
Stage 1	7047340	104.35
1973 Six Exc	7047317	52.35
Auto Trans	7047314	54.80
1974 Six Exc	7047417	52.35
Auto Trans Exc	7047414	54.80
Calif	7047404	54.80
1974 V8-350 2 Bar Carb—		
Century & Regal Exc	7047442	69.90
Calif	7047445	69.90
Apollo Exc	7047446	69.90
Calif	7047447	69.90
1974 V8-455 2 Bar	7047441	69.90
1974 V8-350 4 Bar Carb—		
Century & Regal, Exc	7047435	104.35
Calif	7047437	104.35
Apollo Exc	7047436	104.35
Calif	7047438	104.35
1974 V8-455 4 Bar Carb—		
Exc Below	7047429	104.35
Stage 1	7047439	104.35
Calif	17050670	104.35

2—CARBURETOR OK KIT (ROCHESTER):

Model	Part No.	Price
1968-69 Six	7039147	4.90
1969 V8-350—		
2 Bar. Carb.	7039119	6.75
4 Bar. Carb.	7039165	9.00
1969 V8-400	7039164	9.00
1970 Six	7039166	4.90
1970 V8-350—		
2 Bar. Carb.	7039172	7.70
4 Bar. Carb.	7039165	9.00
1970 V8-455—		
Exc. Stage 1	7039164	9.00
Stage 1	7039189	9.00
1971 Six	7039196	4.90
1971 V8-350, 2 Bar.	7039203	7.70
4 Bar.	7039205	9.00
1971 V8-455	7039219	9.00
1972 V8-350—		
2 Bar Carb	7039228	7.70
4 Bar Carb	7039231	9.00
1972 V8-455	7039230	9.00
1973-74 V8 (2 Bar)	7039245	7.70
4 Bar, Exc	7039247	9.00
V8-455	7039246	9.00
1973-74 Six	7039248	4.90

3—CARBURETOR GASKET KIT (ROCHESTER):

Model	Part No.	Price
1969 Six	7036546	2.40
1969 V8-350—		
2 Bar. Carb.	7016840	2.75
4 Bar. Carb.	7036749	5.85
1969 V8-400	7036749	5.85
1970 Six	7036784	3.35
1970 V8-350—		
2 Bar. Carb	7041810	3.30
4 Bar. Carb.	7036749	5.85
1970 V8-455	7036749	5.85
1971 Six	7041599	2.85
1971 V8-350—		
2 Bar. Carb	7041810	3.30
4 Bar. Carb	7041695	5.05
1971 V8-455	7041695	5.05
1972 V8-350—		
2 Bar Carb	7041969	3.30
4 Bar Carb	7041977	4.90
1972 V8-455	7041977	4.90
1973-74 V8 (2 Bar)	7046659	3.25
4 Bar	7046663	4.90
1973-74 Six	7046679	3.35

4—CHOKE VACUUM CONTROL ASS'Y:

Model	Part No.	Price
1968-69 V8-400	7038237	4.05
1969 V8-350 (2 Bar)	7036766	3.40
1969 V8-350 (4 Bar)	7038237	4.05
1970 V8-455	7038237	4.05
1970 V8-350—		
2 Bar. Carb.—		
Synchro-Mesh	7038036	2.70
Auto Trans	7037911	2.70
4 Bar. Carb.	7038237	4.05
1971 V8-350, 2 Bar	7037911	2.70
4 Bar	7038732	8.40
1971 V8-455	7043720	8.40
1972-74 V8 2 Bar	7037911	2.70
4 Bar	7038237	4.05
1973-74 Six	7030918	8.80

5—DASHPOT:

Model	Part No.	Price
1968-69 Six	1385042	2.71
1968-71 V8—		
Synchro-Mesh	1385042	2.71
Auto. Trans	1376158	2.83

6—FUEL PUMP

Model	Part No.	Price
1968-74 Six	6416502	11.38
1969-74 V8-350—		
L/Air Cond	6417173	16.82
W/Air Cond, Exc	6470694	16.31
Apollo	6470848	16.62
1969 V8-400—		
Exc Below	6470634	16.65
Gran Sport	6470098	16.02
1970-74 V8-455	6470098	16.02

7—FUEL TANK:

Model	Part No.	Price
1968-69—		
Exc. Below	404078	43.95
Sta. Wagon	398168	41.75
1970 (Exc. Sta. Wagon)—		
L/Evap. Emission	1234123	43.95
W/Evap. Emission	1234125	48.35
1970 (Sta. Wagon)—		
L/Evap. Emission	404160	43.95
W/Evap. Emission	404964	50.55
1971-72—		
Exc. Below	1235674	48.35
Sportwagon	231450	46.15
1973 Century & Regal Exc	1244524	48.35
Sta. Wagon	416366	46.15
1973-74 Apollo	344416	48.35
1974 Century & Regal Exc	416216	48.35
Sta Wagon	416366	46.15
1975 Apollo, Skylark	357393	45.70
Sta Wagon	419530	45.70

8—INTAKE MANIFOLD GASKET:
1968-71 V8-400,455 ....1394705 4.21
1968-73 Six 3953746 1.60
1969-74 V8-350 ....1394953 6.25
1972-74 V8-455 ....1242283 4.21
1974 Six 338115 1.60

9—ACCELERATOR PUMP
1970-74, Six 7037597 3.00
1970-74, V8-350, 2 Bar 7036282 4.05
4 Bar 7037504 3.10
1970-74, V8-455, 4 Bar 7037504 3.10
2 Bar (74) 7037495 3.00

10—ACCELERATOR PUMP NEEDLE & SEAT
1970-74, Six 7035133 3.05
1970-72, V8-350, 2 Bar 7035144 3.05
4 Bar 7035140 3.60
1970, V8-455, Exc 7035142 3.30
Stage 1 ....7035134 3.30
1971-72, V8-455 ....7035134 3.30
1973-74, V8, 2 Bar 7035141 3.00
4 Bar, Exc 7035140 3.60
V8-455 ....7035134 3.30

CADILLAC

Time — Emission Controls (Group AB) — Time

OPERATION INDEX

AB1— POSITIVE CRANKCASE VENTILATION VALVE, CLEAN OR RENEW
Renew (0.2) 0.2
Clean (0.3) 0.5

AB2— EXHAUST EMISSION CONTROL, (CCS), CHECK
Includes check & adjust carb. & Timing.
All Models (0.6) 1.0

AB6—AIR PUMP, R & R OR RENEW
1968-69 (0.7) 1.0
1971-75 (0.6) 0.9

—NOTE—
To Replace Diverter Valve, Add (0.2) *0.3*

AB7—DIVERTER VALVE, RENEW (ON CAR)
1969-75 (0.3) 0.3

AB9— HOSES, RENEW
1968-69 (Each) (0.2) 0.2

AB12— CHECK VALVE, RENEW
1968-75 (0.2) 0.2

AB14— AIR PUMP BELT, RENEW
1968-69 (0.3) 0.5

AB16— AIR CLEANER MOTOR, RENEW
1970-75 (0.4) 0.6

AB17— AIR CLEANER SENSOR, RENEW
1970-75 (0.2) 0.3

AB18— FUEL VAPOR CANNISTER, R & R OR RENEW
1970-75 (0.2) 0.3

AB19—TEMPERATURE SENSOR, RENEW (CCS)
1970-75 (0.2) 0.3

AB20—EXHAUST GAS RECIRCULATION VALVE, RENEW
1973-75 (0.3) 0.5

AB21—E G R TIME DELAY VALVE, RENEW
1973-75 (0.2) 0.3

Parts — Emission Controls — Parts

PARTS INDEX

1—AIR INJECTOR REACTOR PUMP:
1969-74 ....7806286 48.05
1975 7817810

2—CHECK VALVE:
1969-75 ....5354987 3.66

3—AIR DIVERTER VALVE:
1969-75 ....7030761 11.60

4—AIR INJECTOR PUMP DRIVE BELT:
—NOTE—
Order By Complete Model Description.

5—CRANKCASE VENTILATOR VALVE:
1969-75 ....6421972 1.94

6—DISTRIBUTOR THERMOSTATIC VACUUM SWITCH:
1969-74 ....3015636 11.20

7—DISTRIBUTOR VACUUM ADVANCE SOLENOID
1970-72 ....1114435 7.60

8—FUEL VAPOR CANNISTER
1970 ....7028045 27.20
1971-74 ....7028131 21.95
1975 ....7043715 21.95

9—AIR CLEANER MOTOR (C.C.S.):
1970-75 ....6484245 3.31

10—AIR CLEANER SENSOR (C.C.S.):
1970-75 ....6486587 4.26

11—ANTI-DIESELING SOLENOID
1972-74 ....1604093 7.40

12—EVAPORATOR EMISSION SEPARATOR
1970 ....7028034 9.50
1971-72 ....407742 14.85

13—EXHAUST GAS RECIRCULATION VALVE
1973—
To Carburetor 1602030 2.03
On Intake Manifold Exc 7040571 16.85
California 7040556 16.85
1974-75
To Carburetor 1604913 2.03
Back Pressure Transducer..1603900 16.45
On Intake Manifold Exc 7049869 16.85
California 7042840 16.85

Time — Tune-Up & Ignition (Group B) — Time

OPERATION INDEX

B1—TUNE-UP, MINOR

Includes: Renew points, condenser & plugs,set spark timing & adjust carb idle. Does not include R & R distributor.

1969-74 Exc Hi Energy Ign (1.4) 1.8

—NOTE—

For Air Injection Add (0.2) *0.2*

B2—TUNE-UP, MAJOR

Includes: Check compression, clean or renew & adjust spark plugs. R&R dist & renew points & condenser. Adjust ignition timing, carburetor & fan belts. Clean battery terminals & service manifold heat control valve. Clean fuel pump sediment bowl & replace or clean fuel line filter.

1969-74 Exc (3.2) 4.0
High Energy Ign (2.7) 3.5
1975 (2.7) 3.5

—NOTE—

To Clean PCV Valve Add (0.3) *0.4*
To Renew PCV Valve Add (0.2) *0.2*
For Air Injection, Add (0.2) *0.2*

B3—TUNE-UP,MAJOR & OVERHAUL CARBURETOR

1969-74 Exc (5.1) 5.9
High Energy Ign (4.6) 5.3
1975 (4.6) 5.3

—NOTE—

For Air Injection, Add (0.3) *0.3*
For Cruise Control Add (0.1) *0.2*
If Air Cond. Obstructs Work Add (0.3) *0.5*

B4—POINTS & CONDENSER, RENEW

Includes set timing. Does not include R & R distributor

1969-74 Exc Hi Energy Ign (0.4) 0.6

—NOTE—

For Air Injection, Add (0.2) *0.2*

B5—SPARK PLUGS, CLEAN & ADJUST OR RENEW

1969-75—
Clean (0.5) 0.6
Renew (0.3) 0.5

—NOTE—

For Air Injection Add (0.2) *0.2*

B6—COMPRESSION, TEST

1969-75—
L/Air Cond. (0.8) 1.0
W/Air Cond. (1.1) 1.2

—NOTE—

For Air Injection, Add (0.2) *0.2*

B7—IGNITION TIMING, SET

All Models (0.3) 0.3

B8—DISTRIBUTOR,R&R OR RENEW

All Models (0.4) 0.5

B9—DISTRIBUTOR, OVERHAUL (UNIT OFF)

1969-75 (0.6) 1.1

B9A— DISTRIBUTOR, ADJUST ON STROBOSCOPE (UNIT OFF)

All Models (0.4) 0.4

B10— DISTRIBUTOR CAP, RENEW

All Models (0.3) 0.4

B11— IGNITION CABLE SET, RENEW

Time allowance covers installation of factory supplied sets.

1969-75 (0.5) 0.7

B12— VACUUM CONTROL UNIT, RENEW

Includes R & R distributor.

1969-75 (0.5) 0.6

B13— IGNITION COIL, RENEW

1969-75 (0.2) 0.2

B14— STARTER & IGNITION SWITCH,RENEW

1969-75 (0.4) 0.5

B16— STEERING & IGNITION LOCK &ACTUATOR, RENEW

1969-75 (1.7) 2.3

Parts — Tune-Up & Ignition — Parts

FIG.1-TUNE-UP & IGNITION

(For Parts Identification Only)

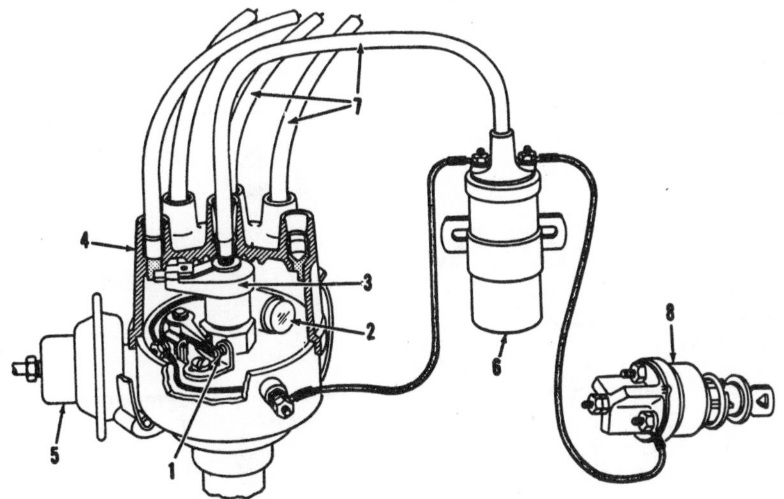

DISTRIBUTOR ASS'Y:

	Part No.	Price
1968-70	1111939	44.05
1971-72	1112108	44.30
1973	1112229	44.30
1974 Exc (See Note)	1112835	43.10
High Energy Ign	1112839	145.00
High Alt Eng, Exc	1112845	43.10
High Energy Ign	1112855	145.00
1975, Exc (See Note)	1112891	145.00
Elec Fuel Inj	1112892	

—NOTE—

For 1974 Models, When Used For California Cars, Use The California Type Vacuum Control Unit.

1—IGNITION POINT SET:

	Part No.	Price
1968-74—		
Clip Type Terminal	1931988	4.40
Screw Type Terminal	1966289	4.40

2—CONDENSER:

	Part No.	Price
1969-75 (Exc Below)	1932004	1.51
1974-75 Capacitor	1876154	2.33

3—ROTOR:

	Part No.	Price
1969-74, Exc	1852722	2.10
High Energy Ign	1875943	3.08

4—DISTRIBUTOR CAP:

	Part No.	Price
1969-74, Exc	800063	6.75
High Energy Ign	1875963	9.50

5—VACUUM CONTROL UNIT:

	Part No.	Price
1968-72	1973409	3.22
1973	1973460	3.22
1974 Exc	1973484	3.32
High Energy Ign	1973487	3.77
Calif, Exc	1973486	3.32
High Energy Ign	1973489	3.77
1975, Exc	1973526	5.40
Calif	1973528	5.40

6—IGNITION COIL:

	Part No.	Price
1969-74, Exc	1115238	13.65
High Energy Ign	1875894	23.10

7—IGNITION CABLE SET:

	Part No.	Price
1969-70	6291064	11.85
1971-74, Exc	8918453	13.00
High Energy Ign	8914949	32.61

8—IGNITION SWITCH:

	Part No.	Price
1969-73—		
Exc.Below	1990095	5.25
Tilt & Tel. Wheel	1990096	5.55
1974-75, Exc	1990098	5.70
Tilt & Teles Wheel	1990099	6.20
Air Cushion Sys	1990100	5.75

Time — Fuel System & Intake Manifold (Group C) — Time

OPERATION INDEX

C1—CARBURETOR, R & R OR RENEW
1969-75 (0.8) 0.9

—NOTE—

For Cruise Control, Add (0.1) *0.2*
For Auto. Level, Add(0.1) *0.2*

C2—CARBURETOR, R & R & OVERHAUL
1969-75 (2.3) 2.6

—NOTE—

For Cruise Control, Add (0.1) *0.2*
For Auto. Level, Add (0.1) *0.2*

C3—AUTOMATIC CHOKE THERMOSTAT, RENEW
Includes: Adjust & check operation.
1969-75 (0.2) 0.2

C4—DASHPOT, RENEW
1969-75 (0.4) 0.4

C5—FUEL PUMP, R & R OR RENEW
1969-75 (0.6) 0.9

—NOTE—

For Auto Level, Add (0.4) *0.5*

C6—FUEL TANK, R & R OR RENEW
1969-75—
R & R (1.0) 1.3
Renew (1.2) 1.5

C7—FUEL SYSTEM, CLEAN
Includes: R & R tank, blow out lines & clean or renew fuel filter.
1969-75 (1.4) 1.7

C8—INTAKE MANIFOLD GASKETS, RENEW
1968-69 (1.0) ②1.5
1970-75 (1.0) ①1.5
①*For Air Cond., Add (0.3)* *0.5*
②*For Air Cond., Add (0.6)* *0.7*

Parts — Fuel System & Intake Manifold — Parts

PARTS INDEX

1—CARBURETOR ASS'Y:
Year	Part No.	Price
1968-69	7016932	94.30
1970	7047030	99.35
1971	7041777	104.35
1972	7047231	104.35
1973	7047331	104.35
1974 Exc	7047430	104.35
California	7047431	104.35
High Alt	17050632	104.35

2—CARBURETOR OFF CAR REPAIR KIT:
Year	Part No.	Price
1967-69	7039144	9.00
1970-74	7039244	9.00

2A—CARBURETOR MAJOR OVERHAUL KIT
Year	Part No.	Price
1968-69	7036338	18.00
1970	7036850	17.90
1971-72	7041765	18.40
1973-74, Exc	7046650	18.40
High Alt	17050633	18.40

3—CARBURETOR GASKET KIT:
Year	Part No.	Price
1967-69	7016751	5.70
1970-72	7036852	5.02
1973-74	7046652	5.40

4—CHOKE COIL & COVER:
Year	Part No.	Price
1968-69	7037711	7.70
1970-71	7038254	10.75
1972	7042091	10.75
1973	7043091	10.75
1974, Exc	7044092	18.80
Calif	7044093	18.80

5—CHOKE VACUUM CONTROL ASS'Y:
Year	Part No.	Price
1969	7037625	6.25
1970	7038309	10.05
1971 (Early)	7046535	8.65
1971 (Late)	7045921	8.65
1972	7045921	8.65
1973-74	7046234	8.65

6—THROTTLE RETURN CHECK ASSEMBLY:
Year	Part No.	Price
1966-70	1483692	7.55

7—FUEL PUMP
Year	Part No.	Price
1969-72—		
Less Air Cond	6470007	18.76
With Air Cond	6417494	18.94
1973-74—		
Less Air Cond	6470782	18.94
With Air Cond	6470781	18.94
1975	6470960	18.98

8—FUEL TANK:
Year	Part No.	Price
1969	3633265	72.05
1970—		
Exc. Below	3633265	72.05
Calif. Prod	3633442	76.45
1971-72	3633537	76.45
1973	3515810	76.45
1974	3516106	76.45
1975, Exc	3516252	74.25
Elec Fuel Inj	3516253	70.20

9—INTAKE MANIFOLD GASKET:
Year	Part No.	Price
1969-75 (Kit)	3633793	7.85

10—ACCELERATOR PUMP
Year	Part No.	Price
1969-74	7029989	3.10

11—ACCEL PUMP NEEDLE & SEAT
Year	Part No.	Price
1969-74	7035142	3.30

12—ELEC FUEL INJ (PARTS)
Part	Part No.
Control Unit	1606013
Support	1606553
Injector	1606771
Switch	1606785
Sensor (Oxygen)	1606014
Sensor (Switch)	1606011
Sensor (Temp)	1606774

CADILLAC ELDORADO

Time — Emission Controls (Group AB) — Time

OPERATION INDEX

AB1—POSITIVE CRANKCASE VENTILATOR (P.C.V.) VALVE, CLEAN OR RENEW
Clean (0.3) 0.5
Renew (0.2) 0.2

AB2—EMISSION CONTROL (CCS), CHECK
Includes: Check & adjust carburetor & ignition timing.
All Models (0.6) 1.0

AB6—AIR PUMP, R & R OR RENEW
1968-69 (0.7) 1.0
1971-75 (0.6) 0.9

—NOTE—

To Replace Diverter Valve, Add (0.2) *0.3*

AB7—DIVERTER VALVE, RENEW (ON CAR)
1969-75 (0.3) 0.3

AB9—HOSES, RENEW
1967-69 (Each) (0.2) 0.2

AB12—CHECK VALVE, RENEW
1969-75 (0.2) 0.2

AB14—AIR PUMP BELT, RENEW
All Models (0.4) 0.5

AB15—INJECTION REACTOR MANIFOLD ASS'Y, R & R OR RENEW
1969-75—
Left Side (0.4) 0.7
Right Side (0.3) 0.5
Both Sides (0.7) 1.1
Crossover (0.2) 0.3

AB16—AIR CLEANER MOTOR, RENEW
1970-75 (0.4) 0.6

AB17—AIR CLEANER SENSOR, RENEW
1970-75 (0.2) 0.3

AB18—FUEL VAPOR CANNISTER, R&R OR RENEW
1970-75 (0.2) 0.3

AB19—TEMPERATURE SENSOR, RENEW (CCS)
1970-75 (0.2) 0.3

AB20—EXHAUST GAS RECIRCULATION VALVE, RENEW
1973-75 (0.3) 0.5

AB21—EGR TIME DELAY VALVE, RENEW
1973-75 (0.2) 0.3

Parts — Emission Controls — Parts

PARTS INDEX

1—AIR INJECTION REACTOR PUMP:
1969-74 .... 7806286 48.05
1975 7817810

2—AIR DIVERTER VALVE:
1969-75 .... 7030761 11.60

3—AIR INJECTION CHECK VALVE:
1969-75 .... 5354987 3.66

4—CRANKCASE VENTILATOR VALVE:
1969-75 .... 6421972 1.94

5—DISTRIBUTOR THERMOSTATIC VACUUM SWITCH:
1969-74 .... 3015636 11.20

6—FUEL VAPOR CANNISTER:
1970 .... 7028045 27.20
1971-74 .... 7028131 21.95
1975 .... 7043715 21.95

7—EVAPORATOR EMISSION SYSTEM SEPARATOR:
1970 .... 7028034 9.50
1971-72 .... 407742 14.85

8—AIR CLEANER MOTOR (C. C. S.):
1970-75 .... 6484245 3.31

9—AIR CLEANER SENSOR (C. C. S.):
1970-75 .... 6486587 4.26

10—DISTRIBUTOR VACUUM ADVANCE SOLENOID:
1970-72 .... 1114435 7.60

11—ANTI-DIESELING SOLENOID:
1972-74 .... 1604093 7.40

12—EXHAUST GAS RECIRCULATION VALVE
1973—
To Carburetor 1602030 2.03
On Intake Manifold Exc 7030695 16.85
California 7040556 16.85
1974-75
To Carburetor 1604913 2.03
Back Pressure Transducer 1603900 16.45
On Intake Manifold Exc 7049869 16.85
California 7042840 16.85

Time — Tune-Up & Ignition (Group B) — Time

OPERATION INDEX

B1—TUNE-UP, MINOR
Includes: Renew points, condenser & plugs, set spark timing and adjust carb. Idle. Does not include R & R distributor.
1969-74 Exc Hi Energy Ign (1.4) 1.8

B2—TUNE-UP, MAJOR
Includes: Check compression, clean or renew and adjust spark plugs. Renew points and condenser. Adjust ignition timing, carburetor and fan belts. Clean battery terminals and service manifold heat control valve and replace or clean fuel line filter. Includes R & R distributor.
1969-74 Exc (3.2) 4.0
High Energy Ign (2.7) 3.5
1975 (2.7) 3.5

—NOTE—
To Clean PCV Valve Add (0.3) 0.4
To Renew PCV Valve, Add (0.2) 0.2

B3—TUNE-UP MAJOR & OVERHAUL CARBURETOR
1969-74 Exc (5.1) 5.9
High Energy Ign (4.6) 5.3
1975 (4.6) 5.3

—NOTE—
For Cruise Control, Or Auto. Level Control Add (0.1) 0.1

B4—POINTS & CONDENSER, RENEW
Includes set timing. Does not include R & R distributor.
1969-74 Exc Hi Energy Ign (0.4) 0.6

B5—SPARK PLUGS, CLEAN & ADJUST OR RENEW
1969-75—
Clean (0.5) 0.6
Renew (0.3) 0.5

B6—COMPRESSION, TEST
1969-75—
L/Air Cond. (0.8) 1.0
W/Air Cond. (1.1) 1.2

B7—IGNITION TIMING, SET
1969-75 (0.2) 0.3

B8—DISTRIBUTOR, R & R OR RENEW
1969-75 (0.4) 0.5

B9—DISTRIBUTOR, OVERHAUL (UNIT OFF)
1969-75 (0.6) 1.1

B9A—DISTRIBUTOR, ADJUST ON STROBOSCOPE (UNIT OFF)
All Models (0.4) 0.4

B10—DISTRIBUTOR CAP, RENEW
1969-75 (0.3) 0.4

B11—IGNITION CABLE SET, RENEW
Time allowance covers installation of factory supplied sets.
1969-75 (0.5) 0.7

B12—VACUUM CONTROL UNIT, RENEW
Includes: R & R distributor.
1969-75 (0.5) 0.6

B13—IGNITION COIL, RENEW
1969-75 (0.2) 0.2

B14—STARTER & IGNITION SWITCH, RENEW
1969-75 (0.4) 0.5

B16—STEERING & IGNITION LOCK & ACTUATOR, RENEW
1969-75—
Exc. Below (1.3) 2.0
Tilt & Telescope (2.1) 3.0

Parts — Tune-Up & Ignition — Parts

FIG. 1-TUNE-UP & IGNITION
(For Parts Identification Only)

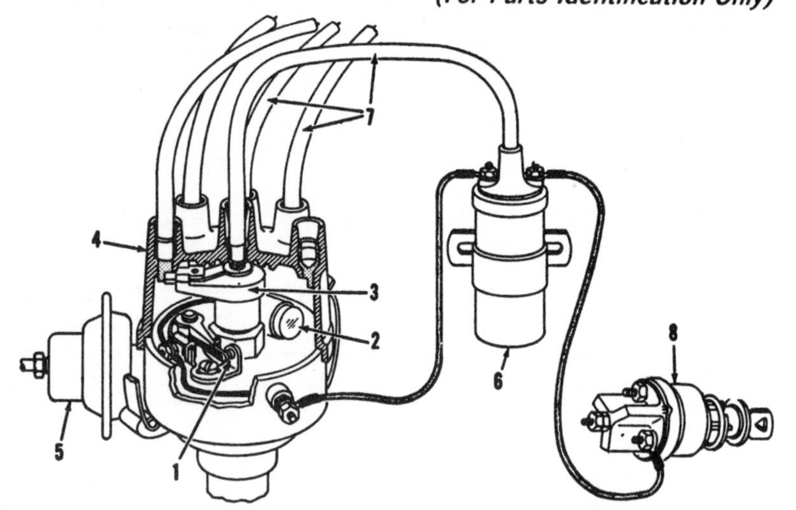

DISTRIBUTOR ASS'Y:

Year	Part No.	Price
1968-70	1111939	44.05
1971-72	1112108	44.30
1973	1112229	44.30
1974, Exc (See Note)	1112837	43.10
High Energy Ign	1112841	145.00
High Alt Eng. Exc	1112845	43.10
High Energy Ign	1112855	145.00
1975, Exc (See Note)	1112891	145.00
Elec Fuel Inj	1112892	

—NOTE—
For 1974 Models, When Used For California Cars, Use The California Type Vacuum Control Unit.

1—IGNITION POINT SET:

Year	Part No.	Price
1968-74—		
Clip Type Terminal	1931988	4.40
Screw Type Terminal	1966289	4.40

2—CONDENSER:

Year	Part No.	Price
1969-74 (Exc Below)	1932004	1.51
1974-75 Capacitor	1876154	2.33

3—ROTOR:

Year	Part No.	Price
1969-74, Exc	1852722	2.10
High Energy Ign	1875943	3.08

4—DISTRIBUTOR CAP:

Year	Part No.	Price
1969-74, Exc	800063	6.75
High Energy Ign	1875963	9.50

5—VACUUM CONTROL UNIT:

Year	Part No.	Price
1968-72	1973409	3.22
1973	1973460	3.22
1974 Exc	1973484	3.32
High Energy Ign	1973487	3.77
Calif, Exc	1973486	3.32
High Energy Ign	1973489	3.77
1975, Exc	1973526	5.40
Calif	1973528	5.40

6—IGNITION COIL:

Year	Part No.	Price
1969-74, Exc	1115238	13.65
High Energy Ign	1875894	23.10

7—IGNITION CABLE SET:

Year	Part No.	Price
1969-70	6291064	11.85
1971-74, Exc	8918453	13.00
High Energy Ign	8914949	32.61

8—IGNITION SWITCH:

Year	Part No.	Price
1969-73—		
Exc. Below	1990095	5.25
Tilt Wheel	1990096	5.55
1974-75, Exc	1990098	5.70
Tilt & Tel Wheel	1990099	6.20
Air Cushion Sys	1990100	5.75

Time — Fuel System & Intake Manifold (Group C) — Time

OPERATION INDEX

Operation	
Carburetor, R & R Or Renew (B)	*C1*
Carburetor, R & R & Overhaul (B)	*C2*
Needle & Seat, Renew (B)	*C2B*
Automatic Choke Thermostat, Renew (B)	*C3*
Dashpot, Renew (B)	*C4*
Fuel Pump, R & R Or Renew (B)	*C5*
Fuel Tank, R & R Or Renew (C)	*C6*
Fuel System, Clean (C)	*C7*
Intake Manifold Gaskets, Renew (B)	*C8*

C1—CARBURETOR, R & R OR RENEW

1969-75 (0.8) 0.9

—NOTE—
For Cruise Control, Add (0.1) 0.2
For Auto. Level Control, Add (0.1) 0.2

C2—CARBURETOR, R & R & OVERHAUL

1969-75 (2.3) 2.6

—NOTE—
For Cruise Control, Add (0.1) 0.2
For Auto. Level Control, Add (0.1) 0.2

C2B—NEEDLE & SEAT, RENEW

—NOTE—
Does Not Include R & R Carburetor

1969-75 (0.7) 0.9

C3—AUTOMATIC CHOKE THERMOSTAT, RENEW

Includes: Adjust & check operation.

1969-75 (0.2) 0.2

C4—DASHPOT, RENEW

1969-75 (0.4) 0.4

C5—FUEL PUMP, R & R OR RENEW

1969-75 (0.6) 0.9

C6—FUEL TANK, R & R OR RENEW

1969-75, R&R (1.0) 1.3
Renew (1.2) 1.5

C7—FUEL SYSTEM, CLEAN

Includes: R & R tank, blow out lines & clean or renew filter.

1969-75 (1.4) 1.7

C8—INTAKE MANIFOLD GASKETS, RENEW

1968-69—
L/Air Cond. (1.0) 1.5
W/Air Cond. (1.6) 2.4
1970-75—
L/Air Cond (1.0) 1.5
W/Air Cond (1.3) 2.1

Parts — Fuel System & Intake Manifold — Parts

PARTS INDEX

Carburetor Ass'y	*1*
Carburetor Off Car Repair Kit	*2*
Carb Major Overhaul Kit	*2A*
Carburetor Gasket Kit	*3*
Choke Coil & Cover	*4*
Throttle Return Check Ass'y	*5*
Choke Vacuum Control Ass'y	*6*
Fuel Pump	*7*
Fuel Tank	*8*
Intake Manifold Gasket	*9*
Accelerator Pump	*10*
Accelerator Pump Needle & Seat	*11*
Elect Fuel Injection	*12*

1—CARBURETOR ASS'Y:

Year	Part No.	Price
1968-69	7016932	94.30
1970	7047030	99.35
1971	7041777	104.35
1972	7047232	104.35
1973	7047332	104.35
1974 Exc	7047432	104.35
California	7047434	104.35
High Alt	17050631	104.35

2—CARBURETOR OFF CAR REPAIR KIT:

Year	Part No.	Price
1967-69	7039144	9.00
1970-74	7039244	9.00

2A—CARBURETOR MAJOR OVERHAUL KIT

Year	Part No.	Price
1969	7036645	18.45
1970	7036850	17.90
1971-72	7041778	18.40
1973-74, Exc	7046651	18.40
High Alt	17050633	18.40

3—CARBURETOR GASKET KIT:

Year	Part No.	Price
1967-69	7016751	5.70
1970-72	7036852	5.02
1973-74	7046652	5.40

4—CHOKE COIL & COVER:

Year	Part No.	Price
1968-69	7037711	7.70
1970-71	7038254	10.75
1972	7042091	10.75
1973 Exc	7043093	10.10
California	7043091	10.75
1974, Exc	7044092	18.80
Calif	7044093	18.80

5—THROTTLE RETURN CHECK ASS'Y:

Year	Part No.	Price
1967-70	1483692	7.55

6—CHOKE VACUUM CONTROL ASS'Y:

1969	7037625	6.25
1970	7038309	10.05
1971	7046535	8.65
1972	7045921	8.65
1973-74	7046234	8.65

7—FUEL PUMP:

1969-72—		
Exc Below	6470007	18.76
Air Cond	6417494	18.94
1973-74—		
Exc Below	6470782	18.94
Air Cond	6470781	18.94
1975	6470960	18.98

8—FUEL TANK:

1967-69	3633287	69.85
1970—		
Exc. California	3633287	69.85
California	3633461	76.45
1971-72	3633538	76.45
1973-74	3515809	76.45
1975, Exc	3516254	70.20
Elec Fuel Inj	3516255	70.20

9—INTAKE MANIFOLD GASKET:

1969-75 (Kit)	3633793	7.85

10—ACCELERATOR PUMP

1969-74	7029989★	3.10

11—ACCEL PUMP NEEDLE & SEAT

1969-74	7035142	3.30

12—ELEC FUEL INJ (PARTS)

Control Unit	1606013
Support	1606553
Injector	1606771
Switch	1606785
Sensor (Oxygen)	1606014
Sensor (Switch)	1606011
Sensor (Temp)	1606774

CAMARO • CHEVELLE • NOVA

Time — Emission Controls (Group AB) — Time

OPERATION INDEX

AB1—CRANKCASE VENT VALVE (PCV),CLEAN OR RENEW

All Models—
Clean (0.3) 0.5
Renew (0.2) 0.2

AB2—EMISSION CONTROL CHECK (CCS)

Includes adjust carburetor idle speed, mixture & ignition timing. Check PCV valve and renew if necessary.
1969-75 (0.5) 0.7

AB3A—DIAPHRAGM ASS'Y., RENEW

1969-71 (0.3) 0.4

AB5—AIR CLEANER TEMP. SENSOR, RENEW

1969-75 (0.3) 0.4

AB6—AIR PUMP, R & R OR RENEW

Includes R & R relief valve
1969-75—
Exc. Below (0.4) 0.6
396, 400, 402, 454 (0.7) 0.9

—NOTE—
To Renew, Add (0.2) *0.2*

AB8—AIR PUMP TUBES, RENEW

Includes R & R pump.
1969-75 (One)—
Exc. Below (0.5) 0.7
396, 400, 402, 454 (0.8) 1.0

AB9—HOSES, RENEW

Does not include R & R pump.
Each (0.2) 0.3

AB10—CONTROL VALVE, RENEW

1969-75 (Each) (0.2) 0.4

AB11—RELIEF VALVE, RENEW

Includes R & R pump.
1969-75—
Exc. Below (0.6) 0.8
396, 400, 402, 454 (0.9) 1.2

AB12—CHECK VALVE, RENEW

1967-73 (0.2) 0.5

AB13A—CENTRIFUGAL FILTER, RENEW

Includes R & R pump pulley.
1969-75 (0.3) 0.5

AB14—AIR PUMP BELT, RENEW

1969-75 (0.2) 0.2

AB15—AIR INJECTION MANIFOLD ASS'Y., R & R OR RENEW

1969-75 Four & Six Cyl. (0.6) 0.7
1969-75 V8—
One (0.6) 0.7
Both (1.0) 1.2

AB18—EXHAUST GAS RECIRCULATION VALVE, RENEW

1973-75 (0.2) 0.4

AB19—TRANS CONTROLLED SPARK SOLENOID, RENEW

1973-75 (0.2) 0.4

AB20—TRANS CONTROLLED SPARK SWITCH, RENEW

1973-75 Exc (0.3) 0.4
TH400 (0.6) 0.8

AB24—FUEL VAPOR CANNISTER, RENEW

1970-73 (0.3) 0.5

AB25—FUEL VAPOR SEPARATOR, RENEW

1970-73 (0.4) 0.6

Parts — Emission Controls — Parts

PARTS INDEX

1—AIR INJECTOR REACTOR PUMP:

1968-72	7806686	46.85
1973-75 Six	7803943	59.95
1973-75 V8	7803948	45.70

2—AIR INJECTOR PUMP DIVERTER VALVE:

1969 Six	7029198	14.45
1969 V8—		
Exc. Below	7029295	14.45
V8-396	7029297	14.45
1970-71—		
Exc. Below	7029297	14.45
Sp. Hi-Perf. V8-350	7029295	14.45
1972-74 Six	7045625	14.45
1972 V8—		
Exc. Below	7029295	14.45
V8-402,454	7029297	14.45
1973-74 V8 Except	7029295	14.45
454	7046328	14.45
1975 Six, Exc	17051182	
Nova	17051180	
1975 V8, Exc	7029295	14.45
Calif Emission	17051179	
V8-454	7046328	14.45

3—EXHAUST GAS RECIRCULATION VALVE

1973 Six Exc	7035171	16.85
W/Auto Trans	7035169	16.85
1973 V8-307	7035170	16.85
V8-350 (Synchro Trans)—		
2 Bar Carb	7040042	16.85
4 Bar Carb Exc	7040318	16.85
Spec Hi Perf	7040299	16.85
V8-350 (Auto Trans)—		
2 Bar Carb	7040437	16.85
4 Bar Carb Exc	7035172	16.85
Spec Hi Perf	7047065	16.85
V8-454	7047066	16.85
1974 Six Exc	7043042	16.85
W/Auto Trans	7035169	16.85
1974 V8-350 (Synchro Trans)—		
2 Bar Carb	7035170	16.85
4 Bar Carb Exc	7040599	16.85
Spec Hi Perf	7040299	16.85
1974 V8-350 (Auto Trans)—		
2 Bar Carb	7040437	16.85
4 Bar Carb	7041409	16.85
1974 V8-400, 2 Bar	7035172	16.85
4 Bar	7041416	16.85
1974 V8-454	7049867	16.85
1975 Six, Exc	7043037	
Auto Trans	7043038	
1975 V8-350—		
Std Trans, Exc	7043133	
Sp Hi-Perf	7043137	
Auto Trans	7043132	
1975 V8-400, Exc	17051418	
Calif Emission	17050494	

4—CHECK VALVE:
1969-75 ....5361992★ 4.41

5—AIR INJECTOR PUMP DRIVE BELT:

—NOTE—
Order By Complete Model Description.

6—CRANKCASE VENTILATOR VALVE:
1969-70 Four ....6422717★ 1.94
1969-70 Six ....6422718★ 1.94
1969-72 V8 ....6423695★ 1.94
1971-72 Six ....6422717★ 1.94
1973 Six ....6487534★ 1.89
V8 Exc 6487532 1.89
Spec Hi Perf 6484525 1.91
1974-75, Six ....6487936★ 2.20
V8, Exc ....6487779★ 2.20
Sp Hi-Perf 6487945 2.20

7—FUEL VAPOR CANISTER:
1970—
2 Bar. Carb 7036964 27.45
4 Bar. Carb ....7030605★ 26.30
Sp. Hi-Perf. 7036968 30.40
1971 ....7030605★ 26.30
1972-75 (Exc Below) ....7030605★ 26.30
1974-75 V8 ....7028131★ 21.95

8—FUEL VAPOR CANISTER FILTER:
1970-74 ....7026014★ 1.05

9—FUEL TANK EVAPORATIVE SEPARATOR:
1970 Camaro ....7028052★ 10.00
1970 Chevelle—
Exc. Below 7028021 9.65
Sta. Wagon ....7028052★ 10.00
1970 Nova ....7028052★ 10.00
1971-72 ....7043728★ 10.45
1973 Camaro ....407742★ 14.85

Time — Tune-Up & Ignition (Group B) — Time

OPERATION INDEX

B1—TUNE-UP (MINOR)
Includes renew points, condenser & plugs, set spark timing and adjust carburetor idle. Does not include R & R distributor.
CAMARO. CHEVELLE:
1968-74—
Six Cyl. (0.9) 1.3
V8 (Exc. Below) (1.3) 1.7
V8-396-402 (1.2) 1.6
NOVA
1969-74—
Exc. V8 (0.9) 1.3
V8 (1.8) 2.0
—NOTE—
For Air Cond., Add (0.2) *0.4*

B2—TUNE-UP, (MAJOR)
Includes check compression, clean or renew & adjust spark plugs, R & R distributor and renew points & condenser, adjust timing, carburetor & fan belts, clean battery terminals and service air cleaner. Check coil and service manifold heat control valve and clean or renew fuel line filter.
CAMARO. CHEVELLE:
1968-74 Six (2.5) 3.0
1968-74 V8—
Exc. Below (2.8) 3.3
396-400-402, 454 (2.7) 3.3
1975 Six (2.0) 2.5
1975 V8 (2.3) 2.8
NOVA
1969-74—
Exc. V8 (2.5) 3.0
V8 (2.8) 3.3
1975 Six (2.0) 2.5
1975 V8 (2.3) 2.8
—NOTE—
For Air Cond, Add (0.2) *0.4*

B3—TUNE-UP MAJOR & OVERHAUL CARBURETOR
CAMARO. CHEVELLE:
1968-74 Six (3.6) 4.3
1968-74 V8—
2 Barrel (4.3) 5.6
4 Barrel—
Exc. Below (5.1) 6.4
Holley 4160 (4.9) 6.2
Quadrajet (4.5) 5.8
1975 Six (3.1) 3.8
1975 V8—
2 Barrel (3.8) 5.1
4 Barrel (4.6) 5.9
NOVA
1968-74 (Exc. V8) (3.7) 4.4
1968-74 V8—
2 Barrel (4.9) 6.2
4 Barrel—
Exc. Below (5.7) 6.9
Quadrajet (5.1) 6.4
1975 Six (3.2) 3.8
1975 V8 (4.3) 5.6
—NOTE—
With Air Cond, Add (0.2) *0.4*

B4—POINTS & CONDENSER, RENEW
1968-74—
Four (0.4) 0.5
Six (0.4) 0.5
V8 (0.5) 0.6

B5—SPARK PLUGS, CLEAN & ADJUST OR RENEW
CAMARO. CHEVELLE:
1969-75 Six (0.3) 0.4
1969-75 V8—
Exc. Below (0.6) 0.7
396, 400, 402, 454 (0.5) 0.6
NOVA
1969-75 Six (0.3) 0.4
1968-70 Four (0.3) 0.4
1969-75 V8 (Exc. Below)—
L/Air Cond. (1.1) 1.3
W/Air Cond. (1.3) 1.5
1969-71 V8-396, 402 (0.5) 0.6

B6—COMPRESSION, TEST
CAMARO. CHEVELLE:
1969-75 Six (0.4) 0.5
1969-75 V8—
Exc. Below (0.7) 0.8
396, 400, 402, 454 (0.6) 0.7
NOVA
1969-75 Six (0.4) 0.5
1967-70 Four (0.4) 0.5
1969-75 V8 (Exc. V8-396-402)—
L/Air Cond. (1.2) 1.4
W/Air Cond. (1.4) 1.6
1969-71 V8-396-402 (0.6) 0.7

B7—IGNITION TIMING, SET
1969-75 (0.3) 0.3

B8—DISTRIBUTOR, R & R OR RENEW
Includes adjust timing.
1969-75 (0.5) 0.5

B9—DISTRIBUTOR, OVERHAUL (UNIT OFF)
1969-75 (0.5) 1.0

B9A—DISTRIBUTOR, ADJUST ON STROBOSCOPE, (UNIT OFF)
All Models (0.4) 0.4

B10—DISTRIBUTOR CAP, RENEW
1969-75 (0.2) 0.3

B11—IGNITION CABLE SET, RENEW
Time allowance covers installation of factory supplied sets only.
1969-75—
Four Or Six (0.3) 0.4
V8 (0.5) 0.6

B12—VACUUM CONTROL UNIT, RENEW
Includes adjust ignition timing & dwell. Does not include R & R distributor.
V8 (0.5) 0.6
Six (0.3) 0.4
Four (0.3) 0.4

B13—IGNITION COIL, RENEW
1969-75 (0.3) 0.3

B14—IGNITION SWITCH, RENEW
CAMARO:
1969 (0.3) 0.4
1970-75 (0.5) 0.7
CHEVELLE:
1969-75 (0.5) 0.7
NOVA
1969 (0.3) 0.4
1970-75 (0.5) 0.7

B16—STEERING & IGNITION LOCK & ACTUATOR, RENEW
1969-75 (0.9) 1.5

Parts — Tune-Up & Ignition — Parts

DISTRIBUTOR ASS'Y:
CAMARO:
1968-69 6-230—
Exc. Below 1110459 34.90
Auto. Trans 1110460 34.90
1968-69 6-250—
Exc. Below 1110465 37.80
Auto. Trans 1110466 37.80
1969 V8-302 ....1111480 43.70
1969 V8-327, 350—
Synchro-Mesh 1111482 40.60
Auto. Trans 1112005 42.55
1969 V8-396—
Exc. Below 1111998 46.25
Hi. Perf 1111999 45.10
Sp. Hi. Perf 1111499 39.80
1970 Six—
Synchro-Mesh 1110465 37.80
Auto. Trans 1110466 37.80
1970 V8-307—
Synchro-Mesh 1111995 43.25
Auto. Trans 1112005 42.55
1970 V8-350—
Synchro-Mesh 1111996 44.30
Auto. Trans.—
Exc. Below 1112002 43.65
Sp. Hi. Perf 1112019 45.50
1970 V8-396—
Exc. Below 1112001 43.75
Hi. Perf.—
Less TH 400 ....1111999 45.10
With TH 400 ....1111998 46.25
Sp. Hi. Perf 1112000 46.20
1971-72 Six 1110489 34.25
1971 V8-307—
Synchro-Mesh 1112005 42.55

Auto. Trans	1112039	42.95
1971 V8-350 (2 Bar. Carb.)—		
Synchro-Mesh	1112042	42.95
Auto. Trans	1112005	42.55
1971 V8-350 (4 Bar. Carb.)—		
Synchro-Mesh—		
Exc. Below	1112044	44.15
Sp. Hi. Perf	1112049	46.20
Auto. Trans.—		
Exc. Below	1112045	42.95
Sp. Hi. Perf	1112074	50.75
1971 V8-400—		
2 Bar. Carb	1112056	44.55
4 Bar. Carb	1112057	44.75
1972 V8-307—		
Synchro-Mesh	1112005	42.55
Auto. Trans.	1112039	42.95
1972 V8-350—		
2 Bar. Carb.	1112005	42.55
4 Bar. Carb.—		
Synchro-Mesh—		
Exc. Below	1112044	44.15
Sp. Hi-Perf.	1112095	47.95
Auto Trans.—		
Exc. Below	1112045	42.95
Sp. Hi-Perf.	1112095	47.95
1972 V8-400	1112099	43.90
1972 V8-402	1112057	44.75
1973-74 Six	1110499	35.25
1973-74 V8-350—		
2 Bar Carb (73)	1112168	42.55
2 Bar Carb (74)	1112844	44.30
4 Bar Carb—		
Except Below	1112093	44.15
Std. Tr. (Sp. Hi-Perf)	1112153	43.65
Auto Trans, Exc	1112094	44.15
W/Spec Hi Perf	1112148	47.95
Calif Emission (74)	1112543	42.95
High Energy Ign.	1112528	145.00
1973 V8-307—		
Synchro-Mesh	1112227	43.75
Auto Trans	1112102	44.15
1975 Six	1112863	118.00
V8-350, 2 Bar	1112880	145.00
4 Bar, Exc	1112888	145.00
Sp Hi-Perf	1112883	145.00
CHEVELLE:		
1968-69 6-230—		
Exc. Below	1110459	34.90
Auto. Trans	1110460	34.90
1968-69 6-250—		
Synchro-Mesh	1110465	37.80
Auto. Trans	1110466	37.80
1969 V8-307, 327	1111995	43.25
1969 V8-396—		
Exc. Below	1111998	46.25
Hi. Perf	1111999	45.10
Sp. Hi. Perf	1111499	39.80
1970 Six—		
Synchro-Mesh	1110465	37.80
Auto. Trans	1110466	37.80
1970 V8-307—		
Synchro-Mesh	1111995	43.25
Auto. Trans	1112005	42.55
1970 V8-350—		
Synchro-Mesh	1112001	43.75
Auto. Trans.—		
Exc. Below	1112002	43.65
Hi- Perf	1111997	43.85
1970 V8-396—		
Exc. Below	1111999	45.10
Spec. Hi- Perf	1112000	46.20
1970 V8-400 (2 Bar. Carb.)—		
Synchro-Mesh	1111492	46.15
Auto. Trans	1111494	44.00
1970 V8-400 (4 Bar.)	1111998	46.25
1970 V8-454—		
Exc. Below	1111963	45.80
Spec. Hi - Perf	1111437	49.15
1971-72 Six	1110489	34.25
1971 V8-307—		
Synchro-Mesh	1112005	42.55
Auto. Trans	1112039	42.95
1971 V8-350 (2 Bar. Carb.)—		
Synchro-Mesh	1112042	42.95
Auto. Trans	1112005	42.55
1971 V8-350 (4 Bar. Carb.)—		
Synchro-Mesh	1112044	44.15
Auto Trans	1112045	42.95
1971 V8-400—		
2 Bar. Carb	1112056	44.55
4 Bar. Carb	1112057	44.75
1971 V8-454—		
Exc. Below	1112163	42.00
Sp. Hi. Perf—		
Std. Trans	1112075	48.20
Auto. Trans	1112054	43.80
1972 V8-307—		
Synchro-Mesh	1112005	42.55
Auto. Trans.	1112039	42.95
1972 V8-350—		
2 Bar Carb	1112005	42.55
4 Bar. Carb.—		
Synchro-Mesh—		
Exc Below	1112044	44.15
Sp Hi Perf	1112095	47.95
Auto. Trans.—		
Exc. Below	1112045	42.95
Sp Hi Perf	1112095	47.95
1972 V8-400	1112099	43.90
1972 V8-402	1112057	44.75
1972 V8-454	1112163	42.00
1973-74 Six	1110499	35.25
1973 V8-307 Exc	1112227	43.75
W/Auto Trans	1112102	44.15
1973-74 V8-350—		
2 Bar (73)	1112168	42.55
2 Bar. (74)	1112844	44.30
4 Bar Exc	1112093	44.15
Auto Trans (73)	1112094	44.15
Calif Emission (74)	1112543	42.95
1973-74 V8-454	1112113	46.20
1974, V8-400, 4 Bar.	1112545	44.75
2 Bar.	1112846	44.75
1975 Six	1112863	118.00
V8-350	1112880	145.00
V8-400	1112882	145.00
V8-454	1112886	145.00
NOVA		
1968-70 6-230—		
Exc. Below	1110459	34.90
Auto. Trans	1110460	34.90
1968-70 6-250—		
Exc. Below	1110465	37.80
Auto. Trans	1110466	37.80
1969-70 Four—		
Synchro-Mesh	1110457	38.00
Auto. Trans	1110458	38.60
1969 V8-307, 327	1111995	43.25
1969 V8-350—		
Synchro-Mesh	1112001	43.75
Auto. Trans	1112002	43.65
1969 V8-396—		
Exc. Below	1111999	45.10
Auto. Trans	1111998	46.25
1970 V8-307—		
Synchro-Mesh	1111995	43.25
Auto. Trans	1112005	42.55
1970 V8-350—		
Synchro-Mesh	1112001	43.75
Auto. Trans	1111997	43.85
1970 V8-396—		
Exc. Below	1111998	46.25
Hi Perf	1111999	45.10
Spec. Hi Perf	1112000	46.20
1971-72 Six	1110489	34.25
1971 V8-307—		
Synchro-Mesh	1112005	42.55
Auto. Trans	1112039	42.95
1971 V8-350 (2 Bar. Carb.)—		
Synchro-Mesh	1112042	42.95
Auto. Trans	1112005	42.55
1971 V8-350 (4 Bar. Carb.)—		
Synchro-Mesh	1112044	44.15
Auto. Trans	1112045	42.95
1971 V8-400—		
2 Bar. Carb	1112056	44.55
4 Bar. Carb	1112057	44.75
1972 V8-307—		
Synchro-Mesh	1112005	42.55
Auto. Trans.	1112039	42.95
1972 V8-350—		
2 Bar. Carb.	1112005	42.55
4 Bar. Carb.—		
Synchro-Mesh—		
Exc. Below	1112044	44.15
Sp. Hi-Perf.	1112095	47.95
Auto. Trans.—		
Exc. Below	1112045	42.95
Sp. Hi-Perf.	1112095	47.95
1973-74 Six	1110499	35.25
1973 V8-307 Exc	1112227	43.75
Auto Trans	1112102	44.15
1973-74 V8-350—		
2 Bar (73)	1112168	42.55
2 Bar (74)	1112844	44.30
4 Bar Exc	1112093	44.15
Auto Trans (73)	1112094	44.15
Calif Emission (74)	1112543	42.95
1975 Six	1112863	118.00
V8-350, 2 Bar	1112880	145.00
4 Bar	1112888	145.00

FIG 1-TUNE-UP & IGNITION

(For Parts Identification Only)

1—IGNITION POINT SET

1969-70 Four	1954557	3.40
1969 V8	1931988	4.40
1969-74 Six	1954557	3.40
1970 V8—		
Exc. Below	1931988	4.40
V8-396 Spec. Hi Perf	1966294	5.05
1971-72 V8—		
Exc. Below	1931988	4.40
V8-350 Spec. Hi-Perf	1966294	5.05
V8-454	1966294	5.05
1973 V8 Exc	1931988	4.40
454 & Spec Hi Perf	1966294	5.05
1974 V8	1876600	7.25

2—CONDENSER:

1969-74 (Exc. Below)	1928111	1.51
1969-74 V8 (Exc Below)	1932004	1.51
1974-75 Capacitor	1876154	2.33

3—ROTOR:

1969-74 (Exc. Below)	800056	1.19
1969-74 V8, Exc	1852722	2.10
High Energy Ign.	1875943	3.08

4—DISTRIBUTOR CAP:

1969-70 Four	1962446	3.60
1969-74 Six	1971324	3.58
1969-74 V8, Exc.	800061	5.95
High Energy Ign.	1875963	9.50
1974-75 Cover	1875960	2.73

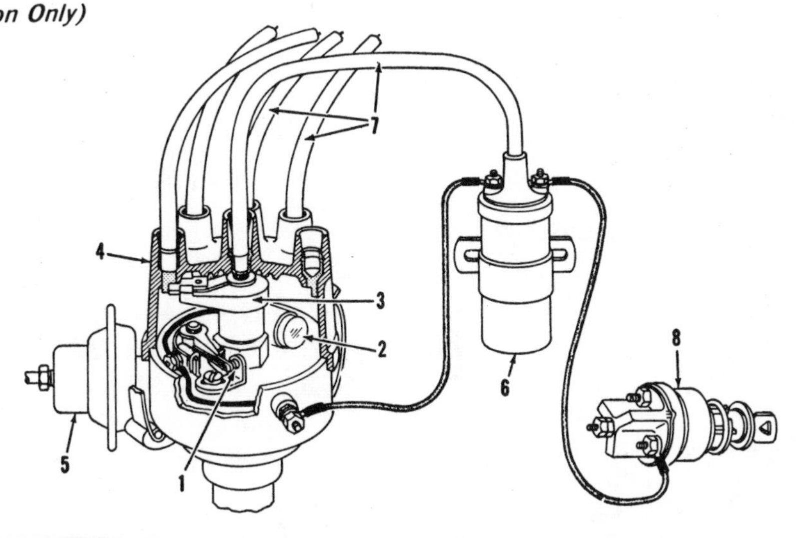

5—VACUUM CONTROL UNIT:

Model	Part No.	Price
1969-70 Four, Six	1116217	3.57
1969 V8-350—		
2 Bar. Carb	1973421	3.21
4 Bar. Carb	1115355	3.19
1969-70 V8-396—		
Exc. Below	1116163	3.05
High Perf	1115355	3.19
1969-70 V8-307—		
Exc. Below	1115355	3.19
Auto. Trans	1115357	3.20
1970 V8-350—		
Exc. Below	1973421	3.21
Hi-Perf.—		
L/Auto. Trans	1968861	3.21
W/Auto. Trans	1115357	3.20
1970 V8-400—		
2 Bar. Carb	1115355	3.19
4 Bar. Carb	1116163	3.05
1970 V8-454	1116163	3.05
1971-72 Six	1973434	3.58
1971-72 V8-307—		
Synchro-Mesh	1115357	3.20
Auto. Trans	1973436	3.16
1971 V8-350 (2 Bar. Carb.)—		
Synchro-Mesh	1973436	3.16
Auto. Trans	1115357	3.20
1971 V8-350 (4 Bar)	1973437	3.16
1971 V8-400—		
2 Bar. Carb	1973438	3.16
4 Bar. Carb	1973436	3.16
1971 V8-454—		
Exc. Below	1973436	3.16
Sp. Hi-Perf	1973439	3.16
1972 V8-350—		
2 Bar. Carb.	1115357	3.20
4 Bar. Carb.	1973437	3.16
1972 V8-400, 402	1973436	3.16
1972 V8-454	1973436	3.16
1973-74 Six	1973428	3.25
1973 V8-307	1973448	3.21
1973-74 V8-350—		
2 Bar Carb	1973469	3.54
4 Bar Carb Exc	1973446	3.16
Spec Hi Perf (73)	1973448	3.21
Spec Hi Perf (74)	1973482	3.60
1973-74 V8-454	1116212	3.52
1974 V8-400, 2 Bar	1973503	3.24
4 Bar., Exc.	1973459	3.29
Calif. Emission	1973437	3.16
2 Bar W Calif Emiss	1973508	5.20

6 IGNITION COIL:

Model	Part No.	Price
1966-69—		
Exc. Below	1115202	13.50
Transistor Ign	1115207	15.45
1970-74—		
W/1.8 Ohm Wire	1115202	13.50
W/1.3 Ohm Wire	1115238	13.65

7—IGNITION CABLE SET:

Model	Part No.	Price
1969-70 Four	2986603	4.92
1969 Six	2986606	7.30
1969 (Exc. Below)	8912493	18.26
1969 V8-396	8909665	17.76
1970-74 Six	8909903	7.54
1970 V8—		
Exc. Below	8912493	18.26
V8-396, 400, 454	8909665	17.76
1971-74 V8—		
Exc. Below	8912493	18.26
V8-400, 402, 454	8909665	17.76
V8-400 (73-74)	8912493	18.26
High Energy Ign. (Harness)—		
V8-350 Sp. Hi-Perf	8918699	28.73
V8-400	8908551	35.20
V8-454	8908553	35.20
1975 Six	8908517	
V8	8908551	35.20

8—IGNITION SWITCH:

Model	Part No.	Price
1969-73—		
L/Tilt Wheel	1990095	5.25
W/Tilt Wheel	1990096	5.55
1974, Exc.	1990098	5.70
W/Tilt Wheel	1990099	6.20

Time — Fuel System & Intake Manifold (Group C) — Time

OPERATION INDEX

C1—CARBURETOR, R & R OR RENEW

1969-75—
Exc. Below (0.5) 0.6
Three Carbs. (0.9) 1.3
One Carter AFB (0.7) 0.9

C2—CARBURETOR, R & R & OVERHAUL

1969-75—
One Barrel (1.2) 2.0
2 Barrel (1.5) 2.4
4 Barrel—
Exc. Below (2.3) 3.5
Holley 4160 (2.1) 3.2
Quadrajet (1.7) 2.7

C2A—ACCELERATOR PUMP, RENEW

1969-75—
Exc. Below (0.6) 0.8
Rochester Mono-Jet (0.4) 0.6

—NOTE—
Does Not Include R & R Carburetor.

C2B—NEEDLE & SEAT, RENEW

1969-75—
Exc. Below (0.6) 0.8
Rochester 4MV (0.8) 1.1

—NOTE—
Does Not Include R & R Carburetor.

C3—AUTO. CHOKE THERMOSTAT, RENEW

1969-75 (0.2) 0.2

C3A—AUTO. CHOKE, CLEAN & ADJUST

1969-75 (0.2) 0.3

C3B—AUTO. CHOKE DIAPHRAGM RENEW

1969-75—
Exc. Below (0.2) 0.3
Two Bar. & Four Bar. (0.3) 0.5

C4—DASHPOT, RENEW

All Models (0.2) 0.3

C4A—IDLE STOP SOLENOID, RENEW

Includes adjust.
1969-75 (0.2) 0.5

C5—FUEL PUMP, R & R OR RENEW

CAMARO:
1969-75 Six (0.3) 0.4
1969-75 V8—
Exc. Below (0.6) .... (1)0.8
396-402 (0.5) .... (1)0.7
(1)For Air Cond., Add (0.2) *0.2*

CHEVELLE:
1969-75—
Six (0.3) 0.4
V8 (0.6) 1.0

NOVA
1969-70 L-4 (0.4) 0.7
1969-75 Six (0.3) 0.4
1969-75 V8 (0.6) 1.0

C5A—FUEL PUMP PUSH ROD, RENEW

Use Opr No C5 "Fuel Pump, renew"

C6—FUEL TANK, R & R OR RENEW

CAMARO:
1969-75 (0.8) 1.2

CHEVELLE:
1969-75—
Exc. Wagon (0.8) 1.2
Sta. Wagon (1.0) 1.7

NOVA
1969-75 (0.7) 1.0

C7—FUEL SYSTEM, CLEAN

Includes R & R tank, blow out lines & clean or renew fuel line filter.

CAMARO:
1967-70 (1.4) 2.1
1971-75 (1.2) 1.9

CHEVELLE:
1969-75—
Exc. Wagon (1.4) 2.1
Sta. Wagon (1.6) 2.5

NOVA
1969-75 (1.2) 1.9

C8—INTAKE MANIFOLD GASKETS, RENEW (V8)

CAMARO:
1967-69—
Exc. Below (2.2) 3.0
V8-396 (2.1) 2.9
1970-75—
Exc. Below (1.0) 1.6
402-454 (2.3) 3.0

CHEVELLE & NOVA
1969-75—
Exc. Below (1.9) 2.8
396, 400, 402, 454 (2.1) 2.9

C8A—MANIFOLD GASKETS, RENEW (FOUR & SIX CYL.)

—NOTE—
For P. Steering, Add (0.3) *0.3*

CAMARO, CHEVELLE:
1969-74 (0.6) 0.9

CHEVY II, NOVA:
1969-74 (0.6) 0.9

Parts — Fuel System & Intake Manifold — Parts

PARTS INDEX

1—CARBURETOR ASS'Y (ROCHESTER):

CAMARO:

Model	Part No.	Price
1969 Six—		
Synchro-Mesh	7016901	48.75
Auto. Trans	7016902	48.75
1969 V8 (2 Bar. Carb.)—		
Exc. V8-350—		
Synchro-Mesh	7016903	56.45
Auto. Trans	7016912	56.45
V8-350—		
Synchro-Mesh	7016915	60.45
Auto. Trans	7016916	60.45

Application	Part No.	Price
1969 V8 (4 Bar. Carb.)—		
Exc. V8-396—		
Synchro-Mesh	7016923	94.30
Auto. Trans	7046904	94.30
V8-396—		
Exc. Below	7046904	94.30
TH 400	7046904	94.30
1970 Six—		
Synchro-Mesh	7047015	50.70
Auto. Trans	7047014	50.70
1970 V8-307—		
Synchro-Mesh	7047013	58.40
Auto. Trans	7047002	58.40
1970 V8-350—		
2 Bar. Carb.—		
Synchro-Mesh	7047029	63.00
Auto. Trans	7047004	63.00
4 Bar. Carb	7047006	96.75
1970 V8-396	7046906	96.75
1971 Six—		
Synchro-Mesh	7047117	52.35
Auto. Trans	7047114	54.80
1971 V8-307—		
Synchro-Mesh	7047111	66.55
Auto. Trans	7047110	66.55
1971 V8-350—		
2 Bar. Carb.—		
Synchro-Mesh	7047127	69.00
Auto. Trans	7047112	69.00
4 Bar Carb	7046984	100.75
1971 V8-400	7047116	100.50
1972 Six—		
Synchro-Mesh	7047223	52.35
Auto. Trans.	7047222	54.80
1972 V8-307—		
Synchro-Mesh	7047203	66.55
Auto. Trans.	7047210	66.55
1972 V8-350 (2 Bar. Carb.)—		
Synchro-Mesh	7047227	69.00
Auto. Trans.	7047212	69.00
1972 V8-350 (4 Bar. Carb.)—		
Exc. Sp. Hi-Perf.—		
Exc. Below	7046589	100.50
Calif Emission	7047221	100.50
1972 V8-402	7046908	100.50
1973 Six Exc	7047317	52.35
Auto Trans	7047314	54.80
1973 V8-307 Exc	7047301	66.55
Auto Trans	7047300	66.55
1973 V8-350 2 Bar Exc	7047311	66.70
Auto Trans	7047302	66.00
1973 V8-350 4 Bar Exc	7047303	100.50
W/Spec Hi Perf	7047328	100.50
1974 Six Exc	7047417	52.35
Auto Trans Exc	7047414	54.80
Calif Emission	7047404	54.80
1974 V8-350—		
2 Bar Exc	7047415	66.70
Auto Trans	7047402	66.00
4 Bar Exc Sp Hi Perf—		
Std. Trans Exc	17050579	97.05
Calif Emission	17050581	97.05
Auto Trans Exc	17050578	97.05
Calif Emission	17050580	97.05
4 Bar Spec Hi Perf—		
Exc Below	17050591	100.45
Auto Trans	17050590	97.05
CHEVELLE:		
1969 Six—		
Synchro-Mesh	7016901	48.75
Auto. Trans	7016902	48.75
1969 V8 (2 Bar. Carb.)—		
Exc. V8-350—		
Synchro-Mesh	7016903	56.45
Auto. Trans	7016912	56.45
V8-350—		
Synchro-Mesh	7016915	60.45
Auto. Trans	7016916	60.45
1969 V8 (4 Bar. Carb.)—		
Exc. V8-396—		
Synchro-Mesh	7016923	94.30
Auto. Trans	7046904	94.30
V8-396—		
Synchro-Mesh	7046904	94.30
Auto. Trans	7016920	80.65
1970 Six—		
Synchro-Mesh	7047015	50.70
Auto. Trans	7047014	50.70
1970 V8-307—		
Synchro-Mesh	7047013	58.40
Auto. Trans	7047002	58.40
1970 V8-350 (2 Bar. Carb.)—		
Synchro-Mesh	7047005	62.35
Auto. Trans	7047016	62.35
1970 V8-350 (4 Bar.)	7047006	96.75
1970 V8-396	7046906	96.75
1970 V8-400 (2 Bar. Carb.)—		
Synchro-Mesh	7047019	63.00
Auto. Trans	7047020	63.00
1970 V8-400 (4 Bar)	7046906	96.75
1970 V8-454—		
Exc. Below	7046906	96.75
Monte Carlo	7046906	96.75
1971 Six—		
Synchro-Mesh	7047117	52.35
Auto. Trans	7047114	54.80
1971 V8-307—		
Synchro-Mesh	7047111	66.55
Auto. Trans	7047110	66.55
1971 V8-350—		
2 Bar. Carb—		
Synchro-Mesh	7047113	69.00
Auto. Trans	7047104	69.00
4 Bar. Carb	7046984	100.75
1971 V8-400—		
2 Bar. Carb.—		
Synchro-Mesh	7047113	69.00
Auto. Trans	7047118	69.00
1971 V8-454	7047116	100.50
1972 Six—		
Synchro-Mesh	7047223	52.35
Auto. Trans.	7047222	54.80
1972 V8-307—		
Synchro-Mesh	7047203	66.55
Auto. Trans.	7047210	66.55
1972 V8-350—		
2 Bar. Carb.—		
Synchro-Mesh	7047213	69.00
Auto. Trans.	7047204	69.00
4 Bar. Carb.—		
Exc Below	7046589	100.50
Calif Emission	7047221	100.50
1972 V8-402, 454	7046908	100.50
1973 Six Exc	7047317	52.35
Auto Trans	7047314	54.80
1973 V8-307 Exc	7047301	66.55
Auto Trans	7047300	66.55
1973 V8-350 2 Bar Exc	7047311	66.70
Auto Trans	7047302	66.00
1973 V8-350 4 Bar	7047303	100.50
1973 V8-454 Exc	7047315	100.50
Auto Trans	7047316	100.50
1974 Six Exc	7047417	52.35
Auto Trans Exc	7047414	54.80
Calif Emission	7047404	54.80
1974 V8-350—		
2 Bar Exc	7047415	66.70
Auto Trans	7047402	66.00
4 Bar Exc	17050581	97.05
Auto Trans	17050580	97.05
1974 V8-400, 2 Bar	7047418	69.00
4 Bar	7047407	100.50
1974 V8-454 Exc	7047401	100.50
Auto Trans Exc	7047403	100.50
Calif Emission	7047405	100.50
NOVA		
1969 Four	7016900	47.55
1969 Six—		
Synchro-Mesh	7016901	48.75
Auto. Trans	7016902	48.75
1969 V8 (2 Bar. Carb.)—		
Exc. V8-350—		
Synchro-Mesh	7016903	56.45
Auto. Trans	7016912	56.45
V8-350—		
Synchro-Mesh	7016915	60.45
Auto. Trans	7016916	60.45
1969 V8 (4 Bar. Carb.)—		
Exc. V8-396—		
Synchro-Mesh	7016923	94.30
Auto. Trans	7046904	94.30
V8-396—		
Exc. Below	7046904	94.30
TH 400	7046904	94.30
1970 Four	7047008	50.70
1970 Six—		
Synchro-Mesh	7047015	50.70
Auto. Trans	7047014	50.70
1970 V8-307—		
Synchro-Mesh	7047013	58.40
Auto. Trans	7047002	58.40
1970 V8-350 (2 Bar.)—		
Synchro-Mesh	7047005	62.35
Auto. Trans	7047016	62.35
1970 V8-350 (4 Bar.)	7047006	96.75
1970 V8-396, 400	7046906	96.75
1971 Six—		
Synchro-Mesh	7047117	52.35
Auto. Trans	7047114	54.80
1971 V8-307—		
Synchro-Mesh	7047111	66.55
Auto. Trans	7047110	66.55
1971 V8-350—		
2 Bar. Carb.—		
Synchro-Mesh	7047113	69.00
Auto. Trans	7047104	69.00
4 Bar. Carb	7046984	100.75
1972 Six—		
Synchro-Mesh	7047223	52.35
Auto. Trans	7047222	54.80
1972 V8-307—		
Synchro-Mesh	7047203	66.55
Auto. Trans.	7047210	66.55
1972 V8-350—		
2 Bar. Carb.—		
Synchro-Mesh	7047213	69.00
Auto. Trans.	7047204	69.00
4 Bar. Carb.—		
Exc. Below	7046589	100.50
Calif Emission	7047221	100.50
1973 Six Exc	7047317	52.35
Auto Trans	7047314	54.80
1973 V8-307 Exc	7047301	66.55
Auto Trans	7047300	66.55
1973 V8-350 2 Bar Exc	7047311	66.70
Auto Trans	7047302	66.00
1973 V8-350 4 Bar	7047303	100.50
1974 Six Exc	7047417	52.35
Auto Trans Exc	7047414	54.80
Calif Emission	7047404	54.80
1974 V8-350—		
2 Bar Exc	7047415	66.70
Auto Trans	7047402	66.00
4 Bar Synchro-Mesh—		
Exc Below	17050579	97.05
Calif Emission	17050581	97.05
4 Bar Automatic—		
Exc Below	17050578	97.05
Calif Emission	17050580	97.05

2—CARBURETOR ASS'Y (HOLLEY):

Application	Part No.	Price
CAMARO:		
1969 V8-302	3923289	95.20
1969 V8-396 Sp. Perf	3959164	117.45
1970 V8-350 (4 Bar. Carb.)—		
Synchro-Mesh—		
L/Evap. Emission	3972121	112.95
W/Evap. Emission	3972123	138.65
Auto. Trans—		
L/Evap. Emission	3972120	112.95
W/Evap. Emission	3972122	135.90
1970 V8-396 (Spec. Hi-Perf)—		
Synchro-Mesh—		
L/Evap. Emission	3967477	112.95
W/Evap. Emission	3967479	138.65
Auto. Trans—		
L/Evap. Emission	3969898	109.50
W/Evap. Emission	3969894	138.65
1971 V8-350 (4 Bar)—		
W/Spec Hi Perf—		
Synchro-Mesh	3989021	114.00
Auto. Trans	3989022	114.00
1972 V8-350 (4 Bar.)—		
W/Spec. Hi-Perf.—		
Synchro-Mesh	3999263	111.25
Auto. Trans.	3997788	106.95
CHEVELLE:		
1969 V8-396 Sp. Perf	3959164	117.45
1970 V8-396 (Sp. Hi-Perf.)—		
L/Fuel Evap. Emission—		
Synchro-Mesh	3967477	112.95
Auto. Trans	3969898	109.50
W/Fuel Evap. Emission—		
Synchro-Mesh	3967479	138.65
Auto. Trans	3969894	138.65
1970 V8-454 (Synchro-Mesh)—		
L/Fuel Evap Emission	3967477	112.95
W/Fuel Evap Emission	3967479	138.65
1970 V8-454 (Auto. Trans)—		
L/Fuel Evap Emission	3969898	109.50
W/Fuel Evap Emission	3969894	138.65
1971 V8-454 (Spec Hi-Perf)—		
Synchro-Mesh	3986195	115.10
Auto. Trans	3986196	115.10
NOVA		
1969 V8-396 Sp. Perf	3959164	117.45
1970 V8-396 (Sp. Hi-Perf.)—		
L/Fuel Evap Emission—		
Synchro-Mesh	3967477	112.95
Auto. Trans	3969898	109.50
W/Fuel Evap Emission—		
Synchro-Mesh	3967479	138.65
Auto. Trans	3969894	138.65

3—CARBURETOR MINOR REPAIR KIT (HOLLEY):

Application	Part No.	Price
1972 V8-350 (4 Bar.)—		
W/Spec. Hi-Perf.	6273915	12.70

4—CARBURETOR MINOR REPAIR KIT (ROCHESTER):

Application	Part No.	Price
CAMARO:		
1969 Six	7039147	4.90
1969 V8—		
2 Bar. Carb	7039148	6.75
4 Bar. (V8-350)	7039149	9.00
4 Bar. (V8-396)	7039150	9.00
1970 Six	7039166	4.90
1970 V8-307	7039167	6.75

Application	Part No.	Price
1970 V8-350—		
2 Bar. Carb	7039169	7.70
4 Bar Carb	7039174	9.00
1970 V8-396	7039171	9.00
1971 Six	7039196	4.90
1971 V8-307	7039197	6.75
1971 V8-350—		
2 Bar. Carb	7039198	7.70
4 Bar. Carb	7039202	9.00
1971 V8-400	7039222	9.00
1972 Six	7039236	4.90
1972 V8-307	7039224	7.70
1972 V8-350—		
2 Bar. Carb.—		
Synchro-Mesh	7039229	7.70
Auto. Trans.	7039226	7.70
4 Bar. Carb.	7039223	9.00
1972 V8-402	7039222	9.00
1973-74 Six	7039248	4.90
1973 V8-307	7039250	7.70
1973 V8-350 Exc	7039251	7.70
W/4 Bar Carb	7039259	9.00
1974 V8-350 Exc	7039267	7.70
W/4 Bar Carb	7039268	9.00
CHEVELLE:		
1969 Six	7039147	4.90
1969 V8—		
2 Bar. Carb	7039148	6.75
4 Bar. (V8-350)	7039149	9.00
4 Bar. (V8-396)	7039150	9.00
1970 Six	7039166	4.90
1970 V8 (2 Bar. Carb.)—		
V8-307	7039167	6.75
V8-350, 400	7039169	7.70
1970 V8 (4 Bar. Carb.)—		
Exc. Below	7039171	9.00
V8-350	7039174	9.00
1971 Six	7039196	4.90
1971 V8-307	7039197	6.75
1971 V8-350—		
2 Bar. Carb	7039198	7.70
4 Bar. Carb	7039202	9.00
1971 V8-400—		
2 Bar. Carb	7039198	7.70
4 Bar. Carb	7039222	9.00
1971 V8-454	7039222	9.00
1972 Six	7039236	4.90
1972 V8-307	7039224	7.70
1972 V8-350—		
2 Bar. Carb.—		
Synchro-Mesh	7039229	7.70
Auto. Trans.	7039226	7.70
4 Bar. Carb.	7039223	9.00
1972 V8-402, 454	7039222	9.00
1973-74 Six	7039248	4.90
1973 V8-307	7039250	7.70
1973 V8-350 Exc	7039251	7.70
W/4.Bar Carb	7039259	9.00
1973 V8-454	7039259	9.00
1974 V8, 2 Bar	7039267	7.70
4 Bar	7039268	9.00
NOVA		
1969 Six	7039147	4.90
1969 V8-350—		
2 Bar. Carb	7039148	6.75
4 Bar. Carb	7039149	9.00
1969 V8-396	7039150	9.00
1970 (Exc. V8)	7039166	4.90
1970 V8 (2 Bar. Carb.)—		
V8-307	7039167	6.75
V8-350, 400	7039169	7.70
1970 V8 (4 Bar. Carb.)—		
Exc. Below	7039171	9.00
V8-350	7039174	9.00
1971 Six	7039196	4.90
1971 V8-307	7039197	6.75
1971 V8-350—		
2 Bar. Carb	7039198	7.70
4 Bar. Carb	7039202	9.00
1972 Six	7039236	4.90
1972 V8-307	7039224	7.70
1972 V8-350—		
2 Bar. Carb.—		
Synchro-Mesh	7039229	7.70
Auto. Trans.	7039226	7.70
4 Bar. Carb.	7039223	9.00
1973-74 Six	7039248	4.90
1973 V8-307	7039250	7.70
1973 V8-350 Exc	7039251	7.70
W/4 Bar Carb	7039259	9.00
1974 V8-350 Exc	7039267	7.70
W/4 Bar Carb	7039268	9.00

5—CARBURETOR GASKET KIT (ROCHESTER):

Application	Part No.	Price
CAMARO:		
1968-69 Six	7036546	2.40
1969 V8	7036565	4.85
1970 Six	7036784	3.35
1970 V8-307	7036797	4.15
1970 V8-350—		
2 Bar Carb	7036801	5.80
4 Bar. Carb	7036814	6.65
1970 V8-396	7036814	6.65
1971 Six	7041599	2.85
1971 V8-307	7041606	3.40
1971 V8-350—		
2 Bar. Carb	7041614	3.60
4 Bar. Carb	7041872	5.65
1971 V8-400	7041872	5.65
1972 V8-307	7041906	3.40
1972 V8-350—		
2 Bar. Carb.	7041929	3.60
4 Bar. Carb.	7041872	5.65
1972 V8-402	7041872	5.65
1973-74 Six	7046679	3.35
1973 V8-307	7046706	3.40
1973 V8-350 Exc	7046717	3.60
W/4 Bar Carb	7046779	5.65
1974 V8-350 Exc	17050519	3.60
W/4 Bar Carb	17050525	5.65
CHEVELLE:		
1968-69 Six	7036546	2.40
1969 V8	7036565	4.85
1970 Six	7036784	3.35
1970 V8 (2 Bar. Carb.)—		
V8-307	7036797	4.15
V8-350, 400	7036801	5.80
1970 V8 (4 Bar.)	7036814	6.65
1971 Six	7041599	2.85
1971 V8-307	7041606	3.40
1971 V8-350—		
2 Bar. Carb	7041614	3.60
4 Bar. Carb	7041872	5.65
1971 V8-400—		
2 Bar. Carb	7041614	3.60
4 Bar. Carb	7041872	5.65
1971 V8-454	7041872	5.65
1972 V8-307	7041906	3.40
1972 V8-350—		
2 Bar. Carb.	7041929	3.60
4 Bar. Carb.	7041872	5.65
1972 V8-402, 454	7041872	5.65
1973-74 Six	7046679	3.35
1973 V8-307	7046706	3.40
1973 V8-350 Exc	7046717	3.60
W/4 Bar Carb	7046779	5.65
1973 V8-454	7046779	5.65
1974 V8, 2 Bar	17050519	3.60
4 Bar	17050525	5.65
NOVA		
1968-69 Six	7036546	2.40
1969 V8	7036565	4.85
1970 (Exc. V8)	7036784	3.35
1970 V8—		
2 Bar. Carb.—		
V8-307	7036797	4.15
V8-350, 400	7036801	5.80
4 Bar. Carb	7036814	6.65
1971 Six	7041599	2.85
1971 V8-307	7041606	3.40
1971 V8-350—		
2 Bar. Carb	7041614	3.60
4 Bar. Carb	7041872	5.65
1972 V8-307	7041906	3.40
1972 V8-350—		
2 Bar. Carb.	7041929	3.60
4 Bar. Carb.	7041872	5.65
1973-74 Six	7046679	3.35
1973 V8-307	7046706	3.40
1973 V8-350 Exc	7046717	3.60
W/4 Bar Carb	7046779	5.65
1974 V8-350 Exc	17050519	3.60
W/4 Bar Carb	17050525	5.65

6—CARBURETOR GASKET KIT (HOLLEY):

Application	Part No.	Price
1972 V8-350 (4 Bar.)—		
W/Spec. Hi-Perf.	3979667	4.53

7—CHOKE VACUUM CONTROL ASS'Y (ROCHESTER):

Application	Part No.	Price
CAMARO:		
1969 Six—		
Synchro-Mesh	7035878	.99
Auto. Trans	7037778	.99
1969 V8 (2 Bar. Carb.)—		
Exc. Below	7036768	3.40
V8-350	7027649	3.05
1969 V8 (4 Bar. Carb.)	7038239	4.05
1970 Six—		
Synchro-Mesh	7040646	.99
Auto. Trans	7040606	.99
1970 V8-307—		
2 Bar. Carb—		
Synchro-Mesh	7040849	3.05
Auto. Trans	7036769	3.05
1970 V8-350, 400	7038037	2.70
1970 V8 (4 Bar. Carb.)	7043676	4.95
1971 Single Carb—		
Synchro-Mesh	7040646	.99
Auto. Trans	7040606	.99
1971 2 Bar Carb	7042715	9.50
1971 4 Bar Carb	7043674	8.55
1972 Six	7030713	8.80
1972 V8—		
2 Bar. Carb.	7042715	9.50
4 Bar. Carb.—		
Exc. Below	7044903	4.95
W/Bracket	7044901	8.55
1973-74 Six	7030918	8.80
1973 V8-307	7042715	9.50
1973-74 V8-350—		
2 Bar	7040238	9.50
4 Bar, 1973	7040181	5.00
4 Bar, 1974 Exc	7048206	5.00
Spec Hi Perf	7048211	5.00
With Bracket (73)	7047878	8.55
CHEVELLE:		
1969 Six—		
Synchro-Mesh	7035878	.99
Auto. Trans	7037778	.99
1969 V8 (2 Bar. Carb.)—		
Exc. Below	7036768	3.40
V8-350	7027649	3.05
1969 V8 (4 Bar. Carb.)	7038239	4.05
1970 Six—		
Synchro-Mesh	7040646	.99
Auto. Trans	7040606	.99
1970 V8 (2 Bar. Carb.)—		
V8-307	7036768	3.40
V8-350, 400	7027662	3.05
1970 V8 (4 Bar.)	7043676	4.95
1971 Single Carb—		
Synchro-Mesh	7040646	.99
Auto. Trans	7040606	.99
1971 2 Bar. Carb	7042715	9.50
1971 4 Bar. Carb	7043674	8.55
1972 Six	7030713	8.80
1972 V8—		
2 Bar. Carb.	7042715	9.50
4 Bar. Carb.—		
Exc. Below	7044903	4.95
W/Bracket	7044901	8.55
1973-74 Six	7030918	8.80
1973 V8-307	7042715	9.50
1973-74 V8-350&400—		
2 Bar	7040238	9.50
4 Bar 350 (73)	7040181	5.00
4 Bar, 1974 Exc	7048206	5.00
Spec Hi Perf	7048211	5.00
W/Bracket (73)	7047878	8.55
1973 V8-454 Exc	7040384	5.00
W/Bracket	7047872	8.55
1974 V8-454	7048200	5.00
NOVA		
1969 Six—		
Synchro-Mesh	7035878	.99
Auto. Trans	7037778	.99
1969 V8 (2 Bar. Carb.)—		
Exc. Below	7036768	3.40
V8-350	7037953	2.45
1969 V8 (4 Bar. Carb.)	7038239	4.05
1970 Four	7040606	.99
1970 Six—		
Synchro-Mesh	7040646	.99
Auto. Trans	7040606	.99
1970 V8 (2 Bar. Carb.)—		
V8-307	7036768	3.40
V8-350, 400	7027662	3.05
1970 V8 (4 Bar.)	7043676	4.95
1971 Single Carb.—		
Synchro-Mesh	7040646	.99
Auto. Trans	7040606	.99
1971 2 Bar. Carb	7042715	9.50
1971 4 Bar. Carb	7043674	8.55
1972 Six	7030713	8.80
1972 V8—		
2 Bar. Carb.	7042715	9.50
4 Bar. Carb.—		
Exc. Below	7044903	4.95
W/Bracket	7044901	8.55
1973-74 Six	7030918	8.80
1973 V8-307	7042715	9.50
1973-74 V8-350—		
2 Bar	7040238	9.50
4 Bar (73) Exc	7040181	5.00
W/Bracket	7047878	8.55
4 Bar (74)	7048206	5.00

8—CHOKE VACUUM CONTROL ASS'Y (HOLLEY):

Application	Part No.	Price
1969-70	3912092	2.71
1972	6273911	7.85

9—FUEL PUMP

Application	Part No.	Price
CAMARO:		
1969-74 Six	6416502	11.38
1969 V8-302, 350	6470779	14.37
1969-70 V8-327	6416712	10.41
V8-396	6470424	12.97

Application	Part No.	Price
1970-73 V8-307	6470422	11.63
1970-72 V8-350—		
2 Bar. Carb	6470779	14.37
4 Bar. Carb—		
Exc. Below	6470310	15.27
Sp. Hi-Perf	6470779	14.37
1971-72 V8-400—		
2 Bar. Carb	6470779	14.37
4 Bar. Carb	6470424	12.97
1973-75 V8-350—		
2 Bar Carb	6470779	14.37
4 Bar Carb	6470310	15.27
CHEVELLE:		
1968-74 Six	6416502	11.38
1969-72 V8-307	6416712	10.41
1969 V8-350	6470779	14.37
V8-396	6470424	12.97
1970 V8-350—		
Exc. Below	6470779	14.37
W/Air Cond	6470306	15.82
1970 V8-396—		
Exc. Below	6470307	15.43
Sp. Hi-Perf	6470424	12.97
1970 V8-400—		
Exc. Below	6470779	14.37
4 Bar. Carb	6470307	15.43
1970 V8-454	6470307	15.43
1971-72 V8-350—		
Exc. Below	6470779	14.37
W/Air Cond	6470569	14.84
1971-72 V8-400—		
2 Bar. Carb	6470779	14.37
4 Bar. Carb	6470570	15.12
1971 V8-454	6470570	15.12
1972 V8-402, 454	6470570	15.12
1973 V8-307	6470778	14.65
1973-75 V8-350—		
Exc Below	6470779	14.37
4 Bar With Air Cond	6470777	15.78
1973-75 V8-454	6470761	15.16
1974-75 V8-400—		
2 Bar Carb Exc	6470779	14.37
W/Air Cond	6470777	15.78
4 Bar Carb	6470777	15.78
NOVA		
1969-74 Four, Six	6416502	11.38
1969-72 V8-307	6416712	10.41
1969-72 V8-350	6470779	14.37
1969-70 V8-396	6470424	12.97
1971 V8-400	6470779	14.37
1973 V8-307	6470778	14.65
1973-75 V8-350—		
2 Bar Carb	6470779	14.37
4 Bar Carb	6470777	15.78

10—FUEL PUMP ROD:

Application	Part No.	Price
1968-74	3704817	1.50

11—FUEL TANK:

Application	Part No.	Price
CAMARO:		
1969	3953844	43.95
1970—		
L/Evap. Emission	6263025	43.95
W/Evap. Emission	6263022	46.15
1971	6263022	46.15
1972-73	6272127	46.15
1974	344427	48.35
1975	357392	45.70
CHEVELLE:		
1969—		
Exc. Below	3940133	43.95
Sta. Wagon	398168	41.75
El Camino	3930806	43.95
1970 (Exc. Below)—		
L/Evap. Emission	3998308	43.95
W/Evap. Emission	3977534	40.95
1970 El Camino—		
L/Evap. Emission	3930806	43.95
W/Evap. Emission	3995767	48.35
1970 Sta. Wagon—		
L/Evap. Emission	398168	41.75
W/Evap. Emission	409384	46.15
1971—		
Exc. Below	3995766	48.35
Monte Carlo	3995765	46.15
Sta. Wagon	409384	46.15
El Camino	3995767	48.35
1972—		
Exc Below	325173	48.35
Monte Carlo	325172	48.35
El Camino	3995767	48.35
Sta Wagon	409384	46.15
1973 Except	415418	46.75
Sta Wagon	416366	46.15
El Camino	6259308	48.35
1974-75, Exc	344417	54.95
El Camino (74)	344486	59.40
Sta Wagon	416366	46.15
El Camino (75)	357385	45.70
NOVA		
1969-70—		
Exc. Below	3998317	43.95
Evap. Emission	3995720	46.15
1971-72	3995720	46.15
1973-74	344416	48.35
1975	357393	45.70

12—INTAKE MANIFOLD GASKET:

Application	Part No.	Price
1969-73 Six	3953746	1.60
1969-70 Four	3788539	.70
1969-71 V8—		
Exc. Below	3957985	2.78
V8-396, 400, 454—		
L/Hi-Perf	6259379	2.92
W/Hi-Perf	3955527	3.57
1972 V8 (Exc. 402, 454)	3957985	2.78
1972 V8-402, 454	6259379	2.92
1973-74 V8 Exc	6258833	2.78
454 (1973)	6259316	2.78
454 (1974)	6260996	2.78
350, 400 (4 Bar) 74	345195	2.78
1974 Six	338115	1.60
1975 Six	352176	1.54
1975 V8, 2 Bar	356801	3.48

13—ACCELERATOR PUMP:

Application	Part No.	Price
1969 Four, Six	7037597	3.00
1969 V8-307, 327 2 Bar.	7031824	3.10
1969 V8-350 (2 Bar.)	7037562	4.05
1969 V8 (4 Bar.)—		
V8-350	7037337	3.10
V8-396	7037327	3.10
1970 Four	7037596	3.00
1970-74 Six	7037597	3.00
1970-71 V8 (2 Bar.)—		
Exc. Below	7036282	4.05
V8-307 (1970)—		
Synchro-Mesh	7042819	3.10
Auto. Trans	7040996	3.10
V8-307 (1971)	7042819	3.10
1970-71 V8 (4 Bar.)—		
Exc. Below	7037327	3.10
V8-350	7037337	3.10
1972-73 V8-307—		
1972 V8-350—		
2 Bar. Carb.—		
Synchro-Mesh	7046028	3.10
Auto. Trans.	7036282	4.05
4 Bar. Carb.	7037327	3.10
1972 V8-402, 454	7037327	3.10
1973 V8-350 Exc	7046028	3.10
W/4 Bar Carb	7040691	2.85
1973 V8-454	7040691	2.85
1974 V8, 2 Bar	7046028	3.10
4 Bar	7047080	3.10

14—ACCELERATOR PUMP NEEDLE & SEAT:

Application	Part No.	Price
1969-74 Four & Six	7035133	3.05
1969 V8-302 (Camaro)	3877165	2.88
1969-72 V8-307, 327	7023809	3.05
1969-72 V8-350—		
2 Bar	7023813	3.05
4 Bar, Exc	7035130	3.05
Sp Hi-Perf (70 & 72)	3877165	2.88
Sp Hi-Perf (71)	3969656	
1969-70 V8-396, 454—		
Exc. Below	7035140	3.60
Sp. Hi-Perf	3877165	2.88
1970-72 V8-400—		
2 Bar	7023813	3.05
4 Bar	7035140	3.60
1971 V8-454—		
Exc. Below	7035140	3.60
Sp. Hi-Perf	3979656	2.82
1972-73 V8-402, 454	7035140	3.60
1973 V8-307	7035132	3.05
1973 V8-350 Exc	7035132	3.05
W/4 Bar Carb	7035140	3.60
1974 V8, 2 Bar	7035132	3.05
4 Bar	7035140	3.60

CHEVROLET • CORVETTE

Time — Emission Controls (Group AB) — Time

OPERATION INDEX

AB1—CRANKCASE VENT VALVE (P.C.V.), CLEAN OR RENEW

All Models—
Clean (0.3) 0.5
Renew (0.2) 0.2

AB2—EMISSION CONTROL CHECK (CCS)

Includes adjust carburetor idle speed, mixture & ignition timing. Check PCV Valve and renew if necessary.
1969-75 (0.7) 0.7

AB3A—DIAPHRAGM ASS'Y., RENEW

1969-75 (0.3) 0.4

AB5—AIR CLEANER TEMP. SENSOR, RENEW

1969-75 (0.3) 0.4

AB6—AIR PUMP, R & R OR RENEW

Includes R & R relief valve
1969-75—
Exc. Below (0.4) 0.6
396, 400, 402, 427, 454 (0.7) 0.9

—NOTE—
To Renew, Add (0.2) 0.2

AB8—AIR PUMP TUBES, RENEW

Includes R & R pump.
1969-75 (One)—
Exc. Below (0.5) 0.7
396, 400, 402, 427, 454 (0.8) 1.0

AB9—HOSES, RENEW

Does not include R & R & pump
Each (0.2) 0.3

AB10—CONTROL VALVE, RENEW

1969-75 (Each) (0.2) 0.4

AB11—RELIEF VALVE, RENEW

Includes R & R pump.
1969-75—
Exc. Below (0.6) 0.7
396, 400, 402, 427, 454 (0.8) 1.0

AB12—CHECK VALVE, RENEW

1969-75 (One) (0.2) 0.2

AB13A—CENTRIFUGAL FILTER, RENEW
Includes R & R pump pulley.
1969-75 (0.5) 0.5

AB14—AIR PUMP, RENEW
1969-75 (0.2) 0.2

AB15—AIR INJECTION MANIFOLD ASS'Y., R & R OR RENEW
1969-75 Six (0.6) 0.7
1969-75 V8—
One (0.5) 0.6
Both (0.7) 0.8

Parts — Emission Controls — Parts

PARTS INDEX

1—AIR INJECTOR REACTOR PUMP:
1968-71 .... 7806686 46.85
1972-75, Six 7803943 59.95
V8 .... 7803948 45.70

2—AIR INJECTOR PUMP RELIEF VALVE:
1968-69 .... 7803286 2.13
1970-74 .... 7029199 14.45

3—EXHAUST GAS RECIRCULATION VALVE
1973, Six, Exc 7035171 16.85
Auto Trans 7035169 16.85
1973 V8-350 Exc Below—
2 Bar Carb Exc 7040042 16.85
Auto Trans 7040437 16.85
4 Bar Carb Exc 7040318 16.85
Auto Trans 7035172 16.85
1973-74 V8-350 Sp Hi Perf—
Exc Below 7040299 16.85
Auto Trans 7047065 16.85
1973 V8-400 Exc 7035172 16.85
Sta Wagon 7040437 16.85
1973 V8-454 .... 7047066 16.85
1974 V8 Chevrolet—
V8-350 Exc Hi Perf 7040437 16.85
V8-400, 2 Bar 7035172 16.85
4 Bar 7041416 16.85
V8-454 .... 7049867 16.85
1974 V8 Corvette—
V8-350 (Exc Hi Perf)—
Std Trans Exc 7041409 16.85
Calif Emission 7040599 16.85
Auto Trans Exc 7041409 16.85
Calif Emission 7040437 16.85
V8-454 Exc 7041411
Calif Emission 7041425 16.85

4—CHECK VALVE:
1968-74 .... 5361992 4.41

5—AIR INJECTOR PUMP DRIVE BELT:
—NOTE—
Order By Complete Model Description.

6—CRANKCASE VENTILATOR VALVE:
1966-69 V8-396, 427 .... 6423695 1.94
1968-70 Six 6422718 1.94
1970-72 V8 (Exc. Below) 6423695 1.94
1970-72 V8 (Hi-Perf.) 6484525 1.91
1971-72 Six 6422717 1.94
1973-74, Six 6487534 1.89
V8, Exc 6487532 1.89
Sp. Hi-Perf.(350) 6484525 1.91
Chevrolet (74) 6487779 2.20

7—FUEL VAPOR CANISTER:
1970 Corvette—
Exc. Below 7030605 26.30
Spec. Hi-Perf 7036969 33.15
1970 Chev., Exc. 7036964 27.45
4 Bar. Carb. 7030605 26.30
1971 Chevrolet 7030605 26.30
1971-72 Corvette 7030605 26.30
1972-73 Chevrolet 7030605 26.30
1973, Corvette 7030605 26.30
1974 .... 7028131 21.95

8—FUEL VAPOR CANISTER FILTER:
1970-74 .... 7026014 1.05

9—FUEL VAPOR SEPARATOR:
1970 Chevrolet 7028021 9.65
1970-74 Corvette 7028035 9.75
1971-72 Chevrolet 407742 14.85

Time — Tune-Up & Ignition (Group B) — Time

OPERATION INDEX

B1—TUNE-UP, (MINOR)
Includes renew points, condenser & plugs, set spark timing and adjust carburetor idle. Does not include R & R distributor.
CHEVROLET:
1968-74—
Six Cyl. (1.0) 1.3
V8 (Exc. Below) (1.3) 1.7
V8-396, 400, 402, 427 (1.2) 1.6
V8-454 (1.2) 1.6
CORVETTE:
1968-74—
Exc. Below (1.8) 2.1
V8-427, 454 (1.4) 1.8

B2—TUNE-UP, (MAJOR)
Includes check compression, clean or renew & adjust spark plugs, r & r distributor and renew points & condenser, adjust timing, carburetor & fan belts, clean battery terminals and service air cleaner, check coil & service manifold heat control valve and clean or renew fuel line filter.
CHEVROLET:
1968-74 Six (2.5) 3.0
1968-74 V8—
Exc. Below (2.8) 3.3
396, 400, 402, 427, 454 (2.7) 3.3
1975 Six (2.0) 2.5
1975 V8-350 (2.3) 2.8
V8-400, 454 (2.2) 2.8
CORVETTE:
1968-74—
V8-327, 350 (2.6) 3.3
V8-427, 454 (3.6) 4.3
1975 (2.1) 2.8

B3—TUNE-UP MAJOR & OVERHAUL CARBURETOR
CHEVROLET:
1968-74 Six (3.6) 4.3
1968-74 V8—
2 Barrel (4.3) 5.6
4 Barrel—
Exc. Below (5.1) 6.4
Holley 4160 (4.9) 6.2
Quadrajet (4.8) 5.8
1975 Six (3.1) 3.8
1975 V8—
2 Barrel (3.8) 5.1
4 Barrel Exc (4.6) 5.9
Quadrajet (4.3) 5.3
CORVETTE:
1968-74—
Holley 4150 (5.5) 7.0
Holley 4160 (4.7) 6.0
Quadrajet (5.2) 6.5
Three Carbs. (6.8) 8.0
1975 Exc (5.1) 6.5
Quadrajet (4.7) 6.0

B4—POINTS & CONDENSER, RENEW
Includes set spark timing. Does not include R & R distributor.
CHEVROLET:
1968-74 Six (0.4) 0.5
1968-74 V8 (0.5) 0.6
CORVETTE:
1968-74 (0.7) 0.9

B5—SPARK PLUGS, CLEAN & ADJUST OR RENEW
CHEVROLET:
1969-75 Six (0.3) 0.4
1969-75 V8—
Exc. Below (0.6) 0.7
396, 400, 402, 427, 454 (0.6) 0.7
CORVETTE:
1969-75—
V8-327, 350 (1.1) 1.2
V8-427, 454 (0.6) 0.7

B6—COMPRESSION, TEST
CHEVROLET:
1969-75 Six (0.4) 0.5
1969-75 V8—
Exc. Below (0.7) 0.8
396, 400, 402, 427, 454 (0.6) 0.7
CORVETTE:
1969-75—
V8-327, 350 (1.2) 1.3
V8-427, 454 (0.6) 0.7

B7—IGNITION TIMING, SET
1969-75 (0.3) 0.3

B8—DISTRIBUTOR, R & R OR RENEW
Includes adjust timing.
CHEVROLET:
1969-75 Six (0.5) 0.5
1969-75 V8 (0.5) 0.5
CORVETTE:
1969-75—
Exc. Below (0.6) 0.6
V8-427,454 (0.7) 0.7

B9—DISTRIBUTOR, OVERHAUL (UNIT OFF)
1969-75 (0.5) 1.0

B9A—DISTRIBUTOR, ADJUST ON STROBOSCOPE, (UNIT OFF)
All Models (0.3) 0.4

B10—DISTRIBUTOR CAP, RENEW
1969-75—
Exc. Below (0.3) 0.4
Corvette (0.4) 0.5

B11—IGNITION CABLE SET, RENEW
Time allowance covers installation of factory supplied sets only.

CHEVROLET:
1969-75—
Six (0.3) 0.4
V8—
Exc. Below (0.3) 0.4
V8-283, 327, 350 (0.6) 0.8
CORVETTE:
1969-75—
V8-327, 350 (1.5) 1.6
V8-427, 454 (0.4) 0.6

B12—VACUUM CONTROL UNIT, RENEW

Includes adjust ignition timing & dwell. Does not include R & R distributor.

CHEVROLET:
1969-75 V8 (0.4) 0.6
1969-75 Six (0.3) 0.4
CORVETTE:
1969-75 (0.7) 0.9

B13—IGNITION COIL, RENEW

1969-75—
Exc. Below (0.3) 0.3
Corvette (0.4) 0.4

B14—IGNITION SWITCH, RENEW

CHEVROLET:
1969 (0.3) 0.4
1970-75 (0.5) 0.7
CORVETTE:
1969-75 (0.5) 0.7

B16—STEERING & IGNITION LOCK & ACTUATOR, RENEW

1969-75—
Exc. Corvette (0.9) 1.5
Corvette (1.1) 1.7

Parts — Tune-Up & Ignition — Parts

DISTRIBUTOR ASS'Y:

CHEVROLET:

Model	Part No.	Price
1969 V8-327	1111995	43.25
1969 V8-350 (2 Bar. Carb.)—		
Synchro-Mesh	1112001	43.75
Auto. Trans	1112002	43.65
1969 V8-350 (4 Bar. Carb.)—		
Synchro-Mesh	1111996	44.30
Auto. Trans	1111997	43.85
1969 V8-396—		
Exc. Below	1111949	46.40
Turbo Hydramatic	1111950	41.10
1969 V8-427—		
Exc. Below	1111925	41.50
Hi Perf	1111499	39.80
1970 Six—		
Synchro-Mesh	1110465	37.80
Auto. Trans	1110466	37.80
1970 V8-350—		
Synchro-Mesh	1112001	43.75
Auto. Trans.—		
Exc. Below	1112002	43.65
Hi-Perf	1111997	43.85
1970 V8-400—		
2 Bar. Carb	1111494	44.00
4 Bar. Carb	1111998	46.25
1970 V8-454—		
L/Hi Perf	1111436	47.45
W/Hi Perf	1111963	45.80
1971-72 Six	1110489	34.25
1971 V8-350—		
2 Bar. Carb.—		
Synchro-Mesh	1112042	42.95
Auto Trans	1112005	42.55
4 Bar. Carb.—		
Synchro-Mesh	1112044	44.15
Auto Trans	1112045	42.95
1971 V8-400—		
2 Bar. Carb	1112056	44.55
4 Bar. Carb	1112057	44.75
1971 V8-454—		
Exc. Below	1112163	42.00
Spec. Hi-Perf.—		
Std. Trans	1112075	48.20
Auto. Trans	1112054	43.80
1972 V8-350—		
2 Bar. Carb	1112005	42.55
4 Bar. Carb—		
Exc. Below	1112044	44.15
Auto Trans	1112045	42.95
W/Sp. Hi-Perf (Auto.)	1112049	46.20
W/Sp.Hi-Perf.(Std)	1112095	47.95
1972 V8-400(4 Bar.)	1112057	44.75
1972, V8-400 (2 Bar.)	1112099	43.90
1972 V8-402	1112057	44.75
1972 V8-454	1112163	42.00
1973 Six	1110499	35.25
V8-350 2 Bar Exc	1112168	42.55
Sta Wagon	1112230	42.55
V8-350 4 Bar Exc	1112093	44.15
Auto Trans Exc	1112094	44.15
Spec Hi Perf	1112148	47.95
V8-400	1112166	43.90
V8-454	1112113	46.20
1974 V8-350 2 Bar	1112844	44.30
4 Bar Exc	1112093	44.15
Sta Wagon	1112094	44.15
Dual Exh	1112543	42.95
1974 V8-400 2 Bar	1112846	44.75
4 Bar Exc	1112250	46.00
Calif Emission	1112545	44.75
1974, V8-454, Exc	1112113	46.20
High Energy Ign	1112527	145.00
1975, V8-350	1112880	145.00
V8-400	1112882	145.00
V8-454	1112886	145.00

CORVETTE:

Model	Part No.	Price
1969 V8-350—		
Exc. Below	1112020	89.30
Hi-Perf	1112021	89.70
1969 V8-427—		
Exc. Below	1111926	90.55
Heavy Duty	1111927	113.00
Sp. Hi-Perf	1111928	115.00
Transistor Ign	1111958	109.75
1970 V8-350—		
Exc. Below	1112020	89.30
Hi-Perf	1112021	89.70
Sp. Hi-Perf.	1111491	114.00
1970 V8-454	1111464	88.85
1971 V8-350—		
Exc. Below	1112050	88.40
Sp. Hi-Perf.	1112038	116.00
1971 V8-454—		
Hi-Perf.	1112051	92.40
Sp. Hi-Perf.—		
Synchro-Mesh	1112076	109.25
Auto. Trans.	1112053	109.25
1972 V8-350—		
Exc. Below	1112050	88.40
Sp. Hi-Perf	1112167	81.40
1972 V8-454	1112051	92.40
1973 V8-350 Exc	1112098	90.20
Sp Hi Perf	1112150	89.45
1973-74 V8-454	1112114	92.40
1974, 350 Sp Hi Per	1112150	89.45
1974, 350 Exc Above—		
Std Trans Exc	1112247	88.50
Calif Emission	1112544	90.35
Auto Trans Exc	1112098	90.20
Calif Emission	1112247	88.50
1975, Exc	1112905	145.00
Spec Hi Perf	1112883	145.00

FIG. 1-TUNE-UP & IGNITION

(For Parts Identification Only)

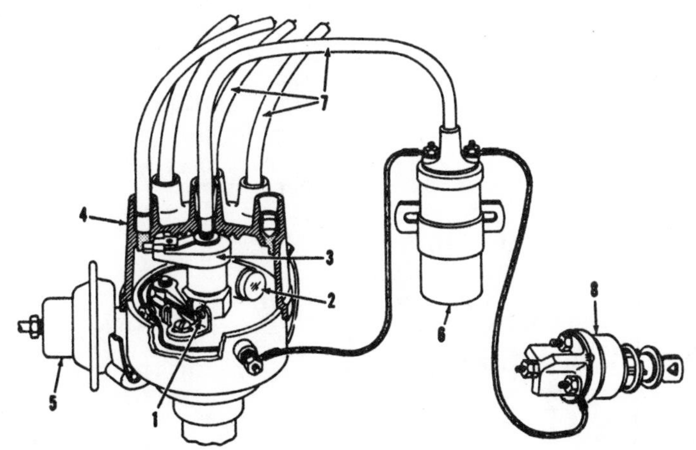

1—IGNITION POINT SET:

Model	Part No.	Price
1967-69 V8 (Exc. 427)	1931988	4.40
1967-73 Six	1954557	3.40
1970-72 V8 (Exc. Below)—		
Exc. Below	1931988	4.40
V8-350 Sp. Hi-Perf.	1966294	5.05
V8-454	1966294	5.05
1972 V8 Contact—		
Ass'y.(W/Capacitor)—		
Exc. Below	1876600	7.25
V8-350 Sp.Hi-Perf;454	1852572	4.60
1973-74 V8 Corvette	1966294	5.05
Chevrolet Exc	1931988	4.40
350 Sp Hi Perf	1966294	5.05
454	1966294	5.05
Contact Assy (74)	1876600	7.25

2—CONDENSER:

Model	Part No.	Price
1968-73 Six	1928111	1.51
1969-75, V8, Exc	1932004	1.51
Capacitor	1876154	2.33

3—ROTOR:

Model	Part No.	Price
1967-73 Six	800056	1.19
1969-74, V8, Exc	1852722	2.10
High Energy Ign	1875943	3.08

4—DISTRIBUTOR CAP:

Model	Part No.	Price
1967-73 Six	1971324	3.58
1969-74, V8, Exc	800061	5.95
High Energy Ign	1875963	9.50
1975	1875960	2.73

5—VACUUM CONTROL UNIT:

Model	Part No.	Price
1968-70 Six	1116217	3.57
1968-69 V8-307	1115355	3.19
1969-70 V8-350—		
Exc. Below	1973421	3.21
Hi-Perf (Chev.)	1115357	3.20
Hi-Perf. (Corvette)	1115360	3.19
Sp. Hi-Perf.	1116163	3.05
1970 V8-400, 454 Chev.,		
Exc.	1116163	3.05
2 Bar. Carb.	1115355	3.19
1970 V8-454 (Corvette)	1115360	3.19
1971-72 Six	1973434	3.58

1971 V8-350—		
2 Bar. Carb.—		
Synchro-Mesh	1973436	3.16
Auto Trans	1115357	3.20
4 Bar. Carb	1973437	3.16
1971 V8-400—		
2 Bar. Carb	1973438	3.16
4 Bar. Carb	1973436	3.16
1971 V8-454—		
Exc. Below	1973436	3.16
Sp. Hi-Perf	1973439	3.16
1972 V8-350—		
2 Bar. Carb	1115357	3.20
4 Bar. Carb	1973437	3.16
1972 V8-400,402	1973436	3.16
1972 V8-454	1973436	3.16
1973-74, Six	1973428	3.25
V8-350, 2 Bar. Exc	1973469	3.54
Sta Wagon	1973472	3.59
V8-350, 4 Bar Exc	1973446	3.16
Sp.Hi-Perf.	1973448	3.21
V8-400, Exc	1973437	3.16
L/Calif Emission (74)—		
2 Bar	1973503	3.24
4 Bar	1973459	3.29
V8-454, Exc	1116212	3.52
High Energy Ign	1973481	3.77

6—IGNITION COIL:

1968-69 Exc	1115202	13.50
Transistor Ign	1115207	15.45
1970-72 Exc	1115238	13.65
W/1.8 Ohm Wire Exc	1115202	13.50
Corvette	1115207	15.45
1973, Six	1115202	13.50
1973-74, V8, Exc	1115238	13.65
High Energy Ign	1875894	23.10

7—IGNITION CABLE SET:

CHEVROLET:		
1967-69 Six	2986606	7.30
1968-69 V8-396, 427	8909665	17.76
1970-73 Six	8909903	7.54
1969-70 V8-350	8912437	18.70
1970-71 V8-400, 454	8909665	17.76
1971 V8-350	8912493	18.26
1972 V8—		
Exc. Below	8912493	18.26
V8-402,454	8909665	17.76
1973-74 V8, Exc.	8912493	18.26
V8-454, Exc	8909665	17.76
High Energy Ign	8908553	35.20
1975	8908551	35.20
CORVETTE:		
1968-69 V8-427—		
Exc. Below	8909665	17.76
Heavy Duty	8909665	17.76
1969-70 V8-350	8912437	18.70
1970-71 V8-454—		
Exc. Below	8909665	17.76
Sp. Hi-Perf	8912284	28.00
1971-72 V8-350	8912437	18.70
1972-74 V8-454	8909665	17.76
1973-74 V8-350	8912437	18.70
1975	8908567	

8—IGNITION SWITCH:

1969-74 (Exc Below)—		
L/Tilt Wheel	1990095	5.25
W/Tilt Wheel	1990096	5.55
1974, Chevrolet, Exc	1990098	5.70
W/Tilt Wheel	1990099	6.20

Time — Fuel System & Intake Manifold (Group C) — Time

OPERATION INDEX

C1—CARBURETOR, R & R OR RENEW

1969-75—
- Exc. Below (0.5) 0.6
- Three Carbs. (0.8) 1.1

C2—CARBURETOR, R & R & OVERHAUL

1969-75—
- One Barrel (1.2) 2.0
- 2 Barrel (1.5) 2.4
- 3 Carbs. (3.3) 4.8
- 4 Barrel—
  - Exc. Below (2.3) 3.5
  - Holley 4160 (2.1) 3.2
  - Quadrajet (1.7) 2.7

C2A—ACCELERATOR PUMP, RENEW

1969-75—
- Exc. Below (0.6) 0.8
- Holley 2 Barrel (0.7) 0.9
- Holley 4 Barrel (0.5) 0.7
- Rochester Mono-Jet (0.4) 0.5

—NOTE—
Does Not Include R & R Carburetor

C2B—NEEDLE & SEAT, RENEW

1969-75—
- Holley 2 Barrel (0.4) 0.5
- Holley 4 Barrel (One Side) (0.4) 0.5
- Rochester Mono-Jet (0.5) 0.7
- Rochester 2GV (0.6) 0.8
- Rochester 4MV (0.8) 1.1

—NOTE—
Does Not Include R & R Carburetor.

C3—AUTO. CHOKE THERMOSTAT, RENEW

1966-69 (0.2) 0.2
1970-75—
- Six Cyl. (0.3) 0.4
- V8 (0.2) 0.2

C3A—AUTO. CHOKE, CLEAN & ADJUST

1969-75 (0.2) 0.3

C3B—AUTO. CHOKE DIAPHRAGM, RENEW

1969-75—
- Exc. Below (0.3) 0.4
- One Bar. (0.2) 0.3

C4—DASHPOT, RENEW

All Models (0.2) 0.3

C4A—IDLE STOP SOLENOID, RENEW

Includes adjust
1969-75 (0.2) 0.5

C5—FUEL PUMP, R & R OR RENEW

CHEVROLET:
1969-75 Six (0.3) 0.5
1969-75 V8 (0.4) .... (1)0.6
(1)*For Air Cond., Add (0.2)* *0.2*
CORVETTE:
1969-75—
- V8-327, 350, (0.8) .... (1)1.1
- V8-427, 454 (0.7) .... (1)1.0

(1)*For Air Cond., Add (0.2)* *0.2*

C5A—FUEL PUMP PUSH ROD, RENEW

Use opr. No. C5 "Fuel Pump, Renew"

C6—FUEL TANK, R & R OR RENEW

CHEVROLET:
1969-75—
- Exc. Wagon (0.8) 1.2
- Sta. Wagon (1.0) 1.7

CORVETTE:
1969-75 (1.8) 2.7

C7—FUEL SYSTEM, CLEAN

Includes R & R tank, blow out lines & clean or renew fuel line filter.
CHEVROLET:
1969-75—
- Exc. Wagon (1.9) 2.1
- Sta. Wagon (2.0) 2.5

CORVETTE:
1969-75 (3.0) 3.6

C8—INTAKE MANIFOLD GASKETS, RENEW (V8)

CHEVROLET:
1969—
- Exc. Below (1.5) 2.1
- V8-396, 427 (2.3) 2.9

1970-71—
- Exc. Below (1.8) 2.4
- 400, 402, 454 (2.1) 2.9

1972-75—
- Exc Below (1.4) 2.0
- 400, 402, 454 (1.6) 2.2

CORVETTE:
1968-71—
- V8-327, 350 (1.8) 2.5
- V8-427, 454 (2.3) 3.0

1972-75—
- V8-327,350(1.6) 2.2
- V8-427,454(2.0) 2.4

—NOTE—
For Tri Carb., Add (0.2) *0.2*

C8A—MANIFOLD GASKETS, RENEW (SIX CYL.)

—NOTE—
For P. Steering, Add (0.3) *0.3*
CHEVROLET:
1967-71 (0.6) 0.9
1972-75 (0.9) 1.2

Parts — Fuel System & Intake Manifold — Parts

PARTS INDEX

1—CARBURETOR ASS'Y (ROCHESTER):

SYNCHRO-MESH		
1969 Six	7016901	48.75
1969 Chev. V8-350—		
2 Bar. Carb	7016915	60.45
4 Bar. Carb	7016923	94.30
1969 Corvette V8-350	7046904	94.30
1969 Chev. V8-327	7016929	60.45
1969 V8-396	7016919	60.45
1969 V8-427	7046904	94.30
1970 Six	7047015	50.70
1970 V8-350 Chevrolet—		
2 Bar. Carb	7047005	62.35
4 Bar. Carb	7047006	96.75

1970 V8-350 Corvette—
Exc. Below 7047006 96.75
Hi-Perf 7046905 99.95
1970 V8-400 7047020 63.00
1970 V8-454—
Chevrolet 7046906 96.75
Corvette 7046906 96.75
1971 V8-350 Corvette 7046984 100.75
1971 V8-454 Corvette 7047116 100.50
1971 Six 7047117 52.35
1971 V8-350 Chevrolet—
2 Bar. Carb 7047113 69.00
4 Bar. Carb 7046984 100.75
1971 V8-400 Chev., Exc. 7047116 100.50
2 Bar. Carb. 7047113 69.00
1971 V8-454 Chevy 7047116 100.50
1972 Six 7047223 52.35
1972 V8-350 Corvette 7046589 100.50
1972 V8-350 Chevrolet—
2 Bar Carb 7047204 69.00
4 Bar Carb—
Exc. Below 7046589 100.50
Emission Control 7047221 100.50
1972 V8-400 7047218 69.00
1972 V8-402 7046908 100.50
1972 V8-454—
Chevrolet 7046908 100.50
Corvette 7047219 94.30
1973 Six 7047317 52.35
1973 V8-350 Chevrolet—
2 Bar. 7047302 66.00
4 Bar. 7047303 100.50
1973 V8-350 Corvette—
Exc. Below 7047303 100.50
Sp. Hi-Perf. 7047328 100.50
1973 V8-400 7047318 69.00
1973 V8-454—
Chevrolet 7047316 100.50
Corvette 7047315 100.50
1974 Corvette—
V8-350 Exc 17050581 97.05
Sp Hi Perf 17050591 100.45
L/Calif Emission 17050579 97.05

AUTO TRANS.

1969 Six 7016902 48.75
1969 V8-327 7016904 60.45
1969 Chev. V8-350—
2 Bar. Carb 7016916 60.45
4 Bar. Carb 7046904 94.30
1969 Corvette V8-350 7016923 94.30
1969 V8-396 7016918 60.45
1969 Chev. V8-427 7016920 80.65
1969 Corvette V8-427 7046904 94.30
1970 Six 7047014 50.70
1970 V8-350 Chevrolet—
2 Bar. Carb 7047016 62.35
4 Bar. Carb 7047006 96.75
1970 V8-350 Corvette 7047006 96.75
1970 V8-400 Chevrolet 7047020 63.00
1970 V8-454 Chevrolet 7046906 96.75
1970 V8-454 Corvette 7046906 96.75
1971 V8-350 Corvette 7046984 100.75
1971 Six 7047114 54.80
1971 V8-350 Chevy, Exc. 7047104 69.00
4 Bar. Carb. 7046984 100.75
1971 V8-400 Chevrolet—
2 Bar. Carb 7047118 69.00
4 Bar. Carb 7047116 100.50
1971 V8-454 7047116 100.50
1972 Six 7047222 54.80
1972 V8-350 Corvette 7046589 100.50
1972 V8-350 Chevrolet—
2 Bar. Carb 7047204 69.00
4 Bar. Carb—
Exc. Below 7046589 100.50
Emission Cont 7047221 100.50
1972 V8-400 7047218 69.00
1972 V8-402 7046908 100.50
1972 V8-454—
Chevrolet 7046908 100.50
Corvette 7047219 94.30
1973 Six 7047317 52.35
1973 V8-350 Chevrolet—
2 Bar. 7047302 66.00
4 Bar. 7047303 100.50
1973 V8-350 Corvette—
Exc. Below 7047303 100.50
Sp. Hi-Perf. 7047328 100.50
1973 V8-400 7047318 69.00
1973 V8-454 7047316 100.50
1974—
V8-350 2 Bar 7047402 66.00
4 Bar Exc 17050580 97.05
Sta Wagon 17050625
Sp Hi Perf 17050590 97.05
L/Calif Emis. (Corvette) 17050578 97.05
V8-400 2 Bar 7047418 69.00
4 Bar Exc 7047406 100.50
Calif Emission 7047407 100.50
V8-454 Exc 7047403 100.50
Calif Emission 7047405 100.50

2—CARBURETOR ASS'Y (HOLLEY):

1969 Corvette V8-427—
Primary—
Synchro-Mesh 3940929 85.60
Auto. Trans 3940930 86.70
Heavy Duty 3955205 220.05
Secondary 3902353 55.30
1970 Corvette V8-350—
L/Fuel Evap. System 3972121 112.95
W/Fuel Evap. System 3972123 138.65
1971 Corvette V8-454—
Exc. Below 3986195 115.10
Auto. Trans. 3986196 115.10
1971 Corvette V8-350 3989021 114.00
1972 Corvette V8-350 3999263 111.25

3—CARBURETOR MINOR REPAIR KIT (ROCHESTER):

1969 Six 7039147 4.90
1969 V8—
2 Bar. Carb 7039148 6.75
4 Bar. Carb.—
V8-350 7039149 9.00
V8-427 7039150 9.00
1970 Six 7039166 4.90
1970 V8—
2 Bar. Carb 7039169 7.70
4 Bar. Carb—
Exc. Below 7039171 9.00
V8-350 7039174 9.00
1971 Six 7039196 4.90
1971 V8—
2 Bar. Carb. 7039198 7.70
4 Bar. Carb.—
Exc. Below 7039222 9.00
V8-350 7039202 9.00
1972 Six 7039236 4.90
1972 V8-350—
2 Bar. Carb—
Exc. Below 7039229 7.70
Auto Trans 7039226 7.70
4 Bar Carb 7039223 9.00
1972 V8-400 7039226 7.70
1972 V8 402,454 7039222 9.00
1973 Six 7039248 4.90
V8, 2 Bar. 7039251 7.70
4 Bar. 7039259 9.00
1974, 2 Bar 7039267 7.70
4 Bar 7039268 9.00

4—CARBURETOR MINOR REPAIR KIT (HOLLEY):

1968-69 Corvette V8-427—
3 Carbs. (Center) 7039689 9.05
Single Carb 7039686 10.25
Heavy Duty 7039687 20.80
1968-69 Chev. V8-427 7039594 11.30
1969 V8-396 3960396 19.85
1970 V8-350—
L/Fuel Evap. System 7039594 11.30
W/Fuel Evap. System 3979637 12.15
1971 3979668 12.65
1972 Corvette 6273915 12.70

5—CARBURETOR GASKET KIT (ROCHESTER):

1969 Six 7036546 2.40
1969 V8—
2 Barrel 7036553 3.60
4 Barrel 7036565 4.85
1970 Six 7036784 3.35
1970 V8-350—
2 Bar. Carb 7036801 5.80
4 Bar. Carb 7036814 6.65
1970 V8-400 7036801 5.80
1970 V8-454 7036814 6.65
1971 Six 7041599 2.85
1971 V8-350, 400—
2 Bar. Carb 7041614 3.60
4 Bar. Carb, Exc. 7041872 5.65
Chev. 7041872 5.65
1971 V8-454, Exc. 7041872 5.65
Chev. 7041872 5.65
1972 Six 7046536 3.35
1972 V8-350—
2 Bar. Carb 7041929 3.60
4 Bar. Carb 7041872 5.65
1972 V8-400 7041929 3.60
1972 V8-402,454 7041872 5.65
1973, Six 7046679 3.35
V8, 2 Bar. 7046717 3.60
4 Bar. 7046779 5.65
1974, 2 Bar 17050519 3.60
4 Bar 17050525 5.65

6—CHOKE VACUUM CONTROL ASS'Y (ROCHESTER):

1969 V8—
2 Barrel 7027649 3.05
4 Barrel 7038239 4.05
1970-71 Six—
Synchro-Mesh 7040646 .99
Auto. Trans 7040606 .99
1970 V8—
2 Bar. Carb 7038037 2.70
4 Bar. Carb 7043676 4.95
4 Bar. Carb (Corvette) 7043674 8.55
1971-72 V8—
2 Bar. Carb 7042715 9.50
4 Bar. Carb(1970-71) 7043674 8.55
4 Bar Carb.(1972) 7044901 8.55
1973 Six 7030918 8.80
1973-74 V8, 2 Bar 7040238 9.50
1973 V8, 4 Bar—
350 Exc 7040181 5.00
W/Bracket 7047878 8.55
Sp Hi Perf 7040386 5.00
454 Exc 7040384 5.00
W/Bracket 7047872 8.55
1974 V8, 4 Bar Exc 7048206 5.00
Spec Hi Perf 7048211 5.00
V8-454 7048200 5.00

7—CHOKE VACUUM CONTROL ASS'Y (HOLLEY):

1967-70 3912092 2.71
1972 6273911 7.85

8—FUEL PUMP (AC):

1967-73 Six 6416502 11.38
1968-69 Chev. V8-427 6470424 12.97
1969 Chev. V8-327 6470779 14.37
1969 Chev. V8-350 6470779 14.37
1969 Corvette V8-350 6470110 14.37
1969 Corvette V8-427—
Exc. Below 6416741 14.08
Hi Perf 6470106 14.37
1969 V8-396 6470424 12.97
1970 V8 Chevrolet—
V8-350, 400 6470779 14.37
V8-454 6470424 12.97
1970-72 Corvette—
V8-350—
Exc. Below 6470308 15.27
Sp. Hi-Perf 6470110 14.37
V8-454 6470309 15.27
1971-72 V8 Chevrolet—
2 Bar. Carb, Exc. 6470779 14.37
V8-400 (W/A.C.) 6470569 14.84
4 Bar. Carb.—
V8-350 6470569 14.84
V8-400,402, 454 6470570 15.12
1973-75, V8-350—
2 Bar Carb 6470779 14.37
4 Bar Exc 6470779 14.37
With Air Cond 6470701 14.77
Corvette 6470308 15.27
1973-75, V8-400, Exc 6470779 14.37
With Air Cond 6470701 14.77
1973-75, V8-454, Exc 6470775 18.35
Corvette 6470309 15.27
1974 V8-350 4 Bar 6470308 15.27

9—FUEL PUMP ROD:

1968-74 V8 3704817 1.50

10—FUEL TANK:

1968-69 Corvette—
Exc. Below 3967741 41.75
High Perf 3967746 41.75
1969 Chevrolet—
Exc. Below 3968731 47.30
Sta. Wagon 3972571 47.30
1970 Chevrolet—
L/Evap. Emission—
Exc. Sta. Wagon 3968731 47.30
Sta. Wagon 3972571 47.30
W/Evap. Emission—
Exc. Sta. Wagon 3982841 57.20
Sta. Wagon 3972572 57.20
1970 Corvette—
V8-350, 454 (L/Sp. Hi-Perf.)—
L/Evap. Emission 3967741 41.75
W/Evap. Emission 3967749 43.95
V8-350, 454 (W/Sp. Hi-Perf.)—
L/Evap. Emission 3967746 41.75
W/Evap. Emission 3967755 43.95
1971-72 Corvette—
Exc. Below 3967749 43.95
W/Spec. Hi-Perf 3967755 43.95
1971-72 Chevrolet—
Exc. Below 3991011 50.55
Sta. Wagon (1971) 412259 43.95
Sta. Wagon(1972) 412259 43.95
1973-74 Chevrolet, Exc. 6259307 59.40
Sta. Wagon (73) 412259 43.95
Sta Wagon (74) 416062 46.15
Exc Sta Wagon (74) 344418 54.95
1973-74 Corvette 3967749 43.95
1975, Exc 357388 51.30
Sta Wag 419531 45.70
Corvette 348366 26.40

11—INTAKE MANIFOLD GASKET:

1969-73 Six	3953746	1.60
1969 V8—		
Exc. Below	3957985	2.78
V8-396, 427	6259379	2.92
Hi-Perf	3955527	3.57
1970-72, V8, Exc	3957985	2.78
V8-400 (4 Bar)	6259379	2.92
V8-402, 454	6259379	2.92
Sp. Hi-Perf	3955527	3.57
1973-74 V8 Exc	6258833	2.78
V8-454 (1973)	6259316	2.78
V8-454 (1974)	6260996	2.78
V8-350, 400 (4 Bar) 74	345195	2.78
1975	356801	3.48

12—ACCELERATOR PUMP:

1969-73 Six	7037597	3.00
1969 V8—		
2 Bar. Carb	7037562	4.05
4 Bar. Carb.—		
V8-350	7037337	3.10
V8-396	7037562	4.05
V8-427	7037327	3.10
1970-72 V8—		
2 Bar. Carb. Exc.	7036282	4.05
Std. Trans. (1972)	7046028	3.10
4 Bar. Carb.—		
V8-350 (1970-71)	7037337	3.10
V8-350,402(1972)	7037327	3.10
V8-400, 454	7037327	3.10
1973-74 V8, 2 Bar.	7046028	3.10
4 Bar. (1973)	7040691	2.85
4 Bar (1974)	7047080	3.10

13—ACCELERATOR PUMP NEEDLE & SEAT:

1968-73 Six	7035133	3.05
1968-69 3 Carbs	3896614	2.78
1969 V8—		
2 Bar. Carb	7023813	3.05
4 Bar. Carb.—		
V8-350	7035130	3.05
V8-396	7023813	3.05
V8-427 (Exc. Below)	7035140	3.60
V8-427 Sp. Hi-Perf.	3877165	2.88
1970-72 V8—		
2 Bar. Carb	7023813	3.05
4 Bar. Carb. (Rochester)—		
V8-350 (Exc. Below)	7035130	3.05
V8-350 Sp. Hi-Perf.	3877165	2.88
V8-400,402,454	7035140	3.60
4 Bar. Carb. (Holley)—		
1970	3877165	2.88
1971	3979656	2.82
1972	3877165	2.88
1973-74 V8 2 Bar.	7035132	3.05
4 Bar.	7035140	3.60

CHEVROLET VEGA

Time — Emission Controls (Group AB) — Time

OPERATION INDEX

AB1—CRANKCASE VENT VALVE (PCV),CLEAN OR RENEW
1971-75 (0.2) 0.2

AB2—EMISSION CONTROL CHECK (CCS)
Includes: Adjust carburetor, idle speed, mixture & ignition timing. Check PCV valve & renew if necessary.
1971-75 (0.5) 0.5

AB3A—DIAPHRAGM ASS'Y, RENEW
1971-75 (0.2) 0.3

AB5—AIR CLEANER TEMP. SENSOR, RENEW
1971-75 (0.2) 0.2

AB6—AIR INJECTION PUMP, R&R OR RENEW
1971-75 (0.4) 0.6

AB8—AIR PUMP TUBES, RENEW
1971-75 Each (0.5) 0.8

AB9—HOSES, RENEW
1971-75 Each (0.3) 0.3

AB17—AIR CLEANER SENSOR, RENEW
1971-75 (0.3) 0.3

AB18—FUEL VAPOR CANISTER, R&R OR RENEW
1971-75 (0.3) 0.5

AB20—TRANS CONTROLLED SPARK SWITCH (T.C.S.) (ENG TEMP) RENEW
1971-75 (0.3) 0.5

AB21—TRANS CONTROLLED SPARK SWITCH (T.C.S.) (TRANS MOUNT) RENEW
1971-75 (0.3) 0.5

AB22—TRANS CONTROLLED SPARK RELAY (T.C.S.) (FIREWALL MOUNT) RENEW
1971-75 (0.2) 0.3

Parts — Emission Controls — Parts

PARTS INDEX

1—CRANKCASE VENTILATOR VALVE:

1971-75	6486964	1.94

2—FUEL EVAPORATOR CONTROL PARTS:

1971-74—		
Canister Assy	7030758	26.30
Filter	7026014	1.05
Separator, 1971	408302	15.75
Separator, 1972-73	6264327	2.66

3—AIR INJECTOR, 1972:

Pump	7803943	59.95
Pulley	6270081	1.70
Bracket	6270083	13.50
Check Valve	5361992	4.41
Relief Diverter Valve	7046171	14.45

4—EXHAUST GAS RECIRCULATION VALVE

1973, 1 Bar Carb—		
Exc Below	7046497	16.85
Automatic Trans	7049875	16.85
1973, 2 Bar Carb—		
Exc Below	7046498	16.85
Automatic Trans	7030880	16.85
1974, 1 Bar Carb—		
Synchro-Mesh Exc	7049873	16.85
Calif Emission	7030879	16.85
Auto Trans Exc	7049873	16.85
Calif Emission	7049875	16.85
1974-75 2 Bar Carb—		
Synchro-Mesh	7043051	16.85
Auto Trans Exc	7048270	16.85
Calif Emission	7043279	16.85
1975, 1 Bar Carb Exc	7043304	
Auto Trans	7043303	

Time	Tune-Up & Ignition (Group B)	Time

OPERATION INDEX

B1—TUNE-UP, (MINOR)

Includes renew points, condenser & plugs, set spark timing and adjust carburetor idle. Does not include R&R distributor.

1971-74 (1.2) 1.7

B2—TUNE-UP, (MAJOR)

Includes check compression, clean or renew & adjust spark plugs, R & R distributor and renew points & condenser, adjust timing, carburetor & fan belts, clean battery terminals and service air cleaner. Check coil and service manifold heat control valve and clean or renew fuel line filter.

1971-74 (2.4) 3.0

1975 (1.9) 2.5

B3—TUNE-UP MAJOR & OVERHAUL CARBURETOR

1971—
Exc Below (3.4) 4.2
2-Barrel (3.9) 4.8
1972-74—
Exc Below (3.8) 4.6
2 Barrel (3.9) 4.8
1975 (3.4) 4.3

B4—POINTS & CONDENSER RENEW

Includes set spark timing. Does not include R & R distributor.

1971-74 (0.4) 0.6

B5—SPARK PLUGS, CLEAN & ADJUST OR RENEW

1971-75 (0.3) 0.4

B6—COMPRESSION, TEST

1971-75 (0.4) 0.6

B7—IGNITION TIMING SET

1971-75 (0.2) 0.2

B8—DISTRIBUTOR, R & R OR RENEW

Includes adjust timing.

1971-75 (0.5) 0.7

B9—DISTRIBUTOR, OVERHAUL (UNIT OFF)

1971-75 (0.5) 0.7

B9A—DISTRIBUTOR, ADJUST ON STROBOSCOPE, (UNIT OFF)

1971-75 (0.3) 0.4

B10—DISTRIBUTOR CAP, RENEW

1971-75 (0.2) 0.2

B11—IGNITION CABLE SET, RENEW

Time allowance covers installation of factory supplied sets only.

1971-75 (0.3) 0.3

B12—VACUUM CONTROL UNIT, RENEW

Includes adjust ignition timing & dwell. Does not include R & R distributor.

1971-75 (0.3) 0.5

B13—IGNITION COIL, RENEW

1971-75 (0.3) 0.3

B14—IGNITION SWITCH, RENEW

1971-75 (0.5) 0.6

Parts	Tune-Up & Ignition	Parts

FIG. 1-TUNE-UP & IGNITION

(For Parts Identification Only)

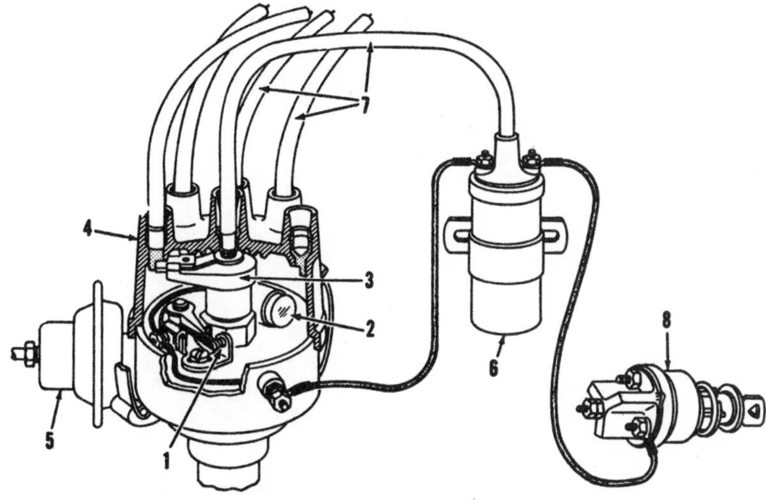

DISTRIBUTOR ASS'Y:

1971 Exc	1110492	37.80
2-BBL Carb W/Auto Tr	1110435	40.30
1972 Exc	1110492	37.80
Calif Emission	1110435	40.30
1973-74 Exc	1110496	40.30
W/2 Bar Carb	1110532	39.80
1975	1112862	118.00

1—IGNITION POINT SET:

1971-74 .... 1954557 — 3.40

2—CONDENSER:

1971-74 .... 1928111 — 1.51

3—ROTOR:

1971-74 .... 800056 — 1.19

4—DISTRIBUTOR CAP:

1971-74 .... 1962446 — 3.60

5—VACUUM CONTROL UNIT:

1971-73	1973428	3.25
1974	1973506	2.99

6—IGNITION COIL:

1971-74	1115202	13.50
1975	1115544	

7—IGNITION CABLE SET:

1971-74 .... 8906932 — 7.74

8—IGNITION SWITCH & CYLINDER:

Switch, 1971-73	1990095	5.25
Switch, 1974	1990098	5.70
Cylinder, 1971	3990946	7.25
Cylinder, 1972	7044844	7.25
Cylinder, 1973	7047678	6.85
Cylinder, 1974-75	345083	7.25

Time — Fuel System & Intake Manifold (Group C) — Time

OPERATION INDEX

C1—CARBURETOR, R & R OR RENEW
1971-75 (0.5) 0.7

C2—CARBURETOR, R & R & OVERHAUL
1971—
- Exc. Below (1.1) 1.7
- 2 Barrel (1.6) 2.2

1972-75—
- Exc Below (1.4) 2.0
- 2 Barrel (1.6) 2.2

C2A—ACCELERATOR PUMP, RENEW
1971-75—
- 1 Barrel (0.4) 0.6
- 2 Barrel (0.6) 0.8

C2B—NEEDLE & SEAT, RENEW
1971-75—
- 1 Barrel (0.5) 0.7
- 2 Barrel (0.6) 0.8

C3—AUTO. CHOKE THERMOSTAT RENEW
1971-75 (0.2) 0.2

C3B—AUTO. CHOKE DIAPHRAGM, RENEW
1971-75—
- Exc. Below (0.2) 0.4
- 2 Barrel (0.3) 0.5

C4A—IDLE STOP SOLENOID, RENEW
Includes adjust.
1971-75 (0.2) 0.3

C5—FUEL PUMP, R & R OR RENEW
Includes R & R tank unit.
1971-75 (0.7) 1.0

C6—FUEL TANK, R & R OR RENEW
1971-75 (0.7) 1.0

C7—FUEL SYSTEM, CLEAN
Includes R & R tank, blow out lines & clean or renew fuel line filter.
1971-75 (1.6) 1.9

C8A—MANIFOLD GASKETS, RENEW
1971—
- L. Power Steering (1.1) 1.6
- W. Power Steering (1.5) 2.1

1972-75—
- L. Power Steering (0.7) 1.0
- W. Power Steering (1.0) 1.4

Parts — Fuel System & Intake Manifold — Parts

PARTS INDEX

1—CARBURETOR ASS'Y:

	Part No.	Price
1971 Single Barrel—		
Synchro-Mesh	7047123	48.20
Auto. Trans	7047124	48.20
1971 Dual Barrel—		
Synchro-Mesh	7041911	62.20
Auto Trans	7041910	62.20
1972 Single Barrel—		
Less Calif. Emission—		
Synchro-Mesh	7046579	48.20
Auto Trans	7046580	48.20
With Calif. Emission—		
Synchro-Mesh	7047257	48.20
Auto Trans	7047254	48.20
1972 Dual Barrel—		
Less Calif. Emission—		
Synchro-Mesh (Early)	7046583	58.35
Synchro-Mesh (Late)	7046631	62.20
Auto Trans (Early)	7046630	62.20
Auto Trans (Late)	7046630	62.20
With Calif. Emission—		
Synchro-Mesh (Early)	7046633	62.20
Synchro-Mesh (Late)	7046633	62.20
Auto Trans (Early)	7046632	62.20
Auto Trans (Late)	7046632	62.20
1973 Single Barrel—		
Synchro-Mesh	7047333	48.20
Automatic	7047334	48.20
1973-75 Dual Barrel—		
Synchro-Mesh, Exc.	6259025	61.85
Calif Emission	6259028	61.85
Automatic Except	6259026	61.85
Calif Emission	6259027	61.85
1974, 1 Bar Carb Exc	7047443	48.20
Auto Trans	17050660	48.20
1974, 2 Bar Carb—		
Synchro-Mesh Exc	345652	64.35
Calif Emission	345654	64.35
Auto Trans Exc	345653	64.35
Calif Emission	345655	64.35

1A—CARBURETOR MAJOR REPAIR KIT:

	Part No.	Price
1971 Single Barrel	7041581	12.90
Dual Barrel	7041866	25.60
1972 Single Barrel	7046524	12.05
Dual Barrel	7041921	25.60
1973-74, 1 Bar	7046682	12.05
1973, 2 Bar	335148	24.95
1974, 2 Bar Exc	345649	14.25
Auto Trans	345651	14.25
1975, 2 Bar Carb	335148	24.95

2—CARBURETOR MINOR REPAIR KIT:

	Part No.	Price
1971—		
Single Barrel	7039194	4.90
Dual Barrel	7039195	6.75
1972—		
Single Barrel	7039235	4.90
Dual Barrel	7039225	7.70
1973-74 Single Barrel	7039249	4.90

3—CARBURETOR GASKET SET:

	Part No.	Price
1971-72—		
Single Barrel	7041582	3.20
Dual Barrel, 1971	7041588	4.30
Dual Barrel, 1972	7041922	4.30
1973-75—		
Single Barrel (73-74)	7046683	30.2
Dual Barrel	335147	4.08

4—FUEL PUMP (NEW):

	Part No.	Price
1971-74 (In Tank) Exc	6470550	15.12

5—FUEL TANK:

	Part No.	Price
1971	3987345	29.55
1972-73	6263069	29.55
1974	345061	46.15

6—INTAKE MANIFOLD GASKET:

	Part No.	Price
1971-75	3977151	.68

CHRYSLER • IMPERIAL

Time — Emission Controls (Group AB) — Time

OPERATION INDEX

AB1—POSITIVE CRANKCASE VENTILATOR (PCV) VALVE, RENEW OR CLEAN
Renew (0.2) 0.3
Clean (0.3) 0.5

AB2—EMISSION CONTROL (CAP), CHECK
Includes adjust idle, timing and distributor vacuum control unit:
All Models (0.6) 1.0

AB3—VACUUM CONTROL UNIT, RENEW
All Models (0.8) 1.2

AB6—AIR PUMP, R&R OR RENEW
1972, Chrysler (0.4) 0.6
Imperial (1.1) 1.5
1973-75 (0.7) 1.1

AB7—AIR PUMP HOSE, RENEW
1972-75 (0.2) 0.3

AB10A—DIVERTER VALVE, RENEW
1972, Chrysler (0.3) 0.7
Imperial (0.7) 1.0
1973-75 (0.7) 1.0

AB12—CHECK VALVE, RENEW
All Models (0.5) 0.8

AB18—FUEL VAPOR CANISTER, R&R OR RENEW
All Models (0.3) 0.5

AB18A—VAPOR CANISTER FILTER, RENEW
All Models (0.2) 0.3

AB20—EXHAUST GAS RECIRCULATION CONTROL VALVE, RENEW
1973-75 (0.3) 0.5

AB21—EXHAUST GAS COOLANT CONTROL VALVE, RENEW
1973-75 (0.3) 0.5

AB22—EGR TIME DELAY TIMER, RENEW
1974-75 (0.2) 0.3

AB23—EGR TIME DELAY SOLENOID, RENEW
1974-75 (0.2) 0.3

AB24—EGR VACUUM AMPLIFIER, RENEW
1973-75 (0.2) 0.3

AB25—ORIFICE SPARK ADVANCE CONTROL VALVE, RENEW
1973-75 (0.3) 0.4

Parts — Emission Controls — Parts

PARTS INDEX

1—CRANKCASE VENTILATOR VALVE:
1966-69 .... 2808622 2.91
1970-75 .... 3671076 2.89

2—DISTRIBUTOR THERMOSTATIC VACUUM SWITCH:
1968-69 V8 .... 2843555 9.17
1970 .... 3549895 14.42

2A—DISTRIBUTOR THERMOSTATIC VACUUM VALVE
1971-72 .... 3614023 6.42
1973-75 .... 3780126 6.76

3—NOX EMISSION CONTROL PARTS:
1971-72—
Vacuum Valve (1971) 3438474 6.01
Vacuum Valve (1972) 3656381 6.01
Control Unit (1971)—
Chrysler—
V8-360 .... 3621803 31.65
V8-383 .... 3621803 31.65
Imperial 3621803 31.65
Control Unit (1972) 3621803 31.65
Thermal Switch 3438465 6.99
Trans. Switch—
1975, Cordoba—
Auto Trans 3438494 15.50

4—FUEL VAPOR SEPARATOR:
1970-71;1972(Early) .... 3466836 .
1972 (Late); 1973 .... 3642105 8.42
1974 .... 3751502 7.35
1975, Exc .... 3870674 .
V8-400, 440 .... 3751502 7.35

5—FILTER INSIDE OF TANK:
1970-75 (Exc Below) 1670694 1.04
1975, V8-400, 440 .... 2534111 .99

6—FUEL VAPOR CANISTER
1972 .... 3577584 26.20
1973-75 .... 3577595 26.20

7—FUEL VAPOR CANISTER FILTER
1972-75 .... 3577586 .74

8—AIR INJECTION PUMP
1973-74 .... 3614985 57.47
1975 3837647

9—DIVERTER VALVE
1973 .... 3698919 10.64
1974 .... 3830624 10.64
1975 3830959

10—EXHAUST GAS RECIRCULATION VALVE
1973, 400 Eng 3671423 10.55
440 Eng 3671420 10.55
1974, 400 Eng—
2 Bar Carb 3769809 13.47
4 Bar Carb Exc 3769670 14.00
Calif Emission 3830120 14.00
1974, 440 Eng—
Wo/Hi Perf Exc 3698886 14.00
Calif Emission 3769669 14.00
W/Hi Perf Exc 3769667 14.00
Calif Emission 3769670 14.00
1975, V8-318, Exc .... 3780189 .
Calif Emission .... 3879709 .
1975, V8-360, Exc .... 3780189 .
Hi-Perf .... 3879728 .
1975, V8-400, Exc .... 3870635 .
Hi-Perf 3698886 14.00
1975, V8-440, Exc 3830120 14.00
Hi-Perf .... 3870630 .

11—EGR TIME DELAY SOLENOID VALVE
1974 Calif Emission 3755450 7.96
1975, Exc .... 3874027 .
Calif Emission (Exc 318) .... 3874030 .

Time — Tune-Up & Ignition (Group B) — Time

OPERATION INDEX

B1—TUNE-UP, MINOR
Includes: Renew or clean & adjust points, condenser & plugs. Set spark timing & adjust carburetor idle.
Standard Ignition (2.2) 2.4
Electronic Ignition (1.7) 1.9
—NOTE—
For 4-Bar Carb, Add (0.2) *0.3*
For C.A.P. Add (0.3) *0.5*

B2—TUNE-UP, MAJOR
Includes: Check compression, clean or renew and adjust spark plugs. R & R distributor, renew points and condenser. Adjust ignition timing, carburetor and fan belts. Clean battery terminals and service air cleaner. Check coil and service manifold heat control valve, and replace or clean fuel line filter.
Standard Ignition—
Exc. Below (2.9) 3.8
4 Bar. (3.2) 4.1
Electronic Ignition—
Exc Below (2.4) 3.3
4 Bar (2.7) 3.6
—NOTE—
To Renew P.C.V. Valve, Add (0.2) *0.3*
To Clean PCVValve, Add (0.3) *0.3*
For C.A.P., Add (0.3) *0.5*

B3—TUNE-UP, MAJOR & OVERHAUL CARBURETOR
Standard Ignition—
Exc. Below (4.9) 5.9
4 Bar. Carb. (6.1) 7.1
Electronic Ignition—
Exc Below (4.4) 5.4
4 Bar (5.6) 6.6
—NOTE—
For C.A.P., Add (0.3) *0.5*
Service P.C.V. Valve, Add (0.3) 0.4

B4—POINTS & CONDENSER, RENEW
Includes: R & R distributor & set spark timing
1968-72 (0.6) 1.0
—NOTE—
For C.A.P. Add (0.3) *0.5*

B5—SPARK PLUGS, CLEAN & ADJUST OR RENEW
1969-75 (0.7) ①0.7
①For V8-440 Hi-Perf., Add (0.5) *0.6*

B6—COMPRESSION TEST
1969-75 (0.8) ①0.8
①For V8-440 Hi Perf., Add (0.5) *0.6*

B7—IGNITION TIMING, SET
1969-75 (0.2) 0.3

B8—DISTRIBUTOR, R & R OR RENEW
1969-71 Exc (0.7) 0.9
W/Electronic Ignition (0.6) 0.8
1972 (0.6) 0.8
1973-75 (0.5) 0.7
—NOTE—
For C.A.P., Add (0.3) *0.5*

B9—DISTRIBUTOR, OVERHAUL (UNIT OFF)
1969-75 (1.0) 1.4

B9A—DISTRIBUTOR ADJUST ON STROBOSCOPE (UNIT OFF)
All Models (0.4) 0.4

B10—DISTRIBUTOR CAP, RENEW
1969-75 (0.3) 0.3

B10A—DISTRUBUTOR RELUCTOR, RENEW
1971-75 (0.3) 0.5

B10B—DIST PICK-UP PLATE & COIL ASSY, RENEW
Distributor removed
1971-75 (0.2) 0.2

B10C—ELECTRONIC IGNITION CONTROL UNIT, RENEW
1971-75 (0.3) 0.5

B11—IGNITION CABLE SET, RENEW
Time Allowance Covers InstallatiON Of Factory Supplied Sets Only.
1969-75—
L/Air Cond. (0.4) 0.6
W/Air Cond. (0.6) 0.8

B12—VACUUM CONTROL UNIT, RENEW
Includes: R & R distributor.
1969-75 (0.6) 0.9

B13—IGNITION COIL, RENEW
All Models (0.3) 0.3

B14—IGNITION SWITCH, RENEW
W/Std Steering Column (1.4) 1.7
W/Tilt Column (0.5) 0.9
W/Tilt-Telescopic Column (0.4) 0.7

B15—IGNITION COIL RESISTOR, RENEW
All Models (0.2) 0.3

Parts — **Tune-Up & Ignition** — Parts

FIG.1-TUNE-UP & IGNITION
(For Parts Identification Only)

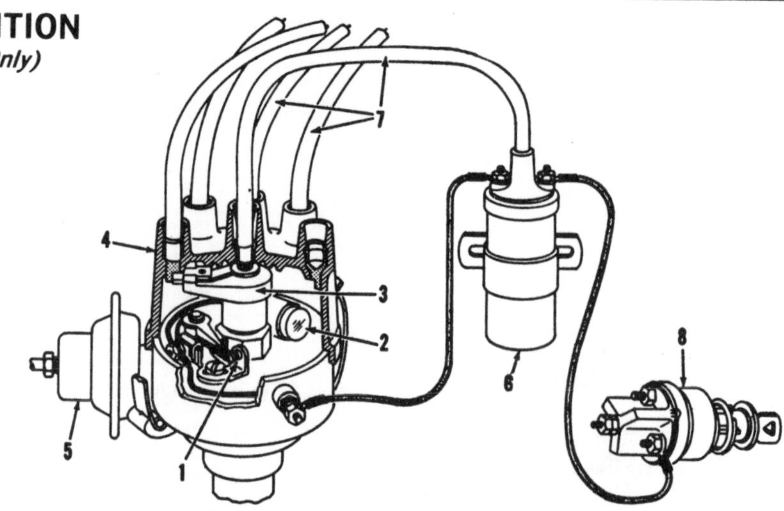

DISTRIBUTOR ASS'Y:

Description	Part No.	Price
1969 V8-383 (2 Bar. Carb.)—		
Synchro-Mesh Trans.	2875743	41.71
Auto. Trans.	2875748	41.71
1969 V8-383 (4 Bar. Carb.)—		
Auto. Trans.	2875732	41.71
1969 V8-440—		
L/Hi Perf.	2875765	44.08
W/Hi.Perf.	2875759	44.08
1970 V8-383—		
2 Bar. Carb.	3438232	41.71
4 Bar. Carb.	3438434	41.71
1970 V8-440—		
L/Hi-Perf.	3438221	44.08
W/Hi-Perf.	3438224	44.08
1971 V8-360—		
Exc. Below	3656273	37.28
Calif. Prod.	3656276	37.28
1971 V8-383—		
2 Bar. Carb.—		
Exc. Below	3438535	41.71
Calif. Prod.	3438545	41.71
4 Bar Carb	3438691	41.71
1971 V8-440—		
L/Hi-Perf.	3438560	44.08
W/Hi-Perf.	3438695	44.08
1972 V8-360—		
Exc. Below	3656273	37.28
Electronic Ign. Exc	3656430	43.01
W/Air Pump	3656436	43.01
1972 V8-400—		
Electronic Ign	3656336	44.08
Exc Above (Early)	3656330	44.08
Exc Above (Late)	3656594	44.08
1972 V8-440—		
Exc. Below	3656345	44.08
Electronic Ign.—		
Exc. Below	3656342	44.08
Emission Cont.	3656348	44.08
1973 V8-400	3656792	44.08
1973 V8-440	3755158	44.08
1974, V8-360	3755476	44.08
V8-400	3755682	44.08
1974, 440 Eng Exc	3755519	44.08
Calif Emission	3755523	44.08
1975, V8-318, Exc	3755473	.
Catalytic Exh	3874091	.
1975, V8-360, Exc	3874146	.
Catalytic Exh	3874116	.
1975, V8-400, 2 Bar	3874102	.
4 Bar, Exc	3755682	44.08
Catalytic Exh	3874111	.
1975, V8-440 (L/Hi-Perf)—		
Exc Below	3874120	.
Catalytic Exh	3874174	.
1975, V8-440 (W/Hi-Perf)—		
Exc Below	3874120	.
Air Pump	3874174	.

ELECTRONIC DISTRIBUTOR PARTS

Description	Part No.	Price
1972—		
Pick-Up	3656025	.
Pick-Up Plate	3656023	3.75
Reluctor	3656017	1.74
1973-75—		
Pick-Up & Plate	3656738	8.77
Reluctor	3656017	1.74

ELECTRONIC IGNITION CONTROL UNIT

Description	Part No.	Price
1973	3656900	50.05
1974	3755550	50.05
1975	3874020	.

1—IGNITION POINT SET:

Description	Part No.	Price
1968-69—		
Single Breaker	2098244	3.20
Double Breaker	2808870	7.40
1970-72	2098244	3.20

2—CONDENSER:

Description	Part No.	Price
1968-69—		
Single Breaker	2098058	1.56
Double Breaker	1818757	1.56
1970-72	3420600	1.56

3—ROTOR:

Description	Part No.	Price
1968-69—		
Single Breaker	1838516	1.18
Double Breaker	1658535	1.15
1970-75	1838516	1.18

4—DISTRIBUTOR CAP:

Description	Part No.	Price
1968-69—		
Single Breaker	2444507	4.44
Double Breaker	2585000	4.21
1970-75	2444507	4.44

5—VACUUM CONTROL UNIT:

Description	Part No.	Price
1969 V8-383—		
2 Bar. Carb.	2875735	4.25
4 Bar. Carb.	2875728	4.25
1969 V8-440—		
L/Hi. Perf.	2875761	4.25
W/Hi. Perf.	2875754	4.25
1970 V8-383—		
2 Bar Carb	3514331	25.47
4 Bar Carb	3514330	25.47
1970 V8-440—		
L/Hi.-Perf.	3514329	25.47
W/Hi.-Perf.	3514330	25.47
1971 V8-360	3438424	4.25
1971 V8-383—		
2 Bar. Carb.	3579239	25.47
4 Bar. Carb.	3579240	25.47
1971 V8-440—		
L/Hi.-Perf.	3579241	25.47
W/Hi.-Perf.	3514330	25.47
1972 V8-360—		
Exc Below	3438424	4.25
Electronic Ign	3656434	4.25
1972 V8-400—		
Electronic Ign	3656304	24.00
All Others (Early)	3656303	24.00
All Others (Late)	3656599	25.47
1972 V8-440—		
Exc Below	3656306	4.25
Elect Ign Exc	3656310	4.25
W/Emission Control	3656304	24.00
1973	3656310	4.25
1974-75, Exc	3755505	4.25
Calif Emission (74)	3755511	24.00
V8-318, 360	3755474	4.25

6—IGNITION COIL:

Description	Part No.	Price
1969-75	2495531	13.28

IGNITION COIL RESISTOR:

Description	Part No.	Price
1969-75, Exc	2275590	2.49
W/Electronic Ign	3656199	2.24

7—IGNITION CABLE SET:

Description	Part No.	Price
1969	3420915	18.52
1970-72—		
Exc. Below	3420915	18.52
V8-360	3004192	11.64
W/Electronic Ign	3620886	17.73
1973-74, Exc	3744973	27.12
V8-360	3780743	13.64

8—IGNITION SWITCH:

Description	Part No.	Price
1969	2864463	5.36
1970-75—		
L/Tilt Wheel (70-74)	2947486	6.34
L/Tilt Wheel (75)	3746938	.
W/Tilt Wheel	2947719	8.96

Time — Fuel System & Intake Manifold (Group C) — Time

OPERATION INDEX

C1—CARBURETOR, R & R OR RENEW

1969-71, 2 Bar (0.5) 0.7
4-Bar, One (0.7) 1.0
4-Bar, Two (1.0) 1.3
1972-75 , 2 Bar (0.7) 0.9
4 Bar (1.0) 1.3

C2—CARBURETOR, R & R & OVERHAUL

1969-718 2 Bar (2.0) 2.4
4 Bar, One (3.0) 3.5
4 Bar, Two (4.5) 5.0
1972-75, 2 Bar (1.7) 2.3
4 Bar (2.4) 3.0

C2A—ACCELERATOR PUMP, RENEW

1969-75 2 Bar. (0.6) 0.8
1969-75 4 Bar. (1.0) 1.3

C2B—NEEDLE & SEAT, RENEW

1969-75 2 Bar. (0.6) 0.7
1969-75 4 Bar. (0.6) 0.8
Thermo-Quad (Two) (1.2) 1.4

C3—AUTOMATIC CHOKE THERMOSTAT, RENEW

Includes: Adjust & check operation.
1969-75—
2 Bar. (0.3) 0.4
4 Bar. (0.4) 0.6

C3B—AUTOMATIC CHOKE VACUUM DIAPHRAGM, RENEW

1969-75—
2 Bar. (0.3) 0.4
4 Bar. (0.4) 0.5
Thermo-Quad (0.9) 1.1

C5—FUEL PUMP, R & R OR RENEW

1969-75 (0.6) 0.8

C5A—FUEL PUMP PUSH ROD, RENEW

1969-75 (0.5) 0.7

—NOTE—

If Air Cond. Obstructs Work, Add (0.2) *0.3*

C6—FUEL TANK, R & R OR RENEW

1969-70 Exc (1.1) 1.7
Station Wagon (1.2) 1.8
1971-72 Exc (1.1) 1.7
Station Wagon (1.5) 1.9
1973-75 Exc (0.8) 1.3
Station Wagon (1.5) 1.9

C7—FUEL SYSTEM, CLEAN

Includes blow out lines & clean or renew fuel line filter after tank is removed.
1969-75 (0.6) 0.8

C8—INTAKE MANIFOLD GASKETS, RENEW

1969-75 (1.3) 1.5

—NOTE—

For Ram Manifold, Add (0.6) *0.7*

Parts — Fuel System & Intake Manifold — Parts

PARTS INDEX

1—CARBURETOR ASS'Y (CARTER)

	Part No.	Price
1969 V8-383 (2 Bar. Carb.)—		
Std. Trans.	3549532	48.56
Auto. Trans.	3549532	48.56
1969 V8-383 (4 Bar. Carb.)—		
Std. Trans.	2946577	76.96
Auto. Trans.	2946591	82.57
1969 V8-440	2946592	84.30
1970 V8-383 (2 Bar. Carb.)—		
Synchro-Mesh—		
Exc. Below	3418526	37.61
California	3418528	43.25
Auto. Trans.	3418529	43.66
1970, V8-383 (4 Bar)	3418541	83.53
1970 V8-440—		
Exc. Below	3418554	.
W/Air Cond.	3418558	.
California	3418558	.
1971 V8-383, 2 Bar	3512825	50.51
4 Bar	3512844	82.75
1971 V8-440	3512831	89.13
1973 V8-440—		
Exc High Perf—		
L/Air Pump	3698334	95.93
W/Air Pump	3698319	95.93
High Perf—		
L/Air Pump	3698336	95.93
W/Air Pump	3698329	95.93
1974, V8-360	3751451	106.12
1970, 400 (Early) Exc	3751452	85.31
Calif Emission	3751453	.
1974, V8-400, Late	3751419	106.12
1974, 440 (Early)—		
L/Hi Perf Exc	3751443	106.12
Calif Emission	3751444	106.12
W/Hi Perf Exc	3751445	85.31
Calif Emission	3751446	85.31
1974, 400, Late, Exc	3830403	71.17
Calif Emission	3830404	92.24
Hi-Perf, Exc	3830415	106.12
Calif Emission	3830416	106.12
1975, V8-318, Exc	3830522	.
Calif Emission	3830524	.
1975, V8-360	3830531	.
1975, V8-400, Exc	3830554	.
Calif Emission	3830535	.
1975, V8-440—		
L/Hi-Perf, Exc	3830536	.
Calif Emission	3830537	.
W/Hi-Perf, Exc	3830538	.
Calif Emission	3830539	.

2—CARBURETOR ASS'Y (HOLLEY):

	Part No.	Price
1969 V8-440 Auto. Trans.	2946582	103.80
1970 V8-383 (2 Bar. Carb.)—		
Exc. Below	3418527	37.55
California	3418528	43.25
1970 V8-440—		
Exc. Below	3418551	136.02
California	3418552	125.92
1971 V8-360	3512823	76.77
1972 V8-360—		
Exc. Below	3614131	75.58
W/NOX Control	3683838	85.99
1972 V8-400—		
Exc. Below	3671748	82.88
Emission Control	3671750	82.88
1972 V8-440—		
Exc. Below	3614140	131.10
W/Air Pump	3621394	125.82
1973 V8-400—		
L/Air Pump	3698331	85.99
W/Air Pump	3698341	85.99
1974, 400 Eng, Early	3751437	71.00
Late	3751490	76.77
1975, V8-360, Exc	3879154	.
Tag No R-7226a	3830563	.
1975, V8-400	3879155	.

3—CARBURETOR MINOR REPAIR KIT (CARTER)

	Part No.	Price
1969 V8-383—		
2 Bar. Carb.	3621286	7.21
4 Bar. Carb.	3621400	9.45
1969-70, V8-440	3621400	9.45
1970 V8-383—		
2 Bar. Carb.	3621286	7.21
4 Bar. Carb.	3621400	9.45
1971 V8-383—		
2 Bar. Carb.	3621286	7.21
4 Bar. Carb.	3621224	10.50
1971 V8-440	3621224	10.50
1973-74, (Early)	3744758	9.62
Late	3837521	7.93

4—CARBURETOR GASKET SET (CARTER)

	Part No.	Price
1969 V8-383—		
2 Bar. Carb.	2933191	1.22
4 Bar. Carb.	2933197	1.39
1969 V8-440	2933197	1.39
1970 V8-383—		
2 Bar. Carb.—		
Exc. Below	3549296	3.84
Auto Trans	2933191	1.22
4 Bar. Carb.	3549297	6.49
1970 V8-440—		
L/Air Cond.	3549273	2.82
W/Air Cond.	3549297	6.49
1971 V8-383—		
2 Bar. Carb.	3549296	3.84
4 Bar. Carb.	3621244	6.49
1971 V8-440	3621244	6.49
1973-74	3744757	2.92

5—THERMOSTATIC COIL & HOUSING ASS'Y (CARTER):

	Part No.	Price
1968-69 V8-440	2863845	10.60
1969 V8-383—		
2 Bar. Carb.	2863846	9.47
4 Bar. Carb.	2863845	10.60
1970-71 V8-383—		
2 Bar	2951652	10.76
4 Bar	2951653	11.19
1970-71, V8-440	2951653	11.19
1972 Exc.	3512872	4.49
V8-440	3512867	4.87
1973 Exc	3698371	7.80
V8-440	3698355	10.16
1974	3751484	10.16

6—ACCELERATOR PUMP

	Part No.	Price
1975 Holley	3621365	4.71

7—ACCEL PUMP NEEDLE & SEAT

	Part No.	Price
1975 Holley	3514730	1.62

8—FUEL PUMP

	Part No.	Price
1969-71—		
Exc. Below	3621675	13.05
V8-360 (1971)	3620795	15.70
1972 V8-400, 440—		
Exc. Below	3621609	15.70
Electric	3642014	86.01
1973-74	3685799	15.70
1975, V8-318, 360	3744806	14.90
V8-400, Exc	3685799	15.70
Emission Cont	3879761	
V8-440, W/Hi-Perf	3685800	15.70
L/Hi-Perf, Exc	3685799	15.70
Emission Cont	3879761	.

9—FUEL TANK:

	Part No.	Price
1969 Chrysler—		
Exc. Below	3404475	56.74
Sta Wagon	2925748	61.31
1969-70, Imperial	3404475	56.74

1970 Chrysler—
Exc. Below ....3404475● 56.74
Sta. Wagon—
L/Evap. Emission ....2925748● 61.31
W/Evap. Emission ....3404225● 70.71
1971 Except ....3466887● 77.72
Sta Wagon ....3404225● 70.71
1972—
Exc. Below ....3583562● 77.72
Sta. Wagon ....3404225● 70.71
1973 Except ....3642156● 77.72
Sta Wagon ....3642175● 68.63
1974-75, Exc ....3726077● 81.57
Sta Wagon ....3726085● 81.57
Cordoba ....3906503¶ .

10—INTAKE MANIFOLD GASKET:
1969-71, V8-440 ....3671575● .
1968-71 V8-383 ....3671874● 3.67
1971-75, V8-360 ....3514187● 4.15
1972-75, V8-400 ....3671874● 3.67
1972 V8-440—
Early ....3671575● .
Late ....3671933● 3.67
1973-75, V8-440, Exc ....3671933● 3.67
Hi-Perf ....3769933¶ 4.27

DODGE

Time — Emission Controls (Group AB) — Time

OPERATION INDEX

AB1—CRANKCASE VENTILATOR VALVE (PCV), CLEAN OR RENEW
Clean (0.3) 0.5
Renew (0.2) 0.3

AB2—EMISSION CONTROL (CAP), CHECK
Includes Adjust Idle, Timing And Distributor Vacuum Control Unit.
All Models (0.6) 1.0

AB3—VACUUM CONTROL UNIT, RENEW
All Models (0.8) 1.2

AB6—AIR PUMP, R & R OR RENEW
1972 (0.4) 0.6
1973 Six Exc (0.4) 0.6
Dart W/Air Cond (0.9) 1.2
1974-75 (0.7) 1.1

AB7—AIR PUMP HOSE, RENEW
1972-75 (0.2) 0.3

AB10A—DIVERTER VALVE, RENEW
1972 (0.3) 0.7
1973 Six (0.3) 0.7
V8 (0.7) 1.0
1974-75 (0.7) 1.0

AB12—CHECK VALVE, RENEW
All Models (0.5) 0.8

AB18—FUEL VAPOR CANISTER, R&R OR RENEW
All Models (0.3) 0.5

AB18A—VAPOR CANISTER FILTER, RENEW
All Models (0.2) 0.3

AB20—EXHAUST GAS RECIRCULATION CONTROL VALVE, RENEW
1973-75 (0.3) 0.5

AB21—EXHAUST GAS COOLANT CONTROL VALVE, RENEW
1973-75 (0.3) 0.5

AB22—EGR TIME DELAY TIMER, RENEW
1974-75 (0.2) 0.3

AB23—EGR TIME DELAY SOLENOID, RENEW
1974-75 (0.2) 0.3

AB24—EGR VACUUM AMPLIFIER, RENEW
1973-75 (0.2) 0.3

AB25—ORIFICE SPARK ADVANCE CONTROL VALVE, RENEW
1973-75 (0.3) 0.4

Parts — Emission Controls — Parts

PARTS INDEX

1—CRANKCASE VENTILATION VALVE:
1967-69 Six 2808441 2.91
1967-69 V8 ....2808622 2.91
1970-75 ....3671076 2.89
1970 V8 ....3671076 2.89

2—DISTRIBUTOR THERMOSTATIC VACUUM SWITCH:
1968-69 V8-426 ....2863739 9.17
1968-69 6-170 ....2843299 9.17

2A—DISTRIBUTOR THERMOSTATIC VACUUM VALVE:
1971-72, Exc. 3614024 6.76
V8-400,440 ....3614023 6.42
1973, V8-360 ....3614023 6.42
V8-400 ....3614024 6.76
V8-440, Exc. 3614024 6.76
W/Air Pump 3614023 6.42
1974-75 ....3780126 6.76

3— "NOX "EXHAUST EMISSION PARTS(1971-72)-
1971-72 Control Unit 3621803 31.65
1971 Vacuum Valve 3438474 6.01
1972 Vacuum Valve 3656381 6.01

1971-72—
Thermal Switch 3438465 6.99
Speed Switch—
Synchro-Mesh 3438472 3.13
Auto. Trans. 3438494 15.50

4—FUEL VAPOR SEPARATOR
DODGE:
1970-71 Polara & Monaco ..3466836 .
1970-71 Challenger 3404183 20.35
1970 Coronet 3404373 20.35
1970 Charger, Exc. 3404365 23.10
Sta.Wagon 3404164 23.10
1971 Coronet & Charger—
Early 3466835 30.46
Late 3466835 30.46
1972 Early—
Polara & Monaco ....3466836 .
Challenger 3404183 20.35
Coronet & Charger 3466835 30.46
1972 Late; 1973 ....3642105 8.42
1974 ....3751502 7.35
1975, Exc ....3870674 .
V8-400, 440 ....3751502 7.35
DART:
1970-71 ....3404351 21.37
1975 ....3870676 .

5—FUEL FILTER (IN TANK):
1970-75—
Exc. Below 1670694 1.04
V8-426, 440 ....2534111 .99

6—FUEL VAPOR CANISTER
1972-73 ....3577584 26.20
1974-75 ....3577595 26.20

7—FUEL VAPOR CANISTER FILTER
1972-75 ....3577586 .74

8—EXHAUST GAS RECIRCULATION VALVE
1973 Six, Std Trans 3671415 7.81
Auto Trans (Exc Calif)—
Early 3751092 7.81
Late 3769218 7.81
Auto Trans (Calif) 3751164 7.81

1973 V8-318 ....3671417 7.81
V8-360, Exc 3671419 7.81
Calif Emission 3751093 7.81
V8-400 ....3671420 10.55
V8-440 ....3671423 10.55
1974 Six Std Trans Exc 3830101 7.81
Calif Emission 3769659 7.81
1974 Six Auto Tr Exc 3769658 7.81
Calif Emission 3769660 7.81
1974 V8-318—
Std Trans, Exc 3830102 7.81
Calif Emission 3769662 7.81
Auto Trans 3830103 7.81

1974 V8-360—
Exc Monaco—
Calif Emission ....3879728 .
Calif Emission 3769661 7.81
Auto Trans, Exc 3769665 7.81
Calif Emission 3769662 7.81
Monaco 3769663 7.81
1974 V8-400—
2 Bar 3769809 13.47
Calif Emission ....3879709 .
4 Bar, Exc 3769670 14.00
4 Speed 3830104 14.00

Auto Tr Hi-Perf 3830105 14.00
Std Trans, Exc 3769664 7.81
1974 V8-440, Exc 3698886 14.00
Calif Emission, Exc 3769667 14.00
Coronet & Charger 3830120 14.00
1975 Six ....3837650 .
V8-318, Exc ....3879713 .
Auto Trans, Exc ....3780189 .
V8-360, 2 Bar ....3780189 .
4 Bar, Exc ....3879711 .
Hi-Perf ....3879728 .

V8-400, Exc ....3870635 .
Hi-Perf 3698886 14.00
V8-440, Exc 3830120 14.00
Hi-Perf ....3870630 .

9—AIR INJECTION PUMP
1972-74 ....3614985 57.47
1975 Six ....3837646 .
V8 ....3837647 .

Time — Tune-Up & Ignition (Group B) — Time

OPERATION INDEX

B1—TUNE-UP, MINOR
Includes renew or clean and adjust points, condenser & plugs, set spark timing and adjust carburetor idle.
Six Cyl—
Standard Ignition (1.3) 1.5
Electronic Ignition (0.8) 1.0
V8 (Standard Ignition)—
Exc. Below (2.0) 2.4
V8-273 (1.6) 2.0
V8-318, 340, 360 (1.5) 2.0
V8-383,400,440 Exc(2.0) 2.4
Polara & Monaco(2.2) 2.6
V8-426 (Hemi) (2.4) ①3.0
V8 (Electronic Ignition)—
Exc Below (1.5) 1.9
V8-318, 340, 360 (1.0) 1.5
V8-383, 400, 440 Exc (1.5) 1.9
Polara & Monaco (1.7) 2.1
V8-426 (Hemi) (1.9) ①2.5
—NOTE—
For Each 4 Barrel Carb., Add (0.2) *0.3*
For Clean Air Package, Add (0.3) *0.5*
①For Power Brake Unit, Add (0.4) *0.5*

B2—TUNE-UP, MAJOR
Includes check compression, clean or renew and adjust spark plugs, R & R distributor, renew points & condenser. Adjust ignition timing, carburetor and fan belts, clean battery terminals and service air cleaner. Check coil and service manifold heat control valve and renew or clean fuel line filter.
Six Cyl—
Standard Ignition (2.1) 2.9
Electronic Ignition (1.6) 2.4
V8 (Standard Ignition)—
Exc. Below (2.9) 3.8
V8-273 (2.6) 3.4
V8-318, 340, 360 (2.4) 3.4
V8-426 (Hemi) (6.3) ①7.5
V8 (Electronic Ignition)—
Exc Below (2.4) 3.3
V8-318, 340, 360 (1.9) 2.9
V8-426 (Hemi) (5.8) ①7.0
—NOTE—
For Each 4 Barrel Carb., Add (0.2) *0.3*
For Cleaner Air Package, Add (0.3) *0.5*
To Renew PCV Valve, Add (0.2) *0.3*
To Clean PCV Valve, Add (0.3) *0.3*
①For Power Brake Unit, Add (0.4) *0.5*

B3—TUNE-UP, MAJOR & OVERHAUL CARBURETOR
Six Cyl—
Standard Ignition (4.1) 5.5
Electronic Ignition (3.6) 5.0
V8 2 Bar & Std Ign—
Exc. Below (5.0) 5.9
V8-273, 318 (4.8) 5.9
V8 2 Bar & Electronic Ign—
Exc Below (4.5) 5.4
V8-273, 318 (4.3) 5.4
V8 4 Bar & Std Ign—
Exc. Below (6.0) ②7.2
V8-273, 318 (5.8) ②6.6
V8-340, 360 (5.5) ②6.3
V8-426 Hemi—
One Carb. (9.4) ①10.9
Two Carbs. (10.8) ①12.6
V8 4 Bar & Electronic Ign—
Exc Below (5.5) ②6.7
V8-273, 318 (5.3) ②6.1
V8-340, 360 (5.0) ②5.8
V8-426 Hemi—
One Carb (8.9) ①10.4
Two Carbs (10.3) ①12.1
—NOTE—
For Cleaner Air Package, Add (0.3) *0.5*
To Service PCV Valve, Add (0.3) *0.4*
①For Power Brake Unit, Add (0.4) *0.5*
②For Two 4 Barrels, Add (1.5) *2.0*

B4—POINTS & CONDENSER, RENEW
Includes R & R distributor & set timing.
1969 Six—
Exc. Below (0.8) 1.2
W/Std. Trans. (1.3) 1.7
1970-72 Six (0.8) 1.2
1969-72 V8 (0.9) ②1.2
②For 1969 V8-426 Hemi W/Std. Trans., Add (0.3) *0.3*

B5—SPARK PLUGS, CLEAN & ADJUST OR RENEW
1969-75 Six (0.4) ②0.5
1968-69 V8—
Exc. Below (0.7) 0.7
V8-440 (Hi-Perf.) (0.9) 1.1
Hemi (1.1) 1.3
1970-75 V8—
Exc. Below (1.1) ②1.3
V8-318, 340, 360 (0.6) ②0.9
②For Air Injection Pump, Low Mount, Add (0.3) *0.4*

B6—COMPRESSION TEST
1969-75 Six (0.5) 0.6
1969-75 V8—
Exc. Below (0.8) 0.8
V8-440 (Hi-Perf.) (1.0) 1.3
Hemi (1.2) 1.5

B7—IGNITION TIMING, SET
All Models (0.2) 0.3

B8—DISTRIBUTOR, R & R OR RENEW
1969-71 Exc (0.7) 0.9
W/Electronic Ignition (0.6) 0.8
1972 (0.6) 0.8
1973-75 (0.5) 0.7
—NOTE—
For Cleaner Air Package, Add (0.3) *0.5*

B9—DISTRIBUTOR, OVERHAUL (UNIT OFF)
1969-75 (1.0) 1.4

B9A—DISTRIBUTOR, ADJUST ON STROBOSCOPE (UNIT OFF)
All Models (0.4) 0.4

B10—DISTRIBUTOR CAP, RENEW
1969-75 (0.3) 0.3

B10A—DISTRIBUTOR RELECTOR, RENEW
1971-75 (0.3) 0.5

B10B—DIST PICK-UP PLATE & COIL ASSY, RENEW
Distributor removed
1971-75 (0.2) 0.2

B10C—ELECTRONIC IGNITION CONTROL UNIT, RENEW
1971-75 (0.3) 0.5

B11—IGNITION CABLE SET, RENEW
Time allowance covers install factory supplied sets only.
1968-69 Six (0.4) ②0.5
1970-75 Six (0.6) 0.8
1968-69 V8—
Exc. Below (0.6) 0.8
Hemi (0.8) ①1.0
1970-71 V8—
Exc. Below (0.6) 0.8
V8-383, 440 (0.8) ③1.1
V8-426 Hemi (1.0) 1.3
1972-75 V8—
Exc. Below (0.5) 0.7
V8-383, 400, 440 (0.6) ③0.9
①For Power Brake Unit, Add (0.4) *0.5*
②For Air Cond., Add (0.5) *0.6*
③For Air Cond., Add (0.4) *0.5*

B12—VACUUM CONTROL UNIT, RENEW
Includes R & R distributor
1969 (0.6) 0.9
1970-71 (0.8) 1.1
1972-75 (0.6) 0.9

B13—IGNITION COIL, RENEW
All Models (0.3) 0.3

B14—IGNITION SWITCH, RENEW
1966-69—
Exc. Below (0.3) 0.5
Monaco (0.4) 0.7
Polara & 880 (0.4) 0.7
1970—
Exc. Below (0.6) 0.9
All Models W/Std. Column (1.4) 1.9
1971-75—
Exc. Below (1.4) 1.9
W/Telescopic Steer. Column (0.4) 0.6
W/Tilt Column (0.5) 0.8

B15—IGNITION COIL RESISTOR, RENEW
All Models (0.2) 0.3

DISTRIBUTOR ASS'Y:

Application	Part No.	Price
DODGE:		
Auto. Trans.	2875181	42.00
1969 Six—		
Synchro-Mesh	2875923	
Auto. Trans.	3656258	32.96
1969 V8-318	2875797	37.28
1969 V8-383 (2 Bar. Carb.)—		
Synchro-Mesh	2875743	41.71
Auto. Trans.	2875748	41.71
1969 V8-383 (4 Bar. Carb.)—		
Synchro-Mesh	2875751	41.71
Auto. Trans.	2875732	41.71
1969 V8-440 (Exc. Hi-Perf)	2875765	44.08
1969 V8-440 (W/Hi-Perf.)—		
Synchro-Mesh	2875773	47.93
Auto. Trans.	2875759	44.08
1970 6-198—		
Synchro-Mesh	3438238	31.95
Auto. Trans.	3656258	32.96
1970 6-225—		
L/Nox Exh. Cont.—		
Synchro-Mesh	3656253	32.96
Auto. Trans.	3656258	32.96
W/Nox Exh. Cont.—		
Synchro-Mesh	3438441	32.96
Auto. Trans.	3438443	32.96
1970 V8-318—		
Synchro-Mesh	3438256	37.28
Auto. Trans.	3656391	37.28
1970 V8-340—		
Synchro-Mesh	3438318	56.98
Auto. Trans.	3438326	39.76
1970 V8-383—		
2 Bar. Carb.	3438232	41.71
4 Bar. Carb.	3438434	41.71
1970 V8-426—		
Synchro-Mesh	2875988	56.98
Auto. Trans.	2875990	56.98
1970 V8-440 (Single Carb.)—		
Exc. Below	3438221	44.08
Hi-Perf.	3438224	44.08
1970 V8-440 (3 Carbs.)—		
Synchro-Mesh	3438316	56.98
Auto. Trans.	2875983	56.98
1971 6-198—		
Exc. Below	3438510	31.95
W/Nox. Exh. Cont.	3438525	31.95
1971 6-225—		
L/Nox Exh. Cont—		
Synchro-Mesh	3656253	32.96
Auto. Trans.	3656258	32.96
W/Nox Exh Cont.—		
Synchro-Mesh	3438441	32.96
Auto. Trans.	3438443	32.96
1971 V8-318—		
Exc. Below	3438256	37.28
Auto Trans.	3656391	37.28
W/Nox. Exh. Cont.	3656276	37.28
1971 V8-340—		
Single Carb.—		
Synchro-Mesh	3438530	60.18
Auto. Trans.	3438520	39.76
3 Carbs.—		
Synchro-Mesh	3438616	60.18
Auto. Trans.	3438618	60.18
1971 V8-360—		
Exc. Below	3656273	37.28
W/Nox. Exh. Cont.	3656276	37.28
1971 V8-383 (2 Bar. Carb.)—		
Exc. Below	3438535	41.71
W/Nox. Exh. Cont.	3438545	41.71
1971 V8-383 (4 Bar.)	3438691	41.71
1971 V8-426—		
Synchro-Mesh	2875988	56.98
Auto. Trans.	3438580	56.98
1971 V8-440—		
Exc. Below	3438560	44.08
4 Bar. Carb	3438695	44.08
3 Carbs.	3438578	56.98
1972 6-198—		
Exc. Below	3656238	31.95
W/Emission Cont.	3656244	31.95
1972 6-225—		
L/Emission Cont.—		
Synchro-Mesh	3656253	32.96
Auto. Trans.	3656258	32.96
W/Emission Cont.—		
Synchro-Mesh	3656261	32.96
Auto. Trans.	3656267	32.96
1972 V8-318—		
L/Emission Cont.—		
Synchro-Mesh	3656273	37.28
Auto. Trans.	3656391	37.28
W/Emission Cont.	3656276	37.28
1972 V8-340, Exc.	3656284	39.76
W/Elect. Ign.	3656279	39.76
1972 V8-360—		
Exc. Below	3656273	37.28
Elect. Ignition	3656430	43.01
1972 V8-400—		
Elect. Ignition	3656336	44.08
L/Emission Cont.—		
Coronet & Charger	3656339	44.08
Polara & Monaco	3656333	44.08
1972 V8-440—		
4 Bar Carb.—		
Synchro-Mesh	3656348	44.08
Auto Trans.—		
Exc. Below	3656342	44.08
Emission Cont.	3656348	44.08
3 Carbs.	3656354	44.08
Hi-Perf.	3656351	44.08
1973-74 Six, Exc.	3755038	32.96
Auto. Trans.	3755043	32.96
1973 V8—		
318	3656764	37.28
340	3656772	39.76
360	3656781	44.08
400, 2 Bar.	3656792	44.08
4 Bar.,Exc.	3755310	44.08
Auto Trans.	3656803	44.08
V8-440	3755158	44.08
1974 V8-318	3656764	37.28
1974 V8-360 Exc	3755487	43.01
Monaco	3755476	44.08
1974 V8-400—		
L/Hi-Perf	3755682	44.08
W/Hi-Perf—		
Less Calif Emission	3755513	44.08
With Calif Emission	3755509	44.08
1974 V8-440 Exc	3755519	44.08
Calif Emission	3755523	44.08
1975 Six, Exc	3874086	
Catalytic Exh	3874083	
1975 V8-318, Exc	3755473	
Catalytic Exh	3874091	
1975 V8-360, Exc	3874146	
Catalytic Exhaust—		
L/Hi-Perf	3874116	
W/Hi-Perf	3874202	
1975 V8-400, 2 Bar	3874102	
4 Bar, Exc	3755682	44.08
Catalytic Exh	3874111	
1975 V8-440—		
Catalytic Exh	3874174	
W/Hi-Perf, Exc	3874120	
Air Pump	3874174	
DART		
1969 6-170—		
Synchro-Mesh	2875814	31.95
Auto. Trans.	2875856	31.95
1969-6-225—		
Synchro-Mesh	3656253	32.96
Auto. Trans.	3656258	32.96
1969 V8-273	2875791	35.80
1969 V8-318	2875797	37.28
1969 V8-340—		
Synchro-Mesh	2875783	56.33
Auto. Trans.	2875780	39.76
1969 V8-383—		
Synchro-Mesh	2875718	48.04
Auto. Trans.	2875847	47.93
1970 6-198	3438238	31.95
1970 6-225—		
Synchro-Mesh	3656253	32.96
Auto. Trans.	3656258	32.96
1970 V8-318—		
Synchro-Mesh	3438256	37.28
Auto. Trans.	3656391	37.28
1970 V8-340—		
Synchro-Mesh	3438318	56.98
Auto. Trans.	3438326	39.76
1971 6-198—		
Exc. Below	3438510	31.95
W/Nox. Exh. Cont.	3438525	31.95
1971 6-225—		
L/Nox. Exh. Cont—		
Synchro-Mesh	3656253	32.96
Auto. Trans.	3656258	32.96
W/Nox. Exh. Cont.—		
Synchro-Mesh	3438441	32.96
Auto. Trans.	3438443	32.96
1971 V8-318—		
Exc. Below	3438256	37.28
W/Nox. Exh. Cont.	3656276	37.28
1971 V8-340—		
Synchro-Mesh	3438530	60.18
Auto. Trans.	3438520	39.76
1972 6-198—		
L/Emission Cont.	3656238	31.95
W/Emission Cont.	3656244	31.95
1972 6-225—		
Exc. Below—		
L/Emission Cont.—		
Synchro-Mesh.	3656253	32.96
Auto. Trans.	3656258	32.96
W/Emission Cont.—		
Synchro-Mesh.	3656261	32.96
Auto. Trans.	3656267	32.96
2 Bar. (A119 Eng. Kit)—		
Synchro-Mesh	3656247	32.96
Auto. Trans.	3656249	32.96
1972 V8-318—		
L/Emission Cont.—		
Synchro-Mesh.	3656273	37.28
Auto. Trans.	3656391	37.28
W/Emission Cont.	3656276	37.28
1972 V8-340	3656279	39.76
1973-74 6-198	3656861	31.95
1973 V8-318	3656764	37.28
V8-340	3656772	39.76
1973-74 V8-360		
1973-74, 6-225—		
Synchromesh Exc	3755038	32.96
Calif Emission	3755468	32.96
Auto Trans Exc	3755043	32.96
Calif Emission	3755471	32.96
1975 Six, Exc	3874232	
Air Pump	3874086	
Catalytic Exh	3874083	
1975 V8-318, Exc	3874239	
Air Pump	3755473	
Catalytic Exh	3874091	
1975 V87-360, Exc	3874098	
Catalytic Exh, Exc	3874116	
Hi-Perf	3874202	

FIG.1-TUNE-UP & IGNITION

(For Parts Identification Only)

ELECTRONIC DISTRIBUTOR PARTS

Application	Part No.	Price
1972—		
Pick-Up	3656025	
Pick-Up Plate	3656023	3.75
Reluctor	3656017	1.74
1973-75		
Pick-Up & Plate Assy—		
6 Cyl	3656866	8.77
V8	3656738	8.77
Reluctor, 6 Cyl	3656862	1.74
Reluctor, V8	3656017	1.74

1—IGNITION POINT SET:

Application	Part No.	Price
DODGE:		
1969-72 (Exc Below)	2098244	3.20
1968-69 V8-426	2808870	7.40
1968-71 V8-440—		
Exc. Hi-Perf.	2098244	3.20
Hi-Perf. (Std. Trans.)	2421173	2.66
Hi-Perf. (Auto. Trans.)	2098244	3.20
1970-72 V8-340, 360,		
Exc,	2098244	3.20
Synchro-Mesh	2421175	2.66
1970 V8-426	2421173	2.66
DART:		
1969-72—		
Exc. Below	2098244	3.20
V8-383	2421173	2.66

2—CONDENSER:

Application	Part No.	Price
1969 (Exc Below)	2098058	1.56
1969 V8-340, 426	1818757	1.56
V8-440 Hi-Perf	1818757	1.56
1970-72 (Exc Below)	3420600	1.56
1970-71 6-225	2098058	1.56

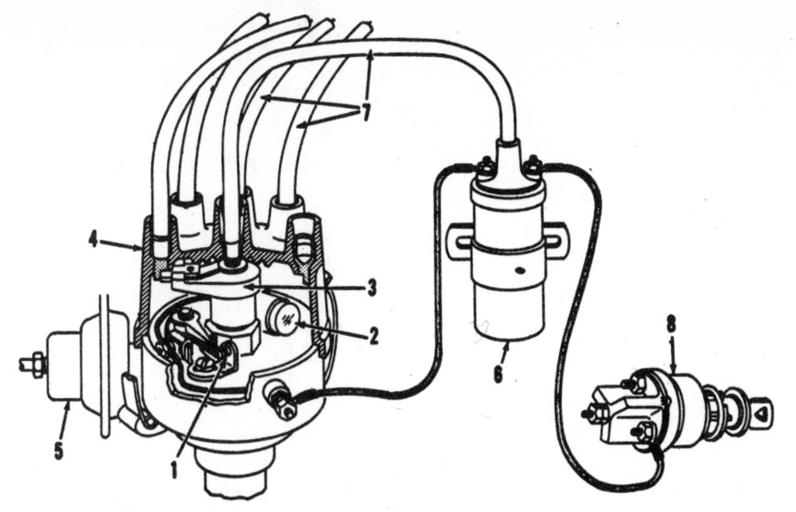

3—ROTOR:

1969-71 Exc	1838516	1.18
V8-340 Std Trans	1658535	1.15
V8-426	1658535	1.15
V8-440 Hi Perf	1658535	1.15
1972-75	1838516	1.18

4—DISTRIBUTOR CAP:

1969-75 Six	2642986	3.81
1968-71 V8-273, 318	2444507	4.44
1968-71 V8-383	2444507	4.44
1968-71 V8-426	2585000	4.21
1969-71 V8-440, Exc	2444507	4.44
W/3 Carbs.	2585000	4.21
1970-71 V8-340, Exc.	2585000	4.21
Auto. Trans.	2444507	4.44
1971 V8-360	2642986	3.81
1972-75 V8	2444507	4.44

5—VACUUM CONTROL UNIT:

DODGE:

1969 V8-426	2808897	3.40
1969 Six—		
Synchro-Mesh	2875818	4.25
Auto. Trans.	2875825	4.25
1969 V8-273	2875786	4.25
1969 V8-318	2875794	4.25
1969 V8-383—		
2 Bar. Carb.	2875735	4.25
4 Bar. Carb.	2875728	4.25
Auto. Trans.	3438229	4.25
1969 V8-440—		
L/Hi-Perf.	2875761	4.25
W/Hi-Perf	2875754	4.25
1970-72 6-198—		
Exc. Below	2875825	4.25
L/Nox Exh. Cont. (1971)	3438514	4.25
1970-72 6-225—		
Synchro-Mesh	2875818	4.25
Auto. Trans. (1970-71)	2875825	4.25
Auto. Trans. (1972)	3438424	4.25
1970-71 V8-318—		
Synchro-Mesh	2875794	4.25
Auto. Trans.	3438229	4.25
Nox Exh. Cont.	3438424	4.25
1970-71 V8-340 (1 Carb.)—		
Synchro-Mesh	3514265	6.20
Auto. Trans. (1970)	3438339	4.25
Auto. Trans. (1971)	3438229	4.25
1970 V8-383, 2 Bar.	3514331	25.47
4 Bar.	3514330	25.47
1970-71 V8-426, Exc.	3514279	7.10
Auto. Trans. (1971)	2808897	3.40
1970 V8-440, Exc.	3514329	25.47
Hi-Perf.	3514330	25.47
Tri-Carbs	3420919	6.75
1971 V8-340 (3 Carbs.)—		
Synchro-Mesh	3420919	6.75
Auto. Trans.	3514265	6.20
1971 V8-360	3438424	4.25
1971 V8-383, 2 Bar.	3579239	25.47
4 Bar.	3579240	25.47
1971 V8-440, Exc.	3579241	25.47
1 Carb.	3514330	25.47
3 Carbs.	3514332	25.47
1972 V8-318—		
Synchro-Mesh.	3438424	4.25
Auto. Trans.	3438229	4.25
1972 V8-340	3656066	4.25
1972 V8-360—		
Exc. Below	3438424	4.25
Elect. Ignition	3656434	4.25
1972 V8-400—		
Elect. Ignition	3656304	24.00
L/Emission Cont.—		
Coronet & Charger	3656310	4.25
Polara & Monaco	3656306	4.25
1972 V8-440—		
Exc. Below	3656304	24.00
Hi-Perf.	3656303	24.00
Auto. (L/Emission)	3656310	4.25
1973-74 Six, Exc.	3755041	4.25
Auto. Trans.	3755036	4.25
1973 V8-318,360	3656766	4.25
V8-340	3656066	4.25
V8-400, Exc.	3656310	4.25
4 Bar.(Std. Trans.)	3656304	24.00
V8-440	3656310	4.25
1974 V8—		
318	3656766	4.25
360 Exc	3755491	4.25
Monaco	3755474	4.25
400 Exc	3755505	4.25
Calif Emission	3755511	24.00
440	3755505	4.25
1975 Six	3755036	4.25
V8-318, 360	3755474	4.25
V8-400, 440	3755505	4.25

DART

1969 6-170	2875809	4.25
1969-71 6-225—		
Std. Trans.	2875818	4.25
Auto. Trans.	2875825	4.25
1969 V8-318	2875794	4.25
1969 V8-273	2875786	4.25
1969 V8-383	2808897	3.40
1970-72 6-198, Exc	2875825	4.25
L/Nox Exh. Cont.	3438514	4.25
1970-71 V8-318—		
Synchro-Mesh	2875794	4.25
Auto. Trans.	3438229	4.25
1972 6-225 (Exc. Below)—		
Synchro-Mesh.	2875818	4.25
Auto. Trans.	2875825	4.25
1972 6-225 (A110 Eng. Kit)—		
Synchro-Mesh.	2875828	4.25
Auto. Trans.	2875832	4.25
1972 V8-318—		
Synchro-Mesh.	3438424	4.25
Auto. Trans.	3438229	4.25
1972 V8-340	3656066	4.25
1973-74 6-198	3755036	4.25
6-225, Exc.	3755041	4.25
Auto. Trans.	3755036	4.25
1973-74 V8-318	3656766	4.25
V8-340	3656066	4.25
V8-360	3755491	4.25
1975 Six, Exc	3755036	4.25
Lean Burn Pkg	3874237	
1975 V8-318, Exc	3855474	
Lean Burn Pkg	3874237	
1975 V8-360	3755474	4.25

6—IGNITION COIL:

1969-75	2495531	13.28

IGNITION COIL RESISTOR:

1967-72—		
Exc. Below	2275590	2.49
Elect. Ignition	3656199	2.24
1973-75	3656199	2.24

7—IGNITION CABLE SET:

DODGE:

1966-71 Six	2495510	8.48
1969-71 V8-426	3420881	27.49
1969-72 V8-318	3004192	11.64
1969 V8-383, 440	3420917	18.89
1970 V8-340, Exc.	3004192	11.64
Tri-Carbs.	3579221	16.23
1970-71 V8-383, 440—		
Coronet & Charger	3420917	18.89
Polara & Monaco	3420915	18.52
1971 V8-340	3579221	16.23
1971-72 V8-360	3004192	11.64
1972 V8-340,360—		
Exc. Below	3004192	11.64
Elect. Ign.	3620886	17.73
1972 V8-400,440—		
Coronet & Charger, Exc.	3420917	18.89
Elect. Ign.	3620887	23.44
Polara & Monaco, Exc.	3420915	18.52
Elect. Ign.	3620888	24.07
1973 Six	3744971	8.48
1973 V8 Exc	3744972	13.64
400&440	3744973	27.12
1974 Six	3780744	8.48
1974 V8 Exc	3780743	13.64
400&440	3744973	27.12
1975 Six	3879330	

DART:

1967-72 Six	2495510	8.48
1969 V8—		
Exc. Below	3004192	11.64
V8-383	3420915	18.52
1970-72, V8-318	3004192	11.64
1970 V8-340	3004192	11.64
1971 V8-340	3579221	16.23
1972 V8 340, Exc.	3004192	11.64
Elect. Ign.	3620886	17.73
1973 Six	3744971	8.48
V8	3744972	13.64
1974 Six	3780744	8.48
V8	3780743	13.64
1975 Six	3879330	

8—IGNITION SWITCH:

1969	2864463	5.36
1970-74 Exc	2947486	6.34
W/Tilt Wheel Exc	2947719	8.96
Coro & Char (71-72)	3488398	10.97
1975 (Exc Dart)—		
Exc Below	3746938	
Tilt Wheel	2947719	8.96
1975 Dart	3746936	

Time — Fuel System & Intake Manifold (Group C) — Time

OPERATION INDEX

C1—CARBURETOR, R & R OR RENEW

1968-69 Six (0.5)	0.7
1970-75 Six (0.7)	0.9
1968-69 V8—	
2 Barrel (0.5)	0.8
One 4 Bar. (0.6)	1.0
Two 4 Bars. (1.0)	1.4
Tri-Carb Center (0.9)	1.2
Tri-Carb Front Or Rear (0.7)	0.9
1970-75 V8—	
2 Barrel (0.7)	0.9
One 4 Bar (0.7)	1.0
Two 4 Bar (1.0)	1.4

Tri-Carb Center (0.9) 1.2
Tri-Carb Front Or Rear (0.7) 0.9
Thermo-Quad (1.0) 1.3

C2—CARBURETOR, R & R & OVERHAUL

1968-71—
One Bar. (2.0) 2.4
Two Bar—
Exc. Below (2.0) 2.4
Rochester (1.4) 1.7
Holley Tri-Carb—
Center (2.1) 2.6
Front Or Rear (1.9) 2.3
All Three (5.5) 6.8
Four Bar—
Exc. Below (3.0) 3.6
Thermo Quad (2.4) 2.9
Two Four Bar (4.5) 5.5

1972—
One Bar—
Exc. Below (1.5) 1.8
Holley (1.4) 1.6
Two Bar—
Exc. Below (1.4) 1.6
Carter (1.6) 1.8
Holley (1.7) 2.0
Holley Tri-Carb—
Center (2.1) 2.6
Front Or Rear (1.9) 2.3
All Three (5.5) 6.8
Four Bar—
Exc. Below (1.7) 2.2
Holley (2.2) 2.7
Thermo-Quad (2.4) 2.9
Two Four Bar. (4.5) 5.5
1973-75—
1 Barrel (1.4) 1.6
2 Barrel (1.7) 2.0
4 Barrel (2.4) 3.0

C2A—ACCELERATOR PUMP, RENEW

1969-75—
Exc. 4 Barrel (0.6) 0.8
4 Barrel—
Exc. Below (0.8) 1.1
Thermo-Quad. (1.0) 1.4

—NOTE—

Does Not Include R & R Carburetor.

C2B—NEEDLE & SEAT, RENEW

1966-69—
Exc. Below (0.4) 0.6
4 Barrel—
Exc. Below (0.6) 0.8
Thermo-Quad. (1.1) 1.5
Tri-Carb. (One) (0.6) 0.8
Tri-Carb-Three (1.0) 1.5
1970-75—
One Bar (0.4) 0.6
Two Bar—
Exc. Below (0.4) 0.6
Holley (0.6) 0.8
Four Bar—
Exc. Below (0.8) ①②1.1
Thermo-Quad (1.1) 1.4
Holley Tri-Carb.—
One (0.6) 0.8
Three (1.0) 1.5

—NOTE—

Does Not Include R & R Carburetor.
①For Holley Secondary Add (0.2) 0.3
②For Holley Primary & Secondary Add (0.4) 0.6

C3—AUTO. CHOKE THERMOSTAT, RENEW

1969-75—
Exc. Below (0.3) 0.4
4 Barrel (0.4) 0.6

C3A—AUTO. CHOKE, OVERHAUL

1969-75—
Exc. Below (0.5) 0.5
4 Barrel (0.7) 1.0

C3B—AUTO. CHOKE VACUUM DIAPHRAGM, RENEW

1966-69—
Exc. Below (0.3) 0.4
4 Barrel (0.4) 0.5
1970-75—
Carter Holley & Rochester—
Exc. Below (0.3) 0.4
Holley-Tri Carb. (0.4) 0.7
Carter-Thermo-Quad (0.9) 1.3

C4—DASHPOT, RENEW

1966-71—
Exc. Below (0.3) 0.3
4 Barrel (0.4) 0.4
1972-75 (0.4) 0.5

C5—FUEL PUMP, R & R OR RENEW

1969-75 Six (0.3) 0.4
1969-75 V8—
Exc. Below (0.5) 0.7
Hemi (0.6) 0.8

C5A—FUEL PUMP PUSH ROD, RENEW

1969-75 V8—
Exc. Below (0.5) 0.7
Hemi (0.6) 0.9

C6—FUEL TANK, R & R OR RENEW

DODGE:
1969-72 Exc (1.1) 1.4
Charger, 70-71 (1.4) 1.8
Charger, 72 (1.1) 1.4
Challenger, 70 (1.4) 1.8
Challenger, 71-72 (1.6) 2.0
Sta Wgn, 70 (1.2) 1.5
Sta Wgn, 71-72 (1.5) 1.9
1973-75 Exc (0.8) 1.2
Challenger (1.6) 2.0
Sta Wgn (1.5) 1.9
DART:
1969-70 (0.8) 1.2
1971-72 (1.4) 1.8
1973-75 (0.8) 1.2

C7—FUEL SYSTEM, CLEAN

Includes blow out lines & clean or renew fuel line filter after tank is removed.
1969-75 (0.6) 0.8

C8—INTAKE MANIFOLD GASKETS, RENEW (V8)

1969-70—
Exc. Below (1.3) 1.5
V8-318 (1.5) 1.8
V8-340 (1.7) 2.0
V8-440 (1.6) 1.9
Hemi (2.0) 2.6
1971-75—
Exc. Below (1.6) 1.9
V8-318 (1.5) 1.8
V8-340, 360, (1.7) 2.0
Hemi (2.0) 2.6

—NOTE—

For V8-426 W/Two Carbs., Add (0.3) 0.5
For V8's 273, 318, 340, 360 With Air Cond., Add (0.4) 0.6

C8A—MANIFOLD GASKETS, RENEW (SIX CYL.)

1969-75 (2.0) 2.3

Parts — Fuel System & Intake Manifold — Parts

PARTS INDEX

1—CARBURETOR ASS'Y (CARTER):

DODGE:
1969 V8-318—
Std. Trans. 2946568 45.39
Auto. Trans. 2946571 41.38
1969 V8-383 2 Bar 3549532 48.56
1969 V8-383 (4 Bar. Carb.)—
Std. Trans. 2946577 76.96
Auto. Trans. 2946591 82.57
1969 V8-426—
Front 2946584 58.55
Rear—
Std. Trans. 2946588 66.46
Auto. Trans. 2899034
1969 V8-440—
Std. Trans. 2946578 76.96
Auto. Trans. 2946592 84.30
1970 V8-318—
L/Fuel Emission—
Synchro-Mesh 3418515 36.47
Auto. Trans., Exc 3418516 45.94
Air Cond. 3462834 35.55
W/Fuel Emission—
Synchro-Mesh 3418517 43.10
Auto. Trans. 3418518 45.61
1970 V8-340—
L/Fuel Emission—
Synchro-Mesh 3462968 74.21
Auto. Trans. 3462969 74.21
W/Air Cond. 3462970 74.21
W/Fuel Emission—
Synchro-Mesh 3462971 79.76
Auto. Trans. 3462972 79.76
1970 V8-383 (2 Bar. Carb.)—
Synchro-Mesh, Exc. 3418527 37.55
W/Fuel Emission 3418528 43.25
Auto. Trans., Exc. 3462835
W/Air Cond. 3418529 43.66
1970 V8-383 4 Bar 3418541 83.53
1970 V8-440—
L/Fuel Emission—
L/Air Cond. 3418554
W/Air Cond. 3418558
W/Fuel Emission—
Synchro-Mesh 3418555 77.16
Auto. Trans. 3418558
1970 V8-426—
Front 3512840 64.41
Rear, Exc. 3418523 75.28
Auto. Trans. 3418524 75.28
1971 6-198, Exc. 3512803 36.43
Auto. Trans. 3512804 36.90
1971 V8-318—
Synchro-Mesh 3512816 40.14
Auto. Trans. 3512817 47.12
1971 V8-340—
Synchro-Mesh 3614122 89.14
Auto. Trans. 3614123 86.24
1971 V8-383—
Synchro-Mesh 3549568 45.15
Auto. Trans., Exc. 3512825 50.51
4 Bar. Carb. 3512844 82.75
1971 V8-440—
Front 3512840 64.41
Rear—
Synchro-Mesh 3512832 83.33
Auto. Trans. 3512833 88.18
1971 V8-426—
Synchro-Mesh 3512838 81.40
Auto. Trans. 3512839 81.40
1972 V8-318—
L/Fuel Emission—
Synchro-Mesh. 3614107 43.20
Auto. Trans. 3614108 43.66
W/Fuel Emission—
Synchro-Mesh. 3614109 44.95
Auto. Trans. 3614110 43.73
1972 V8-340—
Synchro-Mesh 3614122 89.14
Auto. Trans. 3614123 86.24
1972 V8-400—
Synchro-Mesh—
Exc. Below 3614138 86.24
W/Air Pump 3614172 87.02
Auto. Trans.—
Exc. Below 3614139 86.22
W/Air Pump 3614173 86.89

Description	Part No.	Price
1973 V8-318 Synchro-Mesh—		
L/Air Pump	3698325	45.52
W/Air Pump	3698337	45.52
1973 V8-318 Auto.-Trans.—		
L/Air Pump	3698326	43.50
W/Air Pump	3698338	38.00
1973 V8-340 Synchro-Mesh—		
L/Air Pump	3698327	95.93
W/Air Pump	3698339	95.93
1973 V8-340 Auto. Trans.—		
L/Air Pump	3698328	95.93
W/Air Pump	3698340	95.93
1973 V8-400 Synchro-Mesh—		
L/Air Pump	3698332	95.93
W/Air Pump	3698342	95.93
1973 V8-400 A.T. Exc	3698333	95.93
W/Air Pump	3698343	95.93
1973 V8-440 (L/Hi-Perf.)—		
L/Air Pump	3698334	95.93
W/Air Pump	3698319	95.93
1973 V8-440 (W/Hi-Perf.)—		
L/Air Pump	3698336	95.93
W/Air Pump	3698329	95.93
1974 V8-318—		
Synchromesh Exc	3751427	58.22
Calif Emission	3751429	44.07
Auto Trans Exc	3751428	56.04
Calif Emission	3751430	55.35
1974 V8-360 Monaco	3751451	106.12
Exc Monaco—		
Synchromesh Exc	3751433	106.12
Calif Emission	3751435	91.41
Auto Trans Exc	3751434	106.12
Calif Emission	3751436	106.12
1974 V8-400—		
Synchromesh	3751439	106.12
Auto Tr (Less Hi Perf)—		
Exc Below	3751452	85.31
Calif Emission	3751453	
Auto Tr (With Hi Perf)—		
Exc Below	3751440	106.12
Calif Emission	3751442	
1974 V8-440—		
L/High Perf Exc	3751443	106.12
Calif Emission	3751444	106.12
W/High Perf Exc	3751445	85.31
Calif Emission	3751446	85.31
1975 V8-318—		
Std Trans	3830521	
Auto Trans, Exc	3830565	
W/Air Pump	3830522	
W/Calif Emission	3830524	
1975 V8-360	3830531	
V8-400, Exc	3830554	
Calif Emission	3830535	
V8-440 (L/Hi-Perf)—		
Exc Below	3830536	
Calif Emission	3830537	
V8-440 (W/Hi-Perf)—		
Exc Below	3830538	
Calif Emission	3830539	
DART		
Auto. Trans.	2946633	69.77
1969 6-170—		
Std. Trans.	2946552	30.75
Auto. Trans.	2946553	30.15
1969 V8-273—		
Std. Trans.	2946567	39.78
Auto. Trans.	2946570	44 20
1969 V8-318—		
Std. Trans.	2946568	45.39
Auto. Trans.	2946571	41.38
1969 V8-340—		
Std. Trans.	2946576	71.28
Auto. Trans.	2946590	83.53
1969 V8-383—		
Std. Trans.	2946577	76.96
Auto. Trans.	2946591	82.57
1970 6-198 (L/Fuel Emission)—		
Synchro-Mesh	3418503	28.97
Auto. Trans.	3418504	33.59
1970 6-198 (W/Fuel Emission)—		
Synchro-Mesh	3418505	34.36
Auto. Trans.	3418506	32.43
1970 V8-318 (L/Fuel Emission)—		
Synchro-Mesh	3418515	36.47
Auto. Trans.	3418516	45.94
1970 V8-318 (W/Fuel Emission)—		
Synchro-Mesh	3418517	43.10
Auto. Trans.	3418518	45.61
1970 V8-340 (L/Fuel Emission)—		
Synchro-Mesh	3462968	74.21
Auto. Trans.	3462969	74.21
Air Cond.	3462970	74.21
1970 V8-340 (W/Fuel Emission)—		
Synchro-Mesh	3462971	79.76
Auto. Trans.	3462972	79.76
1971 6-198—		
Synchro-Mesh	3512803	36.43
Auto. Trans.	3512804	36.90
1971 V8-318—		
Synchro-Mesh	3512816§	40.14
Auto. Trans.	3512817§	47.12
1971 V8-340—		
Synchro-Mesh	3614122§	89.14
Auto. Trans.	3614123§	86.24
1972 V8-318—		
L/Fuel Emission—		
Synchro-Mesh	3614107§	43.20
Auto. Trans.	3614108§	43.66
W/Fuel Emission—		
Synchro-Mesh	3614109§	44.95
Auto. Trans.	3614110§	43.73
1972 V8-340—		
Synchro-Mesh	3614122§	89.14
Auto. Trans.	3614123§	86.24
1973 V8-318 Synchro-Mesh—		
L/Air Pump	3698325§	45.52
W/Air Pump	3698337§	45.52
1973 V8-318 Auto. Trans.—		
L/Air Pump	3698326§	43.50
W/Air Pump	3698338§	38.00
1973 V8-340 Synchro-Mesh—		
L/Air Pump	3698327§	95.93
W/Air Pump	3698339§	95.93
1973 V8-340 Auto. Trans.—		
L/Air Pump	3698328§	95.93
W/Air Pump	3698340§	95.93
1974 V8-318—		
Synchromesh Exc	3751427§	58.22
Calif Emission	3751429§	44.07
Auto Trans Exc	3751428§	56.04
Calif Emission	3751430§	55.35
1974 V8-360—		
Synchromesh Exc	3751433§	106.12
Calif Emission	3751435§	91.41
Auto Trans Exc	3751434§	106.12
Calif Emission	3751436§	106.12
1975 V8-318—		
Std Trans	3830521	
Auto Trans, Exc	3830565	
W/Air Pump	3830522¶	
W/Calif Emission	3830524¶	
1975 V8-360, Exc	3830531¶	
Hi-Perf	3830529	

2—CARBURETOR ASS'Y (HOLLEY):

Description	Part No.	Price
DODGE:		
1969 6-225—		
Std. Trans.	2946555	36.50
Auto. Trans.	2946557	36.50
1969 V8-383	2946538	109.09
1969 V8-440	2946582	103.80
1970 6-225 (L/Fuel Emission)—		
Synchro-Mesh	3418511	50.97
Auto. Trans.	3418512	39.47
1970 6-225 (W/Fuel Emission)—		
Synchro-Mesh	3418513	52.43
Auto. Trans.	3418514	55.57
1970 V8-340—		
Front	3577185	65.03
Center, Exc.	3577182	109.24
Auto. Trans.	3577183	109.24
Rear	3577185	65.03
1970 V8-383 (2 Bar. Carb.)—		
L/Fuel Emission	3418531	75.52
W/Fuel Emission	3418528	43.25
1970 V8-383 (4 Bar. Carb.)—		
Synchro-Mesh—		
L/Fuel Emission	3418536	127.58
W/Fuel Emission	3418537	121.80
Auto. Trans. (L/Fuel Emission)—		
L/Air Cond.	3418542	117.36
W/Air Cond.	3418562	125.80
Auto. Trans. (W/Fuel Emission)—		
L/Air Cond.	3512975	125.26
W/Air Cond.	3418543	119.80
1970 V8-440 (2 Bar. Carb.)—		
Front—		
L/Fuel Emission	3462845	55.19
W/Fuel Emission	3418544	55.19
Center (Synchro-Mesh)—		
L/Fuel Emission	3418547	75.23
W/Fuel Emission	3418549	79.74
Center (Auto. Trans.)—		
L/Fuel Emission	3418548	79.74
W/Fuel Emission	3418550	88.55
Rear—		
L/Fuel Emission	3462846	55.19
W/Fuel Emission	3462373	55.19
1970 V8-440 (4 Bar. Carb.)—		
L/Fuel Emission	3418551	136.02
W/Fuel Emission	3418552	125.92
1971 6-225—		
Synchro-Mesh	3512805	47.94
Auto. Trans.	3512807	50.82
1971 V8-340 Challenger—		
Front	3577185	65.03
Center—		
Synchro-Mesh	3577182	109.24
Auto. Trans.	3577183	109.24
Rear	3577185	65.03
1971 V8-360 Polara & Monaco—		
Synchro-Mesh	3549566	
Auto. Trans.	3512823	76.77
1971 V8-383 L/Fresh Air Cont—		
Synchro-Mesh	3549994	126.50
Auto. Trans.	3512830	126.50
1971 V8-383 W/Fresh Air Cont.—		
Exc. Below—		
Synchro-Mesh	3549995	119.29
Auto. Trans.	3512842	126.50
Polara & Monaco	3512844	82.75
1971 V8-440—		
Front	3512836	51.19
Center (Std. Trans.)	3512834	94.61
Center (Auto. Trans.)	3512835	72.78
Rear	3512837	48.30
1972 6-225—		
L/Air Pump—		
Synchro-Mesh	3614162	51.36
Auto. Trans.	3614163	50.29
W/Air Pump—		
Synchro-Mesh	3614113	50.29
Auto. Trans.	3614114	50.90
1972 V8-360—		
L/Fuel Emission—		
Synchro-Mesh	3614130	83.54
Auto. Trans.	3614131	75.58
W/Fuel Emission—		
Synchro-Mesh	3683837	85.99
Auto. Trans.	3683838	85.99
1972 V8-400—		
L/Fuel Emission	3671748	82.88
W/Fuel Emission	3671750	82.88
1972 V8-440—		
Coronet & Charger—		
Synchro-Mesh, Exc.	3621387	125.82
W/Air Pump	3621393	125.82
Auto. Trans., Exc.	3621388	125.82
W/Air Pump	3621394	125.82
Polara & Monaco, Exc.	3614140	131.10
W/Air Pump	3614141	131.10
1973 6-225 Synchro-Mesh—		
L/Air Pump	3698346	61.86
W/Air Pump	3698348	61.86
1973 6-225 Auto Trans.—		
L/Air Pump	3698347	63.90
W/Air Pump	3698349	63.90
1973 V8-360, Exc.	3698330	85.68
W/Air Pump	3698318	73.00
1973 V8-400, Exc.	3698331	85.99
W/Air Pump	3698341	85.99
1974, 6-225—		
Synchromesh Exc	3751423	55.57
Calif Emission	3751425	55.57
Auto Trans Exc	3751424	54.25
Calif Emission	3751426	55.57
1974 V8-360	3751431	78.93
V8-400	3751437	71.00
1975 Six, Exc	3830517	
Auto Trans	3830518	
1975 V8-360, Exc	3879154	
Tag R-7226a	3830563	
1975 V8-400	3879155	
DART		
1969 6-225—		
Std. Trans.	2946554	36.50
Auto. Trans.	2946556	36.50
1970 6-225 (L/Fuel Emission)—		
Synchro-Mesh	3418511	50.97
Auto. Trans.	3418512	39.47
1970 6-225 (W/Fuel Emission)—		
Synchro-Mesh	3418513	52.43
Auto. Trans.	3418514	55.57
1971 6-225—		
Synchro-Mesh	3512805	47.94
Auto. Trans.	3512807	50.82
1972 6-198—		
L/Fuel Emission—		
Synchro-Mesh	3671743	52.48
Auto. Trans.	3671744	49.78
W/Fuel Emission—		
Synchro-Mesh	3671745	49.78
Auto. Trans.	3671746	50.34
1972 6-225 (L/Air Pump)—		
Synchro-Mesh	3614162	51.36
Auto. Trans.	3614163	50.29
1972 6-225 (W/Air Pump)—		
Synchro-Mesh	3614113	50.29
Auto. Trans.	3614114	50.90
1973 6-198, Exc.	3698320	64.82
Auto. Trans.	3698321	60.95
1973 6-225 Synchro-Mesh—		
L/Air Pump	3698346	61.86
W/Air Pump	3698348	61.86
1973 6-225 Auto. Trans.—		
L/Air Pump	3698347	63.90
W/Air Pump	3698349	63.90
1974, 6-198 Exc	3751421	38.95
Auto Trans	3751422	

1974, 6-225—
Synchromesh Exc 3751423 55.57
Calif Emission 3751425 55.57
Auto Trans Exc 3751424 54.25
Calif Emission 3751426 55.57
1975 Six—
Std Trans, Exc 3830517
Calif Emission 3830519
Auto Trans, Exc 3830518
Calif Emission 3830520
1975 V8-360, Exc 3879154
Tag R-7226a 3830563

3—CARBURETOR MINOR REPAIR KIT (HOLLEY)

1969 Six 2933125
1969 V8-440&383 3549402
1970 Six Exc 3481677 4.95
With Fuel Emission 3481670
1970-71 V8-340 Exc 3514651 5.33
Center 3514695 7.78
1970 V8-383 (2 Bar)—
Exc Below 3514756
Std Tr W/Fuel Emiss 3514711
1970 V8-383 (4 Bar)—
L/Fuel Emiss Exc 3514816 9.47
W/Air Cond 3514819 9.47
W/Fuel Emission 3514824 9.47
1970 V8-440 (2 Bar)—
Front & Rear 3514651 5.33
Center Exc 3514671
With Fuel Emission 3514695 7.78
1970 V8-440 (4 Bar) 3514801
1971, 6-225 3481670
V8-360 3514711
V8-383 3514824 9.47
V8-440 Exc 3514651 5.33
Center 3514695 7.78
1972, 6-198 3683891 5.99
6-225 3683808
V8-360&400 3683867
V8-440 3683865 11.61
1973, 6-198 Exc 3744792 5.99
Auto Trans 3685804 5.99
1973, 6-225 3685804 5.99
V8-360 3685832 11.07
1974 Six 3837510 5.99
V8 3837507 11.07
1975 Six, Exc 3879164
Auto Trans 3879763
1975 V8 3879767

4—CARBURETOR MINOR REPAIR KIT (CARTER):

DODGE:
1969 V8-318 3621260 7.45
1969 V8-383—
2 Bar. Carb. 3621286 7.21
4 Bar. Carb. 3621400 9.45
1969-70 V8-426 3419503 8.27
1969-70 V8-440 3621400 9.45
1970 V8-318—
L/Fuel Emission 3514466 7.51
W/Fuel Emission 3514467
1970 V8-340 3621400 9.45
1970 V8-383—
2 Bar. Carb. 3621286 7.21
4 Bar. Carb. 3621400 9.45
1971 6-198 3621401 5.51
1971-72 V8-318 3514467
1971 V8-340 3621225 10.27
1971 V8-383, 2 Bar. 3621286 7.21
4 Bar. 3621224 10.50
1971 V8-440 3621224 10.50
1971 V8-426 3419503 8.27
1972 (Exc. V8-318) 3683908 10.27
1973-74 V8 Exc 3744758 9.62
V8-318 (1973) 3744794 7.03
V8-318 (1974) 3837489 7.03

DART:
1969 6-170 3621401 5.51
1969 V8-273 3621260 7.45
1969 V8-318 3621260 7.45
1969-70 V8-340 3621400 9.45
1969 V8-383 3621400 9.45
1970 Six 3621401 5.51
1970 V8-318 3514466 7.51
1971 6-198 3621401 5.51
1971 V8-318 3481688 4.95
1971 V8-340 3621225 10.27
1972 V8-318 3514467
1972 V8-340 3683908 10.27
1973-74 V8 Exc 3744758 9.62
V8-318 (1973) 3744794 7.03
V8-318 (1974) 3837489 7.03

5—CARBURETOR GASKET SET (CARTER):

DODGE:
1969 V8-318 3621245 3.29
1969 V8-383—
2 Bar. Carb. 2933191 1.22
4 Bar. Carb. 2933197 1.39
1969-71 V8-426 3549343 2.11
1969 V8-440 2933197 1.39
1970-72 V8-318 3549295 4.55
1970 V8-340 2933197 1.39
1970 V8-383—
2 Bar. Carb. 3549296 3.84
4 Bar. Carb. 3549297 6.49
1970 V8-440 3549273 2.82
1971 Six 3514475 2.82
1971 V8-340 3621246 2.92
1971 V8-383 3549296 3.84
1971 V8-440 3621244 6.49
1972 V8-340, 400 3683907 2.92
1973 V8-318 3744796 4.92
V8-340 3744757 2.92
1974 V8 Exc 3744757 2.92
318 3837491 3.29

DART
1968-69 V8-273, 318 3621245 3.29
1969 6-170 2933179 1.69
1969-70 V8-340 2933197 1.39
1969 V8-383 2933197 1.39
1970-71 Six 3514475 2.82
1970-72 V8-318 3549295 4.55
1971 V8-340 3621246 2.92
1972 V8-340 3683907 2.92
1973 V8-318 3744796 4.92
V8-340 3744757 2.92
1974 V8-318 3837491 3.29
V8-360 3744757 2.92

6—CARBURETOR GASKET SET (HOLLEY):

DODGE:
1966-69 Six 3683922 1.30
1967-69 V8-440 3549401 4.32
1970 6-225, Exc. 3514827 1.36
Emission Cont. 3683922 1.30
1970-71 V8-340, Exc. 3514652 2.33
Center 3514696 2.59
1970 V8-383 (Exc. Below)—
L/Emission Cont. 3514817
W/Emission Cont. 3514825 5.90
1970 V8-383 Polara & Monaco—
L/Emission Cont. 3514755 2.87
W/Emission Cont. 3514710 3.41
1970 V8-440 (Exc. Below)—
Exc. Center 3514652 2.33
Center, Exc. 3514672 1.90
W/Emission Cont. 3514696 2.59
1970 V8-440 Pol & Mon 3514802 6.27
1971 6-225 3683922 1.30
1971 V8-360 3514199 3.41
V8-383 3514825 5.90
V8-440, Exc. 3514652 2.33
Center 3514696 2.59
1972 Six 3683922 1.30
1972 V8-360, 400 3683871 3.78
1972 V8-440 3683864 6.44
1973 Six 3744791 1.67
V8 3685831 3.78
1974 Six 3837511 1.67
V8 3837508 3.78
1975 Six 3879165
V8 3879766

DART:
1966-69 Six 3683922 1.30
1970 6-225, Exc. 3514827 1.36
W/Emission Cont. 3683922 1.30
1970-71 V8-340, Exc. 3514652 2.33
Center 3514696 2.59
1971 6-225 3683922 1.30
1972 Six 3683922 1.30
1973 Six 3744791 1.67
V8 3685831 3.78
1974 Six 3837511 1.67
V8 3837508 3.78
1975 Six 3879165
V8 3879766

7—THERMOSTATIC COIL & HOUSING ASS'Y (CARTER):

DODGE:
1969 V8-318, 273 2863843 9.30
1969 V8-383—
2 Bar. Carb. 2863846 9.47
4 Bar. Carb. 2863845 10.60
1969-70 V8-426 1826847 7.79
1969 V8-440 2863845 10.60
1970-71 Six 2946548 6.86
1970-72 V8-318 2951651 10.70
1970 V8-340 3462927 9.73
1970-71 V8-383—
2 Bar. Carb. 2951652 10.76
4 Bar. Carb. 2951653 11.19
1970-71 V8-440 2951653 11.19
1971 V8-340 3512875
1971 V8-426 2951653 11.19
1972 V8-340 3614169 8.65
1972 V8-400 3512845 10.16
1973 Exc 3698355 10.16
V8-318 3698353 9.03
1974 Exc 3751484 10.16
V8-318 3751478 9.03

DART:
1968-69 V8-340, 383 2863845 10.60
1969 6-170 2658396 8.76
1969 V8-273, 318 2863843 9.30
1970-72 V8-318 2951651 10.70
1970 V8-340 3462927 9.73
1970-71 6-198 2946548 6.86
1971 V8-340 3512875
1972 V8-340 3614169 8.65
1973-74, See Dodge—

8—CHOKE VACUUM CONTROL ASS'Y (CARTER):

DODGE:
1969 V8-318 2933185 3.85
1969 V8-383 (2 Bar. Carb.) 2933190 5.94
1969 V8-383 (4 Bar. Carb.) 2933196 5.87
1970-71 6-198 2933182 5.22
1970-73 V8-318 2933185 3.85
1970 V8-340 2933199 5.87
1970 V8-383, Exc. 2933199 5.87
W/Air Cond. 2933196 5.87
1970 V8-440, Exc. 2933196 5.87
W/Air Cond. 3514685
W/Emission Cont.—
Synchro-Mesh 3514685
Auto. Trans. 2933196 5.87
1971 V8-340, Exc. 3621209 5.09
Auto. Trans. 3621210 5.09
1971 V8-383, Exc. 2933190 5.94
4 Bar. Carb. 2933196 5.87
1971 V8-440 3621261 3.10
1972-73 V8-340—
Synchro-Mesh 3621209 5.09
Auto. Trans. 3621210 5.09
1972 V8-400 3621210 5.09
1974 V8-318 Exc 3780153 3.85
Auto Trans 3780154 6.19
1974 V8-360 Exc 3621209 5.09
Monaco 3621210 5.09
1974 V8-400 Exc 3621209 5.09
Auto Trans 3621210 5.09
1974 V8-440 3621210 5.09

DART:
1969 6-170 2933182 5.22
1969 V8-273, 318 2933185 3.85
1969 V8-340, 383—
Std. Trans. 2933196 5.87
Auto. Trans. 2933199 5.87
1970-71 6-198 2933182 5.22
1970-73 V8-318 2933185 3.85
1970 V8-340 2933199 5.87
1971-73 V8-340, Exc. 3621209 5.09
Auto. Trans. 3621210 5.09
1974, See Dodge—

9—CHOKE VACUUM CONTROL ASS'Y (HOLLEY):

DODGE:
1969 Six 3419508
1969 V8-440 3621274 2.98
1970-72 Six, Exc. 3419508
Auto. Trans. 3685730 3.90
1970-71 V8-340, Exc. 3514654 2.82
Center, Exc. 3621274 2.98
Auto. Trans. 3621261 3.10
1970-71 V8-383 (Exc. Below)—
Synchro-Mesh 3621274 2.98
Auto. Trans. 3621261 3.10
1970-71 V8-383 Pol & Mon—
Synchro-Mesh 3419508
Auto. Trans. 3419621 3.25
1970 V8-440 (Exc. Below)—
Exc. Center 3514654 2.82
Center, Exc. 3621274 2.98
W/Auto. Trans. 3621261 3.10
1970 V8-440 Pol & Mon 3621274 2.98
1971 V8-360 3549450 3.08
1971 V8-440, Exc. 3514654 2.82
Center 3621274 2.98
1972 V8-360—
Synchro-Mesh 3621272 3.78
Auto. Trans. 3549450 3.08
1972 V8-400 3683874
1972 V8-440
Exc. Below 3621274 2.98
Auto. Trans.(W/Air Pump) 3621261 3.10
1973 Six Exc 3685730 3.90
Std Trans 3685731 3.78
1973 V8 3685732 3.78

1974 Six Exc	3780672	3.90
Std Trans	3780673	3.78
1974 V8-360	3744549	3.90
V8-400	3744550	3.78
1975 Six, Exc	3780673	3.78
Auto Trans	3780672	3.90
1975 V8	3879799	
DART		
1969 6-225—		
Std. Trans.	3419508	
Auto. Trans.	3685730	3.90
1970-72 Six—		
Synchro-Mesh	3419508	
Auto. Trans.	3685730	3.90
1970-71 V8-340, Exc.	3514654	2.82
Center, Exc.	3621274	2.98
W/Auto. Trans.	3621261	3.10
1973-75, See Dodge—		

10—CHOKE KIT (HOLLEY)

1968-69 Six	2658398	4.06
1968-69 V8-440	2843156	3.70
1970-71 V8-340	3614197	4.87
1970-71, 6-225	3614111	4.87
1970 V8-383 (2 Bar)—		
Exc Below	2951652	10.76
Std Tr L/Fuel Emiss	2946537	
1970, V8-383, 4 Bar	2946539	
1970, V8-440, 2 Bar	2946532	
4 Bar	2946539	
1971-72 V8-360	3512872	4.49
1971 V8-383	3512867	4.87
1971 V8-440 Exc	3420255	.16
Auto Trans	2946532	
1972 Six	3614111	4.87
1972 V8-400	2946537	
1972 V8-440	3512867	4.87
1973 Six	3698351	8.00
V8	3698357	
1974 Six	3751476	9.25
V8-360	3751480	9.00
V8-400	3751482	9.05
1975 Six	3830549	
V8-360	3751480	9.00
V8-400	3751482	9.05

11—FUEL PUMP:

DODGE:		
1969 Six	2932798	14.26
1969 V8 Coronet & Charger—		
Exc. Below	2932797	
V8-383	3621675	13.05
V8-426	2585118	13.16
V8-440	3004107	13.28
1969 V8 Polara & Monaco—		
Exc. Below	2932797	
V8-383, 440	3621675	13.05
1970 Six—		
L/Fuel Emission	2932798	14.26
W/Fuel Emission	3420834	14.09
1970-72 V8-318, 340	3620795	15.70
1970 V8-383	3621675	13.05
1970-71 V8-426	2585118	13.16
1970-71 V8-440—		
Exc. Below	3420835	14.09
Polara & Monaco	3621675	13.05
1971 Six	3420834	14.09
1971 V8-383	3621675	13.05
1972 Six	2932798	14.26
1972-73 V8-318	2932797	
1972-73 V8-340, 360	3620795	15.70
1972 V8-400	3621609	15.70
1972 V8-440	3621610	15.70
1973 Six	3621884	14.26
1973 V8-400,440—		
Coronet & Charger	3685800	15.70
1974-75 Six	3685799	15.70
1974 Six	2932798	14.26
1974 V8-318, 360 2 Bar	3744806	14.90
4 Bar	3744805	15.70
1974 V8-400	3685799	15.70
1974 V8-440, Exc	3685800	15.70
Monaco	3685799	15.70
1975 V8-318, 360	3744806	14.90
V8-400, Exc	3685799	15.70
Emission Cont	3879761	
V8-440, Exc	3685799	15.70
Hi-Perf	3685800	15.70
Emission Cont	3879761	
DART		
1969 Six	2932798	14.26
1969 V8—		
Exc. Below	2932797	
V8-383	3621675	13.05
1970 Six—		
L/Fuel Emission	2932798	14.26
W/Fuel Emission	3420834	14.09
1970-71 V8-318, 340	2932797	
1971 Six	3420834	14.09
1972 Six	2932798	14.26
1972-73 V8-318	2932797	
1972-73 V8-340	3620795	15.70
1973 Six	3621884	14.26
1974-75, See Dodge—		

12—FUEL TANK:

DODGE:		
1968-69 Coronet & Charger—		
Exc. Below	2880434	55.89
Charger	2880435	56.74
Sta. Wagon	2880459	46.35
1969 Polara & Monaco—		
Exc. Sta. Wag.	3404475	56.74
Sta. Wagon	2925748	61.31
1970 Challenger—		
L/Fuel Emission	3404510	50.07
W/Fuel Emission	3404494	68.63
1970 Coronet (Exc. Sta. Wagon)—		
L/Fuel Emission	2880434	55.89
W/Fuel Emission	3404392	72.83
1970 Polara & Monaco—		
L/Fuel Emission—		
Exc. Sta. Wag.	3404475	56.74
Sta. Wagon	2925748	61.31
W/Fuel Emission	3404219	77.80
1970 Coronet (Sta. Wagon)—		
L/Fuel Emission	3404497	63.40
W/Fuel Emission	3404394	77.60
1970 Charger—		
L/Fuel Emission	3404492	56.74
W/Fuel Emission	3404393	76.80
1971 Challenger	3404494	68.63
1971-72 Coronet & Charger—		
Exc. Below	3404951	64.83
Sta. Wagon	3466153	57.00
1971 Polara & Monaco—		
Exc. Below	3466887	77.72
Sta. Wagon	2925748	61.31
1972 Challenger	3583570	68.63
1972 Polara & Monaco—		
Exc. Below	3583562	77.72
Sta. Wagon	3404225	70.71
1973-74 Challenger	3642139	75.38
1973 Coronet & Charger—		
Exc. Below	3642103	66.69
Sta. Wagon	3642170	56.74
1973 Polara & Monaco—		
Exc Below	3642156	77.72
Sta. Wagon	3642175	68.63
1974 Coronet & Charger—		
Exc Below	3726425	72.83
Sta Wagon	3642170	56.74
1974-75 Monaco Exc	3726077	81.57
Sta Wagon	3726085	81.57
1975 Coronet & Charger—		
Exc Below	3906503	
Sta Wagon, Exc	3906523	
W/Leaded Full	3906522	
DART:		
1968-69	2880417	49.16
1970-71—		
L/Fuel Emission	3404474	49.16
W/Fuel Emission	3404220	62.49
1972	3583522	49.61
1973-74	3642179	49.16
1975	3906518	

13—FUEL LINE HOSE:

1969-75	3466418	

14—INTAKE MANIFOLD GASKET:

DODGE:		
1967-71 Six	2843279	.28
1967-71 V8-440, Exc.	3671575	
W/Tri-Carbs.	3514186	6.16
1968-71 V8-383	3671874	3.67
1969-74 V8-273, 318	3420027	2.75
1970-71 V8-340—		
1 Carb.	3514187	4.15
3 Carbs.	3514187	4.15
1971 V8-360	3514187	4.15
1970-71 V8-426	2808306	3.19
1972-73 Six (Early 73)	3614387	
1972-74 V8-340, 360	3514187	4.15
1972-74 V8-400	3671874	3.67
1972-74 V8-440 (1 Carb.)—		
Early 1972	3671575	
Late 1972	3671933	3.67
1972 V8-440 (3 Carbs.)	3514186	6.16
1973-74 Six (Late 73)	3751635	.33
1975 Six	3744831	1.03
V8-318	3837605	2.59
V8-400	3671874	3.67
V8-440, Exc	3671933	3.67
Hi-Perf	3769933	4.27
DART:		
1966-71 Six	2843279	.28
1967-69 V8-383	3671874	3.67
1969-74 V8-273, 318	3420027	2.75
1969-71 V8-340	3514187	4.15
1972-73 Six (Early 73)	3614387	
1972-74 V8-340, 360	3514187	4.15
1973-74 Six (Late 73)	3751635	.33
1975 Six	3744831	1.03
V8-318	3837605	2.59

15—ACCELERATOR PUMP

1975 Holley—		
Six, Exc	3879140	
Std Tr (L/Calif)	3514897	.34
V8-360, 400	3621365	

16—ACCEL PUMP NEEDLE & SEAT

1975 Holley—		
Six	2299042	2.59
V8-360, 400	3514730	1.62

FORD

FULL SIZE MODELS

Time	Emission Controls (Group AB)	Time

OPERATION INDEX

AB1—CRANKCASE VENT VALVE (PCV),CLEAN OR RENEW

All Models—
Clean (0.4) 0.5

AB2—EMISSION CONTROL CHECK

Use with IMCO Systems only. Includes adjust carb & ignition timing and check PCV Valve.
All Models (0.6) 0.7

AB6—AIR PUMP, R & R OR RENEW

All Models (0.4) 0.6

Renew (0.2) 0.3

AB10—ANTI-BACKFIRE VALVE, RENEW
1969-75 (0.3) 0.4

AB14—AIR PUMP BELT, RENEW
1969-71 (0.3) 0.4

AB15—EXHAUST GAS RECIRCULATION VALVE, RENEW
1973-75 (0.3) 0.4

AB16—ELECTRONIC SPARK CONTROLS, RENEW
1973-75, Solenoid (0.2) 0.3
Ambient Switch (0.2) 0.3
Delay Control Valve (0.3) 0.3
Modulator Valve (0.3) 0.4

AB19—FUEL VAPOR CANNISTER, RENEW
1970-75 (0.3) 0.4

AB20—AIR CLEANER SENSOR, RENEW
1970-75 (0.2) 0.3

Parts — Emission Controls — Parts

PARTS INDEX

1—THERMACTOR AIR PUMP:
1968-69	C8AZ-9A486C	83.90
1975	D5TZ-9A486C	83.90
1973	C8AZ-9A486C	83.90
1974, Exc	D4AZ-9A486A	83.90
V8-460	D4AZ-9A486B	83.90

2—THERMACTOR AIR PUMP RELIEF VALVE:
1968-70	C8TZ-9B479A	2.40

3—CHECK VALVE:
1968-69 Six	C6AZ-9A487A	2.95
1975, Exc	D4VY-9A487A	5.40
V8-400	D4AZ-9A487A	5.40

4—ANTI-BACKFIRE VALVE:
1968-69 Six	C8AZ-9B289A	16.85
1968-69 V8	C8AZ-9B289B	12.40
1970 V8	C8TZ-9B289A	20.85
1974	D4AZ-9B289A	12.40
1975	D5AZ-9B289C	12.40

5—THERMACTOR PUMP DRIVE BELT:
—NOTE—
Order By Complete Model Description.

6—CRANKCASE VENTILATOR VALVE ASS'Y:
1966-69 Six	DODZ-6A666A	2.05
1967-69 V8-390, 428	C6AZ-6A666A	1.95
1968-69 V8-302, 351	C6AZ-6A666A	1.95
1969 V8-429	C6AZ-6A666A	1.95
1970-72 Six	DODZ-6A666A	2.05
1970-72 V8	DOAZ-6A666A	2.05
1973	D3OZ-6A666A	2.05
1974-75, Exc	D4AZ-6A666A	2.05
V8-351-W, 460	D3OZ-6A666A	2.05

7—DISTRIBUTOR VACUUM ADVANCE CONTROL VALVE:
1968-72 Six	C8AZ-12A111A	8.20
1968-72 V8 Exc	C8AZ-12A111A	8.20
V8-429 (68)	C8UZ-12A111B	8.20
V8-429 (69)	C9AZ-12A111A	8.20

8—DISTRIBUTOR VACUUM CONTROL VALVE:
1968-72	C8AZ-12A091A	11.15
1973-74 Exc	D3FZ-12A091B	4.05
1975, Exc	C8AZ-12A091A	11.15
V8-460	D5VY-12A091A	11.15

9—AIR CLEANER FILTER ASSY:
1971-72 Six	D1AZ-9D695A	1.80
1971-75, V8	D1ZZ-9D695A	1.90

10—AIR CLEANER SENSOR ASSY:
1971-75, Exc	DOZZ-9E607B	2.60

11—FUEL VAPOR CANNISTER:
1970-72 Six	DOAZ-9D653C	22.55
1970 V8—		
Exc. Below	DOAZ-9D653C	22.55
V8-390	DOAZ-9D653B	17.35
1971-73 V8	D1AZ-9D653A	18.35
1974-75, Exc	D4AZ-9D653A	22.05
W/Thermactor	D4DZ-9D653A	22.05

Time — Tune-Up & Ignition (Group B) — Time

OPERATION INDEX

B1—TUNE-UP, MINOR
Includes renew points, plugs and condenser, set spark timing and adjust carburetor idle.
1968-74—
Six (1.2) 1.6
V8 (1.4) 1.8
1975 (0.9) 1.2

B2—TUNE-UP, MAJOR
Includes check compression, clean & adjust or renew spark plugs. R&R distributor, renew points & condenser and adjust ignition timing, carburetor and fan belts. Clean battery terminals, service air cleaner, check coil & clean or renew fuel line filter.
1967-72 Six (2.4) 3.1
1968-74 V8 (2.7) 3.7
1975 (2.2) 3.2

—NOTE—
To Clean PCV Valve, Add (0.4) *0.4*
To Replace PCV Valve, Add (0.2) *0.2*

B3—TUNE-UP, MAJOR & OVERHAUL CARBURETOR
1966-69 Six (3.0) 4.3
1970-72 Six (3.2) 4.5
1967-71 V8—
2 Barrel (3.4) 4.6
4 Barrel—
Exc. Below (3.9) 5.2
Rochester (3.6) 4.8
Autolite, Motorcraft (3.7) 5.0
1972-74 V8 (3.9) 5.3
1975 (3.4) 4.8

—NOTE—
To Renew PCV Valve, Add (0.4) *0.4*
To Replace PCV Valve, Add (0.2) *0.2*

B4—POINTS & CONDENSER, RENEW
Does not include R & R distributor
1968-74 (0.4) 0.6

B5—SPARK PLUGS, CLEAN & ADJUST OR RENEW
1966-72 Six (0.4) 0.5
1968-75 V8 (0.6) 0.8

—NOTE—
To Clean And Adjust, Add (0.2) *0.2*

B6—COMPRESSION TEST
1966-72 Six (0.5) 0.6
1968-75 V8 (0.7) 0.9

B7—IGNITION TIMING, SET
1969-75 (0.3) 0.3

B8—DISTRIBUTOR, R & OR RENEW
1969-75 (0.4) 0.5

B9—DISTRIBUTOR, OVERHAUL (UNIT OFF)
Includes: Adjust on stroboscope.
1966-72 Six (0.8) 1.2
1969-75 V8 (1.1) 1.6

B9A—DISTRIBUTOR, ADJUST ON STROBOSCOPE (UNIT OFF)
All Models (0.3) 0.4

B10—DISTRIBUTOR CAP, RENEW
All Models (0.3) 0.3

B11—IGNITION CABLE SET, RENEW
Time allowance covers installation of factory supplied sets only.
1969-75 (0.4) 0.5

B12—VACUUM CONTROL UNIT, RENEW
Includes R & R distributor
1969-75 (0.7) 0.9

B13—IGNITION COIL, RENEW
Includes: Test coil.
1969-75 (0.3) 0.6

B14—IGNITION SWITCH, RENEW
1968-69 (0.4) 0.6
1970-75 (0.5) 0.7

Parts — Tune-Up & Ignition — Parts

DISTRIBUTOR ASS'Y (LESS CAP & ROTOR):

Application	Part No.	Price
1968-71 Six—		
Std. Trans	D2UZ-12127A	33.15
Auto. Trans.	D2AZ-12127B	33.15
1969 V8-302—		
Std. Trans	C8AZ-12127E	31.30
Auto. Trans—		
L/Air Cond	C9AZ-12127M	34.00
W/Air Cond	C9AZ-12127R	34.00
1969 V8-351	DOOZ-12127M	34.00
1969 V8-390 (2 Bar. Carb.)—		
Std. Trans	C9AZ-12127B	34.00
Auto. Trans	C7AZ-12127D	33.15
1969 V8-390 (4 Bar. Carb.)—		
Std. Trans	C9AZ-12127B	34.00
Auto. Trans	C7AZ-12127L	33.15
1969 V8-428	C8AZ-12127J	33.15
1969 V8-429—		
Std. Trans	C9AZ-12127F	34.00
Auto. Trans	C8VY-12127C	31.30
1970-71 V8-302—		
Std. Trans	DOAZ-12127Y	34.00
Auto. Trans	DOOZ-12127AL	31.30
1970 V8 351—		
Std. Trans	DOAZ-12127H	34.00
Auto. Trans	DOAZ-12127V	34.00
1970 V8-390 (2 Bar. Carb.)—		
Std. Trans	C8AZ-12127M	33.15
Auto. Trans	C7AZ-12127D	33.15
1970 V8-429—		
Std. Trans	C9AZ-12127Y	34.00
Auto. Trans	C9AZ-12127F	34.00
1971 V8-351—		
Std. Trans	D1AZ-12127G	34.00
Auto Trans—		
Exc. Calif	D1AZ-12127H	34.00
Calif	D1AZ-12127K	34.00
1971 V8-390 (2 Bar. Carb.)—		
Exc. Below	D1AZ-12127L	33.15
C6 Trans	C7AZ-12127D	33.15
Calif	C7AZ-12127D	33.15
1971 V8-390 (4 Bar)	C7AZ-12127L	33.15
1971 V8-400—		
Exc. Calif	DOOZ-12127U	34.00
Calif	D2ZZ-12127C	34.00
1971 V8-429 (2 Bar. Carb.)—		
Exc. Below	C9AZ-12127F	34.00
W/Imco Emission	C8VY-12127C	31.30
Calif	D1MY-12127F	34.00
1971 V8-429 (4 Bar)	D1AZ-12127N	45.65
1972 Six	D2AZ-12127B	33.15
1972 V8-302—		
Exc. Calif	D2AZ-12127C	27.20
Calif	D2AZ-12127D	31.30
1972 V8-351 Cleveland Eng—		
Synchro-Mesh	D2ZZ-12127A	31.30
Auto. Trans—		
Exc. Calif	D2AZ-12127K	34.00
Calif	D2ZZ-12127C	34.00
1972 V8-351 Windsor Eng—		
Synchro-Mesh—		
Exc. Calif	D2MY-12127B	34.00
Calif	D2MY-12127B	34.00
Auto Trans—		
Exc. Calif	D2MY-12127B	34.00
Calif	D2MY-12127G	34.00
1972 V8-400—		
Exc. Calif	D2AZ-12127E	34.00
Calif	D2AZ-12127F	34.00
1972 V8-429—		
Exc. Calif	D2AZ-12127J	45.65
Calif	D2AZ-12127H	34.00
1973 V8-351—		
Cleveland Eng.	D3ZZ-12127B	31.30
Windsor Eng.	D3AZ-12127A	34.00
1973 V8-400	D3AZ-12127B	34.00
V8-429	D3SZ-12127A	
1974, V8-351, Cleve—		
L/Breakerless Ign—		
Early	D3MY-12127G	34.00
Late	D3ZZ-12127G	34.00
W/Breakerless Ign	D4AZ-12127A	41.60
1974, V8-351, Windsor—		
L/Breakerless Ign	D3AZ-12127A	34.00
W/Breakerless Ign	D4AZ-12127C	41.60
1974, V8-400	D4OZ-12127C	41.60
1974, V8-460	D4VY-12127C	41.60
1975, Exc	D5AZ-12127B	41.60
V8-400, Exc	D5AZ-12127B	41.60
Calif	D5AZ-12127D	41.60
V8-460	D4VY-12127C	41.60

DISTRIBUTOR REPAIR KIT:

Includes: Points, Rotor And Condenser.

Application	Part No.	Price
1968-72 Six	C5AZ-12000D	7.00
1968-74 V8	COTZ-12000A	7.00

FIG.1-TUNE-UP & IGNITION
(For Parts Identification Only)

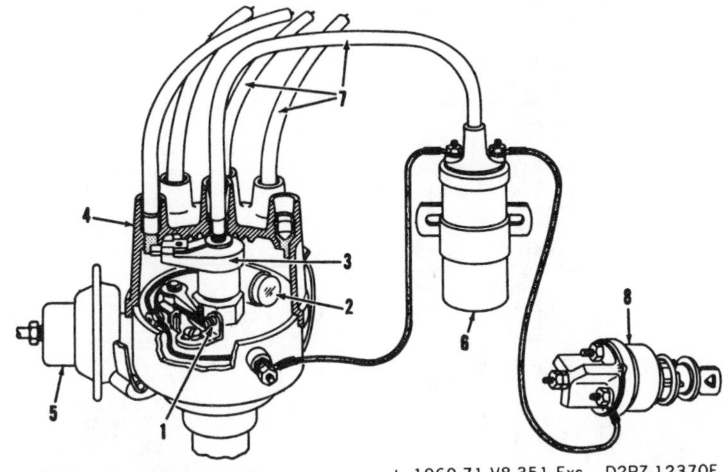

1—IGNITION POINT SET

Application	Part No.	Price
1966-72 Six	C9AZ-12171B	4.40
1968-74 V8	B8Q-12171A	4.40

2—CONDENSER:

Application	Part No.	Price
1966-72 Six	C9AZ-12300A	1.50
1968-74 V8	C9AZ-12300A	1.50

3—ROTOR:

Application	Part No.	Price
1968-74 V8	B7A-12200A	1.10
1968-72 Six	C5TZ-12200B	1.10
1975	D5AZ-12200A	1.50

4—DISTRIBUTOR CAP:

Application	Part No.	Price
1966-72 Six	7HA-12106	5.15
1968-74 V8	B7A-12106A	5.75
1975	D5AZ-12106A	10.05

5—VACUUM CONTROL UNIT:

Application	Part No.	Price
1968-72 Six Exc	D2UZ-12370A	16.70
Auto Trans	D2AZ-12370F	16.70
1968-71 V8-302 Exc	D2PZ-12370L	16.70
Auto Trans	C5AZ-12370A	5.40
1968-71 V8-390,427,428—		
Exc Below	C5AZ-12370A	5.40
Std Trans	D2AZ-12370L	16.70
1969-71 V8-351 Exc	D2PZ-12370F	16.70
Std Trans	D2PZ-12370D	16.70
1969 V8-429 Exc	C5AZ-12370A	5.40
Std Trans	D2VY-12370C	16.70
1970 V8-429 Exc	D2PZ-12370L	16.70
Std Trans	D2DZ-12370F	16.70
1971 V8-429 Exc	D2MY-12370A	16.70
With IMCO	C5AZ-12370A	5.40
4 Bar Carb	D2PZ-12370F	16.70
1971 V8-400	C5AZ-12370A	5.40
1972 V8-351C Exc	D2AZ-12370L	16.70
Auto Trans	D2AZ-12370E	16.70
Calif	D2AZ-12370K	16.70
1972 V8-351W Exc	D2MY-12370D	16.70
Calif	D2MY-12370D	16.70
1972 V8-400 Exc	D2AZ-12370K	16.70
Calif	D2AZ-12370J	16.70
1972 V8-429	D2AZ-12370G	16.70
1973 V8-351 Exc	D2VY-12370B	16.70
Windsor Eng	D2TZ-12370J	16.70
1973 V8-400	D2VY-12370B	16.70
1973 V8-429	D3SZ-12370A	16.70
1974, V8-351, Cleve—		
L/Breakerless Ign—		
Early	D3MY-12370C	16.70
Late	D2VY-12370B	16.70
W/Breakerless Ign	D4AZ-12370C	11.10
1974, V8-351, Windsor—		
L/Breakerless Ign	D2TZ-12370J	16.70
W/Breakerless Ign	D4OZ-12370A	11.10
1974-75, V8-351, 400	D4OZ-12370A	11.10
1974-75, V8-460	D3AZ-12370C	11.10

6—IGNITION COIL:

Application	Part No.	Price
1968-74—		
Exc. Below	B6A-12029B	13.50
W/Transistor	C3TZ-12029A	12.90
Breakerless Ign	D4AZ-12029A	14.85
1975	D5AZ-12029A	14.85

IGNITION COIL RESISTOR:

Application	Part No.	Price
1969-70	C9AZ-12250A	2.50
1971-75	D1AZ-12250A	2.50

7—IGNITION CABLE SET:

Application	Part No.	Price
1968-72 Six	D1AZ-12259D	12.55
1968-72 V8-302 Exc	D1AZ-12259A	16.70
Transistor (68)	D1AZ-12259H	16.70
1968-70 V8-390,428	D1AZ-12259G	18.05
1969-72 V8-429	D1AZ-12259J	17.00
1969-72 V8-351W	D1OZ-12259B	17.00
1971 V8-390	D1AZ-12259G	18.05
1971 V8-351C,400	D1AZ-12259J	17.00
1972 V8-351C,400	D4PZ-12259B	16.70
1973 V8-351&400 Exc	D4PZ-12259B	16.70
V8-351 Windsor	D3AZ-12259C	16.70
1973 V8-429	D3AZ-12259B	15.40
1974, V8-351C & 400		
Exc Below	D4PZ-12259B	16.70
V8-351 Windsor	D4PZ-12259M	24.00
1974 V8-460	D4PZ-12259E	20.15
1975, Exc	D5PZ-12259B	38.10
V8-460	D5PZ-12259G	35.10

8—IGNITION SWITCH:

Application	Part No.	Price
1968-69	D1AZ-11572C	10.75
1970	DOAZ-11572B	4.85
1971-72	D1AZ-11572B	4.55
1973-75	D3AZ-11572A	5.90

Time — Fuel System & Intake Manifold (Group C) — Time

OPERATION INDEX

C1—CARBURETOR, R & R OR RENEW

1969-75 (0.5) 0.8

C2—CARBURETOR, R & R & OVERHAUL

1966-72 Six Cyl.—
- Exc. Below (1.1) 1.6
- 1970-72 Carter (1.3) 1.8

1967-71 V8—
- 2 Barrel (1.2) 1.7
- 4 Barrel—
  - Exc. Below (1.7) 2.4
  - Autolite, Motorcraft (1.5) 2.1
  - Rochester (1.4) 1.9

1972-75 V8 (1.5) 2.1

C2A—ACCELERATOR PUMP, RENEW

1966-72 Six Cyl.—
- Exc. Below (0.6) 0.8
- Autolite, Motorcraft (0.4) 0.5

1969-75 V8—
- 2 Barrel (0.3) 0.4
- 4 Barrel (0.5) 0.7

—NOTE—
Does Not Include R & R Carburetor.

C2B—NEEDLE & SEAT, RENEW

1966-72 Six Cyl.—
- Autolite, Motorcraft (0.4) 0.5
- Carter Y. F. (0.5) 0.7
- Carter R. B. S. (0.6) 0.8

1969-75 V8—
- 2 Barrel (0.4) 0.5
- 4 Barrel—
  - Autolite, Motorcraft (0.6) 0.8
  - Carter (0.5) 0.7
- Holley—
  - One (0.5) 0.7
  - Both (0.7) 0.9
- Rochester (0.7) 0.9

—NOTE—
Does Not Include R & R Carburetor.

C3—AUTO. CHOKE THERMOSTAT, RENEW

All Models (0.3) 0.5

C3A—AUTO. CHOKE, OVERHAUL

1969-75—
- V8 (0.4) 0.6
- Six Cyl. (0.6) 0.9

C4—DASHPOT, RENEW

All Models (0.3) 0.3

C5—FUEL PUMP, R & R OR RENEW

1969-75—
- Exc. Below (0.3) ①0.4
- V8-400 (0.4) 0.6
- V8-429, 460 (0.5) 0.8

①For Air Cond. On V8-390, 428, Add (0.2) *0.2*

C6—FUEL TANK, R & R OR RENEW

1969-75—
- Exc. Wagon (0.8) 1.2
- Sta. Wagon (0.9) 1.4

—NOTE—
To Renew Tank, Add (0.2) *0.2*

C7—FUEL SYSTEM, CLEAN

Includes R & R tank, blow out lines and clean or renew fuel filter.

1969-75—
- Exc. Wagon (1.3) 1.8
- Sta. Wagon (1.4) 2.0

C8—INTAKE MANIFOLD GASKETS, RENEW

Use for V8 models only. For six cyl., see Opr C8A.

1969-75—
- Exc. Below (1.6) 2.1
- V8-390, 428 (2.7) 3.5
- V8-429, 460 (2.2) 3.0

—NOTE—
For Thermactor, Add (0.2) *0.3*

C8A—MANIFOLD GASKETS, RENEW

Use for six cyl. Models only. For V8, use Opr C8.

1966-72 Six (1.1) 2.0

Parts — Fuel System & Intake Manifold — Parts

PARTS INDEX

1—CARBURETOR ASS'Y:

Application	Part No.	Price
1968-69 6-240, Exc	DOPZ-9510N	48.45
Std Trans	D2TZ-9510N	56.20
1968-72 V8-302	D2AZ-9510P	68.10
1969-70 V8-390	D2AZ-9510P	68.10
1969 V8-351	D2AZ-9510P	68.10
1969-70 V8-429, Exc	D2AZ-9510P	68.10
4-Bar Carb	D2AZ-9510M	97.90
1970 6-240, Exc	D2TZ-9510N	56.20
W/IMCO	D2TZ-9510N	56.20
1970 V8-351, Exc	D2AZ-9510P	68.10
Std Trans	D2AZ-9510P	68.10
1971 6-240, Exc	D2TZ-9510N	56.20
L/Air Cond	D2TZ-9510P	56.20
1971 V8-390	D2AZ-9510P	68.10
1971-72 V8-351 Exc	D2AZ-9510P	68.10
Cleveland	D2AZ-9510C	68.10
1971 V8-429, Exc	D2AZ-9510P	68.10
4 Bar Carb	D2AZ-9510M	97.90
1971 V8-400	D2AZ-9510C	68.10
1972 6-240	D2TZ-9510P	56.20
1972 V8-429, Exc	D2AZ-9510M	97.90
Calif	D3ZZ-9510E	137.15
1973 V8-351, Exc	D3AZ-9510E	68.10
W/4-Bar Carb	D3ZZ-9510E	137.15
1973 V8-400	D3AZ-9510E	68.10
1973 V8-429, 460	D3AZ-9510G	97.90
1974, V8-351-C, Exc	D4AZ-9510F	68.10
D4AE-KA, D4PE-HA	D4AZ-9510H	68.10
1974, V8-351-W, Exc	D4AZ-9510H	68.10
D4PE-VA, D4OE-FA	D4AZ-9510F	68.10
1974, V8-400, Exc	D4AZ-9510H	68.10
W/Therm	D4AZ-9510F	68.10
1974, V8-460, Exc	D4OZ-9510G	97.90
W/Therm	D4AZ-9510B	101.25
1975, V8-351, Exc	D5OZ-9510B	68.10
Calif	D5OZ-9510C	68.10
1975, V8-400, Exc	D5AZ-9510A	68.10
Calif	D5MY-9510B	68.10
Colorado	D5MY-9510A	68.10
1975, V8-460, Exc	D5VY-9510A	97.90
Calif	D5VY-9510B	97.90

2—CARBURETOR TUNE-UP KIT

Application	Part No.	Price
1968-72 6-240, Exc	DOTZ-9A586A	4.65
Auto Trans	C8OZ-9A586D	6.75
1968-72 302&390 Exc	D2AZ-9A586A	7.15
390 4 Bar (68)	D2AZ-9A586D	8.60
1969-72 V8-351	D2AZ-9A586A	7.15
1969-71 V8-429, Exc	D2AZ-9A586A	7.15
4-Bar Carb	D2AZ-9A586D	8.60
1971 V8-400	D2AZ-9A586A	7.15
1972 V8-429, Exc	D2AZ-9A586D	8.60
Calif	D2AZ-9A586C	10.60
1973 V8-351, 400	D2AZ-9A586B	7.30
1973 V8-429,460	D2AZ-9A586A	7.15
1974, Exc	D4AZ-9A586A	7.90
V8-460	D3AZ-9A586A	8.60

3—CARBURETOR GASKET KIT:

Application	Part No.	Price
1968-72 6-240, Exc	DODZ-9502A	2.00
Auto Trans	C8AZ-9502A	2.25
1968-72 V8-302	D2AZ-9502A	2.75
1968-71 390&429 Exc	D2AZ-9502A	2.75
4-Bar Carb	D3AZ-9502A	2.65
1969-72 V8-351, Exc	D2AZ-9502A	2.75
Cleve Eng (71-72)	D1AZ-9502A	2.20
1971 V8-400	D2AZ-9502C	2.55
1972 V8-429,Exc	D3AZ-9502A	2.65
Calif	D2AZ-9502C	2.55
1973 V8-351,400	D2AZ-9502A	2.75
1973 V8-429,460	D2AZ-9502A	2.75
1974, V8-351, 400	D4AZ-9502A	2.75
1974, V8-460, Exc	D3AZ-9502A	2.65
W/Therm	D4AZ-9502B	9.35

4—CHOKE THERMOSTAT HOUSING:

Application	Part No.	Price
1968-69 Six Exc	C5AZ-9848A	4.25
1 Bar Carter	DOBZ-9848A	8.85
1968-69 V8-302	C4AZ-9848B	3.95
1968-71 390 2 Bar Exc	C4AZ-9848A	3.95
Auto Trans	C6AZ-9848A	4.25
1969-70 V8-351, Exc	C6AZ-9848A	4.25
W/Air Cond	C4AZ-9848B	3.95
1969-72 429 2 Bar	DOAZ-9848D	4.25
2 Bar. Carb	C6AZ-9848A	4.25
1970-72 Six, Exc	DOTZ-9848B	11.15
Std Trans (70)	DOTZ-9848A	8.05
1970 V8-302	C6AZ-9848A	4.25
1971 V8-302	D1AZ-9848C	4.25
1971 V8-351,Exc	D1AZ-9848B	4.25
Std Trans	D1AZ-9848C	4.25
V8-351-C	D1AZ-9848A	4.25
1971 V8-429 (2 Bar)	D1AZ-9848B	4.25
1971-72 V8-400	D1AZ-9848A	4.25
1972 V8-302, Exc	DOAZ-9848G	4.25
Std Trans	D2AZ-9848B	5.15
1973 V8-351, Exc	D3AZ-9848N	10.35
Windsor Eng	D1AZ-9848B	4.25
1973 V8-400	D1AZ-9848B	4.25
1973 V8-429	DOAZ-9848D	4.25
1973 V8-460	D1AZ-9848F	4.25
1974 V8-351,400	D4AZ-9848A	10.35
1974, V8-460, Exc	D4VY-9848A	10.35
W/Therm	D4AZ-9848F	11.65
1975	D5AZ-9848A	10.35

5—FUEL PUMP

Application	Part No.	Price
1966-69 V8-352, 390	C6AZ-9350B	16.60
1968-69 V8-302, 351	C5AZ-9350B	16.80
1968 Six	C3AZ-9350Y	17.95
1969 Six—		
Early	C5UZ-9350C	17.95
Late	C9DZ-9350A	15.85
1969 V8-429	DOVY-9350A	16.15
1970-72 Six	D3TZ-9350A	17.95
1970-72 V8-302	D3OZ-9350B	17.95
1970-73 V8-351, Exc.	DOAZ-9350C	16.15
Cleveland Eng.	DOAZ-9350A	16.15
1970-71 V8-390	D4TZ-9350A	17.55
1970-73 V8-429	DOVY-9350A	16.15
1971-74, V8-400	DOAZ-9350A	16.15
1974, V8-351w, Exc	DOAZ-9350C	16.15
W/Therm	D4OZ-9350B	17.55
1973-75, V8-351-C	DOAZ-9350A	16.15
1975, V8-460	D4VY-9350A	
1974, 429&460 Exc	D3VY-9350B	16.60
L/Fuel Vapor Tubes	DOVY-9350A	16.15

6—FUEL TANK:

Application	Part No.	Price
1969,Exc	DOAZ-9002B	49.15
Sta Wgn	C9AZ-9002B	49.15
1970, Exc	DOAZ-9002B	49.15
W/Fuel Emission	DOAZ-9002A	49.15
1970 Sta Wgn, Exc	DOAZ-9002C	54.45
W/Fuel Emission	DOAZ-9002E	68.40
1971-73,Exc	D1AZ-9002A	56.15
From 11/29/71	D2AZ-9002B	56.15
Sta Wgn	D2AZ-9002A	58.20
1974,Exc	D4AZ-9002A	56.15
Sta Wgn	D4AZ-9002D	58.20

1975, Exc Sta Wag—		
L/Aux Tank	D5AZ-9002A	61.20
W/Aux Tank	D5AZ-9002B	61.20
1975, Sta Wag, Exc	D5AZ-9002F	58.20
W/Aux Tank	D5AZ-9002C	58.20
1975, Auxilliary Tank		
Exc Below	D5AZ-9002E	31.80
Sta Wag	D5AZ-9002D	32.30

7—INTAKE MANIFOLD GASKET SET:

1968-71 V8-390,428	C3AZ-9433G	3.45
1968-72 V8-302	D1AZ-9433B	2.95
1969-73 351 Exc	D1AZ-9433C	3.55
Cleve Eng (71-73)	DOAZ-9433B	7.50
1969-73, V8-429	C9AZ-9433A	10.25
1971-73 V8-400	D1AZ-9433A	9.15
1974, V8-351, Exc	D1AZ-9433C	3.55
Cleve Eng, Exc	DOAZ-9433B	7.50
W/Therm	DOAZ-9433A	7.50
1974, V8-400	D4AZ-9433B	9.15
1974, V8-460	C9AZ-9433A	10.25
1975, Exc	D1AZ-9433C	3.55
V8-351	D5AZ-9433A	9.15
V8-460	D5AZ-9433C	10.75

8—INTAKE MANIFOLD GASKET:

1968-71 V8-390	C8AZ-9441A	1.55
1968-73 V8-302	C3AZ-9441D	1.35
1969-74, V8-351-W, Exc	C9OZ-9441A	1.45
W/Therm	D4OZ-9441A	2.05
1969-74 V8-429	C8SZ-9441A	4.35
1974, V8-460	C8SZ-9441A	4.35

FORD

INTERMEDIATE AND COMPACT MODELS

Time — Emission Controls (Group AB) — Time

OPERATION INDEX

AB1—CRANKCASE VENT VALVE (PCV),CLEAN OR RENEW

1969-75—
Renew (0.2) 0.3
Clean (0.4) 0.6

AB2—IMCO EMISSION CONTROL, CHECK

Includes adjust carburetor & ignition timing and check PCV Valve.
1969-75 (0.4) 0.7

AB6—AIR PUMP, R & R OR RENEW

1969-75 (0.4) 0.6

AB10—ANTI-BACKFIRE VALVE, RENEW

1969-75 (0.3) 0.4

AB14—AIR PUMP BELT, RENEW

1969-75—
Exc. Below (0.3) 0.5
V8-429,460 (0.6) 0.9

Parts — Emission Controls — Parts

PARTS INDEX

1—THERMACTOR AIR PUMP:

FAIRLANE. FALCON. TORINO.		
1968-70	C8AZ-9A486C	83.90
1973	C8AZ-9A486C	83.90
1974 Exc	D4AZ-9A486B	83.90
V8-460	D4AZ-9A486A	83.90
1975	D5TZ-9A486C	83.90
MUSTANG:		
1968-73	C8AZ-9A486C	83.90
1974 Four	D4TZ-9A486D	85.30
Six	D4FZ-9A486B	83.90
1975	D5TZ-9A486C	83.90
MAVERICK, GRANADA		
1973	C8AZ-9A486C	83.90
1974 Six	D4AZ-9A486A	83.90
V8	D4AZ-9A486B	83.90
1975	D5TZ-9A486C	83.90

2—THERMACTOR AIR PUMP RELIEF VALVE:

1968-71	C8TZ-9B479A	2.40

3—CHECK VALVE:

1968-71	C8AZ-9A487A	2.90
1974-75—		
Torino Exc	D4VY-9A487A	5.40
V8-400	D4AZ-9A487A	5.40
Maverick, Granada Exc	D4VY-9A487A	5.40
V8-302	D4DZ-9A487A	5.40
Mustang Exc	D4FZ-9A487A	5.40
6-171, V8-302	D4VY-9A487A	5.40
4-140 (75)	D5FZ-9A487A	5.40

4—AIR BY PASS VALVE:

FAIRLANE. FALCON. TORINO:		
1968-70 V8	C8AZ-9B289B	12.40
1974-75 Exc	D4AZ-9B289A	12.40
W/Unleaded Fuel	D5AZ-9B289C	12.40
MUSTANG:		
1968-69 V8	C8AZ-9B289B	12.40
1970 V8-428	C8AZ-9B289B	12.40
1970 V8-429	C8AZ-9B289A	16.85
1974-75 Exc	D4AZ-9B289A	12.40
6-171, Exc.	C8TZ-9B289A	20.85
Calif.	D4VY-9B289A	11.90
4-140 (75)	D4VY-9B289A	11.90
V8-302	D5AZ-9B289C	12.40
MAVERICK:		
1974, Exc.	C8TZ-9B289A	20.85
6-250	D4AZ-9B289A	12.40
V8-302	D4TZ-9B289A	12.40
1975 6-250 Exc	D4VY-9B289A	11.90
Calif	D4AZ-9B289A	12.40
Granada	C8TZ-9B289A	20.85
1975 V8-302	D5AZ-9B289C	12.40
1975 V8-351	D4VY-9B289A	11.90

5—THERMACTOR PUMP DRIVE BELT:

—NOTE—

Order By Complete Model Description.

6—CRANKCASE VENTILATOR VALVE:

FAIRLANE & TORINO:		
1968-69 V8-302, 351	C6AZ-6A666A	1.95
1968-69 V8-427	C7OZ-6A666A	2.05
1968-69 V8-428	C8OZ-6A666B	2.05
1969 6-250	C8OZ-6A666A	2.05
1969 V8-390	C7OZ-6A666A	2.05
1970-75 6-250, Exc.	DODZ-6A666A	2.05
W/T.E.	D4DZ-6A666A	2.05
1970-72 V8-302, 351	DOAZ-6A666A	2.05
1970 V8-428—		
Exc. Below	DOAZ-6A666A	2.05
Cobra Jet	C8OZ-6A666B	2.05
1970 V8-429—		
Exc. Below	DOAZ-6A666A	2.05
Cobra Jet	C1TZ-6A666A	2.95
1971-72 V8-429—		
Exc. Below	DOAZ-6A666A	2.05
Super Cobra Jet	C9TZ-6A666A	2.05
1973-75 V8, Exc.	D3OZ-6A666A	2.05
Cleve. Eng	D4AZ-6A666A	2.05
FALCON:		
1968-70 V8-302	C6AZ-6A666A	1.95
1969 Six—		
Std. Trans.	C8OZ-6A666A	2.05
Auto. Trans.	C9DZ-6A666A	2.05
1970 Six	DODZ-6A666A	2.05
1970 V8-351	DOAZ-6A666A	2.05
MAVERICK, GRANADA		
1970-75 Exc	DODZ-6A666A	2.05
W/Thermactor (74)	D4DZ-6A666A	2.05
V8-302, 351	D3OZ-6A666A	2.05
MUSTANG:		
1968-69 V8-390, 427	C7OZ-6A666A	2.05
1968-69 V8-428	C8OZ-6A666B	2.05
1969 6-200—		
Std. Trans	C8OZ-6A666A	2.05
Auto. Trans	C9DZ-6A666A	2.05
1969 6-250	C8OZ-6A666A	2.05
1969 V8-302—		
Exc. Below	C6AZ-6A666A	1.95
Boss (4 Bar.)	C7OZ-6A666A	2.05
1969 V8-351	C6AZ-6A666A	1.95
1969-70 V8-429	C1TZ-6A666A	2.95
1970-73 Six	DODZ-6A666A	2.05
1970-72 V8-302—		
Early	DOAZ-6A666A	2.05
Late	DOOZ-6A666A	2.05
1970-72 V8-351	DOAZ-6A666A	2.05
1970 V8-390, 428	DOOZ-6A666A	2.05
1971 V8-429—		
Exc. Below	DOAZ-6A666A	2.05
Super Cobra Jet	C9TZ-6A666A	2.05
1973 V8-302,351	D3OZ-6A666A	2.05
1974 Four	D4FZ-6A666A	1.65
Six	D2RY-6A666A	2.05
1975 Exc	D5FZ-6A666A	1.65
V8-302	D3OZ-6A666A	2.05

7—FUEL VAPOR CANISTER:

FAIRLANE, TORINO & GRANADA		
1970-71—		
Exc. Below	DOAZ-9D653C	22.55
6-250	DOAZ-9D653C	22.55
1972-73	D1AZ-9D653A	18.35
1974-75 Exc	D4AZ-9D653A	22.05
W/Thermactor	D4DZ-9D653A	22.05
MAVERICK:		
1970-72	DOAZ-9D653C	22.55
1973-75, See Torino—		
MUSTANG:		
1970-71—		
Exc. Below	DOAZ-9D653C	22.55
6-200, 250	DOAZ-9D653C	22.55
1972-73	D1AZ-9D653A	18.35
1974-75 Four	D4FZ-9D653A	18.35
Six (74)	D4FZ-9D653B	18.35
Six (75)	D5ZZ-9D653A	18.35
V8-302	D4DZ-9D653A	22.05

8—EXHAUST GAS RECIRCULATION VALVE:

FAIRLANE & TORINO:

1973 Six, Exc	D3DZ-9D475A	16.45
Std Trans	D3DZ-9D475D	14.10
1973-74 V8-302, Exc	D3OZ-9D475D	14.10
Std Trans	D3OZ-9D475B	16.60
1973 V8-351-W, Exc	D3OZ-9D475C	14.10
Auto Trans	D3DZ-9D475A	16.45
1973 V8-351-C, Exc	D3ZZ-9D475C	17.00
Auto Trans	D3ZZ-9D475B	18.90
Sta Wag	D3AZ-9D475F	27.75
1973-74 V8-400, Exc	D3AZ-9D475G	14.10
W/C-6 Trans (73)	D3AZ-9D475N	17.00
1973 V8-429, Exc	D3AZ-9D475K	24.45
Auto Trans	D3SZ-9D475A	24.80
1974 Six	D4DZ-9D475H	17.05
1974 V8-351, Exc	D3AZ-9D475F	27.75
Cleve Eng, Exc	D4AZ-9D475F	17.05
W/Te	D3AZ-9D475F	27.75
1974 V8-460, Exc	D4AZ-9D475B	17.90
Sta Wag, Exc	D4AZ-9D475A	25.30
W/Te	D4VY-9D475A	
1975 V8-351	D5AZ-9D475A	15.90
V8-400	D3OZ-9D475C	14.10
V8-460 Exc	D5VY-9D475D	23.20
Calif	D5VY-9D475C	23.20

MAVERICK:

1973-74 6-200	D3OZ-9D475D	14.10
1973 6-250	D3OZ-9D475C	14.10
1973 V8-302, Exc	D3OZ-9D475D	14.10
Std Trans	D3OZ-9D475B	16.60
1974 6-250, Exc	D3DZ-9D475A	16.45
W/Te	D4DZ-9D475A	17.05
1974 V8-302, Exc	D3DZ-9D475D	14.10
Std Trans	D3OZ-9D475B	16.60
1975 6-250	D5DZ-9D475A	15.90
V8-302 Exc	D5OZ-9D475A	15.90
Calif	D5TZ-9D475D	15.90

MUSTANG:

1973 Six	D3DZ-9D475D	14.10
1973 V8-302, Exc	D3OZ-9D475D	14.10
Std Trans	D3OZ-9D475B	16.60
1973 V8-351, Exc	D3ZZ-9D475B	18.90
Std Trans	D3ZZ-9D475A	18.90
1973 V8-400	D3AZ-9D475G	14.10
1974 Four, Exc	D4FZ-9D475J	22.20
W/Te	D4FZ-9D475F	22.20
Std Trans	D4FZ-9D475G	22.20
1974 Six—		
Auto Trans, Exc	D4ZZ-9D475F	24.45
W/Te	D4ZZ-9D475D	24.45
Std Trans, Exc	D4ZZ-9D475A	24.45
W/Te	D4ZZ-9D475B	24.45
1975 4-140—		
Auto Trans Exc	D5FZ-9D475G	
Calif	D5FZ-9D475D	20.80
Std Trans Exc	D5FZ-9D475F	
Calif	D5FZ-9D475E	
1975 6-171	D5ZZ-9D475A	15.90
1975 V8-302 Exc	D5OZ-9D475A	15.90
Calif	D5TZ-9D475D	15.90

GRANADA

1975 6-250	D5DZ-9D475A	15.90
1975 V8-302 Exc	D3OZ-9D475B	16.60
Auto Trans	D5OZ-9D475A	15.90
Calif	D5TZ-9D475D	15.90
1975 V8-351 Exc	D5AZ-9D475A	15.90
Calif	D5TZ-9D475D	15.90

Time — Tune-Up & Ignition (Group B) — Time

OPERATION INDEX

B1—TUNE-UP, MINOR

Includes: Renew points, condenser and plugs. Set spark timing and adjust carburetor idle.

1968-74 Six (1.2) 1.6
1968-74 V8—
Exc. Below (1.5) 1.9
Mustang—
V8-302 (1.4) 1.8
V8-351 (1.8) 2.2
V8-390, 428 (2.2) 2.7
1974 Mustang Four (1.2) 1.8
1974 Mustang V6 (2.0) 2.6
1975 Four (0.8) 1.2
1975 Six Exc (0.9) 1.4
Mustang (1.3) 1.8
1975 V8-302 (1.0) 1.4
V8-351, 400 (1.3) 1.8
V8-460 (1.5) 2.0

—NOTE—
For V8-390, 428 Equipped With Thermactor Add (1.0) *1.5*

B2—TUNE-UP, MAJOR

Includes check compression, clean and adjust or renew spark plugs, R&R dist, renew points and condenser and adjust ignition timing, carburetor and fan belts. Clean battery terminals and service air cleaner. Check coil & replace or clean fuel line filter.

1968-74 Six (2.0) 3.0
1968-74 V8 (2.2) 3.3
1974 Mustang Four (2.4) 2.9
1974 Mustang V6 (3.0) 3.6
1975 Four (2.0) 2.5
1975 Six Exc (2.0) 2.5
Mustang (2.2) 2.8
1975 V8 (2.0) 2.8

—NOTE—
To Service PCV Valve, Add (0.5) *0.5*
For V8-390, 428 With Thermactor, Add (1.0) *1.5*

B3—TUNE-UP MAJOR & OVERHAUL CARBURETOR

1968-74 Six (3.0) 4.3
1968-74 V8—
2 Barrel (3.4) 4.6
4 Barrel—
Exc. Below (3.9) 4.8
Autolite Motorcraft (3.7) 4.8
1974 Mustang Four (3.3) 4.3
1974 Mustang V6 (3.9) 4.8
1975 Four (2.8) 3.8
1975 Six Exc (2.8) 3.8
Mustang (3.2) 4.2
1975 V8—
2 Barrel (3.0) 4.2
4 Barrel (3.5) 4.7

—NOTE—
To Service PCV Valve, Add (0.5) *0.5*
For V8-390, 428 With Thermactor, Add (1.0) *1.5*

B4—POINTS & CONDENSER, RENEW

Does not include R & R distributor.

1968-74 (0.4) 0.6

B5—SPARK PLUGS, CLEAN & ADJUST OR RENEW

1969-75 Six (0.4) 0.5
1969-75 V8 (0.6) 0.8
1974-75 Mustang Four (0.3) 0.4
1974-75 Mustang V6 (0.5) 0.6

—NOTE—
To Clean And Adjust, Add (0.2) *0.2*
For 1968-70 V8-390, 428 W/Thermactor, Add (1.0) *1.0*

B6—COMPRESSION, TEST

1969-75 Six (0.5) 0.6
1969-75 V8 (0.7) 0.9
1974-75 Mustang Four (0.3) 0.4
1974-75 Mustang V6 (0.5) 0.6

—NOTE—
For 1968-70 V8-390, 428 W/Thermactor, Add (1.0) *1.0*

B7—IGNITION TIMING, SET

1969-75 (0.3) 0.3

B8—DISTRIBUTOR, R & R OR RENEW

1969-75 (0.4) 0.5

B9—DISTRIBUTOR, OVERHAUL (UNIT OFF)

1969-75 Six (0.8) 1.0
1969-75 V8—
Exc. Below (1.1) 1.4
Transistor Ign. (0.7) 0.9
1974 Mustang II (0.8) 1.0

B9A—DISTRIBUTOR, ADJUST ON STROBOSCOPE (UNIT OFF)

All Models (0.3) 0.4

B10—DISTRIBUTOR CAP, RENEW

All Models (0.3) 0.4

B11—IGNITION CABLE SET, RENEW

Time allowance covers installation of factory supplied sets only.

1969-75 (0.4) 0.5

B12—VACUUM CONTROL UNIT, RENEW

Includes R & R distributor.

1969-75 (0.7) 0.9

B13—IGNITION COIL, RENEW

1969-75 (0.4) 0.6

B14—IGNITION SWITCH, RENEW

1966-69 (0.3) 0.5
1970—
Exc. Below (0.5) 0.8
Maverick—
Before 11/03/69 (0.3) 0.5
After 11/03/69 (0.6) 0.9
Falcon—
Before 01/01/70 (0.3) 0.5
After 01/01/70 (0.5) 0.8
1971—
Exc. Below (0.5) 0.8
Maverick (0.6) 0.9
1972-73—
Exc. Below (0.5) 0.8
Maverick (0.6) 0.9
Torino (0.6) 0.9
1974-75 Exc (0.6) 0.9
Mustang (0.4) 0.6

Parts — Tune-Up & Ignition — Parts

DISTRIBUTOR ASS'Y:

FAIRLANE & TORINO:

1969 6-250—		
Synchro-Mesh	C9OZ-12127A	34.00
Auto. Trans	C9OZ-12127V	34.00
1969 V8-302—		
Synchro-Mesh	C8AZ-12127E	31.30
Auto. Trans.—		
L/Air Cond.	C9AZ-12127M	34.00
W/Air Cond.	C9AZ-12127R	34.00
1969 V8-351—		
2 Bar. Carb	DOOZ-12127M	34.00
4 Bar. Carb.—		
Std. Trans	DOOZ-12127N	34.00
Auto. Trans	DOOZ-12127R	34.00
1969 V8-390—		
2 Bar. Carb	C7AZ-12127D	33.15
4 Bar. Carb.—		
Std. Trans	C9AZ-12127D	34.00
Auto. Trans	C7AZ-12127L	33.15
1969 V8-427	C8OZ-12127G	33.15
1969 V8-428—		
Synchro-Mesh	C8OZ-12127D	31.30
Auto. Trans	C8OZ-12127J	36.50

1970 Six	D2OZ-12127P	31.30
1970 V8-302—		
Synchro-Mesh	DOAZ-12127Y	34.00
Auto. Trans	DOOZ-12127AL	31.30
1970 V8-351—		
2 Bar. Carb	D2ZZ-12127A	31.30
4 Bar. Carb	DOOZ-12127G	34.00
1970 V8-428	C8OZ-12127D	31.30
1970 V8-429 (W/Imco)—		
Synchro-Mesh	C9AZ-12127Y	34.00
Auto. Trans	C8VY-12127G	33.60
1970 V8-429 (W/Thermactor)—		
Synchro-Mesh	DOOZ-12127J	36.50
Auto. Trans	DOOZ-12127K	45.65
1971 Six—		
Exc. Calif	D2OZ-12127P	31.30
Calif—		
Std. Trans	D1OZ-12127A	33.15
Auto. Trans	D1OZ-12127B	33.15
1971-72 V8-302 (2 Bar. Carb.)—		
Synchro-Mesh	DOAZ-12127Y	34.00
Auto. Trans	DOOZ-12127AL	31.30
1971-72 V8-302 (4 Bar.)	D1ZZ-12127A	44.25
1971 V8-351 (2 Bar. Carb.)—		
Synchro-Mesh	D2ZZ-12127A	31.30
Auto. Trans.—		
Exc. Calif	DOOZ-12127U	34.00
Calif	D2ZZ-12127C	34.00
1971 V8-351 (4 Bar. Carb.)—		
Synchro-Mesh	DOOZ-12127V	34.00
Auto. Trans.—		
Exc. Calif	DOOZ-12127T	34.00
Calif	D1OZ-12127L	34.00
1971 V8-429 (2 Bar. Carb.)—		
Exc. Calif	C9AZ-12127F	34.00
Calif	D1MY-12127F	34.00
1971 V8-429 (4 Bar. Carb.)—		
Exc. Cobra Jet—		
Exc. Calif	C9AZ-12127F	34.00
Calif	D1MY-12127F	34.00
Cobra Jet—		
Std. Trans	DOOZ-12127J	36.50
1972 Six—		
Exc. Calif	D2OZ-12127D	33.15
Calif	D2OZ-12127E	27.20
1972 V8-351 (2 Bar. Carb)—		
Exc. Calif	D2ZZ-12127A	31.30
Calif	D2ZZ-12127C	34.00
1972 V8-351 (4 Bar Carb)—		
Synchro-Mesh—		
Exc. Calif	D2ZZ-12127E	34.00
Calif	D2ZZ-12127F	34.00
Auto. Trans.—		
Exc. Calif	D2ZZ-12127G	34.00
Calif	D2ZZ-12127H	34.00
1972 V8-400	D2AZ-12127F	34.00
1972 V8-429	D2AZ-12127J	45.65
1973 Six	D3OZ-12127A	33.15
1973 V8-302—		
Std. Tran.	D3OZ-12127E	
Auto. Tran.	D3OZ-12127E	
1973 V8-351—		
Cleveland Eng.	D3ZZ-12127B	31.30
Windsor Eng.	D3AZ-12127A	34.00
1973 V8-351 C.J.—		
Std. Tran.	D3OZ-12127F	34.00
Auto. Tran.	D3OZ-12127G	34.00
1973 V8-400	D3AZ-12127B	34.00
1973 V8-429	D3SZ-12127A	
1974 Six	D3OZ-12127R	31.30
1974 V8-302—		
Std Trans	D3BZ-12127D	34.00
Auto Trans Exc	D3OZ-12127H	34.00
W/Thermactor	D4DZ-12127M	41.60
1974 V8-351c Exc	D3MY-12127G	34.00
Breakerless Ign	D4AZ-12127A	41.60
1974 V8-351-W, Exc.	D3AZ-12127A	34.00
W/Breakerless Ign.	D4AZ-12127C	41.60
1974 V8-351 (4 Bar), Exc.	D3OZ-12127G	34.00
W/Man. Trans.	D3OZ-12127F	34.00
1974-75 V8-460	D4VY-12127C	41.60
1975 V8-351 Exc	D5DZ-12127H	41.60
351-M	D5AZ-12127B	41.60
1975 V8-400 Exc	D5AZ-12127B	41.60
Calif	D5AZ-12127D	41.60

FALCON:

1968-69 6-200—		
Synchro-Mesh	C8DZ-12127C	25.60
Auto. Trans	C8DZ-12127D	25.60
1969 6-170—		
Synchro-Mesh	D2DZ-12127A	36.50
Auto. Trans	C8DZ-12127J	25.60
1969 V8-302—		
Synchro-Mesh	C8AZ-12127E	31.30
Auto. Trans.—		
L/Air Cond.	C9AZ-12127M	34.00
W/Air Cond	C9AZ-12127R	34.00
1970 6-200	C4OZ-12127F	24.15
1970 V8-302	C8AZ-12127E	31.30

MAVERICK & GRANADA

1970-71 6-170—		
Synchro-Mesh	D2DZ-12127A	36.50
Auto. Trans	DODZ-12127B	25.60
1970 6-200	DODZ-12127C	25.60
1971 6-200—		
Exc. Calif	DODZ-12127C	25.60
Calif—		
Std. Trans	D2DZ-12127C	25.60
Auto. Trans	D1DZ-12127G	34.00
1971 6-250—		
Exc. Calif	D2OZ-12127P	31.30
Calif—		
Std. Trans	D1OZ-12127A	33.15
Auto. Trans	D1OZ-12127B	33.15
1972 6-170—		
Exc. Calif	D2DZ-12127A	36.50
Calif	D2DZ-12127B	34.00
1972 6-200—		
Synchro Mesh—		
Exc. Calif	D2DZ-12127C	25.60
Calif	D2DZ-12127E	34.00
Auto Trans—		
Exc Calif	D2DZ-12127D	25.60
Calif.	D2DZ-12127F	34.00
1972 6-250	D2OZ-12127D	33.15
1972 V8-302—		
Synchro-Mesh	DOAZ-12127Y	34.00
Auto Trans.	DOOZ-12127AL	31.30
1973 6-200—		
Std. Tran.	D3DZ-12127B	25.60
Auto. Tran.	D3DZ-12127A	25.60
1973 6-250	D3OZ-12127A	33.15
1973 V8-302—		
Std. Tran.	D3OZ-12127E	
Auto. Tran.	D3OZ-12127E	
1974, 6-200—		
Std Trans	D4DZ-12127H	34.00
Auto Trans Exc	D4DZ-12127K	24.90
Breakerless Ign	D4DZ-12127F	41.60
1974, 6-250—		
Std Trans Exc	D3OZ-12127B	33.15
Breakerless Ign	D4DZ-12127B	
Auto Trans Exc	D3OZ-12127R	31.30
Breakerless Ign	D4DZ-12127B	
1974 V8-302	D4DZ-12127M	41.60
1975 6-250 Exc	D5DZ-12127D	41.60
Auto Trans	D5DZ-12127A	41.60
1975 V8-302 Exc	D5DZ-12127L	41.60
Auto Trans Exc	D5DZ-12127K	41.60
Granada	D5DZ-12127J	41.60
Calif	D5DZ-12127B	41.60
1975 V8-351 Exc	D5DZ-12127H	41.60
Calif	D5DZ-12127M	41.60

MUSTANG:

1968-69 6-200—		
Synchro-Mesh	C8DZ-12127C	25.60
Auto. Trans	C8DZ-12127D	25.60
1968-69 V8-427	C8OZ-12127G	33.15
1969 6-250—		
Synchro-Mesh	C9OZ-12127A	34.00
Auto. Trans	C9OZ-12127V	34.00
1969 V8-302—		
Synchro-Mesh	C8AZ-12127E	31.30
Auto. Trans.—		
L/Air Cond	C9AZ-12127M	34.00
W/Air Cond	C9AZ-12127R	34.00
1969 V8-351—		
2 Bar. Carb	DOOZ-12127M	34.00
4 Bar. Carb	DOOZ-12127N	34.00
1969 V8-390—		
2 Bar. Carb	C7AZ-12127D	33.15
4 Bar. Carb	C9OZ-12127A	34.00
1969 V8-428—		
Synchro-Mesh	C8OZ-12127D	31.30
Auto. Trans	C7OZ-12127F	33.15
1969 V8-429	C9ZZ-12127D	59.70
1970 6-250	D2OZ-12127P	31.30
1970 V8-302—		
Synchro-Mesh	C8AZ-12127E	31.30
Auto. Trans	DOOZ-12127AL	31.30
1970 V8-351—		
2 Bar. Carb	DOAZ-12127H	34.00
4 Bar. Carb	DOOZ-12127G	34.00
1970 V8-390—		
Synchro-Mesh	C9AZ-12127D	34.00
Auto. Trans	C7AZ-12127L	33.15
1970 V8-428	C8OZ-12127D	31.30
1970 V8-429—		
Synchro-Mesh	DOZZ-12127C	62.55
Auto. Trans	DOZZ-12127D	62.55
1971 6-250—		
Exc. Calif	D2OZ-12127P	31.30
Calif—		
Std. Trans	D1OZ-12127A	33.15
Auto. Trans	D1OZ-12127B	33.15
1971-72 V8-302 (2 Bar. Carb.)—		
Synchro-Mesh	DOAZ-12127Y	34.00
Auto. Trans	DOOZ-12127AL	31.30
1971-72 V8-302 (4 Bar.)	D1ZZ-12127A	44.25
1971 V8-351 (2 Bar. Carb.)—		
Synchro-Mesh	D2ZZ-12127A	31.30
Auto. Trans.—		
Exc. Calif	DOOZ-12127U	34.00
Calif	D2ZZ-12127C	34.00
1971 V8-351 (4 Bar. Carb.)—		
Synchro-Mesh	DOOZ-12127V	34.00
Auto. Trans.—		
Exc. Calif	DOOZ-12127T	34.00
Calif	D1OZ-12127L	34.00
1971 V8-429—		
Exc. Super Cobra Jet—		
Std. Trans	DOOZ-12127J	36.50
Auto. Trans	DOOZ-12127K	45.65
1972 Six—		
Exc. Calif	D2OZ-12127D	33.15
Calif	D2OZ-12127E	27.20
1972 V8-351 (2 Bar Carb)—		
Exc. Calif	D2ZZ-12127A	31.30
Calif	D2ZZ-12127C	34.00
1972 V8-351 (4 Bar Carb)—		
Synchro-Mesh—		
Exc. Calif	D2ZZ-12127E	34.00
Calif	D2ZZ-12127F	34.00
Auto Trans—		
Exc Calif	D2ZZ-12127G	34.00
Calif	D2ZZ-12127H	34.00
1973 6-250	D3OZ-12127A	33.15
1973 V8-302—		
Std. Tran.	D3OZ-12127E	
Auto. Tran.—		
Exc. Below	D3OZ-12127E	
C/M Type	D3ZZ-12127A	
1973 V8-351—		
2 Bar. Carb.	D3ZZ-12127B	31.30
4 Bar. Carb.	D3ZZ-12127D	
1973 V8-351 C.J.—		
Std. Tran.	D3OZ-12127F	34.00
Auto. Tran.	D3OZ-12127G	34.00
1974 Four Exc	D4ZZ-12127D	32.30
Auto Trans, Exc.	D4ZZ-12127B	32.30
Calif.	D4ZZ-12127B	32.30
1974 Six Exc	D4ZZ-12127S	45.35
Calif.	D4ZZ-12127L	45.35
Auto Trans	D4ZZ-12127M	45.35
1975 4-140 Exc	D5FZ-12127C	41.60
Calif	D5ZZ-12127A	41.60
1975 V8-302 Exc	D5DZ-12127K	41.60
Calif	D5DZ-12127B	41.60
1975 6-171	D5ZZ-12127D	

DISTRIBUTOR REPAIR KIT:

—NOTE—

Includes Rotor, Points And Condenser

FAIRLANE & TORINO:

1968-74 V8	COTZ-12000A	7.00
1968-74 Six	C5AZ-12000D	7.00

FALCON:

1966-70 V8	COTZ-12000A	7.00
1968-69 Six	C5AZ-12000D	7.00

MAVERICK:

1970-72	C5AZ-12000D	7.00
1973-74—		
Exc. Below	C5AZ-12000D	7.00
V8-302	COTZ-12000A	7.00

MUSTANG:

1967-73 V8	COTZ-12000A	7.00
1969-74 Six	C5AZ-12000D	7.00
1974 Four	D4ZZ-12200A	1.10

FIG. 1-TUNE-UP & IGNITION

(For Parts Identification Only)

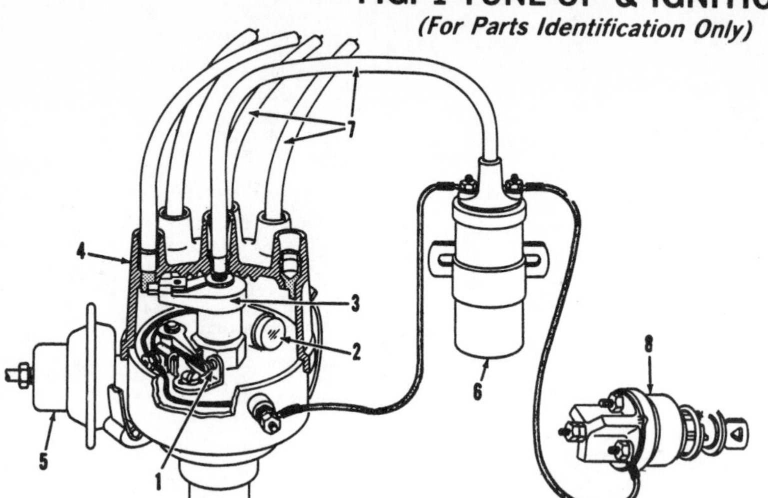

1—IGNITION POINT SET:

Application	Part No.	Price
FAIRLANE & TORINO:		
1966-70 Six	C9AZ-12171B	4.40
1966-70 V8	B8Q-12171A	4.40
1971-74 Six	C9AZ-12171B	4.40
1971-72 V8-302—		
2 Bar. Carb	C5AZ-12171A	4.40
4 Bar. Carb	C9AZ-12171A	4.40
1971-72 V8-351 (2 Bar. Carb.)—		
Synchro-Mesh	C5AZ-12171A	4.40
Auto. Trans	B8Q-12171A	4.40
1971-72 V8-351 (4 Bar.)	C5AZ-12171A	4.40
1971-72 V8-429	C5AZ-12171A	4.40
1973-74 V8—		
Exc. Below	B8Q-12171A	4.40
V8-351 C.J.	C9AZ-12171A	4.40
FALCON:		
1966-70 Six	C9AZ-12171B	4.40
1966-70 V8	B8Q-12171A	4.40
MAVERICK:		
1970 Six	C9AZ-12171B	4.40
1971-72	C9AZ-12171A	4.40
1973-74—		
6-200,250	C9AZ-12171B	4.40
V8-302	B8Q-12171A	4.40
MUSTANG:		
1966-70 Six	C9AZ-12171B	4.40
1969-70 V8—		
Exc. Below	B8Q-12171A	4.40
V8-429	C9AZ-12171A	4.40
1971-73 Six	C9AZ-12171B	4.40
1971-72 V8-302—		
2 Bar. Carb.	C5AZ-12171A	4.40
4 Bar. Carb.	C9AZ-12171A	4.40
1971-72 V8-351 (2 Bar. Carb.)—		
Synchro-Mesh	C5AZ-12171A	4.40
Auto. Trans	B8Q-12171A	4.40
1971-72 V8-351 (4 Bar-)	C5AZ-12171A	4.40
1971-72 V8-429	C5AZ-12171A	4.40
1973 V8—		
Exc. Below	B8Q-12171A	4.40
V8-351 C.J.	C9AZ-12171A	4.40
1974 Four	D4ZZ-12171A	4.40
Six	D4RY-12171A	4.40

2—CONDENSER:

Application	Part No.	Price
FAIRLANE & TORINO:		
1968-70	C9AZ-12300A	1.50
1971-72 Six	C9AZ-12300A	1.50
1971-72 V8	C9AZ-12300A	1.50
1973-74	C9AZ-12300A	1.50
FALCON:		
1968-70	C9AZ-12300A	1.50
MAVERICK:		
1970-72	C9AZ-12300A	1.50
1973-74	C9AZ-12300A	1.50
MUSTANG:		
1966-70 Six—		
L/Thermactor	7RA-12300C	1.50
W/Thermactor	C9AZ-12300A	1.50
1967-70 V8	C9AZ-12300A	1.50
1971-72 Six	C9AZ-12300A	1.50
1971-72 V8	C9AZ-12300A	1.50
1973	C9AZ-12300A	1.50
1974 Four	D4ZZ-12300A	1.50
Six	D4ZZ-12300B	1.50

3—ROTOR:

Application	Part No.	Price
FAIRLANE & TORINO:		
1968-74 V8	B7A-12200A	1.10
1969-74 Six	C5TZ-12200B	1.10
1975 V8	D5AZ-12200A	1.50
FALCON:		
1966-70 V8	B7A-12200A	1.10
1968-70 Six	C5TZ-12200B	1.10
MAVERICK & GRANADA		
1970-72 Six	C5TZ-12200B	1.10
1973-74—		
Exc. Below	C5TZ-12200B	1.10
V8-302	B7A-12200A	1.10
1975 Six	D5DZ-12200A	1.50
1975 V8	D5AZ-12200A	1.50
MUSTANG:		
1967-73 V8	B7A-12200A	1.10
1966-72 Six—		
L/Thermactor	FAA-12200B	1.10
W/Thermactor	C5TZ-12200B	1.10
1973 Six	B7A-12200A	1.10
1974 Four	D4ZZ-12200A	1.10
Six	D2RY-12200A	1.30
1975 Four	D5FZ-12200A	1.50
Six	D5FZ-12200B	1.50
V8-302	D5AZ-12200A	1.50

4—DISTRIBUTOR CAP:

Application	Part No.	Price
FAIRLANE & TORINO:		
1968-74 Six	7HA-12106	5.15
1968-74 V8	B7A-12106A	5.75
1975	D4AZ-12106A	
FALCON:		
1966-70 Six	7HA-12106	5.15
1966-70 V8	B7A-12106A	5.75
MAVERICK & GRANADA		
1970-74 Six	7HA-12106	5.15
1972-74 V8	B7A-12106A	5.75
1975 Six	D5DZ-12106A	9.75
V8	D5AZ-12106A	10.05
MUSTANG:		
1967-73 Six	7HA-12106	5.15
1967-73 V8	B7A-12106A	5.75
1974 Six	D2RY-12106A	3.85
1974 Four	D4ZZ-12106A	4.15
1975 Four	D5FZ-12106A	8.15
Six	D5DZ-12106A	9.75
V8-302	D5AZ-12106A	10.05

5—VACUUM CONTROL UNIT:

Application	Part No.	Price
FAIRLANE & TORINO:		
1968-69 V8-302	D2PZ-12370L	16.70
1969 V8-390	C5AZ-12370A	5.40
1969 V8-427	C5AZ-12370A	5.40
1969 V8-428—		
Synchro-Mesh	D2PZ-12370M	16.70
Auto. Trans	C5AZ-12370A	5.40
1970-71 Six—		
Exc. Calif.	D2PZ-12370A	16.70
Calif.	C5TZ-12370A	3.35
1970-71 V8-302—		
2 Bar. Carb.—		
Std. Tran.	D2PZ-12370L	16.70
Auto. Tran.	D2PZ-12370M	16.70
4 Bar. Carb.	D2ZZ-12370G	16.70
1970 V8-351—		
2 Bar. Carb.	D2PZ-12370M	16.70
4 Bar. Carb.	D2PZ-12370M	16.70
1970 V8-428	D2PZ-12370M	16.70
1970 V8-429—		
W/Imco	D2DZ-12370F	16.70
W/Thermactor—		
Std. Tran.	D1AZ-12370A	11.10
Auto. Tran.	D2PZ-12370F	16.70
1971-72 V8-351—		
2 Bar. Carb.—		
Std. Tran.	D2PZ-12370M	16.70
Auto. Tran.	C5AZ-12370A	5.40
4 Bar. Carb.	D2PZ-12370L	16.70
1971-72 V8-429—		
Exc. Cobra Jet—		
Exc. Calif.	D2VY-12370C	16.70
Calif.	D2PZ-12370E	16.70
Cobra Jet	D1AZ-12370A	11.10
1972 Six—		
Exc. Calif.	D2OZ-12370A	16.70
Calif.	D2OZ-12370D	16.70
1972 V8-351—		
2 Bar. Carb.—		
Exc. Calif.	D2AZ-12370L	16.70
Calif.	D2AZ-12370K	16.70
4 Bar. Carb.	D2ZZ-12370A	16.70
1972 V8-400	D2AZ-12370J	16.70
1972 V8-429	D2AZ-12370G	16.70
1973 V8-302—		
Std. Tran.	D3OZ-12370A	16.70
Auto. Tran.	D3OZ-12370A	16.70
1973 V8-351—		
Cleveland Eng.	D2VY-12370B	16.70
Windsor Eng.	D2TZ-12370J	16.70
Cobra Jet	D3AZ-12370A	16.70
1973 V8-400	D2VY-12370B	16.70
1973 V8-429	D3SZ-12370A	16.70
1974 Six	D2OZ-12370D	16.70
1974 V8-302—		
Std Trans	D3OZ-12370C	16.70
Auto Trans Exc	D3OZ-12370E	16.70
W/Thermactor	D4VY-12370A	11.10
1974 V8-351 Exc	D2TZ-12370J	16.70
Breakerless Ign	D3MY-12370C	16.70
1975 V8-351 Exc	D5DZ-12370C	16.70
351-M	D4OZ-12370A	11.10
1975 V8-400 Exc	D4OZ-12370A	11.10
Calif	D5AZ-12370A	16.70
1975 V8-460	D3AZ-12370C	11.10
MAVERICK & GRANADA		
1970-71(6-170)—		
Std. Tran.	D2PZ-12370A	16.70
Auto. Tran.	D2PZ-12370B	16.70
1970-71 (6-200)	D2PZ-12370A	16.70
1971(6-250)—		
Exc. Calif.	D2PZ-12370A	16.70
Calif.	C5TZ-12370A	3.35
1972(6-170)	D2UZ-12370A	16.70
1972(6-200)—		
Std. Tran.	D2UZ-12370A	16.70
Auto. Tran.—		
Exc. Calif.	D2TZ-12370A	16.70
Calif.	D2DZ-12370A	16.70
1972(6-250)	D2OZ-12370A	16.70
1972 V8-302—		
Std. Tran.	D2PZ-12370L	16.70
Auto. Tran.	D2PZ-12370M	16.70
1973(6-200)—		
Std. Tran.	D3DZ-12370B	16.70
Auto. Tran.	D3DZ-12370A	16.70
1973 V8-302—		
Std. Tran.	D3OZ-12370A	16.70
Auto. Tran.	D3OZ-12370A	16.70
1974 6-200 Exc	D3DZ-12370B	16.70
Auto Trans Exc	D3DZ-12370A	16.70
Breakerless Ign	D4DZ-12370D	11.10
1974 6-250 Exc	D3DZ-12370C	11.10
Breakerless Ign	D4DZ-12370E	11.10
1974 V8-302	D4VY-12370A	11.10
1975 6-250 Exc	D5DZ-12370B	16.70
Auto Trans	D5DZ-12370A	16.70
1975 V8-302 Exc	D5DZ-12370E	16.70
Auto Trans Exc	D5OZ-12370A	16.70
Calif	D4VY-12370A	11.10
1975 V8-351 Exc	D5DZ-12370D	16.70
Calif	D5DZ-12370C	16.70
MUSTANG:		
1969 V8-302, 390	D2PZ-12370L	16.70
1969 V8-428—		
Synchro-Mesh	D2PZ-12370L	16.70
Auto. Trans	C5AZ-12370A	5.40
1970 6-250	D2PZ-12370A	16.70
1970 V8-302—		
Std. Tran.	D2AZ-12370N	16.70
Auto. Tran.	D2PZ-12370M	16.70
1970 V8-351—		
2 Bar. Carb.	D2PZ-12370H	16.70
4 Bar. Carb.	D2PZ-12370M	16.70
1970 V8-390	C5AZ-12370A	5.40
1970 V8-428	D2PZ-12370M	16.70
1970 V8-429—		
Std. Tran.	DOZZ-12370B	11.10
Auto. Tran.	C5AZ-12370A	5.40

Application	Part No.	Price
1971 6-250—		
Exc. Calif.	D2PZ-12370A★	16.70
Calif.	C5TZ-12370A★	3.35
1971 V8-302—		
2 Bar. Carb.—		
Std. Tran.	D2PZ-12370L★	16.70
Auto. Tran.	D2PZ-12370M★	16.70
4 Bar. Carb.	D2ZZ-12370G★	16.70
1971 V8-351—		
2 Bar. Carb.—		
Std. Tran.	D2PZ-12370G★	16.70
Auto. Tran.—		
Exc. Calif.	C5AZ-12370A★	5.40
Calif.	D2PZ-12370L★	16.70
4 Bar. Carb.	D2PZ-12370L★	16.70
1971 V8-429—		
Std. Tran.	D1AZ-12370A★	11.10
Auto. Tran.	D2PZ-12370F	16.70
1972 6-250—		
Exc. Calif.	D2OZ-12370A★	16.70
Calif.	D2OZ-12370D★	16.70
1972 V8-302—		
Std. Tran.	D2OZ-12370C★	16.70
Auto. Tran.	D2AZ-12370A★	16.70
1972 V8-351—		
2 Bar. Carb.—		
Exc. Calif.	D2AZ-12370L★	16.70
Calif.	D2AZ-12370K★	16.70
4 Bar. Carb.	D2ZZ-12370A★	16.70
1973 V8-302—		
Std. Tran.	D3OZ-12370A★	16.70
Auto. Tran.	D3OZ-12370A★	16.70
1973 V8-351—		
Cleveland Eng.	D2VY-12370B	16.70
Windsor Eng.	D2TZ-12370J	16.70
Cobra Jet	D3AZ-12370A★	16.70
1974 Four	D4ZZ-12370C	11.10
Six Exc	D3RY-12370A	11.10
Auto Trans	D3RY-12370B	11.10
1975 Four (Calif)	D5FZ-12370B	16.70
1975 V8-302 Exc	D5OZ-12370A★	16.70
Calif	D4VY-12370A★	11.10

6—IGNITION COIL:

Application	Part No.	Price
1968-74 Exc	B6A-12029B★	13.50
Breakerless Ign	D4AZ-12029A★	14.85
1975	D5AZ-12029A★	14.85

IGNITION COIL RESISTOR:

FAIRLANE & FALCON:

Application	Part No.	Price
1966-69 (Wire)	COLF-12250A★	2.70
1973-75	C9OZ-12250A★	2.50

MAVERICK & GRANADA

Application	Part No.	Price
1970	COLF-12250A★	2.70
1973-75 Exc	C9OZ-12250A★	2.50
Granada	COLF-12250A★	2.70

MUSTANG:

Application	Part No.	Price
1966-69 (Wire)	COLF-12250A★	2.70
1970-73	C9OZ-12250A★	2.50
1975 Exc	C9AZ-12250A★	2.50
W/Tachometer	COLF-12250A★	2.70

7—IGNITION CABLE SET:

FAIRLANE & TORINO:

Application	Part No.	Price
1966-72 Six	D1AZ-12259A★	16.70
1969-72 V8	D1AZ-12259B★	15.05
1973 Six	D1AZ-12259B★	15.05
1973 V8-302	D3OZ-12259B★	16.70
1973 V8-351—		
Windsor Eng.	D4PZ-12259B	16.70
Cleveland Eng.	D4PZ-12259B	16.70
1973 V8-400	D4PZ-12259B	16.70
1973 V8-429	D3AZ-12259B★	15.40
1974 Six	D4PZ-12259G★	15.05
V8-302	D4PZ-12259J★	24.00
V8-351 Exc	D4PZ-12259B★	16.70
Windsor Eng	D4PZ-12259M★	24.00
V8-400	D4PZ-12259B★	16.70
V8-460	D4PZ-12259E★	20.15
1975 Exc	D5PZ-12259M★	35.10
351-M, 400	D5PZ-12259B★	38.10
460	D5PZ-12259G★	35.10

FALCON:

Application	Part No.	Price
1966-70 Six	D1AZ-12259B★	15.05
1969-70	D1AZ-12259B★	15.05

MAVERICK & GRANADA

Application	Part No.	Price
1970-72	D1AZ-12259B★	15.05
1973 Six	D1AZ-12259B★	15.05
1973 V8-302	D3DZ-12259A★	16.70
1974 Six	D4PZ-12259G★	15.05
V8	D4PZ-12259J★	24.00
1975 Exc	D5PZ-12259K★	15.95
302	D5PZ-12259L★	35.10
351	D5PZ-12259M★	35.10

MUSTANG:

Application	Part No.	Price
1966-72 Six	D1AZ-12259A★	16.70
1968-69 V8-390	C5AZ-12259F★	18.05
1969-72 V8	D1AZ-12259B★	15.05
1973 6-250	D1AZ-12259B★	15.05
1973 V8-302	D3OZ-12259B★	16.70
1973 V8-351	D4PZ-12259B	16.70
1974 Four	D4PZ-12259F	12.70
Six	D4ZZ-12259A	16.80
1975 Four	D5PZ-12259H	16.65
Six	D5PZ-12259J	22.00
302	D5PZ-12259L★	35.10

8—IGNITION SWITCH:

FAIRLANE & TORINO:

Application	Part No.	Price
1968-69	D1AZ-11572C★	10.75
1970	DOAZ-11572B★	4.85
1971	D4DZ-11572A	5.30
1972-75	D2OZ-11572A★	4.55

FALCON:

Application	Part No.	Price
1968-70	D1AZ-11572C★	10.75

MAVERICK & GRANADA

Application	Part No.	Price
1970 Six—		
Early	D1AZ-11572C★	10.75
Late	DOAZ-11572A★	4.20
1971-73	D4DZ-11572A	5.30
1974-75 Exc	D4DZ-11572A★	5.30
Granada	D2OZ-11572A★	4.55

MUSTANG:

Application	Part No.	Price
1968-69	D1AZ-11572C★	10.75
1970	DOAZ-11572A★	4.20
1971-72	D4DZ-11572A	5.30
1973	D1AZ-11572B★	4.55
1974-75	D2OZ-11572A★	4.55
1974 V8-400	D4OZ-12127C★	41.60

Time — Fuel System & Intake Manifold (Group C) — Time

OPERATION INDEX

C1—CARBURETOR, R & R OR RENEW

Application	Time
1969-75 Six (0.4)	0.6
1969-75 V8 (0.5)	0.7
1974-75 Mustang (0.5)	0.7

C2—CARBURETOR, R & R & OVERHAUL

Application	Time
1966-69 Six (1.0)	1.5
1970-75 Six (1.2)	1.8
1969-75 V8—	
2 Barrel (1.2)	1.7
4 Barrel—	
Exc. Below (1.7)	2.2
Autolite, Motorcraft (1.5)	2.2
Rochester (1.4)	2.2
1974-75 Mustang (1.1)	1.6

C2A—ACCELERATOR PUMP, RENEW

Application	Time
1969-75 Six Cyl.—	
Exc. Below (0.6)	0.8
Autolite, Motorcraft (0.4)	0.5
1969-75 V8—	
2 Barrel (0.3)	0.4
4 Barrel (0.5)	0.7
1974-75 Mustang (0.4)	0.6

—NOTE—
Does Not Include R & R Carburetor.

C2B—NEEDLE & SEAT, RENEW

Application	Time
1969-75 Six Cyl.—	
Autolite-Motorcraft (0.4)	0.5
Carter Y.F. (0.5)	0.7
Carter R.B.S. (0.6)	0.8
1969-75 V8—	
2 Barrel (0.4)	0.5
4 Barrel—	
Autolite-Motorcraft (0.6)	0.8
Carter (0.5)	0.7
Holley—	
One (0.5)	0.7
Both (0.7)	0.9
Rochester (0.7)	0.9
1974-75 Mustang (0.5)	0.7

—NOTE—
Does Not Include R & R Carburetor.

C3—AUTOMATIC CHOKE THERMOSTAT, RENEW

Application	Time
All Models Exc (0.3)	0.6
1974-75 Mustang (0.5)	0.6

C3A—AUTOMATIC CHOKE, OVERHAUL

Application	Time
1969-75—	
Exc. Below (0.4)	0.6
Carter (0.6)	0.9
Mustang II (0.7)	0.9

C5—FUEL PUMP, R & R OR RENEW

Application	Time
1966-69—	
Exc. Below (0.3)	0.5
390, 428 W/AC (0.5)	0.8
1970-71—	
Exc. Below (0.3)	0.5
V8-390, 428 W/AC (0.5)	0.8
V8-429—	
Exc. Below (0.7)	1.0
Mustang (0.6)	0.9
1972-75 Torino (0.5)	0.8
Maverick Six (0.3)	0.5
Maverick V8—	
L/Power Steering (0.4)	0.6
W/Power Steering (0.5)	0.8
Granada Six (0.3)	0.5
Granada V8—	
L/Power Steering (0.4)	0.6
W/Power Steering (0.5)	0.8
Mustang (72-73)—	
Six (0.3)	0.5
V8 (0.4)	0.6
Mustang (74-75) (0.4)	0.6

C6—FUEL TANK, R & R OR RENEW

Application	Time
MUSTANG & MUSTANG II	
1969-75 (0.8)	1.2
FAIRLANE. TORINO:	
1966-71 (0.9)	1.4
1972-75 (0.8)	1.2
FALCON:	
1967-70—	
Exc. Below (0.9)	1.4
Sta. Wagon—	
Before 01/01/70 (0.7)	1.1
After 01/01/70 (0.9)	1.4
MAVERICK:	
1970 (0.9)	1.4
1971-75 (1.1)	1.6
GRANADA	
1975 (1.1)	1.6

C7—FUEL SYSTEM, CLEAN

Includes R & R tank, blow out lines and clean or renew fuel filter.

Application	Time
MUSTANG & MUSTANG II-	
1969-75 (1.6)	2.5
FAIRLANE. TORINO:	
1969-75 (1.6)	2.5

FALCON:
1966-71—
Exc. Below (1.7) ... 2.6
Sta. Wagon—
Before 01/01/70 (1.5) ... 2.3
After 01/01/70 (1.7) ... 2.6
MAVERICK:
1970 (1.7) ... 2.6
1971-75 (1.9) ... 2.9
GRANADA
1975 (1.9) ... 2.9

C8—INTAKE MANIFOLD GASKETS, RENEW

MUSTANG & MUSTANG II
1967-73—
Exc. Below (1.6) ... 2.4
V8-302 Boss (1.7) ... 2.6
V8-351-W (1.9) ... 2.9
V8-351-C-Boss (2.0) ... 3.1
V8-390 (2.8) ... 3.9
V8-428 (2.9) ... 4.0
V8-429 (2.2) ... 3.4
1974-75 Four (1.0) ... 1.5

FAIRLANE, TORINO:
1966-69—
Exc. Below (1.6) ... 2.4
V8-390 (2.6) ... 3.6
V8-428 (2.8) ... 3.9
1970-71—
Exc. Below (1.6) ... 2.4
V8-351-W (2.0) ... 3.1
V8-351-C, 400 (2.5) ... 2.2
V8-429 (2.2) ... 3.4
1972-75—
Exc. Below (1.7) ... 2.6
V8-351-C-M, 400 (1.5) ... 2.2
V8-429,460 (2.3) ... 3.5
MAVERICK:
1971-75 V8 (1.7) ... 2.6
GRANADA
1975 V8 (1.7) ... 2.6

—NOTE—
For Thermactor, Add (0.2) ... 0.2

Parts — Fuel System & Intake Manifold — Parts

PARTS INDEX

1—CARBURETOR ASS'Y:

FAIRLANE & TORINO:
1969 6-250 (L/Air Cond.)—
Synchro-Mesh ... DOPZ-9510T 48.45
Auto. Trans ... DOPZ-9510T 48.45
1969 6-250 (W/Air Cond.)—
Synchro-Mesh ... DOPZ-9510T 48.45
Auto. Trans ... DOPZ-9510T 48.45
1969 V8-302—
Synchro-Mesh ... D2AZ-9510P 68.10
Auto. Trans ... D2AZ-9510P 68.10
1969 V8-351 (2 Bar. Carb.)—
Synchro-Mesh ... D2AZ-9510P 68.10
Auto Trans ... D2AZ-9510P 68.10
1969 V8-351 (4 Bar. Carb.)—
Auto. Trans ... C9OZ-9510D 97.90
Synchro-Mesh ... D2AZ-9510M 97.90
1969 V8-427 ... C9OZ-9510N 113.85
1969 V8-428—
Synchro-Mesh ... C9AZ-9510U 108.85
Auto. Trans ... C9AZ-9510U 108.85
1970 Six—
Synchro-Mesh—
L/Air Cond ... DOZZ-9510AA 51.20
W/Air Cond. ... DOZZ-9510AA 51.20
Auto. Trans.—
L/Air Cond ... DOZZ-9510AA 51.20
W/Air Cond ... DOZZ-9510AA 51.20
1970 V8-302—
Synchro-Mesh ... D2AZ-9510P 68.10
Auto. Trans.—
L/Air Cond ... D2AZ-9510P 68.10
W/Air Cond ... D2AZ-9510P 68.10
1970 V8-351 (2 Bar. Carb.)—
Synchro-Mesh ... D2AZ-9510C 68.10
Auto. Trans.—
L/Air Cond ... D2AZ-9510C 68.10
W/Air Cond ... D2AZ-9510C 68.10
1970 V8-351 (4 Bar. Carb.)—
Synchro-Mesh—
L/Air Cond ... D2AZ-9510M 97.90
W/Air Cond ... D2AZ-9510M 97.90
Auto. Trans.—
L/Air Cond ... D2AZ-9510M 97.90
W/Air Cond ... D2AZ-9510M 97.90
1970 V8-429 (Exc. Cobra Jet)—
Synchro-Mesh ... D2AZ-9510M 97.90
Auto. Trans ... D2AZ-9510M 97.90
1970 V8-429 Cobra Jet—
Synchro-Mesh.
L/Air Cond ... DOOZ-9510B 124.35
W/Air Cond ... DOOZ-9510B 124.35
Auto. Trans.—
L/Air Cond ... DOOZ-9510B 124.35
W/Air Cond ... DOOZ-9510B 124.35
1970 V8-429 Super Cobra Jet—
Synchro-Mesh ... DOOZ-9510N 116.40
Auto. Trans ... DOOZ-9510R 116.40
1971 Six—
Synchro-Mesh—
Exc. Calif ... D1ZZ-9510B 49.10
Calif ... D1ZZ-9510B 49.10
Auto. Trans. (L/Air Cond.)—
Exc. Calif ... D1ZZ-9510B 49.10
Calif ... D1ZZ-9510B 49.10
Auto. Trans. (W/Air Cond.)—
Exc. Calif ... D1ZZ-9510B 49.10
Calif ... D1ZZ-9510B— 49.10
1971 V8-302 (2 Bar. Carb.) ... D2AZ-9510P 68.10
1971 V8-302 (4 Bar.) ... DOPZ-9510U
1971 V8-351 (2 Bar. Carb.)—
Synchro-Mesh ... D2AZ-9510C 68.10
Auto. Trans ... D2AZ-9510C 68.10
1971 V8-351 (4 Bar. Carb.)—
Holley ... DOPZ-9510U
Auto-Lite ... D2AZ-9510M 97.90
1971 V8-429—
Exc. Cobra Jet ... D2AZ-9510M 97.90
1972 6-250 ... D2OZ-9510A 49.10
1972 V8-302 ... D2AZ-9510P 68.10
1972 V8-351—
2 Bar. Carb. ... D2AZ-9510C 68.10
4 Bar. Carb.—
1972 V8-400 ... D2AZ-9510C 68.10
1973 6-250—
Std. Tran. ... D3OZ-9510B 49.05
Auto. Tran. ... D3OZ-9510C 49.05
1973 V8-302 ... D3OZ-9510D 68.10
1973 V8-351—
Windsor Eng. ... D3AZ-9510E 68.10
Cleveland Eng. ... D3AZ-9510E 68.10
Cobra Jet ... D3ZZ-9510E 137.15
1973 V8-400 ... D3AZ-9510E 68.10
1973 V8-429 ... D3AZ-9510G 97.90
1974 Six ... D4DZ-9510TA 50.80
1974 V8-302 ... D4OZ-9510H 68.10
1974 V8-351, Exc. ... D4AZ-9510F 68.10
Windsor Eng. ... D4AZ-9510H 68.10
1974 V8-400 ... D4AZ-9510H 68.10
1974 V8-460, Exc. ... D4OZ-9510G 97.90
W/T.E. ... D4AZ-9510B 101.25
1975 V8-351 Exc ... D5OZ-9510A 68.10
351-M Exc ... D5OZ-9510B 68.10
Calif ... D5OZ-9510C 68.10
1975 V8-400 Exc ... D5AZ-9510A 68.10
Calif ... D5MZ-9510F 68.10
Colorado ... D5MY-9510A 68.10
1975 V8-460 Exc ... D5VY-9510A 97.90
Calif ... D5VY-9510B 97.90

FALCON:
1969 6-170—
Synchro-Mesh ... C8DZ-9510A 52.10
Auto. Trans ... C8DZ-9510A 52.10
1969 6-200—
Synchro-Mesh ... DOPZ-9510G 48.45
Auto. Trans ... DOPZ-9510G 48.45
1969 V8-302—
Synchro-Mesh ... D2AZ-9510P 68.10
Auto. Trans ... D2AZ-9510P 68.10
1970 6-200—
Synchro-Mesh ... D1DZ-9510A 53.50
Auto. Trans ... D1DZ-9510A 53.50
1970 V8-302 ... D2AZ-9510P 68.10

MAVERICK & GRANADA
1970 6-170—
L/Air Cond.—
Synchro-Mesh ... D1DZ-9510A 53.50
Auto. Trans ... D1DZ-9510A 53.50
W/Air Cond.—
Synchro-Mesh ... D1DZ-9510A 53.50
Auto. Trans ... D1DZ-9510A 53.50
1970 6-200—
L/Air Cond.—
Synchro-Mesh ... D1DZ-9510A 53.50
Auto. Trans ... D1DZ-9510A 53.50
W/Air Cond.—
Synchro-Mesh ... D1DZ-9510A 53.50
Auto. Trans ... D1DZ-9510A 53.50
1971 6-200—
Synchro-Mesh—
L/Air Cond ... D1DZ-9510B 53.50
W/Air Cond ... D1DZ-9510A— 53.50
Auto. Trans. (Exc. Calif)—
L/Air Cond ... D1DZ-9510B 53.50
W/Air Cond ... D1DZ-9510A 53.50
Auto. Trans. (Calif)—
L/Air Cond ... D1DZ-9510B 53.50
W/Air Cond ... D1DZ-9510A 53.50
1971 6-250—
Synchro-Mesh—
Exc. Calif ... D1ZZ-9510B 49.10
Calif ... D1ZZ-9510B 49.10
Auto. Trans. (L/Air Cond.)—
Exc. Calif ... D1ZZ-9510B 49.10
Calif ... D1ZZ-9510B 49.10
Auto. Trans. (W/Air Cond.)—
Exc. Calif ... D1ZZ-9510B 49.10
Calif ... D1ZZ-9510B 49.10
1971 V8-302 ... D2AZ-9510P 68.10
1972 6-170 ... D2DZ-9510F 53.50
1972 6-200—
Synchro Mesh—
L/Air Cond ... D2DZ-9510F 53.50
W/Air Cond ... D2DZ-9510G 53.50
Auto Trans—
L/Air Cond ... D2DZ-9510F 53.50
W/Air Cond ... D2DZ-9510G 53.50
1972 6-250 ... D2OZ-9510A 49.10
1972 V8-302 ... D2AZ-9510P 68.10
1973 6-200—
Std. Tran.—
L/Air Cond. ... D3DZ-9510F 53 50
W/Air Cond. ... D3DZ-9510G
Auto. Tran.—
L/Air Cond. ... D3DZ-6510F 53.50
W/Air Cond. ... D3DZ-9510G
1973 6-250—
Std. Tran. ... D3OZ-9510B 49.05
Auto. Tran. ... D3OZ-9510C 49.05
1973 V8-302 ... D3OZ-9510D 68.10
1974 6-200—
Std. Trans., Exc. ... D4DZ-9510AB 58.90
W/Air Cond. ... D4DZ-9510HA 61.15
Auto. Trans., Exc ... D4DZ-9510J 63.65
W/Air Cond., Exc. ... D4DZ-9510FA
L/T.E. ... D4DZ-9510K 50.95
W/2.79, 3.00 Axle ... D4DZ-9510EA 50.95
1974 6-250—
Auto. Trans., Exc. ... D4DZ-9510E 58.90
W/T.E. ... D4DZ-9510AA 58.90
Std. Trans, Exc. ... D4DZ-9510S 50.80
W/T.E. ... D4DZ-9510BA 44.15
1974, V8-302, Exc. ... D4OZ-9510H 68.10
W/T.E. ... D4DZ-9510C 68.10
1975 6-200 Exc ... D5DZ-9510N 63.65
Auto Trans ... D5DZ-9510R 50.95
1975 6-250—
Std Trans Exc ... D5DZ-9510E 58.90
Calif ... D5DZ-9510F 58.90
W/Catalyst ... D5DZ-9510Z 58.90
Auto Trans Exc ... D5DZ-9510G 58.90
Calif ... D5DZ-9510D 58.90
W/Catalyst ... D5DZ-9510Y 58.90
1975 V8-302—
Auto Trans Exc ... D5ZZ-9510J 68.10
Granada Exc ... D5DZ-9510A 68.10
Calif ... D5DZ-9510J 68.10
Std Trans ... D5DZ-9510B 68.10
1975 V8-351 Exc ... D5OZ-9510A 68.10
351-M Exc ... D5DZ-9510U 68.10
Calif ... D5OZ-9510E 68.10

MUSTANG:
1969 6-200—
Synchro-Mesh ... DOPZ-9510G 48.45
Auto. Trans ... DOPZ-9510G 48.45
1969 6-250 (L/Air Cond.)—
Synchro-Mesh ... DOPZ-9510T 48.45
Auto. Trans ... DOPZ-9510T— 48.45

1969 6-250 (W/Air Cond.)—		
Synchro-Mesh	DOPZ-9510T	48.45
Auto. Trans	DOPZ-9510T	48.45
1969 V8-302—		
Synchro-Mesh—		
Exc. Below	D2AZ-9510P	68.10
Boss 302	DOZZ-9510Z	135.00
Auto. Trans.—		
Exc. Below	D2AZ-9510P	68.10
C6 Trans	D2AZ-9510P	68.10
1969 V8-351 (2 Bar. Carb)—		
Synchro-Mesh	D2AZ-9510P	68.10
Auto. Trans	D2AZ-9510P	68.10
1969 V8-351 (4 Bar. Carb.)—		
Synchro-Mesh	D2AZ-9510M	97.90
Auto. Trans	D2AZ-9510M	97.90
1969 V8-390 (Ford Type)—		
Synchro-Mesh	D2AZ-9510M	97.90
Auto. Trans	D2AZ-9510M	97.90
1969 V8-427	C9OZ-9510N	113.85
1969 V8-428—		
Synchro-Mesh	C9AZ-9510U	108.85
Auto. Trans	C9AZ-9510U	108.85
1969 V8-429	C9AZ-9510S	119.35
1970 6-200—		
Synchro-Mesh—		
L/Air Cond	D1DZ-9510A	53.50
W/Air Cond	D1DZ-9510A	53.50
Auto. Trans.—		
L/Air Cond	D1DZ-9510A	53.50
W/Air Cond	D1DZ-9510A	53.50
1970 6-250—		
Synchro-Mesh—		
L/Air Cond	DOZZ-9510AA	51.20
W/Air Cond	DOZZ-9510AA	51.20
Auto. Trans.—		
L/Air Cond	DOZZ-9510AA	51.20
W/Air Cond	DOZZ-9510AA	51.20
1970 V8-302 (2 Bar. Carb.)—		
Synchro-Mesh	D2AZ-9510P	68.10
Auto. Trans.—		
L/Air Cond	D2AZ-9510P	68.10
W/Air Cond	D2AZ-9510P	68.10
1970 V8-302 (4 Bar. Carb.)	DOZZ-9510Z	135.00
1970 V8-351 (2 Bar. Carb.)—		
Synchro-Mesh	D2AZ-9510P	68.10
Auto. Trans.—		
L/Air Cond	D2AZ-9510P	68.10
W/Air Cond	D2AZ-9510P	68.10
1970 V8-351 (4 Bar. Carb.)—		
Synchro-Mesh—		
L/Air Cond	D2AZ-9510M	97.90
W/Air Cond	D2AZ-9510M	97.90
Auto. Trans.—		
L/Air Cond	D2AZ-9510M	97.90
W/Air Cond	D2AZ-9510M	97.90
1970 V8-428 CJ	DOZZ-9510H	135.00
1971 Six—		
Synchro-Mesh—		
Exc. Calif	D1ZZ-9510B	49.10
Calif	D1ZZ-9510B	49.10
Auto. Trans. (L/Air Cond.)—		
Exc. Calif	D1ZZ-9510B	49.10
Calif	D1ZZ-9510B	49.10
Auto. Trans. (W/Air Cond.)—		
Exc. Calif	D1ZZ-9510B	49.10
Calif	D1ZZ-9510B	49.10
1971 V8-302 (2 Bar. Carb.)	D2AZ-9510P	68.10
1971 V8-302 (4 Bar. Carb.)—		
Exc. Below	DOPZ-9510U	
"Boss" Eng	DOZZ-9510Z	135.00
1971 V8-351 (2 Bar. Carb.)	D2AZ-9510C	68.10
1971 V8-351 (4 Bar. Carb.)—		
Holley	DOPZ-9510U	
Auto-Lite—		
1972 Six	D2OZ-9510A	49.10
1972 V8-302—		
Synchro-Mesh	D2AZ-9510P	68.10
Auto Trans	D2AZ-9510P	68.10
1972 V8-351—		
2 Bar. Carb	D2AZ-9510C	68.10
4 Bar. Carb	D3ZZ-9510E	137.15
1973 6-250—		
Std. Tran.	D3OZ-9510B	49.05
Auto. Tran.	D3OZ-9510C	49.05
1973 V8-302	D3OZ-9510D	68.10
1973 V8-351—		
Windsor Eng.	D3AZ-9510E	68.10
Cleveland Eng.	D3AZ-9510E	68.10
Cobra Jet Or H.O.	D3ZZ-9510E	137.15
1974, Four, Exc.	D4FZ-9510C	71.00
W/Std. Trans.	D4FZ-9510D	81.70
1974 Six—		
Auto. Trans, Exc.	D4ZZ-9510B	80.35
W/T.E.	D4ZZ-9510B	80.35
Std. Trans., Exc.	D4ZZ-9510D	80.35
W/T.E.	D4ZZ-9510C	80.35
1975 Four—		
Auto Trans Exc	D5ZZ-9510F	71.00
Calif	D5ZZ-9510E	71.00
Std Trans Exc	D5ZZ-9510H	71.00
Calif	D5ZZ-9510G	71.00
1975 6-171 Exc	D5ZZ-9510C	
Auto Trans	D5ZZ-9510D	
1975 V8-302 Exc	D5ZZ-9510J	68.10
Calif	D5DZ-9510J	68.10

2—CARBURETOR TUNE UP KIT:

FAIRLANE & TORINO:

1968-69 V8-427	C8ZZ-9A586D	14.00
1969 Six	C8OZ-9A586D	6.75
1969 V8-302—		
Synchro-Mesh	D2AZ-9A586D	8.60
Auto. Trans	D2AZ-9A586A	
1969 V8-351—		
2 Bar. Carb	D2AZ-9A586A	
4 Bar. Carb	D2AZ-9A586D	8.60
1969 V8-390	D2AZ-9A586D	8.60
1969 V8-428	C8OZ-9A586C	
1970 Six	DOZZ-9A586B	8.75
1970 V8-302	D2AZ-9A586D	8.60
1970 V8-351—		
2 Bar. Carb	D2AZ-9A586D	8.60
4 Bar. Carb	D2AZ-9A586D	8.60
1970 V8-429—		
Exc. Below	D2AZ-9A586D	8.60
Cobra Jet	DOOZ-9A586B	9.95
Super CJ	C8OZ-9A586C	
1973 Six	DOZZ-9A586B	8.75
1973 V8-302, 400	D2AZ-9A586B	7.30
1973 V8-351 Exc	D2AZ-9A586B	7.30
4 Bar Carb	D3OZ-9A586A	8.20
1973 V8-429	D3AZ-9A586A	8.60
1974 Six	DOZZ-9A586B	8.75
1974 V8-351, 400	D4AZ-9A586A	7.90
1974 V8-460, Exc.	D3AZ-9A586A	8.60
W/T.E.	D4AZ-9A586B	9.05

FALCON:

1968-69 6-170	C7DZ-9A586C	6.20
1969 6-200	C8OZ-9A586D	6.75
1969 V8-302	D2AZ-9A586A	
1970 Six	DODZ-9A586B	6.90
1970 V8-302	D2AZ-9A586D	8.60

MAVERICK:

1970 6-170	DODZ-9A586B	6.90
1970 6-200—		
L/Air Cond.—		
Synchro-Mesh	DODZ-9A586B	6.90
Auto. Trans	D2AZ-9A586D	8.60
W/Air Cond	DODZ-9A586B	6.90
1973 Six	DODZ-9A586B	6.90
1973 V8-302	DOZZ-9A586B	8.75
1974 Six, Exc.	DODZ-9A586B	6.90
6-250	DOZZ-9A586B	8.75

MUSTANG:

1969 6-200	C8OZ-9A586D	6.75
1969 6-250	C8OZ-9A586D	6.75
1969 V8-302—		
Synchro-Mesh—		
Exc. Below	D2AZ-9A586D	8.60
Boss 302	C8OZ-9A586C	
Auto. Trans	D2AZ-9A586D	8.60
1969 V8-351—		
2 Bar. Carb	D2AZ-9A586A	
4 Bar. Carb	D2AZ-9A586D	8.60
1969 V8-390—		
Synchro-Mesh	D2AZ-9A586D	8.60
Auto. Trans	D2AZ-9A586A	
1969 V8-427	D2AZ-9A586A	
1969 V8-428	C8OZ-9A586C	
1969 V8-429	D2AZ-9A586D	8.60
1970 6-200—		
Exc. Below	DODZ-9A586B	6.90
Auto. Trans. W/A.C	D2AZ-9A586D	8.60
1970 6-250	DOZZ-9A586B	8.75
1970 V8-302—		
2 Bar. Carb	D2AZ-9A586D	8.60
4 Bar. Carb	C8OZ-9A586C	
1970 V8-351—		
2 Bar. Carb	D2AZ-9A586D	8.60
4 Bar. Carb	D2AZ-9A586D	8.60
1970 V8-428	C8OZ-9A586C	
1973 V8-302, 351—		
Exc Below	D2AZ-9A586B	7.30
4 Bar 351	D3OZ-9A586A	8.20

3—CARBURETOR GASKET SET:

FAIRLANE & TORINO:

1968-69 V8-302—		
Std. Trans	D2AZ-9502A	2.75
Auto. Trans	D2AZ-9502A	2.75
1968-69 V8-427	C8ZZ-9502A	8.45
1969 Six	C8AZ-9502A	2.25
1969 V8-302	D2AZ-9502A	2.75
1969 V8-351	D3AZ-9502A	2.65
1969 V8-390	D3AZ-9502A	2.65
1969 V8-428	C8ZZ-9502D	7.15
1970 Six	DOZZ-9502A	2.00
1970 V8-302	D2AZ-9502A	2.75
1970 V8-351—		
2 Bar. Carb	DOOZ-9502A	8.45
4 Bar. Carb	D3AZ-9502A	2.65
1970 V8-429—		
Exc. Below	D3AZ-9502A	2.65
Cobra Jet	DOOZ-9502A	8.45
Super CJ	C8ZZ-9502D	7.15
1973 Six	DOZZ-9502A	2.00
V8-302, 400	D2AZ-9502A	2.75
V8-351 Exc	D2AZ-9502A	2.75
4 Bar	D3OZ-9502A	2.55
V8-429	D3OZ-9502A	2.55
1974 Six	DOZZ-9502A	2.00
1974 V8-351, 400	D4AZ-9502A	2.75
1974 V8-460, Exc.	D4AZ-9502A	2.75
W/T.E.	D4AZ-9502B	9.35

FALCON:

1968-69 V8-302	D3AZ-9502A	2.65
1969 6-170	DODZ-9502A	2.00
1969 6-200—		
Synchro-Mesh	C8AZ-9502A	2.25
Auto. Trans	C8AZ-9502A	2.25
1970 Six—		
Synchro-Mesh	DODZ-9502A	2.00
Auto. Trans	D2AZ-9502A	2.75
1970 V8-302	D2AZ-9502A	2.75

MAVERICK:

1970 6-170	DODZ-9502A	2.00
1970 6-200—		
L/Air Cond.—		
Synchro-Mesh	DODZ-9502A	2.00
Auto. Trans	D2AZ-9502A	2.75
W/Air Cond	DODZ-9502A	2.00
1973, 6-200	DODZ-9502A	2.00
6-250	DOZZ-9502A	2.00
V8-302	D2AZ-9502A	2.75
1974 Six, Exc.	DODZ-9502A	2.00
6-250	DOZZ-9502A	2.00

MUSTANG:

1969 6-200—		
Synchro-Mesh	C8AZ-9502A	2.25
Auto. Trans	C8AZ-9502A	2.25
1969 6-250	C8AZ-9502A	2.25
1969 V8-302—		
Synchro-Mesh—		
Exc. Below	D2AZ-9502A	2.75
Boss 302	C8ZZ-9502D	7.15
Auto. Trans	D2AZ-9502A	2.75
1969 V8-351—		
2 Bar. Carb	D2AZ-9502A	2.75
4 Bar. Carb	D3AZ-9502A	2.65
1969 V8-390	D3AZ-9502A	2.65
1969 V8-427	D2AZ-9502A	2.75
1969 V8-428	C8ZZ-9502D	7.15
1969 V8-429	D3AZ-9502A	2.65
1970 6-200—		
Synchro-Mesh	DODZ-9502A	2.00
Auto. Trans.—		
L/Air Cond	D2AZ-9502A	2.75
W/Air Cond	DODZ-9502A	2.00
1970 6-250	DOZZ-9502A	2.00
1970 V8-302—		
2 Bar. Carb	D2AZ-9502A	2.75
4 Bar. Carb	C8ZZ-9502D	7.15
1970 V8-351—		
2 Bar. Carb	D2AZ-9502A	2.75
4 Bar. Carb	D3AZ-9502A	2.65
1970 V8-428	C8ZZ-9502D	7.15
1973 V8-302	D2AZ-9502A	2.75
1973 V8-351 Exc	D2AZ-9502A	2.75
4 Bar	D3OZ-9502A	2.55

5—FUEL PUMP (NEW):

FAIRLANE & TORINO:

1968-73 Six	D3TZ-9350A	17.95
1969 V8-302, 351	D3OZ-9350B	17.95
1969 V8-390	D4TZ-9350A	17.55
1969 V8-427, 428	C7AZ-9350A	22.50
1970-73 V8-302	D3OZ-9350B	17.95
1970-72 V8-351	DOAZ-9350A	16.15
1970 V8-429—		
Exc. Below	DOVY-9350A	16.15
Cobra Jet	DOOZ-9350A	20.95
Super Cobra Jet	C9AZ-9350A	29.90
1971 V8-429	DOOZ-9350A	20.95
1972-73 V8-429	DOVY-9350A	16.15
1973 V8-351,400—		
Exc. Below	DOAZ-9350A	16.15
V8-351 Cleveland	DOAZ-9350C	16.15
1974 Six	D3DZ-9350A	17.95
V8-302	D3OZ-9350B	17.95
V8-351 Exc	DOAZ-9350C	16.15
Windsor Eng	D3OZ-9350C	
V8-400	DOAZ-9350A	16.15
V8-429 & 460 Exc	D3VY-9350B	16.60
L/Vapor Tubes	DOVY-9350A	16.15
1975—		
302	D5OZ-9350B	16.15
351, 400 Exc	D5OZ-9350B	16.15
Windsor Eng	DOAZ-9350A	16.15
460	D4VY-9350A	

FALCON:

1968-70 Six	D3TZ-9350A	17.95
1968-69 V8	D3OZ-9350B	17.95
1970 V8-302	D3OZ-9350B	17.95

1970 V8-351 ... DOAZ-9350A 16.15
1970 V8-429—
Exc. Below ... DOVY-9350A 16.15
Cobra Jet ... DOOZ-9350A 20.95
Super Cobra Jet ... C9AZ-9350A 29.90

MAVERICK & GRANADA
1970-73 Six ... D3TZ-9350A 17.95
1971-73 V8 ... D3OZ-9350B 17.95
1974 Six ... D3DZ-9350A 17.95
V8 ... D3OZ-9350B 17.95
1975 Six ... D5DZ-9350D 17.95
V8 ... D5OZ-9350B 16.15

MUSTANG:
1968-72 Six ... C5AZ-9350B 16.80
1969 V8-302—
Exc. Below ... D3OZ-9350B 17.95
Boss 302 ... C9ZZ-9350A 17.20
1969 V8-351 ... D3OZ-9350B 17.95
1969 V8-390 ... D4TZ-9350A 17.55
1969 V8-427, 428 ... C7AZ-9350A 22.50
1969 V8-429 ... C9AZ-9350A 29.90
1970 V8-302 ... C9ZZ-9350A 17.20
1970 V8-351—
2 Bar Carb ... DOAZ-9350C 16.15
4 Bar. Carb ... DOAZ-9350A 16.15
1970 V8-428 ... C7AZ-9350A 22.50
1971-72 V8-302—
2 Bar. Carb ... D3OZ-9350B 17.95
4 Bar. Carb ... DOOZ-9350A 20.95
1971-72 V8-351 ... DOAZ-9350A 16.15
1971 V8-429 ... DOOZ-9350A 20.95
1973 6-250 ... D3TZ-9350A 17.95
1973 V8-302 ... D3OZ-9350B 17.95
1973 V8-351 ... DOAZ-9350A 16.15
1974-75 Four ... D4FZ-9350A 17.55
Six (74) ... D4ZZ-9350A 17.55
V8-302 ... D5OZ-9350B 16.15

6—FUEL TANK:

FAIRLANE & TORINO:
1969—
Exc. Sta. Wag ... C6OZ-9002K 48.40
Sta. Wagon ... DOOZ-9002F 39.90
1970—
Exc. Sta. Wag. & Ranchero—
L/Fuel Emission ... DOOZ-9002D 48.40
W/Fuel Emission ... DOOZ-9002E 50.85
Sta. Wagon.—
L/Fuel Emission ... DOOZ-9002F 39.90
W/Fuel Emission ... DOOZ-9002G 48.35
Ranchero—
L/Fuel Emission ... DOOZ-9002A 31.80
W/Fuel Emission ... DOOZ-9002B 65.05
1971—
Exc. Below ... D1OZ-9002B 60.35
Sta. Wagon ... D1OZ-9002A 42.60
Ranchero ... D1OZ-9002C 34.00
1972—
Exc. Below ... D2OZ-9002D 60.35
Sta. Wagon ... D2OZ-9002C 46.90
Ranchero ... D2OZ-9002B 40.80
1973—
Exc. Below ... D2OZ-9002D 60.35
Sta. Wagon ... D2OZ-9002C 46.90
Ranchero ... D2OZ-9002B 40.80
1974 Exc ... D4OZ-9002H 60.35
Sta Wagon ... D4OZ-9002G 48.05
Ranchero ... D4OZ-9002J 48.05
1975 Exc ... D5OZ-9002D 60.35
Sta Wag ... D5OZ-9002A 48.05
Ranchero ... D5OZ-9002E 48.05

FALCON:
1968-69—
Exc. Sta. Wag ... C6DZ-9002B 30.95
Sta. Wagon ... DOOZ-9002C 51.35
1970—
Exc. Sta. Wagon ... C6DZ-9002B 30.95
Sta. Wagon ... DOOZ-9002C 51.35

MAVERICK & GRANADA
1970 Six—
Exc. Below ... DODZ-9002A 28.95
Calif. Prod.—
Early ... DODZ-9002D 87.35
Late ... DODZ-9002D 87.35
1971-72 ... D3DZ-9002A 44.55
1973-74 ... D3DZ-9002A 44.55
1975 Exc ... D5DZ-9002B 47.50
Granada ... D5DZ-9002A 58.70

MUSTANG:
1969 ... C9ZZ-9002A 49.15
1970—
L/Fuel Emission ... DOZZ-9002A 49.15
W/Fuel Emission ... DOZZ-9002B 49.15
1971-73 ... D1ZZ-9002A 58.70
1974 ... D4ZZ-9002A 28.45
1975 ... D5ZZ-9002B

7—INTAKE MANIFOLD GASKET SET:

FAIRLANE & TORINO:
1968-70 V8-289, 302 ... D1AZ-9433B 2.95
1968-69 V8-427, 428 ... C3AZ-9433G 3.45
1969 V8-351 ... D1AZ-9433C 3.55
1969 V8-390 ... C3AZ-9433G 3.45
1970-71 V8-351—
2 Bar. Carb ... DOAZ-9433B 7.50
4 Bar. Carb ... DOAZ-9433A 7.50
1970 V8-429 ... C9AZ-9433A 10.25
1971 V8-302 ... D1AZ-9433B 2.95
1971 V8-429 ... DOOZ-9433A 10.35
1972-75 V8-302 ... D1AZ-9433B 2.95
1972-73 V8-351—
2 Bar. Carb. ... DOAZ-9433B 7.50
4 Bar. Carb. ... DOAZ-9433A 7.50
1973 V8-400 ... D1AZ-9433A 9.15
1972-74 V8-429 ... C9AZ-9433A 10.25
1974-75 V8-351 Exc ... D1AZ-9433C 3.55
Cleve. Eng, Exc. ... DOAZ-9433B 7.50
W/T.E. ... DOAZ-9433A 7.50
1974 V8-400 ... D4AZ-9433B 9.15
1974 V8-460 ... C9AZ-9433A 10.25
1975 351-M, 400 ... D5AZ-9433A 9.15
1975 460 ... D5AZ-9433C 10.75

FALCON:
1968-70 V8 ... D1AZ-9433B 2.95

MAVERICK & GRANADA
1971-73 V8-302 ... D1AZ-9433B 2.95
1974-75 V8-302 ... D4DZ-9433A 3.45

MUSTANG:
1968-69 V8-390 ... C3AZ-9433G 3.45
1969-70 V8-302—
Exc. Below ... D1AZ-9433B 2.95
Boss 302 ... D1ZZ-9433A 3.25
1969 V8-351 ... D1AZ-9433C 3.55
1969 V8-390 ... C3AZ-9433G 3.45
1969 V8-427, 428 ... C3AZ-9433G 3.45
1969 V8-429 ... C9ZZ-9433B 10.25
1970-71 V8-351—
2 Bar. Carb—
Exc. Below ... D1AZ-9433C 3.55
Cleveland Eng ... DOAZ-9433B 7.50
4 Bar. Carb ... DOAZ-9433A 7.50
1971 V8-302—
Exc. Below ... D1AZ-9433B 2.95
"Boss Eng" ... D1ZZ-9433A 3.25
1971 V8-429 ... DOOZ-9433A 10.35
1972-73 V8-302 ... D1AZ-9433B 2.95
1972-73 V8-351—
2 Bar. Carb. ... DOAZ-9433B 7.50
4 Bar. Carb. ... DOAZ-9433A 7.50

FORD PINTO

Time — Emission Controls (Group AB) — Time

OPERATION INDEX

AB1—CRANKCASE VENT VALVE (PCV), CLEAN OR RENEW

1971-75—
Clean (0.4) ... 0.4
Renew (0.2) ... 0.2

AB2—EMISSION CONTROL CHECK

Use with IMCO Systems only. Includes adjust carburetor & ignition timing and check PCV Valve.
All Models (0.4) ... 0.7

Parts — Emission Controls — Parts

PARTS INDEX

1—CRANKCASE VENTILATOR VALVE:

1971 ... D1FZ-6A666A 1.65
1972 Exc ... D1FZ-6A666A 1.65
122 Eng ... D2FZ-6A666A 1.65
1973-74, 122 Eng ... D2FZ-6A666A 1.65
1974, 140 Eng ... D4FZ-6A666A 1.65
1975 ... D5FZ-6A666A 1.65

2—EXHAUST EMISSION PUMP:

1971-72 ... D1FZ-9A486A 72.50
1974 Exc ... D4FZ-9A486B 83.90
140 Eng ... D4TZ-9A486D 85.30
1975 ... D5TZ-9A486C 83.90

3—FUEL VAPOR CANISTER ASS'Y:

1971-73 ... D1AZ-9D653A 18.35
1974-75 Exc ... D4FZ-9D653B 18.35
140 Eng ... D4FZ-9D653A 18.35
171 Eng ... D5ZZ-9D653A 18.35

4—DISTRIBUTOR VACUUM CONTROL VALVE:

1971 122 C.I.D.—
Early ... C8AZ-12A091A 11.15
Late ... D1FZ-12A091A 10.15
1972 122 C.I.D.—
Exc. Calif ... D1FZ-12A091A 10.15
Calif ... D1FZ-12A091B
1973 Except ... D2OZ-12A091B 4.05
122 C.I.D. W/AC—
In Thermo Hsg ... D1FZ-12A091A 10.15
1974 (Exc Below) ... D3FZ-12A091A 4.05
W/140 Eng, Exc ... D1FZ-12A091A 10.15
W/T. E. ... D3FZ-12A091B 4.05
Calif ... D3AZ-12A091B 4.05
1975 Exc ... D5FZ-12A091A 11.15
6-171 ... D3FZ-12A091B 4.05

Time — Tune-Up & Ignition (Group B) — Time

OPERATION INDEX

B1—TUNE-UP, MINOR

Includes renew points, plugs and condenser, set spark timing and adjust carburetor idle.

1971-74—
- L/Air Cond (1.0) 1.5
- W/Air Cond (1.2) 1.8

1975 Four—
- L/Air Cond (0.8) 1.2
- W/Air Cond (1.0) 1.4

1975 V6 (1.3) 1.8

B2—TUNE-UP, MAJOR

Includes check compression, clean and adjust or renew spark plugs, R & R distributor, renew points and condenser and adjust ignition timing, carburetor and fan belts. Clean battery terminals and service air cleaner. Check coil and replace or clean fuel line filter.

1971-74—
- L/Air Cond (2.2) 2.6
- W/Air Cond (2.4) 2.9

1975 Four—
- L/Air Cond (1.7) 2.1
- W/Air Cond (1.9) 2.5

1975 V6 (2.1) 2.7

B3—TUNE-UP, MAJOR & OVERHAUL CARBURETOR

—NOTE—

For Air Cond, Add (0.2) *0.3*

1971-74—
- 1600 Eng. (3.5) 4.5
- 2000 & 2300 Eng. (3.3) 4.3

1975 Four (2.8) 3.8
1975 V6 (3.2) 4.2

B4—POINTS & CONDENSER, RENEW

Does not include R & R distributor.

1971-74 (0.4) 0.6

B5—SPARK PLUGS, CLEAN & ADJUST OR RENEW

1971-75 Four (0.3) 0.4
1975 V6 (0.5) 0.6

B6—COMPRESSION TEST

1971-75 Four (0.3) 0.4
1975 V6 (0.5) 0.6

B7—IGNITION TIMING, SET

1971-75 (0.3) 0.3

B8—DISTRIBUTOR, R & R OR RENEW

1971-75 (0.4) 0.5

B9—DISTRIBUTOR, OVERHAUL (UNIT OFF)

1971-75 (0.8) 1.0

B9A—DISTRIBUTOR, ADJUST ON STOBOSCOPE (UNIT OFF)

1971-75 (0.3) 0.4

B10—DISTRIBUTOR CAP, RENEW

1971-75 (0.3) 0.4

B11—IGNITION CABLE SET, RENEW

Time allowance covers installation of factory supplied sets only.

1971-75 Four (0.4) 0.4
1975 V6 (0.5) 0.5

B12—VACUUM CONTROL UNIT, RENEW

Includes R & R distributor.

1971-75—
- L/Air Cond (0.7) 0.9
- W/Air Cond (0.9) 1.2

B13—IGNITION COIL, RENEW

1971-75 (0.4) 0.6

B14—IGNITION SWITCH, RENEW

1971-75 (0.4) 0.6

Parts — Tune-Up & Ignition — Parts

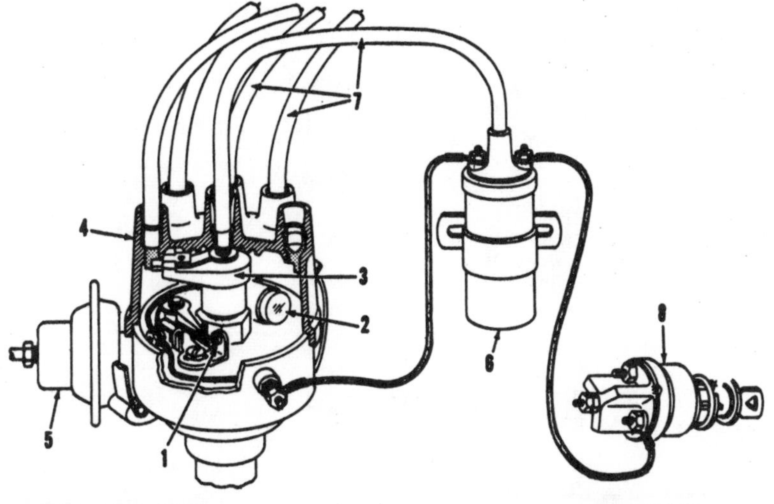

FIG.1-TUNE-UP & IGNITION

DISTRIBUTOR ASS'Y:

Application	Part No.	Price
1971 98 C.I.D.	D1FZ-12127B	28.35
1971 122 C.I.D.—		
Exc. Below	D1FZ-12127A	32.30
Calif (Auto Tran)	D1FZ-12127C	32.30
1972 98 C.I.D.—		
Exc. Calif	D2FZ-12127A	28.35
Calif	D2FZ-12127B	32.30
1972 122 C.I.D.—		
Auto Trans—		
Exc. Below	D3FZ-12127B	32.30
Calif	D2FZ-12127E	32.30
1973 98 C.I.D.	D2FZ-12127G	32.30
1973 122 C.I.D.—		
Manual Trans	D3FZ-12127A	32.30
Auto Trans Exc	D3FZ-12127B	32.30
Calif	D2FZ-12127E	32.30
1974—		
122 Eng Exc	D4FZ-12127B	45.35
Std Trans	D4FZ-12127A	45.35
140 Eng Exc	D4ZZ-12127A	32.30
Runabout	D4ZZ-12127K	32.30
L/Calif	D4ZZ-12127B	32.30
Std Trans	D4ZZ-12127D	32.30
1975, 4-140 Exc	D5FZ-12127C	41.60
Calif	D5ZZ-12127A	41.60
1975, 6-171 Exc	D5ZZ-12127AA	
Auto Trans	D5ZZ-12127BA	

1—IGNITION POINT SET:

Application	Part No.	Price
1971, 98	C5AZ-12171A	4.40
1971-72, 122	D1FZ-12171A	4.40
1972, 98	D1RY-12171B	4.40
1973-74, 122	D1FZ-12171A	4.40
1974, 140	D4ZZ-12171A	4.40

2—CONDENSER:

Application	Part No.	Price
1971-73 98 C.I.D.	DORY-12300A	1.45
1971-73 122 C.I.D.	D1FZ-12300A	2.55
1974, 122	D4FZ-12300A	1.50
140	D4ZZ-12300A	1.50

3—ROTOR:

Application	Part No.	Price
1971-73 98 C.I.D.	DORY-12200B	1.15
1971-74 122 C.I.D.	D1FZ-12200A	1.30
1974, 140	D4ZZ-12200A	1.10
1975, Exc	D5FZ-12200A	1.50
6-171	D5FZ-12200B	1.50

4—DISTRIBUTOR CAP:

Application	Part No.	Price
1971-73 98 C.I.D.	DORY-12106A	3.85
1971-74 122 C.I.D.	D1FZ-12106A	3.85
1974, 140 Eng	D4ZZ-12106A	4.15
1975 Exc	D5FZ-12106A	8.15
6-171	D5DZ-12106A	9.75

5—VACUUM CONTROL UNIT:

Application	Part No.	Price
1971-72 98 C.I.D.	DORY-12370B	6.30
1971-72 122 C.I.D.	D1FZ-12370B	6.95
1973 98 C.I.D.	D2FZ-12370C	6.30
1973 122 C.I.D.—		
Manual Trans	D2FZ-12370B	6.95
Auto Trans Exc	D2FZ-12370A	6.95
Calif	D2FZ-12370B	6.95
1974, 122 Exc	D4FZ-12370A	11.10
Std Trans	D3FZ-12370B	6.95
1974, 140, Exc	D4ZZ-12370C	11.10
Runabout	D4ZZ-12370B	11.10

6— IGNITION COIL:

Application	Part No.	Price
1971-74	B6A-12029B	13.50
1975	D5AZ-12029A	14.85

IGNITION COIL RESISTOR:

Application	Part No.	Price
1971-75	COLF-12250A	2.70

7—IGNITION CABLE SET:

Application	Part No.	Price
1971-73 98 C.I.D.	D1FZ-12259A	10.35
1971-73 122 C.I.D.	D1FZ-12259B	11.35
1974, 140	D4PZ-12259F	12.70
1974, 122 Eng	D4FZ-12259A	12.70
1975 Exc	D5PZ-12259H	16.65
6-171	D5PZ-12259J	22.00

8—IGNITION SWITCH:

Application	Part No.	Price
1971 (Early)	D1FZ-11572A	4.15
1971 (Late)	D1FZ-11572B	4.15
1972-73	D1FZ-11572B	4.15
1974-75	D4FZ-11572A	4.15

Time — Fuel System & Intake Manifold (Group C) — Time

OPERATION INDEX

C1—CARBURETOR, R & R OR RENEW

1971-75 (0.5) 0.7

C2—CARBURETOR, R & R & OVERHAUL

1971-74—
1600 Eng. (1.3) 1.9
2000 & 2300 Eng. (1.1) 1.6
1975 (1.1) 1.6

C2A—ACCELERATOR PUMP, RENEW

1971-74—
1600 Eng. (0.5) 0.7
2000 & 2300 Eng. (0.4) 0.6
1975 (0.4) 0.6

—NOTE—
Does Not Include R & R Carburetor.

C2B—NEEDLE & SEAT, RENEW

1971-74—
1600 Eng. (0.7) 0.9
2000 & 2300 Eng. (0.5) 0.7
1975 (0.5) 0.7

—NOTE—
Does Not Include R & R Carburetor.

C3—AUTO. CHOKE THERMOSTAT, RENEW

1971-75 (0.5) 0.6

C3A—AUTO. CHOKE, OVERHAUL

1971-75 (0.7) 0.9

C5—FUEL PUMP, R & R OR RENEW

1971-75 (0.4) 0.6

C6—FUEL TANK, R & R OR RENEW

1971-75 (0.8) 1.2

C7—FUEL SYSTEM, CLEAN

Includes R & R tank, blow out lines and clean or renew fuel filter.
1971-75 (1.6) 2.5

C8—INTAKE MANIFOLD GASKETS, RENEW

1971-74—
1600 Eng. (0.8) 1.2
2000 & 2300 Eng.—
L/Air Cond. (0.8) 1.2
W/Air Cond. (1.0) 1.5
1975 Four—
L/Air Cond (0.8) 1.2
W/Air Cond (1.0) 1.5

Parts — Fuel System & Intake Manifold — Parts

PARTS INDEX

1—CARBURETOR ASS'Y:

1971 98 C.I.D	D2FZ-9510P	65.20
1971 122 C.I.D	D2FZ-9510E	71.00
1972 98 C.I.D.	D2FZ-9510F	65.20
1972 122 C.I.D.—		
Synchro-Mesh	D2FZ-9510E	71.00
Auto Trans—		
Exc. Below	D2FZ-9510J	71.00
Calif	D2FZ-9510J	71.00
1973 98 C.I.D.	D3FZ-9510F	53.50
1973 122 C.I.D.—		
Manual Trans	D3FZ-9510B	71.00
Auto Trans	D3FZ-9510C	71.00
1974, 122 Eng—		
Std Trans Exc	D4FZ-9510E	81.70
Tag D42E-EB	D4FZ-9510J	71.00
W/Thermactor	D4FZ-9510F	81.70
Auto Trans	D4FZ-9510G	71.00
1974, 140 Eng—		
Auto Trans, Exc	D4FZ-9510C	71.00
Tag D42E-GA	D4FZ-9510L	71.00
L/T. E.	D4FZ-9510A	71.00
Man Trans, Exc	D4FZ-9510D	81.70
L/T. E.	D4FZ-9510B	71.00
1975, 4-140—		
Auto Trans Exc	D5FZ-9510B	71.00
Calif	D5FZ-9510A	71.00
Std Trans Exc	D5FZ-9510D	71.00
Calif	D5FZ-9510C	71.00

2—CARBURETOR GASKET SET:

1971-72 98 C.I.D.	D1FZ-9502B	1.65
1971-74 122 C.I.D.	D1FZ-9502A	1.95

3—NEEDLE & SEAT ASS'Y:

1971-72	D1FZ-9541A	.73
1973-75	D2FZ-9564A	4.35

4—ACCELERATOR PUMP DIAPHRAGM:

1971-72, 98 Eng	DORY-9B559A	3.60
1971-72, 122 Exc	D1FZ-9B559A	3.45
Calif	D2FZ-9B559A	3.45
1973-75	D2FZ-9B559A	3.45

5—CARBURETOR TUNE-UP KIT:

1971-72 98 C.I.D.	D1FZ-9A586C	6.60
1971-72 122 Exc	D1FZ-9A586D	12.55
Calif	D1FZ-9A586D	12.55

6—FUEL TANK:

1971-72	D1FZ-9002A	25.30
1973 Except	D1FZ-9002A	25.30
12 Gal Capacity	D2FZ-9002A	27.85
1974 Exc	D4FZ-9002A	30.15
Sta Wagon	D4FZ-9002B	27.85
1975 Exc	D5FZ-9002B	28.45
Sta Wag	D5FZ-9002A	33.40

7—FUEL PUMP:

1971-73—		
98 C.I.D.	DORY-9350C	17.55
122 C.I.D.	D1FZ-9350C	17.55
1974-75, 122	D3FZ-9350A	17.55
140	D4FZ-9350A	17.55

8—INTAKE MANIFOLD GASKET:

1971-73 98 C.I.D.	DORY-9441A	.95
1971-74 122 C.I.D.	D1FZ-9441A	1.30
1974-75, 140	D4FZ-9441A	.67
6-171	D5ZZ-9441A	4.40

FORD THUNDERBIRD

Time — Emission Controls (Group AB) — Time

OPERATION INDEX

AB1—CRANKCASE VENT VALVE (PCV),CLEAN OR RENEW

All Models—
Renew (0.2) 0.3
Clean (0.4) 0.5

AB2—EMISSION CONTROL CHECK

Use with imco systems only. Includes adjust carburetor & ignition timing and check PCV Valve.
All Models (0.4) 0.7

AB6—AIR PUMP, R & R OR RENEW

1968-71 (0.4) 0.6

AB10—ANTI-BACKFIRE VALVE, RENEW

1969-75 (0.3) 0.4

AB14—AIR PUMP BELT, RENEW

1966-69 (0.4) 0.6
1970-71 (0.6) 0.9

AB15—EXHAUST GAS RECIRCULATION VALVE, RENEW

1973-75 (0.3) 0.4

AB16—EXHAUST GAS RECIRCULATION SWITCH, RENEW

1973-75 (0.3) 0.4

AB17—EGR VACUUM CONTROL VALVE, RENEW

1973-75 (0.3) 0.4

AB18—ELECTRONIC SPARK CONTROLS, RENEW

1973-75, Solenoid (0.2) 0.3
Modulator Valve (0.3) 0.3
Ambient Switch (0.3) 0.4
Delay Control Valve (0.3) 0.3

AB19—FUEL VAPOR CANNISTER, RENEW

1970-75 (0.3) 0.3

Parts — Emission Controls — Parts

PARTS INDEX

1—ANTI-BACKFIRE VALVE:

1970	C8TZ-9B289A★	20.85
1974	D4AZ-9B289A★	12.40

2—THERMACTOR PUMP DRIVE BELT:

—NOTE—

Order By Complete Model Discription.

9—CRANKCASE VENTILATOR VALVE

1966-69	C6AZ-6A666A	1.95
1970-72	DOAZ-6A666A	2.05
1973-75	D3OZ-6A666A	2.05

4—DISTRIBUTOR VACUUM CONTROL VALVE:

1968-73	C8AZ-12A091A	11.15
1974	D3FZ-12A091B	4.05
1975	D5VY-12A091A	11.15

5—FUEL VAPOR CANISTER:

1970-72	DOAZ-9D653C	22.55
1973	D1AZ-9D653A	18.35
1974-75 Exc	D4AZ-9D653A	22.05
With Thermactor	D4DZ-9D653A	22.05

6—AIR CLEANER SENSOR ASS'Y:

1971-73	DOZZ-9E607B	2.60
1974	D3ZZ-9E607A	2.70
1975	DOZZ-9E607B	2.60

7—AIR CLEANER FILTER ASS'Y:

1971-75	D1ZZ-9D695A	1.90

8—EXHAUST GAS RECIRCULATION VALVE

1973 Exc	D3OZ-9D475C	14.10
V8-460	D3VY-9D475A	24.00
3.25 Axle	D3BZ-9D475A	17.00
1974 Exc	D4AZ-9D475H	.
W/Thermactor	D4VY-9D475A	.
3.25 Axle	D4AZ-9D475A	25.30
1975 Exc	D5VY-9D475D	23.20
Calif.	D5VY-9D475C	23.20

Time — Tune-Up & Ignition (Group B) — Time

OPERATION INDEX

B1—TUNE-UP, MINOR

Includes: Renew points, plugs and condenser, set spark timing and adjust carburetor idle.

1969-72 (1.6) 1.8
1973-75 (1.0) 1.2

—NOTE—

For Thermactor Add (0.3) *0.3*

B2—TUNE-UP, MAJOR

Includes check compression, clean & adjust or renew spark plugs, renew points and condenser and adjust ignition timing, carburetor and fan belts. Clean battery terminals, service air cleaner, check coil and clean or renew fuel line filter.

1969-72 (2.6) 3.3
1973-75 (2.1) 2.8

—NOTE—

To Service PCV Valve, Add (0.5) *0.5*
For Thermactor Add (0.3) *0.3*

B3—TUNE-UP MAJOR & OVERHAUL CARBURETOR

1969-72 (3.9) 4.8
1973-75 (3.4) 4.3

—NOTE—

For Thermactor Add (0.3) *0.3*

B4—POINTS & CONDENSER, RENEW

Does not include R & R distributor

1968-73 (0.4) 0.6

B5—SPARK PLUGS, CLEAN & ADJUST OR RENEW

1969-75 (0.6) 0.8

—NOTE—

For Thermactor Add (0.3) *0.3*

B6—COMPRESSION, TEST

1969-75 (0.7) 0.9

—NOTE—

For Thermactor Add (0.3) *0.3*

B7—IGNITION TIMING, SET

1969-75 (0.3) 0.3

B8—DISTRIBUTOR, R & R OR RENEW

1969-75 (0.4) 0.5

B9—DISTRIBUTOR, OVERHAUL (UNIT OFF)

Includes: Adjust on stroboscope.

1969-75 (1.1) 1.6

B9A—DISTRIBUTOR, ADJUST ON STROBOSCOPE (UNIT OFF)

All Models (0.3) 0.4

B10—DISTRIBUTOR CAP, RENEW

All Models (0.3) 0.3

B11—IGNITION CABLE SET, RENEW

Time allowance covers installation of factory supplied sets only.

1969-75 (0.4) 0.5

B12—VACUUM CONTROL UNIT, RENEW

Includes R & R distributor.

1969-75 (0.7) 0.9

B13—IGNITION COIL, RENEW

1969-75 (0.4) 0.6

B14—IGNITION SWITCH, RENEW

1966-69 (0.3) 0.6
1970-75 (0.7) 1.0

FIG.1-TUNE-UP & IGNITION

(For Parts Identification Only)

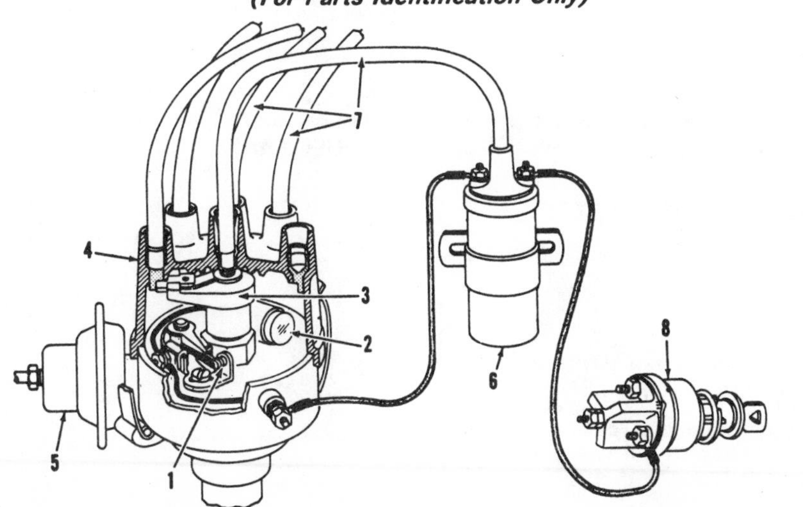

DISTRIBUTOR ASS'Y:

1968-69 V8-429	C8VY-12127C	31.30
1970-71 V8-429	DOAZ-12127Z	31.30
1972 V8-400—		
Exc. Calif	D2SZ-12127E	45.65
Calif	D2AZ-12127F	34.00
1972 V8-429—		
Exc. Calif	D2AZ-12127J	45.65
Calif	D2AZ-12127H	34.00
1973—		
V8-429	D3SZ-12127A	.
V8-460	D3VY-12127A	33.60
1974-75	D4VY-12127C	41.60

DISTRIBUTOR REPAIR KIT:

Includes Points, Rotor And Condenser.

1967-73	COTZ-12000A	7.00

1—IGNITION POINT SET:

1967-72 (Exc. Below)	C5AZ-12171A	4.40
1972 V8-400	B8Q-12171A	4.40
1973	B8Q-12171A	4.40

2—CONDENSER:

1969-73	C9AZ-12300A	1.50

3—ROTOR:

1968-74	B7A-12200A	1.10
1975	D5AZ-12200A	1.50

4—DISTRIBUTOR CAP:

Year	Part No.	Price
1969-74—		
Exc. Below	B7A-12106A	5.75
Transistor	B7AZ-12106A	9.00
1975	D5AZ-12106A	10.05

5—VACUUM CONTROL UNIT:

Year	Part No.	Price
1966-72	C5AZ-12370A	5.40
1973	D3SZ-12370A	16.70
1974-75	D3AZ-12370C	11.10

6—IGNITION COIL:

Year	Part No.	Price
1967-73	B6A-12029B	13.50
1974	D4AZ-12029A	14.85
1975	D5AZ-12029A	14.85

IGNITION COIL RESISTOR

Year	Part No.	Price
1968-72	COLF-12250A	2.70
1973-75	C9AZ-12250A	2.50

7—IGNITION CABLE SET:

Year	Part No.	Price
1968-70 V8-429	D1AZ-12259J	17.00
1971-72 V8-429	D1AZ-12259J	17.00
1973	D3AZ-12259B	15.40
1974	D4PZ-12259E	20.15
1975	D5PZ-12259G	35.10

8—IGNITION SWITCH:

Year	Part No.	Price
1968-69	D1AZ-11572C	10.75
1970	DOAZ-11572B	4.85
1971	DOAZ-11572A	4.20
1972-75	D2OZ-11572A	4.55

Time — Fuel System & Intake Manifold (Group C) — Time

OPERATION INDEX

C1—CARBURETOR, R & R OR RENEW

1969-71 (0.5) 0.7
1972-75 (0.6) 0.9

C2—CARBURETOR, R & R & OVERHAUL

1969-75 (1.7) 2.2

C2A—ACCELERATOR PUMP, RENEW

1969-75 (0.5) 0.7

—NOTE—
Does Not Include R & R Carburetor

C2B—NEEDLE & SEAT, RENEW

1969-75—
Autolite-Motorcraft (0.6) 0.8
Rochester (0.7) 0.9

—NOTE—
Does Not Include R & R Carburetor

C3—AUTO. CHOKE THERMOSTAT, RENEW

All Models (0.3) 0.5

C3A—AUTO. CHOKE, OVERHAUL

All Models (0.5) 0.8

C4—DASHPOT, RENEW

All Models (0.3) 0.3

C5—FUEL PUMP, R & R OR RENEW

1966-71 (0.5) 0.7
1972-75 (0.4) 0.6

C6—FUEL TANK, R & R OR RENEW

1967-71 (0.9) ①1.5
1972-75 (0.7) ①1.2

—NOTE—
To Renew Tank, Add(0.1)* *0.2*
①Includes Drain And Refill.

C7—FUEL SYSTEM, CLEAN

Includes: R & R tank, blow out lines and clean or renew fuel filter.
1969-75 (1.8) 2.3

C8—INTAKE MANIFOLD GASKETS, RENEW

1968-69—
V8-390, (3.0) 3.5
V8-429 (2.7) 3.1
1970-71 (2.4) 2.9
1972-75—
V8-400 (1.6) 2.3
V8-429 (2.3) 3.1
460 (2.1) 2.8

—NOTE—
For Thermactor Pkg., Add (0.2) *0.3*

Parts — Fuel System & Intake Manifold — Parts

PARTS INDEX

1—CARBURETOR ASS'Y:

Year	Part No.	Price
1968-69 V8-429	D2AZ-9510M	97.90
1970 V8-429	D2AZ-9510M	97.90
1971 V8-429	D2AZ-9510M	97.90
1972 V8-400	D2AZ-9510C	68.10
1972 V8-429, 460	D2AZ-9510M	97.90
1973	D3AZ-9510G	97.90
1974 Exc	D4OZ-9510G	97.90
With Thermactor	D4AZ-9510B	101.25
1975 Exc	D5VY-9510A	97.90
Calif.	D5VY-9510B	97.90

2—CARBURETOR TUNE-UP KIT:

Year	Part No.	Price
1968-71	D2AZ-9A586D	8.60
1972	C8OZ-9A586C	
1973-74	D3AZ-9A586A	8.60

3—CARBURETOR GASKET KIT:

Year	Part No.	Price
1968-72 V8-429, 460	D3AZ-9502A	2.65
1972 V8-400	D2AZ-9502A	2.75
1973-74	D3AZ-9502A	2.65

4—CHOKE THERMOSTAT HOUSING:

Year	Part No.	Price
1969-71	DOAZ-9848D	4.25
1972—		
V8-400	C8AZ-9848C	4.25
V8-429	C7OZ-9848D	3.40
1973	D3AZ-9848N	10.35
1974 Exc	D4VY-9848A	10.35
With Thermactor	D4AZ-9848A	10.35

5—CARBURETOR DASHPOT:

Year	Part No.	Price
1967-71	C1AZ-9B549A	3.05

6—FUEL PUMP (NEW):

Year	Part No.	Price
1968-72 V8-429	DOVY-9350A	16.15
1972 V8-400	DOAZ-9350A	16.15
1973	DOVY-9350A	16.15
1974 Exc	DOVY-9350A	16.15
With Thermactor	D3VY-9350B	16.60
1975	D4VY-9350A	

7—FUEL TANK:

Year	Part No.	Price
1967-69	C7AZ-9002B	48.40
1970—		
L/Fuel Emission	C7AZ-9002B	48.40
W/Fuel Emission	DOSZ-9002C	48.40
1971	D1SZ-9002A	51.75
1972	D2OZ-9002D	60.35
1973	D2OZ-9002D	60.35
1974	D4SZ-9002C	60.35
1975	D5SZ-9002A	60.35

8—INTAKE MANIFOLD GASKET SET:

Year	Part No.	Price
1968-72 V8-429	C9AZ-9433A	10.25
1972 V8-400	D1AZ-9433A	9.15
1973-74	C9AZ-9433A	10.25
1975	D5AZ-9433C	10.75

LINCOLN

Time — Emission Controls (Group AB) — Time

OPERATION INDEX

AB1—CRANKCASE VENT VALVE (PCV);CLEAN OR RENEW

1969-75, Renew (0.2) 0.3
Clean (0.4) 0.5

AB2—EMISSION CONTROL CHECK

Use with IMCO Systems only. Includes adjust carb. & Ignition timing and check PCV Valve.
All Models (0.4) 0.7

AB6—AIR PUMP, R & R OR RENEW

1970-71 (0.4) 0.6

AB10—ANTI-BACKFIRE VALVE, RENEW

1968-71 (0.3) 0.4

AB15—EXHAUST GAS RECIRCULATION VALVE, RENEW

1973-75 (0.3) 0.4

AB16—EXHAUST GAS RECIRCULATION SWITCH, RENEW

1973-75 (0.3) 0.4

AB17—EGR VACUUM CONTROL VALVE, RENEW

1973-75 (0.3) 0.4

AB18—ELECTRONIC SPARK CONTROLS, RENEW

1973-75, Solenoid (0.2) 0.3
Modulator Valve (0.3) 0.3
Ambient Switch (0.3) 0.4
Delay Control Valve (0.3) 0.3

AB19—FUEL VAPOR CANNISTER, RENEW

1970-75 (0.3) 0.3

Parts — Emission Controls — Parts

PARTS INDEX

1—THERMACTOR AIR PUMP:

1970-71 ....C8AZ-9A486C 83.90
1974 ....D4AZ-9A486A 83.90

4—THERMACTOR AIR PUMP RELIEF VALVE:

1970-71 ....C8TZ-9B479A 2.40

5—CHECK VALVE:

1970-71 ....C6AZ-9A487A 2.95
1974 ....D4VY-9A487A 5.40

6—ANTI-BACKFIRE VALVE:

1970-72 ....C8TZ-9B289A 20.85
1974 ....D4VY-9B289A 11.90
1975 ....D5AZ-9B289C 12.40

8—THERMACTOR PUMP DRIVE BELT:

—NOTE—
Order By Complete Model Description.

9—CRANKCASE VENTILATOR VALVE:

1968-69 ....C6AZ-6A666A 1.95
1970-72 ....DOAZ-6A666A 2.05
1973-75 ....D3OZ-6A666A 2.05

10—DISTRIBUTOR VACUUM CONTROL VALVE:

1968-74 ....C8AZ-12A091A 11.15
1975 ....D5VY-12A091A 11.15

11—FUEL VAPOR CANISTER:

1970-71 ....DOAZ-9D653C 22.55
1972-73 ....D1AZ-9D653A 18.35
1974-75 Exc D4AZ-9D653A 22.05
With Thermactor D4DZ-9D653A 22.05

12—FUEL VAPOR SEPARATOR:

1971-73 ....D1AZ-9B328A 1.40
1974-75 ....D4AZ-9B328A 1.40

13—EXH. GAS RECIRCULATION VALVE:

1973, Exc. D3OZ-9D475C 14.10
W/3.25 Axle D3UZ-9D475C 16.60
1974, Exc. Below D4VY-9D475A 23.20
Mark IV Exc D4AZ-9D475H 16.75
W/Thermactor D4VY-9D475A 23.20
W/3.25 Axle D4AZ-9D475A 25.30
1975, Exc. D5VY-9D475D 23.20
Calif. D5VY-9D475C 23.20

14—EXH. GAS RECIRCULATION VACUUM CONT. VALVE:

1973-74 ....D3TZ-9D473A 7.45

15—EXH. AIR SUPPLY PUMP ASSY:

1974-75 ....D4TZ-9C472A 1.85

Time — Tune-Up & Ignition (Group B) — Time

OPERATION INDEX

B1—TUNE-UP, MINOR

Includes: Renew points, condenser and plugs. Set spark timing and adjust carburetor idle.
1969-72 (1.6) 1.8
1973-75 (1.0) 1.2

B2—TUNE-UP MAJOR

Includes: Check compression, clean or renew and adjust spark plugs. Renew points and condenser. Adjust ignition timing, carburetor and fan belts. Clean battery terminals and service air cleaner. Check coil and service manifold heat control valve and replace or clean fuel line filter.
1969-72 (2.6) 3.0
1973-75 (2.1) 2.5

—NOTE—
To Service PCV Valve
Add (0.5) 0.5

B3—TUNE-UP, MAJOR & OVERHAUL CARBURETOR

1969-72 (4.2) 5.0
1973-75 (3.7) 4.5

—NOTE—
To Service PCV Valve
Add (0.5) 0.5

B4—POINTS & CONDENSER, RENEW

Does not include R & R distributor.
1969-72 (0.4) 0.6

B5—SPARK PLUGS, CLEAN & ADJUST OR RENEW
1969-75 (0.6) 0.8
—NOTE—
To Clean & Adjust, Add (0.2) 0.2

B6—COMPRESSION, TEST
1969-75 (1.0) 1.2

B7—IGNITION TIMING, SET
1969-75 (0.3) 0.3

B8—DISTRIBUTOR, R & R OR RENEW
1969-75 (0.4) 0.5

B9—DISTRIBUTOR, OVERHAUL (UNIT OFF)
1969-75 (1.1) 1.4

B9A—DISTRIBUTOR, ADJUST ON STROBOSCOPE (UNIT OFF)
All Models (0.4) 0.4

B10—DISTRIBUTOR CAP, RENEW
All Models (0.3) 0.3

B11—IGNITION CABLE SET, RENEW
Time allowance covers installment of factory supplied sets only.
1969-75 (0.4) 0.5

B12—VACUUM CONTROL UNIT RENEW
Includes R & R distributor
1969-75 (0.7) 0.9

B13—IGNITION COIL, RENEW
1969-75 (0.4) 0.6

B14—STARTER & IGNITION SWITCH, RENEW
1966-69 (0.4) 0.6
1970-75—
Exc. Below (0.6) 0.9
Mark III & Mark IV (0.7) 1.0

Parts — Tune-Up & Ignition — Parts

FIG.1-TUNE-UP & IGNITION
(For Parts Identification Only)

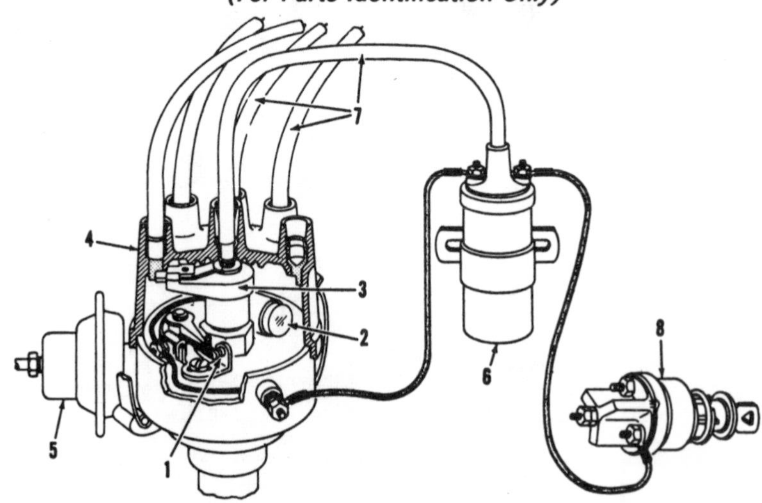

DISTRIBUTOR ASS'Y:

Year	Part No.	Price
1968-69 V8-460	C8VY-12127G	33.60
1970-71	DOVY-12127A	33.60
1972—		
Exc. Calif	D2VY-12127A	33.60
Calif	D2VY-12127B	33.60
1973	D3VY-12127A	33.60
1974-75	D4VY-12127C	41.60

1—IGNITION POINT SET:

Year	Part No.	Price
1968-70	C5AZ-12171A	4.40
1971-72	B8Q-12171A	4.40

2—CONDENSER:

Year	Part No.	Price
1966-72	C9AZ-12300A	1.50

3—ROTOR:

Year	Part No.	Price
1968-74	B7A-12200A	1.10
1975	D5AZ-12200A	1.50

4—DISTRIBUTOR CAP:

Year	Part No.	Price
1968-74 Exc	B7A-12106A	5.75
Transistor (68-69)	B7AZ-12106A	9.00
1975	D5AZ-12106A	10.05

5—VACUUM CONTROL UNIT:

Year	Part No.	Price
1966-72	C5AZ-12370A	5.40
1973-75, Exc.	D3VY-12370A	16.70
W/Breakerless Ign.	D3AZ-12370C	11.10

6—IGNITION COIL:

Year	Part No.	Price
1967-73	B6A-12029B	13.50
1974	D4AZ-12029A	14.85
1975	D5AZ-12029A	14.85

IGNITION COIL RESISTOR:

Year	Part No.	Price
1967-69	COLF-12250A	2.70
1970-74	C9AZ-12250A	2.50

7—IGNITION CABLE SET:

Year	Part No.	Price
1966-72	D1AZ-12259J	17.00
1973	D3AZ-12259B	15.40
1974	D4PZ-12259E	20.15
1975	D5PZ-12259G	35.10

8—IGNITION SWITCH:

Year	Part No.	Price
1968-69	D1AZ-11572C	10.75
1970	DOAZ-11572B	4.85
1971-72	D4DZ-11572A	5.30
1973, Exc.	D4DZ-11572A	5.30
Mark IV	D2OZ-11572A	4.55
1974-75 Exc	D4DZ-11572A	5.30
Mark IV	D2OZ-11572A	4.55

Time — Fuel System & Intake Manifold (Group C) — Time

OPERATION INDEX

C1—CARBURETOR, R & R OR RENEW
1969-75 (0.6) 0.8

C2—CARBURETOR, R & R & OVERHAUL
1969-75 (1.8) 2.2

C2A—ACCELERATOR PUMP, RENEW
1969-75 (0.5) 0.7
—NOTE—
Does Not Include R & R Carburetor

C2B—NEEDLE & SEAT, RENEW
1969-75 (0.6) 0.8
—NOTE—
Does Not Include R & R Carburetor.

C3A—AUTOMATIC CHOKE, OVERHAUL
1969-75 (0.4) 0.8

C4—DASHPOT, RENEW
All Models (0.3) 0.3

C5—FUEL PUMP, R & R OR RENEW
LINCOLN CONTINENTAL:
1966-69—
V8-460 (0.6) 0.9
V8-462 (0.4) 0.6
1970-75 (0.5) 0.8
MARK III:
1969-71 (0.6) 0.9

MARK IV:
1972-75 (0.4) 0.7

C6—FUEL TANK, RENEW

LINCOLN CONTINENTAL:
1966-69 (1.2) 1.5
1970-75 (1.0) 1.2

MARK III:
1969-71 (1.1) 1.5

MARK IV:
1972-75 (0.9) 1.2

C7—FUEL SYSTEM, CLEAN

Includes: R & R tank, blow out lines and clean fuel filter

LINCOLN CONTINENTAL:
1966-69 (1.8) 2.5
1970-75 (1.6) 2.3

MARK III:
1969-71 (1.6) 2.4

MARK IV:
1972-75 (1.4) 2.3

C8—INTAKE MANIFOLD GASKETS, RENEW

LINCOLN CONTINENTAL:
1966-69—
V8-460 (2.6) 3.2
V8-462 (1.9) 2.3
1970-75 (2.3) 2.8

MARK III:
1969 (2.7) 3.4
1970-71 (2.4) 3.0

MARK IV:
1972-75 (2.3) 3.0

Parts — Fuel System & Intake Manifold — Parts

PARTS INDEX

1—CARBURETOR ASS'Y:

1968-72 Exc	D2AZ-9510M	97.90
V8-462	C6VY-9510F	87.30
1973	D3AZ-9510G	97.90
1974 Exc	D4OZ-9510G	97.90
W/Thermactor	D4AZ-9510B	101.25
1975, Exc	D5VY-9510A	97.90
Calif.	D5VY-9510B	97.90

2—CARBURETOR TUNE-UP KIT:

1969-70	D2AZ-9A586D	8.60
1971-72	D2AZ-9A586D	8.60

3—CARBURETOR GASKET KIT:

1969-72	D3AZ-9502A	2.65

4—CHOKE THERMOSTAT HOUSING:

1968-69 V8-460	C8SZ-9848A	4.25
1970-73	DOAZ-9848D	4.25
1974	D4VY-9848A	10.35

6—CARBURETOR DASH POT:

1966-72	C1AZ-9B549A	3.05

7—FUEL PUMP

1968-69 (V8-460)	DOVY-9350A	16.15
1970-73	DOVY-9350A	16.15
1974 Exc	DOVY-9350A	16.15
W/Thermactor	D4VY-9350A	.
1975	D4VY-9350A	.

9—FUEL TANK:

1969—		
Exc. Mark III	C6VY-9002B	60.40
Mark III	C8LY-9002B	49.85
1970—		
Exc. Mark III—		
L/Fuel Emission	DOAZ-9002B	49.15
W/Fuel Emission	DOAZ-9002A	49.15
Mark III		
L/Fuel Emission	C8LY-9002B	49.85
W/Fuel Emission	DOSZ-9002C	48.40
1971 (Exc. Mark III)	D1AZ-9002A	56.15
1971 Mark III	D1SZ-9002A	51.75
1972-73, Exc	D2AZ-9002B	56.15
Mark IV	D2OZ-9002D	60.35
1974 Exc	D4AZ-9002A	56.15
Mark IV	D4SZ-9002C	60.35
1975	D5SZ-9002A	60.35

10—INTAKE MANIFOLD GASKET:

1968-74 V8-460	C8SZ-9441A	4.35

MERCURY

FULL SIZE MODELS

Time — Emission Controls (Group AB) — Time

OPERATION INDEX

AB1—CRANKCASE VENT VALVE (PCV),CLEAN OR RENEW

All Models—
Clean (0.4) 0.5
Renew (0.2) 0.3

AB2—EMISSION CONTROL CHECK (IMCO)

Use with IMCO Systems only. Includes adjust carburetor & ignition timing and check PCV Valve.
All Models (0.6) 0.7

AB6—AIR PUMP, R & R OR RENEW

All Models (0.4) 0.6

AB10—ANTI-BACKFIRE VALVE, RENEW

1969-75 (0.3) 0.4

AB14—AIR PUMP BELT, RENEW

1969-75 (0.3) 0.4

AB15—EXHAUST GAS RECIRCULATION VALVE, RENEW

1973-75 (0.3) 0.4

AB16—ELECTRONIC SPARK CONTROLS, RENEW

1973-75, Solenoid (0.2) 0.3
Ambient Switch (0.2) 0.3
Delay Control Valve (0.3) 0.3
Modulator Valve (0.3) 0.4

AB19—FUEL VAPOR CANNISTER, RENEW

1970-75 (0.3) 0.4

AB20—AIR CLEANER SENSOR, RENEW

1970-75 (0.2) 0.3

Parts — Emission Controls — Parts

PARTS INDEX

1—THERMACTOR PUMP ASS'Y:

1974 Exc	D4AZ-9A486B	83.90
V8-460	D4AZ-9A486A	83.90

2—CHECK VALVE:

1974-75, Exc	D4AZ-9A487A	5.40
V8-460	D4VY-9A487A	5.40

3—ANTI-BACKFIRE VALVE:

1970 V8-429	C8TZ-9B289A	20.85
1974	D4AZ-9B289A	12.40
1975, Exc.	D5AZ-9B289C	12.40
W/Air Cond.	D5AZ-9B289B	.

4—THERMACTOR PUMP DRIVE BELT:

—NOTE—
Order By Complete Model Description.

5—CRANKCASE VENTILATOR VALVE:

1966-69	C6AZ-6A666A	1.95
1970 V8-390	DOOZ-6A666A	2.05
1970 V8-429	DOAZ-6A666A	2.05
1971-72	DOAZ-6A666A	2.05
1973-75 V8-460	D3OZ-6A666A	2.05
1974-75 V8-400	D4AZ-6A666A	2.05

6—DISTRIBUTOR VACUUM CONTROL VALVE:

1968-74	C8AZ-12A091A	11.15
1975	D5VY-12A091A	11.15

7—FUEL VAPOR CANISTER:

1971-73	D1AZ-9D653A	18.35

1974 Exc	D4AZ-9D653A	22.05
With Thermactor	D4DZ-9D653A	22.05
1975	D4DZ-9D653A	22.05

8—FUEL VAPOR SEPARATOR:

1971-73	D1AZ-9B328A	1.40
1974-75	D4AZ-9B328A	1.40

9—EXH. GAS RECIRCULATION VALVE:

1973 V8-351	D3ZZ-9D475B	18.90
V8-400	D3AZ-9D475G	14.10
V8-429, 460—		
Std. Trans.	D3AZ-9D475B	18.25
Auto. Trans.	D3DZ-9D475B	
1974 V8-400	D3AZ-9D475G	14.10
V8-460	D4VY-9D475A	24.80
1975 Exc.	D3OZ-9D475C	14.10
V8-460,Exc.	D5VY-9D475D	23.20
Calif.	D5VY-9D475C	23.20

10—EXH. GAS RECIRCULATION VACUUM CONT. VALVE:

1973-74, Exc.	D3TZ-9D473A	7.45
W/T.E.	D3OZ-9D473A	7.45
1975, Exc	D5AZ-9D473A	7.45
V8-460	D5VY-9D473A	7.45

11—EXH. AIR SUPPLY PUMP:

1973	C8TZ-9C472A	1.85
1974-75	D4TZ-9C472A	1.85

Time — Tune-Up & Ignition (Group B) — Time

OPERATION INDEX

B1—TUNE-UP, MINOR

Includes renew points, plugs and condenser, set spark timing and adjust carburetor idle.

1969-73 (1.4) 1.8
1974-75 (0.9) 1.2

B2—TUNE-UP, MAJOR

Includes check compression, clean & adjust or renew spark plugs. R & R distributor, renew points & condenser and adjust ignition timing, carburetor & fan belts. Clean battery terminals, service air cleaner, check coil & clean or renew fuel line filter

1969-73 (2.7) 3.7
1974-75 (2.2) 3.2

—NOTE—
To Service PCV Valve, Add (0.5) *0.5*

B3—TUNE-UP, MAJOR & OVERHAUL CARBURETOR

1966-71—
2 Barrel Carb (3.4) 4.6
4 Barrel Carb—
Exc Below (3.9) 5.2
Autolite-Motorcraft (3.7) 5.0
Rochester (3.6) 4.8
1972-73 (3.9) 5.3
1975 (3.4) 4.8

—NOTE—
To Clean PCV Valve, Add (0.4) *0.4*
To Replace PCV Valve, Add (0.2) *0.2*

B4—POINTS & CONDENSER, RENEW

Does not include R & R distributor
1968-73 (0.4) 0.6

B5—SPARK PLUGS, CLEAN & ADJUST OR RENEW

1969-75 (0.6) 0.8

—NOTE—
To Clean And Adjust, Add (0.2) *0.2*

B6—COMPRESSION, TEST 1969-75 (0.7)

1968-74 (0.7) 0.9

B7—IGNITION TIMING, SET

1969-75 (0.3) 0.3

B8—DISTRIBUTOR, R & R OR RENEW

1969-75 (0.4) 0.5

B9—DISTRIBUTOR, OVERHAUL (UNIT OFF)

Includes: Adjust on stroboscope.
1969-75 (1.1) 1.6

B9A—DISTRIBUTOR, ADJUST ON STROBOSCOPE (UNIT OFF)

All Models (0.3) 0.4

B10—DISTRIBUTOR CAP, RENEW

All Models (0.3) 0.3

B11—IGNITION CABLE SET, RENEW

Time allowance covers installation of factory supplied sets only.
1969-75 (0.4) 0.5

B12—VACUUM CONTROL UNIT, RENEW

Includes R & R distributor.
1969-75 (0.7) 0.9

B13—IGNITION COIL, RENEW

Includes: Test coil.
1969-75 (0.4) 0.6

B14—IGNITION SWITCH, RENEW

1969 (0.3) 0.5
1970-75 (0.5) 0.8

Parts — Tune-Up & Ignition — Parts

FIG.1-TUNE-UP & IGNITION

(For Parts Identification Only)

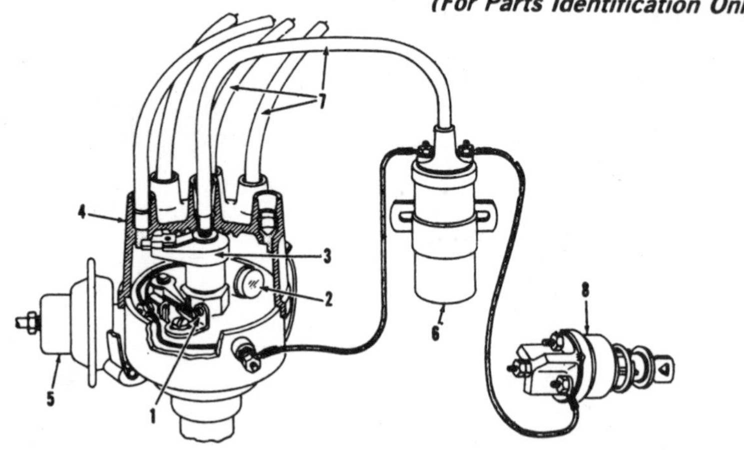

DISTRIBUTOR ASS'Y:

1969 V8-390—		
Std. Trans	C9AZ-12127B	34.00
Auto Trans	C8AZ-12127R	31.30
1969 V8-429	C8VY-12127C	31.30
1970 V8-390—		
Std. Trans	C8AZ-12127M	33.15
Auto. Trans	C7AZ-12127D	33.15
1970 V8-429—		
L/Fuel Emission	C8VY-12127C	31.30
W/Fuel Emission	C9AZ-12127F	34.00
1971 V8-351—		
Synchro-Mesh	D1AZ-12127G	34.00
Auto. Trans	D1AZ-12127H	34.00
1971 V8-400—		
Exc. California	DOOZ-12127U	34.00
California	D2ZZ-12127C	34.00
1971 V8-429 (2 Bar. Carb.)—		
Exc. California	C9AZ-12127F	34.00
California	D1MY-12127F	34.00
1971 V8-429 (4 Bar. Carb.)—		
Exc. California	C9AZ-12127D	34.00
California	D1MY-12127F	34.00
1972 V8-351—		
Exc Calif	D2AZ-12127K	34.00
Calif	D2ZZ-12127C	34.00
1972 V8-400—		
Exc. Calif	D2AZ-12127E	34.00
Calif	D2AZ-12127F	34.00
1972 V8-429—		
Exc. Calif	D2AZ-12127J	45.65
Calif	D2AZ-12127H	34.00
1973 V8-351	D3ZZ-12127B	31.30
V8-400	D3AZ-12127B	34.00
V8-429	D3SZ-12127A	
V8-460	D3VY-12127A	33.60
1974 V8-400	D4OZ-12127C	41.60
V8-460	D4VY-12127C	41.60
1975 Exc.	D4VY-12127C	41.60
V8-400 Exc.	D5AZ-12127B	41.60
Calif	D5AZ-12127D	41.60

1—IGNITION POINT SET:

1966-70	B8Q-12171A	4.40
1971-72	C5AZ-12171A	4.40
1973	B8Q-12171A	4.40

2—CONDENSER:

1966-72	C9AZ-12300A	1.50
1973	C9AZ-12300A	1.50

3—ROTOR:

1968-74	B7A-12200A	1.10
1975	D5AZ-12200A	1.50

4—DISTRIBUTOR CAP:

1968-74	B7A-12106A	5.75
1975	D5AZ-12106A	10.05

5—VACUUM CONTROL UNIT:

1966-72	C5AZ-12370A	5.40
1973, Exc.	D2VY-12370B	16.70
V8-429	D3SZ-12370A	16.70
1974-75 V8-400,Exc	D4OZ-12370A	11.10
Calif	D5AZ-12370A	16.70
V8-460	D3AZ-12370C	11.10

6—IGNITION COIL:

1969-74, Exc.	B6A-12029B	13.50
W/Breakerless Ign.	D4AZ-12029A	14.85
1975	D5AZ-12029A	14.85

IGNITION COIL RESISTOR:

1966-69	COLF-12250A	2.70
1970	C9AZ-12250A	2.50
1971-75	D1AZ-12250A	2.50

7—IGNITION CABLE SET:

1969 V8-429	D1AZ-12259J	17.00
1970 V8-390	C5AZ-12259F	18.05
1970 V8-429	D1AZ-12259J	17.00
1971-72 V8-351	D1OZ-12259B	17.00
1971-72 V8-400, 429	D1AZ-12259J	17.00
1973, Exc.	D4PZ-12259B	16.70
V8-429, 460	D3AZ-12259B	15.40
1974 V8-400	D4PZ-12259B	16.70
V8-460	D4PZ-12259E	20.15
1975, Exc.	D5PZ-12259B	38.10
V8-460	D5PZ-12259G	35.10

8—IGNITION SWITCH:

1968-69	D1AZ-11572C	10.75
1970	DOAZ-11572B	4.85
1971-72	D1AZ-11572B	4.55
1973-75	D3AZ-11572A	5.90

Time — Fuel System & Intake Manifold (Group C) — Time

OPERATION INDEX

C1—CARBURETOR, R & R OR RENEW

1969-75 (0.5) 0.8

C2—CARBURETOR, R & R & OVERHAUL

1966-71—
- 2 Barrel (1.2) 1.7
- 4 Barrel—
  - Exc. Below (1.7) 2.4
  - Autolite-Motorcraft (1.5) 2.2
  - Rochester (1.4) 2.0

1972-75 (1.5) 2.1

C2A—ACCELERATOR PUMP, RENEW

1968-74—
- 2 Barrel (0.3) 0.4
- 4 Barrel (0.5) 0.7

—NOTE—
Does Not Include R & R Carburetor

C2B—NEEDLE & SEAT, RENEW

1969-75—
- 2 Barrel (0.4) 0.5
- 4 Barrel—
  - Autolite, Motorcraft (0.6) 0.8
  - Carter (0.5) 0.7
  - Holley—
    - One (0.5) 0.7
    - Both (0.7) 0.9
  - Rochester (0.7) 0.9

—NOTE—
Does Not Include R & R Carburetor.

C3—AUTO CHOKE THERMOSTAT, RENEW

All Models (0.3) 0.5

C3A—AUTO. CHOKE, OVERHAUL

All Models (0.4) 0.6

C4—DASHPOT, RENEW

All Models (0.3) 0.3

C5—FUEL PUMP, R & R OR RENEW

1969-75—
- Exc. Below (0.4) 0.5
- V8-429, 460 (0.5) 0.8

—NOTE—
For Air Cond. On V8-390, 428, Add (0.2) *0.3*

C6—FUEL TANK, R & R OR RENEW

1969-75—
- Exc. Below (0.8) 1.2
- Sta. Wagon (0.9) 1.4

—NOTE—
To Replace Tank, Add (0.2) *0.2*

C7—FUEL SYSTEM, CLEAN

Includes R & R tank, blow out lines and clean or renew fuel filter.

1969-75—
- Exc. Wagon (1.3) 1.7
- Sta. Wagon (1.4) 2.1

C8—INTAKE MANIFOLD GASKETS, RENEW

1969-75—
- Exc. Below (2.7) 3.7
- V8-400 (1.6) 2.4
- V8-429, 460 (2.2) 3.2

Parts — Fuel System & Intake Manifold — Parts

PARTS INDEX

1—CARBURETOR ASS'Y:

1969 V8-390—		
Std. Trans	D2AZ-9510P	68.10
Auto Trans.—		
Regular Fuel	D2AZ-9510P	68.10
Premium Fuel	D2AZ-9510P	68.10
1969 V8-429—		
2 Bar. Carb	D2AZ-9510P	68.10
4 Bar. Carb	D2AZ-9510M★	97.90
1970 V8-390—		
Std. Trans.—		
L/Air Cond	D2AZ-9510P	68.10
W/Air Cond	D2AZ-9510P	68.10
Auto. Trans.—		
L/Air Cond	D2AZ-9510P	68.10
W/Air Cond	D2AZ-9510P	68.10
1970 V8-429—		
2 Bar. Carb.—		
L/Air Cond	D2AZ-9510P	68.10
W/Air Cond	D2AZ-9510P	68.10
4 Bar. Carb	D2AZ-9510M★	97.90
1971 V8-351	D2AZ-9510P	68.10
1971 V8-400	D2AZ-9510C★	68.10
1971 V8-429—		
2 Bar. Carb	D2AZ-9510P	68.10
4 Bar. Carb	D2AZ-9510M★	97.90
1972 V8-351	D2AZ-9510P	68.10
1972 V8-400	D2AZ-9510C★	68.10
1972 V8-429	D2AZ-9510M	97.90
1973 V8-351, 400	D3AZ-9510E	68.10
V8-429	D3AZ-9510G	97.90
V8-460	D3AZ-9510G	97.90
1974 V8-400, Exc.	D4AZ-9510H	68.10
With Thermactor	D4AZ-9510F	68.10
1974 V8-460 Exc	D4OZ-9510G	97.90
With Thermactor	D4AZ-9510B	101.25
1975 V8-400 Exc	D5AZ-9510A	68.10
Calif	D5MY-9510B	68.10
Colorado	D5MY-9510A	68.10
1975 V8-460, Exc	D5VY-9510A	97.90
Calif	D5VY-9510B	97.90

2—CARBURETOR TUNE UP-KIT:

1969 V8—		
Exc. Below	D2AZ-9A586A	
V8-429 (4 Bar.)	D2AZ-9A586D	8.60
1970	D2AZ-9A586D	8.60
1971—		
2 Bar. Carb	D2AZ-9A586D	8.60
4 Bar. Carb	D2AZ-9A586D	8.60
1972-73, Exc.	D2AZ-9A586A	
V8-429	D2AZ-9A586D	8.60

3—CARBURETOR GASKET KIT:

1969 V8—		
Exc. Below	D2AZ-9502A	2.75
V8-429 (4 Bar.)	D3AZ-9502A	2.65
1970	D2AZ-9502A	2.75
1971—		
2 Bar. Carb	D2AZ-9502A	2.75
4 Bar. Carb	D3AZ-9502A	2.65
1972-73, Exc.	D2AZ-9502A	2.75
V8-429	D3AZ-9502A	2.65

4—CHOKE THERMOSTAT HOUSING:

1969-70 V8-390—		
Std. Trans	C4AZ-9848A	3.95
Auto. Trans	C6AZ-9848A	4.25
1969 V8-429—		
2 Barrel	C6AZ-9848A	4.25
4 Barrel	C8SZ-9848A	4.25
1970 V8-429—		
2 Barrel	C6AZ-9848A	4.25
4 Barrel	DOAZ-9848D	4.25
1971—		
2 Bar. Carb	C6AZ-9848A	4.25
4 Bar. Carb	DOAZ-9848D	4.25
1972, Exc.	DOAZ-9848G	4.25
V8-429	DOAZ-9848D	4.25
1974 V8-400	D4AZ-9848A	10.35
V8-460	D4VY-9848A	10.35
1975 V8-400	D5AZ-9848A	10.35

5—CARBURETOR DASHPOT:

1966-69	C1AZ-9B549A	3.05
1970 V8-390	C8AZ-9B549A	2.90
1970 V8-429—		
2 Bar. Carb	C8AZ-9B549A	2.90
4 Bar. Carb	C1AZ-9B549A	3.05
1971—		
2 Bar. Carb	C8AZ-9B549A	2.90
4 Bar. Carb	C1AZ-9B549A	3.05
1972	C8AZ-9B549A	2.90

6—FUEL PUMP

1969 V8-390	C6AZ-9350B	16.60
1969 V8-429	DOVY-9350A	16.15
1970 V8-390	D4TZ-9350A	17.55
1970-72 V8-429	DOVY-9350A	16.15
1971-72 (Exc. V8-429)—		
V8-351	DOAZ-9350C	16.15
V8-400	DOAZ-9350A	16.15
1973, Exc.	DOAZ-9350A	16.15
V8-429, 460	DOVY-9350A	16.15
1974-75 V8-400	DOAZ-9350A	16.15
V8-460 Exc	DOVY-9350A	16.15
W/Thermactor	D3VY-9350B	16.60
1975 V8-460	D4VY-9350A	

7—FUEL TANK:

Model	Part No.	Price
1969—		
Exc. Sta. Wag	DOAZ-9002B	49.15
Sta. Wagon	C9AZ-9002B	49.15
1970 (Exc. Sta. Wag.)—		
L/Fuel Emission	DOAZ-9002B	49.15
W/Fuel Emission	DOAZ-9002A	49.15
1970 Sta. Wag.—		
L/Fuel Emission	DOAZ-9002C	54.45
W/Fuel Emission	DOAZ-9002E	68.40
1971-72 (Early)—		
Exc. Below	D1AZ-9002A	56.15
Sta. Wagon	D2AZ-9002A	58.20
1972 (Late);73—		
Exc. Below	D2AZ-9002B	56.15
Sta. Wagon	D2AZ-9002A	58.20
1974 Exc	D4AZ-9002A	56.15
Sta Wagon	D4AZ-9002D	58.20
1975 Exc Sta. Wag	D5AZ-9002A	61.20
W/Auxiliary Tank	D5AZ-9002B	61.20
1975 Sta. Wag, Exc	D5AZ-9002F	58.20
W/Auxiliary Tank	D5AZ-9002C	58.20
1975 Auxiliary Tank Exc	D5AZ-9002E	31.80
Sta. Wag	D5AZ-9002D	32.30

8—INTAKE MANIFOLD GASKET:

Model	Part No.	Price
1969 V8-390—		
Early	C8AZ-9441A	1.55
Late	C8AZ-9441A	1.55
1969 V8-429	C8SZ-9441A	4.35
1970 V8-390	C8AZ-9441A	1.55
1970-73 V8-429, 460	C8SZ-9441A	4.35
1971-72 V8-351	C9OZ-9441A	1.45
1974 V8-460	C8SZ-9441A	4.35

9—INTAKE MANIFOLD GASKET & SEAL KIT:

Model	Part No.	Price
1969 V8-390—		
Early	C3AZ-9433G	3.45
Late	C3AZ-9433G	3.45
1969 V8-429—		
2 Bar. Carb	C9AZ-9433A	10.25
4 Bar. Carb	C9AZ-9433A	10.25
1970 V8-390	C3AZ-9433G	3.45
1970-72 V8-429	C9AZ-9433A	10.25
1971-72 (Exc. V8-429)—		
V8-351	D1AZ-9433C	3.55
V8-400	D1AZ-9433A	9.15
1973 V8-351	DOAZ-9433B	7.50
V8-400	D1AZ-9433A	9.15
V8-429, 460	C9AZ-9433A	10.25
1974 V8-400 Exc	D1AZ-9433A	9.15
W/Thermactor	D4AZ-9433B	9.15
1974 V8-460	C9AZ-9433A	10.25
1975 Exc	D5AZ-9433A	9.15
V8-460	D5AZ-9433C	10.75

10—ACCELERATOR PUMP NEEDLE & SEAT

Model	Part No.	Price
1975	D2AZ-9564A	2.95

MERCURY

INTERMEDIATE AND COMPACT MODELS

Time — Emission Controls (Group AB) — Time

OPERATION INDEX

AB1—CRANKCASE VENT VALVE (PCV),CLEAN OR RENEW

1968-75—
Renew (0.2) 0.3
Clean (0.4) 0.6

AB2—IMCO EMISSION CONTROL, CHECK

Includes adjust carburetor & ignition timing and check PCV Valve.
1969-75 (0.4) 0.7

AB6—AIR PUMP, R & R OR RENEW

1969-75 (0.4) 0.6

AB10—ANTI-BACKFIRE VALVE, RENEW

1969-75 (0.3) 0.4

AB14—AIR PUMP BELT, RENEW

1968-74—
Exc. Below (0.3) 0.5
V8-429, 460 (0.6) 0.9

Parts — Emission Controls — Parts

PARTS INDEX

1—THERMACTOR AIR PUMP:

Model	Part No.	Price
1968-70	C8AZ-9A486C	83.90
1974 Exc	D4AZ-9A486B	83.90
V8-460	D4AZ-9A486A	83.90
1975	D5TZ-9A486C	83.90

2—THERMACTOR AIR PUMP RELIEF VALVE:

Model	Part No.	Price
1968-70	C8TZ-9B479A	2.40

3—CHECK VALVE:

Model	Part No.	Price
1968-70	C8AZ-9A487A	2.90
1974-75 Exc	D4VY-9A487A	5.40
351-M, 400	D4AZ-9A487A	5.40

4—ANTI BACKFIRE VALVE:

Model	Part No.	Price
COMET & MONTEGO. MONARCH		
1969-70 V8-427, 428	C8AZ-9B289B	12.40
1975 Six	D4AZ-9B289A	12.40
V8-351, 400, 460	D5AZ-9B289C	12.40
COUGAR:		
1969-70 V8-427, 428	C8AZ-9B289B	12.40
1975	D5AZ-9B289C	12.40

5—THERMACTOR PUMP DRIVE BELT:

—NOTE—

Order By Complete Model Description.

6—CRANKCASE VENTILATOR VALVE:

Model	Part No.	Price
COMET. COUGAR. MONTEGO:		
1968-69, 289, 302, 351	C6AZ-6A666A	1.95
1968-69 V8-390, 427	C7OZ-6A666A	2.05
1969 Six	C8OZ-6A666A	2.05
1969 V8-428	C8OZ-6A666B	2.05
1969 V8-429	C1TZ-6A666A	2.95
1970-72 Six	DODZ-6A666A	2.05
1970 V8-302—		
Exc. Below	C6AZ-6A666A	1.95
Eliminator	C7OZ-6A666A	2.05
1970-72 V8-351	DOAZ-6A666A	2.05
1970 V8-428	DOOZ-6A666A	2.05
1970 V8-429—		
Exc. Below	DOAZ-6A666A	2.05
Cobra Jet	C1TZ-6A666A	2.95
1971-72 V8-302	DOAZ-6A666A	2.05
1971-72 V8-429	DOAZ-6A666A	2.05
1973-75 Six Exc	DODZ-6A666A	2.05
W/Thermactor	D4DZ-6A666A	2.05
1973-75 V8-302	D3OZ-6A666A	2.05
1973 V8-351	D3OZ-6A666A	2.05
1974-75 V8-351, 400—		
Exc Below	D4AZ-6A666A	2.05
Windsor Eng	D3OZ-6A666A	2.05
1973-75 V8-429,460	D3OZ-6A666A	2.05

7—FUEL VAPOR CANISTER:

Model	Part No.	Price
1970-71 (Exc. Below)	DOAZ-9D653C	22.55
1971 Comet	D1AZ-9D653A	18.35
1972-73	D1AZ-9D653A	18.35
1974 Exc	D4AZ-9D653A	22.05
W/Thermactor	D4OZ-9D653A	
1975	D4DZ-9D653A	22.05

8—FUEL VAPOR SEPARATOR:

Model	Part No.	Price
1972-73, Exc.	D1AZ-9B328A	1.40
Sta. Wag.	D2OZ-9B328A	1.50
1974-75 Exc	D4AZ-9B328A	1.40
Comet	D1AZ-9B328A	1.40

9—EXHAUST GAS RECIRCULATION VALVE:

1973 Comet & Montego—
Six Std. Trans. D3AZ-9D475E
Six Auto Trans. (200) D3DZ-9D475B
Six Auto Trans. (250) D3DZ-9D475C
V8-302—
Exc. Below D3OZ-9D475B 16.60
Auto. Trans. D3DZ-9D475B
V8-351 C D3ZZ-9D475B 18.90
V8-351 W D3DZ-9D475A 16.45
V8-351 C.J. D3ZZ-9D475A 18.90
V8-400 ....D3AZ-9D475G 14.10
V8-429-460 ....D3DZ-9D475B

1973 Cougar—
V8-351 C D3ZZ-9D475B 18.90
V8-351 C.J. D3ZZ-9D475A 18.90
1974 Six ....D3OZ-9D475A .
1974 V8-302 Exc D3OZ-9D475D 14.10
W/Thermactor ....D4TZ-9D475C .
1974 V8-351-W Exc D3AZ-9D475F 27.75
W/Thermactor ....D4OZ-9D475F .
1974 V8-351-C Exc D3ZZ-9D475C 17.00
W/Thermactor D3AZ-9D475G 14.10
1974 V8-400 ....D3AZ-9D475G 14.10
1974 V8-460 ....D4VY-9D475A 24.80
1975 Montego & Cougar—
351 ....D3OZ-9D475D 14.10
400 ....D3OZ-9D475C 14.10
460 ....D5VY-9D475D 23.20
1975 Comet & Monarch—
6-250 ....D5DZ-9D475A 15.90

302 Exc D5OZ-9D475A 15.90
Man Trans D3OZ-9D475B 16.60
351 ....D5TZ-9D475D 15.90

10—EXH. GAS RECIR. VAC. CONT. VALVE:

1973-75 Comet—
Six Std. Trans. D3TZ-9D473A 7.45
Six Auto. Trans. D3DZ-9D473A 7.45
V8—
1973-75 Montego—
Six D3DZ-9D473A 7.45
V8, Exc. Below D3TZ-9D473A 7.45
V8-302 ....D3OZ-9D473A 7.45
1973-75 Cougar D3TZ-9D473A 7.45

11—EXH. AIR SUPPLY PUMP:

1973 ....C8TZ-9C472A 1.85
1974-75 ....D4TZ-9C472A 1.85

Time — Tune-Up & Ignition (Group B) — Time

OPERATION INDEX

B1—TUNE-UP, MINOR

Includes: Renew points, condenser and plugs. Set spark timing and adjust carburetor idle.

1968-74 Six (1.2) 1.6
1968-74 V8—
Exc. Cougar (1.5) 1.9
Cougar—
V8-302 (1.4) 1.8
V8-351, 429, 460 (1.8) 2.2
V8-390, 428 (2.2) 2.7
1975 Six (0.9) 1.4
1975 V8-302 (1.0) 1.4
V8-351, 400 (1.3) 1.8
V8-460 (1.5) 2.0

—NOTE—
For V8-390, 428 Equipped With Thermactor, Add (1.0) *1.5*

B2—TUNE-UP, MAJOR

Includes check compression, clean and adjust or renew spark plugs, R&R dist, renew points and condenser and adjust ignition timing, carburetor and fan belts. Clean battery terminals and service air cleaner. Check coil & clean or renew fuel line filter.

1968-74 Six (2.0) 3.0
1968-74 V8 (2.2) 3.3
1975 Six (2.0) 2.5
1975 V8 (2.0) 2.8

—NOTE—
To Service PCV Valve, Add (0.5) *0.5*
For V8-390, 428 With Thermactor, Add (1.0) *1.5*

B3—TUNE-UP, MAJOR & OVERHAUL CARBURETOR

1968-74 Six (3.0) 4.3
1968-74 V8—
2 Barrel (3.4) 4.6
4 Barrel—
Exc. Below (3.9) 4.8
Autolite, Motorcraft (3.7) 4.8
1975 Six (2.8) 3.8
1975 V8—
2 Barrel (3.0) 4.2
4 Barrel (3.5) 4.7

—NOTE—
To Service PCV Valve, Add (0.5) *0.5*
For V8-390, 428 With Thermactor, Add (1.0) *1.5*

B4—POINTS & CONDENSER, RENEW

Does not include R & R distributor.
1968-73 (0.4) 0.6

B5—SPARK PLUGS, CLEAN & ADJUST OR RENEW

1969-75 Six (0.4) 0.5
1969-75 V8 (0.6) 0.8

—NOTE—
To Clean And Adjust, Add (0.2) *0.2*
For 1968-70 V8-390, 428 W/Thermactor, Add (1.0) *1.0*

B6—COMPRESSION, TEST

1969-75 Six (0.5) 0.6
1969-75 V8 (0.7) 0.9

—NOTE—
For 1968-70 V8-390, 428 W/Thermactor, Add (1.0) *1.0*

B7—IGNITION TIMING SET

1969-75 (0.4) 0.3

B8—DISTRIBUTOR, R & R OR RENEW

1969-75 (0.4) 0.5

B9—DISTRIBUTOR, OVERHAUL (UNIT OFF)

1969-75 Six (0.8) 1.0
1969-75 V8—
Exc. Below (1.1) 1.4
Transistor Ign. (0.7) 0.9

B9A—DISTRIBUTOR, ADJUST ON STROBOSCOPE (UNIT OFF)

All Models (0.3) 0.4

B10—DISTRIBUTOR CAP, RENEW

All Models (0.3) 0.4

B11—IGNITION CABLE SET, RENEW

Time allowance covers installation of factory supplied sets only.
1969-75 (0.4) 0.5

B12—VACUUM CONTROL UNIT, RENEW

Includes R & R distributor.
1969-75 (0.7) 0.9

B13—IGNITION COIL, RENEW

1969-75 (0.4) 0.6

B14—IGNITION SWITCH, RENEW

1967-69 (0.3) 0.5
1970-75 Comet (0.6) 0.9
1970-75 Cougar (0.5) 0.8
1970-71 Montego (0.5) 0.8
1972-75 Montego (0.6) 0.9
1975 Monarch (0.6) 0.9

Parts — Tune-Up & Ignition — Parts

DISTRIBUTOR ASS'Y.:

1969 Six—
Std. Trans. C9OZ-12127A 34.00
Auto. Trans. C9OZ-12127V 34.00
1969 V8-302—
2 Bar. Carb.—
L/Air Cond. C9AZ-12127M 34.00
W/Air Cond. C9AZ-12127R 34.00
4 Bar. Carb. D1ZZ-12127A 44.25
1969 V8-351—
2 Bar. Carb. DOOZ-12127M 34.00
4 Bar. Carb.—
Std. Trans. DOOZ-12127N 34.00
Auto. Trans. DOOZ-12127R 34.00

1969 V8-390—
Std. Trans. C9AZ-12127D 34.00
Auto. Trans.—
Exc. GT C7AZ-12127L 33.15
GT C7OZ-12127F 33.15
1969 V8-428—
W/Thermactor—
Std. Trans. C8OZ-12127H 34.00
Auto. Trans. C8OZ-12127J 36.50
W/Imco C7OZ-12127F 33.15
1969 V8-429 ....C9ZZ-12127D 59.70
1970 Six D2OZ-12127P 31.30
1970 V8-302—
Synchro-Mesh DOAZ-12127Y 34.00
Auto. Trans. DOOZ-12127AL 31.30

1970 V8-351 (2 Bar. Carb.)—
Synchro-Mesh C9AZ-12127R 34.00
Auto. Trans. DOOZ-12127U 34.00
1970 V8-351 (4 Bar.) .C8UZ-12127L 34.00
1970 V8-428—
Synchro-Mesh DOZZ-12127C 62.55
Auto. Trans. DOZZ-12127D 62.55
1970 V8-429 (Exc. Cobra Jet)—
Synchro-Mesh C9AZ-12127Y 34.00
Auto Trans. C9AZ-12127F 34.00
1970 V8-429 (Cobra Jet)—
Synchro-Mesh DOOZ-12127J 36.50
Auto. Trans. DOOZ-12127K 45.65
1971 6-200—
Exc. Calif. DODZ-12127C 25.60
Calif.—
Exc. Below D2DZ-12127C 25.60
Auto. Trans. D1DZ-12127G 34.00

FIG. 1-TUNE-UP & IGNITION

(For Parts Identification Only)

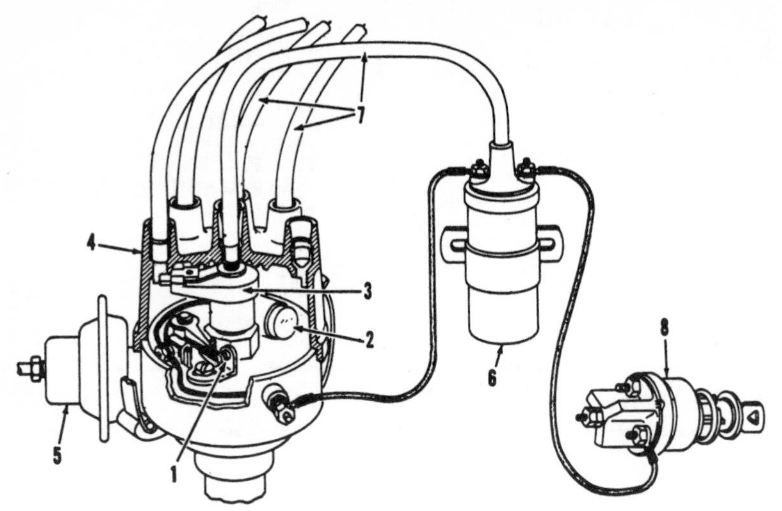

Application	Part No.	Price
1971 6-250—		
Exc. Calif.	D1OZ-12127C	33.15
Calif.—		
Exc. Below	D1OZ-12127A	33.15
Auto. Trans.	D1OZ-12127B	33.15
1971-72 V8-302—		
L/Emission Control—		
Exc. Below	DOAZ-12127Y	34.00
Auto. Trans.	DOOZ-12127AL	31.30
W/Emission Control—		
Exc. Below	DOAZ-12127Y	34.00
Auto. Trans.	D2OZ-12127H	34.00
1971 V8-351 (2 Bar. Carb.)—		
L/Emission Control—		
Exc. Calif.	DOOZ-12127U	34.00
Calif.—		
Exc. Below	D2ZZ-12127A	31.30
Auto. Trans.	D2ZZ-12127C	34.00
W/Emission Control—		
Exc. Below	D2ZZ-12127A	31.30
Auto. Trans.	DOOZ-12127U	34.00
1971 V8-351 (4 Bar. Carb.)—		
Exc. Calif.	DOOZ-12127T	34.00
Calif.—		
Exc. Below	DOOZ-12127V	34.00
Auto. Trans.	D1OZ-12127L	34.00
1971 V8-429—		
L/Emission Control—		
Exc. Calif.	C9AZ-12127F	34.00
Calif.	D1MY-12127F	34.00
W/Emission Control—		
Exc. Below	DOOZ-12127J	36.50
Auto. Trans.	DOOZ-12127K	45.65
1972 Six—		
Exc. Calif	D2OZ-12127D	33.15
Calif—		
Std. Trans	D2OZ-12127E	27.20
Auto Trans	D2OZ-12127E	27.20
1972 V8-351 (2 Bar. Carb)—		
Synchro-Mesh	D2ZZ-12127A	31.30
Calif	D2ZZ-12127C	34.00
1972 V8-351 (4 Bar Carb)—		
Synchro-Mesh—		
Exc. Calif	D2ZZ-12127E	34.00
Calif	D2ZZ-12127F	34.00
Auto Trans—		
Exc. Calif	D2ZZ-12127G	34.00
Calif	D2ZZ-12127H	34.00
1972 V8-400—		
Exc. Calif	D2AZ-12127E	34.00
Calif	D2AZ-12127F	34.00
1972 V8-429—		
Exc. Calif	D2AZ-12127J	45.65
Calif	D2AZ-12127H	34.00
1973 Six—		
200 Std. Trans.	D3DZ-12127B	25.60
200 Auto. Trans.	D3DZ-12127A	25.60
250	D3OZ-12127A	33.15
1973 V8—		
302 Std. Trans.	D3OZ-12127E	
302 Auto. Trans.	D3OZ-12127E	
351c	D3ZZ-12127B	31.30
351w	D3AZ-12127A	34.00
351cobra Jet—		
Exc. Below	D3OZ-12127F	34.00
Auto. Trans.	D3OZ-12127G	34.00
400	D3AZ-12127B	34.00
429	D3SZ-12127A	
1974 Comet—		
6-200 Exc	D3DZ-12127B	25.60
Auto Trans Exc	D3DZ-12127A	25.60
Breakerless Ign	D4DZ-12127F	41.60
6-250 Std Trans—		
Exc Below	D4DZ-12127L	41.60
Breakerless Ign	D3OZ-12127B	33.15
6-250 Auto Trans—		
Exc Below	D3OZ-12127R	31.30
Breakerless Ign	D4DZ-12127B	
V8-302 Exc	D3BZ-12127D	34.00
Auto Trans Exc	D3OZ-12127H	34.00
Breakerless Ign	D4DZ-12127M	41.60
1974 Montego—		
6-250	D3OZ-12127R	31.30
V8-302 Exc	D3BZ-12127D	34.00
Auto Trans Exc	D3OZ-12127H	34.00
Breakerless Ign	D4DZ-12127M	41.60
V8-351-C 2 Bar Carb—		
Exc Below	D3MY-12127G	34.00
Breakerless Ign	D4AZ-12127A	41.60
V8-351-C 4 Bar Carb—		
Exc Below	D3OZ-12127F	34.00
Auto Trans	D3OZ-12127G	34.00
V8-351-W	D3AZ-12127A	34.00
V8-400	D4OZ-12127C	41.60
V8-460	D4VY-12127C	41.60
1974 Cougar—		
V8-400	D4OZ-12127C	41.60
V8-351, See Montego—		
V8-460	D4VY-12127C	41.60
1975 Six Exc	D5DZ-12127D	41.60
Auto Trans	D5DZ-12127A	41.60
1975 V8-302 Exc	D5DZ-12127L	41.60
Auto Trans Exc	D5DZ-12127K	41.60
Monarch	D5DZ-12127J	41.60
Calif	D5DZ-12127B	41.60
1975 V8-351 Exc	D5AZ-12127B	41.60
Windsor Eng Exc	D5DZ-12127H	41.60
Calif	D5DZ-12127M	41.60
1975 V8-400	D5AZ-12127D	41.60
1975 V8-460	D4VY-12127C	41.60

DISTRIBUTOR REPAIR KIT:

—NOTE—

Includes Rotor, Points And Condenser.

COMET. COUGAR. MONTEGO:

Application	Part No.	Price
1969-74 Six	C5AZ-12000D	7.00
1969-70 V8—		
Exc. Below	COTZ-12000A	7.00
V8-427	C5ZZ-12000A	12.30
1971-74 V8	COTZ-12000A	7.00

1—IGNITION POINT SET:

Application	Part No.	Price
1966-70 Six	C9AZ-12171B	4.40
1966-70 V8	B8Q-12171A	4.40
1971-74 Six	C9AZ-12171B	4.40
1971-72 V8-302, 351—		
Exc. Below	C5AZ-12171A	4.40
W/Emission Control	B8Q-12171A	4.40
1971-72 V8-429—		
Exc. Below	C9AZ-12171A	4.40
Auto. Trans.	C5AZ-12171A	4.40
1973-74 Exc. Below	B8Q-12171A	4.40
351 Cobra Jet	C9AZ-12171A	4.40

2—CONDENSER:

Application	Part No.	Price
1966-70 Six	7RA-12300C	1.50
1966-70 V8	C9AZ-12300A	1.50
1971-72 Six	C9AZ-12300A	1.50
1971-72 V8—		
Exc. Below	C9AZ-12300A	1.50
V8-429	C9AZ-12300A	1.50
1973-74	C9AZ-12300A	1.50

3—ROTOR:

Application	Part No.	Price
1969-74 V8	B7A-12200A	1.10
1971-74 Six	C5TZ-12200B	1.10
1975 Six	D5DZ-12200A	1.50
V8	D5AZ-12200A	1.50

4—DISTRIBUTOR CAP:

Application	Part No.	Price
1968-74 Six	7HA-12106	5.15
1966-70 V8—		
Exc. Below	B7A-12106A	5.75
Transistor	B7AZ-12106A	9.00
1971-74 V8	B7A-12106A	5.75
1975 Six	D5DZ-12106A	9.75
V8	D5AZ-12106A	10.05

5—VACUUM CONTROL UNIT:

Application	Part No.	Price
1973 Six—		
Std. Trans.	D3DZ-12370B	16.70
Auto. Trans.	D3DZ-12370A	16.70
1973 V8—		
V8-302—		
Std. Trans.	D3OZ-12370A	16.70
Auto. Trans.	D3OZ-12370A	16.70
V8-351—		
Cleveland	D2VY-12370B	16.70
Windsor	D2TZ-12370J	16.70
Cobra Jet (Auto)	D3AZ-12370A	16.70
V8-400	D2VY-12370B	16.70
V8-429	D3SZ-12370A	16.70

6—IGNITION COIL:

Application	Part No.	Price
1969-73	B6A-12029B	13.50
1974	D4AZ-12029A	14.85
1975	D5AZ-12029A	14.85

IGNITION COIL RESISTOR:

Application	Part No.	Price
1969-75	C9OZ-12250A	2.50

7—IGNITION CABLE SET:

Application	Part No.	Price
1966-70 Six	D1AZ-12259B	15.05
1968-69 V8-302—		
Exc. Below	D1AZ-12259A	16.70
Auto. Trans.	C8AZ-12259B	15.95
1968-70 V8-390, 427	C5AZ-12259F	18.05
1968-70 V8-428	D1PZ-12259P	14.15
1970-72 V8-302	D1AZ-12259A	16.70
1970-72 V8-351	D1AZ-12259J	17.00
1971-72 V8-429	D1AZ-12259J	17.00
1971-73 Six	D1AZ-12259B	15.05
1973 V8-302—		
Comet	D3DZ-12259A	16.70
Montego	D3OZ-12259B	16.70
1973 V8-351—		
Exc. Below	D3AZ-12259C	16.70
351c, 400	D4PZ-12259B	16.70
1973 V8-429	D3AZ-12259B	15.40
1974 Six	D4PZ-12259G	15.05
1974 V8-302 Exc	D4PZ-12259J	24.00
Comet	D4PZ-12259H	23.25
1974 V8-351 Exc	D4PZ-12259D	20.15
Windsor Eng	D4PZ-12259M	24.00
1974 V8-400	D4PZ-12259B	16.70
1974 V8-400	D4PZ-12259E	20.15
1975 Six	D5PZ-12259K	15.95
302	D5PZ-12259L	35.10
351, 400 Exc	D5PZ-12259B	38.10
351-W	D5PZ-12259M	35.10
460	D5PZ-12259G	35.10

8—IGNITION SWITCH:

Application	Part No.	Price
1968-69	D1AZ-11572C	10.75
1970—		
Exc. Below	DOAZ-11572B	4.85
Cougar	DOAZ-11572A	4.20
1971	D4DZ-11572A	5.30
1972	D2OZ-11572A	4.55
1973—		
Montego	D2OZ-11572A	4.55
Comet	D4DZ-11572A	5.30
Cougar	D1AZ-11572B	4.55
1974-75—		
Comet	D4DZ-11572A	5.30
Montego & Monarch	D2OZ-11572A	4.55
Cougar	D2OZ-11572A	4.55

Time — Fuel System & Intake Manifold (Group C) — Time

OPERATION INDEX

C1—CARBURETOR, R & R OR RENEW

1969-75 Six (0.4) 0.6
1969-75 V8 (0.5) 0.7

C2—CARBURETOR, R & R & OVERHAUL

1966-69 Six (1.0) 1.5
1970-75 Six (1.2) 1.8
1969-75 V8—
- 2 Barrel (1.2) 1.7
- 4 Barrel—
  - Exc. Below (1.7) 2.2
  - Autolite, Motocraft (1.5) 2.2
  - Rochester (1.4) 2.2

C2A—ACCELERATOR PUMP, RENEW

1969-75 Six Cyl.—
- Exc. Below (0.6) 0.8
- Autolite, Motocraft (0.4) 0.5

1969-75 V8—
- 2 Barrel (0.3) 0.4
- 4 Barrel (0.5) 0.7

—NOTE—

Does Not Include R & R Carburetor.

C2B—NEEDLE & SEAT, RENEW

1969-75 Six Cyl.—
- Autolite, Motocraft (0.4) 0.5
- Carter Y. F. (0.5) 0.7
- Carter R. B. S. (0.6) 0.8

1969-75 V8—
- 2 Barrel (0.4) 0.5
- 4 Barrel—
  - Autolite, Motocraft (0.6) 0.8
  - Holley—
    - One (0.5) 0.7
    - Two (0.7) 0.9
  - Rochester (0.7) 0.9

—NOTE—

Does Not Include R & R Carburetor.

C3—AUTOMATIC CHOKE THERMOSTAT, RENEW

All Models (0.4) 0.6

C3A—AUTOMATIC CHOKE, OVERHAUL

1969-75 (0.5) 0.8

C4—DASHPOT, RENEW

All Models (0.3) 0.3

C5—FUEL PUMP, R & R OR RENEW

1969-75 Six (0.3) 0.5
1966-71 V8—
- Exc. Below (0.4) 0.6
- V8-390, 428 W/AC (0.5) 0.8
- V8-429 (0.7) 1.0

1972-75 V8—
- Exc. Below (0.4) 0.6
- V8-429 (0.6) 0.9
- Comet V8-302 W/PS (0.5) 0.8
- Monarch W/Pwr Strg (0.5) 0.8

C6—FUEL TANK, R & R OR RENEW

1969-75 (Exc Below (0.9) 1.2
1971-75 Comet (1.1) 1.5
1972-75 Montego—
- Exc Sta Wagon (0.7) 1.0
- Sta Wagon (0.8) 1.2

1975 Monarch (1.1) 1.6

C7—FUEL SYSTEM, CLEAN

Includes R & R tank, blow out lines and clean or renew fuel line filter.

1966-71 (2.1) 2.6
1972-75—
- Exc. Wagon (1.9) 2.4
- Sta. Wagon (2.0) 2.5

C8—INTAKE MANIFOLD GASKETS, RENEW

COUGAR:

1969-75—
- Exc. Below (1.6) 2.4
- V8-302 Boss (1.7) 2.6
- V8-351-W (1.9) 2.9
- V8-351-C-Boss (2.0) 3.1
- V8-390 (2.8) 3.9
- V8-400 (1.6) 2.4
- V8-428 (2.9) 4.0
- V8-429, 460 (2.2) 3.4

MONTEGO:

1967-69—
- Exc. Below (1.6) 2.4
- V8-390 (2.6) 3.6
- V8-428 (2.8) 3.9

1970-71—
- Exc. Below (1.6) 2.4
- V8-351-W (2.0) 3.1
- V8-351-C, 400 (1.5) 2.2
- V8-429 (2.2) 3.4

1972-75—
- Exc. Below (1.7) 2.6
- V8-351-C-M, 400 (1.5) 2.2
- V8-429, 460 (2.3) 3.5

COMET:

1971-75 V8 (1.7) 2.6

MONARCH

1975 V8 (1.7) 2.6

—NOTE—

For Thermactor, Add (0.2) *0.2*

Parts — Fuel System & Intake Manifold — Parts

PARTS INDEX

1—CARBURETOR ASS'Y:

COMET & MONTEGO & MONARCH:

Application	Part No.	Price
1968-69 V8-427	C9OZ-9510N★	113.85
1969 Six (Std. Trans.)—		
L/Air Cond.	DOPZ-9510T★	48.45
W/Air Cond.	DOPZ-9510T★	48.45
1969 Six (Auto Trans.)—		
L/Air Cond.	DOPZ-9510T★	48.45
W/Air Cond.	DOPZ-9510T★	48.45
1969 V8-302—		
Std. Trans.	D2AZ-9510P	68.10
Auto. Trans.	D2AZ-9510P	68.10
1969 V8-351 (2 Bar. Carb.)—		
Std. Trans.	D2AZ-9510P	68.10
Auto. Trans.	D2AZ-9510P	68.10
1969 V8-351 (4 Bar. Carb.)—		
Std. Trans.	D2AZ-9510M★	97.90
Auto. Trans.	C9OZ-9510D★	97.90
1969 V8-390 (Ford Type)—		
Std. Trans.	D2AZ-9510M★	97.90
Auto. Trans.	D2AZ-9510M★	97.90
1969 V8-428—		
Std. Trans.	C9AZ-9510U★	108.85
Auto. Trans.	C9AZ-9510U★	108.85
1970 Six (Synchro-Mesh)—		
L/Air Cond.	DOZZ-9510AA★	51.20
W/Air Cond.	DOZZ-9510AA★	51.20
1970 Six (Auto. Trans.)—		
L/Air Cond.	DOZZ-9510H★	135.00
W/Air Cond.	DOZZ-9510AA★	51.20
1970 V8-302—		
Synchro-Mesh	D2AZ-9510P	68.10
Auto. Trans.—		
L/Air Cond.	D2AZ-9510P	68.10
W/Air Cond.	D2AZ-9510P	68.10
1970 V8-351 (2 Bar. Carb.)—		
Synchro-Mesh	D2AZ-9510C★	68.10
Auto. Trans.—		
L/Air Cond.	D2AZ-9510C★	68.10
W/Air Cond.	D2AZ-9510C★	68.10
1970 V8-351 (4 Bar. Carb.)—		
Synchro-Mesh—		
L/Air Cond.	D2AZ-9510M★	97.90
W/Air Cond.	D2AZ-9510M★	97.90
Auto. Trans.—		
L/Air Cond.	D2AZ-9510M★	97.90
W/Air Cond.	D2AZ-9510M★	97.90
1970 V8-429 (Exc. Cobra Jet)—		
Synchro-Mesh	D2AZ-9510M★	97.90
Auto. Trans.	D2AZ-9510M★	97.90
1970 V8-429 Cobra Jet—		
Synchro-Mesh—		
L/Air Cond.	DOOZ-9510B★	124.35
W/Air Cond.	DOOZ-9510B★	124.35
Auto. Trans.—		
L/Air Cond.	DOOZ-9510B★	124.35
W/Air Cond.	DOOZ-9510B★	124.35
1970 V8-429 Super Cobra Jet—		
Synchro-Mesh	DOOZ-9510N★	116.40
Auto. Trans.	DOOZ-9510R★	116.40
1971 6-170	D1DZ-9510B★	53.50
1971 6-200—		
Synchro-Mesh—		
L/Air Cond.	D1DZ-9510B★	53.50
W/Air Cond.	D1DZ-9510A★	53.50
Auto. Trans—		
L/Air Cond.	D1DZ-9510B★	53.50
W/Air Cond.	D1DZ-9510A★	53.50
Calif. Only—		
Auto. Trans.—		
L/Air Cond.	D1DZ-9510B★	53.50
W/Air Cond.	D1DZ-9510A★	53.50
1971 6-250 (Exc. Calif.)—		
Synchro-Mesh	D1ZZ-9510B★	49.10
Auto. Trans.—		
L/Air Cond.	D1ZZ-9510B★	49.10
W/Air Cond.	D1ZZ-9510B★	49.10
1971 6-250 (Calif.)—		
Synchro-Mesh	D1ZZ-9510B★	49.10
Auto. Trans.—		
L/Air Cond.	D1ZZ-9510B	49.10
W/Air Cond.	D1ZZ-9510B	49.10
1971 V8-302	D2AZ-9510P	68.10
1971 V8-351 (2bar. Carb.)—		
Synchro-Mesh	D2AZ-9510C	68.10
Auto. Trans.	D2AZ-9510C	68.10
1971 V8-351 (4 Bar Carb.)—		
Syncho-Mesh	D2AZ-9510M	97.90
Auto. Trans.	D2AZ-9510M	97.90
1971 V8-429—		
Exc. Cobra Jet	D2AZ-9510M	97.90
Cobra Jet	DOOZ-9510B	124.35
1972 6-200—		
Synchro-Mesh—		
L/Air Cond	D2DZ-9510F	53.50
W/Air Cond	D2DZ-9510G	53.50
Auto Trans—		
L/Air Cond	D2DZ-9510F	53.50
W/Air Cond	D2DZ-9510G	53.50
1972 6-250—		
Synchro-Mesh	D2OZ-9510A	49.10
Auto Trans	D2OZ-9510A	49.10
1972 V8-302—		
Synchro-Mesh	D2AZ-9510P	68.10
Auto Trans	D2AZ-9510P	68.10
1972 V8-351—		
2 Bar Carb—		
Exc. Below	D2AZ-9510C	68.10
Auto Trans	D2AZ-9510C	68.10
4 Bar Carb	D3ZZ-9510E	137.15
1972 V8-400	D2AZ-9510C	68.10
1973 Six 200—		
Std. Trans.		
L/Air Cond.	D3DZ-9510F	53.50
W/Air Cond.	D3DZ-9510G	.
Auto. Trans.		
L/Air Cond.	D3DZ-6510F	53.50
W/Air Cond.	D3DZ-9510G	.
1973 Six 250—		
Std. Trans.	D3OZ-9510B	49.05
Auto. Trans.	D3OZ-9510C	49.05
1973 V8—		
V8-302	D3OZ-9510D	68.10
V8-351c	D3AZ-9510E	68.10
V8-351w	D3AZ-9510E	68.10
V8-351 Cobra Jet	D3ZZ-9510E	137.15

Application	Part No.	Price
V8-400	D3AZ-9510E	68.10
V8-429	D3AZ-9510G	97.90
1974 6-200—		
Std Trans Exc	D4DZ-9510AB	58.90
W/Air Cond Exc	D4DZ-9510DA	45.85
W/Thermactor	D4DZ-9510HA	61.15
Auto Trans Exc	D4DZ-9510EA	50.95
W/Air Cond	D4DZ-9510FA	38.20
1974 6-250 Exc	D4DZ-9510BA	44.15
W/Auto Trans	D4DZ-9510AA	58.90
1974 V8-302 Exc	D4DZ-9510C	68.10
W/Auto Trans	D4DZ-9510C	68.10
1974 V8-351-C—		
Std Trans	D4AZ-9510F	68.10
Cruisomatic	D4AZ-9510F	68.10
C4	D4AZ-6510F	68.10
C6	D4AZ-9510F	68.10
1974 V8-351-W	D4AZ-9510H	68.10
1974 V8-351 4 Bar—		
Std Trans	D4OZ-9510F	137.15
Auto Trans	D4OZ-9510F	137.15
1974 V8-400 Exc	D4AZ-9510F	68.10
W/3.25 Axle	D4AZ-9510F	68.10
W/3.00 Axle	D4AZ-9510F	68.10
1974 V8-460 Exc	D4OZ-9510G	97.90
W/Thermactor	D4AZ-9510B	101.25
1975 Six—		
Std Trans Exc	D5DZ-9510E	58.90
Calif	D5DZ-9510F	58.90
Auto Trans Exc	D5DZ-9510G	58.90
Calif	D5DZ-9510D	58.90
1975 V8-302 Exc	D5DZ-9510B	68.10
Auto Trans Exc	D5DZ-9510A	68.10
Calif	D5DZ-9510J	68.10
Colorado	D5DZ-9510C	
1975 V8-351 Exc	D5OZ-9510A	68.10
351-M Exc	D5OZ-9510B	68.10
Calif	D5OZ-9510C	68.10
1975 V8-400 Exc	D5AZ-9510A	68.10
Calif	D5MY-9510B	68.10
Colorado	D5MY-9510A	
1975 V8-460 Exc	D5VY-9510A	97.90
Calif	D5VY-9510B	97.90
COUGAR:		
1968-69 V8-427	C9OZ-9510N	113.85
1969 V8-302	D2AZ-9510P	68.10
1969 V8-351 (2 Bar. Carb.)—		
Std. Trans.	D2AZ-9510P	68.10
Auto. Trans.	D2AZ-9510P	68.10
1969 V8-351 (4 Bar. Carb.)—		
Std. Trans.	D2AZ-9510M	97.90
Auto. Trans.	D2AZ-9510M	97.90
1969 V8-390 (Ford Type)—		
Std. Trans.	D2AZ-9510M	97.90
Auto. Trans.	D2AZ-9510M	97.90
1969 V8-428—		
Std. Trans.	C9AZ-9510U	108.85
Auto. Trans.	C9AZ-9510U	108.85
1969 V8-429	C9AZ-9510S	119.35
1970 V8-302	DOZZ-9510Z	135.00
1970 V8-351 (2 Bar. Carb.)—		
Synchro-Mesh	D2AZ-9510P	68.10
Auto. Trans.—		
L/Air Cond.	D2AZ-9510P	68.10
W/Air Cond.	D2AZ-9510P	68.10
1970 V8-351 (4 Bar. Carb.)—		
Synchro-Mesh—		
L/Air Cond.	D2AZ-9510M	97.90
W/Air Cond.	D2AZ-9510M	97.90
Auto. Trans.—		
L/Air Cond.	D2AZ-9510M	97.90
W/Air Cond.	D2AZ-9510M	97.90
1970 V8-428	DOZZ-9510H	135.00
1971 V8-351 (2 Bar. Carb.)	D2AZ-9510C	68.10
1971 V8-351 (4 Bar. Carb.)	D2AZ-9510M	97.90
1971 V8-429	DOOZ-9510B	124.35
1972 Six	D2OZ-9510A	49.10
1972 V8-302	D2AZ-9510P	68.10
1972 V8-351—		
2 Bar. Carb—		
Exc. Below	D2AZ-9510C	68.10
Auto Trans	D2AZ-9510C	68.10
4 Bar. Carb	D3ZZ-9510E	137.15
1973—		
Exc. Below	D3AZ-9510E	68.10
V8-351 Cobra Jet	D3ZZ-9510E	137.15
1974-75 See Montego—		

2—CARBURETOR TUNE-UP KIT:

COMET. COUGAR. MONTEGO:

Application	Part No.	Price
1971 V8-351 (4 Bar. Carb.)	D2AZ-9A586D	8.60
1971 V8-429—		
Exc. Below	D2AZ-9A586D	8.60
Cobra Jet	DOOZ-9A586B	9.95

3—CARBURETOR GASKET KIT:

Application	Part No.	Price
1971 V8-351 (4 Bar. Carb.)	D3AZ-9502A	2.65
1971 V8-429—		
Exc. Below	D3AZ-9502A	2.65
Cobra Jet	DOOZ-9502A	8.45
COUGAR:		
1968 V8-302—		
2 Bar. Carb.	D2AZ-9502A	2.75
4 Bar. Carb.	D3AZ-9502A	2.65
1968 V8-390—		
2 Bar. Carb.	D2AZ-9502A	2.75
4 Bar. Carb.	B7AZ-9502G	5.75
1968 V8-427	C8ZZ-9502A	8.45
1971 V8-351 (4 Bar. Carb.)	D3AZ-9502A	2.65
1971 V8-429	DOOZ-9502A	8.45

4—CHOKE CONTROL (OR COVER) ASS'Y.:

COMET. COUGAR. MONTEGO:

5—FUEL PUMP

Application	Part No.	Price
1968-73 Six	D3TZ-9350A	17.95
1968-69 V8-302, 351—		
Exc. Below	D3OZ-9350B	17.95
Eliminator	C9ZZ-9350A	17.20
1968-69 V8-390	D4TZ-9350A	17.55
1968-70 V8-427, 428	C7AZ-9350A	22.50
1969 V8-429	DOVY-9350A	16.15
1970-73 V8-302—		
Exc. Below	D3OZ-9350B	17.95
Eliminator	C9ZZ-9350A	17.20
1970-72 V8-351	DOAZ-9350A	16.15
1970 V8-429	DOVY-9350A	16.15
1971 V8-429	DOOZ-9350A	20.95
1972 V8-429	DOVY-9350A	16.15
1973—		
V8-351w	DOAZ-9350C	16.15
V8-351c&400	DOAZ-9350A	16.15
V8-429	DOVY-9350A	16.15
1974 Six	D3DZ-9350A	17.95
V8-302 Exc	D3OZ-9350B	17.95
W/Thermactor	D4OZ-9350B	17.55
V8-351-W Exc	DOAZ-9350C	16.15
W/Thermactor	D4OZ-9350B	17.55
V8-351-C, 400	DOAZ-9350A	16.15
V8-460	D4VY-9350A	
1975 Six	D5DZ-9350D	17.95
V8-302, 351 Exc	D5OZ-9350B	16.15
351-M, 400	DOAZ-9350A	16.15
V8-460	D4VY-9350A	

6—FUEL TANK:

COMET & MONTEGO:

Application	Part No.	Price
1968-69—		
Exc. Sta. Wag.	C6GY-9002C	30.65
Sta. Wagon	DOOZ-9002F	39.90
1970 (Exc. Sta. Wagon)—		
L/Fuel Emission	DOOZ-9002D	48.40
W/Fuel Emission	DOOZ-9002E	50.85
1970 Sta. Wagon—		
L/Fuel Emission	DOOZ-9002F	39.90
W/Fuel Emission	DOOZ-9002G	48.35
1971 Montego—		
Exc. Sta. Wagon	D1OZ-9002B	60.35
Sta. Wagon	D1OZ-9002A	37.60
1971-72 Comet	D3DZ-9002A	44.55
1972 Montego—		
Exc. Sta. Wagon	D2OZ-9002D	60.35
Sta. Wagon	D2OZ-9002C	46.90
1973 Montego—		
Exc. Sta. Wag.	D2OZ-9002D	60.35
Sta. Wagon	D2OZ-9002C	46.90
1973-74 Comet	D3DZ-9002A	44.55
1974 Montego Exc	D4OZ-9002H	60.35
Sta Wagon	D4OZ-9002G	48.05
1975 Montego Exc	D5OZ-9002D	60.35
Sta Wag	D5OZ-9002A	48.05
1975 Comet & Monarch—		
Exc Below	D5DZ-9002B	47.50
Monarch	D5DZ-9002A	58.70
COUGAR:		
1967-68	C5ZZ-9002D	37.15
1969	C9ZZ-9002A	49.15
1970—		
L/Fuel Emission	DOZZ-9002A	49.15
W/Fuel Emission	DOZZ-9002B	49.15
1971-73	D1WY-9002A	58.70
1974	D4OZ-9002H	60.35
1975	D5OZ-9002D	60.35

7—INTAKE MANIFOLD GASKET SET:

Application	Part No.	Price
1968-69 V8-427, 428	C3AZ-9433G	3.45
1969-70 V8-302—		
Exc. Below	D1AZ-9433B	2.95
Eliminator	D1ZZ-9433A	3.25
1969 V8-351	D1AZ-9433C	3.55
1969 V8-390	C3AZ-9433G	3.45
1969 V8-429	C9ZZ-9433B	10.25
1970-73 V8-351—		
2 Bar. Carb.	DOAZ-9433B	7.50
4 Bar. Carb.	DOAZ-9433A	7.50
1971-73 V8-302	D1AZ-9433B	2.95
1971-73 V8-429—		
Exc. Below	C9AZ-9433A	10.25
Cobra Jet	DOOZ-9433A	10.35
1973 V8-400	D1AZ-9433A	9.15
1974—		
V8-302 Exc	D1AZ-9433B	2.95
W/Thermactor	D4DZ-9433A	3.45
V8-351-C, 2 Bar—		
Exc Below	DOAZ-9433B	7.50
W/Thermactor	DOAZ-9433B	7.50
V8-351-W, 2 Bar—		
Exc Below	D1AZ-9433C	3.55
W/Thermactor	D4OZ-9433A	
V8-351, 4 Bar	DOAZ-9433A	7.50
V8-400 Exc	D1AZ-9433A	9.15
W/Thermactor	D4AZ-9433B	9.15
V8-460	C9AZ-9433A	10.25

OLDSMOBILE

FULL SIZE MODELS

Time	Emission Controls (Group AB)	Time

OPERATION INDEX

AB1—POSITIVE CRANKCASE VENTILATION VALVE, CLEAN OR RENEW

All Models—
Clean (0.4) 0.5
Renew (0.2) 0.2

AB2—CONTROLLED COMBUSTION SYSTEM, CHECK

Includes check & adjust timing, dwell, idle speed & mixture. Check operation of positive crankcase ventilation valve.
1969-75 (0.4) 0.6

AB4—AIR CLEANER MOTOR, RENEW

1969-75 (0.2) 0.3

AB5—AIR CLEANER SENSOR, RENEW

1969-75 (0.2) 0.3

Parts — Emission Controls — Parts

PARTS INDEX

1—CRANKCASE VENTILATING VALVE:

1968-74 .... 6421972 — 2.08

2—DISTRIBUTOR VACUUM SWITCH:

1968-70 .... 1230500 — 8.15
1971-72 .... 410052 — 8.90
1973-74 .... 413473 — 9.00
1975 .... 419591 — 8.80

3—FUEL VAPOR CANISTER

1970 .... 7036967 — 29.10
1971-74 .... 7028131 — 23.25
1975 .... 7043715 — 23.25

4—FUEL VAPOR CANISTER ELEMENT

1970-74 .... 7026014 — 1.10

5—FUEL VAPOR SEPARATOR

1970 .... 7028074 — 10.60

6—EXHAUST GAS RECIRCULATION VALVE

1973-74, Exc .... 7040452 — 16.85
Calif (74) .... 7041437 — 16.85
1975 V8-350, Exc 7043522
Calif 7043523
1975 V8-455, Exc 7043521
Calif 7043526

7—EXHAUST GAS RECIRCULATION CONTROL VALVE

1973-74 .... 413158 — 2.23
1975 .... 419459 — 2.15

8—BACK PRESSURE TRANSDUCER VALVE

1974 Calif Cars .... 416502 — 11.20

Time — Tune-Up & Ignition (Group B) — Time

OPERATION INDEX

B1—TUNE-UP, MINOR

Includes: Renew points, condenser and plugs. Set spark timing and adjust carburetor idle

—NOTE—

To Renew Or Clean PCV Valve, Add (0.2) *0.2*
1968-74 (1.1) 1.4

—NOTE—

For Pwr Steering, Add (0.2) *0.2*
For Air Cond., Add (0.2) *0.2*

B2—TUNE-UP, MAJOR

Includes: Check compression, clean or renew and adjust spark plugs. R & R distributor, renew points and condenser. Adjust ignition timing, carburetor and fan belts. Clean battery terminals and service air cleaner. Check coil and manifold heat control valve and replace or clean fuel line filter.

—NOTE—

To Service PCV Valve Add (0.2) *0.2*
For Air Cond., Add (0.2) *0.2*
For Power Steering, Add (0.2) *0.2*
1969-74 (2.5) 3.0
1975 (2.0) 2.5

B3—TUNE-UP, MAJOR & OVERHAUL CARBURETOR

—NOTE—

To Service PCV Valve, Add (0.2) *0.2*
For Power Steering, Add (0.2) *0.2*
For Air Cond., Add (0.2) *0.2*
1969-74—
2 Barrel (4.4) 5.5
4 Barrel (4.8) 5.8
1975—
2 Barrel (3.9) 5.0
4 Barrel (4.3) 5.3

B4—POINTS & CONDENSER, RENEW

Includes R & R distributor and set spark timing.
All Models (0.4) 0.6

B5—SPARK PLUGS, CLEAN & ADJUST OR RENEW

1969-75 (0.3) 0.5

—NOTE—

For Power Steering, Add (0.2) *0.2*

B6—COMPRESSION, TEST

1969-75 (0.6) 0.7

—NOTE—

For Power Steering, Add (0.2) *0.2*
For Air Cond., Add (0.2) *0.2*

B7—IGNITION TIMING, SET.

All Models (0.2) 0.2

B8—DISTRIBUTOR, R & R OR RENEW

All Models (0.3) 0.3

B9—DISTRIBUTOR, OVERHAUL (UNIT OFF)

All Models (0.5) 0.9

B9A—DISTRIBUTOR, ADJUST ON STROBOSCOPE (UNIT OFF)

All Models (0.4) 0.4

B10—DISTRIBUTOR CAP, RENEW

All Models (0.3) 0.3

B11—IGNITION CABLE SET, RENEW

Time allowance covers installation of factory supplied sets.
1969-75 (0.4) 0.5

B12—VACUUM CONTROL UNIT, RENEW

All Models (0.4) 0.5

B13—IGNITION COIL, RENEW

All Models (0.2) 0.2

B14—IGNITION SWITCH, RENEW

1969-75 (0.3) 0.5

B16—STEERING & IGNITION LOCK & ACTUATOR, RENEW

1969-75 (1.2) 1.8

FIG. 1- TUNE-UP & IGNITION
(For Parts Identification Only)

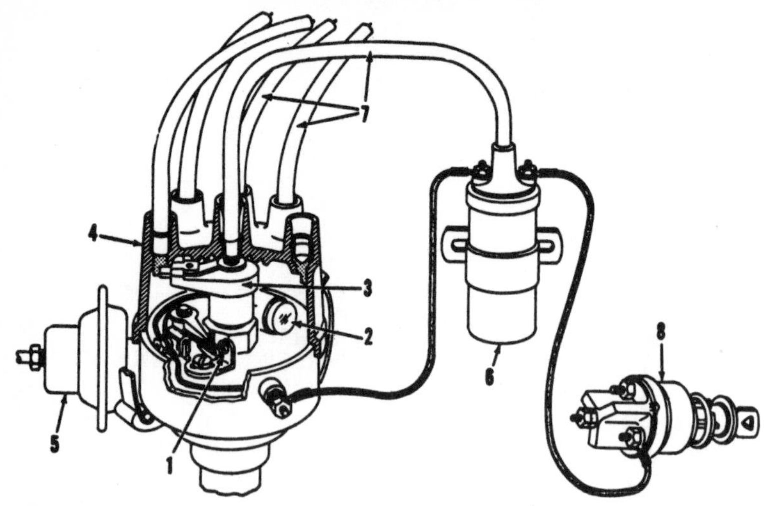

DISTRIBUTOR ASS'Y:

	Part No.	Price
1969 V8-350	1111961	51.85
1969 V8-455—		
2 Bar. Carb	1111980	51.80
4 Bar. Carb.—		
Exc. Below	1111935	52.80
Hi Perf	1111936	52.70
1970 V8-350—		
2 Bar. Carb	1111976	52.85
4 Bar. Carb	1111975	52.30
1970 V8-455—		
2 Bar. Carb	1111980	51.80
4 Bar. Carb.—		
Exc. Below	1111978	50.70
Hi Perf	1111982	54.20
1971 V8-350	1112079	51.85
1971-72 V8-455	1112033	50.70
1972 V8-350—		
Exc. Below	1112079	51.85
Calif	1112106	51.40
4 Bar.	1112085	52.80
1973, V8-350, Exc	1112226	55.50
4 Bar	1112225	51.85
1973 V8-455, Exc	1112197	52.10
Unit Ign System	1112506	159.50
1974, 350 Exc	1112225	51.85
Unit Ign System	1112524	159.50
1974, 455 (Exc Calif)—		
Exc Below	1112197	52.10
Unit Ign System	1112506	159.50
1974, 455 (Calif)—		
Exc Below	1112531	52.85
Unit Ign System	1112532	159.50
1975 V8-350	1112907	
V8-455, Exc	1112908	
Calif	1112937	170.50

1—IGNITION POINT SET:

	Part No.	Price
1968-74—		
Exc. Below	1931988	4.65
Screw Terminal	1966289	4.65

2—CONDENSER:

	Part No.	Price
1969-74 (Exc Below)	1932004	1.61
1973-75 Capacitor	1876154	2.49

3—ROTOR:

	Part No.	Price
1969-74 Exc Below	1852722	2.20
1973-74 Unit Ign Sys	1875943	3.40

4—DISTRIBUTOR CAP:

	Part No.	Price
1968-74 (Exc. Below)	800061	6.20
1967-69 Transistor	800062	7.45
1973-75 Unit Ign System—		
Cap	1875963	10.85
Cover	1875960	2.89

5—VACUUM CONTROL UNIT:

	Part No.	Price
1968-69 V8-350, 2 Bar.	1973408	3.58
4 Bar.	1115361	3.98
1968-69 V8-455, Exc.	1973408	3.58
2 Bar. (1969)	1973407	3.58
1970 V8, 2 Bar.	1973408	3.58
4 Bar.	1115361	3.98
1971-72 V8-350	1973407	3.58
1971-72 V8-455	1973408	3.58
1973 V8-350	1973468	3.81
1973-74 V8-455 (Exc Calif)—		
Exc Below	1116232	3.43
Unit Ignition Sys	1973474	4.33
1974 V8-350, Exc	1973453	3.58
Unit Ign System	1973499	13.80
1974 V8-455 (Calif)—		
Exc Below	1973496	13.65
Unit Ignition Sys	1973499	13.80
1975 V8-350	1973542	.
V8-455	1963531	.

6—IGNITION COIL:

	Part No.	Price
1969, Exc	1115238	14.65
Transistor	1115248	14.90
1970-74 V8 Exc	1115238	14.65
Unit Ignition Sys	1876209	25.40

7—IGNITION CABLE SET:

	Part No.	Price
1968-73	6292319	11.93
1974 Exc	8918402	13.21
Calif Cars	8918400	14.45
Unit Ign Sys, Right	8913748	14.67
Left	8913749	15.21

8—IGNITION & STARTER SWITCH:

	Part No.	Price
1969-73, Exc	1990095	5.25
Tilt Wheel	1990096	5.55
1974, Exc	1990098	5.90
Tilt Wheel	1990099	6.50
Air Cushion System	1990100	6.05

Time — Fuel System & Intake Manifold (Group C) — Time

OPERATION INDEX

C1—CARBURETOR, R & R OR RENEW
1969-75 (0.5) 0.6

C2—CARBURETOR, R & R & OVERHAUL
1969-75—
2-Barrel (1.4) 1.8
4-Barrel (1.6) 2.1

C2A—ACCELERATOR PUMP, RENEW
1969-75 (0.6) 0.8

—NOTE—
Does Not Include R & R Carburetor.

C2B—NEEDLE & SEAT, RENEW
1969-75 (0.5) 0.7

—NOTE—
Does Not Include R & R Carburetor.

C3A—AUTOMATIC CHOKE, OVERHAUL
1969-75 (0.4) 0.5

C3B—AUTOMATIC CHOKE VACUUM DIAPHRAM, RENEW
1969-75 (0.2) 0.2

C4—DASHPOT, RENEW
1969-75 (0.2) 0.3

C4A—IDLE STOP SOLENOID, RENEW
All Models (0.3) 0.5

C5—FUEL PUMP, R & R OR RENEW
—NOTE—
For Power Steering, Add (0.1) *0.1*
For Air Cond., Add (0.2) *0.2*
For Air Injection, Add (0.2) *0.2*
1969-75 (0.3) 0.5

C6—FUEL TANK, R & R OR RENEW
1969-75 (0.6) 1.0

C7—FUEL SYSTEM, CLEAN
Includes R & R tank, blow out lines and clean or replace fuel filter.
1969-75 (1.1) 1.6

C8—INTAKE MANIFOLD GASKETS, RENEW (V8)
1969-75—
L/Air Cond. (1.4) 2.1
W/Air Cond. (1.6) 2.3

—NOTE—
For Power Steering, Add (0.3) *0.3*

Parts — Fuel System & Intake Manifold — Parts

PARTS INDEX

1—CARBURETOR ASS'Y (ROCHESTER):

2 BARREL

	Part No.	Price
1968-69 V8-350	7016956	78.00
1968-69 V8-455	7016959	78.00
1970 V8	7047059	78.00
1971 V8-350	7047156	78.00
1971 V8-455	7047159	78.00
1972 V8-350, Exc	7047256	78.00
Std Trans	7047255	78.00
1973	7047355	82.00

4 BARREL

	Part No.	Price
1969 V8-350—		
L/Air Induction	7016937	112.00
W/Air Induction	7016955	112.00
1969 V8-455	7016937	112.00
1970 V8-455, Exc	7047051	120.00
Hi-Perf	7041327	
1971 V8-455	7047151	120.00
1972 V8-350, Exc	7047250	120.00
V8-455, Exc	7047253	120.00
Auto Trans	7047251	120.00
1973 V8-350	7047350	101.65
1973-74, V8-455 Exc	7047351	120.00
Calif (74)	7047456	120.00
1974 V8-350	7047450	120.00

2—CARB MINOR REPAIR KIT (ROCHESTER):

	Part No.	Price
1969 V8—		
2 Bar. Carb	7039158	6.40
4 Bar. Carb	7039163	9.45
1970 V8—		
2 Bar. Carb	7039206	7.35
4 Bar. Carb	7039181	9.45
1971-72 V8—		
2 Bar. Carb	7039206	7.35
4 Bar. Carb	7039258	9.45
1973, 2 Bar.	7039260	7.35
4 Bar.	7039258	9.45
1974	7039258	9.45

3—CARBURETOR GASKET KIT (ROCHESTER):

	Part No.	Price
1969 (2 Bar. Carb.)	7036611	5.40
1969 (4 Bar. Carb.)	7036699	8.20
1970 (2 Bar. Carb.)	7036859	4.15
1970 (4 Bar. Carb.)	7036885	9.00
1971-72 V8—		
2 Bar. Carb	7041711	5.15
4 Bar. Carb	7046766	8.50
1973, 2 Bar.	7046797	5.15
4 Bar.	7046766	8.50
1974	7046766	8.50

4—THERMOSTATIC COIL & COVER:

	Part No.	Price
1969, V8-350	7036609	6.00
V8-455	7036726	6.00
1970 V8—		
2 Bar. Carb	7036857	5.95
4 Bar. Carb	7036948	4.55
1971-72 V8—		
2 Bar. Carb	7041709	5.95
4 Bar. Carb	7036881	4.55
1973-74 V8-350, 2 Bar	7041709	5.95
4 Bar.	7036948	4.55
1973-74 V8-455	7036881	4.55

5—CHOKE VACUUM CONTROL ASS'Y. (ROCHESTER):

	Part No.	Price
1967-69 (4 Bar.)	7038238	4.25
1969 (2 Bar.)	7027641	3.20
1970 (2 Bar. Carb.)	7026125	8.60
1970 4 Bar. Carb.	7043732	8.85
1971 V8—		
2 Bar. Carb	7035996	10.00
4 Bar. Carb	7043732	8.85
1972 V8-350, 2 Bar.	7046047	10.00
4 Bar.	7024218	8.85
1972 V8-455	7043732	8.85
1973-74 V8-350, 2 Bar	7040034	10.00
4 Bar	7040100	8.85
1973-74 V8-455, Exc	7040031	8.85
Calif (74)	17050396	8.85

6—DASHPOT

	Part No.	Price
1968-70	401159	3.48
1971-72 V8	412277	3.48

7—FUEL PUMP

	Part No.	Price
1969 V8-350—		
Exc. Below	6470036	15.43
W/Air Cond	6470086	17.05
1969 V8-455—		
L/Air Cond	6470037	15.28
W/Air Cond	6416836	16.87
1970 V8-350—		
L/Air Cond	6470331	17.10
W/Air Cond	6470332	18.40
1970-74 V8-455—		
L/Air Cond	6470329	17.10
W/Air Cond	6470330	18.66
1971-72 V8-350	6470331	17.10
1973-74 V8-350, 4 Bar	6470330	18.66
2 Bar	6470842	18.66

8—FUEL TANK:

	Part No.	Price
1969—		
Exc. Below	405150	49.50
"98"	405151	49.50
1970 (Exc. Ser. "98")—		
Exc. Below	405150	49.50
Fuel Emission	405018	59.40
1970 Ser. "98"—		
Exc. Below	405151	49.50
Fuel Emission	405019	59.40
1971-72—		
Exc. Below	408077	59.40
Sta. Wagon	412259	43.95
1973, Delta	415426	59.40
Sta. Wagon	412259	43.95
Ser. 98	417382	59.40
1974, Delta	416217	59.40
Sta Wagon	416062	46.15
98	415427	47.10
1975 Sta Wagon	416062	46.15

9—FUEL GAUGE FILTER (IN TANK):

	Part No.	Price
1969-74, Exc	5651422	1.67
Sta. Wagon	5651702	1.11

10—INTAKE MANIFOLD GASKET:

	Part No.	Price
1969-72 V8-455	230110	7.00
1969-72 V8-350	230522	4.99
1973-75 V8-350	231464	4.99
V8-455	231465	7.00

11—ACCELERATOR PUMP

	Part No.	Price
1969-74 4 Bar	7035031	3.50
1969 2 Bar, Exc	7037920	3.13
Hvy Duty	7037562	4.25
1970-73 2 Bar	7037562	4.25

12—ACCEL PUMP NEEDLE & SEAT

	Part No.	Price
1969-74, 2 Bar	7035386	2.70
4 Bar	7035142	3.45

OLDSMOBILE TORONADO

Time — Emission Controls (Group AB) — Time

OPERATION INDEX

AB1—CRANKCASE VENT VALVE, (PCV), CLEAN OR RENEW

All Models—
Clean (0.3) 0.4
Renew (0.2) 0.3

AB2—EMISSION CONTROL CHECK

Includes: Adjust timing, dwell angle, idle speed and mixture and check PCV Valve.
All Models (0.4) 0.6

AB3—VACUUM CONTROL UNIT, RENEW

All Models (0.6) 0.7

AB4—AIR CLEANER MOTOR, RENEW

All Models (0.6) 0.8

AB5—AIR CLEANER SENSOR, RENEW

All Models (0.5) 0.7

Parts — Emission Controls — Parts

PARTS INDEX

1—CRANKCASE VENTILATOR VALVE:
1968-74 .... 6421972 2.08

2—DISTRIBUTOR THERMOSTATIC VACUUM SWITCH:
1968-70 .... 1230500 8.15
1971-72 .... 410052 8.90
1973-74 .... 413473 9.00

3—FUEL VAPOR CANISTER:
1970 .... 7036967 29.10
1971-74 .... 7028131 23.25
1975 .... 7043715 23.25

4—FUEL VAPOR CANISTER FILTER ELEMENT
1970-74 .... 7026014 1.10

5—FUEL VAPOR SEPARATOR:
1970 .... 405924 7.05

6—EXHAUST GAS RECIRCULATION VALVE
1973 .... 7040452 16.85
1974 .... 7048215 16.85

7—EXHAUST GAS RECIRCULATION CONTROL VALVE
1973-74 .... 413158 2.23

8—BACK PRESSURE TRANSDUCER VALVE
1974 (Calif Cars) 416504 11.20
1975 .... 419920 16.45

Time — Tune-Up & Ignition (Group B) — Time

OPERATION INDEX

B1—TUNE-UP, MINOR
Includes: Renew points, condenser and plugs. Set timing and adjust carburetor idle.
1968-74 (1.4) 1.8

B2—TUNE-UP, MAJOR
Includes: Check compression, clean or renew and adjust spark plugs. R & R distributor, renew points and condenser. Adjust ignition timing, carburetor and fan belts. Clean battery terminals and service air cleaner. Check coil and service manifold heat control valve & replace or clean fuel line filter.
1968-74 (2.6) 3.0
1975 (2.1) 2.6

B3—TUNE-UP, MAJOR & OVERHAUL CARBURETOR
1968-74 (3.5) 4.1
1975 (3.0) 3.6

B4—POINTS & CONDENSER, RENEW
Includes: Set timing.
1968-74 (0.4) 0.6

B5—SPARK PLUGS, CLEAN & ADJUST OR RENEW
1969-75—
Clean & Adjust (0.5) 0.7
Renew (0.3) 0.5

B6—COMPRESSION, TEST
1969-75 (0.5) 0.6

B7—IGNITION TIMING, SET
All Models (0.2) 0.3

B8—DISTRIBUTOR, R & R OR RENEW
1969-75—
Std. Ign. (0.3) 0.5
U.H.V. Ign. (0.5) 0.7

B9—DISTRIBUTOR, OVERHAUL (UNIT OFF)
1969-75—
Std. Ign. (0.5) 0.9
U.H.V. Ign. (0.3) 0.6

B9A—DISTRIBUTOR, ADJUST ON STROBOSCOPE
Unit removed from engine.
All Models (0.4) 0.4

B10—DISTRIBUTOR CAP, RENEW
1969-75 (0.3) 0.3

B11—IGNITION CABLE SET, RENEW
Time allowance covers installation of factory supplied sets only.
1969-75 (0.4) 0.5

B12—VACUUM CONTROL UNIT, RENEW
Does not include R & R distributor.
All Models (0.2) 0.3

B13—IGNITION COIL, RENEW
1969-75 (0.2) 0.3

B14—STARTER & IGNITION SWITCH, RENEW
1969-75 (0.5) 0.5

B16—STEERING & IGNITION LOCK AND ACTUATOR, RENEW
1969-75 (1.2) 1.9

Parts — Tune-Up & Ignition — Parts

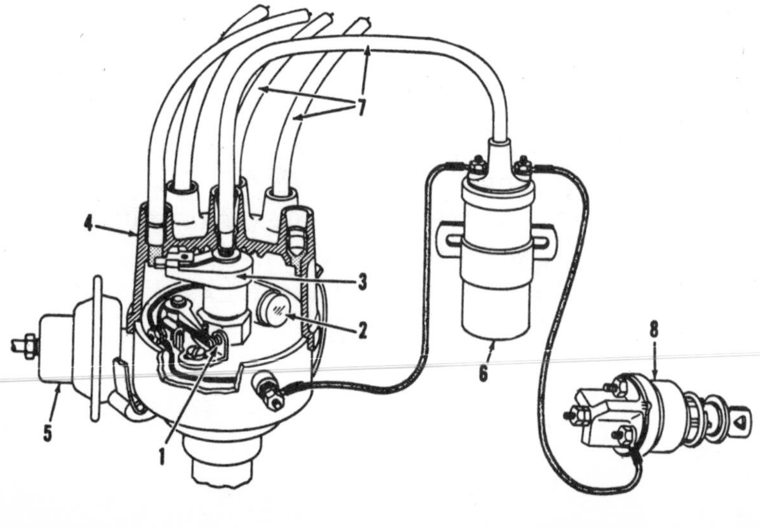

FIG 1- TUNE-UP & IGNITION
(For Parts Identification Only)

DISTRIBUTOR ASS'Y:

1969—		
L/Hi Perf	1111935	52.80
W/Hi Perf	1111936	52.70
1970—		
L/Hi Perf	1111978	50.70
W/Hi Perf	1111982	54.20
1971—		
2.73 Axle	1112033	50.70
3.07 Axle	1112078	52.10
1972	1112172	52.10
1973 Except	1112198	52.10
Unit Ign System	1112815	159.50
1974 (Exc Calif)—		
Exc Below	1112827	52.85
Unit Ign System	1112830	159.50
1974 Calif Cars—		
Exc Below	1112825	52.85
Unit Ign System	1112829	159.50
1975	1112909	

1—IGNITION POINT SET:

1968-74—		
Clip On Type	1931988	4.65
Screw Type	1966289	4.65

2—CONDENSER:

1969-74 (Exc Below)	1932004	1.61
1973-74 Capacitor	1876154	2.49

3—ROTOR:

1969-74, Exc	1852722	2.20
Unit Ign System	1875943	3.40

4—DISTRIBUTOR CAP:

1969-74 Except	800061	6.20
Unit Ignition System—		
Cap	1875963	10.85
Cover	1875960	2.89

5—VACUUM CONTROL UNIT:

1968-69	1973408	3.58
1970—		
2 Bar. Carb	1973408	3.58
4 Bar. Carb	1115361	3.98
1971-72	1973408	3.58
1973, Exc	1973466	3.58
Unit Ign System	1973490	13.65
1974, Exc	1973496	13.65
Unit Ign, Exc	1973500	13.80
Calif	1973499	13.80
1975	1973535	13.65

6—IGNITION COIL:

1968-74 (Exc. Below)	1115238	14.65
1968-69 Transistor	1115248	14.90
1973-74 Unit Ign Sys	1875894	25.40

7—IGNITION CABLE SET:

1968-73	6292319	11.93
1974 Exc	8918401	14.02
Calif	8918400	14.45
Unit Ign Sys, Right	8915052	14.67
Left	8915053	15.21

8—IGNITION SWITCH:

1969-73—		
L/Tilt Wheel	1990095	5.25
W/Tilt Wheel	1990096	5.55
1974, Exc	1990098	5.90
W/Tilt Wheel	1990099	6.50
W/Air Cushion	1990100	6.05

Time — Fuel System & Intake Manifold (Group C) — Time

OPERATION INDEX

C1—CARBURETOR, R & R OR RENEW
1969-75 (0.5) 0.8

C2—CARBURETOR, R & R & OVERHAUL
1969-75 (1.6) 2.4

C2A—ACCELERATOR PUMP, RENEW
1969-75 (0.6) 0.8

—NOTE—
Does Not Include R & R Carburetor

C2B—NEEDLE & SEAT, RENEW
1969-75 (0.5) 0.7

—NOTE—
Does Not Include R & R Carburetor

C3—CHOKE THERMOSTAT, RENEW
1969-75 (0.2) 0.3

C3B—CHOKE DIAPHRAGM, RENEW
1969-75 (0.2) 0.3

C4—DASHPOT, RENEW
1969-75 (0.2) 0.4

C5—FUEL PUMP, R & R OR RENEW
1969-75 (0.3) 0.5

C6—FUEL TANK, R & R OR RENEW
1969-75 (0.7) 1.0

C7—FUEL SYSTEM, CLEAN
Includes: R & R tank, blow out lines and clean or renew fuel line filter.
1969-75 (1.3) 1.6

C8—INTAKE MANIFOLD GASKETS, RENEW
1969-75 (1.4) 2.1

—NOTE—
For Air Cond., Add (0.2) *0.3*

Parts — Fuel System & Intake Manifold — Parts

PARTS INDEX

1—CARBURETOR ASS'Y:

1968-69	7016952	112.00
1970-71	7047052	120.00
1972	7047252	120.00
1973	7047352	120.00
1974 Exc	7047352	120.00
Calif	7047455	120.00

2—CARBURETOR GASKET KIT:

1969	7036699	8.20
1970	7036885	9.00
1971-74	7046766	8.50

3—CARBURETOR MINOR REPAIR KIT:

1969	7039163	9.45
1970	7039181	9.45
1971-74	7039258	9.45

4—CHOKE HOUSING:

1968-69	7029094	8.70
1970	7036963	5.35
1971-74	7036880	5.35

5—DASH POT:

1968-70	401446	4.70
1971	412277	3.48

6—CHOKE VACUUM CONTROL ASS'Y

1969	7038238	4.25
1970-72	7043732	8.85
1973-74, Exc	7040031	8.85
Calif	17050396	8.85

7—FUEL PUMP:

1968-69	6416836	16.87
1970-72	6470330	18.66
1973-74	6470725	24.80

8—FUEL TANK:

1969-70—		
L/Fuel Emission	405107	46.75
W/Fuel Emission	405081	54.95
1971-72	408589	59.40
1973-74	415429	59.40

9—INTAKE MANIFOLD GASKET:

1969-72 (Set)	230110	7.00
1973-74 (Set)	231465	7.00

10—ACCELERATOR PUMP

1969-74	7035031	3.50

11—ACCEL PUMP NEEDLE & SEAT

1969-74	7035142	3.45

OLDSMOBILE

INTERMEDIATE MODELS

Time — Emission Controls (Group AB) — Time

OPERATION INDEX

AB1—POSITIVE CRANKCASE VENTILATION VALVE, CLEAN OR RENEW

All Models—
Clean (0.4) 0.5
Renew (0.2) 0.2

AB2—CONTROLLED COMBUSTION SYSTEM, CHECK

Includes: Check & adjust timing, dwell idle speed & mixture. Check operation of positive crankcase ventilation valve.
1969-75 (0.4) 0.6

AB4—AIR CLEANER MOTOR, RENEW

1969-75 (0.2) 0.3

AB5—AIR CLEANER SENSOR, RENEW

1969-75 (0.2) 0.4

AB6—AIR INJECTOR PUMP, R&R OR RENEW

1973-75 (0.3) 0.5

AB7—AIR PUMP DIVERTER VALVE, RENEW

1973-75 (0.2) 0.3

AB12—CHECK VALVE, RENEW

1973-75 (0.2) 0.3

AB20—EXHAUST GAS RECIRCULATION VALVE, RENEW

1973-75 (0.2) 0.4

AB24—TRANS CONTROLLED SPARK SOLENOID, RENEW

1971-75 (0.2) 0.3

AB25—TRANS CONTROLLED SPARK SWITCH, RENEW

1971-75 (0.3) 0.5

Parts — Emission Controls — Parts

PARTS INDEX

1—AIR INJECTION REACTOR PUMP:

1973-75 Six Exc .... 7817574 — 59.95
V8-260 .... 7803948 — 48.00

2—CRANKCASE VENTILATING VALVE:

1968-74 V8 .... 6421972 — 2.08
1968-70 Six .... 6422718 — 2.08
1971-73 Six .... 6422717 — 2.08
1974-75 .... 6487936 — 2.33

3—DISTRIBUTOR VACUUM SWITCH:

1968-70 .... 1230500 — 8.15
1971-72 .... 410052 — 8.90
1973-74 .... 413473 — 9.00
1975 .... 419591 — 8.80

4—FUEL VAPOR CANNISTER:

1970 .... 7036967 — 29.10
1971 Six .... 7030605 — 26.50
1971-74 V8 .... 7028131 — 23.25
1973-75 Six .... 7030605 — 27.90
1975 V8 .... 7043715 — 23.25

5—FUEL VAPOR CANNISTER FILTER ELEMENT

1970-74 .... 7026014 — 1.10

6—FUEL VAPOR SEPARATOR:

1970 .... 7028074 — 10.60

7—FUEL VAPOR CANNISTER FILTER

1973 Six .... 7021739 — 3.50

8—EXHAUST GAS RECIRCULATION VALVE

Six Cylinder—
1973, Exc .... 7035171 — 16.85
Automatic Trans .... 7035169 — 16.85
1974, Exc .... 7043042 — 16.85
Automatic Trans Exc .... 7043039 — 16.85
Calif .... 7043041 — 16.85
V8-350—
Std Trans, Omega .... 7040350 — 16.85
Cutlass Supreme .... 7040528 — 16.85
Vista-Cruiser .... 7040528 — 16.85
Auto Trans, Omega .... 7040497 — 16.85
4-Bar Carb .... 7040452 — 16.85
Calif Cars .... 7041437 — 16.85
V8-455—
Exc Below .... 7040350 — 16.85
4 Bar Auto Tr .... 7040452 — 16.85
Calif Cars .... 7041437 — 16.85
1975—
Six Exc 7043037
Auto Trans Exc 7043058
Calif 7043038
V8-350 Exc 7043522
Calif 7043523
V8-455 Exc 7043521
Calif 7043526

9—EXHAUST GAS RECIRCULATION CONTROL VALVE

1973-74 V8 .... 413158 — 2.23
1975 .... 419459 — 2.15

10—CARB & EGR VALVE PKG

1973 Sta Wgn .... 231645 — 24.50

11—BACK PRESSURE TRANSDUCER VALVE

1974 Calif Cars—
V8-350 .... 416502 — 11.20
V8-455 .... 416503 — 11.20

Time — Tune-Up & Ignition (Group B) — Time

OPERATION INDEX

B1—TUNE-UP, MINOR

Includes: Renew points, condenser and plugs. Set spark timing and adjust carburetor idle.

—NOTE—

To Renew Or Clean PCV Valve, Add (0.2) *0.2*

1969-74 Six—
L/Air Cond (1.2) 1.6
W/Air Cond (1.4) 1.8
1969-74 V8—
Exc Below (1.2) 1.6
V8-400, 455 (1.4) 1.8

B2—TUNE-UP, MAJOR

Includes check compression, clean or renew and adjust spark plugs, R & R distributor, renew points and condenser. Adjust ignition timing, carburetor and fan belts, clean battery terminals and service air cleaner. Check coil & service manifold heat control valve and replace or clean fuel line filter.

—NOTE—

To Service PCV Valve, Add (0.2) *0.2*

1969-74 Six—
L/Air Cond (1.7) 2.3
W/Air Cond (1.9) 2.5
1969-74 V8—
Exc Below (1.9) 2.5
V8-400, 455 (2.1) 2.7
1975 Six—
L/Air Cond (1.4) 2.0
W/Air Cond (1.6) 2.2
1975 V8—
Exc Below (1.5) 2.3
V8-455 (1.7) 2.5

B3—TUNE-UP, MAJOR & OVERHAUL CARBURETOR

—NOTE—
To Service PCV Valve, Add (0.2) *0.2*
1968-74—
Exc. Below (3.2) 3.9
2 Barrel Carb. (3.4) 4.1
4 Barrel Carb. (3.8) 4.5
Quadrajet (3.6) 4.3
1975 Six (3.0) 3.7
1975 V8—
2 Barrel (2.9) 3.6
4 Barrel (3.3) 4.0

B4—POINTS & CONDENSER, RENEW

Includes R & R distributor and set spark timing.
1968-74 (0.4) ①0.6
①For Six Cyl. W/Air Cond., Add (0.3) *0.3*

B5—SPARK PLUGS, CLEAN & ADJUST OR RENEW

1969-75 Six (0.5) 0.7
1969-75 V8 (0.6) 0.8

B6—COMPRESSION, TEST

1969-75 Six (0.4) 0.5
1969-75 V8 (0.5) 0.6

B7—IGNITION TIMING, SET

All Models (0.3) 0.3

B8—DISTRIBUTOR, R & R OR RENEW

All Models (0.4) 0.4

B9—DISTRIBUTOR, OVERHAUL (UNIT OFF)

1969-75 (0.5) 0.9

B9A—DISTRIBUTOR, ADJUST ON STROBOSCOPE (UNIT OFF)

All Models (0.4) 0.4

B10—DISTRIBUTOR CAP, RENEW

All Models (0.3) 0.3

B11—IGNITION CABLE SET, RENEW

Time allowance covers installation of factory supplied sets.

1969-75 (0.5) 0.6

B12—VACUUM CONTROL UNIT, RENEW

1969-75 (0.3) 0.4

B13—IGNITION COIL, RENEW

All Models (0.2) 0.3

B14—IGNITION SWITCH, RENEW

1969-75 (0.3) 0.5

B16—STEERING & IGNITION LOCK & ACTUATOR, RENEW

1969-75 (1.2) 1.8

Parts — **Tune-Up & Ignition** — Parts

FIG.1-TUNE-UP & IGNITION

(For Parts Identification Only)

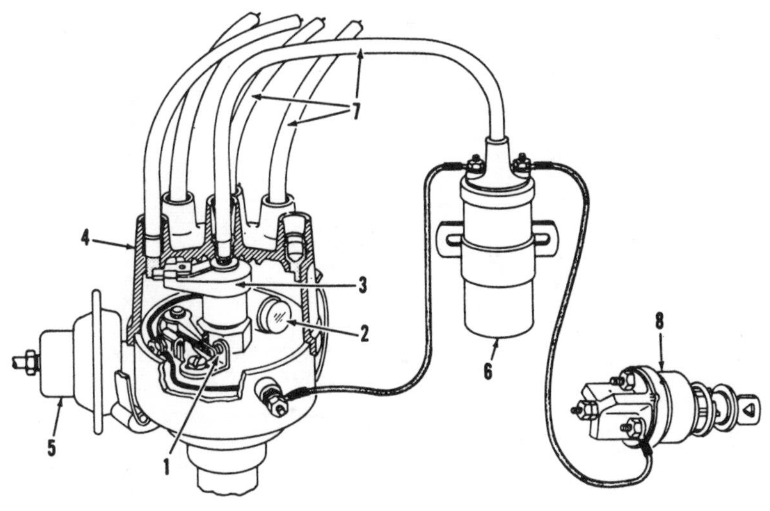

DISTRIBUTOR ASS'Y:

1969-71 Six—
Std. Trans. .... 1110465 .... 40.40
Auto. Trans. .... 1110466 .... 40.40
1969 V8-350—
2 Bar. Carb. .... 1111961 .... 51.85
4 Bar. Carb. .... 1111975 .... 52.30
1969 V8-400—
Exc. .... 1111932 .... 49.30
Transistor .... 1111341 .... 76.10
1969 Hurst .... 1111989 .... 39.85
1970 V8-350—
2 Bar. Carb. .... 1111976 .... 52.85
4 Bar. Carb. .... 1111975 .... 52.30
1970 V8-455—
Exc. Below .... 1111978 .... 50.70
W/Air Induction (4-4-2)—
Std. Trans. .... 1111977 .... 51.70
Auto. Trans. .... 1111979 .... 54.00
L/Air Induction (4-4-2) .... 1111982 .... 54.20
1971 V8-350—
2 Bar. Carb. .... 1112079 .... 51.85
4 Bar. Carb.—
Std. Trans. .... 1112079 .... 51.85
Auto. Trans. .... 1111976 .... 52.85
1971-72 V8-455—
Exc. Below .... 1112033 .... 50.70
W/Air Induction—
Std. Trans. .... 1112036 .... 50.75
Auto. Trans. .... 1112034 .... 54.50
1972 V8-350 (Exc. Calif.)—
Synchro-Mesh .... 1112079 .... 51.85
Auto. Trans. .... 1112085 .... 52.80
1972 V8-350 Calif. .... 1112106 .... 51.40
1973 Six .... 1110499 .... 37.70
V8-350 Exc. .... 1112195 .... 51.85
W/Std. Trans. .... 1112222 .... 54.80
V8-455 .... 1112197 .... 52.10
1974 Six .... 1110499 .... 37.70
V8-350, Omega .... 1112226 .... 55.50
V8-350, Cutlass—
Exc .... 1112195 .... 51.85
Sta Wagon .... 1112225 .... 51.85
Calif Cars .... 1112828 .... 52.85
V8-455—
Exc Below .... 1112197 .... 52.10
Calif Cars .... 1112531 .... 52.85
1975—
Six Exc .... 1112863 .... 129.75
Calif .... 1110650 .... 129.75
V8-260 .... 1112934 .... 155.00
V8-350 .... 1112907 .... .
V8-455 Exc .... 1112908 .... .
Calif .... 1112934 .... 155.00

1—IGNITION POINT SET:

1968-74 Six .... 1954557 .... 3.50
1968-74 V8—
Screw Type .... 1966289 .... 4.65
Clip Type .... 1931988 .... 4.65

2—CONDENSER:

1968-74 Six .... 1928111 .... 1.61
1968-74 V8 .... 1932004 .... 1.61

3—ROTOR:

1968-74 V8 .... 1971247 .... 1.87
1968-74 Six .... 800056 .... 1.24

4—DISTRIBUTOR CAP:

1968-74 Six .... 1971324 .... 3.75
1969-75 V8—
Exc. Below .... 800061 .... 6.20
Transistor (1968-69) .... 800062 .... 7.45
Unit Ignition System—
Cap .... 1875963 .... 10.85
Cover .... 1875960 .... 2.89

5—VACUUM CONTROL UNIT:

1968-70 V8-350—
2 Bar. Carb. .... 1973408 .... 3.58
4 Bar. Carb. .... 1115361 .... 3.98
1968-69 V8-400—
2 Bar. Carb. .... 1973407 .... 3.58
4 Bar. Carb.—
Synchro-Mesh .... 1973408 .... 3.58
Auto. Trans. .... 1973418 .... 3.51
1969-71 Six .... 1116217 .... 3.74
1970 V8-455—
2 Bar. Carb. .... 1973427 .... 3.47
4 Bar. Carb. .... 1115361 .... 3.98
1971 V8-350 .... 1973407 .... 3.58
1971 V8-455—
L/Air Induction—
Std. Trans. .... 1973408 .... 3.58
Auto. Trans. .... 1973427 .... 3.47
W/Air Induction .... 1973407 .... 3.58
1972—
Exc. Below .... 1973407 .... 3.58
V8-455 .... 1973408 .... 3.58
1973 Six .... 1973428 .... 3.47
V8-350 (Exc.) .... 1973453 .... 3.58
W/2 Bar. Carb. .... 1973468 .... 3.81
V8-455 .... 1116232 .... 3.43
1975 V8-350 .... 1973542 .... .
V8-455 .... 1963531 .... .

6—IGNITION COIL:

1968-74 Six .... 1115202 .... 14.50
1966-69 V8—
Exc. Below .... 1115238 .... 14.65
Transistor .... 1115248 .... 14.90
1970-74 V8 .... 1115238 .... 14.65

7—IGNITION CABLE SET:

1966-69 Six—
L/Air Cond. .... 2986606 .... 7.30
W/Air Cond. .... 6292334 .... 7.92
1967-73 V8 .... 6292319 .... 11.93
1970-74 Six .... 8909903 .... 7.54
1974 V8 Exc .... 8918402 .... 13.21
Calif Cars .... 8918400 .... 14.45

8—IGNITION & STARTER SWITCH:

1969-74—
Exc. Below .... 1990095 .... 5.25
Tilt Wheel .... 1990096 .... 5.55

Time — Fuel System & Intake Manifold (Group C) — Time

OPERATION INDEX

C1—CARBURETOR, R & R OR RENEW

1969-75—
- 1 Barrel (0.4) ... 0.5
- 2 Barrel (0.4) ... 0.5
- 4 Barrel (0.5) ... 0.6

C2—CARBURETOR, R & R & OVERHAUL

1969-75—
- Single Barrel (1.2) ... 1.6
- 2 Barrel (1.4) ... 1.8
- 4 Barrel (1.6) ... 2.1

C2A—ACCELERATOR PUMP, RENEW

1969-75 (0.6) ... 0.8

—NOTE—
Does Not Include R & R Carburetor.

C2B—NEEDLE & SEAT, RENEW

1969-75 (0.5) ... 0.7

—NOTE—
Does Not Include R & R Carburetor.

C3A—AUTOMATIC CHOKE, OVERHAUL

1969-75 (0.4) ... 0.5

C3B—AUTOMATIC CHOKE VACUUM DIAPHRAGM, RENEW

1969-75 (0.2) ... 0.2

C3D—AUTOMATIC CHOKE HEAT TUBE (IN MANIFOLD), RENEW

1969-75—
- L/Air Cond. (2.4) ... 3.5
- W/Air Cond. (3.0) ... 4.5

—NOTE—
For Power Steering, Add (0.2) ... *0.2*

C4—DASHPOT, RENEW

1969-75 (0.2) ... 0.3

C4A—IDLE STOP SOLENOID, RENEW

All Models (0.3) ... 0.5

C5—FUEL PUMP, R & R OR RENEW

—NOTE—
For Power Steering, Add (0.1) ... *0.1*
For Air Cond., Add (0.2) ... *0.2*
For Air Injection, Add (0.2) ... *0.2*
1969-75 (0.3) ... 0.5

C6—FUEL TANK, R & R OR RENEW

1969-75—
- Exc. Wagon (0.6) ... 1.1
- Sta. Wagon (1.1) ... 1.6

C7—FUEL SYSTEM, CLEAN

Includes R & R tank, blow out lines and clean or replace fuel filter.
1969-75—
- Exc Wagon (1.4) ... 1.9
- Sta. Wagon (1.7) ... 2.2

C8—INTAKE MANIFOLD GASKETS, RENEW (V8)

1969-75—
- L/Air Cond. (1.4) ... 2.1
- W/Air Cond. (1.6) ... 2.3

—NOTE—
For Power Steering. Add (0.3) ... *0.3*

C8A—MANIFOLD GASKETS, RENEW (SIX CYL.)

1969-75 (0.6) ... 1.0

Parts — Fuel System & Intake Manifold — Parts

PARTS INDEX

1—CARBURETOR ASS'Y (ROCHESTER):

Application	Part No.	Price
1969 Six	7016957	60.00
1969 V8-350—		
2 Bar. Carb.	7016956	78.00
4 Bar. Carb.—		
Exc. Below	7016937	112.00
Air Induction	7016955	112.00
1969 V8-400—		
Synchro-Mesh	7016937	112.00
Auto. Trans.	7016937	112.00
1970 Six—		
Synchro-Mesh	7047015	60.00
Auto. Trans.	7047014	60.00
1970 V8-350—		
2 Bar. Carb.	7047059	78.00
4 Bar. Carb.—		
Exc. Below	7036931	120.00
Auto. Trans	7047050	100.60
1970 V8-455—		
Synchro-Mesh	7041326	120.00
Auto. Trans.	7041346	78.00
1971 Six—		
Synchro-Mesh	7047117	60.00
.Auto. Trans.	7047114	60.00
1971 V8-350—		
2 Bar. Carb—		
Exc. Below—		
Std. Trans.	704715	78.00
Auto. Trans.	704715	78.00
4 Bar. Carb.	704715	120.00
1971 V8-455—		
2 Bar. Carb.	7047159	78.00
4 Bar. Carb.—		
Exc. Below	7047151	120.00
4-4-2—		
Std. Trans.	7047153	120.00
Auto. Trans.	7047157	120.00
1972 V8-350—		
2 Bar. Carb.—		
Std. Trans.	7047255	78.00
Auto. Trans.	7047256	78.00
4 Bar. Carb.	7047250	120.00
1972 V8-455—		
Std. Trans.	7047253	120.00
Auto. Trans.	7047251	120.00
1973-(Exc. Below)—		
V8-350 (Exc.)	7047356	70.20
4 Bar. Carb.	7047350	101.65
V8-455 (Exc.)	7047353	120.00
Auto. Trans	7047351	120.00
1973 Omega—		
Six (Exc.)	7047317	62.00
Auto. Trans.	7047314	62.00
V8-350 (Exc.)	7047357	120.00
4bar. Carb.	7047356	70.20
1974 Six, Exc	7047714	
Auto Trans Exc	7047414	62.00
Calif	7047404	62.00
1974 V8-350—		
Omega	7047357	120.00
Cutlass Exc	7047450	120.00
Sta Wagon	7047350	101.65
1974 V8-455 Exc	7047351	120.00
Calif	7047456	120.00

2—CARBURETOR KLEANOUT KIT (ROCHESTER):

Application	Part No.	Price
1968-69 Six	7039147	5.15
1969 V8—		
2 Bar. Carb.	7039158	6.40
4 Bar. Carb.	7039163	9.45
1970 Six	7039166	5.15
1970 V8—		
2 Bar. Carb.	7039206	7.35
4 Bar. Carb.	7039181	9.45
1971 Six	7039196	5.15
1971-72 V8—		
2 Bar. Carb.	7039206	7.35
4 Bar. Carb.	7039258	9.45
1973-74 Six	7039248	5.15
V8-350 (Exc.)	7039260	7.35
4 Bar. Carb.	7039258	9.45
V8-455	7039258	9.45

3—CARBURETOR GASKET KIT (ROCHESTER):

Application	Part No.	Price
1968-69 Six	7036546	2.50
1969 V8—		
2 Bar. Carb.	7036611	5.40
4 Bar. Carb.	7036699	8.20
1970 Six	7036784	3.50
1970 V8—		
2 Bar. Carb.	7036859	4.15
4 Bar. Carb.	7036885	9.00
1971 Six	7041599	3.00
1971-72 V8—		
2 Bar. Carb.	7041711	5.15
4 Bar. Carb.	7046766	8.50
1973 Six	7046679	3.50
V8-350 (Exc.)	7046797	5.15
W/4 Bar. Carb.	7046766	8.50
V8-455	7046766	8.50
1974 Six	7046679	3.50
V8	7046766	8.50

4—THERMOSTATIC COIL & COVER:

Application	Part No.	Price
1968-71 Six—		
Synchro-Mesh	3927770	3.11
Auto. Trans.	3927772	2.63
1969 2 Bar.	7036609	6.00
1969 4 Bar.	7036726	6.00
1970 V8—		
2 Bar. Carb.	7036857	5.95
4 Bar. Carb.	7036948	4.55
442 (W/Turbo-Hydro.)	7036881	4.55
1971 V8—		
2 Bar. Carb.	7041709	5.95
4 Bar. Carb.—		
Exc. Below	7036948	4.55
442 (W/A.T.)	7036881	4.55
1972 V8-350	7041709	5.95
V8-455—		
Std. Trans.	7036948	4.55
Auto. Trans.	7036881	4.55
1973-74 Six	3998944	.67
V8-350 Exc.	7041709	5.95
4 Bar. Carb.	7036948	4.55
V8-455	7036881	4.55

5—CHOKE VACUUM CONTROL ASS'Y. (ROCHESTER):

Application	Part No.	Price
1967-69 (4 Bar.)	7038238	4.25
1969 (2 Bar.)	7027641	3.20
1970 (2 Bar. Carb.)	7026125	8.60
1970 4 Bar. Carb.—		
Exc. Below	7043732	8.85
W/Air Induction	7040697	3.20
1971 V8—		
2 Bar. Carb.	7035996	10.00
4 Bar. Carb.	7043732	8.85
1972 V8-350 (Exc.)	7046047	10.00
4 Bar. Carb.	7024218	8.85
V8-455	7043732	8.85

1973-74 Six 7030918 9.25
V8-350 (Exc.) 7040034 10.00
4 Bar. Carb. 7040100 8.85
V8-455 (1973) 7040031 8.85
V8-455 (1974) 17050396 8.85

6—DASHPOT:
1968-70 ....401159 3.48
1971-72 ....412277 3.48

7—FUEL PUMP
1968-74 Six 6416502 14.09
1966-69 V8-400 ....6416836 16.87
1969 V8-350—
Exc. Below 6470036 15.43
W/Air Cond. 6470086 17.05
1970 V8-350—
Exc. Below 6470331 17.10
T. H. (2 Bar.) Air Cond. 6470332 18.40
Air Induction 6470332 18.40
1970 V8-455—
Exc. Below 6470329 17.10
W/Air Cond. 6470330 18.66
1971 V8—
Exc. Below 6470331 17.10
V8-455—
2 Bar. Carb.—
L/Air Cond. 6470329 17.10
W/Air Cond. 6470330 18.66
4 Bar. Carb. 6470330 18.66
1972 V8—
V8-350 ....6470331 17.10
V8-455 ....6470330 18.66
Air Induction 6470725 24.80
1973-74 V8-350—
Omega 6470330 18.66
Cutlass Exc 6470841 17.27
Air Cond 6470330 18.66
1973-74 V8-455 ....6470330 18.66
1975 Omega V8-350 ....6416502 14.09

8—FUEL TANK:
1969—
Exc. Below 404078 43.95
Sta. Wagon 404160 43.95
1970 (Exc. Sta. Wagon)—
L/Fuel Emission 405109 43.95
W/Fuel Emission 405010 48.35
1970 Sta. Wagon—
L/Fuel Emission 404160 43.95
W/Fuel Emission 404964 50.55
1971-72—
Exc. Below 408082 48.35
Sta. Wagon 408439 49.25
1973-74 Omega 344416 55.60
1973 Cutlass Exc 411827 40.65
Sta Wagon 409873 49.25
1974 Cutlass Exc 416216 48.35
Sta Wagon (74-75) 416366 46.15
1974 Six 338115 1.68

9—FUEL GAUGE FILTER (IN TANK):
1968-70—
Exc. Below ....5651264 .99
V8-400 ....5651418 1.38
1971-74 ....5651702 1.11

10—INTAKE MANIFOLD GASKET:
1967-73 Six 3953746 1.68
1967-72 V8-400, 455 ....230110 7.00
1968-72 V8-350 ....401477 1.24
1973-75 V8-350 ....231464 4.99
V8-455 (74) 231465 7.00
1975 V8-260 ....231464 4.99

11—ACCELERATOR PUMP
1969 Six, Exc 7037595 3.15
Auto Trans 7037597 3.15
1969 V8 2 Bar, Exc 7037920 3.13
Hvy Duty 7037562 4.25
1969-74 V8, 4 Bar 7035031 3.50
1970-74 Six 7037597 3.15
V8, 2 Bar 7037562 4.25

12—ACCEL PUMP NEEDLE & SEAT
1969-74 Six 7035133 3.20
V8, 2 Bar 7035386 2.70
4 Bar 7035142 3.45

PLYMOUTH

Time — Emission Controls (Group AB) — Time

OPERATION INDEX

AB1—CRANKCASE VENT VALVE (PCV),CLEAN OR RENEW
All Models—
Clean (0.3) 0.5
Renew (0.2) 0.3

AB2—EMISSION CONTROL, CHECK (C.A.P.)
Includes adjust idle, timing and distributor vacuum control unit.
All Models (0.6) 1.0

AB3—VACUUM CONTROL UNIT, RENEW
All Models (0.8) 1.2

AB6—AIR PUMP, R & R OR RENEW
1972 (0.4) 0.6
1973 Six Exc (0.4) 0.6
Valiant W/Air Cond (0.9) 1.2
1974-75 (0.7) 1.1

AB7—AIR PUMP HOSE, RENEW
1972-75 (0.2) 0.3

AB10A—DIVERTER VALVE, RENEW
1972 (0.3) 0.7
1973 Six (0.3) 0.7
V8 (0.7) 1.0
1974-75 (0.7) 1.0

AB12—CHECK VALVE, RENEW
All Models (0.5) 0.8

AB18—FUEL VAPOR CANISTER, R & R OR RENEW
All Models (0.3) 0.5

AB18A—FUEL VAPOR CANISTER FILTER, RENEW
All Models (0.2) 0.3

AB20—EXHAUST GAS RECIRCULATION CONTROL VALVE, RENEW
1973-75 (0.3) 0.5

AB21—EXHAUST GAS COOLANT CONTROL VALVE, RENEW
1973-75 (0.3) 0.5

AB22—EGR TIME DELAY TIMER, RENEW
1971-75 (0.2) 0.3

AB23—EGR TIME DELAY SOLENOID, RENEW
1971-75 (0.2) 0.3

AB24—EGR VACUUM AMPLIFIER, RENEW
1973-75 (0.2) 0.3

AB25—ORIFICE SPARK ADVANCE CONTROL VALVE, RENEW
1973-75 (0.3) 0.4

Parts — Emission Controls — Parts

PARTS INDEX

1—CRANKCASE VENTILATOR VALVE:
1966-69 V8 ....2808622 2.91
1967-69 Six 2808441 2.91
1970-75 ....3671076 2.89

2—DISTRIBUTOR THERMOSTATIC VACUUM SWITCH:
1969 Six, V8-318 ....2843299 9.17
1968-69 V8-426 ....2863739 9.17
1968-69 V8-440 ....2843555 9.17

3—DISTRIBUTOR THERMOSTATIC VACUUM VALVE
1971-72 (Exc Below) 3614024 6.76
1972 Fury 3614023 6.42
1973 V8-360 ....3614023 6.42
1973 V8-400 ....3614024 6.76
1973 V8-440 Exc 3614024 6.76
W/Air Pump 3614023 6.42
1974-75 ....3780126 6.76

4—NOX EXHAUST EMISSION PARTS
1971-72—
Control Unit 3621803 31.65
Vacuum Valve (1971) 3438474 6.01
Vacuum Valve (1972) 3656381 6.01
Thermal Switch 3438465 6.99
Speed Switch Exc 3438472 3.13
Auto Trans 3438494 15.50

5—FUEL VAPOR SEPARATOR
PLYMOUTH
1970 Belvedere Exc 3404373 20.35
Sta Wagon 3404164 23.10
1970-72 Fury (Early 72) 3466836 24.88
1971 Satellite Exc 3466835 30.46

Sta Wagon	3466835	30.46
1972 Satellite, Early	3466835	30.46
Late	3642105	8.42
1972 Fury (Late)	3642105	8.42
1973	3642105	8.42
1974	3751502	7.35
1975, Exc	3870674	6.10
V8-400, 440	3751502	7.35

VALIANT & BARRACUDA

1970-71 Valiant	3404351	21.37
Barracuda	3404183	20.35
1972	3404183	20.35
1973	3642105	8.42
1974	3751502	7.35
1975	3870674	6.10

6—FUEL VAPOR CANISTER

1972-73	3577584	26.20
1974	3769254	.
1975	3577595	26.20

7—FUEL VAPOR CANISTER FILTER

1972-75	3577586	.74

8—FUEL FILTER (IN TANK)

1970-75 Exc	1670694	1.04
V8-426, 400, 440	2534111	.99

Time — Tune-Up & Ignition (Group B) — Time

OPERATION INDEX

B1—TUNE-UP (MINOR)

Includes renew or clean & adjust points, condenser & plugs, set spark timing & adjust carburetor idle.

Six Cyl—
- Standard Ignition (1.3) 1.5
- Electronic Ignition (0.8) 1.0

V8 (Standard Ignition)—
- Exc. Below (2.0) 2.4
- V8-273 (1.6) 2.0
- V8-318, 340, 360 (1.6) 2.0
- V8-383,400,440—
  - Except Below(2.0) 2.4
  - Fury(2.2) 2.6
- V8-426 Hemi (2.4) ①3.0

V8 (Electric Ignition)—
- Exc Below (1.5) 1.9
- V8-318, 340, 360 (1.0) 1.5
- V8-383, 400, 440 Exc (1.5) 1.9
  - Fury (1.7) 2.1
- V8-426 (Hemi) (1.9) ①2.5

—NOTE—

For Each 4 Barrel Carb., Add (0.2) *0.3*
For Clean Air Package, Add (0.3) *0.5*
①For Power Brake Unit, Add (0.4) *0.5*

B2—TUNE-UP, (MAJOR)

Includes check compression, clean or renew & adjust spark plugs, R&R dist, renew points & condenser. Adjust ignition timing, carburetor & fan belts, clean battery terminals and service manifold heat control valve. Check coil, service air cleaner & clean or renew fuel line filter

Six Cyl—
- Standard Ignition (2.1) 2.9
- Electronic Ignition (1.6) 2.4

V8 (Standard Ignition)—
- Exc. Below (2.9) 3.8
- V8-273 (2.6) 3.4
- V8-318, 340, 360 (2.6) 3.4
- V8-426 (Hemi) (6.3) ①7.5

V8 (Electronic Ignition)—
- Exc Below (2.4) 3.3
- V8-318, 340, 360 (1.9) 2.9
- V8-426 (Hemi) (5.8) ①7.0

—NOTE—

For Each 4 Barrel Carb., Add (0.2) *0.3*
For Cleaner Air Package, Add (0.3) *0.5*
To Renew P.C.V., Add (0.2) *0.3*
To Clean P.C.V., Add (0.3) *0.3*
①For Power Brake Unit, Add (0.4) *0.5*

B3—TUNE-UP, MAJOR & OVERHAUL CARBURETOR

Six Cyl—
- Standard Ignition (4.1) 5.5
- Electronic Ignition (3.6) 5.0

V8 2 Bar & Std Ignition—
- Exc. Below (5.0) 5.9
- V8-273, 318 (4.8) 5.9

V8 2 Bar & Electronic Ign—
- Exc Below (4.5) 5.4
- V8-273, 318 (4.3) 5.4

V8 4 Bar & Std Ignition—
- Exc. Below (6.0) ②7.2
- V8-273, 318 (5.8) ②6.6
- V8-340, 360 (5.5) ②6.3
- V8-426 Hemi—
  - One Carb. (9.4) ①10.9
- V8-426 Hemi—

V8 4 Bar & Electronic Egn—
- Exc Below (5.5) ②6.7
- V8-273, 318 (5.3) ②6.1
- V8-340, 360 (5.0) ②5.8
  - One Carb (8.9) ①10.4
  - Two Carbs (10.3) ①12.1

—NOTE—

For Cleaner Air Package, Add (0.3) *0.5*
①For Power Brake Unit, Add (0.4) *0.5*
②For Two 4 Barrels, Add (1.5) *2.0*

B4—POINTS & CONDENSER, RENEW

Includes R & R distributor & set timing.

1969 Six—
- Exc. Below (0.8) 1.2
- W/Std. Trans. (1.3) 1.7

1970-72 Six (0.8) 1.2
1969-72 V8 (0.9) ②1.2
②For 1969 V8-426 W/Std. Trans., Add (0.3) *0.3*

B5—SPARK PLUGS, CLEAN & ADJUST OR RENEW

1969-75 Six (0.4) ②0.5

1968-69 V8—
- Exc. Below (0.7) 0.7
- V8-440 (Hi-Perf.) (0.9) 1.1
- Hemi (1.1) 1.3

1970-75 V8—
- Exc. Below (1.1) ①1.3
- V8-318, 340, 360 (0.6) ②0.9

①For Power Brake Unit, Add (0.4) *0.5*
②For Air Injection Pump, Low Mount, Add (0.3) *0.4*

B6—COMPRESSION TEST

1969-75 Six (0.5) 0.6

1969-75 V8—
- Exc. Below (0.8) 0.8
- V8-440 (Hi-Perf.) (1.0) 1.3
- Hemi (1.2) 1.5

B7—IGNITION TIMING, SET

All Models (0.2) 0.3

B8—DISTRIBUTOR, R & R OR RENEW

1969-71 Exc (0.7) 0.9
- W/Electronic Ignition (0.6) 0.8

1972 (0.6) 0.8
1973-75 (0.5) 0.7

—NOTE—

For Cleaner Air Package, Add (0.3) *0.5*

B9—DISTRIBUTOR, OVERHAUL (UNIT OFF)

1969-75 (1.0) 1.4

B9A—DISTRIBUTOR ADJUST ON STROBOSCOPE (UNIT OFF)

All Models (0.4) 0.4

B10—DISTRIBUTOR CAP, RENEW

1969-75 (0.3) 0.3

B10A—DISTRBUTOR RELUCTOR, RENEW

1971-75 (0.3) 0.5

B10B—DIST PICK-UP PLATE & COIL ASSY, RENEW

Distributor removed

1971-75 (0.2) 0.2

B10C—ELECTRONIC IGNITION CONTROL UNIT, RENEW

1971-75 (0.3) 0.5

B11—IGNITION CABLE SET, RENEW

Time allowance covers installation of factory supplied sets ony.

1968-69 Six (0.4) ②0.5
1970-75 Six (0.6) 0.8

1968-69 V8—
- Exc. Below (0.6) ②0.8
- Hemi (0.8) ②1.0

1970-71 V8—
- Exc. Below (0.6) 0.8
- V8-383, 440 (0.8) ③1.1
- V8-426 Hemi (1.0) 1.3

1972-75 V8—
- Exc. Below (0.5) 0.7
- V8-383, 400, 440 (0.6) ③0.9

②For Air Cond., Add (0.5) *0.6*
③For Air Cond., Add (0.4) *0.5*

B12—VACUUM CONTROL UNIT, RENEW

Includes R & R distributor.

1969 (0.6) 0.9
1970-71 (0.8) 1.1
1972-75 (0.6) 0.9

B13—IGNITION COIL, RENEW

All Models (0.3) 0.3

B14—IGNITION SWITCH, RENEW

1966-69—
- Exc. Below (0.3) 0.5
- Fury (0.4) 0.7

1970—
- Exc. Below (0.6) 0.9
- All Models-W/Std. Column (1.4) 1.9

1971-75—
- Exc. Below (1.4) 1.9
- W/Telescopic Steer Column (0.4) 0.6
- W/Tilt Column (0.5) 0.8

B15—IGNITION COIL RESISTOR, RENEW

All Models (0.2) 0.3

DISTRIBUTOR ASS'Y:

PLYMOUTH:

Description	Part No.	Price
1969 Six—		
Synchro-Mesh	3656253	34.95
Auto. Trans	3656258	34.95
1969 V8-318	2875797	39.50
1969 V8-383 (2 Bar. Carb.)—		
Synchro-Mesh	2875743	44.20
Auto. Trans	2875748	44.20
1969 V8-383 (4 Bar. Carb.)—		
Synchro-Mesh	2875751	44.20
Auto. Trans	2875732	44.20
1969 V8-426	2875141	54.00
1969 V8-440—		
L/Hi-Perf	2875765	46.70
W/Hi-Perf.—		
Std. Trans	2875773	50.80
Auto. Trans	2875759	46.70
1970 Six—		
Synchro-Mesh	3656253	34.95
Auto. Trans	3656258	34.95
1970 V8-318—		
Synchro-Mesh	3438256	39.50
Auto. Trans	3656391	39.50
1970-71 V8-340 (W/Elect Ign)—		
Synchro-Mesh	3656153	44.95
Auto Trans	NOTSOLD	
1970 V8-383—		
2 Bar. Carb	3438232	44.20
4 Bar. Carb	3438434	44.20
1970 V8-426—		
Synchro-Mesh	2875988	60.40
Auto. Trans	2875990	56.98
1970 V8-440—		
Single Breaker—		
Exc. Below	3438221	46.70
Hi-Perf	3438224	46.70
Dual Breaker—		
Synchro-Mesh (Early)	3438316	60.40
Synchro-Mesh (Late)	3438355	55.80
Auto. Trans (Early)	2875983	60.40
Auto Trans (Late)	3438356	55.80
1971 Six (Exc Below)—		
Synchro-Mesh	3656253	34.95
Auto. Trans	3656258	34.95
1971 6-225 (W/Nox Exh Sys)—		
Synchro-Mesh	3438441	34.95
Auto Trans	3438443	34.95
1971 V8-318—		
Synchro-Mesh	3438256	39.50
Auto. Trans	3656391	39.50
W/Nox Exh System	3656276	39.50
1971 V8-340—		
Synchro-Mesh	3438530	63.80
Auto. Trans	3438520	42.15
1971 V8-360—		
Exc. Below	3656273	39.50
W/Nox Eht. Cont	3656276	39.50
1971 V8-383 (2 Bar. Carb.)—		
Exc. Below	3438535	44.20
W/Nox Eht. Cont	3438545	44.20
1971 V8-383 (4 Bar)	3438691	44.20
1971 V8-426—		
Synchro-Mesh	2875988	60.40
Auto. Trans	3438580	60.40
1971 V8-440—		
Exc. Below	3438560	46.70
4 Bar. Carb	3438695	46.70
3 Carbs	3438578	60.40
1972 6-225—		
L/Emission Cont.—		
Synchro-Mesh	3656253	34.95
Auto. Trans.	3656258	34.95
W/Emission Cont.—		
Synchro-Mesh	3656261	34.95
Auto. Trans.	3656267	34.95
1972 V8-318 (Exc Below)—		
L/Emission Cont.—		
Synchro-Mesh	3656273	39.50
Auto Trans	3656391	39.50
W/Emission Cont.	3656276	39.50
1972 V8-318 (W/Elect Ign)—		
Synchro-Mesh	3656430	43.01
Auto Trans	3656588	39.50
1972 V8-340	3656279	42.15
1972 V8-360—		
Exc. Below	3656273	39.50
Elect. Ignition	3656430	43.01
1972 V8-400—		
Elect Ignition	3656336	46.70
L/Emission Cont.—		
Satellite	3656339	46.70
Fury	3656333	46.70
1972 V8-440—		
4 Bar. Carb.—		
Synchro-Mesh	3656348	46.70
Auto Trans.—		
Exc. Below	3656342	46.70
Emission Cont.	3656348	46.70
3 Carbs.	3656354	46.70
Hi-Perf	3656351	46.70
1973-74 Six Exc	3755038	34.95
Auto Trans	3755043	34.95
1973 V8—		
318	3656764	39.50
340	3656772	42.15
360	3656781	46.70
400 (2 Bar)	3656792	46.70
400 (4 Bar), Fury	3656803	46.70
Exc Fury, Synchromesh	3755310	46.70
Exc Fury, Auto Tr	3656803	46.70
440	3755158	46.70
1974 V8-318	3656764	39.50
V8-360 Exc	3755487	45.60
Fury	3755476	46.70
V8-400, 2 Bar	3755682	46.70
4 Bar (L/Hi Perf)—		
L/Calif Emission	3755504	39.78
W/Calif Emission	3755687	
4 Bar (W/Hi Perf)—		
L/Calif Emission	3755513	46.70
W/Calif Emission	3755509	46.70
V8-440 Exc	3755519	46.70
Calif Emission	3755523	46.70
1975 Six, Exc	3874086	34.95
Catalytic Exh	3874083	34.95
1975 V8-318, Exc	3755473	33.64
Catalytic Exh	3874091	39.50
1975 V8-360—		
L/Hi-Perf, Exc	3874146	46.70
Catalytic Exh	3874116	45.60
W/Hi-Perf	3874202	
1975 V8-400, 2 Bar	3874102	46.70
4 Bar, Exc	3755682	46.70
Catalytic Exh	3874111	46.70
1975 V8-440—		
L/Hi-Perf, Exc	3874120	46.70
Catalytic Exh	3874174	46.70
W/Hi-Perf, Exc	3874120	46.70
Air Pump	3874174	46.70

VALIANT & BARRACUDA:

Description	Part No.	Price
1969 6-170—		
Std. Trans	2875814	33.85
Auto. Trans	2875856	33.85
1969 6-225—		
Std. Trans	3656253	34.95
Auto. Trans	3656258	34.95
1969 V8-273	2875791	36.05
1969 V8-318	2875797	39.50
1969 V8-340—		
Std. Trans	2875783	59.70
Auto. Trans	2875780	42.15
1969 V8-383—		
Std. Trans	2875718	50.90
Auto. Trans	2875847	50.80
1970 6-198 Exc	3438238	33.85
W/Auto Trans	3656258	34.95
1970 6-225—		
Synchro-Mesh	3656253	34.95
Auto. Trans	3656258	34.95
1970 V8-318—		
Synchro-Mesh	3438256	39.50
Auto. Trans	3656391	39.50
1970 V8-340 (Exc Below)—		
Synchro-Mesh	3438318	60.40
Auto. Trans	3438326	42.15
1970 V8-340 (Tri Carbs)—		
Synchro-Mesh	3438530	63.80
Auto Trans	3438532	63.80
1970-71 V8-340 (W/Elect Ign)—		
Synchro-Mesh	3656153	44.95
Auto Trans (Not Sold)		
1971 6-198—		
Exc. Below	3438510	33.85
W/Nox Eht. Cont	3438525	33.85
1971 6-225—		
Synchro-Mesh Exc	3656253	34.95
W/Nox Exh Sys	3438441	34.95
Auto. Trans	3656258	34.95
W/Nox Exh Sys	3438443	34.95
1971 V8-318—		
Synchro-Mesh	3438256	39.50
Auto. Trans	3656391	39.50
W/Nox Exh Sys	3656276	39.50
1971 V8-340 (Exc Below)—		
Synchro-Mesh	3438530	63.80
Auto. Trans	3438520	42.15
1971 V8-340 (Tri Carbs)—		
Synchro-Mesh	3438616	63.80
Auto Trans	3438618	63.80
1971 V8-383 (2 Bar. Carb.)—		
Exc. Below	3438535	44.20
W/Nox Eht. Cont	3438545	44.20
1971 V8-383 (4 Bar.)	3438691	44.20
1971 V8-426 (Exc Below)—		
Synchro-Mesh	2875988	60.40
Auto. Trans	3438580	60.40
1971 V8-440	3438578	60.40
1972 6-198—		
L/Emission Cont.	3656238	33.85
W/Emission Cont.	3656244	33.85
1972, 6-225—		
L/Emission Control—		
Synchro-Mesh	3656253	34.95
Auto Trans	3656258	34.95
W/Emission Control—		
Synchro-Mesh	3656261	34.95
Auto Trans	3656267	34.95
1972 V8-318 (L/Elect Ign)—		
Synchro-Mesh	3656273	39.50
Auto Trans	3656391	39.50
1972 V8-318 (W/Elect Ign)—		
Synchro-Mesh	3656430	43.01
Auto Trans	3656588	39.50
1972 V8-340 Exc	3656284	42.15
W/Electronic Ignition	3656279	42.15
1973-74, 6-198	3656861	33.85
1973-74, 6-225—		
Synchromesh Exc	3755038	34.95
Calif Emission	3755468	34.95
Automatic Trans Exc	3755043	34.95
Calif Emission	3755471	34.95
1973-74 V8-318	3656764	39.50
1973 V8-340	3656772	42.15
1974 V8-360	3755487	45.60
1975 Six, Exc	3874086	34.95
Catalytic Exh	3874083	34.95
Lean Burn Pkg	3874232	
1975 V8-318, Exc	3755473	33.64
Catalytic Exh	3874091	39.50
Lean Burn Pkg	3874239	
1975 V8-360, Exc	3874116	45.60
Hi-Perf, Exc	3874098	45.60
Catalytic Exh	3874202	

FIG 1-TUNE-UP & IGNITION

(For Parts Identification Only)

ELECTRONIC DISTRIBUTOR PARTS

Description	Part No.	Price
1972—		
Pick-Up	3656025	4.81
Pick-Up Plate	3656023	3.75
Reluctor	3656017	1.74
1973-75—		
Pick-Up & Plate Assy—		
6 Cyl	3656866	8.77
V8	3656738	8.77
Reluctor, 6 Cyl	3656862	1.74
V8	3656017	1.74

1—IGNITION POINT SET:

PLYMOUTH:

Description	Part No.	Price
1966-72 Six	2098244	3.20
1966-72 V8-318	2098244	3.20
1966-69 V8-273	2098244	3.20
1968-71 V8-383	2098244	3.20
1969-71 V8-426	2421173	2.66
1969-71 V8-440 Exc	2098244	3.20
W/Dual Breaker	2421173	2.66
1971 V8-340 Exc	2421175	2.66
Auto Trans	2098244	3.20
1971-72 V8-360	2098244	3.20
1972 V8-400, 440	2098244	3.20

VALIANT & BARRACUDA:

Description	Part No.	Price
1969-72 (Exc. Below)	2098244	3.20
1969-71 V8-426, 440	2421173	2.66
1970-71 V8-340	2421175	2.66

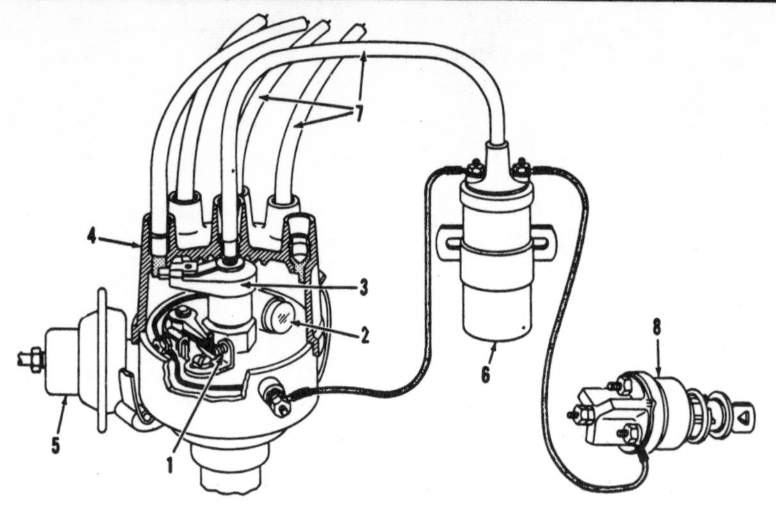

2—CONDENSER:

PLYMOUTH:

Application	Part No.	Price
1966-71 Six Exc	2098058	1.56
W/Nox Exh Sys	3420600	1.56
1966-71 V8-318	3420600	1.56
1966-71 V8-383	3420600	1.56
1967-69 V8-426	1818757	1.56
1968-69 V8-440—		
L/Hi-Perf	2098058	1.56
W/Hi-Perf	1818757	1.56
1970-71 V8-426,440	3420600	1.56
1971 V8-340,360	3420600	1.56
1972	3420600	1.56

VALIANT & BARRACUDA:

Application	Part No.	Price
1969-70 Six Except	2098058	1.56
Synchro-Mesh (6-198)	3420600	1.56
1969 V8	2098058	1.56
1970-71 V8	3420600	1.56
1971 Six Except	3420600	1.56
6-225 (L/Nox Exh)	2098058	1.56
1972	3420600	1.56

3—ROTOR:

Application	Part No.	Price
1968-71 Exc	1838516	1.18
V8-340 (Std Trans)	1658535	1.15
V8-426	1658535	1.15
V8-440 (Hi Perf)	1658535	1.15
1972-74	1838516	1.18

4—DISTRIBUTOR CAP:

PLYMOUTH:

Application	Part No.	Price
1968-71 V8-318 & 383	2444507	4.44
1968-71 V8-426	2585000	4.21
1969-75 Six	2642986	3.81
1968-71 V8-440—		
L/Hi-Perf	2444507	4.44
W/Hi-Perf	2585000	4.21
1971 V8-340 Exc	2585000	4.21
Auto Trans	2444507	4.44
1971 V8-360	2444507	4.44
1972-75 V8	2444507	4.44

VALIANT & BARRACUDA:

Application	Part No.	Price
1969-75 Six	2642986	3.81
1968-71 V8—		
Exc. Below	2444507	4.44
V8-340 (Synchro-Mesh)	2585000	4.21
W/Tri Carbs	2585000	4.21
W/Elect Ign	2444507	4.44
V8-426 (L/Elect Ign)	2585000	4.21
V8-440	2585000	4.21
1972-75 V8	2444507	4.44

5—VACUUM CONTROL UNIT:

PLYMOUTH:

Application	Part No.	Price
1968-69 V8-426	2808897	3.40
1969-72 Six—		
Synchro-Mesh	2875818	4.25
Auto. Trans	2875825	4.25
1969 V8-318	2875794	4.25
1969 V8-383—		
2 Bar. Carb	2875735	4.25
4 Bar. Carb	2875728	4.25
1969 V8-440—		
L/Hi-Perf	2875761	4.25
W/Hi-Perf	2875754	4.25
1970-71 V8-318—		
Synchro-Mesh	2875794	4.25
Auto. Trans	3438229	4.25
W/Nox Exh System	3438424	4.25
1970-71 V8-340—		
Synchro-Mesh	3514265	6.20
Auto. Trans	3438229	4.25
1970-71 V8-383 Exc	3579239	25.47
4 Bar Carb	3579240	25.47
1970-71 V8-426 Exc	3514279	7.10
Auto Trans	2808897	3.40
1970 V8-440 (1 Carb.)—		
Exc. Hi-Perf	3514329	25.47
Hi-Perf	3514330	25.47
1970 V8-440 (3 Carbs.)—		
Synchro-Mesh	3420919	6.75
Auto. Trans	3420919	6.75
1971 V8-360	3438424	4.25
1971 V8-440 Exc	3579241	25.47
4 Bar Carb	3514330	25.47
3 Carb	3514332	25.47
1972 V8-318 (L/Elect Ign)—		
Synchro-Mesh	3438424	4.25
Auto. Trans.	3438229	4.25
1972 V8-318 (W/Elect Ign)—		
Synchro-Mesh	3656434	4.25
Auto Trans	3656586	4.25
1972 V8-340	3656066	4.25
1972 V8-360—		
Exc. Below	3438424	4.25
Elect. Ignition	3656434	4.25
1972 V8-400—		
Elect. Ignition	3656304	24.00
L/Emission Cont.—		
Satellite	3656310	4.25
Fury	3656306	4.25
1972 V8-440—		
Exc. Below	3656304	24.00
Hi-Perf.	3656303	24.00
Auto. (L/Emission)	3656310	4.25
1973-74 Six Exc	3755041	4.25
Auto Trans	3755036	4.25
1973 V8-318,360	3656766	4.25
1973 V8-340	3656066	4.25
1973 V8-400 Exc	3656310	4.25
4 Bar (Manual)	3656304	24.00
1973 V8-440	3656310	4.25
1974 V8-318	3656766	4.25
V8-360 Exc	3755491	4.25
Fury	3755474	4.25
V8-400 Exc	3755505	4.25
Calif Emission	3755511	24.00
V8-440	3755505	4.25

VALIANT & BARRACUDA:

Application	Part No.	Price
1969 6-170	2875809	4.25
1969-71 6-225—		
Std. Trans	2875818	4.25
Auto. Trans	2875825	4.25
1969 V8-273	2875786	4.25
1969 V8-318	2875794	4.25
1969 V8-340	2875776	4.25
1969 V8-383	2808897	3.40
1970-71, 6-198	2875825	4.25
1970-71 V8-318 (Exc Below)—		
Synchro-Mesh	2875794	4.25
Auto Trans	3438229	4.25
1970-71 V8-340—		
L/Elect Ignition—		
Synchro-Mesh	3514265	6.20
Auto Trans Exc	3438339	4.25
W/Tri Carb	3620704	6.20
W/Elect Ignition—		
Synchro-Mesh	3656156	4.25
Auto Trans	3656066	4.25
1971 V8-318 (W/Nox Exh)	3438424	4.25
1971 V8-383, 2 Bar	3579239	25.47
4 Bar	3579240	25.47
1971 V8-426 (L/Elect Ign)—		
Synchro-Mesh	3514279	7.10
Auto Trans	2808897	3.40
1971 V8-440	3514332	25.47
1972 6-198	3438514	4.25
1972 6-225		
Synchro-Mesh	2875818	4.25
Auto Trans	2875825	4.25
1972 V8-318 (L/Elect Ign)—		
Synchro-Mesh	3438424	4.25
Auto Trans.	3438229	4.25
1972 V8-318 (W/Elect Ign)—		
Synchro-Mesh	3656434	4.25
Auto Trans	3656586	4.25
1972 V8-340	3656066	4.25
1973-74, 6-198	3755036	4.25
1973-74, 6-225 Exc	3755041	4.25
Auto Trans	3755036	4.25
1973-74 V8-318	3656766	4.25
1973 V8-340	3656066	4.25
1974 V8-360	3755474	4.25

6—IGNITION COIL:

Application	Part No.	Price
1968-74	2495531	13.28

IGNITION COIL RESISTOR:

Application	Part No.	Price
1967-69	2275590	2.49
1970-72—		
Exc. Below	2275590	2.49
Elect Ignition	3656199	2.24
1973-74	3656199	2.24

7—IGNITION CABLE SET:

PLYMOUTH:

Application	Part No.	Price
1967-72 Six	2495510	10.30
1969 V8 Belvedere—		
V8-318	3004192	11.64
V8-383, 440	3420917	18.89
V8-426	3420881	27.49
1969 V8 Fury—		
Exc. Below	3420915	18.52
V8-318	3004192	11.64
1970 V8 Belvedere—		
Exc. Below	3420917	18.89
V8-318	3004192	11.64
V8-426	3420881	27.49
1970 Fury V8—		
Exc. Below	3004192	11.64
V8-383, 440	3420915	18.52
1971-72 V8 Satellite—		
Exc. Below	3004192	11.64
V8-318, 340 (Elect)	3620886	17.73
V8-383, 400, 440 Exc	3420917	18.89
W/Elect Ign	3620887	23.44
V8-426	3420881	27.49
1971-72 V8 Fury—		
Exc. Below	3004192	11.64
V8-318, 360 (Elect)	3620886	17.73
V8-383, 400, 440 Exc	3420915	18.52
W/Elect Ign	3620888	24.07
1973 Six	3744971	10.30
V8 Exc	3744972	14.32
400 & 440	3744973	27.12
1974 Six	3780744	10.30
V8 Exc	3780743	14.32
400 & 440	3744973	27.12

VALIANT & BARRACUDA:

Application	Part No.	Price
1967-72 Six	2495510	10.30
1969 V8—		
Valiant	3004192	11.64
Barracuda—		
Exc. V8-383	3004192	11.64
V8-383	3420915	18.52
1970-71 V8—		
Exc. Below	3004192	11.64
V8-340 Valiant (1971)	3579221	16.23
V8-340 (W/3 Carbs)	3579221	16.23
V8-383, 440	3420917	18.89
V8-426	3420881	27.49
1972 V8 Exc	3004192	11.64
W/Electronic Ignition	3620886	17.73
1973-74, See Plymouth—		

8—IGNITION SWITCH:

Application	Part No.	Price
1969	2864463	5.36
1970-74 Exc	2947486	6.34
W/Tilt Wheel Exc	2947719	8.96
Satellite (71-72)	3488398	10.97
1975, Exc	3746938	6.34
Valiant	3746936	6.34
Tilt Wheel	2947719	8.96

Time — Fuel System & Intake Manifold (Group C) — Time

OPERATION INDEX

C1—CARBURETOR, R & R OR RENEW

1968-69 Six (0.5) 0.7
1970-75 Six (0.7) 0.9
1968-69 V8—
  2 Barrel (0.5) 0.8
  One 4 Bar. (0.6) 1.0
  Two 4 Bar. (1.0) 1.4
  Tri-Carb Center (0.9) 1.2
  Tri-Carb Front Or Rear (0.7) 0.9
1970-75 V8—
  2 Barrel (0.7) 0.9
  One 4 Bar. (0.7) 1.0
  Two 4 Bars. (1.0) 1.4
  Tri-Carb Center (0.9) 1.2
  Tri-Carb Front Or Rear (0.7) 0.9
  Thermo-Quad (1.0) 1.3

C2—CARBURETOR, R & R & OVERHAUL

1966-71—
  One Bar (2.0) 2.4
  Two Bar.—
    Exc. Below (2.0) 2.4
    Rochester (1.4) 1.7
  Holley Tri-Carb—
    Center (2.1) 2.6
    Front Or Rear (1.9) 2.3
    All Three (5.5) 6.8
  Four Bar.—
    Exc. Below (3.0) 3.6
    Thermo Quad (2.4) 2.9
  Two Four Bar. (4.5) 5.5
1972—
  One Bar.—
    Exc. Below (1.5) 1.8
    Holley (1.4) 1.6
  Two Bar.—
    Exc. Below (1.4) 1.6
    Carter (1.6) 1.8
    Holley (1.7) 2.0
  Holley Tri-Carb—
    Center (2.1) 2.6
    Front Or Rear (1.9) 2.3
    All Three (5.5) 6.8
  Four Bar.—
    Exc. Below (1.7) 2.0
    Holley (2.2) 2.7
    Thermo-Quad (2.4) 2.9
    Two Four Bar. (4.5) 5.5
1973-75—
  1 Barrel (1.4) 1.6
  2 Barrel (1.7) 2.0
  4 Barrel (2.4) 3.0

C2A—ACCELERATOR PUMP, RENEW

1969-75—
  Exc. 4 Barrel (0.6) 0.8
  4 Barrel—
    Exc. Below (0.8) 1.1
    Thermo-Quad. (1.0) 1.4

—NOTE—

Does Not Include R & R Carburetor.

C2B—NEEDLE & SEAT, RENEW

1966-69—
  Exc. Below (0.4) 0.6
  4 Barrel—
    Exc. Below (0.4) 0.6
    Thermo-Quad. (1.1) 1.5
  Tri-Carb. (One) (0.6) 0.8
  Tri-Carb.-Three (1.0) 1.5
1970-75—
  One Bar (0.4) 0.6
  Two Bar—
    Exc. Below (0.4) 0.6
    Holley (0.6) 0.8
  Four Bar—
    Exc. Below (0.8) ①②1.1
    Thermo-Quad (1.1) 1.4
  Holley Tri-Carb.—
    One (0.6) 0.8
    Three (1.0) 1.5

—NOTE—

Does Not Include R & R Carburetor.
①For Holley Secondary, Add (0.2) *0.3*
②For Holley Primary & Secondary, Add (0.4) *0.6*

C3—AUTO. CHOKE THERMOSTAT, RENEW

1969-75—
  Exc. Below (0.3) 0.4
  4 Barrel (0.4) 0.6

C3A—AUTO. CHOKE, OVERHAUL

1969-75—
  Exc. Below (0.5) 0.6
  4 Barrel (0.7) 1.0

C3B—AUTO. CHOKE VACUUM DIAPHRAGM, RENEW

1966-69—
  Exc. Below (0.3) 0.4
  4 Barrel (0.4) 0.5
1970-75—
  Carter, Holley & Rochester—
    Exc. Below (0.3) 0.4
    Holley-Tri-Carb (0.4) 0.7
    Carter-Thermo-Quad (0.9) 1.3

C4—DASHPOT, RENEW

1966-71—
  Exc. Below (0.3) 0.3
  4 Barrel (0.4) 0.4
1972-75 (0.4) 0.5

C5—FUEL PUMP, R & R OR RENEW

1969-75 Six (0.3) 0.4
1969-75 V8—
  Exc. Below (0.5) 0.7
  Hemi (0.6) 0.8

C5A—FUEL PUMP PUSH ROD, RENEW

1969-75 V8—
  Exc. Below (0.5) 0.7
  Hemi (0.6) 0.9

C6—FUEL TANK, R & R OR RENEW

1969-72 Exc (1.1) 1.4
  Valiant (0.8) 1.2
  Barracuda, 70 (1.4) 1.8
  Barracuda, 71-72 (1.6) 2.0
  Sta Wgn, 70 (1.2) 1.5
  Sta Wgn, 71-72 (1.5) 1.9
1973-75 Exc (0.8) 1.2
  Barracuda (1.6) 2.0
  Sta Wgn (1.5) 1.9

C7—FUEL SYSTEM, CLEAN

Includes blow out lines & clean or renew fuel line filter after tank is removed.
1969-75 (0.6) 0.8

C8—INTAKE MANIFOLD GASKETS, RENEW (V8)

1969-70—
  Exc. Below (1.3) 1.5
  V8-318 (1.5) 1.8
  V8-340 (1.7) 2.0
  V8-440 (1.6) 1.9
  Hemi (2.0) 2.6
1971-75—
  Exc. Below (1.6) 1.9
  V8-318 (1.5) 1.8
  V8-340, 360 (1.7) 2.0
  Hemi (2.0) 2.6

—NOTE—

For V8-426 With Two Carbs., Add (0.3) *0.5*
For V8-273, 318, 340, 360 With Air Cond., Add (0.4) *0.6*

C8A—MANIFOLD GASKETS, RENEW (SIX CYL.)

1969-75 (2.0) 2.3

Parts — Fuel System & Intake Manifold — Parts

PARTS INDEX

1—CARBURETOR ASS'Y (CARTER):

PLYMOUTH:

	Part No.	Price
1969 V8-318—		
Std. Trans	2946568	45.39
Auto. Trans	2946571	41.38
1969 V8-383 (2 Bar. Carb.)—		
Std. Trans	3549532	48.56
Auto. Trans	3549532	48.56
1969 V8-383 (4 Bar. Carb.)—		
Std. Trans	2946577	76.96
Auto. Trans	2946591	82.57
1969 V8-440—		
Std. Trans	2946578	76.96
Auto. Trans	2946592	84.30
1969 V8-426—		
Front	2946584	58.55
Rear—		
Std. Trans	2946588	66.46
Auto. Trans	2899034	66.35
1970 V8-318—		
Synchro-Mesh—		
L/Fuel Emission	3418515	36.47
W/Fuel Emission	3418517	43.10
Auto. Trans.—		
L/Fuel Emission Exc	3418516	45.94
W/Air Cond	3462834	35.55
W/Fuel Emission	3418518	45.61
1970 V8-383 (2 Bar. Carb.)—		
Synchro-Mesh—		
L/Fuel Emission	3418526	37.61
W/Fuel Emission	3418528	43.25
Auto. Trans.	3418529	43.66
1970 V8-383 (4 Bar. Carb.)—		
L/Fuel Emission—		
L/Air Cond	3418541	83.53
W/Air Cond	3418541	83.53
W/Fuel Emission	3418541	83.53
1970 V8-426—		
Front	3512840	64.41
Rear—		
Synchro-Mesh	3418523	75.28
Auto. Trans	3418524	75.28
1970 V8-440 (Synchro-Mesh)—		
L/Fuel Emission	3418553	75.84
W/Fuel Emission	3418555	77.16
1970 V8-440 (Auto. Trans.)—		
L/Fuel Emission—		
L/Air Cond	3418554	78.45
W/Air Cond	3418558	79.80
W/Fuel Emission	3418558	79.80
1971 V8-318—		
Synchro-Mesh	3512816	40.14
Auto. Trans	3512817	47.12
1971 V8-340 Exc	3614122	89.14
Auto Trans.	3614123	86.24
1971 V8-383 (2 Bar)—		
Synchro-Mesh	3549568	
Auto. Trans	3512825	50.51
1971 V8-383 (4 Bar)	3512844	82.75
1971 V8-426—		
Front	3512840	64.41
Rear—		

Synchro-Mesh	3512838	81.40
Auto. Trans	3512839	81.40
1971 V8-440—		
Synchro-Mesh	3512832	83.33
Auto. Trans	3512833	88.18
1972 V8-318—		
L/Fuel Emission—		
Synchro-Mesh	3614107	43.20
Auto Trans	3614108	43.66
W/Fuel Emission—		
Synchro-Mesh	3614109	44.95
Auto. Trans.	3614110	43.73
1972 V8-340—		
Synchro-Mesh	3614122	89.14
Auto Trans	3614123	86.24
1972 V8-400—		
Synchro-Mesh—		
Exc. Below	3614138	86.24
W/Air Pump	3614172	87.02
Auto Trans.—		
Exc. Below	3614139	86.22
W/Air Pump	3614173	86.89
1973 V8-318—		
L/Air Pump Exc	3698325	45.52
Auto Trans	3698326	43.50
W/Air Pump Exc	3698337	45.52
Auto Trans	3698338	38.00
1973 V8-340—		
L/Air Pump Exc	3698327	95.93
Auto Trans	3698328	95.93
W/Air Pump Exc	3698339	95.93
Auto Trans	3698340	95.93
1973 V8-400—		
L/Air Pump Exc	3698332	95.93
Auto Trans	3698333	95.93
W/Air Pump Exc	3698342	95.93
Auto Trans	3698343	95.93
1973 V8-440—		
Exc High Perf—		
L/Air Pump	3698334	95.93
W/Air Pump	3698319	95.93
High Perf—		
L/Air Pump	3698336	95.93
W/Air Pump	3698329	95.93
1974 V8-318 Synchro-Mesh—		
Exc Below	3751427	58.22
Calif Emission	3751429	44.07
1974 V8-318 Auto Trans—		
Exc Below	3751428	56.04
Calif Emission	3751430	55.35
1974 V8-360 Fury	3751451	106.12
Satellite (Snychro-Mesh)—		
Exc Below	3751433	106.12
Calif Emission	3751435	91.41
Satellite (Auto Trans)—		
Exc Below	3751434	106.12
Calif Emission	3751436	106.12
1974 V8-400—		
Synchro-Mesh	3751439	106.12
Auto Tr (Less H/Perf)—		
Exc Below	3751452	85.31
Calif Emission	3751453	85.31
Auto Tr (With H/Perf)—		
Exc Below	3751440	106.12
Calif Emission	3751442	85.31
1974 V8-440 (L/Hi Perf)—		
Exc Below	3751443	106.12
Calif Emission	3751444	106.12
1974 V8-440 (W/Hi Perf)—		
Exc Below	3751'45	85.31
Calif Emission	3751446	85.31
1975 V8-318—		
Std Trans	3830521	56.04
Auto Trans, Exc	3830565	55.35
Calif Emission	3830524	55.35
Air Pump	3830522	55.35
1975 V8-360	3830531	106.12
V8-400, Exc	3830554	106.10
Calif Emission	3830535	106.12
V8-440 (L/Hi-Perf)—		
Exc Below	3830536	106.12
Calif Emission	3830537	106.12
V8-440 (W/Hi-Perf)—		
Exc Below	3830538	106.12
Calif Emission	3830539	106.12

VALIANT & BARRACUDA

1969 6-170—		
Std. Trans	2946552	30.75
Auto. Trans	2946553	30.15
1969 V8-273—		
Std. Trans	2946567	39.78
Auto. Trans	2946570	44.20
1969 V8-318—		
Std. Trans	2946568	45.39
Auto. Trans	2946571	41.38
1969 V8-340—		
Std. Trans	2946576	71.28
Auto. Trans	2946590	83.53
1969 V8-383—		
Std. Trans	2946577	76.96
Auto. Trans	2946591	82.57
1970 6-198 (Synchro-Mesh)—		
L/Fuel Emission	3418503	28.97
W/Fuel Emission	3418505	34.36
1970 6-198 (Auto. Trans.)—		
L/Fuel Emission	3418504	33.59
W/Fuel Emission	3418506	32.43
1970 V8-318—		
Synchro-Mesh—		
L/Fuel Emission	3418515	36.47
W/Fuel Emission	3418517	43.10
Auto. Trans.—		
L/Fuel Emission Exc	3418516	45.94
W/Air Cond	3462834	35.55
W/Fuel Emission	3418518	45.61
1970 V8-340 (Synchro-Mesh)—		
L/Fuel Emission	3462968	74.21
W/Fuel Emission	3462971	79.76
1970 V8-340 (Auto. Trans.)—		
L/Fuel Emission—		
L/Air Cond	3462969	74.21
W/Air Cond	3462970	74.21
W/Fuel Emission	3462972	79.76
1970 V8-383 (2 Bar)	3418529	43.66
1970 V8-383 (4 Bar. Carb.)—		
L/Fuel Emission—		
L/Air Cond	3418541	83.53
W/Air Cond	3418541	83.53
W/Fuel Emission	3418541	83.53
1970 V8-426—		
Front	3512840	64.41
Rear—		
Synchro-Mesh	3418523	75.28
Auto. Trans	3418524	75.28
1970 V8-440 (Synchro-Mesh)—		
L/Fuel Emission	3418553	75.84
W/Fuel Emission	3418555	77.16
1970 V8-440 (Auto. Trans.)—		
L/Fuel Emission—		
L/Air Cond	3418554	78.45
W/Air Cond	3418558	79.80
W/Fuel Emission	3418558	79.80
1971 6-198—		
Synchro-Mesh	3512803	36.43
Auto. Trans	3512804	36.90
1971 V8-318—		
Synchro-Mesh	3512816	40.14
Auto. Trans	3512817	47.12
1971 V8-340—		
Synchro-Mesh	3614122	89.14
Auto. Trans	3614123	86.24
1971 V8-383	3512825	50.51
1971 V8-426—		
Front	3512840	64.41
Rear—		
Synchro-Mesh	3512838	81.40
Auto. Trans	3512839	81.40
1971 V8-440—		
Synchro-Mesh	3512832	83.33
Auto. Trans	3512833	88.18
1972 V8-318—		
L/Fuel Emission—		
Synchro-Mesh	3614107	43.20
Auto. Trans.	3614108	43.66
W/Fuel Emission—		
Synchro-Mesh	3614109	44.95
Auto. Trans	3614110	43.73
1972 V8-340—		
Synchro-Mesh	3614122	89.14
Auto Trans	3614123	86.24
1973 V8-318—		
L/Air Pump Exc	3698325	45.52
Auto Trans	3698326	43.50
W/Air Pump Exc	3698337	45.52
Auto Trans	3698338	38.00
1973 V8-340—		
L/Air Pump Exc	3698327	95.93
Auto Trans	3698328	95.93
W/Air Pump Exc	3698339	95.93
Auto Trans	3698340	95.93
1974 V8-318 Synchromesh—		
Exc Below	3751427	58.22
Calif Emission	3751429	44.07
1974 V8-318 Auto Trans—		
Exc Below	3751428	56.04
Calif Emission	3751430	55.35
1974 V8-360 Synchromesh—		
Exc Below	3751433	106.12
Calif Emission	3751435	91.41
1974 V8-360 Auto Trans—		
Exc Below	3751434	106.12
Calif Emission	3751436	106.12
1975 V8-318—		
Std Trans	3830521	56.04
Auto Trans, Exc	3830565	55.35
Calif Emission	3830524	55.35
Air Pump	3830522	55.35
1975 V8-360, Exc	3830529	106.12
Calif Emission	3830531	106.12

2—CARBURETOR ASS'Y (HOLLEY):

PLYMOUTH:

1969 Six—		
Std. Trans	2946555	36.50
Auto. Trans	2946557	36.50
1969 V8-440	2946582	103.80
1970 6-225 (L/Fuel Emission)—		
Std. Trans	3418511	50.97
Auto. Trans	3418512	39.47
1970 6-225 (W/Fuel Emission)—		
Std. Trans	3418513	52.43
Auto. Trans	3418514	55.57
1970 V8-383 (2 Bar. Carb.)—		
Synchro-Mesh—		
L/Fuel Emission	3418527	37.55
W/Fuel Emission	3418528	43.25
Auto. Trans	3418531	75.52
1970 V8-383 (4 Bar. Carb.)—		
Synchro-Mesh—		
L/Fuel Emission	3418536	127.58
W/Fuel Emission	3418537	121.80
Auto. Trans.—		
L/Fuel Emission—		
L/Air Cond	3418542	117.36
W/Air Cond	3418562	125.80
W/Fuel Emission	3418543	119.80
1970 V8-440 (2 Bar. Carb.)—		
Front—		
L/Fuel Emission	3462845	55.19
W/Fuel Emission	3418544	55.19
Center (Synchro-Mesh)—		
L/Fuel Emission	3418547	75.23
W/Fuel Emission	3418549	79.74
Center (Auto. Trans.)—		
L/Fuel Emission	3418548	79.74
W/Fuel Emission	3418550	88.55
Rear—		
L/Fuel Emission	3462846	55.19
W/Fuel Emission	3462373	55.19
1970 V8-440 (4 Bar. Carb.)—		
L/Fuel Emission	3418551	136.02
W/Fuel Emission	3418552	125.92
1971 6-225—		
Synchro-Mesh	3512805	47.94
Auto. Trans	3512807	50.82
1971 V8-360 Exc	3549566	
Auto Trans	3512823	76.77
1971 V8-383 (L/Fresh Air Pkg)—		
Synchro-Mesh	3549994	126.50
Auto. Trans	3512830	126.50
1971 V8-383 (W/Fresh Air Pkg)—		
Synchro-Mesh	3549995	119.29
Auto. Trans	3512842	126.50
1971 V8-440—		
Front	3512836	51.19
Center—		
Synchro-Mesh	3512834	94.61
Auto. Trans	3512835	72.78
Rear	3512837	48.30
1972 6-225—		
L/Air Pump—		
Synchro-Mesh	3614162	51.36
Auto. Trans	3614163	50.29
W/Air Pump—		
Synchro-Mesh	3614113	50.29
Auto Trans	3614114	50.90
1972 V8-360—		
L/Fuel Emission—		
Synchro-Mesh	3614130	83.54
Auto. Trans	3614131	75.58
W/Fuel Emission—		
Synchro-Mesh	3683837	85.99
Auto Trans	3683838	85.99
1972 V8-400—		
L/Fuel Emission	3671748	82.88
W/Fuel Emission	3671750	82.88
1972 V8-440 (Synchro-Mesh)—		
Satellite Exc	3621387	125.82
W/Fresh Air	3621389	125.82
W/Air Pump Exc	3621393	125.82
W/Fresh Air, Not Sold—		
1972 V8-440 (Auto Trans)—		
W/Air Pump	3621394	125.82
W/Fresh Air Exc	3621390	125.82
W/Air Pump, Not Sold—		
1973, 6-225—		
L/Air Pump Exc	3698346	61.86
Auto Trans	3698347	63.90
W/Air Pump Exc	3698348	61.86
Auto Trans	3698349	63.90
1973 V8-360 Exc	3698330	85.68
W/Air Pump	3698318	73.00
1973 V8-400 Exc	3698331	85.99
W/Air Pump	3698341	85.99
1974 6-225 Synchromesh—		
Exc Below	3751423	55.57
Calif Emission	3751425	55.57
1974 6-225 Auto Trans—		
Exc Below	3751424	54.25
Calif Emission	3751426	55.57

Application	Part No.	Price
1974 V8-360	3751431	78.93
400	3751437	71.00
1975 Six, Exc	3830517	55.57
Auto Trans	3830518	55.57
1975 V8-360, Exc	3879154	79.64
Code R-7226-A	3830563	78.95
1975 V8-400	3879155	76.76
VALIANT & BARRACUDA		
1969 Six—		
Std. Trans	2946554	36.50
Auto. Trans	2946556	36.50
1970 6-225 (L/Fuel Emission)—		
Std. Trans	3418511	50.97
Auto. Trans	3418512	39.47
1970 6-225 (W/Fuel Emission)—		
Std. Trans	3418513	52.43
Auto. Trans	3418514	55.57
1970 V8-340—		
Front, Not Sold—		
Center Exc	3577182	109.24
Auto Trans	3577183	109.24
Rear	3577185	65.03
1970 V8-383 (2 Bar. Carb.)—		
Synchro-Mesh	3418527	37.55
Auto. Trans	3418531	75.52
1970 V8-383 (4 Bar. Carb.)—		
Synchro-Mesh—		
L/Fuel Emission	3418536	127.58
W/Fuel Emission	3418537	121.80
Auto. Trans.—		
L/Fuel Emission—		
L/Air Cond	3418542	117.36
W/Air Cond	3418562	125.80
W/Fuel Emission	3418543	119.80
1970 V8-440 (2 Bar. Carb.)—		
Front—		
L/Fuel Emission	3462845	55.19
W/Fuel Emission	3418544	55.19
Center (Synchro-Mesh)—		
L/Fuel Emission	3418547	75.23
W/Fuel Emission	3418549	79.74
Center (Auto. Trans.)—		
L/Fuel Emission	3418548	79.74
W/Fuel Emission	3418550	88.55
Rear—		
L/Fuel Emission	3462846	55.19
W/Fuel Emission	3462373	55.19
1971 6-225—		
Synchro-Mesh	3512805	47.94
Auto. Trans	3512807	50.82
1971 V8-340 (Tri-Carb.)—		
Front	3577185	65.03
Center—		
Synchro-Mesh	3577182	109.24
Auto. Trans	3577183	109.24
Rear	3577185	65.03
1971 V8-383 (L/Fresh Air Pkg)—		
Synchro-Mesh	3549994	126.50
Auto. Trans	3512830	126.50
1971 V8-383 (W/Fresh Air Pkg)—		
Synchro-Mesh	3549995	119.29
Auto. Trans	3512842	126.50
1971 V8-440—		
Front	3512836	51.19
Center—		
Synchro-Mesh	3512834	94.61
Auto. Trans	3512835	72.78
Rear	3512837	48.30
1972 6-198—		
L/Fuel Emission—		
Synchro-Mesh	3671743	52.48
Auto. Trans.	3671744	49.78
W/Fuel Emission—		
Synchro-Mesh	3671745	49.78
Auto Trans	3671746	50.34
1972 6-225 (L/Air Pump)—		
Synchro-Mesh	3614162	51.36
Auto. Trans.	3614163	50.29
1972 6-225 (W/Air Pump)—		
Synchro-Mesh	3614113	50.29
Auto. Trans	3614114	50.90
1973, 6-198 Exc	3698320	64.82
Auto Trans	3698321	60.95
1973, 6-225—		
L/Air Pump Exc	3698346	61.86
Auto Trans	3698347	63.90
W/Air Pump Exc	3698348	61.86
Auto Trans.	3698349	63.90
1974, 6-198 Exc	3751421	38.95
Auto Trans	3751422	36.03
1974, 6-225 Synchromesh—		
Exc Below	3751423	55.57
Calif Emission	3751425	55.57
1974, 6-225 Auto Trans—		
Exc Below	3751424	54.25
Calif Emission	3751426	55.57
1975 Six, Std Trans—		
Exc Below	3830517	55.57
Calif Emission	3830519	55.57
1975 Six, Auto Trans—		
Exc Below	3830518	55.57
Calif Emission	3830520	55.57

3—CARBURETOR ZIP KIT (CARTER):

Application	Part No.	Price
PLYMOUTH:		
1969 V8-318	3621260	7.45
1969 V8-383—		
2 Bar. Carb	3621286	7.21
4 Bar. Carb	3621400	9.45
1969 V8-426	3621260	7.45
1969 V8-440	3621400	9.45
1970 V8-318—		
L/Fuel Emission	3514466	7.51
W/Fuel Emission	3514467	6.94
1970 V8-383—		
2 Bar. Carb Exc	3621286	7.21
L/Fuel Emission	3621286	7.21
4 Bar. Carb	3621400	9.45
1970-71 V8-426	3419503	8.27
1970 V8-440 Exc	3621400	9.45
W/Air Cond	3621400	9.45
1971-72 V8-318	3514467	6.94
1971 V8-340	3621225	10.27
1971 V8-383 (2 Bar Carb)	3621286	7.21
Synchro-Mesh 4 Bar Carb	3621224	10.50
1971 V8-440	3621224	10.50
1972 V8 (Exc. V8-318)	3683908	10.27
1973-74 V8 Exc	3744758	9.62
318 (1973)	3744794	7.03
318 (1974)	3837489	7.03
VALIANT & BARRACUDA:		
1969 6-170	3621401	5.51
1969 V8-273	3621260	7.45
1969 V8-318	3621260	7.45
1969 V8-340	3621400	9.45
1969 V8-383	3621400	9.45
1970 V8-318 Exc	3514466	7.51
W/Fuel Emission	3514467	6.94
1970 V8-340	3621400	9.45
1970 6-198	3621401	5.51
1971 V8-383, 2 Bar	3621286	7.21
4 Bar	3621400	9.45
1970-71 V8-426	3419503	8.27
1970 V8-440	3621400	9.45
1971, 6-225	2933043	6.34
1971, 6-198	3621401	5.51
1971, V8-383	3621286	7.21
1971, V8-440	3621224	10.50
1971-72 V8-318	3514467	6.94
1971 V8-340	3621225	10.27
1972 V8-340	3683908	10.27
1973-74 V8 Exc	3744758	9.62
318 (1973)	3744794	7.03
318 (1974)	3837489	7.03

4—CARBURETOR MINOR REPAIR KIT (HOLLEY):

Application	Part No.	Price
1969 Six	3683923	6.45
1969 V8-440 & 383	3549402	11.09
1970 Six Exc	3481677	4.95
W/Fuel Emission	3481670	6.02
1970-71 V8-340 Exc.	3514651	5.33
Center	3514695	7.78
1970 V8-383 (2 Bar)—		
Exc Below	3514756	9.05
Std Trans W/Fuel Emiss	3514711	9.45
1970 V8-383 (4 Bar)—		
L/Fuel Emission Exc	3514816	9.47
W/Air Cond	3514819	9.47
W/Fuel Emission	3514824	9.47
1970 V8-440 (2 Bar)—		
Front & Rear	3514651	5.33
Center Exc	3514695	7.78
W/Fuel Emission	3514695	7.78
1970 V8-440 (4 Bar)—		
L/Fuel Emission	3683935	14.25
W/Fuel Emission	3683935	14.25
1971, 6-225	3481670	6.02
1971 V8-360	3514711	9.45
1971 V8-383	3514824	9.47
1971 V8-440 Exc	3514651	5.33
Center	3514695	7.78
1972, 6-198	3683891	5.99
1972, 6-225	3683891	5.99
1972 V8-360,400	3683867	9.45
1972 V8-440	3683865	11.61
1973, 6-198 Exc	3744792	5.99
Auto Trans	3685804	5.99
1973, 6-225	3685804	5.99
1973 V8-360	3685853	
1974 Six	3837510	5.99
1974 V8	3837507	11.07

5—CARBURETOR GASKET KIT (CARTER):

Application	Part No.	Price
PLYMOUTH:		
1968-69 V8-273, 318	3621245	3.59
1969 V8-383—		
2 Bar. Carb	2933191	1.22
4 Bar. Carb	2933197	1.39
1969 V8-426	3549343	2.11
1969 V8-440	2933197	1.39
1970-72 V8-318	3549295	4.55
1970 V8-383—		
2 Bar. Carb. Exc	3549296	3.84
Auto Trans	2933191	1.22
4 Bar. Carb	3549297	6.49
1970-71 V8-426	3549343	2.11
1970 V8-440 Exc	3549273	2.82
Auto Trans W/Air Cond	3549297	6.49
1971 V8-340	3621246	2.92
1971 V8-383 Exc	3549296	3.84
4-Bar Carb	3621244	6.49
1971 V8-440	3621244	6.49
1972 V8-340, 400	3683907	2.92
1973 V8-318	3744796	4.92
V8-340	3744757	2.92
1974 V8 Exc	3744757	2.92
V8-318	3837491	3.29
VALIANT & BARRACUDA:		
1968-69 V8-273, 318	3621245	3.59
1969 6-170	2933179	1.69
1969-70 V8-340	2933197	1.39
1969 V8-383	2933197	1.39
1970-72 V8-318	3549295	4.55
1970-71 6-198	3514475	2.82
1970 V8-383, 2 Bar	2933191	1.22
4 Bar	3549297	6.49
1970-71 V8-426	3549343	2.11
1970 V8-440 Exc	3549273	2.82
Auto Trans W/Air Cond	3549297	6.49
1971, 6-225	3621245	3.59
1971, V8-383	3549296	3.84
1971, V8-440	3621244	6.49
1971 V8-340	3621246	2.92
1972 V8-340	3683907	2.92
1974, See Plymouth—		

6—CARBURETOR GASKET KIT (HOLLEY):

Application	Part No.	Price
1966-69 Six	3683922	1.30
1969 V8-440	2933197	1.39
1972 Six	3683922	1.30
1972 V8-360, 400	3683871	3.78
1970-71 V8-340 Exc	3514652	2.33
Center	3514696	2.59
1970, 6-225 Exc	3514827	1.36
W/Fuel Emission	3683922	1.30
1970 V8-383 (2 Bar)—		
Exc Below	3514755	2.87
Std Trans W/Fuel Emiss	3514710	3.41
1970 V8-383 (4 Bar)—		
L/Fuel Emission Exc	3514817	5.45
W/Air Cond	3514818	6.27
W/Fuel Emission	3514825	5.90
1970 V8-440 (2 Bar)—		
Front & Rear	3514652	2.33
Center Exc	3514672	1.90
W/Fuel Emission	3514696	2.59
1970 V8-440 (4 Bar)—		
Exc Below	3514802	6.27
W/Fuel Emission	3514802	6.27
1971, 6-225	3683922	1.30
1971 V8-360	3514199	3.41
1971 V8-383	3514825	5.90
1971 V8-440 Exc	3514652	2.33
Center	3514696	2.59
1972 V8-440	3683864	6.44
1973 Six	3744791	1.67
V8	3685831	3.78
1974 Six	3837511	1.67
V8	3837508	3.78

7—THERMOSTATIC COIL & HOUSING ASS'Y (CARTER):

Application	Part No.	Price
PLYMOUTH:		
1968-69 V8-440	2863845	10.60
1969 V8-318	2863843	9.30
1969 V8-383—		
2 Bar. Carb	2863846	9.47
4 Bar. Carb	2863845	10.60
1969-70 V8-426	1826847	7.79
1970-72 V8-318	2951651	10.70
1970-71 V8-383—		
2 Bar. Carb	2951652	10.76
4 Bar. Carb	2951653	11.19
1970-71 V8-440	2951653	11.19
1971 V8-340	3512875	8.00
1972 V8-340	3614169	8.65
1972 V8-400	3512845	10.16
1973 Exc	3698355	10.16
V8-318	3698353	9.03
1974 Exc	3751484	10.16
V8-318	3751478	9.03
VALIANT & BARRACUDA:		
1968-69 V8-340, 383	2863845	10.60
1969 Six	2658396	8.76
1969 V8-273, 318	2863843	9.30
1970-72 V8-318	2951651	10.70
1970 V8-340	3462927	9.73
1970 V8-383, 2 Bar	2951652	10.76
4 Bar	2951653	11.19
1970 V8-426	1826847	7.79

1970-71 V8-440	2951653	11.19
1970-71, 6-198	2946548	6.86
1971, 6-225	2809286	6.69
1971 V8-340	3512875	8.00
1971, V8-383	2951652	10.76
1972 V8-340	3614169	8.65
1973-74, See Plymouth—		

8—CARBURETOR CHOKE KIT (HOLLEY):

1966-69 Six	2658398	4.06
1967-69 V8-440	2843156	3.70
1970-71 V8-340	3614197	4.87
1970-71, 6-225	3614111	4.87
1970 V8-383 (2 Bar)—		
Exc Below	2951652	10.76
Std Trans L/Fuel Emiss	3512872	4.49
1970 V8-383 (4 Bar)	2946539	4.50
1970 V8-440 (2 Bar)	2946532	4.77
4 Bar	2946539	4.50
1971-72 V8-360	3512872	4.49
1971 V8-383	3512867	4.87
1971 V8-440 Exc	3420255	.16
Auto Trans	2946532	4.77
1972 Six	3614111	4.87
1972 V8-400	3512872	4.49
1973 Six	3698351	8.00
V8	3698357	4.50
1974 Six	3751476	9.25
V8-360	3751480	9.00
V8-400	3751482	9.05

9—CHOKE VACUUM CONTROL ASS'Y (CARTER):

PLYMOUTH:

1969-71 V8-383 (2 Bar)	2933190	5.94
1969-71 V8-383 (4 Bar)—		
Exc Below	2933199	5.87
1971	2933196	5.87
1969-73 V8-318	2933185	3.85
1969-70 V8-440 Exc	2933196	5.87
Auto Trans	3514865	3.84
1971-73 V8-340—		
Synchro-Mesh	3621209	5.09
Auto. Trans	3621210	5.09
1971 V8-440	3514865	3.84
1972 V8-400	3621210	5.09
1974 V8-318 Exc	3780153	3.85
Auto Trans	3780154	6.19
1974 V8-360 Exc	3621209	5.09
Fury	3621210	5.09
1974 V8-400 Exc	3621209	5.09
Auto Trans	3621210	5.09
1974 V8-440	3621210	5.09

VALIANT & BARRACUDA:

1969 6-170	2933182	5.22
1969 V8-383 (4 Bar.)	3420457	3.63
1969 V8-273, 318	2933185	3.85
1969-70 V8-340	2933199	5.87
1970-72 V8-318	2933185	3.85
1970-71, 6-198	2933182	5.22
1970-71 V8-383—		
2 Bar	2933190	5.94
4 Bar	2933199	5.87
1970 V8-440 Exc	2933196	5.87
Auto Trans Exc	2933196	5.87
W/Fuel Emission & AC	3514865	3.84
1971-73 V8-340—		
Synchro-Mesh	3621209	5.09
Auto. Trans	3621210	5.09
1971 V8-440	3514865	3.84
1974 V8-318 Exc	3780153	3.85
Auto Trans	3780154	6.19
1974 V8-360	3621209	5.09

10—CHOKE VACUUM CONTROL ASS'Y (HOLLEY):

PLYMOUTH:

1969 6-225	3419508	2.77
1969 V8-383	3621261	3.10
1969 V8-440	3621274	2.98
1970-72, 6-225—		
Synchro-Mesh	3419508	2.77
Auto. Trans.	3685730	3.90
1970 V8-383 (2 Bar)—		
Exc Below	3419621	3.25
Std Trans W/Fuel Emiss	3419508	2.77
1971 V8-383 (4 Bar)—		
Synchro-Mesh	3621274	2.98
Auto Trans	3621261	3.10
1970 V8-440 (3 Carbs)—		
Front & Rear	3514654	2.82
Center Exc	3621274	2.98
Auto Trans	3621261	3.10
1970 V8-440 (4 Bar)	3621274	2.98
1971 V8-360	3549450	3.08
1971 V8-440 Exc	3514654	2.82
Center	3621274	2.98
1972 V8-360—		
Synchro-Mesh	3621272	3.78
Auto. Trans.	3549450	3.08
1972 V8-400	3683874	3.40
1972 V8-440 (4 Bar.)—		
Synchro-Mesh	3621274	2.98
Auto. Trans.	3621261	3.10
1973 Six Exc	3685730	3.90
Std Trans	3685731	3.78
1973 V8-360	3685732	3.78
1974 Six Exc	3780672	3.90
Std Trans	3780673	3.78
1974 V8-360	3744549	3.90
V8-400	3744550	3.78

VALIANT & BARRACUDA:

1969 6-225—		
Std. Trans	3419508	2.77
Auto. Trans	3419621	3.25
1970-72 Six—		
Synchro-Mesh	3419508	2.77
Auto Trans	3685730	3.90
1970-71 V8-340—		
Front & Rear	3514654	2.82
Center Exc	3621274	2.98
Auto Trans	3621261	3.10
1970-72 V8-360,383,440—		
1973-74, See Plymouth—		

11—FUEL PUMP:

PLYMOUTH:

1966-69 Six	2932798	14.26
1969-70 V8-318	2932797	13.78
1969-70 V8-383	3621675	13.05
1969-71 V8-426	2585118	13.16
1969 V8-440—		
Belvedere	3004107	13.28
Fury	3621675	13.05
1970 Six—		
L/Fuel Emission	2932798	14.26
W/Fuel Emission	3420834	14.09
1970 V8-440—		
Fury	3621675	13.05
Belvedere & Satellite	3420835	14.09
1971 Six	3420834	14.09
1971 V8-318,340,360	3620795	15.70
1971 V8-383,440	3621675	13.05
1972 Six	2932798	14.26
1972-73 V8-318	2932797	13.78
1972-73 V8-340,360	3620795	15.70
1972 V8-400	3621609	15.70
1972 V8-440	3621610	15.70
1973 Six	3621884	14.26
1973 V8-400, 440—		
Fury	3685799	15.70
Satellite	3685800	15.70
1974-75 Six	2932798	14.26
V8-318 & 360, 2 Bar	3744806	14.90
4 Bar	3744805	15.70
V8-400	3685799	15.70
V8-440 Exc	3685800	15.70
Fury	3685799	15.70

VALIANT & BARRACUDA:

1966-69 Six	2932798	14.26
1969 V8—		
Exc. Below	2932797	13.78
V8-383	3621675	13.05
1970-71 Six—		
L/Fuel Emission	2932798	14.26
W/Fuel Emission	3420834	14.09
1970-71 V8—		
Exc. Below	3620795	15.70
V8-383	3621675	13.05
V8-426	2585118	13.16
V8-440	3420835	14.09
1972 Six	2932798	14.26
1972-73 V8, Exc	2932797	13.78
V8-340	3620795	15.70
1973 Six	3621884	14.26
1974-75, See Plymouth—		

12—FUEL TANK:

PLYMOUTH:

1968-69 Belvedere—		
Exc. Sta. Wag	2880434	55.89
Station Wagon	2880459	46.35
1968-69 Fury—		
Exc. Sta. Wag	3404475	56.74
Station Wagon (1968)	2856347	61.31
Station Wagon (1969)	2925748	61.31
1970 Belvedere—		
Exc. Sta. Wagon—		
L/Fuel Emission	2880434	55.89
W/Fuel Emission	3404392	72.83
Sta. Wagon—		
L/Fuel Emission	3404497	63.40
W/Fuel Emission	3404394	77.60
1970 Fury—		
Exc.	3404475	56.74
W/Fuel Emission	3404219	77.80
Sta. Wagon	2925748	61.31
1971-72 Satellite—		
Exc. Below (Early)	3404951	64.83
Late	3642103	66.69
Sta. Wagon (Early)	3466153	57.00
Late	3642170	56.74
1971 Fury—		
Exc. Below	3466887	77.72
Sta. Wagon	3404225	70.71
1972 Fury—		
Exc. Below	3583562	77.72
Sta. Wagon	3404225	70.71
1973 Fury Exc	3642156	77.72
Sta Wagon	3642175	68.63
1973 Satellite Exc	3642103	66.69
Sta Wagon	3642170	56.74
1974 Satellite Exc	3726425	72.83
Sta Wagon	3642170	56.74
1974 Fury Exc	3726077	81.57
Sta Wagon	3726085	81.57
1975 Fury, Exc	3906503	72.85
Sta Wagon, Exc	3906523	86.15
W/Leaded Fuel	3906522	82.50
1975 Gran Fury, Exc	3726077	81.57
Sta Wagon	3726085	81.57

VALIANT & BARRACUDA:

1968-69	2880417	49.16
1970-71—		
L/Fuel Emission—		
Exc Barracuda	3404474	49.16
Barracuda	3404509	55.56
W/Fuel Emission—		
Exc. Barracuda	3404220	62.49
Barracuda	3404493	64.70
1972 Barracuda, Early	3583569	64.70
Late	3642138	75.35
1972 Valiant, Early	3583522	49.61
Late	3642179	49.16
1973-74 Valiant	3642179	49.16
1973-74 Barracuda	3642138	75.35
1975	3906518	56.50

13—INTAKE MANIFOLD GASKET:

PLYMOUTH:

1966-71 Six	2843279	.40
1966-69 V8-440	3671575	3.40
1968-71 V8-383	3671874	3.67
1968-69 V8-426	2780680	.82
1969-74 V8-273, 318	3420027	2.75
1970-71 V8-340 Exc	3514187	4.15
W/3 Carbs	3514187	4.15
1970-71 V8-440	3514186	6.16
1970-71 V8-426	2808306	3.19
1971 V8-360	3514187	4.15
1972-73 Six (Early 73)	3614387	.32
1972 V8-340, 360	3514187	4.15
1972-74 V8-400	3671874	3.67
1972-74 V8-440	3514186	6.16
1973-74 Six (Late 73)	3751635	.40
1973-74 V8-440	3671933	3.67

VALIANT & BARRACUDA:

1969-71 Six	2843279	.40
1969 V8-273, 318 (Set)	3420027	2.75
1967-71 V8-383	3671874	3.67
1969 V8-340 (Set)	3514187	4.15
1970-71 V8-340—		
1 Carb	3514187	4.15
3 Carbs	3514187	4.15
1970-74 V8-318	3420027	2.75
1970-71 V8-426	2808306	3.19
1970-71 V8-440	3514186	6.16
1972-73 Six (Early 73)	3614387	.32
1972-74 V8-340 & 360	3514187	4.15
1973-74 Six (Late 73)	3751635	.40

PONTIAC

FULL SIZE MODELS

Time — Emission Controls (Group AB) — Time

OPERATION INDEX

AB1—POSITIVE CRANKCASE VENTILATION VALVE, CLEAN OR RENEW

1969-75 (0.3) 0.3

AB2—CONTROLLED COMBUSTION SYSTEM, CHECK

Includes: Check & adjust carb idle speed & mixture & ignition timing.

1969-75 (0.3) 0.7

AB3—VACUUM CONTROL UNIT, RENEW

1969-75 (0.2) 0.4

AB4—AIR CLEANER MOTOR, RENEW

1969-75 (0.4) 0.6

AB5—AIR CLEANER SENSOR, RENEW

1969-75 (0.4) 0.5

AB5A—THERMOSTATIC VACUUM SWITCH, RENEW

1969-75 (0.3) 0.4

Parts — Emission Controls — Parts

PARTS INDEX

1—AIR INJECTOR REACTOR PUMP:

1972 ....7803948 48.00

2—AIR INJECTOR PUMP DRIVE BELT:

—NOTE—

Order By Complete Model Description.

3—CRANKCASE VENTILATING VALVE:

1966-74 ....6421972 2.08

4—DISTRIBUTOR THERMOSTATIC VACUUM SWITCH:

1968-69 ....3016754 9.90

1970-71 ....6490152 9.55

1972 ....6490384 10.12

1973-74 ....6490440 4.89

5—FUEL VAPOR CANNISTER:

1970 ....7027658 29.10

1971-74 ....7028131 23.25

6—FUEL VAPOR CANNISTER ELEMENT:

1970-74 ....7026014 1.10

Time — Tune-Up & Ignition (Group B) — Time

OPERATION INDEX

B1—TUNE-UP, MINOR

Includes: Renew points, condenser and plugs, set spark timing and adjust carburetor idle.

1968-74 (1.4) 1.7

—NOTE—

For Air Cond., Add (0.1) 0.3
For Power Steering, Add (0.1) 0.2

B2—TUNE-UP, MAJOR

Includes: Check compression, clean or renew and adjust spark plugs. R&R dist, renew points and condenser. Adjust ignition timing, carburetor and fan belts. Clean battery terminals and service air cleaner. Check coil and service manifold heat control valve. Clean or replace fuel line filter.

1969-75 (2.7) 3.2
1975 (2.2) 2.7

—NOTE—

For Air Cond., Add (0.1) 0.3
For Power Steering, Add (0.2) 0.2
To Renew PCV Valve, Add (0.3) 0.3

B3—TUNE-UP MAJOR & OVERHAUL CARBURETOR

1968-74—
2 Barrel (4.1) 5.0
4 Barrel (4.4) 5.3
1975—
2 Barrel (3.7) 4.7
4 Barrel (4.0) 5.0

—NOTE—

For Air Cond., Add (0.1) 0.3
For Power Steering, Add (0.2) 0.2
To Renew PCV Valve, Add (0.3) 0.3

B4—POINTS & CONDENSER, RENEW

Does not include R & R distributor.

1969-75 (0.5) 0.8

B5—SPARK PLUGS, CLEAN & ADJUST OR RENEW

1969-75 (0.4) 0.6

—NOTE—

For Air Cond., Add (0.1) 0.3
For Power Steering, Add (0.2) 0.2
To Clean Plugs, Add (0.3) 0.3

B6—COMPRESSION, TEST

1969-75 (0.8) 1.0

—NOTE—

For Air Cond., Add (0.1) 0.3
For Power Steering, Add (0.2) 0.2

B7—IGNITION TIMING, SET

1969-75 (0.2) 0.3

B8—DISTRIBUTOR, R & R OR RENEW

1969-75 (0.5) 0.7

B9—DISTRIBUTOR, OVERHAUL (UNIT OFF)

1969-75 (0.6) 1.0

B9A—DISTRIBUTOR, ADJUST ON STROBOSCOPE (UNIT OFF)

All Models (0.4) 0.4

B10—DISTRIBUTOR CAP, RENEW

1969-75 (0.3) 0.4

B11—IGNITION CABLE SET, RENEW

Time covers installation of factory supplied sets.

1969-75 (0.3) 0.8

B12—VACUUM CONTROL UNIT, RENEW

Includes R & R distributor & set spark timing.

1969-75 (0.8) 0.9

B13—IGNITION COIL, RENEW

1969-75 (0.3) 0.3

B14—STARTER & IGNITION SWITCH, RENEW

1969-75—
L/Air Cond. (0.2) 0.3
W/Air Cond. (0.5) 0.8

B16—STEERING & IGNITION LOCK & ACTUATOR, RENEW

1969-75 (1.2) 1.8

FIG.1—TUNE-UP & IGNITION
For parts identification only

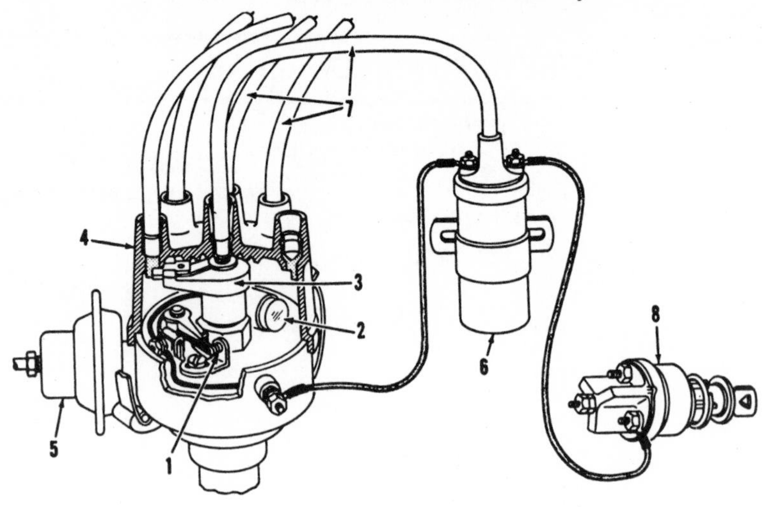

DISTRIBUTOR ASS'Y:

Application	Part No.	Price
1968 V8-400—		
Synchro-Mesh	1111448	39.70
Auto. Trans.—		
2 Bar. Carb.	1111272	49.25
4 Bar. Carb.	1111300	52.00
1968 V8-428 (Exc. Hi Output)—		
Synchro-Mesh	1111450	45.20
Auto. Trans.	1111435	49.95
1968 V8-428 Hi Output—		
Synchro-Mesh	1111449	50.70
Auto. Trans.	1111270	50.70
1969 V8-400—		
2 Bar. Carb.	1111940	40.95
4 Bar. Carb.—		
Std. Trans.	1111952	48.15
Auto. Trans.	1111253	48.95
1969 V8-428—		
Exc. Hi-Output—		
Std. Trans.	1111960	45.55
Auto. Trans.	1112009	51.15
Hi-Output—		
Std. Trans.	1111952	48.15
Auto. Trans.	1111946	48.95
1970 V8-350	1112008	49.50
1970 V8-400—		
Exc. Grand Prix—		
Exc. Below	1112007	49.40
290 H.P.	1112008	49.50
Grand Prix—		
350 H.P. (Std. Tra.)	1111176	52.30
350 H.P. (Auto. Tra.)	1111148	51.15
370 H.P.	1112024	49.20
1970 V8-455—		
Exc. Below	1112012	54.70
350 H.P. (Auto. Tra.)	1111105	50.70
1971 V8-350—		
Std. Trans.	1112083	49.50
Auto. Trans.	1112090	50.70
1971 V8-400—		
2 Bar. Carb.	1112089	50.70
4 Bar. Carb.	1112070	53.05
1971 V8-455—		
2 Bar. Carb.	1112071	48.45
4 Bar. Carb.	1112072	53.75
1972 V8-350 2 Bar. Carb.—		
Synchro-Mesh	1112140	53.15
Auto. Trans.—		
Exc. Calif.	1112118	52.40
Calif.	1112117	
1972 V8-350 (4 Bar)	1112120	
1972 V8-400—		
2 Bar. Carb.	1112119	44.10
4 Bar. Carb.—		
Synchro-Mesh	1112120	
Auto. Trans.	1112121	53.10
1972 V8-455—		
2 Bar. Carb.	1112122	42.80
4 Bar. Carb.	1112145	53.20
1973 V8-350—		
Std. Trans.	1112202	53.15
Auto Trans.	1112201	53.20
1973 V8-400—		
2 Bar. Carb.—		
L/Alt. Perf.	1112199	52.40
W/Alt. Perf.	1112224	52.95
4 Bar. Carb.—		
L/Alt. Perf.	1112231	44.70
W/Alt. Perf.	1112232	51.65
W/Unit. Dist.	1112233	166.75
1973 V8-455—		
Exc. Below	1112191	53.20
W/Alt. Perf.	1112220	53.75
W/Unit. Dist.	1112203	166.75
1973 V8-455(Super Duty)	1112205	90.35
1974, V8-400 2 Bar—		
Exc Below	1112805	44.10
W/Alt Perf	1112809	54.05
1974, V8-400 4 Bar—		
Exc Below	1112814	44.70
L/Alt Perf Exc	1112231	44.70
W/Auto Trans	1112813	46.45
1974 V8-455 Exc	1112807	44.80
W/Alt Perf	1112811	44.80
W/Unit Ign	1112810	190.50

1—IGNITION POINT SET:

Application	Part No.	Price
1966-68—		
Clip Type	1931988	4.65
Screw Type	1966289	4.65
1969-70—		
Synchro-Mesh	1966294	5.25
Auto. Trans.	1931988	4.65
1971-74—		
2 Bar. Carb.	1931988	4.65
4 Bar. Carb.	1966294	5.25

2—CONDENSER:

Application	Part No.	Price
1968-74	1932004	1.61

3—ROTOR:

Application	Part No.	Price
1968-74 Exc	1971247	1.87
Unit Ign	1847993	2.20

4—DISTRIBUTOR CAP:

Application	Part No.	Price
1968-74	800061	6.20

5—VACUUM CONTROL UNIT:

Application	Part No.	Price
1968 V8-400—		
2 Bar. Carb.—		
Synchro-Mesh	1973412	7.20
Auto. Trans.	1973411	7.20
4 Bar. Carb.	1973412	7.20
1968 V8-428—		
Synchro-Mesh	1973411	7.20
Auto. Trans.	1973412	7.20
1969 V8-400	1115374	3.21
1969 V8-428	1115365	3.37
1970 V8-350	1115364	3.26
1970 V8-400—		
Synchro-Mesh	1115365	3.37
Auto. Trans.	1115364	3.26
1970-72 V8-455	1115365	3.37
1971-72 V8-350, 400	1115364	3.26
1973 V8-350	1973471	3.37
1973 V8-400—		
2 Bar. Carb.—		
Exc. Below	1973455	3.37
W/Alt. Perf.	1973464	3.37
4 Bar. Carb.	1973458	3.37
1973 V8-455—		
Exc. Below	1973470	3.37
V8-455(Super Duty)	1973458	3.37
1974, V8-400 Exc	1115365	3.37
W/Alt Perf Exc	1973461	3.45
4 Bar Carb	1973471	3.37
1974, V8-455 Exc	1973464	3.37
W/Unit Ign Exc	1973470	3.37
W/Alt Perf	1973471	3.37

6—IGNITION COIL:

Application	Part No.	Price
1968-74	1115238	14.65

7—IGNITION CABLE SET:

Application	Part No.	Price
1968-72	6296271	12.22
1973-74	8914141	18.11

8—IGNITION SWITCH (LESS CYLINDER):

Application	Part No.	Price
1968	1116692	7.85
1969—		
Less Tilt Wheel	1990091	6.90
With Tilt Wheel	1990093	7.40
1970—		
Less Tilt Wheel	1990091	6.90
With Tilt Wheel	1990093	7.40
1971-72—		
Exc. Below	1990095	5.25
Catalina (W/Synchro-Mesh)	3986841	2.08
W/Tilt Wheel	1990096	5.55
1973-74—		
L/Tilt Wheel	1990095	5.25
W/Tilt Wheel	1990096	5.55

Time — Fuel System & Intake Manifold (Group C) — Time

OPERATION INDEX

C1—CARBURETOR, R & R OR RENEW

1969-75 (0.7) 0.9

C2—CARBURETOR, R & R & OVERHAUL

1969-75—
- 2 Barrel (1.9) 2.3
- 4 Barrel—
  - Exc. Below (2.2) 2.6
  - Quadrajet (1.8) 2.2

C2A—ACCELERATOR PUMP, RENEW

1969-75—
- 2 Barrel (0.9) 1.2
- 4 Barrel (1.1) 1.4

—NOTE—

Does Not Include R & R Carburetor.

C2B—NEEDLE & SEAT, RENEW

1969-75—
- 2 Barrel (0.8) 1.1
- 4 Barrel (1.0) 1.3

—NOTE—

Does Not Include R & R Carburetor.

C4A—IDLE STOP SOLENOID, RENEW

1969-75 (0.3) 0.5

C4B—VACUUM BRAKE ASS'Y, RENEW

1969-75 (0.2) 0.4

C5—FUEL PUMP, R & R OR RENEW

1969-75 (0.4) 0.6

C6—FUEL TANK, R & R OR RENEW

1969-75—
- Exc. Below (1.2) 1.6
- Grand Prix (1.0) 1.4

C7—FUEL SYSTEM, CLEAN

Includes: R & R tank, blow out lines and clean or renew all filters.

1969-75—
- Exc. Below (1.6) 2.4
- Sta. Wagon (1.4) 2.2

C8—INTAKE MANIFOLD GASKETS, RENEW

1969-75 (1.6) 2.3

—NOTE—

For Air Cond., Add (0.1) *0.2*
For Air Injection, Add (0.4) *0.5*

Parts — Fuel System & Intake Manifold — Parts

PARTS INDEX

1—CARBURETOR ASS'Y (ROCHESTER):

Application	Part No.	Price
1968 (2 Bar. Carb.)—		
Synchro-Mesh	7036366	74.00
Auto. Trans.	7036360	74.00
1968 V8-400 (4 Bar. Carb.)—		
Synchro-Mesh	7036827	44.15
Auto. Trans.	7016826	112.00
1968 V8-428 (4 Bar. Carb.)—		
Synchro-Mesh	7036331	
Auto. Trans.	7036332	88.45
1969 V8 (2 Bar. Carb.)—		
Synchro-Mesh	7036366	74.00
Auto. Trans.	7016946	74.00
1969 V8 (4 Bar. Carb.)—		
V8-400—		
Synchro-Mesh	7016933	88.45
Auto. Trans.	7046901	94.30
V8-428—		
Exc. Below	7046901	112.00
Hi-Output	7046901	94.30
1970 V8-350 (2 Bar. Carb.)—		
Synchro-Mesh—		
L/Fuel Emission	7047034	74.00
W/Fuel Emission	7047031	74.00
Auto. Trans.—		
L/Fuel Emission	7047033	74.00
W/Fuel Emission	7047036	74.00
1970 V8-400 (2 Bar. Carb.)—		
Synchro-Mesh—		
L/Fuel Emission	7047037	74.00
W/Fuel Emission	7047039	74.00
Auto. Trans.—		
L/Fuel Emission	7047035	74.00
W/Fuel Emission	7047038	74.00
1970 V8-400 (4 Bar. Carb.)—		
Exc. Grand Prix—		
L/Fuel Emission	7047048	94.20
W/Fuel Emission	7047049	112.00
Grand Prix—		
L/Fuel Emission	7046927	100.40
W/Fuel Emission	7036917	112.00
1970 V8-455 (Synchro-Mesh)—		
L/Fuel Emission	7047057	94.20
W/Fuel Emission	7047058	112.00
1970 V8-455 (Auto. Trans.)—		
L/Hi-Perf—		
L/Fuel Emission	7046927	112.00
W/Fuel Emission	7047055	112.00
W/Hi-Perf.—		
L/Fuel Emission	7047056	94.20
W/Fuel Emission	7047053	112.00
1971 (2 Bar. Carb.)—		
Synchro-Mesh	7047149	74.00
V8-350 (Auto.)	7047148	74.00
V8-400 (Auto.)	7047158	74.00
V8-455 (Auto.)	7047138	74.00
1971 (4 Bar. Carb.)—		
V8-400—		
Exc. Below	7041743	98.15
Auto. Trans.	7041743	98.15
V8-455—		
1972-(2 Bar. Carb.)—		
V8-350	7047200	74.00
V8-400—		
Exc. Below	7047258	74.00
Calif.	7046636	70.00
V8-455	7047238	74.00
1972(4 Bar. Carb.)—		
V8-400—		
Std. Trans.	7047235	112.00
Auto. Trans.	7047236	112.00
V8-455—		
L/Hi Perf.	7047234	112.00
W/Hi Perf.—		
Std. Trans.	7047239	112.00
Auto. Trans.	7047246	112.00
1973(2 Bar. Carb.)—		
V8-350—		
Std. Trans.	7046771	82.00
Auto. Trans.—		
L/Alt. Perf.	7047349	82.00
W/Alt. Perf.	7046752	82.00
1973(2 Bar. Carb.)—		
V8-400—		
Exc. Below	7047358	82.00
Alt. Perf.	7047359	82.00
Calif.	7046750	82.00
1973 V8-400 4 Bar—		
Std Trans	7047335	120.00
Auto Trans Exc	7047330	120.00
L/Alt Perf, Early	7047336	120.00
Late	7046936	120.00
1973 V8-455 4 Bar—		
Std Trans Exc	7047337	120.00
Super Duty	7047339	120.00
Auto Trans Exc	7047338	120.00
W/Alt Perf	7047329	120.00
Super Duty	7047346	120.00
1974 V8-400 —		
2 Bar Exc	7047453	82.00
W/Alt Perf	7046750	82.00
Calif	7047448	82.00
4 Bar Exc	7047335	120.00
Auto Trans Exc	7047428	120.00
W/Alt Perf	17050508	120.00
1974 V8-455—		
4 Bar Exc	7047427	120.00
W/Alt Perf	17050507	120.00

2—CARBURETOR OK KLEANOUT KIT (ROCHESTER):

Application	Part No.	Price
1968-69—		
2 Bar. Carb.—		
Std. Trans.	7039128	7.10
Auto. Trans.	7039127	7.10
4 Bar. Carb.	7039162	9.45
1970—		
2 Bar. Carb.—		
Std. Trans.	7039180	7.20
Auto. Trans.	7039238	8.10
4 Bar. Carb.	7039183	9.45
1971—		
2 Bar. Carb.	7039238	8.10
4 Bar. Carb.	7039232	9.45
1972—		
2 Bar. Carb.—		
Exc. Below	7039238	8.10
Calif.	7039242	8.10
4 Bar. Carb.—		
Std. Trans.	7039232	9.45
Auto. Trans.	7039243	9.45
Hi Perf.	7039237	9.45
1973-74 V8-350	7039255	8.10
1973-74 V8-400	7039252	8.10
1973-74 4 Bar Carb—		
Exc Below	7039262	9.45
W/Alt Perf	7039263	9.45

3—CARBURETOR GASKET KIT (ROCHESTER):

Application	Part No.	Price
1968	7016848	6.45
1969 V8—		
2 Bar. Carb.	7016844	2.70
4 Bar. Carb.	7016848	6.45
1970-71 (2 Bar. Carb.)	7036873	5.30
1970-71 (4 Bar. Carb.)	7046511	7.90
1972—		
2 Bar. Carb.	7036873	5.30
4 Bar. Carb.	7046511	7.90
1973-74—		
2 Bar Carb	7046726	5.15
4 Bar Carb	7046825	8.50

4—THERMOSTATIC COIL & COVER ASS'Y (ROCHESTER):

Application	Part No.	Price
1968-70—		
2 Bar. Carb.—		
Synchro-Mesh	7028295	6.55
Auto. Trans.	7028293	6.90
4 Bar. Carb.	7041094	8.20
1971 (2 Bar. Carb.)—		
Exc. Below	482125	9.80
V8-350 (Auto.)	482124	9.80
1971 (4 Bar. Carb.)—		
Exc. Below	482128	9.80
V8-400 (Std.)	482127	9.80
1972—		
2 Bar. Carb.—		
V8-350—		
Std. Trans.	488074	9.80
Auto. Trans.	486249	9.80
V8-400—		
Exc. Below	488073	9.80
Calif.	486250	9.80
4 Bar. Carb.	487112	9.80
1973-74—		
V8-350	7046739	5.95
V8-400	7041709	5.95

5—CHOKE VACUUM CONTROL ASS'Y (ROCHESTER):

1968 V8—		
2 Bar.	7036539	3.45
4 Bar.	7038237★	4.25
1969 V8 (2 Bar. Carb.)	7036539	3.45
1969 V8 (4 Bar. Carb.)	7038237★	4.25
1970—		
2 Bar. Carb.	7038942	3.20
4 Bar. Carb.	7026214	9.15
1971 (2 Bar. Carb.)—		
V8-350, 400	7042687	7.80
V8-455	7043773	7.80
1971 (4 Bar. Carb.)—		
Exc. Below	7043898	9.40
W/Bracket	7043988	14.20
1972—		
2 Bar. Carb.	7045915	9.10
4 Bar. Carb.	7045931	14.20
1973-74—		
2 Bar Carb Exc	7030987	9.10
Calif	17050084	9.10
4 Bar Carb Exc	7047864	10.05
Super Duty	7048193	10.05

6—FUEL PUMP

1968 V8-400	6417211	13.81
1968 V8-428	6417212	13.81
1969—		
Exc. Grand Prix—		
L/Vapor Return	6417420	13.15
W/Vapor Return	6417419	13.03
Grand Prix	6417418	13.15
1970 2 Bar. Carb.—		
Exc. Below	6417419	13.03
Grand Prix	6417418	13.15
1970 4 Bar. Carb.—		
Exc. Below—		
Early	6470222	17.10
Late	6470513	17.75
Grand Prix	6470222	17.10
1971 (Exc. Grand Prix)—		
2 Bar. Carb.—		
L/Air Cond.	6470498	12.68
W/Air Cond.	6470497	13.40
4 Bar. Carb.—		
L/Air Cond.	6470498	12.68
W/Air Cond.	6470499	16.03
1971 Grand Prix	6470513	17.75
1972 (Exc. Grand Prix)—		
2 Bar. Carb.—		
L/Air Cond.	6470668	15.45
W/Air Cond.	6470669	15.91
4 Bar. Carb.	6470670	25.61
1972 Grand Prix	6470513	17.75
1973—		
L/Air. Cond.	6470670	25.61
W/Air. Cond.	6470669	15.91
1974, 4 Bar Carb	6470670	25.61
2 Bar Exc	6470668	15.45
W/Air Cond	6470669	15.91

7—FUEL TANK:

1968—		
Exc. Below	9790794	52.25
Sta. Wagon	3972571★	47.30
1969 (Exc. Grand Prix)—		
Exc. Below	480645	52.25
Sta. Wagon	3972571★	47.30
1969-70 Grand Prix	478116	43.95
1970 (Exc. Sta. Wag. & Grand Prix)-		
L/Fuel Emission	480645	52.25
W/Fuel Emission	480648	59.40
1970 Sta. Wagon—		
L/Fuel Emission	3972571★	47.30
W/Fuel Emission—		
Steel Tank	3972572★	65.80
Plastic Tank	9799774	61.55
1971 (Exc. Grand Prix)—		
Exc. Below	408077★	59.40
Sta. Wagon	412259★	43.95
1971-72 Grand Prix	484471	59.40
1972 (Exc. Grand Prix)—		
Exc. Below	408077★	59.40
Sta. Wagon	412259★	43.95
1973(Exc. Below)	411934	47.10
1973(Sta. Wagon)	412259★	43.95
1974 Exc	495331	59.40
Sta Wgn	416062★	46.15
Grand Prix	495333	59.40

8—FUEL TANK FILTER:

1967-72 (Sta. Wagon)	5651264	.99
1973	5651422★	1.67

9—INTAKE MANIFOLD GASKET:

1966-71	479433	2.08
1972-74 Exc	9780358	.50
455 Super Duty	493405	2.08

PONTIAC

INTERMEDIATE AND COMPACT MODELS EXCEPT ASTRE

Time — Emission Controls (Group AB) — Time

OPERATION INDEX

AB1—POSITIVE CRANKCASE VENTILATION VALVE, CLEAN OR RENEW

1969-75 (0.3) 0.3

AB2—CONTROLLED COMBUSTION SYSTEM, CHECK

Includes check & adjust carb idle speed & mixture & ignition timing

1969-75 (0.3) 0.7

AB3—VACUUM CONTROL UNIT, RENEW

1969-75 (0.2) 0.4

AB4—AIR CLEANER MOTOR, RENEW

1969-75 (0.4) 0.6

AB5—AIR CLEANER SENSOR, RENEW

1969-75 (0.3) 0.5

AB5A—THERMOSTATIC VACUUM SWITCH, RENEW

1969-75 (0.3) 0.4

AB6—AIR PUMP, RENEW

1972-75 (0.4) 0.6

AB7—AIR PUMP VALVE, RENEW

1972-75, Relief (0.4) 0.8
By-Pass (0.3) 0.4
Check (0.3) 0.4

AB8—EXHAUST GAS RECIRCULATION VALVE, RENEW

1972-75 (0.2) 0.4

AB9—EGR SOLENOID, RENEW

1972-75 (0.2) 0.3

AB10—EGR TRANSMISSION SWITCH, RENEW

1972-75 (0.3) 0.4

AB11—THERMAL DELAY SWITCH, RENEW

1972-75 (0.2) 0.3

AB12—FUEL VAPOR CANNISTER, RENEW

1970-75 (0.2) 0.4

AB13—FUEL VAPOR SEPARATOR, RENEW

1970 (0.7) 0.9

Parts — Emission Controls — Parts

PARTS INDEX

1—AIR INJECTOR REACTOR PUMP:

FIREBIRD:

1972	7803948	48.00
1972-74, 6-250	7803943	62.95
1973-74 V8	7803948	48.00

2—AIR INJECTOR PUMP SEAL:

1967-68	7801092—	1.45

3—AIR INJECTOR PUMP RELIEF VALVE:

1966-68	5696639	2.13

4—AIR INJECTOR PUMP DRIVE BELT:

—NOTE—

Order By Complete Model Description.

5—CRANKCASE VENTILATING VALVE:

FIREBIRD:

1967-69 Six 6423581 2.90
1968-74 V8 ....6421972 2.08
1970-72 Six 6422717 2.08
1973 Six 6487534 2.00
1974 Six 6487936 2.33

TEMPEST. GTO. LEMANS. T-37:

1968-74 V8 ....6421972 2.08
1966-69 Six 6423581 2.90
1970-72 Six 6422717 2.08
1973 Six 6487534 2.00
1974 Six 6487936 2.33

VENTURA II:

1971-72 Six 6422717 2.08
1971-74 V8 6427972
1973 Six 6487534 2.00
1974 Six 6487936 2.33
1973-74 Six 1110499 37.70

1973-74 V8-350—
Exc Below 1112806 44.75
Auto Trans Exc 1112804 44.80
W/Alt Perf 1112808 54.25
1973 V8-455 Exc 1112191 53.20
W/Alt Perf 1112220 53.75
1974 V8-400 2 Bar—
Exc 1112805 44.10
W/Alt Perf 1112809 54.05
1974 V8-400 4 Bar—
W/Alt Perf 1112814 44.70
L/Alt Perf Exc 1112231 44.70
Auto Trans 1112813 46.45

6—DISTRIBUTOR THERMOSTATIC VACUUM SWITCH

1968-71 ....3016754 9.90
1972—
Six 6489903 6.31
V8 ....6490384 10.12
1973 (6-250)—
Std. Trans. 6490555 5.84
Auto. Trans. 6490454 5.84
1973-74 (V8) 6490440 4.89

7—FUEL VAPOR CANNISTER:

1970 Six 7027659 23.25
1970 V8 ....7027658 29.10
1971 Six 7030605 26.50
1971-72 V8—
Exc. Below 7028131 23.25
V8-307 ....7030605 26.50
1973-74—
Six 7030605 27.90
V8 ....7028131 23.25

8—FUEL VAPOR CANNISTER ELEMENT:

1970-74 ....7026014 1.10

9—FUEL VAPOR SEPARATOR:

FIREBIRD:

1970 ....7028052 10.60

TEMPEST. GTO. LEMANS. T-37:

1970 Six 7028202 11.70
1970 V8 ....7028073 10.60

Time — Tune-Up & Ignition (Group B) — Time

OPERATION INDEX

B1—TUNE UP, MINOR

Includes: Renew points, condenser and plugs, set spark timing and adjust carburator idle

1968-74—
Six Cyl. (1.2) 1.5
V8 (1.4) 1.7
1975 Six (0.9) 1.3
1975 V8 (1.1) 1.5

—NOTE—

For Air Cond. On Tempest 6 Cyl., Add (0.2) *0.3*
For Air Cond. On Firebird Add (0.3) *0.3*

B2—TUNE UP, MAJOR

Includes: Check compression, clean or renew and adjust spark plugs. R&R dist, renew points and condenser. Adjust ignition timing, carburetor and fan belts. Clean battery terminals and service air cleaner. Check coil and service manifold heat control valve. Clean or replace fuel line filter.

1968-74—
Six Cyl (2.3) 3.0
V8 (2.7) 3.3
1975 Six (1.8) 2.5
1975 V8 (2.2) 2.7

—NOTE—

For Air Cond. On Tempest Six Cyl., Add (0.2) *0.3*
For Air Cond. On Firebird, Add (0.3) *0.3*
To Renew PCV Valve Add (0.3) *0.3*

B3—TUNE UP MAJOR & OVERHAUL CARBURETOR

1968-74 Six Cyl.—
One Barrel (3.6) 4.3
Quadrajet (3.8) 4.5
1968-74 V8—
2 Barrel (4.1) 4.8
4 Barrel—
Exc. Below (4.4) 5.1
Quadrajet (4.0) 4.5
1975 Six (3.1) 3.8
1975 V8 Exc (3.9) 4.6
Quadrajet (3.5) 4.0

—NOTE—

For Air Cond. On Tempest 6 Cyl., Add (0.2) *0.3*
For Air Cond. On Firebird Add (0.3) *0.3*
To Renew PCV Valve, Add (0.3) *0.3*

B4—PLUGS, POINTS & CONDENSER, RENEW OR CLEAN & ADJUST

Includes: R & R distributor & set spark timing

1968-74 Six Cyl. (1.3) 1.3
1968-74 V8 (1.4) 1.7

—NOTE—

For Air Cond. On 6 Cyl., Add (0.2) *0.3*
For Air Cond. On Firebird, Add (0.3) *0.3*

B5—SPARK PLUGS, CLEAN & ADJUST OR RENEW

1969-75—
Six Cyl. (0.3) 0.4
V8 (0.5) 0.6

—NOTE—

For Air Cond. On Tempest 6 Cyl., Add (0.2) *0.3*
For Air Cond. On Firebird, Hoist Car, And Add (0.3) *0.3*
To Clean Plugs, Add (0.3) *0.3*

B6—COMPRESSION TEST

1969-75—
Six Cyl. (0.6) 0.9
V8 (0.9) 1.0

—NOTE—

For Air Cond. On Tempest 6 Cyl., Add (0.2) *0.3*
For Air Cond. On Firebird, Hoist Car, And Add (0.3) *0.3*

B7—IGNITION TIMING SET

1969-75 (0.2) 0.3

B8—DISTRIBUTOR, R & R OR RENEW

1969-75 (0.5) 0.7

—NOTE—

For Tempest Six Cyl. W/Air Cond., Add (0.1) *0.3*

B9—DISTRIBUTOR, OVERHAUL (UNIT OFF)

1969-75 (0.6) 1.0

B9A—DISTRIBUTOR, ADJUST ON STROBOSCOPE (UNIT OFF)

All Models (0.4) 0.4

B10—DISTRIBUTOR CAP, RENEW

1969-75 (0.3) 0.4

B11—IGNITION CABLE SET, RENEW

Time covers installation of factory supplied sets.

1969-75 Six (0.2) 0.4
1969-75 V8 (0.3) 0.8

B12—VACUUM CONTROL UNIT, RENEW

Includes R & R distributor & set spark timing.

1969-75 (0.8) 0.9

B13—IGNITION COIL, RENEW

1969-75 (0.3) 0.3

B14—STARTER & IGNITION SWITCH, RENEW

1969-75 (0.2) 0.3

—NOTE—

For Air Cond., Add (0.3) *0.3*

B16—STEERING & IGNITION LOCK & ACTUATOR, RENEW

1969-75 (1.2) 1.8

Parts — Tune-Up & Ignition — Parts

DISTRIBUTOR ASS'Y:

FIREBIRD:

1968 Six—
1 Bar. Carb 1110430 50.05
4 Bar. Carb.—
Exc. Below 1110449 48.45
Std. Trans. 1110431 45.85
1968 V8-350—
2 Bar. Carb 1111281 45.85
4 Bar. Carb.—
Synchro-Mesh 1111447 44.85
Auto. Trans 1111282 45.85

1968 V8-400—
Synchro-Mesh 1111449 50.70
Auto. Trans 1111270 50.70
1969 Six—
1 Bar. Carb 1110475 46.80
4 Bar. Carb 1110474 47.55
1969 V8-350—
Synchro-Mesh—
2 Bar. Carb 1111960 45.55
4 Bar. Carb 1111966 51.50
Auto. Trans.—
2 Bar. Carb 1111942 44.20
4 Bar. Carb 1111965 48.95

1969 V8-400—
Exc. Below 1111946 48.95
Ram AirIII 1111952 48.15
Ram AirIV 1111941 51.15
1970 V8-350 ....1112008 49.50
1970 V8-400—
Std. Trans 1112011 52.75
Auto. Trans 1112009 51.15
1971 V8-350—
Std. Trans 1112083 49.50
Auto. Trans 1112090 50.70
1971 V8-400—
2 Bar. Carb 1112089 50.70

Application	Part No.	Price
4 Bar. Carb	1112070	53.05
1971 V8-455 (Exc. Hi-Perf.)—		
2 Bar. Carb	1112071	48.45
4 Bar. Carb	1112072	53.75
1971 V8-455 (Hi-Perf)	1112073	53.75
1972 V8-350 (2 Bar. Carb)—		
Synchro-Mesh	1112140	53.15
Auto. Trans	1112118	52.40
1972 V8-400—		
2 Bar. Carb	1112119	44.10
4 Bar. Carb	1112121	53.10
1972 V8-455—		
2 Bar. Carb	1112122	42.80
4 Bar. Carb—		
Exc. Below	1112145	53.20
Hi-Perf	1112126	54.20
TEMPEST. GTO. LEMANS. T-37:		
1968 Six—		
1 Bar. Carb	1110430	50.05
4 Bar. Carb.—		
Std. Trans.	1110431	45.85
Auto. Trans.	1110449	48.45
1968 V8-350—		
2 Bar. Carb. (Std. Tra.)	1111281	45.85
2 Bar. Carb. (Auto. Trans.)—		
(W/3 Hose Harness)	1111165	48.20
(W/5 Hose Harness)	1111281	45.85
4 Bar. Carb.—		
Synchro-Mesh	1111447	44.85
Auto. Trans	1111282	45.85
1968 V8-400—		
Synchro-Mesh	1111449	50.70
Auto. Trans.—		
2 Bar. Carb	1111272	49.25
4 Bar. Carb	1111270	50.70
1969 Six—		
1 Bar. Carb	1110475	46.80
4 Bar. Carb	1110474	47.55
1969 V8-350—		
Synchro-Mesh—		
2 Bar. Carb	1111960	45.55
4 Bar. Carb	1111966	51.50
Auto. Trans.—		
2 Bar. Carb	1111942	44.20
4 Bar. Carb	1111965	48.95
1969 V8-400—		
2 Bar. Carb	1111940	40.95
4 Bar. Carb.—		
Ram AirIV	1111941	51.15
1970 Six—		
Synchro-Mesh	1110465	40.40
Auto. Trans	1110466	40.40
1970 V8-350	1112008	49.50
1970 V8-400—		
Exc. Below	1112007	49.40
350 H.P. (Std. Tra)	1111176	52.30
350 H.P. (Auto Tra)	1111148	51.15
370 H.P.	1112024	49.20
1970 V8-455	1112012	54.70
1971 V8-400—		
2 Bar. Carb	1112089	50.70
4 Bar. Carb	1112070	53.05
1972 V8-350 2 Bar. Carb.—		
Synchro-Mesh	1112140	53.15
Auto. Trans.—		
Exc. Below	1112118	52.40
1972 V8-350 4 Bar. Carb.—		
1972 V8-400—		
2 Bar. Carb	1112119	44.10
4 Bar. Carb—		
Auto. Trans	1112121	53.10
1972 V8-455 (2 Bar.)	1112122	42.80
1972 V8-455 4 Bar.—		
Exc. Below	1112145	53.20
Engine Prefix "Ya"	1112127	166.75
High Output	1112133	166.75
1973—		
6-250	1110499	37.70
V8-350—		
Std. Trans.	1112202	53.15
Auto. Trans.—		
L/Alt. Perf.	1112201	53.20
W/Alt. Perf.	1112216	53.75
V8-400—		
2 Bar. Carb.—		
L/Alt. Perf.	1112199	52.40
W/Alt. Perf.	1112224	52.95
4 Bar. Carb—		
W/Alt. Perf.	1112232	51.65
Unit. Dist.	1112233	166.75
V8-455—		
Exc. Below—		
L/Alt. Perf.	1112191	53.20
W/Alt. Perf.	1112220	53.75
Unit. Dist.	1112203	166.75
V8-455 S.D.	1112206	
1973-74, See Firebird—		
VENTURA II:		
1971-72 Six	1110489	36.60
1971-72 V8-307—		
Synchro-Mesh	1112005	45.95
Auto. Trans	1112039	46.35
1973-74 (6-250)	1110499	37.70

FIG.1-TUNE UP & IGNITION

(For Parts Identification Only)

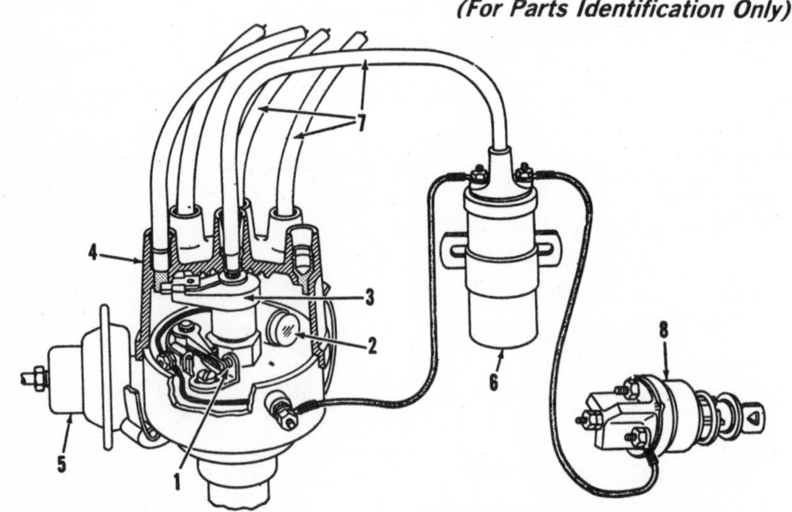

1—IGNITION POINT SET:

Application	Part No.	Price
FIREBIRD:		
1967-74 Six	1954557	3.50
1967-68 V8	1931988	4.65
1969-74 V8—		
2 Bar. Carb	1931988	4.65
4 Bar. Carb	1966294	5.25
TEMPEST. GTO. LEMANS. T-37:		
1966-68 V8	1931988	4.65
1966-74 Six	1954557	3.50
1969-74 V8—		
2 Bar. Carb	1931988	4.65
4 Bar. Carb	1966294	5.25

2—CONDENSER:

Application	Part No.	Price
FIREBIRD:		
1967-74 Six	1928111	1.61
1967-74 V8	1932004	1.61
TEMPEST. GTO. LEMANS. T-37:		
1966-72 V8	1932004	1.61
1966-72 Six	1928111	1.61

3—ROTOR:

Application	Part No.	Price
FIREBIRD:		
1967-72 Six	800056	1.24
1968-74 V8 Exc	1971247	1.87
Unit Dist	1847993	2.20
TEMPEST. GTO. LEMANS. T-37:		
1966-72 V8	1971247	1.87
1966-72 Six	800056	1.24

4—DISTRIBUTOR CAP:

Application	Part No.	Price
FIREBIRD:		
1967-74 Six	1971324	3.75
1967-74 V8	800061	6.20
TEMPEST. GTO. LEMANS. T-37:		
1966-74 V8	800061	6.20
1966-74 Six	1971324	3.75

5—VACUUM CONTROL UNIT:

Application	Part No.	Price
FIREBIRD:		
1968 Six—		
1 Bar. Carb	1973413	9.35
4 Bar. Carb.—		
Std. Trans	1973414	9.35
Auto. Trans	1973413	9.35
1968 V8-350	1973411	7.20
1968 V8-400—		
2 Bar. Carb	1973411	7.20
4 Bar. Carb	1973412	7.20
1969 Six	1973419	3.43
1969 V8-350—		
2 Bar. Carb.—		
Std. Trans	1115365	3.37
Auto. Trans	1115364	3.26
4 Bar. Carb	1115365	3.37
1969-70 V8-400	1115365	3.37
1970 Six	1116217	3.74
1970 V8-350	1115364	3.26
1971-72 Six	1973434	3.75
1971-72 V8	1115364	3.26
1973-74 V8-350—		
Exc Below	1115364	3.26
W/Alt Perf	1973464	3.37
1973-74 V8-400—		
2 Bar Carb Exc	1115365	3.37
W/Alt Perf	1973461	3.45
4 Bar Carb Exc	1973458	3.37
W/Alt Perf	1973471	3.37
TEMPEST. GTO. LEMANS. T-37:		
1968 Six—		
1 Bar. Carb	1973413	9.35
4 Bar. Carb.—		
Std. Trans	1973414	9.35
Auto. Trans	1973413	9.35
1968 V8-350	1973411	7.20
1968 V8-400—		
2 Bar. Carb	1973411	7.20
4 Bar. Carb	1973412	7.20
1969 Six	1973419	3.43
1969 V8-350—		
2 Bar. Carb.—		
Std. Trans	1115365	3.37
Auto. Trans	1115364	3.26
4 Bar. Carb	1115365	3.37
1969-70 V8-400	1115365	3.37
1970 Six	1116217	3.74
1970 V8-350	1115364	3.26
1970 V8-455	1115365	3.37
1971-72 Six	1973434	3.75
1971-72 V8	1115364	3.26
1973-74 Six	1973428	3.47
1973-74 V8, See Firebird—		

6—IGNITION COIL:

Application	Part No.	Price
FIREBIRD:		
1967-68 V8	1115238	14.65
1968 Six	1115202	14.50
1969 Six	1115238	14.65
1969 V8—		
Exc. Below	1115238	14.65
Ram AirIV	1115421	
1970-74 V8	1115238	14.65
1970-74 Six	1115202	14.50
TEMPEST. GTO. LEMANS. T-37:		
1968 Six	1115202	14.50
1968 V8	1115238	14.65
1969-70 Six	1115238	14.65
1969 V8—		
Exc. Below	1115238	14.65
Ram AirV	1115421	
1970-74 V8	1115238	14.65
1971-74 Six	1115202	14.50
VENTURA II:		
1971-74 Six	1115202	14.50
1971-74 V8	1115238	14.65

7—IGNITION CABLE SET:

Application	Part No.	Price
FIREBIRD:		
1967-69 Six	2986606	7.30
1967-68 V8	6293790	13.12

1969-72 V8 ...6296271 12.22
1970-74 Six ...8909903 7.54
1973-74 V8 ...8914141 18.11

TEMPEST. GTO. LEMANS. T-37:
1966-68 V8 ...6289618 11.90
1967-69 Six ...2986606 7.30
1969-72 V8 ...6296271 12.22
1970-74 Six ...8909903 7.54
1973-74 V8 ...8914141 18.11

VENTURA II:
1971-74 Six ...8909903 7.54

1971-72 V8 ...8912493 18.26
1973-74 V8 ...8914141 18.11

8—IGNITION SWITCH (LESS CYLINDER):

FIREBIRD:
1968 ...1116694 5.95
1969—
Less Tilt Wheel ...1990091 6.90
With Tilt Wheel ...1990093 7.40
1971-74—
L/Tilt Wheel ...1990095 5.25
W/Tilt Wheel ...1990096 5.55

TEMPEST. GTO. LEMANS. T-37:
1968 ...1116693 6.60
1969—
Less Tilt Wheel ...1990091 6.90
With Tilt Wheel ...1990093 7.40
1970—
Less Tilt Wheel ...1990091 6.90
With Tilt Wheel ...1990093 7.40
1971-74—
L/Tilt Wheel ...1990095 5.25
W/Tilt Wheel ...1990096 5.55

Time — Fuel System & Intake Manifold (Group C) — Time

OPERATION INDEX

C1—CARBURETOR, R & R OR RENEW

1969-75—
Single Barrel (0.6) ...0.9
2 Or 4 Barrel (0.7) ...0.9

C2—CARBURETOR, R & R & OVERHAUL

1969-75—
Single Barrel (1.5) ...1.9
2 Barrel (1.9) ...2.3
4 Barrel—
Exc. Below (2.2) ...2.6
Quadrajet (1.8) ...2.2

C2A—ACCELERATOR PUMP, RENEW

1969-75—
1 Barrel (0.7) ...0.9
2 Barrel (0.9) ...1.1
4 Barrel (1.1) ...1.4

—NOTE—

Does Not Include R & R Carburetor

C2B—NEEDLE & SEAT, RENEW

1969-75—
1 Barrel (0.6) ...8.0
2 Barrel (0.8) ...1.0
4 Barrel (1.0) ...1.3

—NOTE—

Does Not Include R & R Carburetor

C4A—IDLE STOP SOLENOID, RENEW

1969-75 (0.3) ...0.5

C4B—VACUUM BRAKE ASS'Y, RENEW

1969-75 (0.2) ...0.4

C5—FUEL PUMP, R & R OR RENEW

1969-75 (0.4) ...0.6

C6—FUEL TANK R & R OR RENEW

FIREBIRD:
1969-75 (1.1) ...1.5

TEMPEST-GTO LEMANS. T-37:
1969-75—
Exc. Below (1.0) ...1.4
Sta Wgn (1.2) ...1.6

VENTURA II:
1971-75 (0.7) ...1.0

C7—FUEL SYSTEM, CLEAN

Includes: R & R tank, blow out lines and clean or renew all filters.

FIREBIRD:
1969-75 (1.5) ...2.3

TEMPEST. GTO. LEMANS. T37:
1969-75—
Exc. Below (1.4) ...2.2
Sta. Wagon (1.6) ...2.4

VENTURA II:
1971-75 (1.1) ...1.5

C8—INTAKE MANIFOLD GASKETS, RENEW (V8)

1969-75 (1.6) ...2.0

—NOTE—

For Air Cond, Add (0.1) ...0.2
For Air Injection Add (0.4) ...0.5

C8A—MANIFOLD GASKETS (SIX CYL.), RENEW

1967-69 (0.8) ...1.0
1970-75 (0.9) ...1.0

—NOTE—

For Power Steering, Add (0.3) ...0.4
For Air Injection Add (0.4) ...0.5

Parts — Fuel System & Intake Manifold — Parts

PARTS INDEX

1—CARBURETOR ASS'Y (ROCHESTER):

1968 Six (1 Bar. Carb.)—
Synchro-Mesh ...7036350 60.00
Auto. Trans ...7016812 55.00
1968 Six (4 Bar. Carb.)—
Synchro-Mesh ...7046899 94.30
Auto. Trans ...7016854 88.45
1968 V8-350 (2 Bar. Carb.)—
Synchro-Mesh ...7016821 74.00
Auto. Trans ...7016820 74.00
1968 V8-350 (4 Bar. Carb.)—
Synchro-Mesh ...7036337 112.00
Auto. Trans ...7046900 94.30
1968 V8-400 (Exc. Hi Output, Ram Air)—
Synchro-Mesh ...7036333
Auto. Trans ...7036334 94.30
1968 V8-400 Ram Air—
Synchro-Mesh ...7036345
Auto. Trans ...7036344
1968 V8-400 Hi Output ...7036335
1969 Six (1 Bar. Carb.)—
Synchro-Mesh ...7016935 60.00
Auto. Trans ...7016934 60.00
1969 Six (4 Bar. Carb.)—
Synchro-Mesh ...7016931 112.00
Auto. Trans ...7016948 112.00
1969 V8 (2 Bar. Carb.)—
Synchro-Mesh ...7016821 74.00
Auto. Trans ...7016936 74.00
1969 V8-350 (4 Bar. Carb.)—
Synchro-Mesh ...7016933 88.45
Auto. Trans ...7046901 94.30
1969 V8-400—
Exc. Ram Air & Hi Output—
Synchro-Mesh ...7016933 88.45
Auto. Trans ...7046901 94.30
Ram-Air & Hi Output—
Synchro-Mesh ...7046901 94.30
Auto. Trans ...7046901 112.00
1970 Six—
Synchro-Mesh ...7047015 60.00
Auto Trans ...7047014 60.00
1970 V8-350 (2 Bar. Carb.)—
Synchro-Mesh—
L/Emission Cont. ...7047034 74.00
W/Emission Cont. ...7047031 74.00
Auto. Trans.—
L/Emission Cont ...7047033 74.00
W/Emission Cont ...7047036 74.00
1970 V8 (4 Bar. Carb.) (Exc. Ram Air)—
Synchro-Mesh—
L/Fuel Emission ...7046927 100.40
W/Fuel Emission ...7036917 112.00
Auto. Trans.—
L/Fuel Emission ...7047048 94.20
W/Fuel Emission ...7047049 112.00
1970 V8 (4 Bar. Carb.) (Ram-Air)-
Synchro-Mesh—
L/Fuel Emission ...7036912 108.65
W/Fuel Emission ...7036915 112.00
Auto. Trans.—
L/Fuel Emission ...7036912 112.00
W/Fuel Emission ...7036913 112.00
1971 Six (1 Bar. Carb.)—
Synchro-Mesh ...7047117 60.00
Auto. Trans ...7047114 60.00
1971 V8-350 (2 Bar. Carb.)—
Synchro-Mesh ...7047149 74.00
Auto. Trans ...7047148 74.00
1971 V8-400 (2 Bar. Carb.)—
Synchro-Mesh ...7047149 74.00
Auto. Trans ...7047158 74.00
1971 V8-400 (4 Bar. Carb.)—
Synchro-Mesh ...7041743 98.15
Auto. Trans ...7041743 98.15
1971 V8-455 (4. Bar. Carb.)—
Exc. High Performance ...7041762 112.00
High Performance—
Synchro-Mesh ...7041749 98.15
Auto. Trans ...7041748 98.15
1972 (Six) (1 Bar.)—
W/Air. Injector—
Std. Trans. ...7047223 62.00
Auto. Trans. ...7047222 62.00
L/Air. Injector—
Std. Trans. ...7046578 62.00
Auto. Trans. ...7046577 62.00
1972 (V8-350)—
Std. Trans. ...488062 65.05
Auto. Trans. ...7047248 74.00
1972 (V8-400) ...7047258 74.00
1972 (V8-455) ...7047238 74.00
1973 (Six) (1 Bar.)—
Std. Trans. ...7047317 62.00
Auto. Trans. ...7047314 62.00
1973-74 (V8-350) (2 Bar)—
Exc. Below ...7046771 82.00
L/Alt. Perf. ...7047348 82.00
W/Alt. Perf. ...7046752 82.00
Calif. (73) ...7047349 82.00
Calif (74) ...7047449 82.00
1973 (V8-400) (2 Bar)—
L/Alt. Perf. ...7047358 82.00
W/Alt. Perf. ...7046750 82.00
Calif. ...7047359 82.00
1973 V8-400 (4 Bar)—
Exc Below ...7047335 120.00

W/Alt Perf 7047330 120.00
1974 V8-400 (4 Bar)—
Exc Below 7047335 120.00
W/Alt Perf 17050508 120.00
1974 V8-400 (2 Bar)—
Exc Below 7047453 82.00
W/Alt Perf 7046750 82.00
Calif 7047448 82.00

TEMPEST. GTO. LEMANS. T-37:
1968 Six (1 Bar. Carb.)—
Synchro-Mesh 7036350 60.00
Auto. Trans 7016812 55.00
1968 Six (4 Bar. Carb.)—
Synchro-Mesh 7046899 94.30
Auto. Trans 7016854 88.45
1968 V8-350 (2 Bar. Carb.)—
Synchro-Mesh 7016821 74.00
Auto. Trans 7016820 74.00
1968 V8-350 (4 Bar. Carb.)—
Synchro-Mesh 7036337 112.00
Auto. Trans 7046900 94.30
1968 V8-400 (2 Bar. Carb.) 7036360 74.00
1968 V8-400 (4 Bar. Carb.)—
Exc. Hi Output Ram Air—
Synchro-Mesh 7016827 112.00
Auto. Trans 7036332 88.45
Ram Air—
Synchro-Mesh 7036343
Auto. Trans 7036344
Hi Output—
Synchro-Mesh 7036331
Auto. Trans 7036342
1969 Six (1 Bar. Carb.)—
Synchro-Mesh 7016935 60.00
Auto. Trans 7016934 60.00
1969 Six (4 Bar. Carb.)—
Synchro-Mesh 7016931 112.00
Auto. Trans 7016948 112.00
1968-69 V8 (2 Bar. Carb.)—
Synchro-Mesh 7016821 74.00
Auto. Trans 7016936 74.00
1969 V8-350 (4 Bar. Carb.)—
Exc. Ram Air & Hi Output—
Synchro-Mesh 7016933 88.45
Auto. Trans 7046901 94.30
Ram Air & Hi Output—
Synchro-Mesh 7046901 94.30
Auto. Trans 7046901 112.00
1970 Six—
Synchro-Mesh 7047015 60.00
Auto. Trans 7047014 60.00
1970 V8-350 (2 Bar. Carb.)—
Synchro-Mesh—
L/Fuel Emission 7047034 74.00
W/Fuel Emission 7047031 74.00
Auto. Trans.—
L/Fuel Emission 7047033 74.00
W/Fuel Emission 7047036 74.00
1970 V8-400 (2 Bar. Carb.)—
Synchro-Mesh—
L/Fuel Emission 7047037 74.00
W/Fuel Emission 7047039 74.00
Auto Trans—
L/Fuel Emission 7047035 74.00
W/Fuel Emission 7047038 74.00
1970 V8-400 (4 Bar. Carb.) (Exc. Ram-Air)—
Synchro-Mesh—
L/Fuel Emission 7046927 100.40
W/Fuel Emission 7036917 112.00
Auto. Trans.—
L/Fuel Emission 7047048 94.20
W/Fuel Emission 7047049 112.00
1970 V8-400 (4 Bar. Carb.) (Ram-Air)—
Synchro-Mesh—
L/Fuel Emission 7036912 108.65
W/Fuel Emission 7036915 112.00
Auto. Trans.—
L/Fuel Emission 7036912 112.00
W/Fuel Emission 7036913 112.00
1970 V8-455 (Synchro-Mesh)—
L/Fuel Emission—
L/Hood Air Inlet 7047057 94.20
W/Hood Air Inlet 7036912 108.65
W/Fuel Emission—
L/Hood Air Inlet 7047058 112.00
W/Hood Air Inlet 7036915 112.00
1970 V8-455 (Auto. Trans.)—
L/Fuel Emission—
L/Hood Air Inlet 7047056 94.20
W/Hood Air Inlet 7036912 112.00
W/Fuel Emission—
L/Hood Air Inlet 7047053 112.00
W/Hood Air Inlet 7036913 112.00
1971 Six—
Synchro-Mesh 7047117 60.00
Auto. Trans 7047114 60.00
1971 V8-400 (2 Bar. Carb.)—
Synchro-Mesh 7047149 74.00
Auto. Trans 7047158 74.00
1971 V8-400 (4 Bar. Carb.)—
Synchro-Mesh 7041743 98.15
Auto. Trans 7041743 98.15
1972 V8-400 (4 Bar.)—
Std. Trans. 7047235 112.00
Auto. Trans. 7047236 112.00
1972 V8-455 (Exc. Below) 7047234 112.00
V8-455 H.O.—
Std. Trans. 7047239 112.00
Auto. Trans. 7047246 112.00
1973 (Six)—
Std. Trans. 7047317 62.00
Auto. Trans. 7047314 62.00
1974 Six—
Exc Below 7047417 62.00
Auto Trans Exc 7047414 62.00
Calif 7047404 62.00
1973-74 V8, See Firebird—

2—CARBURETOR OK KLEANOUT KIT (ROCHESTER):

FIREBIRD:
1968 Six (1 Bar. Carb.)—
Synchro-Mesh 7039159 5.15
Auto. Trans 7039079 5.15
1968 Six (4 Bar.) 7039132 8.45
1968-69 V8 (2 Bar. Carb.)—
Synchro-Mesh 7039128 7.10
Auto. Trans 7039127 7.10
1968 V8 (4 Bar.) 7039132 8.45
1969 Six—
1 Bar. Carb 7039159 5.15
4 Bar. Carb 7039160 9.45
1969 V8 (4 Bar.)—
Exc. Below 7039162 9.45
Ram Air 7039161 9.45
1970 Six 7039166 5.15
1970 V8 (2 Bar. Carb.)—
Synchro-Mesh 7039180 7.20
Auto. Trans 7039238 8.10
1970 V8 (4 Bar. Carb.)—
Exc. Ram Air 7039183 9.45
Ram Air 7039185 9.45
1971 Six 7039196 5.15
1971 V8 (2 Bar. Carb.) 7039238 8.10
1971 V8 (4 Bar. Carb.)—
Exc. Below 7039232 9.45
High Performance 7039217 9.45
1972 (Six) 7039236 5.15
1972 (V8-350)—
Std. Trans. 7039241 8.10
1972 V8-400 (2 Bar.) 7039238 8.10
1972 V8-400 (4 Bar.)
Std. Trans. 7039232 9.45
Auto. Trans. 7039240 9.45
1972 V8-455 (Exc. H.O.) 7039238 8.10
V8-455 H.O. 7039237 9.45
1973-74 Six 7039248 5.15
V8-350 .... 7039255 8.10
V8-400 (2 Bar) 7039252 8.10
4 Bar Exc 7039262 9.45
W/Alt Perf 7039263 9.45

TEMPEST. GTO. LEMANS. T-37:
1968 Six (1 Bar. Carb.)—
Synchro-Mesh 7039159 5.15
Auto. Trans 7039079 5.15
1968 Six (4 Bar.) 7039132 8.45
1968-69 V8 (2 Bar. Carb.)—
Synchro-Mesh 7039128 7.10
Auto. Trans 7039127 7.10
1968 V8 (4 Bar.) 7039132 8.45
1969 Six—
1 Bar. Carb 7039159 5.15
4 Bar. Carb 7039160 9.45
1969 V8 (4 Bar. Carb.)—
Exc. Below 7039162 9.45
Hi Perf 7039142 9.45
Ram Air 7039161 9.45
1970 Six 7039166 5.15
1970 V8 (2 Bar. Carb.)—
Synchro-Mesh 7039180 7.20
Auto. Trans 7039238 8.10
1970 V8 (4 Bar. Carb.)—
Exc. Ram Air 7039183 9.45
Ram Air 7039185 9.45
1971 Six 7039196 5.15
1971 V8 (2 Bar. Carb.) 7039238 8.10
1971 V8 (4 Bar. Carb.) 7039232 9.45
1972 (Six) 7039236 5.15
1972 (V8-350)—
Std. Trans. 7039241 8.10
Auto. Trans. 7039239 8.10
1972 V8-400 (2 Bar. Carb.) 7039238 8.10
1972 V8-400 (4 Bar. Carb.)—
Std. Trans. 7039232 9.45
Auto. Trans. 7039240 9.45
1972 V8-455 (Exc. Below) 7039238 8.10
V8-455 Hi Perf. 7039237 9.45
1973-74, See Firebird—

VENTURA II:
1971 Six 7039196 5.15
1971 V8 .... 7039197 7.10
1972 (Six) 7039236 5.15
1972 (V8) 7039224 8.10
1973-74 Six 7039248 5.15

3—CARBURETOR GASKET KIT (ROCHESTER):

FIREBIRD:
1968 Six (1 Bar. Carb.) .... 7036019 .28
1968-69 Six (4 Bar.) 7016848 6.45
1968-69 V8 (2 Bar.) 7016844 2.70
1968-69 V8 (4 Bar.) 7016848 6.45
1969 Six (1 Bar.) 7036619 3.90
1970 Six 7036784 3.50
1970 V8 (2 Bar.) 7036873 5.30
1971 Six 7041599 3.00
1971 V8 (2 Bar.) 7036873 5.30
1972 (Six) 7046536 3.50
1972 (V8-350)—
Std. Trans. 489246 1.55
Auto. Trans. 7036873 5.30
1973-74 Six 7046679 3.50
1973-74 V8exc 7046726 5.15
4 Bar 7046825 8.50

TEMPEST. GTO. LEMANS. T-37:
1968 Six (1 Bar. Carb.) 7036352
1968-69 Six (4 Bar.) 7016848 6.45
1968-69 V8 (2 Bar.) 7016844 2.70
1968-69 V8 (4 Bar.) 7016848 6.45
1969 Six (1 Bar.) 7036619 3.90
1970 Six 7036784 3.50
1971 V8 (2 Bar.) Exc 7036873 5.30
W/Fuel Emission 7046511 7.90
1971 Six 7041599 3.00
1971 V8 (2 Bar) 7036873 5.30
1972 (Six) 7046536 3.50
1972 (V8-350)—
Std. Trans. 489246 1.55
Auto. Trans. 7036873 5.30
1972 V8-400, 455—
2 Bar. Carb. 7036873 5.30
4 Bar. Carb. 7046511 7.90
1973-74 6-250 (1 Bar. Carb.) 7046679 3.50
1973-74 V8, Exc 7046726 5.15
4 Bar 7046825 8.50

VENTURA II:
1971 Six 7041599 3.00
1971 V8 .... 7041606 3.55
1972 (Six) 7046536 3.50
1972 (V8) 7041906 3.55
1973-74 (1 Bar. Carb.) 7046679 3.50
1973-74 (2 Bar. Carb.) 7046726 5.15

4—THERMOSTATIC COIL & COVER ASS'Y (ROCHESTER)

FIREBIRD:
1968 Six (1 Bar. Carb.)—
Std. Trans 9792129 3.76
Auto. Trans 9792133 3.76
1968 Six (4 Bar. Carb.)—
Std. Trans 7029624 9.85
Auto. Trans 7029778 9.85
1968 V8 (2 Bar. Carb.)—
Std. Trans 7028295 6.55
Auto. Trans 7028294 6.95
1968 V8 (4 Bar.) 7041094 8.20
1969 Six (1 Bar. Carb.)—
Std. Trans 9797797 3.65
Auto. Trans 9797798 3.65
1969 Six (4 Bar. Carb.)—
Std. Trans 7029090 8.50
Auto. Trans 7029091 8.50
1969 V8 (2 Bar. Carb.)—
Std. Trans 7028295 6.55
Auto. Trans 7028294 6.95
1969 V8 (4 Bar. Carb.)—
Exc. Below 7041094 8.20
Ram Air 7029099 6.45
1970-71 Six—
Synchro-Mesh 3927770 3.11
Auto. Trans 3927772 2.63
1970 V8-350—
Synchro-Mesh 7028295 6.55
Auto. Trans 7028293 6.90
1970 V8-400—
2 Bar. Carb 7028295 6.55
4 Bar. Carb. (Synchro-Mesh)—
Exc. Below 7040097 7.10
Ram. AirIV 7029099 6.45
4 Bar. Carb. (Auto. Trans.)—
L/Emission Cont 7041094 8.20
W/Emission Cont 7040097 7.10
1971 V8-350—
Synchro-Mesh 482125 9.80
Auto. Trans 482124 9.80
1971 V8-400—
2 Bar. Carb 482125 9.80

4 Bar. Carb.—
Synchro-Mesh 482127 9.80
Auto. Trans 482128 9.80
1971 V8-455—
Exc. Below 482128 9.80
Hi. Performance 7041094 8.20
1972-74 (Six) .... 3998944 .67
1972 V8-350 (2 Bar. Carb.)—
Std. Trans. 488074 9.80
Auto. Trans. 486249 9.80
1972 V8-400, 455 (2 BC) 488073 9.80
1972 (4 Bar. Carb.) 487112 9.80
1973-74 Exc 7036881 4.55
W/Alt Perf 7046822 4.60

TEMPEST. GTO. LEMANS. T-37:

1968 Six (1 Bar. Carb.)—
Std. Trans 9792129 3.76
Auto. Trans 9792133 3.76
1968 Six (4 Bar. Carb.)—
Std. Trans 7029624 9.85
Auto. Trans 7029778 9.85
1968 V8 (2 Bar. Carb.)—
Std. Trans 7028295 6.55
Auto. Trans.—
Exc. Below 7028294 6.95
Turbo H.M. 7028293 6.90
1968 V8 (4 Bar.) 7041094 8.20
1969 Six (1 Bar. Carb.)—
Std. Trans 9797797 3.65
Auto. Trans 9797798 3.65
1969 Six (4 Bar. Carb.)—
Std. Trans 7029090 8.50
Auto. Trans 7029091 8.50
1969 V8 (2 Bar. Carb.)—
Std. Trans 7028295 6.55
Auto. Trans.—
Exc. Below 7028294 6.95
Turbo H-Matic 7028293 6.90
1969 V8 (4 Bar. Carb.)—
Exc. Below 7041094 8.20
Ram. Air 7029099 6.45
1970-71 Six—
Synchro-Mesh 3927770 3.11
Auto. Trans 3927772 2.63
1970 V8-350—
Synchro-Mesh 7028295 6.55
Auto. Trans 7028293 6.90
1970 V8-400—
2 Bar. Carb 7028295 6.55
4 Bar. Carb.—
Exc. Below 7040097 7.10
Ram AirIII 7041094 8.20
Ram AirIV 7029099 6.45
1971 V8-400—
2 Bar. Carb 482125 9.80
4 Bar. Carb.—
Synchro-Mesh 482127 9.80
Auto. Trans 482128 9.80
1972-74 (Six) .... 3998944 .67
1972 V8-350 (2 Bar.)—
Std. Trans. 488074 9.80
Auto. Trans. 486249 9.80
1972 V8-400 (2 Bar.) 488073 9.80
1972 V8-455 (2 Bar.) 486250 9.80
1972 (4 Bar Carb) 487112 9.80
1973-74 Exc 7036881 4.55
W/Alt Perf 7046822 4.60

5—CHOKE VACUUM CONTROL ASS'Y (ROCHESTER):

1968 Six—
1 Bar 7028644 3.20
4 Bar 7038239 4.25
1968 V8 (4 Bar.) 7038237 4.25
1969 Six (4 Bar.) 7038239 4.25
1969 V8—
2 Bar. Carb 7036539 3.45
4 Bar. Carb.—
Exc. Below 7038237 4.25
Ram Air 7037835 8.70
1970 V8—
2 Bar. Carb 7038941 4.10
4 Bar. Carb.—
Exc. Below 7026214 9.15
Ram Air 7042595 4.25
1971 V8—
2 Bar. Carb 7042687 7.80
4 Bar. Carb—
Exc. Below 7043988 14.20
Hi. Performance 7042641 14.20
1972 (2 Bar. Carbs.) 7045915 9.10
4 Bar. Carbs. 7045931 14.20
1973 (1 Bar. Carb.) 7030918 9.25
2 Bar. Carb. 7030987 9.10
4 Bar Carb 7047864 10.05

TEMPEST. GTO. LEMANS. T-37:

1966-68 Six (1 Bar.) 7028644 3.20
1968-69 Six (4 Bar.) 7038239 4.25
1968 V8 (2 Bar.) 7036539 3.45
1968 V8 (4 Bar.) 7038237 4.25
1969 V8—
2 Bar. Carb 7036539 3.45
4 Bar. Carb.—
Exc. Below 7038237 4.25
Ram Air 7037835 8.70
1970 V8—
2 Bar. Carb. 7038941 4.10
4 Bar. Carb.—
Exc. Below 7038718 10.55
Ram Air 7042604 8.70
1971 V8—
2 Bar. Carb 7042687 7.80
4 Bar. Carb 7043988 14.20
1972 (2 Bar. Carbs.) 7045915 9.10
1972 (4 Bar. Carbs.) 7045931 14.20
1973-74, See Firebird—

6—FUEL PUMP

FIREBIRD:

1968 Six (1 Bar. Carb.) 6416909 12.85
1968 Six (4 Bar. Carb.) 6416912 11.49
1968 V8 (2 Bar. Carb.) 6417211 13.81
1968 V8 (4 Bar. Carb.) 6417212 13.81
1969 Six 6416912 11.49
1969 V8—
Exc. Below 6417420 13.15
W/Vapor Return 6417419 13.03
1970-74 Six 6416502 14.09
1970-71 V8 (2 Bar. Carb.)—
L/Air Cond 6470498 12.68
W/Air Cond 6470497 13.40
1970-71 V8 (4 Bar. Carb.) 6470499 16.03
1972-73 V8 (2 Bar. Carb)—
L/Air Cond 6470668 15.45
W/Air Cond 6470669 15.91
1972-73 V8 (4 Bar) 6470670 25.61
1974 V8—
2 Bar Carb Exc 6470668 15.45
Air Cond 6470669 15.91
4 Bar Carb 6470670 25.61

TEMPEST. GTO. LEMANS. T-37:

1967-68 Six (1 Bar. Carb.) 6416909 12.85
1967-68 Six (4 Bar. Carb.) 6416912 11.49
1968 V8 (2 Bar. Carb.) 6417211 13.81
1968 V8 (4 Bar. Carb.) 6417212 13.81
1969 Six 6416912 11.49
1969 V8—
Exc. Below 6417420 13.15
W/Vapor Return 6417419 13.03
1970-74 Six 6416502 14.09
1970 V8 (2 Bar. Carb.) 6417419 13.03
1970 V8 (4 Bar. Carb)—
Early 6470222 17.10
Late 6470513 17.75
1971-72 V8 (2 Bar Carb)—
L/Air Cond. 6417420 13.15
W/Air Cond 6417419 13.03
1971-72 V8 (4 Bar. Carb.) 6470513 17.75
1973 (2 Bar. Carb.)—
L/Air Cond. 6470669 15.91
W/Air Cond. 6470668 15.45
1973 (4 Bar. Carb.) 6470670 25.61
1974 V8, See Firebird—

VENTURA II:

1971-74 Six 6416502 14.09
1971 V8 .... 6416712 11.64
1972-74 V8, See Firebird—

7—FUEL TANK:

FIREBIRD:

1967-68 .... 3912377 50.55
1969 .... 3953844 50.55
1970—
L/Fuel Emission 6263025 50.55
W/Fuel Emission 6263022 53.05
1971 .... 6263022 53.05
1972-73 .... 6272127 53.05
1974 .... 344427 55.60

TEMPEST. GTO. LEMANS. T-37:

1968—
Exc. Below 9790355 43.95
Sta. Wagon 398168 41.75
1969—
Exc. Below 487116 11.00
Sta. Wagon 398168 41.75
1970 (Exc. Sta. Wagon)—
L/Fuel Emission 478116 43.95
W/Fuel Emission 478119 48.35
1970 Sta. Wagon—
L/Fuel Emission 404160 43.95
W/Fuel Emission 404964 50.55
1971-72
Exc. Below 485131 48.35
Sta. Wagon 408439 49.25
1973 (Exc. Below) 489966 48.35
Sta. Wagon 409873 49.25
1974 Exc 495332 48.35
Grand AM 495334 59.40
Sta Wagon 416366 46.15

VENTURA II:

1971-72 .... 3995720 53.05
1973-74 .... 6259306 39.75

8—FUEL TANK FILTER:

TEMPEST. GTO. LEMANS. T-37:

1967-73 .... 5651264 .99

9—INTAKE MANIFOLD GASKET:

FIREBIRD:

1967-69 Six—
1 Bar. Carb .... 329604 .27
4 Bar. Carb .... 9773574 .39
1967-68 V8 .... 479433 2.08
1969 V8—
Exc. Below 479433 2.08
Ram Air 9796613 2.08
1970-71 Six .... 329604 .27
1970 V8—
Exc. Below .... 9780358 .50
Ram AirIV 9796613 2.08
1971—
Exc. Below 479433 2.08
V8-455 Hi. Performance 9796613 2.08
1972-73 Six 3953746 1.68
1972-74 V8 .... 493404 1.68
1974 Six 338115 1.68

TEMPEST. GTO. LEMANS. T-37:

1966-68 V8 .... 479433 2.08
1967-70 Six—
1 Bar. Carb .... 329604 .27
4 Bar. Carb .... 9773574 .39
1969-70 V8—
Exc. Below 479433 2.08
Ram Air 9796613 2.08
1971 Six .... 329604 .27
1971 V8 .... 479433 2.08
1972-74 See Firebird—

VENTURA-II:

1971-72 Six 3953746 1.68
1971-72 V8 .... 3957985 2.92
1973-74 See Firebird—

MOTOR'S

Time/Dollar Conversion Table

HOURS Labor Time	LABOR RATES PER HOUR $6.00	$6.50	$7.00	$7.50	$8.00	$9.00	$10.00	$11.00	$12.00	$13.00	$14.00	$15.00	$16.00	$17.00	$18.00	$19.00	$20.00
0.1	.60	.65	.70	.75	.80	.90	1.00	1.10	1.20	1.30	1.40	1.50	1.60	1.70	1.80	1.90	2.00
0.2	1.20	1.30	1.40	1.50	1.60	1.80	2.00	2.20	2.40	2.60	2.80	3.00	3.20	3.40	3.60	3.80	4.00
0.3	1.80	1.95	2.10	2.25	2.40	2.70	3.00	3.30	3.60	3.90	4.20	4.50	4.80	5.10	5.40	5.70	6.00
0.4	2.40	2.60	2.80	3.00	3.20	3.60	4.00	4.40	4.80	5.20	5.60	6.00	6.40	6.80	7.20	7.60	8.00
0.5	3.00	3.25	3.50	3.75	4.00	4.50	5.00	5.50	6.00	6.50	7.00	7.50	8.00	8.50	9.00	9.50	10.00
0.6	3.60	3.90	4.20	4.50	4.80	5.40	6.00	6.60	7.20	7.80	8.40	9.00	9.60	10.20	10.80	11.40	12.00
0.7	4.20	4.55	4.90	5.25	5.60	6.30	7.00	7.70	8.40	9.10	9.80	10.50	11.20	11.90	12.60	13.30	14.00
0.8	4.80	5.20	5.60	6.00	6.40	7.20	8.00	8.80	9.60	10.40	11.20	12.00	12.80	13.60	14.40	15.20	16.00
0.9	5.40	5.85	6.30	6.75	7.20	8.10	9.00	9.90	10.80	11.70	12.60	13.50	14.40	15.30	16.20	17.10	18.00
1.0	6.00	6.50	7.00	7.50	8.00	9.00	10.00	11.00	12.00	13.00	14.00	15.00	16.00	17.00	18.00	19.00	20.00
1.1	6.60	7.15	7.70	8.25	8.80	9.90	11.00	12.10	13.20	14.30	15.40	16.50	17.60	18.70	19.80	20.90	22.00
1.2	7.20	7.80	8.40	9.00	9.60	10.80	12.00	13.20	14.40	15.60	16.80	18.00	19.20	20.40	21.60	22.80	24.00
1.3	7.80	8.45	9.10	9.75	10.40	11.70	13.00	14.30	15.60	16.90	18.20	19.50	20.80	22.10	23.40	24.70	26.00
1.4	8.40	9.10	9.80	10.50	11.20	12.60	14.00	15.40	16.80	18.20	19.60	21.00	22.40	23.80	25.20	26.60	28.00
1.5	9.00	9.75	10.50	11.25	12.00	13.50	15.00	16.50	18.00	19.50	21.00	22.50	24.00	25.50	27.00	28.50	30.00
1.6	9.60	10.40	11.20	12.00	12.80	14.40	16.00	17.60	19.20	20.80	22.40	24.00	25.60	27.20	28.80	30.40	32.00
1.7	10.20	11.05	11.90	12.75	13.60	15.30	17.00	18.70	20.40	22.10	23.80	25.50	27.20	28.90	30.60	32.30	34.00
1.8	10.80	11.70	12.60	13.50	14.40	16.20	18.00	19.80	21.60	23.40	25.20	27.00	28.80	30.60	32.40	34.20	36.00
1.9	11.40	12.35	13.30	14.25	15.20	17.10	19.00	20.90	22.80	24.70	26.60	28.50	30.40	32.30	34.20	36.10	38.00
2.0	12.00	13.00	14.00	15.00	16.00	18.00	20.00	22.00	24.00	26.00	28.00	30.00	32.00	34.00	36.00	38.00	40.00
2.1	12.60	13.65	14.70	15.75	16.80	18.90	21.00	23.10	25.20	27.30	29.40	31.50	33.60	35.70	37.80	39.90	42.00
2.2	13.20	14.30	15.40	16.50	17.60	19.80	22.00	24.20	26.40	28.60	30.80	33.00	35.20	37.40	39.60	41.80	44.00
2.3	13.80	14.95	16.10	17.25	18.40	20.70	23.00	25.30	27.60	39.90	32.20	34.50	36.80	39.10	41.40	43.70	46.00
2.4	14.40	15.60	16.80	18.00	19.20	21.60	24.00	26.40	28.80	31.20	33.60	36.00	38.40	40.80	43.20	45.60	48.00
2.5	15.00	16.25	17.50	18.75	20.00	22.50	25.00	27.50	30.00	32.50	35.00	37.50	40.00	42.50	45.00	47.50	50.00
2.6	15.60	16.90	18.20	19.50	20.80	23.40	26.00	28.60	31.20	33.80	36.40	39.00	41.60	44.20	46.80	49.40	52.00
2.7	16.20	17.55	18.90	20.25	21.60	24.30	27.00	29.70	32.40	35.10	37.80	40.50	43.20	45.90	48.60	51.30	54.00
2.8	16.80	18.20	19.60	21.00	22.40	25.20	28.00	30.80	33.60	36.40	39.20	42.00	44.80	47.60	50.40	53.20	56.00
2.9	17.40	18.85	20.30	21.75	23.20	26.10	29.00	31.90	34.80	37.70	40.60	43.50	46.40	49.30	52.20	55.10	58.00
3.0	18.00	19.50	21.00	22.50	24.00	27.00	30.00	33.00	36.00	39.00	42.00	45.00	48.00	51.00	54.00	57.00	60.00
3.1	18.60	20.15	21.70	23.25	24.80	27.90	31.00	34.10	37.20	40.30	43.40	46.50	49.60	52.70	55.80	58.90	62.00
3.2	19.20	20.80	22.40	24.00	25.60	28.80	32.00	35.20	38.40	41.60	44.80	48.00	51.20	54.40	57.60	60.80	64.00
3.3	19.80	21.45	23.10	24.75	26.40	29.70	33.00	36.30	39.60	42.90	46.20	49.50	52.80	56.10	59.40	62.70	66.00
3.4	20.40	22.10	23.80	25.50	27.20	30.60	34.00	37.40	40.80	44.20	47.60	51.00	54.40	57.80	61.20	64.60	68.00
3.5	21.00	22.75	24.50	26.25	28.00	31.50	35.00	38.50	42.00	45.50	49.00	52.50	56.00	59.50	63.00	66.50	70.00
3.6	21.60	23.40	25.20	27.00	28.80	32.40	36.00	39.60	43.20	46.80	50.40	54.00	57.60	61.20	64.80	68.40	72.00
3.7	22.20	24.05	25.90	27.75	29.60	33.30	37.00	40.70	44.40	48.10	51.80	55.50	59.20	62.90	66.60	70.30	74.00
3.8	22.80	24.70	26.60	28.50	30.40	34.20	38.00	41.80	45.60	49.40	53.20	57.00	60.80	64.60	68.40	72.20	76.00
3.9	23.40	25.35	27.30	29.25	31.20	35.10	39.00	42.90	46.80	50.70	54.60	58.50	62.40	66.30	70.20	74.10	78.00
4.0	24.00	26.00	28.00	30.00	32.00	36.00	40.00	44.00	48.00	52.00	56.00	60.00	64.00	68.00	72.00	76.00	80.00
4.1	24.60	26.65	28.70	30.75	32.80	36.90	41.00	45.10	49.20	53.30	57.40	61.50	65.60	69.70	73.80	77.90	82.00
4.2	25.20	27.30	29.40	31.50	33.60	37.80	42.00	46.20	50.40	54.60	58.80	63.00	67.20	71.40	75.60	79.80	84.00
4.3	25.80	27.95	30.10	32.25	34.40	38.70	43.00	47.30	51.60	55.90	60.20	64.50	68.80	73.10	77.40	81.70	86.00
4.4	26.40	28.60	30.80	33.00	35.20	39.60	44.00	48.40	52.80	57.20	61.60	66.00	70.40	74.80	79.20	83.60	88.00
4.5	27.00	29.25	31.50	33.75	36.00	40.50	45.00	49.50	54.00	58.50	63.00	67.50	72.00	76.50	81.00	85.50	90.00
4.6	27.60	29.90	32.20	34.50	36.80	41.40	46.00	50.60	55.20	59.80	64.40	69.00	73.60	78.20	82.80	87.40	92.00
4.7	28.20	30.55	32.90	35.25	37.60	42.30	47.00	51.70	56.40	61.10	65.80	70.50	75.20	79.90	84.60	89.30	94.00
4.8	28.80	31.20	33.60	36.00	38.40	43.20	48.00	52.80	57.60	62.40	67.20	72.00	76.80	81.60	86.40	91.20	96.00
4.9	29.40	31.85	34.30	36.75	39.20	44.10	49.00	53.90	58.80	63.70	68.60	73.50	78.40	83.30	88.20	93.10	98.00
5.0	30.00	32.50	35.00	37.50	40.00	45.00	50.00	55.00	60.00	65.00	70.00	75.00	80.00	85.00	90.00	95.00	100.00
5.1	30.60	33.15	35.70	38.25	40.80	45.90	51.00	56.10	61.20	66.30	71.40	76.50	81.60	86.70	91.80	96.90	102.00
5.2	31.20	33.80	36.40	39.00	41.60	46.80	52.00	57.20	62.40	67.60	72.80	78.00	83.20	88.40	93.60	98.80	104.00
5.3	31.80	34.45	37.10	39.75	42.40	47.70	53.00	58.30	63.60	68.90	74.20	79.50	84.80	90.10	95.40	100.70	106.00
5.4	32.40	35.10	37.80	40.50	43.20	48.60	54.00	59.40	64.80	70.20	75.60	81.00	86.40	91.80	97.20	102.60	108.00
5.5	33.00	35.75	38.50	41.25	44.00	49.50	55.00	60.50	66.00	71.50	77.00	82.50	88.00	93.50	99.00	104.50	110.00
5.6	33.60	36.40	39.20	42.00	44.80	50.40	56.00	61.60	67.20	72.80	78.40	84.00	89.60	95.20	100.80	106.40	112.00
5.7	34.20	37.05	39.90	42.75	45.60	51.30	57.00	62.70	68.40	74.10	79.80	85.50	91.20	96.90	102.60	108.30	114.00
5.8	34.80	37.70	40.60	43.50	46.40	52.20	58.00	63.80	69.60	75.40	81.20	87.00	92.80	98.60	104.40	110.20	116.00
5.9	35.40	38.35	41.30	44.25	47.20	53.10	59.00	64.90	70.80	76.70	82.60	88.50	94.40	100.30	106.20	112.10	118.00

Time/Dollar Conversion Table—Continued

HOURS Labor Time	LABOR RATES PER HOUR $6.00	$6.50	$7.00	$7.50	$8.00	$9.00	$10.00	$11.00	$12.00	$13.00	$14.00	$15.00	$16.00	$17.00	$18.00	$19.00	$20.00
6.0	36.00	39.00	42.00	45.00	48.00	54.00	60.00	66.00	72.00	78.00	84.00	90.00	96.00	102.00	108.00	114.00	120.00
6.1	36.60	39.65	42.70	45.75	48.80	54.90	61.00	67.10	73.20	79.30	85.40	91.50	97.60	103.70	109.80	115.90	122.00
6.2	37.20	40.30	43.40	46.50	49.60	55.80	62.00	68.20	74.40	80.60	86.80	93.00	99.20	105.40	111.60	117.80	124.00
6.3	37.80	40.95	44.10	47.25	50.40	56.70	63.00	69.30	75.60	81.90	88.20	94.50	100.80	107.10	113.40	119.70	126.00
6.4	38.40	41.60	44.80	48.00	51.20	57.60	64.00	70.40	76.80	83.20	89.60	96.00	102.40	108.80	115.20	121.60	128.00
6.5	39.00	42.25	45.50	48.75	52.00	58.50	65.00	71.50	78.00	84.50	91.00	97.50	104.00	110.50	117.00	123.50	130.00
6.6	39.60	42.90	46.20	49.50	52.80	59.40	66.00	72.60	79.20	85.80	92.40	99.00	105.60	112.20	118.80	125.40	132.00
6.7	40.20	43.55	46.90	50.25	53.60	60.30	67.00	73.70	80.40	87.10	93.80	100.50	107.20	113.90	120.60	127.30	134.00
6.8	40.80	44.20	47.60	51.00	54.40	61.20	68.00	74.80	81.60	88.40	95.20	102.00	108.80	115.60	122.40	129.20	136.00
6.9	41.40	44.85	48.30	51.75	55.20	62.10	69.00	75.90	82.80	89.70	96.60	103.50	110.40	117.30	124.20	131.10	138.00
7.0	42.00	45.50	49.00	52.50	56.00	63.00	70.00	77.00	84.00	91.00	98.00	105.00	112.00	119.00	126.00	133.00	140.00
7.1	42.60	46.15	49.70	53.25	56.80	63.90	71.00	78.10	85.20	92.30	99.40	106.50	113.60	120.70	127.80	134.90	142.00
7.2	43.20	46.80	50.40	54.00	57.60	64.80	72.00	79.20	86.40	93.60	100.80	108.00	115.20	122.40	129.60	136.80	144.00
7.3	43.80	47.45	51.10	54.75	58.40	65.70	73.00	80.30	87.60	94.90	102.20	109.50	116.80	124.10	131.40	138.70	146.00
7.4	44.40	48.10	51.80	55.50	59.20	66.60	74.00	81.40	88.80	96.20	103.60	111.00	118.40	125.80	133.20	140.60	148.00
7.5	45.00	48.75	52.50	56.25	60.00	67.50	75.00	82.50	90.00	97.50	105.00	112.50	120.00	127.50	135.00	142.50	150.00
7.6	45.60	49.40	53.20	57.00	60.80	68.40	76.00	83.60	91.20	98.80	106.40	114.00	121.60	129.20	136.80	144.40	152.00
7.7	46.20	50.05	53.90	57.75	61.60	69.30	77.00	84.70	92.40	100.10	107.80	115.50	123.20	130.90	138.60	146.30	154.00
7.8	46.80	50.70	54.60	58.50	62.40	70.20	78.00	85.80	93.60	101.40	109.20	117.00	124.80	132.60	140.40	148.20	156.00
7.9	47.40	51.35	55.30	59.25	63.20	71.10	79.00	86.90	94.80	102.70	110.60	118.50	126.40	134.30	142.20	150.10	158.00
8.0	48.00	52.00	56.00	60.00	64.00	72.00	80.00	88.00	96.00	104.00	112.00	120.00	128.00	136.00	144.00	152.00	160.00
8.1	48.60	52.65	56.70	60.75	64.80	72.90	81.00	89.10	97.20	105.30	113.40	121.50	129.60	137.70	145.80	153.90	162.00
8.2	49.20	53.30	57.40	61.50	65.60	73.80	82.00	90.20	98.40	106.60	114.80	123.00	131.20	139.40	147.60	155.80	164.00
8.3	49.80	53.95	58.10	62.25	66.40	74.70	83.00	91.30	99.60	107.90	116.20	124.50	132.80	141.10	149.40	157.70	166.00
8.4	50.40	54.60	58.80	63.00	67.20	75.60	84.00	92.40	100.80	109.20	117.60	126.00	134.40	142.80	151.20	159.60	168.00
8.5	51.00	55.25	59.50	63.75	68.00	76.50	85.00	93.50	102.00	110.50	119.00	127.50	136.00	144.50	153.00	161.50	170.00
8.6	51.60	55.90	60.20	64.50	68.80	77.40	86.00	94.60	103.20	111.80	120.40	129.00	137.60	146.20	154.80	163.40	172.00
8.7	52.20	56.55	60.90	65.25	69.60	78.30	87.00	95.70	104.40	113.10	121.80	130.50	139.20	147.90	156.60	165.30	174.00
8.8	52.80	57.20	61.60	66.00	70.40	79.20	88.00	96.80	105.60	114.40	123.20	132.00	140.80	149.60	158.40	167.20	176.00
8.9	53.40	57.85	62.30	66.75	71.20	80.10	89.00	97.90	106.80	115.70	124.60	133.50	142.40	151.30	160.20	169.10	178.00
9.0	54.00	58.50	63.00	67.50	72.00	81.00	90.00	99.00	108.00	117.00	126.00	135.00	144.00	153.00	162.00	171.00	180 00
9.1	54.60	59.15	63.70	68.25	72.80	81.90	91.00	100.10	109.20	118.30	127.40	136.50	145.60	154.70	163.80	172.90	182.00
9.2	55.20	59.80	64.40	69.00	73.60	82.80	92.00	101.20	110.40	119.60	128.80	138.00	147.20	156.40	165.60	174.80	184.00
9.3	55.80	60.45	65.10	69.75	74.40	83.70	93.00	102.30	111.60	120.90	130.20	139.50	148.80	158.10	167.40	176.70	186.00
9.4	56.40	61.10	65.80	70.50	75.20	84.60	94.00	103.40	112.80	122.20	131.60	141.00	150.40	159.80	169.20	178.60	188.00
9.5	57.00	61.75	66.50	71.25	76.00	85.50	95.00	104.50	114.00	123.50	133.00	142.50	152.00	161.50	171.00	180.50	190.00
9.6	57.60	62.40	67.20	72.00	76.80	86.40	96.00	105.60	115.20	124.80	134.40	144.00	153.60	163.20	172.80	182.40	192.00
9.7	58.20	63.05	67.90	72.75	77.60	87.30	97.00	106.70	116.40	126.10	135.80	145.50	155.20	164.90	174.60	184.30	194.00
9.8	58.80	63.70	68.60	73.50	78.40	88.20	98.00	107.80	117.60	127.40	137.20	147.00	156.80	166.60	176.40	186.20	196.00
9.9	59.40	64.35	69.30	74.25	79.20	89.10	99.00	108.90	118.80	128.70	138.60	148.50	158.40	168.30	178.20	188.10	198.00
10.0	60.00	65.00	70.00	75.00	80.00	90.00	100.00	110.00	120.00	130.00	140.00	150.00	160.00	170.00	180.00	190.00	200.00
10.5	63.00	68.25	73.50	78.75	84.00	94.50	105.00	115.50	126.00	136.50	147.00	157.50	168.00	178.50	189.00	199.50	210.00
11.0	66.00	71.50	77.00	82.50	88.00	99.00	110.00	121.00	132.00	143.00	154.00	165.00	176.00	187.00	198.00	209.00	220.00
11.5	69.00	74.75	80.50	86.25	92.00	103.50	115.00	126.50	138.00	149.50	161.00	172.50	184.00	195.50	207.00	218.50	230.00
12.0	72.00	78.00	84.00	90.00	96.00	108.00	120.00	132.00	144.00	156.00	168.00	180.00	192.00	204.00	216.00	228.00	240.00
12.5	75.00	81.25	87.50	93.75	100.00	112.50	125.00	137.50	150.00	162.50	175.00	187.50	200.00	212.50	225.00	237.50	250.00
13.0	78.00	84.50	91.00	97.50	104.00	117.00	130.00	143.00	156.00	169.00	182.00	195.00	208.00	221.00	234.00	247.00	260.00
13.5	81.00	87.75	94.50	101.25	108.00	121.50	135.00	148.50	162.00	175.50	189.00	202.50	216.00	229.50	243.00	256.50	270.00
14.0	84.00	91.00	98.00	105.00	112.00	126.00	140.00	154.00	168.00	182.00	196.00	210.00	224.00	238.00	252.00	266.00	280.00
14.5	87.00	94.25	101.50	108.75	116.00	130.50	145.00	159.50	174.00	188.50	203.00	217.50	232.00	246.50	261.00	275.50	290.00
15.0	90.00	97.50	105.00	112.50	120.00	135.00	150.00	165.00	180.00	195.00	210.00	225.00	240.00	255.00	270.00	285.00	300.00
15.5	93.00	100.75	108.50	116.25	124.00	139.50	155.00	170.50	186.00	201.50	217.00	232.50	248.00	263.50	279.00	294.50	310.00
16.0	96.00	104.00	112.00	120.00	128.00	144.00	160.00	176.00	192.00	208.00	224.00	240.00	256.00	272.00	288.00	304.00	320.00
16.5	99.00	107.25	115.50	123.75	132.00	148.50	165.00	181.50	198.00	214.50	231.00	247.50	264.00	280.50	297.00	313.50	330.00
17.0	102.00	110.50	119.00	127.50	136.00	153.00	170.00	187.00	204.00	221.00	238.00	255.00	272.00	289.00	306.00	323.00	340.00
17.5	105.00	113.75	122.50	131.25	140.00	157.50	175.00	192.50	210.00	227.50	245.00	262.50	280.00	297.50	315.00	332.50	350.00
18.0	108.00	117.00	126.00	135.00	144.00	162.00	180.00	198.00	216.00	234.00	252.00	270.00	288.00	306.00	324.00	342.00	360.00
18.5	111.00	120.25	129.50	138.75	148.00	166.50	185.00	203.50	222.00	240.50	259.00	277.50	296.00	314.50	333.00	351.50	370.00
19.0	114.00	123.50	133.00	142.50	152.00	171.00	190.00	209.00	228.00	247.00	266.00	285.00	304.00	323.00	342.00	361.00	380.00
19.5	117.00	126.75	136.50	146.25	156.00	175.50	195.00	214.50	234.00	253.50	273.00	292.50	312.00	331.50	351.00	370.50	390.00
20.0	120.00	130.00	140.00	150.00	160.00	180.00	200.00	220.00	240.00	260.00	280.00	300.00	320.00	340.00	360.00	380.00	400.00
30.0	180.00	195.00	210.00	225.00	240.00	270.00	300.00	330.00	360.00	390.00	420.00	450.00	480.00	510.00	540.00	570.00	600.00
40.0	240.00	260.00	280.00	300.00	320.00	360.00	400.00	440.00	480.00	520.00	560.00	600.00	640.00	680.00	720.00	760.00	800.00
50.0	300.00	325.00	350.00	375.00	400.00	450.00	500.00	550.00	600.00	650.00	700.00	750.00	800.00	850.00	900.00	950.00	1000.00

SUMMARY OF FEDERAL MOTOR VEHICLE EMISSION CONTROL RULES & REGULATIONS

All regulations previous to those concerning 1975 model year vehicles remain the same as printed in your Emission Control Manual Volume I beginning on page 748.

1975-1976 MODEL YEAR VEHICLES

(except Light Duty Trucks and truck derivatives under 6000 lbs.)

Emission standards

1. Exhaust emissions from 1975 model year vehicles shall not exceed:
   HYDROCARBONS—1.5 grams per vehicle mile.
   (California 0.9 gm/mi)
   CARBON MONOXIDE—15 grams per vehicle mile.
   (California 9 gm/mi)
   OXIDES OF NITROGEN—3.1 grams per vehicle mile.
   (California 2 gm/mi)
2. Fuel evaporative emissions shall not exceed:
   HYDROCARBONS—2 grams per test.
3. No crankcase emissions shall be discharged into the ambient atmosphere.

Mileage accumulation and emission measurements

Same as 1973-74.

Test procedures

Same as 1973-74. With the addition that a catalytic converter may be serviced once during 50,000 miles if an audible or visual signal approved by EPA alerts the vehicle operator to the need for maintenance.

Compliance with emission standards

Same as 1973-74.

1977 Model Year Vehicles Emission standards

Exhaust emissions shall not exceed:
HYDROCARBONS—0.41 gram per vehicle mile.
CARBON MONOXIDE—3.4 grams per vehicle mile.
OXIDES OF NITROGEN—2.0 grams per vehicle mile.

EMISSION STANDARDS FOR 1975 GASOLINE OPERATED AND DIESEL/ LIGHT DUTY TRUCKS AND TRUCK DERIVATIVES UNDER 6000 LBS.

HYDROCARBONS—2 gpm
CARBON MONOXIDE—28 gpm
OXIDES OF NITROGEN—3.1 gpm
EVAPORATIVE EMISSIONS—2 grams per test

EXHAUST EMISSION STANDARDS FOR LIGHT DUTY DIESEL-POWERED VEHICLES FOR 1976 MODEL YEAR

HYDROCARBONS—2 gpm
CARBON MONOXIDE—20 gpm
OXIDES OF NITROGEN—3.1 gpm

HIGH ALTITUDE VEHICLE CERTIFICATION

Beginning with the 1977 model year, all gasoline or diesel powered light duty vehicles offered for sale in high altitude (over 4000 ft.) regions in the U.S. must be certified for compliance with federal emission standards at high altitude.

ENGINE SMOKE AND GASEOUS EMISSION REGULATIONS FOR DIESEL AND GAS HEAVY DUTY VEHICLES

No changes. Consult your Emission Control Manual page 753 for information.

SUMMARY OF STATE MOTOR VEHICLE EMISSION CONTROL RULES & REGULATIONS

There are some states which have had no changes made in their Emission Control laws since the publication of the Emission Control Manual. In such cases, we have indicated here that there is no change. To get the regulations for such states, refer to the Emission Control Law Summary beginning on page 755 in your Emission Control Manual. Where there have been changes, we have printed here a synopsis of the complete new law.

ALABAMA

No changes.

ALASKA

No changes.

ARIZONA

State law prohibits, subsequent to the first sale, 1968 and later model year motor vehicles equipped with an emission control system or device in accordance with Federal law from discharging into the atmosphere air contaminants in quantities in excess of the following:

Engine piston displacement over 140 cubic inches—
- 3.0% of carbon monoxide
- 300 parts per million of hydrocarbons

Engine piston displacement of 140 cubic inches or less—
- 4.0% of carbon monoxide
- 400 parts per million of hydrocarbons

For passenger type motor vehicles of the 1963 through 1967 model years the exhaust emission standards are the following:

Engine piston displacement over 140 cubic inches—
- 4.5% of carbon monoxide
- 500 parts per million of hydrocarbons

Engine piston displacement of 140 cubic inches or less—
- 5.0% of carbon monoxide
- 600 parts per million of hydrocarbons

For passenger type motor vehicles of the 1962 model year and older the exhaust emission standards are the following:

Engine piston displacement over 140 cubic inches—
- 5.0% of carbon monoxide
- 600 parts per million of hydrocarbons

Engine displacement of 140 cubic inches or less—
- 6.0% of carbon monoxide
- 800 parts per million of hydrocarbons

The law further prohibits the emission into the atmosphere from any gasoline-powered vehicle of any visible air contaminant for a period greater than ten consecutive seconds, or from any diesel-powered motor vehicle of any visible air contaminant for more than ten consecutive seconds which is a shade or density equal to but not darker than No. 2 on the Ringelmann chart. This regulation does not apply to emissions from diesel-powered vehicles that are the direct result of cold engine startup, nor to off-highway diesel-powered vehicles.

Inspection

Exhaust emissions are measured by the Arizona vehicle-in-use inspection test to determine that a motor vehicle complies with the standards. The vehicle is run on a chassis dynamometer at speeds corresponding to 50 mph, 30 mph and idle, in that order. At each of the three test conditions, exhaust hydrocarbon and carbon monoxide readings are taken. The results for the hydrocarbon and carbon monoxide emissions are expressed as an average of the readings taken at the three test conditions. All tests are run with the engine at normal operating temperature.

Any vehicle having a positive crankcase ventilation valve must be inspected to see that the system is connected and operating. The inspection consists of placing a vacuum gauge over the oil filler opening. A negative pressure at idle speed is required in order to pass.

Beginning with motor vehicles and motor vehicle engines of model year 1968, no certificate of title or registration, including permission to install or exchange blocks or engines, can be issued, transferred or renewed unless the application is accompanied by a sworn affidavit that the vehicle or engine is equipped with approved emission control devices that are both connected and operating.

Beginning on January 1, 1976 there will be a mandatory emissions inspection program in Maricopa and Pima Counties.

Alteration of Emission Control Devices

Any person who removes or alters a motor vehicle emission control device to impair the effectiveness of the device is guilty of a misdemeanor. This regulation does not apply to motor vehicles that are used exclusively for competition and not operated on public streets or highways.

ARKANSAS

State law requires that all types of required emission control systems (crankcase, exhaust and evaporative) be maintained in good operable condition, and prohibits intentionally making the system inoperable or removing it.

The law prohibits the emission of air contaminants from motor vehicles of a density exceeding 30% opacity (No. 1.5 on the Standard Smoke Chart), except during acceleration and gear shifting for periods not to exceed five seconds (water vapor excepted).

Inspection

Arkansas State Police safety inspection stations examine the condition of the positive crankcase ventilation valve on all 1968 and later model motor vehicles.

CALIFORNIA

General motor vehicle pollution control requirements applicable to passenger cars and light commercial vehicles registered in California:

1. Light Duty Vehicles of American Manufacture
   (*a*) 1971 and later model American-manufactured vehicles must be equipped with crankcase, exhaust and fuel evaporative loss control systems.
   (*b*) 1970 model American-manufactured vehicles first sold and registered in California must be equipped with crankcase, exhaust and fuel evaporative loss control systems.
   (*c*) 1970 model American-manufactured vehicles first sold and registered outside California require only crankcase and exhaust emission control systems.
   (*d*) 1968 and 1969 model American-manufactured vehicles must be equipped with crankcase and exhaust emission control systems.
   (*e*) 1966 and 1967 model American-manufactured vehicles first sold and registered in California must be equipped with crankcase and exhaust emission control systems.
   (*f*) 1966 and 1967 model American-manufactured vehicles first sold and registered outside California require only a crankcase control device upon initial registration in California.
   (*g*) 1963 through 1965 model American-manufactured vehicles require only a crankcase control device.
   (*h*) 1955 through 1962 model American-manufactured vehicles currently registered in California must be equipped with crankcase control devices upon transfer of ownership and registration to an owner residing in one of the counties listed in 1 (i).
   (*i*) 1955 through 1962 model vehicles previously registered outside California are required, upon initial registration in this state, to be equipped with a crankcase device if the registered owner resides in one of the following counties:

Alameda	San Diego
Contra Costa	San Francisco
Los Angeles	San Mateo
Marin	Santa Clara
Napa	Sonoma
Orange	Ventura
Santa Barbara	

Portions of Riverside, San Bernardino, and Solano Counties

2. Light Duty Vehicles of Foreign Manufacture
   (*a*) 1971 and later model foreign-manufactured vehicles first sold and registered in the United States must be equipped with crankcase, exhaust and fuel evaporative loss control systems upon initial registration in California.
   (*b*) 1970 model foreign-manufactured vehicles first sold and registered in California must be equipped with crankcase, exhaust and fuel evaporative loss control systems.
   (*c*) 1968 and 1969 model foreign-manufactured vehicles first sold and registered in the United States must be equipped with crankcase and exhaust control systems.
   (*d*) 1965 through 1967 model foreign-manufactured vehicles first sold and registered in the United States must be equipped with a crankcase control device.
   (*e*) 1965 and later model foreign-manufactured vehicles first sold and registered in a foreign country must be equipped with a crankcase control device upon initial registration in California. These vehicles are not required to be equipped with ex-

CALIFORNIA

NEW VEHICLE EMISSION STANDARDS SUMMARY

Light-duty Vehicles (under 6000 lbs)

Year①	Hydrocarbons	Carbon Monoxide	Oxides of Nitrogen
Prior to controls	850 ppm (11 gm/mi)	3.4% (80 gm/mi)	1000 ppm (4 gm/mi)
1966-1967	275 ppm	1.5%	—
1968-1969			
50-100 CID	410 ppm	2.3%	—
101-140 CID	350 ppm	2.0%	—
Over 140 CID	275 ppm	1.5%	—
1970	2.2 gm/mi	23 gm/mi	—
1971	2.2 gm/mi	23 gm/mi	4 gm/mi
1972	1.5 gm/mi	23 gm/mi	3 gm/mi
1972	3.2 gm/mi	39 gm/mi	3.2 gm/mi②
1973	3.2 gm/mi	39 gm/mi	3 gm/mi
1974	3.2 gm/mi	39 gm/mi	2 gm/mi
1975	0.9 gm/mi	9 gm/mi	2.0 gm/mi
1976	0.9 gm mi	9 gm/mi	2.0 gm/mi

①—A 7-mode 137-second driving cycle test is used up to 1972. From 1972-1976 a Constant Volume Sample cold star test is used. The changeover was in midyear.

②—A hot 7-mode test is used.

Heavy-duty Vehicles (over 6000 lbs.)

Year	Hydrocarbons	Carbon Monoxide	Oxides of Nitrogen
1969-1971 (gasoline powered)	275 ppm	1.5%	—
1972 (gasoline powered)	180 ppm	1.0%	—
1973-1974 (gasoline & diesel powered)	Hydrocarbons + Oxides of Nitrogen = 16 gm/BHP hr		
	Carbon monoxide = 40 gm/BHP hr		
1975 & Later (gasoline & diesel powered)	Hydrocarbons + Oxides of Nitrogen = 10 gm/BHP hr		
	Carbon monoxide = 30 gm/BHP hr		

gm/BHP hr—grams per brake horsepower-hour.
ppm—parts per million gm/mi—grams per mile CID—cubic inch displacement.

QUICK REFERENCE CHART

Emission Control Laws

Light Duty Vehicle (≤6000# GVW)

Regulatory Emission Control Requirements

	PRE-CONTROL	1968 ('68 CALIF.)	1970	1971	1972	1973	1974	** 1975-76	** 1977	** 1978
		1970 FTP (TAILPIPE CONCENTRATION)			1972 FTP gpm (CVS)			1975 FTP gpm		
HC	11 gpm	275 ppm	2.2 gpm		3.4 (C) 3.2			1.5 (C) 0.9	0.41*	
CO	80 gpm	1.5%	23 gpm		39			15 (C) 9	3.4*	
NO_x	4 gpm	NR		(C) 4 gpm	(C) 3 gpm (on 1970 FTP)	3	(C) 2	3.1 (C) 2	2.0	0.4*
EVAP.	g/test by Trap:		(C) 6	6	2					

NOTES:

FTP = Federal Test Procedure
ppm = parts per million
NR = No Requirement
gpm = grams/mile
(C) Means California Only
CVS = constant volume sampler (true mass meas.)

*Less severe NO_x requirements proposed to Congress by EPA, 1977 HC/CO subject to 1 year suspension by EPA.

**Except Light Duty Trucks and Truck Derivatives ≤6000#, see Additional Light Duty Vehicle Requirements.

15% Allowance in exhaust req'ts. for off-road utility vehicles through 1974 (1973 in Calif.).

Equivalent Test Results for different test procedure (based on 1970-71 cars, not applicable to pre-control cars):

	1970 FTP		1972 FTP		1975 FTP
HC	2.2 gpm	=	4.6 gpm	=	4.1 gpm
CO	23 gpm	=	47 gpm	=	34 gpm
NO_x	4.0 gpm	=	6.0 gpm	=	6.2 gpm

ADDITIONAL LIGHT DUTY VEHICLE REQUIREMENTS

1974 No Crankcase Emissions Allowed
- Mfr. or Dealer, $10,000 Fine for Tampering with System
- 50,000 Mile Warranty Req't.; Recall Provision

1975 Fuel Filter Design to Exclude Leaded Fuel Nozzle (Cars with catalyst)
- Light Duty Trucks and Truck Derivatives ≤6000#: Exh. HC 2.0, CO 28, NO_x 3.1 gpm; Evap. 2 g/test
- Exhaust Standards for 1975 apply to Diesel LDV w/Test Procedure Change

197X Assembly Line Test Requirement

CANADIAN REQUIREMENTS DIFFERING FROM U.S.

1975 LDV (Incl. L. D. Trucks) Exh. HC 2.0, CO 25.0, NO_x 3.1 gpm by 1975 FTP

CALIFORNIA—IN ADDITION TO FED. REQUIREMENTS

1974 End-of-line Exhaust Tests:
- 100% Steady State (Idle) Test
  - Stds. Based on $\bar{x} + 2\sigma$ of Prior Sample
- 2% Cold Start Audit
  - >10% Failures (Cert. Stds.); Possible Cert. Loss
- Octane Requirements may not Exceed 91 RON
- Dealership Inspection: Specs. Check, Functional & Idle Test

1975 End-of-line Exhaust Test Program to Continue
- Light Duty Trucks and Truck Derivatives ≤6000#: Exh. HC 2.0, CO 20.0, NO_x 2.0 gpm

1976 Light Duty Trucks and Truck Derivatives ≤6000#: Exh. HC 0.9, CO 17.0, NO_x 2.0 gpm

haust or evaporative loss control systems.

(*f*) Foreign-manufactured vehicles of 1964 and prior year models do not require pollution control equipment.

Heavy Duty Vehicles

All non resident heavy duty vehicles powered by gasoline engines manufactured after Jan. 1, 1970 require factory installed exhaust emission controls.

Heavy duty vehicles powered by diesel engines 1973 and later first sold in California require factory installed exhaust emission controls.

Smoke Emission, Heavy Duty Vehicles

Vehicles sold before 1971—

Discharge up to 10 seconds, smoke no darker than Ringelmann No. 2 or 40% opacity.

1971 and later—

Discharge up to 10 seconds, smoke no darker than Ringelmann No. 1 or 20% opacity.

Crankcase Emission

Zero for all new light duty vehicles since 1968, and heavy duty vehicles since 1970.

Evaporative Hydrocarbon Emissions

For light duty vehicles—

1970-1971—6 grams per test

1972 —2 grams per test

For heavy duty gasoline-powered vehicles—

1973 —2 grams per test

These standards are also applicable to motor vehicles which have been modified or altered to use a fuel other than gasoline or diesel.

Emission standards for Light Duty Trucks (under 6000 lbs GVW)

	HC	CO	NO_x
1975	2.0 gm/mi	20 gm/mi	2.0 gm/mi
1976	0.9 gm/mi	17 gm/mi	2.0 gm/mi

Emission standards for Heavy Duty trucks

1975-1976	Hydrocarbons Oxides of Nitrogen	= 10 gm/bhp hr
	Carbon Monoxide	= 30 gm/bhp hr
1977	Hydrocarbons Oxides of Nitrogen	= 5 gm/bhp hr
	Carbon Monoxide	= 25 gm/bhp hr

Permanent Tag Requirement

California law requires that new 1972 model year vehicles be equipped with a permanent type label within the engine compartment showing the following information:

(*a*) Heading: Vehicle Emission Control Information.

(*b*) Full corporate name and trademark of manufacturer.

(*c*) Engine size (in cubic inches).

(*d*) Exhaust emission control type.

(*e*) Engine tuneup specifications and adjustments, as recommended by the manufacturer, including specified idle speed, ignition timing, and air/fuel mixture setting and/or idle carbon monoxide setting. These specifications should indicate the proper transmission position during tuneups and what accessories, if any, should be in operation.

(*f*) A statement to the effect that: This vehicle conforms to California regulations applicable to 1972 model year new motor vehicles.

Certification of Compliance

California requires upon initial registration, or transfer of ownership and registration, of any motor vehicle subject to the law a valid certificate of compliance from a licensed motor vehicle pollution control device installation and inspection station indicating that the vehicle is properly equipped with a pollution control device or devices in proper operating condition.

Official Installation and Inspection Stations

Class A licensed motor vehicle pollution control device installation and inspection stations must be adequately equipped to install, repair and inspect all certified devices to control the emission of pollutants from crankcases, exhausts and fuel systems of vehicles. These stations must have the necessary tools to inspect or repair all motor vehicle pollution control devices, and the necessary instruments for major engine tuneup analysis, including the following or equivalent:

Ignition analyzer-oscilloscope
Ammeter
Ohmmeter
Voltmeter
Tachometer
Vacuum gauge
Pressure gauge (0-10 psi)
Cam angle dwell meter
Ignition timing light
Engine exhaust combustion analyzer or carbon monoxide analyzer with a range readout of 0-10%
Compression tester
Distributor advance tester

Each licensed station must maintain the *Bureau of Automotive Repair Handbook for Installation and Inspection Stations* in addition to appropriate manuals, bulletins and instructions issued by the bureau and by the manufacturers of motor vehicle pollution control devices.

No person other than a licensed motor vehicle pollution control device installer employed in a licensed motor vehicle pollution control device installation and inspection station shall complete or sign a certificate of compliance.

Class A official motor vehicle pollution control device installers' licenses are issued to persons who have passed an installation and inspection exam prescribed by the bureau and have submitted certificates of competence from the station licensee to demonstrate that they are qualified to perform automotive engine tuneup procedures in accordance with accepted industry practices. The bureau may accept in lieu of certificates evidence of competence that applicants have satisfactorily completed a course of instruction in automotive tuneup procedures conducted by a vehicle manufacturer, a tuneup equipment manufacturer, an industrial or trade school, a public high school, a junior college, or by more than one of these.

Application for licensing official stations and installers should be made to the California Consumer Affairs Bureau of Automotive Repair.

Inoperable or Modified Pollution Control Devices

California prohibits the operation or leaving standing on any highway of any motor vehicle which is required by law to be equipped with a pollution control device unless the device is correctly installed and in operating condition. Disconnecting, modifying or altering any such required device, unless approved by the State Air Resources Board, is prohibited.

Exempted Vehicles

The California Air Resources Board has exempted certain vehicles from motor vehicles pollution control requirements.

Vehicles Exempted from All Requirements

The following vehicles are either not required by law to be equipped or have been exempted from all motor vehicle pollution control device requirements by Air Resources Board action:

Asphalt Spreaders
Bituminous Mixers
Bucket Loaders
Caterpillars
Ditchers
Earth Moving Scrapers
Mobile Cranes
Motorcycles & Motor-driven Cycles
Motor Graders
Paving Mixers
Power Shovels and Draglines
Fork Lift Trucks
Highway Finishing Machines
Implements of Husbandry
Leveling Graders
Road Rollers
Skip Loaders
Speed Swings
Street Sweepers
Weed Mowers
Agricultural Water-Well Boring Rigs.
All foreign-made vehicles, both commercial and passenger, manufactured prior to the 1965 model year.
All vehicles manufactured prior to the 1955 model year.
Racing vehicles defined as competition vehicles not used on public roads or highways.
Vehicles equipped with two-cycle engines.
Vehicles which qualify for special license plates under Section 5004 of the Vehicle Code.
Vehicles of 1963 and prior year models equipped with fuel injection, supercharger and/or multiple carburetors.
All vehicles not subject to State registration requirements.

Partial Exemption from Requirements

Refer to the General Summary of Motor Vehicle Pollution Control Requirements for vehicles exempted from certain state requirements.

COLORADO

State law prohibits visible emissions from 4-stroke gasoline engines. Emissions up to 20% opacity are permitted from 2-stroke engines. The law prohibits emissions of 30% or greater opacity from diesel engines operating below 8000 feet, and prohibits emissions of 40% or greater opacity from diesel engines operating above 8000 feet.

Further, the law prohibits the disconnecting, modifying or altering of manufacturer installed air pollution control devices.

CONNECTICUT

State law prohibits the removal, dismantling or making inoperative of any operational element of the air pollution control system of a motor vehicle required by regulations of the commissioner of environmental protection and federal law. In addition, the air pollution control system must be maintained in good working order.

Further, no visible emissions from gasoline-powered motor vehicles are permitted for longer than five consecutive seconds. No visible emissions equal to or darker than No. 1 on the Ringelmann chart, or 20% opacity, from diesel-powered motor vehicles for more than 10 consecutive seconds during which time the maximum shade or density of emissions shall be no darker than No. 2 on the Ringelmann chart, or 40% opacity.

Exceptions are for water vapor, antique vehicles over 30 years old, vehicles used exclusively for racing, and vehicles being repaired. No motor vehicle engine may idle more than three minutes with the following exceptions: in order to bring the engine up to the manufacturer's recommended operating temperature; when the vehicle is forced to remain motionless because of traffic conditions or mechanical difficulties over which the operator has no control; when necessary to operate heating, cooling or auxiliary equipment and when the vehicle is being repaired.

DELAWARE

No changes.

FLORIDA

State law requires that motor vehicles be inspected for excessive visible emissions, and that emission control devices required by federal law be in place and in operating condition.

The law also prohibits the emission of smoke (exclusive of water vapor) within the proximity of the engine exhaust outlet from motor vehicles on public roadways.

GEORGIA

State law requires that motor vehicles be inspected to ensure that all exhaust emission and air pollution control systems as required by federal law be in place and in good working order.

Further, it is unlawful to operate a motor vehicle if any pollution control device which has been placed on the vehicle by the manufacturer has been removed or made unserviceable. Modifications are allowed if they will improve emission control, such as converting to liquified petroleum gas operation. The law prohibits visible emissions from gasoline-powered vehicles for more than ten consecutive seconds or 1000 feet of operation. Emissions from diesel-powered vehicles equal to or exceeding 30% opacity are prohibited except during acceleration and deceleration for periods of not more than 10 consecutive seconds or a distance not exceeding 1000 feet.

IDAHO

State law prohibits anyone from removing, disabling or disconnecting any emission control device (crankcase, exhaust or evaporative) which has been installed on the motor vehicle in accordance with Federal laws and regulations.

The law prohibits the discharge of any visible emission from any motor vehicle which is darker than No. 2 on the Ringelmann Smoke Chart or of greater opacity than is smoke designated as No. 2 on the Ringelmann Smoke Chart (water vapor excepted).

The law also requires the engine and power mechanism of every motor vehicle be so equipped and adjusted as to prevent the escape of excessive fumes or smoke.

ILLINOIS

State law prohibits the removal or making inoperative of any equipment that is an operational part of the air pollution control system of a motor vehicle as required by state and federal law. In addition, the air pollution control system is required to be maintained in good working order.

Air pollution control devices are required to be inspected in accordance with standards set by the Illinois Air Pollution Control Board in order for a motor vehicle to receive an inspection sticker.

The law prohibits any visible emissions of smoke from gasoline-powered motor vehicles.

Diesel engines manufactured before January 1, 1970, must not emit smoke which is equal to or greater than 30% opacity, except for individual puffs of smoke not exceeding 15 seconds in duration. Diesel engines must be operated only on specific fuels as specified by the manufacturer.

Alternative Fuel Use

Vehicles converted to the use of liquid petroleum gas (LPG) must have the excess air injection system (where such systems have been installed by the manufacturers) made inoperative when operating on LPG, but the system must be operative when operating on gasoline in dual-fuel systems. The intake manifold heat riser system to the carburetor must be operational at all times the vehicle is operating.

SPECIAL REGULATIONS PERTAINING TO THE CITY OF CHICAGO

Chicago city ordinance requires that after June 1, 1973 every motor vehicle registered in the city be inspected and tested annually for compliance with the following emission standards:

Type of Vehicle	Model Year	Idle Exhaust Emission Standard: Hydro-carbons	Idle Exhaust Emission Standard: Carbon Monoxide
A. Non-fleet	Pre-1968	1000 ppm	6.0%
Same	1968-1969	600	5.0
Same	1970 through 1974	500	4.0
Same	1975 and subsequent years	250	1.4
B. Fleet Vehicles	Pre-1968	600	5.0%
Same	1968-1969	400	4.5
Same	1970 through 1974	300	3.5
Same	1975 and subsequent years	150	1.3
C. Passenger Carriers for Hire	Pre-1968	400	3.0
Same	1968-1969	300	2.0
Same	1970 through 1974	300	1.5
Same	1975 and subsequent years	100	0.8

The City of Chicago prohibits diesel powered motor vehicles from emitting smoke darker than 20% opacity in the lugging mode and 40% opacity in the accelerating mode. All spark ignition powered motor vehicles are prohibited from emitting smoke darker than No. 1 on the Ringelmann Chart.

INDIANA

No changes.

IOWA

State law requires inspection of motor vehicles to check that none of the factory installed emission control devices required by federal law have been removed or made inoperable.

Further, gasoline-powered vehicles may not emit visible emissions for longer than five consecutive seconds, and diesel-powered vehicle emissions may not exceed a shade or density darker than No. 2 on the Ringelmann Chart or 40% opacity.

KANSAS

No changes.

KENTUCKY

No changes.

LOUISIANA

State law requires that the automotive emission control devices installed on motor vehicles produced and sold after model year 1968 in compliance with Federal law be inspected annually to check that the devices are operative and have not been tampered with.

MAINE

No changes.

MARYLAND

State law prohibits the removal or altering of any pollution control device which has been installed as a requirement of Federal law or regulation.

The law prohibits the operation of a motor vehicle originally equipped with Federally required air pollution control devices unless those devices are in place and in operating condition.

Exceptions to the above regulations apply to vehicles which have been modified to use a fuel other than gasoline and the resulting emissions still comply with state and federal standards.

MASSACHUSETTS

State law requires inspection of gasoline- and diesel-powered motor vehicles for visible exhaust emissions.

Gasoline-powered vehicles must not, at normal operating temperature, at any constant speed over 15 mph, produce visible exhaust emissions, excluding water vapor.

Diesel-powered vehicles must not, at normal operating temperature, at any constant speed over 15 mph, produce visible steady black exhaust emissions or constant blue emissions indicating bypassing of engine lubricant through the combustion chambers.

Further, the law prohibits the removal, alteration or making inoperative of any air pollution control device installed on a vehicle in compliance with state and federal regulations, except for reasonable maintenance periods or unexpected and unavoidable failure of equipment.

MICHIGAN

No changes.

MINNESOTA

No changes.

MISSISSIPPI

No changes.

MISSOURI

No changes.

MONTANA

No changes.

NEBRASKA

No changes.

NEW HAMPSHIRE

No changes.

NEVADA

No changes.

NEW JERSEY

Gasoline-Fueled Vehicles
Visible Emissions

State law prohibits the operation of any light duty gasoline-fueled motor vehicle on public highways that emits visible smoke in the exhaust or crankcase emissions.

Exhaust Emission Standards

The following exhaust emission standards apply to light duty gasoline-fueled vehicles subject to inspection by the Division of Motor Vehicles, except for motor vehicles with an engine displacement of less than 50 cubic inches and motorcycles:

New motor vehicle dealers are required to inspect all new light duty gasoline-fueled motor vehicles to verify conformance with the emission specifications prescribed by the manufacturer to assure proper functioning of emission control devices.

The Director, Division of Motor Vehicles, may waive emission inspection standards for any model year of vehicle up to and including 1967 which, because of their design, cannot meet the standards no matter how well they are tuned.

Diesel-Powered Vehicles

For diesel-powered vehicles subject to inspection by the Division of Motor Vehicles, the opacity of smoke emissions may not exceed 20% in either of the following tests:

1. With the vehicle running on a chassis dynamometer under no load, in a gear that produces a speed of 45-60 mph at governed rpm, apply a load to the dynamometer until the engine rpm is reduced to 80% of the governed speed. The peak smoke opacity in a 5-to-10 second period with the engine under this load is the measured smoke opacity.
2. Drive the vehicle in a gear which produces a speed of 10-15 mph at governed engine rpm. Apply the brakes until the engine rpm is lugged down to 80% of the governed rpm, and measure the peak smoke opacity over a 5-to-10 second period.

For vehicles subject to inspection by the Public Utilities Commission (busses), the opacity of smoke emissions may not exceed 40% in a test of maximum acceleration to 20 mph.

All of the above tests are made with the engine at normal operating temperature.

NEW MEXICO

No changes.

NEW YORK

Gasoline-Powered Vehicles

State law prohibits the operation or registration of 1964 through 1967 gasoline-powered motor ve-

New Jersey Standards

Model Year of Vehicle	Effective July 5, 1972		Effective February 1, 1975		Effective February 1, 1976	
	CO(%)	HC(PPM)	CO(%)	HC(PPM)	CO(%)	HC(PPM)
Up to and including 1967	10.0	1600	8.5	1400	7.5	1200
1968-1969	8.0	800	7.0	700	5.0	600
1970-1974	6.0	600	5.0	500	4.0	400

hicles not equipped with an emission control device that will return at least 80% of crankcase emissions (as determined in a specified sampling procedure) to the induction system.

No 1968 or later model year gasoline-powered vehicle may be registered or operated that is not equipped with emission control devices or systems to return all crankcase emissions to the induction system and limit exhaust emissions as originally required by Federal regulation.

Aftermarket Control Devices

No aftermarket crankcase or exhaust emission control device or system can be sold unless such items have been approved by the Commissioner of the Environmental Protection Agency. Nor may any part of a crankcase emission control device or system be replaced except with items approved by the Commissioner.

Emission Standards

No light duty gasoline-powered motor vehicle that exceeds the following exhaust emission standards may be operated:

Exemption from emission control standards are granted to persons engaged in research or development of new or improved motor vehicle emission control devices who receive a waiver from the Commissioner.

Visible Emissions

It is unlawful to operate a gasoline-powered motor vehicle on a highway that emits blue, black or blue-black emissions for more than five continuous seconds.

Tampering

The law prohibits the removing, dismantling or making inoperative of any part of an air pollution control system that is required by state or federal law, except by persons engaged in research of new or improved air pollution control systems or devices and who receive a waiver from the Commissioner.

New York Standards

Motor Vehicle Model Year	Exhaust Emission Control Type*	Effective Jan. 1, 1974 CO(%)	HC(PPM)
1967 & earlier	—	6.5	1000
1968 & 1969	AI	4.0	500
	EM	5.0	600
1970 & later	AI	3.0	350
	EM	4.0	450

*AI—Air injection type emission control system
EM—Engine modification type emission control system

Diesel-Powered Motor Vehicles

The law prohibits operation of a diesel-powered vehicle in such a manner that the opacity of blue, black or grey exhaust emissions exceeds No. 1 on the Ringelmann chart or another acceptable standard for more than five continuous seconds.

It is unlawful to idle the engine of a diesel-powered vehicle for more than five consecutive minutes except where required by traffic conditions; or in compliance with federal, state or local regulations on maintenance of a specific temperature for passenger comfort; to provide power for an auxiliary service; or for fire, police or public utility trucks performing emergency services, vehicles used by persons engaged in mining and quarrying operations on their own property or a vehicle remaining motionless for more than two hours when the ambient temperature is continuously below 25 degrees.

NORTH CAROLINA

State law prohibits the operation of a motor vehicle registered in the state which has been manufactured after 1967 unless it is equipped with required factory installed air pollution control devices. Vehicles converted to operate on natural or liquified petroleum gas are exempt from the above regulation provided that such modification has first been approved by the Department of Water and Air Resources.

Required air pollution control devices have to be in place on 1967 and later vehicles before an approval certificate is issued by a safety equipment inspection station.

The law prohibits visible emissions from any gasoline-powered motor vehicle for longer than five consecutive seconds.

Further, diesel-powered motor vehicles are prohibited from emitting for longer than five consecutive seconds under any mode of operation visible emissions which are equal to or darker than No. 1 on the Ringelmann Chart or 20% opacity.

NORTH DAKOTA

No changes.

OHIO

No changes.

OKLAHOMA

No changes.

OREGON

State law prohibits anyone from disconnecting or altering a factory-installed motor vehicle air pollution device in such a way as to decrease its efficiency or effectiveness in controlling air pollution.

The law prohibits anyone from willfully allowing such devices from becoming or remaining inoperative.

The law allows the disconnection or altering of air pollution devices for the purpose of conversion to gaseous fuels like liquified petroleum gases. Beginning July 1975, Oregon requires mandatory annual motor vehicle emission control inspection for vehicles registered in the greater Portland Metro area.

The law also prohibits the operation of motor vehicles without required air pollution control certificate of compliance.

No gasoline-powered motor vehicle may be operated on public streets or roads that emits any visible emission into the atmosphere.

It is unlawful to operate a diesel-powered motor vehicle at elevations of less than 3000 feet on public roads that emits visible emissions into the atmosphere of an opacity greater than 40% or an opacity of 10% or greater for a period exceeding seven consecutive seconds. At elevations over 3000 feet, visible emissions into the atmosphere may not be of an opacity greater than 60%, or an opacity of 20% or greater for a period exceeding seven consecutive seconds.

The above regulations are exclusive of water vapor.

PENNSYLVANIA

State law requires that motor vehicles be inspected annually to insure that exhaust emission and air pollution control devices required by Federal law are in place and have not been tampered with or altered, and that the engine and air pollution control systems are in good working order.

RHODE ISLAND

No changes.

SOUTH CAROLINA

No changes.

SOUTH DAKOTA

No changes.

TENNESSEE

No changes.

TEXAS

State law requires that any person owning or operating a motor vehicle incorporating a system for the control of emissions from the crankcase or exhaust system, or for the control of evaporative emissions, as required by Federal law, maintain the system in good operable condition and use it at all times the vehicle is operated. The operator of a motor vehicle is expressly prohibited from removing or making the system inoperable except to install a proper replacement.

The law requires all parts of required air pollution control systems be replaced by a like part or one that is designated as a replacement for the specific make and model vehicle or engine.

The law further prohibits excessive visible emissions from motor vehicles for more than ten consecutive seconds.

Inspection of System

The law requires the inspection of the exhaust emission system on those 1968 and later model year motor vehicles so equipped by the manufacturer, to check that the system has not been removed or made inoperative.

UTAH

State law requires that any person owning or operating a motor vehicle that is equipped with a system or device for the control of crankcase emissions or exhaust emissions in compliance with Federal regulation maintain the system or device in operable condition and use it at all times the motor vehicle is operated. The law expressly prohibits the removal or rendering inoperative of the system or device except for the purpose of installing another system or device which is equally or more effective in reducing atmospheric emissions from the vehicle.

The law further prohibits emissions from gasoline-powered vehicles that are a shade or density equal to or darker than No. 1 on the Ringelmann Chart except for starting motion limited to 100 yards. Stationary operation of vehicles is limited to three minutes in any one hour.

VERMONT

State law prohibits the removal or making inoperative Federally required pollution control devices. Further, no visible emissions are permitted, with the exception of water vapor, for periods exceeding five seconds.

VIRGINIA

No changes.

WASHINGTON

No changes.

WEST VIRGINIA

No changes.

WASHINGTON D.C.

The law requires that the exhaust emission and air pollution control system as required by Federal law be in place and in good working order. The PCV valve on all 1968 and later model year motor vehicles must be in good working order.

The law further prohibits the removal or making inoperative air pollution control devices installed by manufacturers in compliance with law.

The law prohibits visible smoke emissions from engines or exhaust systems of gasoline-powered vehicles. Emissions of 20% opacity are permitted for periods not exceeding five consecutive seconds from diesel-powered vehicles.

Inspection

All government vehicles are required to have a complete check of their emission control systems.

Engine Idling

The law prohibits engine idling of a gasoline or diesel-powered vehicle for more than three minutes with the following exceptions: to permit the operation of power takeoff equipment, to permit the operation for 15 minutes of air conditioning equipment on buses with an occupancy of 12 or more persons and to permit the operation of heating equipment when the local temperature is 32° F or below.

Gasoline Sales

In addition, after July 4, 1974, all gasoline service stations must offer for sale at least one grade of regular gasoline which contains no more than .03 gram of lead per gallon. After January 1, 1974 no gasoline containing more than 2.0 grams of lead per gallon is to be sold. After January 1, 1976 no gasoline containing more than 1.0 grams of lead per gallon is to be sold.

WISCONSIN

No changes.

WYOMING

State law prohibits the removal, altering or making inoperative of an exhaust emission control, crankcase ventilation or any other pollution control device or system installed on a motor vehicle as required by Federal law or regulation. Further, no motor vehicle originally equipped with air pollution devices or systems as required by Federal law or regulation may be operated unless they are in place and in operating condition.

Visible Emissions

The law prohibits visible emissions from gasoline engines for periods exceeding five consecutive seconds.

Diesel engine emissions are limited to 30% opacity below 7500 feet elevation except for periods not exceeding 10 consecutive seconds. This limitation does not apply during a reasonable period of warmup following a cold start or where the vehicle is undergoing repairs and adjustment following a malfunction.

Cadillac 1975 Electronic Fuel Injection System

As we were going to press with this book, we received preliminary word from Cadillac Motor Division that they were about to announce the availability of an electronic fuel injection system.

The new system, which is offered as an option on all models, is comprised of Cadillac, Delco and Bendix Corporation components, all of which comply to Cadillac engineering test and development specifications.

The brain of the Cadillac electronic fuel injection system is an analog computer, called the Electronic Control Unit, or ECU for short. This unit determines the precise amount of fuel to be delivered to each cylinder after receiving several bits of operating data from other components. By sensing several operating variables, the ECU is designed to accurately meter the fuel delivery under such changing conditions as high altitude, and cold or warm engine temperatures.

The ECU utilizes highly reliable, long lasting integrated circuits. In addition, a laser beam process is used to trim resistors to exact predetermined values to assure uniform system performance.

According to Cadillac, the new electronic fuel injection system was designed to offer optimized fuel economy over a wide variety and range of driving conditions and driver habits. It also contributes to a cleaner running engine and emission control results are very good with the system. Cadillac also claims faster starting throughout a wide variety of conditions, good throttle response after either a hot or cold start, smooth engine idle, quick engine response at all speeds, consistent performance over a period of time due to the stability of the electronic controls and fewer required maintenance operations and lengthened maintenance intervals.

The electronic fuel injection system is a $600 option and production is scheduled to begin in Detroit the first week of February, 1975.

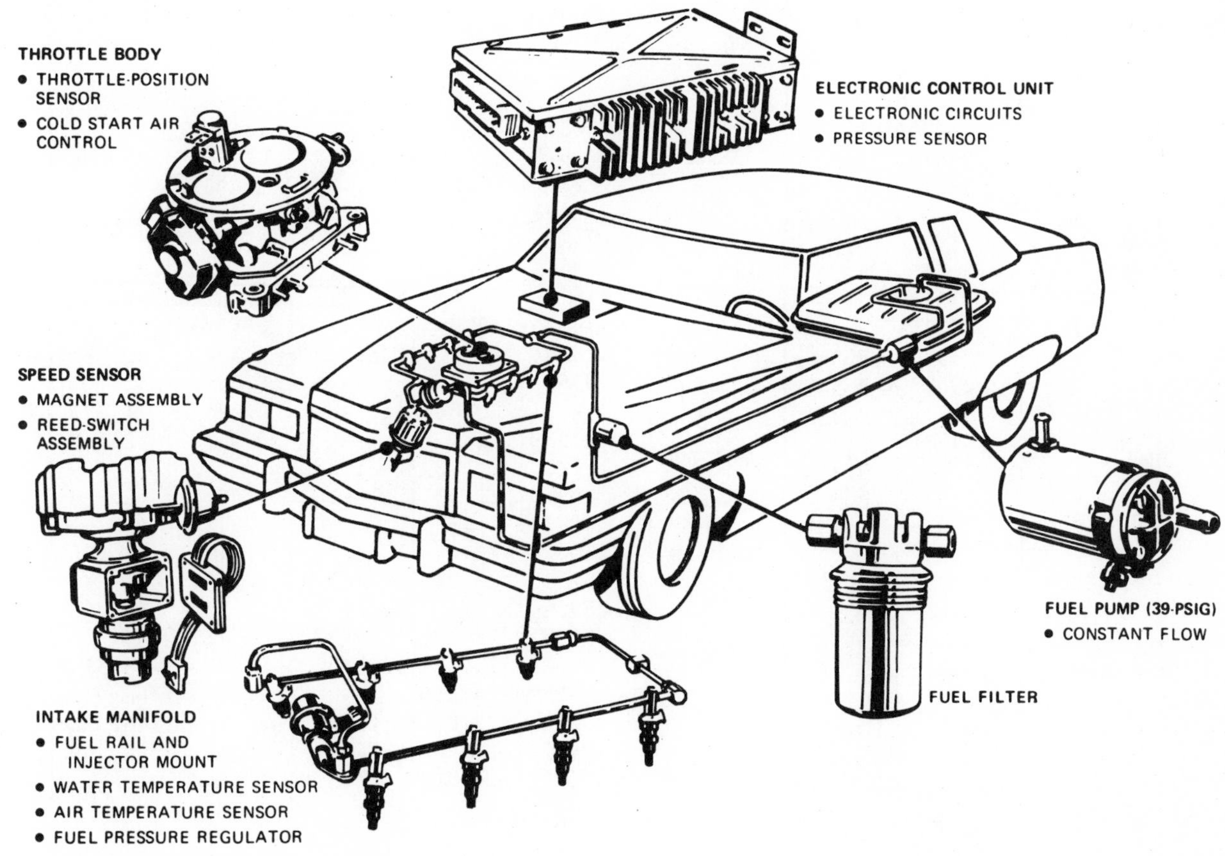

CONVERSION TABLE

INCH FRACTIONS AND DECIMALS TO METRIC EQUIVALENTS

INCHES		m m	INCHES		m m	INCHES		m m
Fractions	Decimals		Fractions	Decimals		Fractions	Decimals	
-	.0004	.01	-	.4331	11	31/32	.96875	24.606
-	.004	.10	7/16	.4375	11.113	-	.9843	25
-	.01	.25	29/64	.4531	11.509	1	1.000	25.4
1/64	.0156	.397	15/32	.46875	11.906	-	1.0236	26
-	.0197	.50	-	.4724	12	1 1/32	1.0312	26.194
-	.0295	.75	31/64	.48437	12.303	1 1/16	1.062	26.988
1/32	.03125	.794	-	.492	12.5	-	1.063	27
-	.0394	1	1/2	.500	12.700	1 3/32	1.094	27.781
3/64	.0469	1.191	-	.5118	13	-	1.1024	28
-	.059	1.5	33/64	.5156	13.097	1 1/8	1.125	28.575
1/16	.0625	1.588	17/32	.53125	13.494	-	1.1417	29
5/64	.0781	1.984	35/64	.54687	13.891	1 5/32	1.156	29.369
-	.0787	2	-	.5512	14	-	1.1811	30
3/32	.094	2.381	9/16	.5625	14.288	1 3/16	1.1875	30.163
-	.0984	2.5	-	.571	14.5	1 7/32	1.219	30.956
7/64	.1093	2.776	37/64	.57812	14.684	-	1.2205	31
-	.1181	3	-	.5906	15	1 1/4	1.250	31.750
1/8	.1250	3.175	19/32	.59375	15.081	-	1.2598	32
-	.1378	3.5	39/64	.60937	15.478	1 9/32	1.281	32.544
9/64	.1406	3.572	5/8	.6250	15.875	-	1.2992	33
5/32	.15625	3.969	-	.6299	16	1 5/16	1.312	33.338
-	.1575	4	41/64	.6406	16.272	-	1.3386	34
11/64	.17187	4.366	-	.6496	16.5	1 11/32	1.344	34.131
-	.177	4.5	21/32	.65625	16.669	1 3/8	1.375	34.925
3/16	.1875	4.763	-	.6693	17	-	1.3779	35
-	.1969	5	43/64	.67187	17.066	1 13/32	1.406	35.719
13/64	.2031	5.159	11/16	.6875	17.463	-	1.4173	36
-	.2165	5.5	45/64	.7031	17.859	1 7/16	1.438	36.513
7/32	.21875	5.556	-	.7087	18	-	1.4567	37
15/64	.23437	5.953	23/32	.71875	18.256	1 15/32	1.469	37.306
-	.2362	6	-	.7283	18.5	-	1.4961	38
1/4	.2500	6.350	47/64	.73437	18.653	1 1/2	1.500	38.100
-	.2559	6.5	-	.7480	19	1 17/32	1.531	38.894
17/64	.2656	6.747	3/4	.7500	19.050	-	1.5354	39
-	.2756	7	49/64	.7656	19.447	1 9/16	1.562	39.688
9/32	.28125	7.144	25/32	.78125	19.844	-	1.5748	40
-	.2953	7.5	-	.7874	20	1 19/32	1.594	40.481
19/64	.29687	7.541	51/64	.79687	20.241	-	1.6142	41
5/16	.3125	7.938	13/16	.8125	20.638	1 5/8	1.625	41.275
-	.3150	8	-	.8268	21	-	1.6535	42
21/64	.3281	8.334	53/64	.8281	21.034	1 21/32	1.6562	42.069
-	.335	8.5	27/32	.84375	21.431	1 11/16	1.6875	42.863
11/32	.34375	8.731	55/64	.85937	21.828	-	1.6929	43
-	.3543	9	-	.8662	22	1 23/32	1.719	43.656
23/64	.35937	9.128	7/8	.8750	22.225	-	1.7323	44
-	.374	9.5	57/64	.8906	22.622	1 3/4	1.750	44.450
3/8	.3750	9.525	-	.9055	23	-	1.7717	45
25/64	.3906	9.922	29/32	.90625	23.019	1 25/32	1.781	45.244
-	.3937	10	59/64	.92187	23.416	-	1.8110	46
13/32	.4062	10.319	15/16	.9375	23.813	1 13/16	1.8125	46.038
-	.413	10.5	-	.9449	24	1 27/32	1.844	46.831
27/64	.42187	10.716	61/64	.9531	24.209	-	1.8504	47

CONVERSION TABLE

INCH FRACTIONS AND DECIMALS TO METRIC EQUIVALENTS

INCHES		m m	INCHES		m m	INCHES		m m
Fractions	Decimals		Fractions	Decimals		Fractions	Decimals	
1 7/8	1.875	47.625	-	3.0709	78	-	4.7244	120
-	1.8898	48	-	3.1102	79	4 3/4	4.750	120.650
1 29/32	1.9062	48.419	3 1/8	3.125	79375	4 7/8	4.875	123.825
-	1.9291	49	-	3.1496	80	-	4.9212	125
1 15/16	1.9375	49.213	3 3/16	3.1875	80.963	5	5.000	127
-	1.9685	50	-	3.1890	81	-	5.1181	130
1 31/32	1.969	50.006	-	3.2283	82	5 1/4	5.250	133.350
2	2.000	50.800	3 1/4	3.250	82.550	5 1/2	5.500	139.700
-	2.0079	51	-	3.2677	83	-	5.5118	140
-	2.0472	52	-	3.3071	84	5 3/4	5.750	146.050
2 1/16	2.062	52.388	3 5/16	3.312	84.1377	-	5.9055	150
-	2.0866	53	-	3.3464	85	6	6.000	152.400
2 1/8	2.125	53.975	3 3/8	3.375	85.725	6 1/4	6.250	158.750
-	2.126	54	-	3.3858	86	-	6.2992	160
-	2.165	55	-	3.4252	87	6 1/2	6.500	165.100
2 3/16	2.1875	55.563	3 7/16	3.438	87.313	-	6.6929	170
-	2.2047	56	-	3.4646	88	6 3/4	6.750	171.450
-	2.244	57	3 1/2	3.500	88.900	7	7.000	177.800
2 1/4	2.250	57.150	-	3.5039	89	-	7.0866	180
-	2.2835	58	-	3.5433	90	-	7.4803	190
2 5/16	2.312	58.738	3 9/16	3.562	90.4877	7 1/2	7.500	190.500
-	2.3228	59	-	3.5827	91	-	7.8740	200
-	2.3622	60	-	3.622	92	8	8.000	203.200
2 3/8	2.375	60.325	3 5/8	3.625	92.075	-	8.2677	210
-	2.4016	61	-	3.6614	93	8 1/2	8.500	215.900
2 7/16	2.438	61.913	3 11/16	3.6875	93.663	-	8.6614	220
-	2.4409	62	-	3.7008	94	9	9.000	228.600
-	2.4803	63	-	3.7401	95	-	9.0551	230
2 1/2	2.500	63.500	3 3/4	3.750	95.250	-	9.4488	240
-	2.5197	64	-	3.7795	96	9 1/2	9.500	241.300
-	2.559	65	3 13/16	3.8125	96.838	-	9.8425	250
2 9/16	2.562	65.088	-	3.8189	97	10	10.000	254.000
-	2.5984	66	-	3.8583	98	-	10.2362	260
2 5/8	2.625	66.675	3 7/8	3.875	98.425	-	10.6299	270
-	2.638	67	-	3.8976	99	11	11.000	279.400
-	2.6772	68	-	3.9370	100	-	11.0236	280
2 11/16	2.6875	68.263	3 15/16	3.9375	100.013	-	11.4173	290
-	2.7165	69	-	3.9764	101	-	11.8110	300
2 3/4	2.750	69.850	4	4.000	101.600	12	12.000	304.800
-	2.7559	70	4 1/16	4.062	103.188	13	13.000	330.200
-	2.7953	71	4 1/8	4.125	104.775	-	13.7795	350
2 13/16	2.8125	71.438	-	4.1338	105	14	14.000	355.600
-	2.8346	72	4 3/16	4.1875	106.363	15	15.000	381
-	2.8740	73	4 1/4	4.250	107.950	-	15.7480	400
2 7/8	2.875	73.025	4 5/16	4.312	109.538	16	16.000	406.400
-	2.9134	74	-	4.3307	110	17	17.000	431.800
2 15/16	2.9375	74.613	4 3/8	4.375	111.125	-	17.7165	450
-	2.9527	75	4 7/16	4.438	112.713	18	18.000	457.200
-	2.9921	76	4 1/2	4.500	114.300	19	19.000	482.600
3	3.000	76.200	-	4.5275	115	-	19.6850	500
-	3.0315	77	4 9/16	4.562	115.888	20	20.000	508
3 1/16	3.062	77.788	4 5/8	4.625	117.475	21	21.000	533.400

Books Published by MOTOR

For the Automotive Service Trade

Motor's Service Trade Manuals are available through Motor's local independent Publishers Representative. If you are unable to contact him, write to MOTOR, 1790 Broadway, New York, N.Y. 10019.

Auto Repair Manual

Mechanical specifications and service procedures for 1969-75 American built cars. Special sections on Engine Service, Wiper Motor Service, Emission System Service, Oscilloscopes, Power Steering, Power Brakes, Rear Axles.

Imported Car Repair Manual

Includes specifications and service procedures for 25 popular imports plus a valuable parts and tool availability list. An additional feature is the Operational Time Guide for these popular models.

Truck & Diesel Repair Manual

Mechanical specifications and service procedures on 1962-75 models of popular trucks plus special Diesel Engine section. Also includes Farm Tractor and Stock Engine specifications.

Emission Control Manual

Covers servicing and specifications of 1968-73 car and truck emission systems. Special sections on Retrofit Emission Control Equipment, Alternative Fuel Systems, Emission Control Law Summary, Imported Cars. Also includes a valuable Time and Parts Guide.

Parts & Time Guide

Part numbers and manufacturers suggested retail prices for American built cars from 1969-75. Interchangeable Parts information is provided for G.M., Ford and Chrysler cars. Operational Times for all cars listed plus popular truck models.

Automatic Transmission Manual

Covers hydraulic oil circuits (most in full color), describes operation of unit and details complete servicing and Trouble Shooting. Also covers popular truck units.

Vacuum & Wiring Diagrams

Lists fuse and lamp bulb data and flasher locations in addition to schematic diagrams of vacuum and electrical circuits. A large 10″ x 13″ book containing 800 pages.

Air Conditioner Service Manual

Covers basic theory, explains Automatic Temperature Control systems, Maintenance, Diagnosis & Testing, Unit Replacement, Compressor Service, vacuum and wiring diagrams. Special sections on aftermarket hang-on units, and truck and trailer refrigeration systems. Complete with parts listings and operational times.

Automobile Trouble Shooter

Lists more than 2000 causes of car and truck troubles on engines, fuel and electrical systems, clutches, transmissions, brakes, rear axles, suspension and more. Pocket size edition.